RUCCIAN ART VOL1
Gray Tone Version

Mario D. Rucci

First Edition (2019)

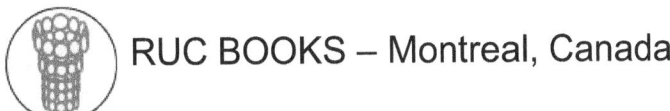

RUC BOOKS – Montreal, Canada

RUCCIAN ART VOL1
Gray Tone Version
by Mario D. Rucci

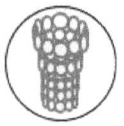

Published by:
RUC™ BOOKS
Post Office Box 20002
Montreal, QC H1H 5W5 Canada
Orders from RucBooks.com

Copyright © 2019 by Mario D. Rucci

All rights reserved. No part of this book may be reproduced or transmitted in any form or by any means, electronic or mechanical, including photocopying, recording, or by any information storage and retrieval system, without the written permission from the author, except for the inclusion of brief quotations in a review.

ISBN, PDF ed.   978-1-989504-13-0
ISBN, print ed.   978-1-989504-14-7
ISBN, print ed. gray tone   978-1-989504-15-4

First Printing 2019

DISCLAIMER: The purpose of these volumes is to educate and entertain. The author and RUC BOOKS shall have neither liability nor responsibility to any person or entity with respect to any loss or damage caused, or alleged to have been caused, directly or indirectly, by the information contained in these volumes. If you do not wish to be bound by the aforesaid, you may return this book to the publisher for a full refund.

DEDICATION

To…

ALL MY SITTERS

(Relatives, Friends, and Acquaintances)

TABLE OF CONTENTS

ABOUT THE AUTHOR	vi
INTRODUCTION	vii
1. INACTIVE DEPICTION	1
2. ANIMAL DEPICTION	21
HUMAN DEPICTION ...	37
3. Head Imitation	37
4. Head Observation, Acquaintances	63
5. Head Observation, Friends	101
6. Head Observation, Relatives	119
7. Head Observation, Self-Portraits	161
8. Head Obs/Vis, At School	193
9. Head Visualization, Other Times	219
10. Torso	271
11. Extremities	283
12. Full Figure, Imitation	311
13. Full Figure, Observation	343
14. Full Figure, Obs/Vis, At School	367
15. Full Figure, Visualization, Other Times	389
16. HUMAN Composition	403
17. HUMAN & ANIMAL Composition	441
18. HUMAN & DIVINE Composition	465

ABOUT THE AUTHOR

Mario D. Rucci ...
Is the 5th child of Nicola Rucci and Cristina Maria Del Russo
Was born in 1948 in Sepino, Campobasso, Molise, Italy
Moved to Canada with family in 1966, when he was 18 years old
Was a teacher for 30 years: taught fine arts in High School and all subjects in Elementary School
Retired from teaching in 2006, at the age of 58, to work full time on PHILOSOPHY
Worked on PHILOSOPHY for another 12 years, until 2018 (age 70)

Over the course of his life **Mario D. Rucci** has been a painter, writer, teacher, computer expert, house builder, inventor, theoretical physicist, and philosopher – and he has excelled in whatever he happened to tackle.

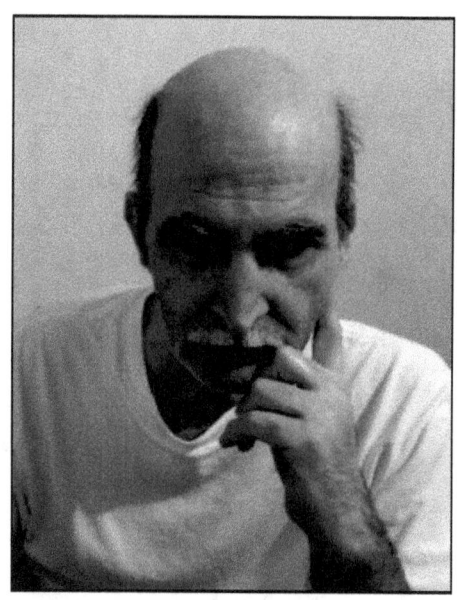

INTRODUCTION

I wanted to have a more affordable version. This is it: a gray tone version. Most of the art work is made up of drawings; so, this is not very drastic. And, besides, we do not need color to enjoy the form.

PICTORIAL ACTIVITIES
There are 3 pictorial activities one can engage in:
Depiction (Still/Static): Drawing, Painting, Printing (convex, concave, stencil by carving, scratching, masking)
Animation: hand-drawn, computer-interpolated, computer-generated (CG)
Motion Picture/Movie: film, video, flash drive

[+] PICTORIAL ACTIVITIES

	Depiction:	Animation:	Motion Picture/Movie:
Method 1	drawing	hand-drawn	film
Method 2	painting	computer-interpolated	video
Method 3	printing (stencil)	computer-generated	flash drive

Just as with a work of literature, a picture can be **factual**, **fictional**/probable, or **fantastic**/unreal. And, the production of a picture can be **manual** (using a depicter*), mechanical/**photographic** (using a camera), and digital/**CG** (using a computer). This is what we need to classify Depiction, Animation, and Motion Picture/Movie, as shown in the following table.
* depicter: pencil, pen, brush

[+] PICTORIAL ACTIVITIES CLASSIFICATION
Factual, Fictional, Fantastic ...

	Depiction:	Animation:	Motion Picture/Movie:
Manual	factual, manual depiction	factual, manual animation	factual, manual movie
Photographic	factual photography	factual, photographic animation	factual cinematography
CG	factual, CG depiction	factual, CG animation	factual, CG movie

RUCCIAN PICTORIAL ACTIVITIES
During the time I was doing art, I got involved with the following pictorial activities:
Factual, Manual Depiction: drawing, painting, printing (depicting pictures)
Fictional, CG/Digital Depiction: photo manipulation (manipulating pictures)
Fantastic, Manual Animation: hand-drawn animation (animating pictures)

FACTUAL, MANUAL DEPICTION
This book is about **Factual, Manual Depiction** (drawing, painting, printing). Depiction classification is in relation to form, extent, and position. The **form** is inactive, animal (equine, in my case), or human. The **extent** is a body part, a full figure (arrangement of body parts), or a composition (arrangement of figures). And, the **position*** used when producing the depiction is from imitation, from observation, or from visualization.
* position: posture, approach, method

Form: **INACTIVE** (inanimate, vegetal, artificial), **ANIMAL, HUMAN**
   Plus: **HUMAN & ANIMAL** (man & horse) and **HUMAN & DIVINE**
Extent: Body Part (**head, torso, extremities**), **Full Figure, Composition**
   Head Models: **acquaintances, friends, relatives, self-portraits**
Position: **Imitation, Observation, Visualization**

In Depiction, we get 27 sections/chapters, like the following table shows.

[+] FACTUAL, MANUAL DEPICTION
INACTIVE, ANIMAL, **HUMAN**...

	Imitation:	Observation:	Visualization:
Body Part	human body part imitation	human body part observation	human body part visualization
Full Figure	human full figure imitation	human full figure observation	human full figure visualization
Composition	human composition imitation	human composition observation	human composition visualization

RUCCIAN ART VOL1 - Factual, Manual Depiction

During the time I was drawing, painting, and printing, I did not cover to the same extent all the possible topics in depiction. What motivated me predominantly was the human form. So, still following the above classification system, for this book, I have partitioned my pictures into the following 18 chapters:

1. INACTIVE DEPICTION
2. ANIMAL DEPICTION
  HUMAN DEPICTION ...
3. Head Imitation
4. Head Observation, Acquaintances
5. Head Observation, Friends
6. Head Observation, Relatives
7. Head Observation, Self-Portraits
8. Head Obs/Vis, At School
9. Head Visualization, Other Times
10. Torso
11. Extremities
12. Full Figure, Imitation
13. Full Figure, Observation
14. Full Figure, Obs/Vis, At School
15. Full Figure, Visualization, Other Times
16. HUMAN Composition
17. HUMAN & ANIMAL Composition
18. HUMAN & DIVINE Composition

PICTORIAL PROFICIENCY

The TOC of this book is structured by taking into account Pictorial Proficiency*. Pictorial Proficiency is in relation to Depiction, Animation, and Motion Picture; type of Form, Extent, Position; and type of Body Part, Full Figure, Composition.
* proficiency: skill, ability, competence

Depiction is a higher proficiency than Animation; whereas, Motion Picture is a lower proficiency than Animation. Manual Depiction is a higher proficiency than Mechanical Depiction; whereas, Digital Depiction is a lower proficiency than Mechanical Depiction. Manual printing (cutting a design) is a higher proficiency than mechanical printing (developing film); whereas, digital printing (using the computer) is a lower proficiency than mechanical printing.

Depicting inactive (inanimate and vegetal) objects, as in landscapes, is a lower proficiency than depicting animals; whereas, depicting humans is a higher proficiency than depicting animals. Depicting body parts is a lower proficiency than depicting the full figure; whereas, depicting a composition of figures is a higher proficiency than depicting isolated figures. And, depicting from imitation (when using a photo of an art work or a photo of a model) is a lower proficiency than depicting from observation (when using a live model); whereas, depicting from visualization (when using one's memory, inspiration, or imagination) is a higher proficiency than depicting from observation.

[+] DETERMINING PROFICIENCY by Form, Extent, Position

	Form:	**Extent:**	**Position:**
Level 1	inactive	body part	imitation/photo
Level 2	animal	full figure	observation/model
Level 3	human	composition	visualization/imagination

x

1. INACTIVE DEPICTION

There are 3 main forms: the inactive, the animal, and the human form. The inactive form is the easiest. By inactive, we mean the inanimate, both natural and artificial, and the vegetal forms. Depicting a mountain, a tree, or a vase is the easiest way when we undertake the *factual, manual depiction* of forms. This is so because there are more variations, more possibilities in the inactive form than in the animal and human forms.

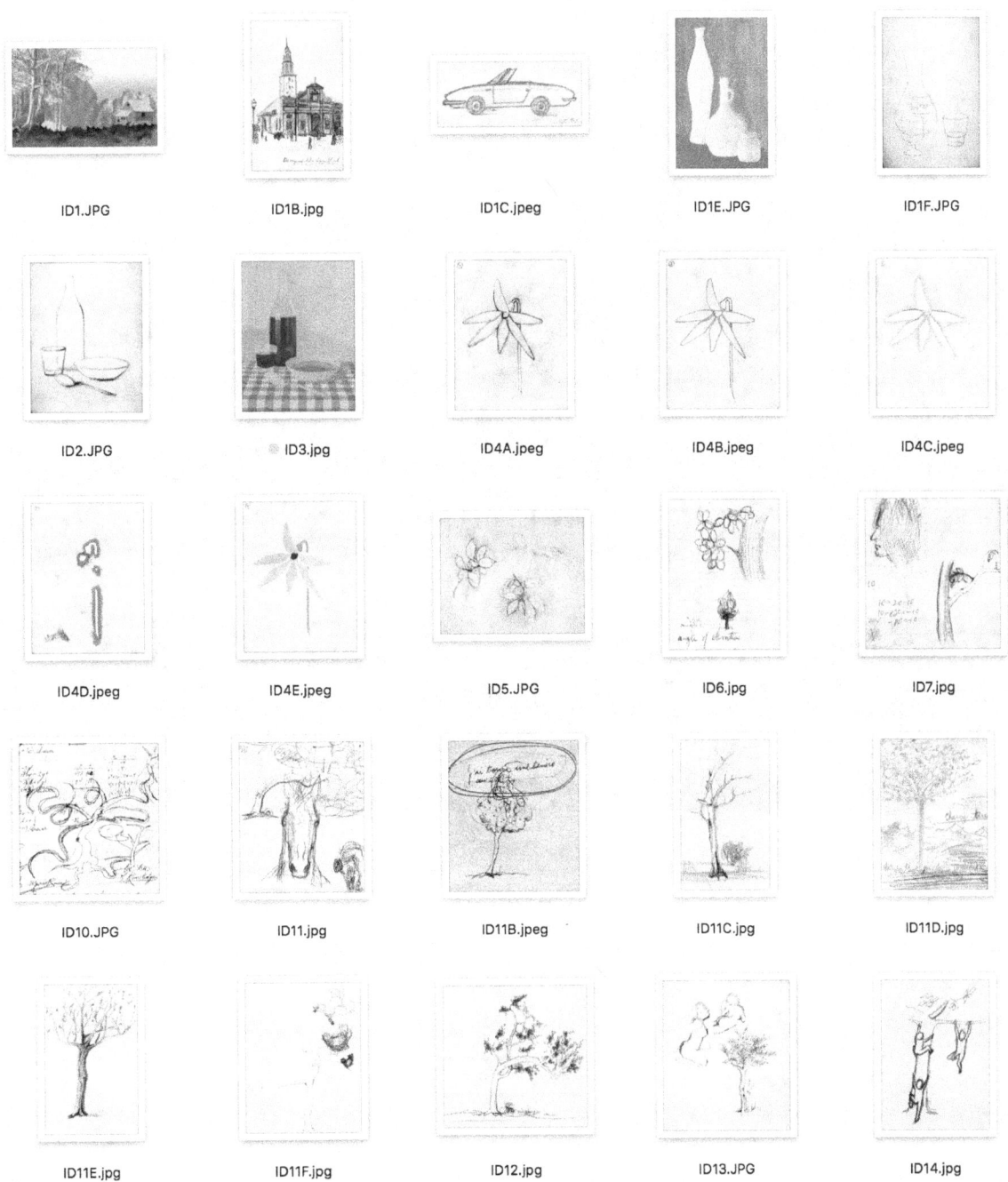

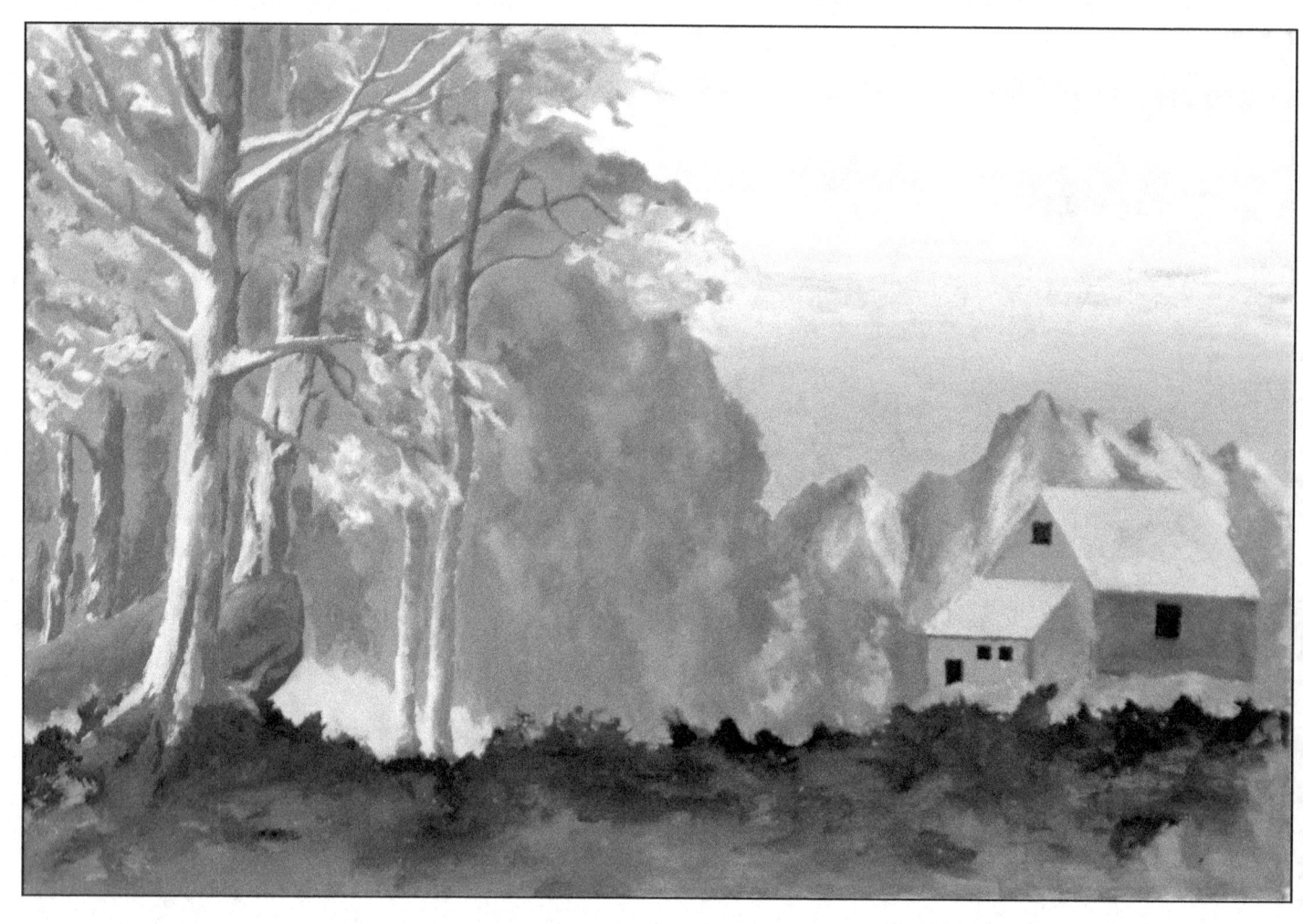

Acrylic on Cardboard

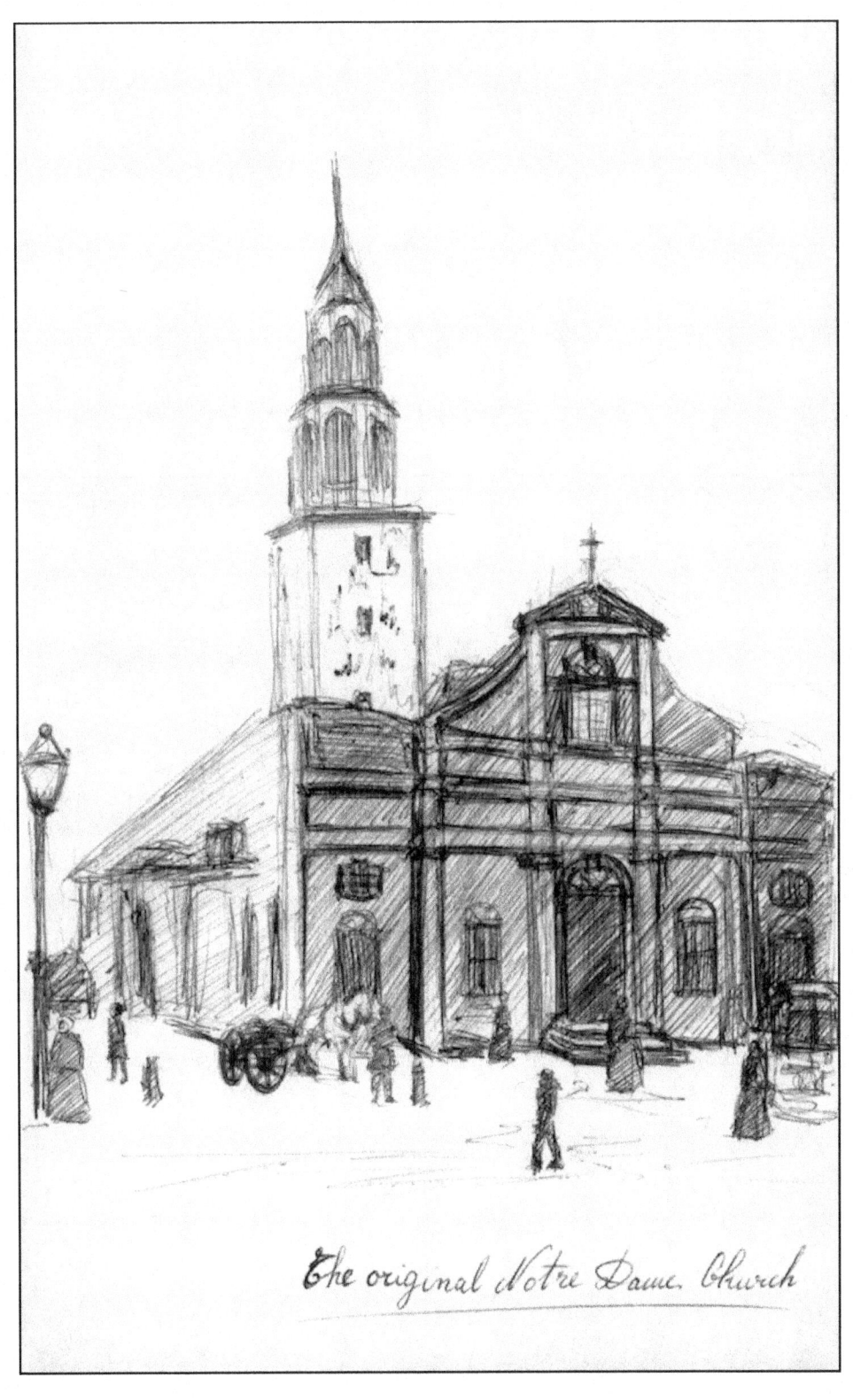

Ballpoint-Pen Drawing on a 5"x8" Notepad

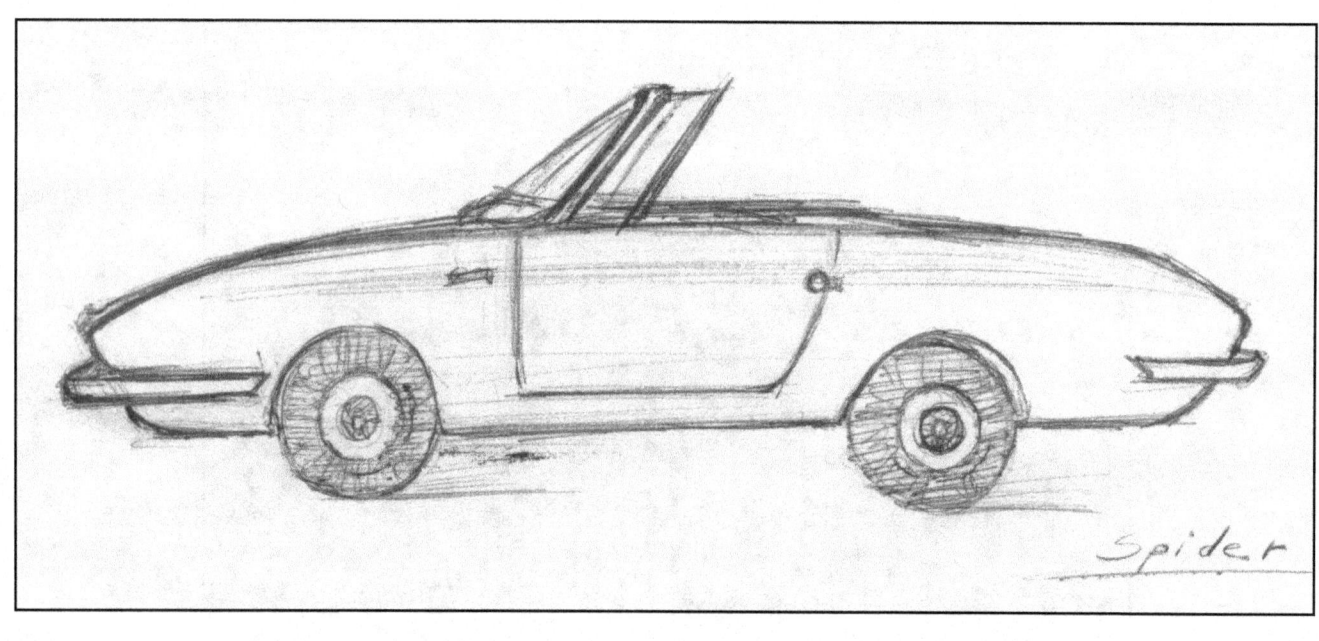

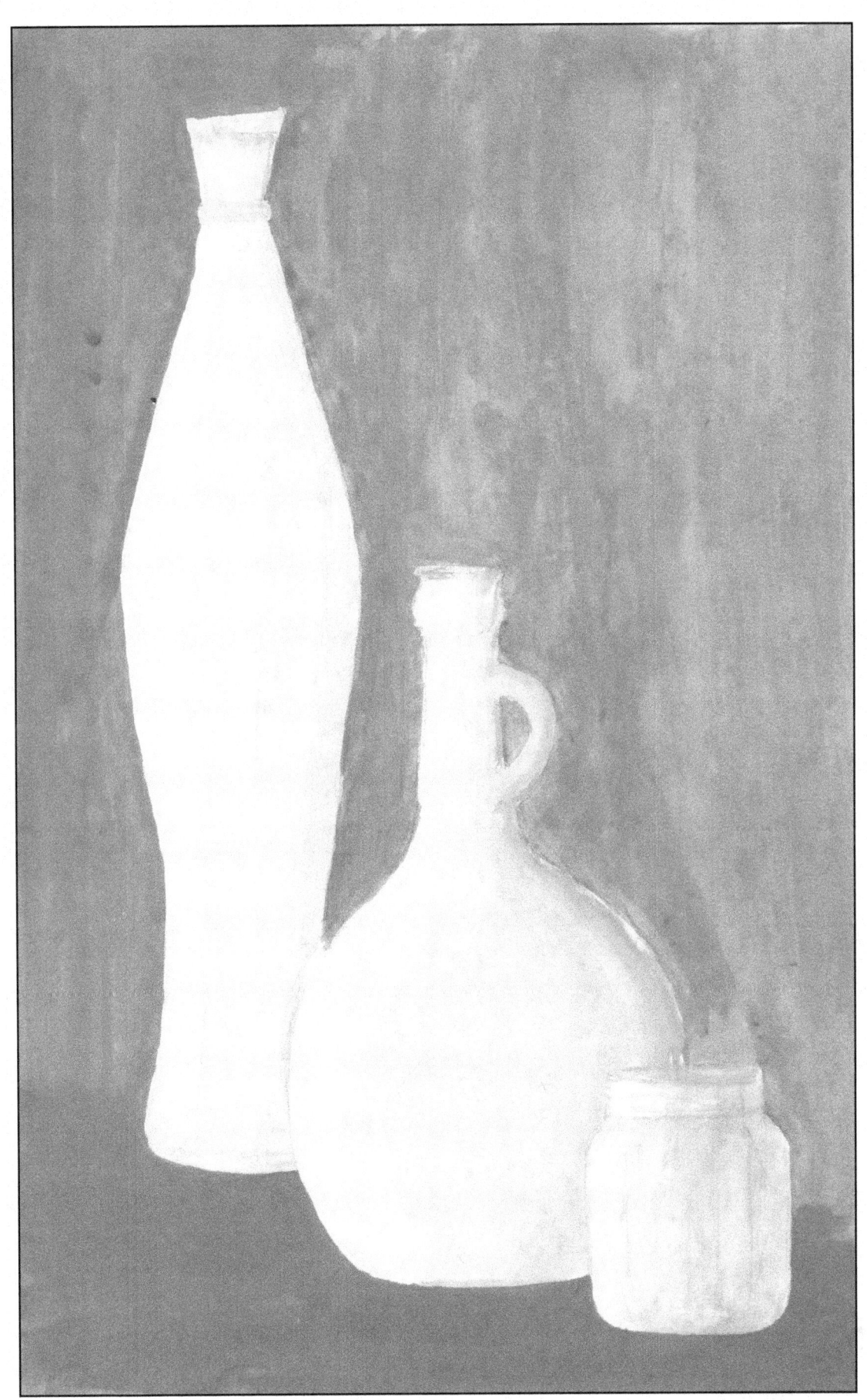

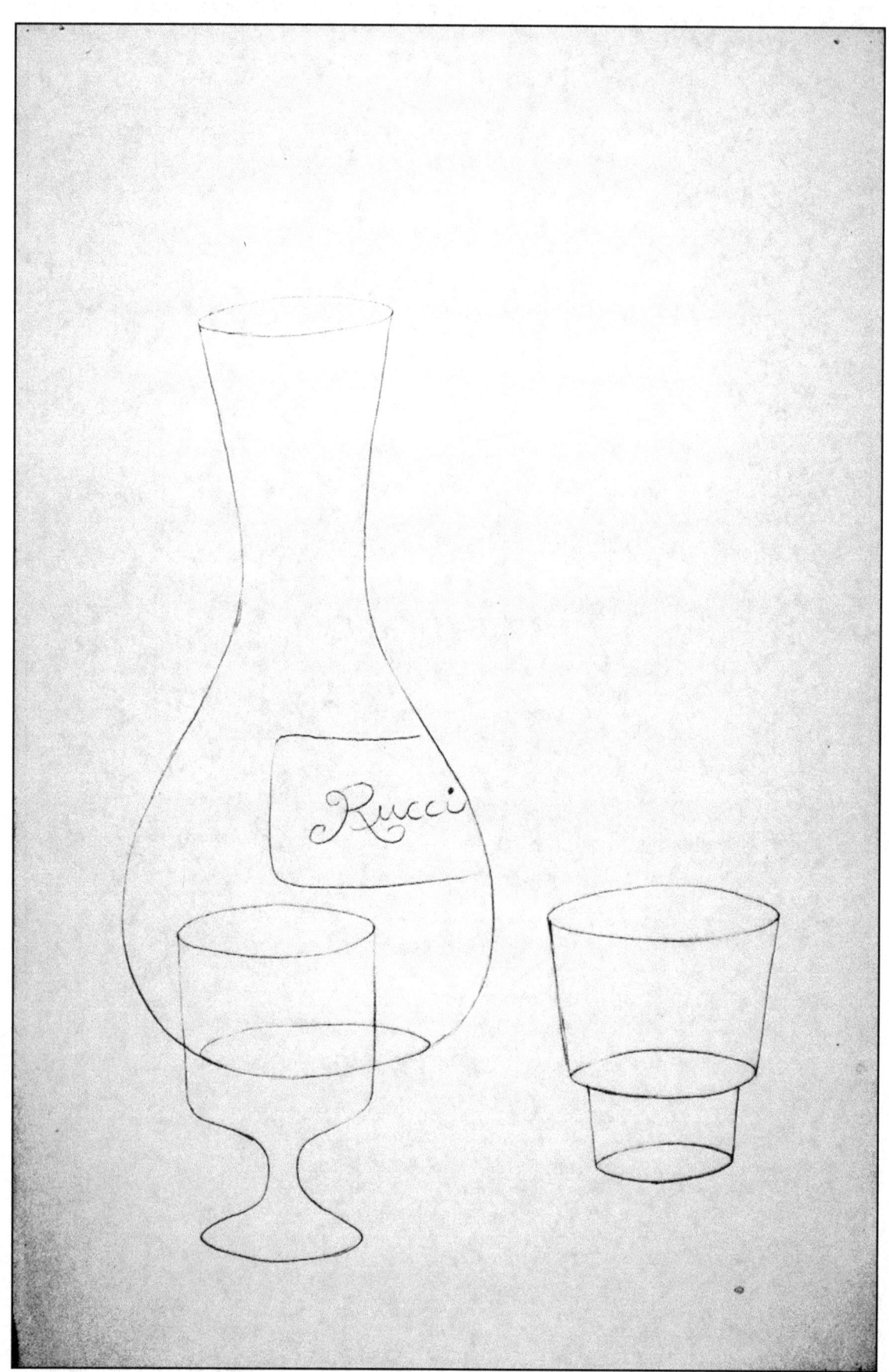

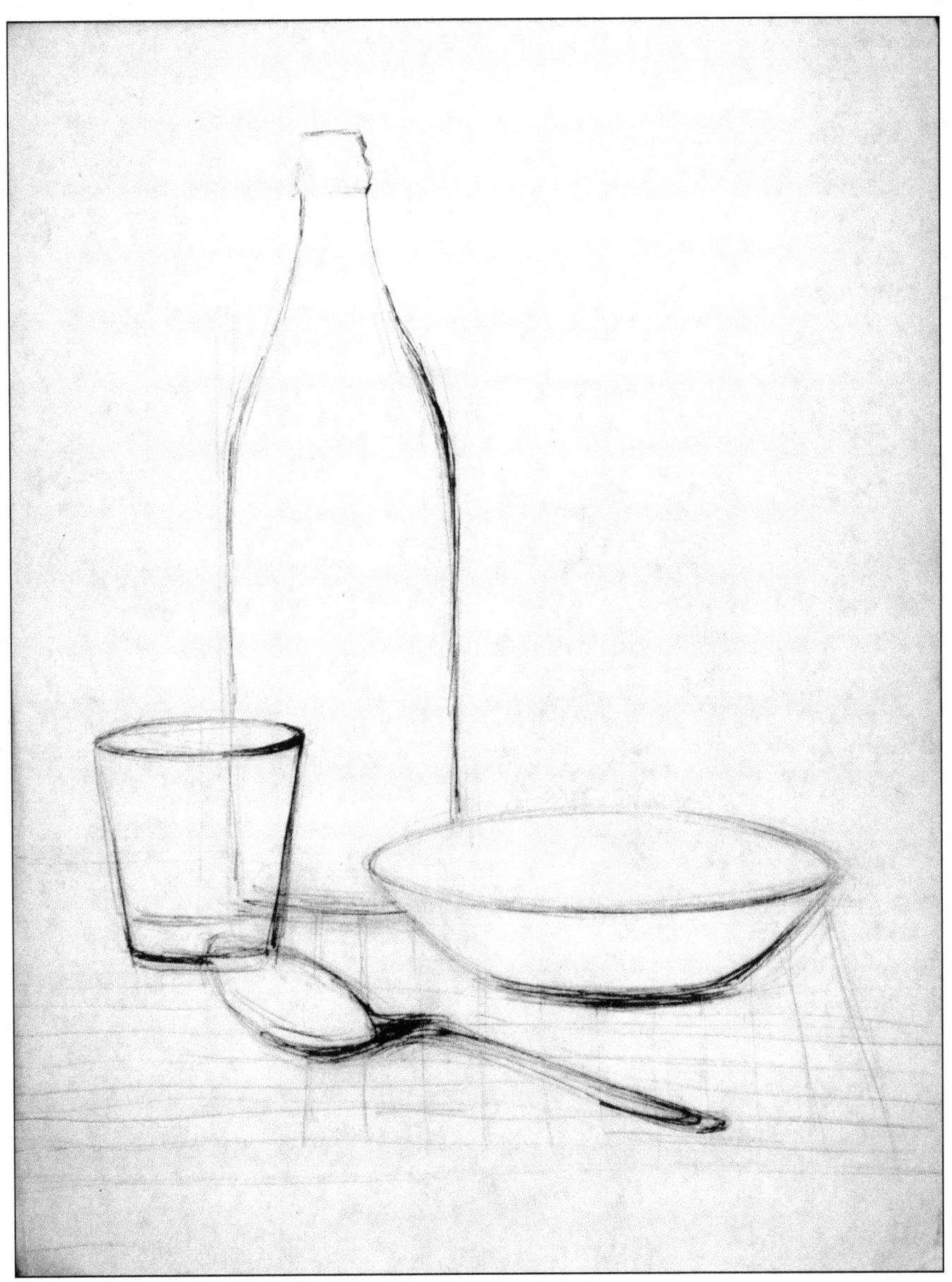

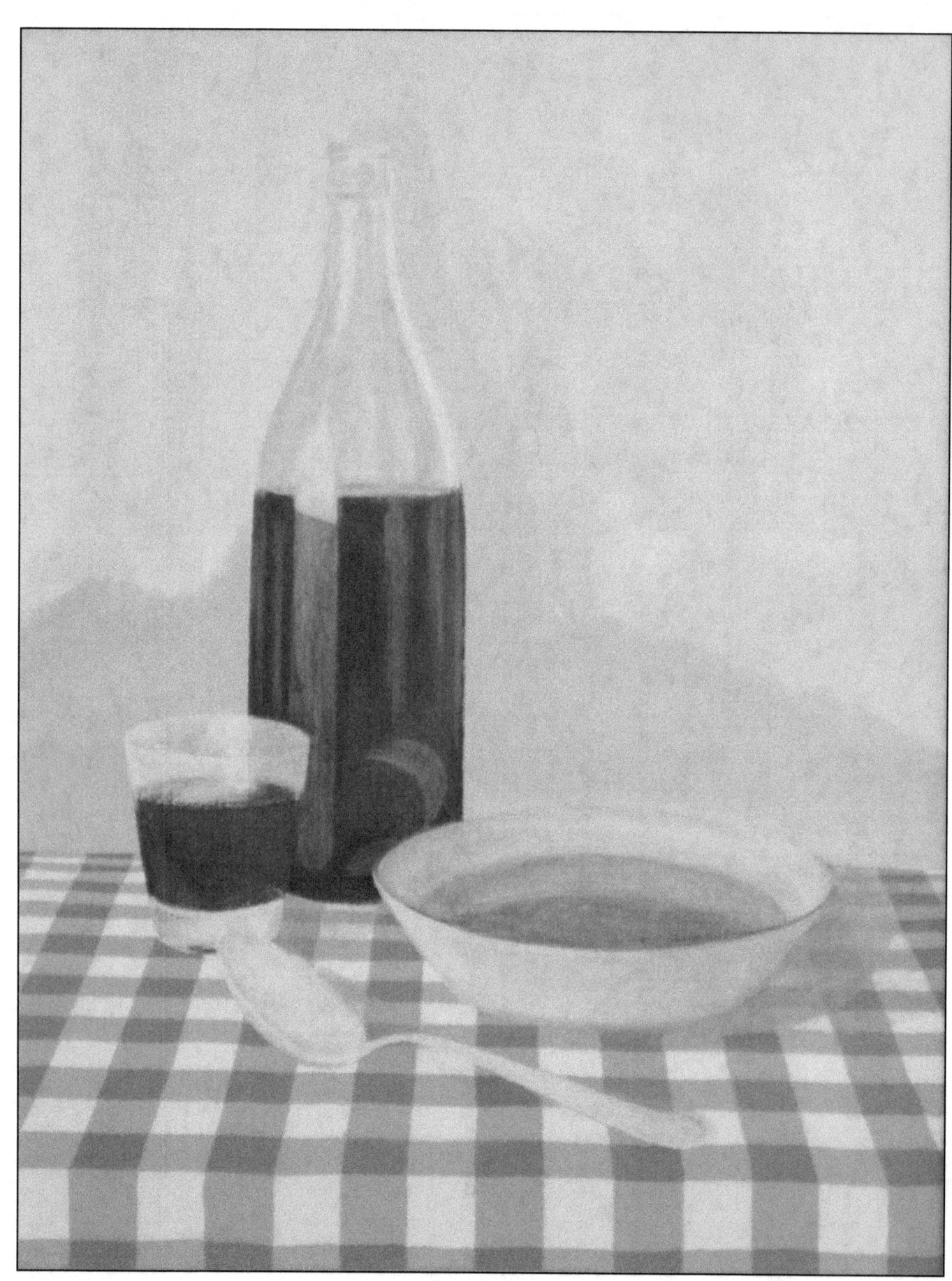

Acrvlic on 12"x18" Canvas

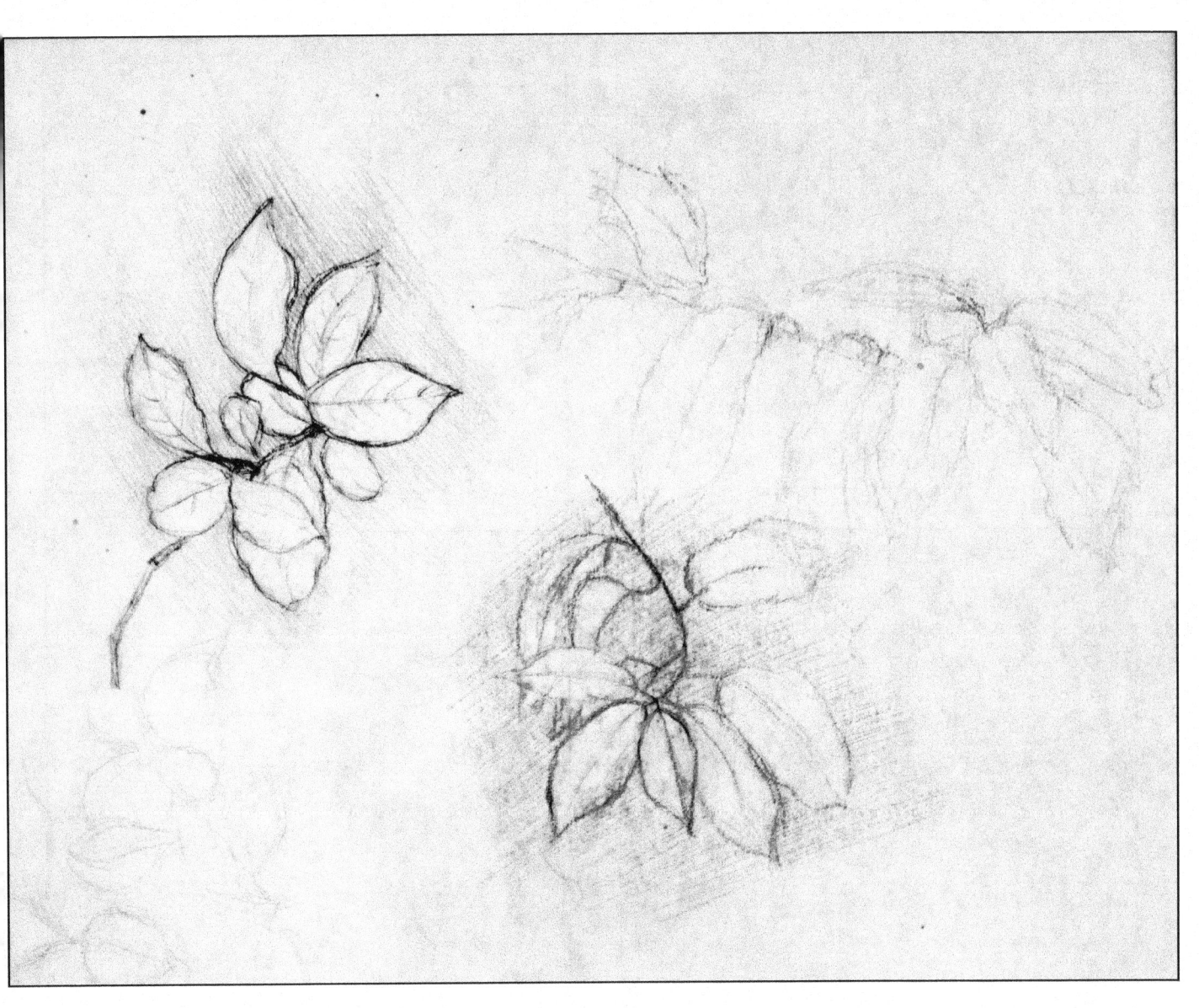

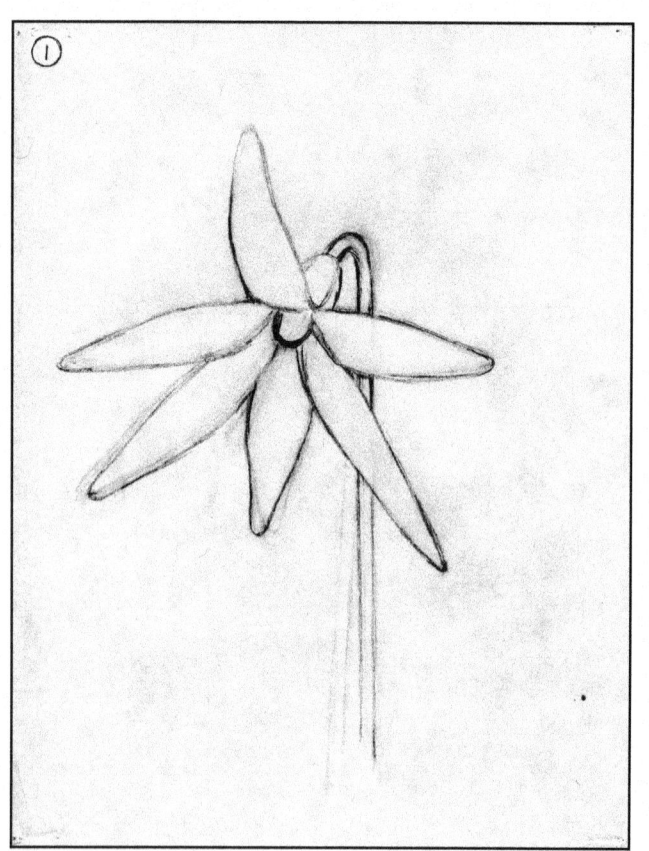
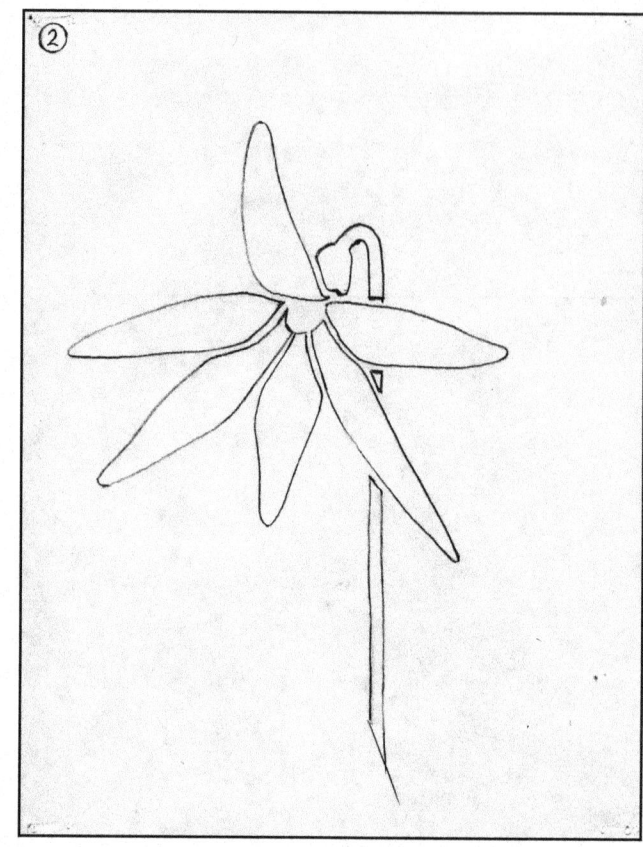
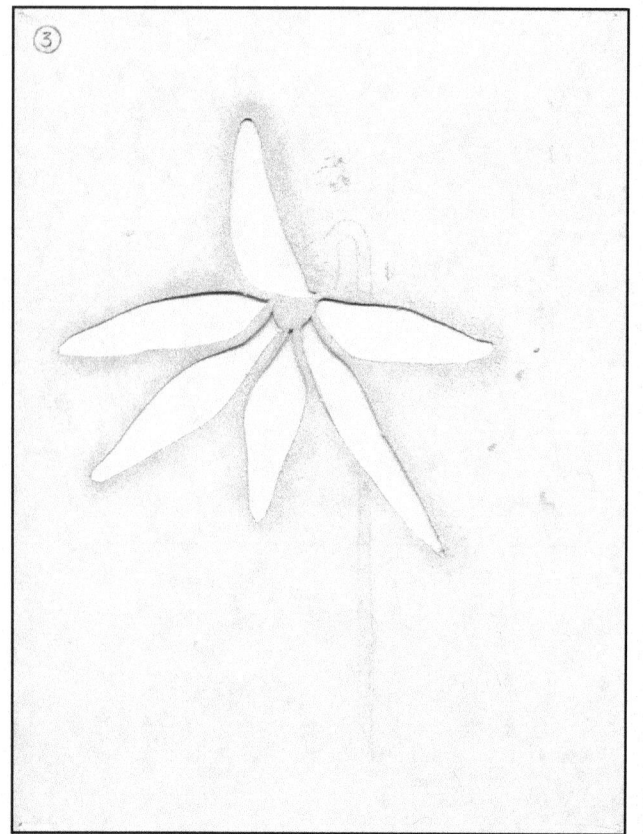
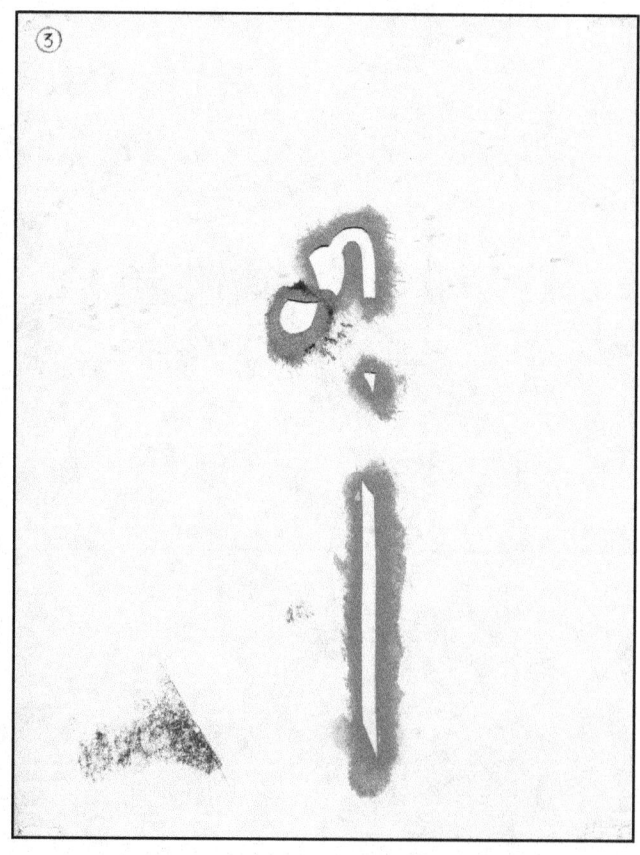

Steps in the preparing of a stencil

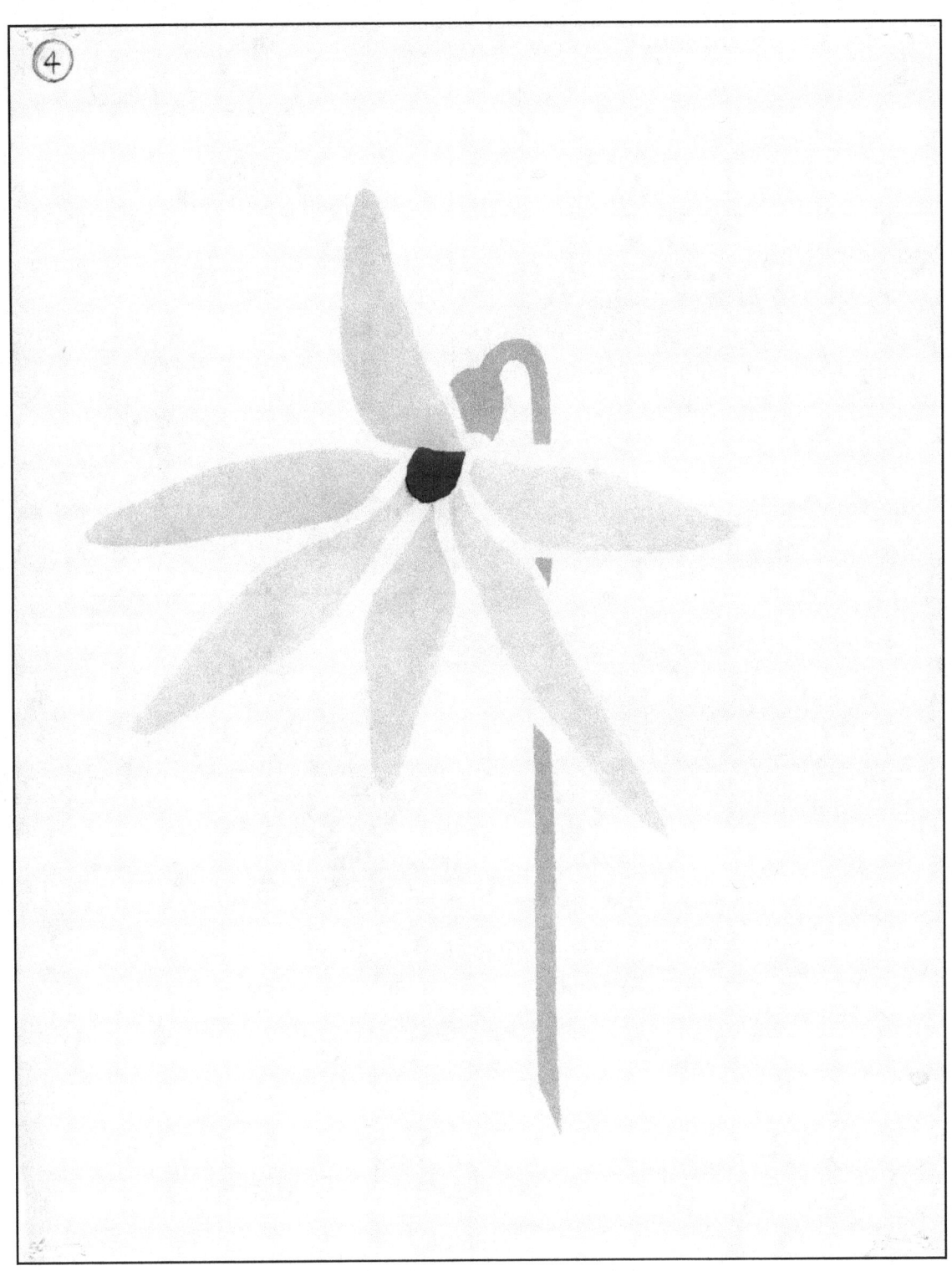

Final print from preceding stencils

**In High School,
in class,
in the math copybook**

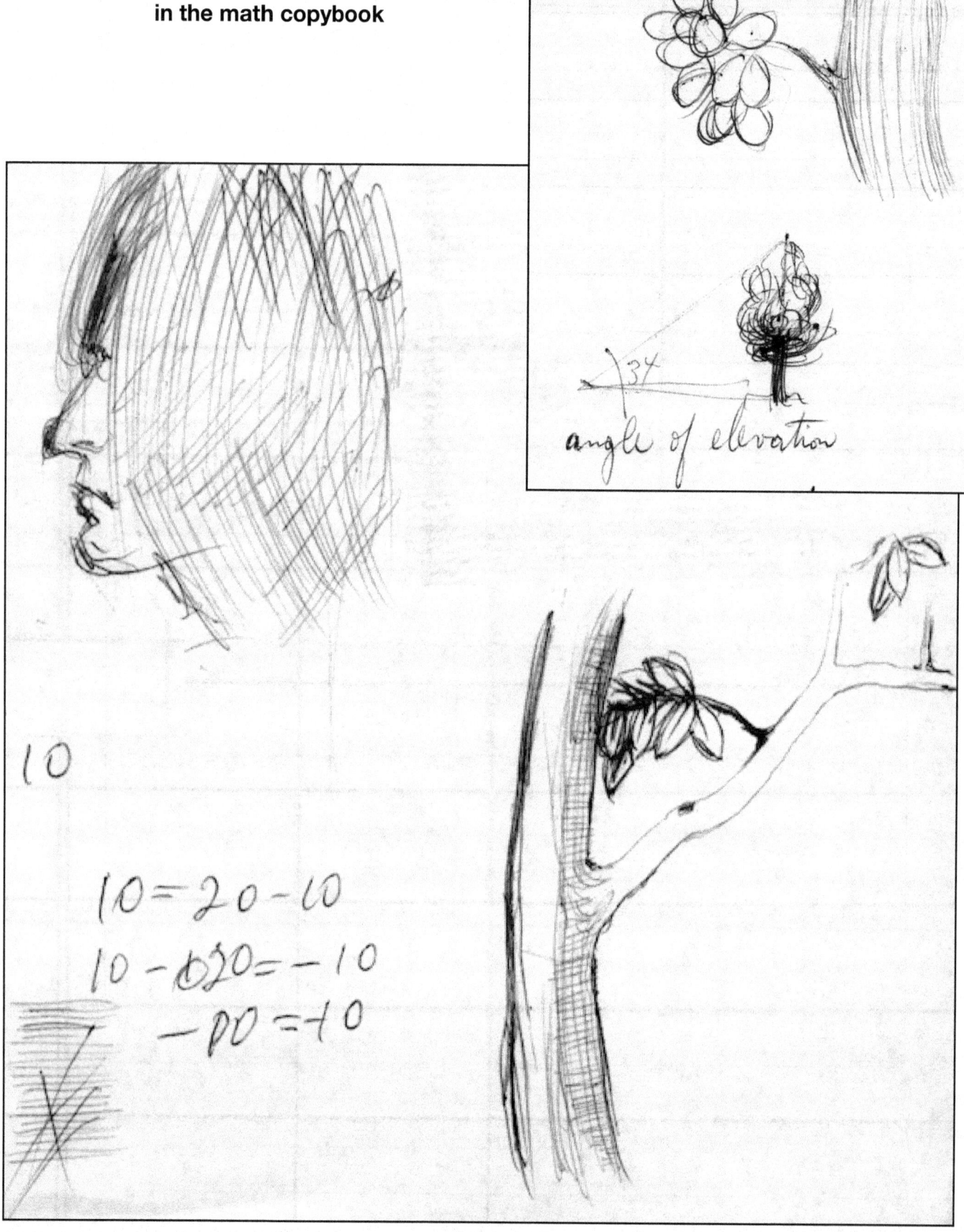

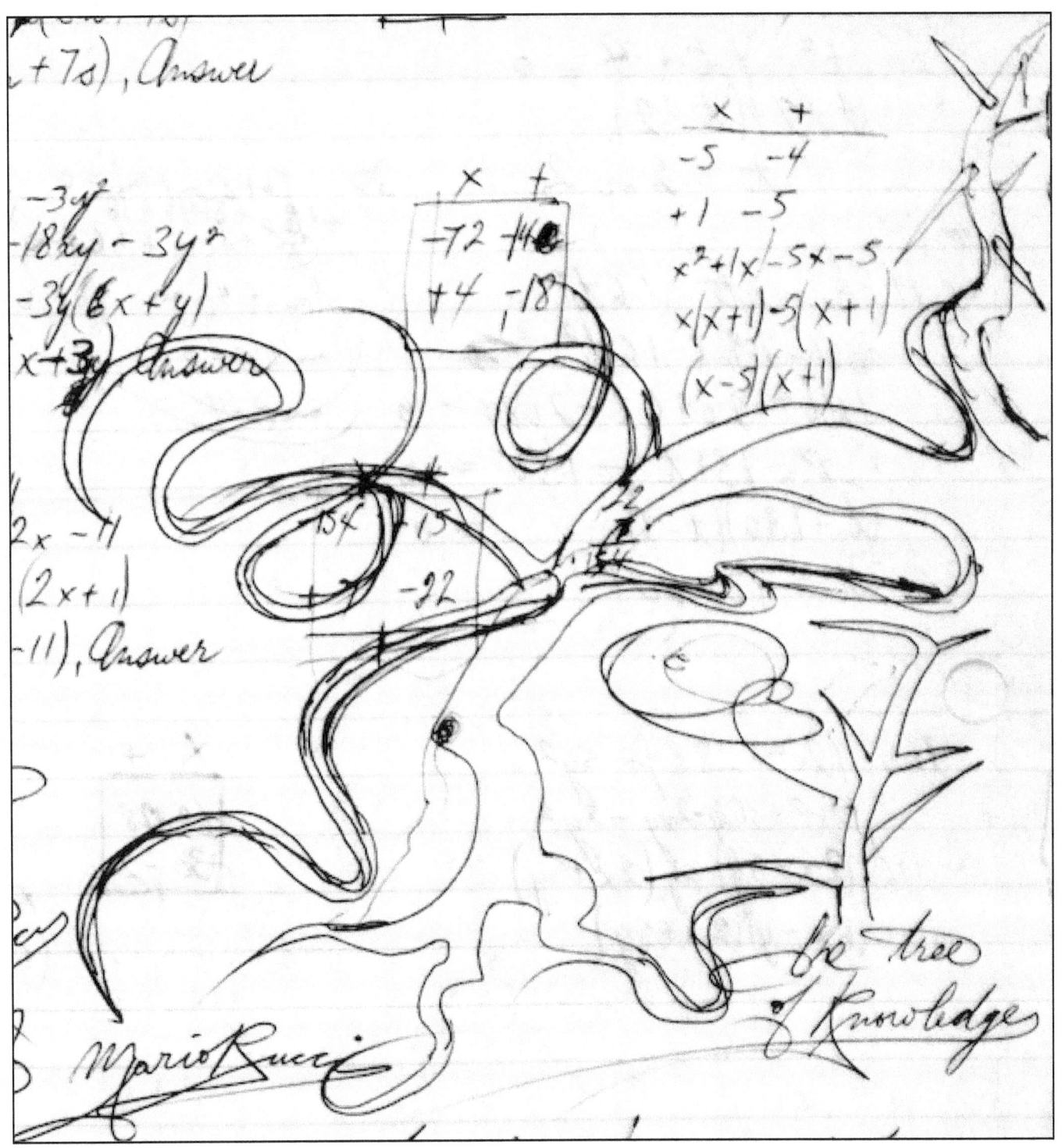

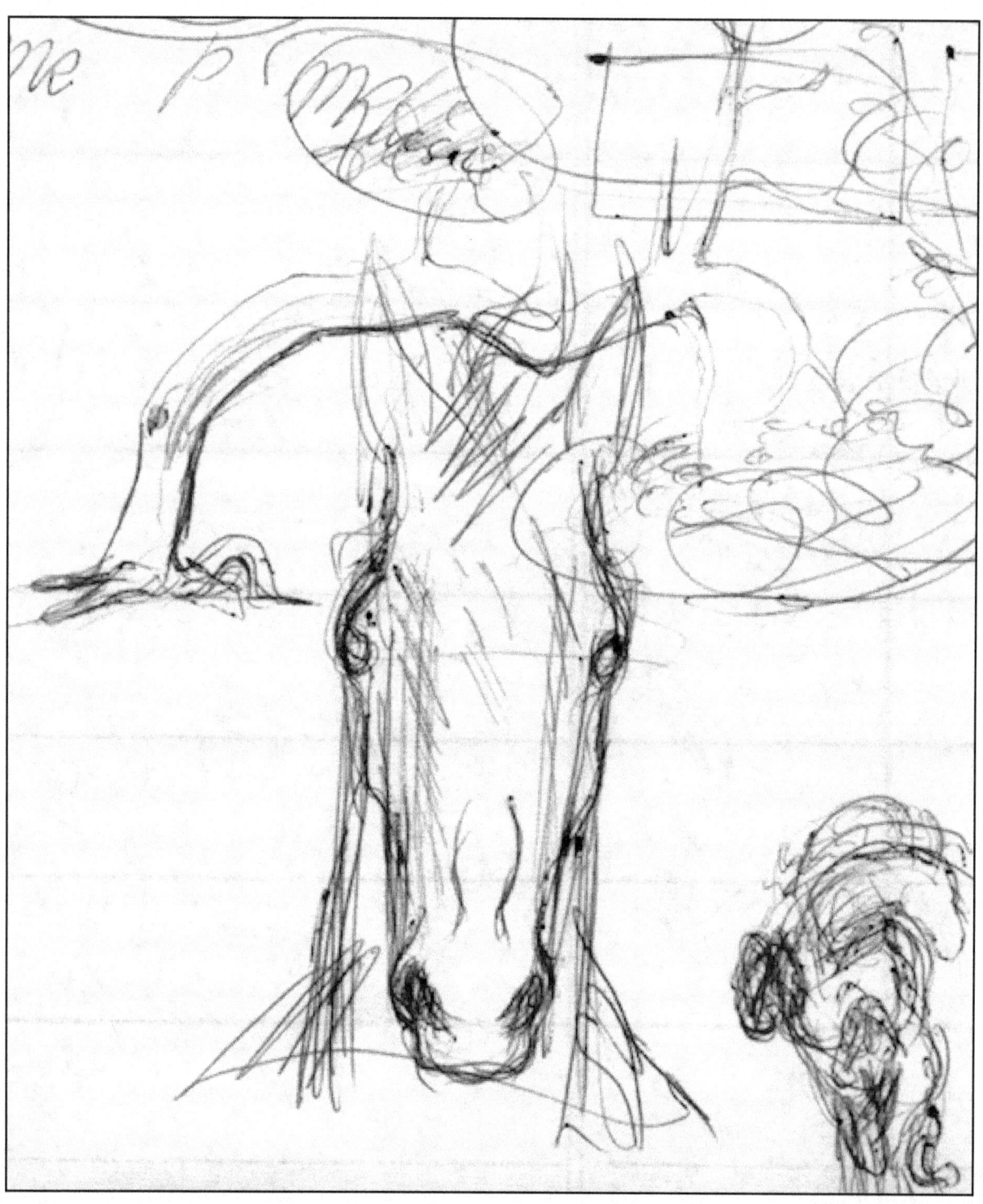

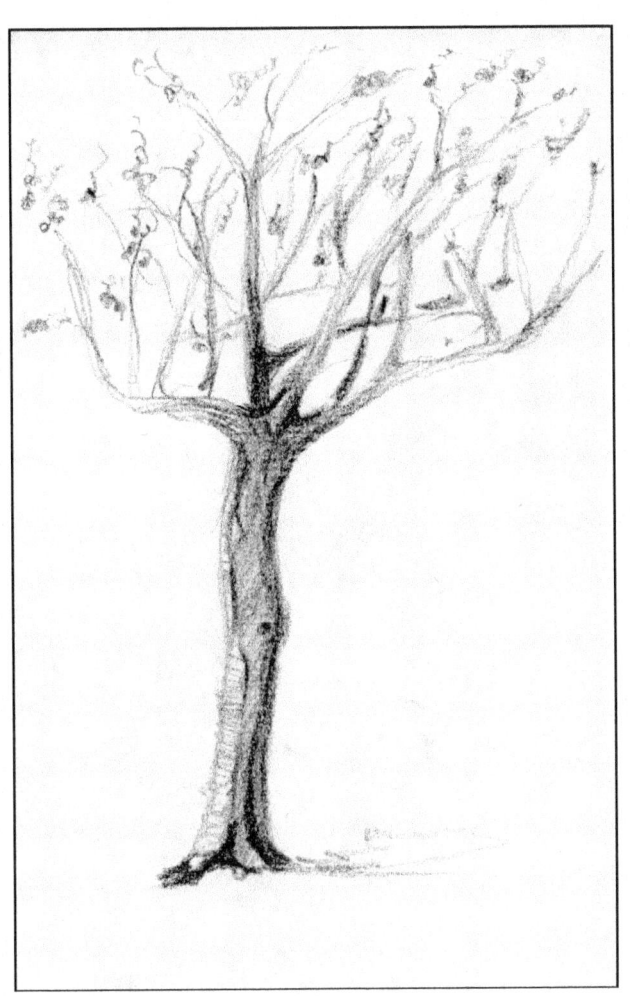
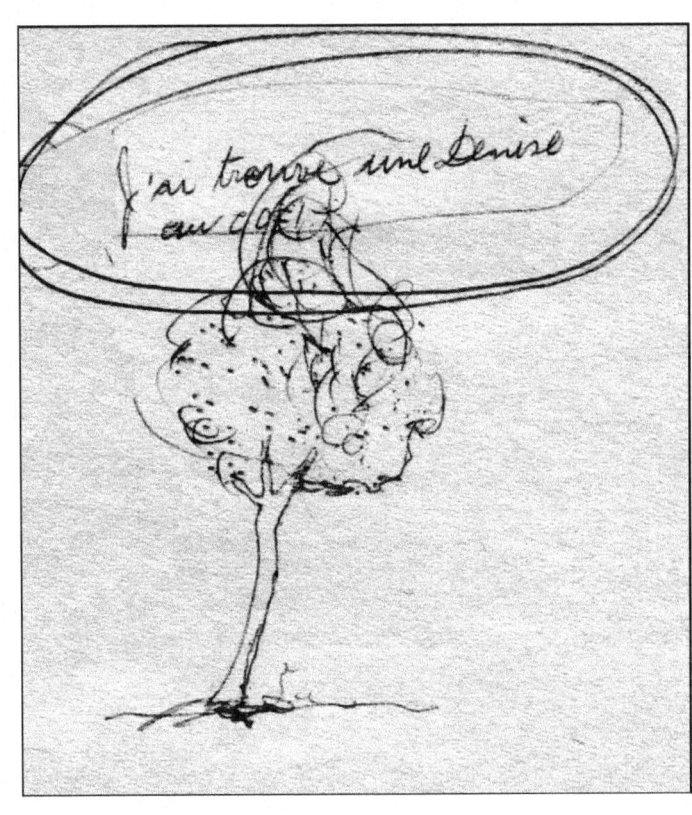
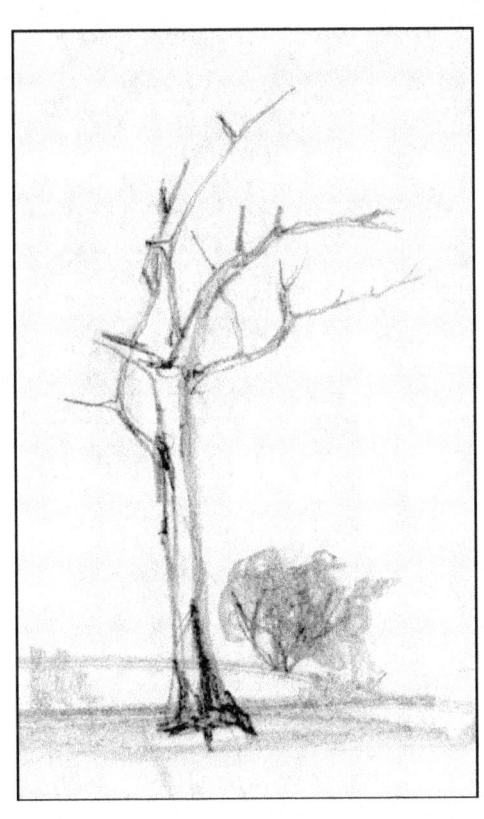
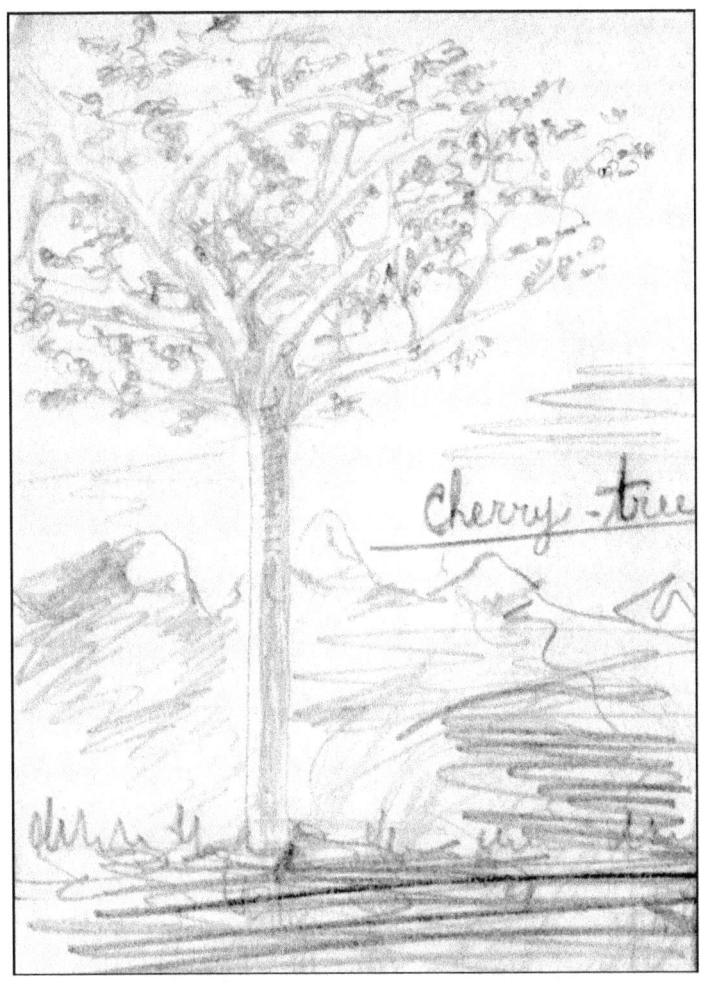

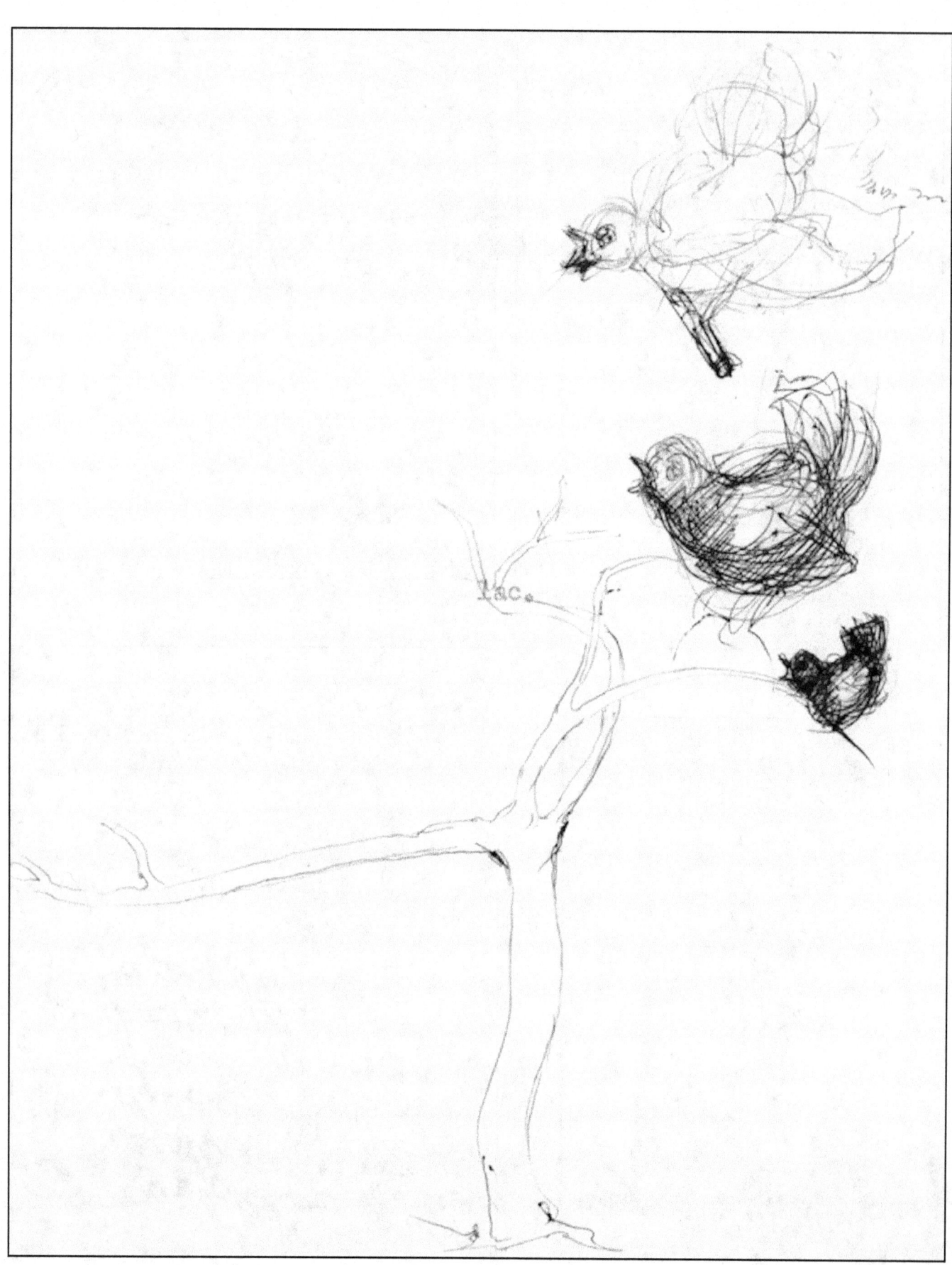

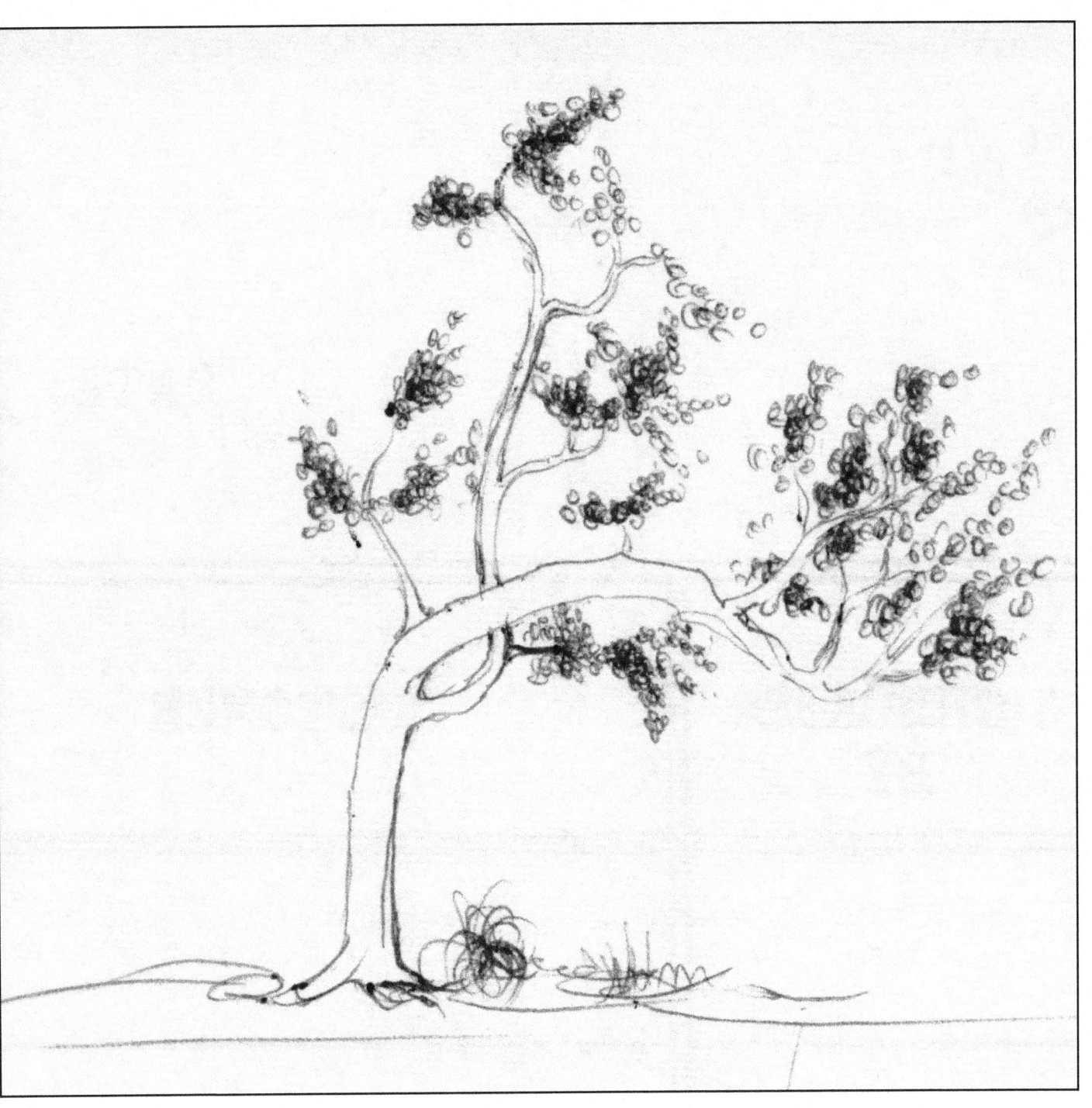

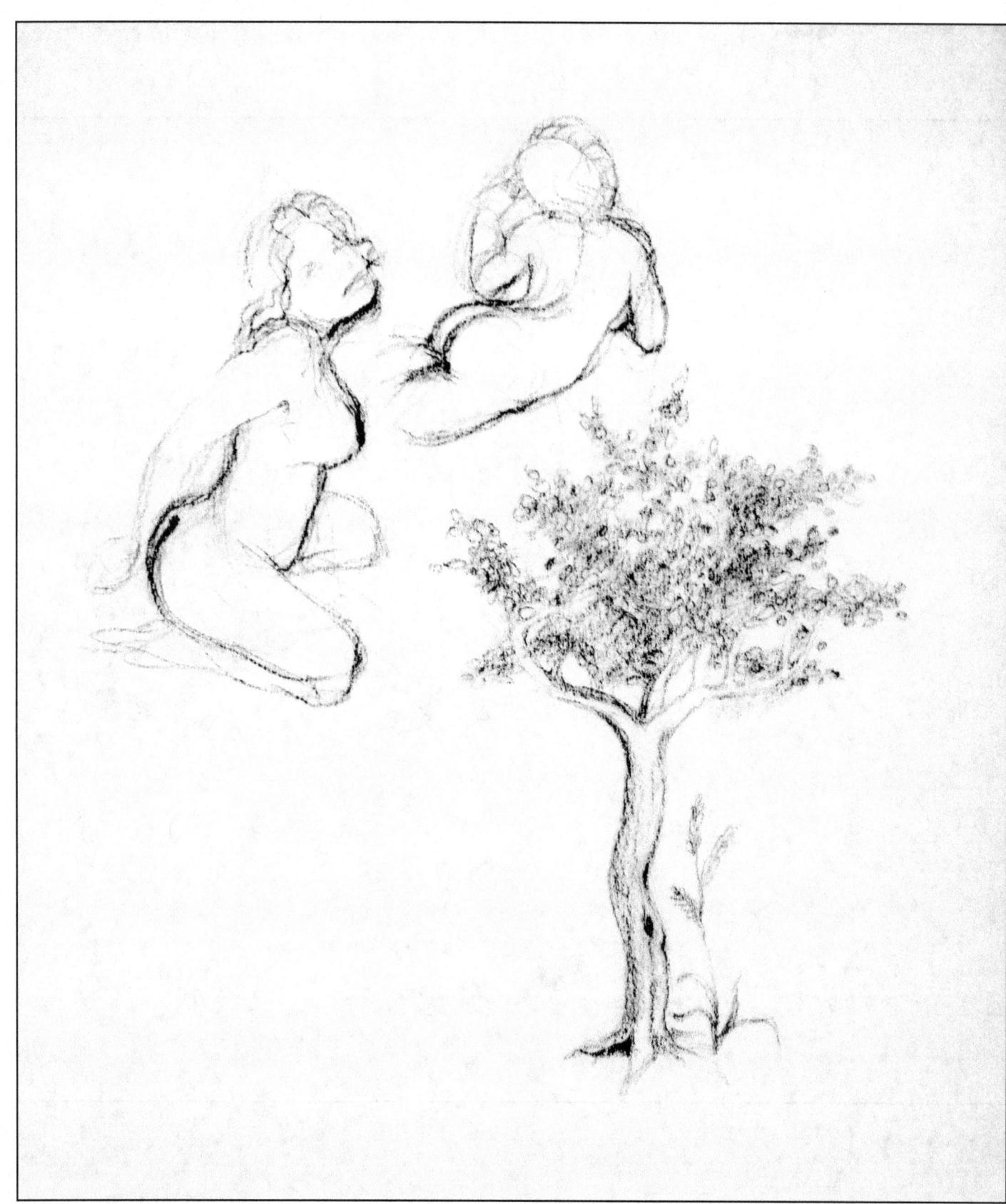

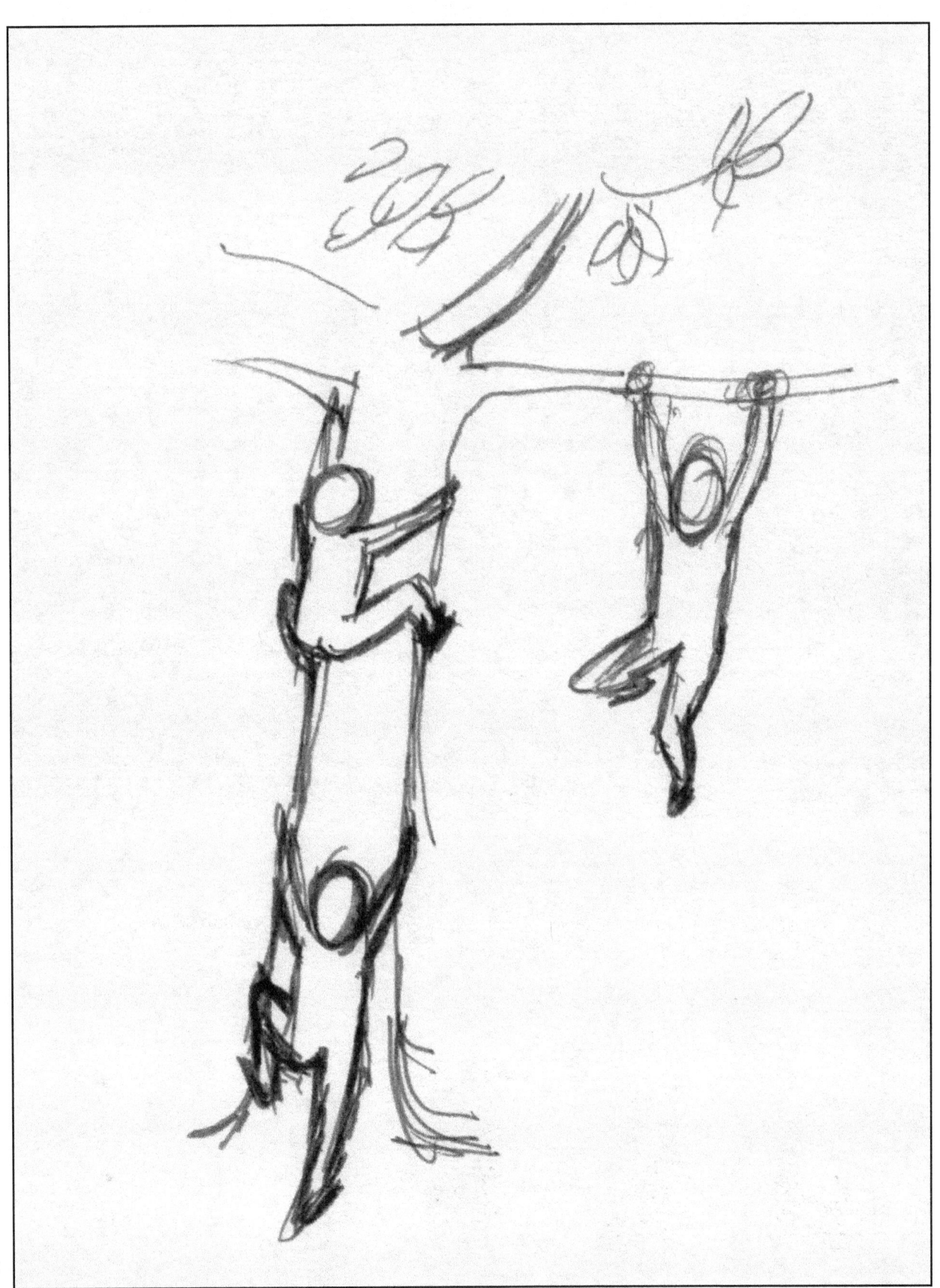

2. ANIMAL DEPICTION

The animal form is more difficult to depict than the inactive form; but, it is less difficult than the human form. As said before, the reason for this is that there are more variations and possibilities in the animal form than in the human form. However, there is another reason: We can tell if something is amiss more easily with the human form than with the animal form, because we are more knowledgeable of the human form.

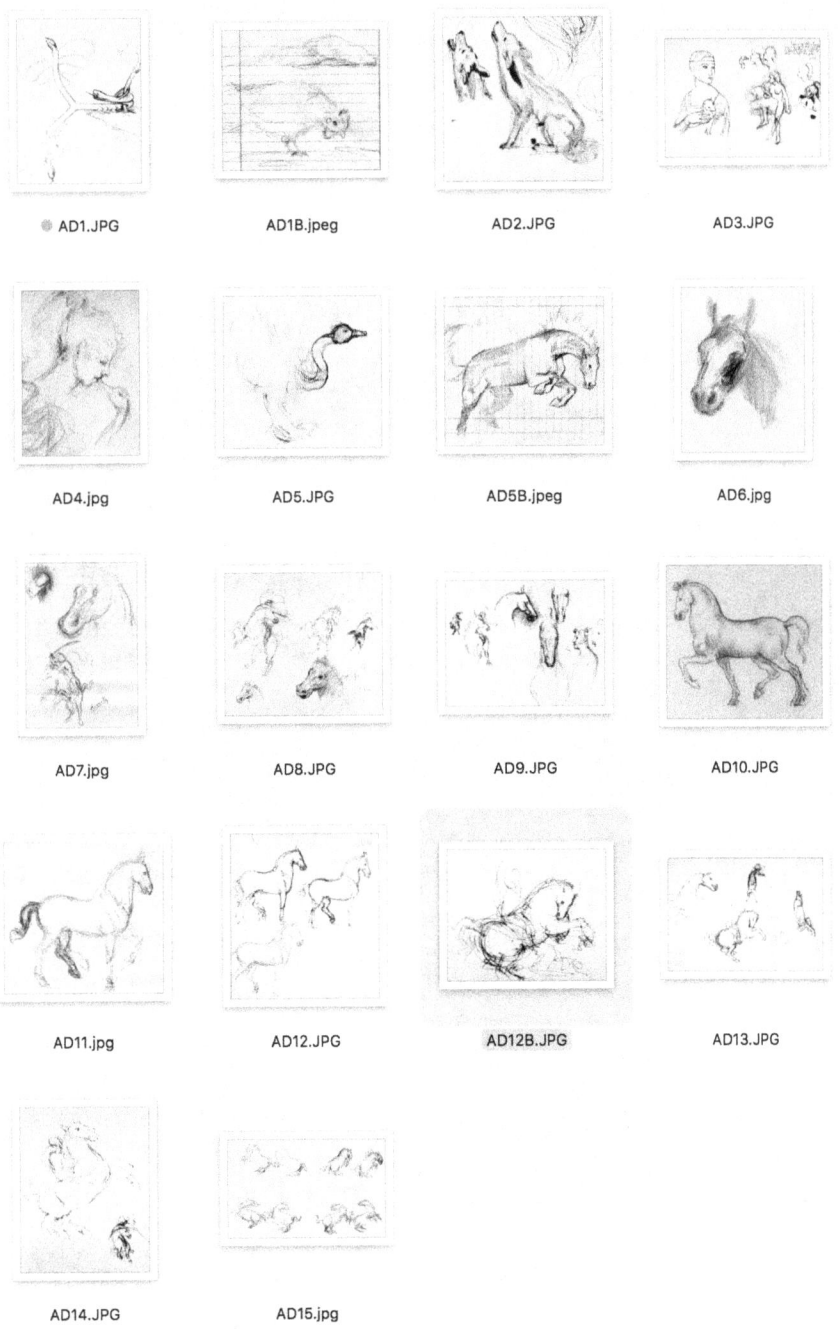

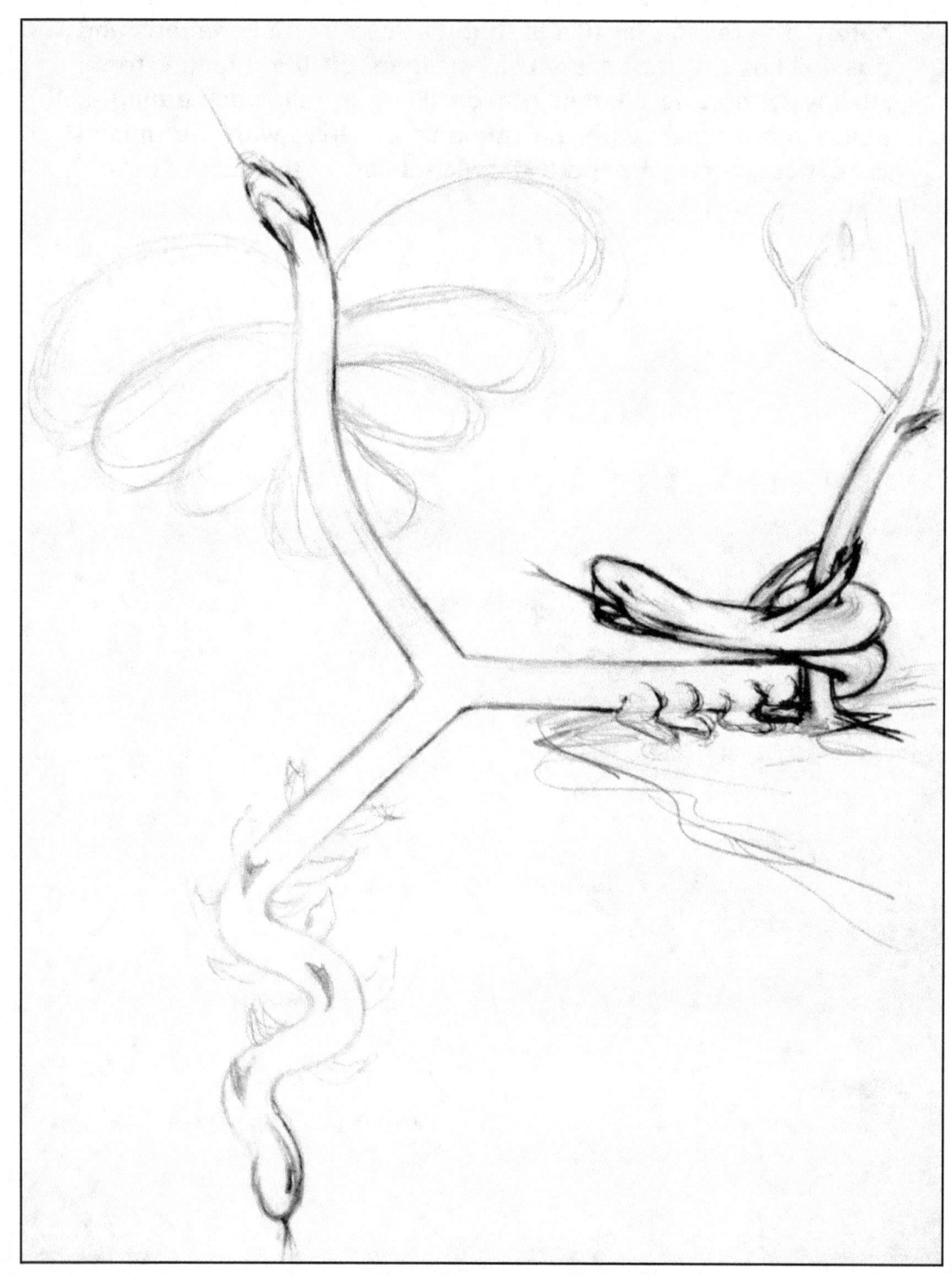

An idea on evolution

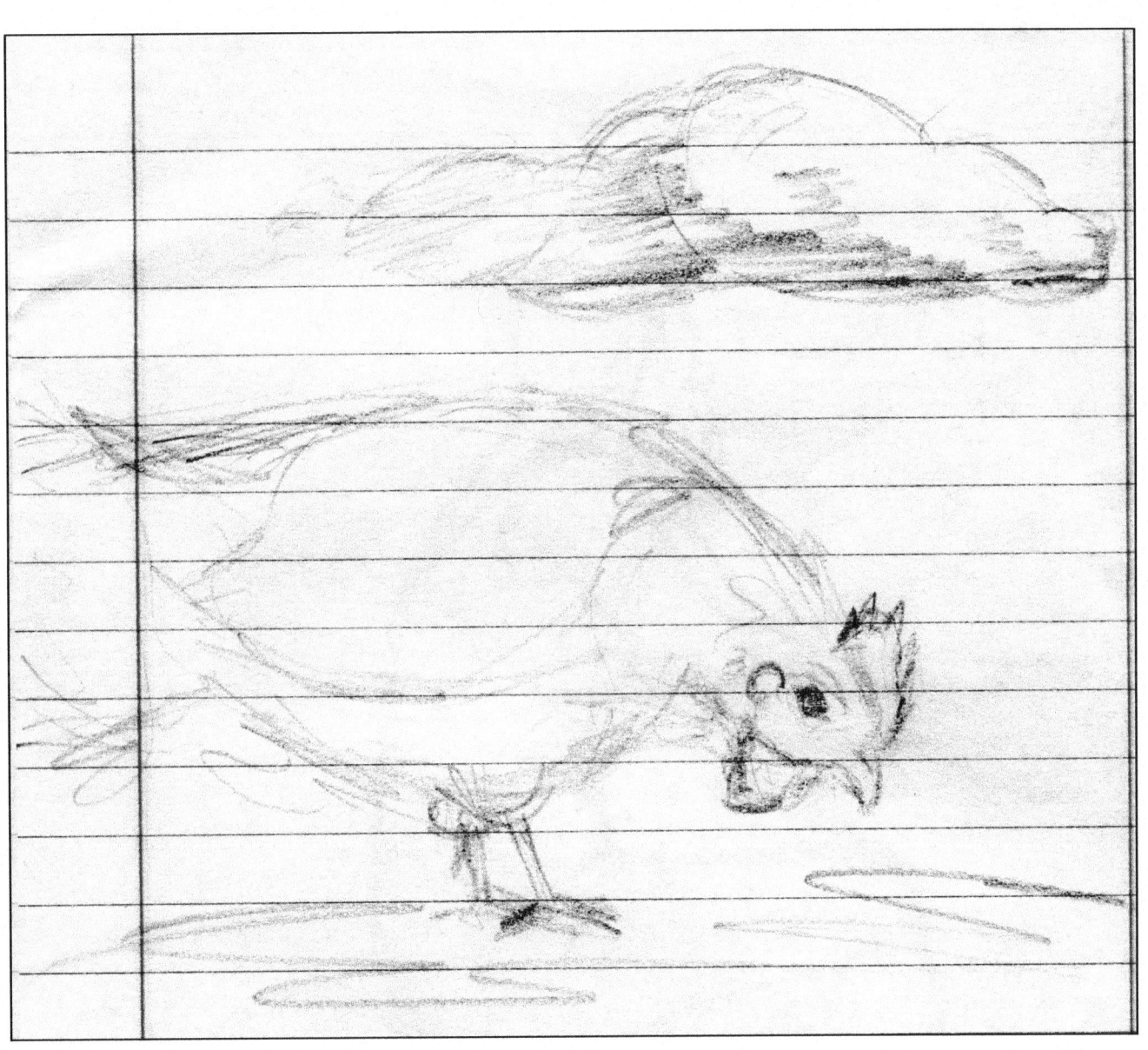

When I was in grade 2, I realized I could draw more than everybody in the class. I drew a hen and chicks from our textbook. The teacher came to my desk to check and, then, declared, "Yeah, he traced it!"

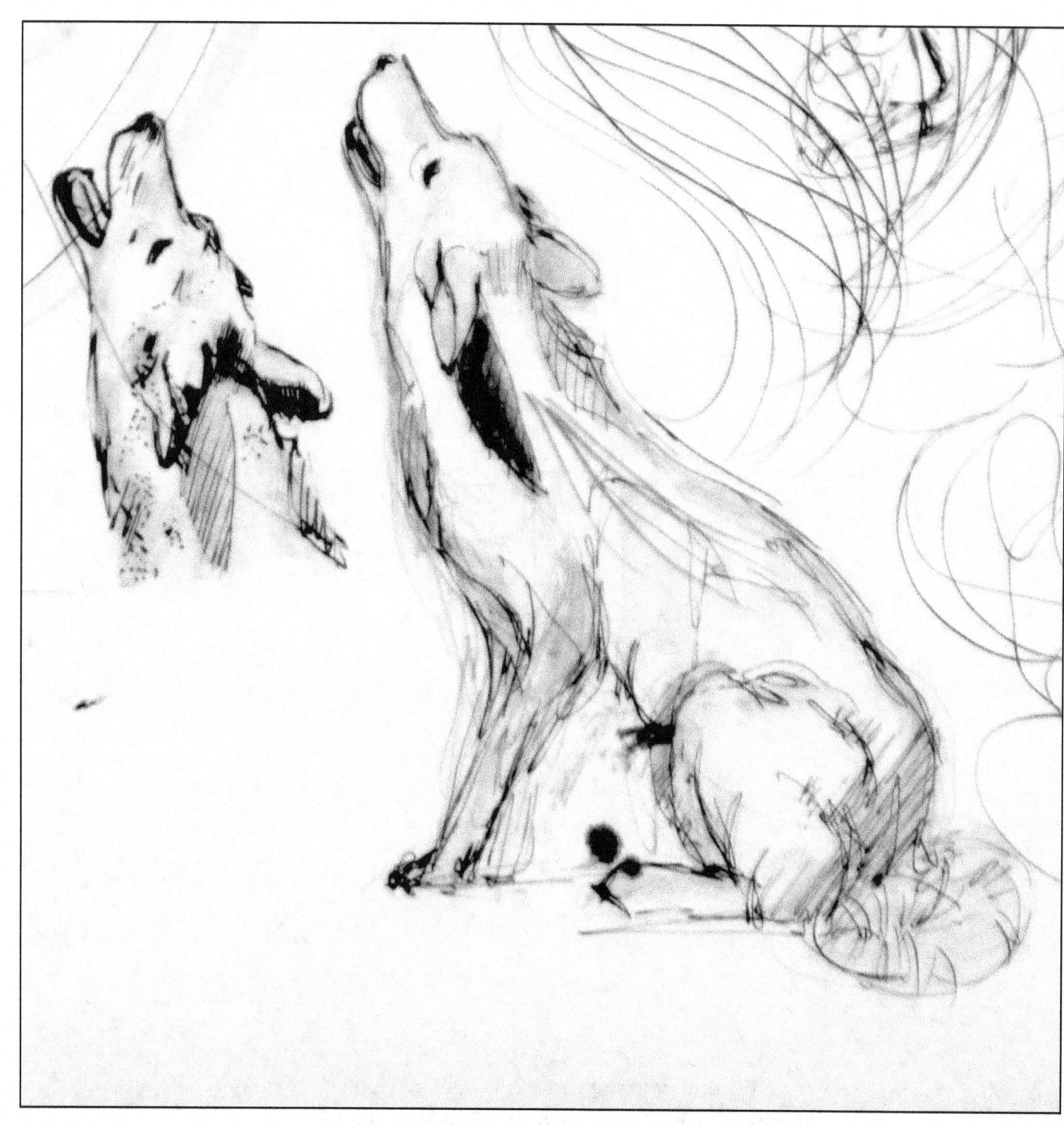

After my newly-discovered talent, because paper was scarce, I got in trouble at home for drawing the wolf on the walls of the house.

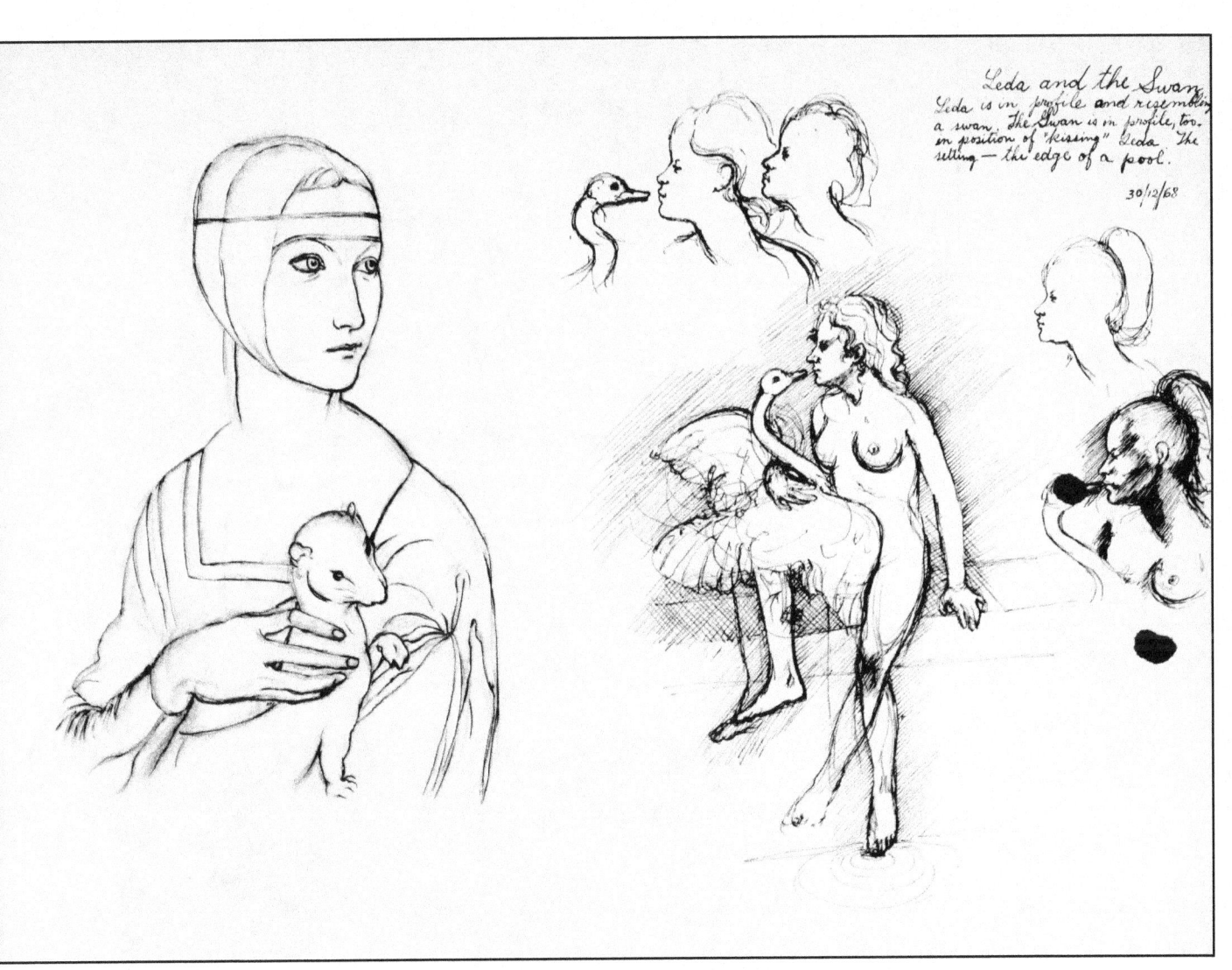

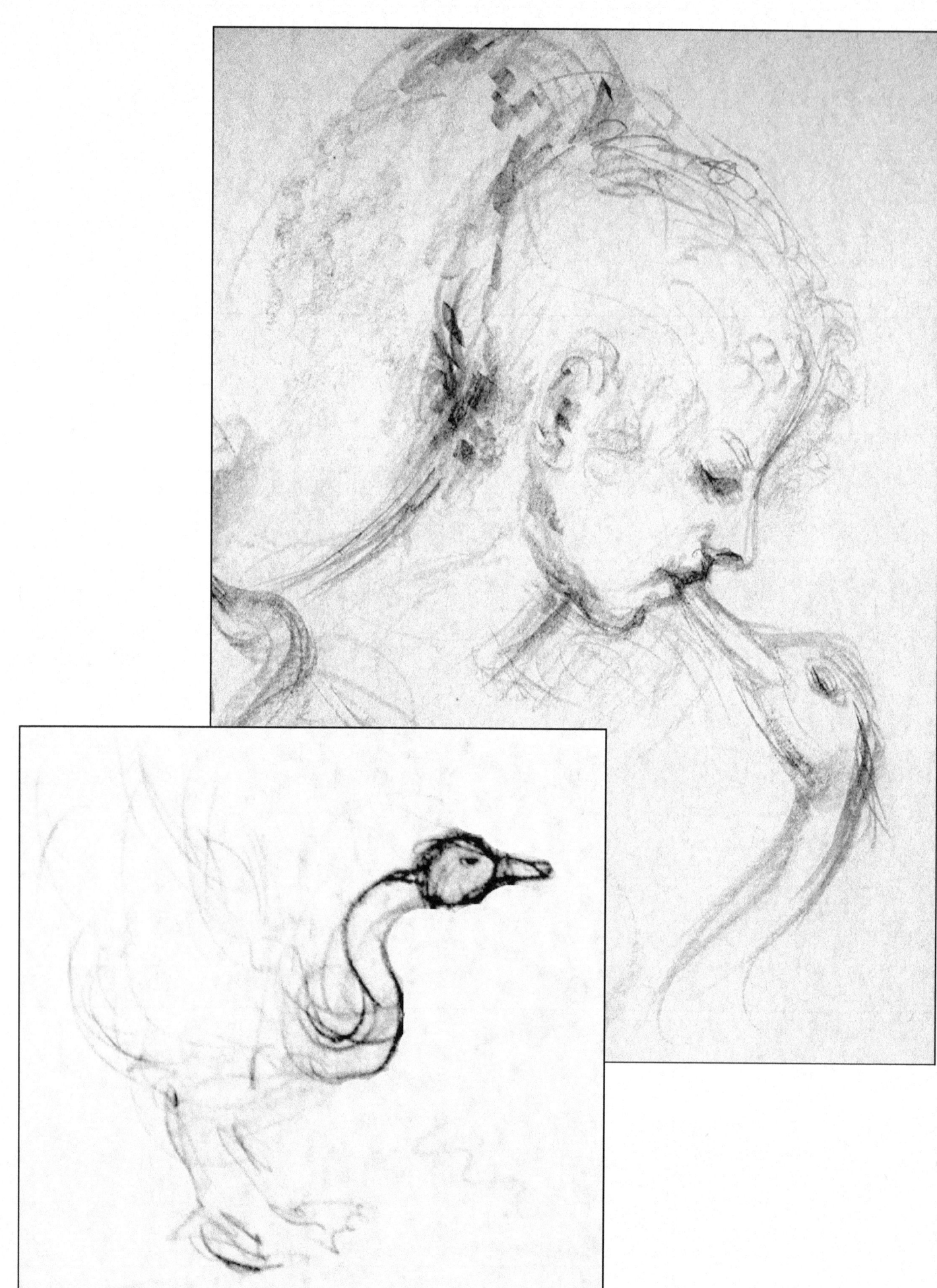

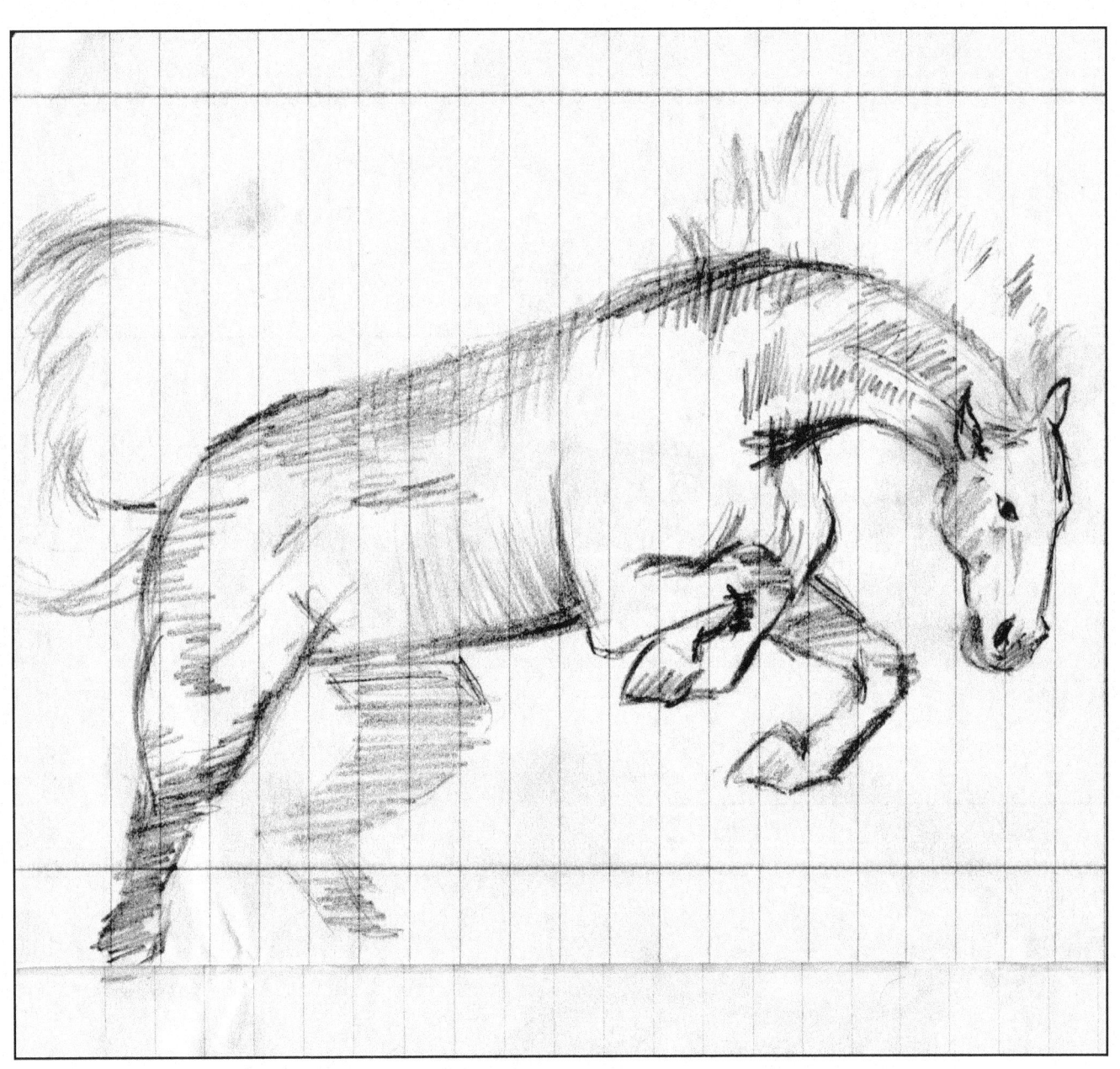

Because of my love for Westerns, I was drawing the horse before Leonardo's horse.

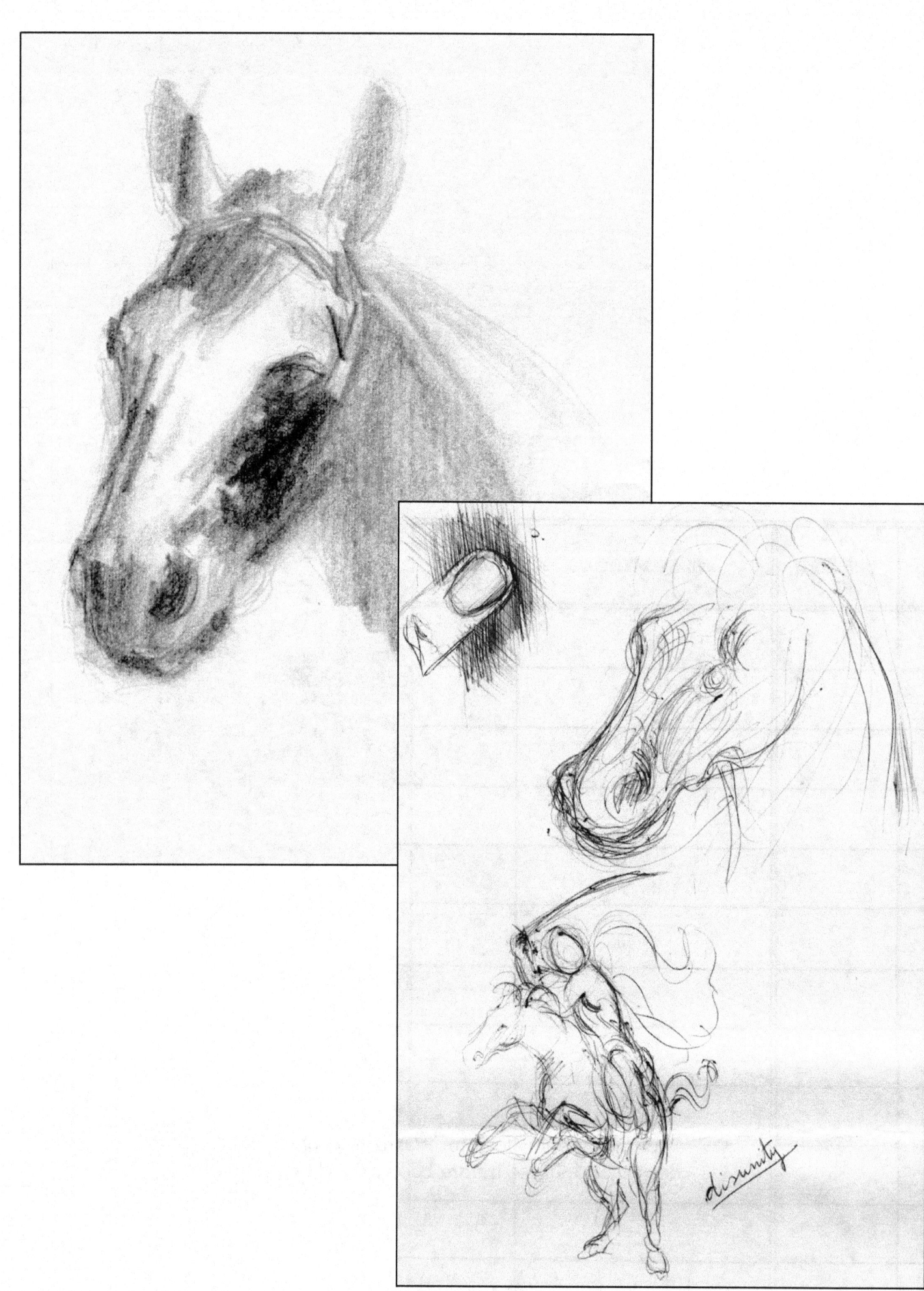

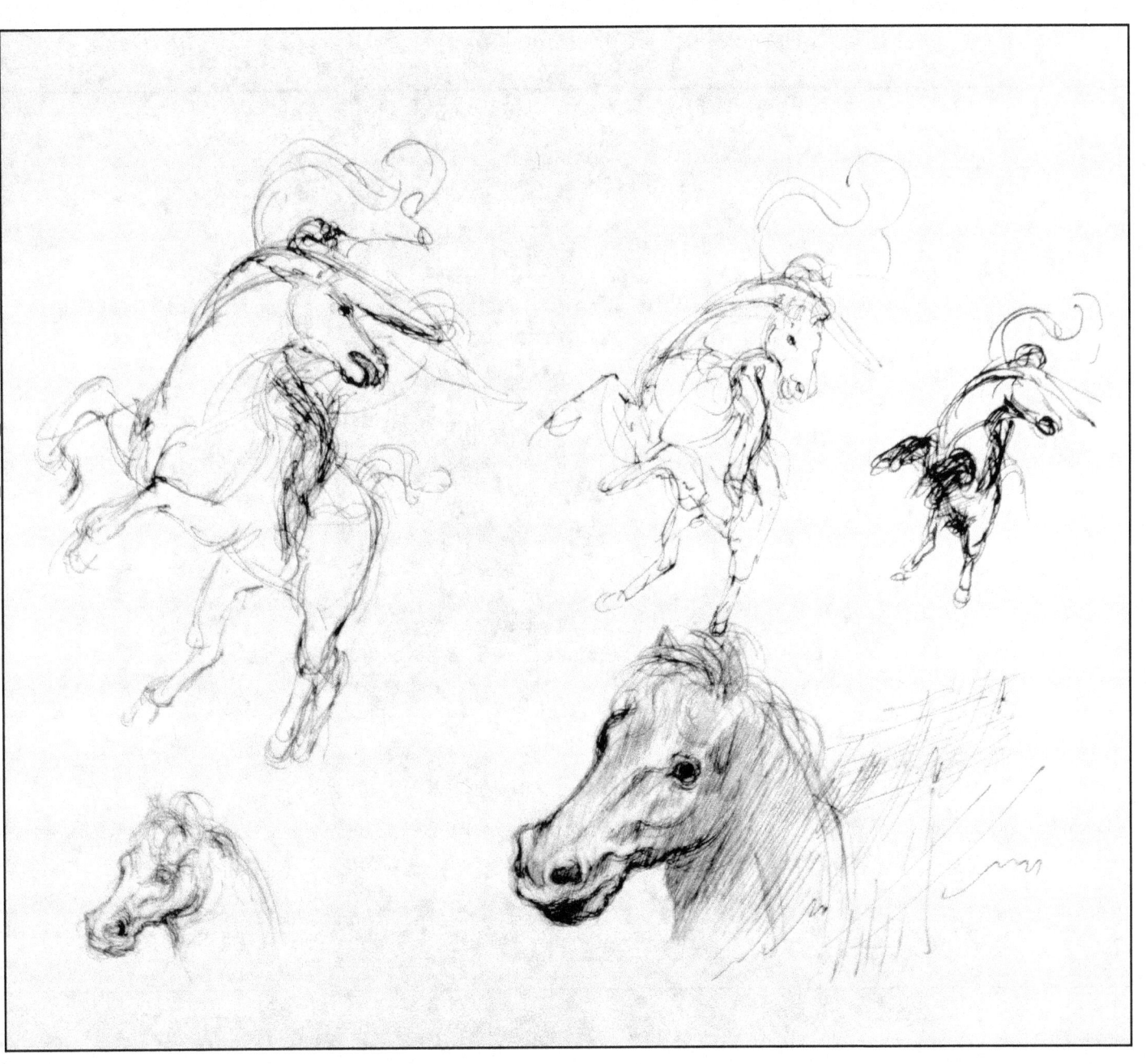

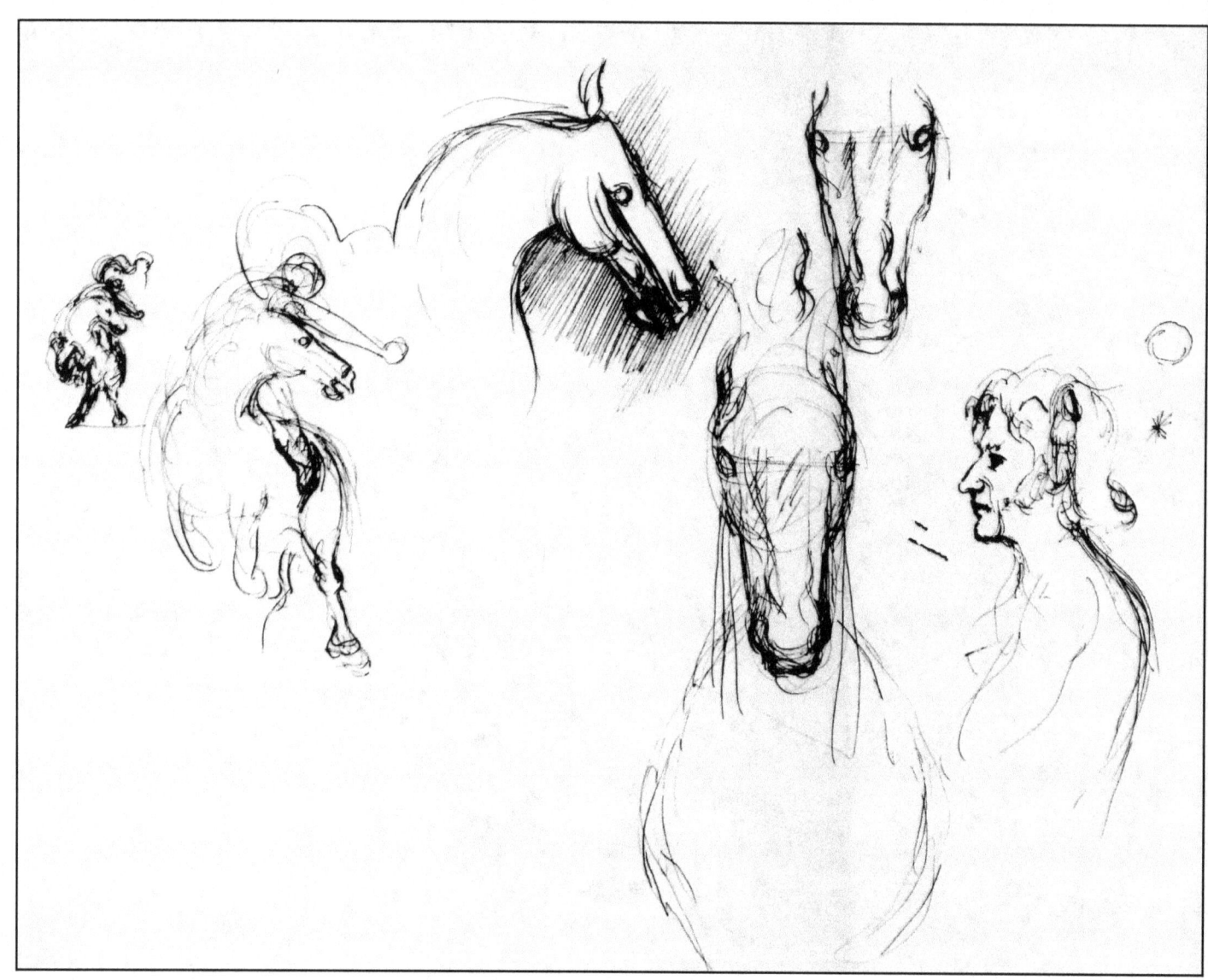

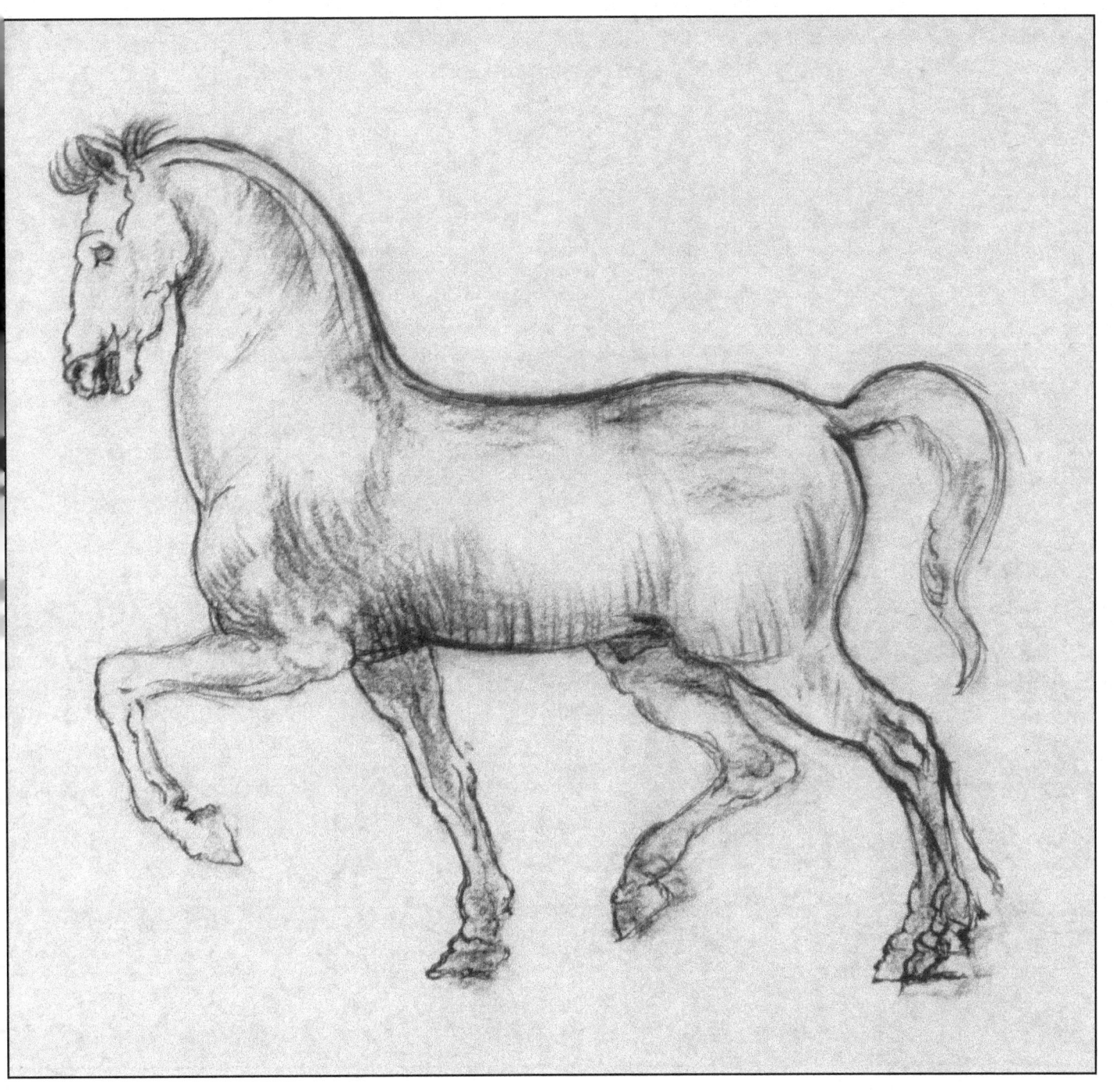

From Picture

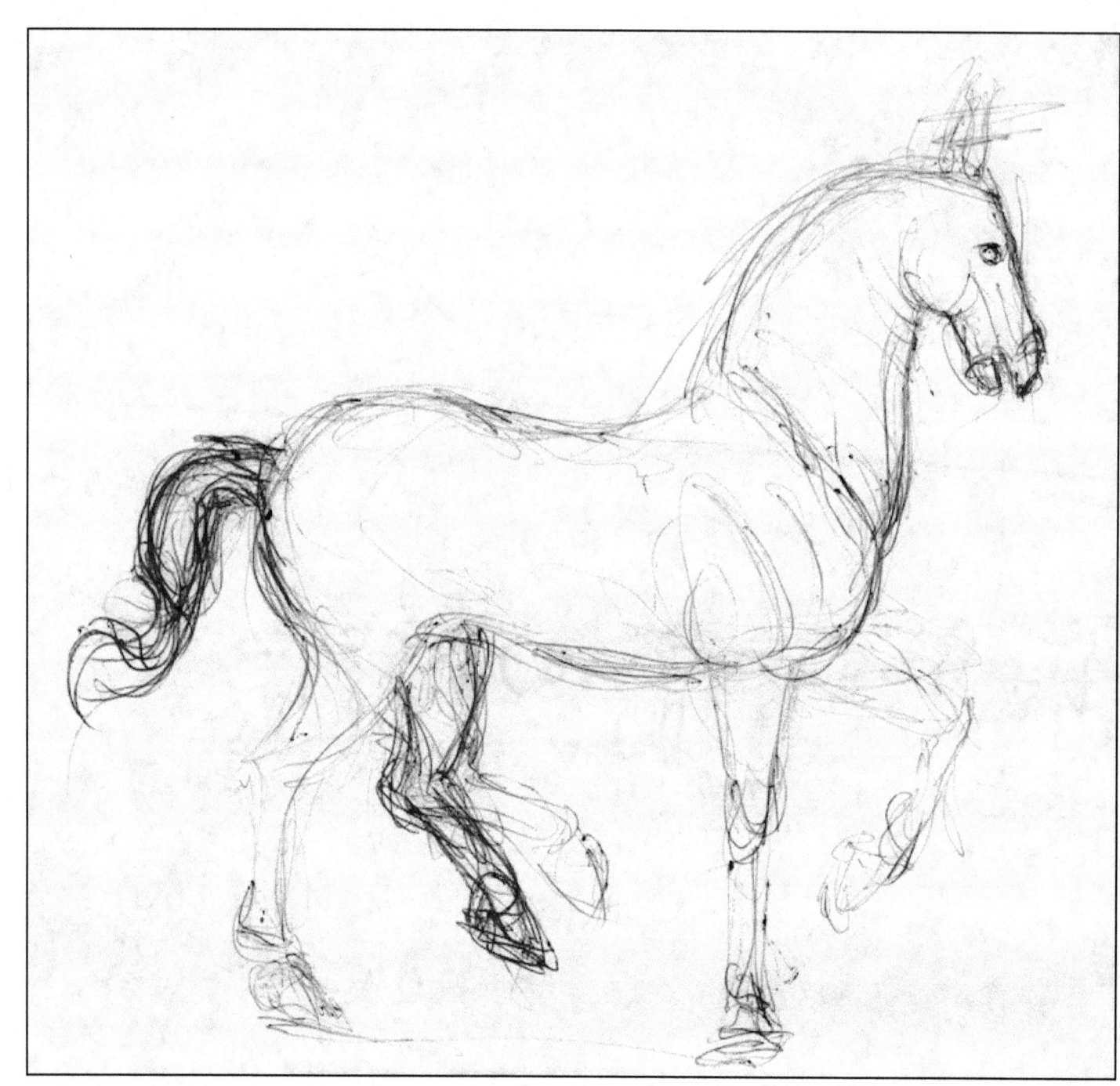

From Memory

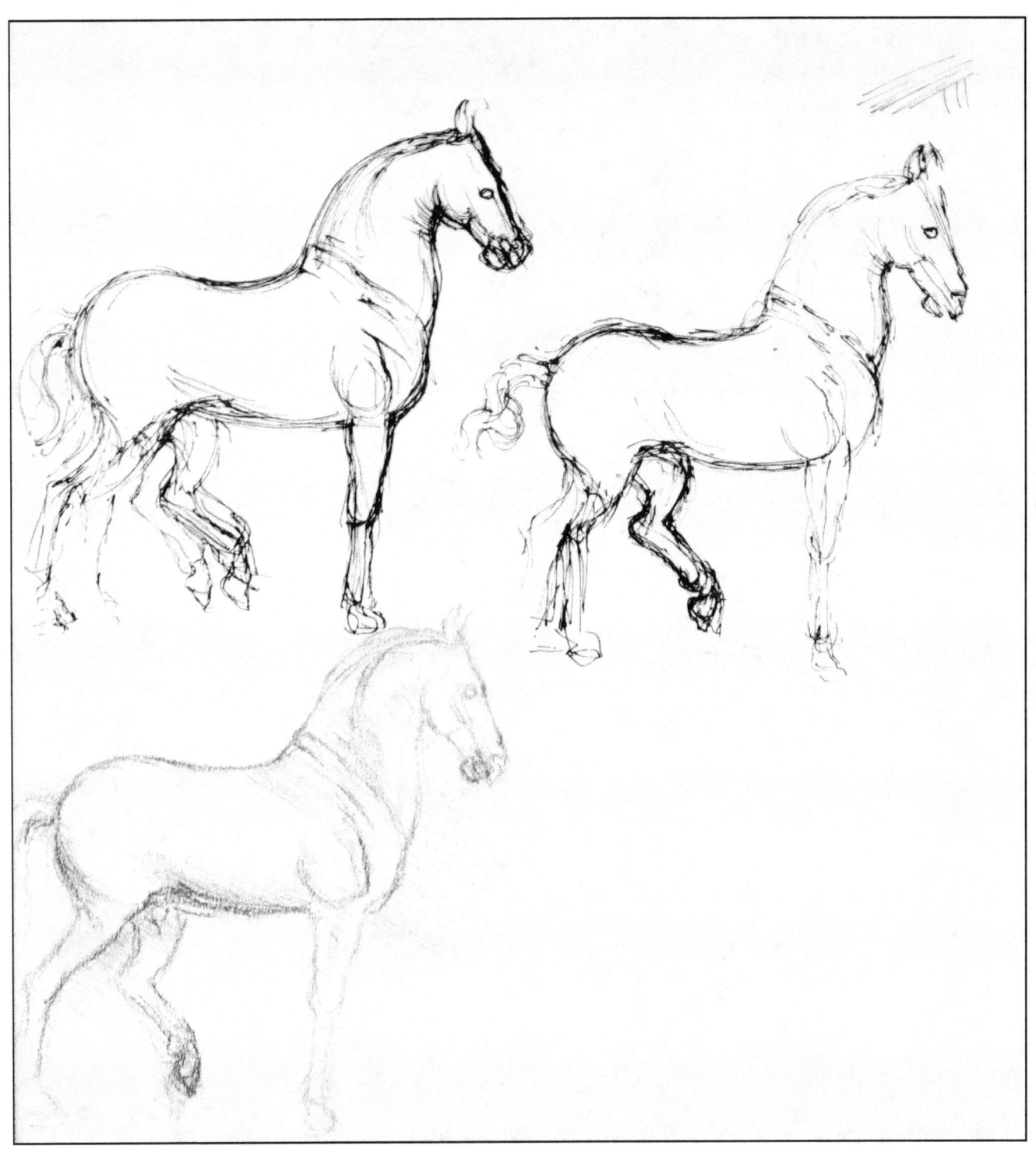

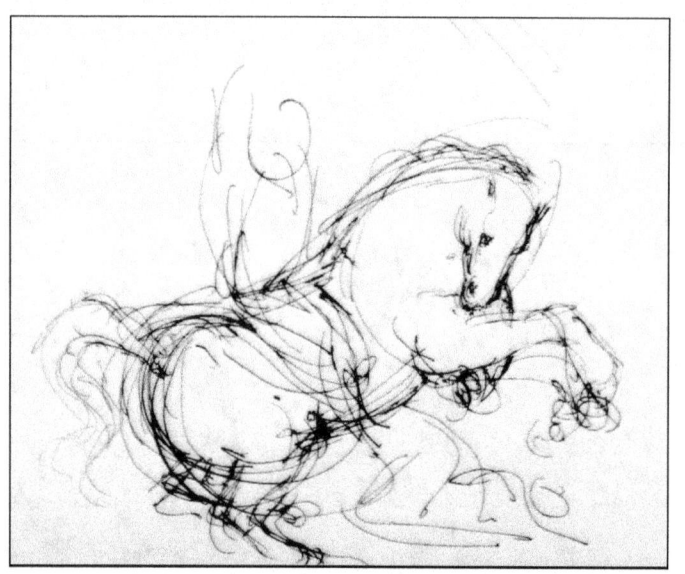

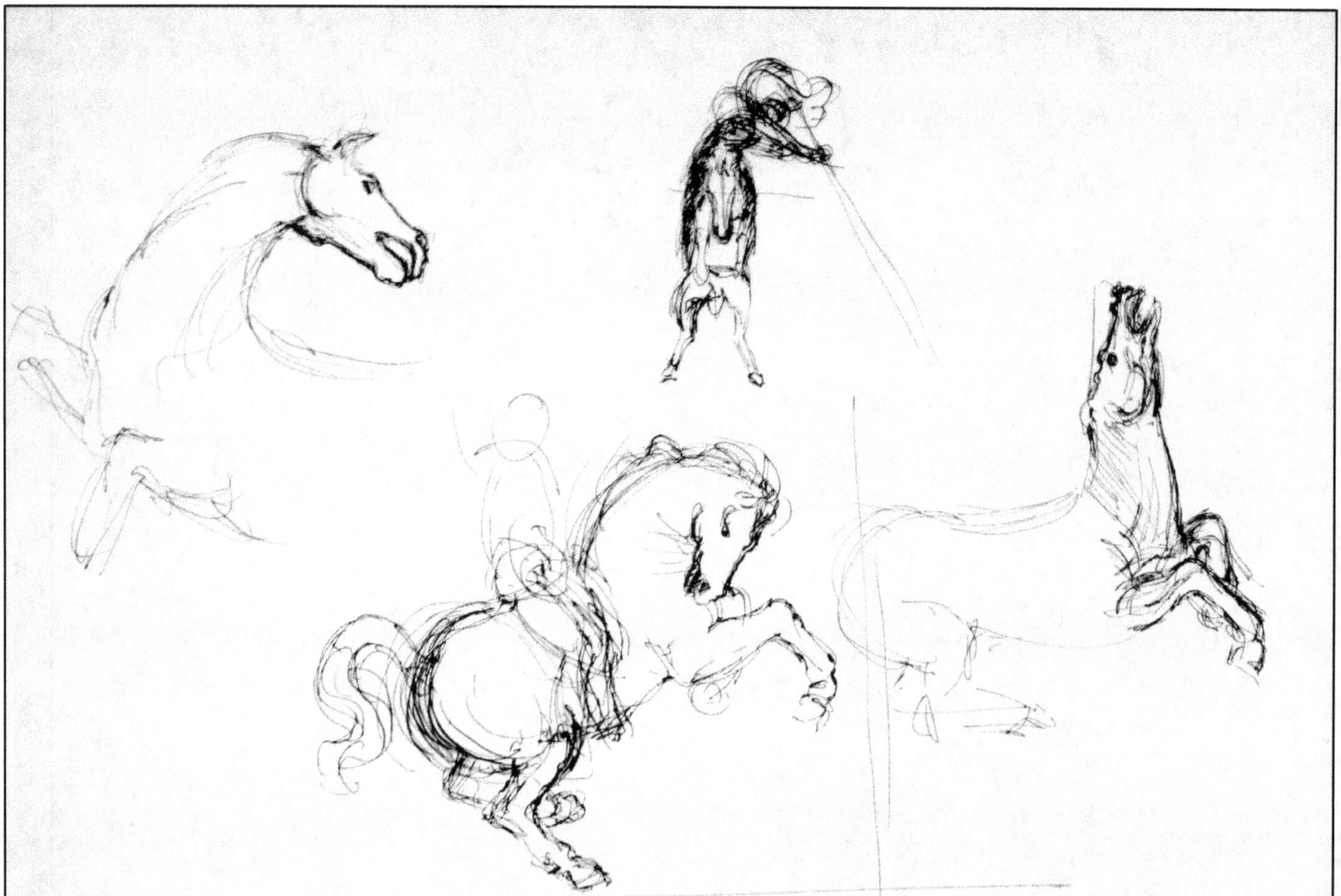

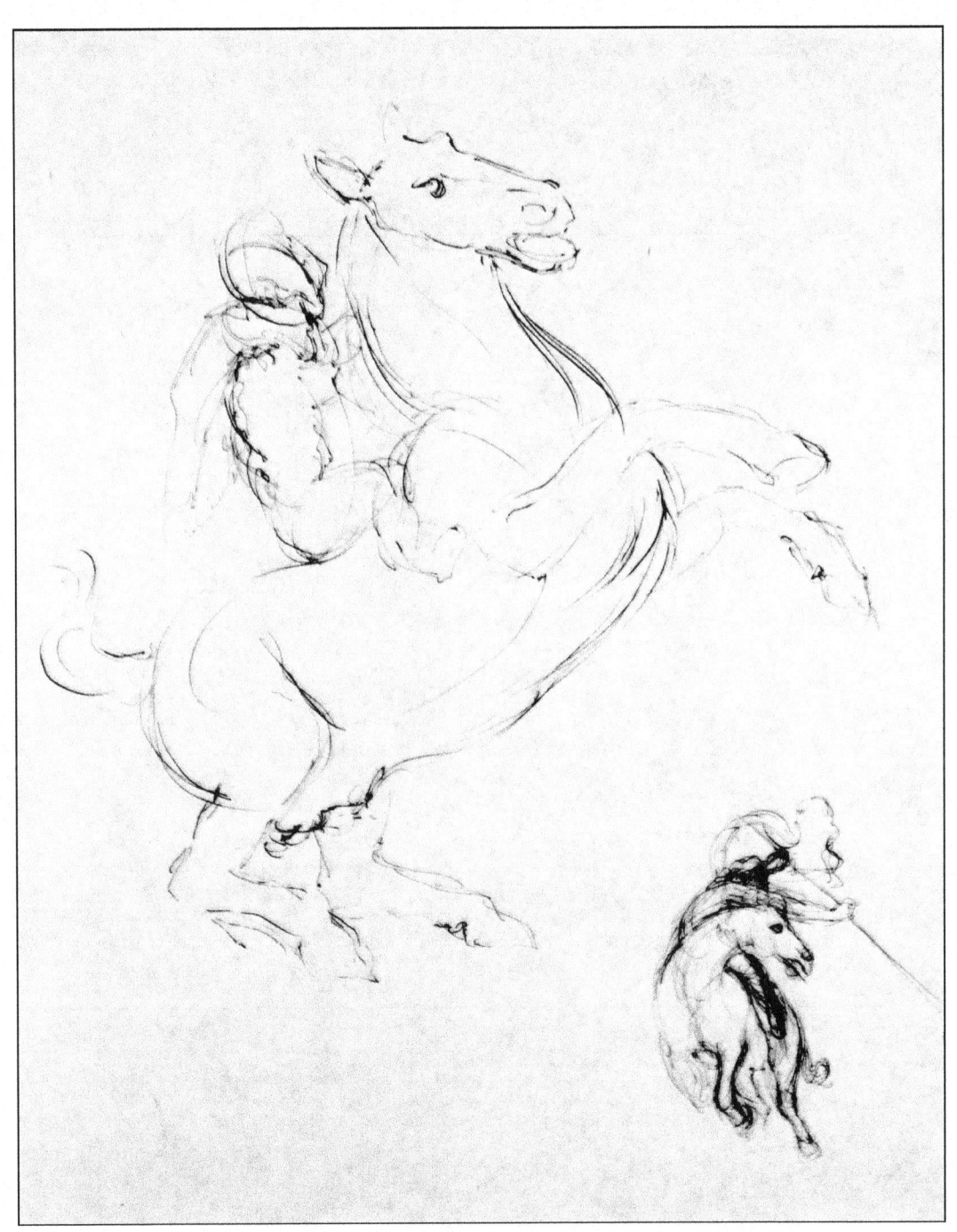

The Horse and Rider, at the top, is from a bronze statuette from Leonardo's Workshop.

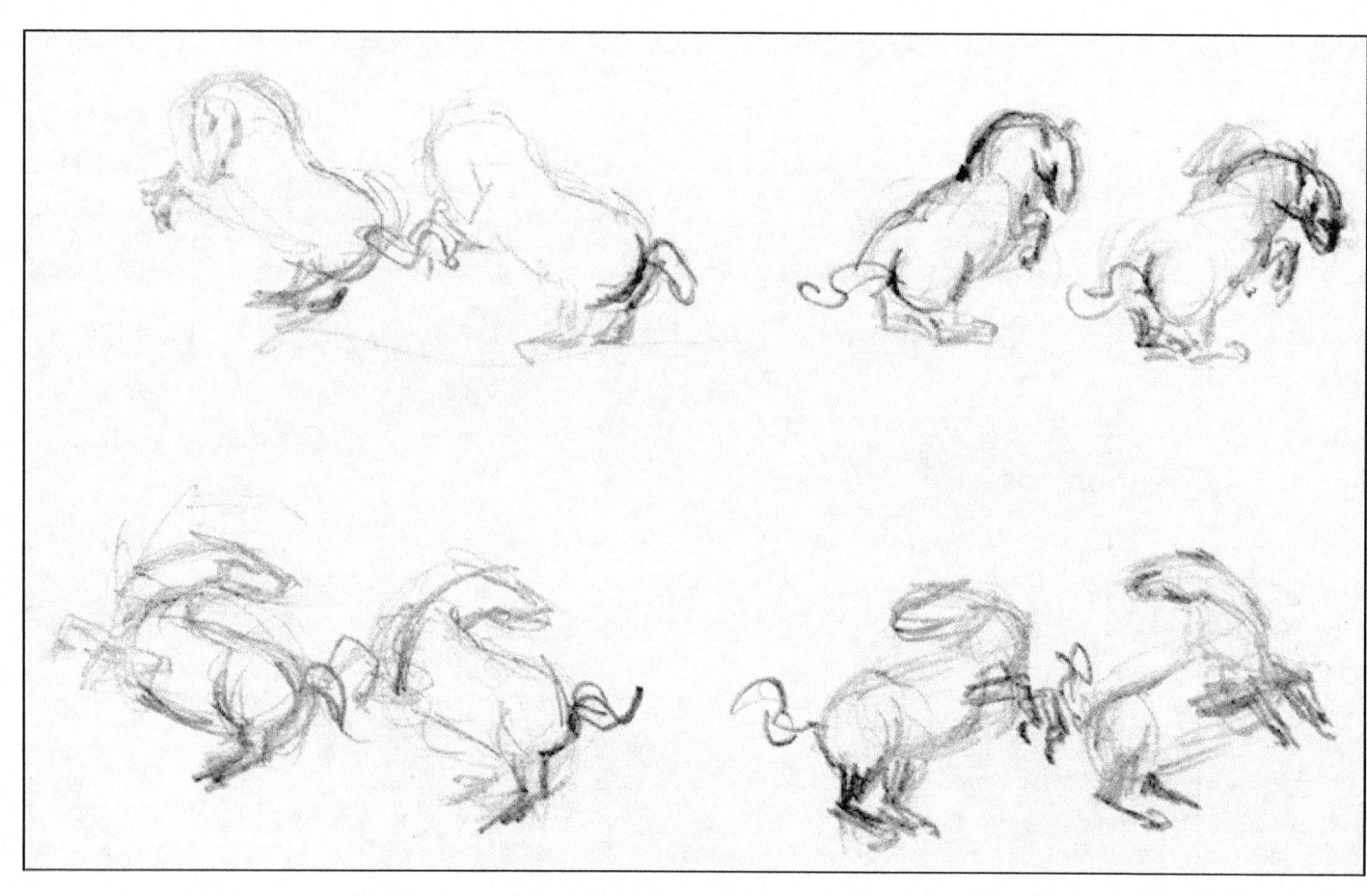

HUMAN DEPICTION ...

Another aspect that renders the *factual, manual depiction* of forms progressively more difficult is the position or approach taken. The position or approach is from imitation, from observation, or from visualization. *From imitation* means that we use pictures. *From observation* means that we have to reduce the 3-D world we see to a virtual 3-D image. And, *from visualization* means that we use our powers of recollection and imagination.

3. Head Imitation

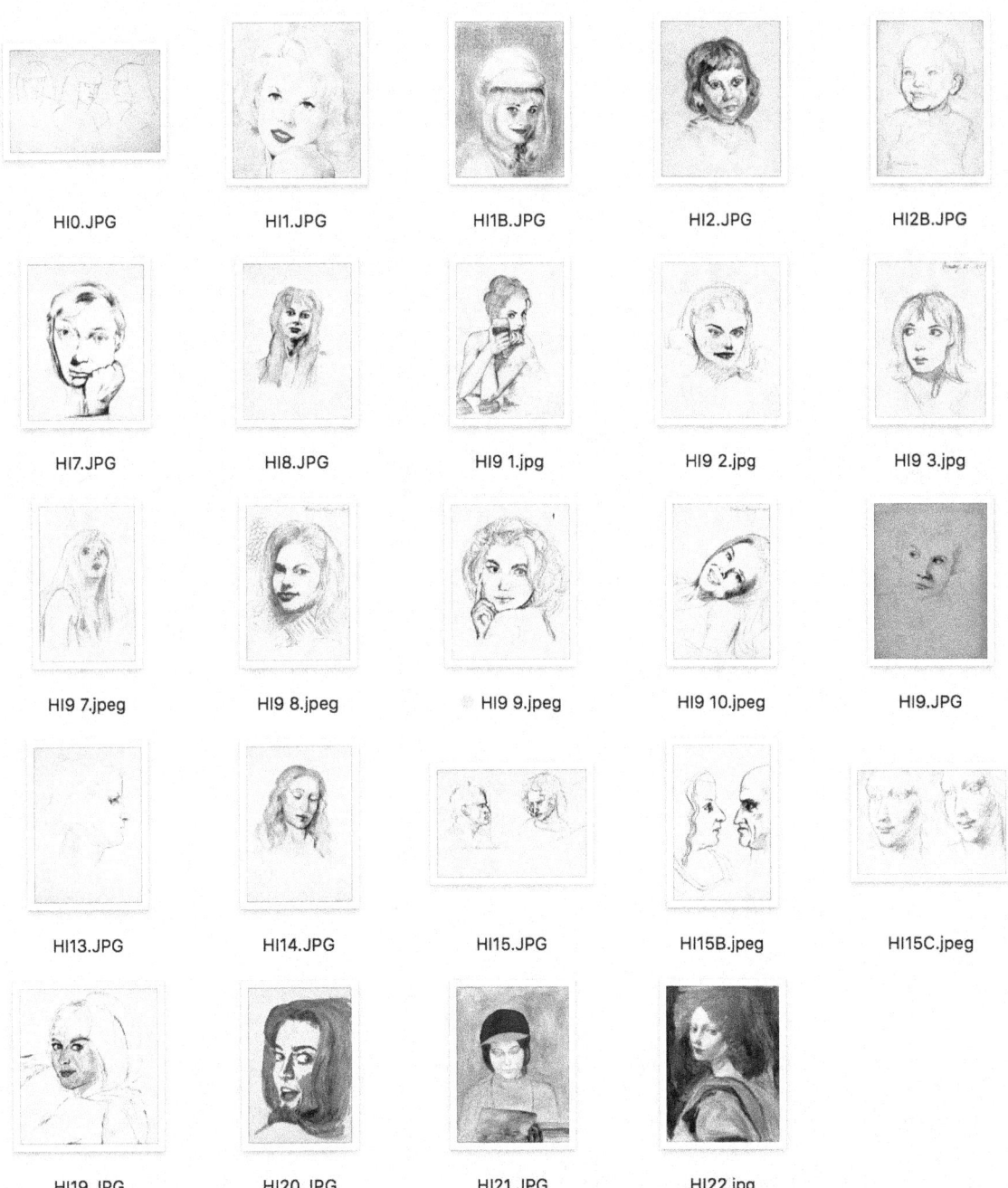

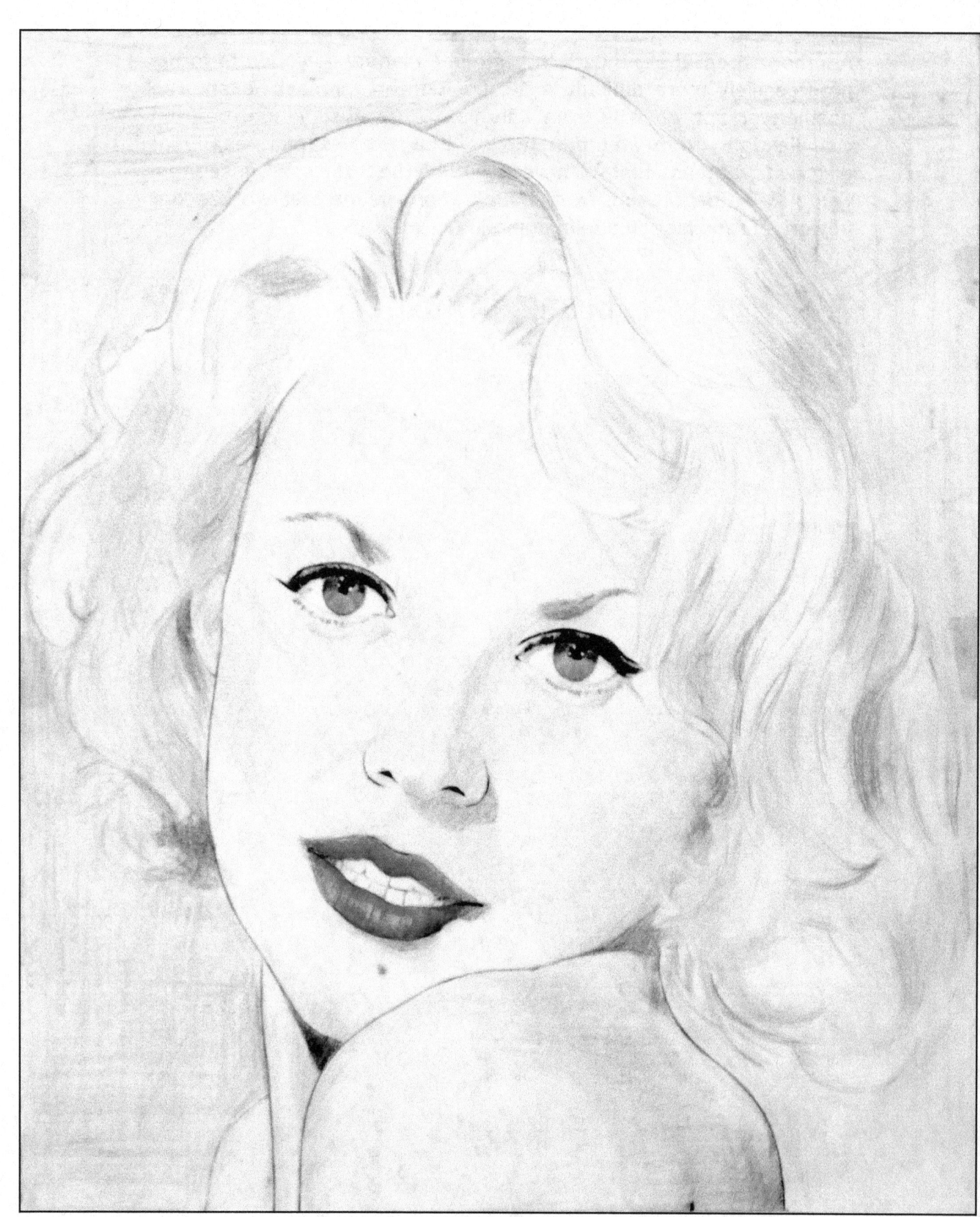

Carroll Baker as Jean Harlow, pencil painting from Italy

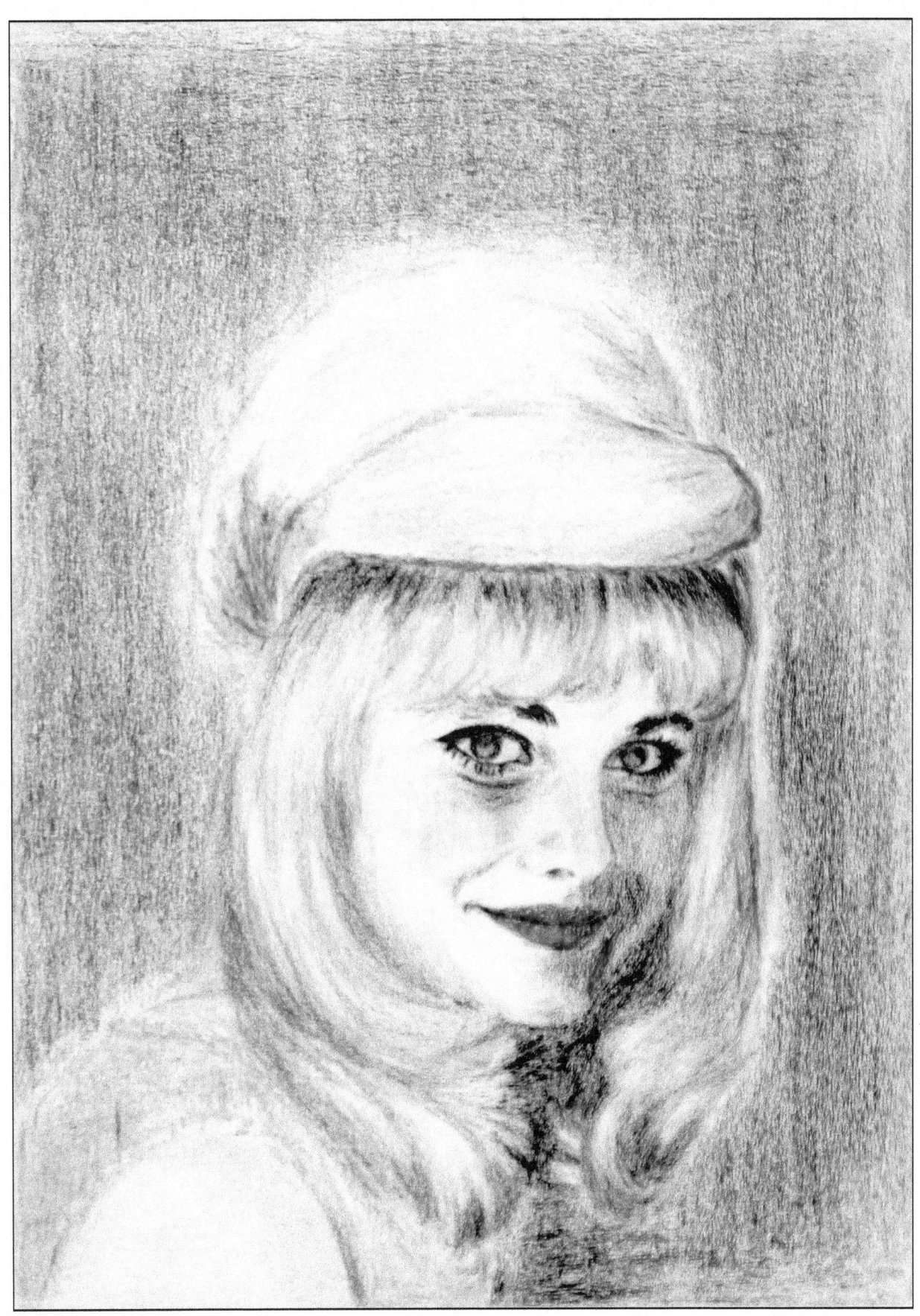

Wax Crayon

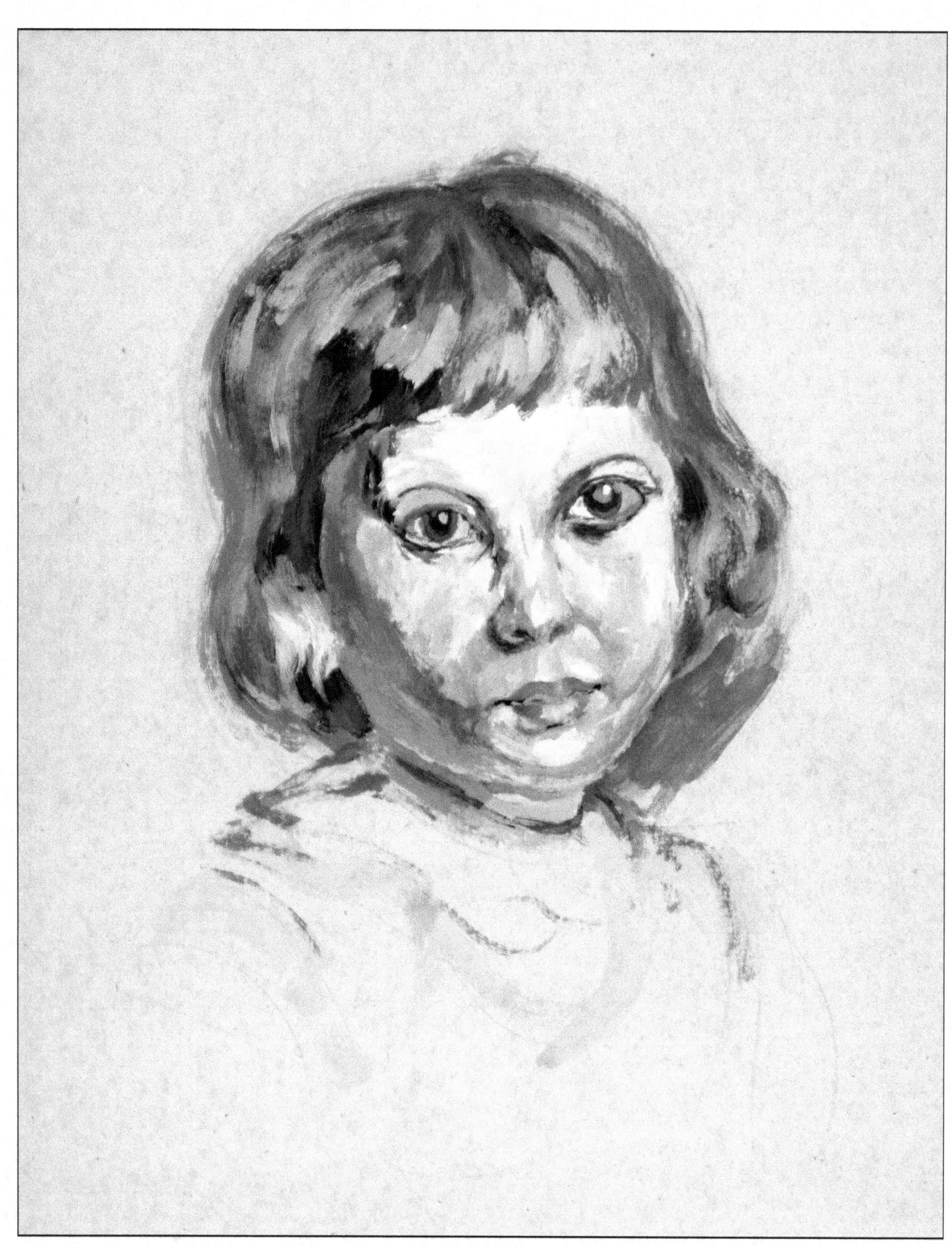

Acrylic on Cardboard

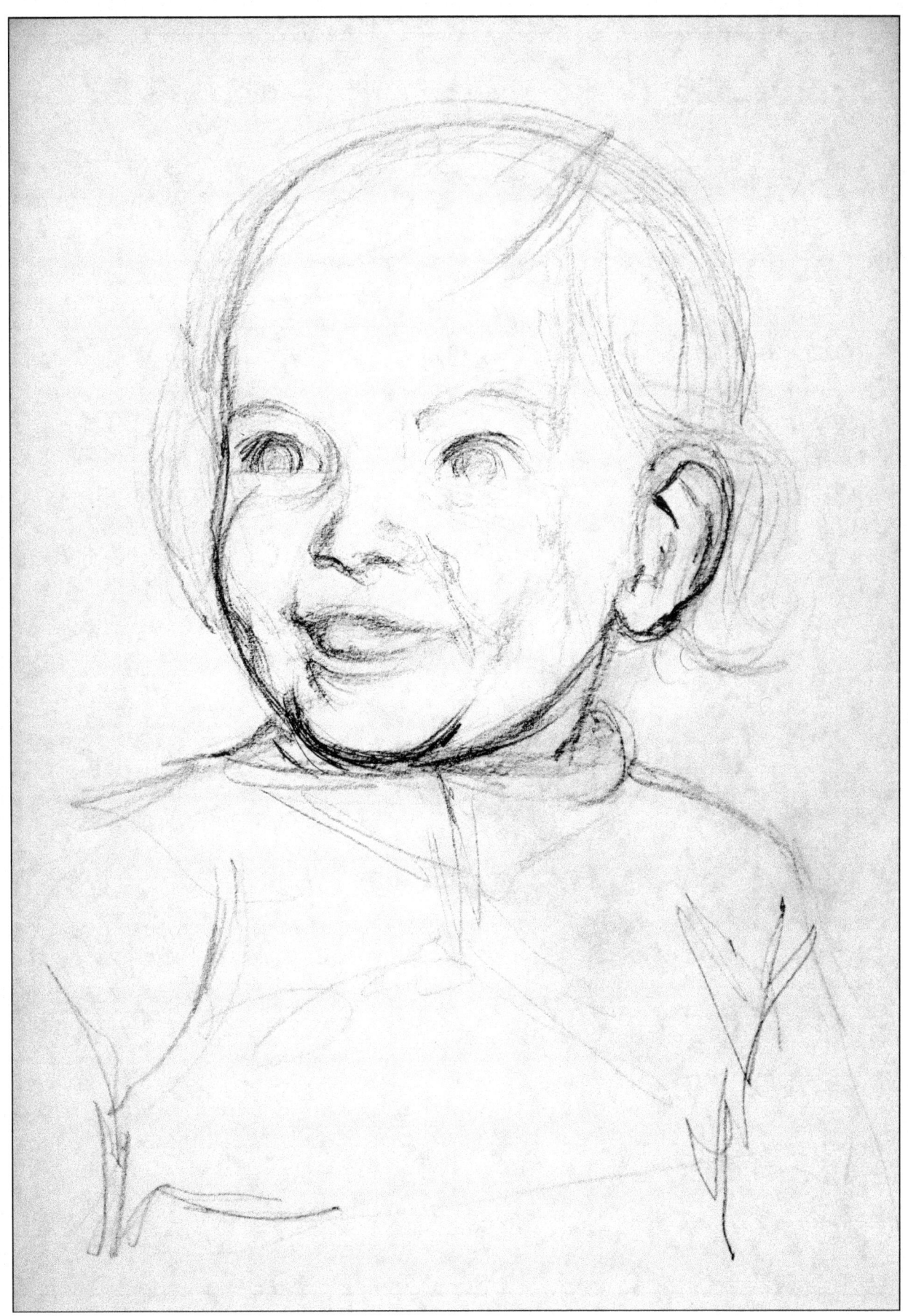

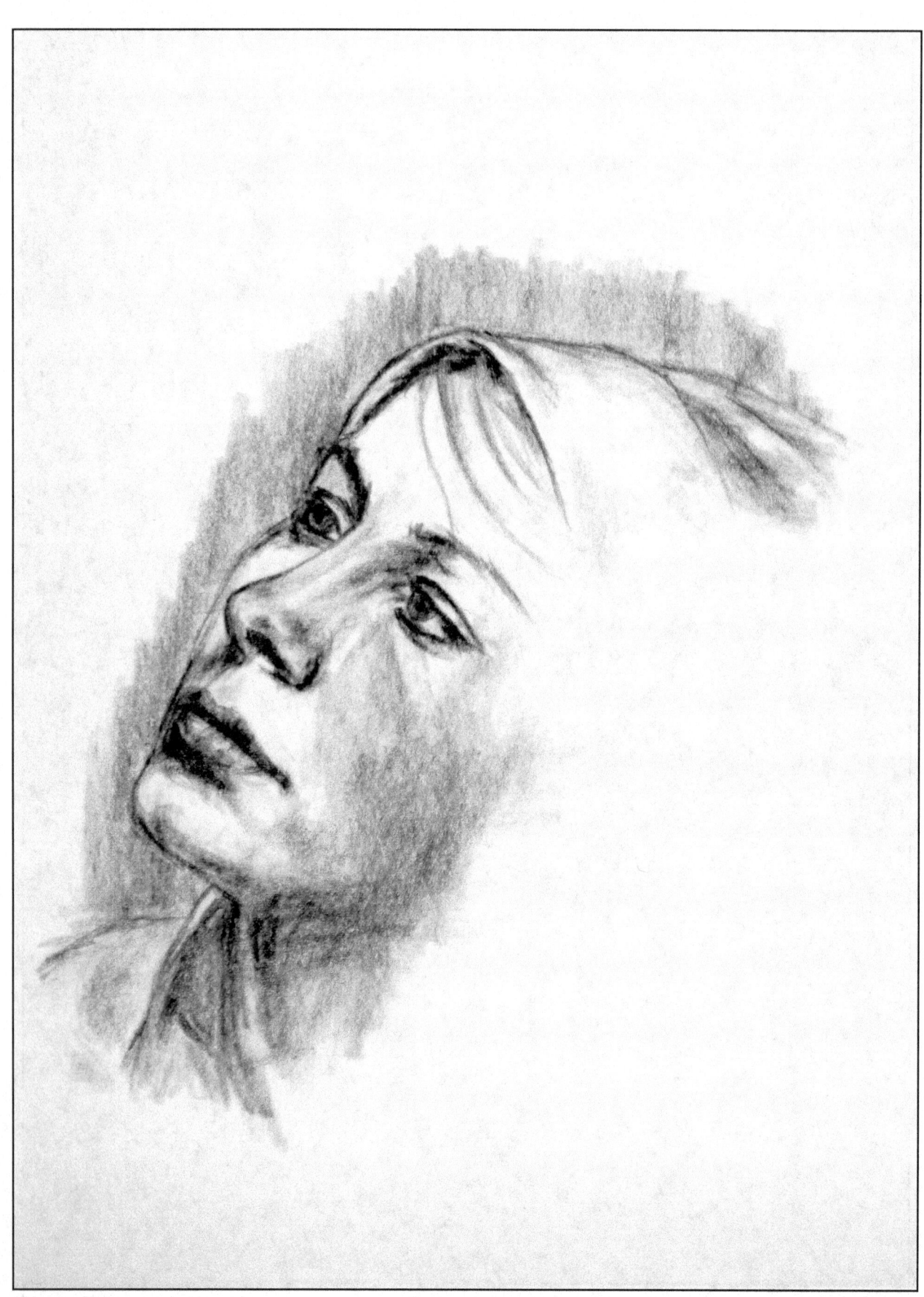

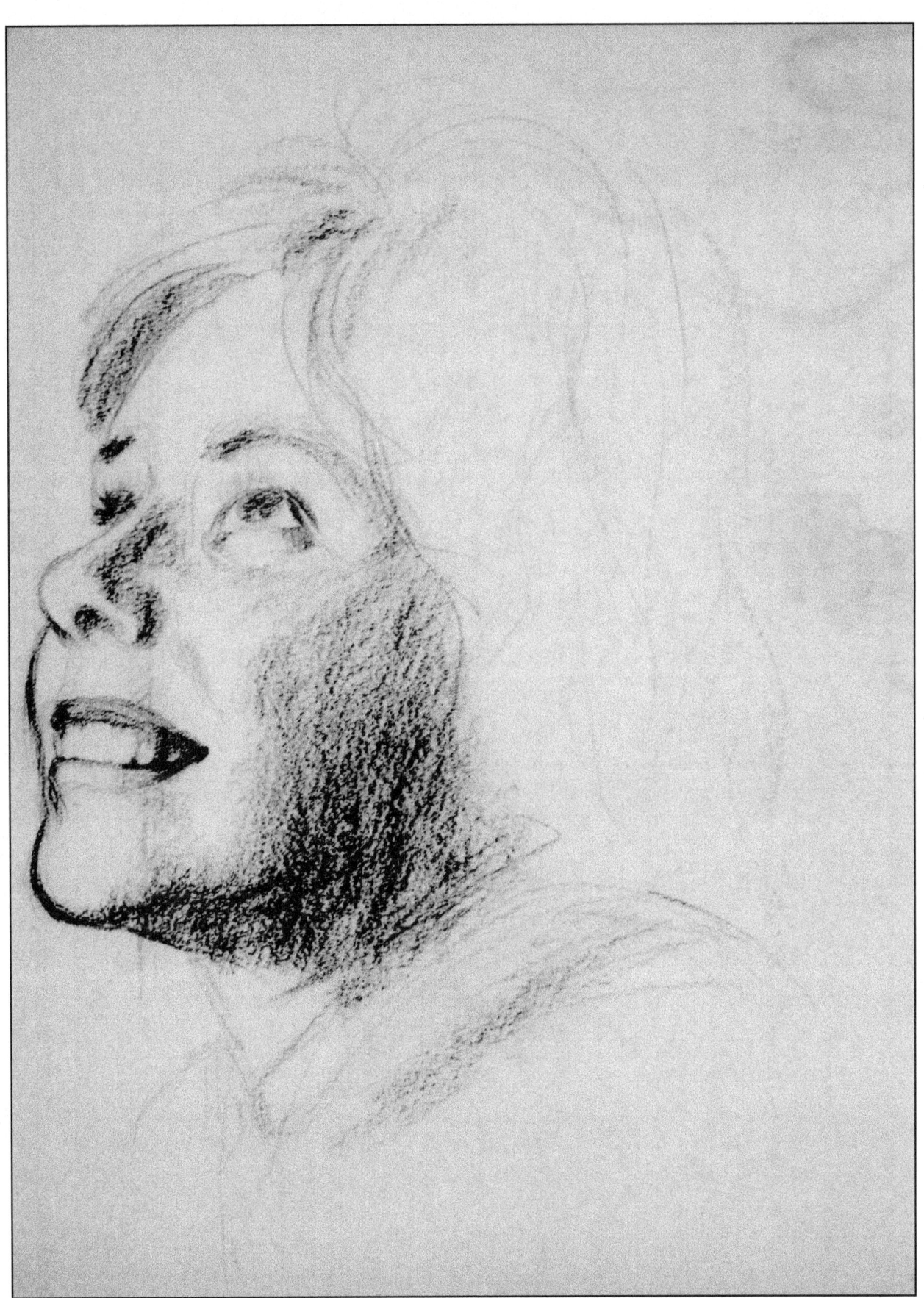

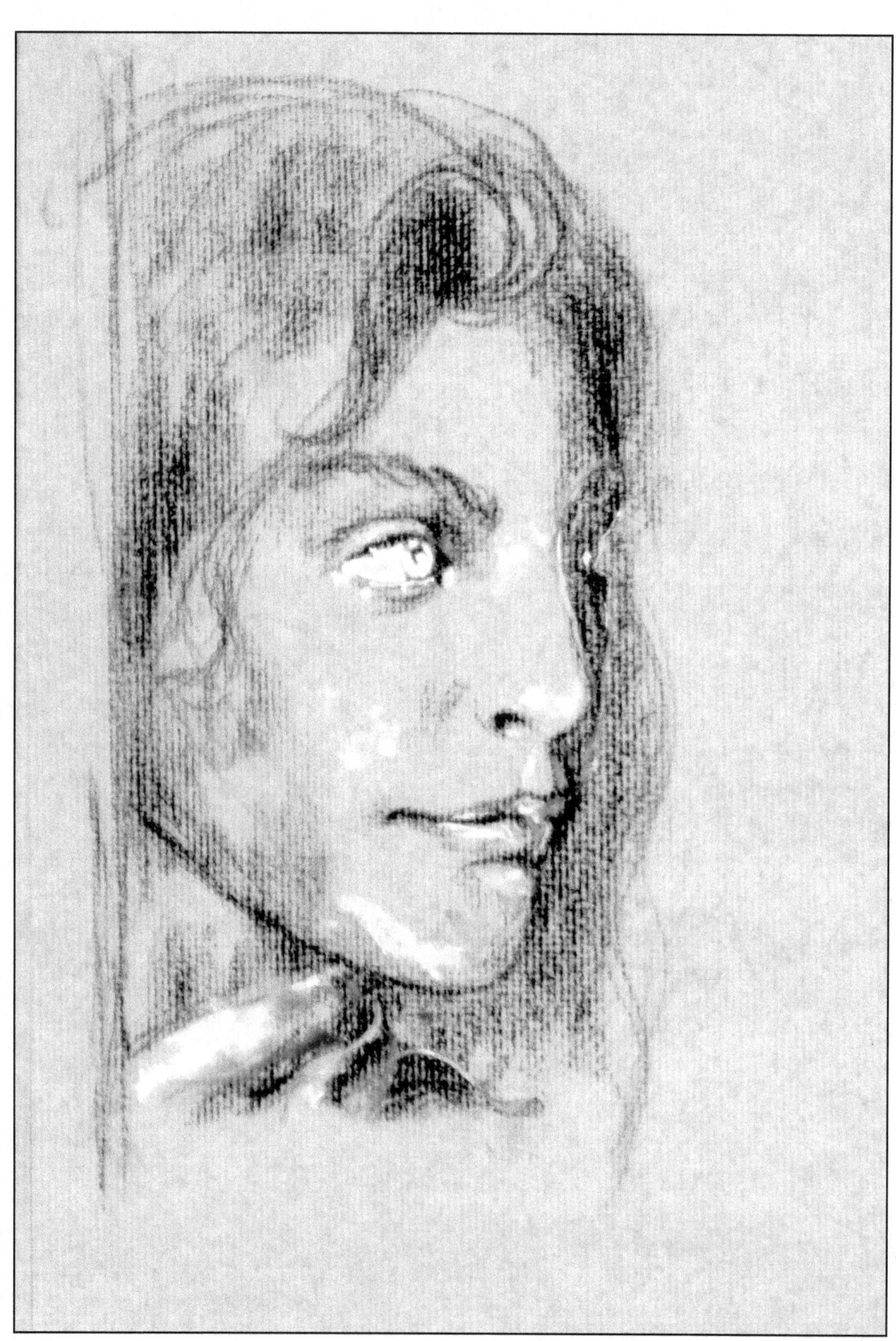

Chalk and Paint on canvas paper

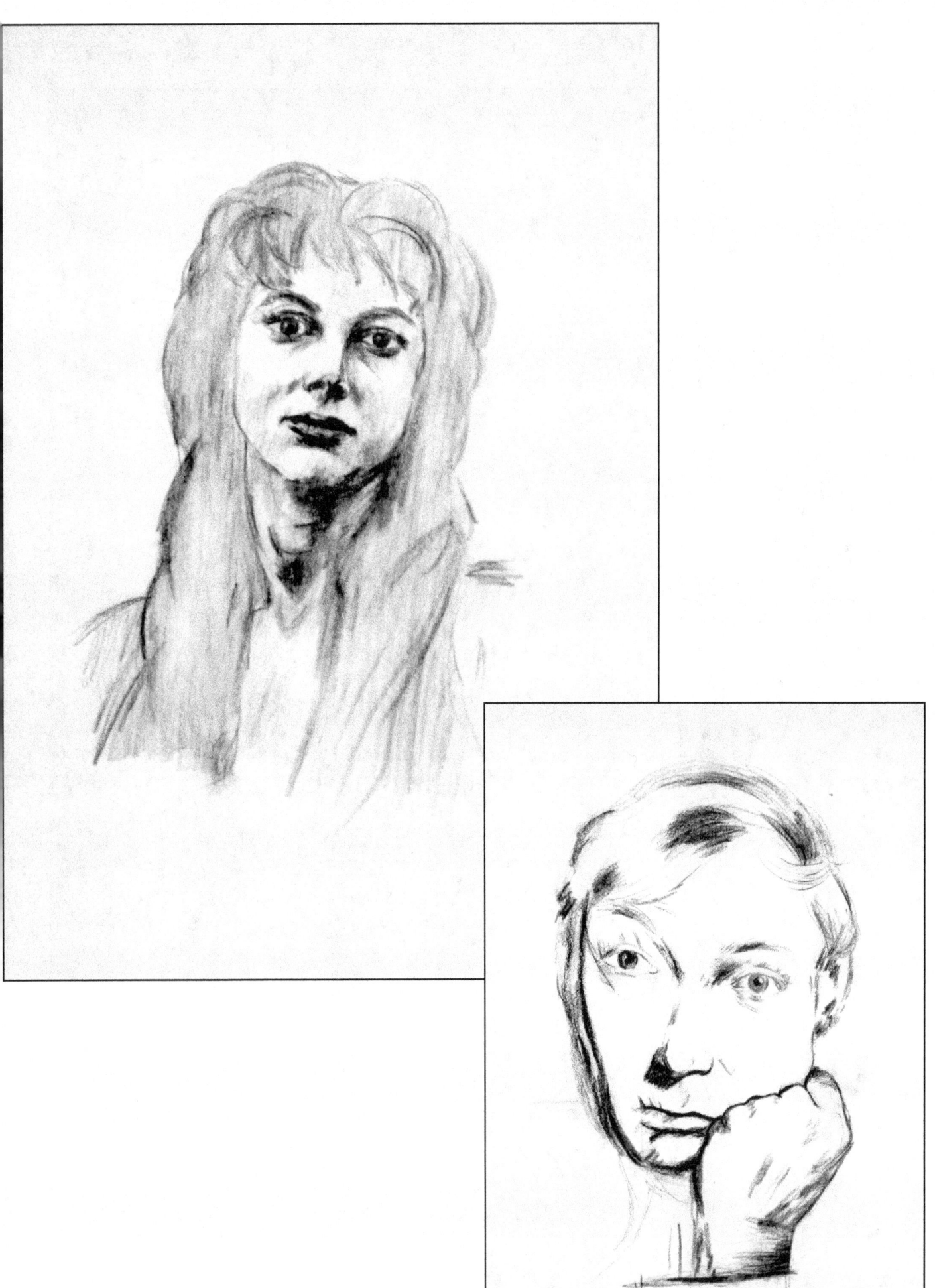

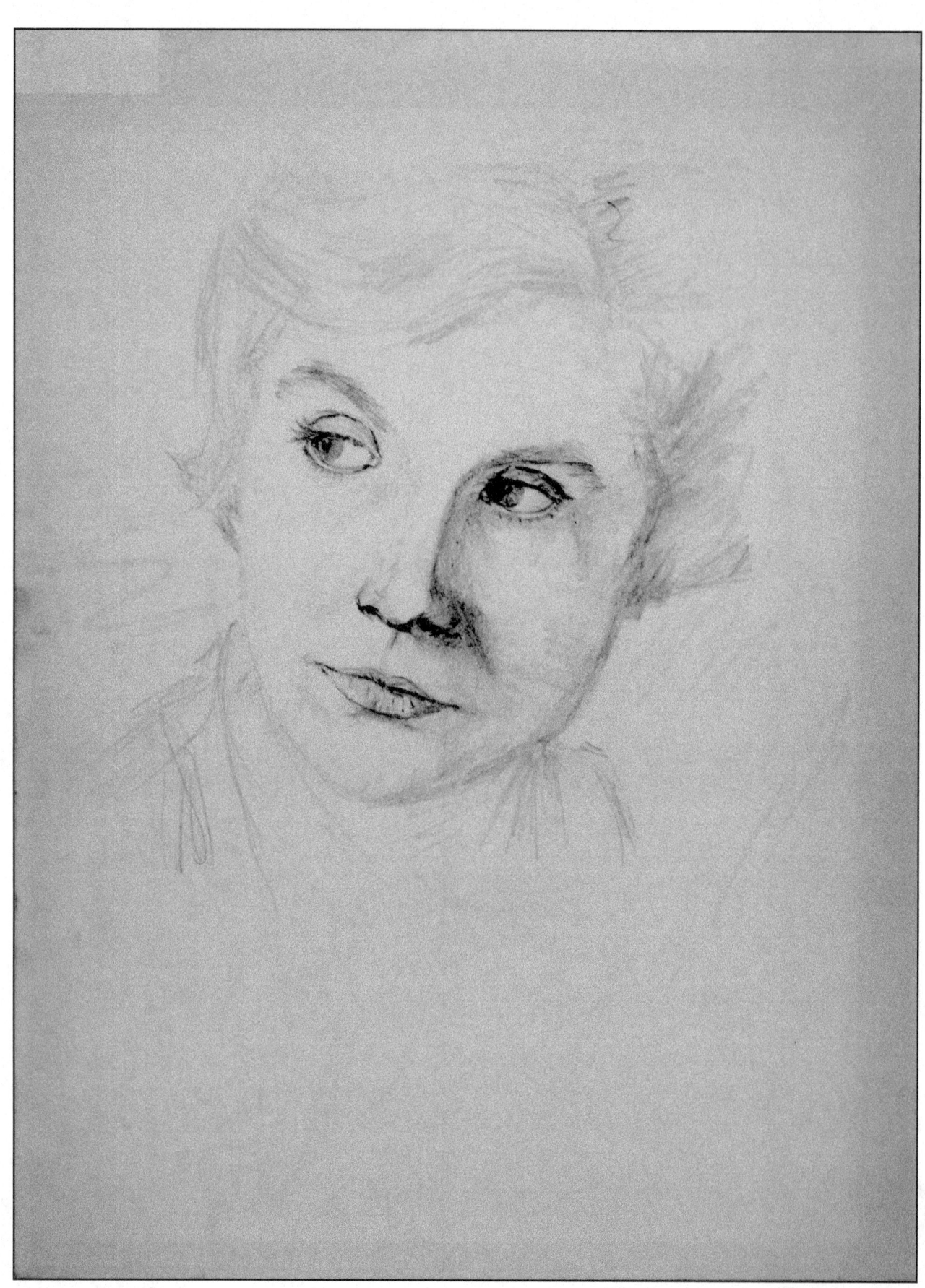

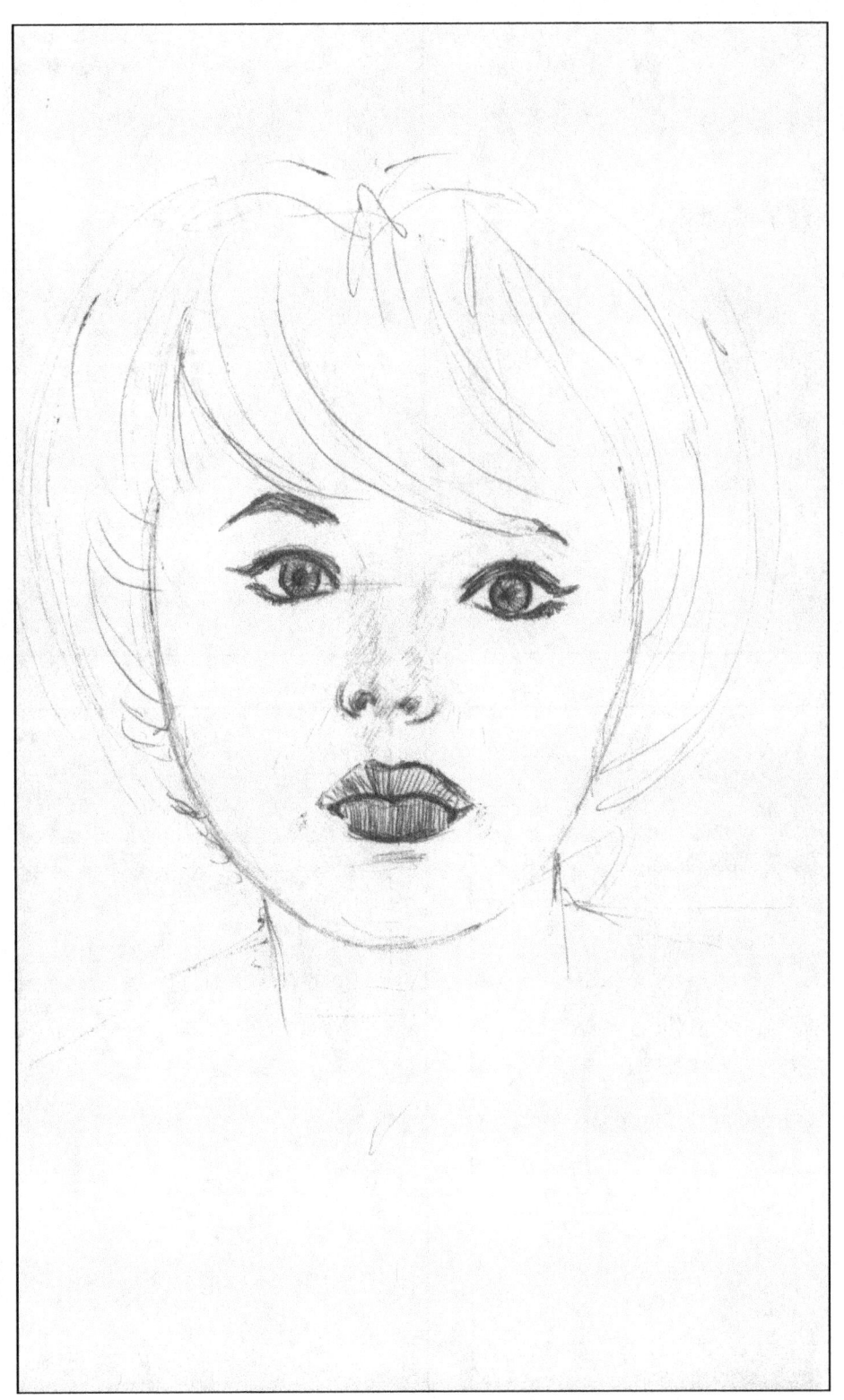

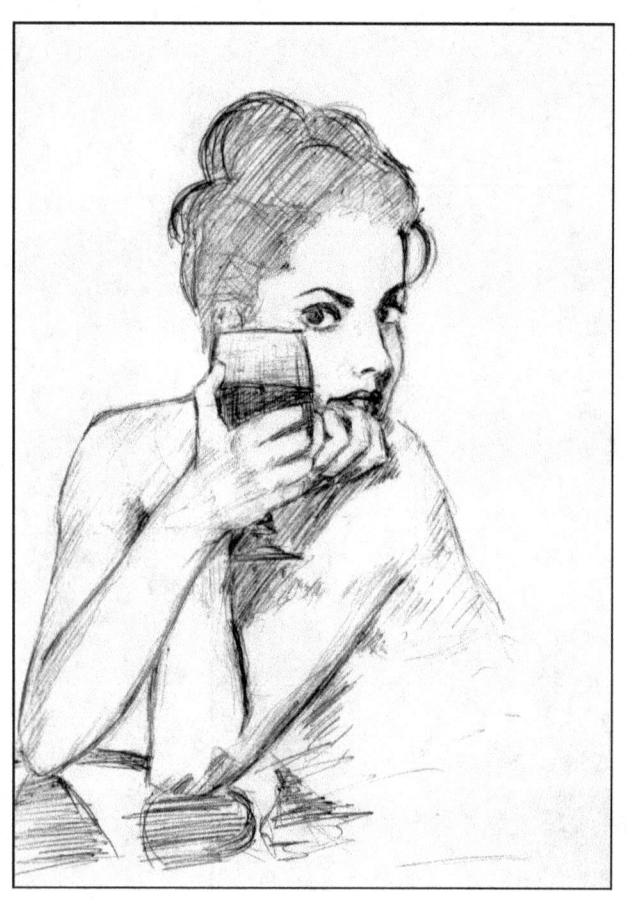
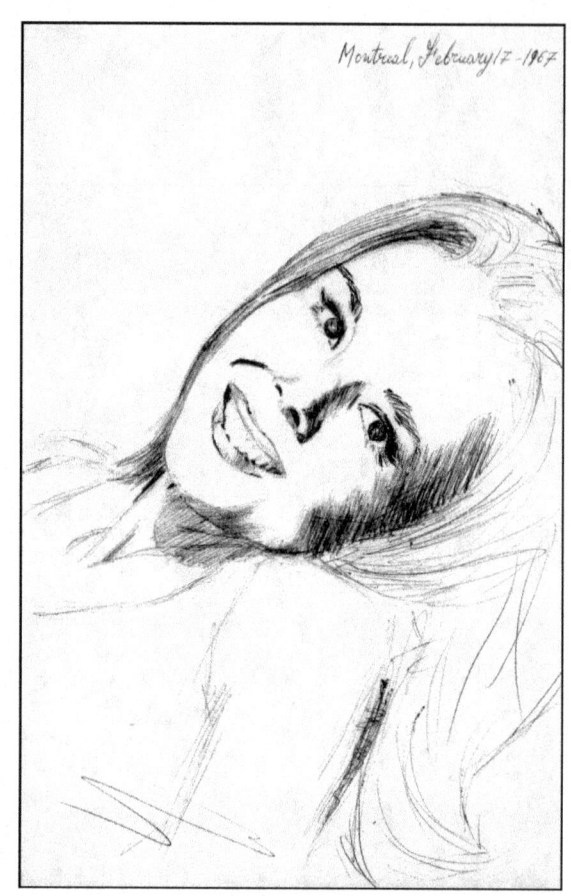
Montreal, February 17-1967

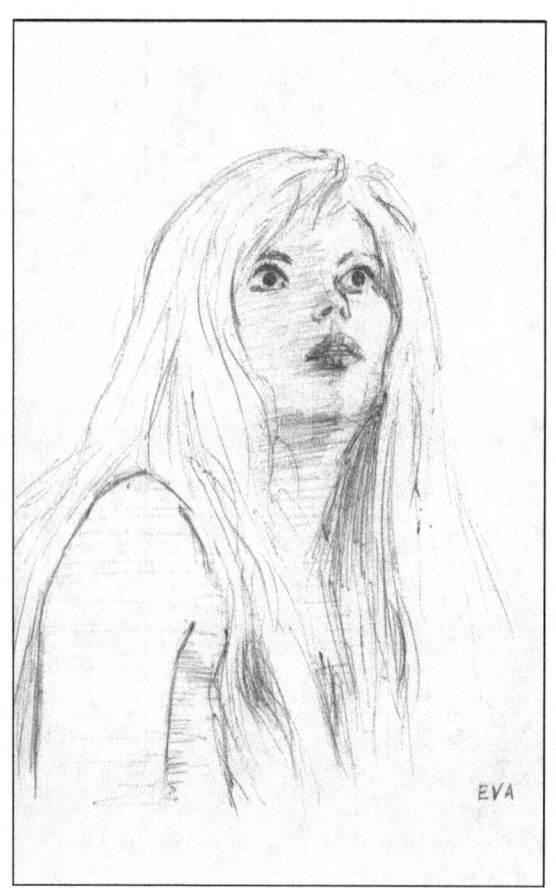
EVA

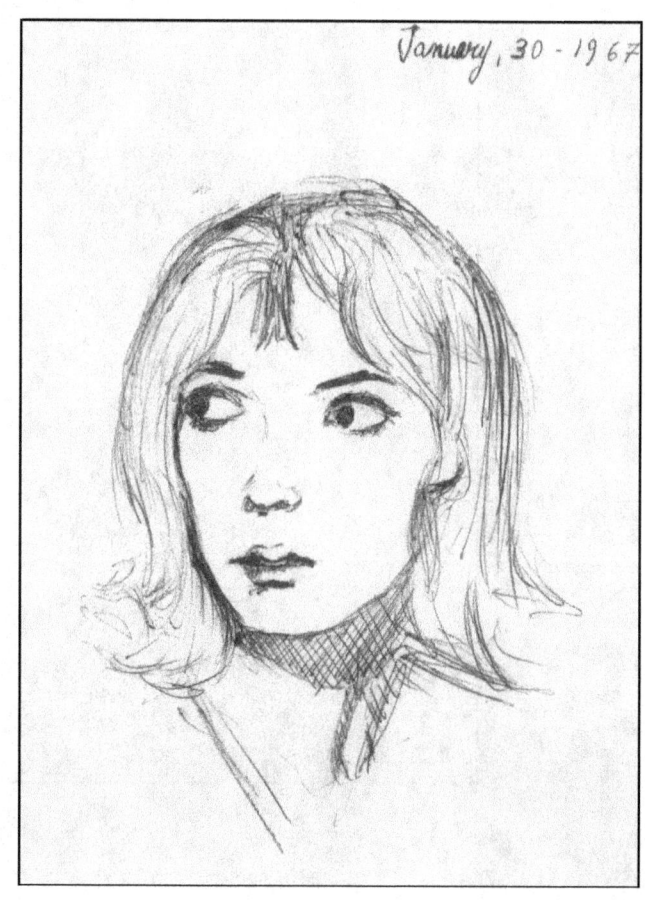
January, 30 - 1967

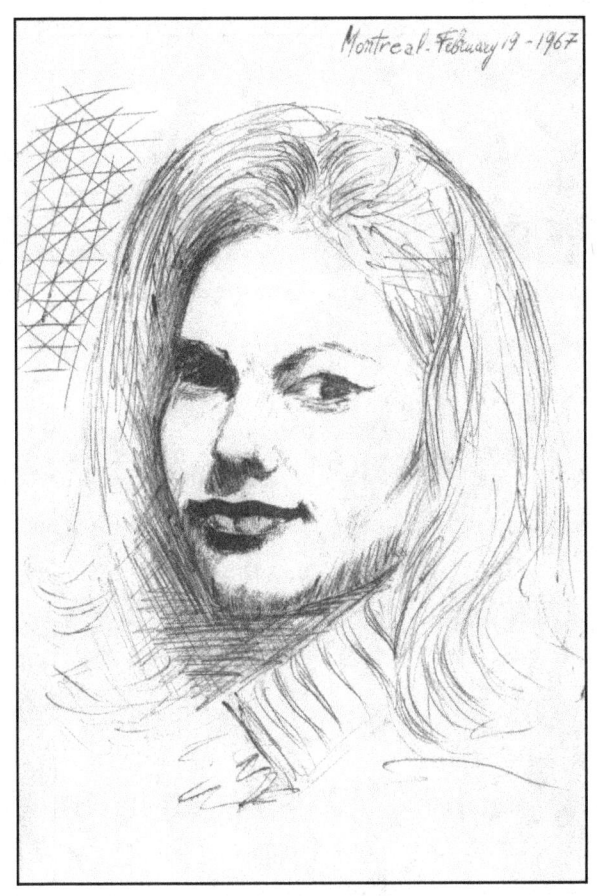
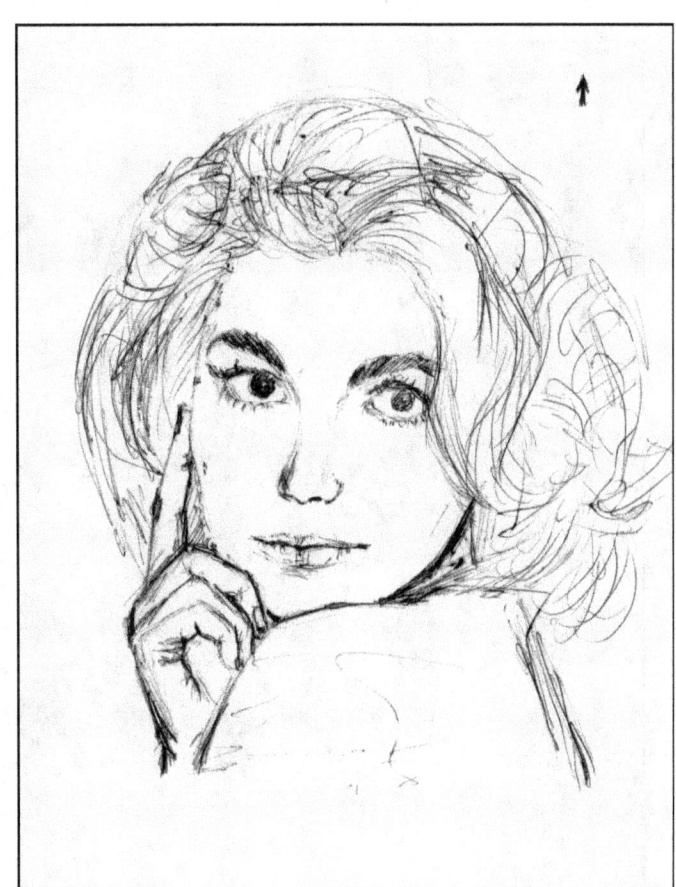
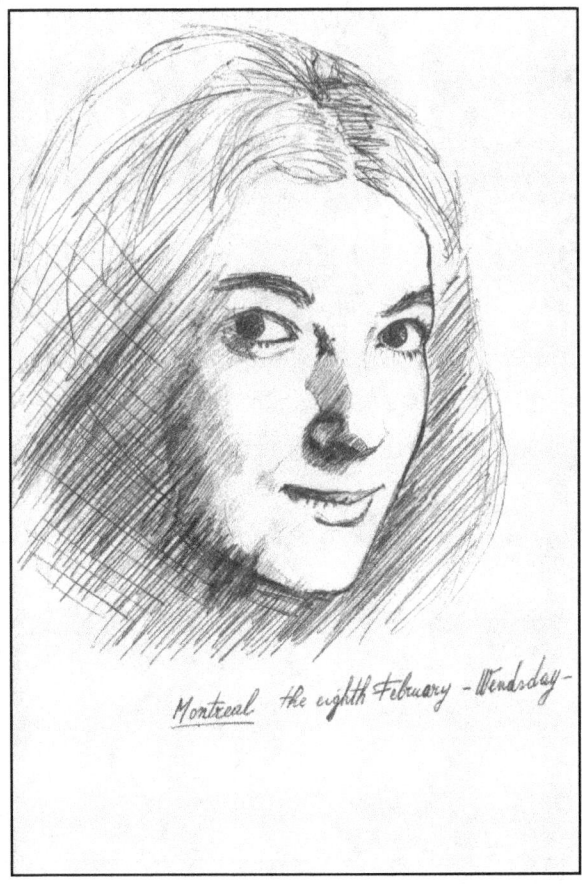
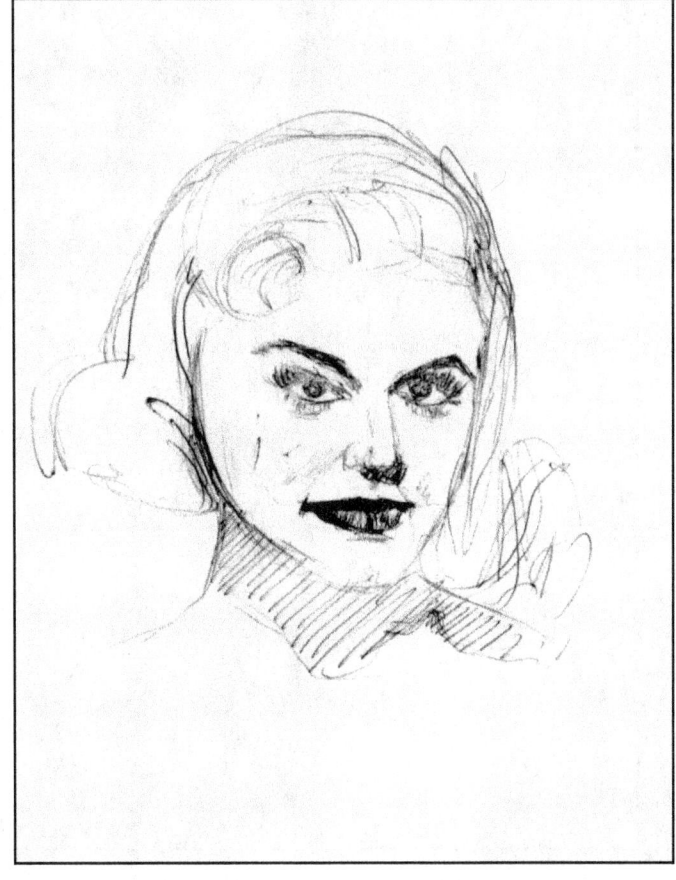

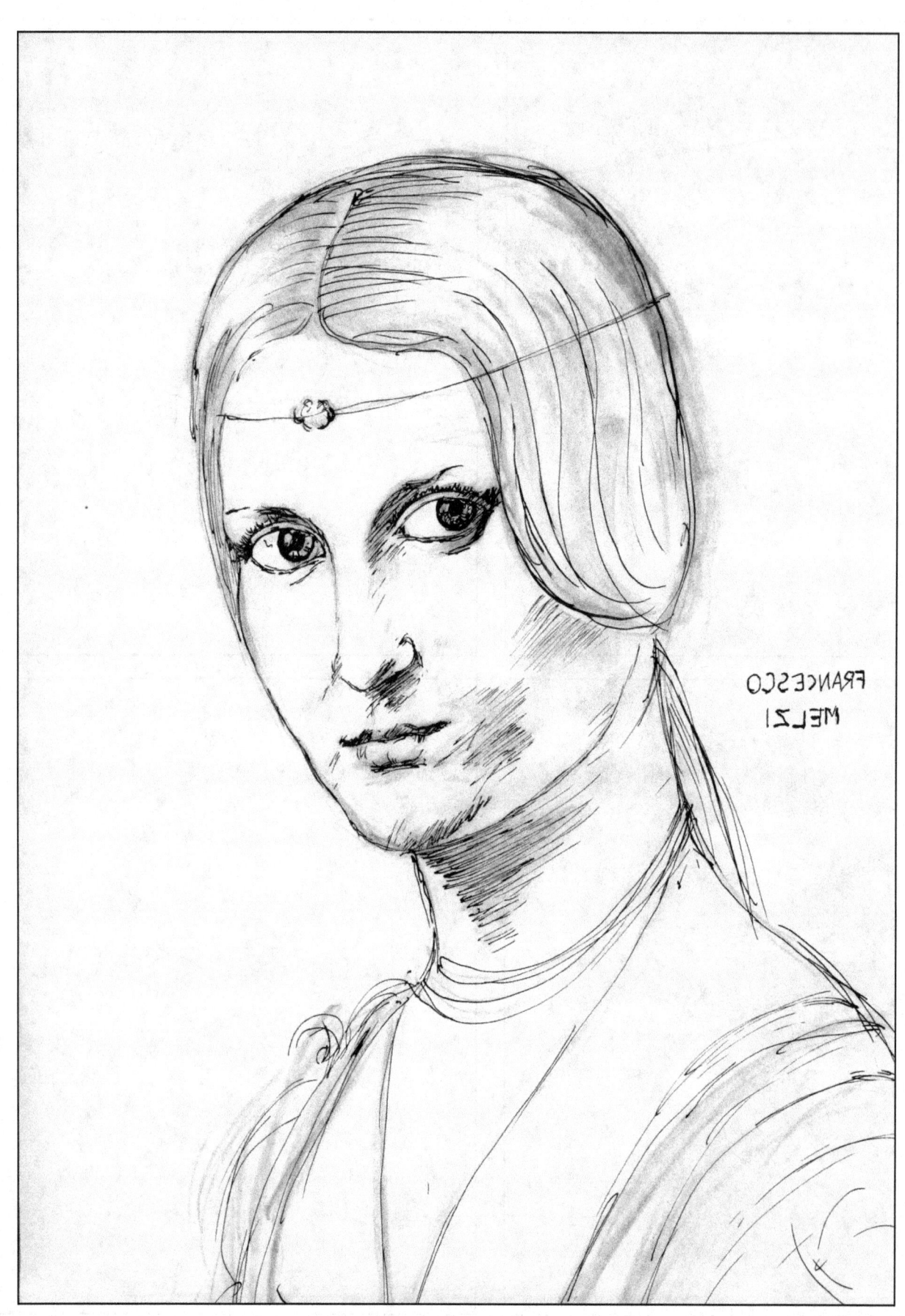

La Belle Ferronniere after Francesco Melzi

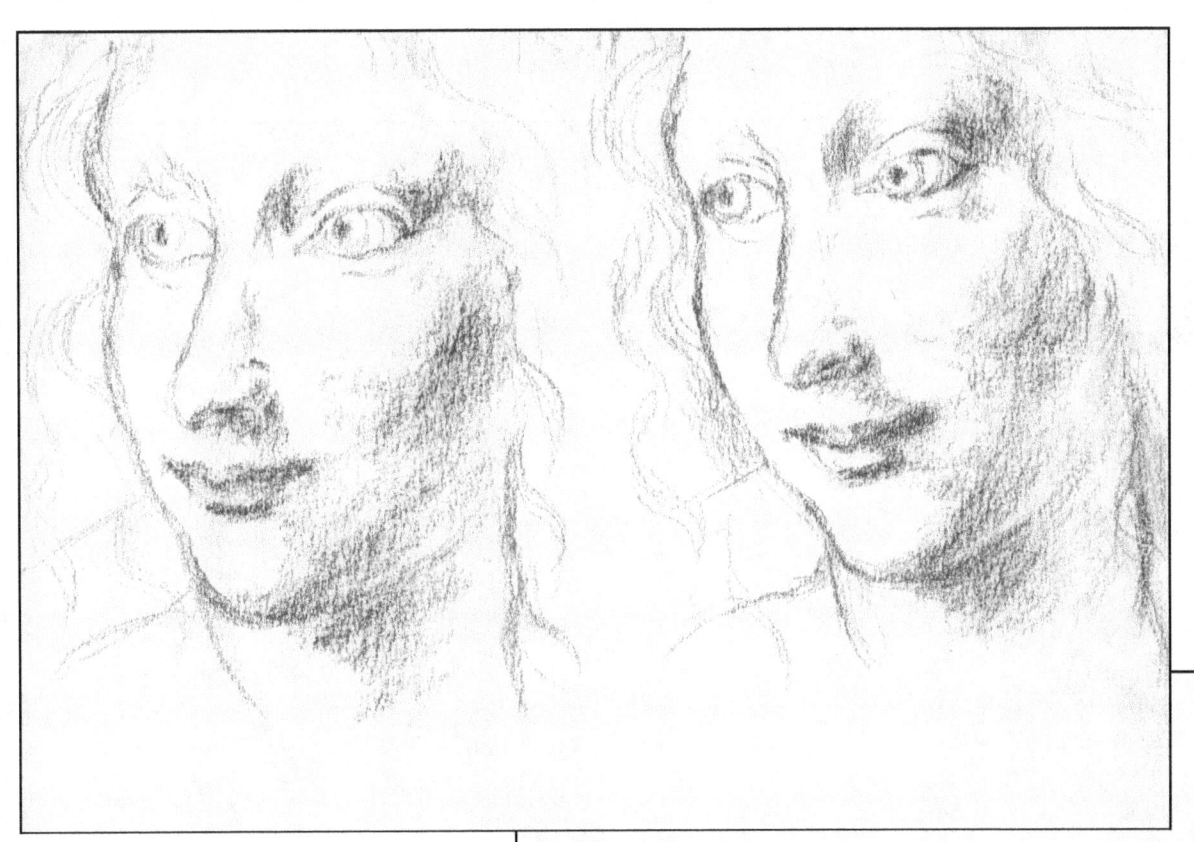
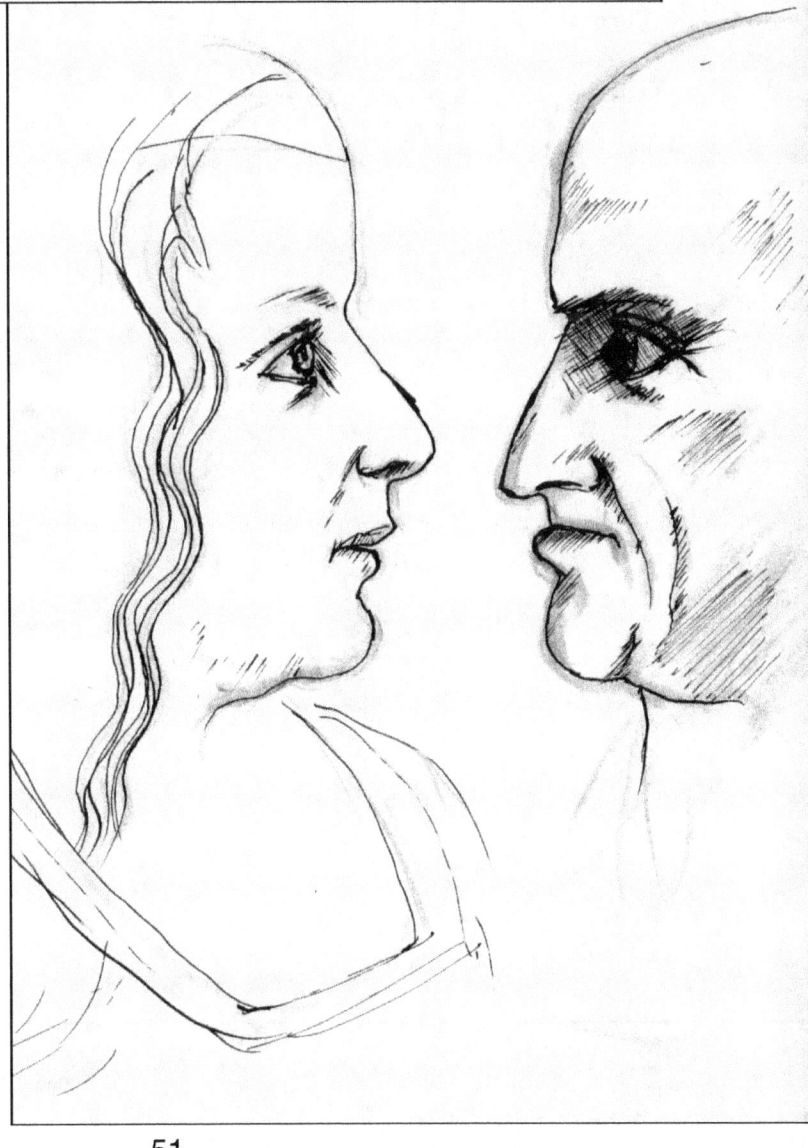

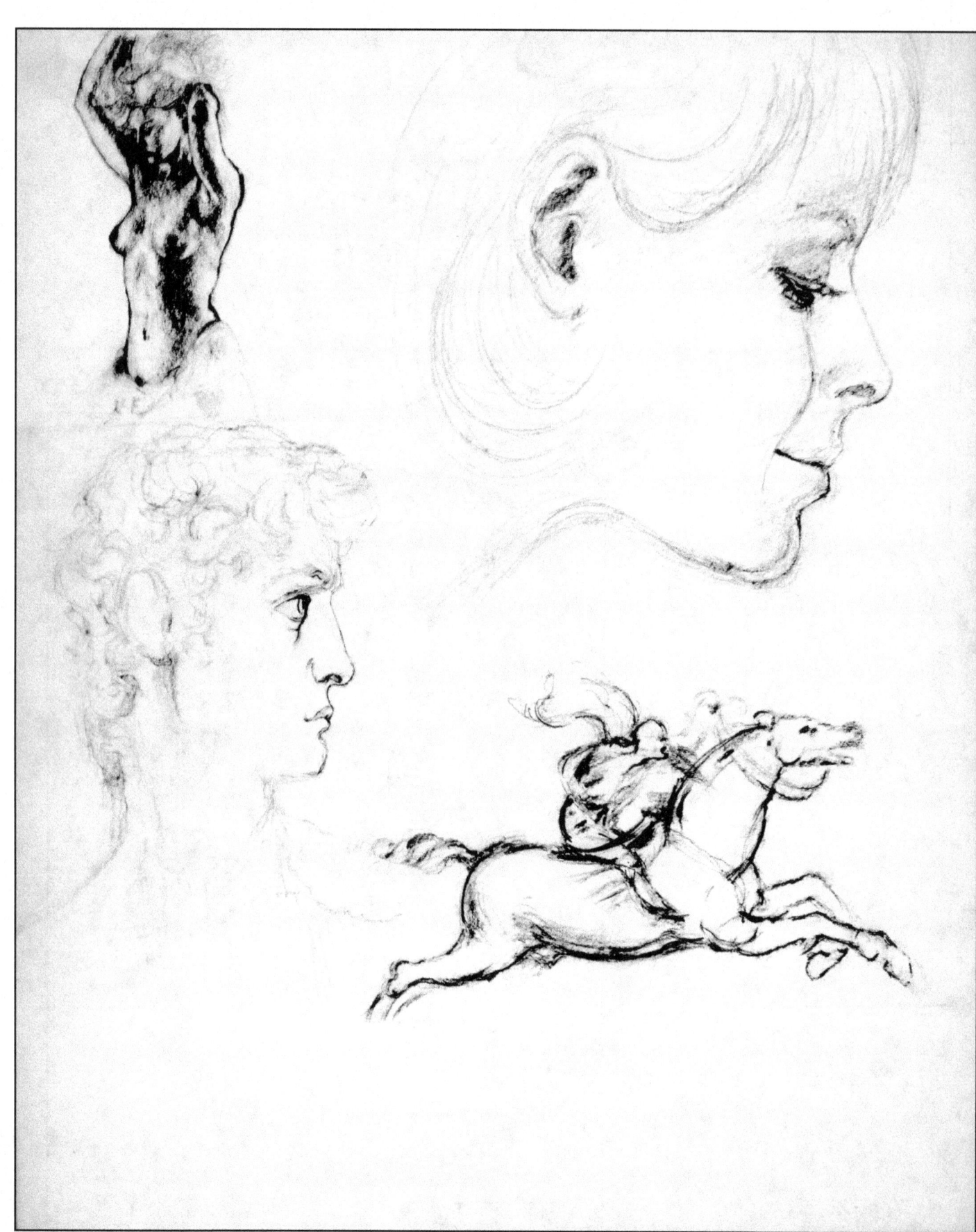

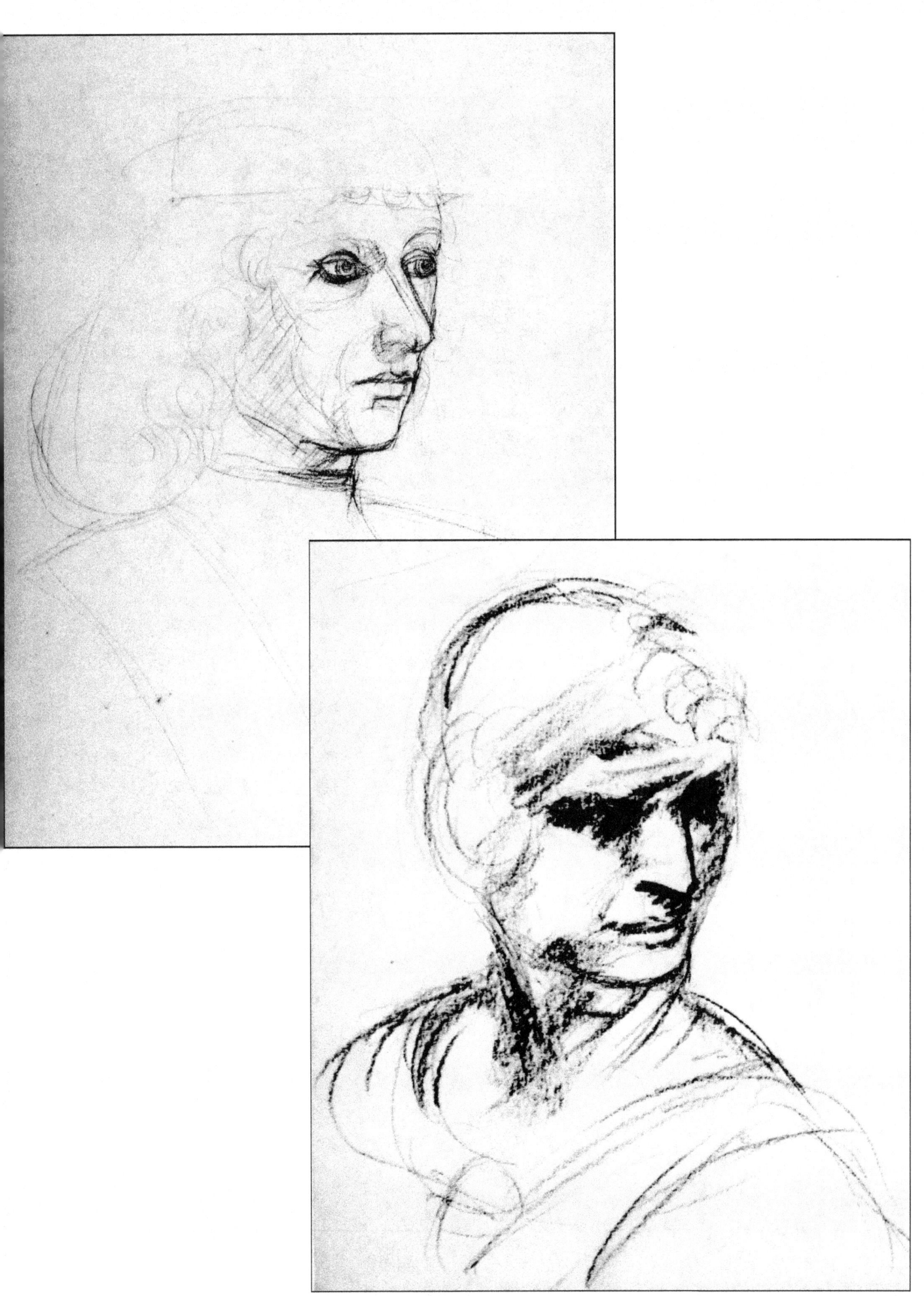

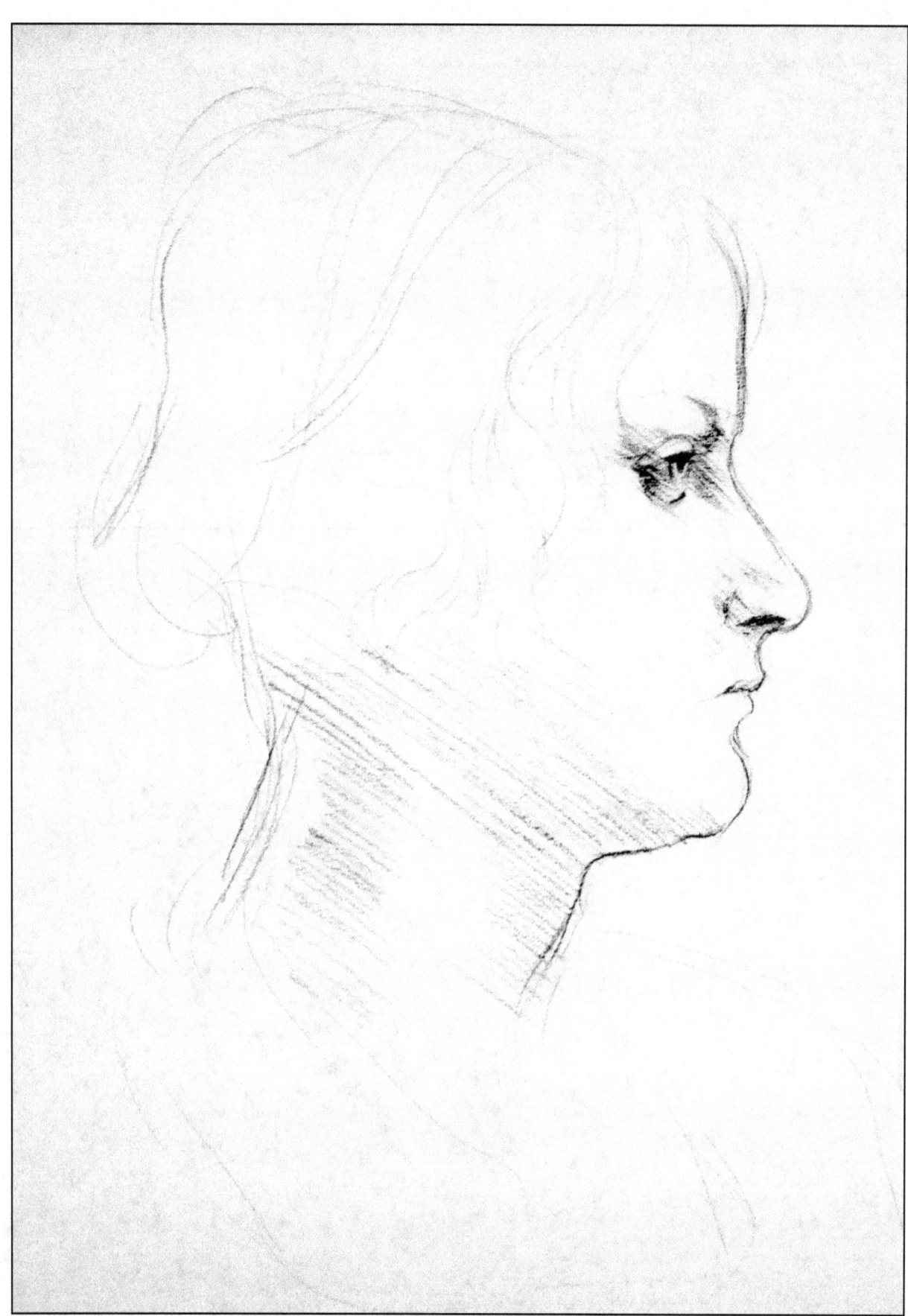

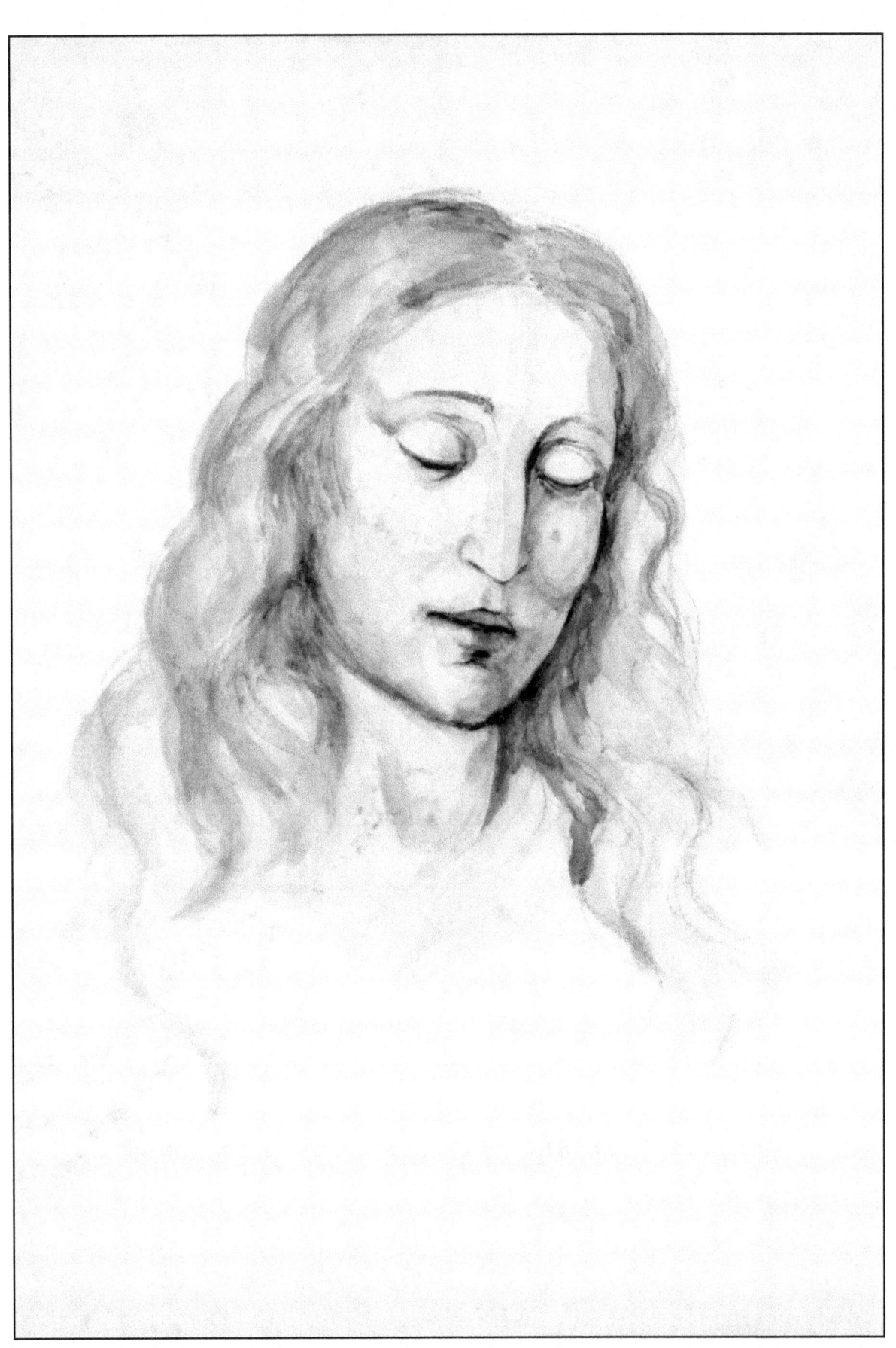

Christ in THE LAST SUPPER, after Leonardo, Watercolor

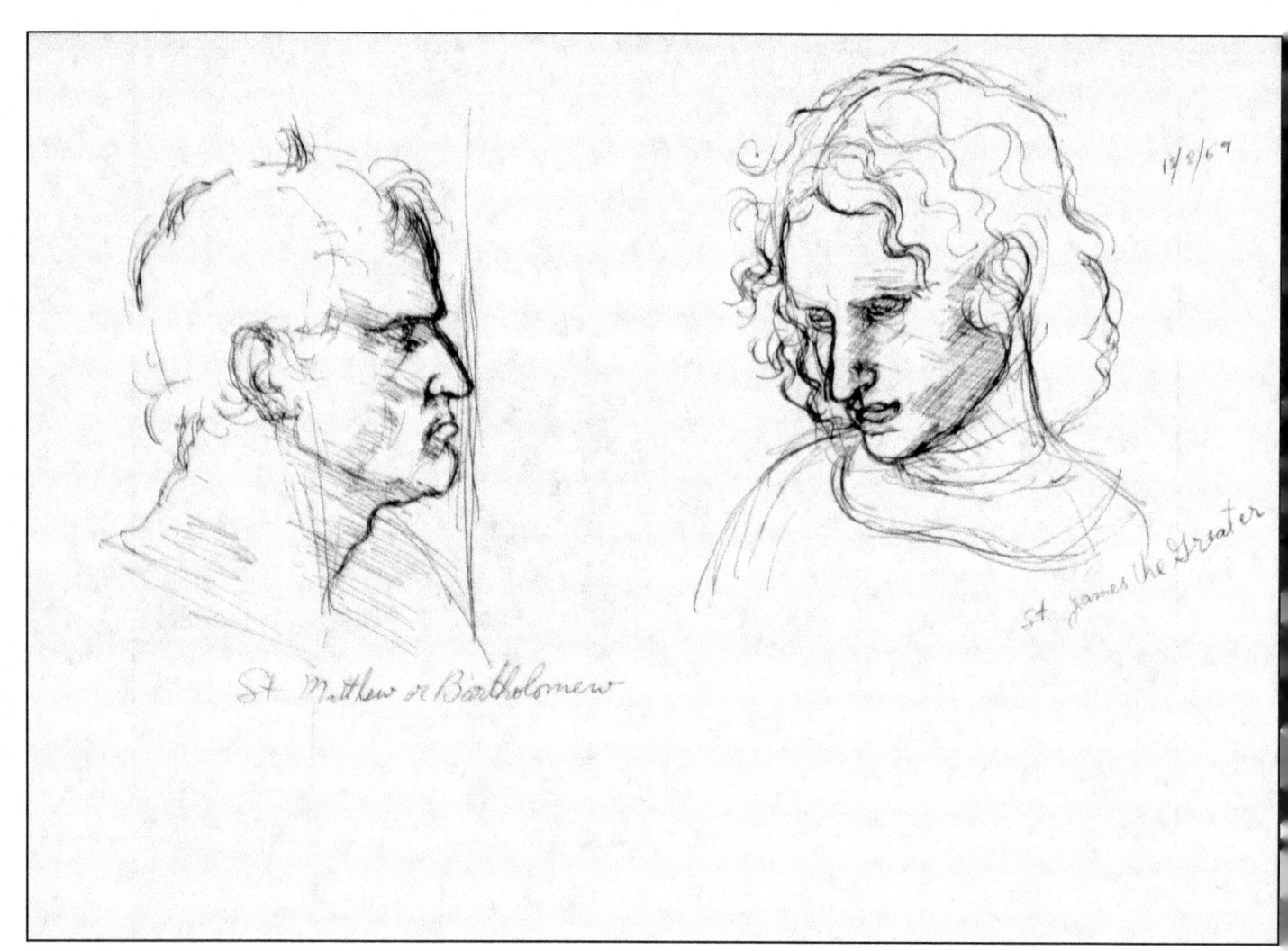

Apostles in THE LAST SUPPER, after Leonardo, pen and ink

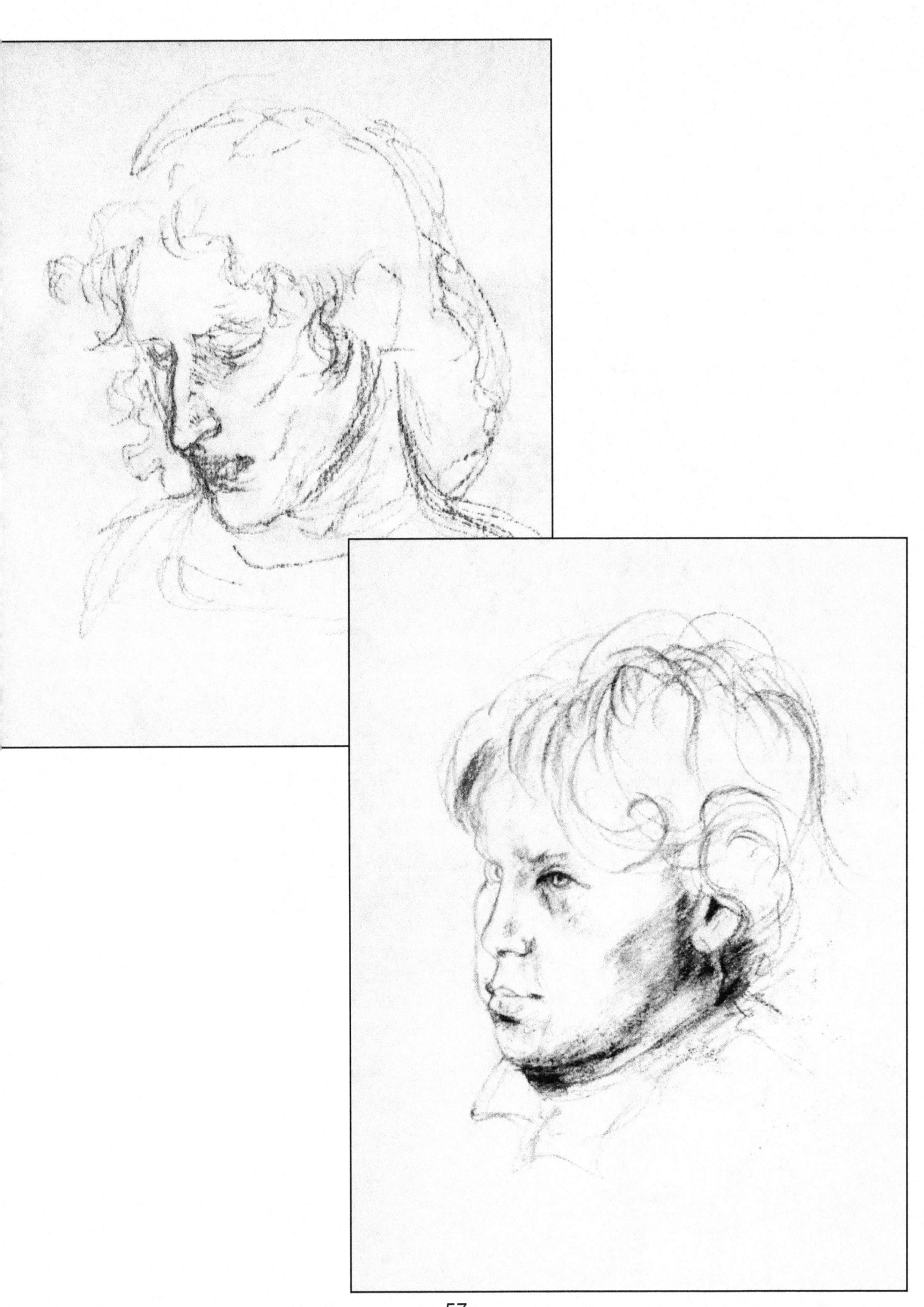

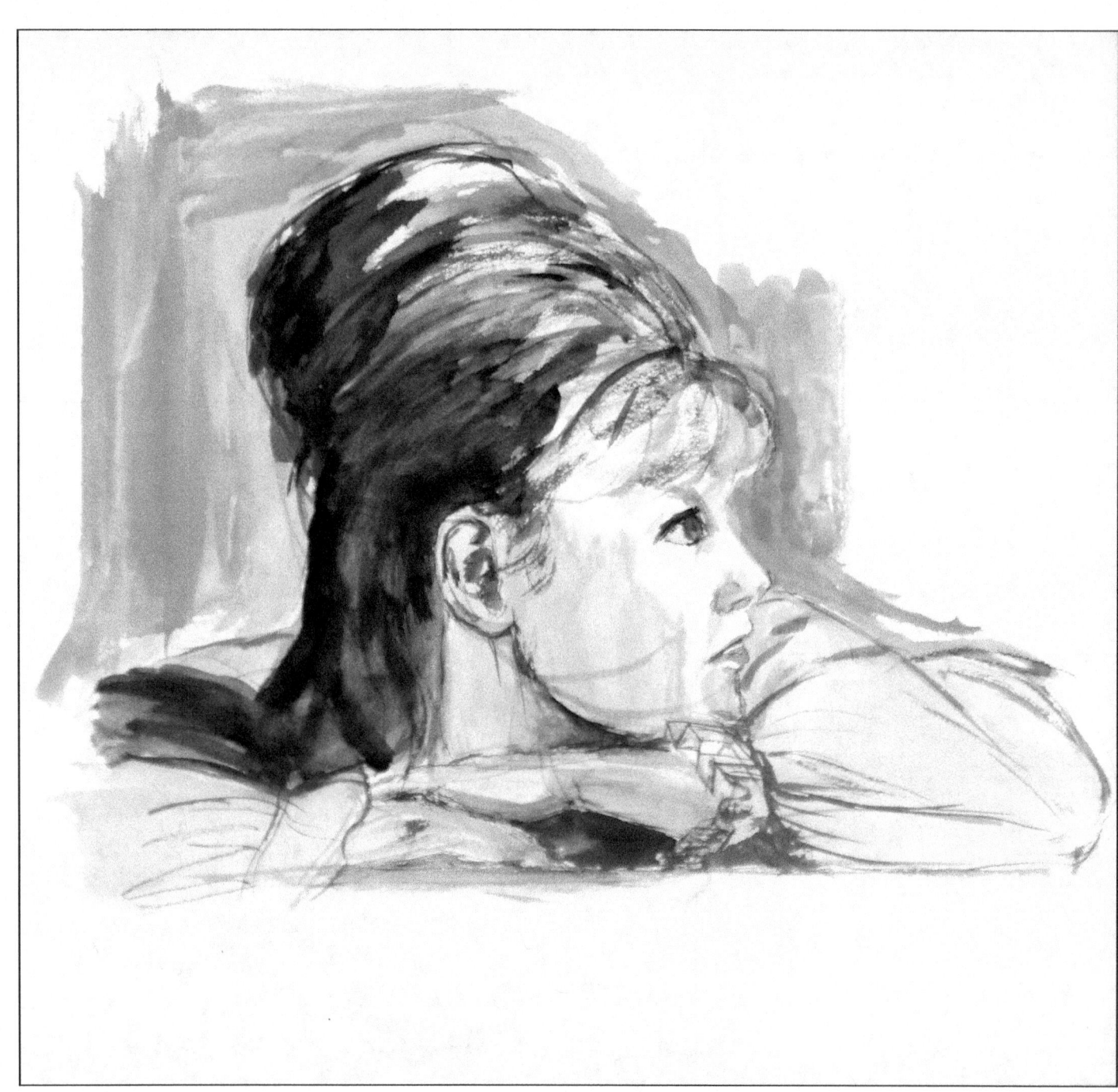

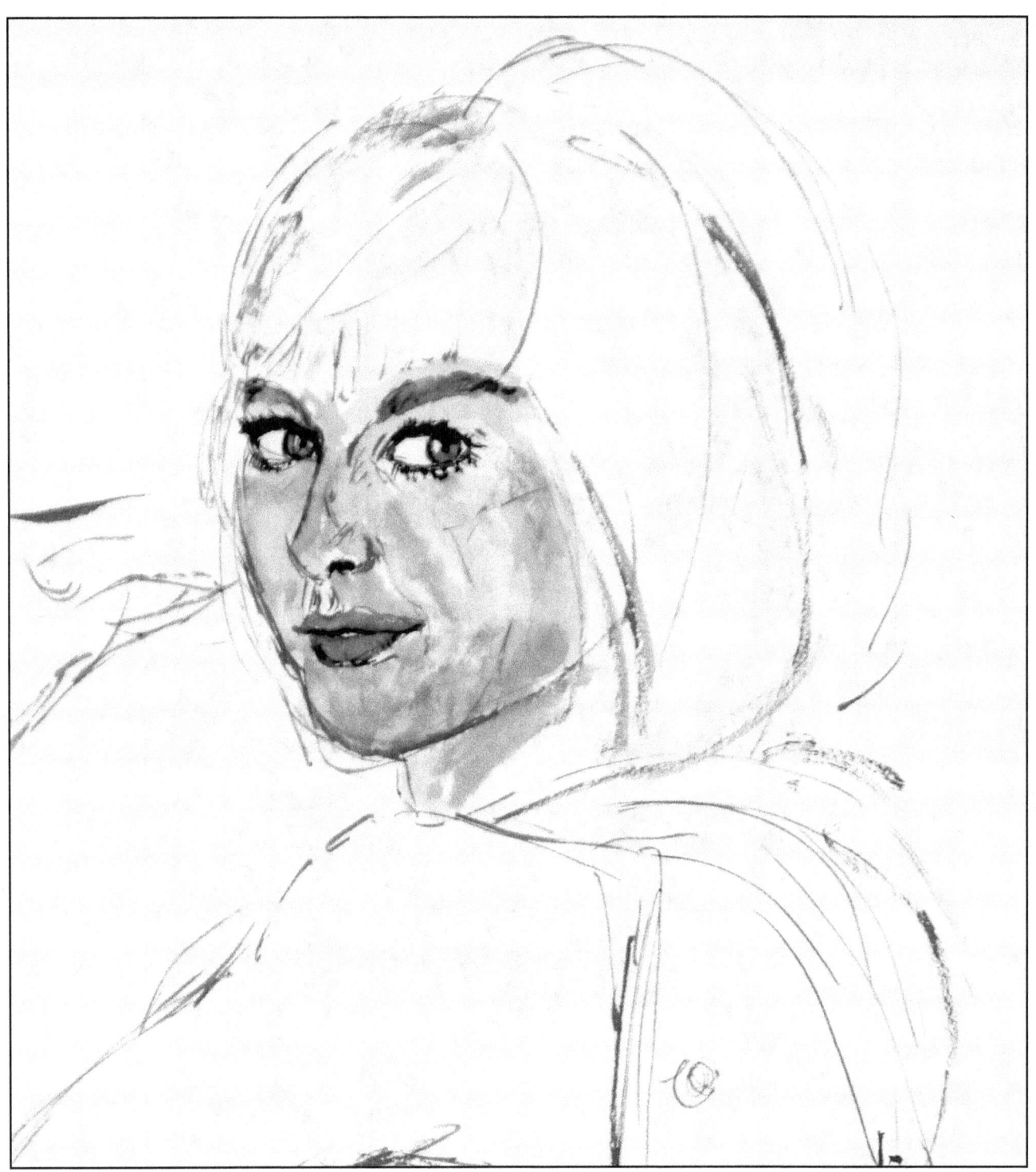

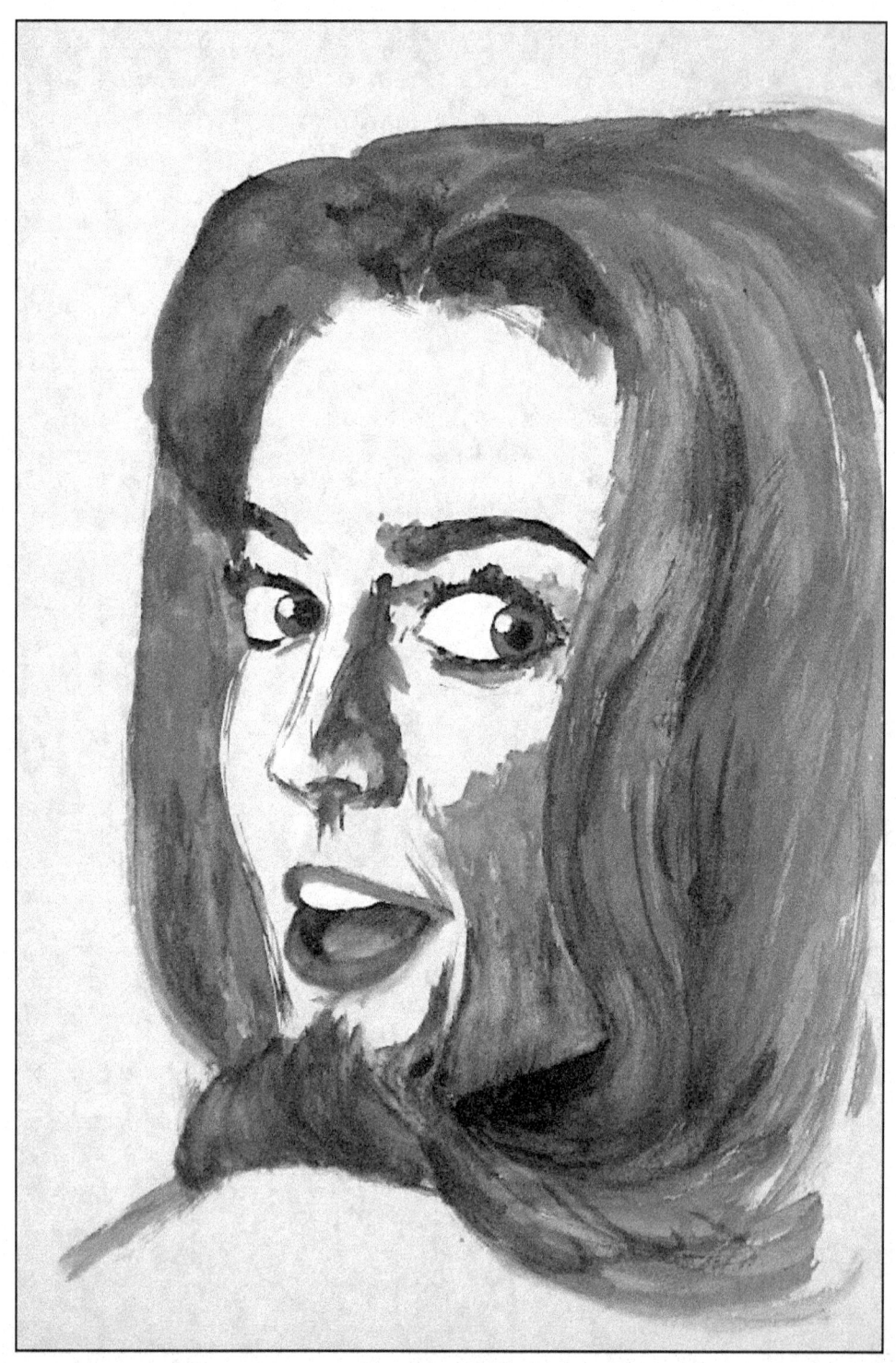

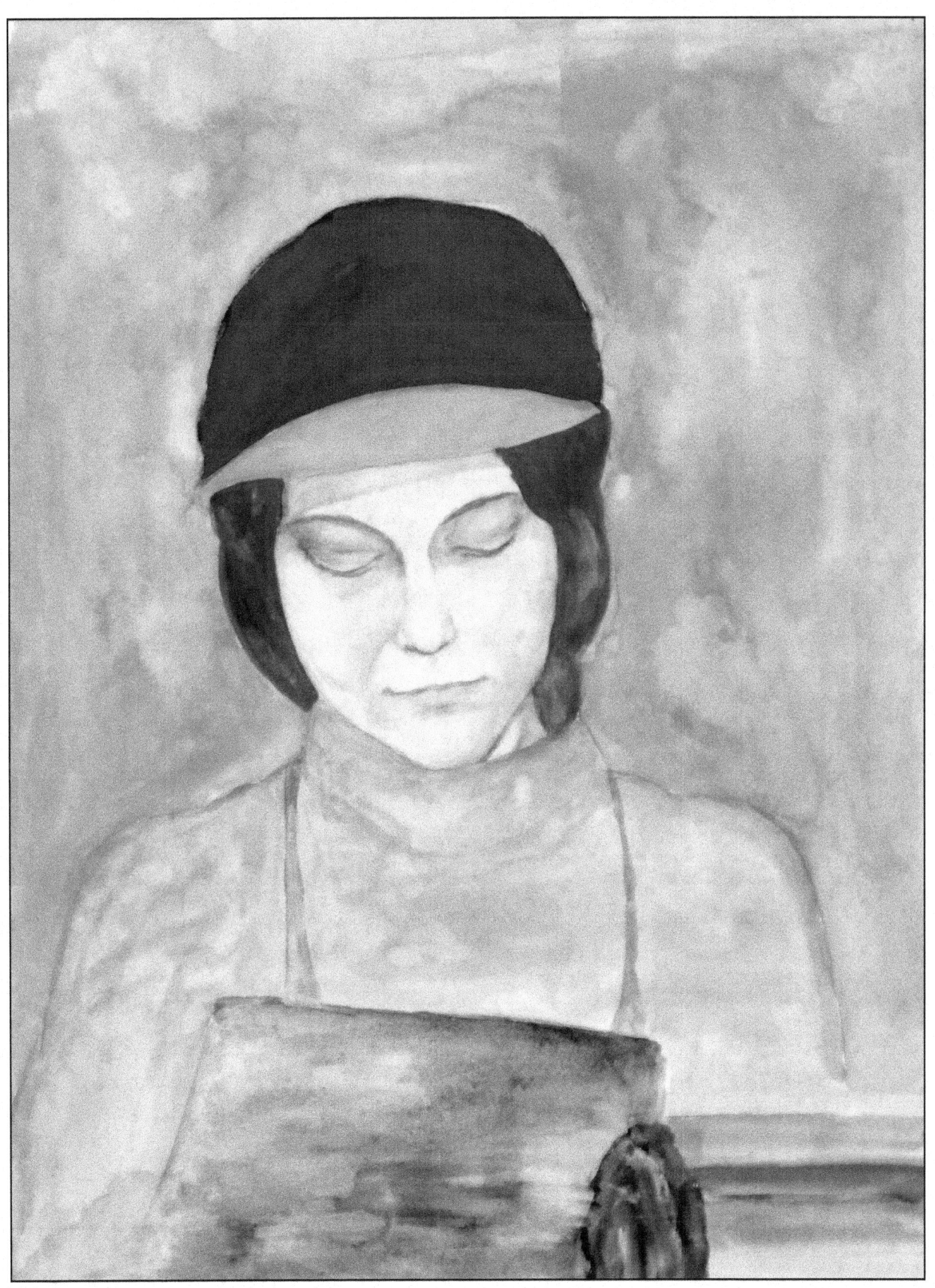

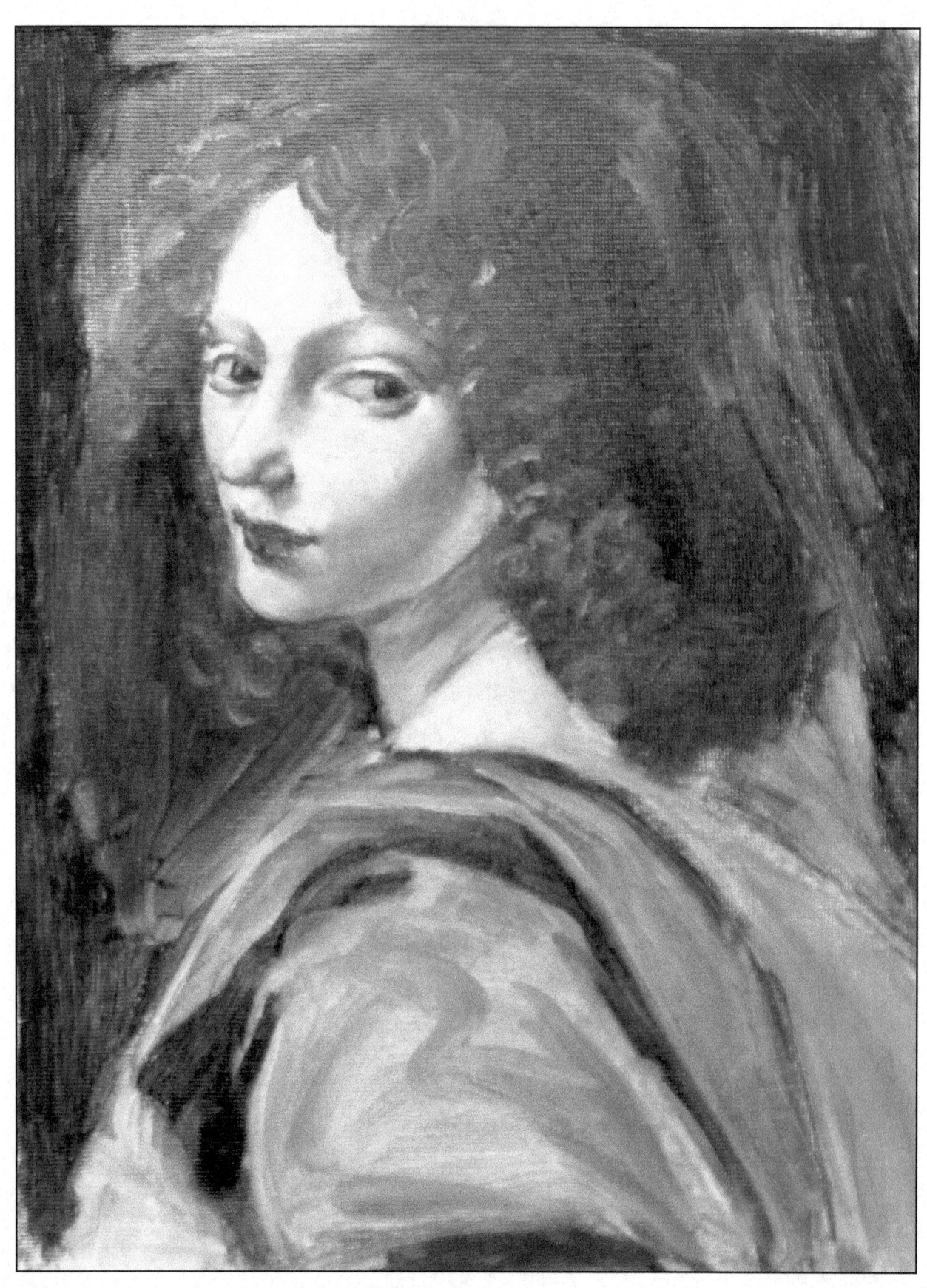

Angel in MADONNA OF THE ROCKS, after Leonardo, oil

4. Head Observation, Acquaintances

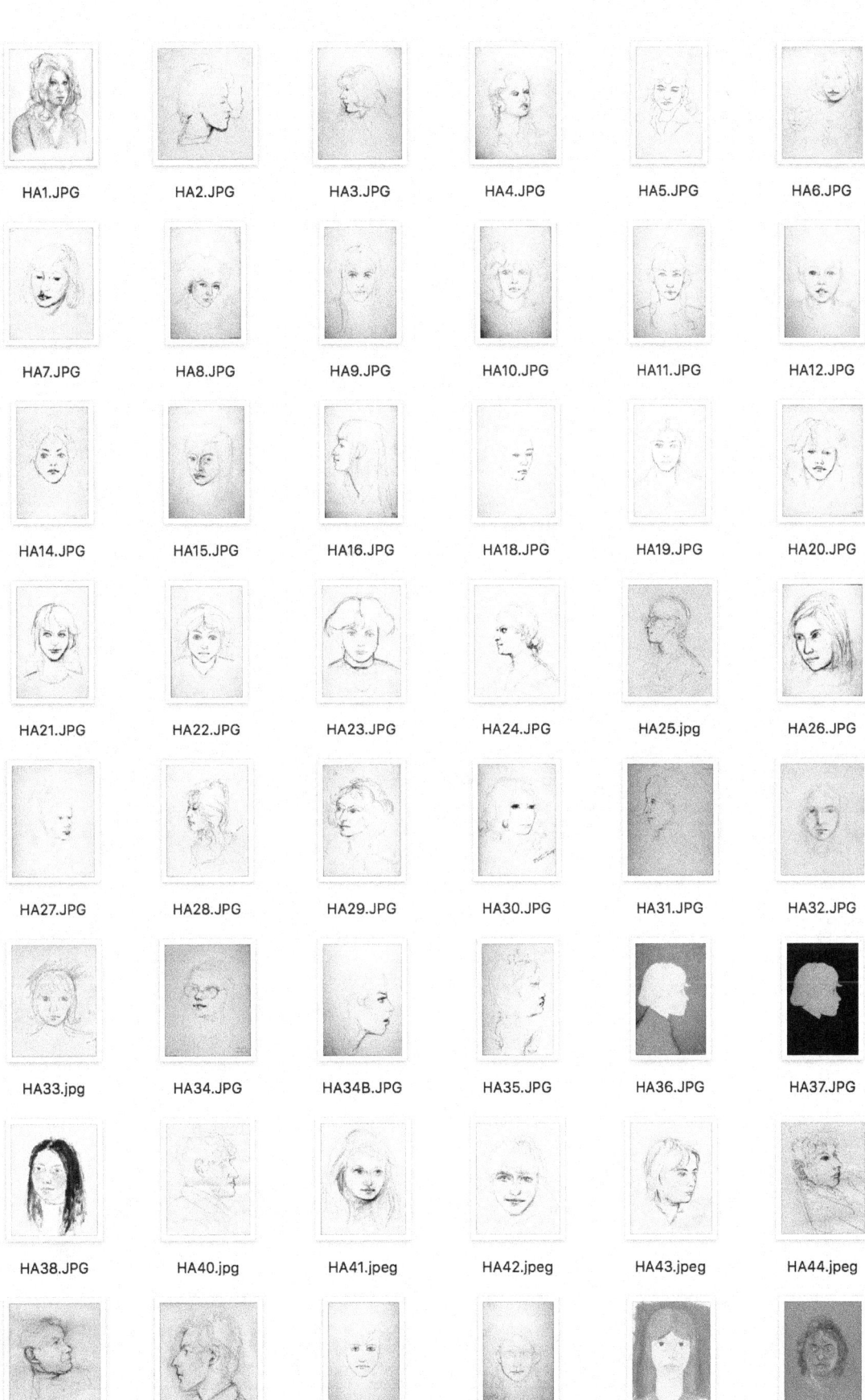

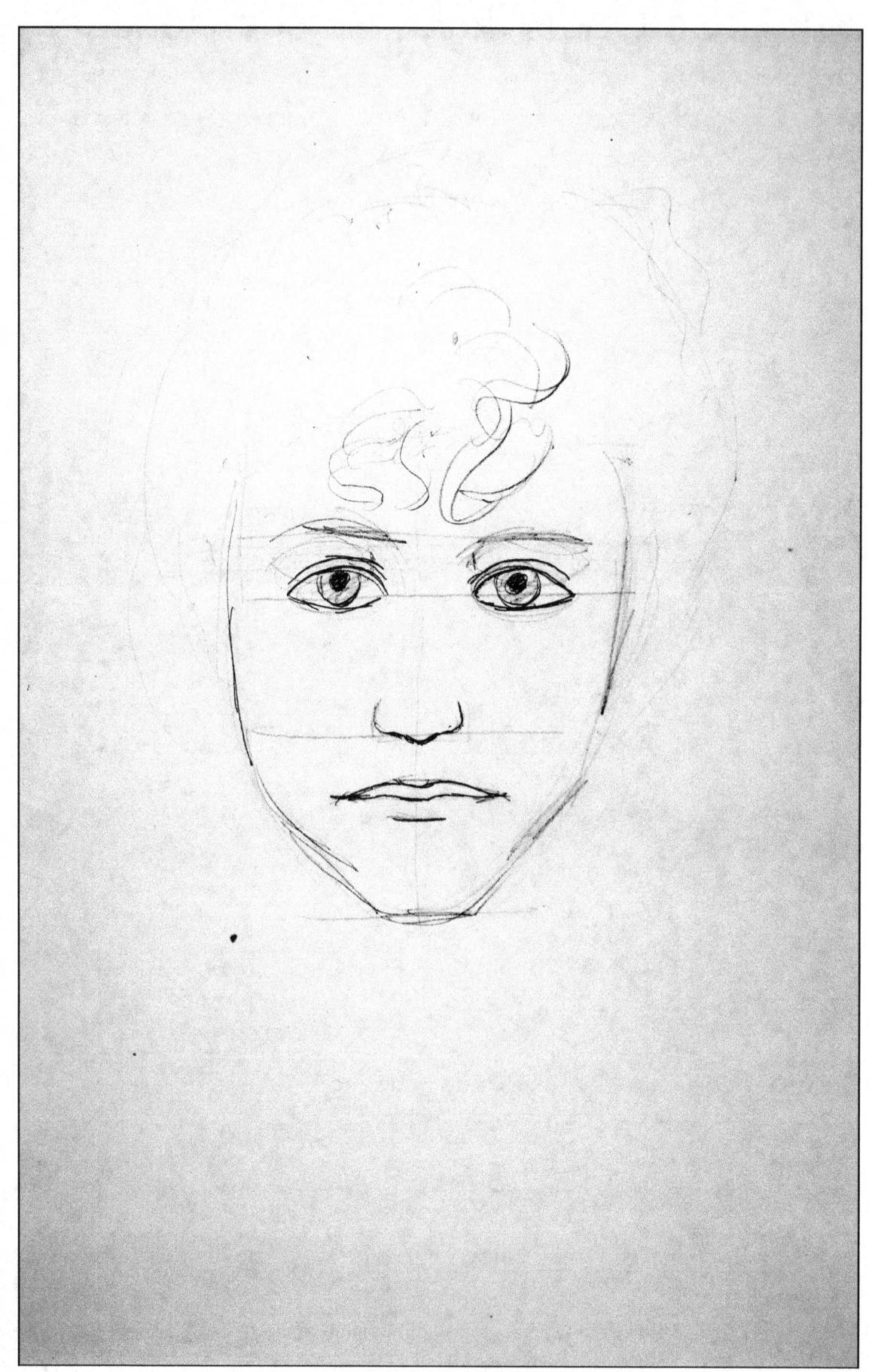

Face Proportions

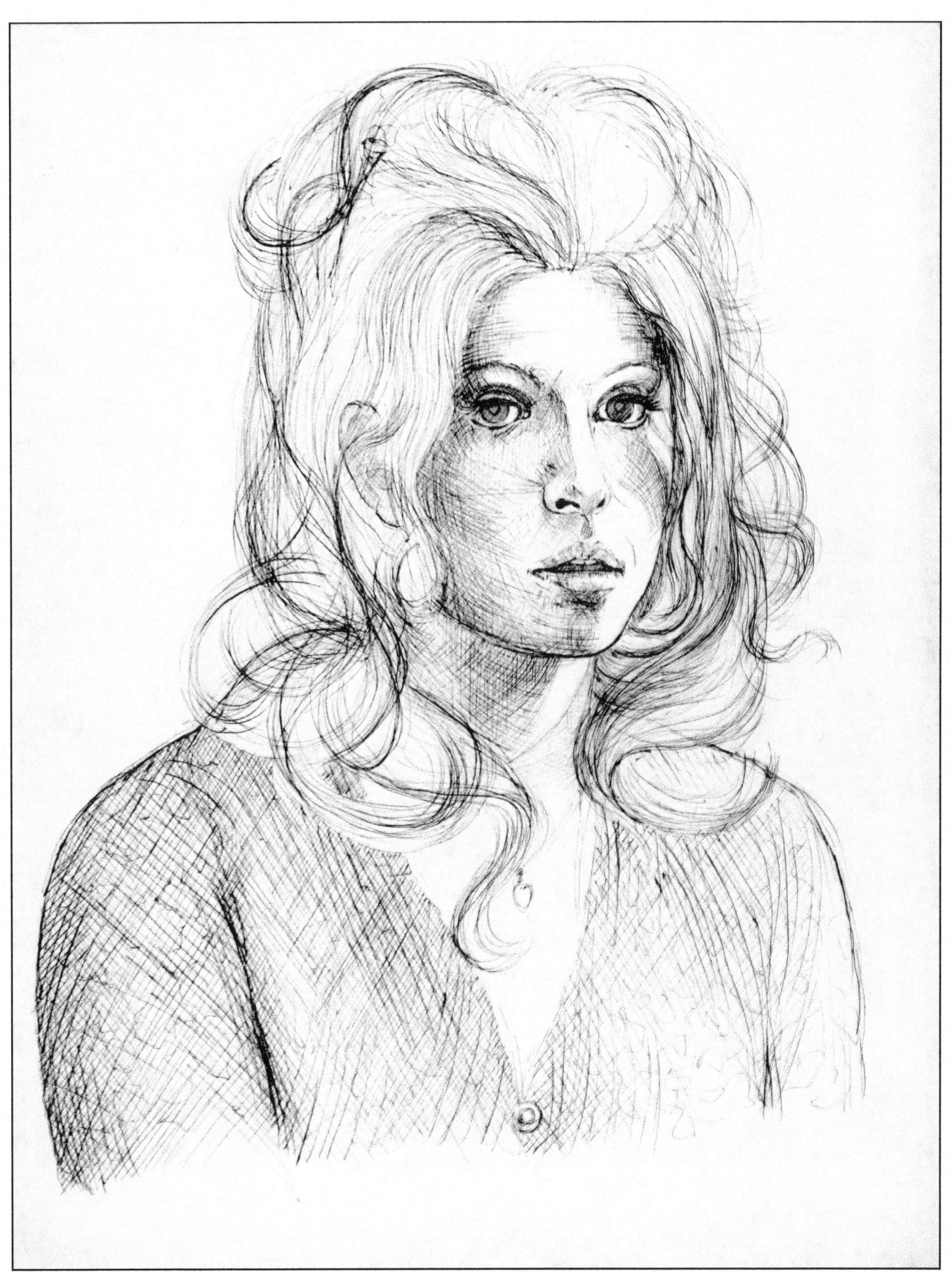

Pen and Ink

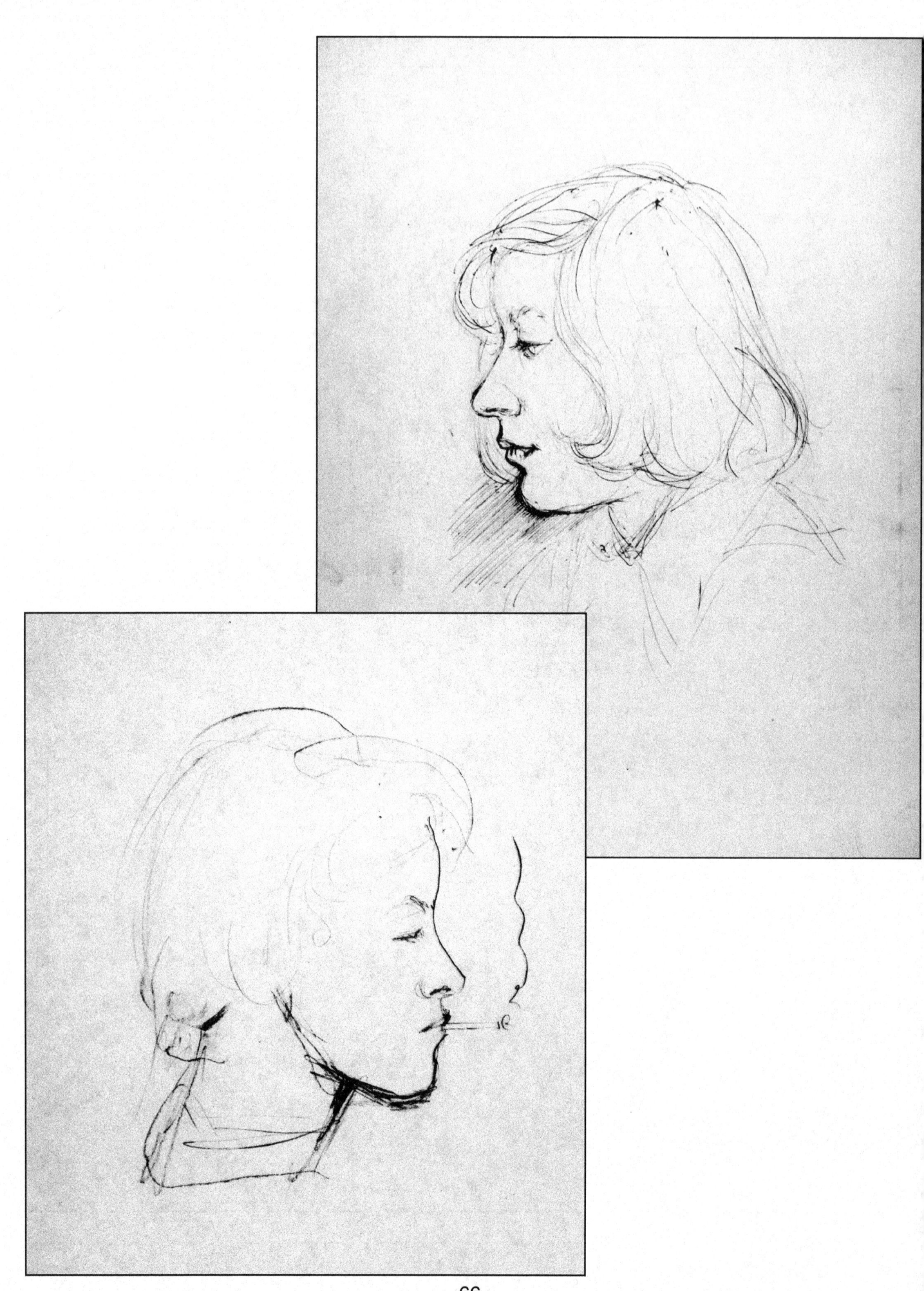

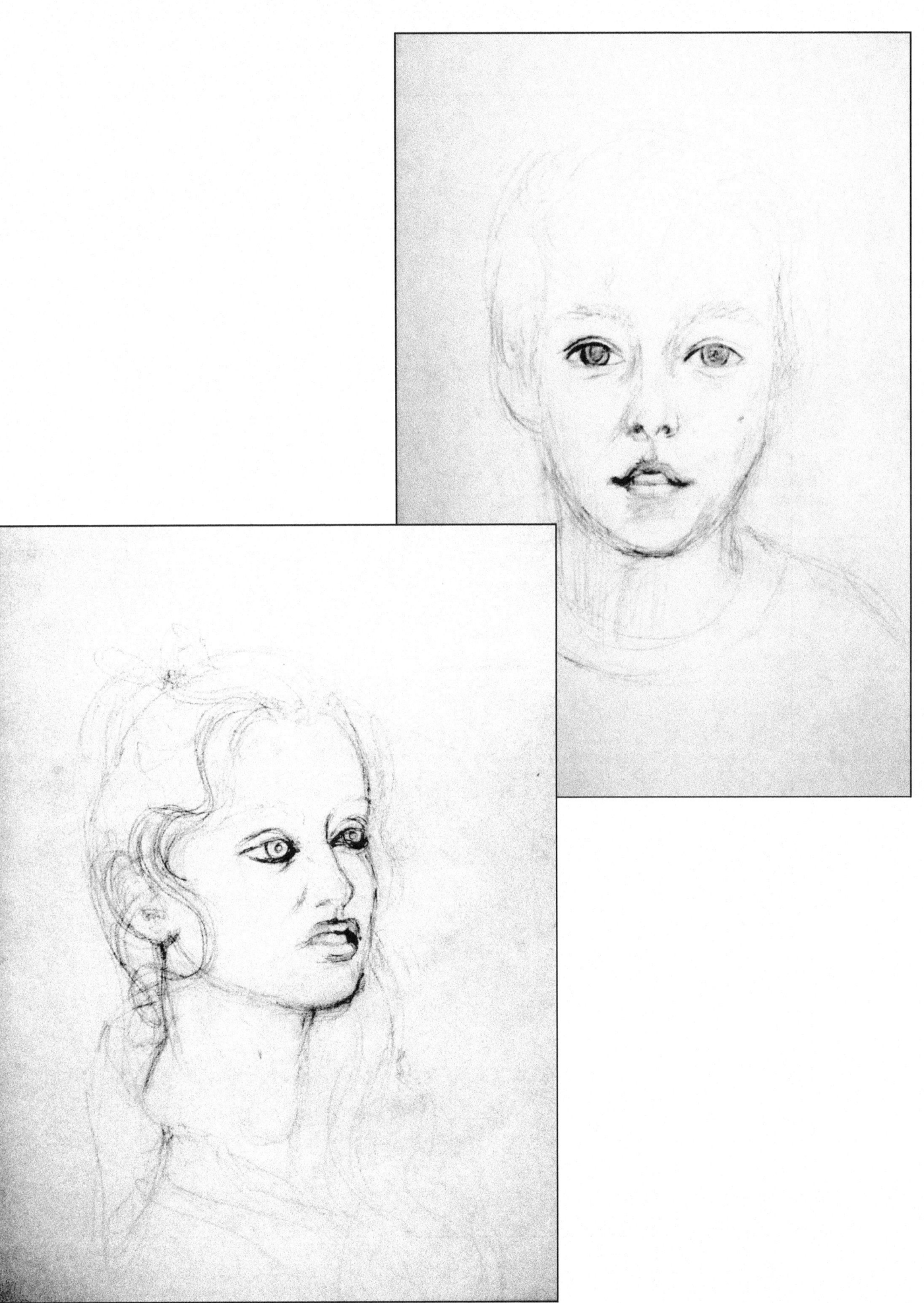

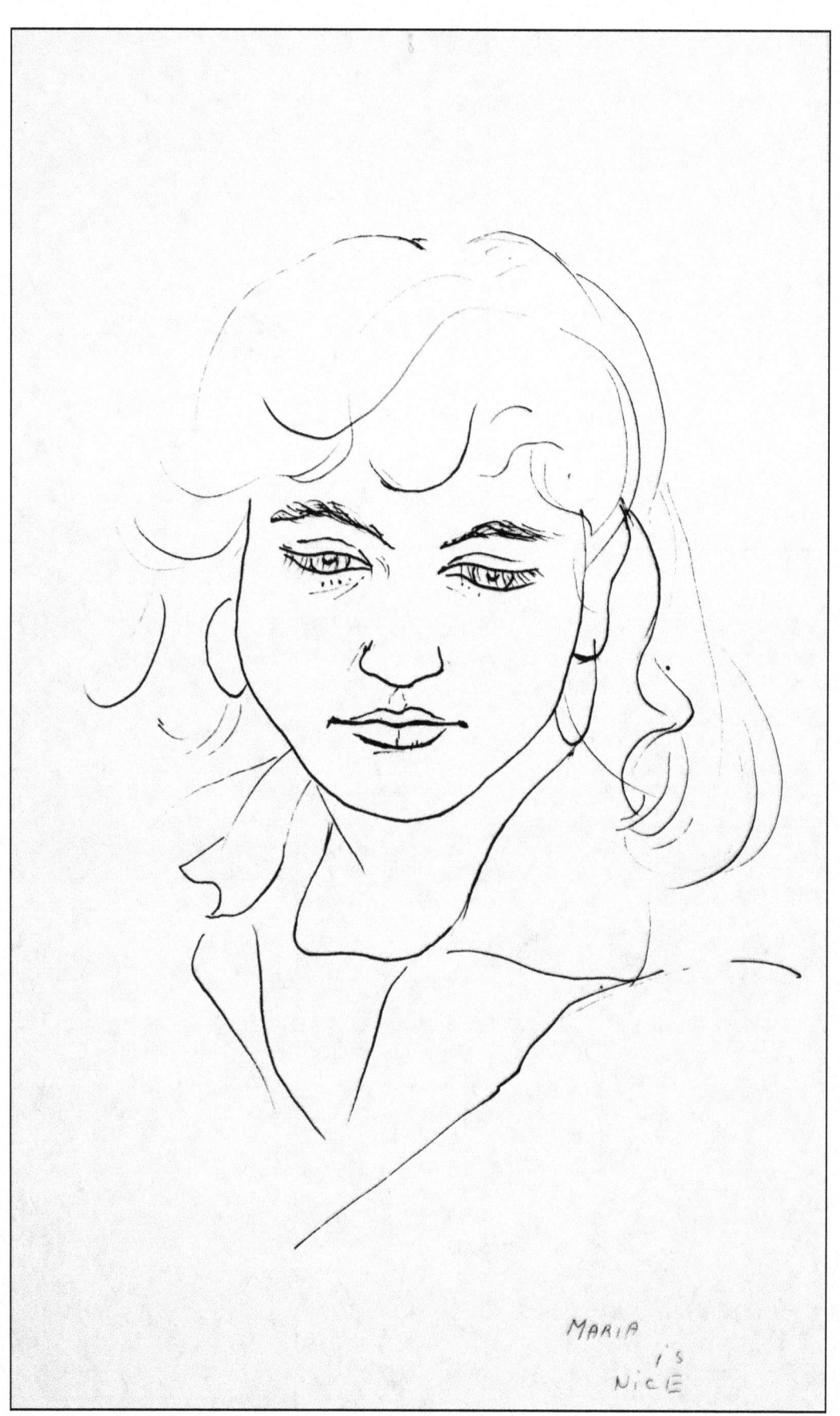

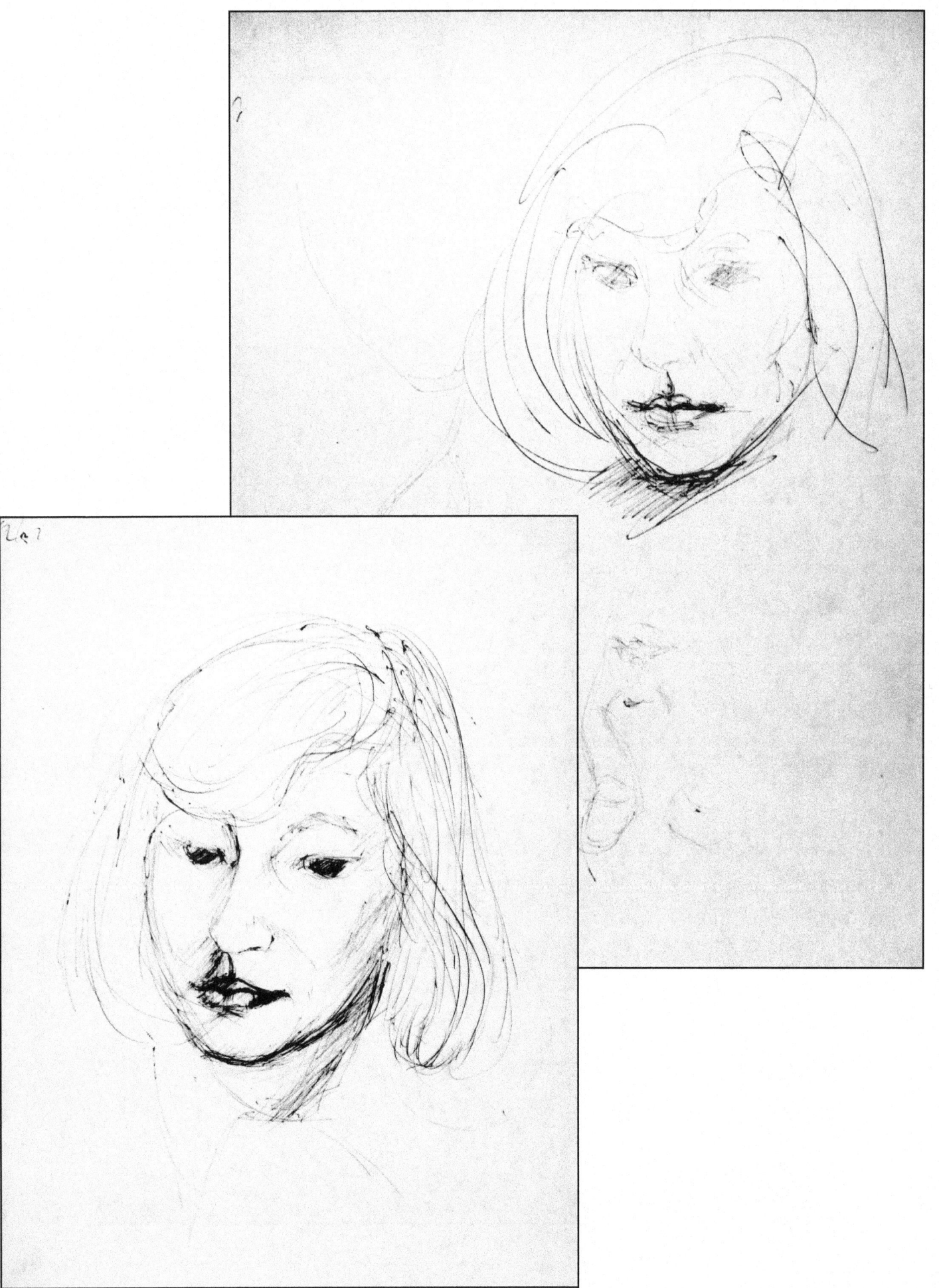

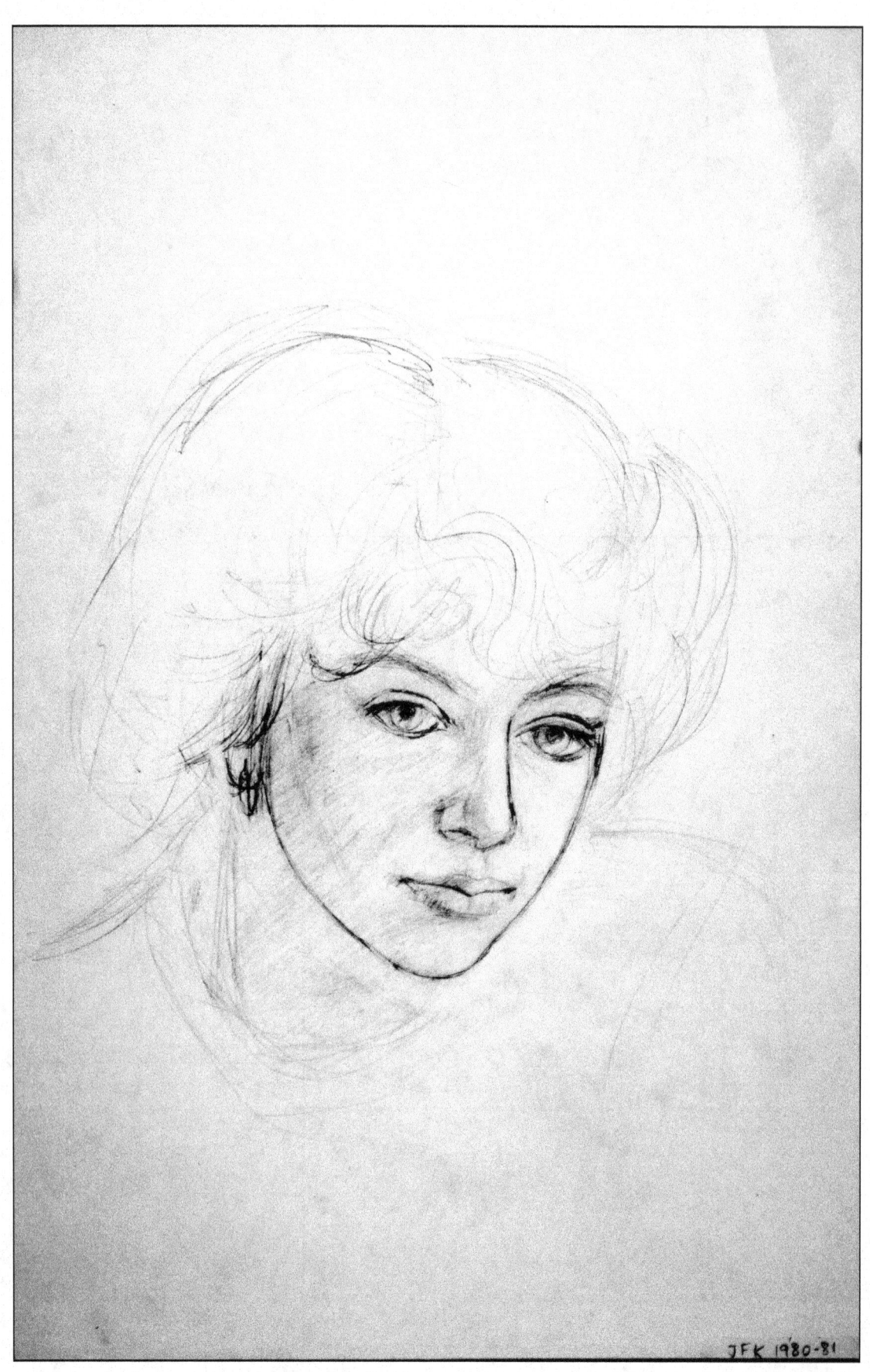

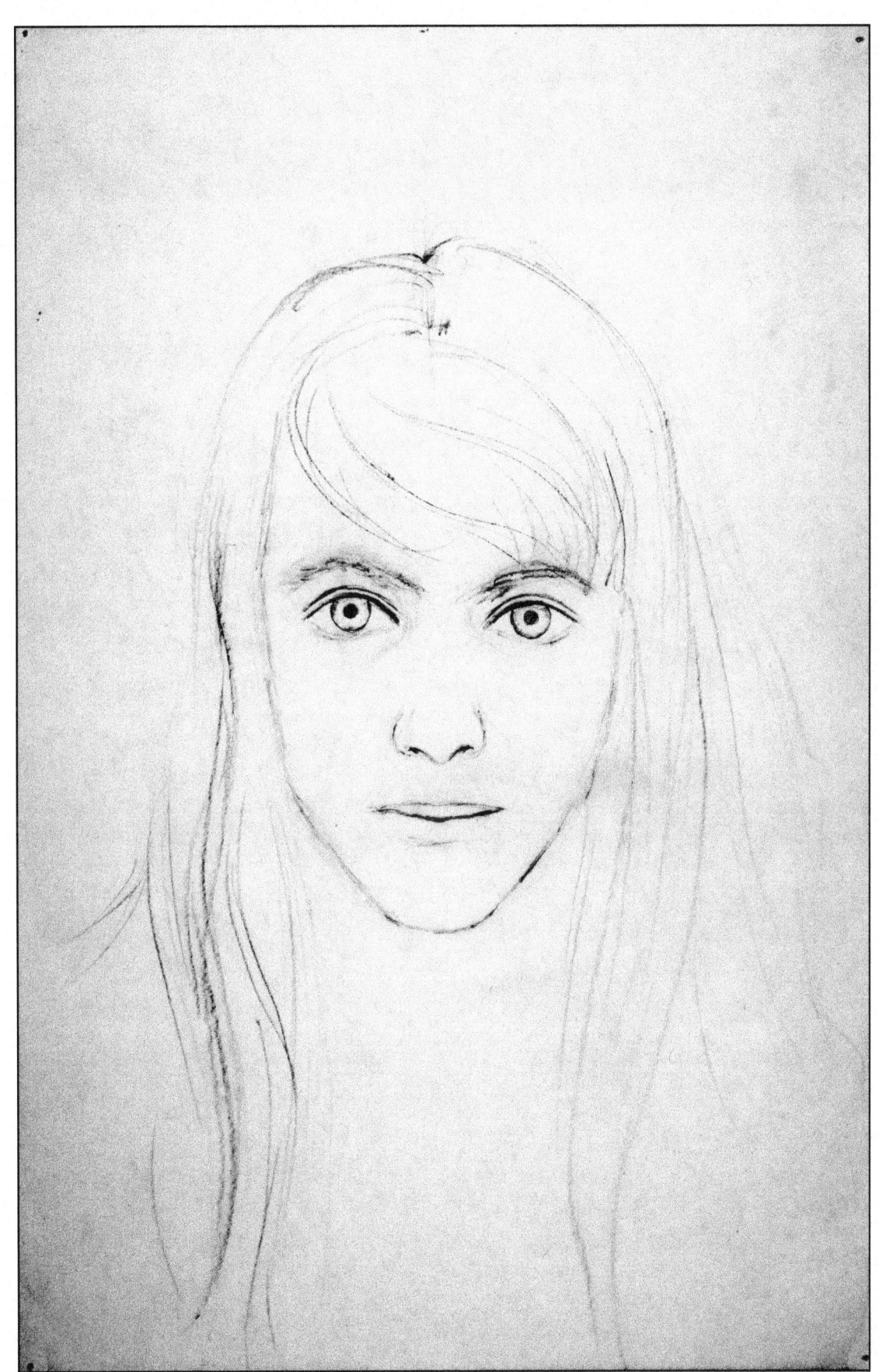

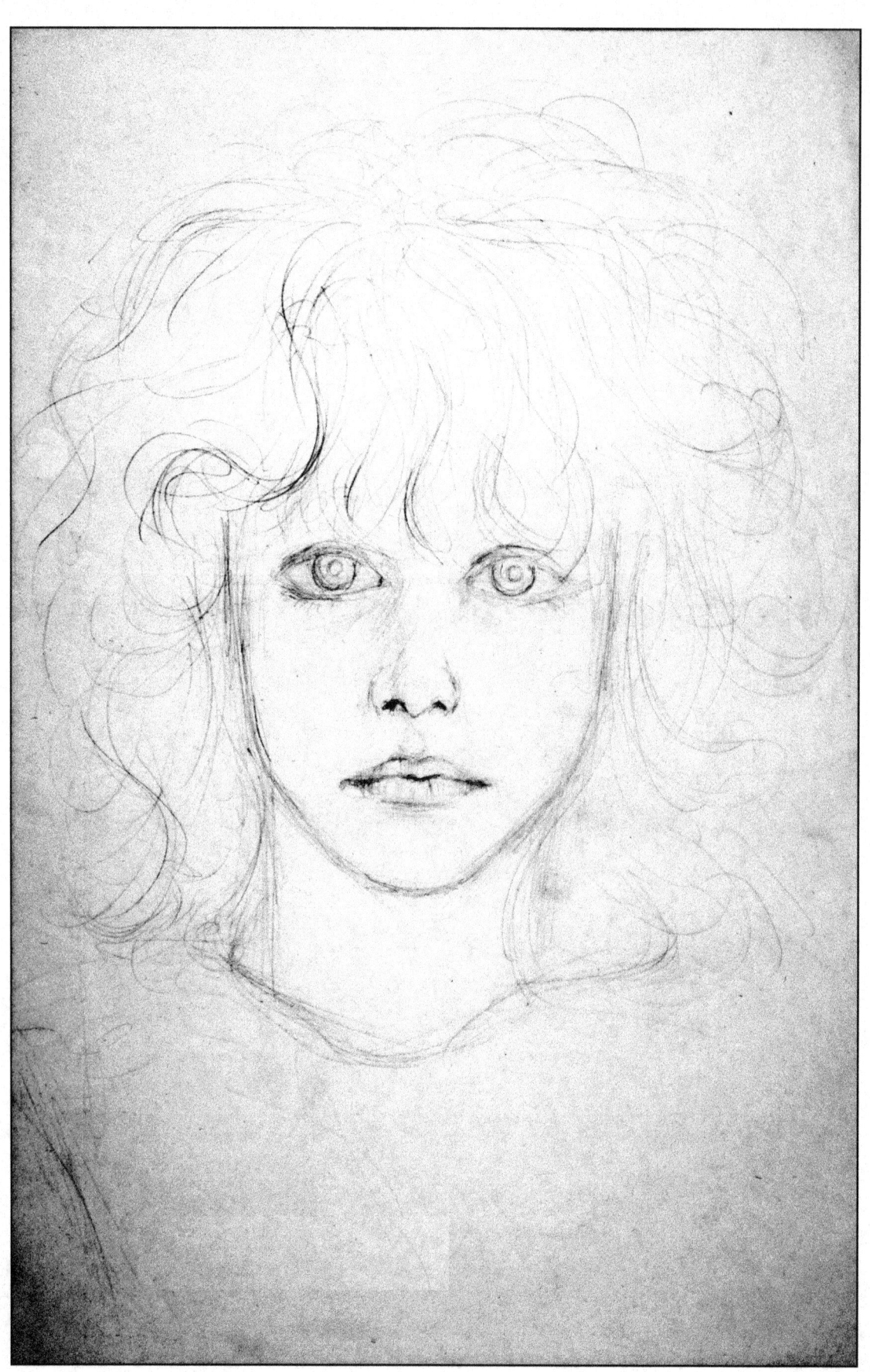

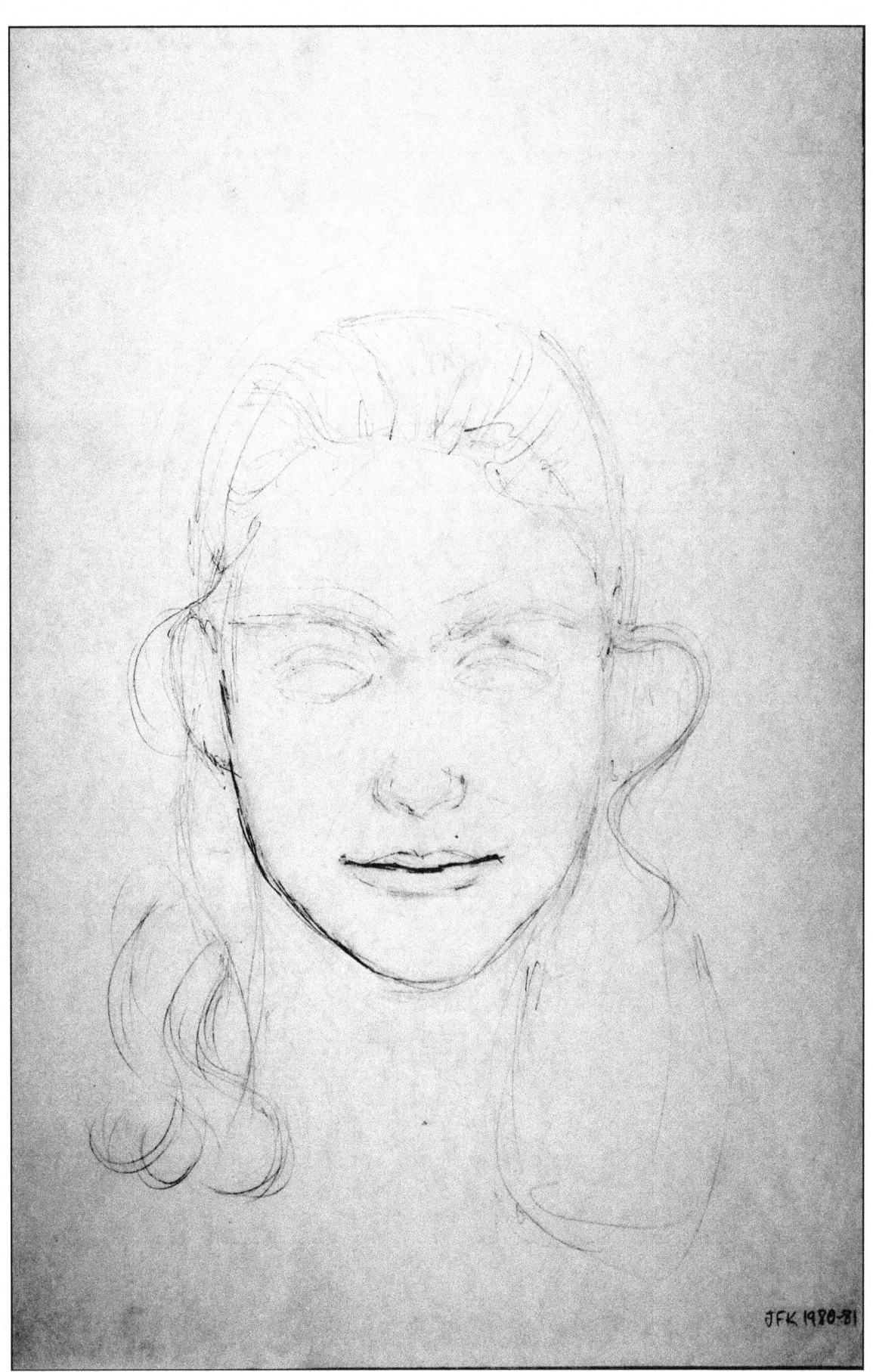

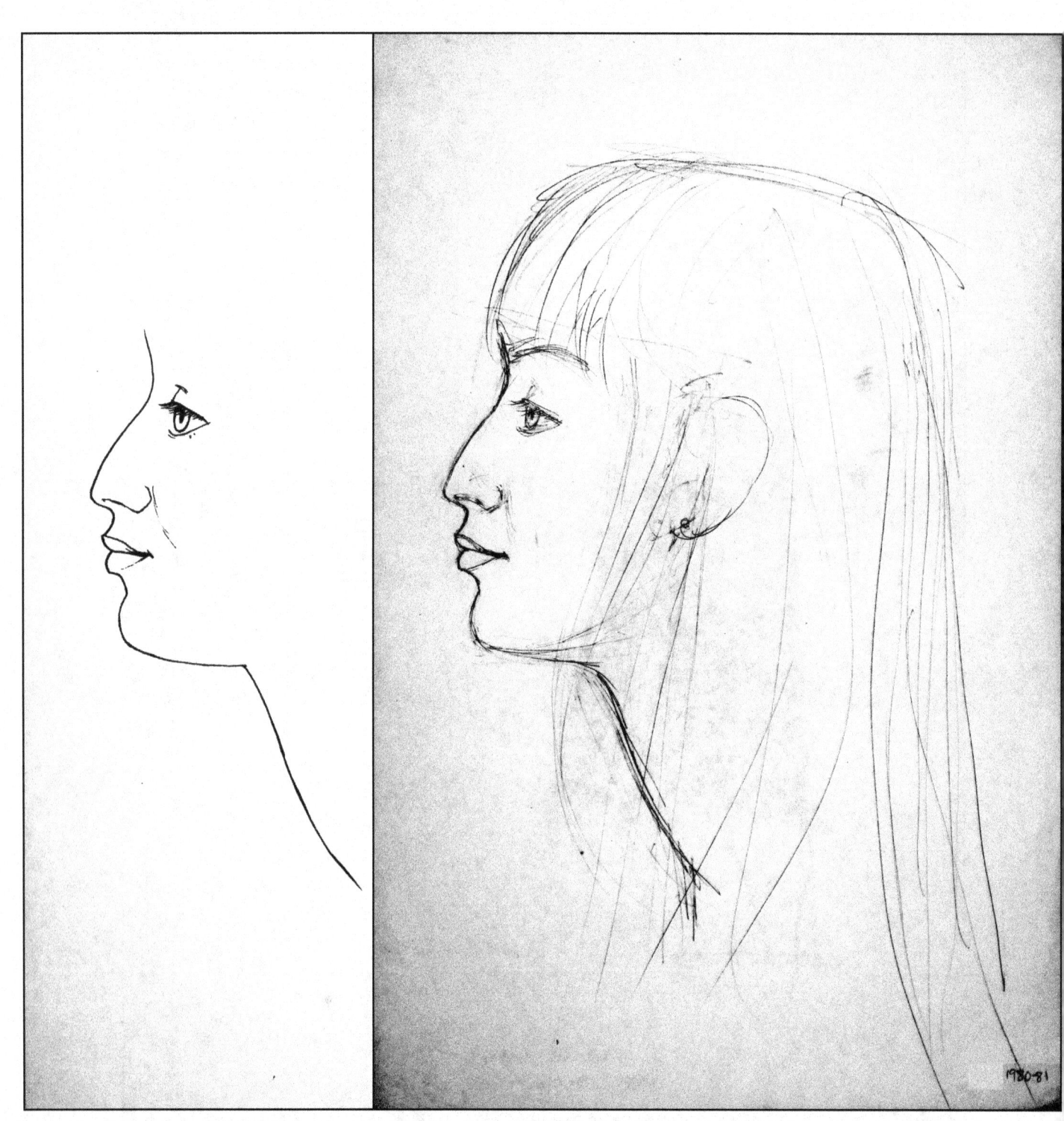

Pen-and-Ink Tracing (on the left) of Pencil Drawing (on the right)

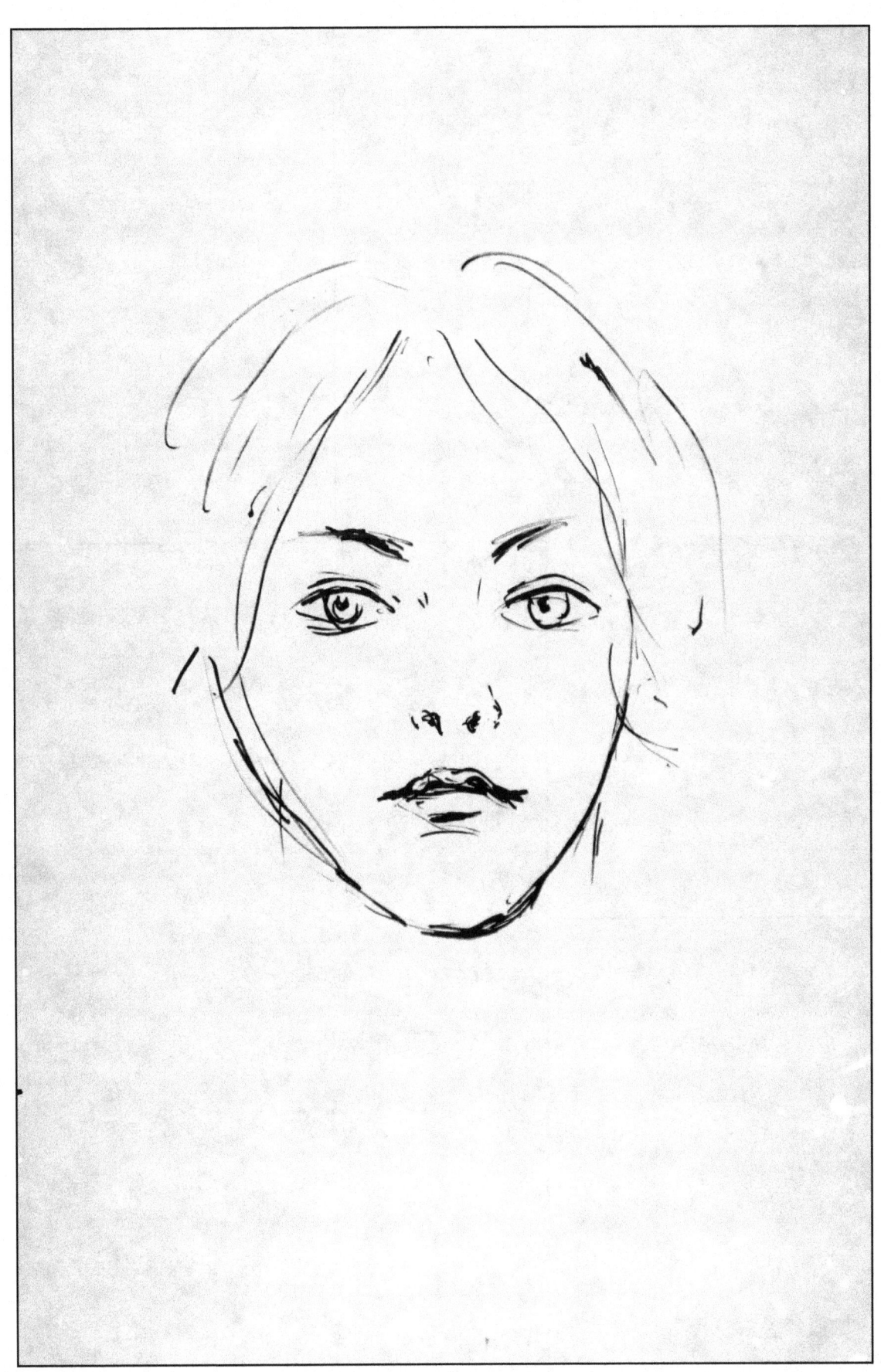

Felt-Tipped-Pen Drawing

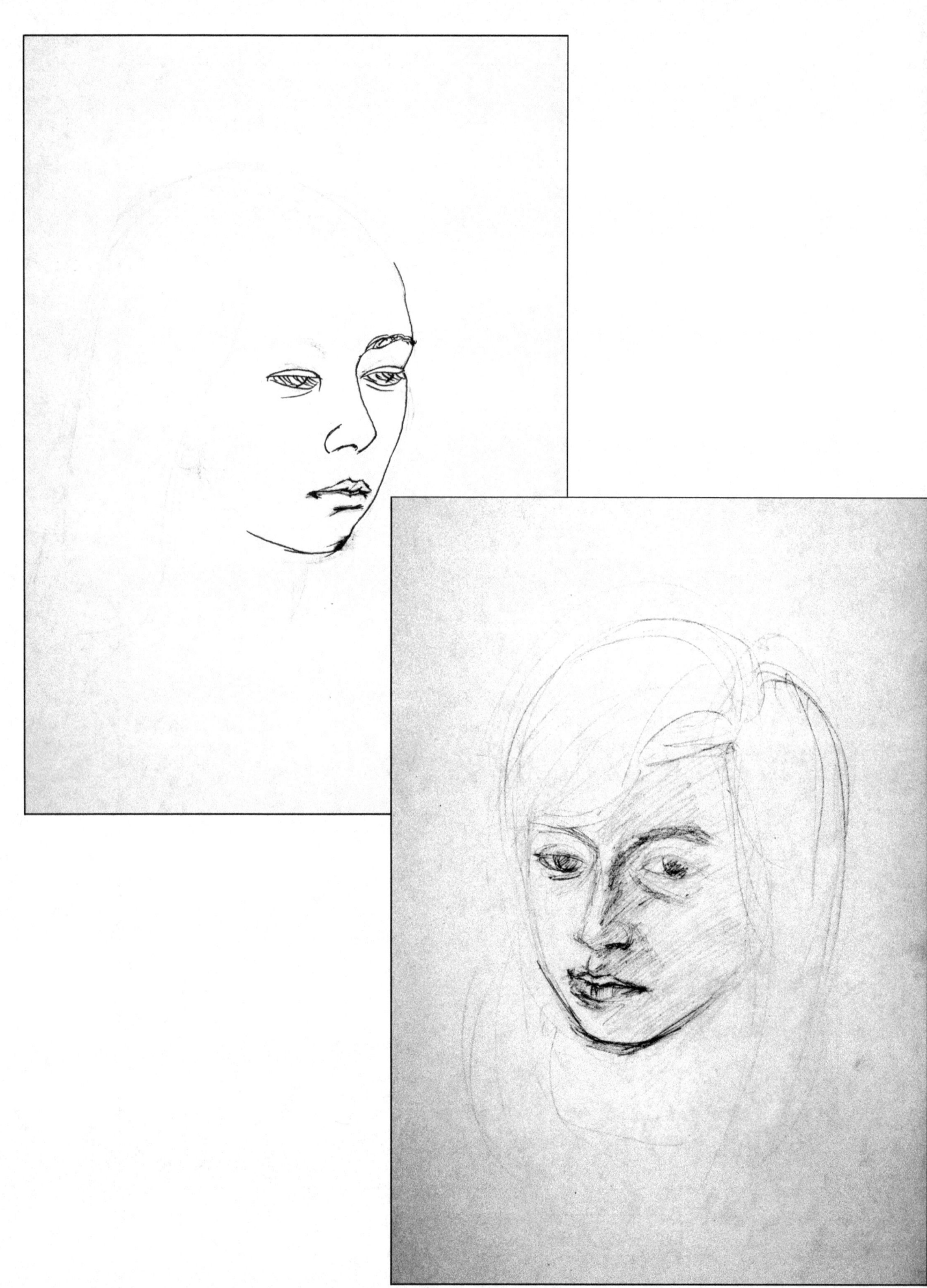

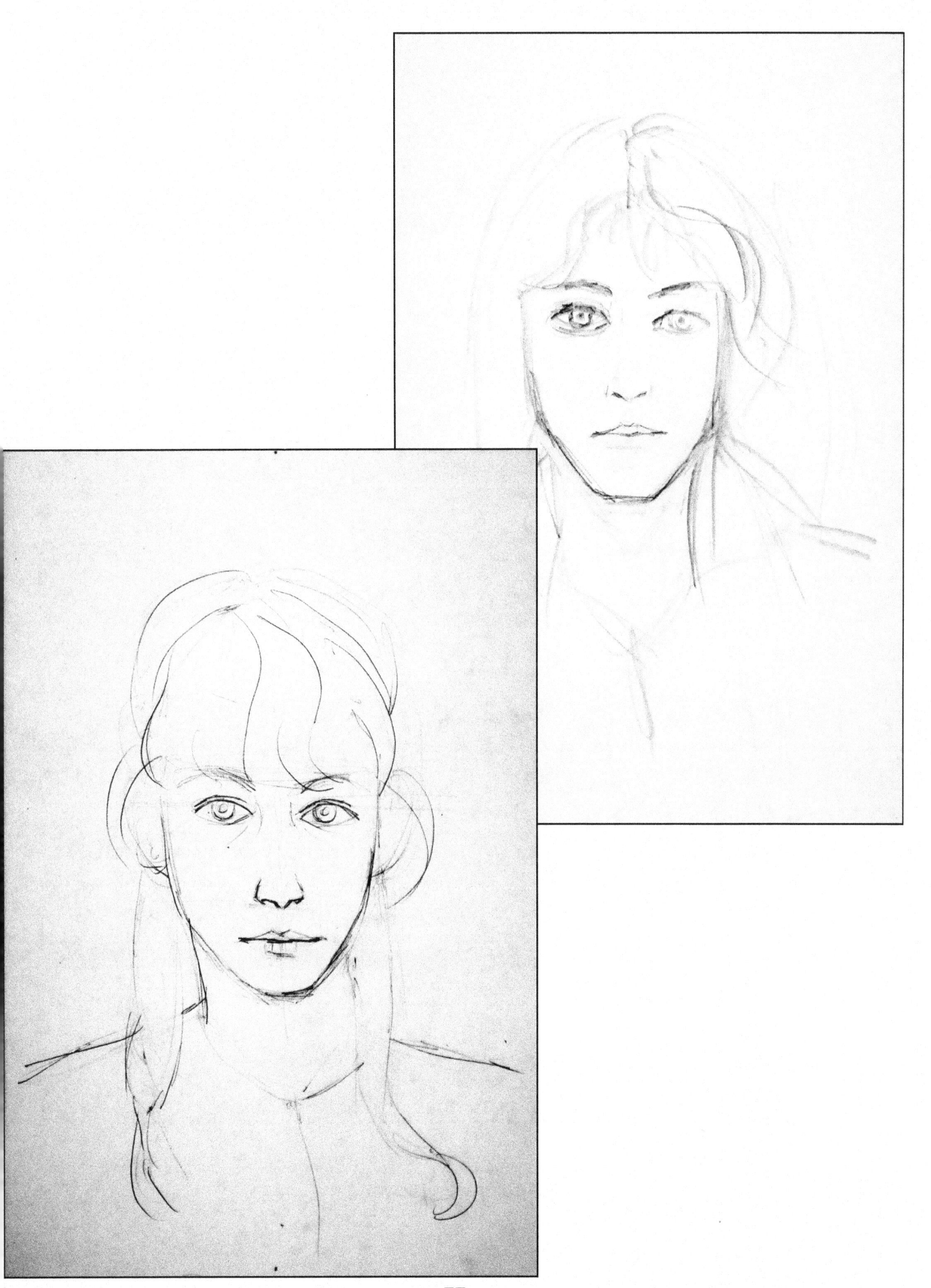

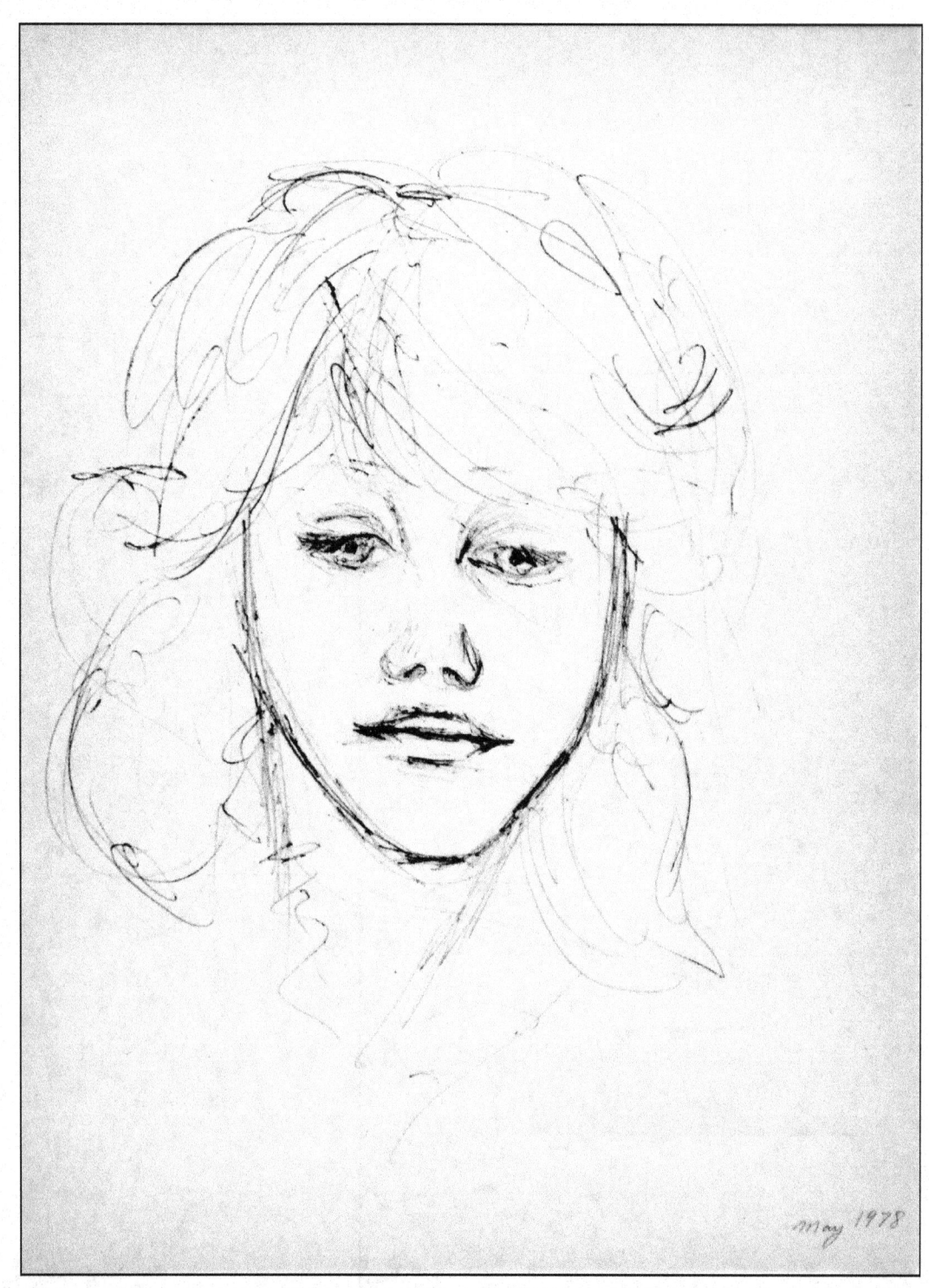

Ballpoint-Pen Drawing

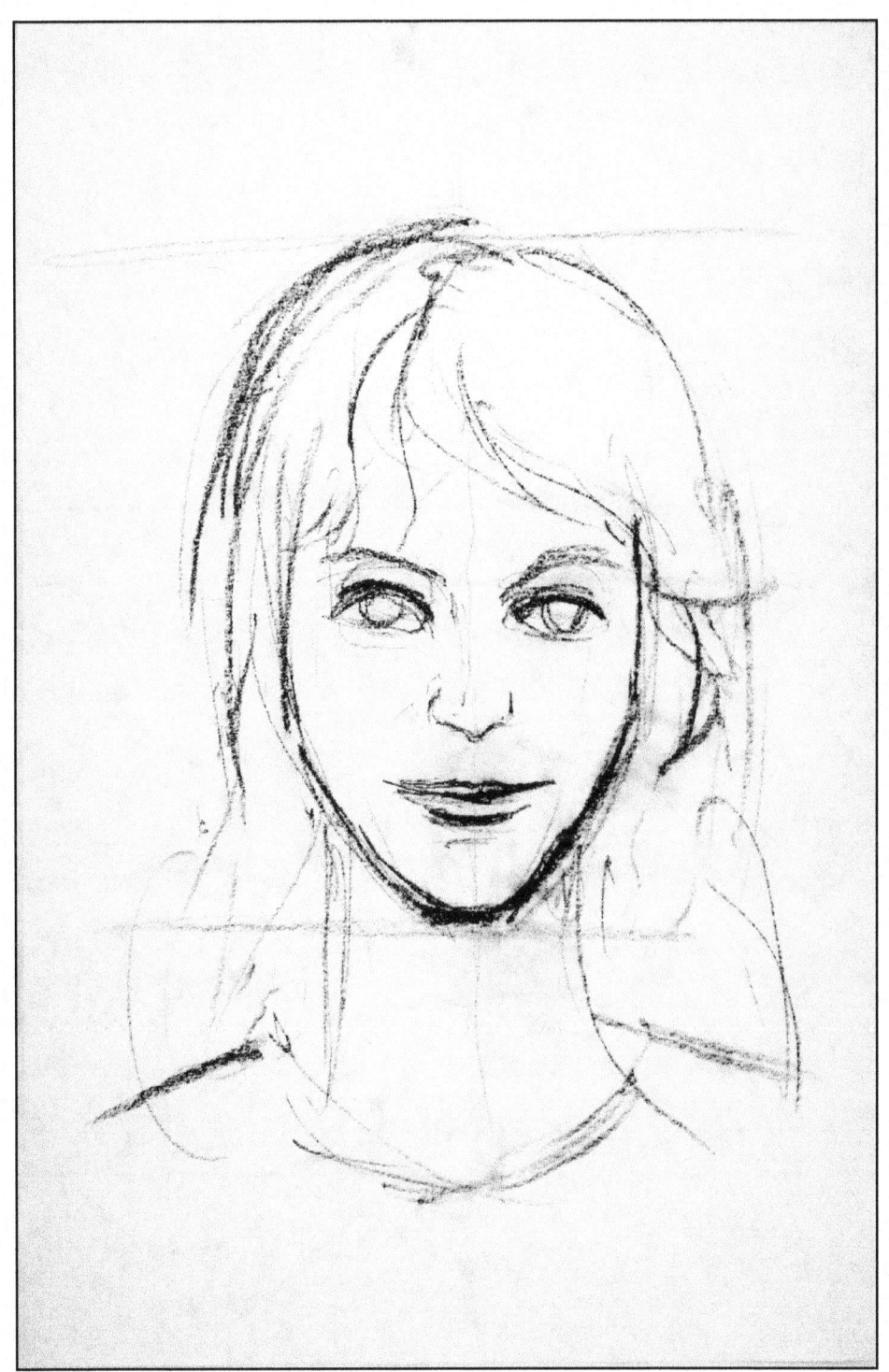

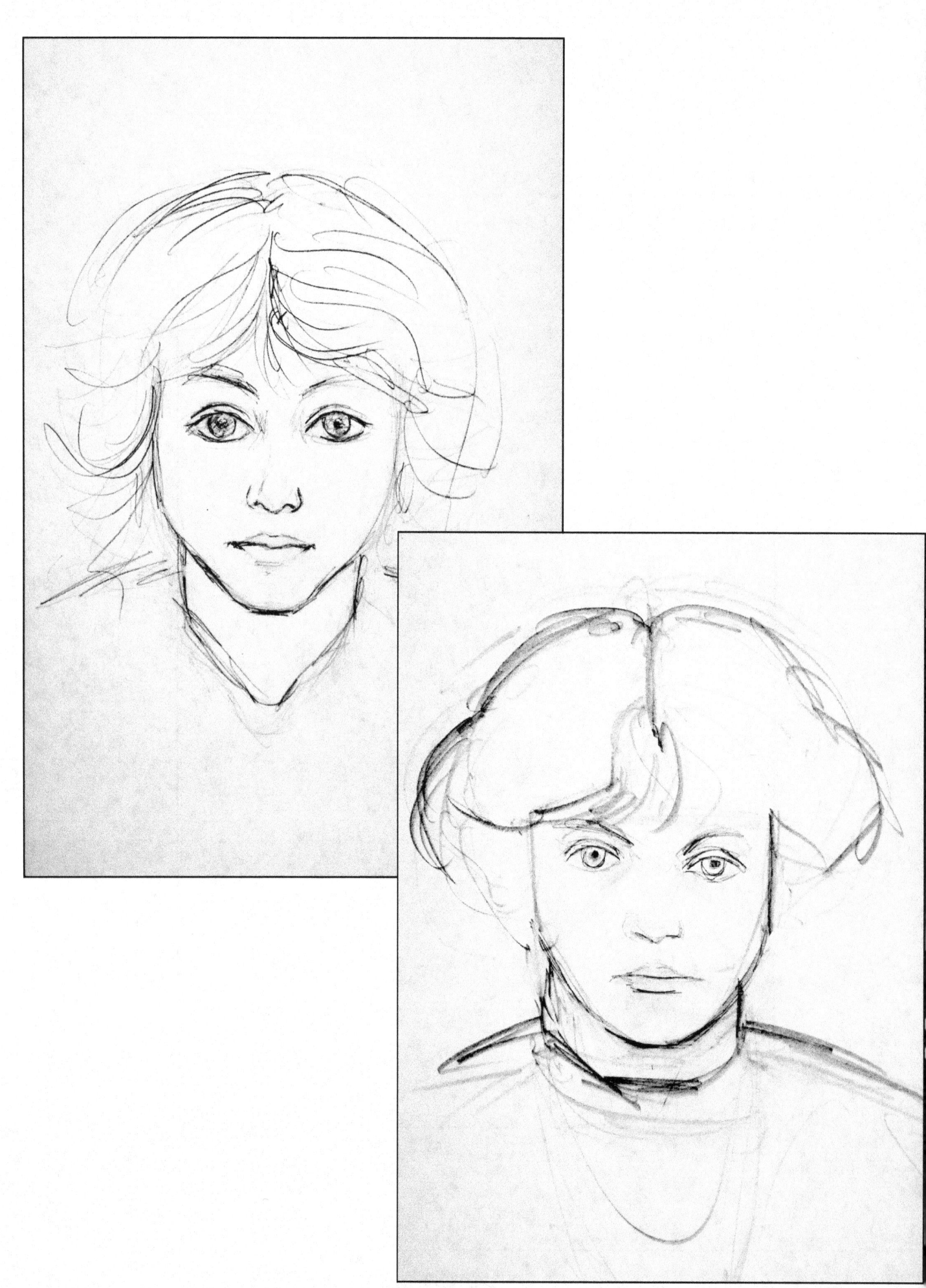

Ballpoint-Pen Drawings

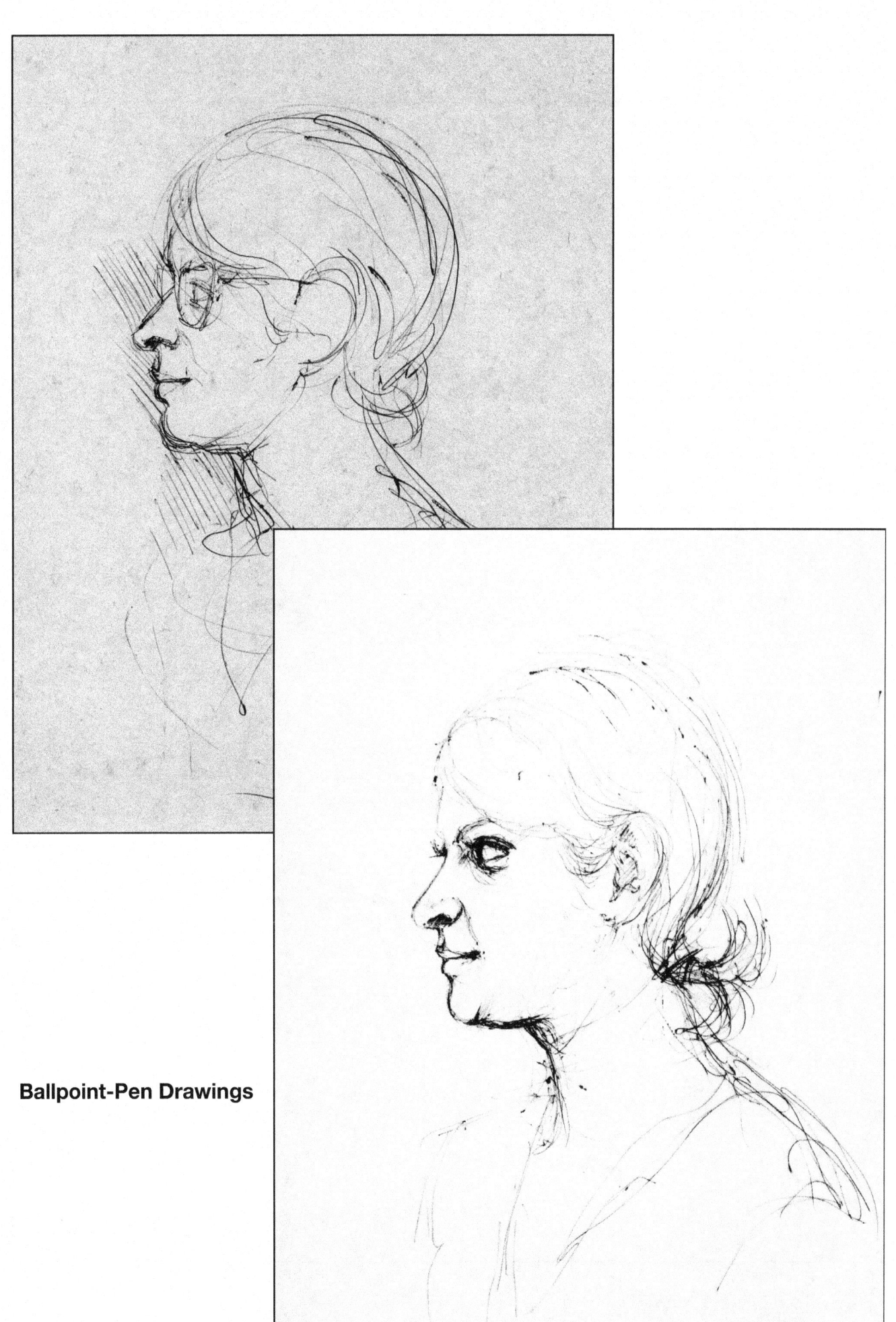

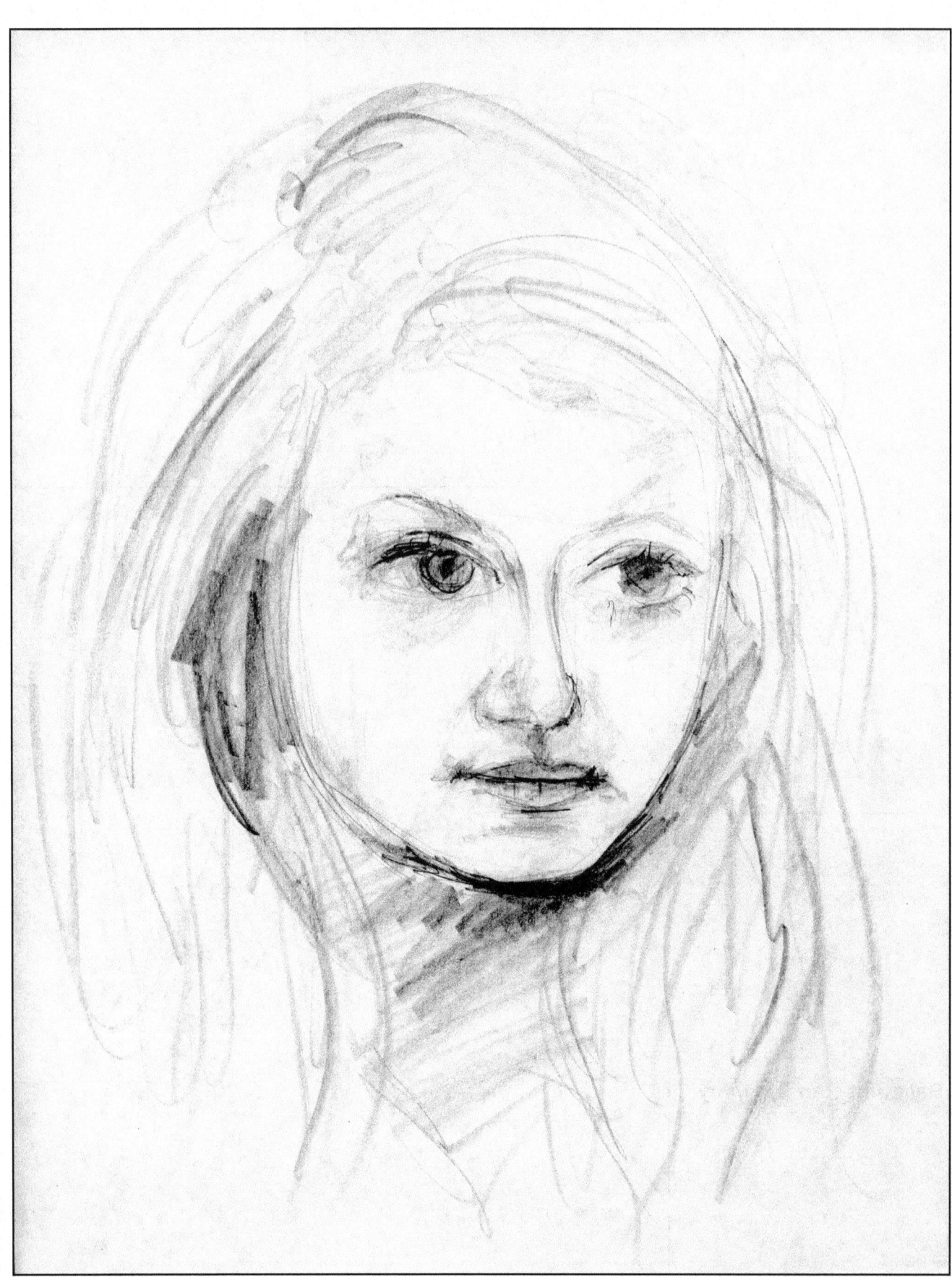

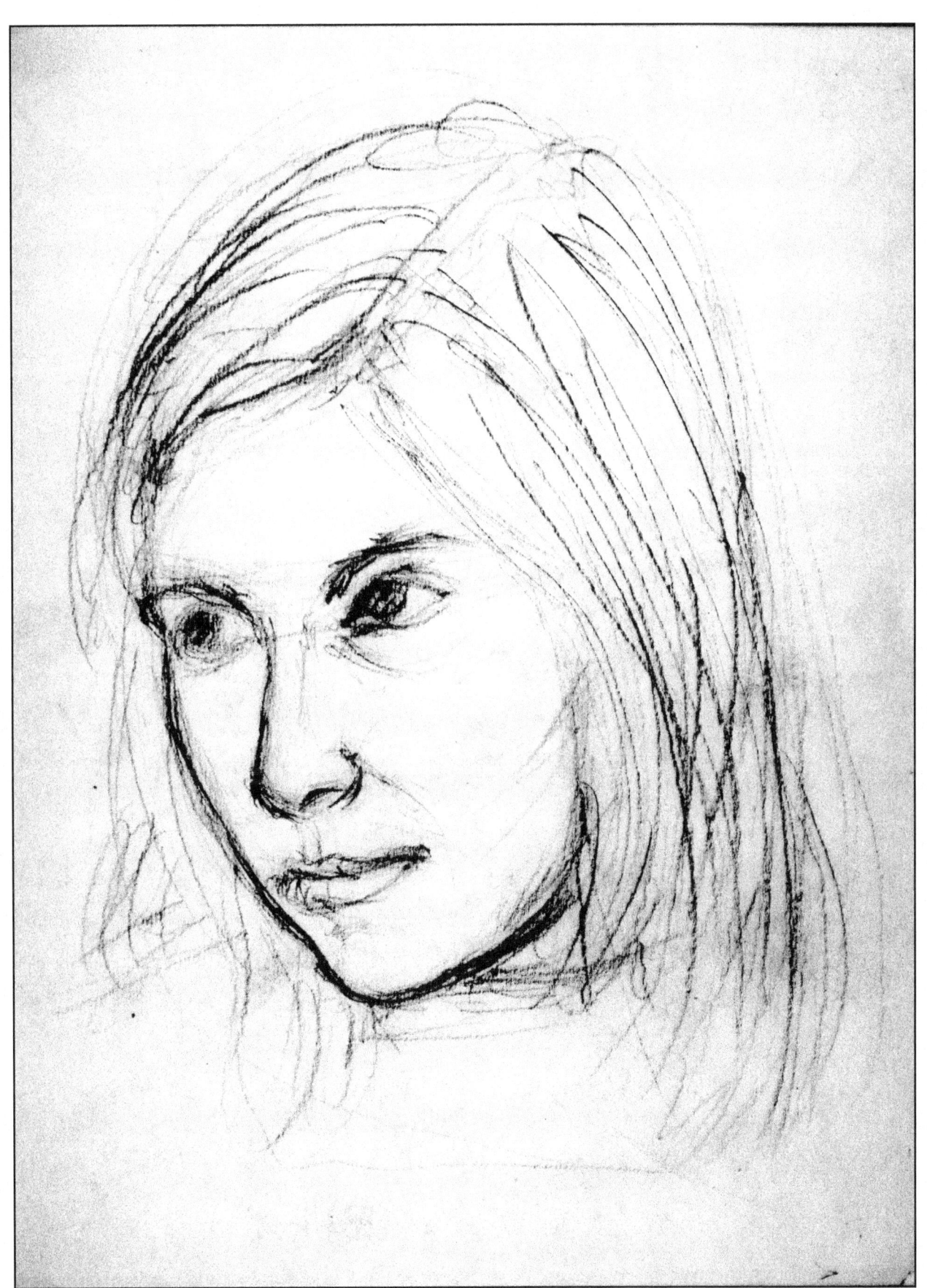

Charcoal

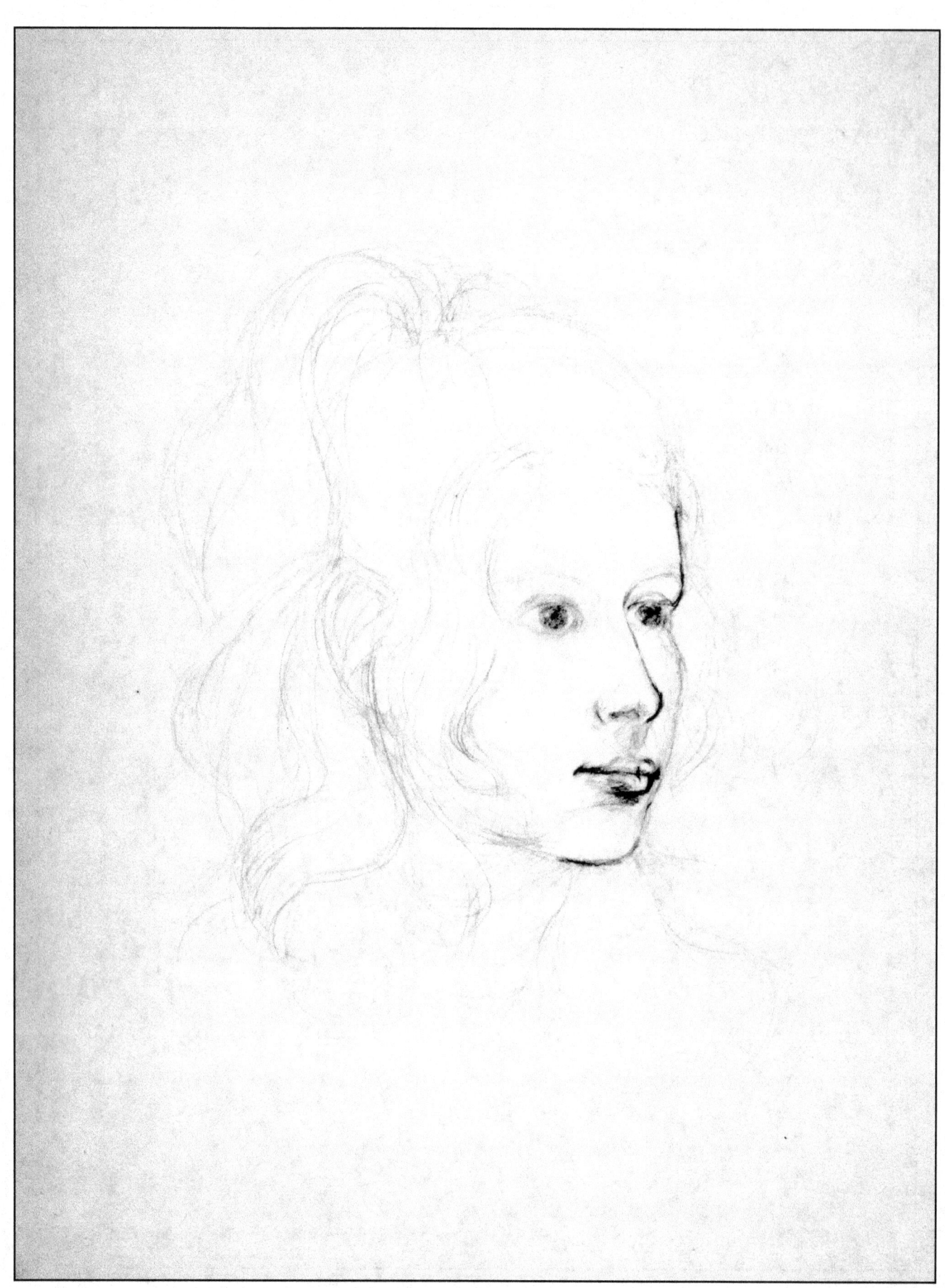

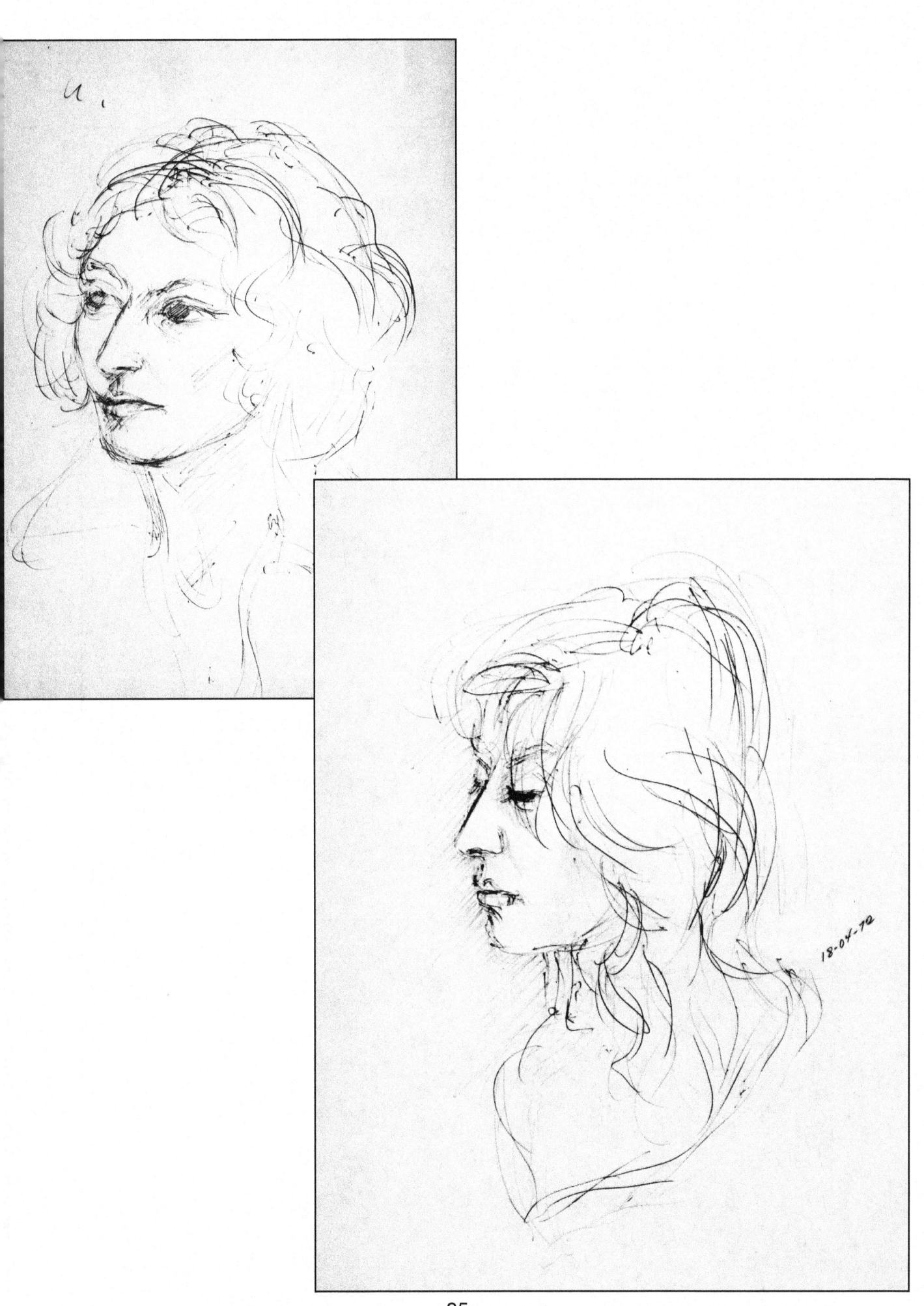

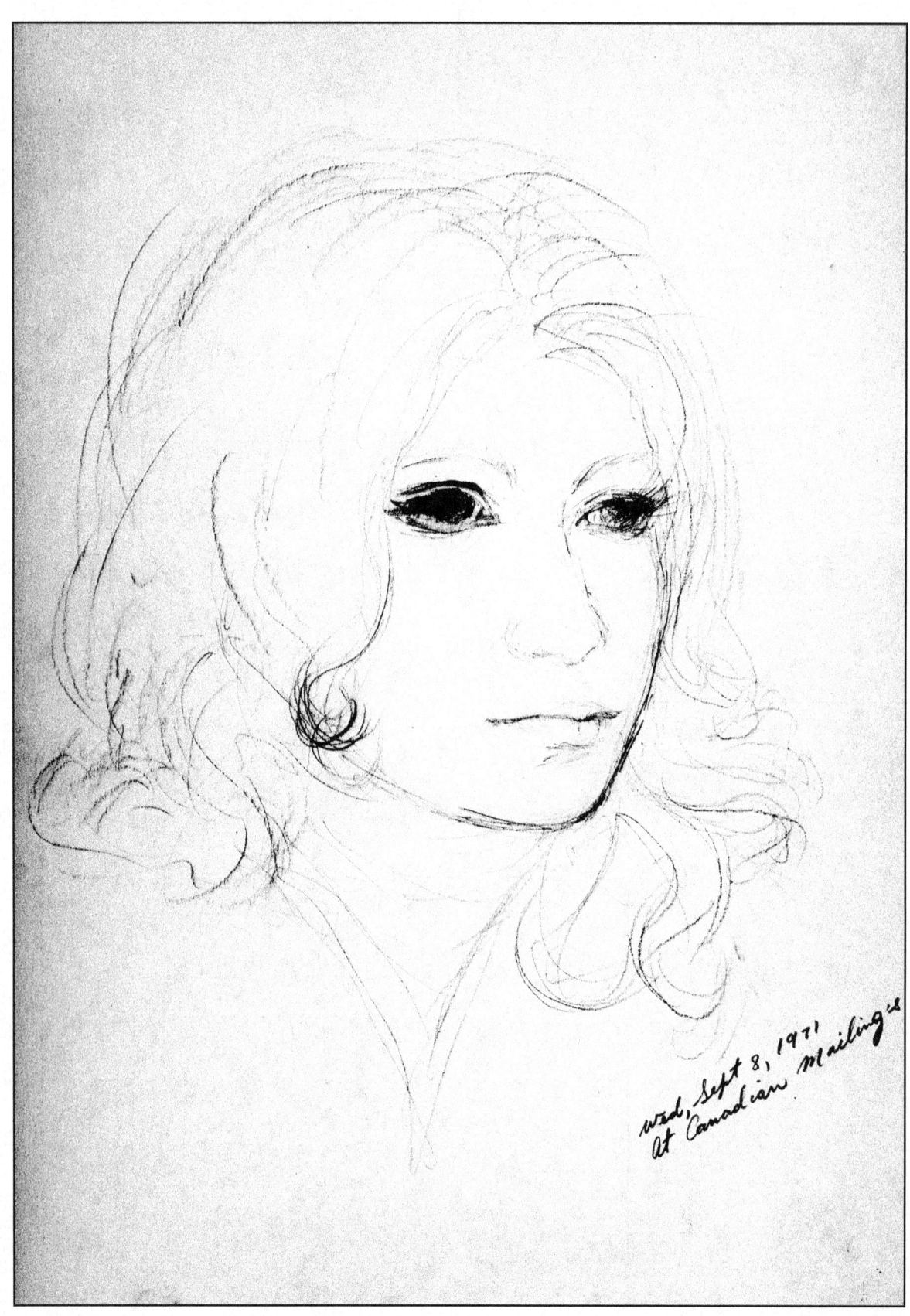

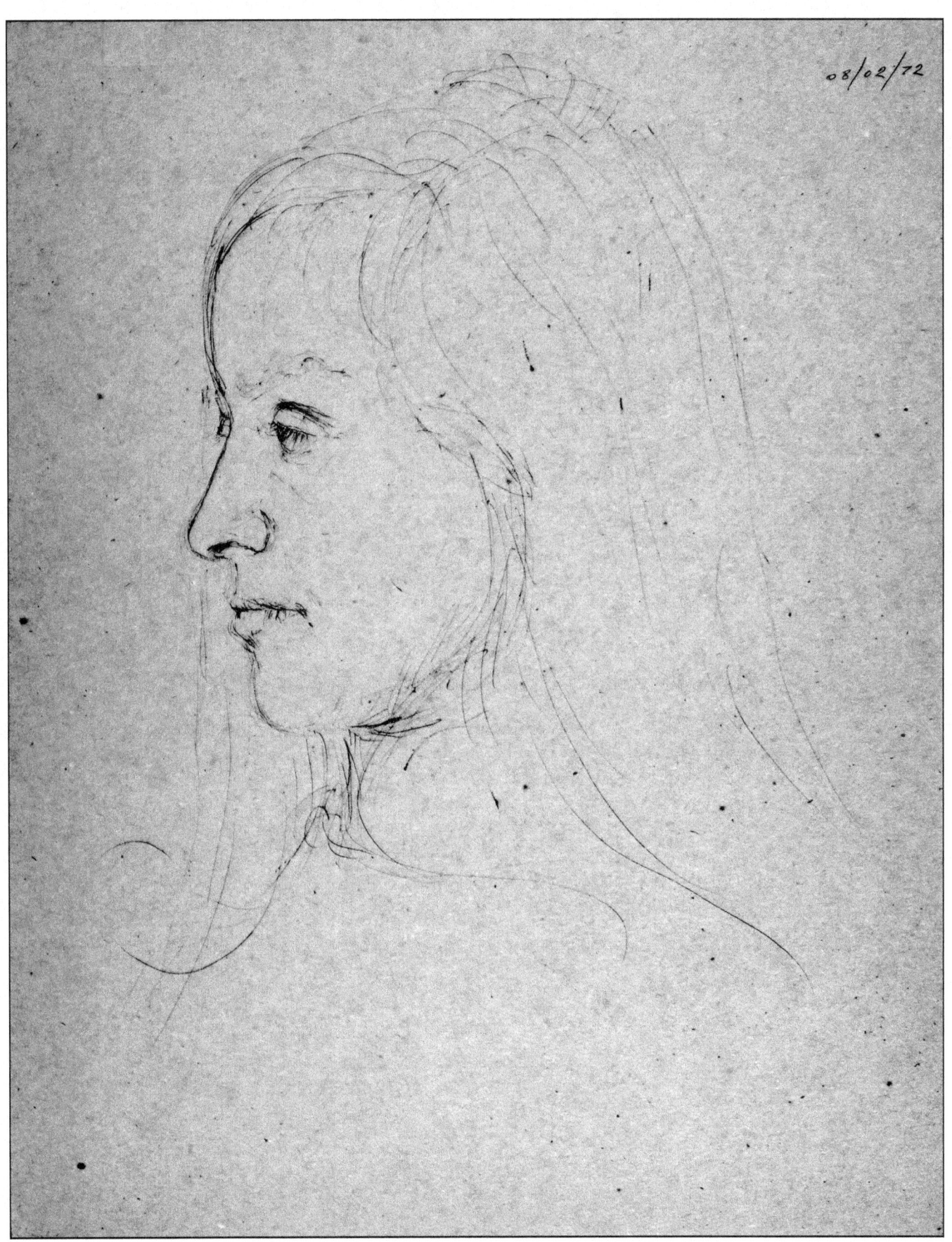

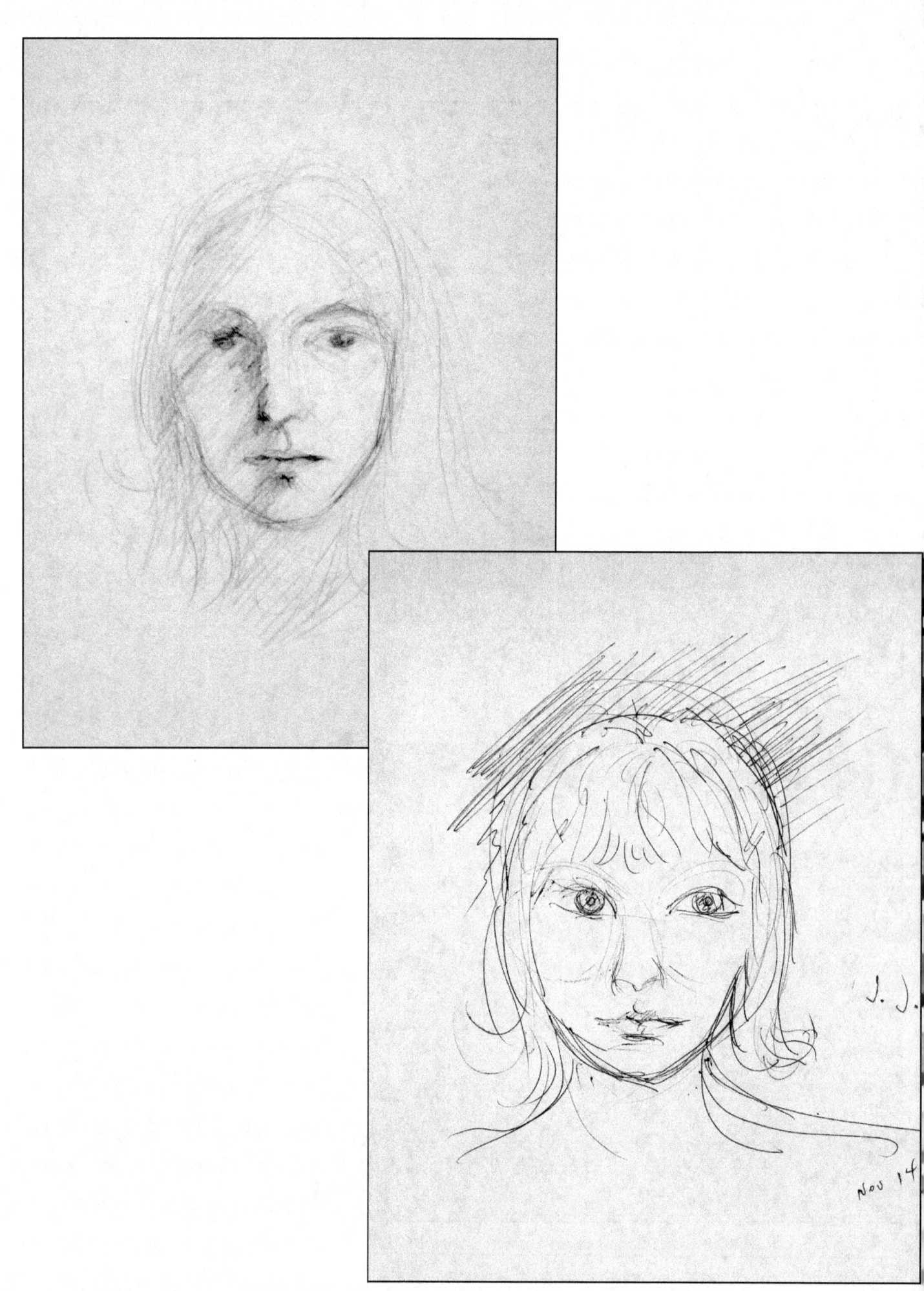

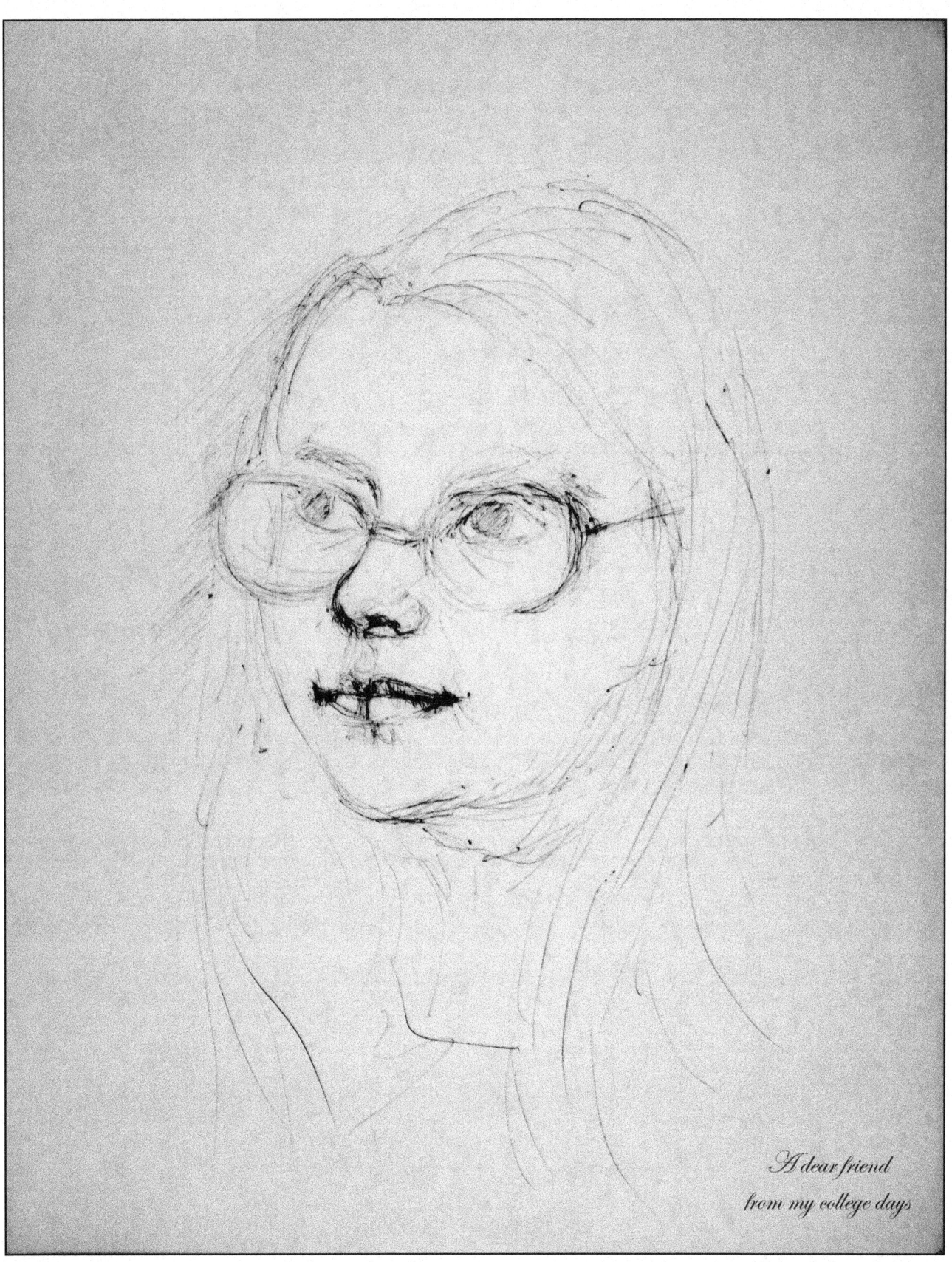

A dear friend from my college days

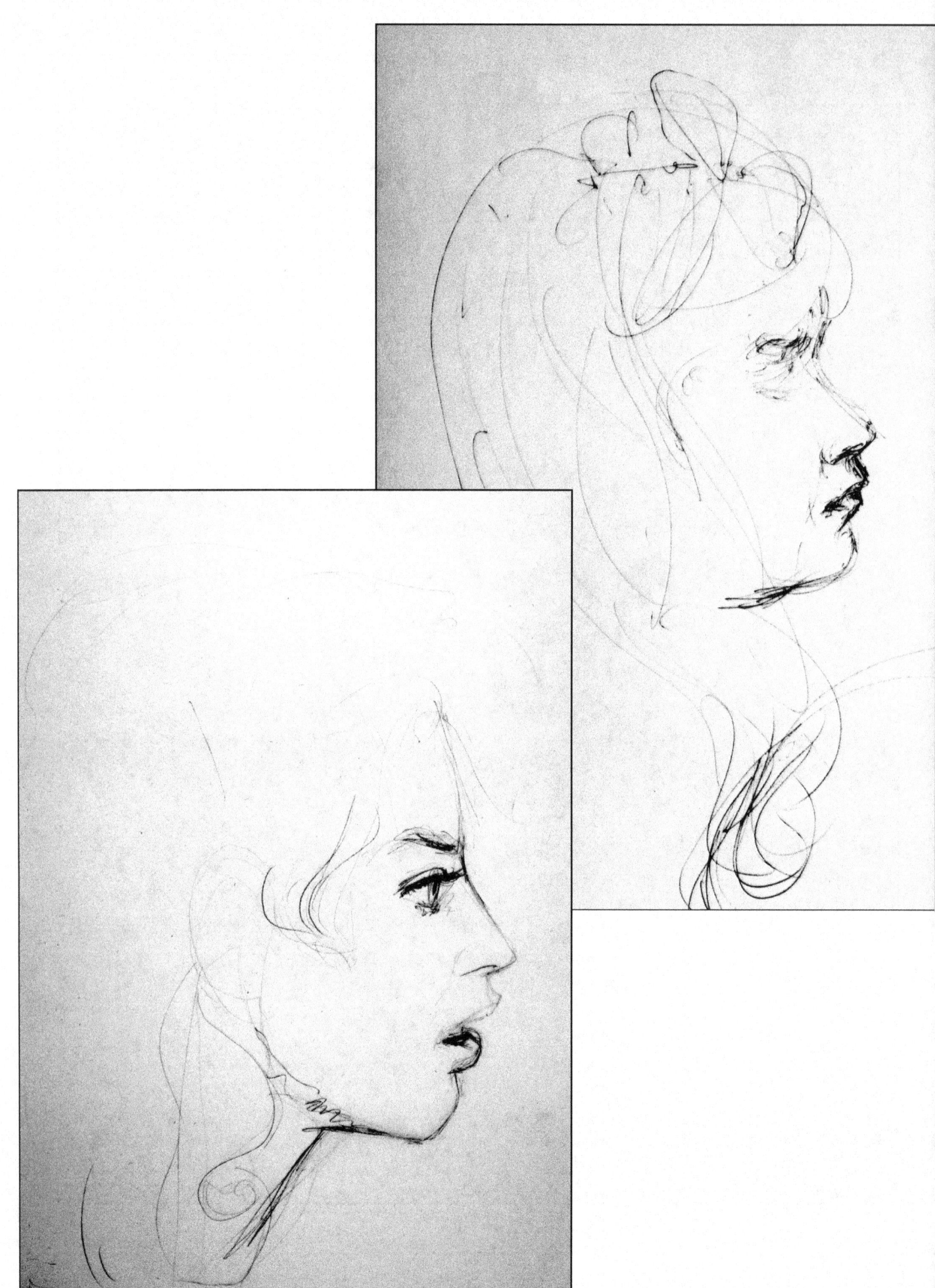

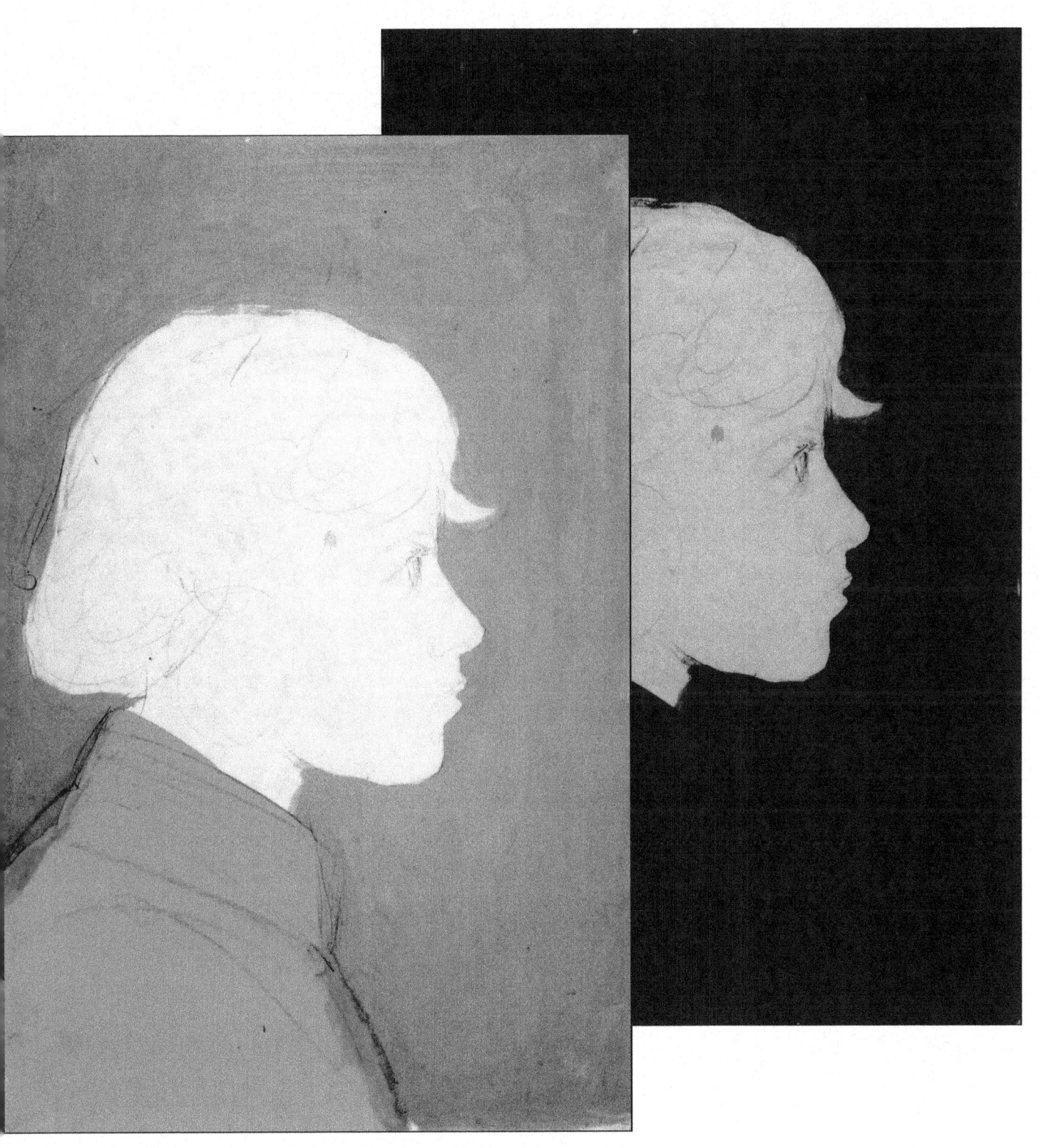

Watercolor (on the left) and CG Imagery (on the right)

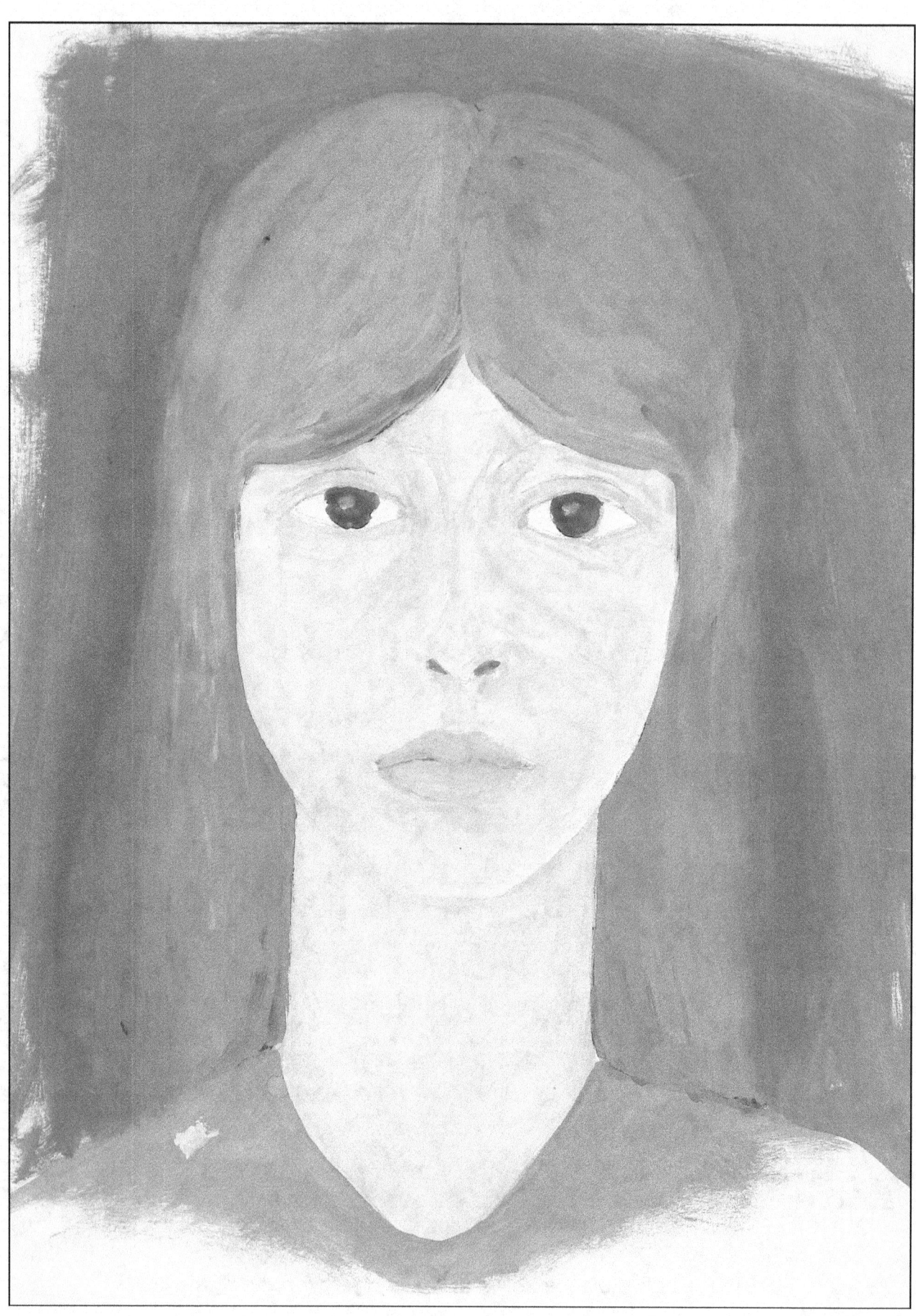

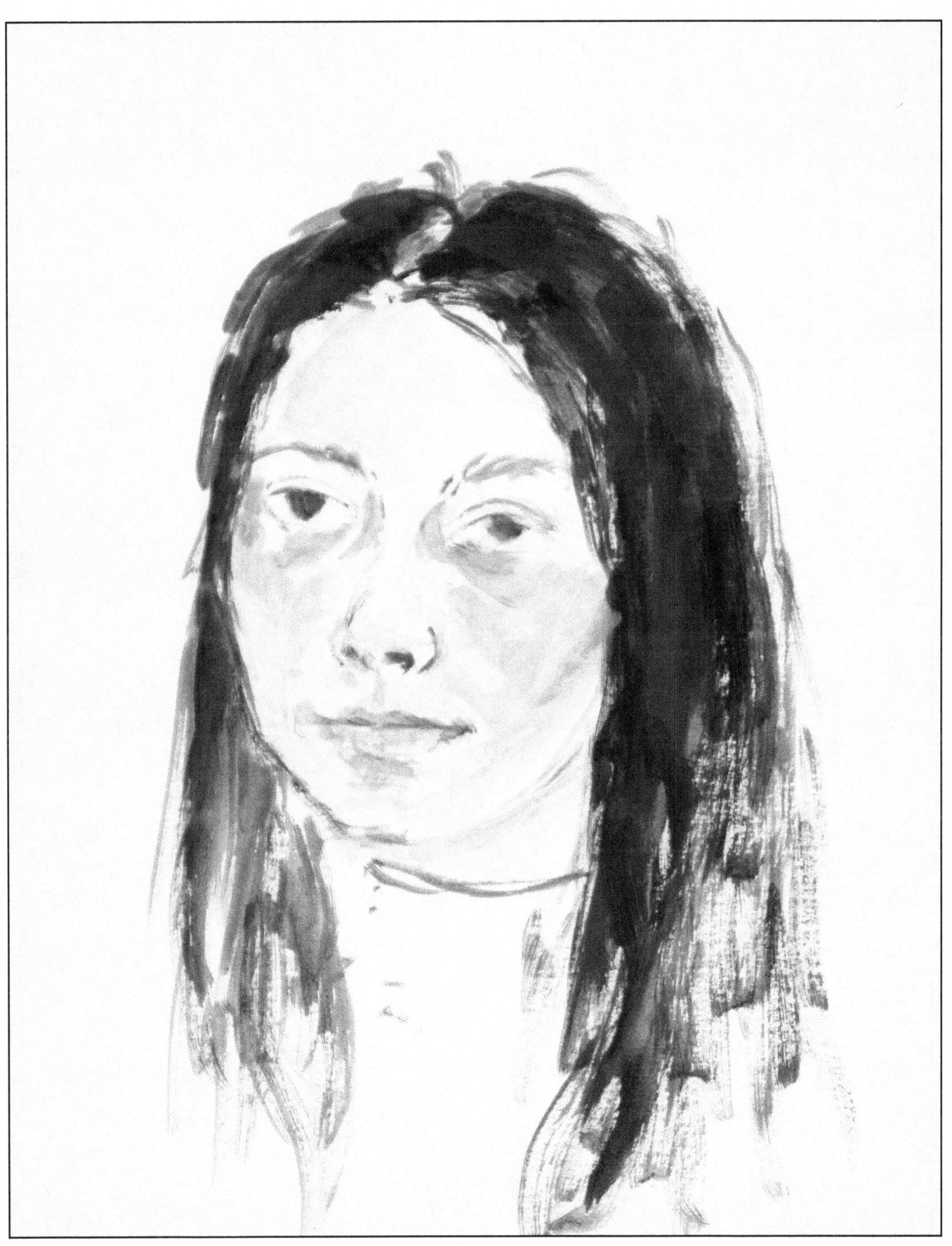

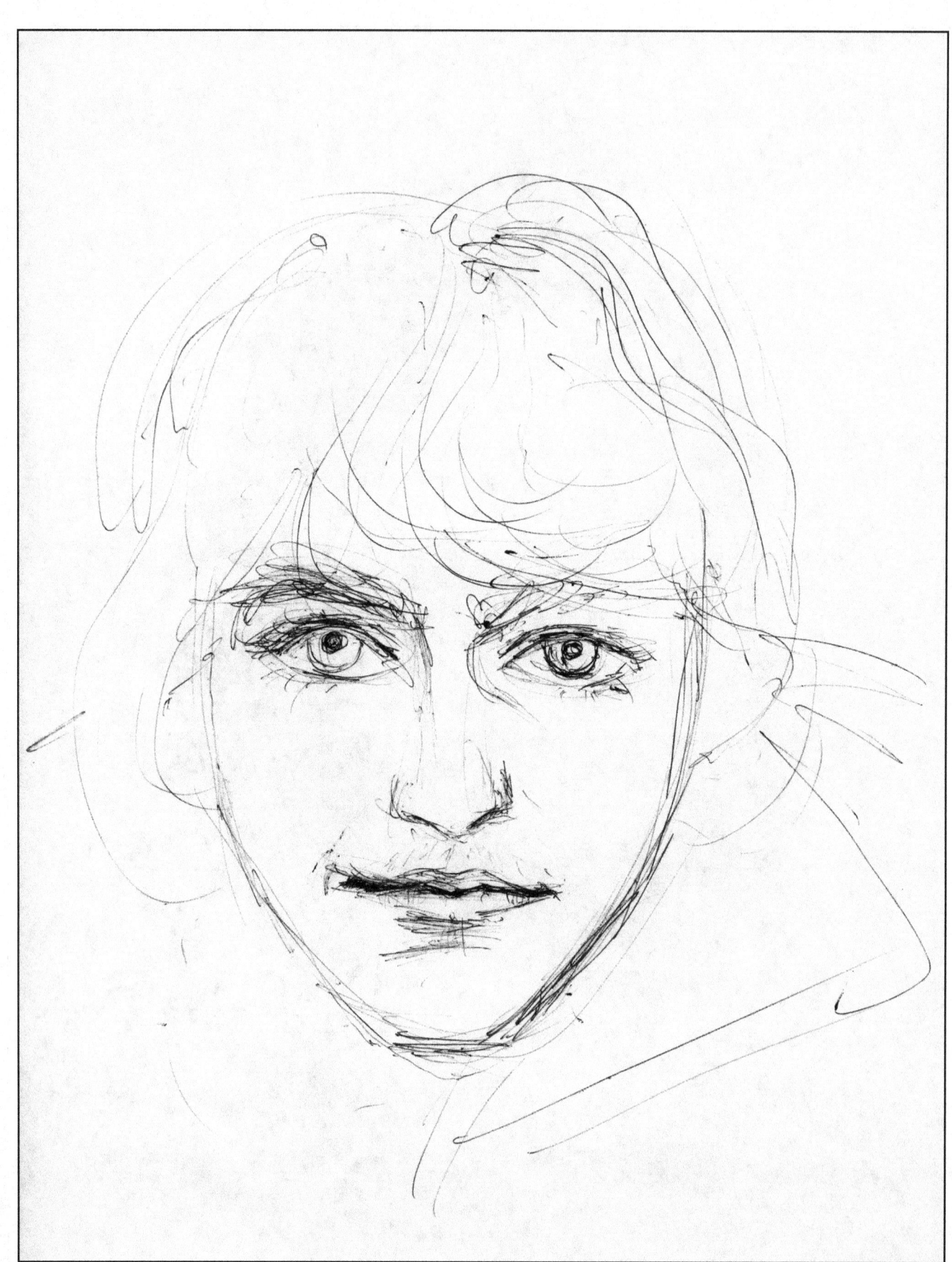

Ballpoint-Pen Drawing

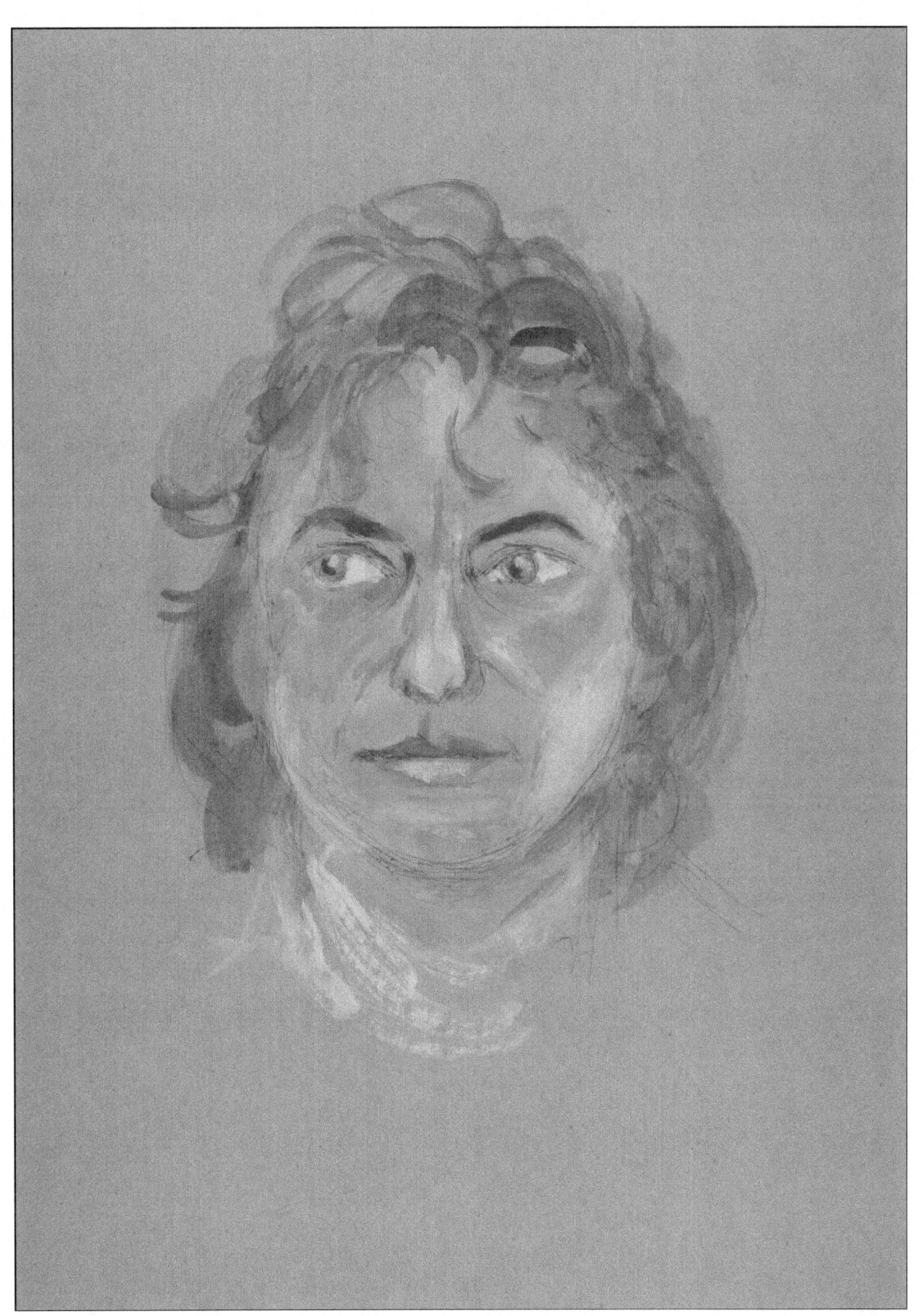

Acrylic on cardboard

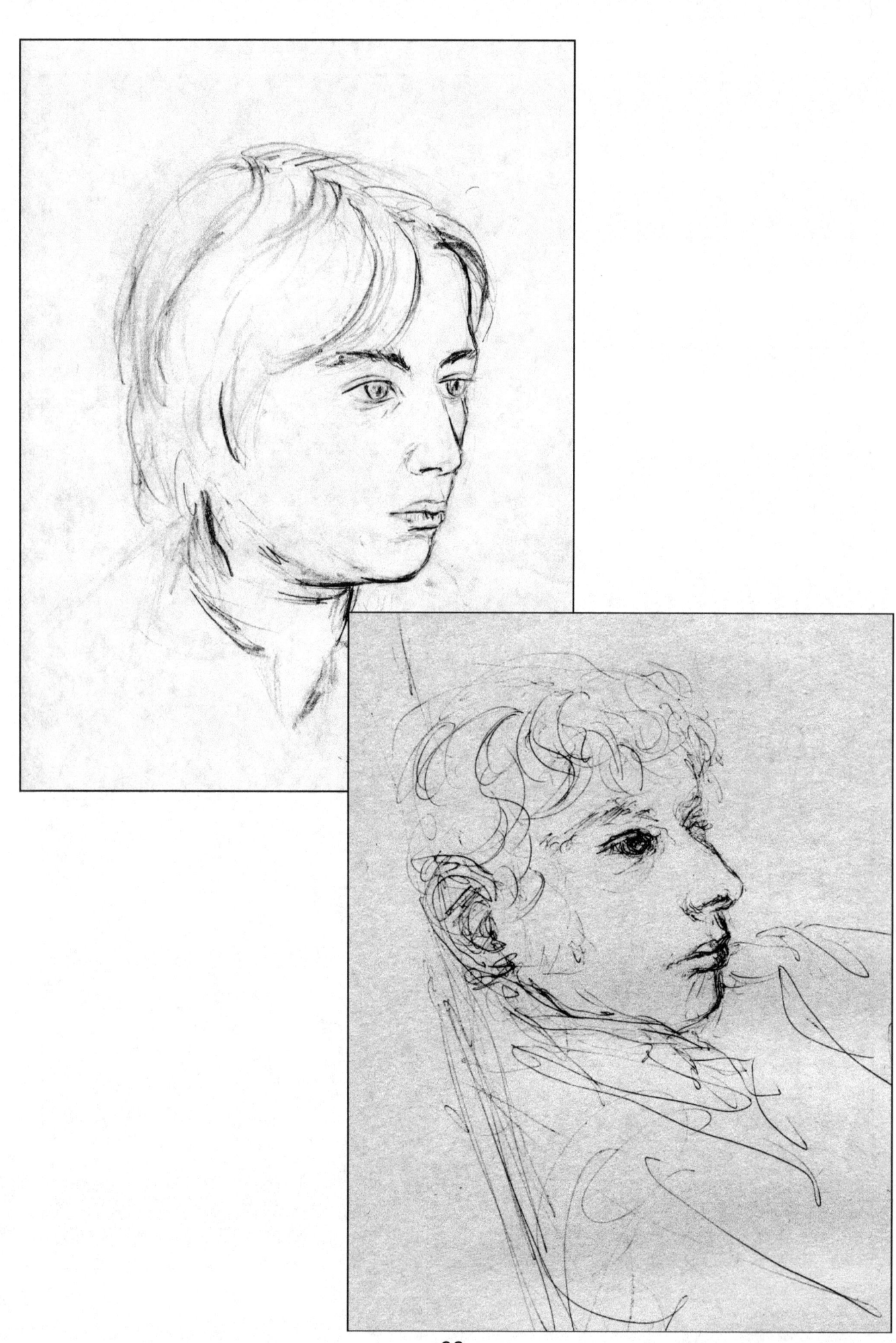

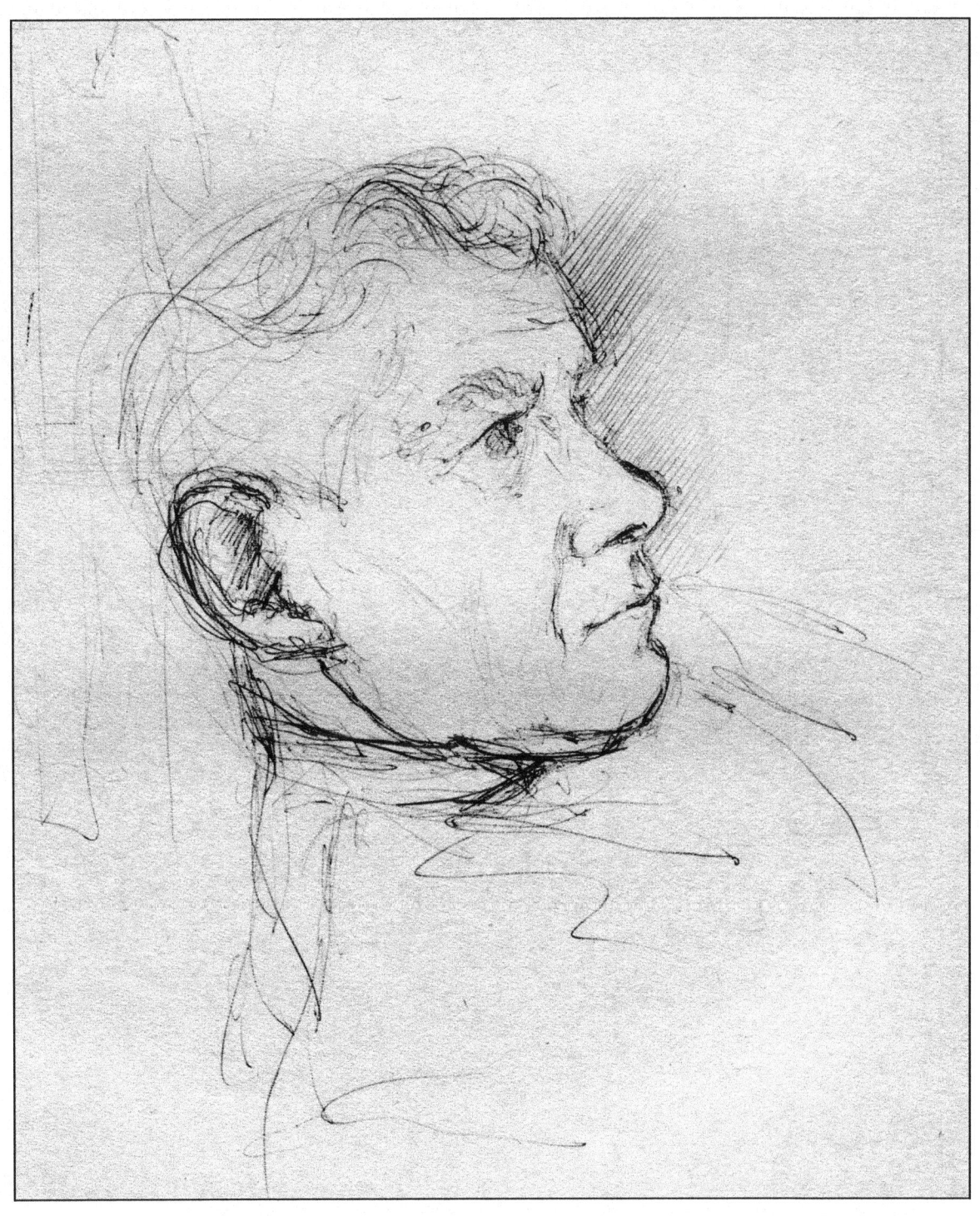

Ballpoint-Pen Drawing

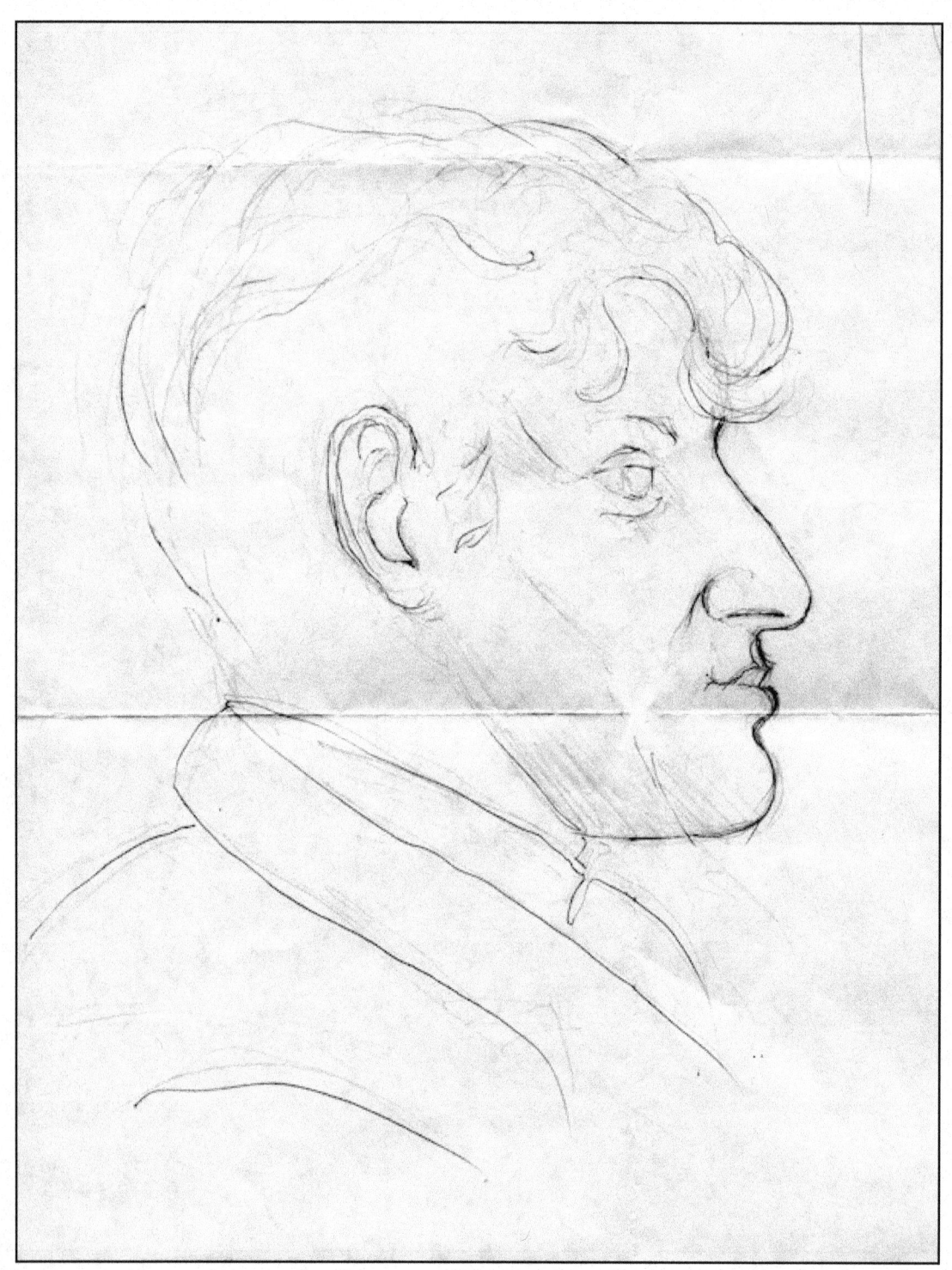

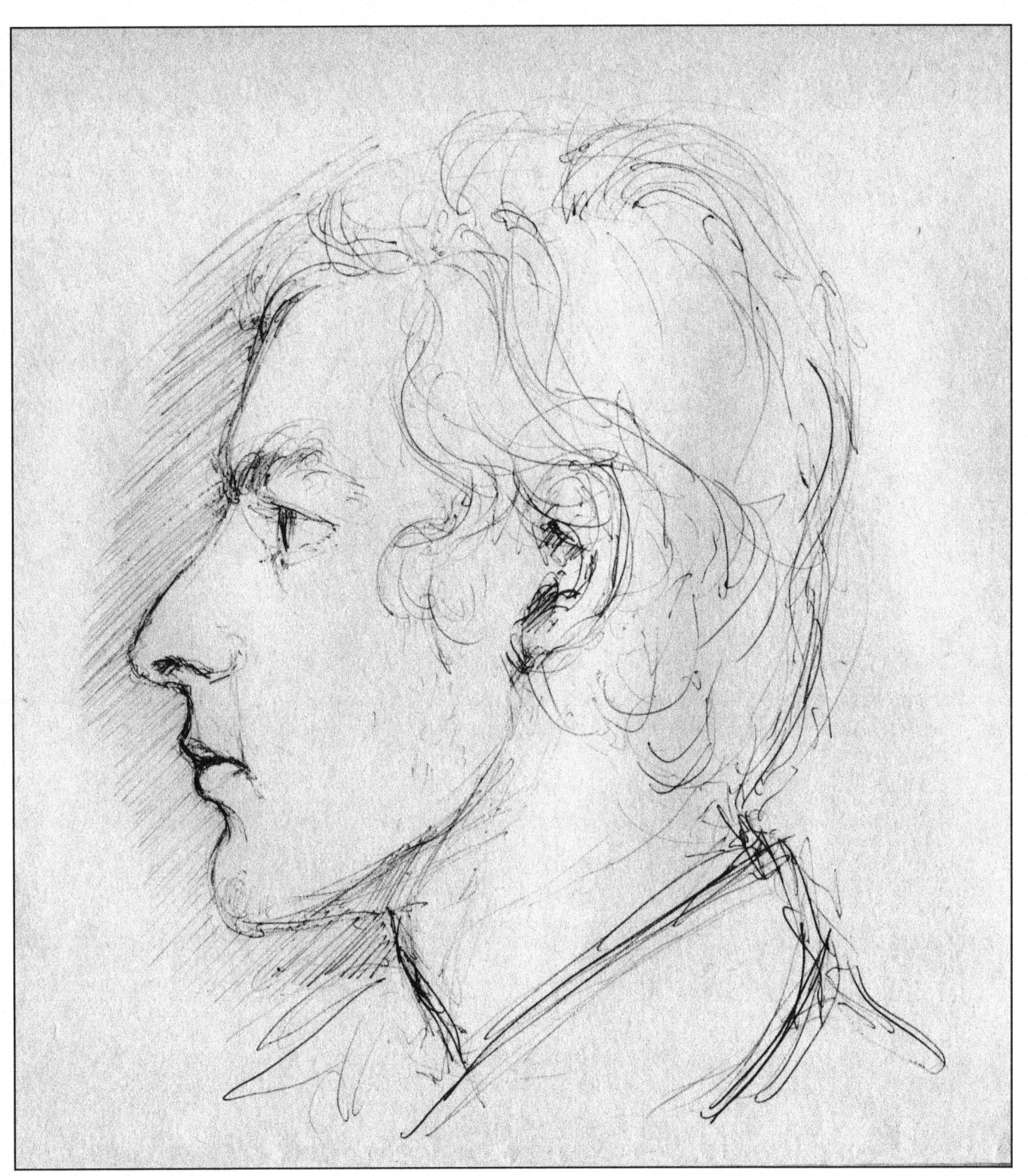

Ballpoint-Pen Drawing

5. Head Observation, Friends

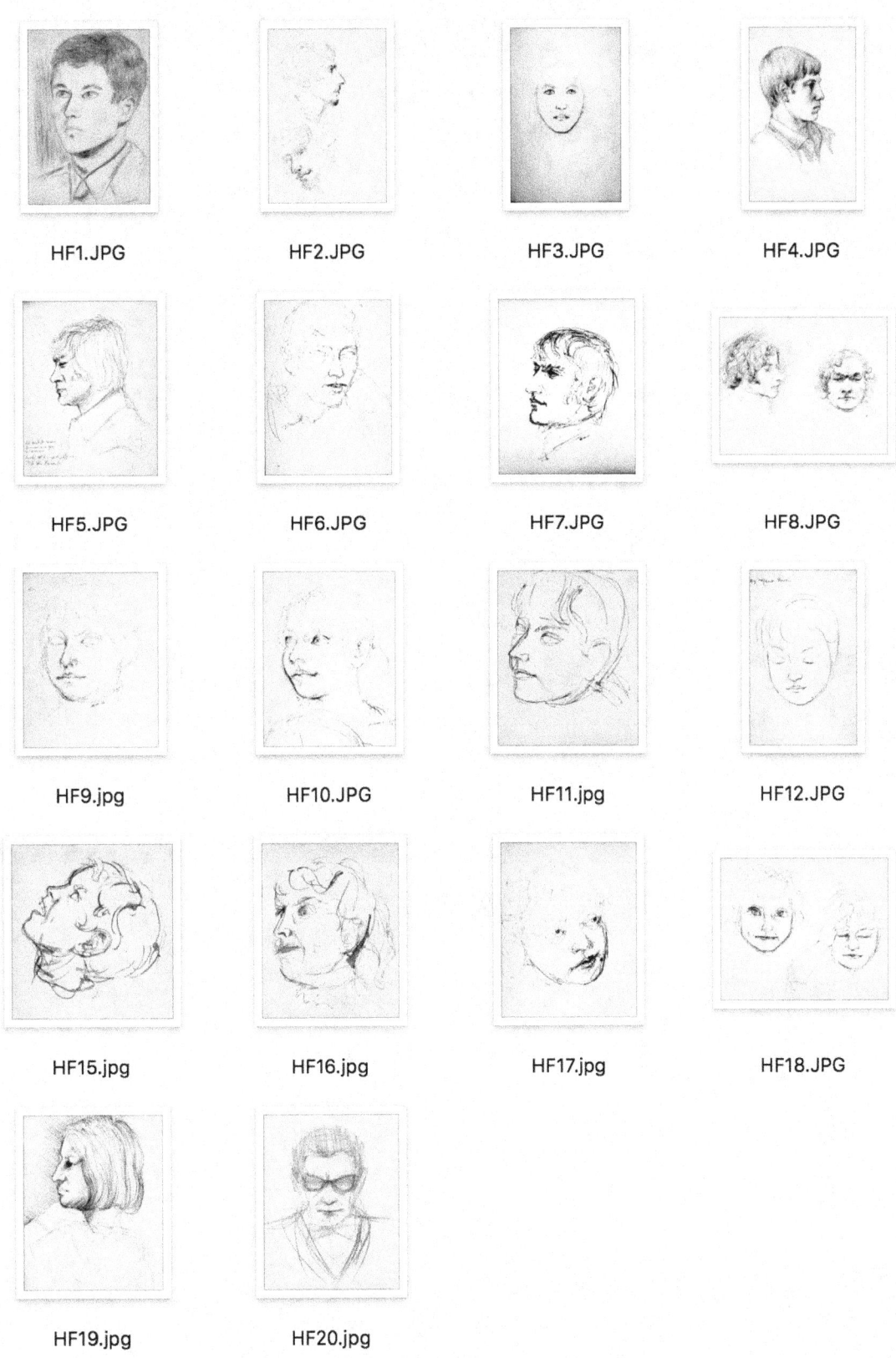

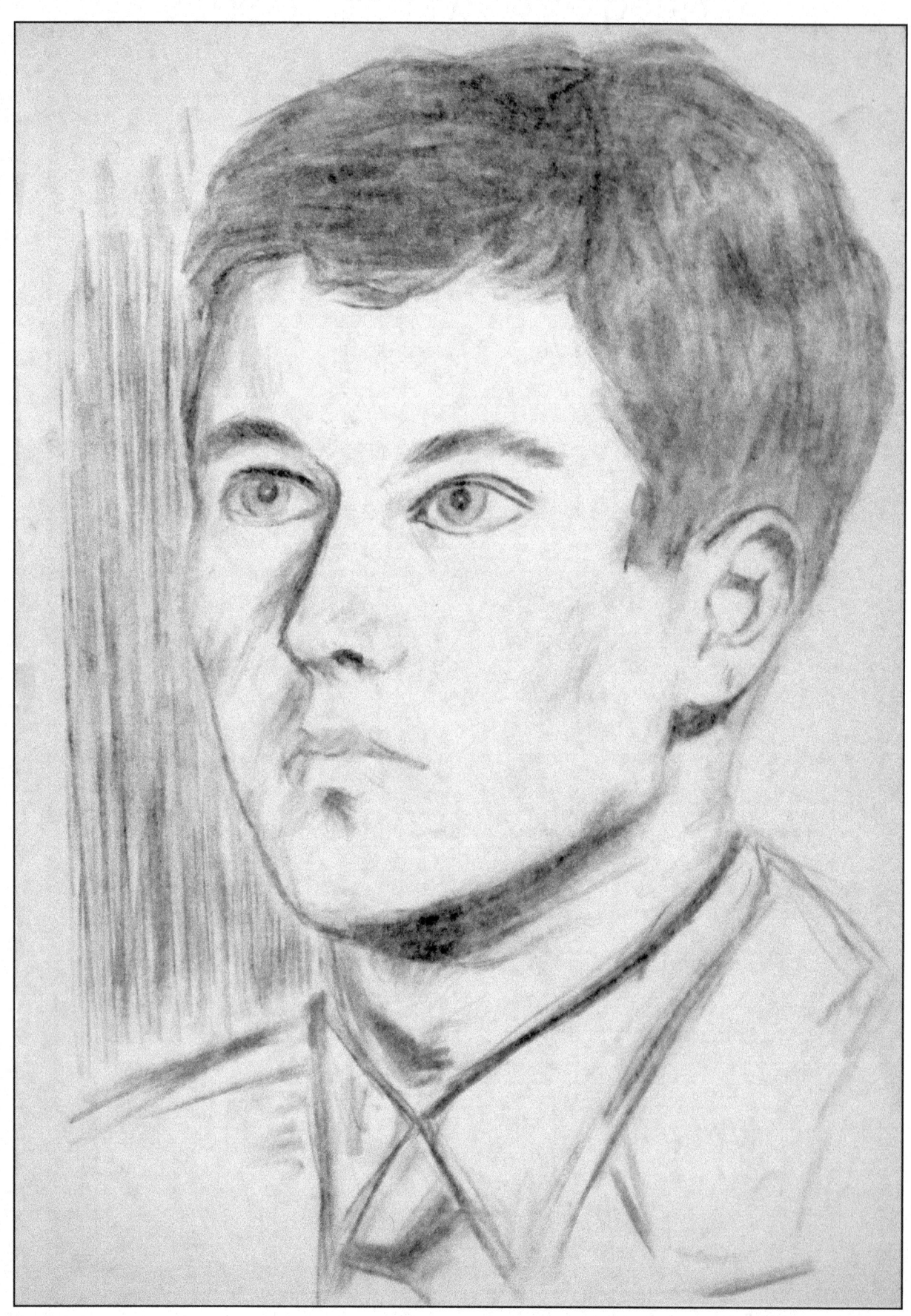

Alan

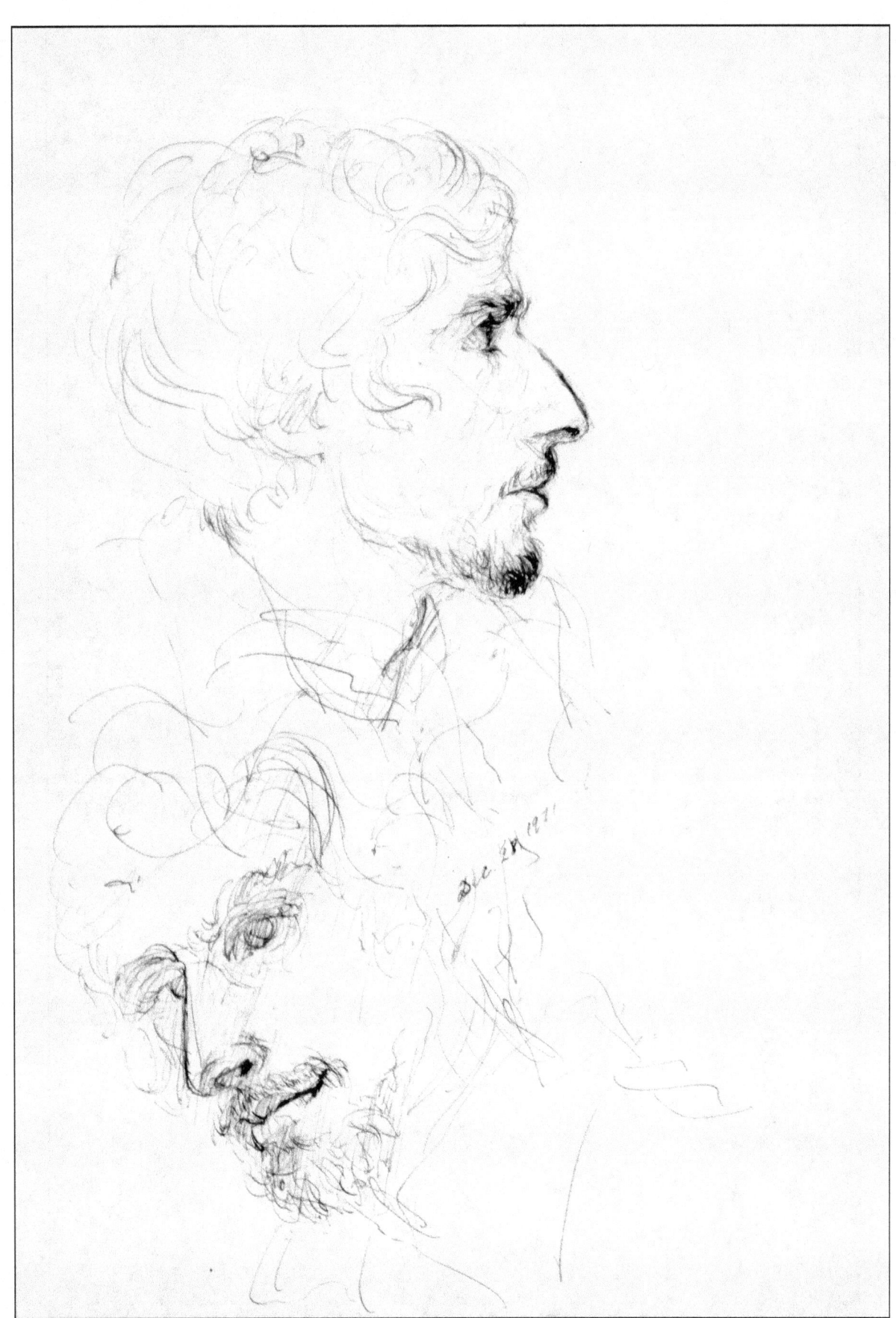

Franco

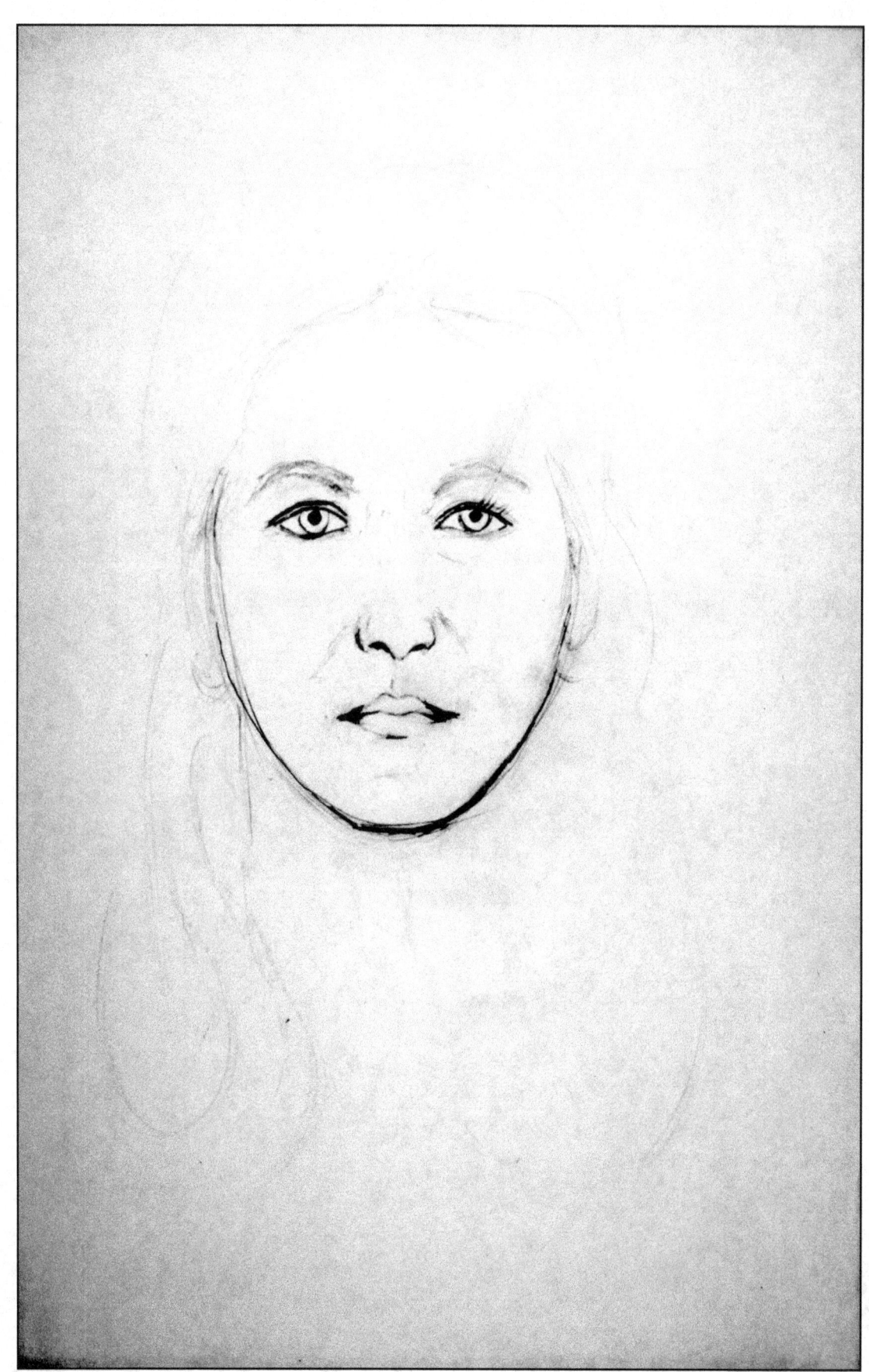

Gaby

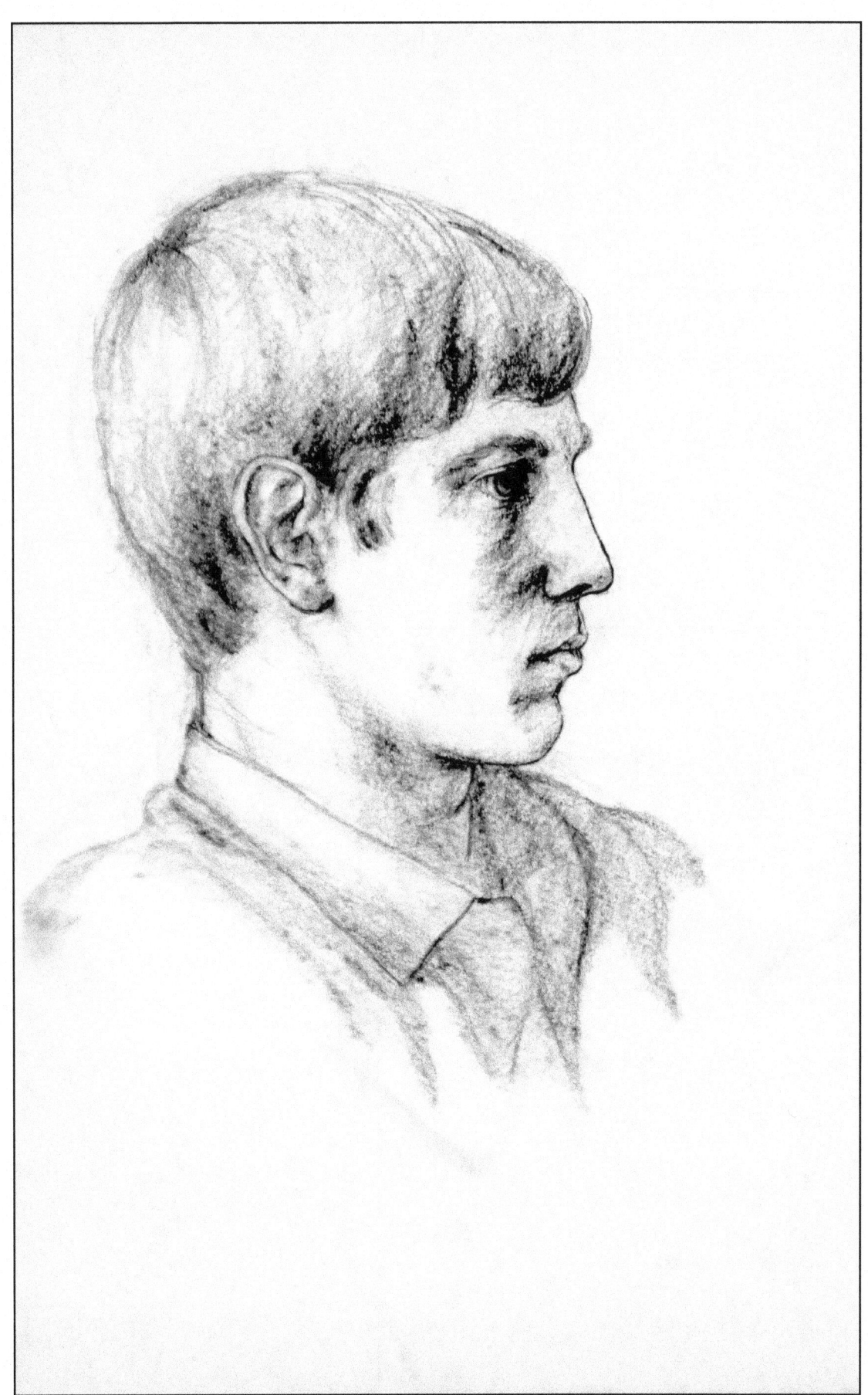

Rick

Giovanni ->

<- Raffaele

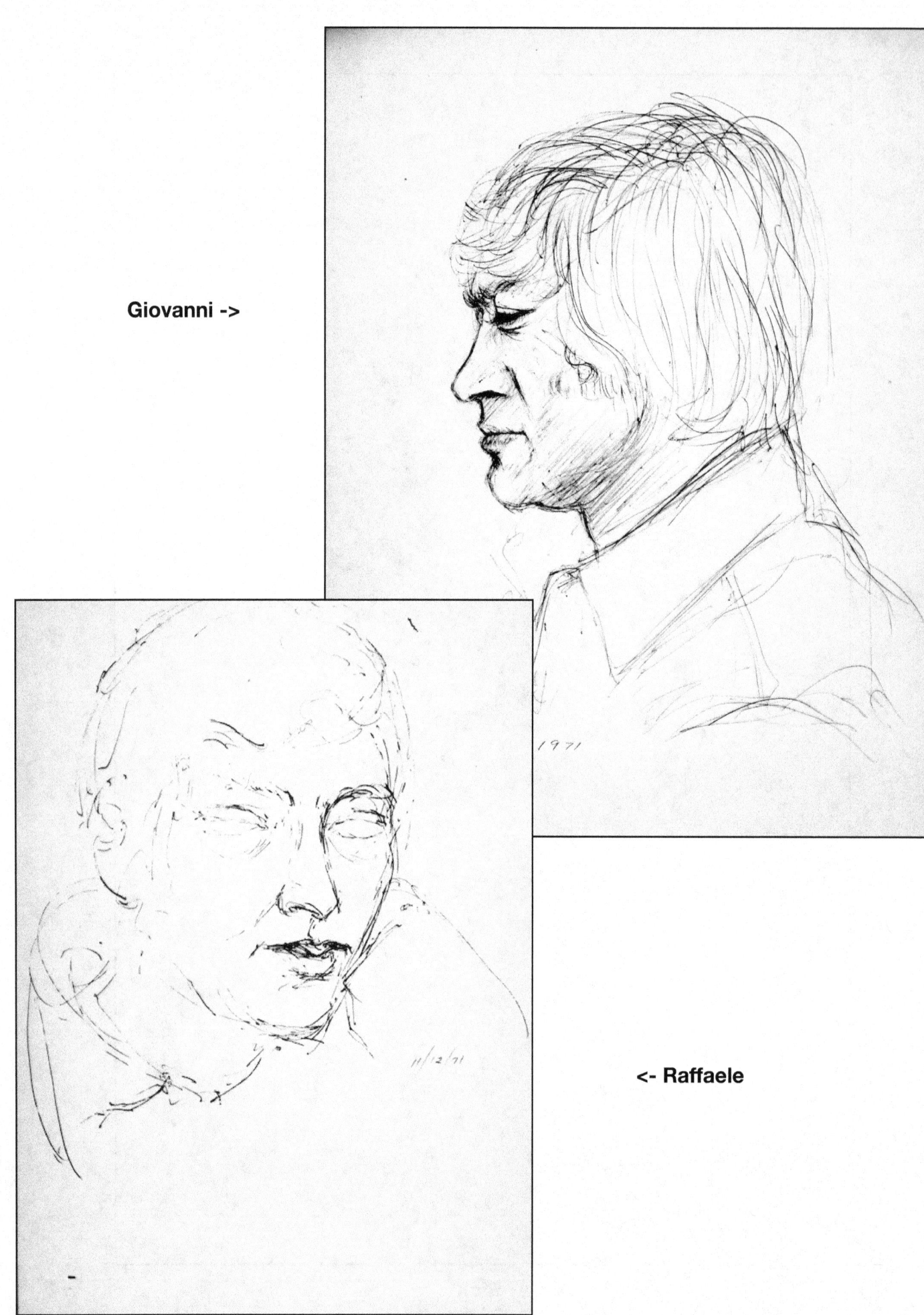

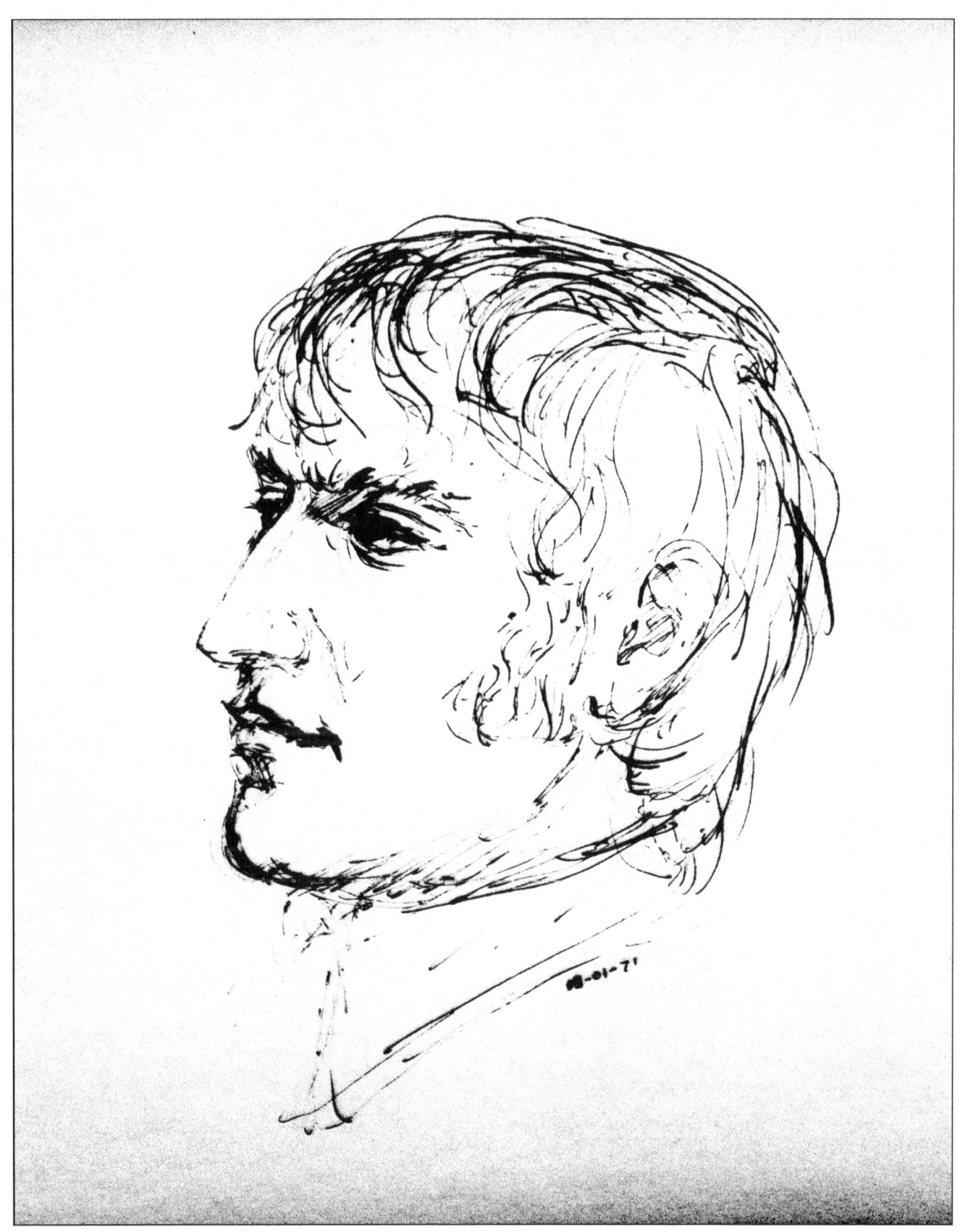

Mario

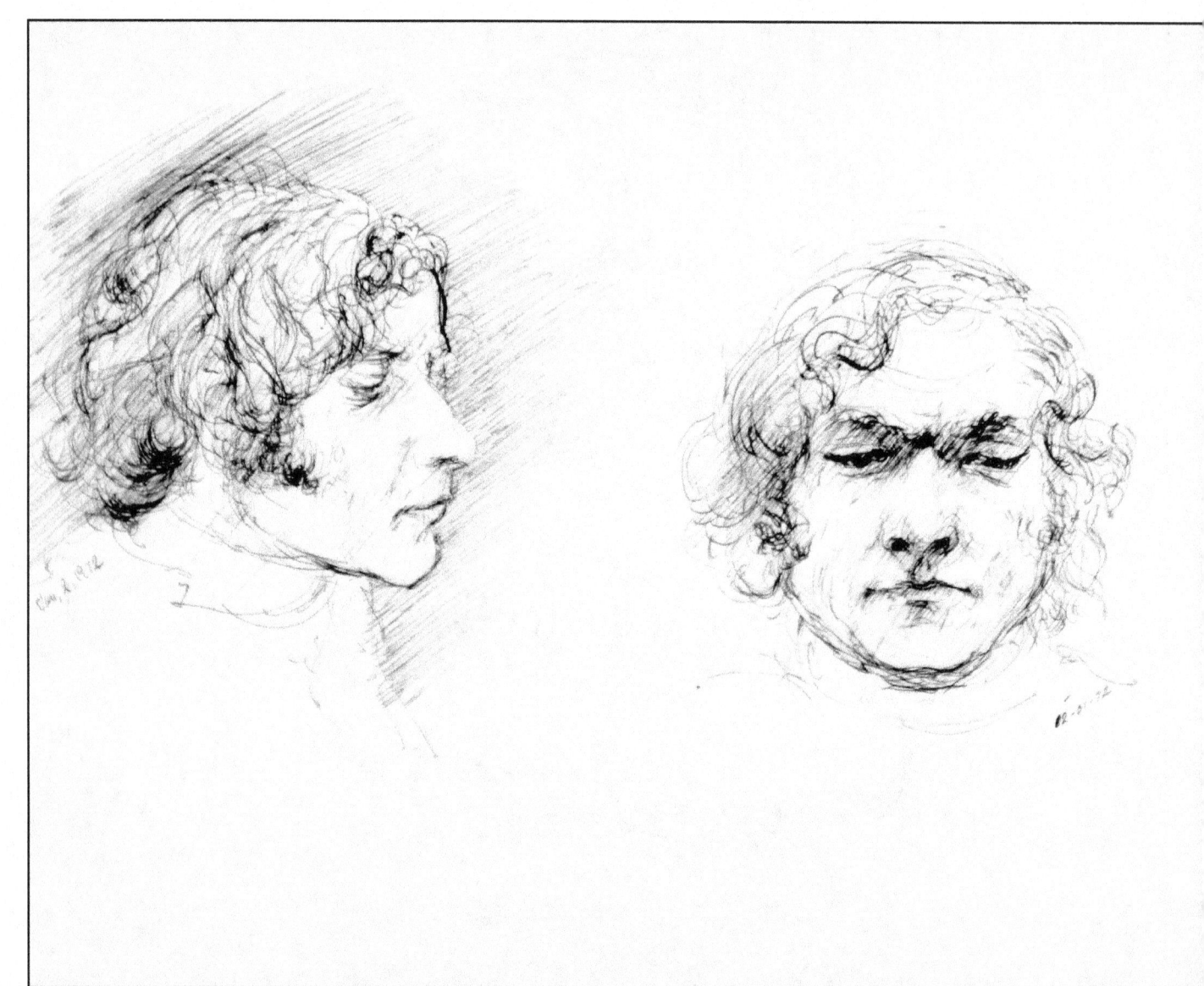

Biase

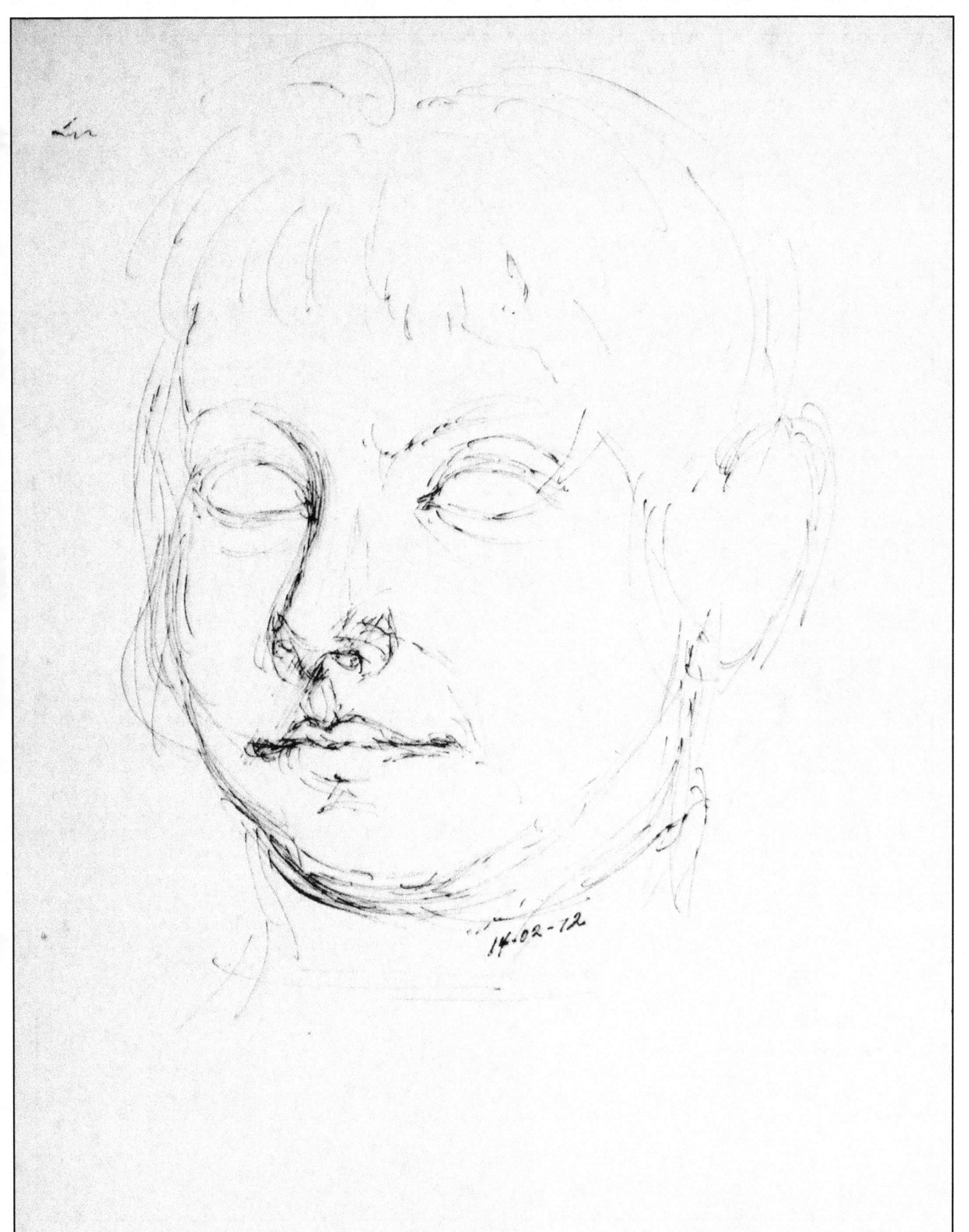

Bella

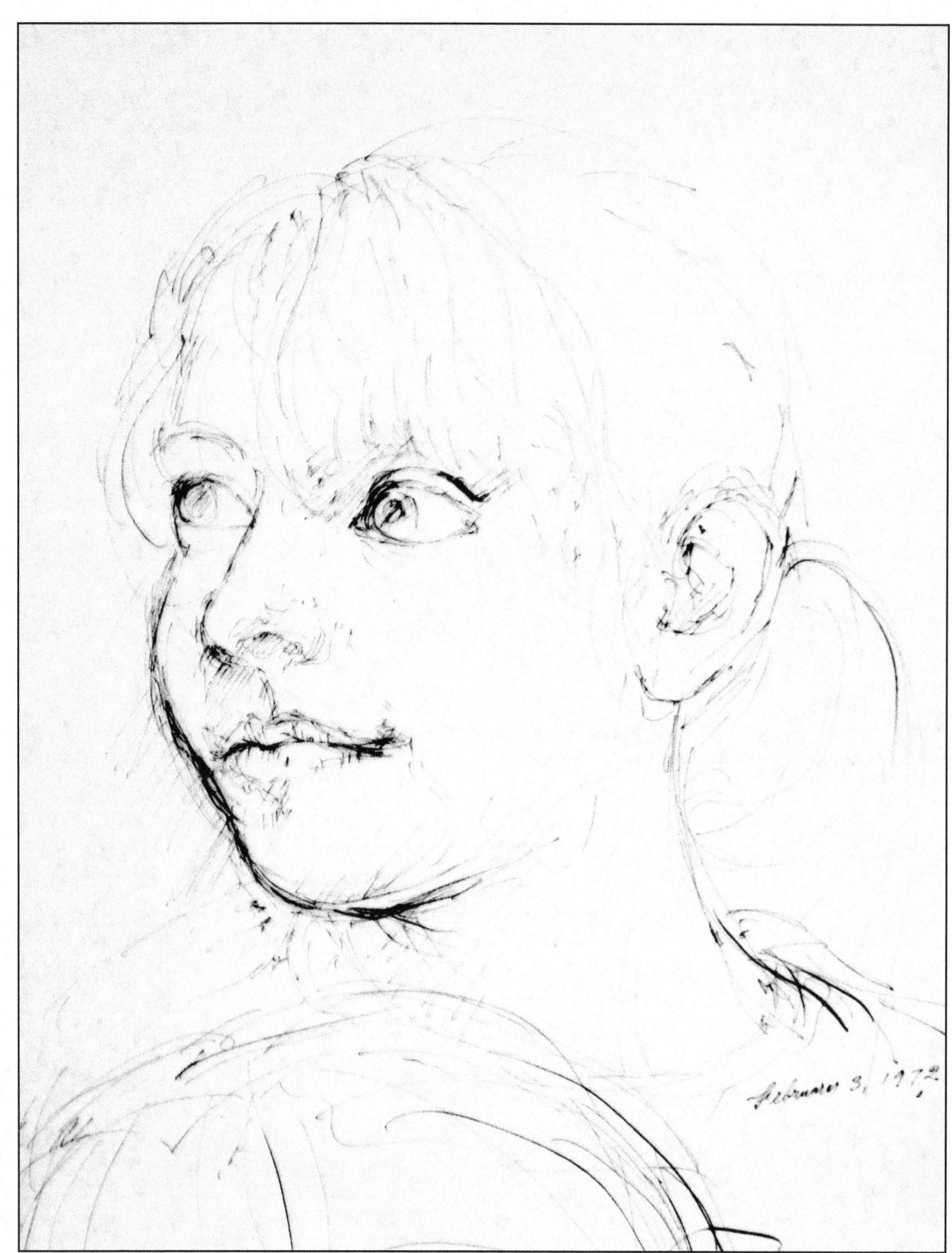

Bella

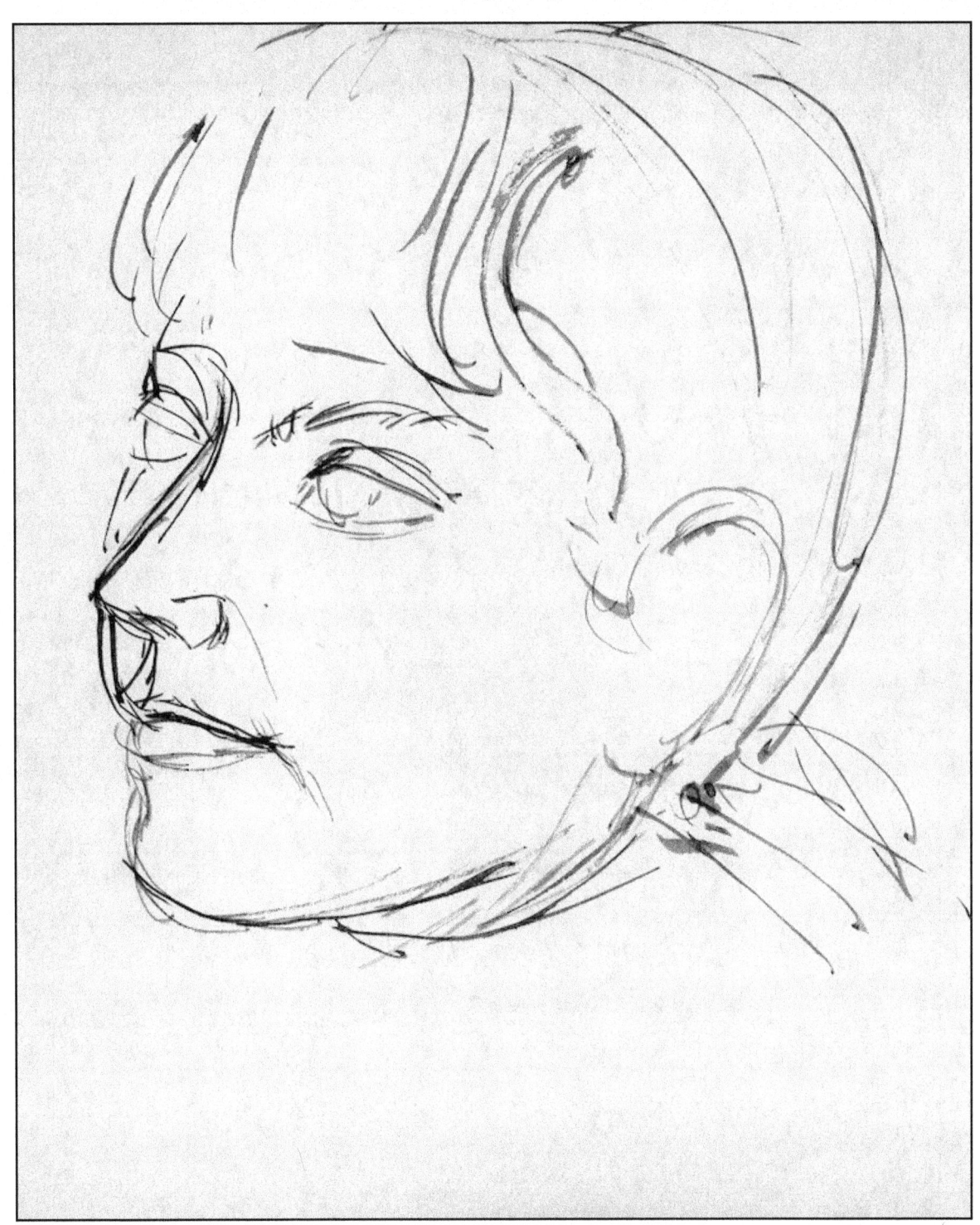

Bella

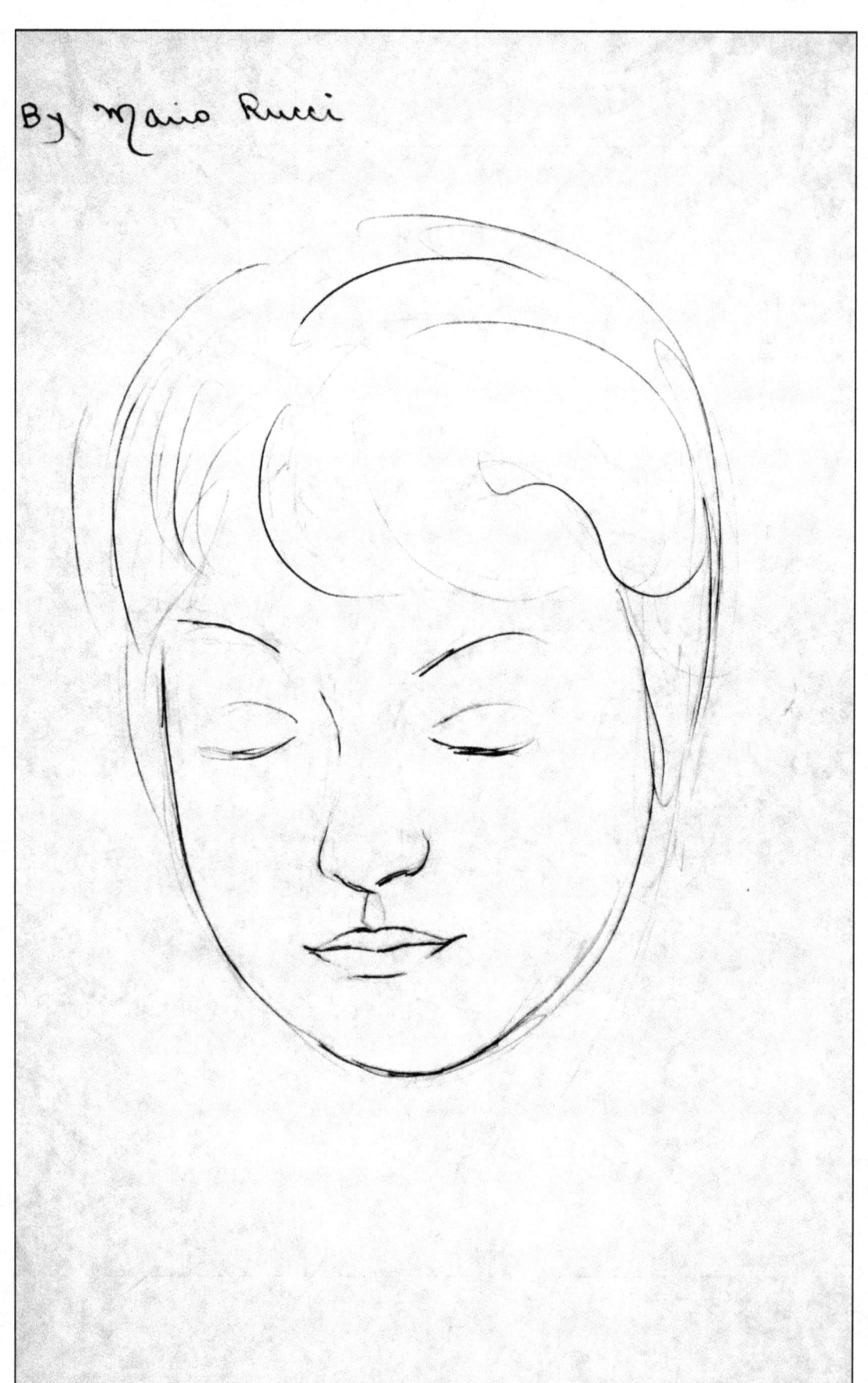

Bella

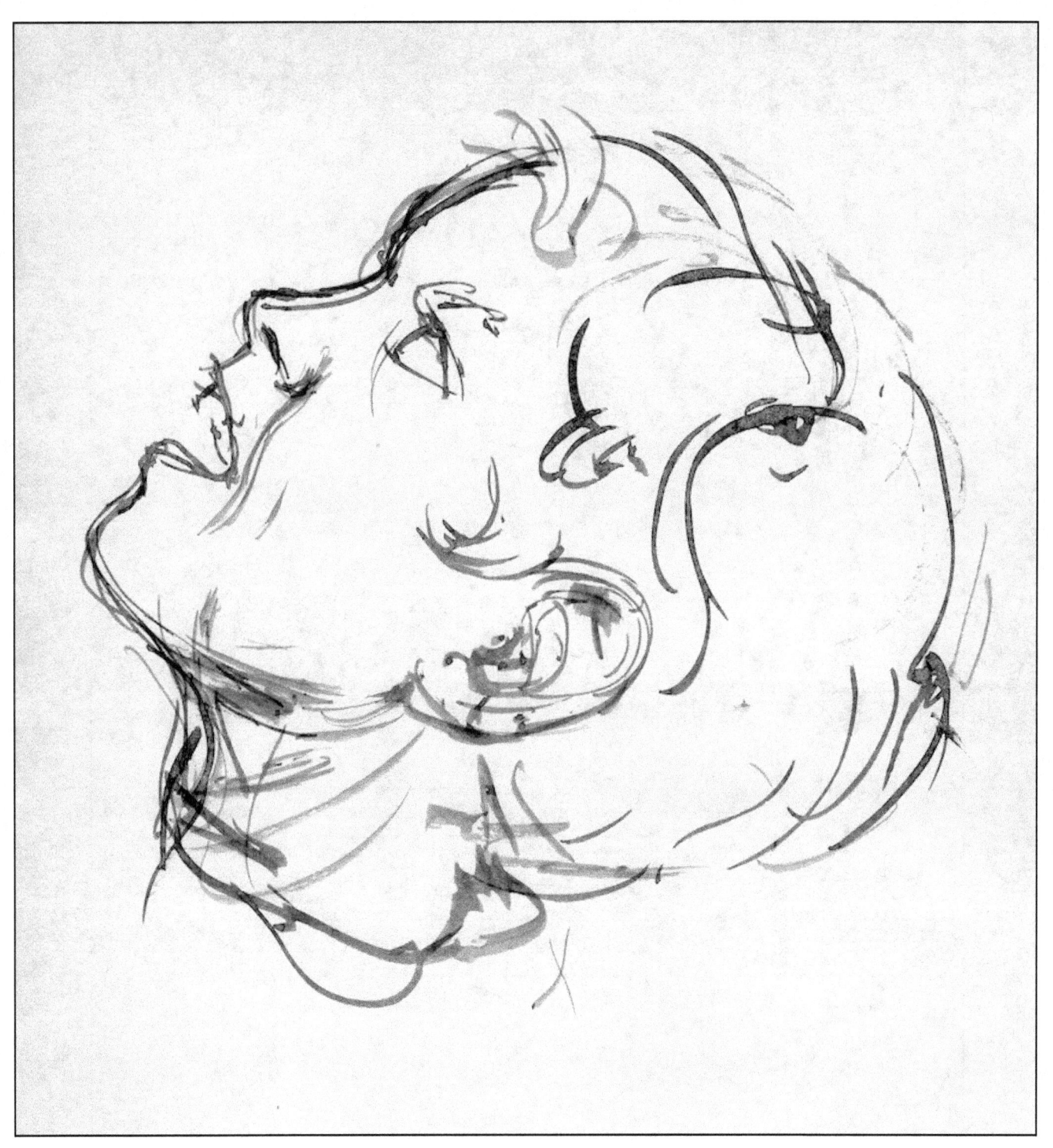

Max

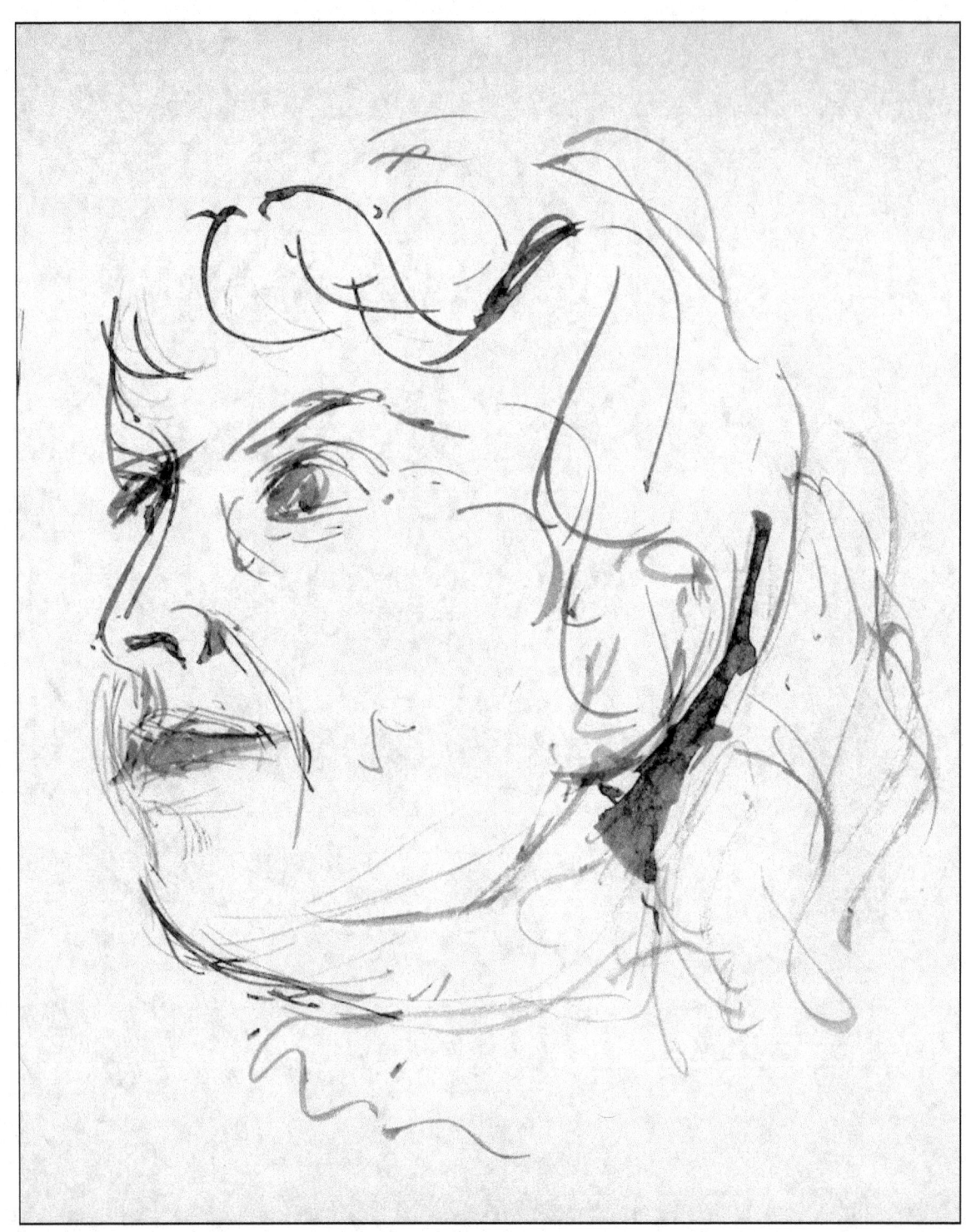

Elle

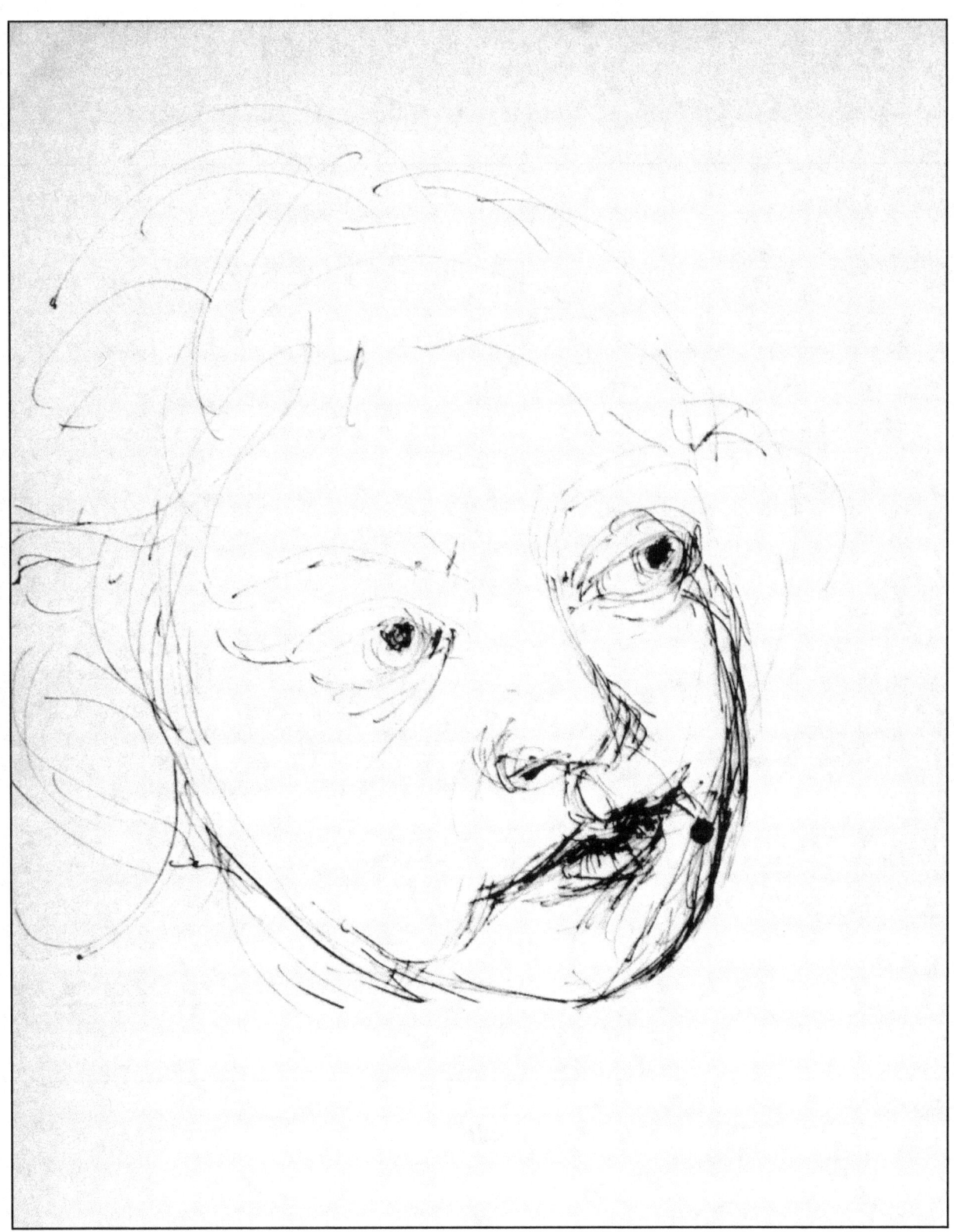

Elle

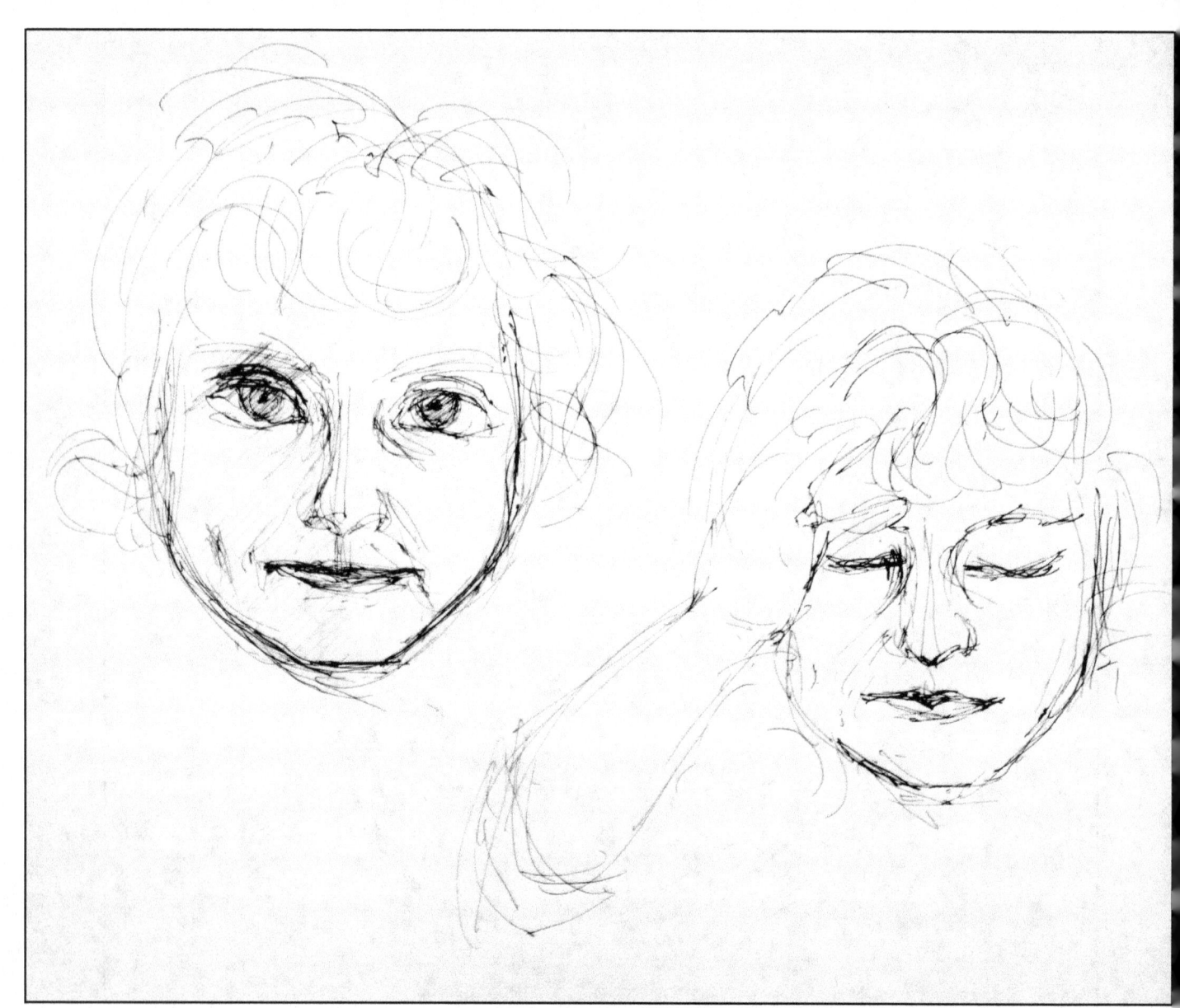

Elle

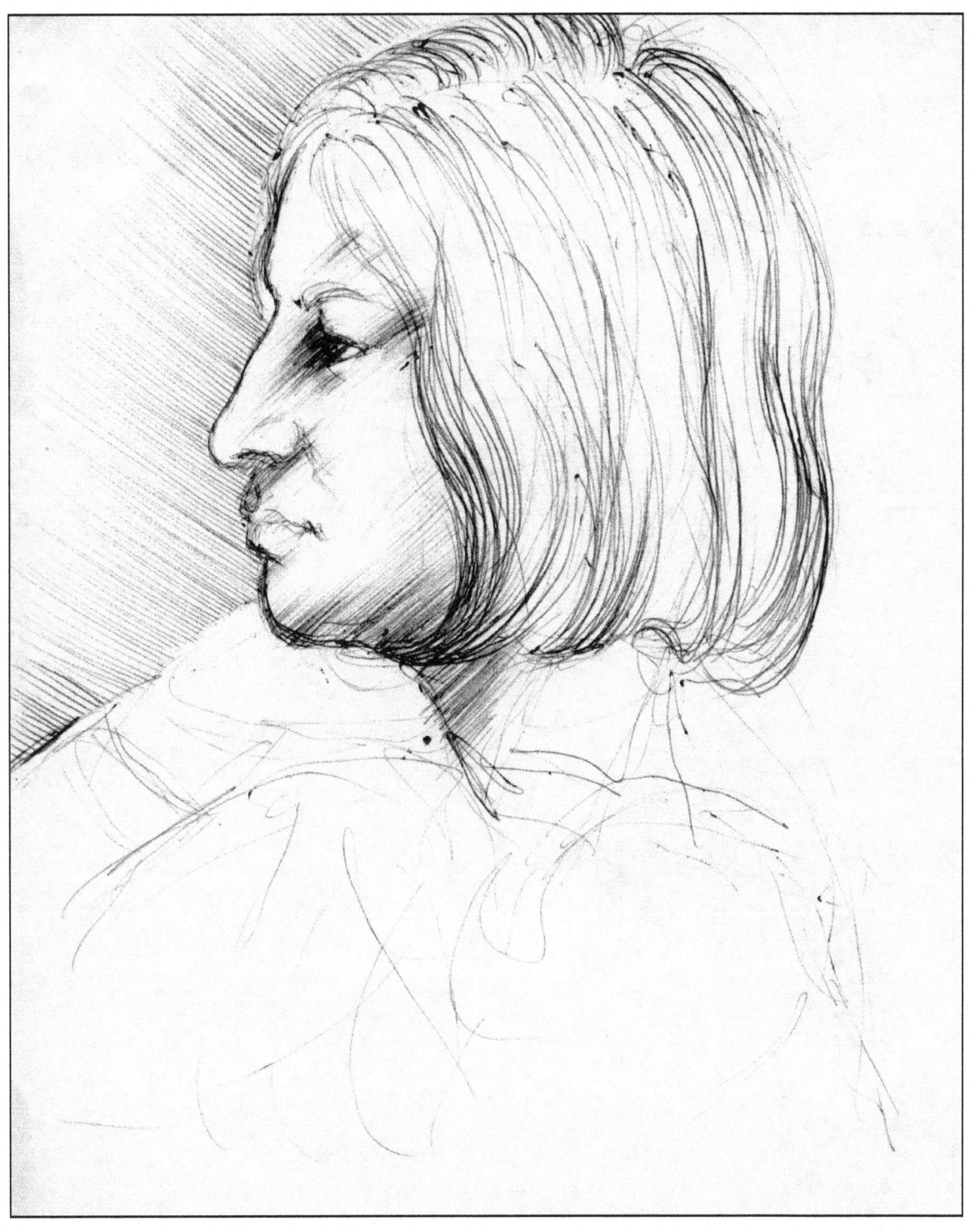

Maria

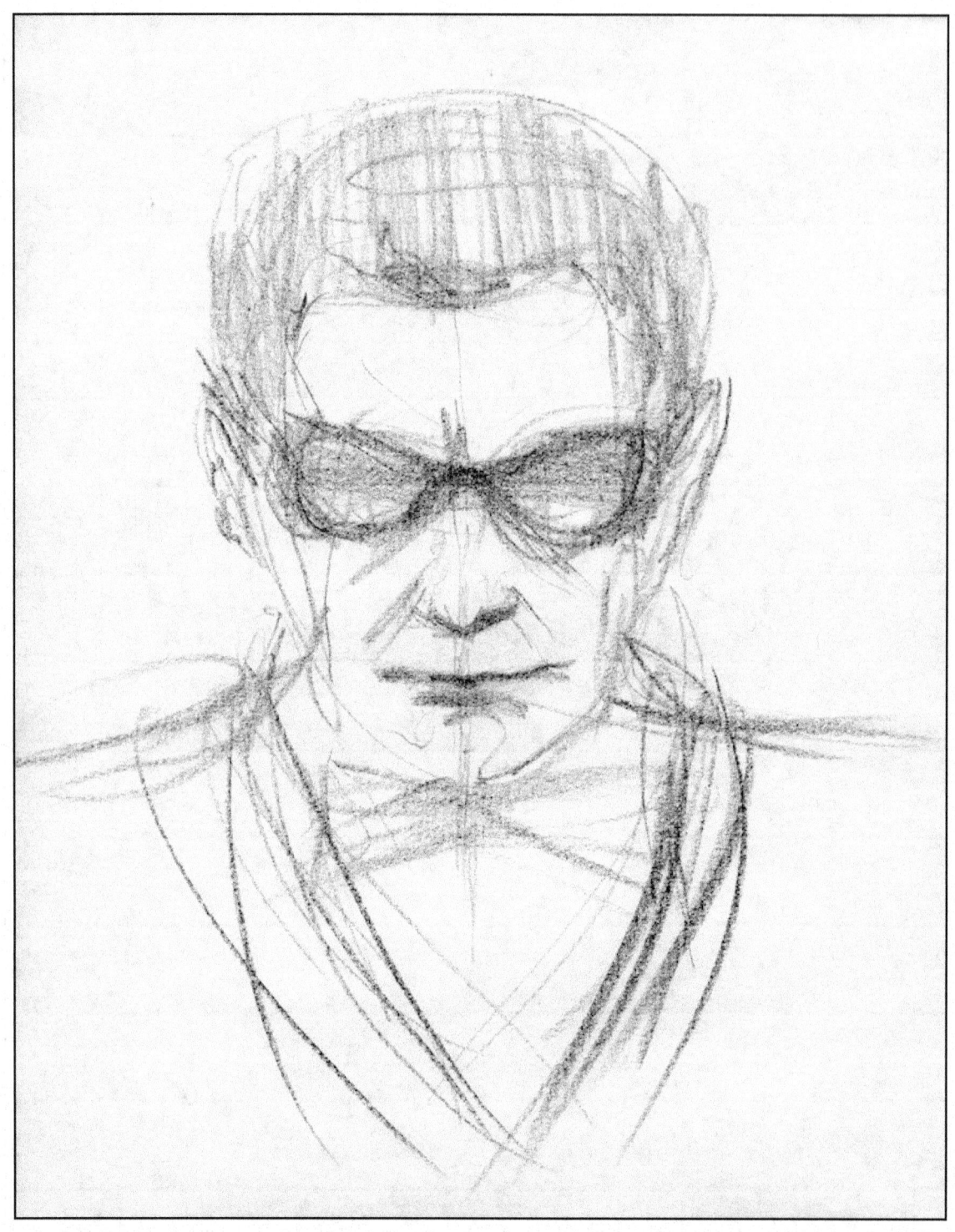

Giulio

6. Head Observation, Relatives

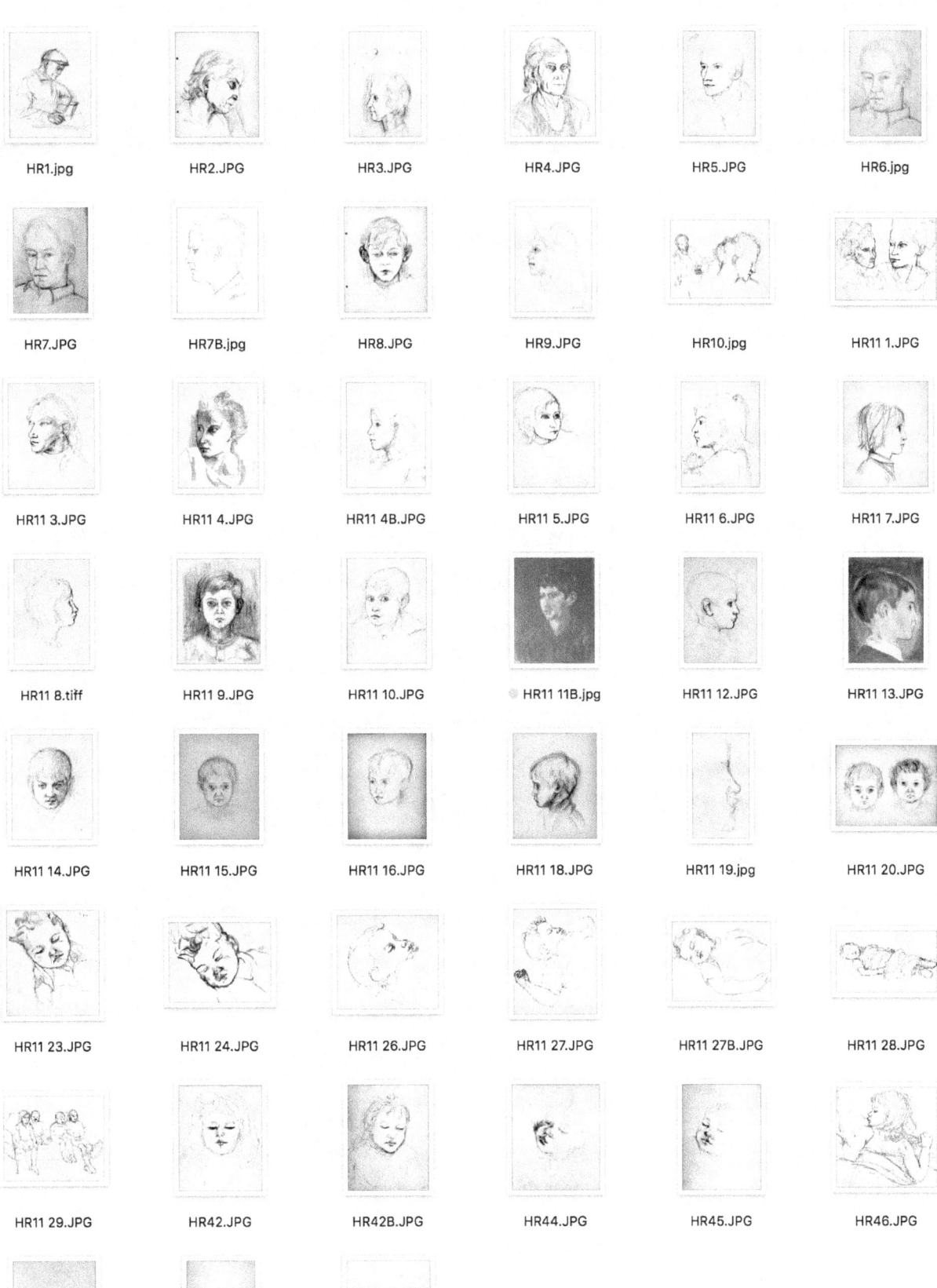

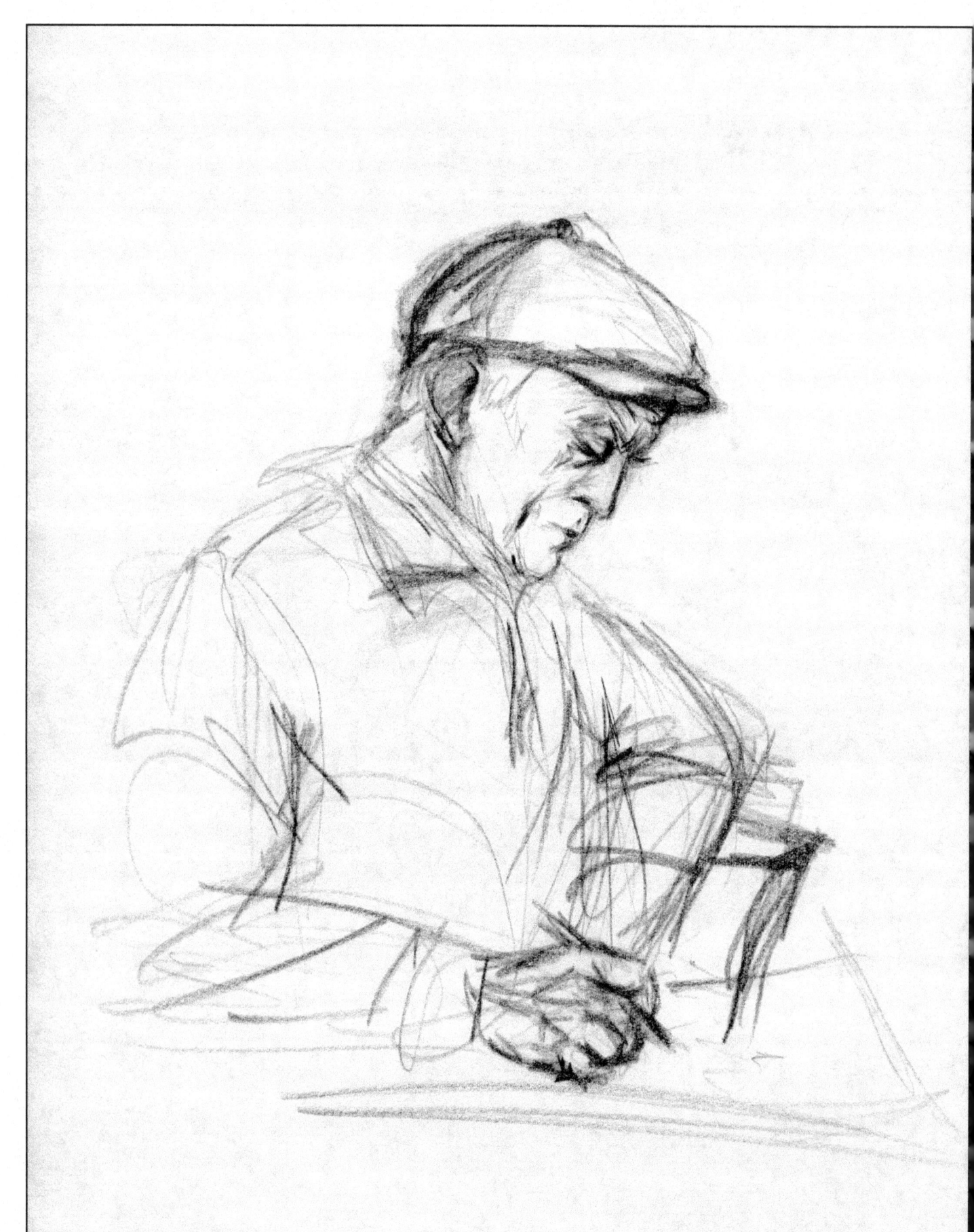

My Father

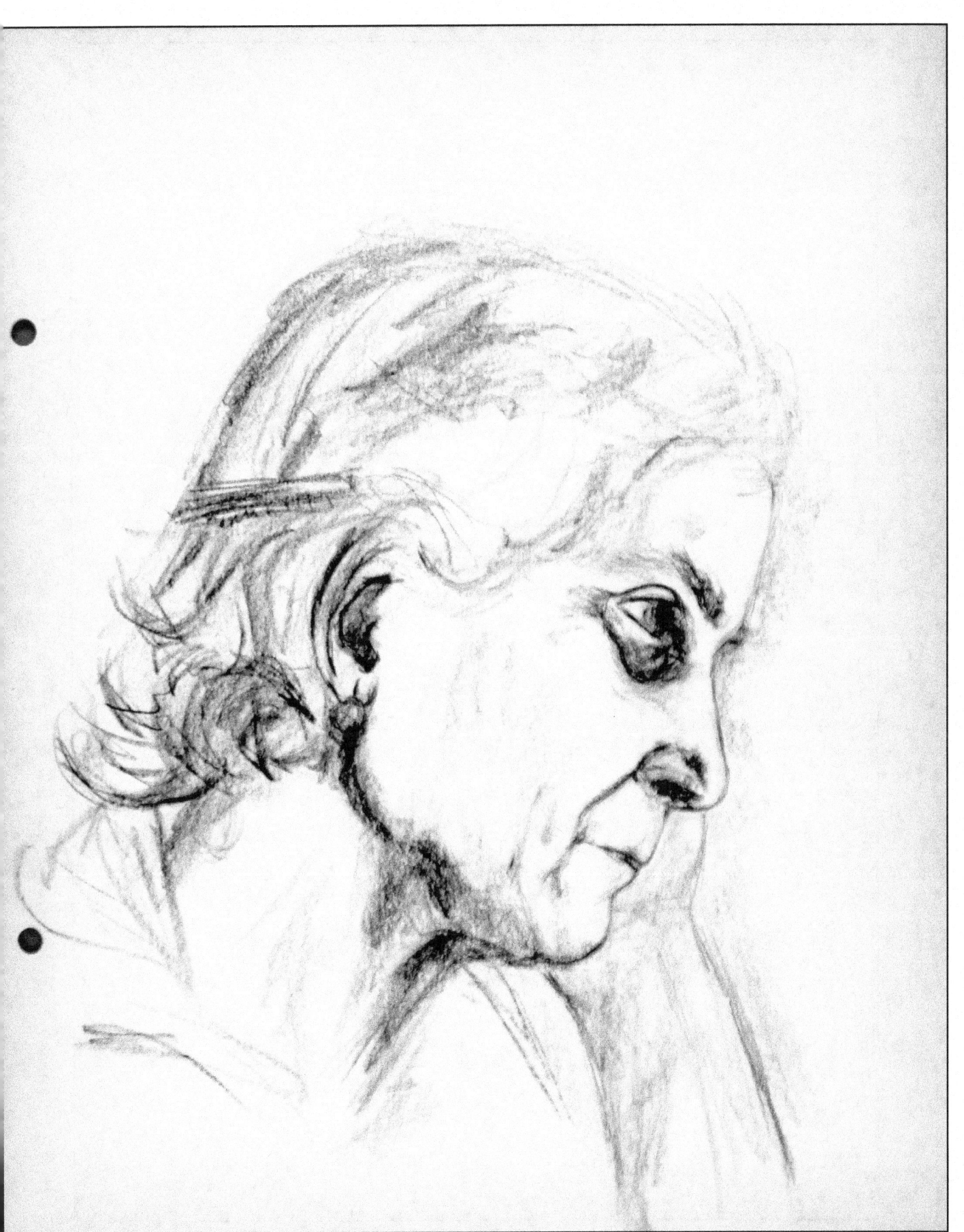

My Mother

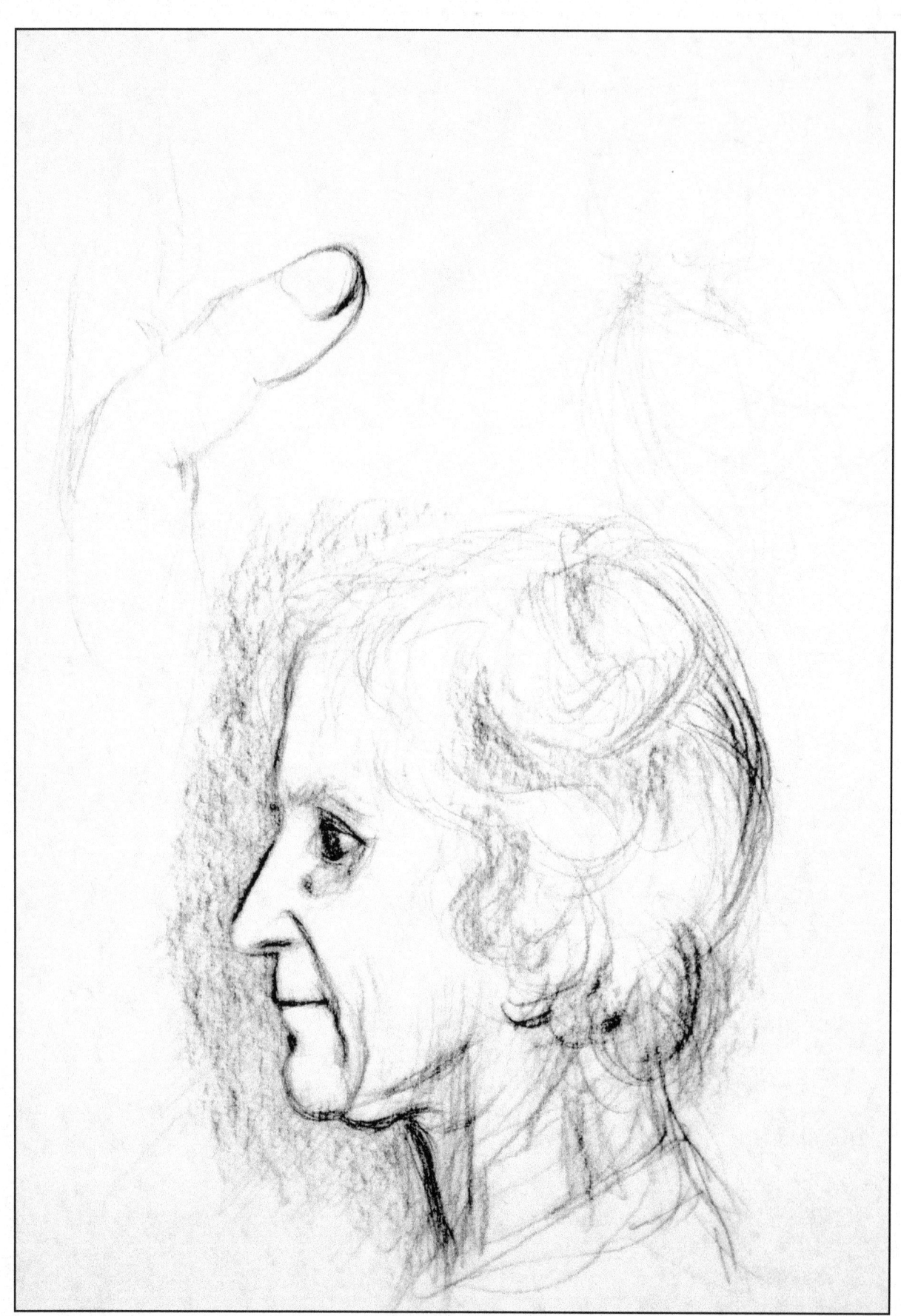

My Mother

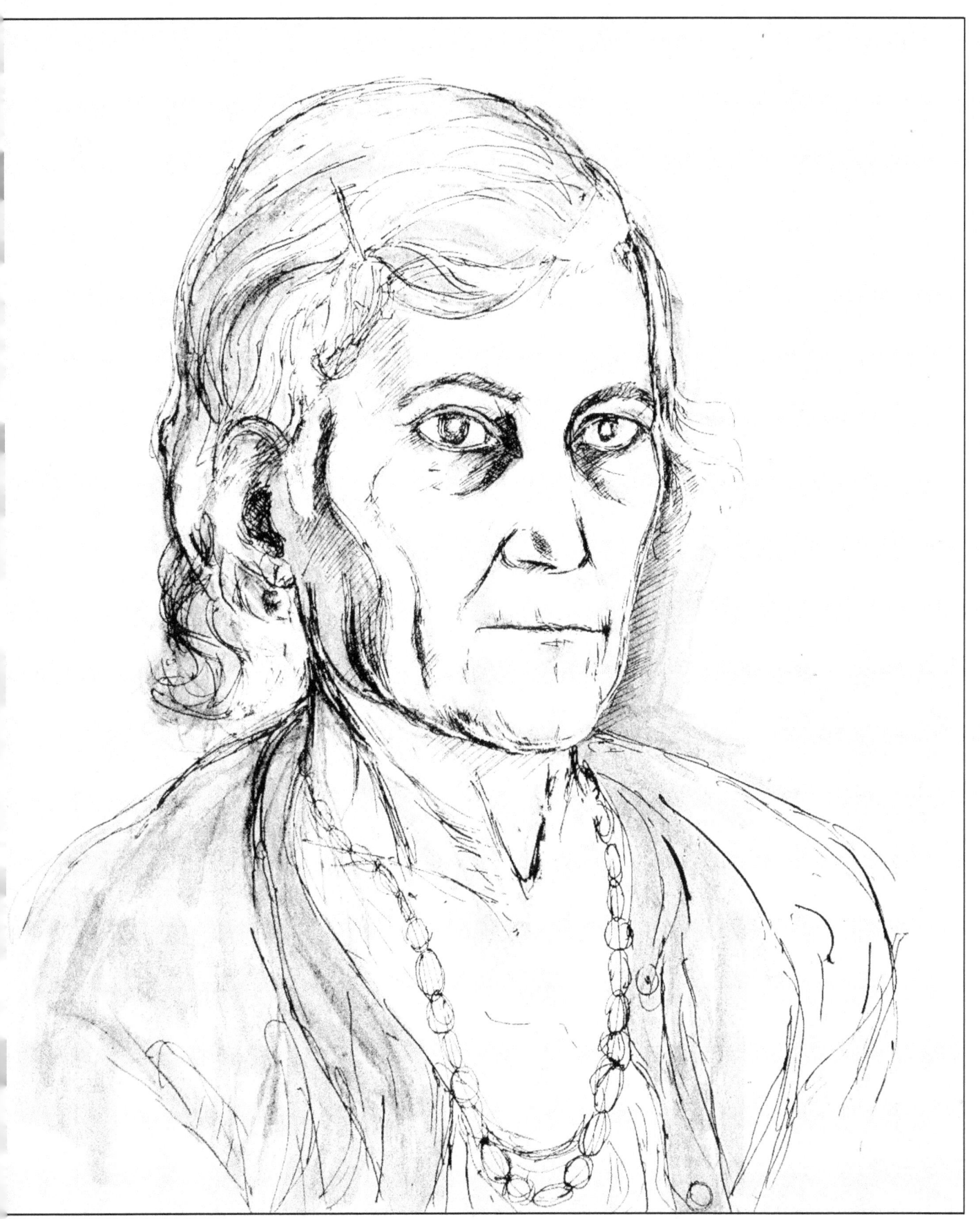

My Mother

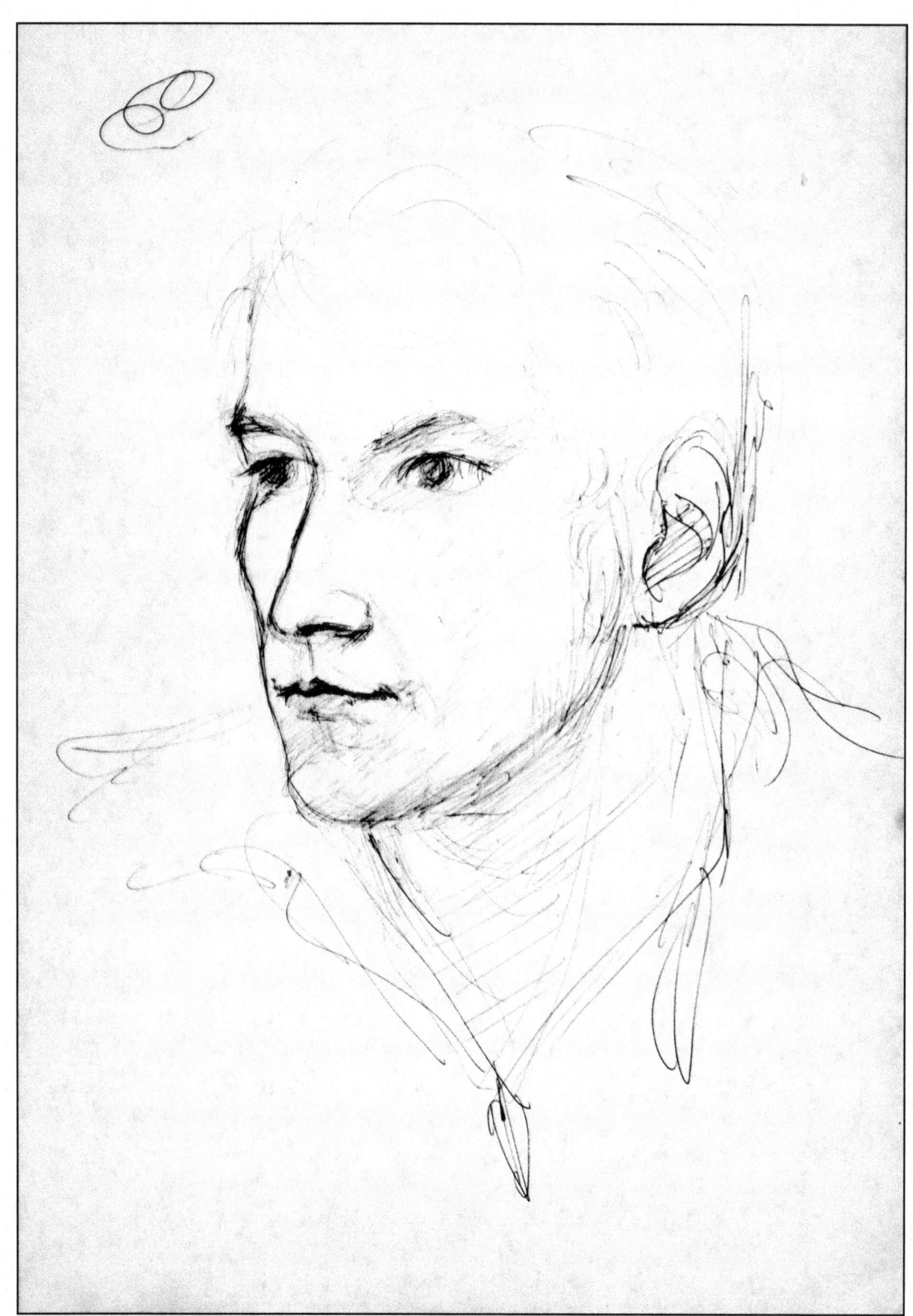

Raffaele

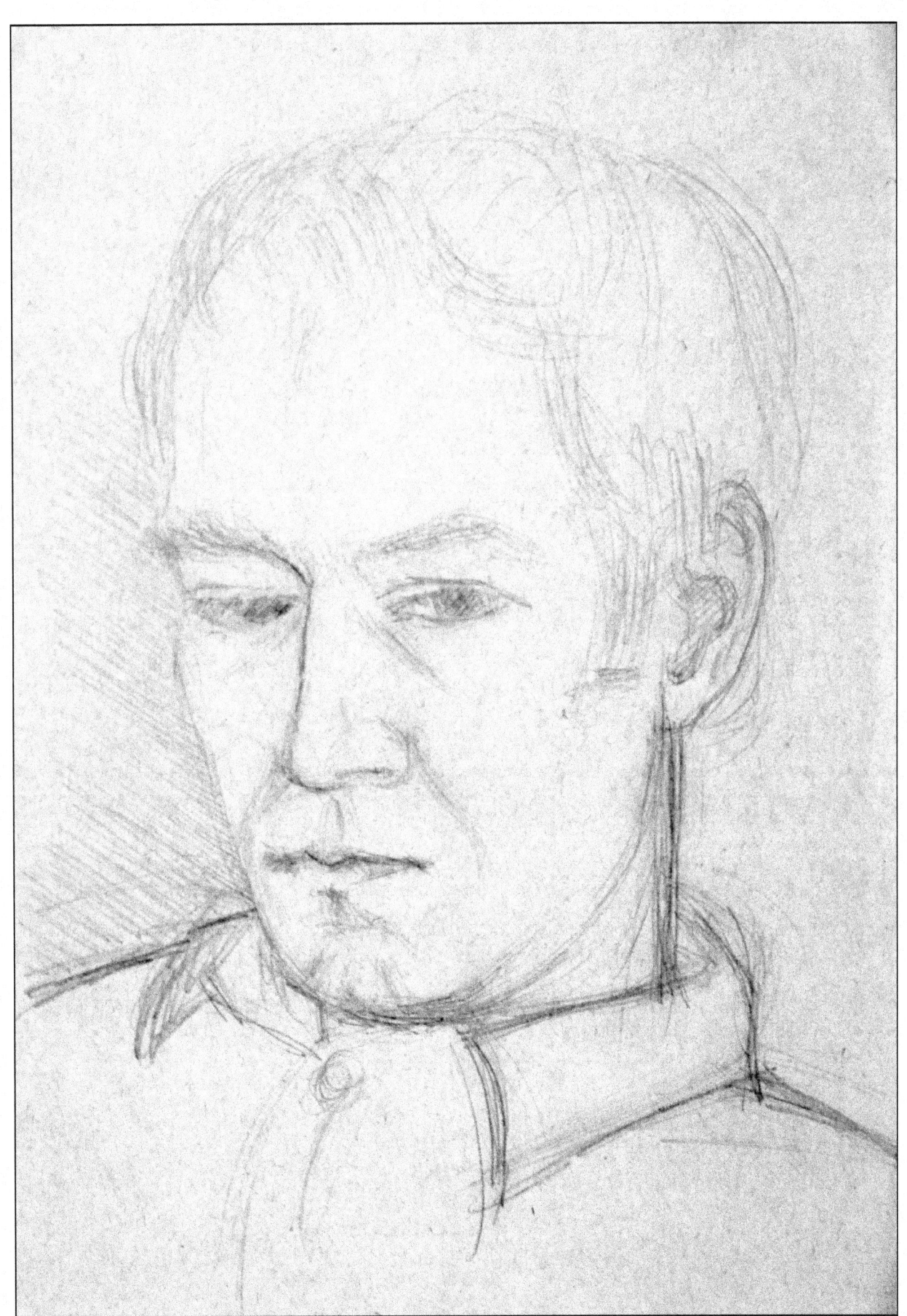

Raffaele

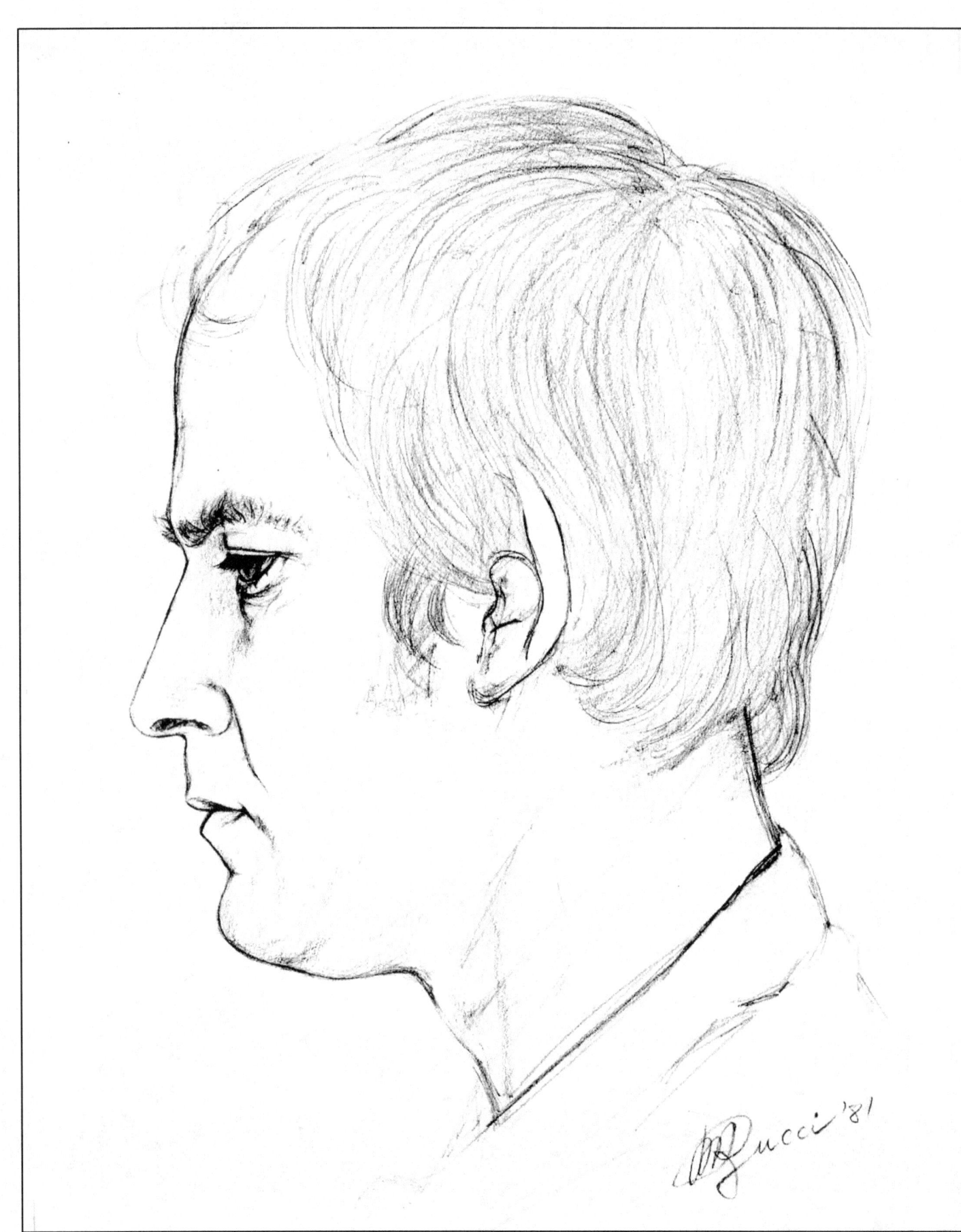

Raffaele (the original hangs in Bruno's office)

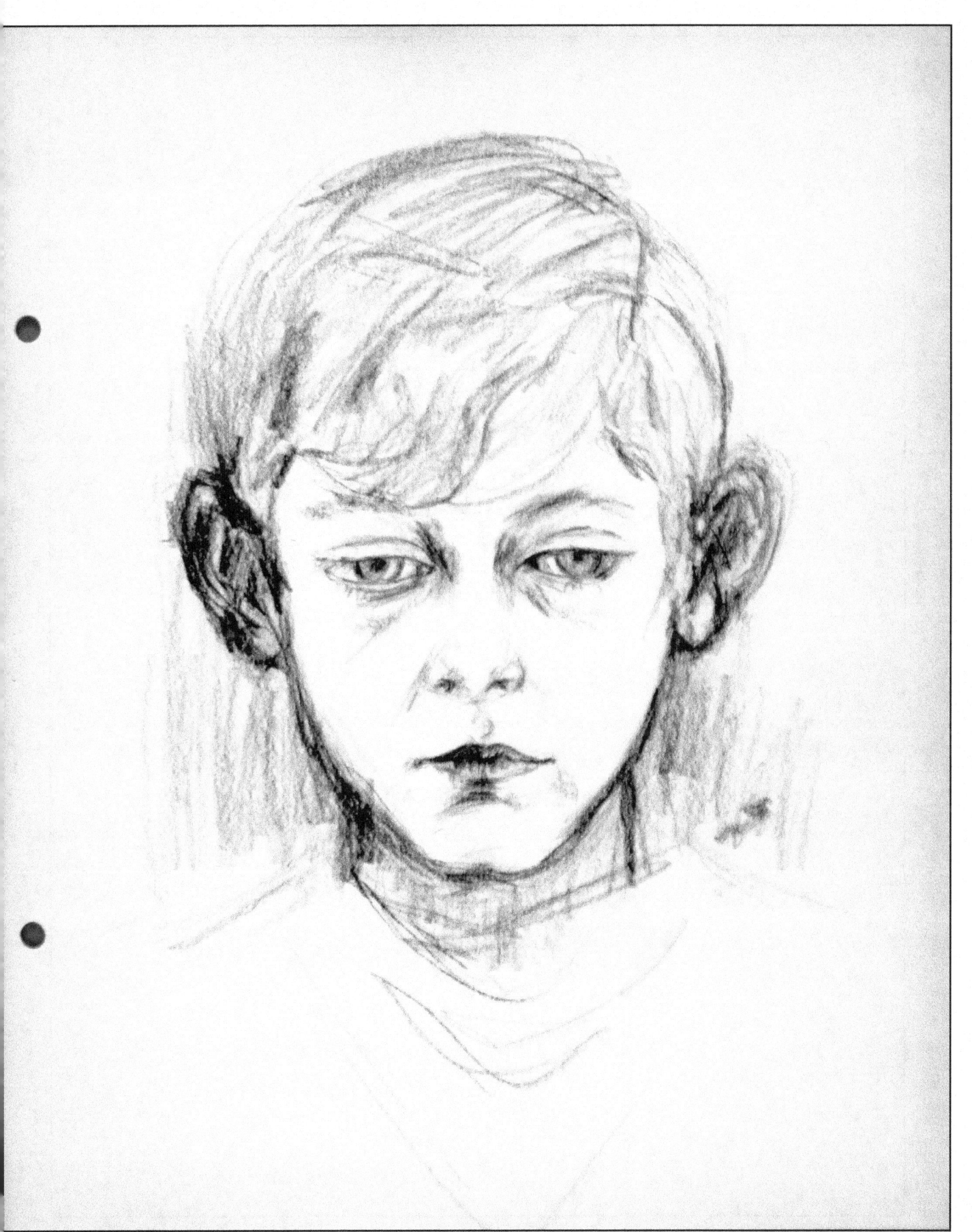

Giuseppe

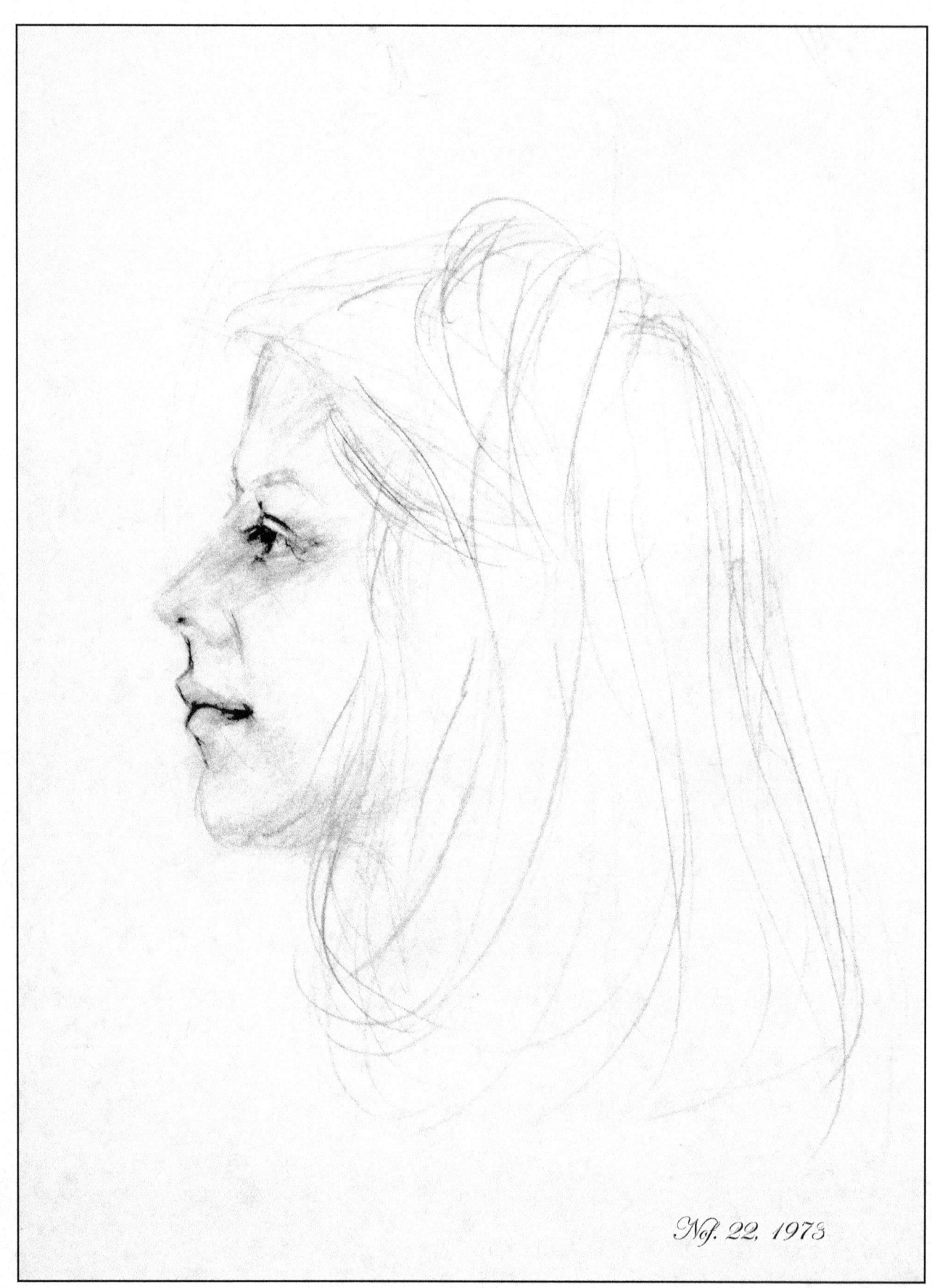

Oriana

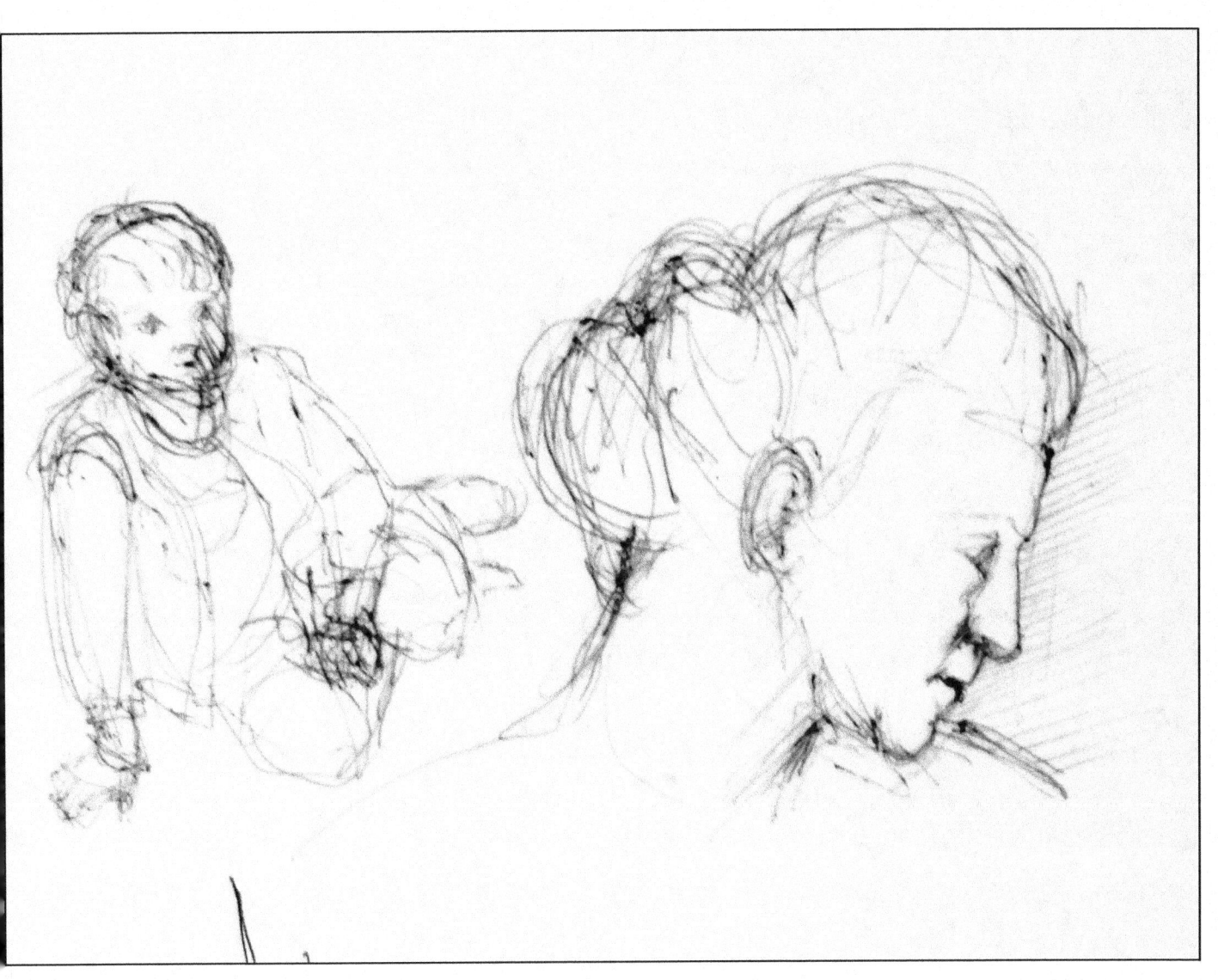

Ilda

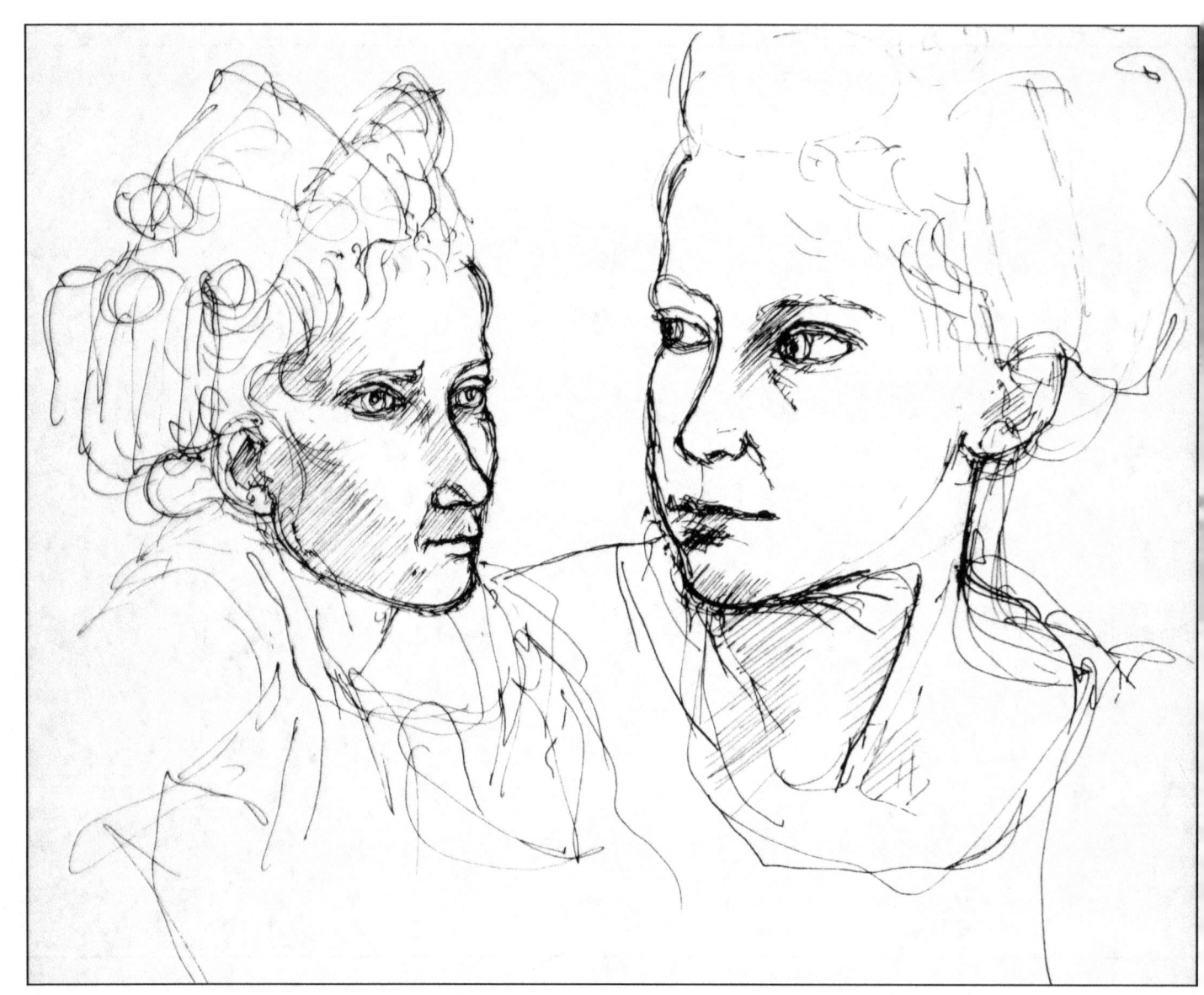

Nella

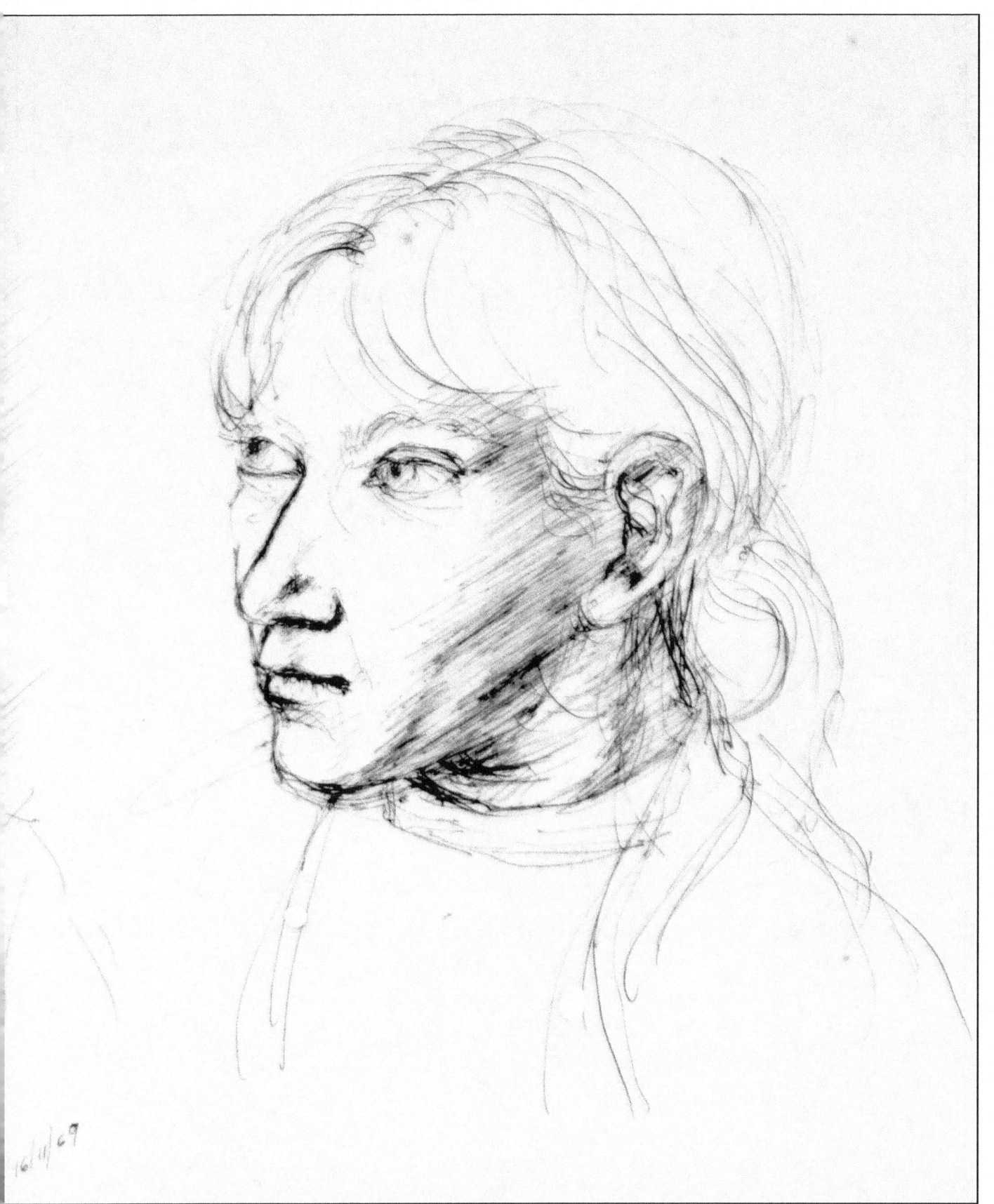

Nella

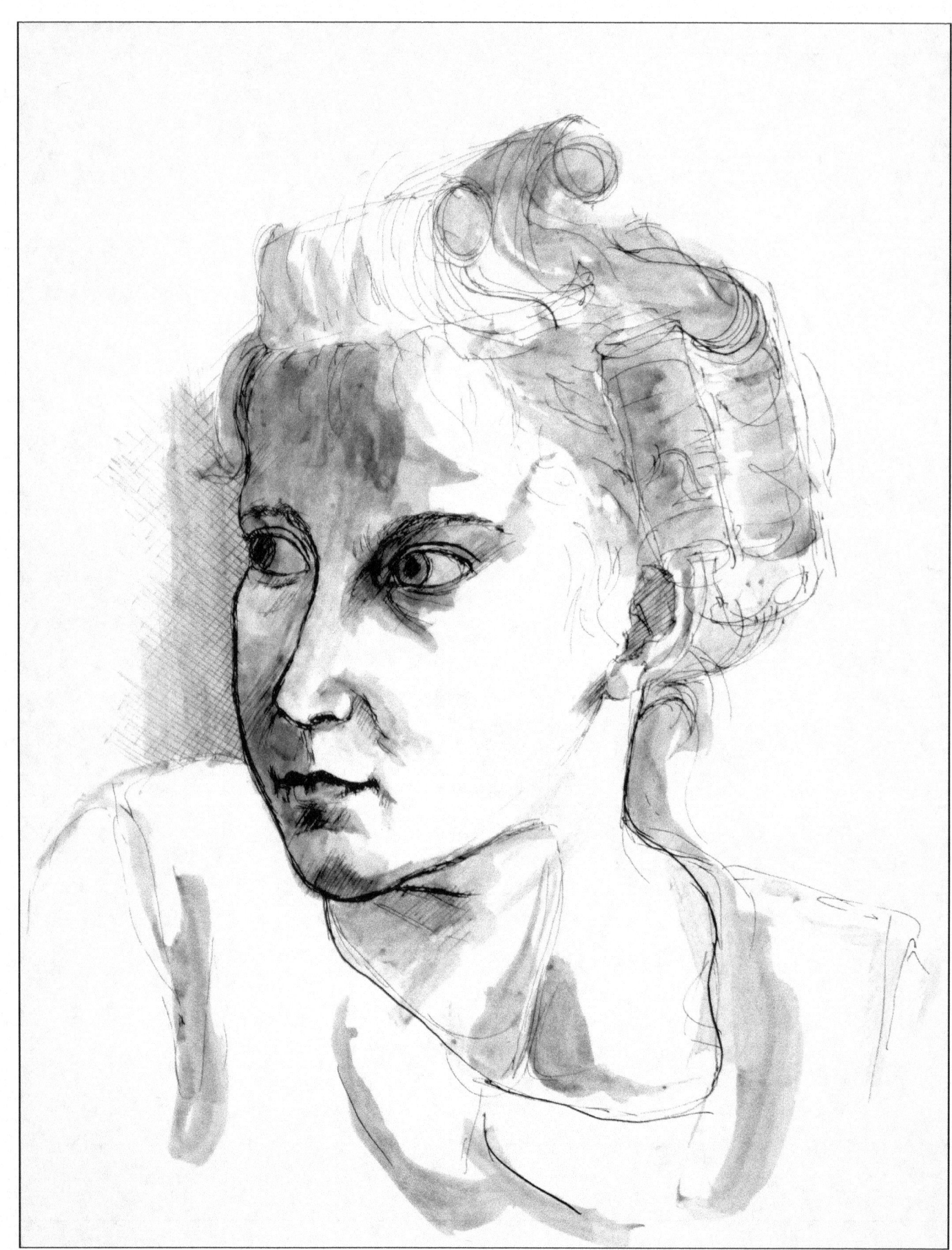

Nella

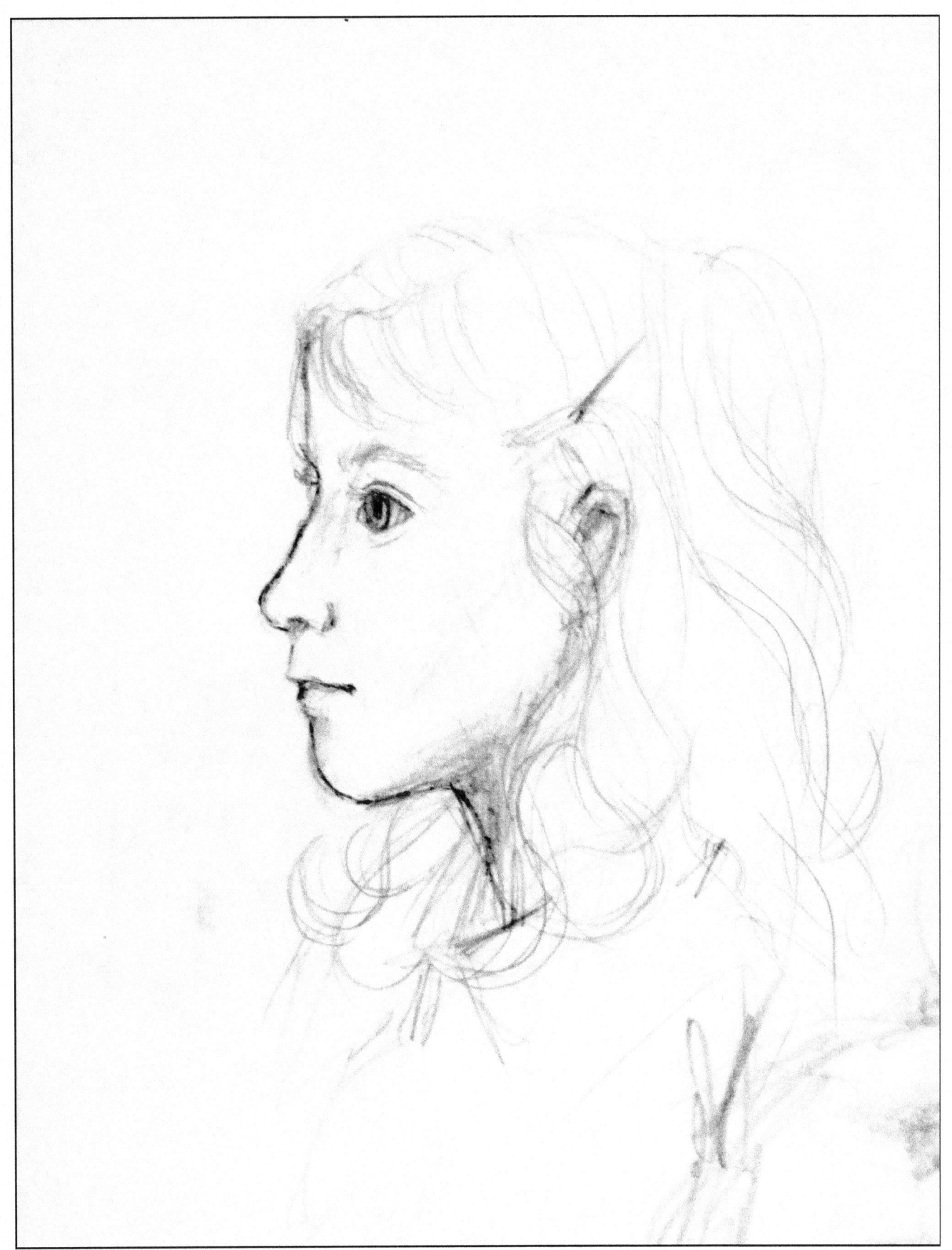

Nella

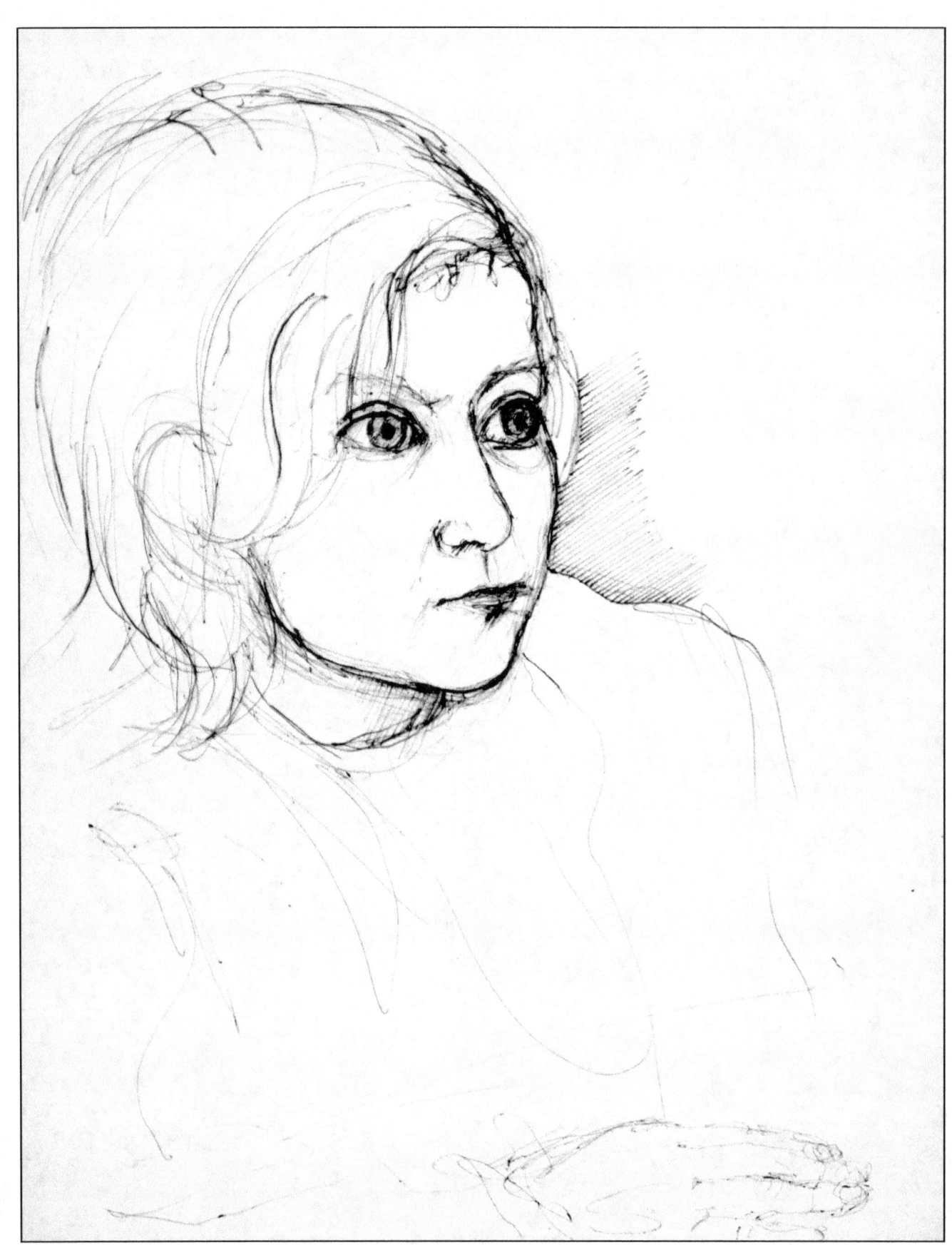

Margherita

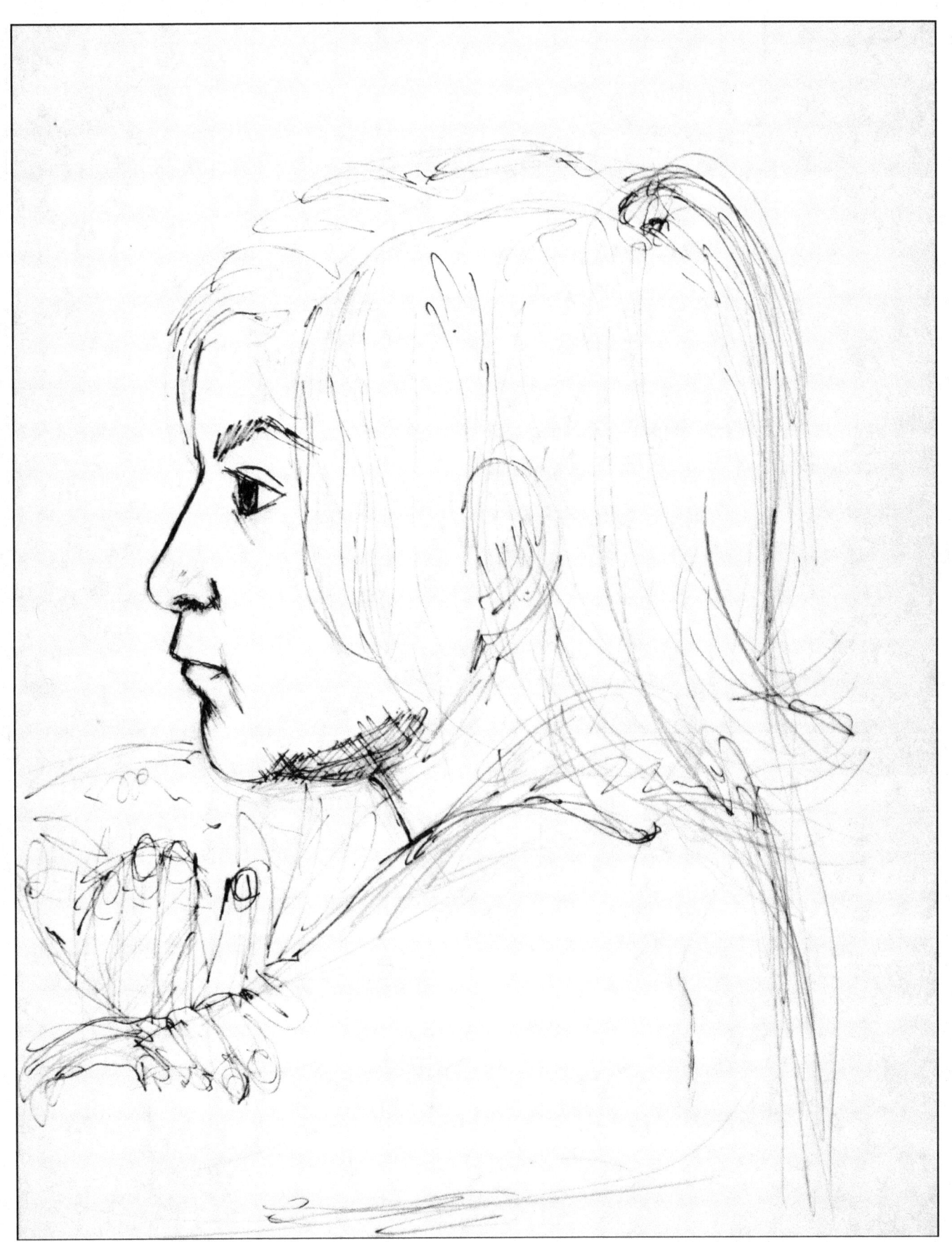

Margherita

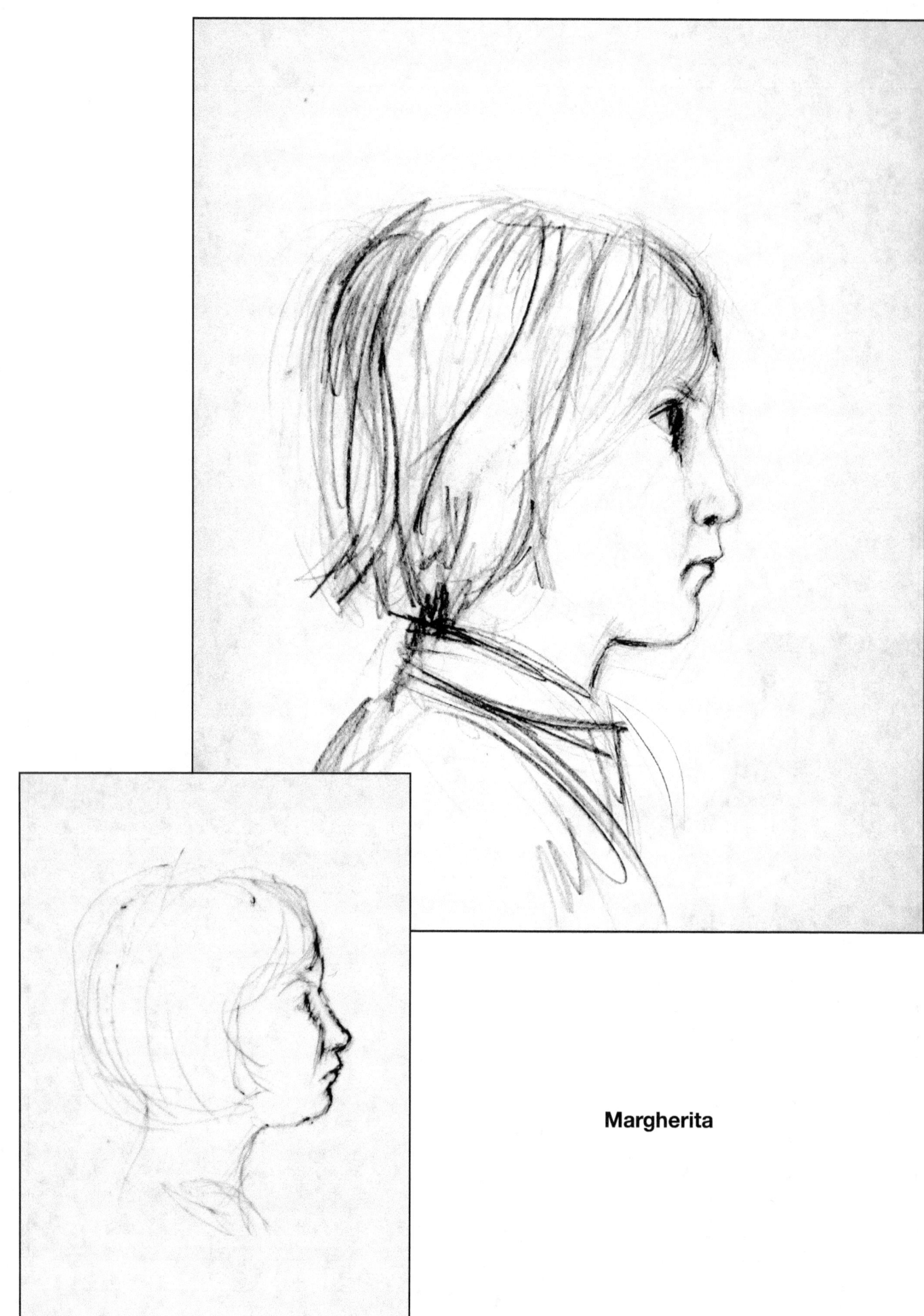

Margherita

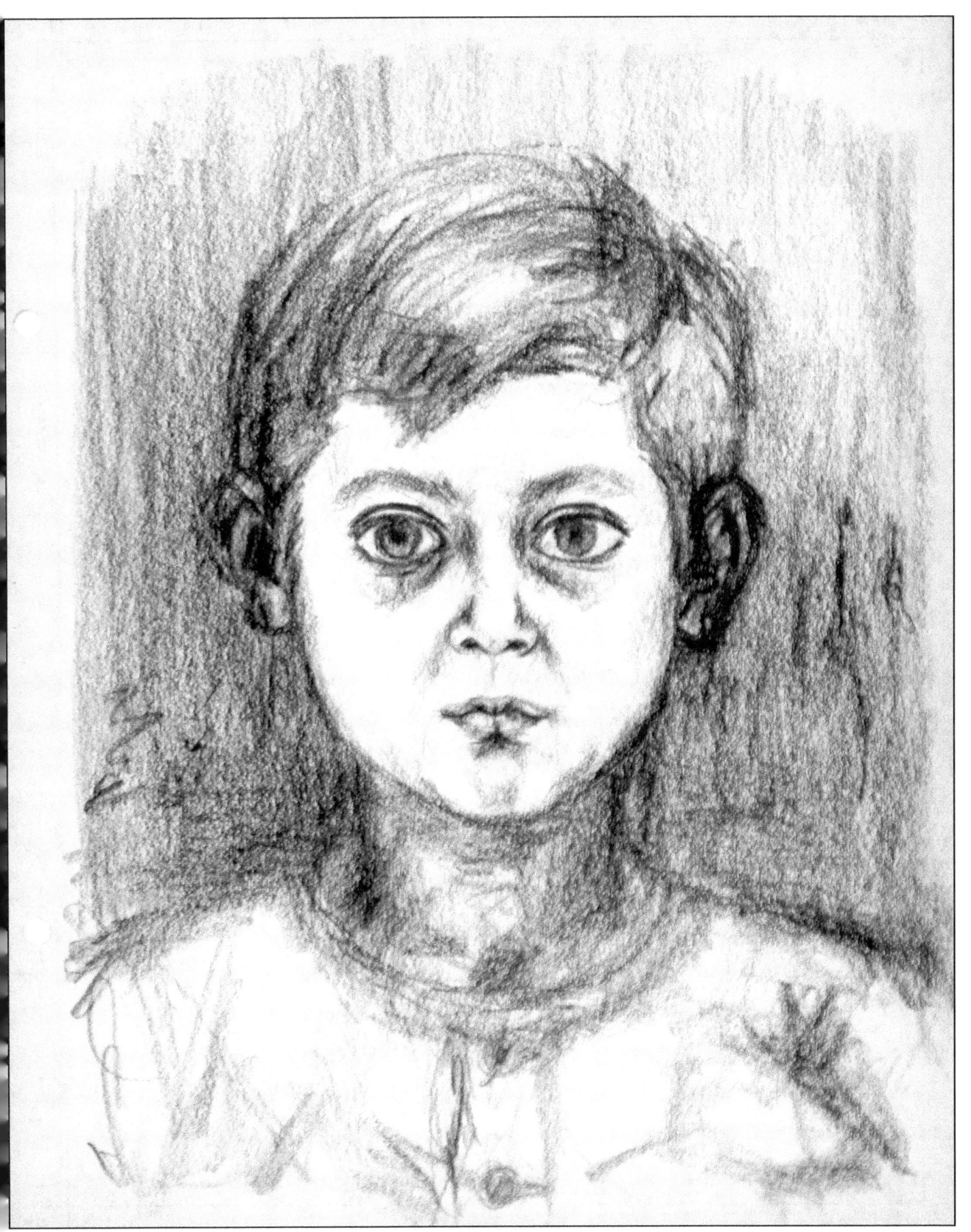
Giancarlo

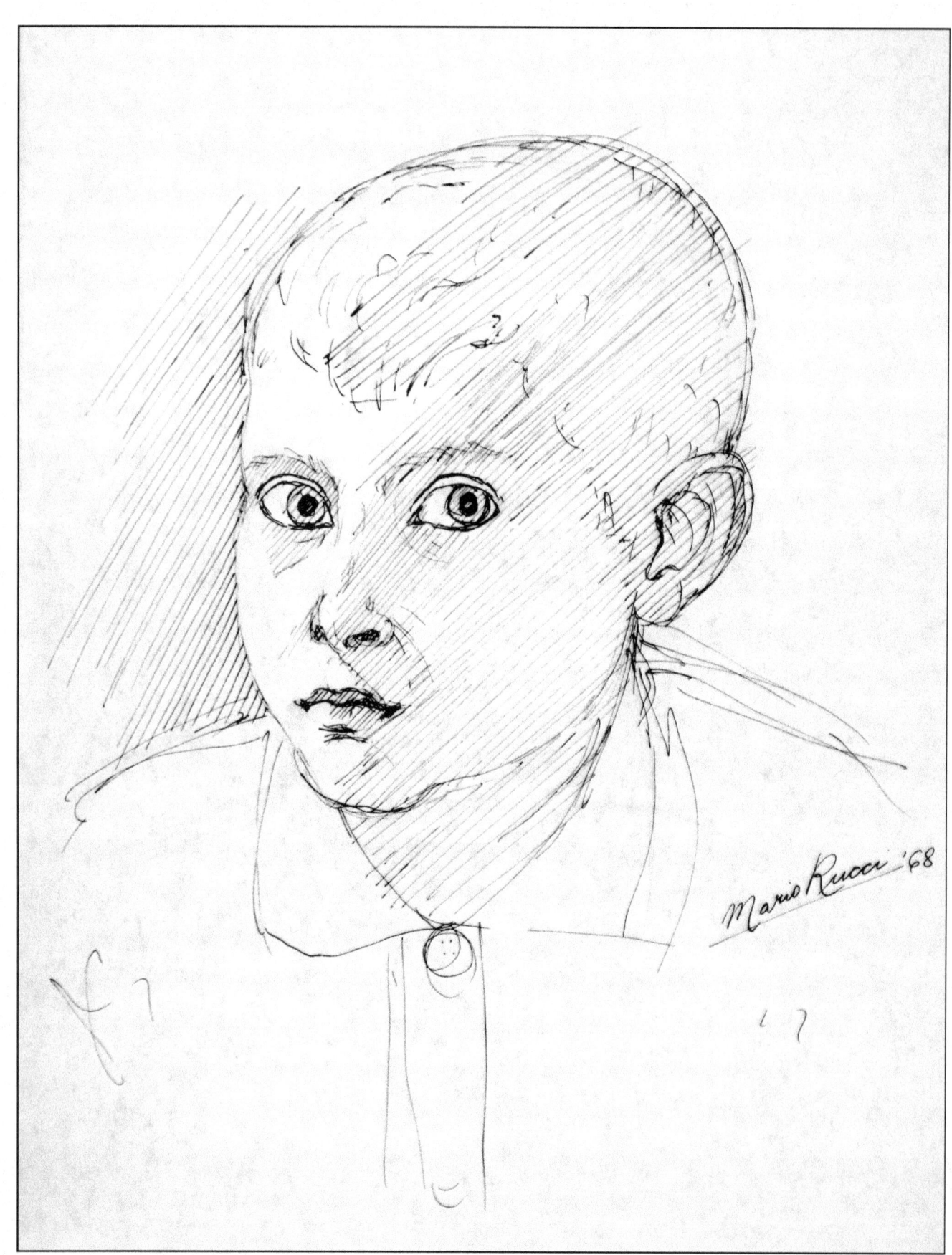

Giancarlo

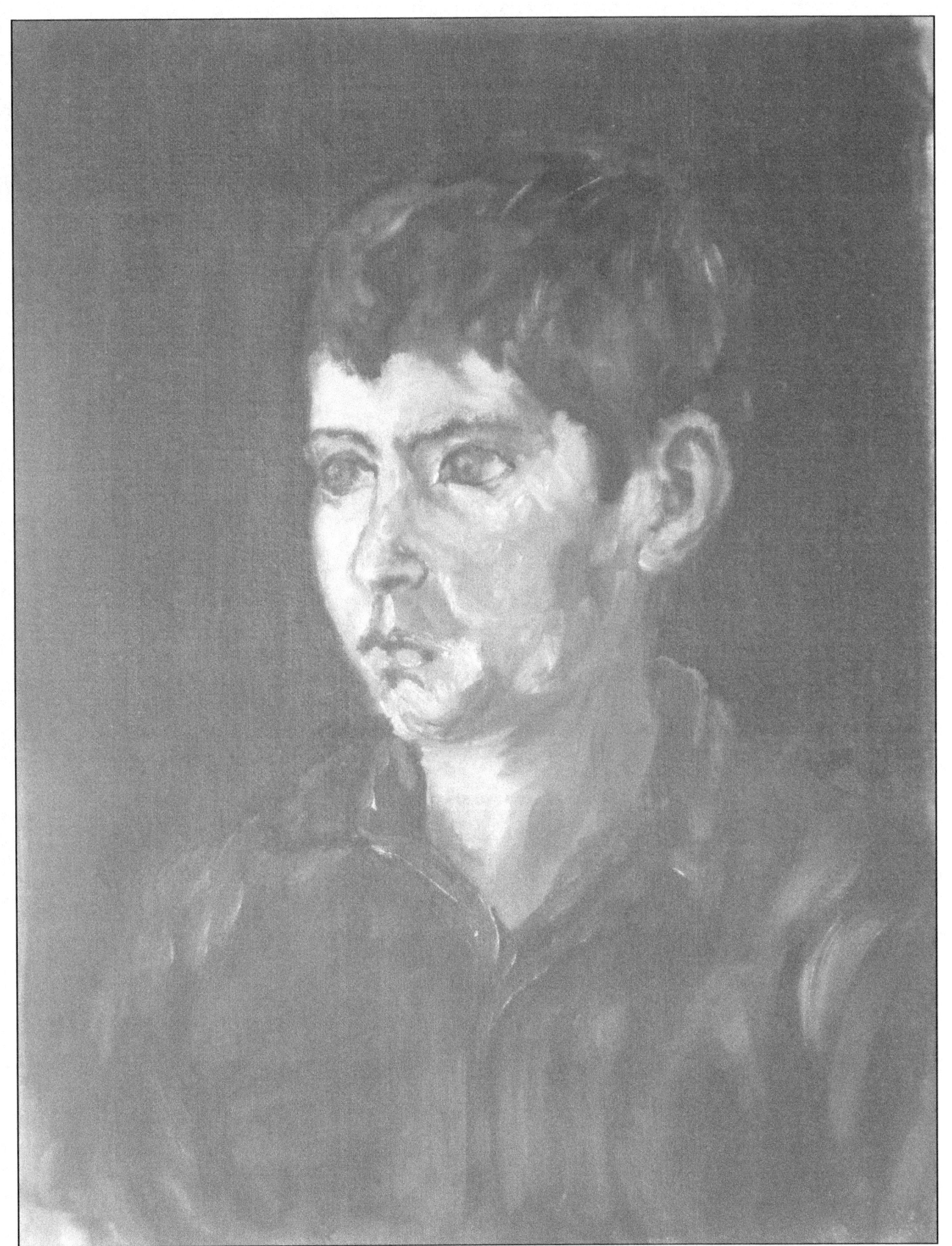

Giancarlo

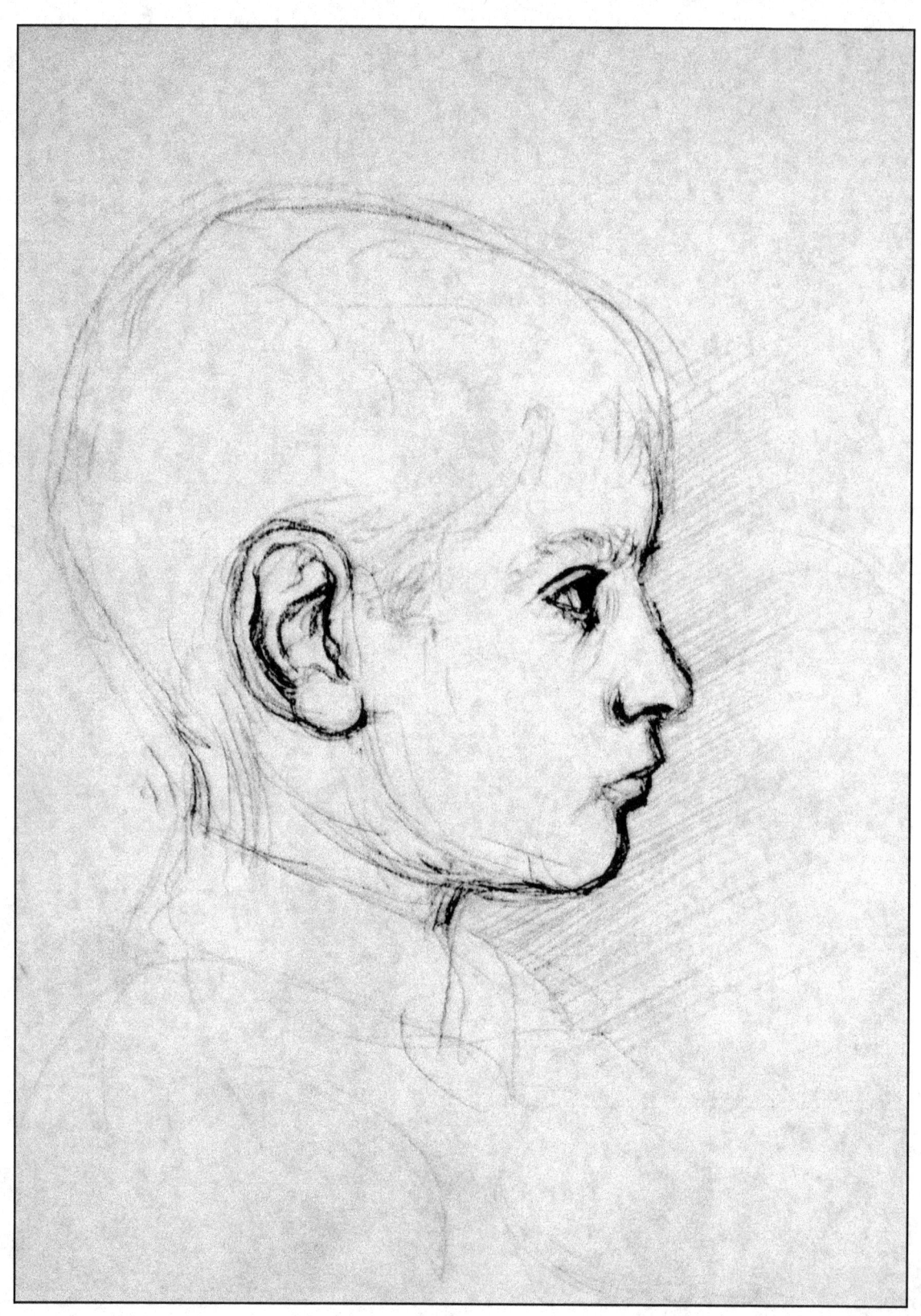

Giancarlo

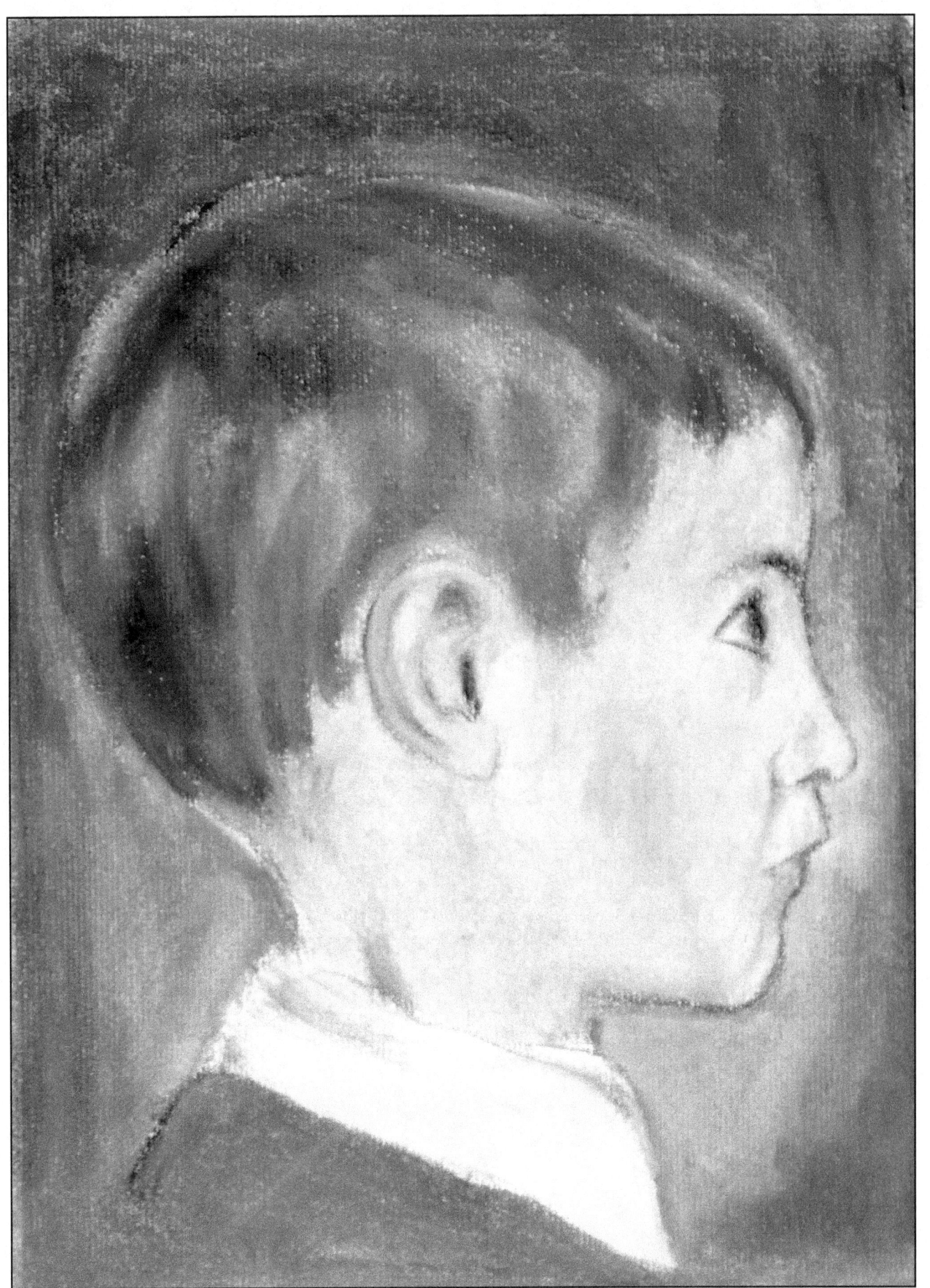

Giancarlo

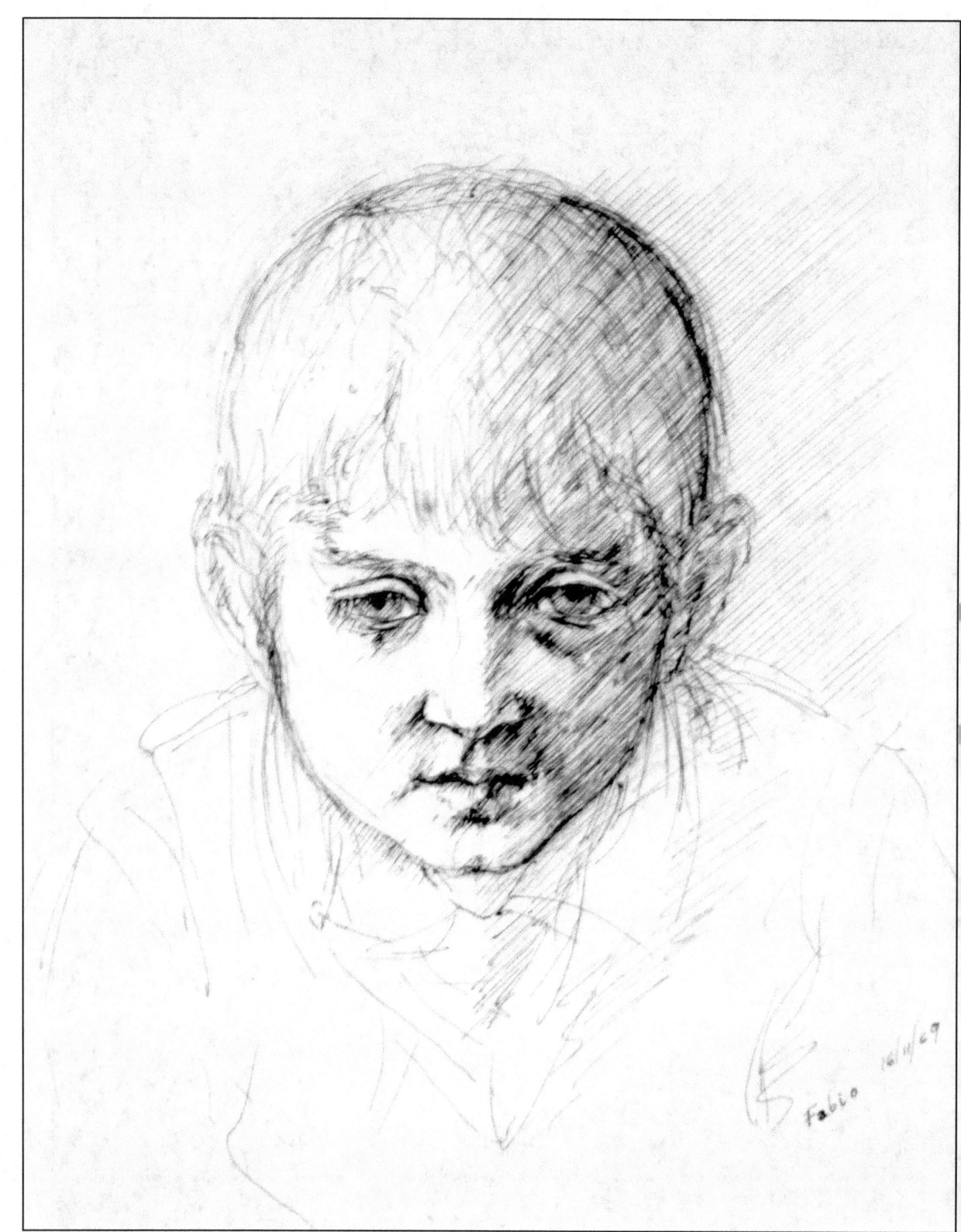

Fabio

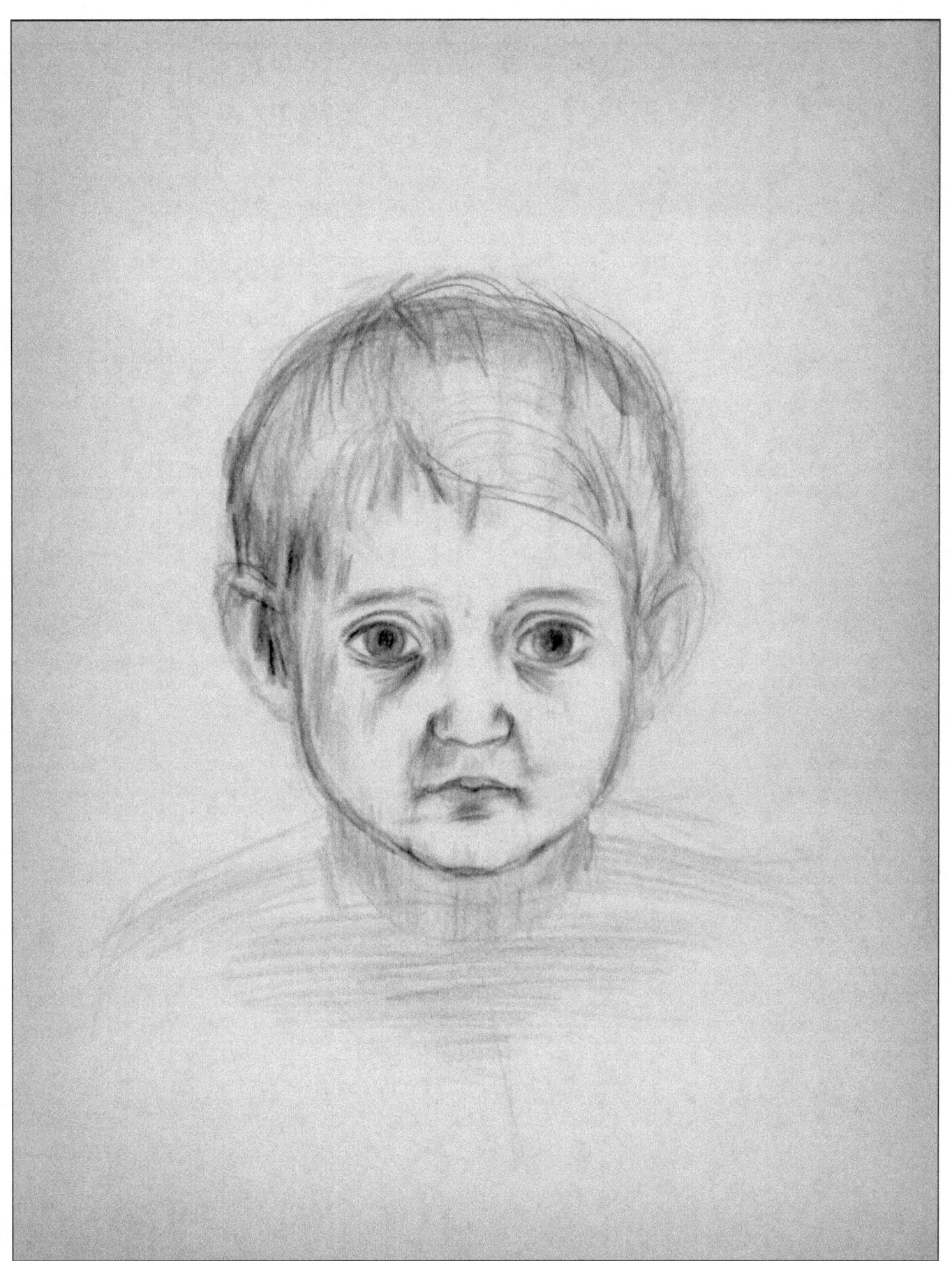

Fabio

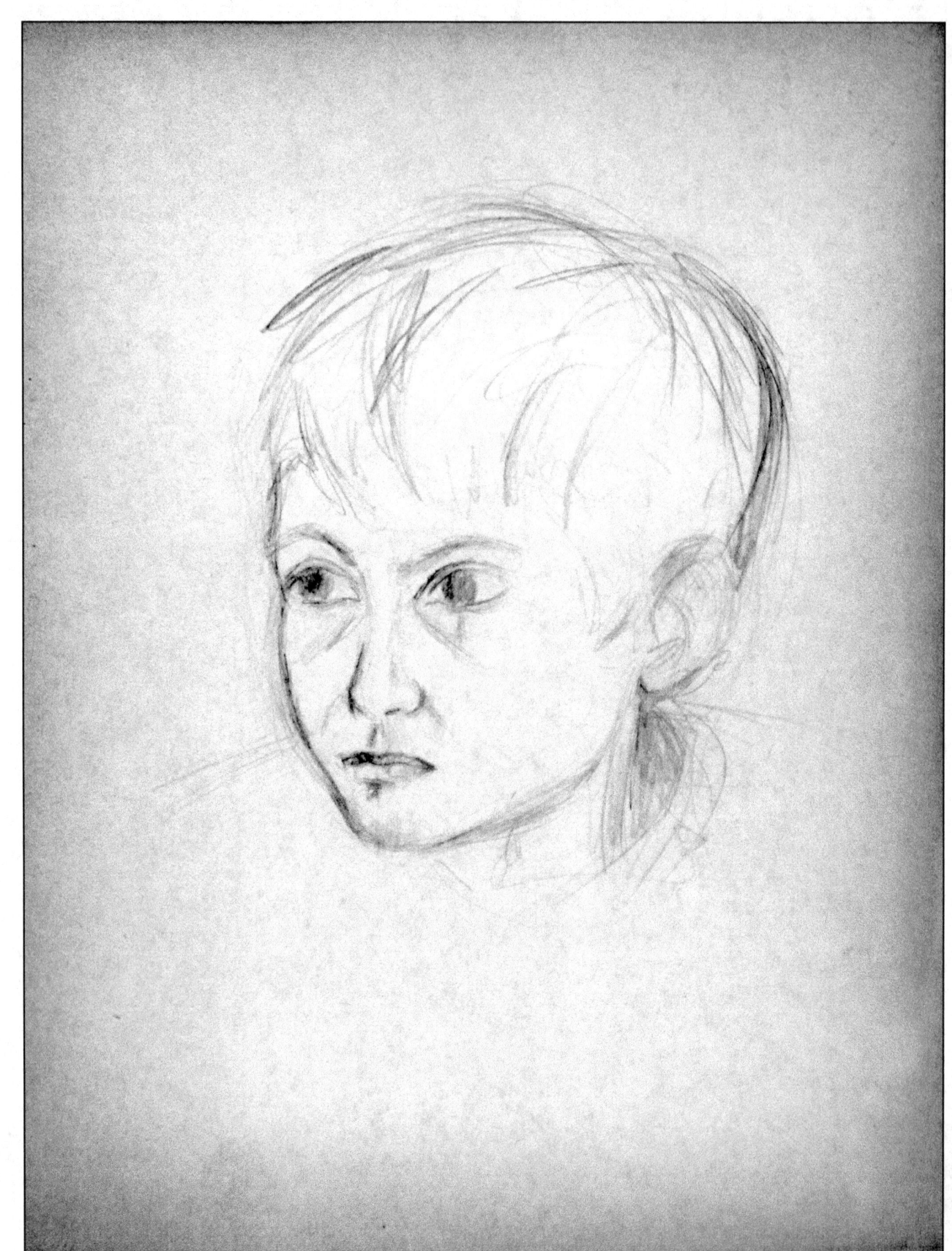
Fabio

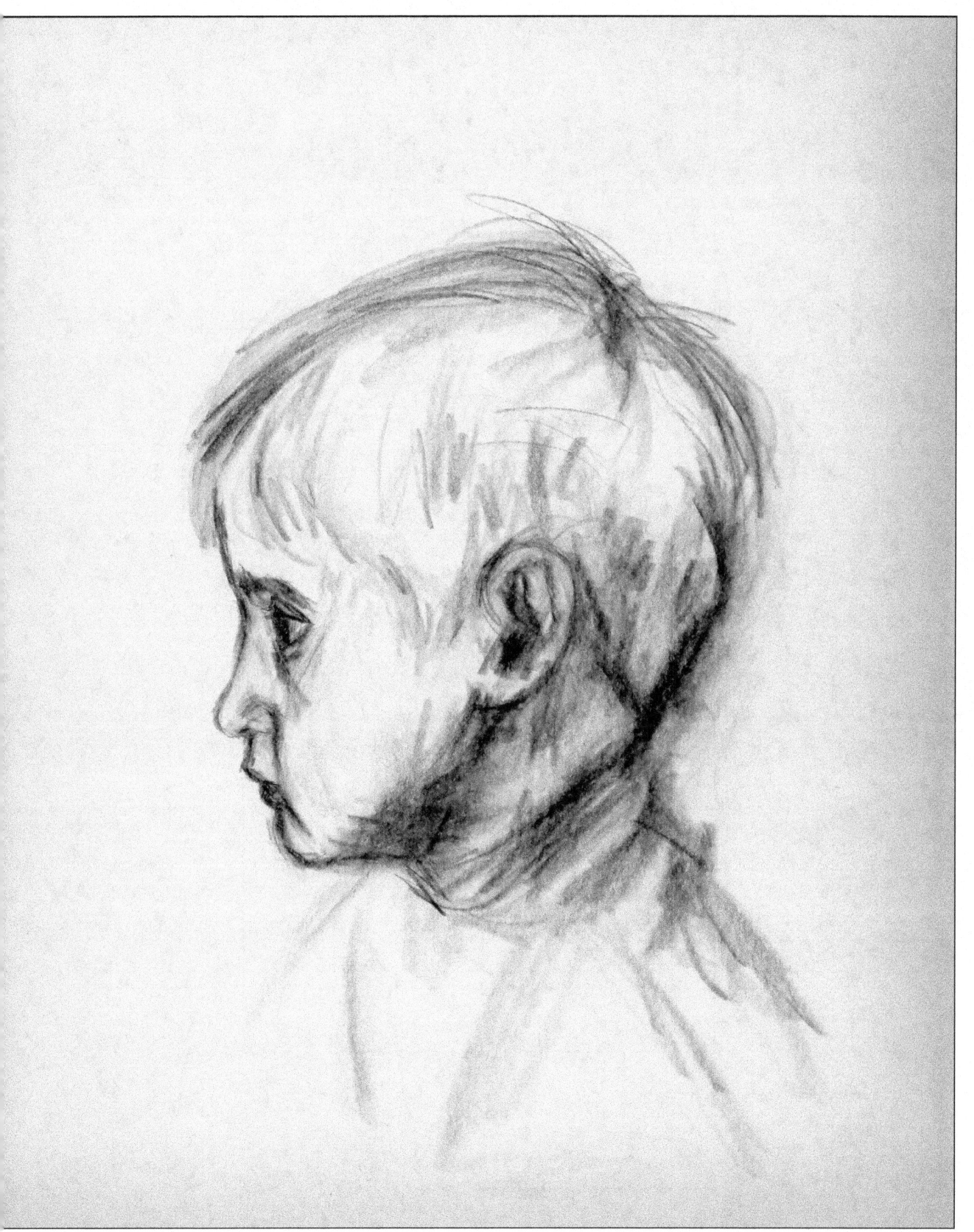

Fabio

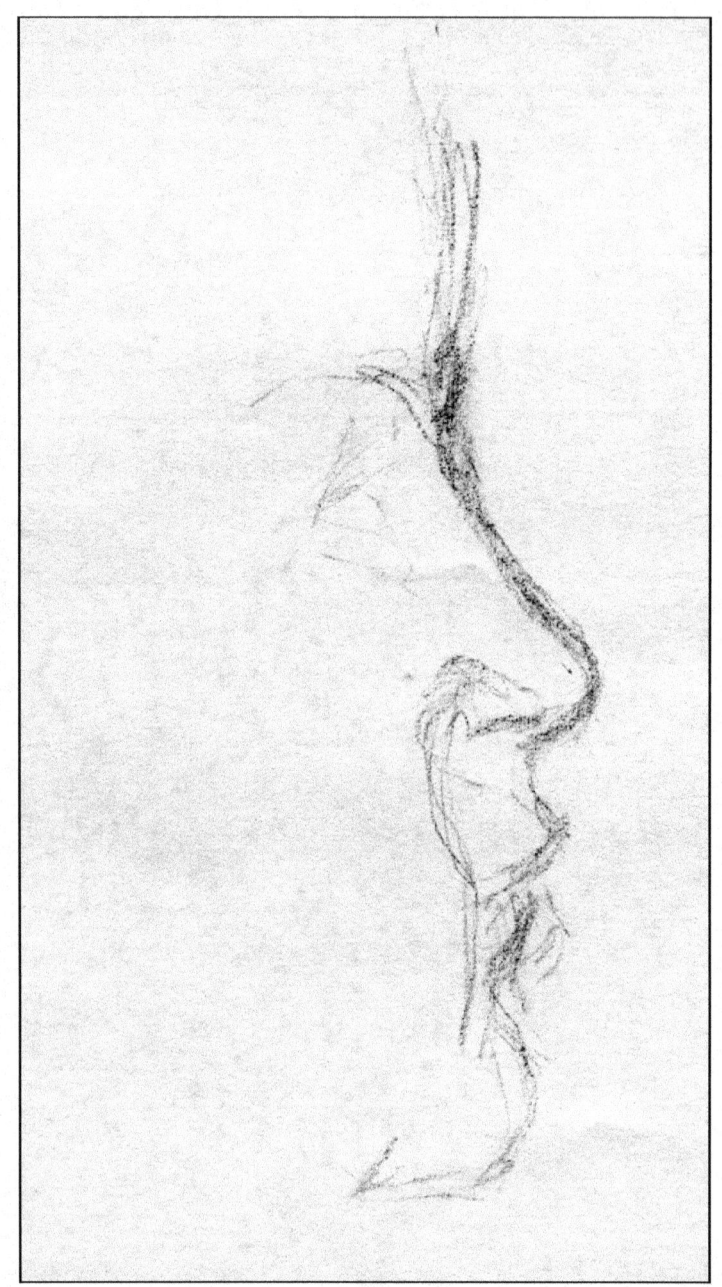

Fabio

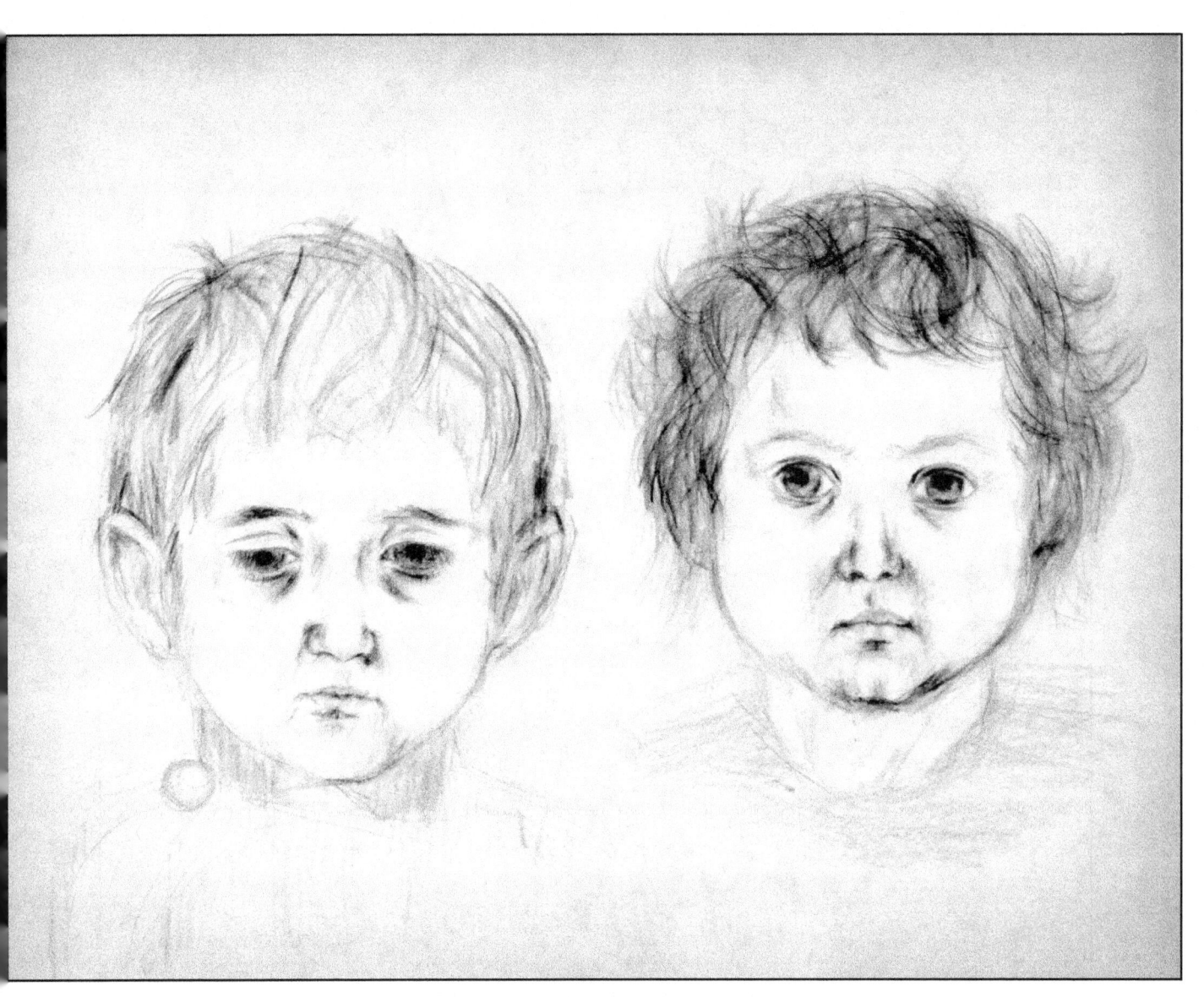

Fabio and Natalie

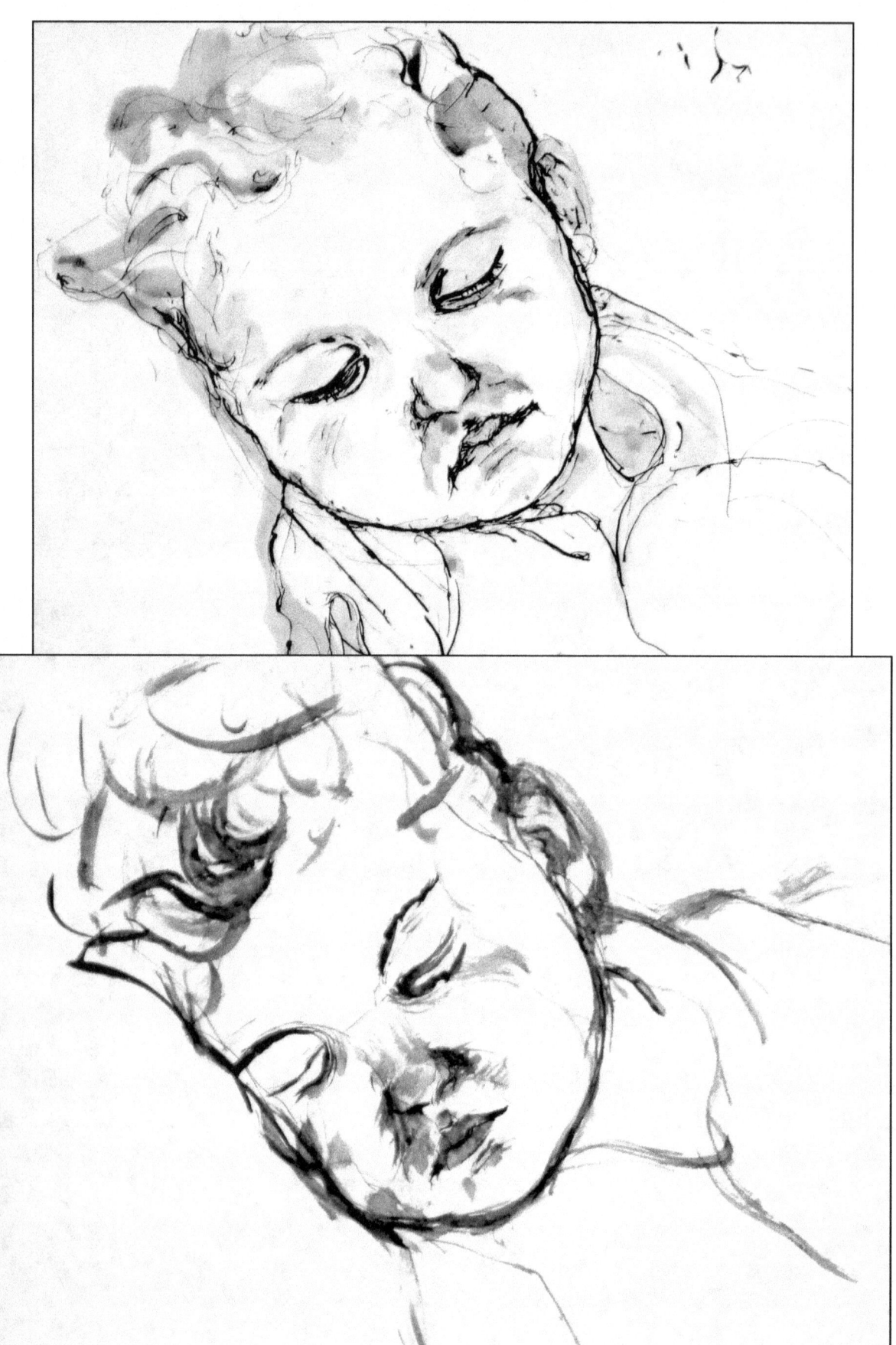

Natale

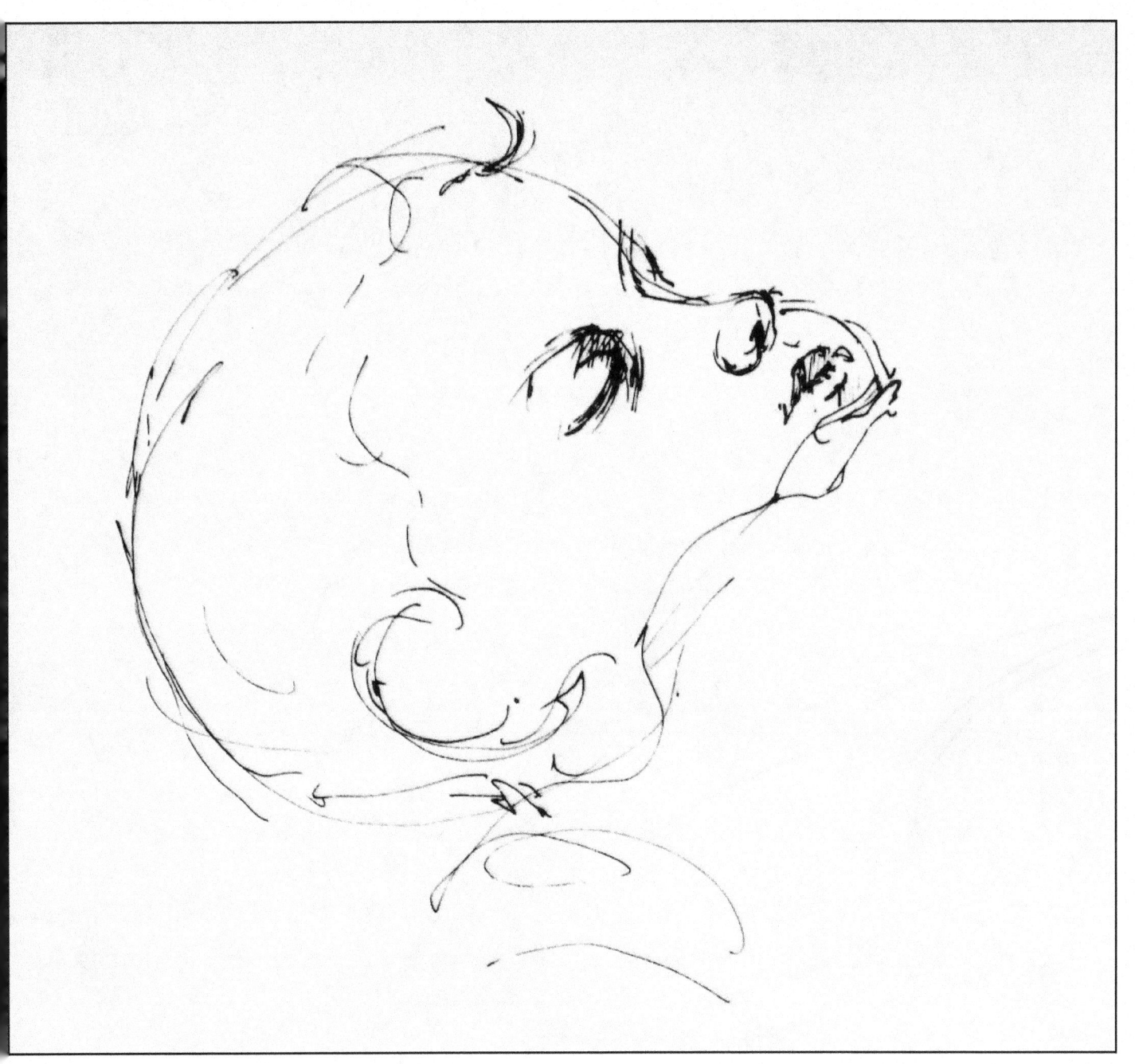

Natale

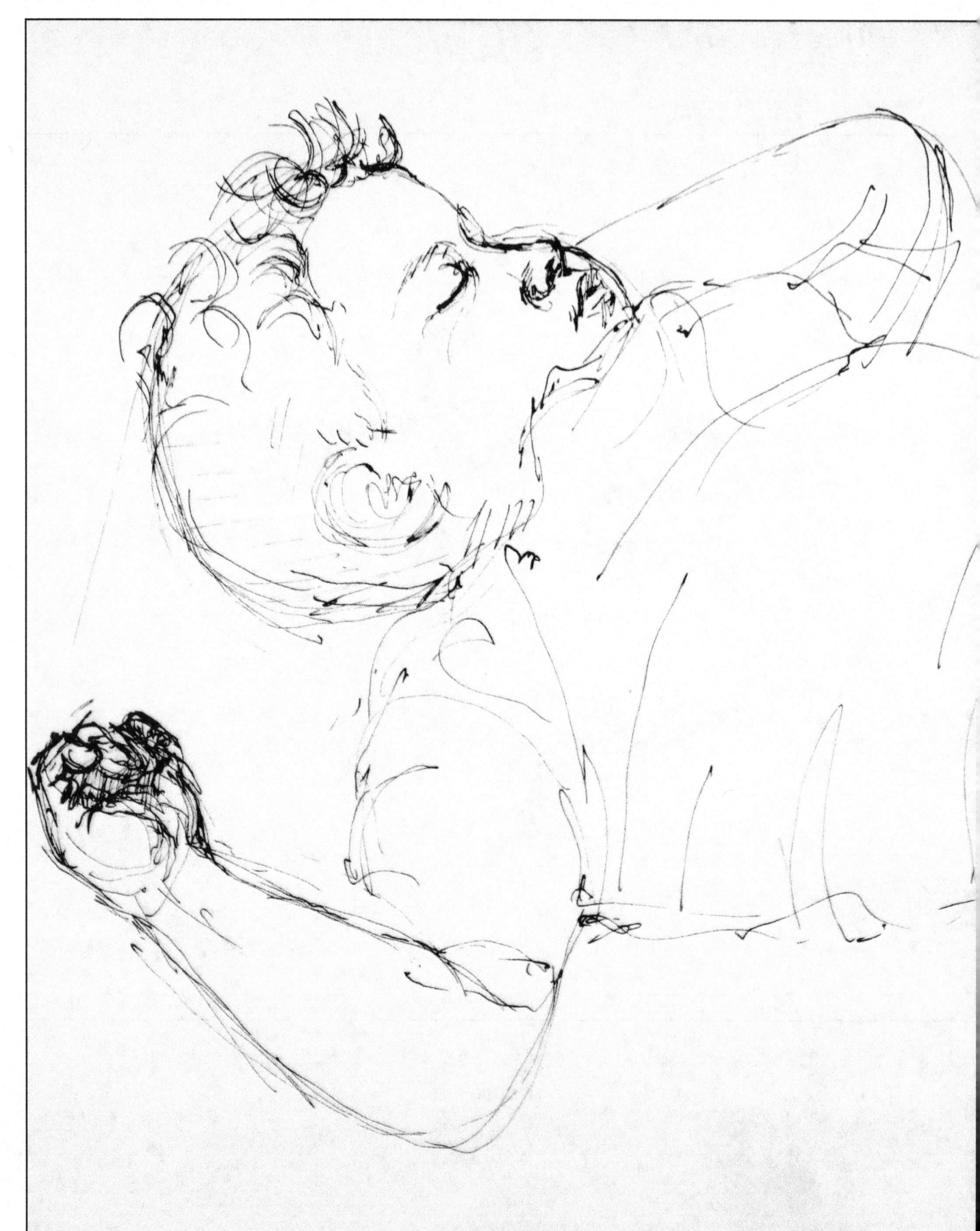

Natalie

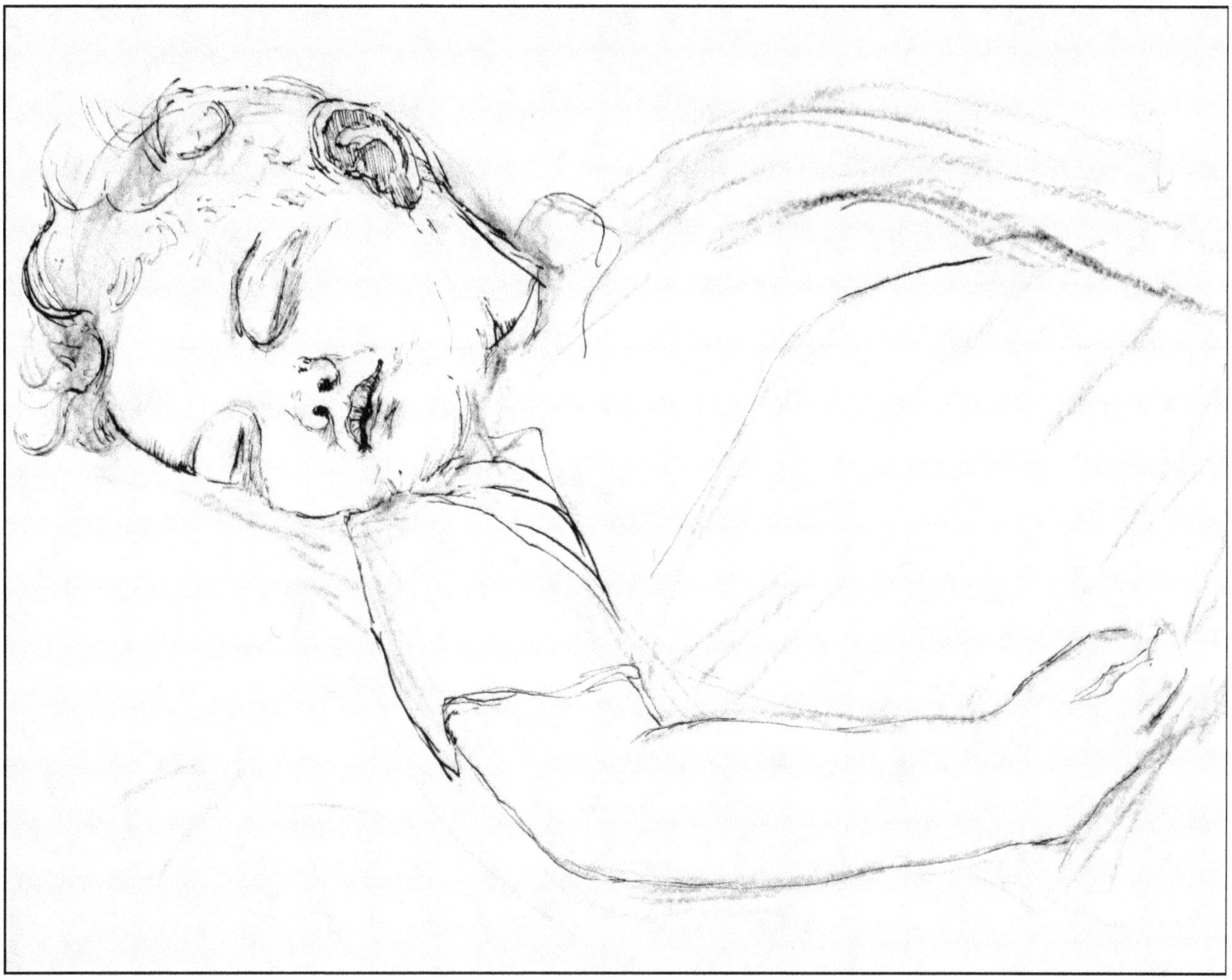

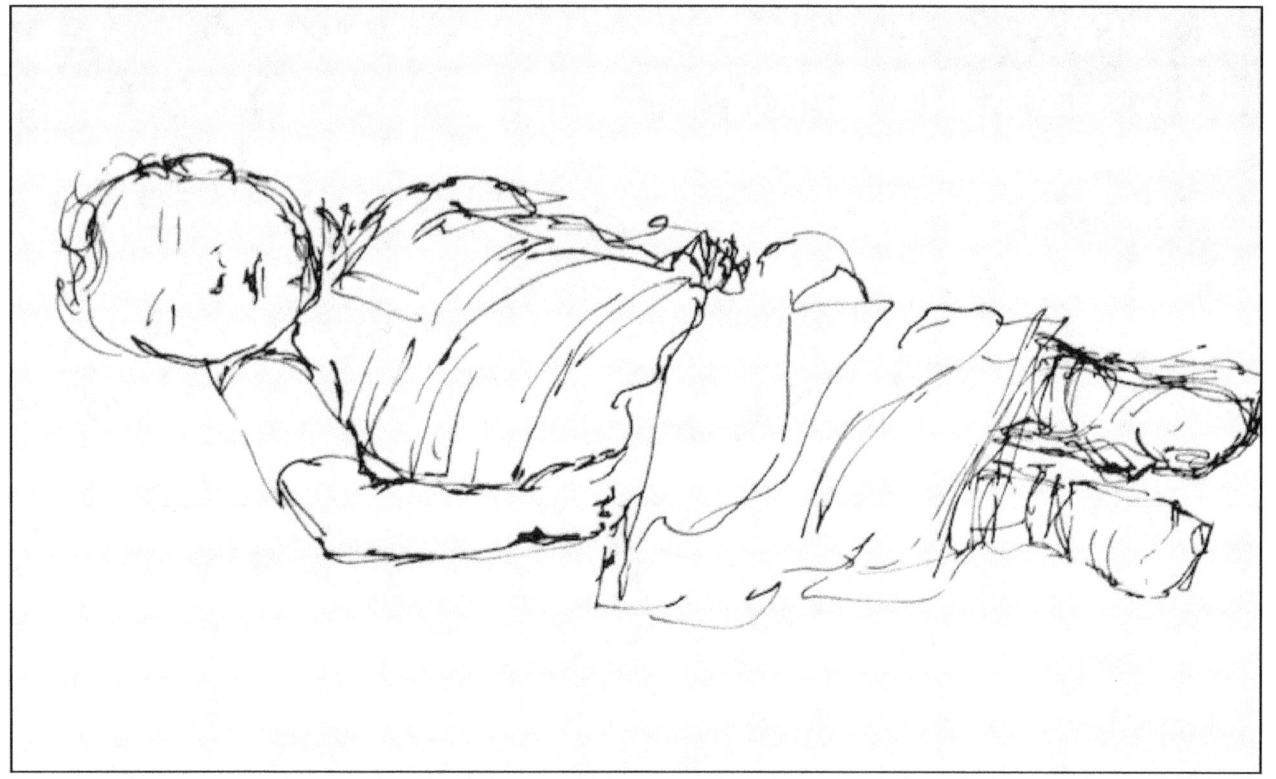

Natale

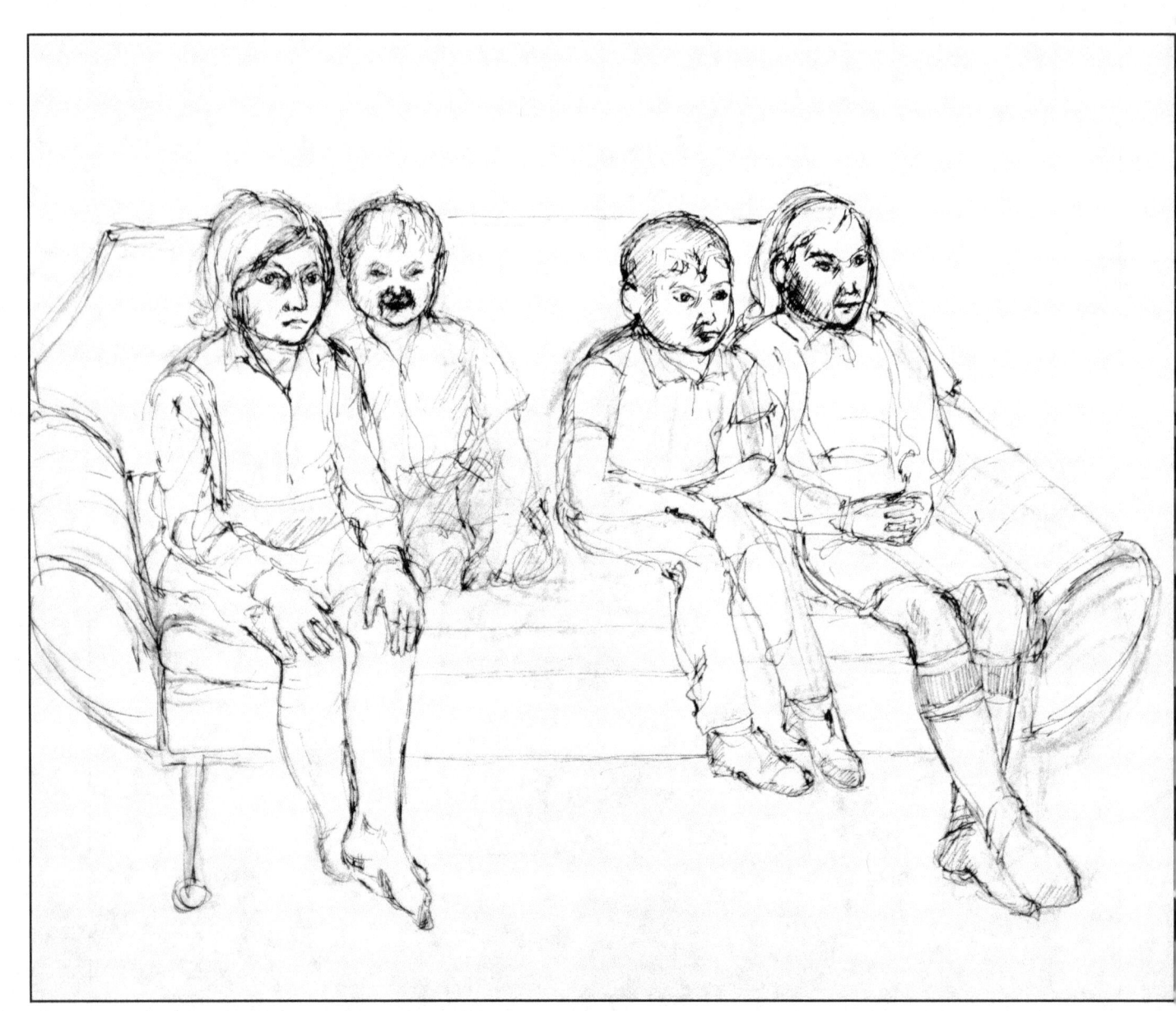

Margherita, Fabio, Giancarlo, and Nella

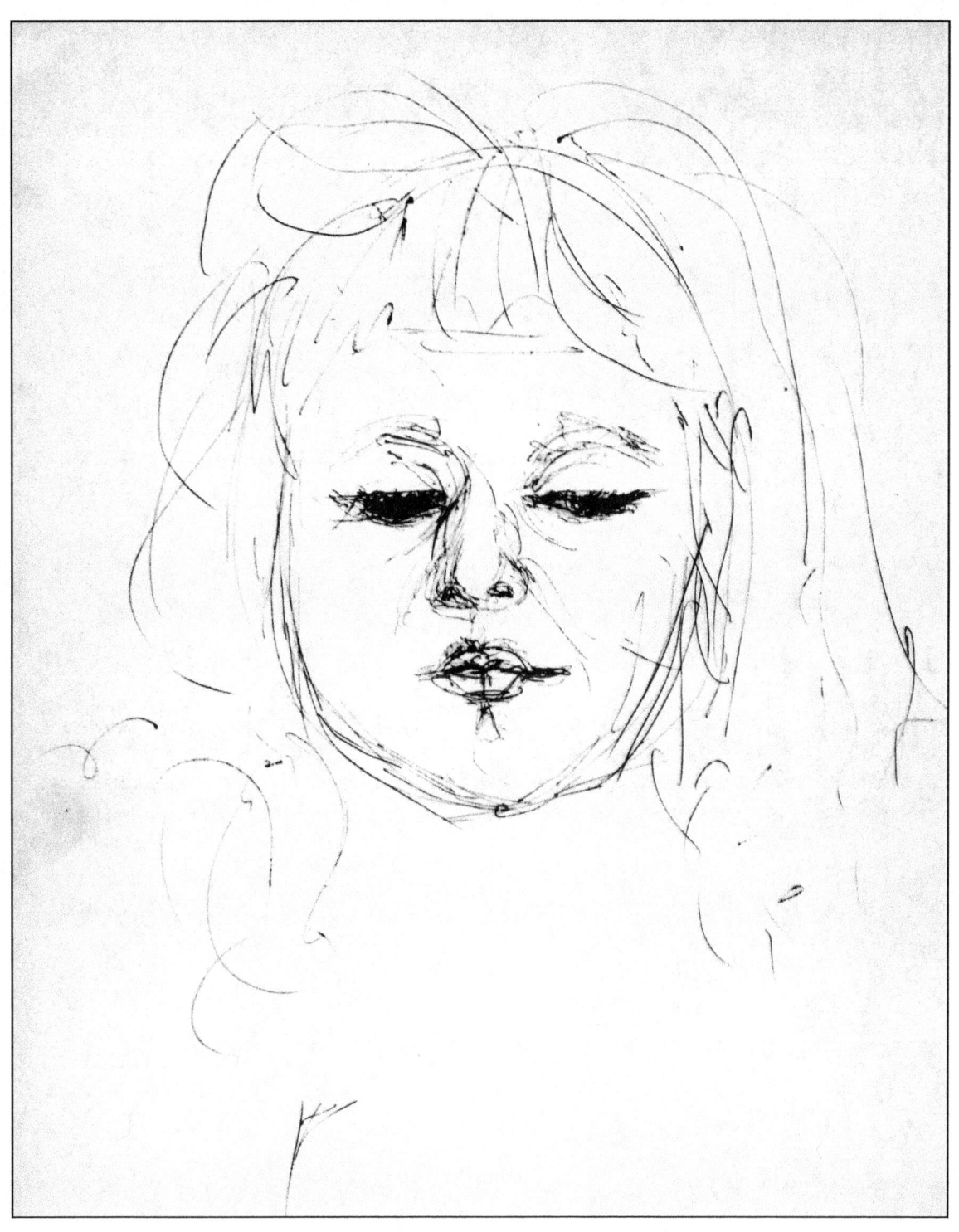

Patrizia

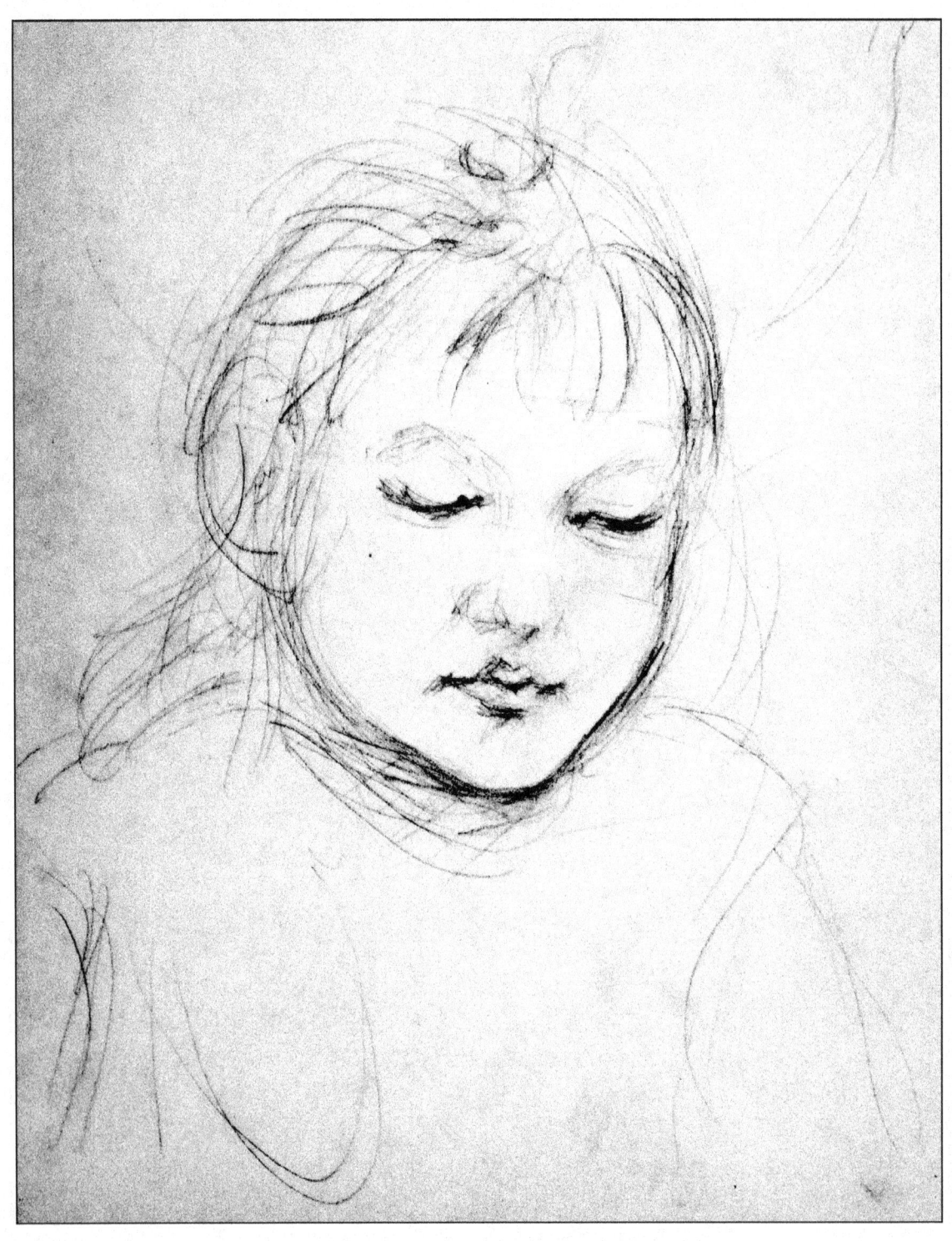

Patrizia

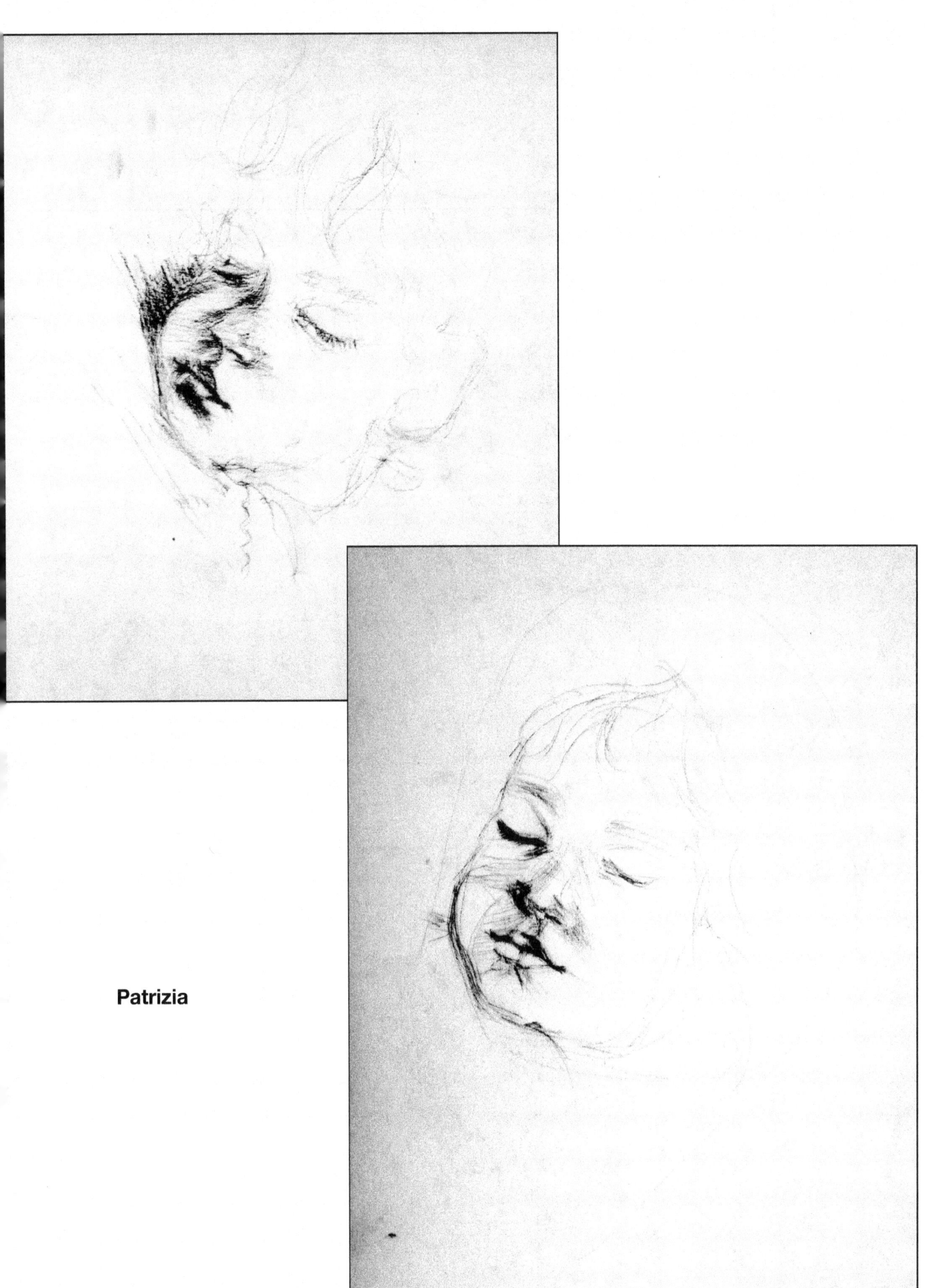

Patrizia

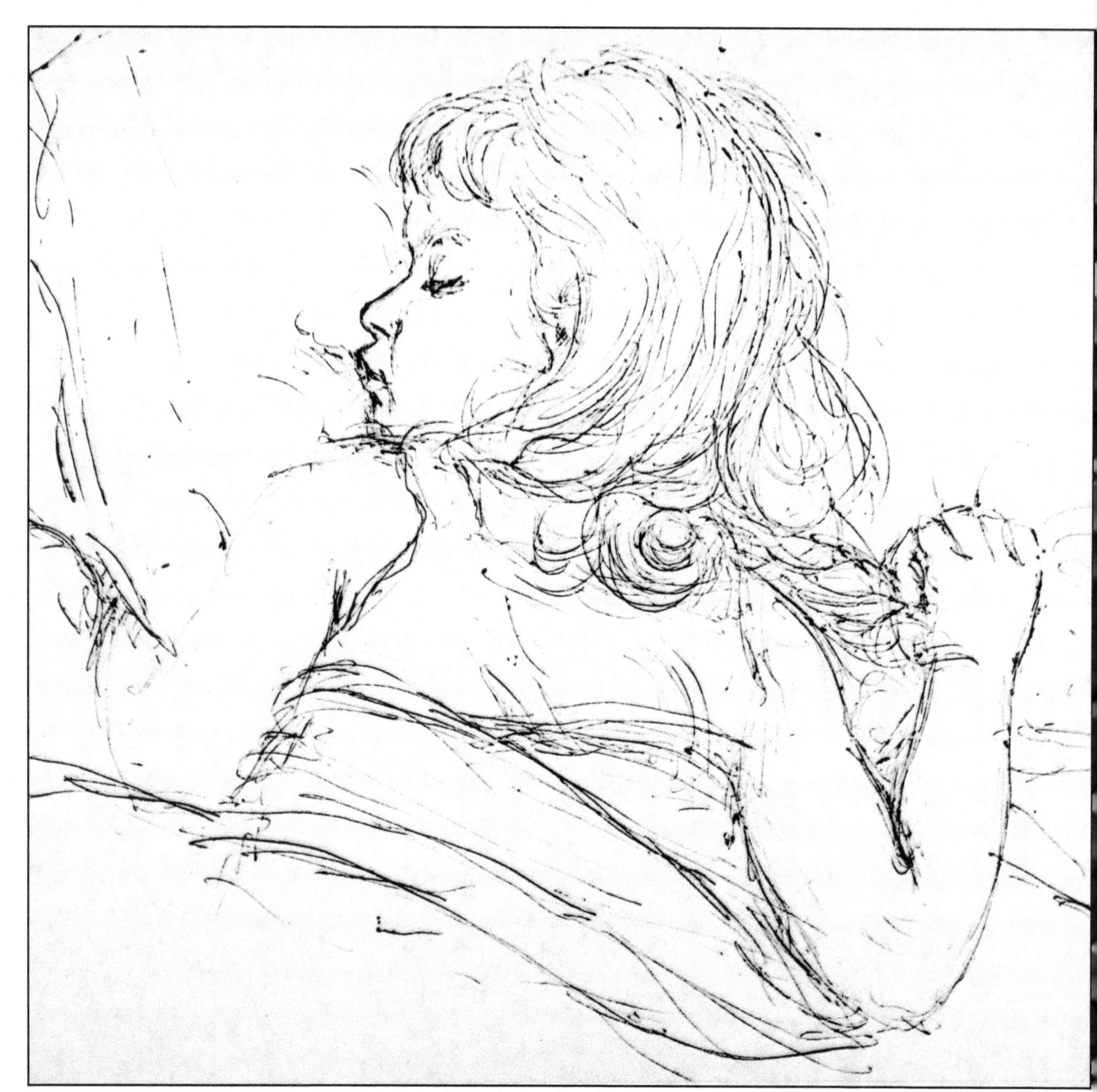

Patrizia, Xerox copy of the original

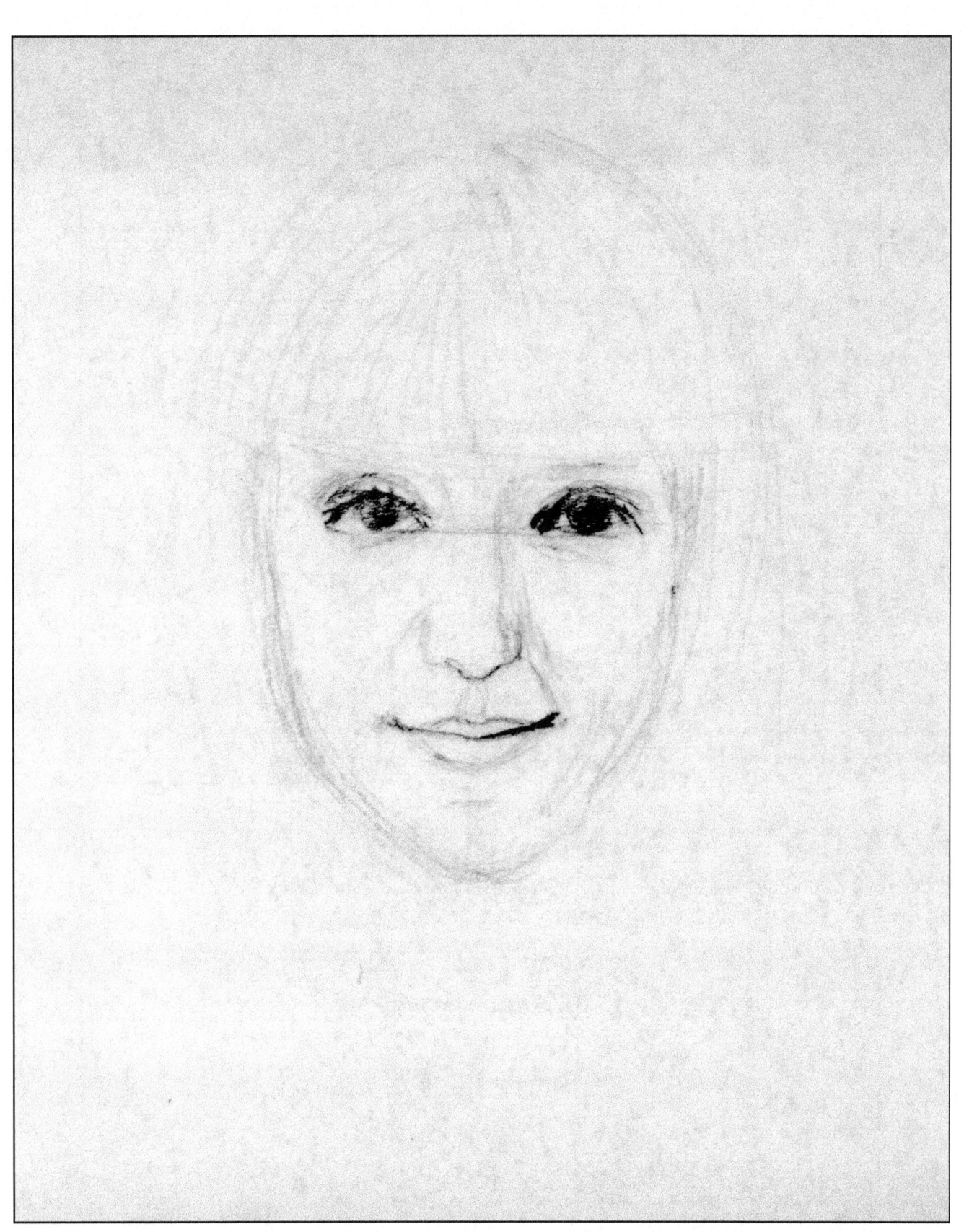

Patrizia, from posing

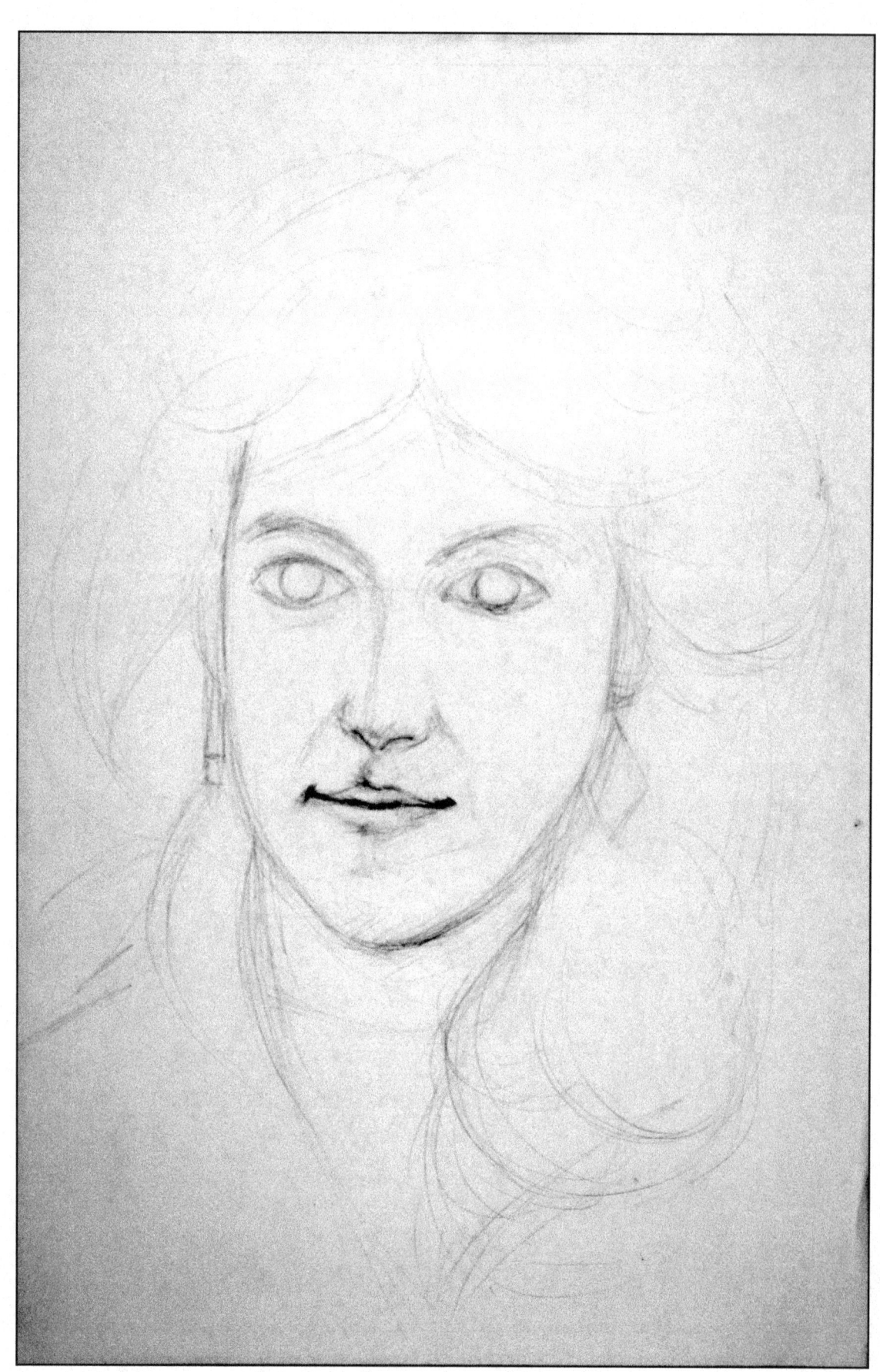

Patrizia, from posing

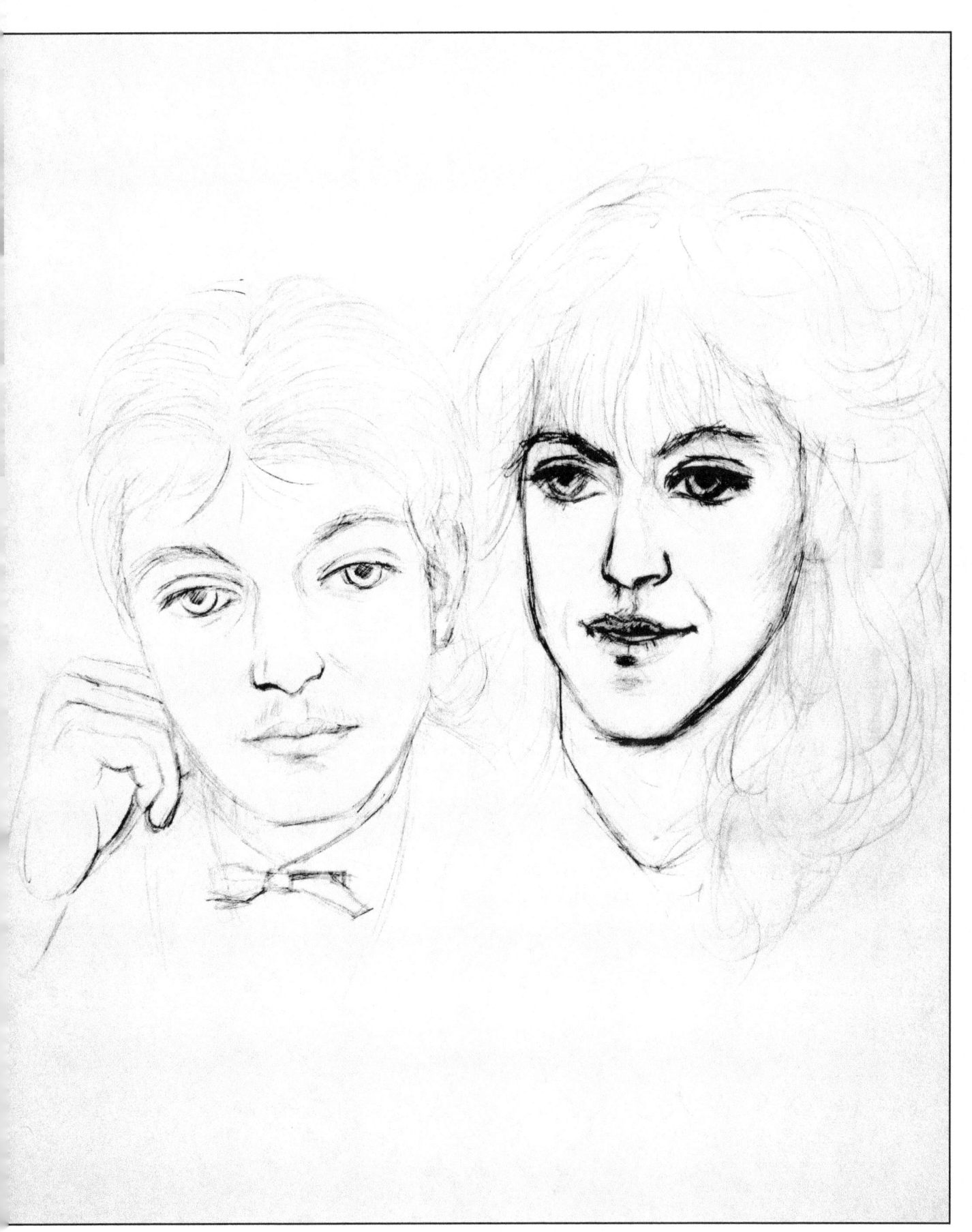

Patrizia and Guerino, from photograph

7. Head Observation, Self-Portraits

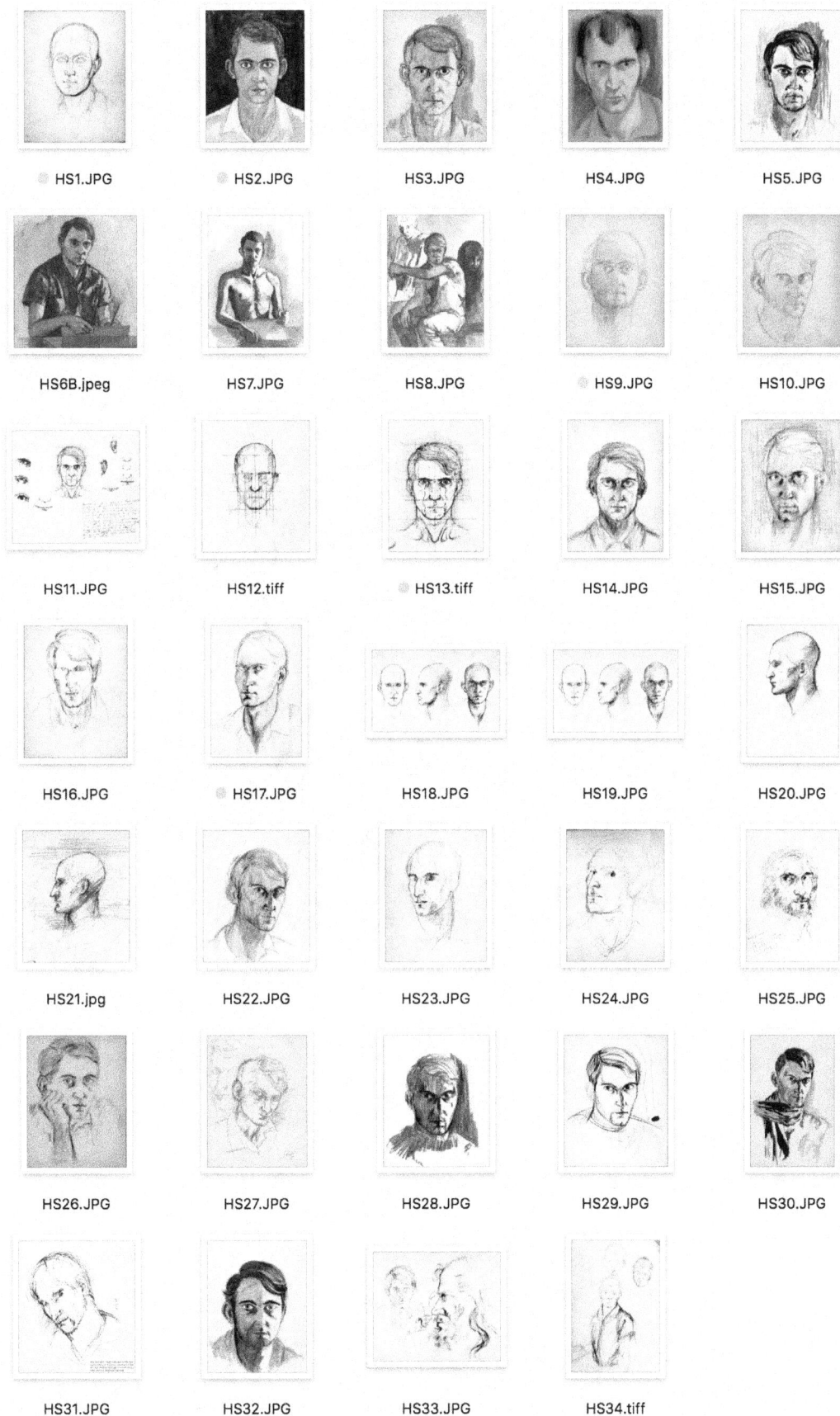

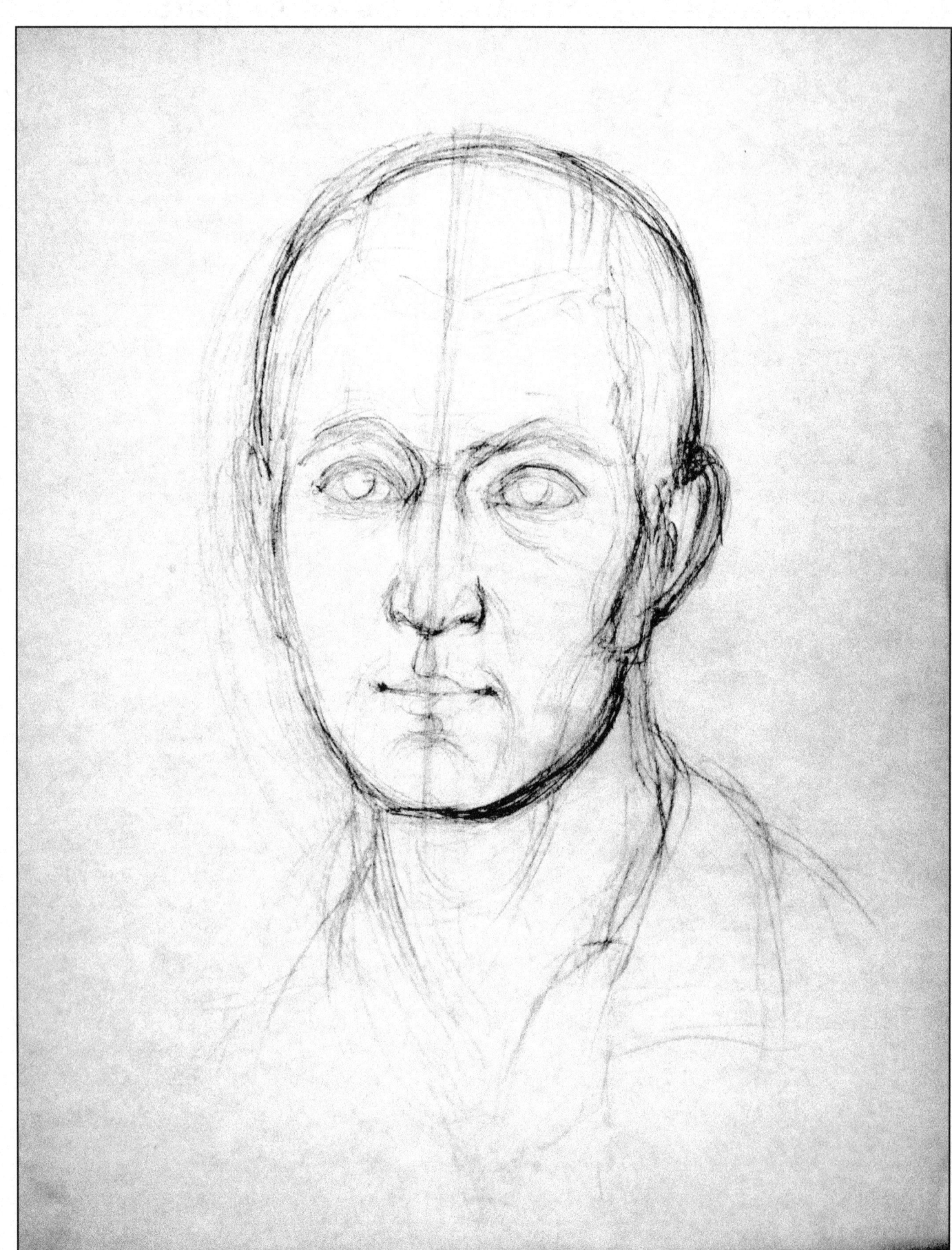

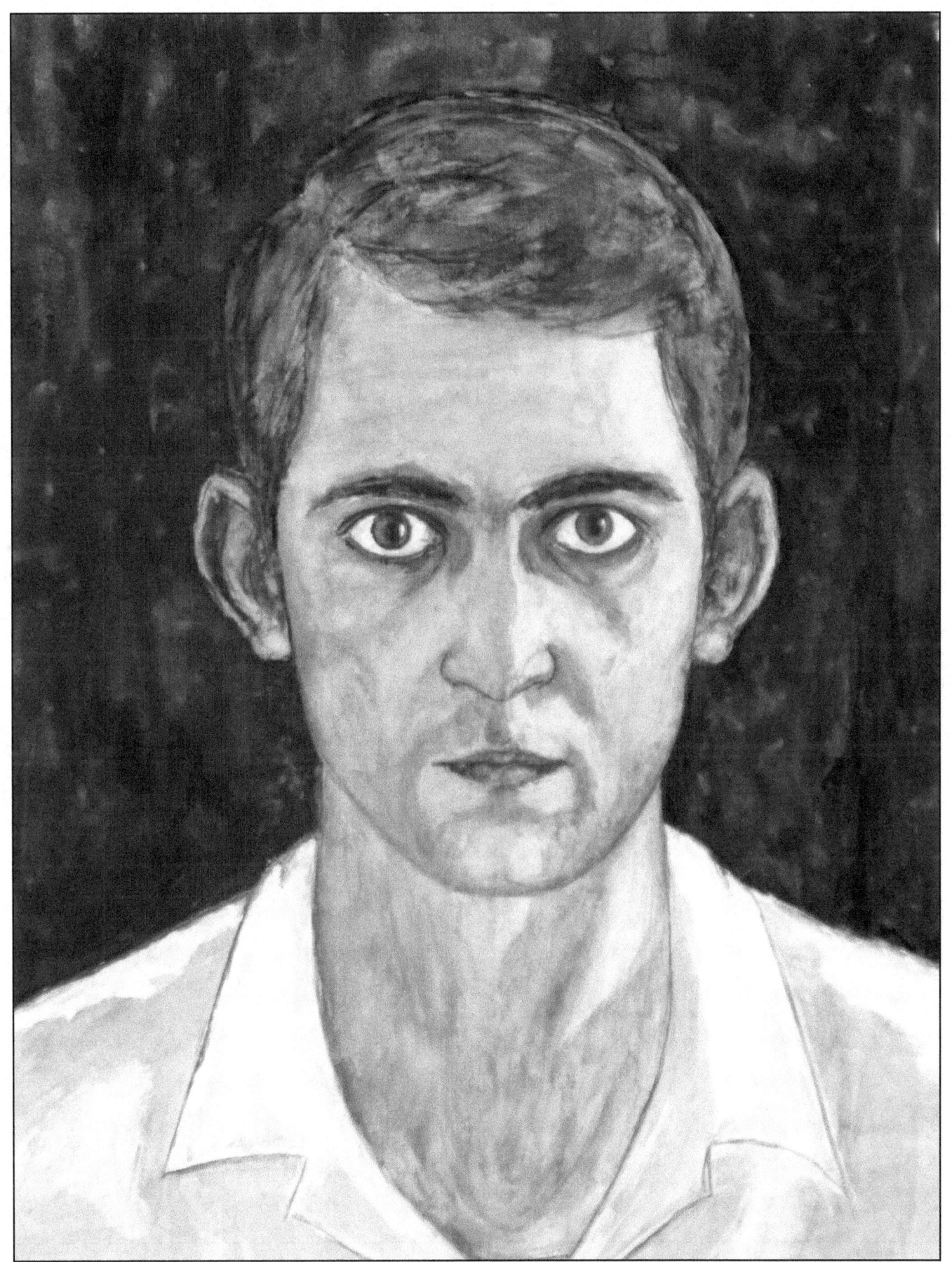

Watercolor

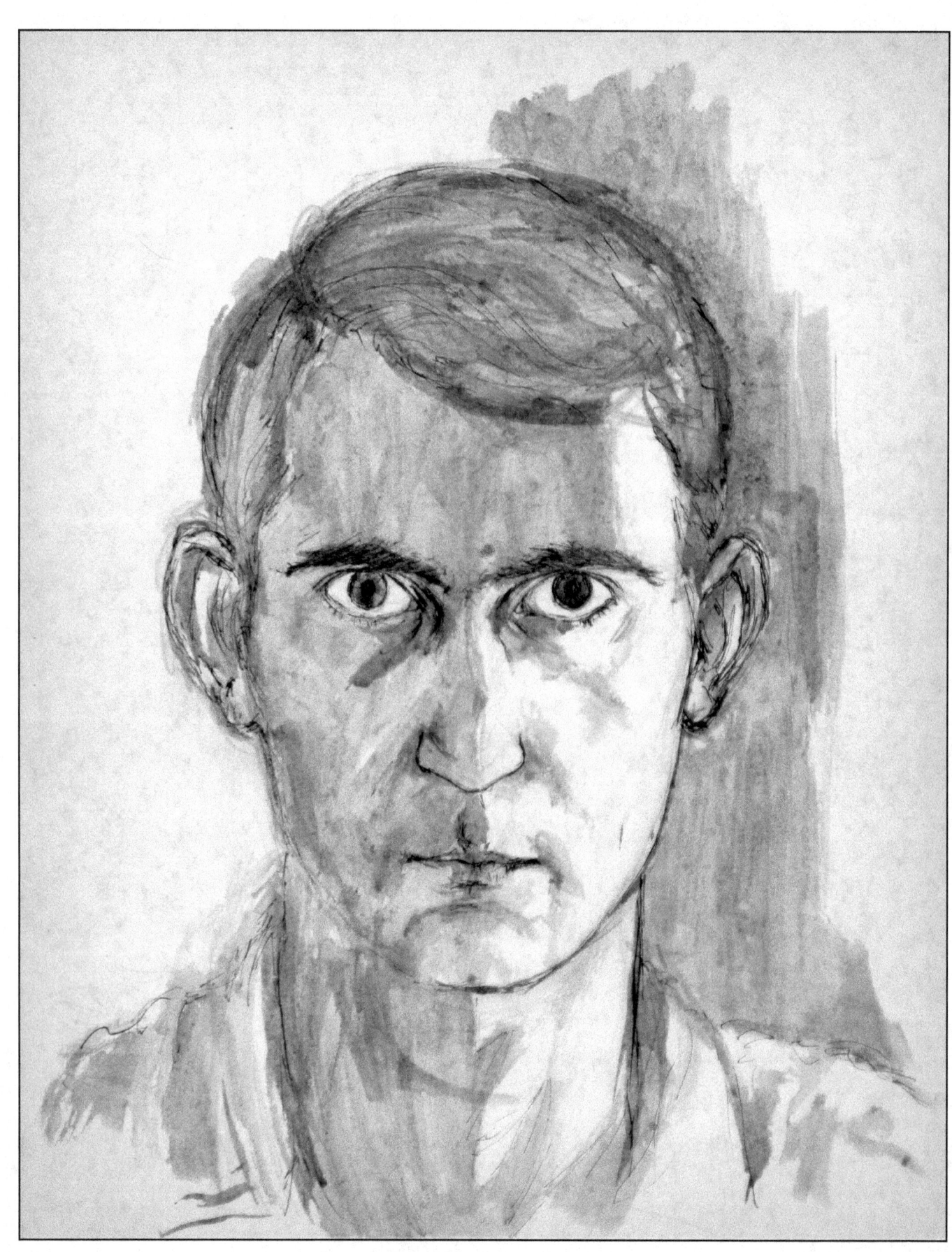

Ink: Pen and Brush

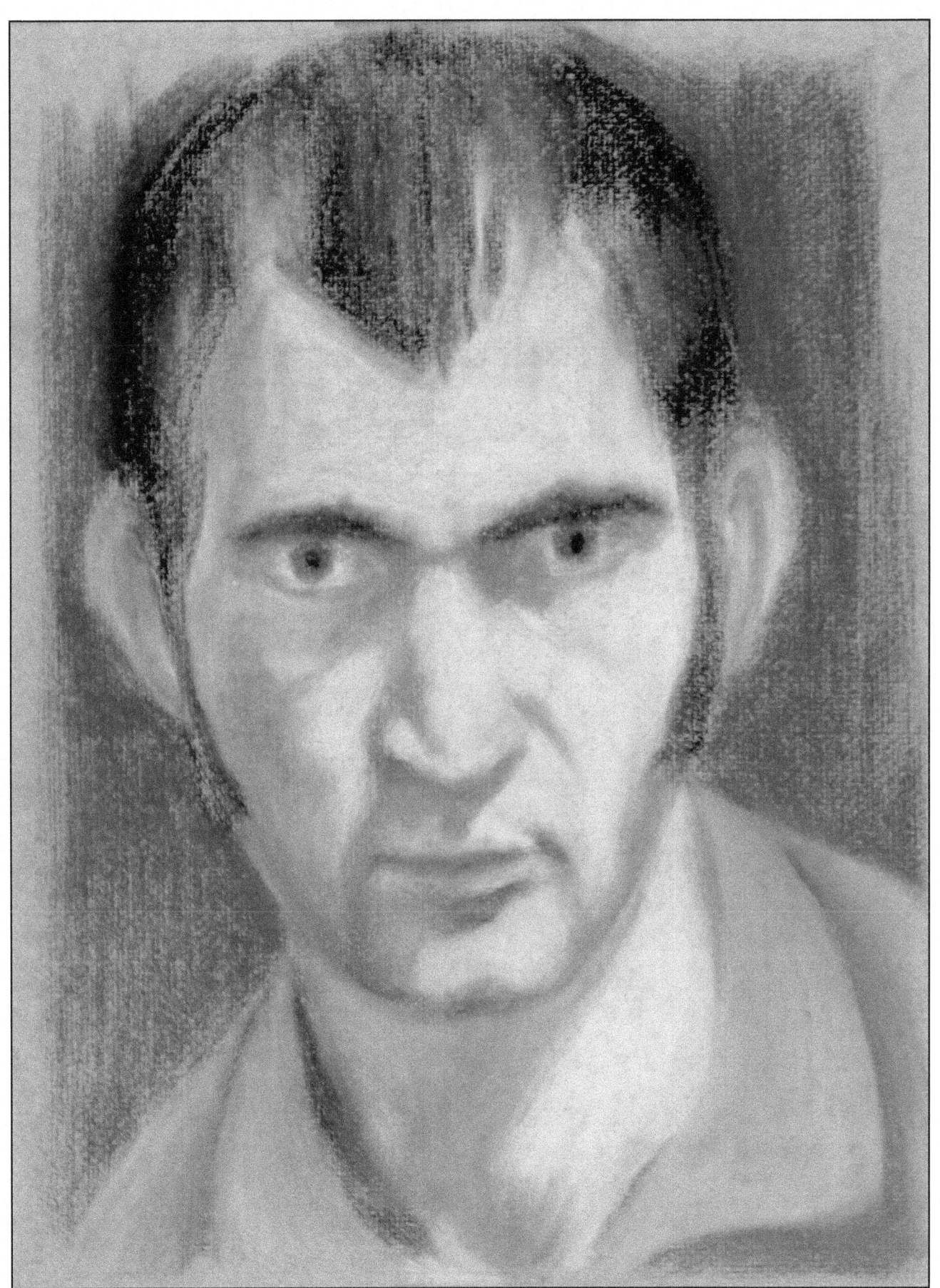

Chalk

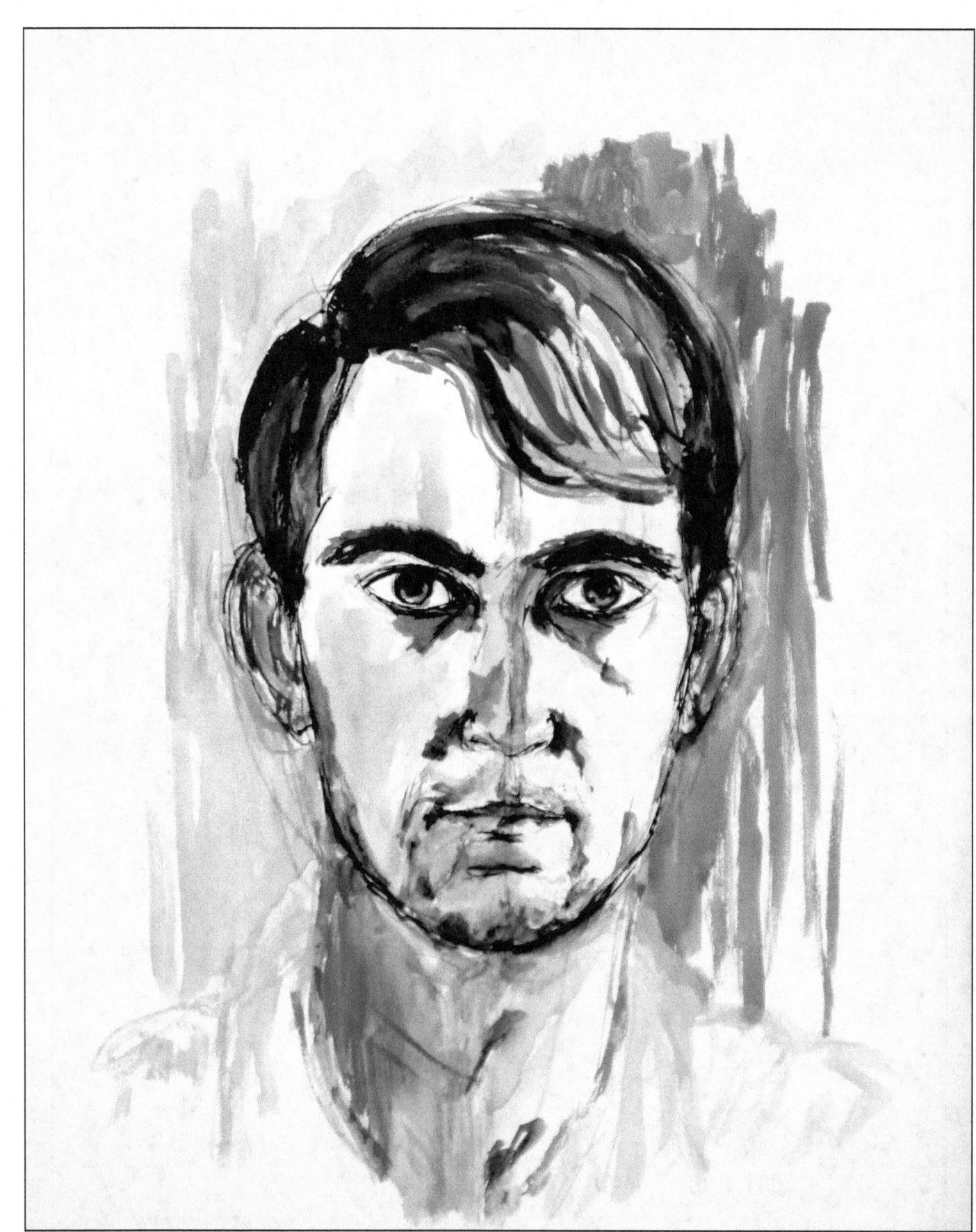

Watercolor

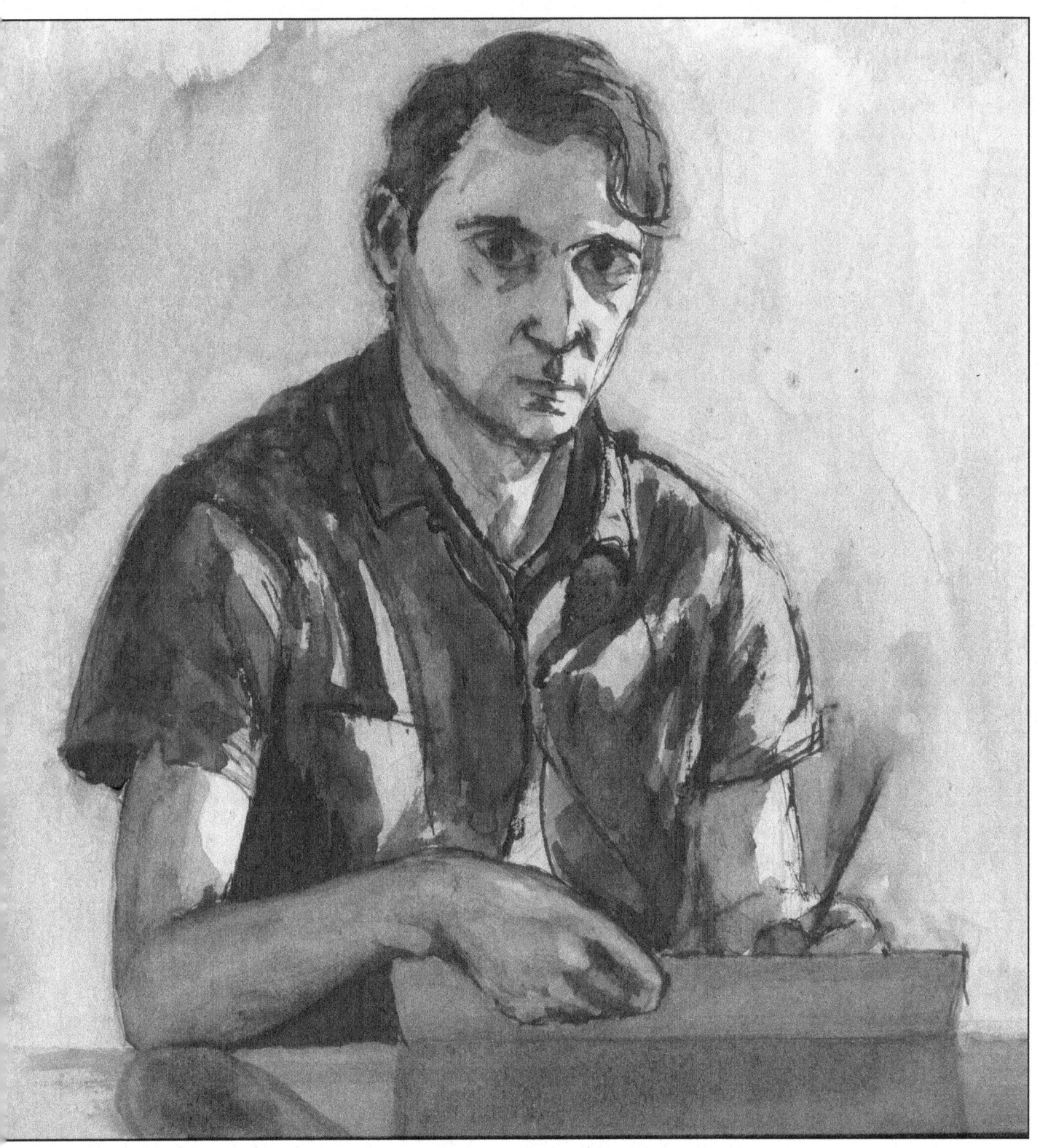

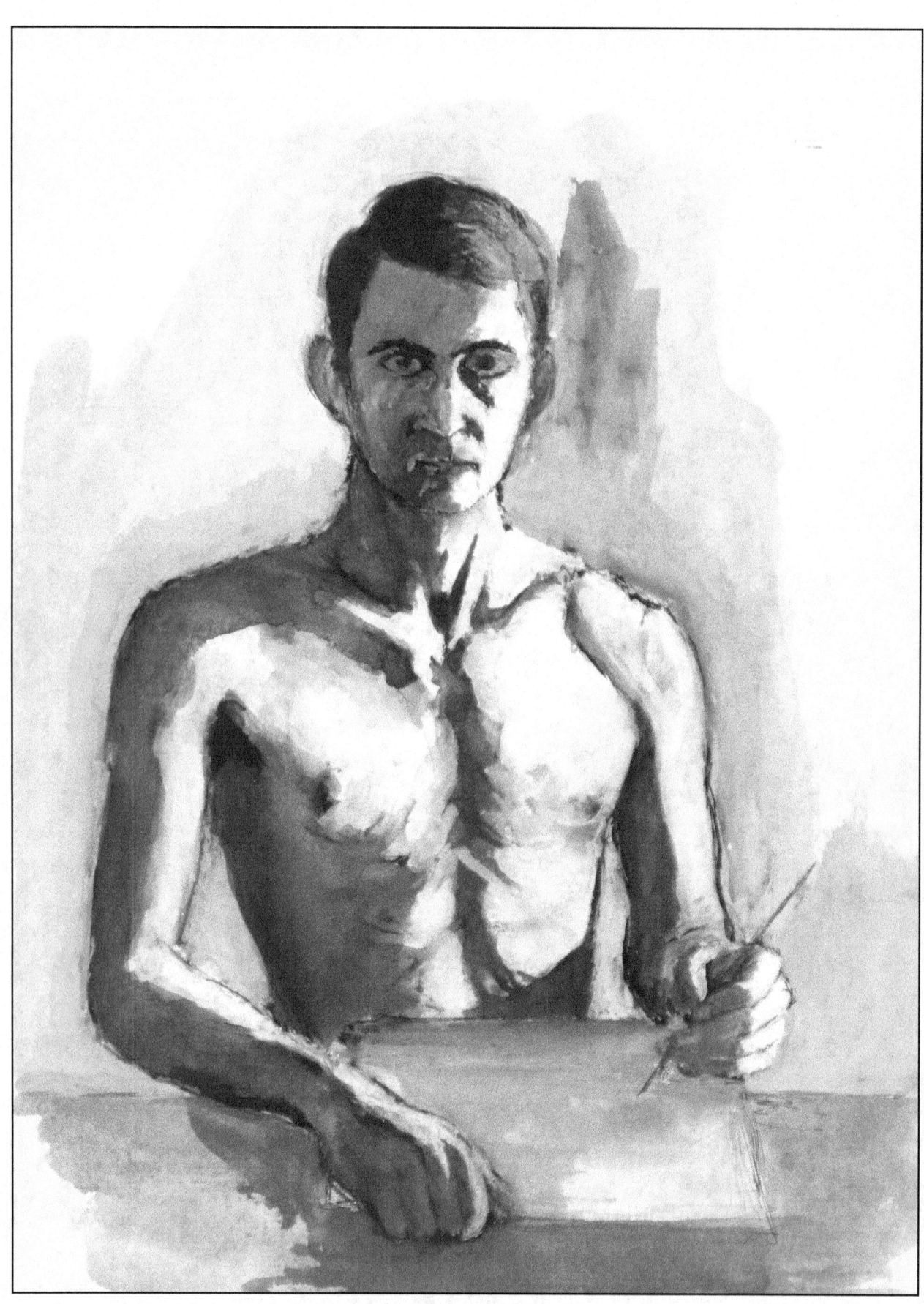

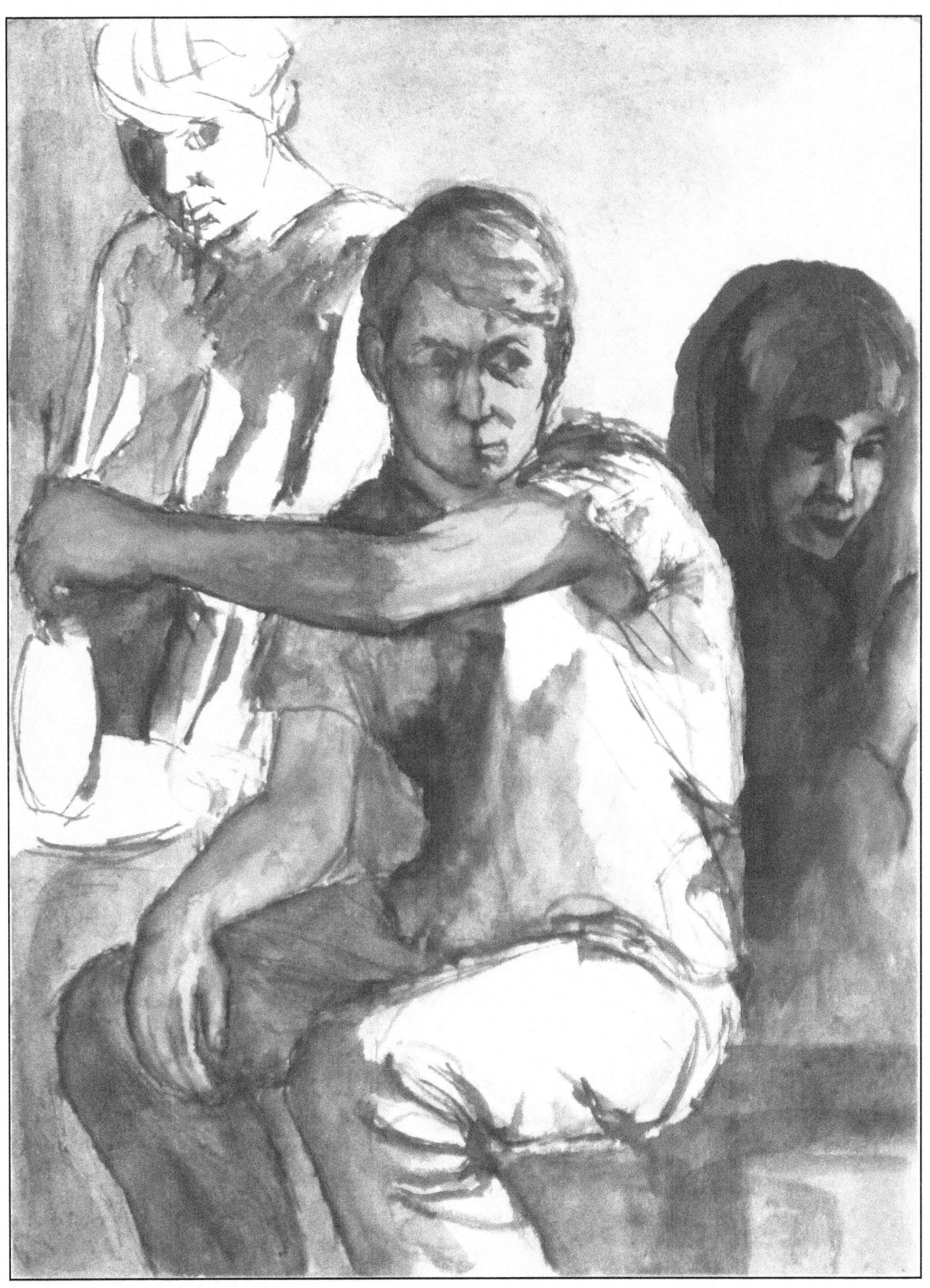

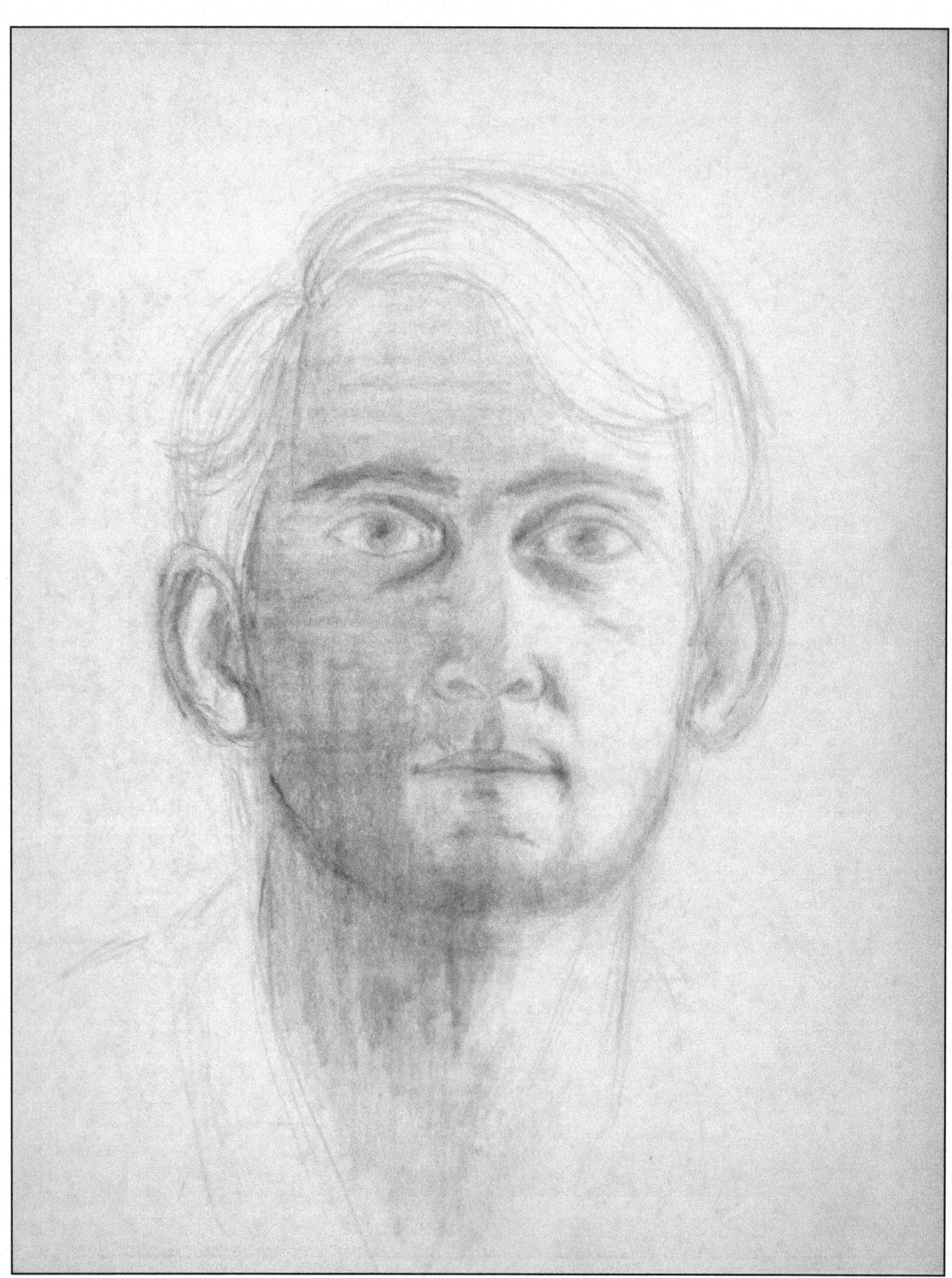

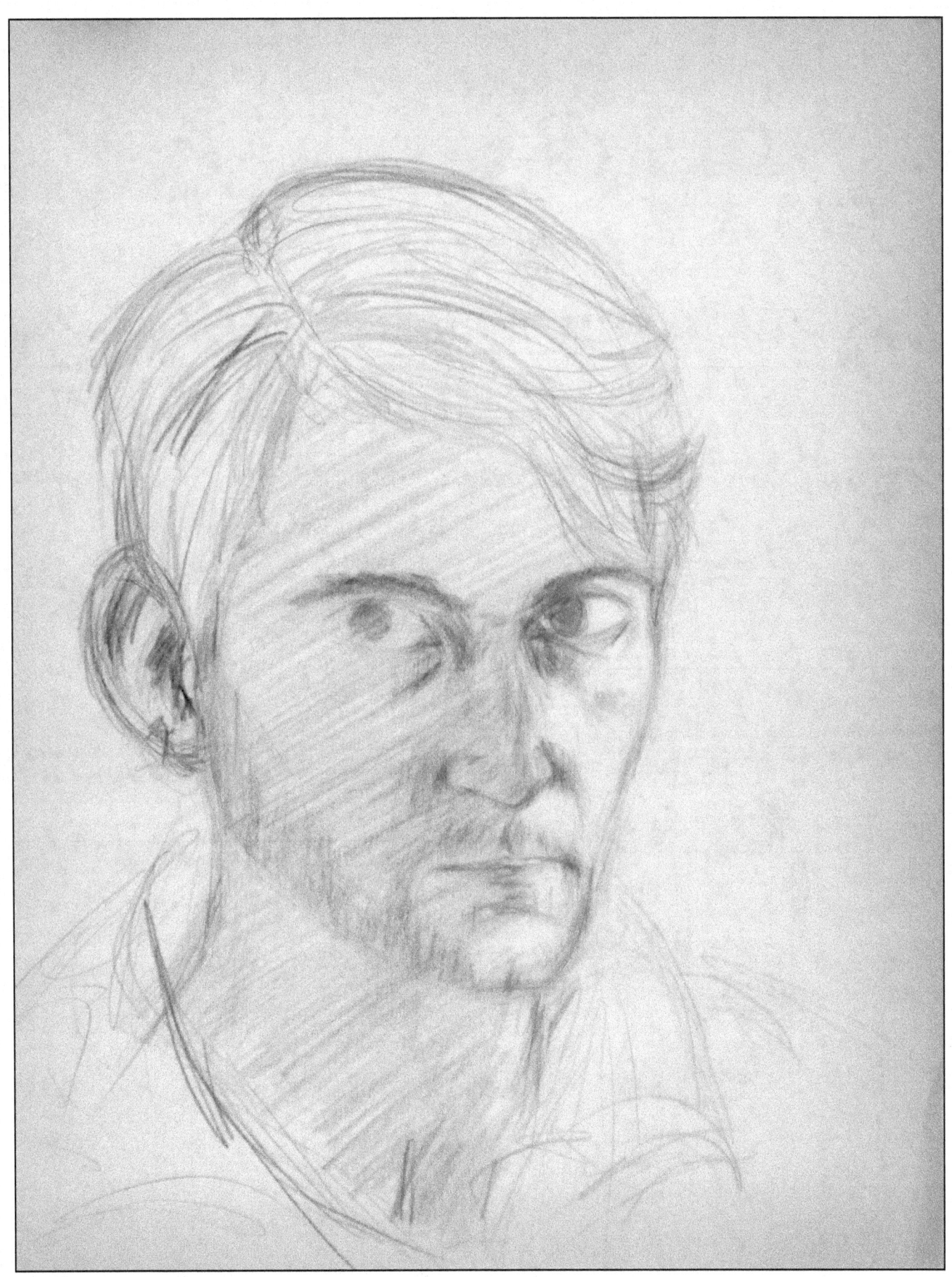

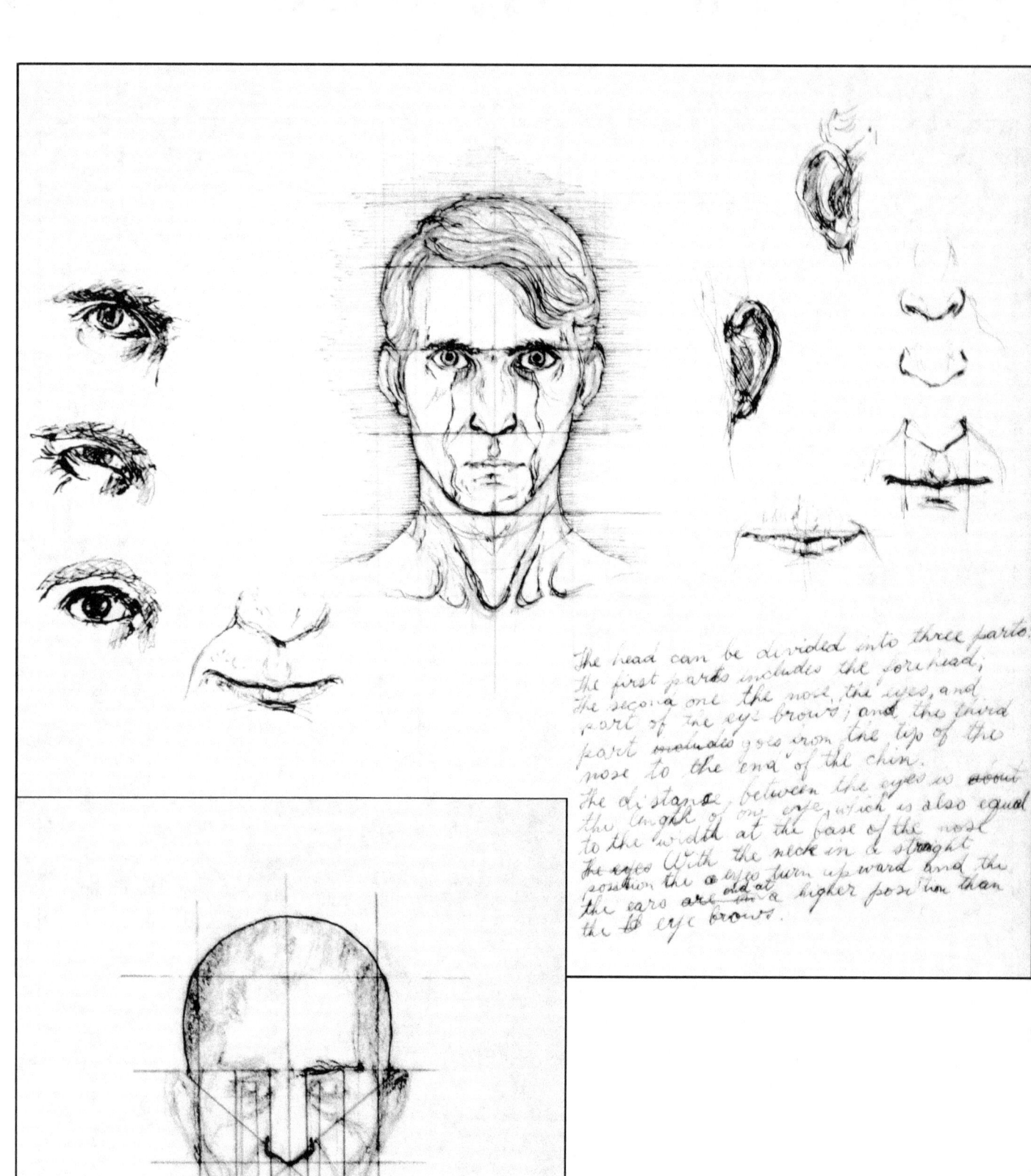

The head can be divided into three parts. The first part includes the forehead; the second one the nose, the eyes, and part of the eye brows; and the third part goes from the tip of the nose to the end of the chin.
The distance between the eyes is about the length of my eye, which is also equal to the width at the base of the nose. With the neck in a straight position the eyes turn up ward and the ears are in a higher position than the eye brows.

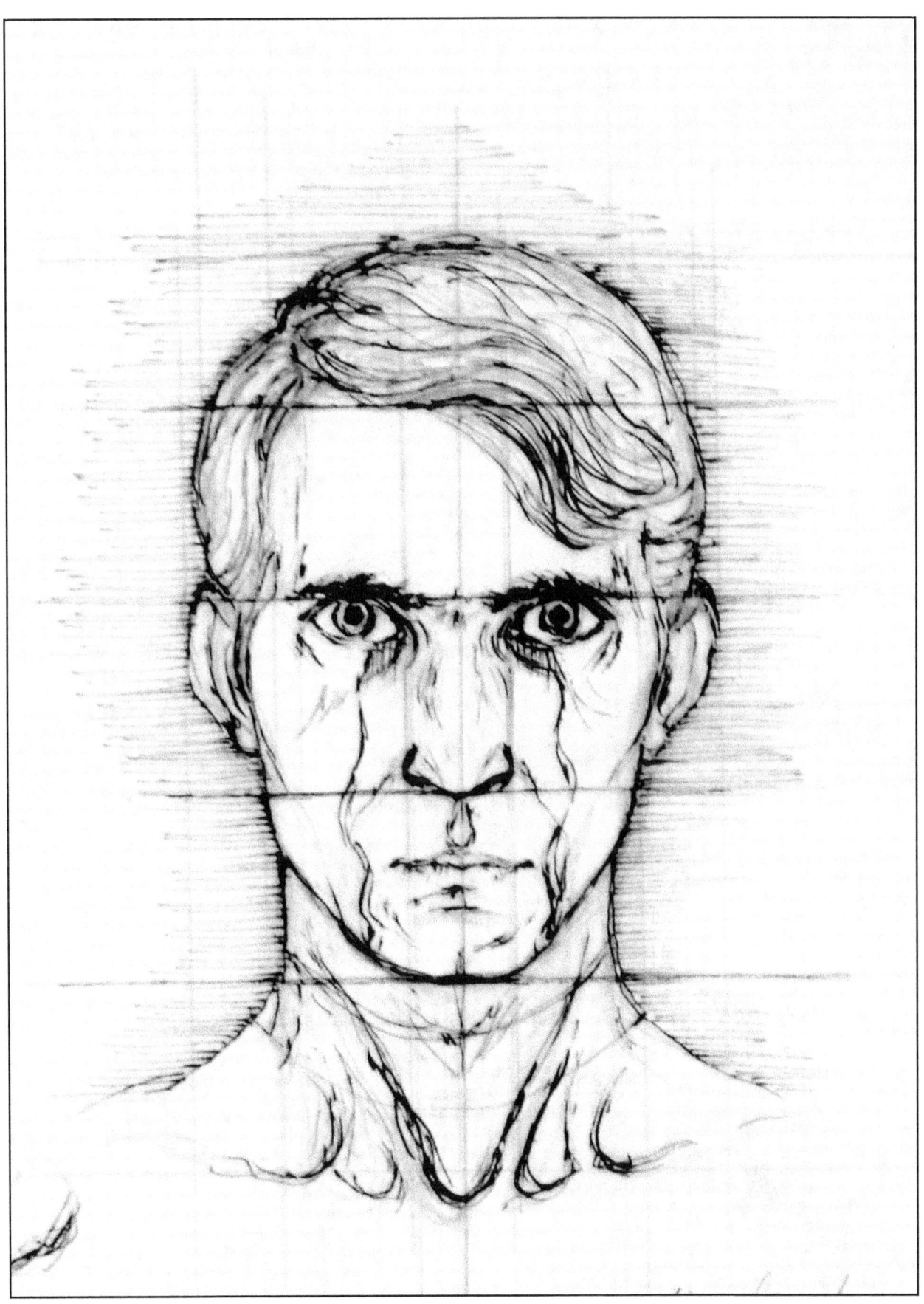

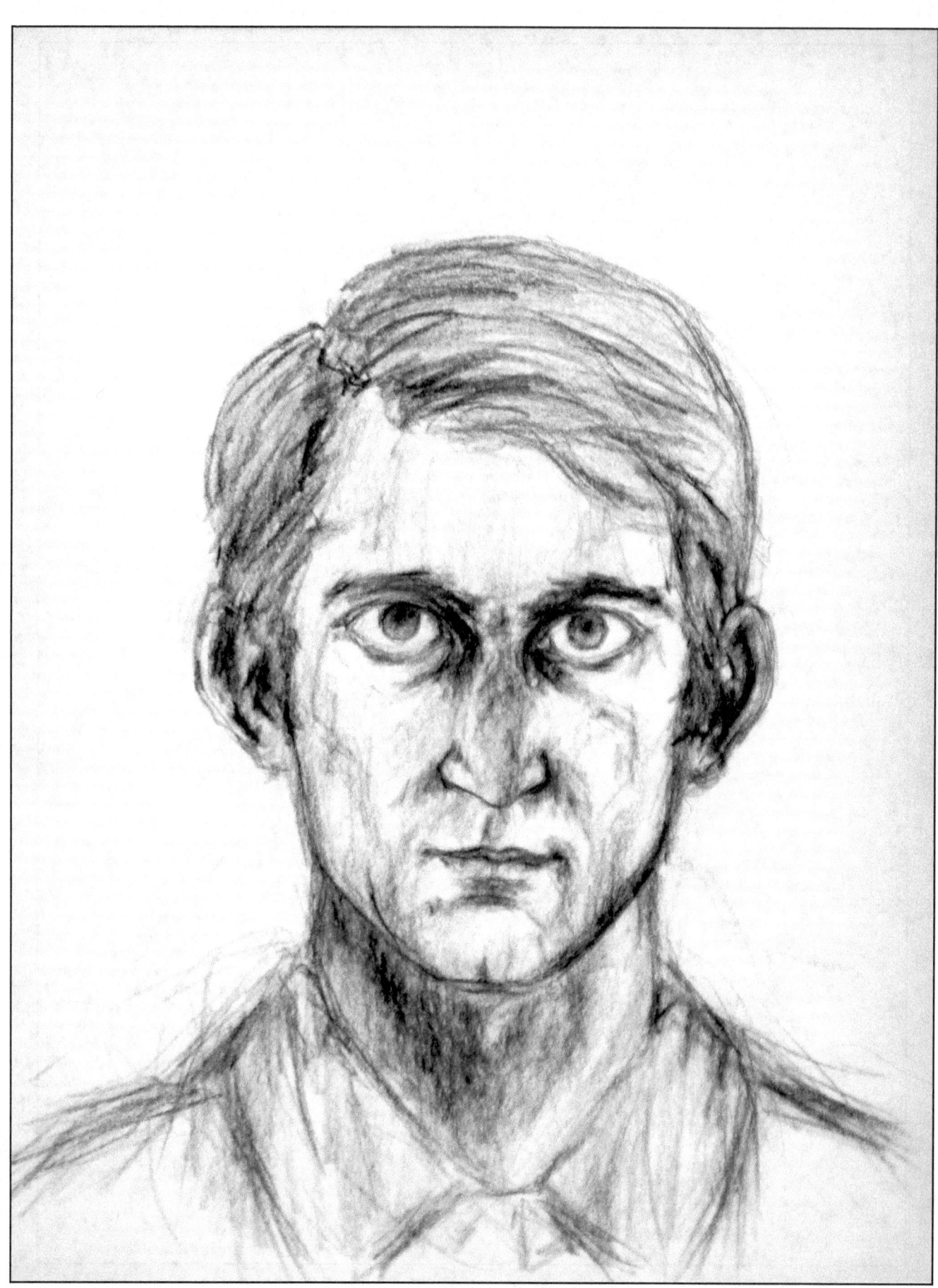

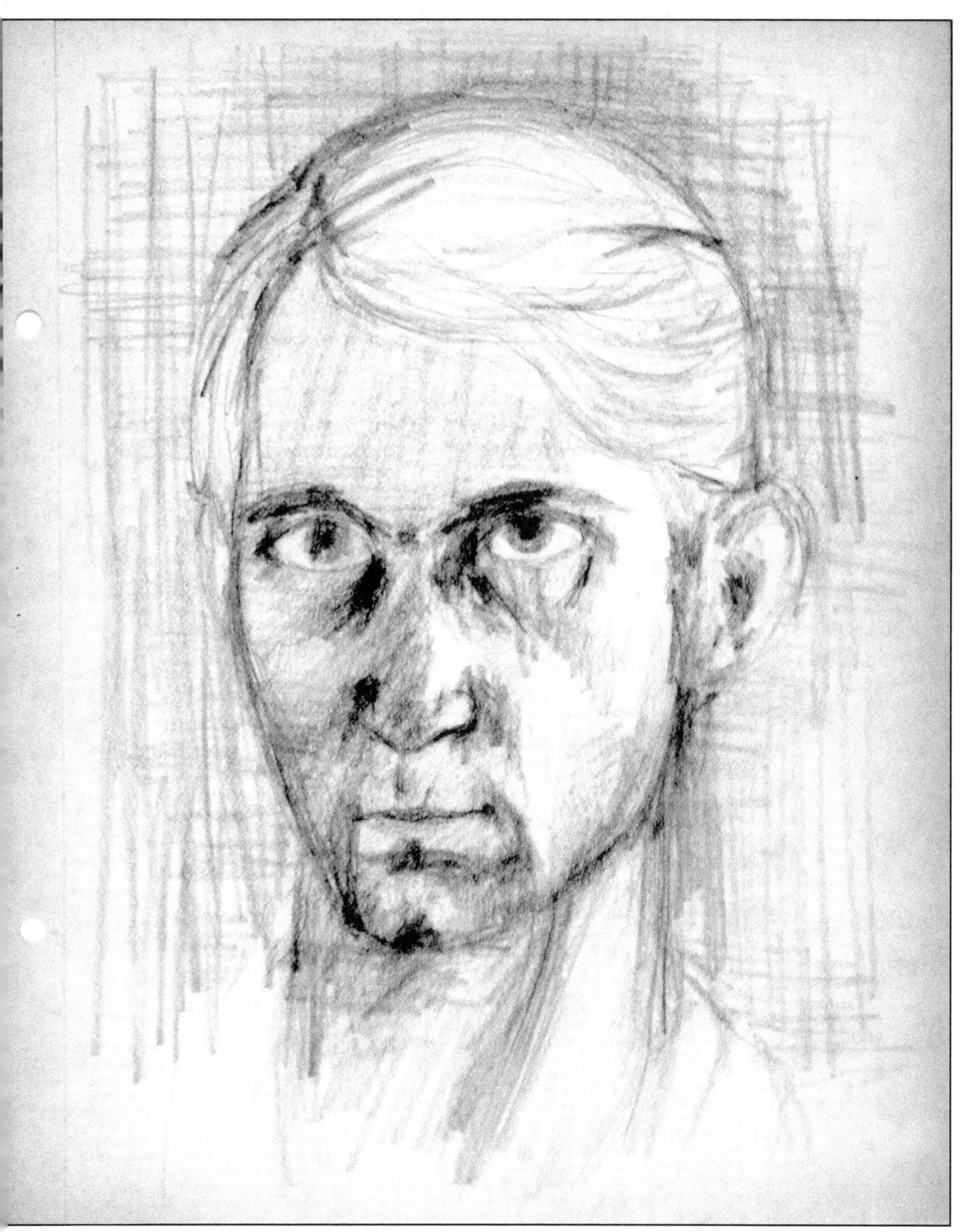

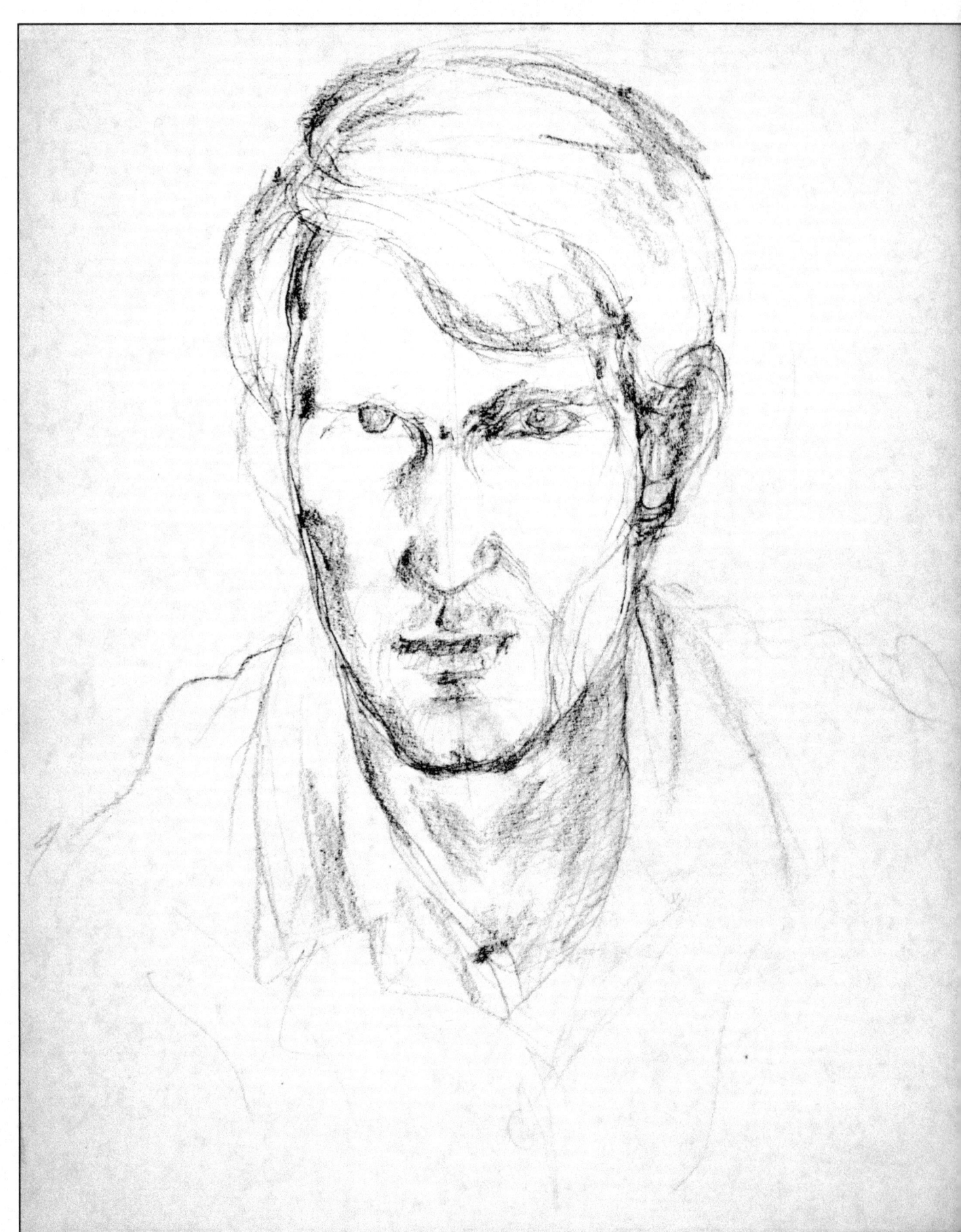

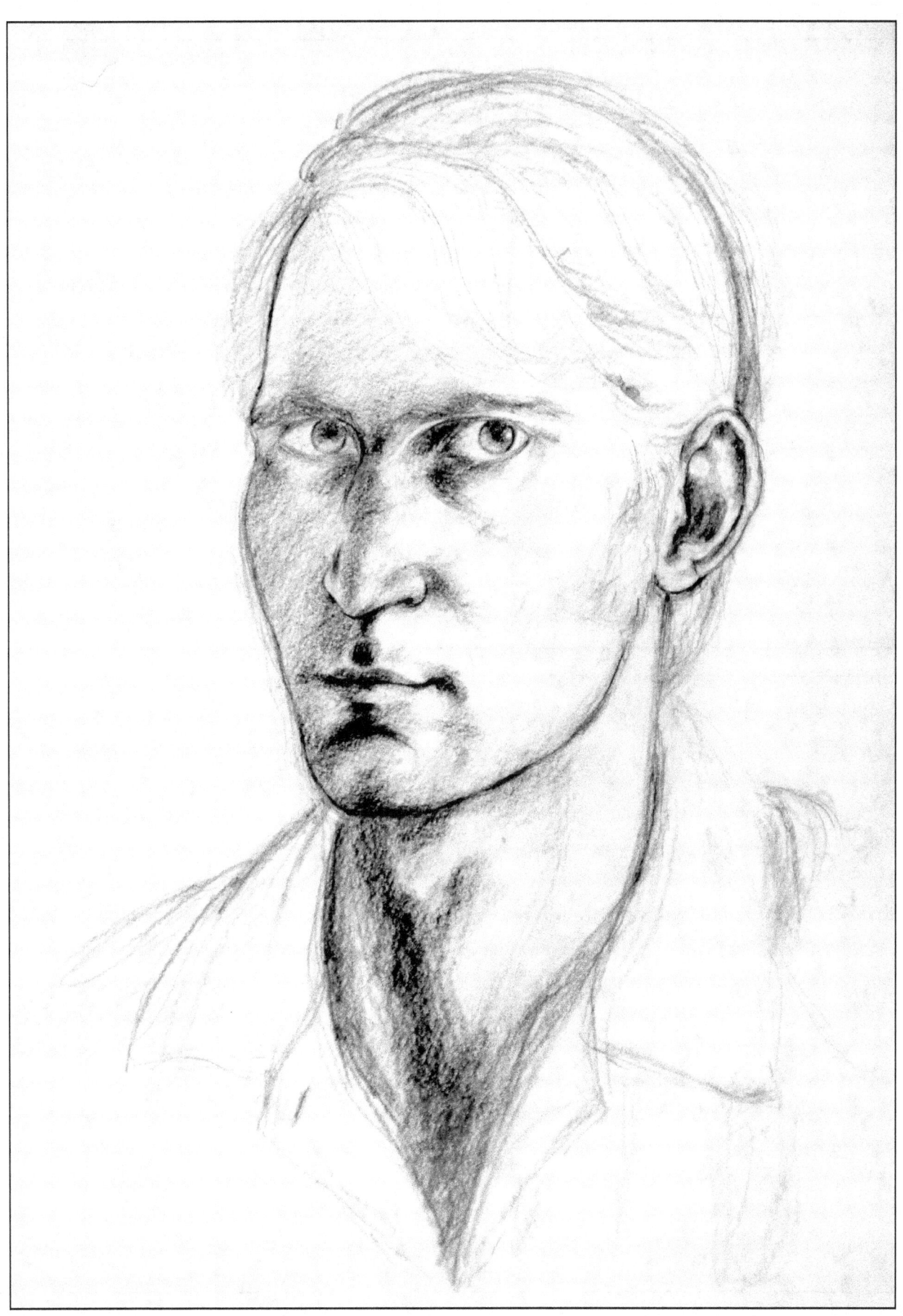

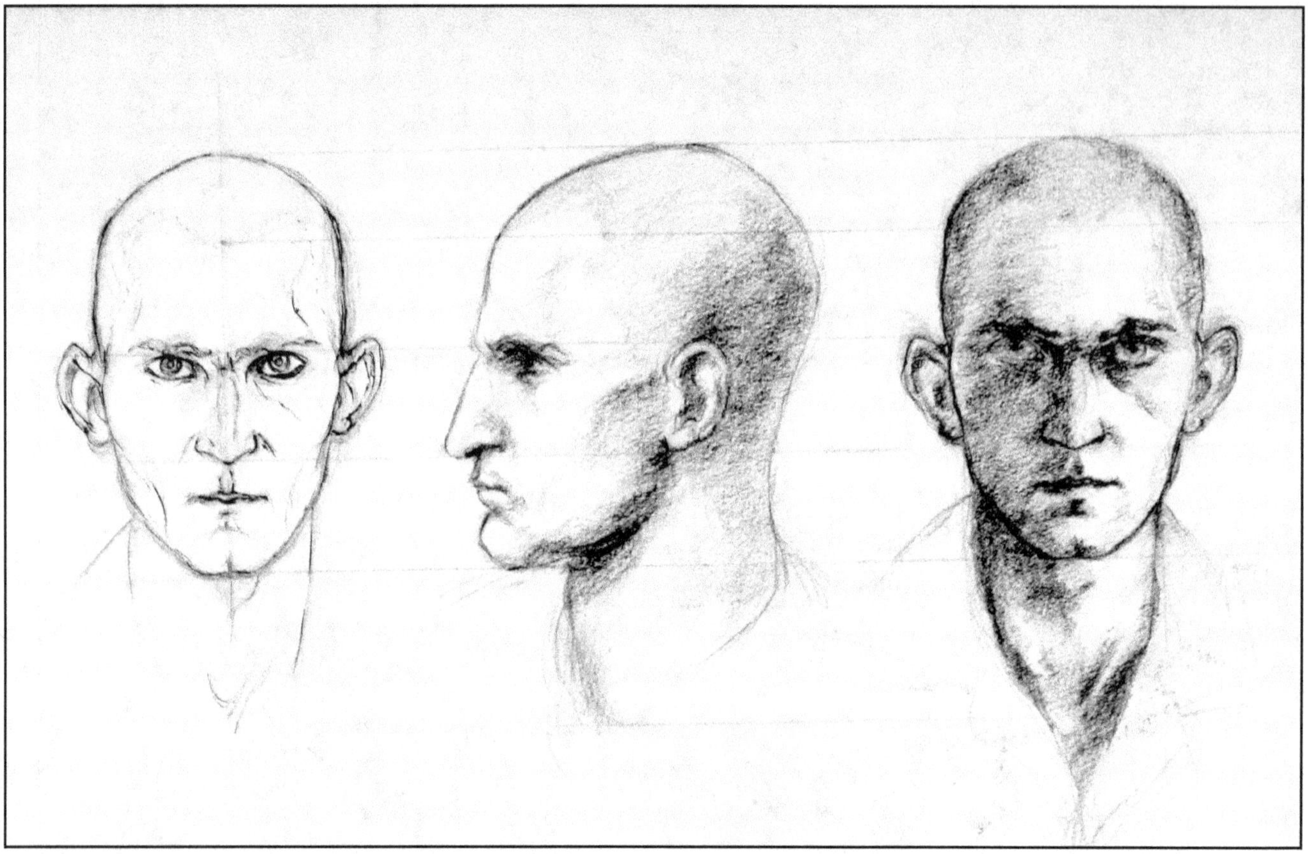

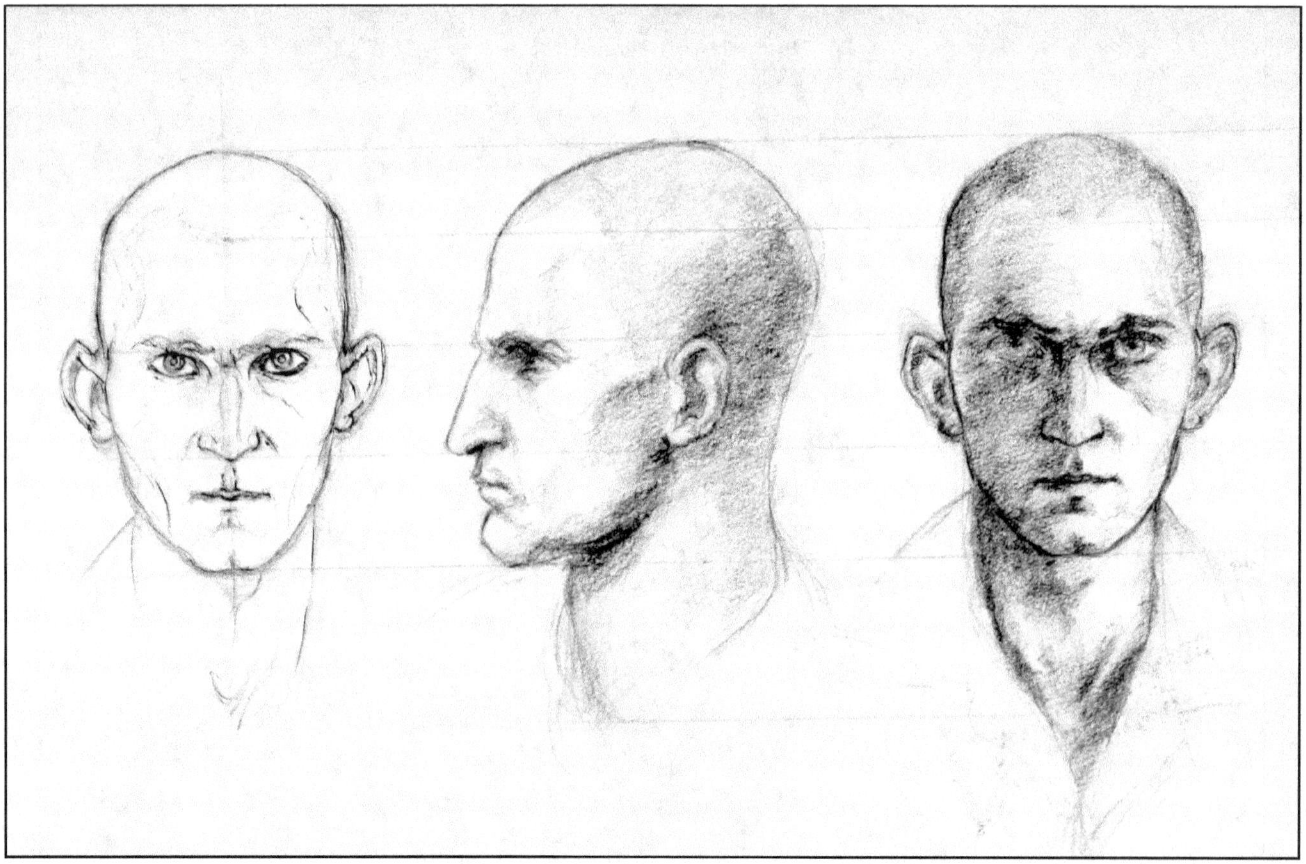

2 Tones of the Same Version

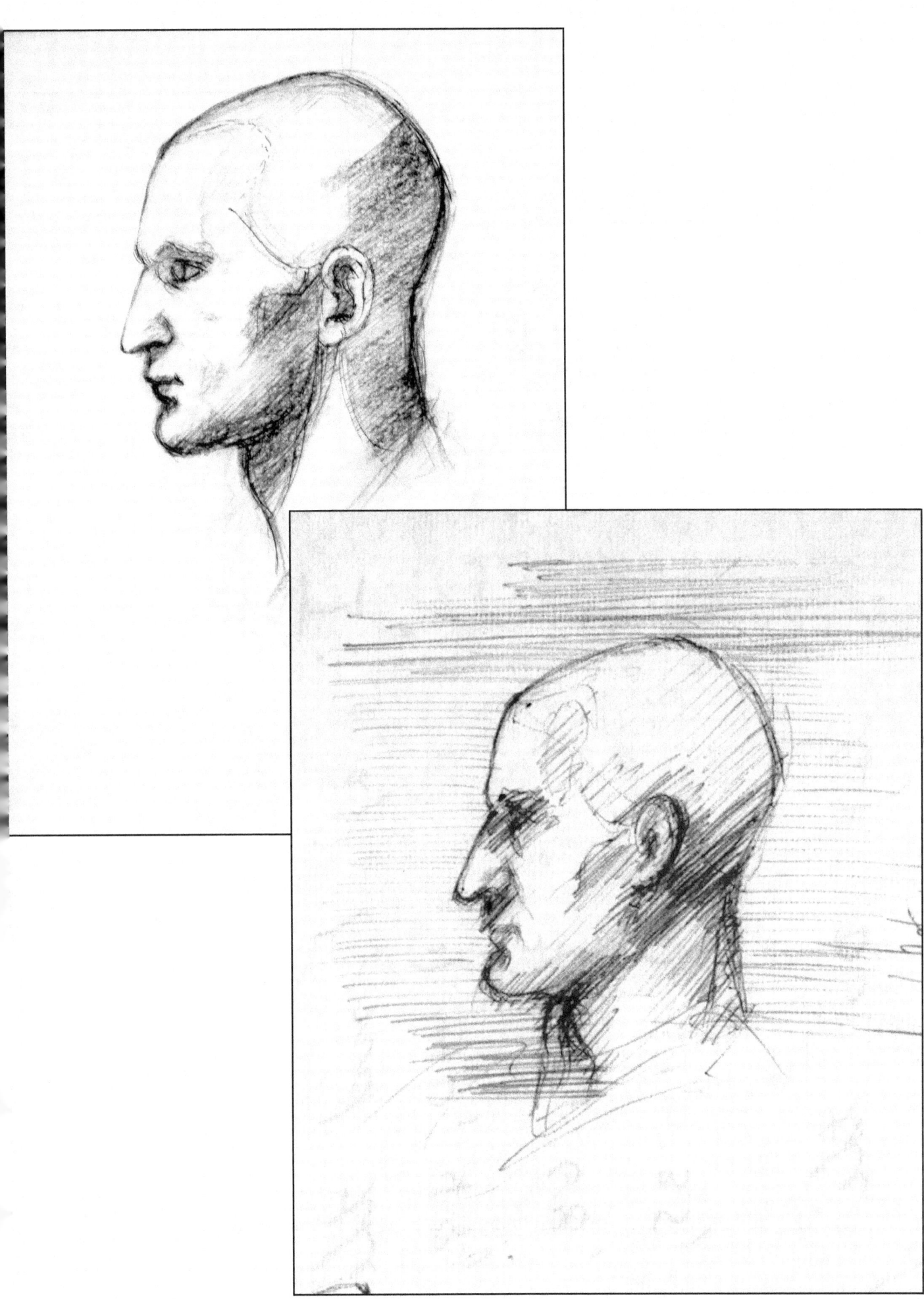

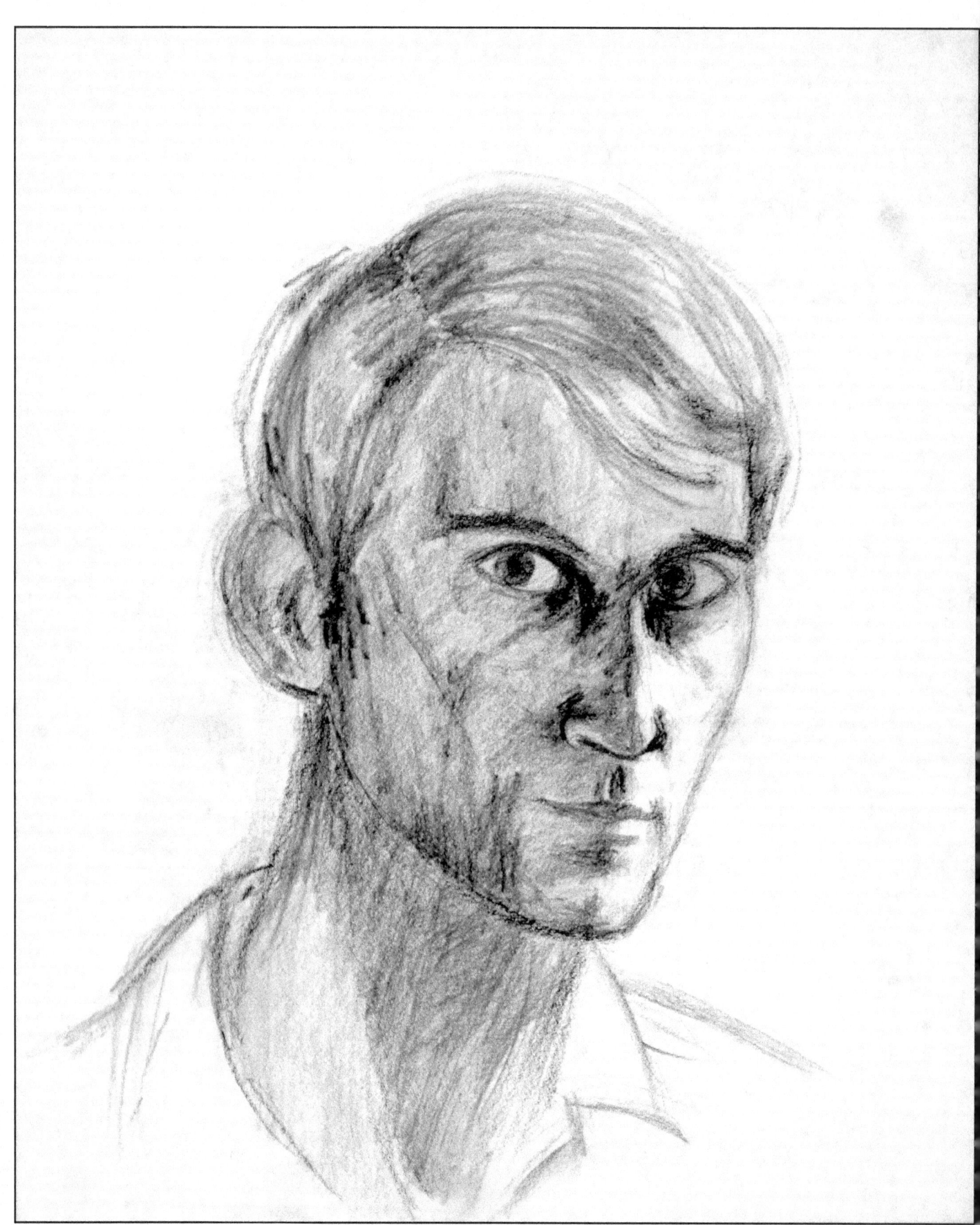

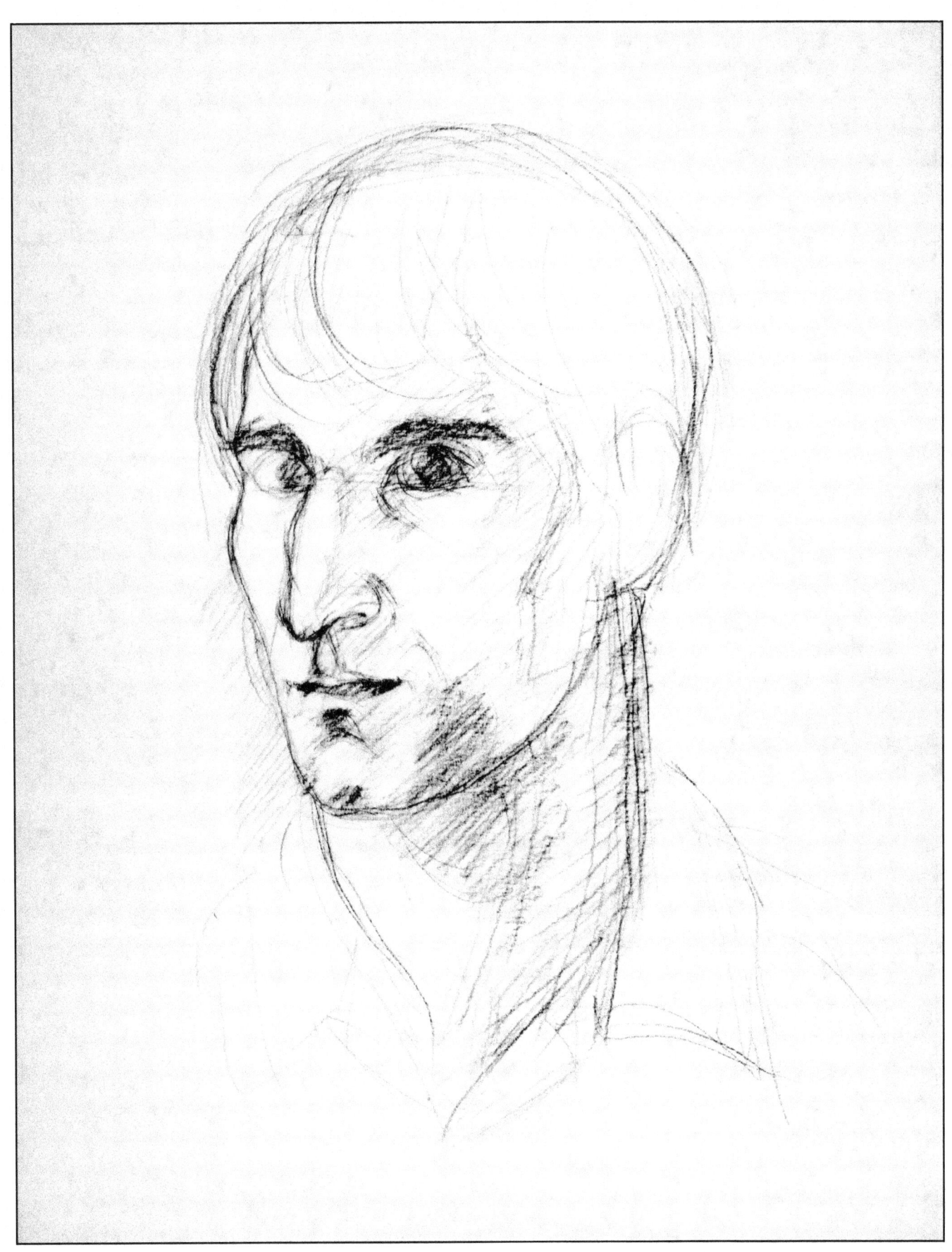

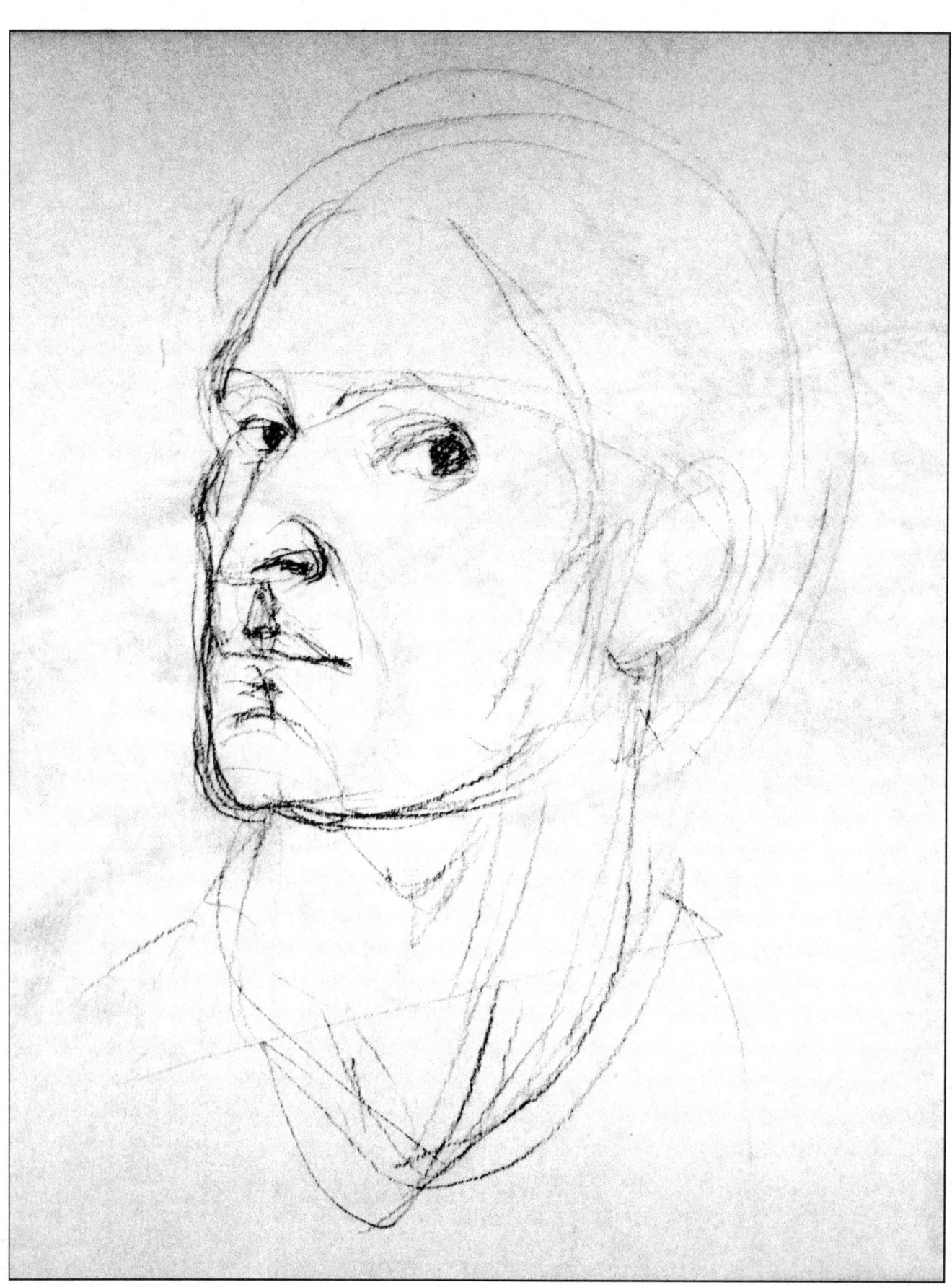

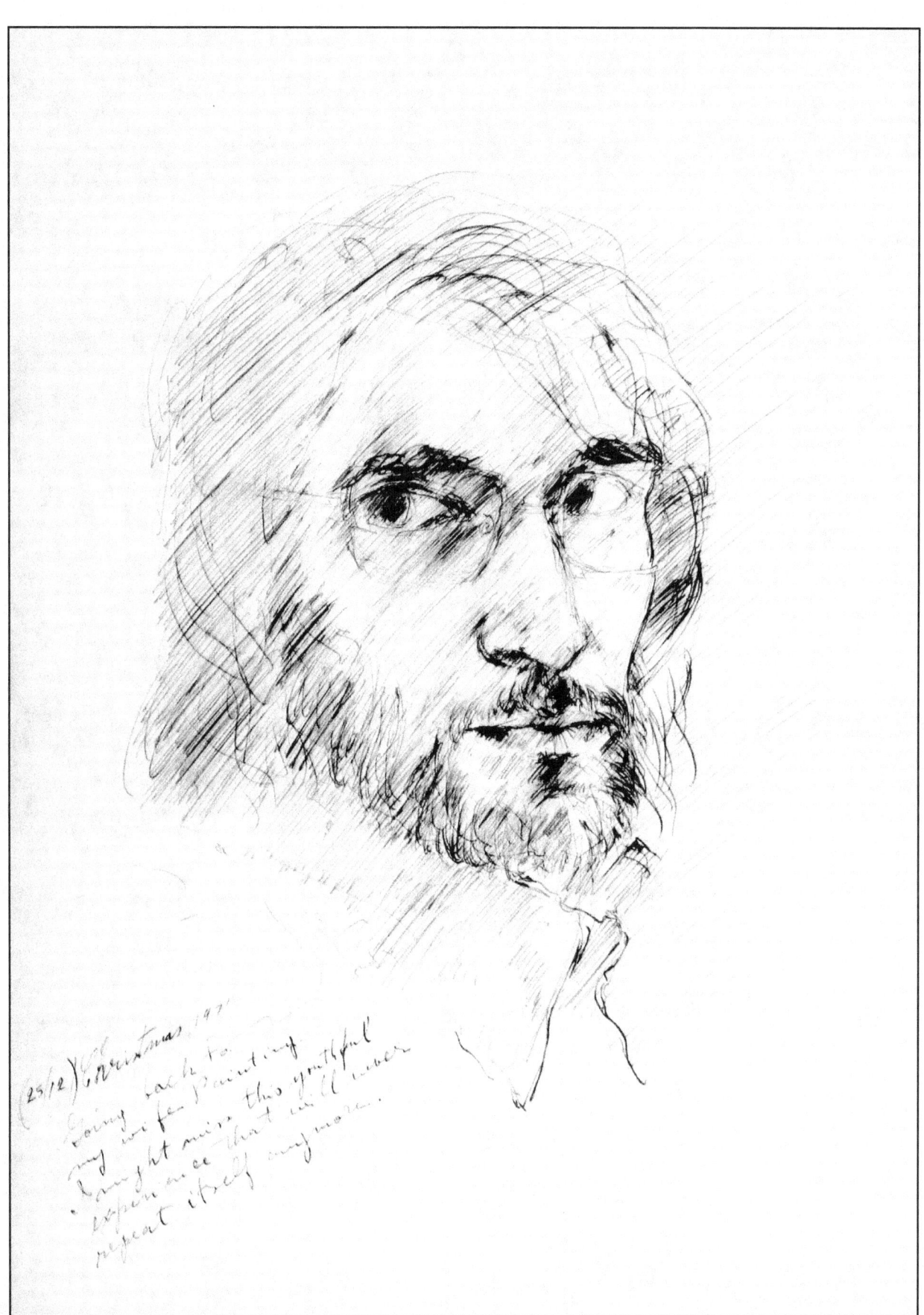

(25/12) Christmas 1977
Going back to
my life for painting
I might miss this youthful
experience that will never
repeat itself anymore.

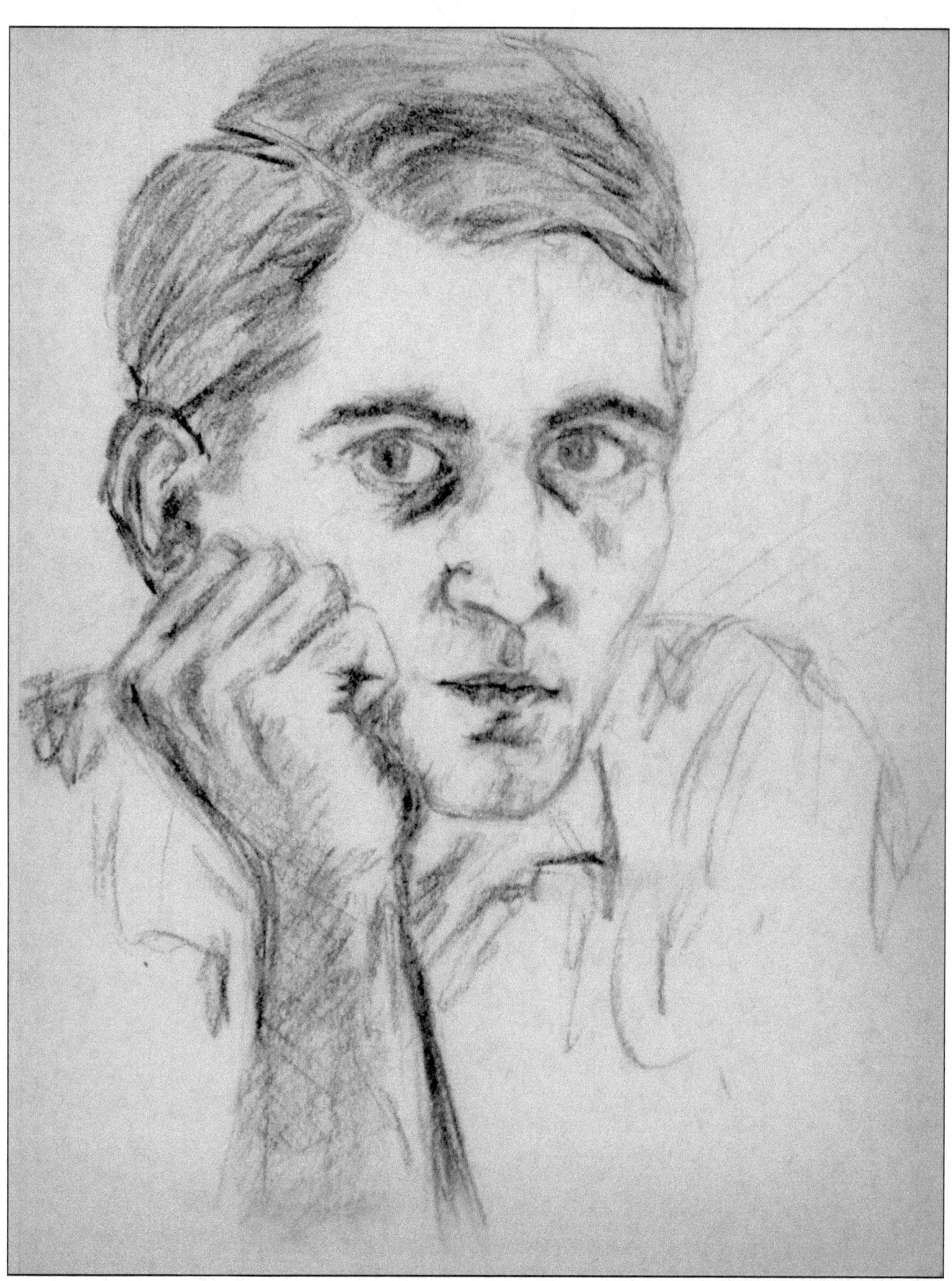

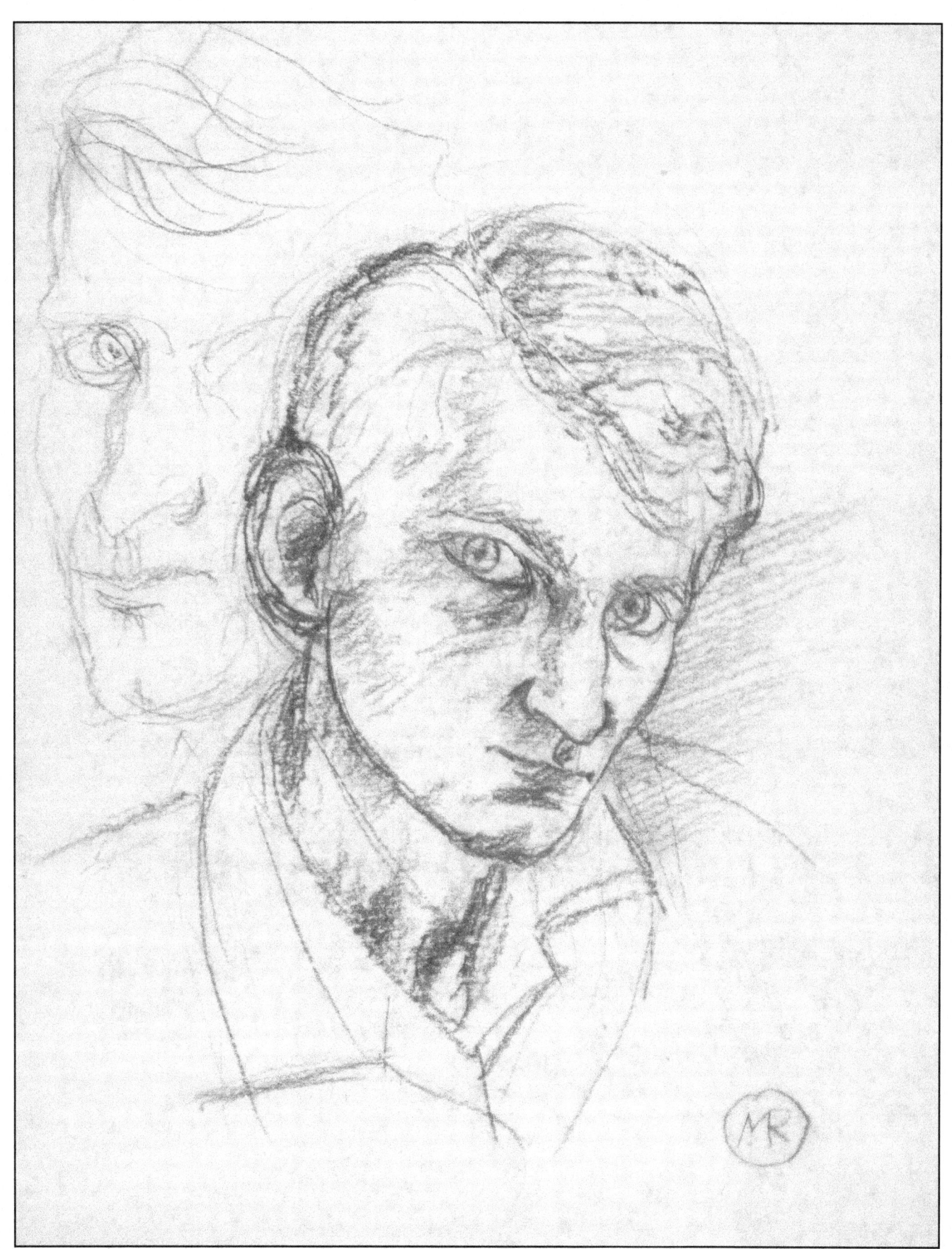

Red Chalk

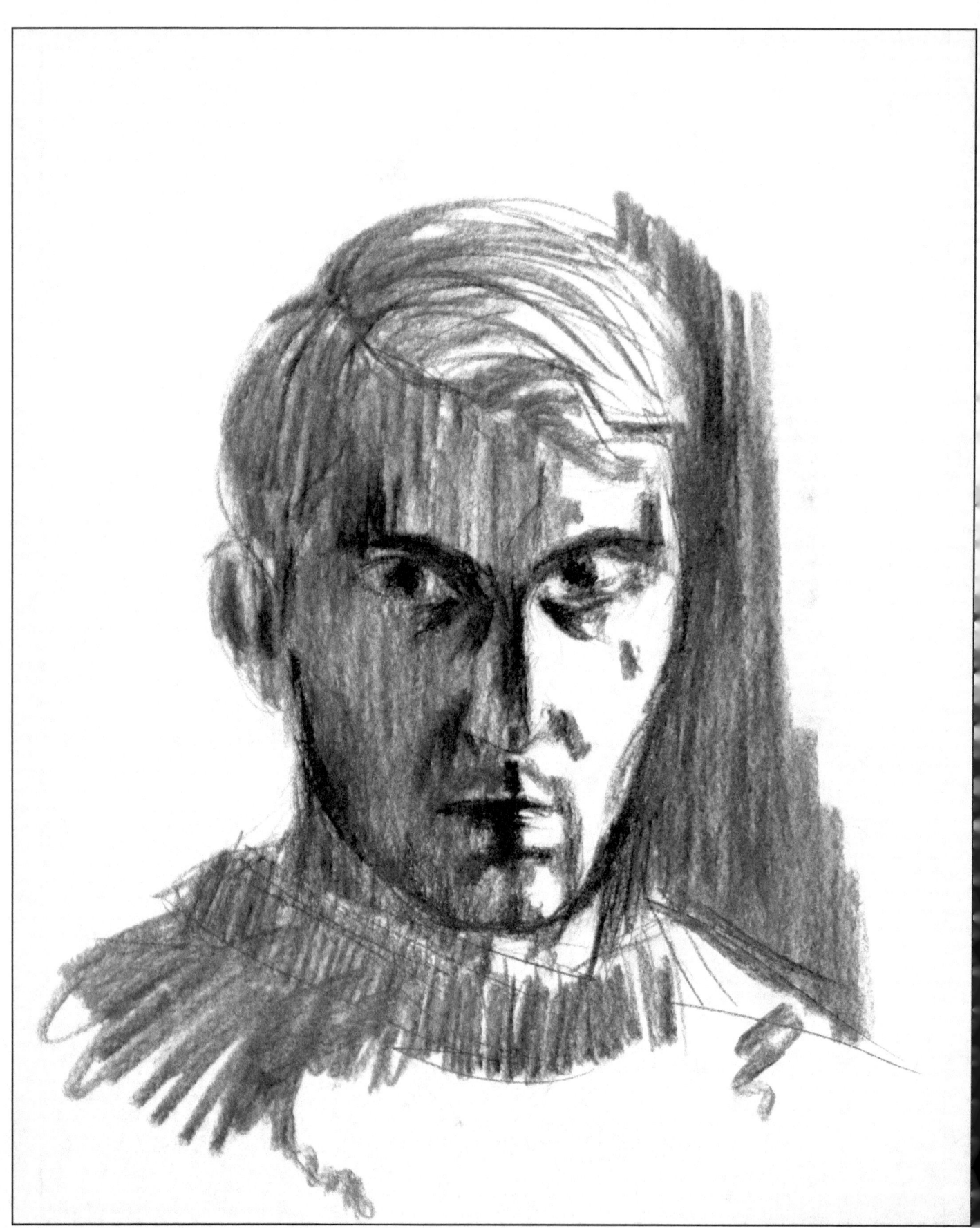

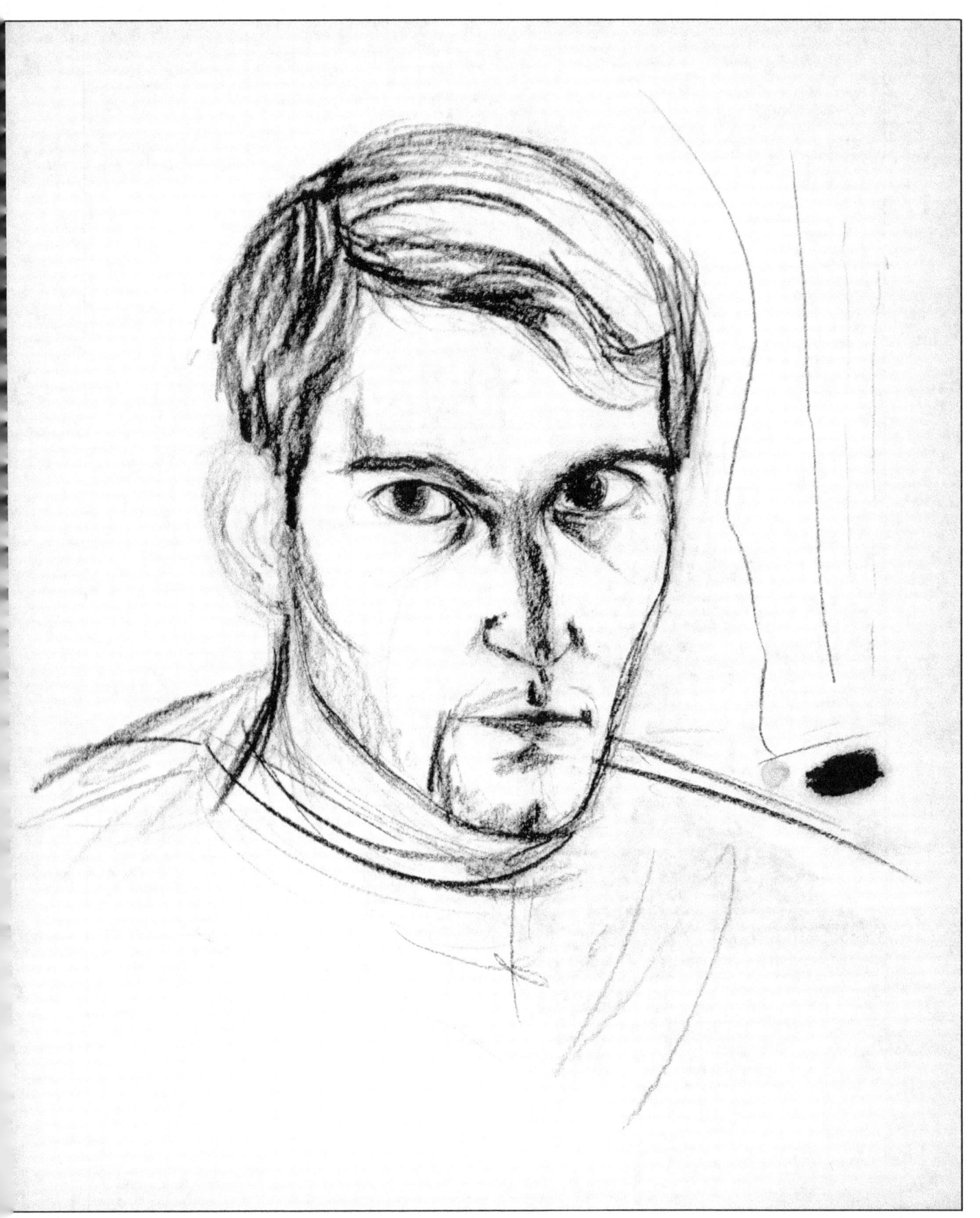

Charcoal

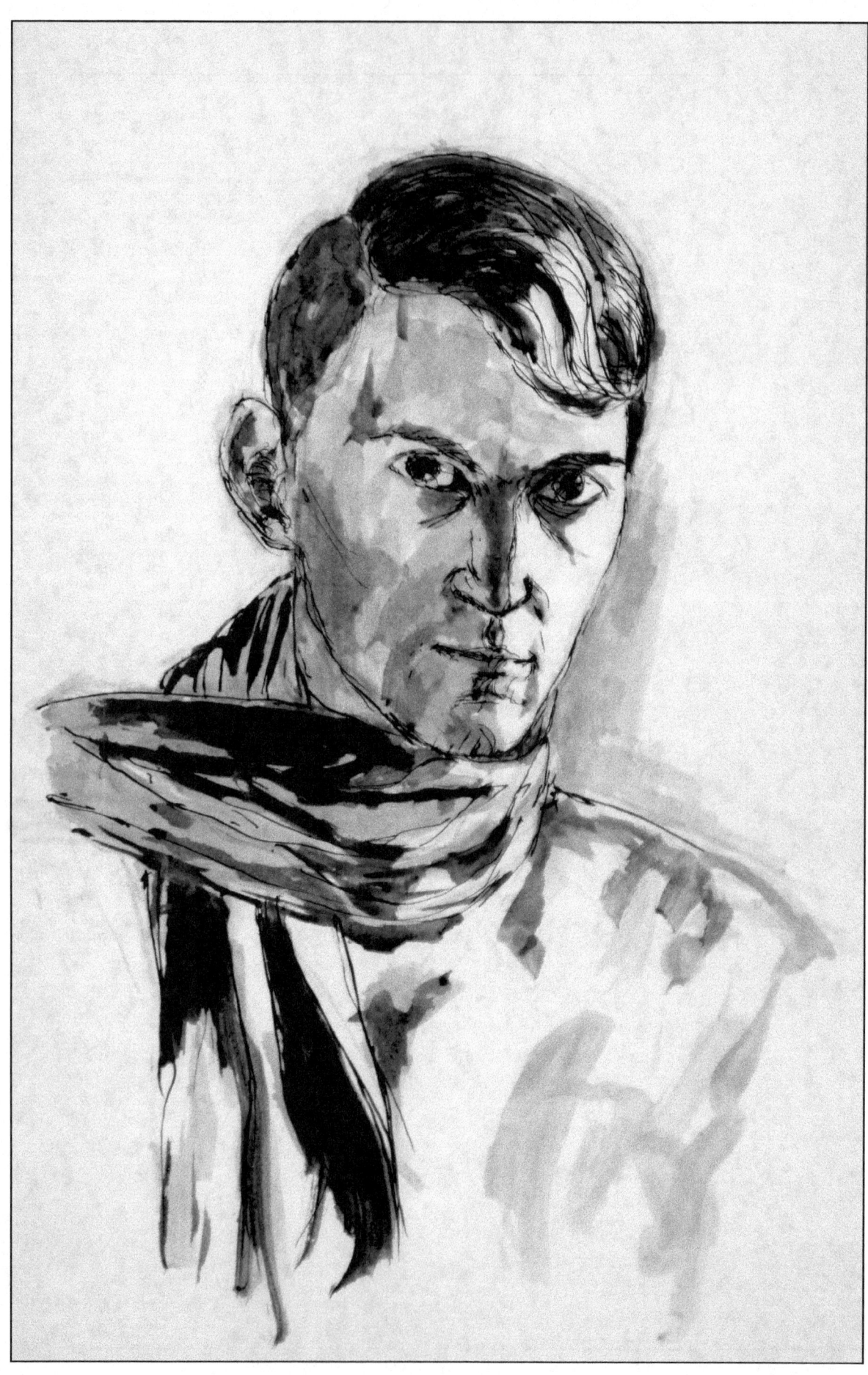

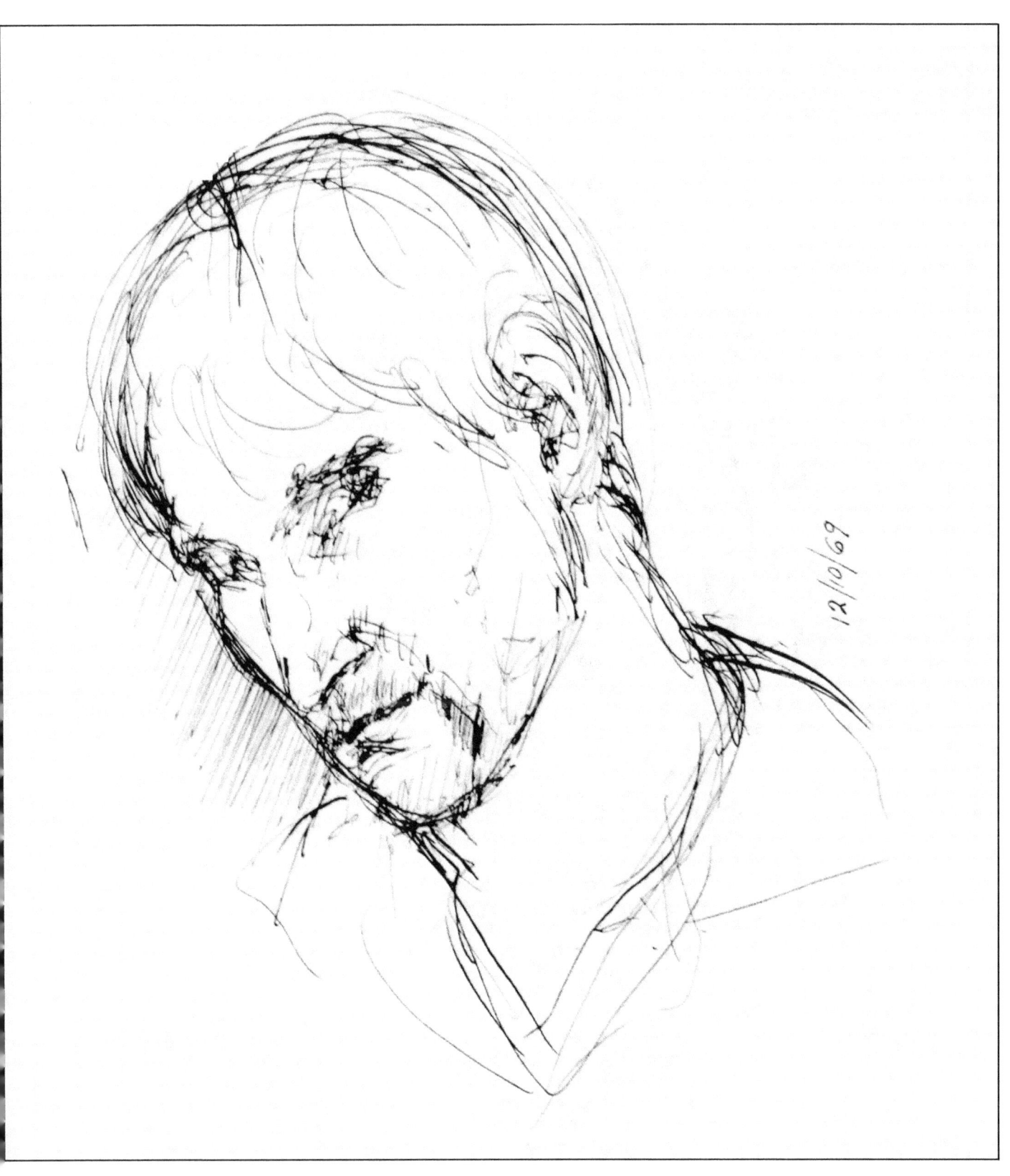

Any face with proper lighting is beautiful. Light coming from above is the best to get the best shades.

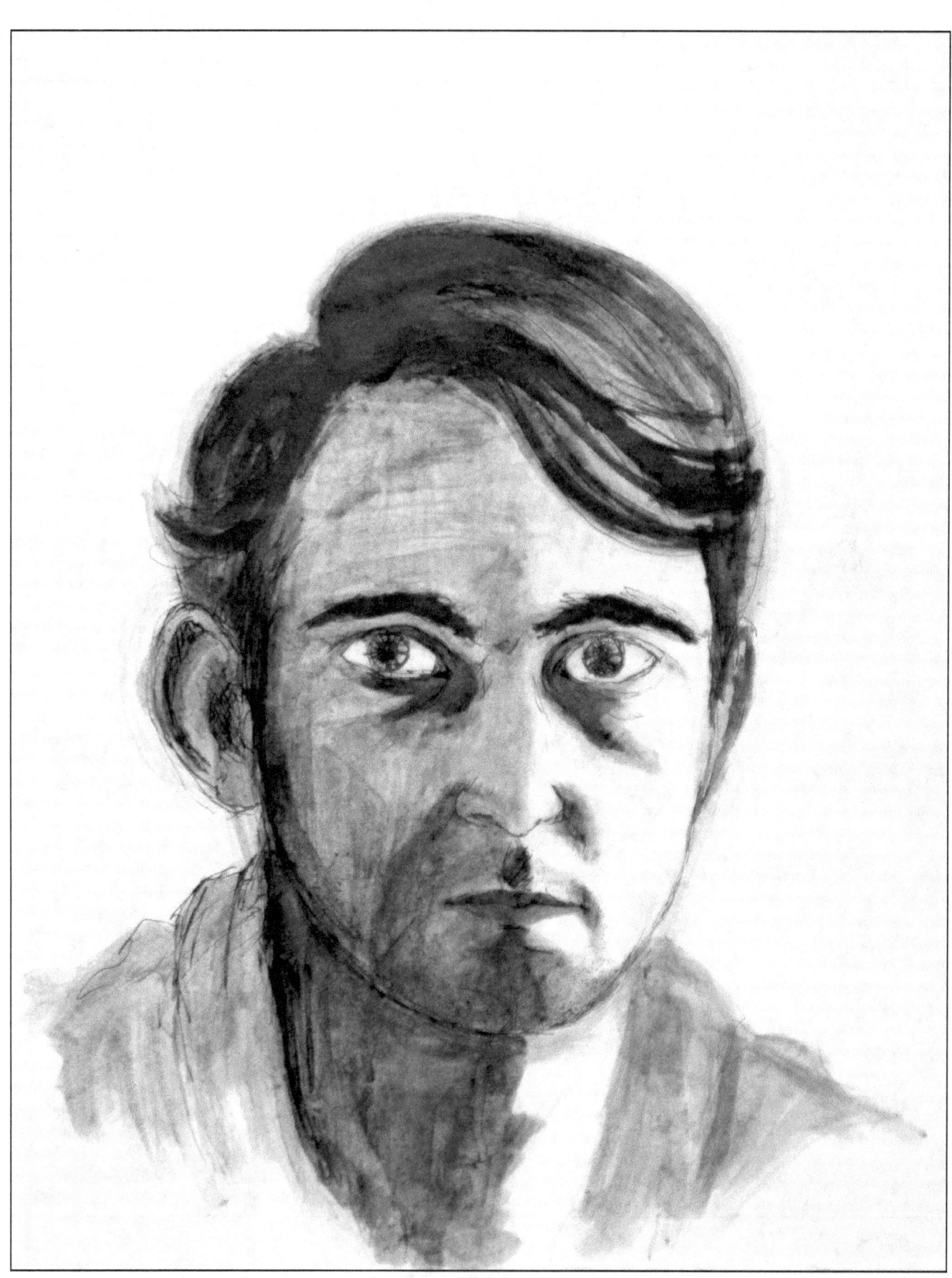

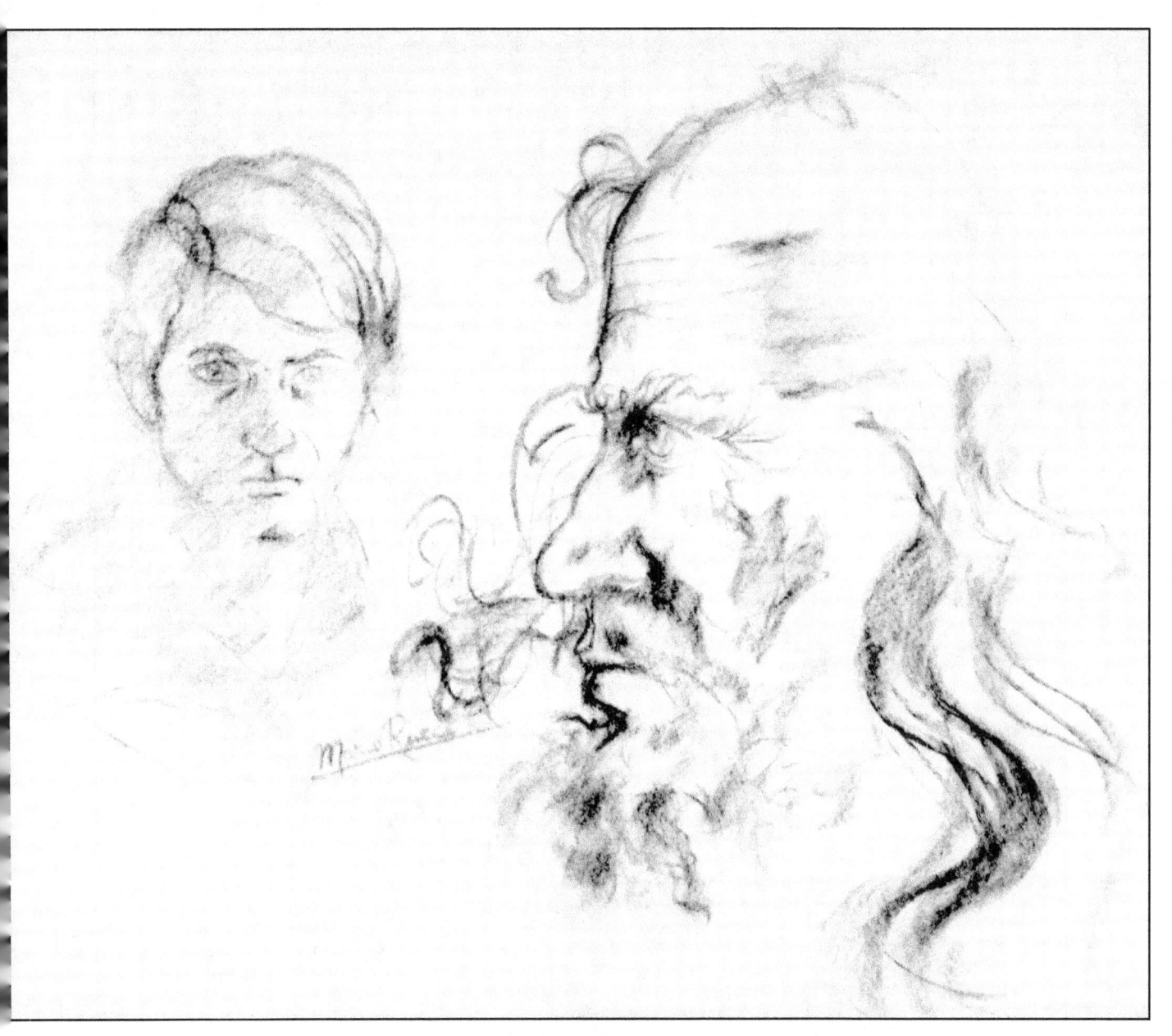

Charcoal

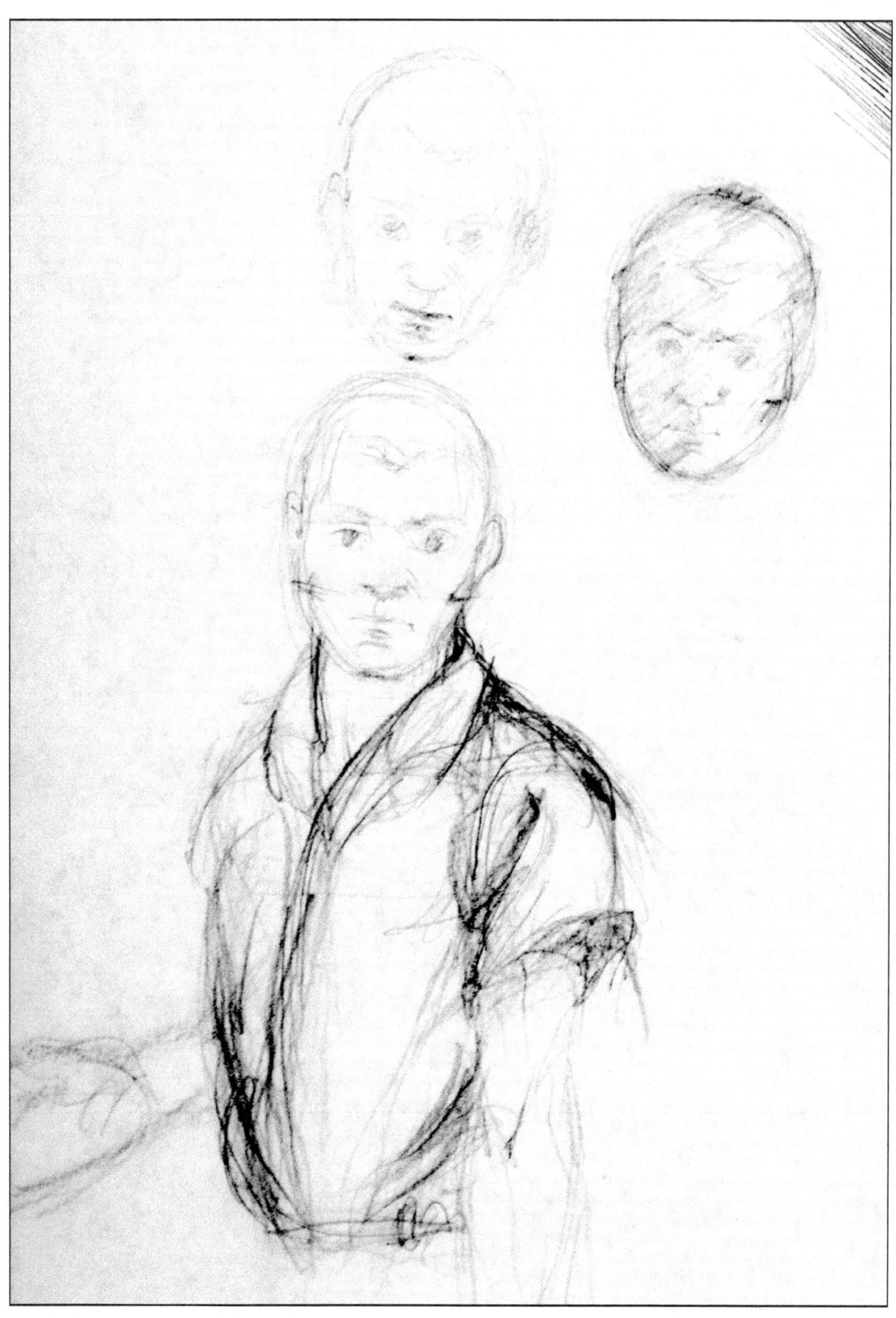

8. Head Obs/Vis, At School

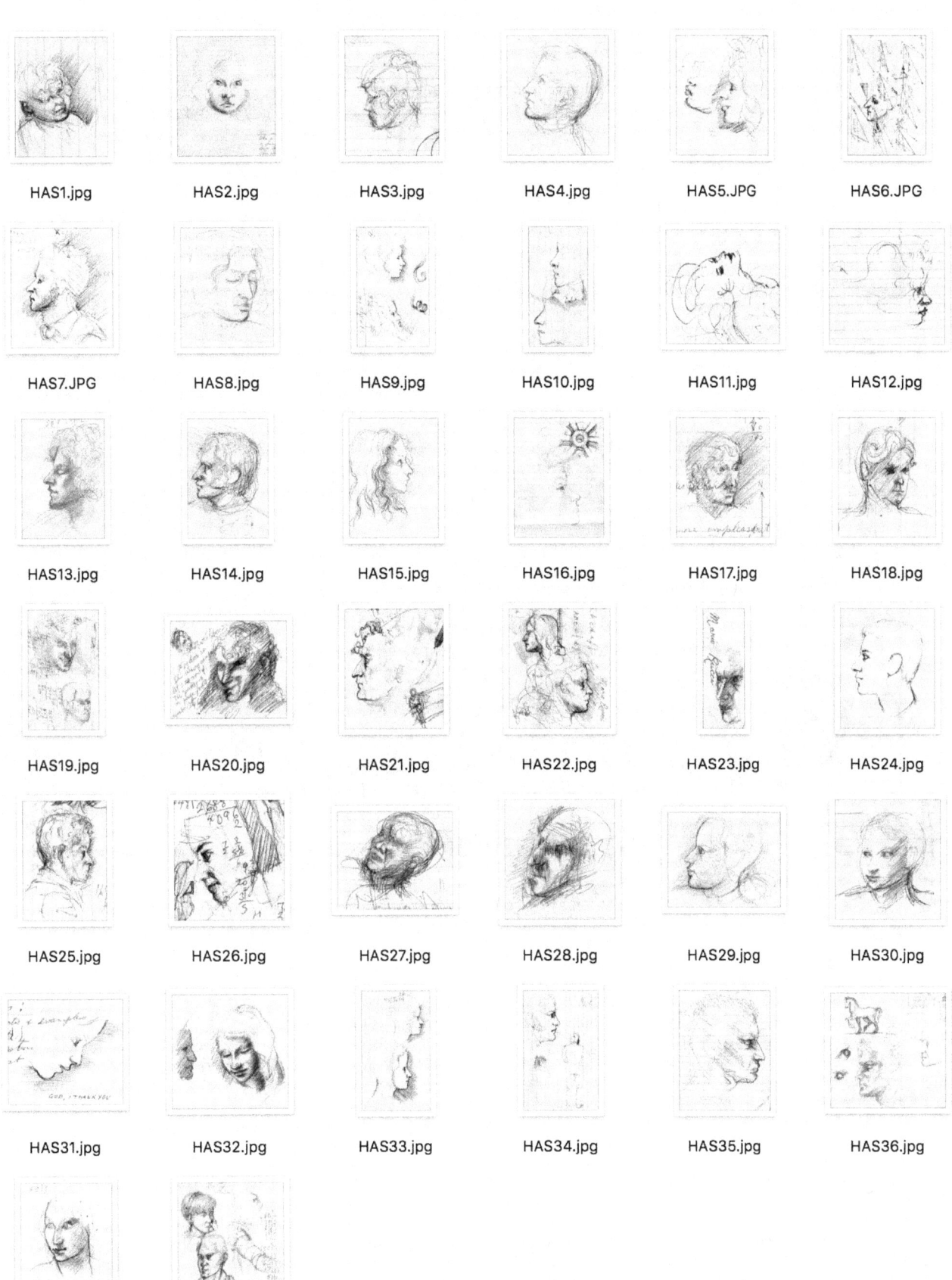

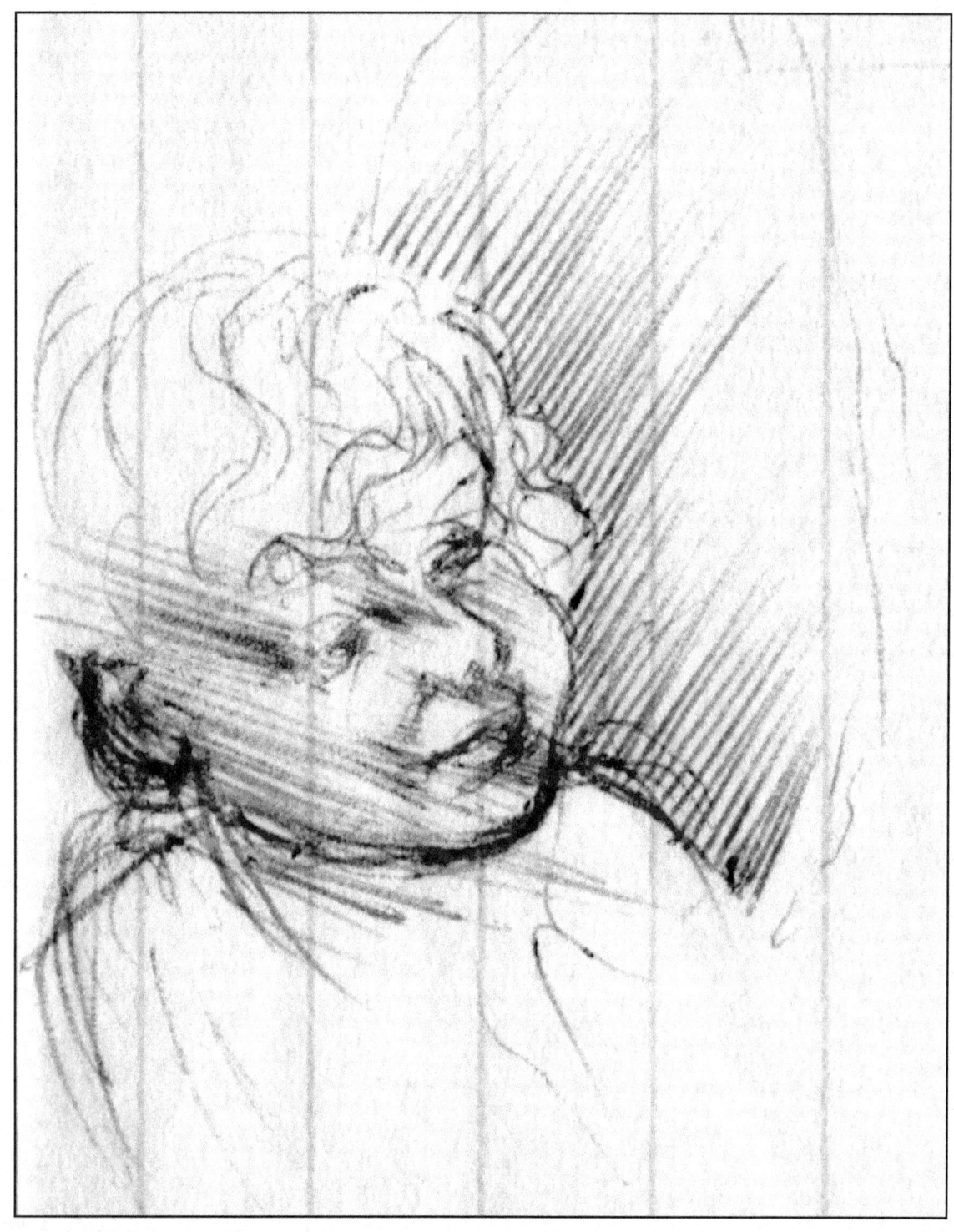

Ballpoint Pen

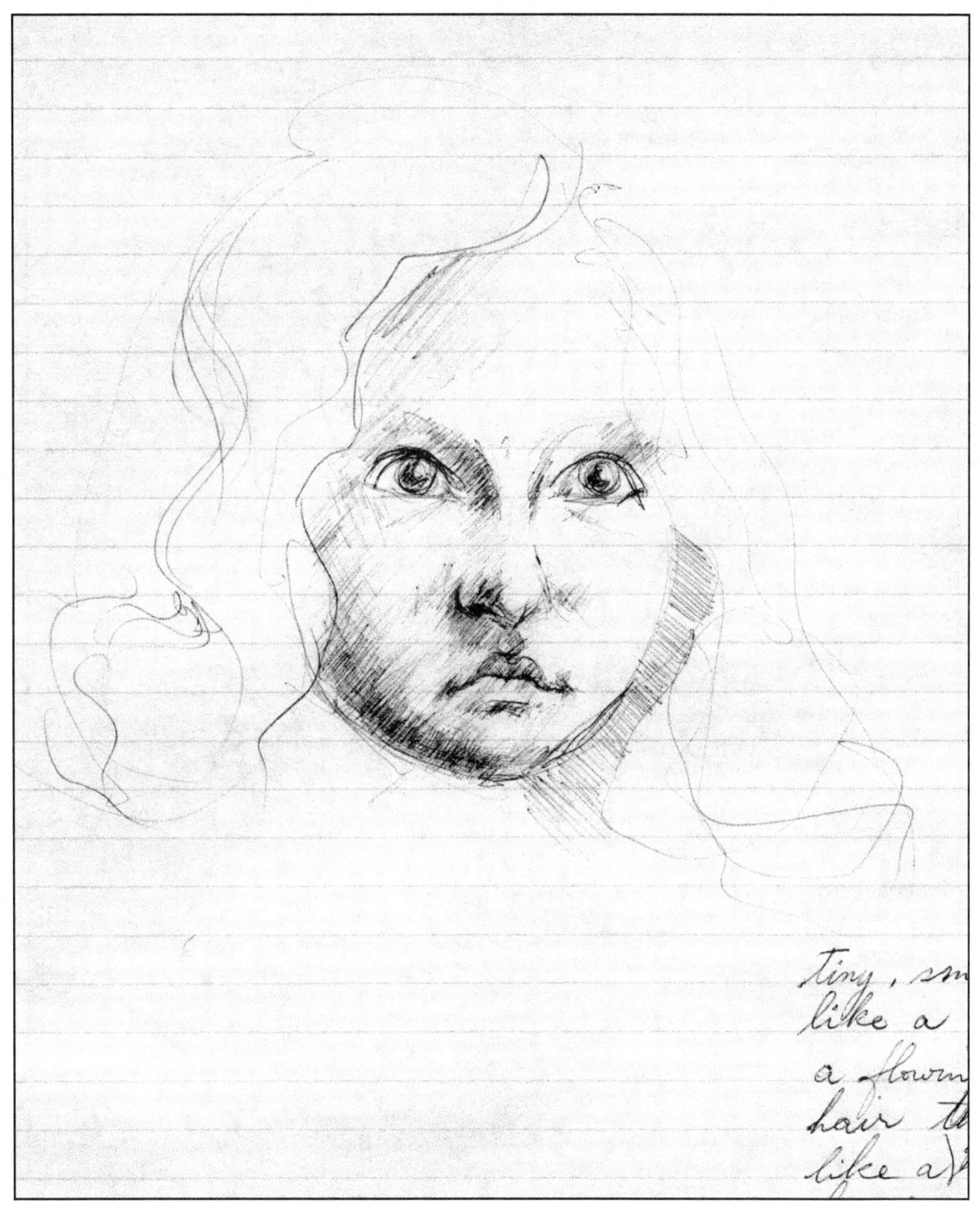

Ballpoint Pen

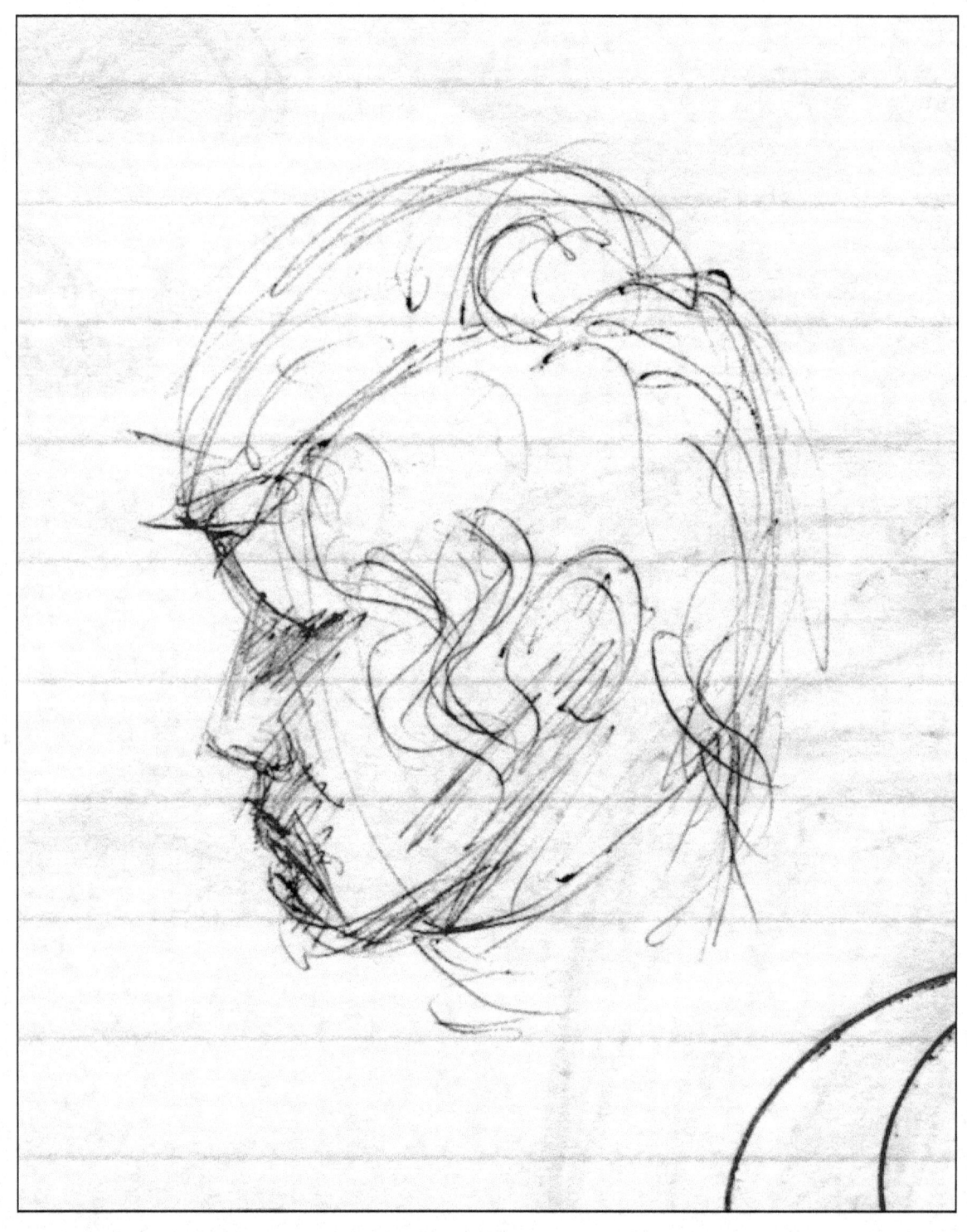

Ballpoint Pen

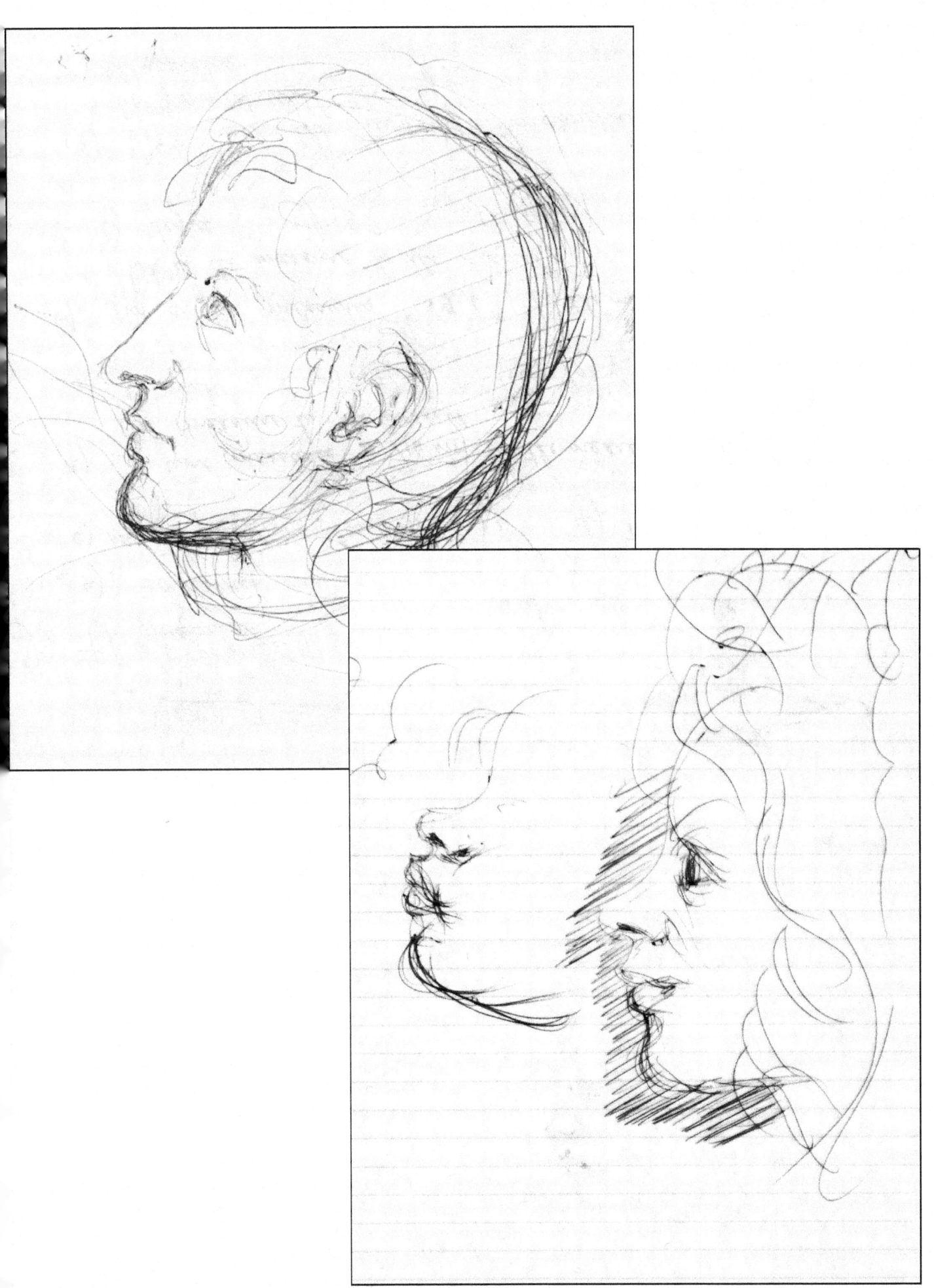

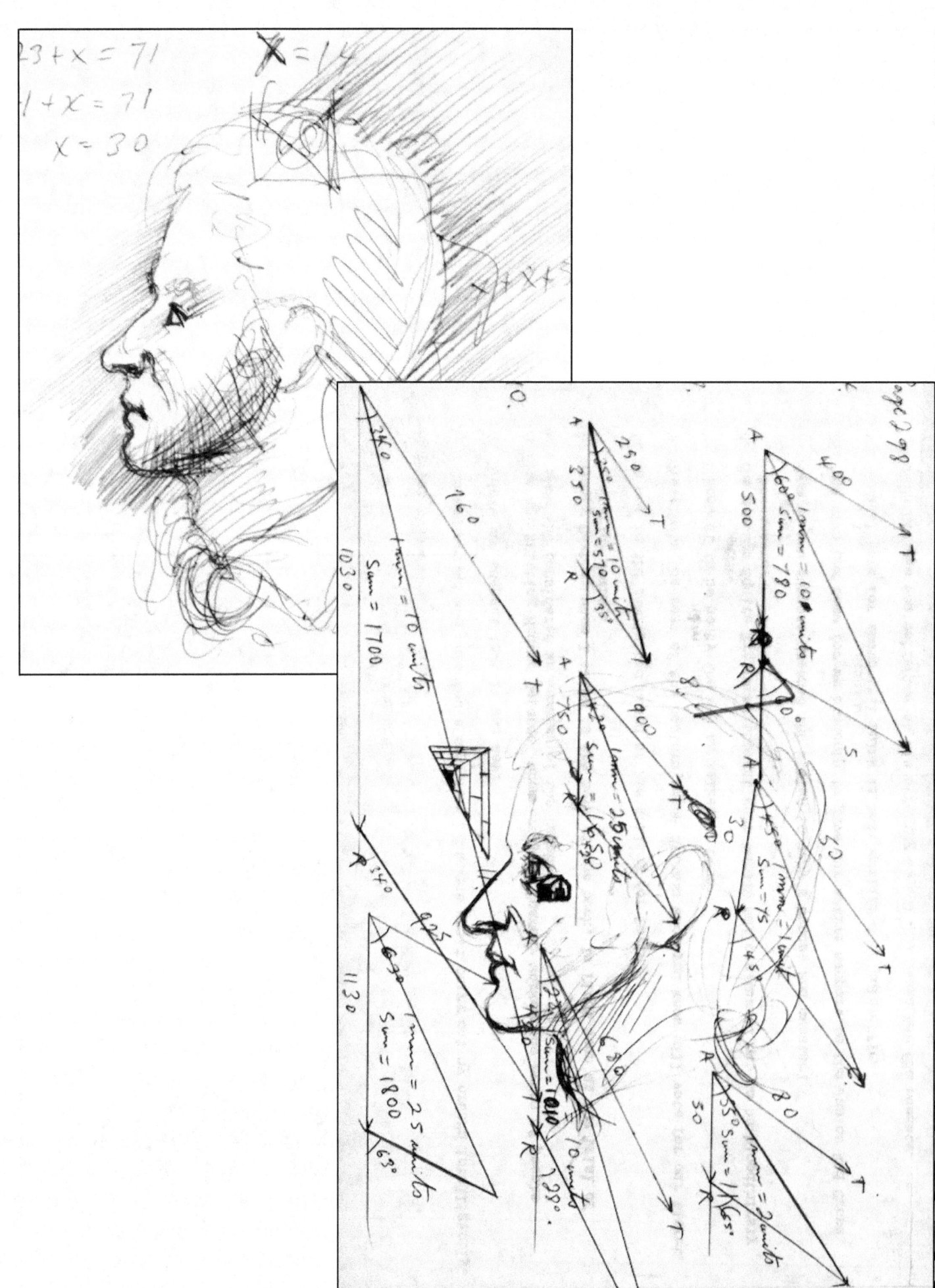

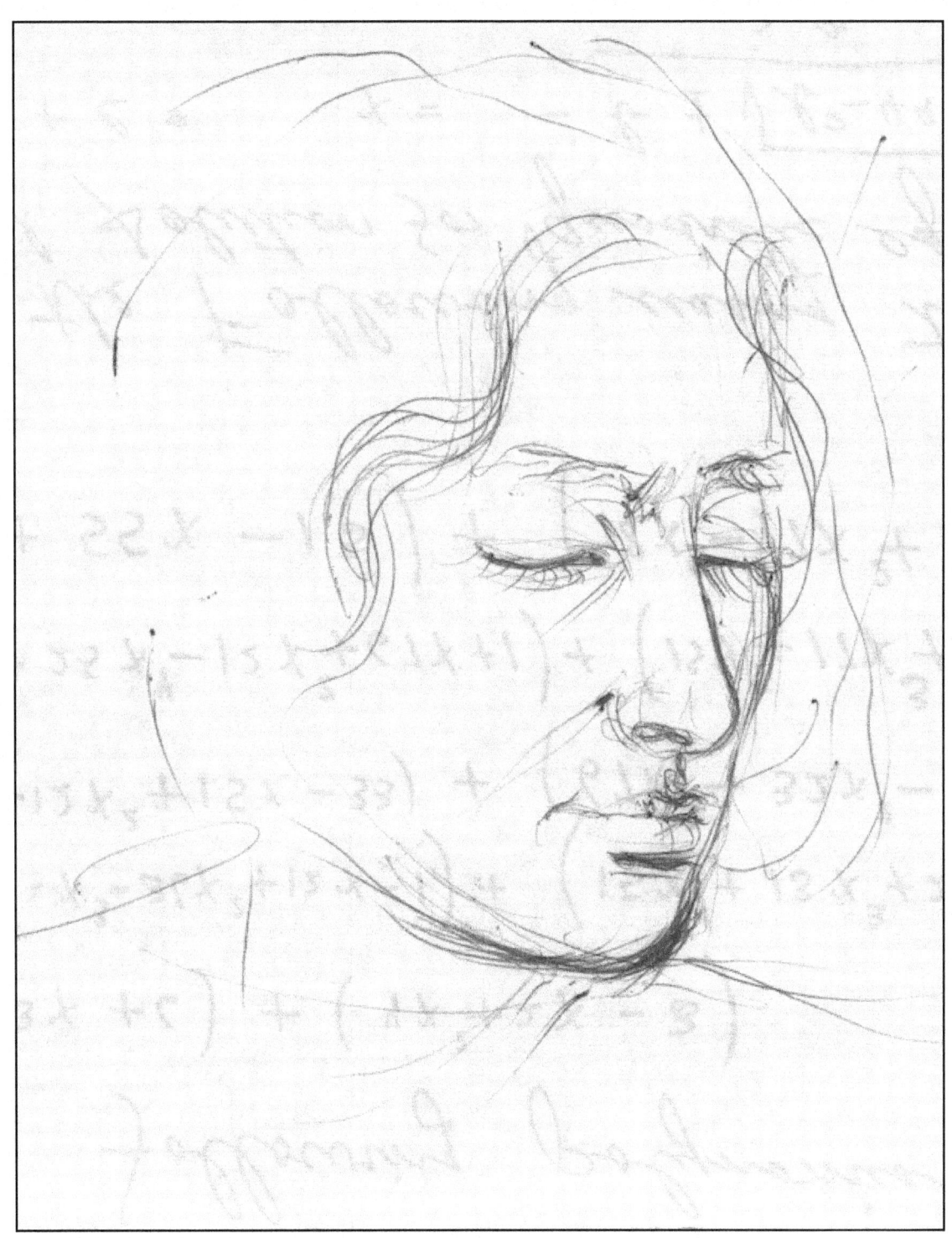

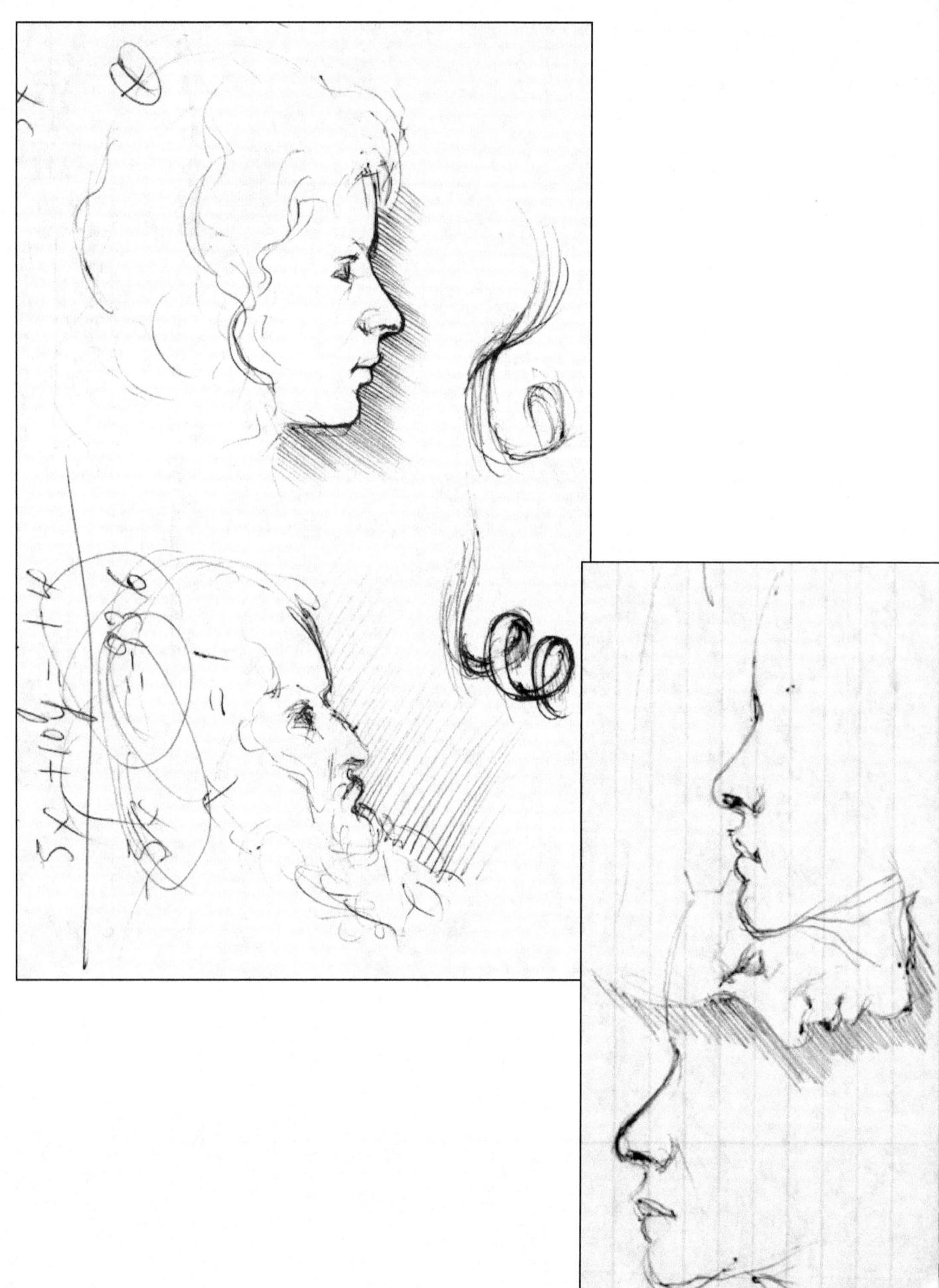

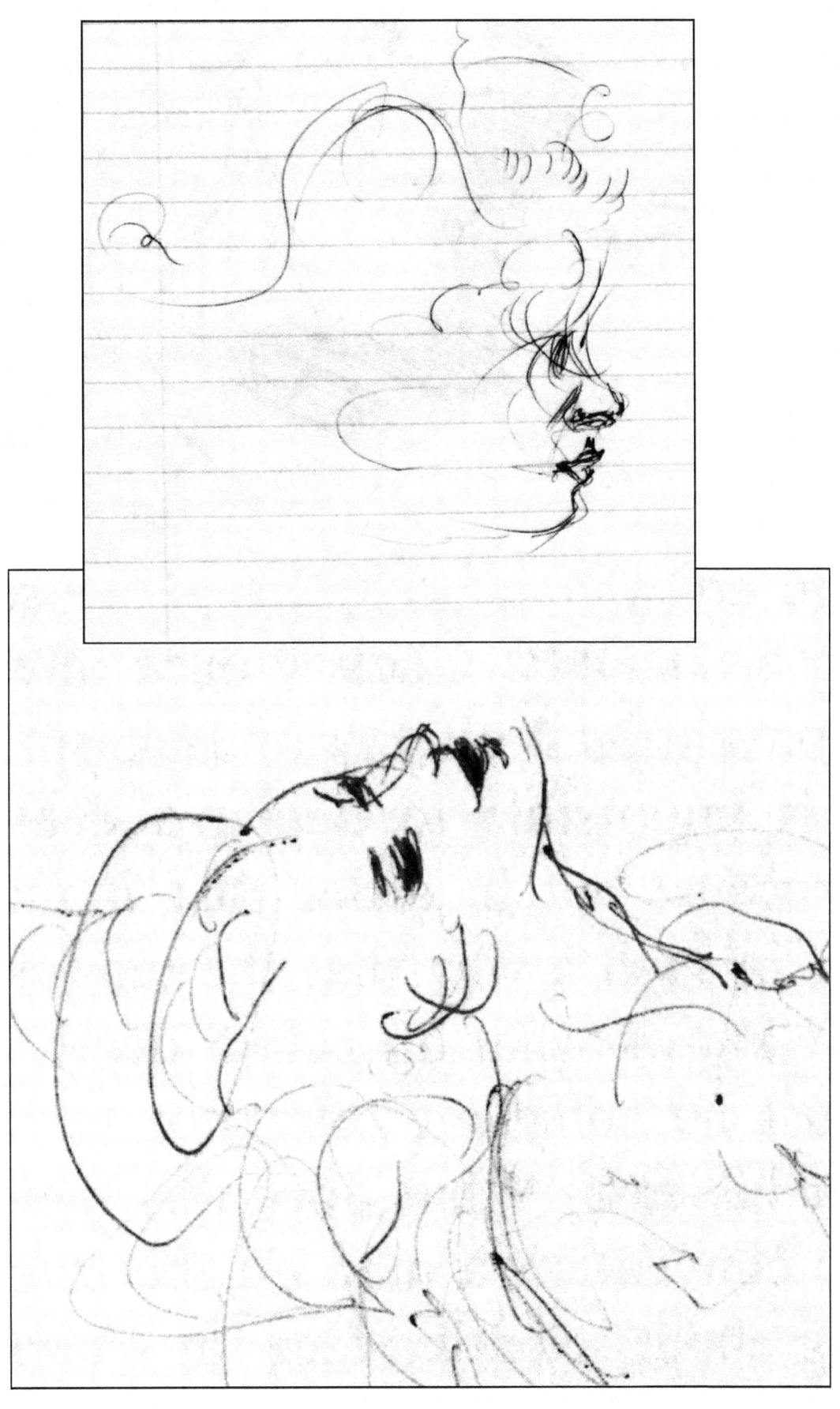

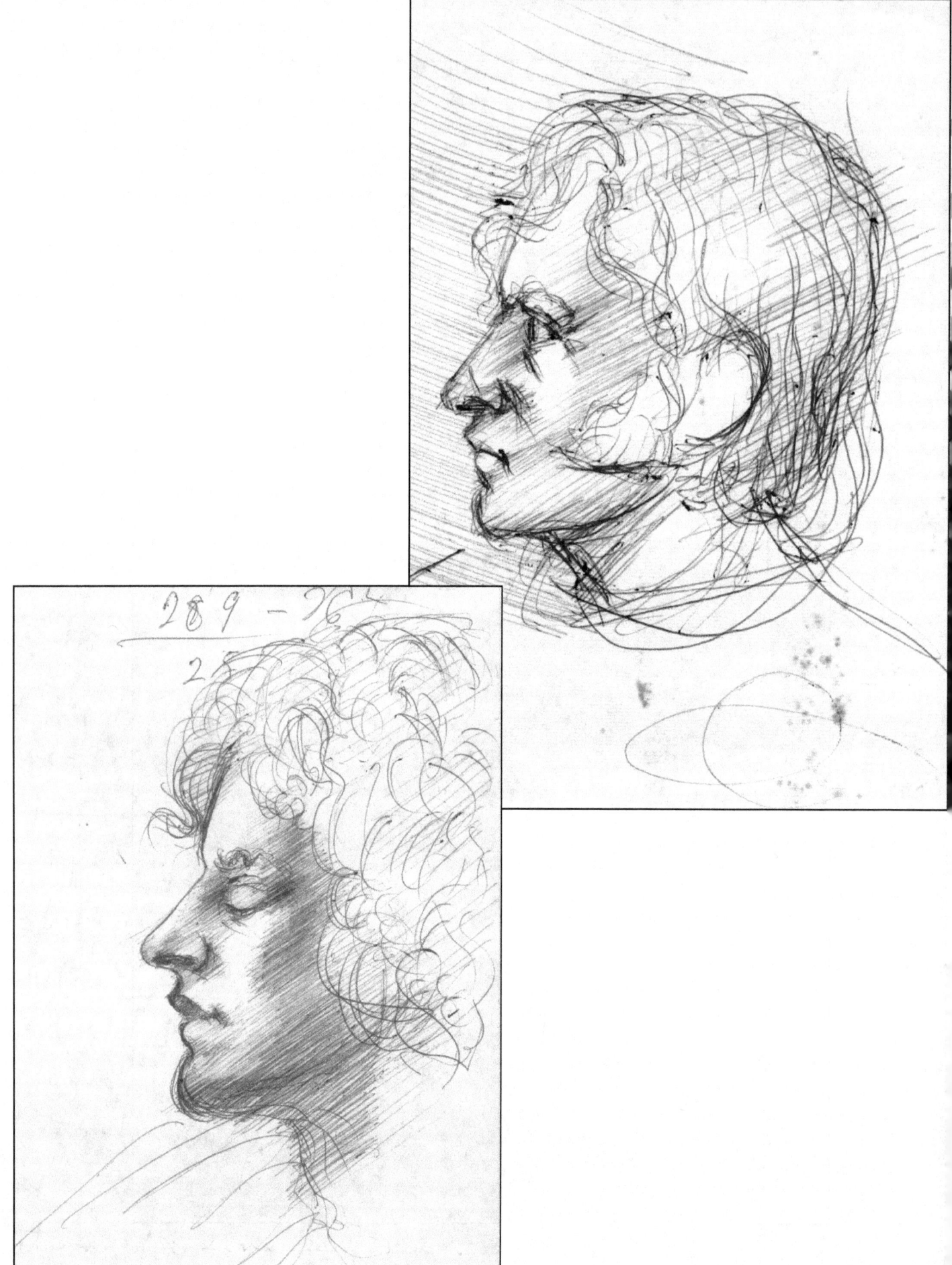

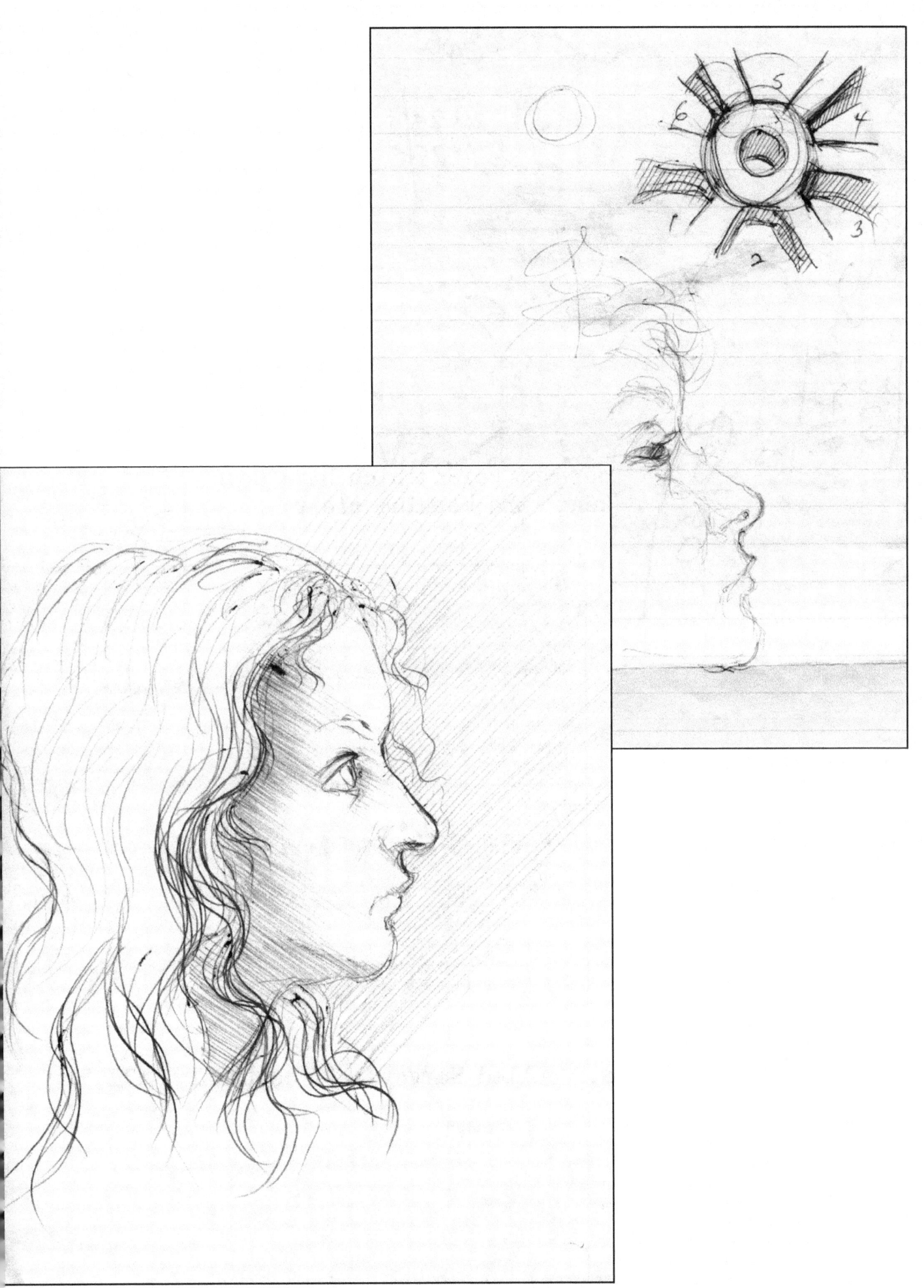

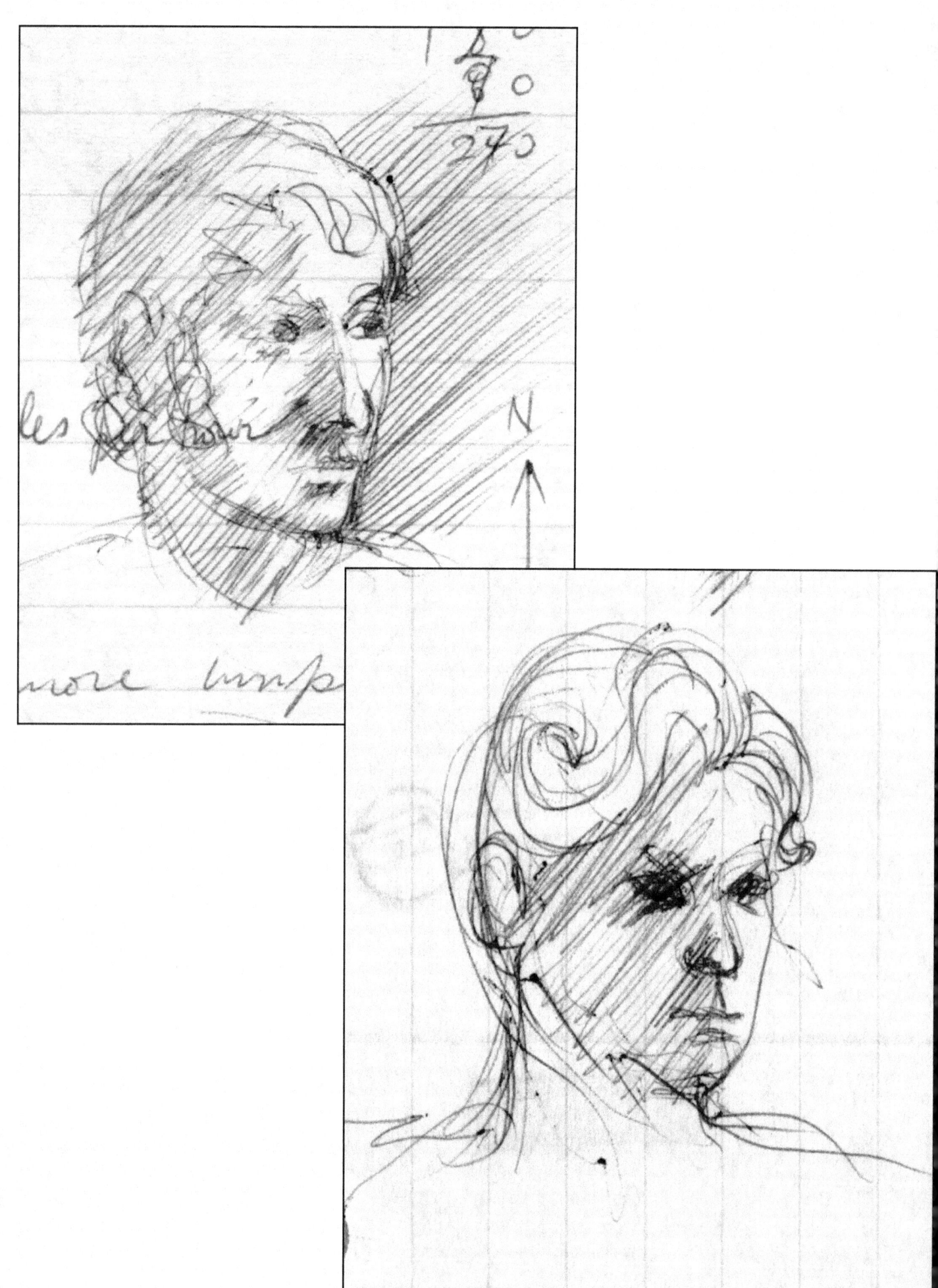

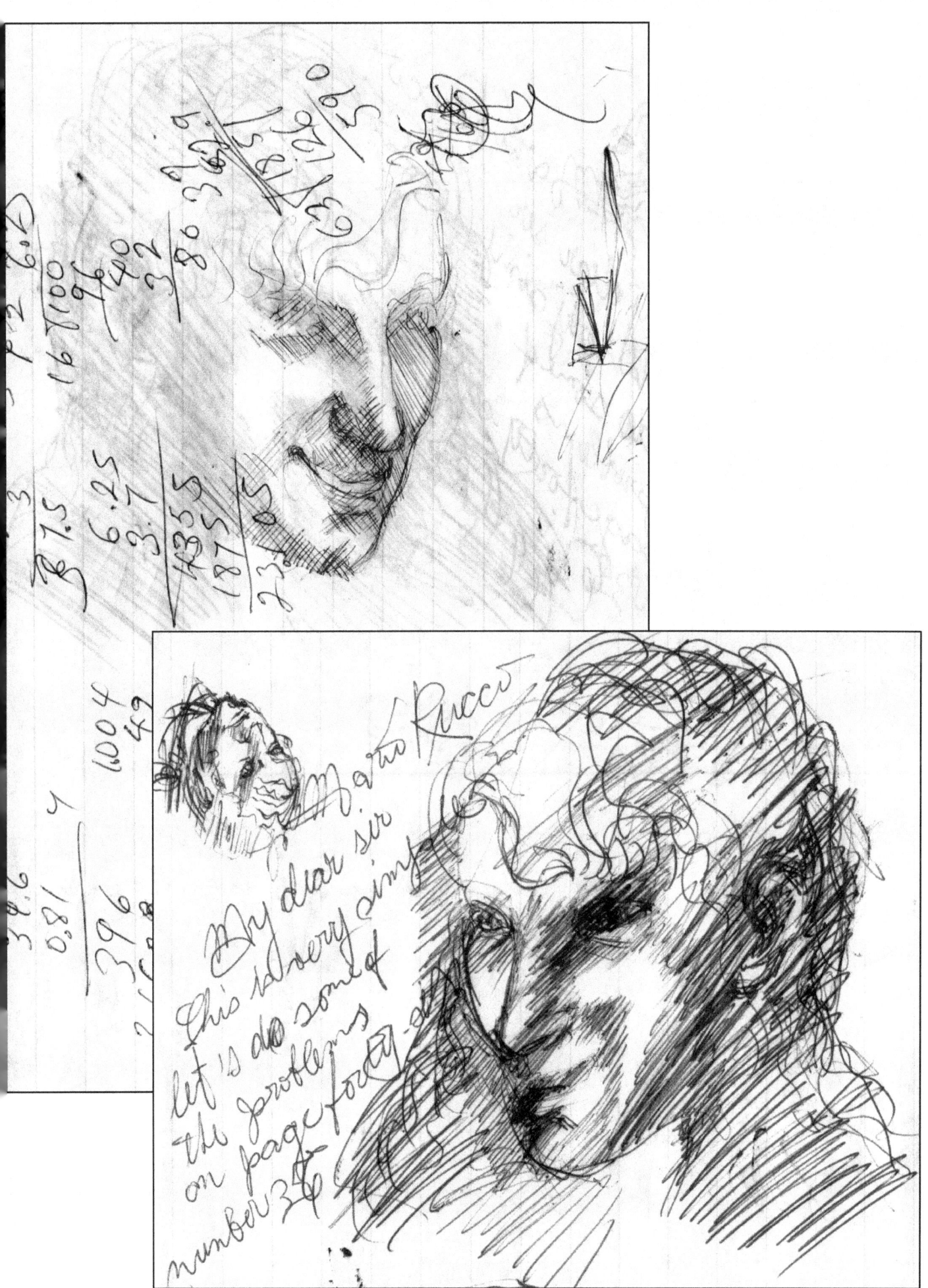

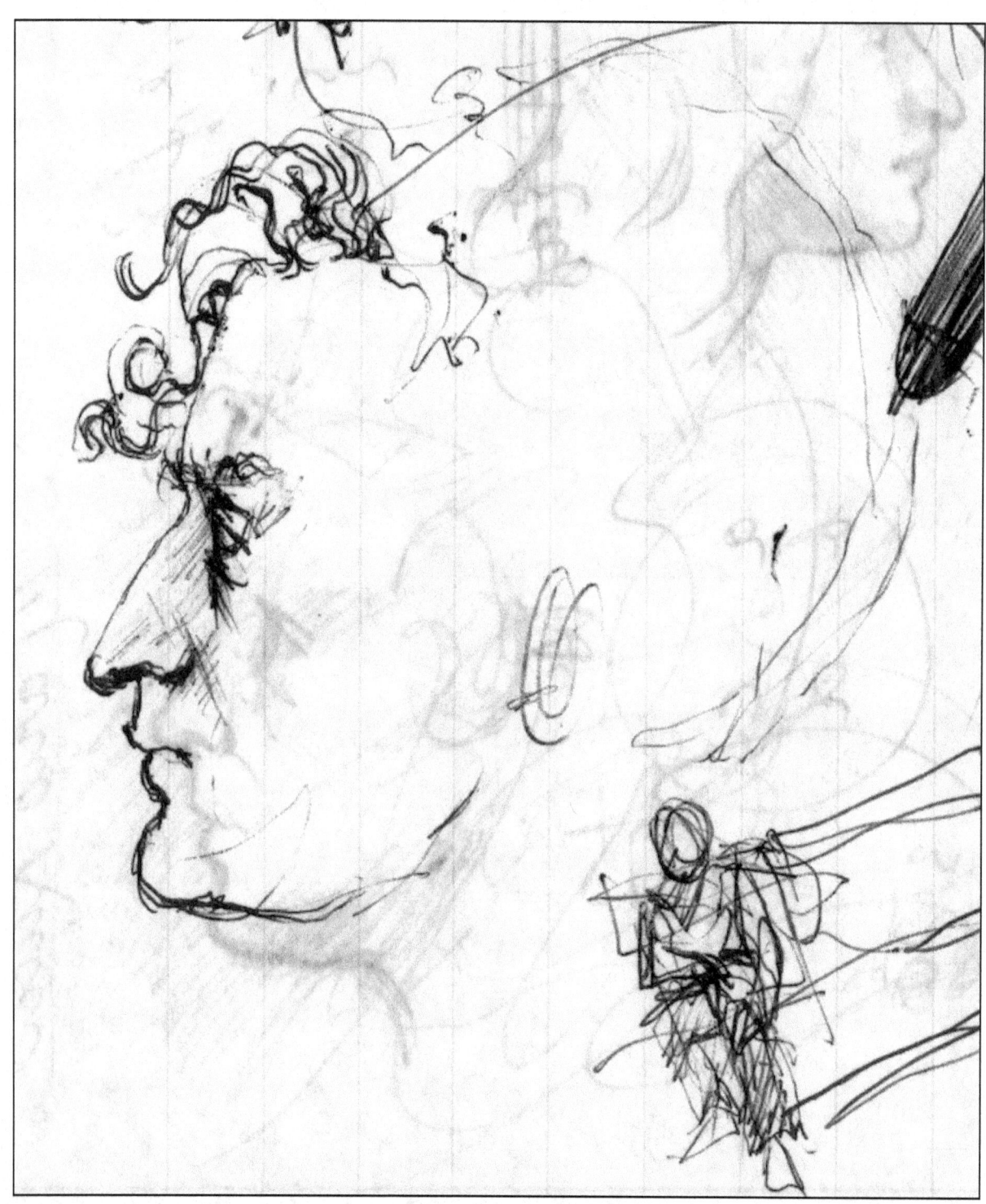

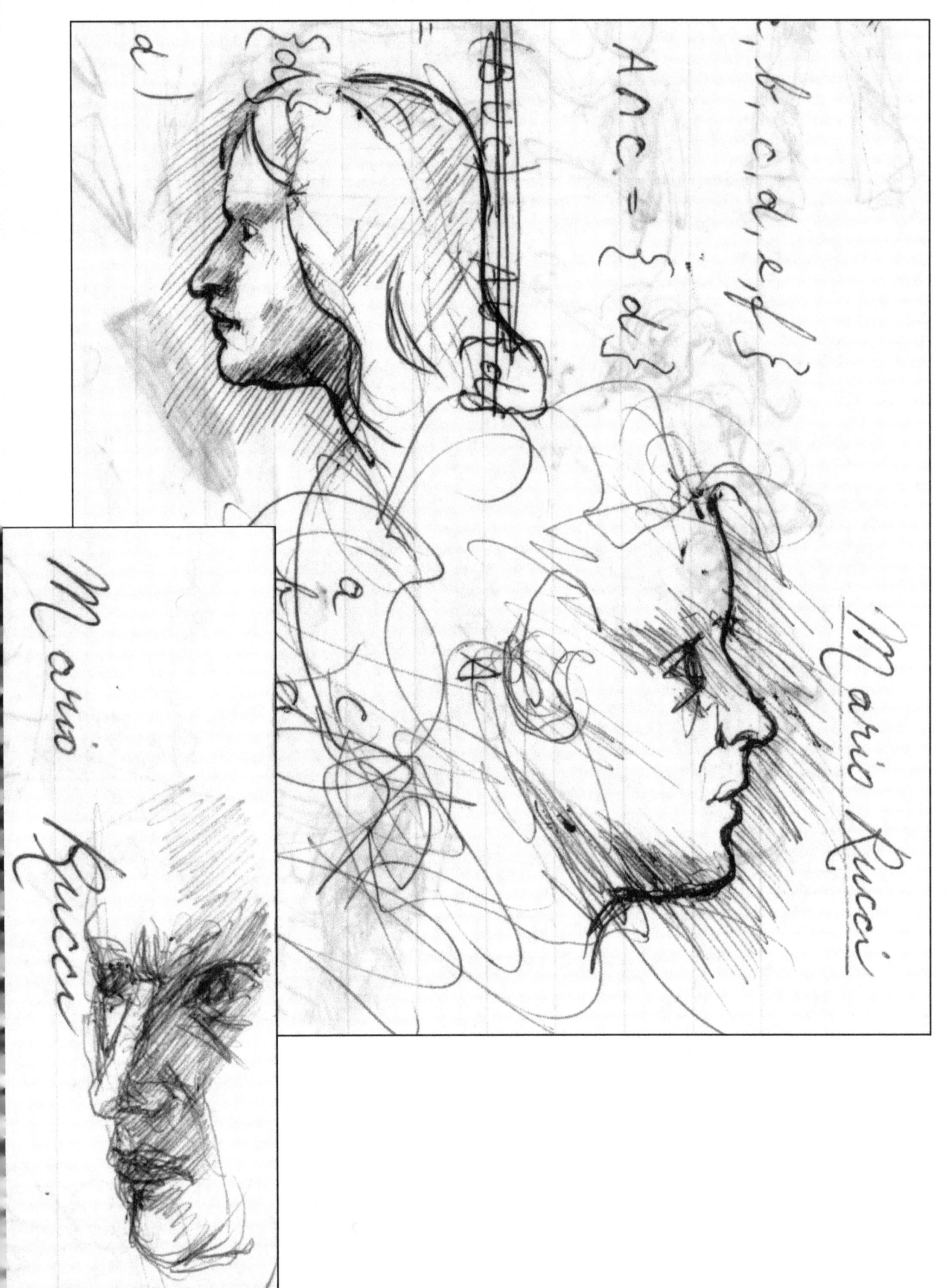

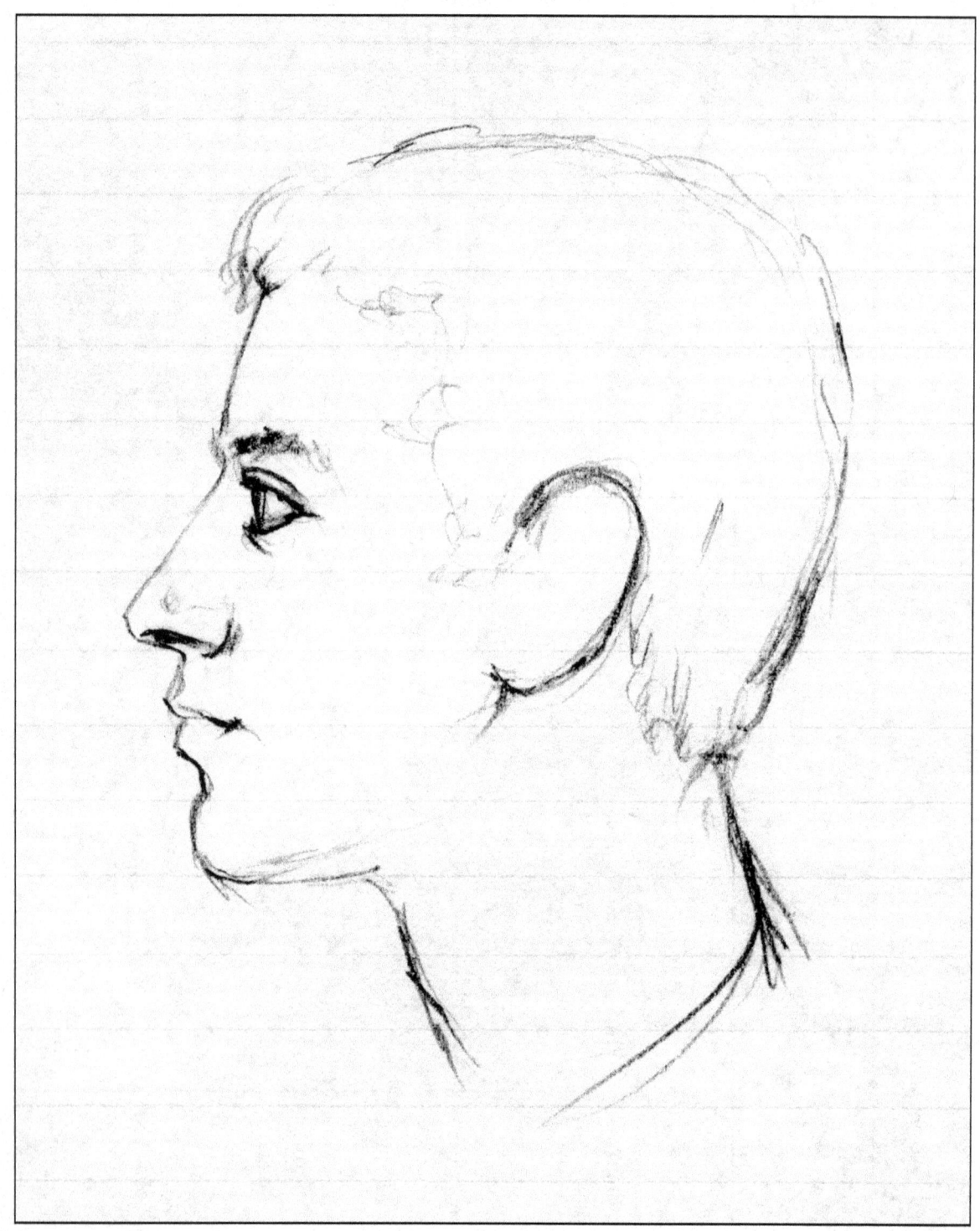

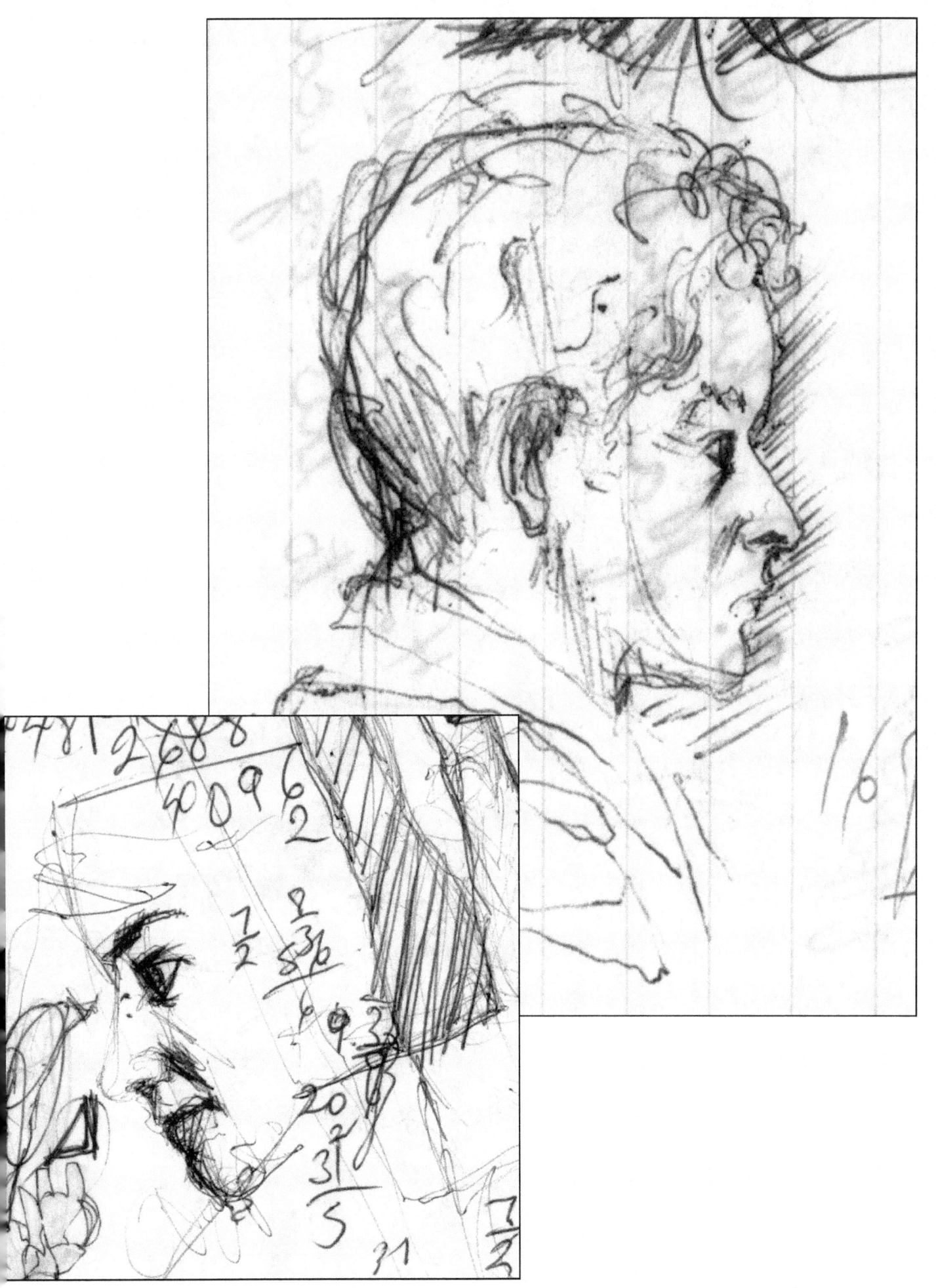

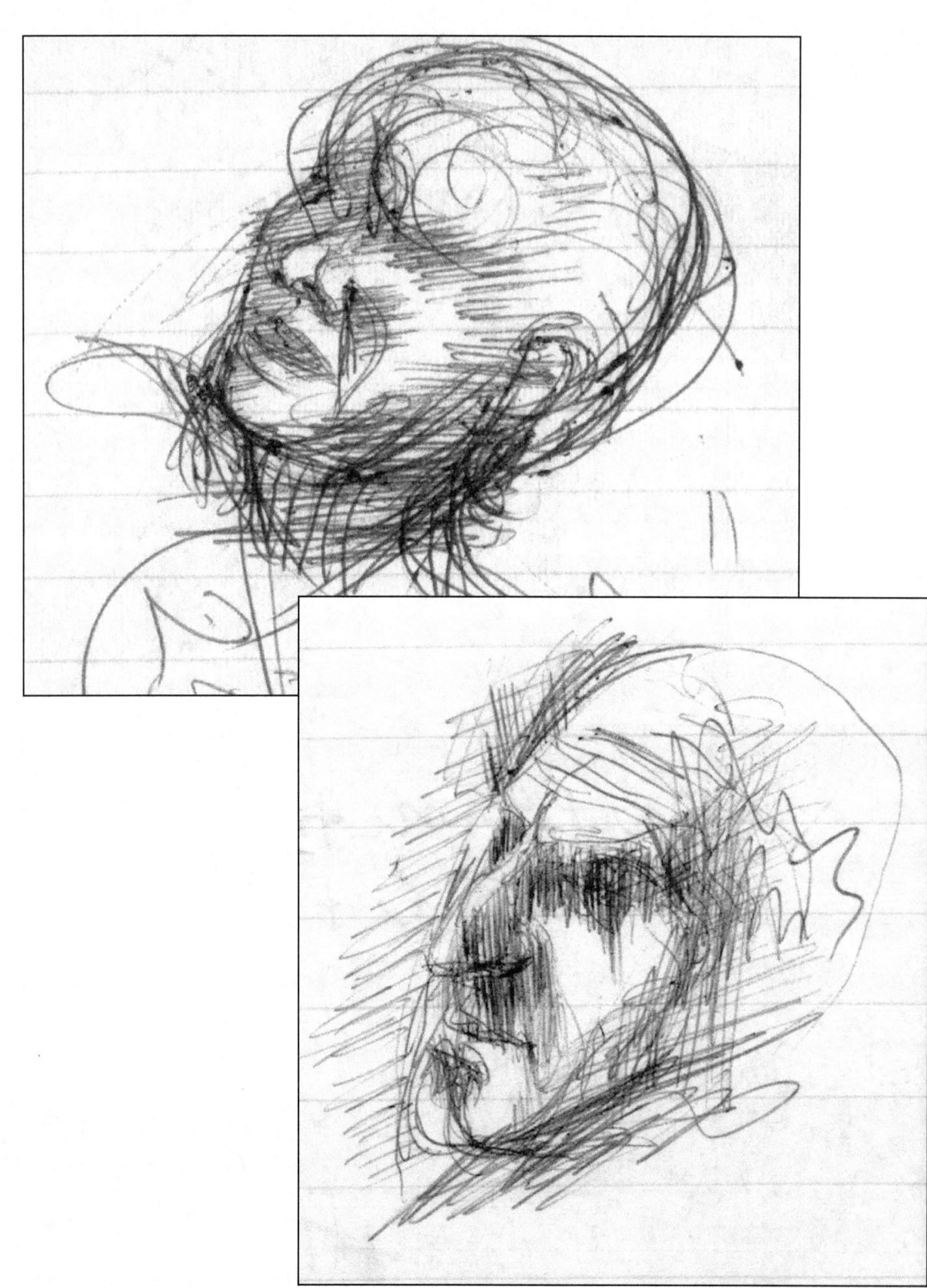

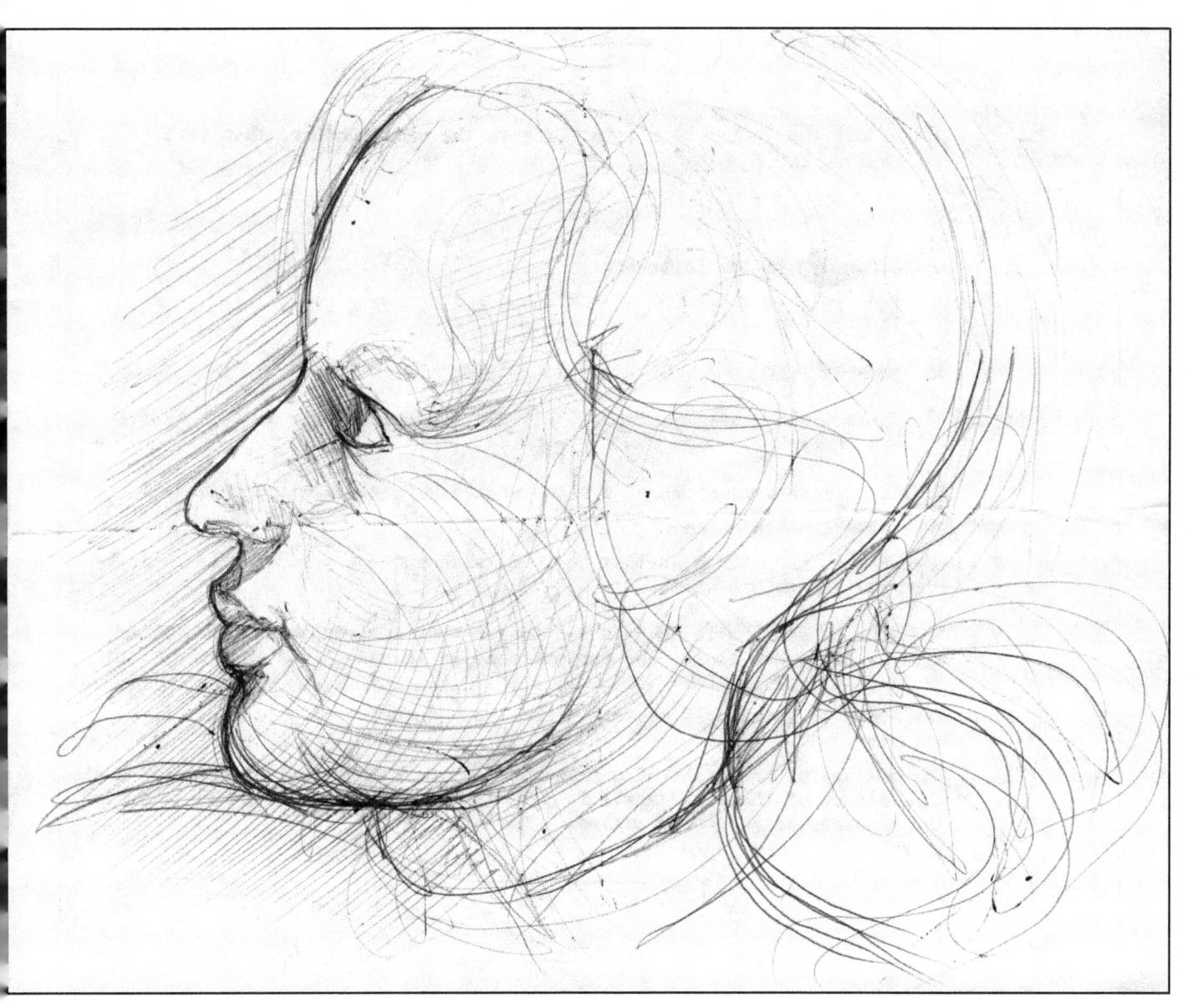

Ballpoint Pen

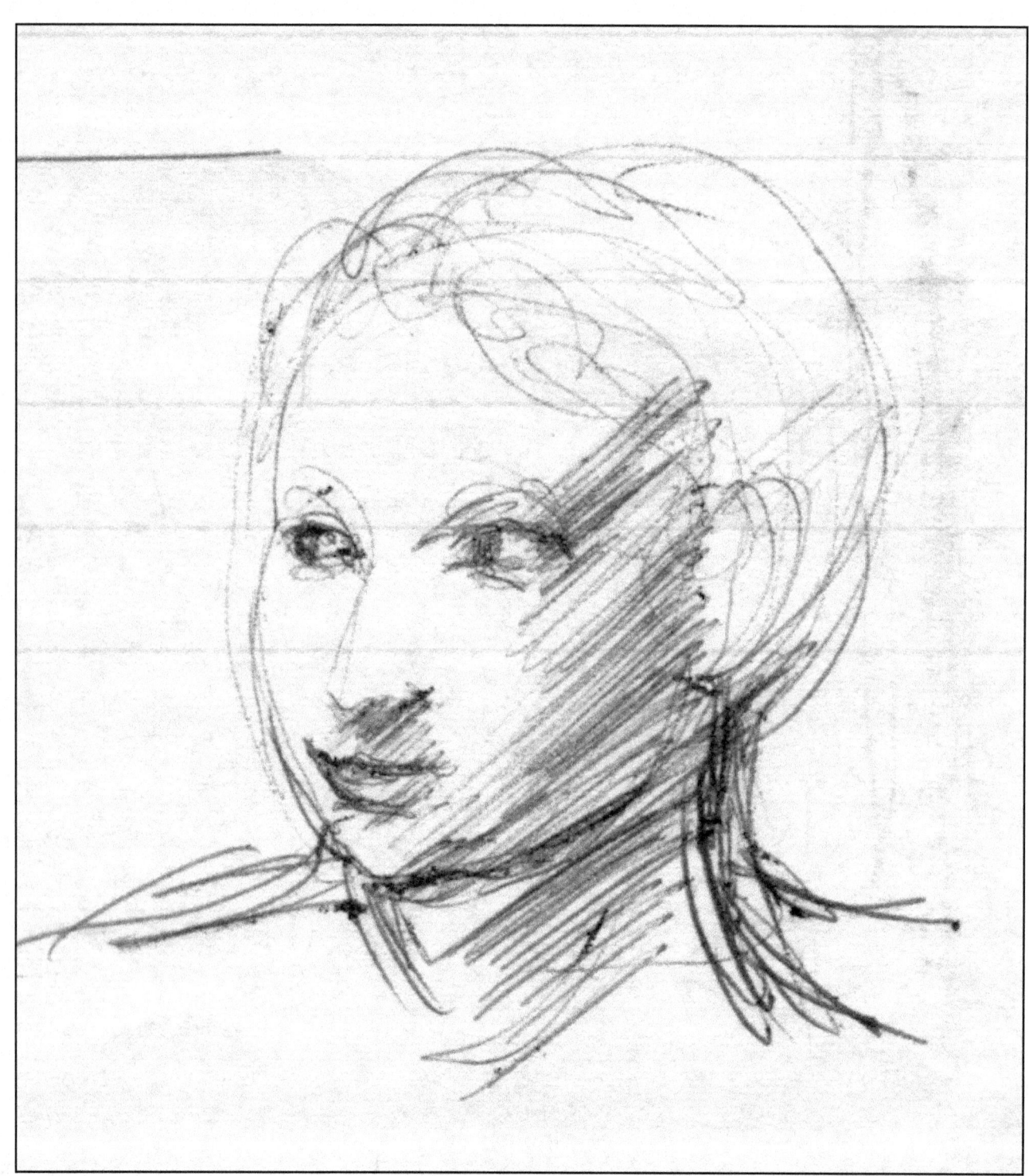

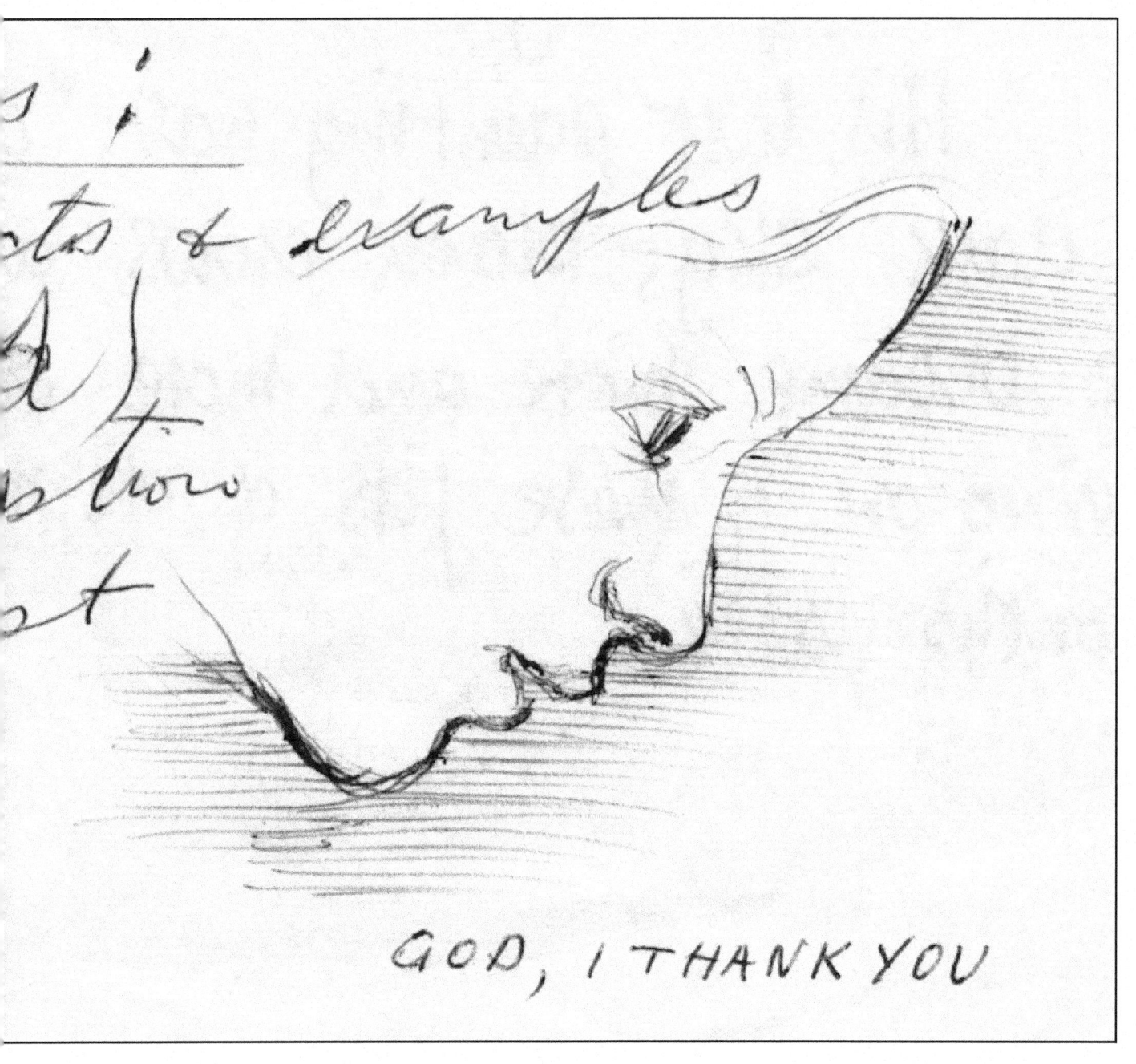

Thank you, God, for letting me see beauty
and giving me the talent to depict it.

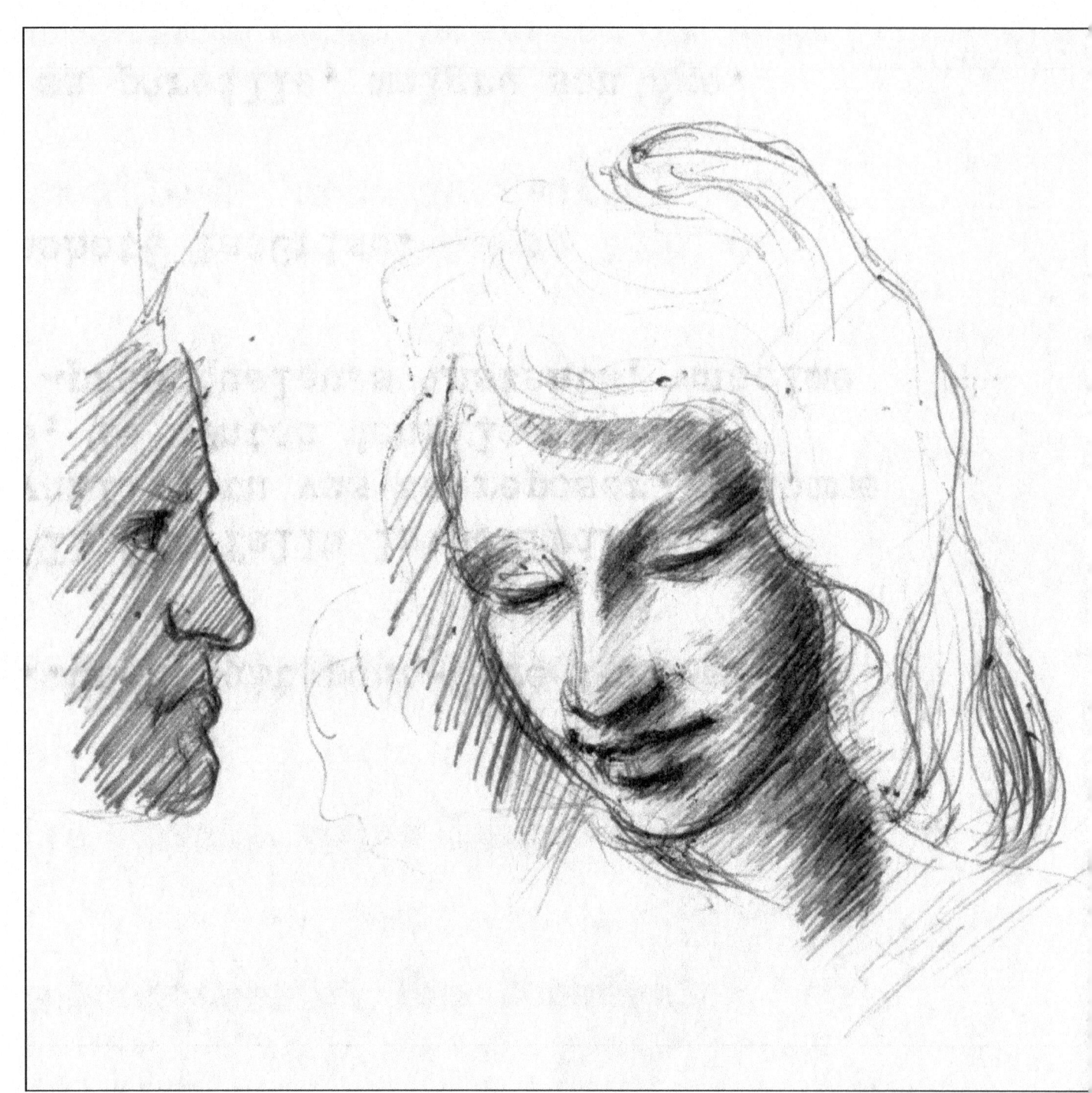

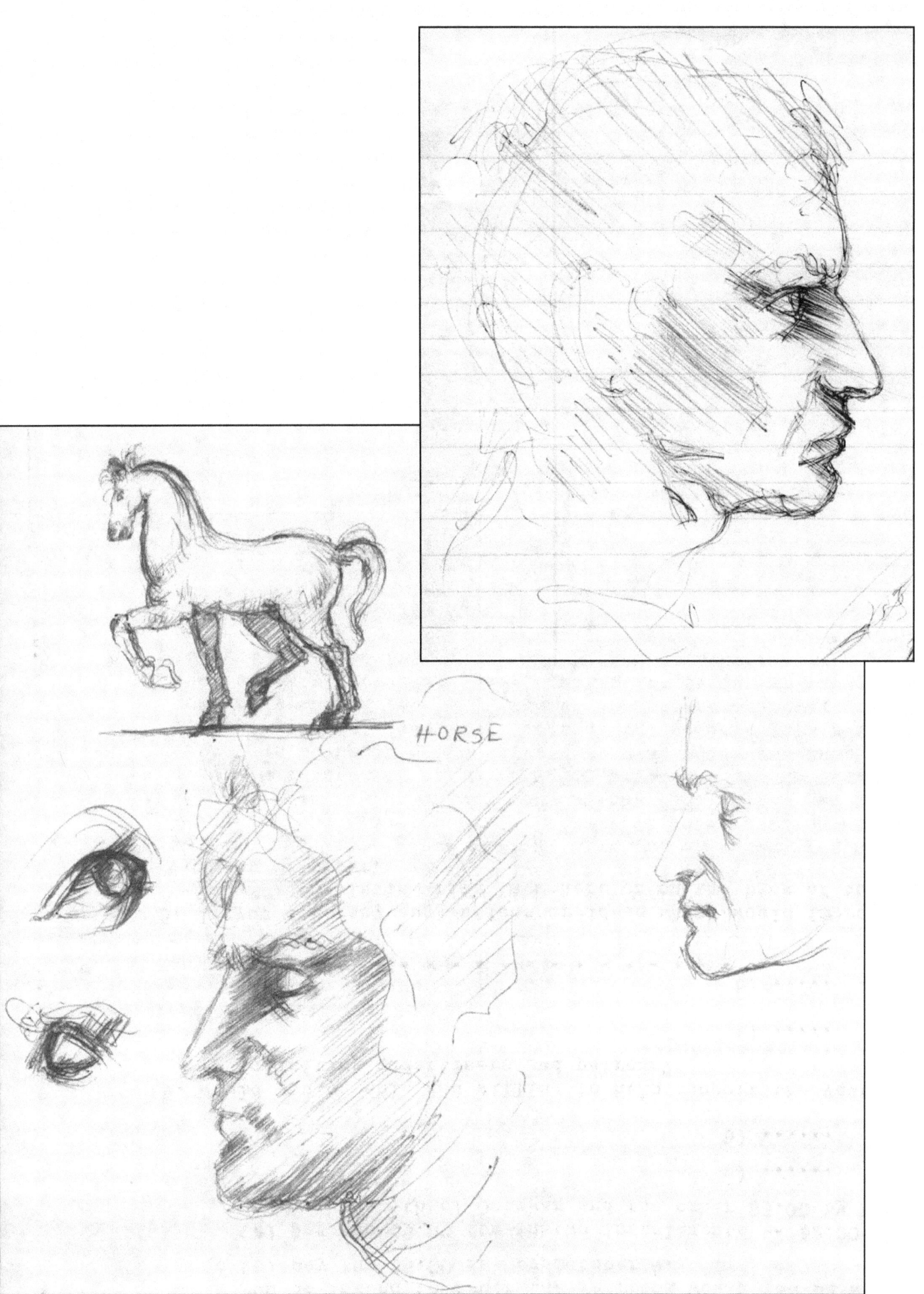

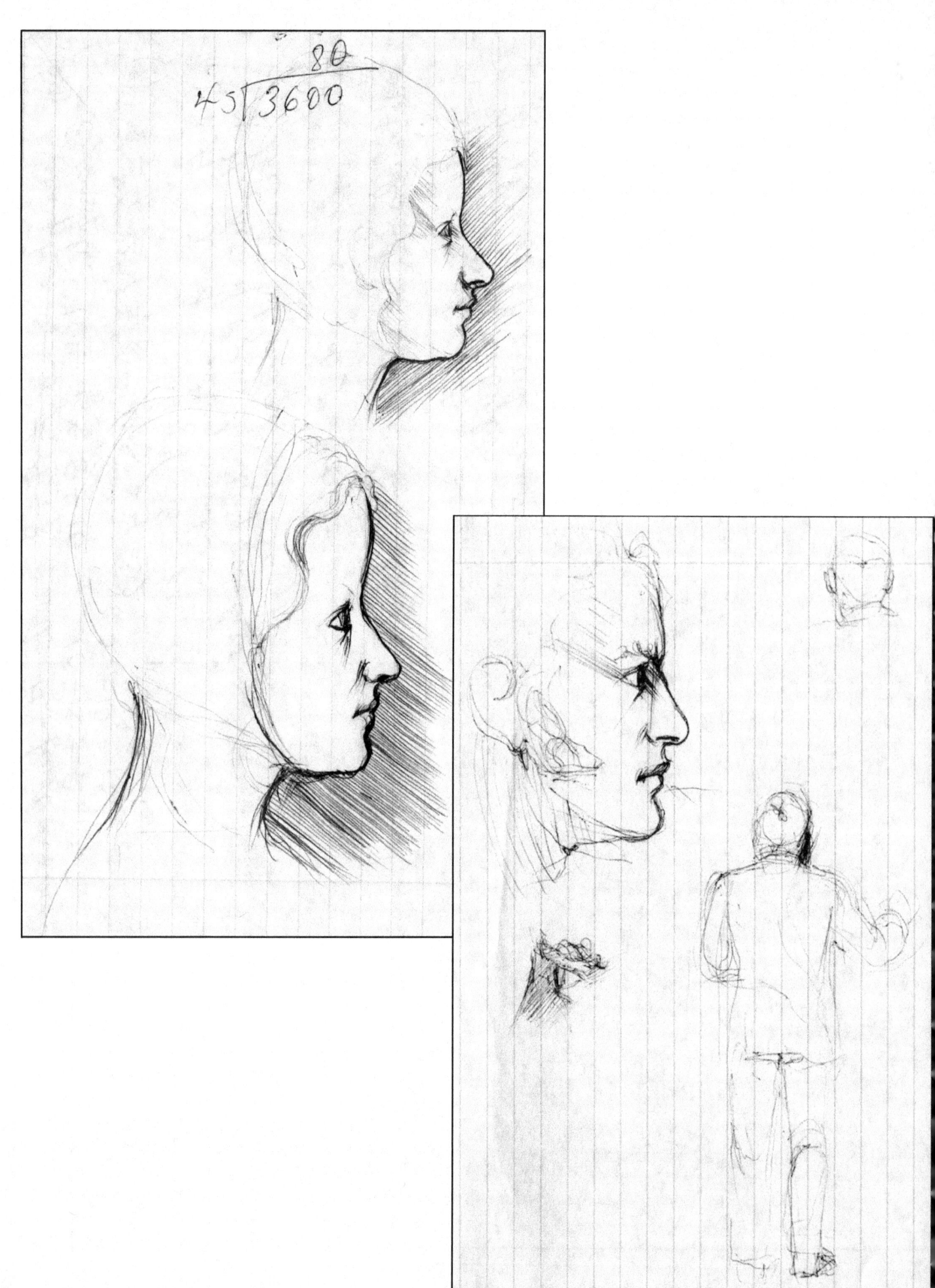

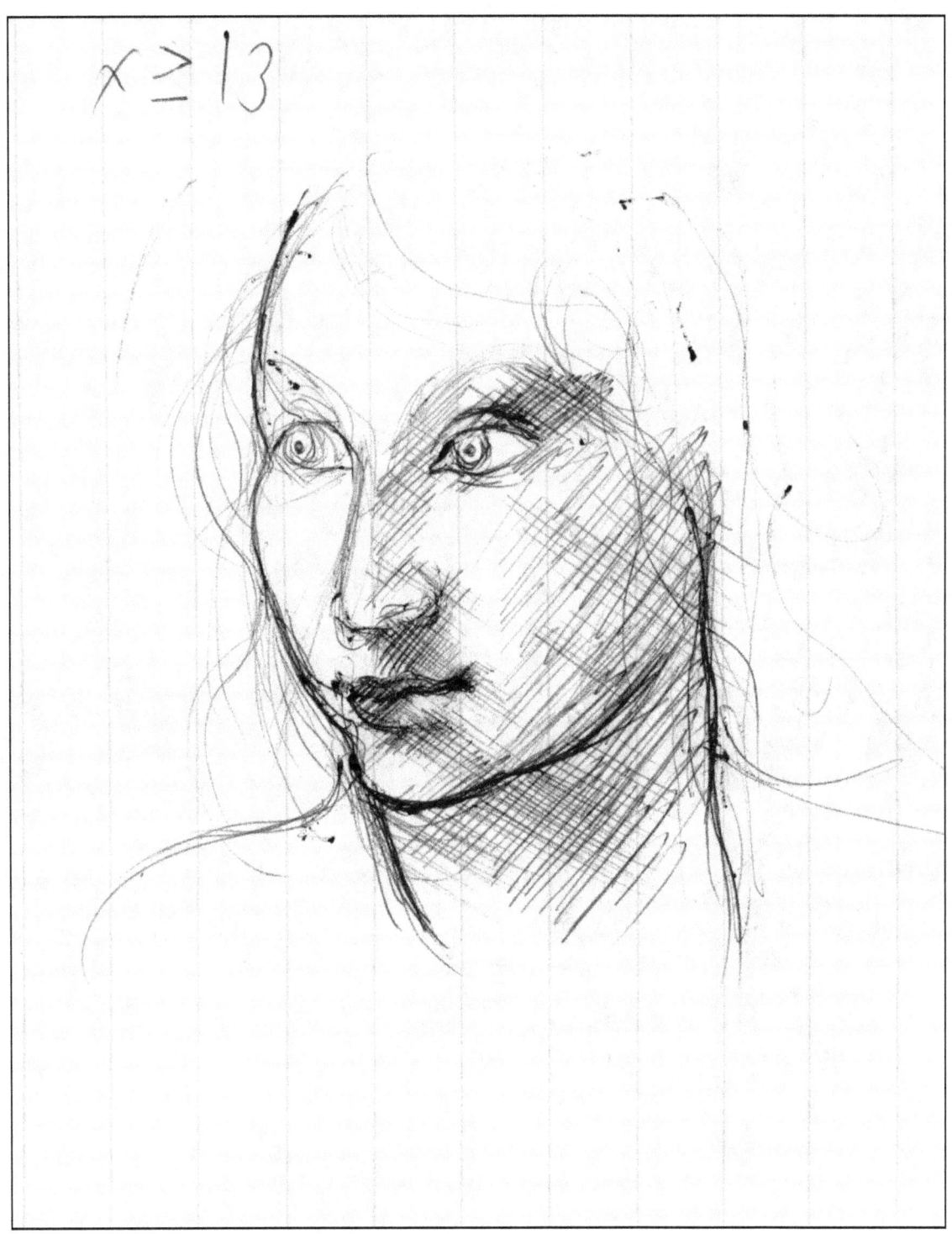

Ballpoint Pen

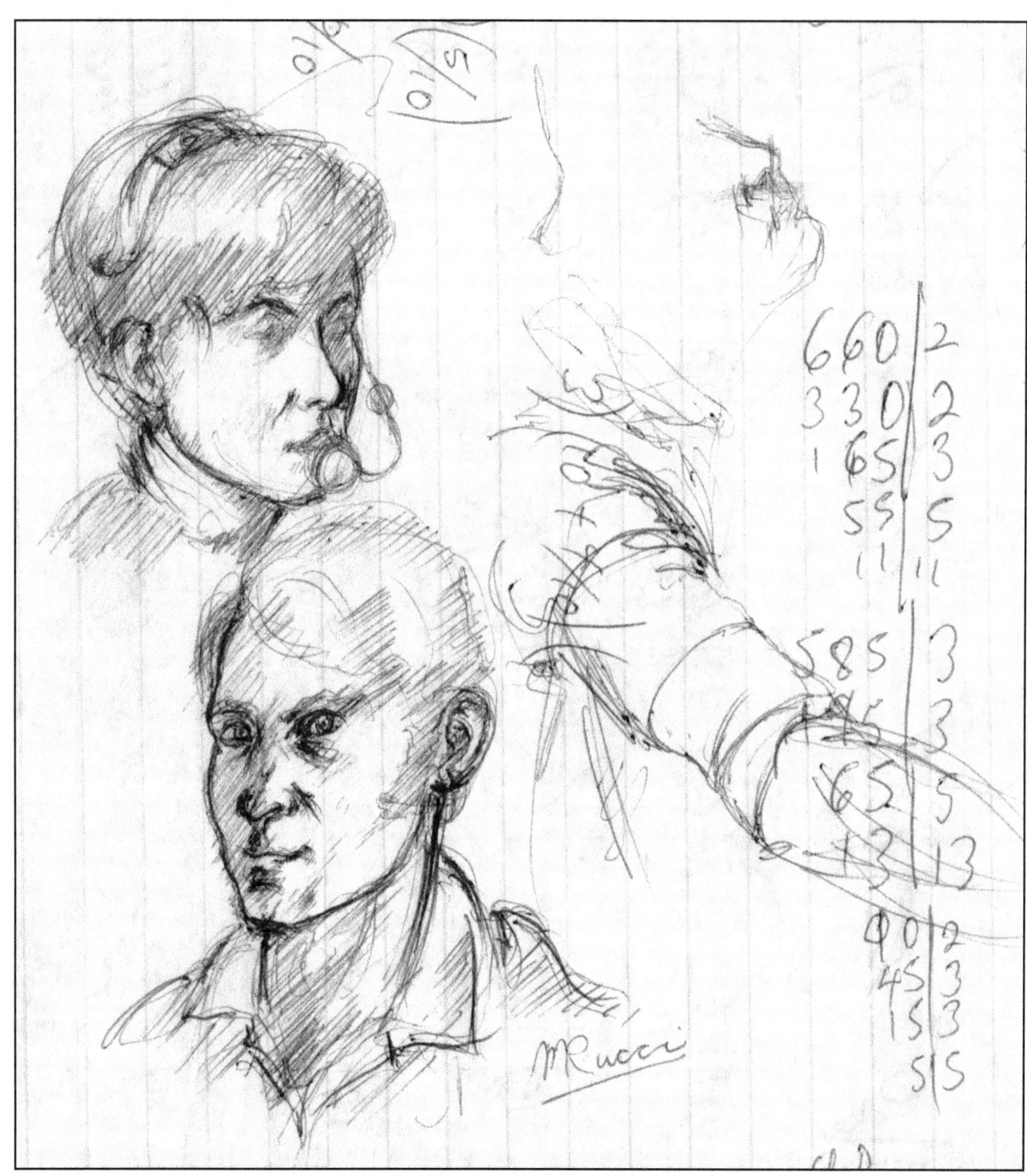

9. Head Visualization, Other Times

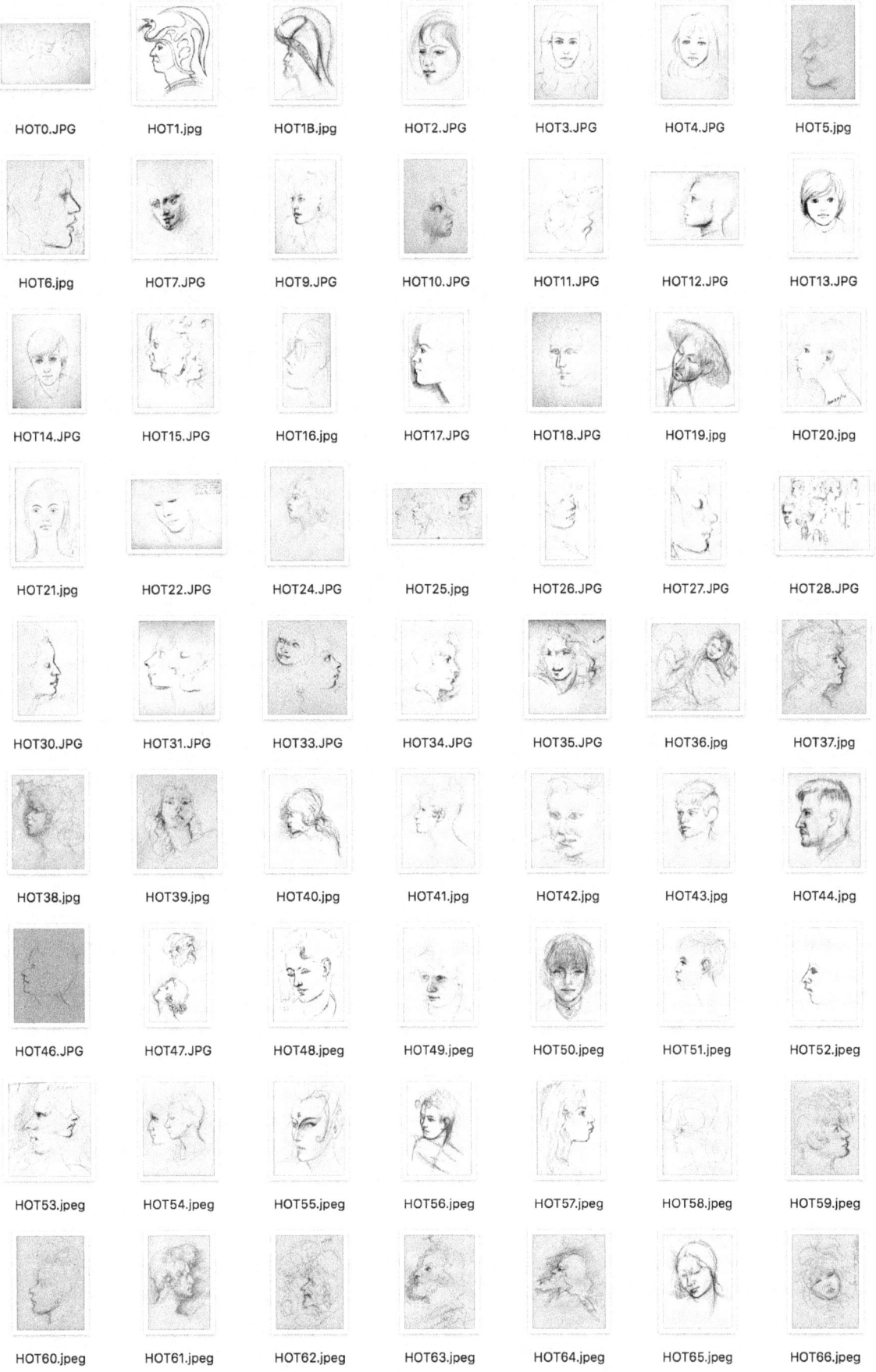

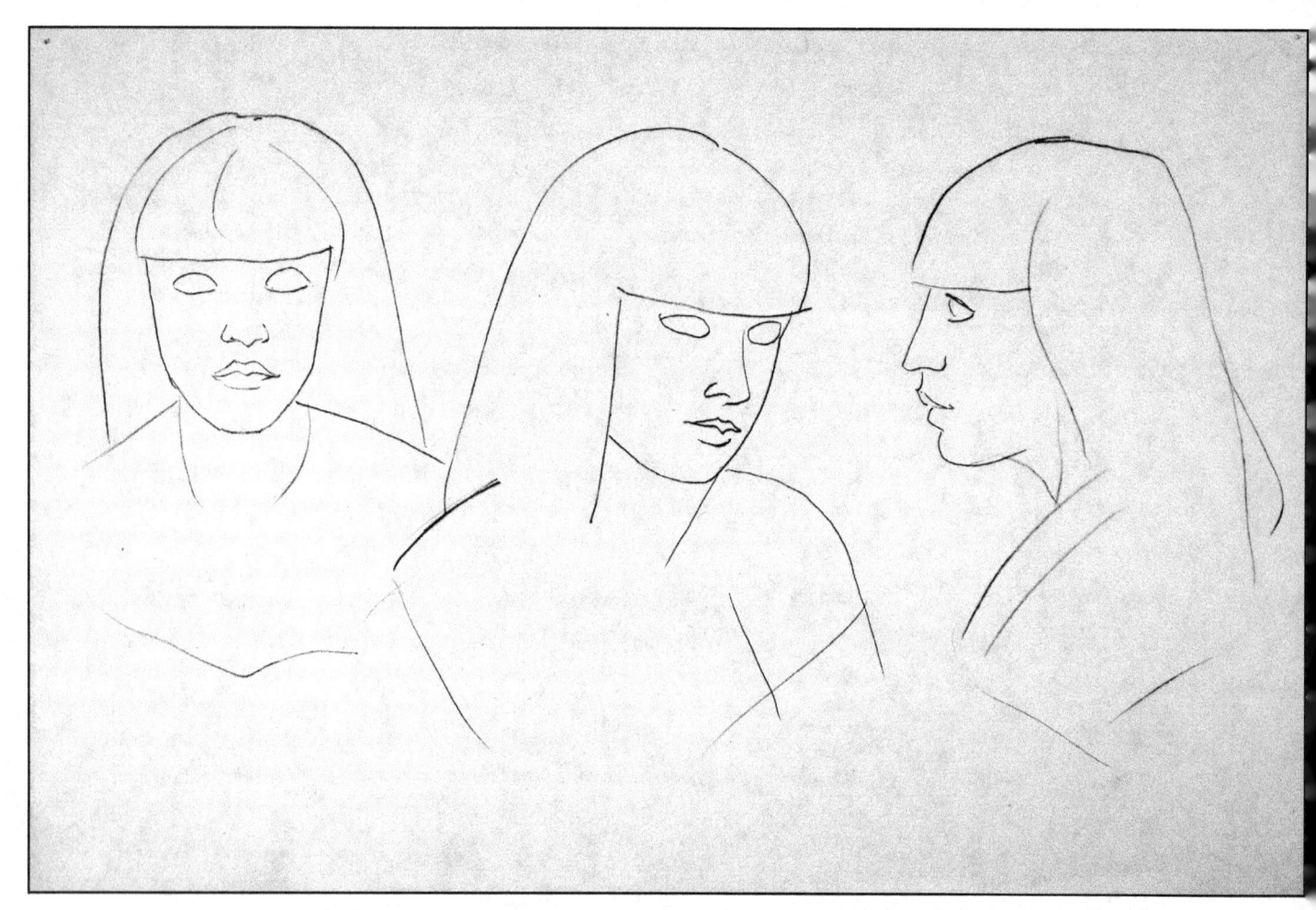

The 3 Views of the Head/Face: front, 3/4, and side View

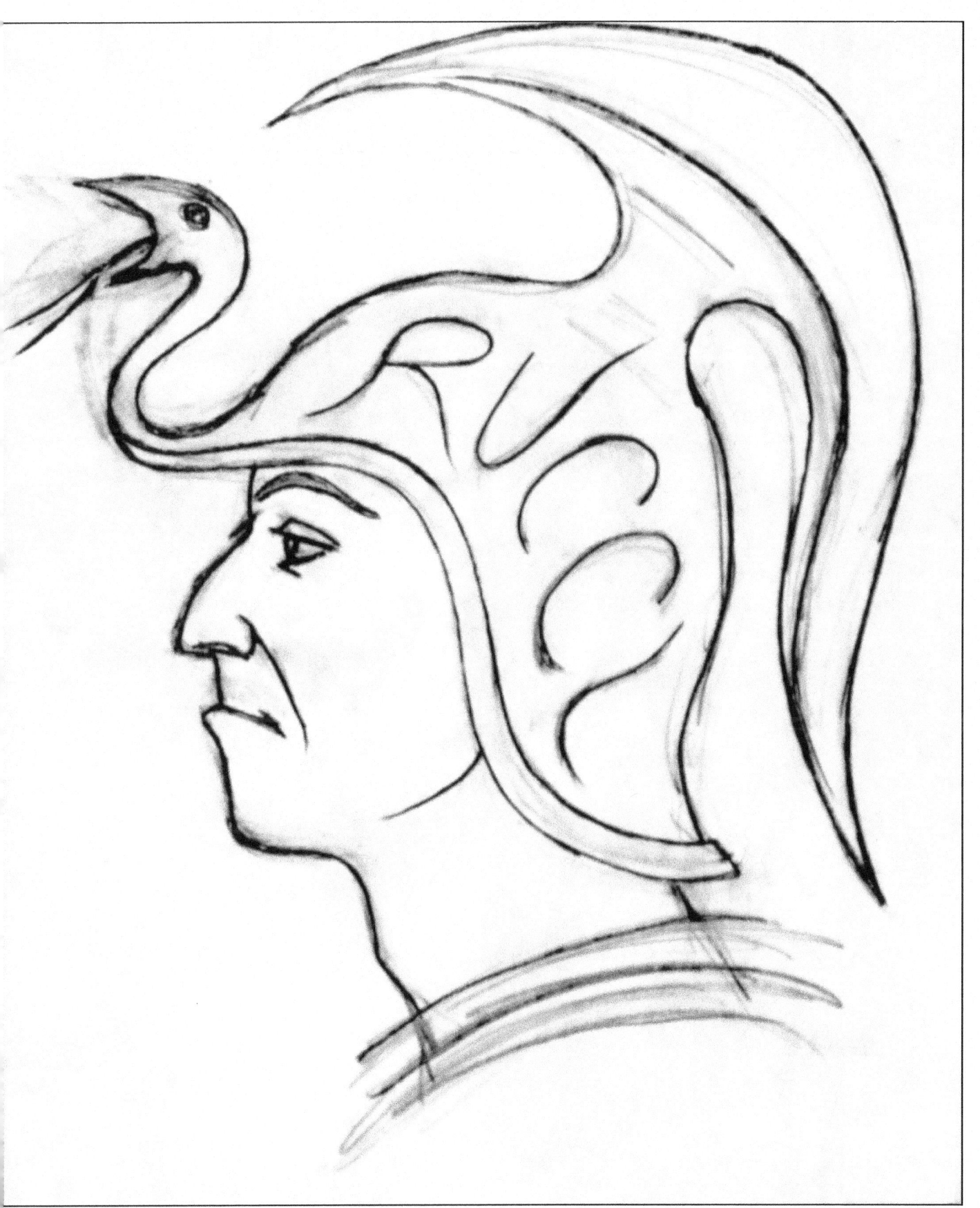

Blueprint for an Aluminum Foil Low Relief

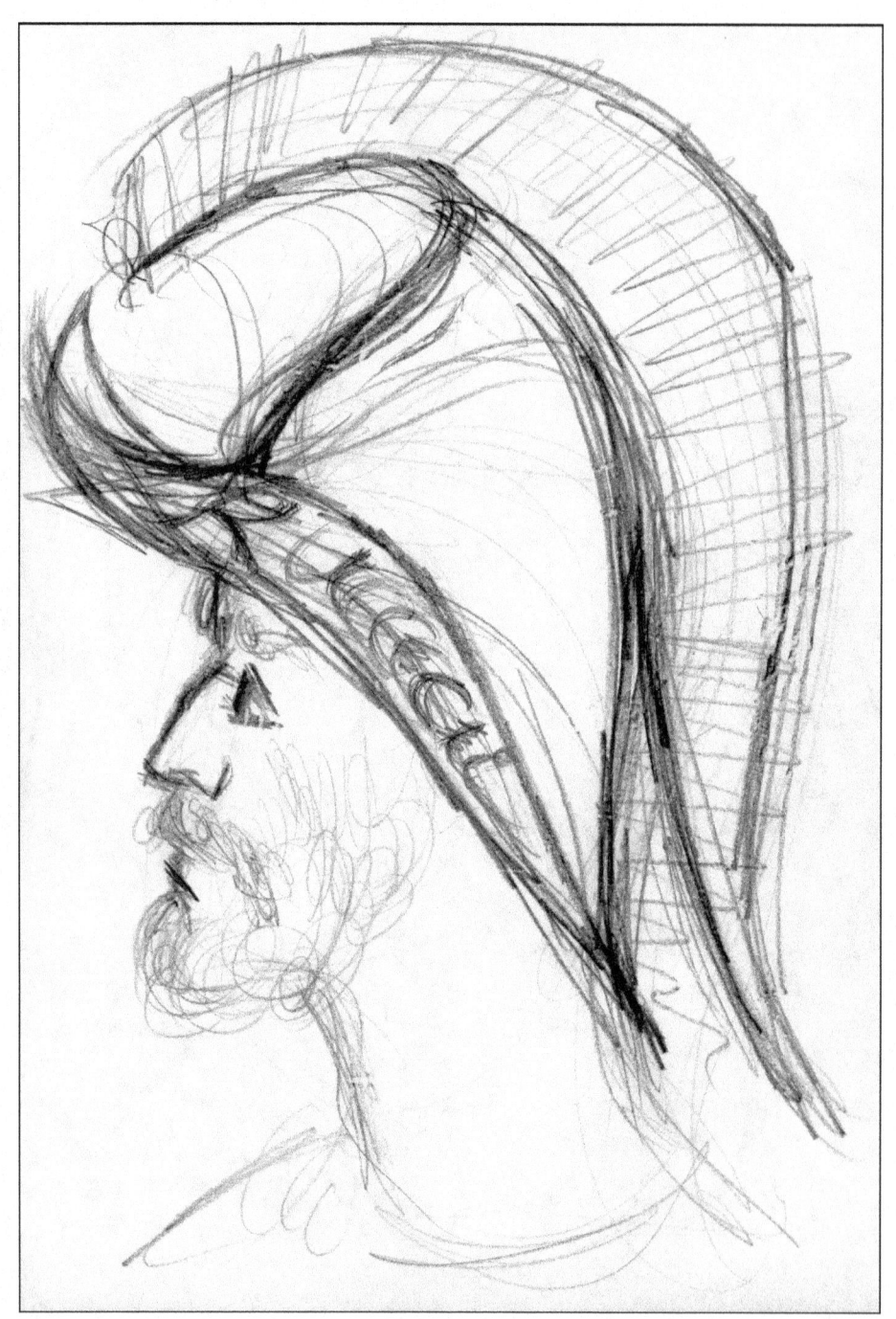

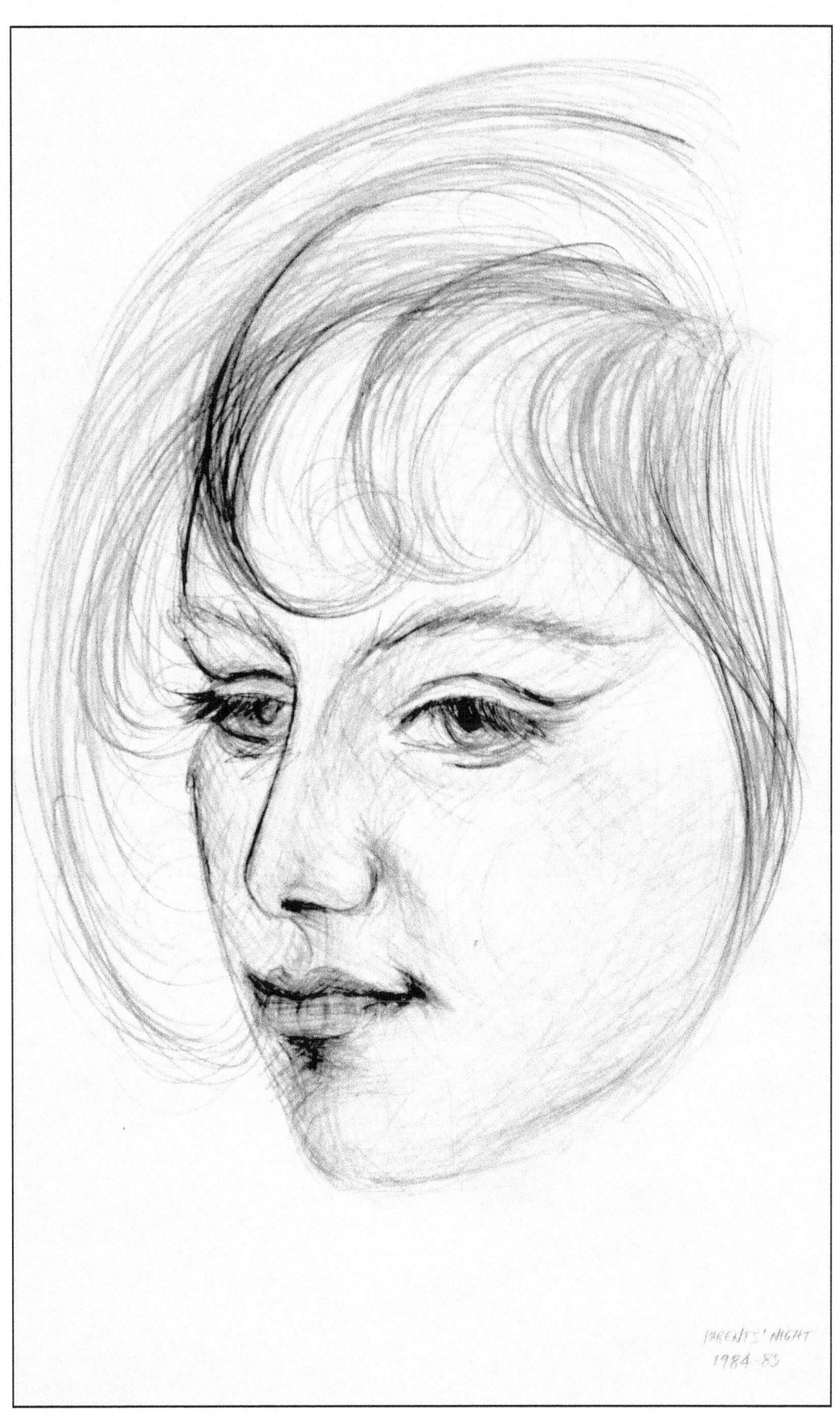

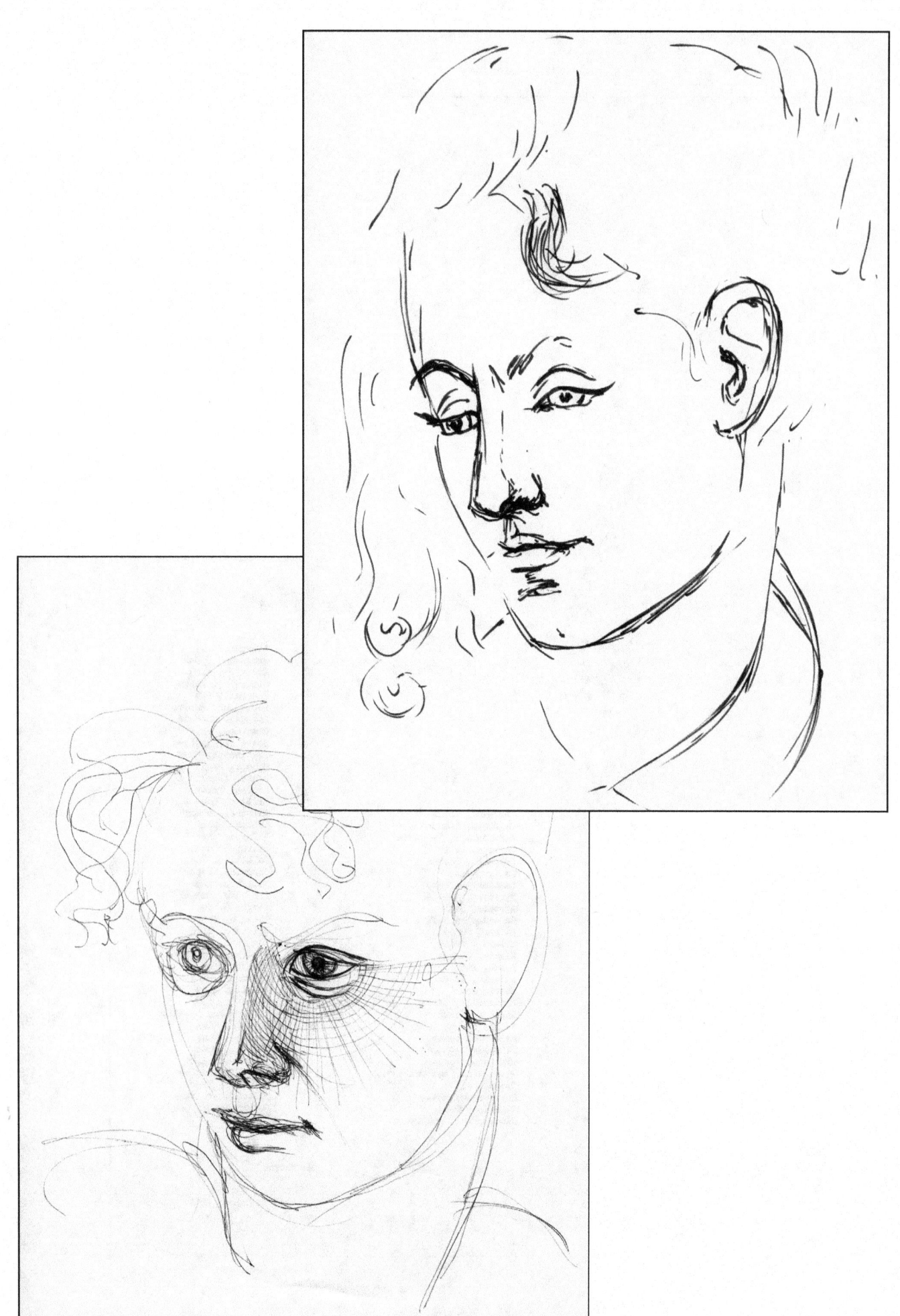

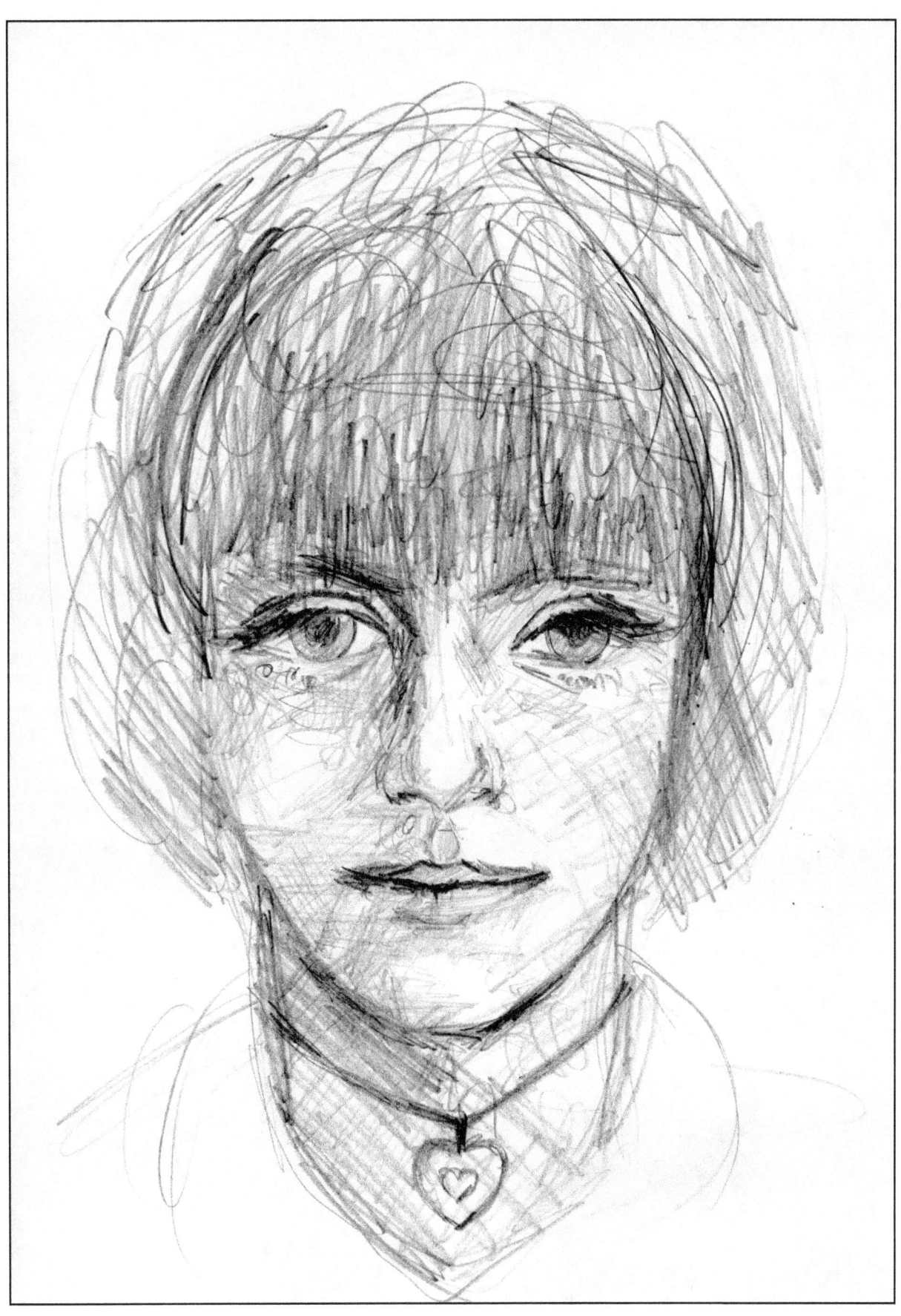

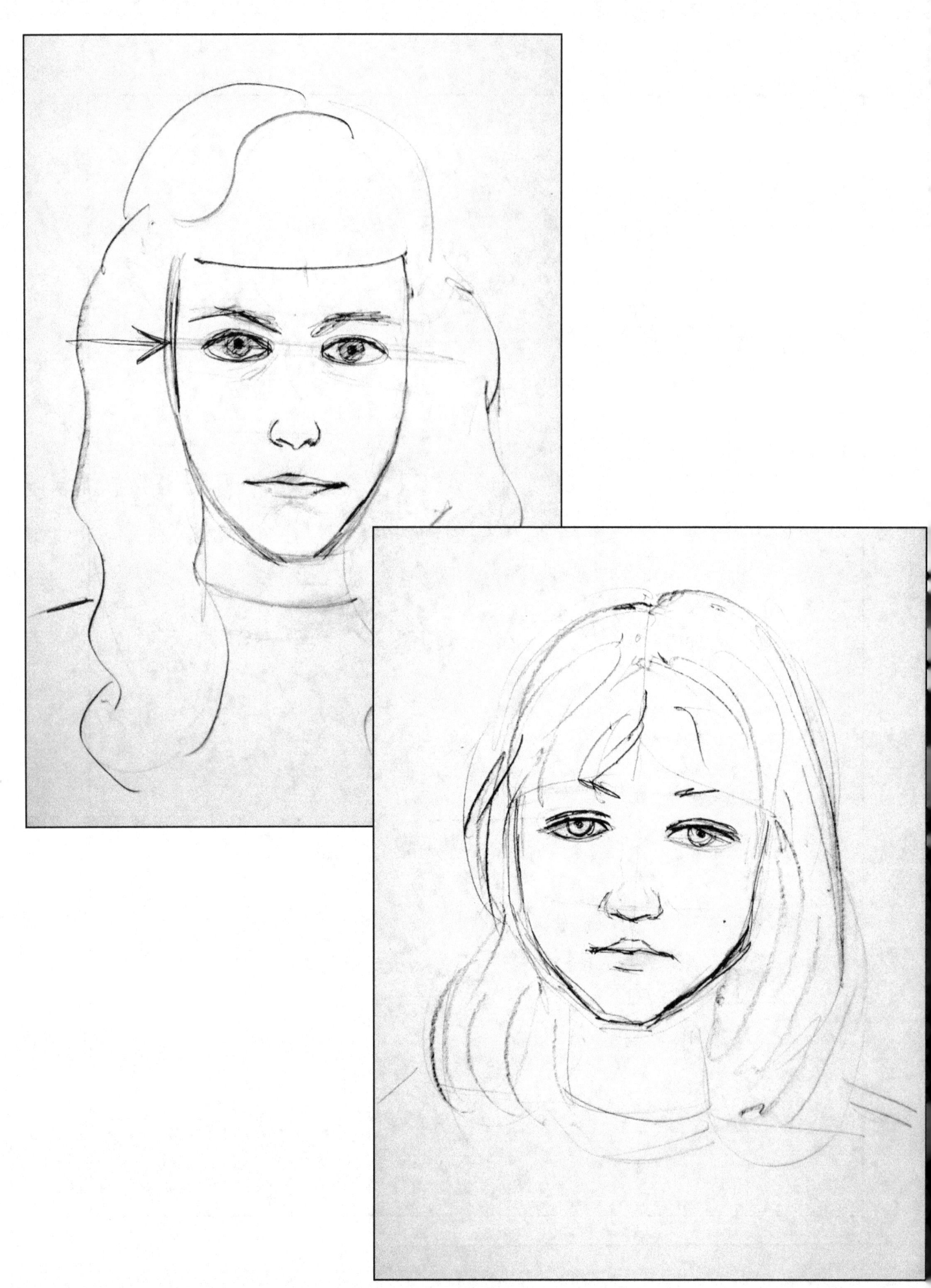

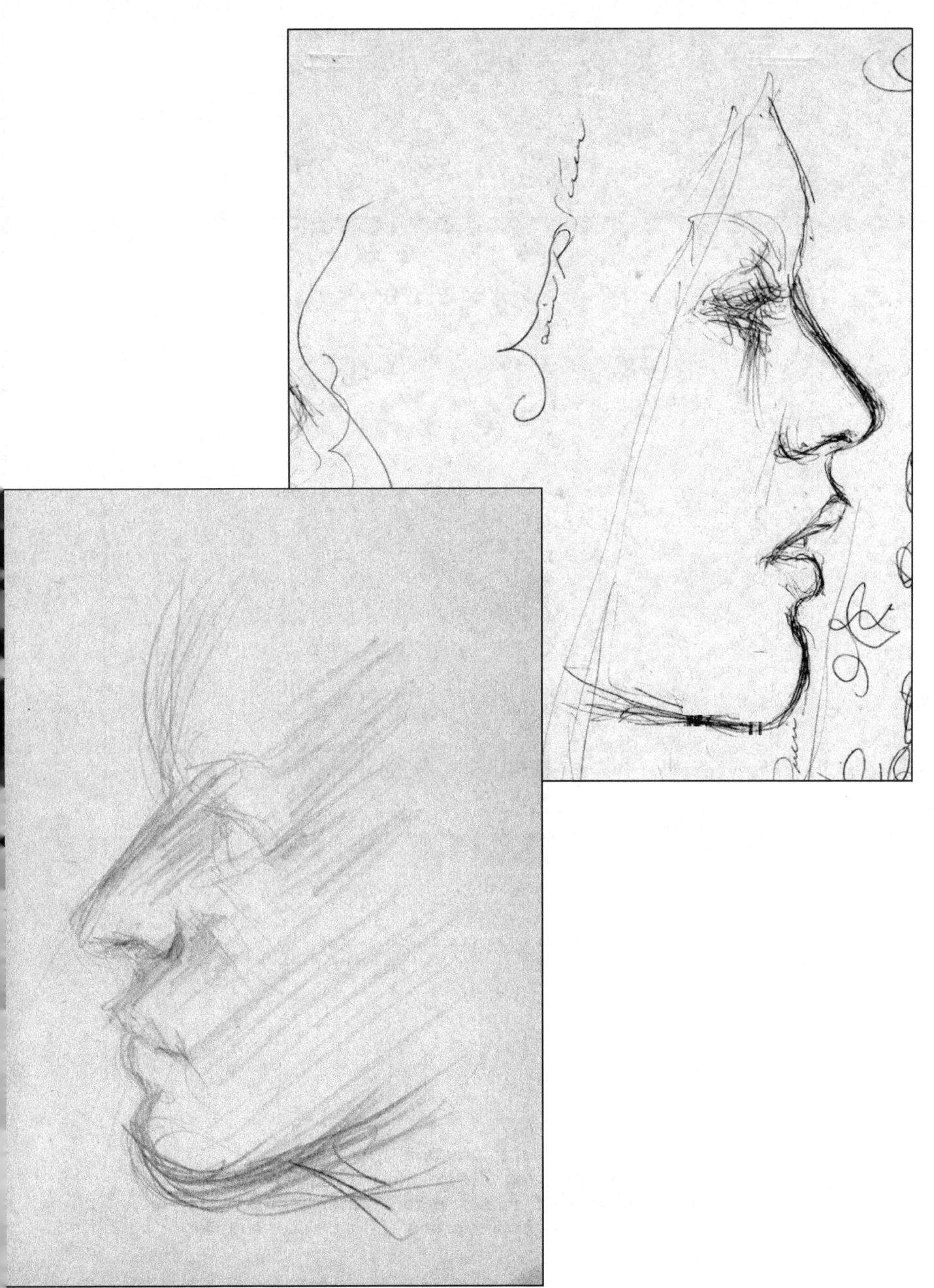

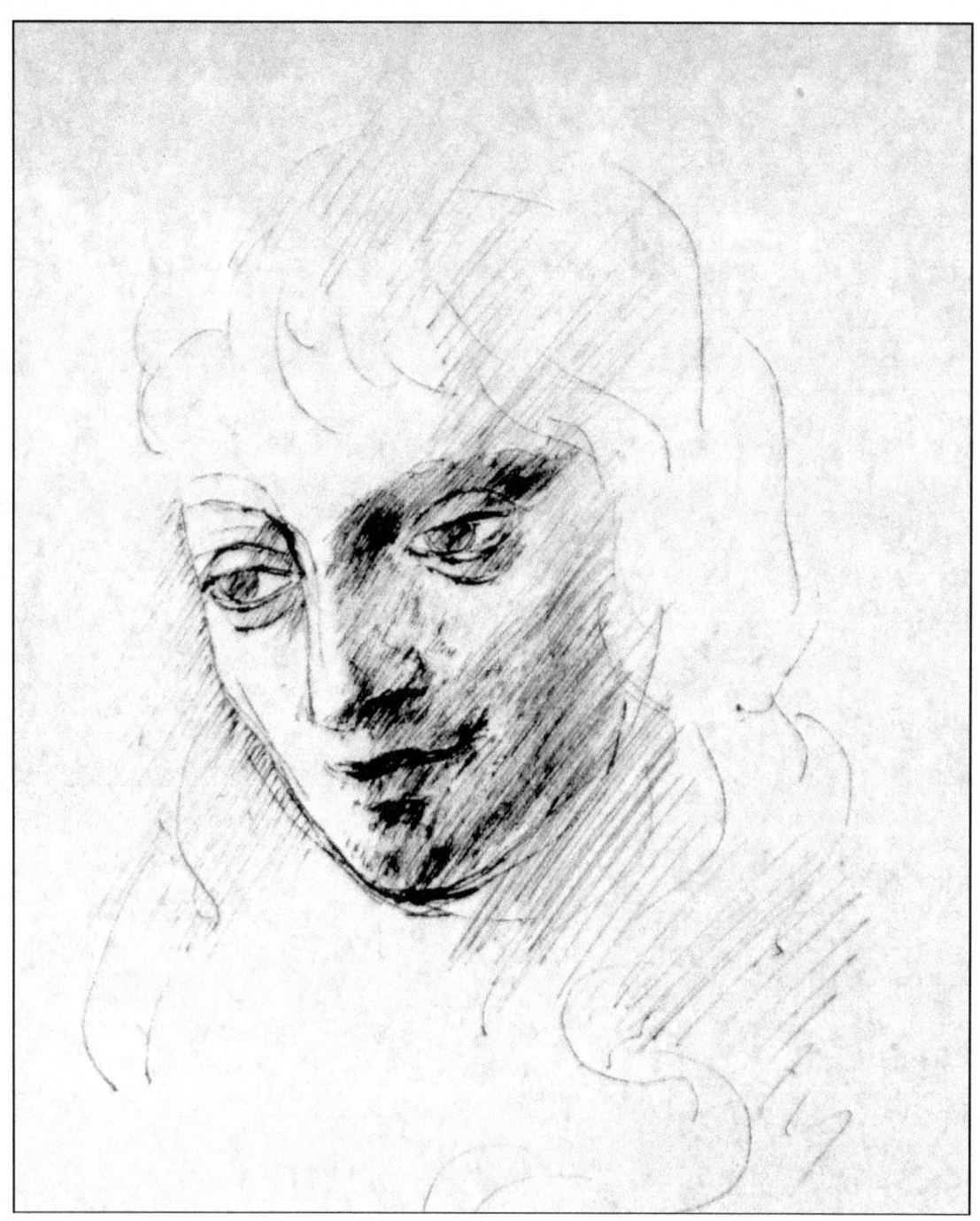

Dec. 28, 1971
- to experiment, not just to practice
- to get the whole of your picture, the big shape of what you are to draw, in a few lines, before starting with details or determining the right proportion of the smaller shapes

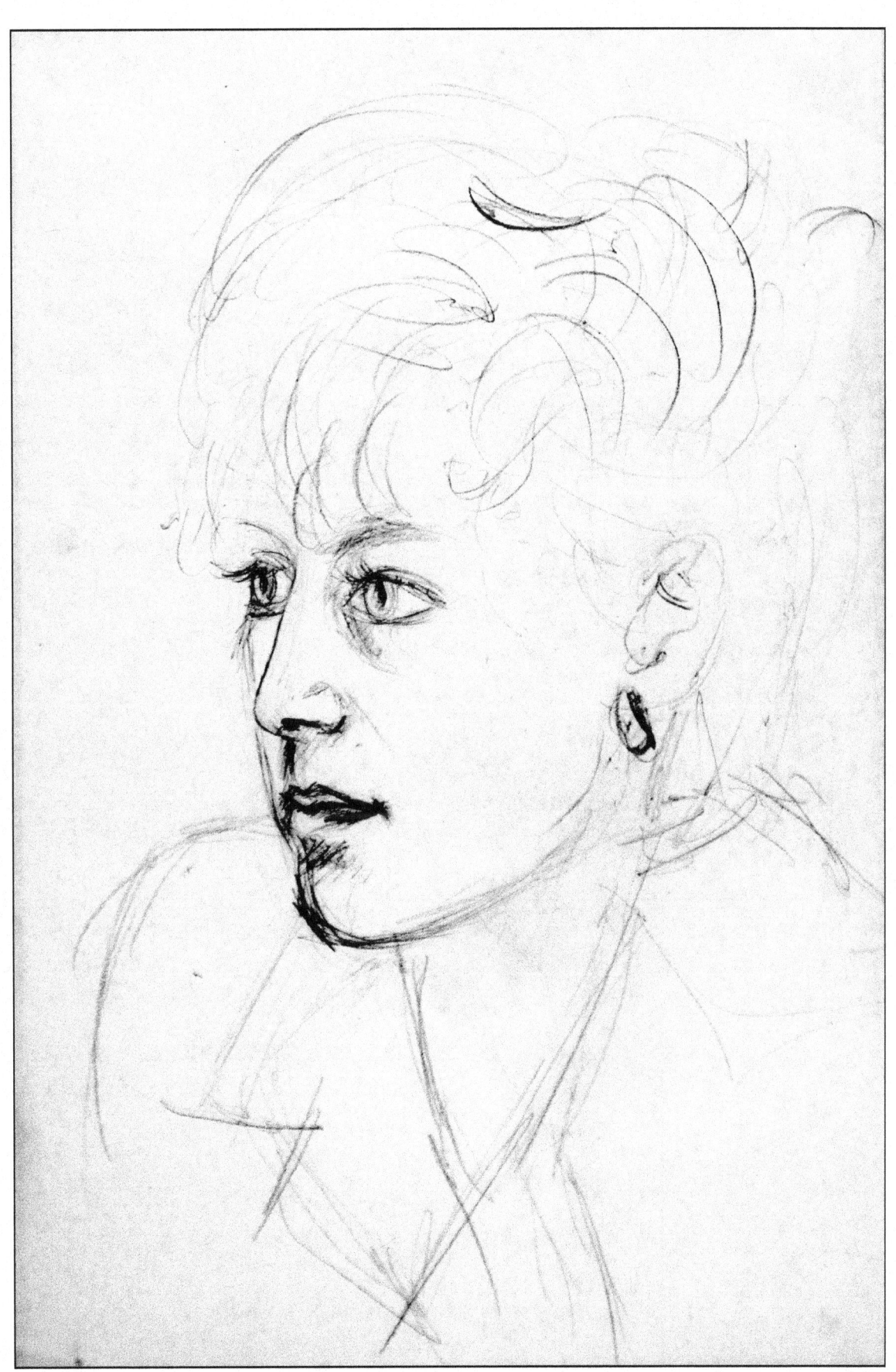

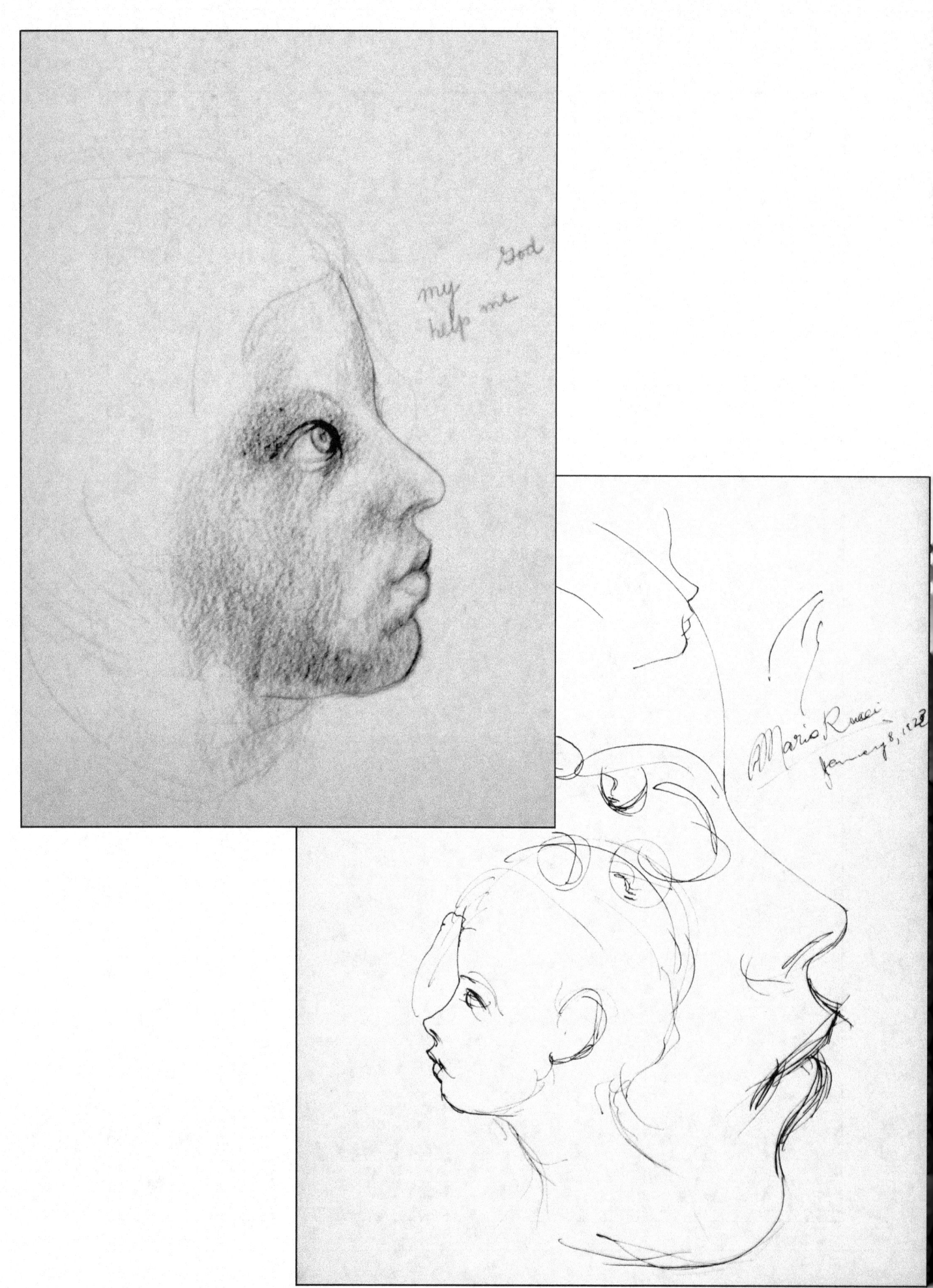

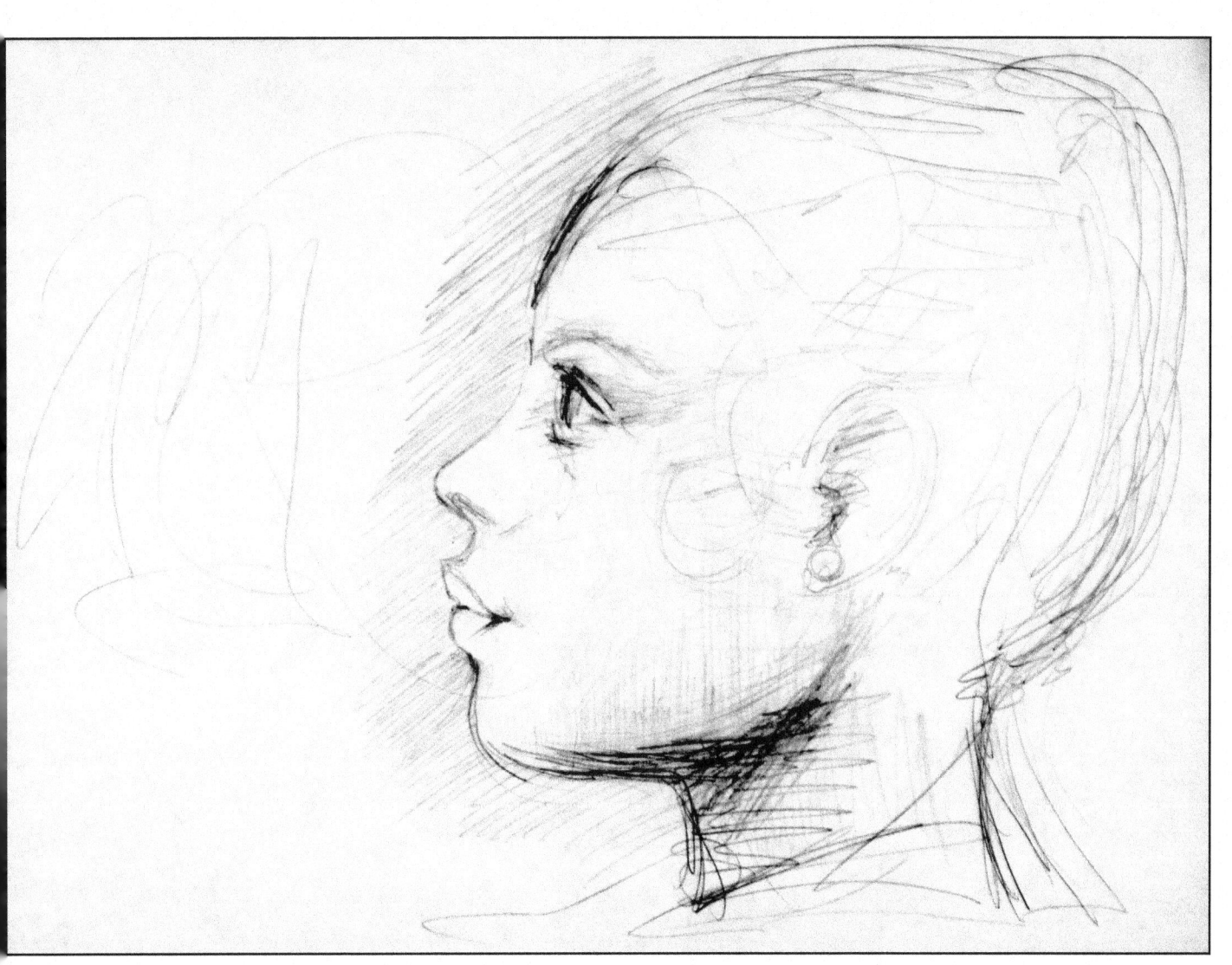

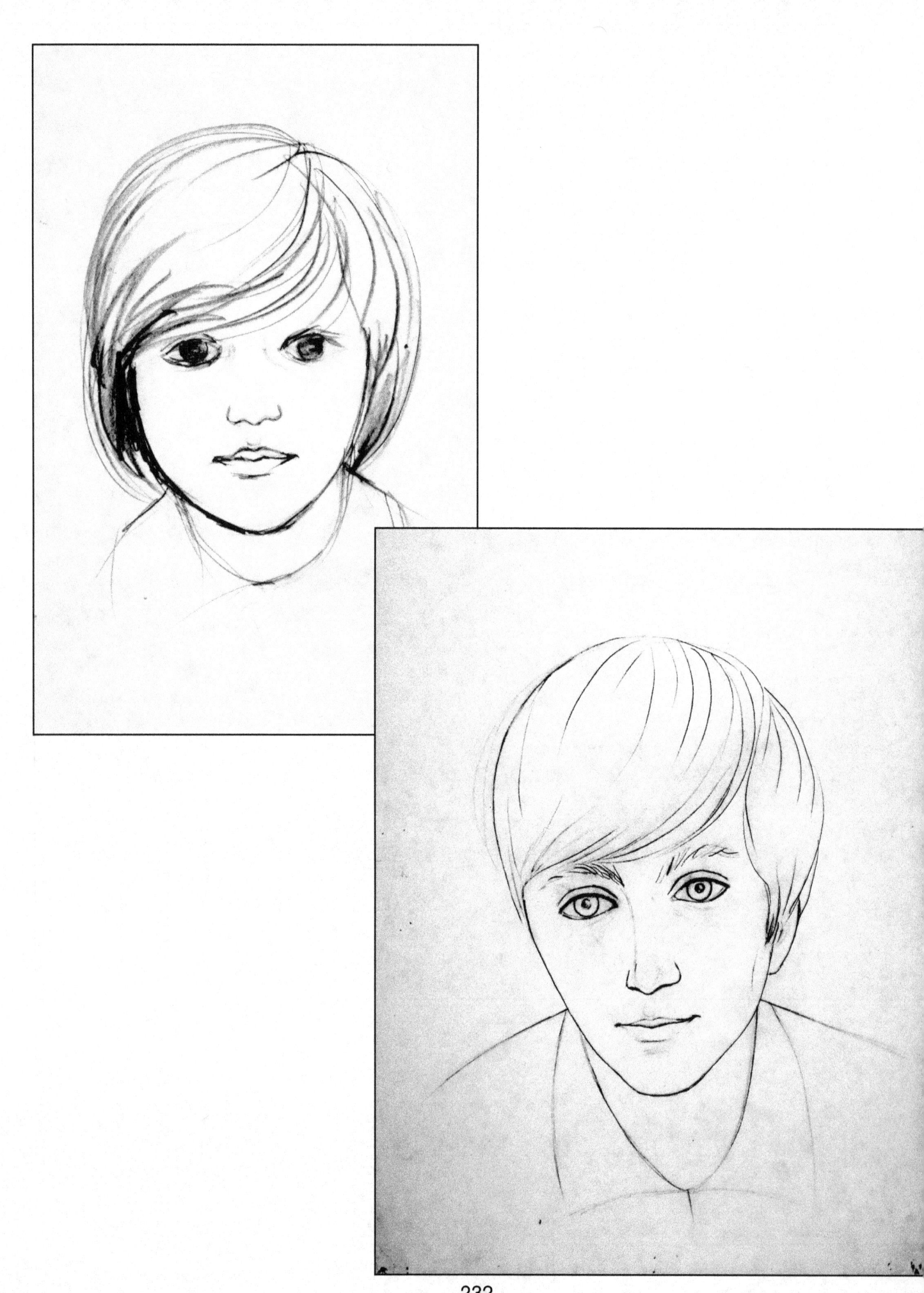

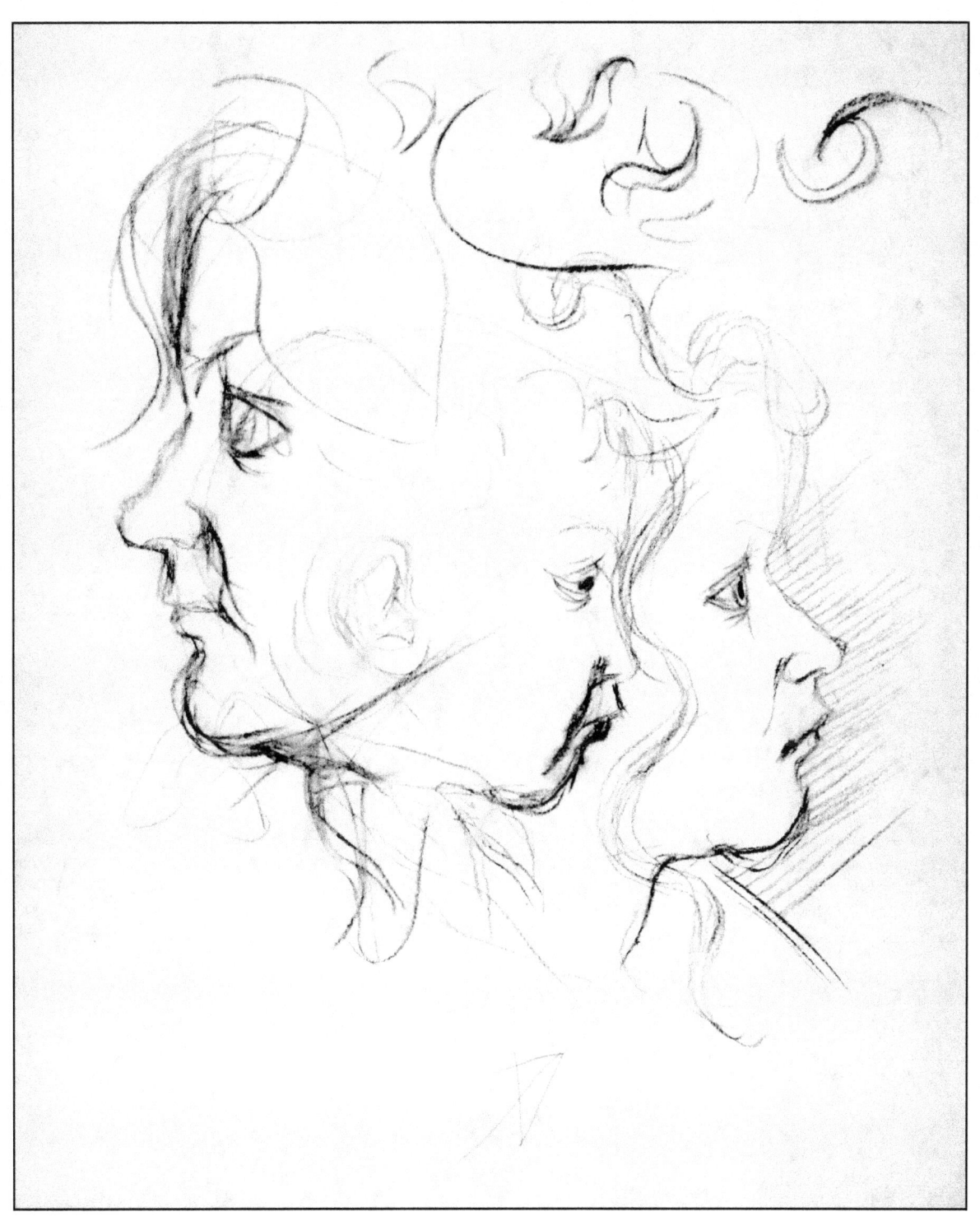

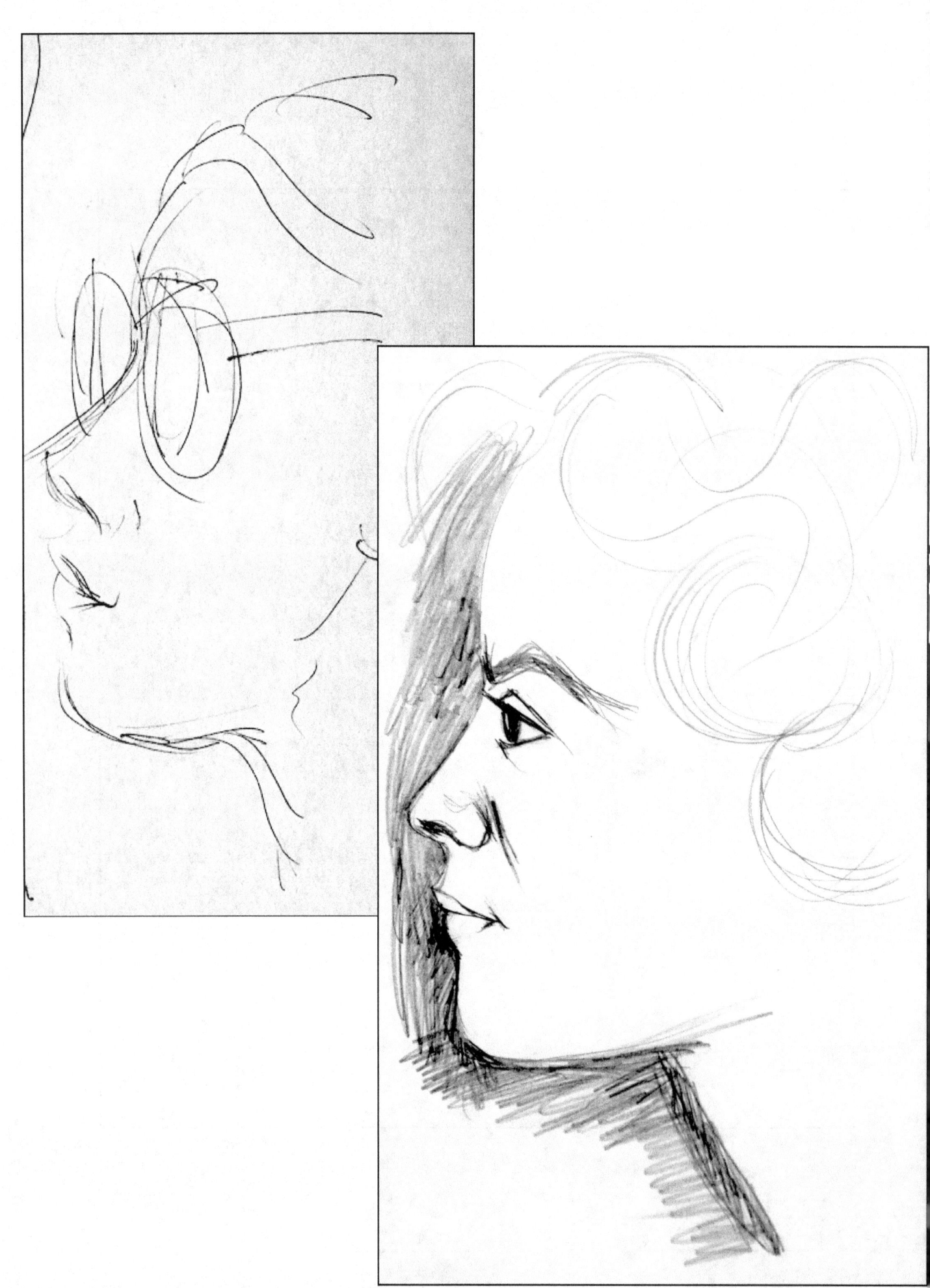

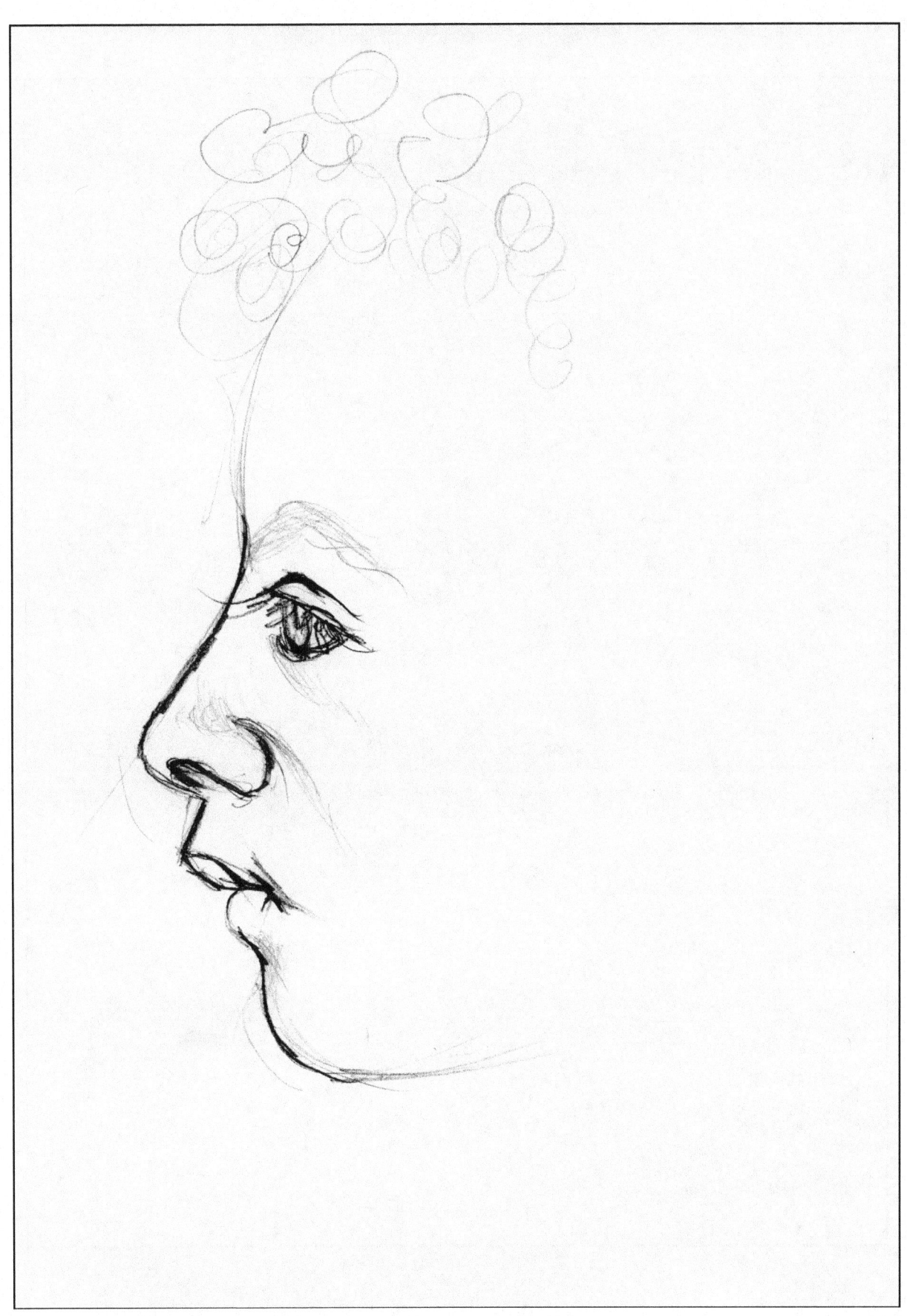

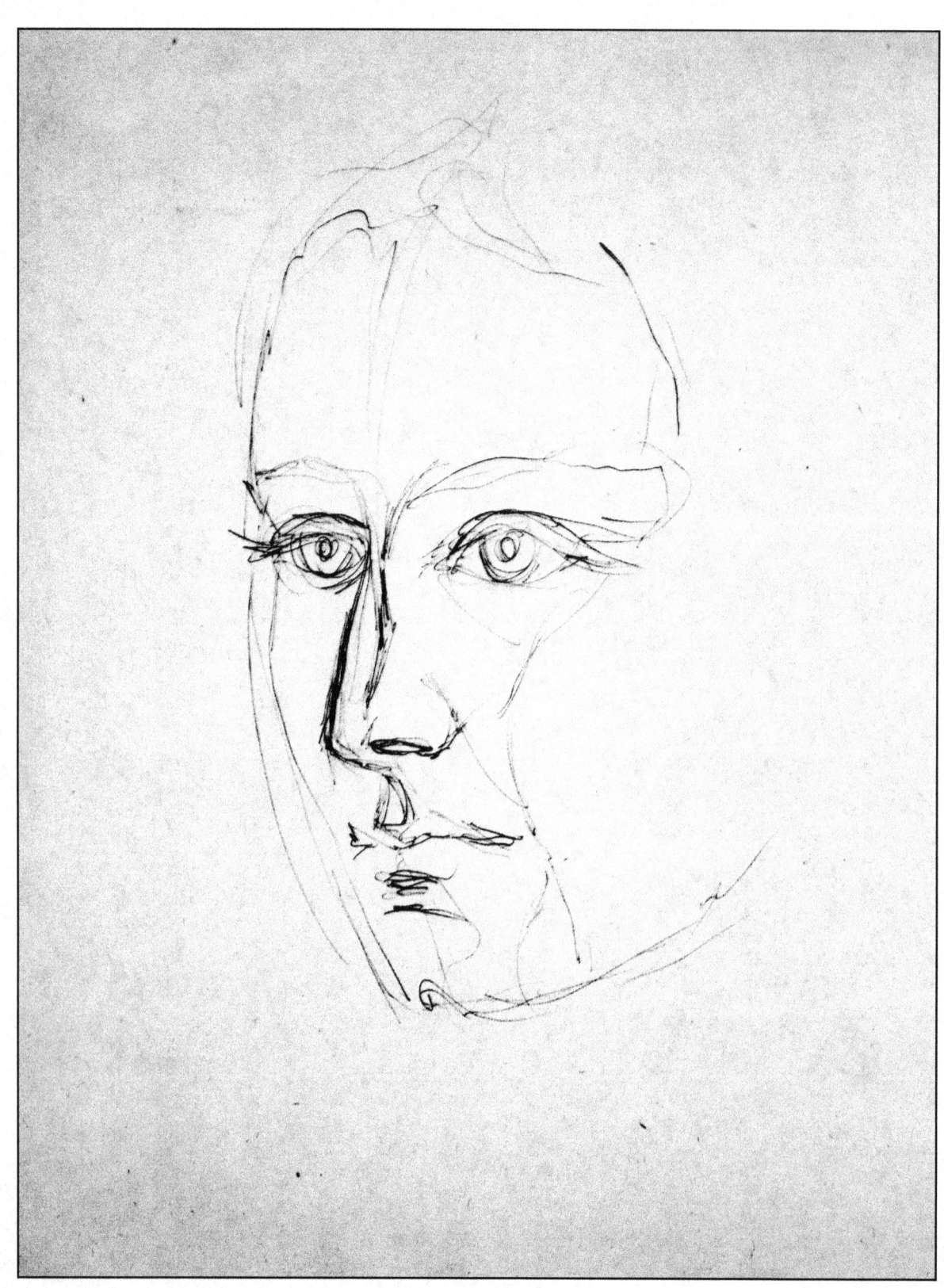

Nib Pen Drawing

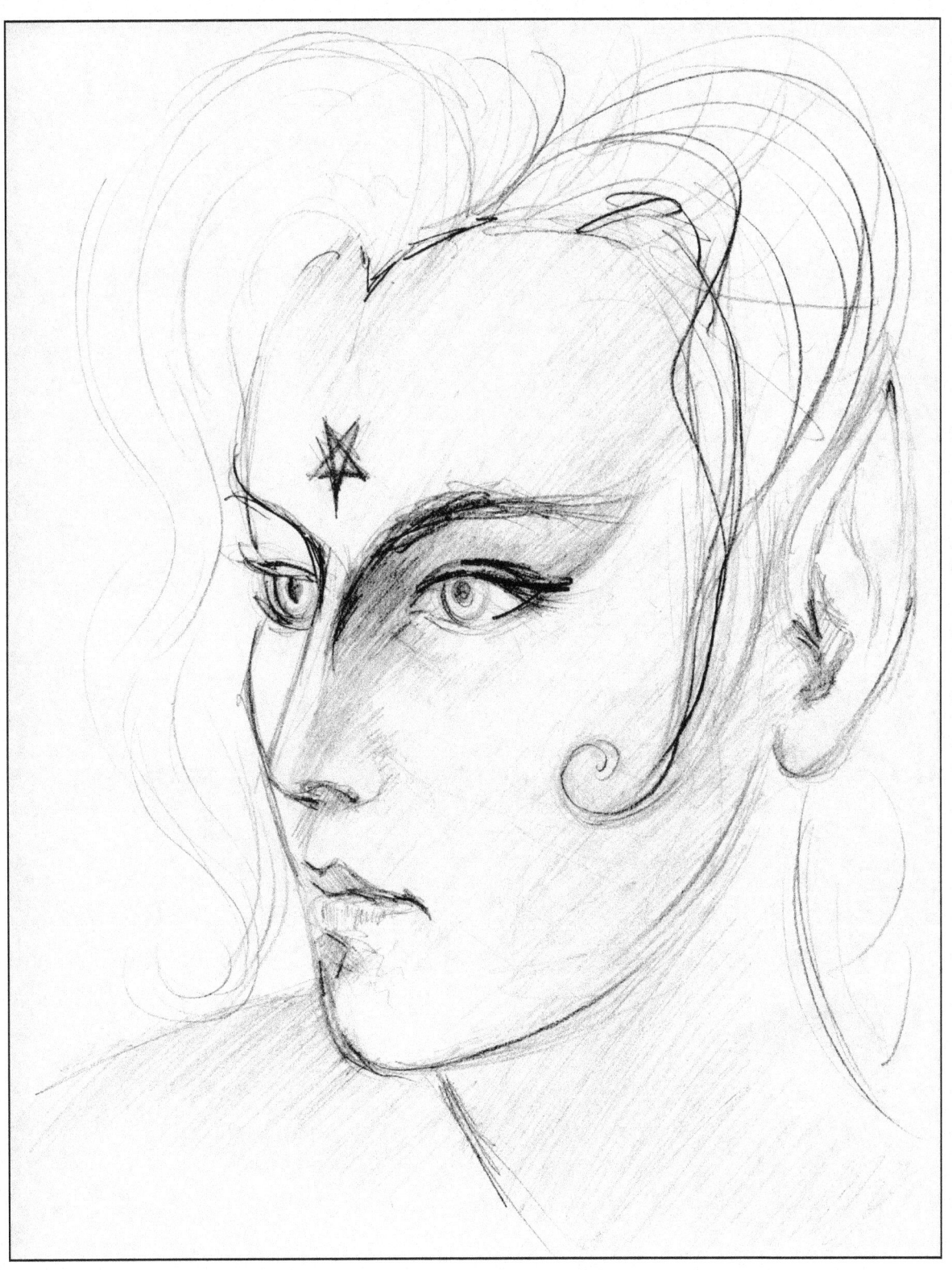

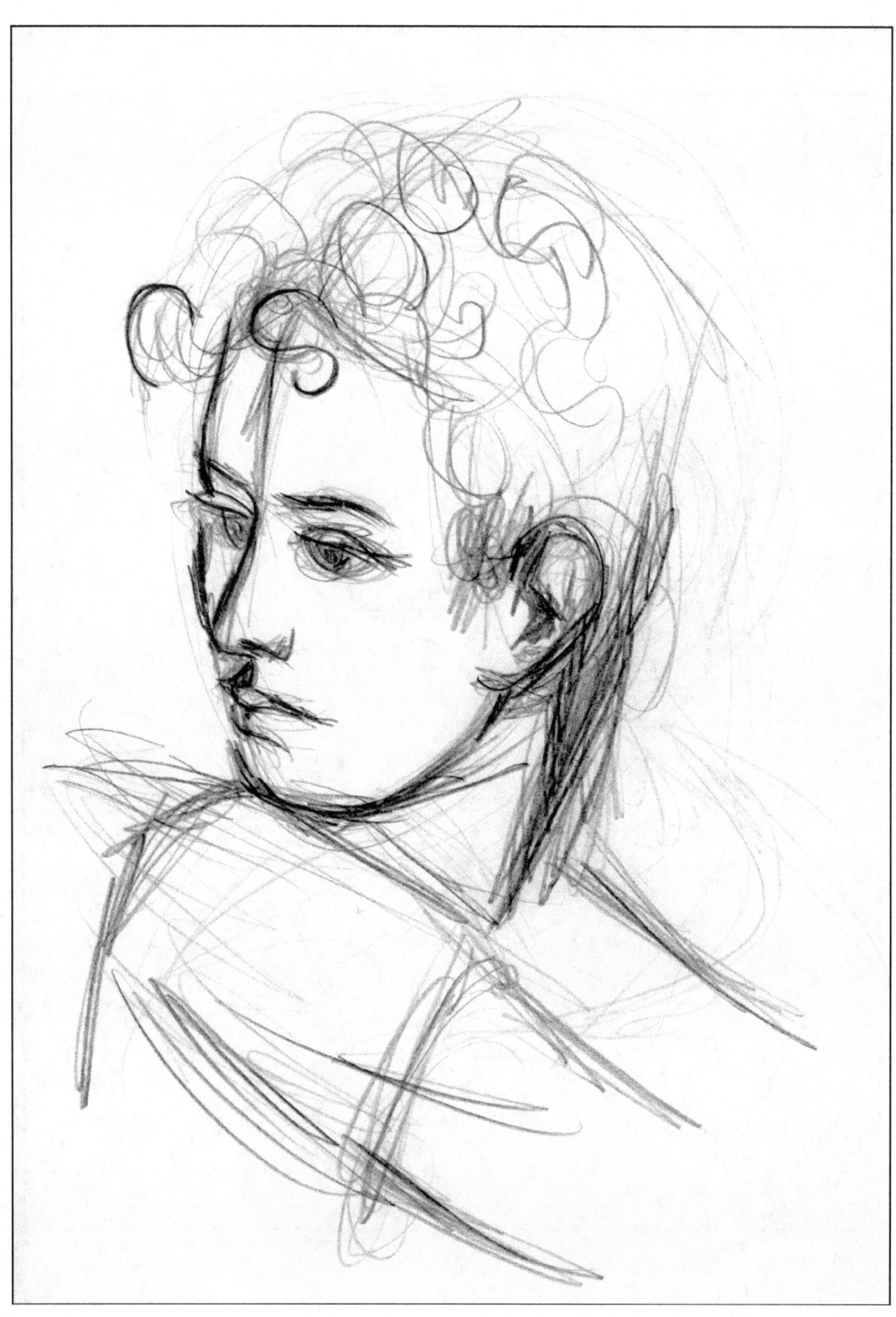

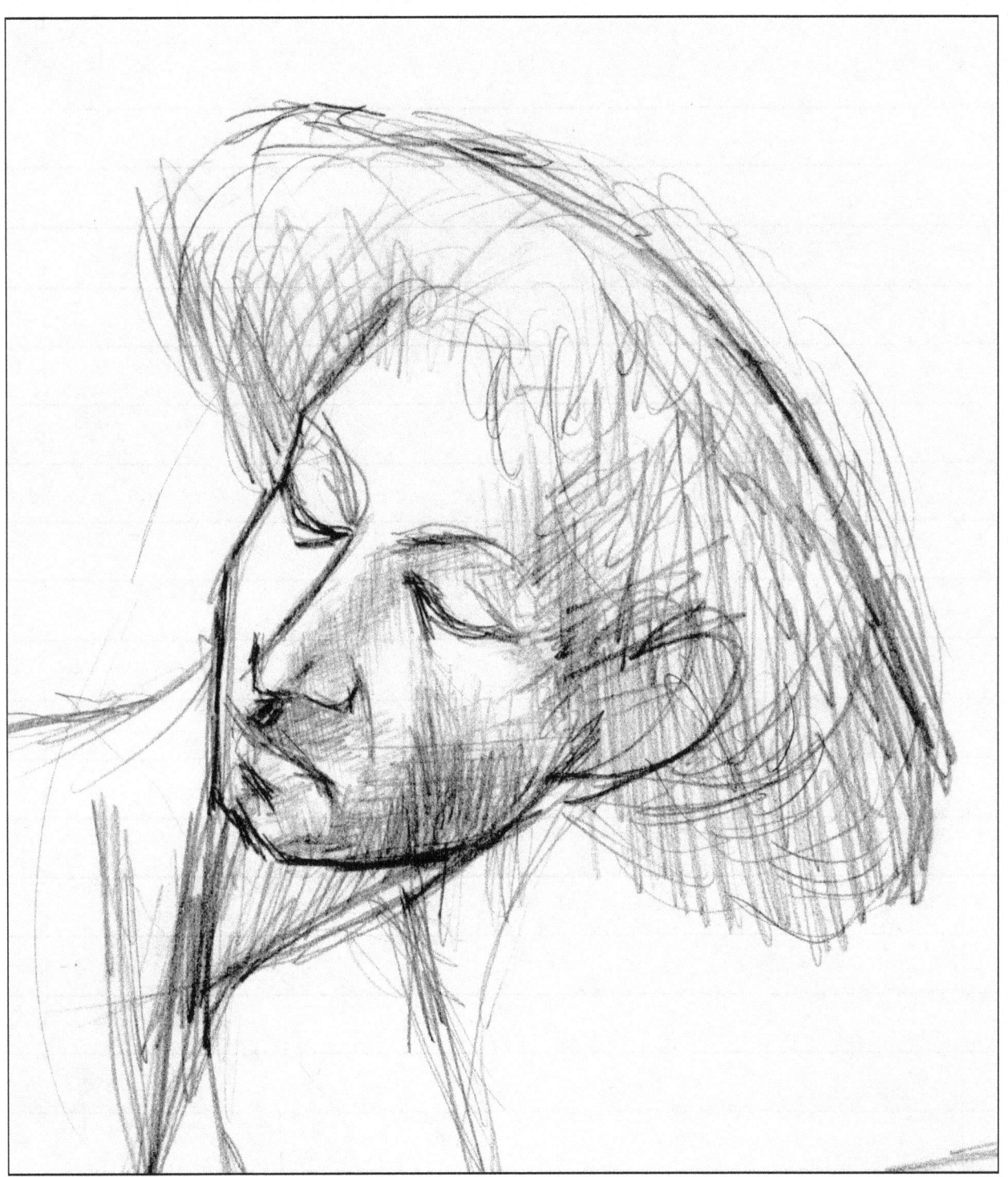

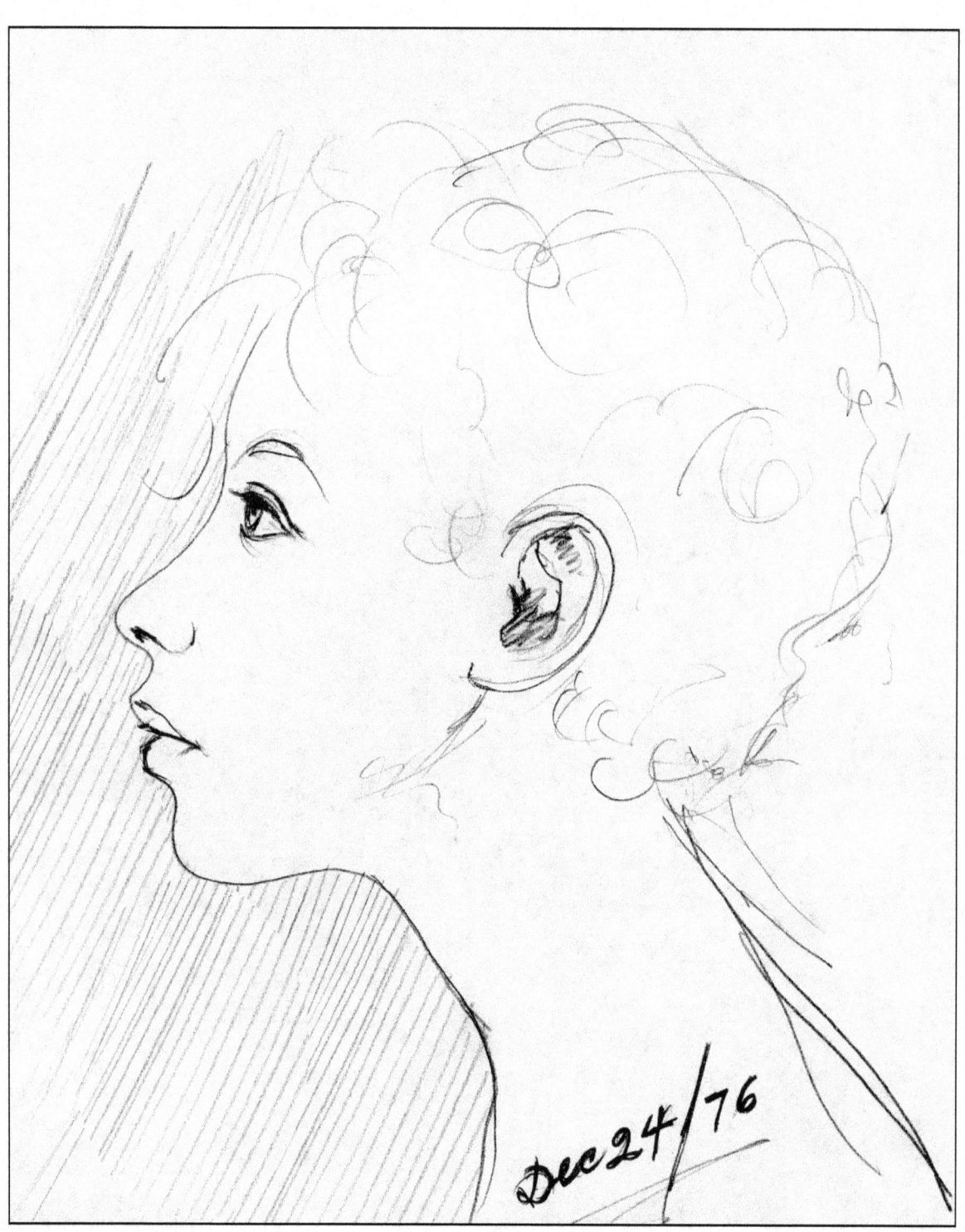

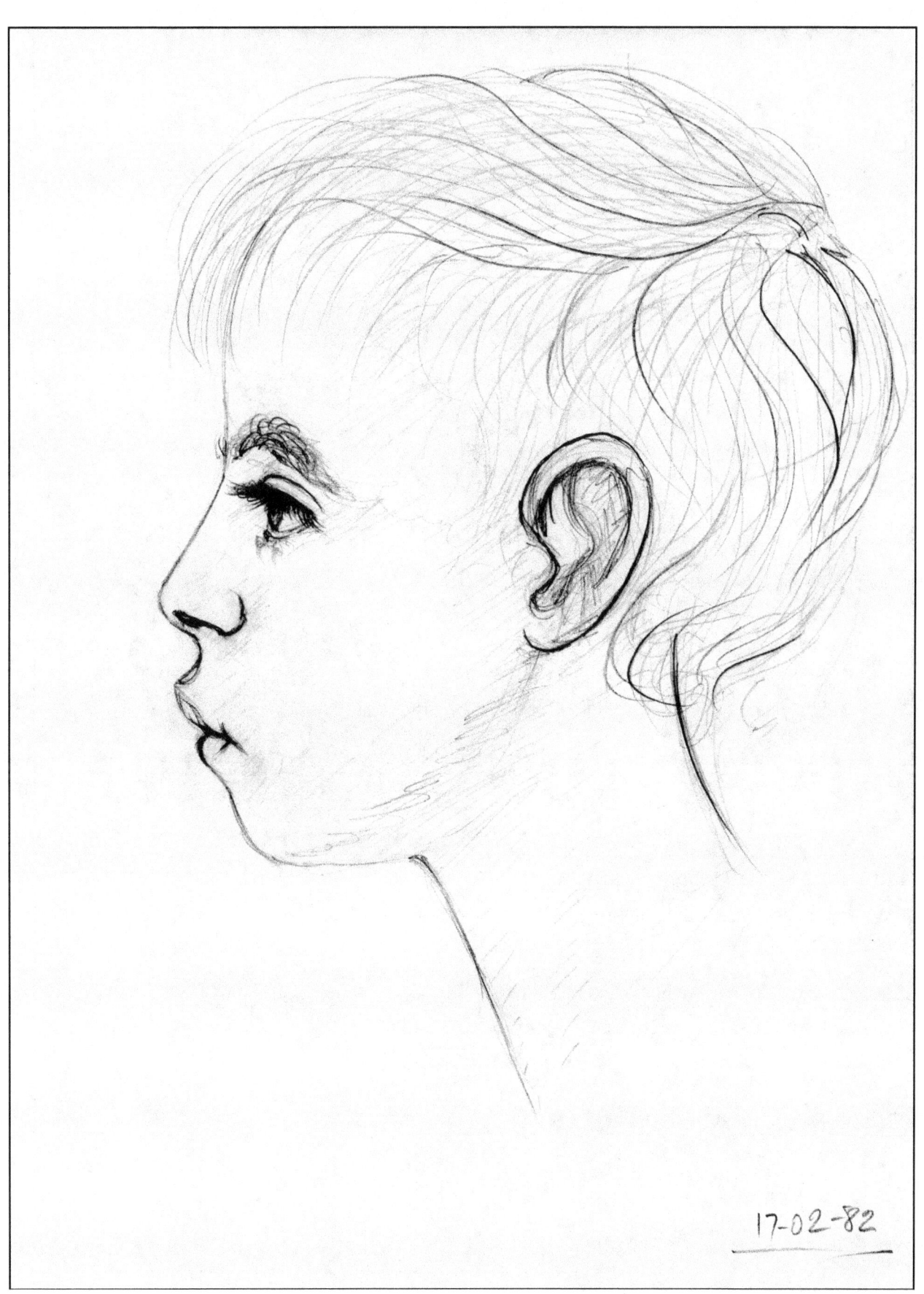

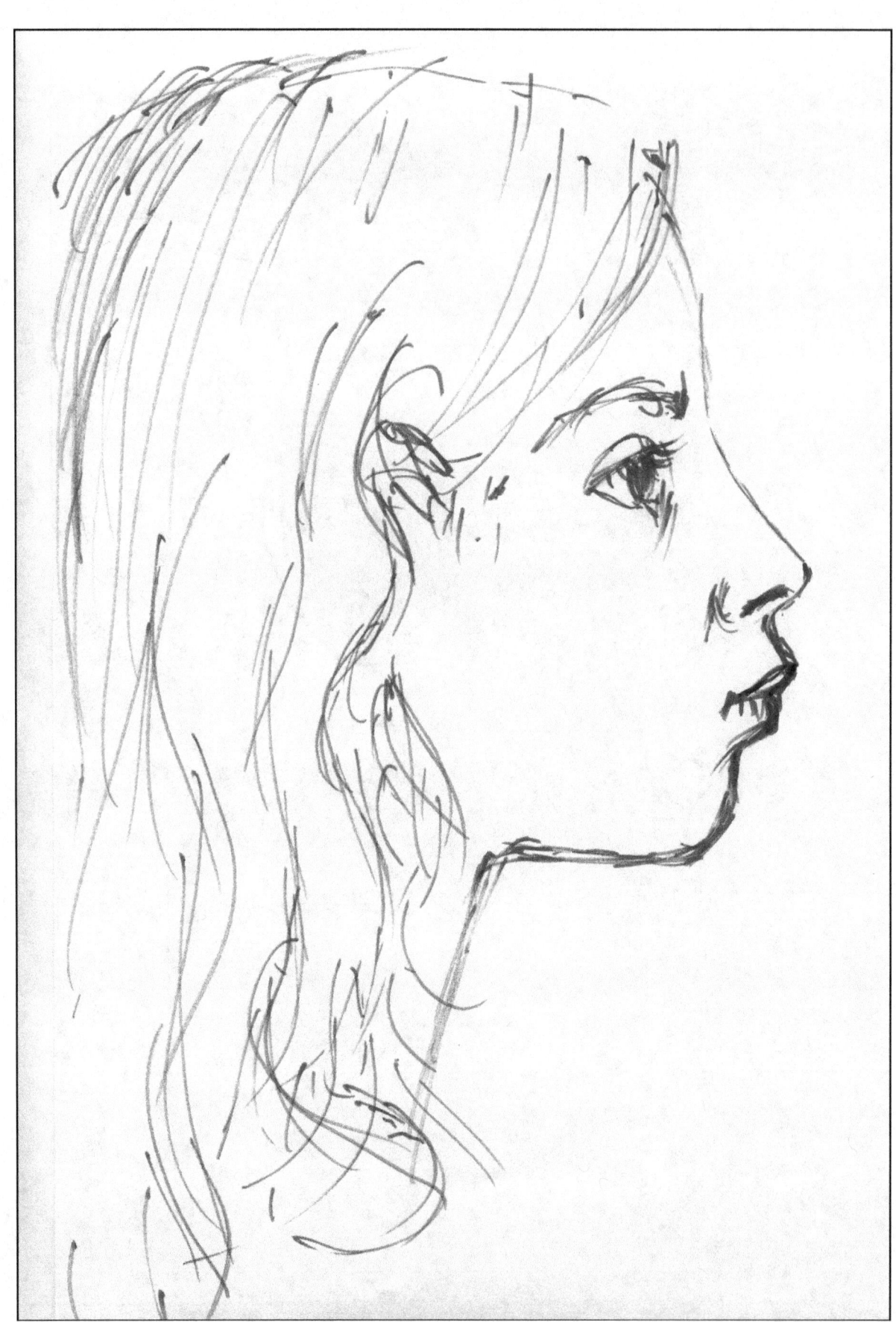

Ballpoint Pen

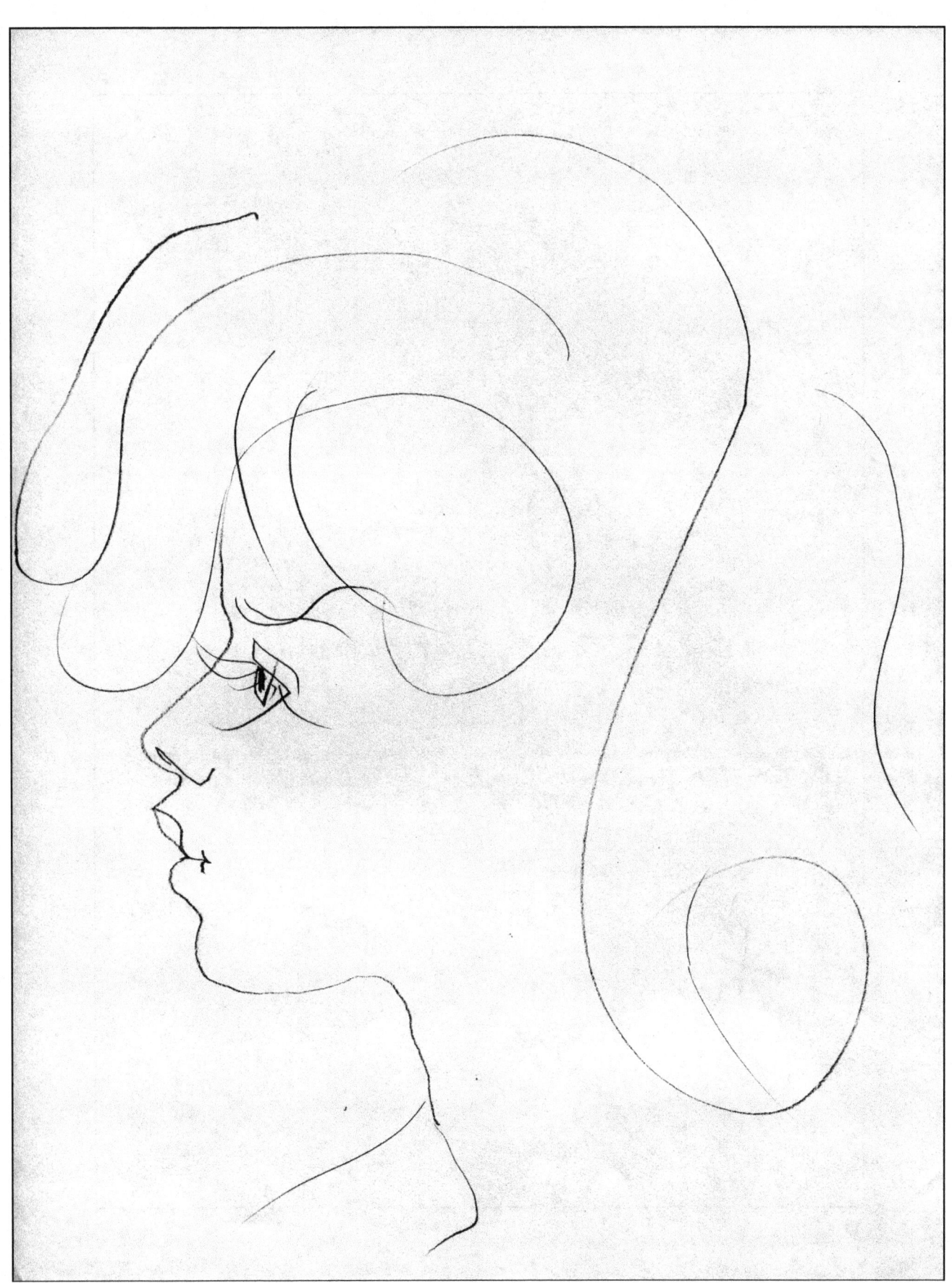

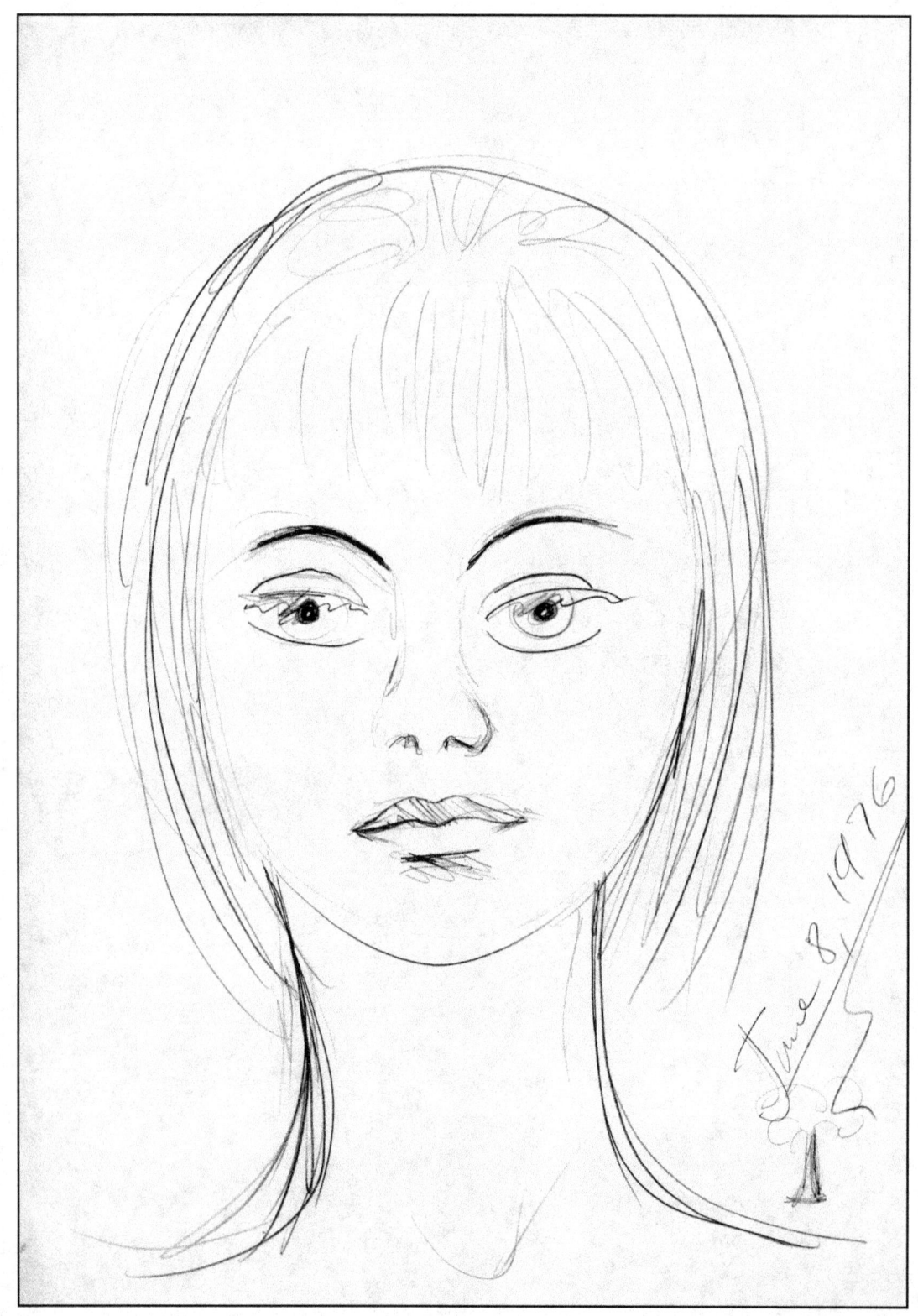

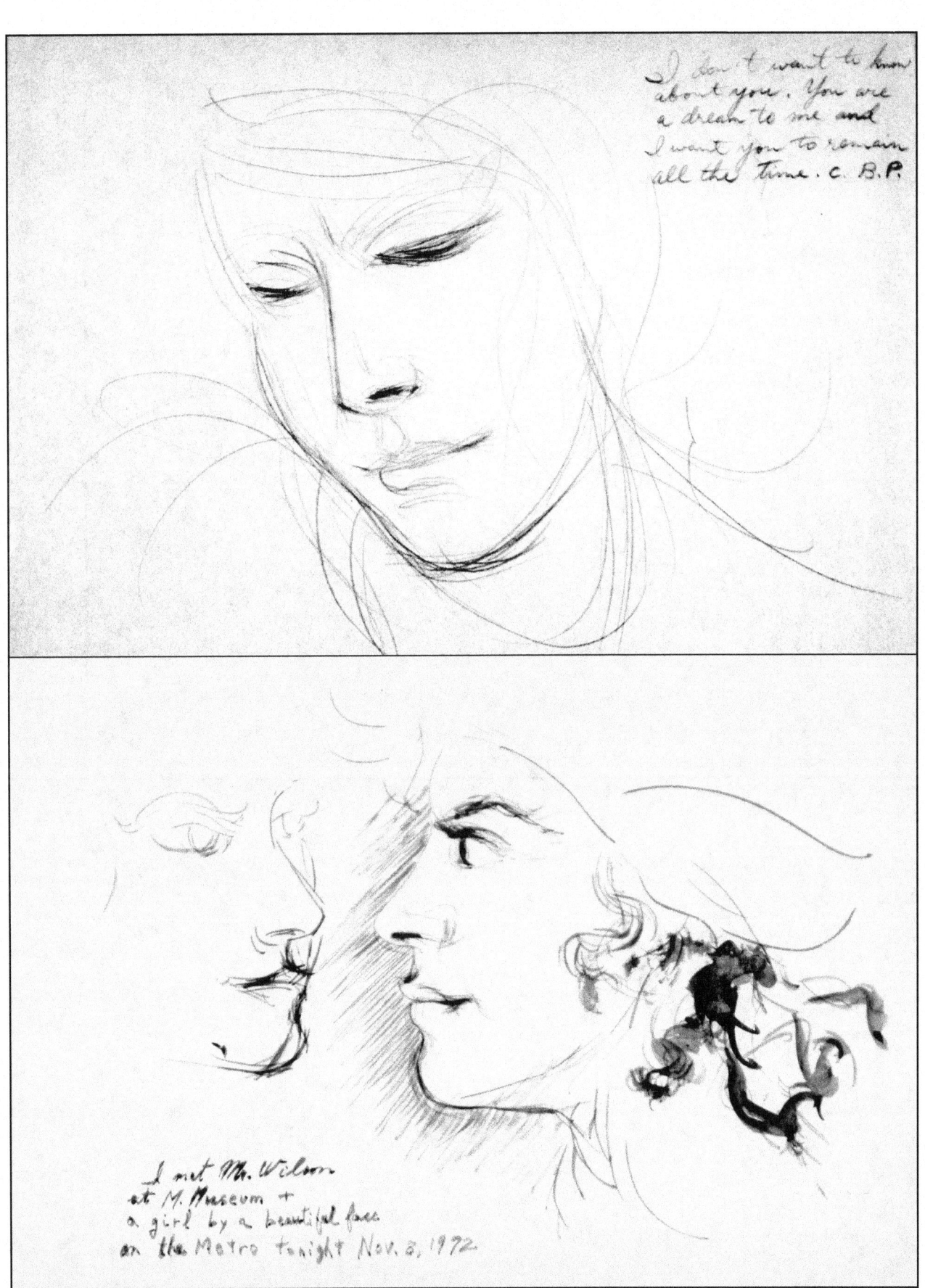

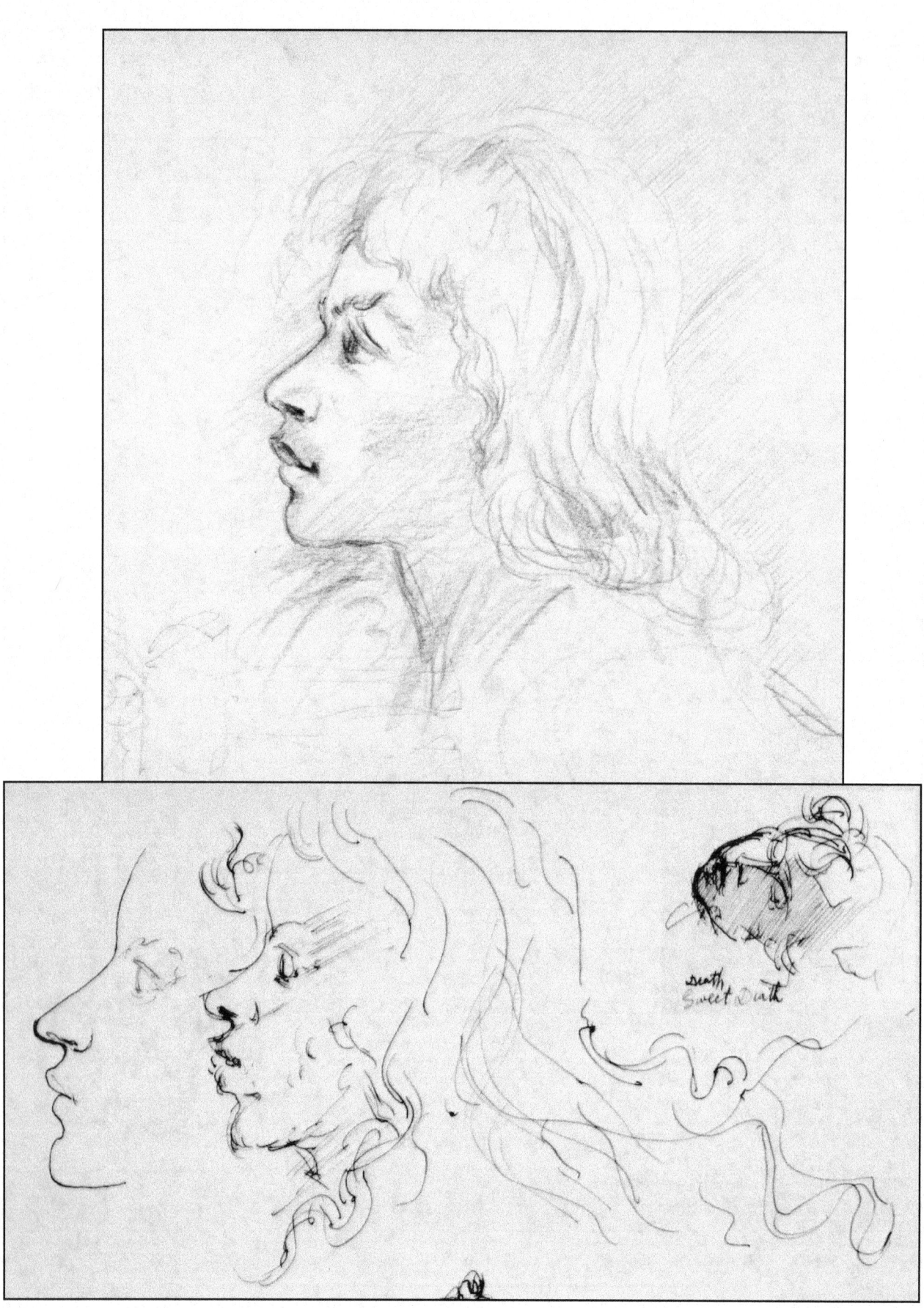

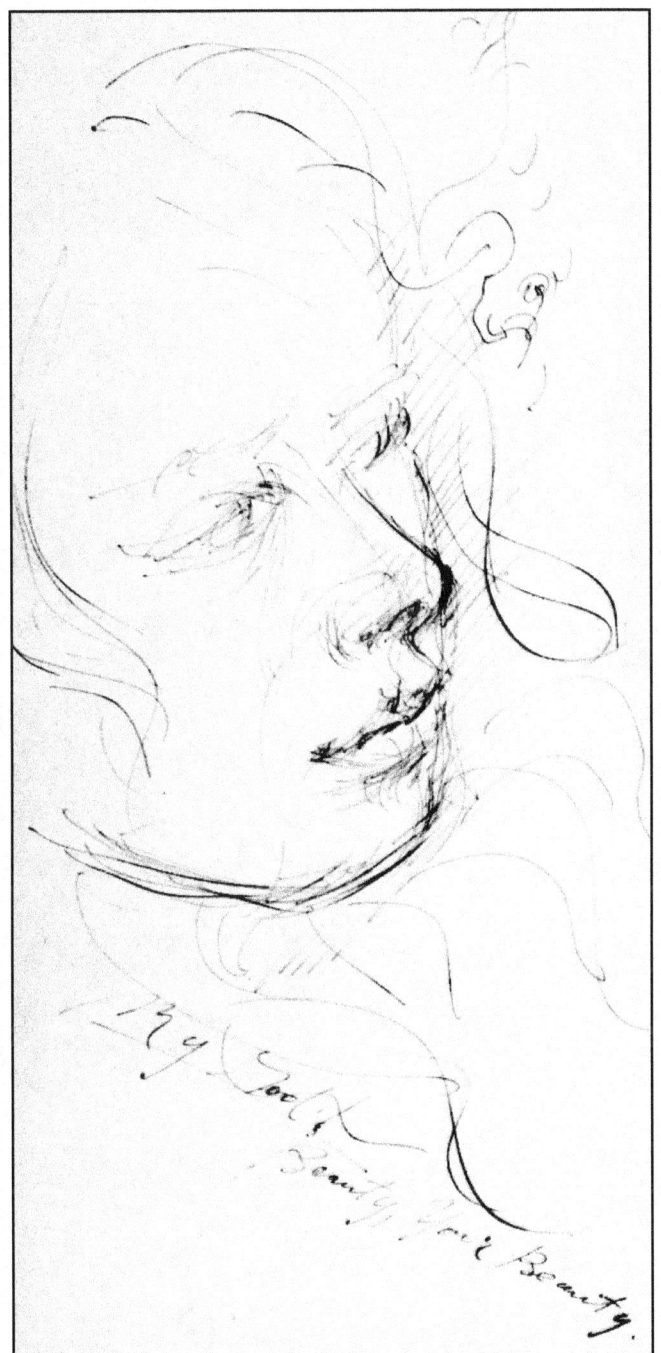
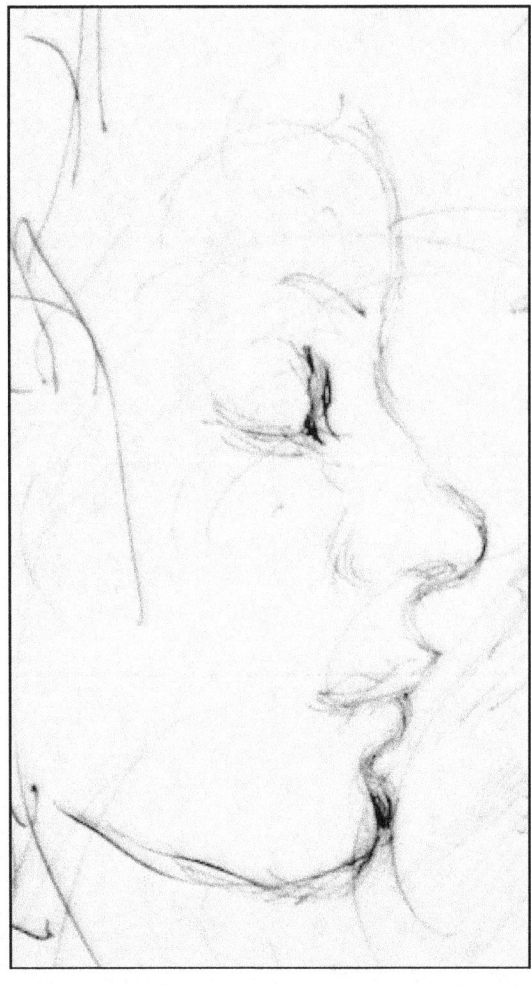

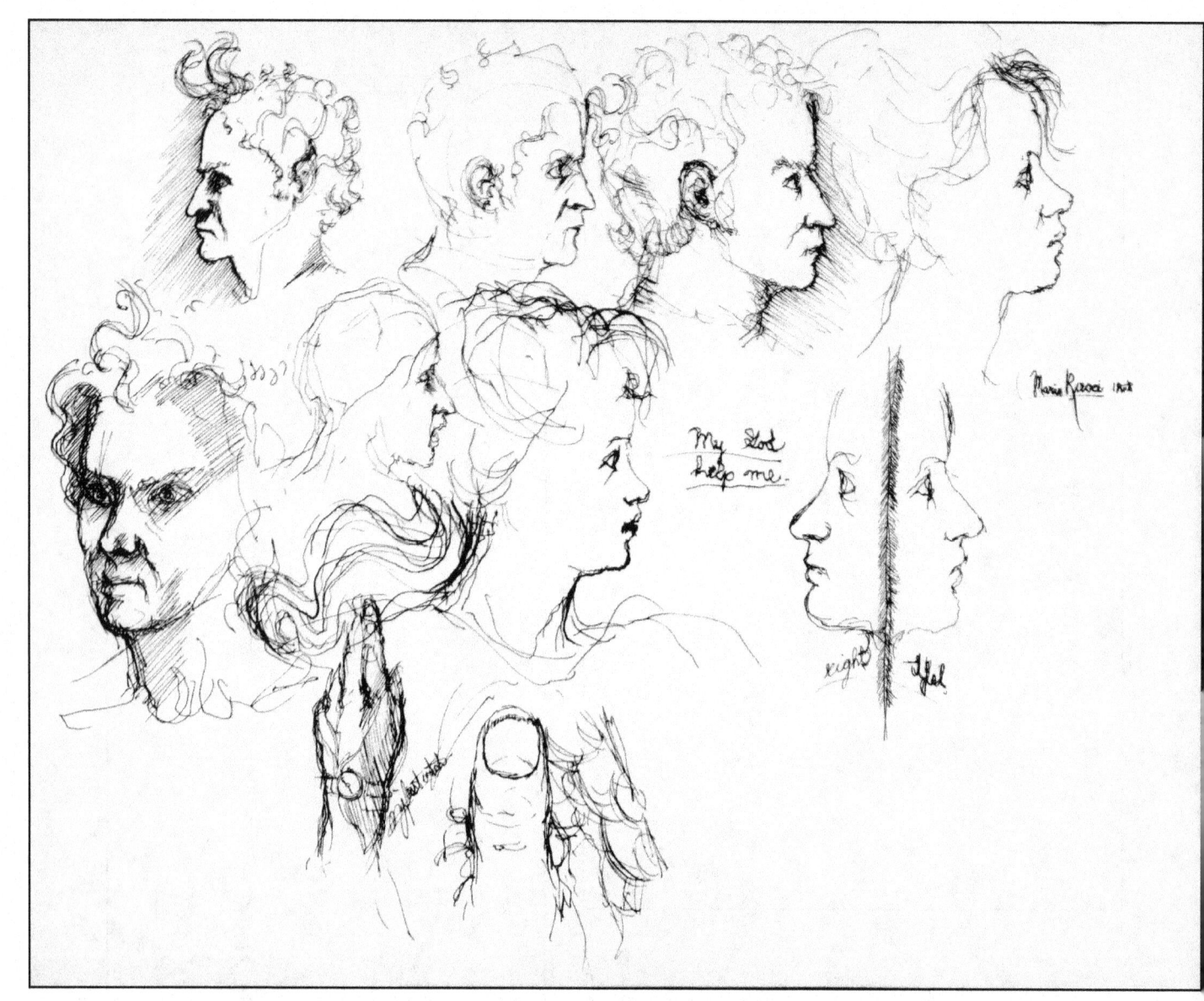

Nib Pen Drawings

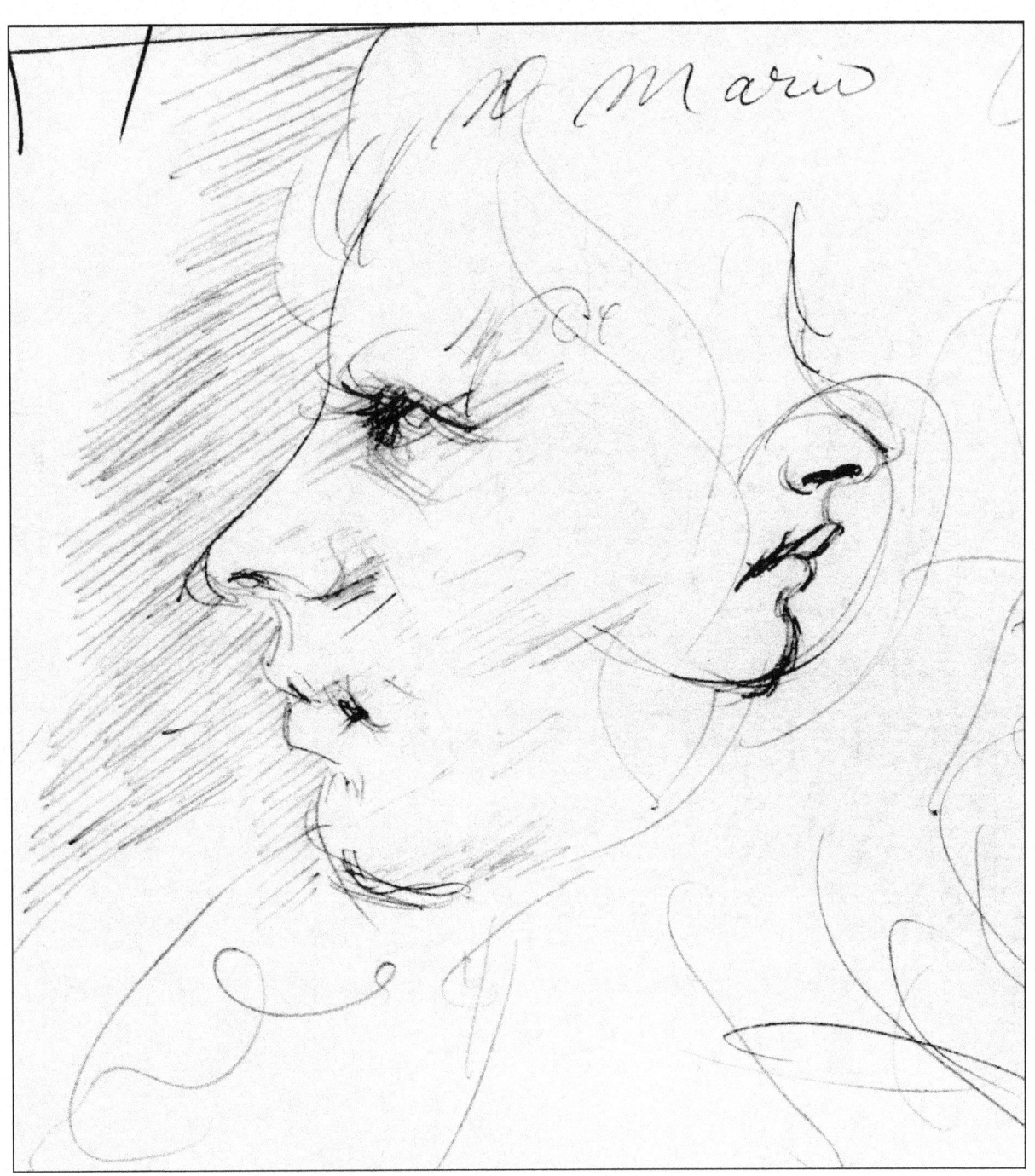

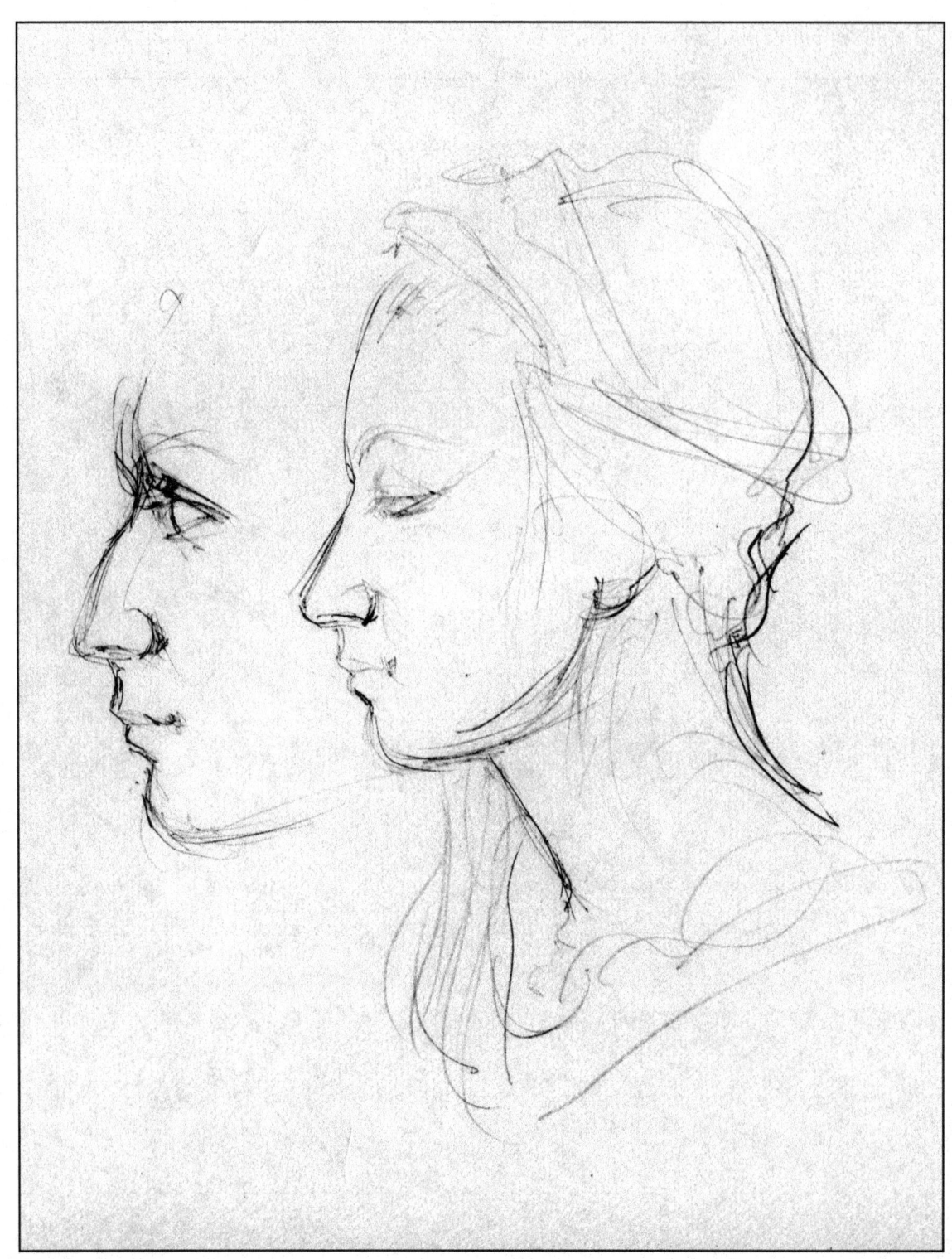

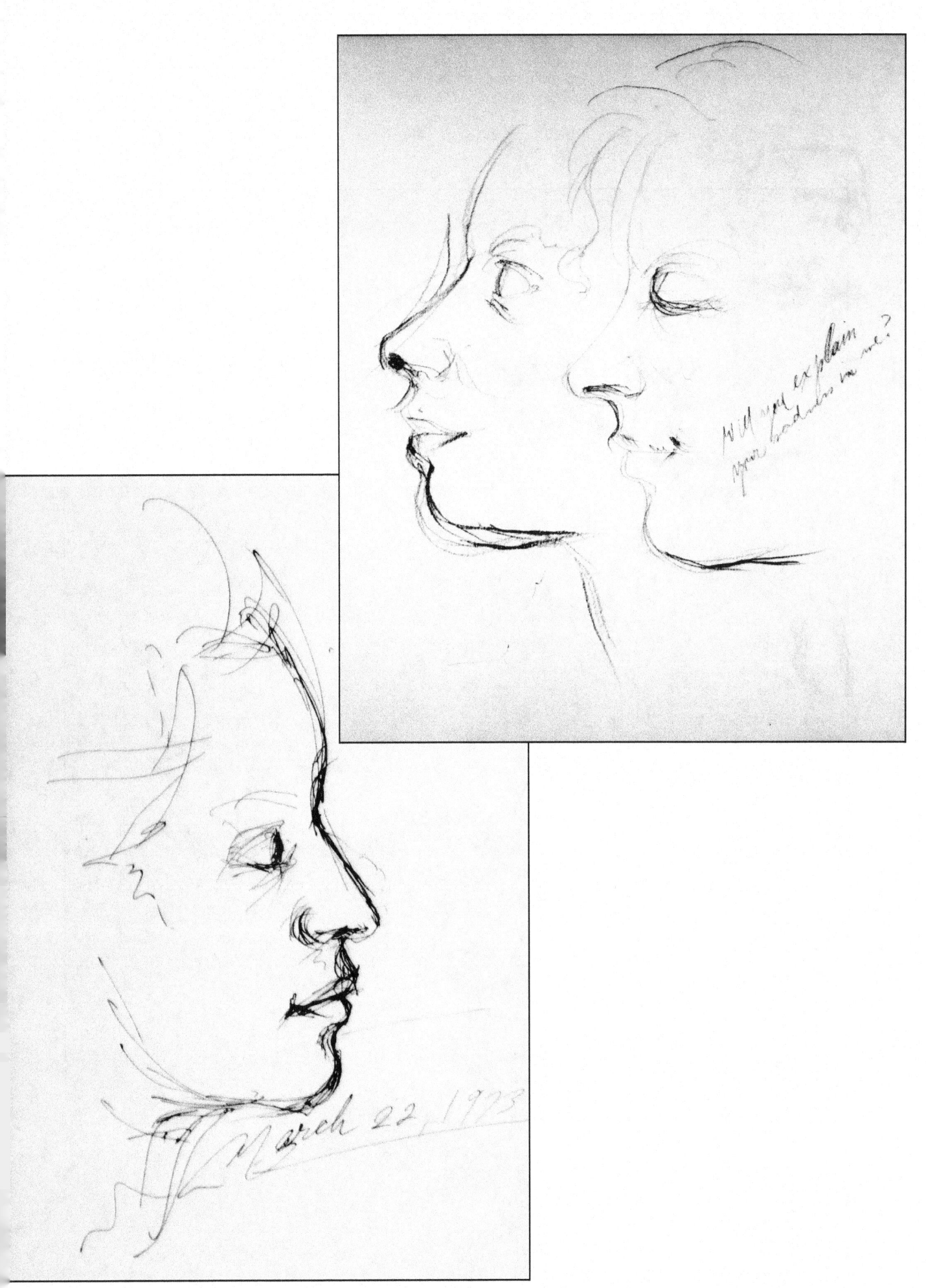

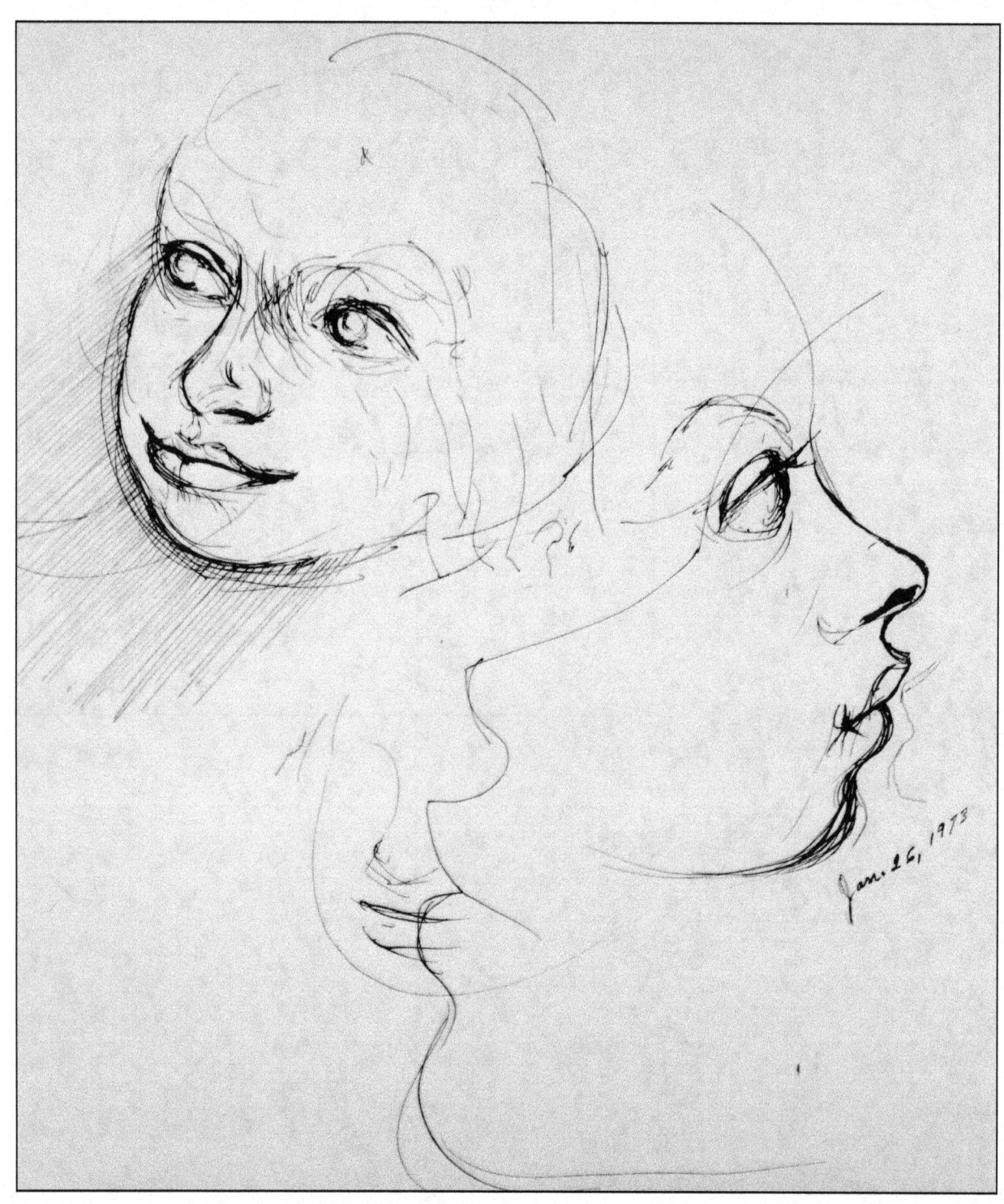

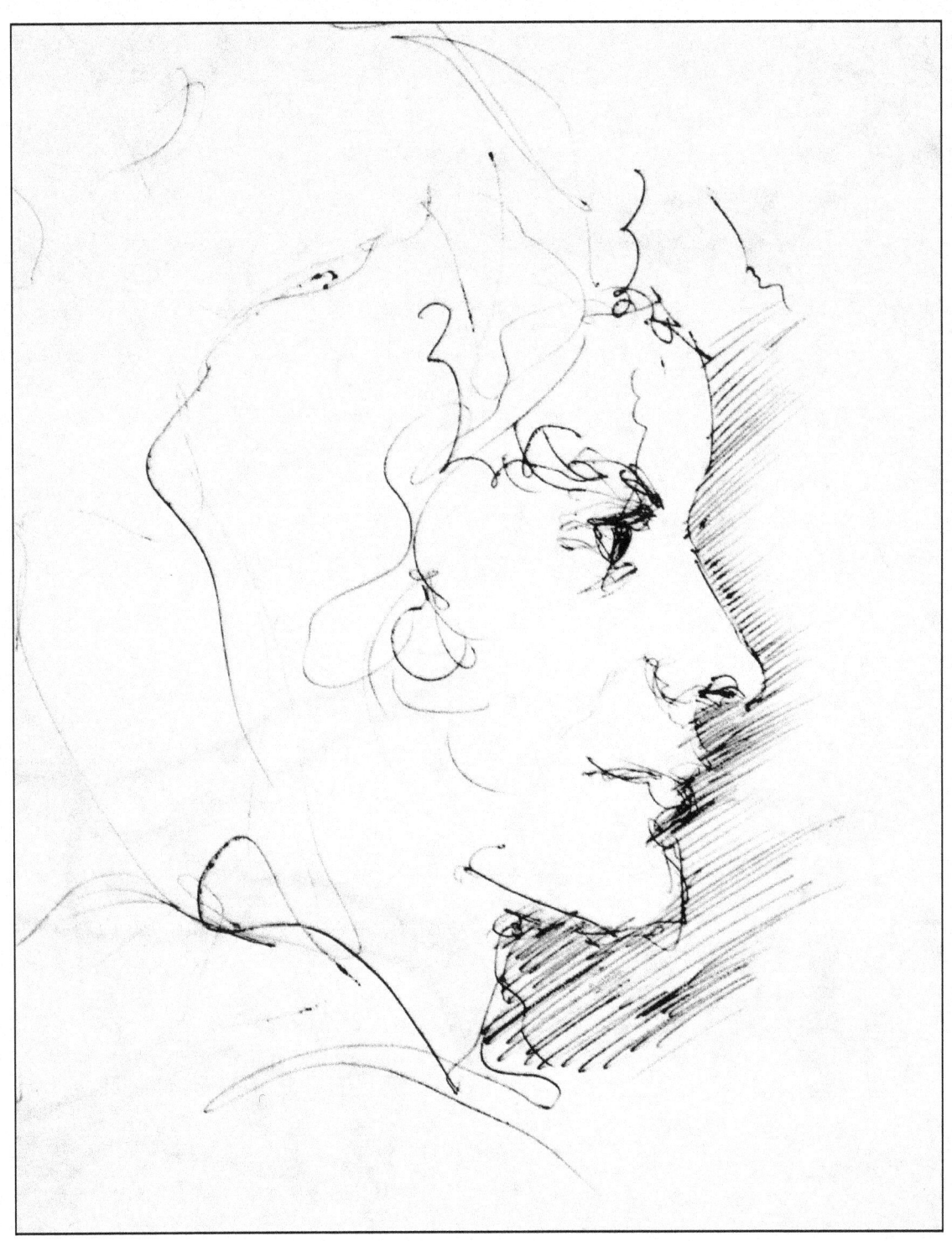

Drawing done with my left hand

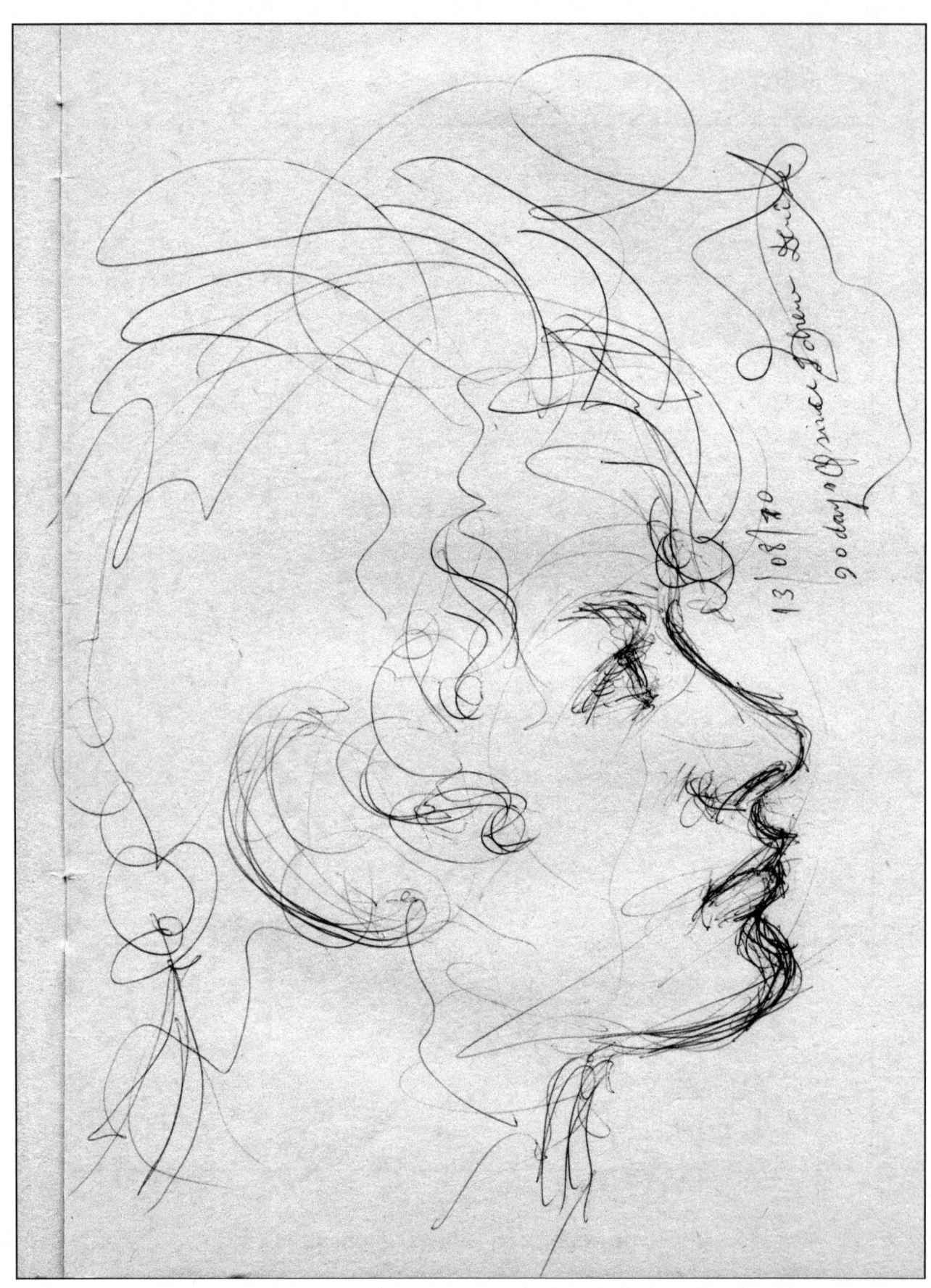

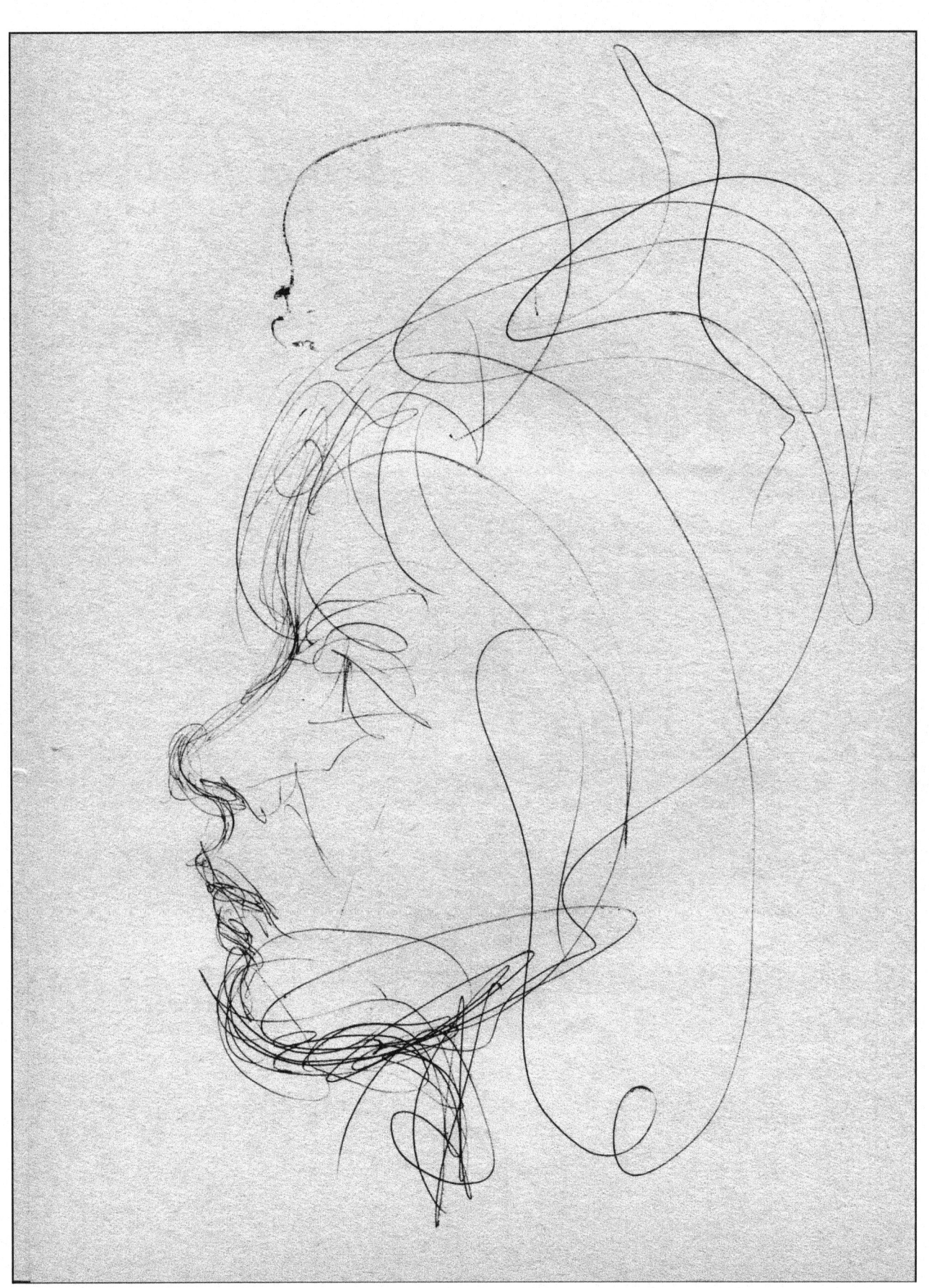

This ballpoint-pen drawing shows how confident I was.

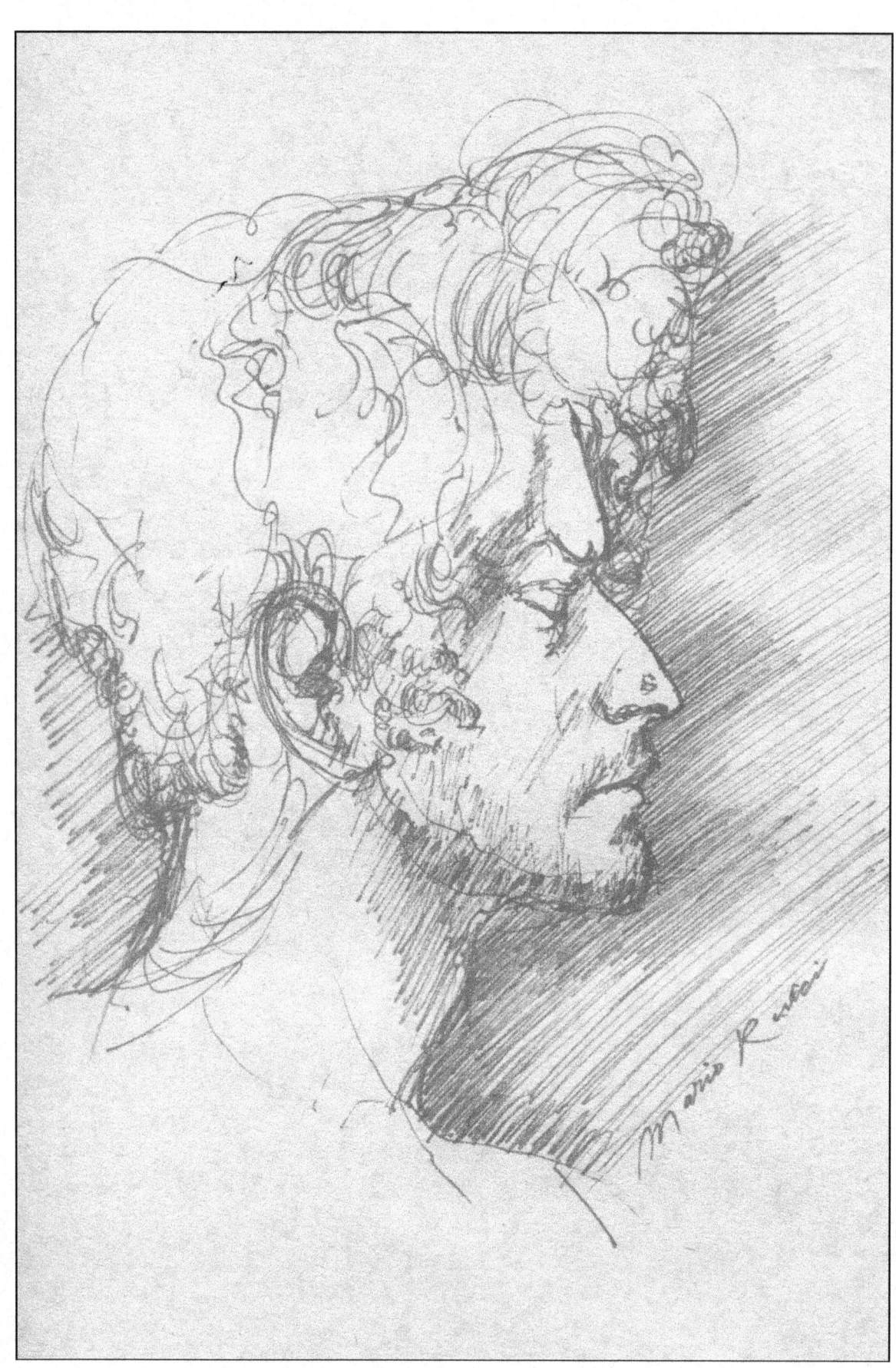

Red Ballpoint-Pen Drawing

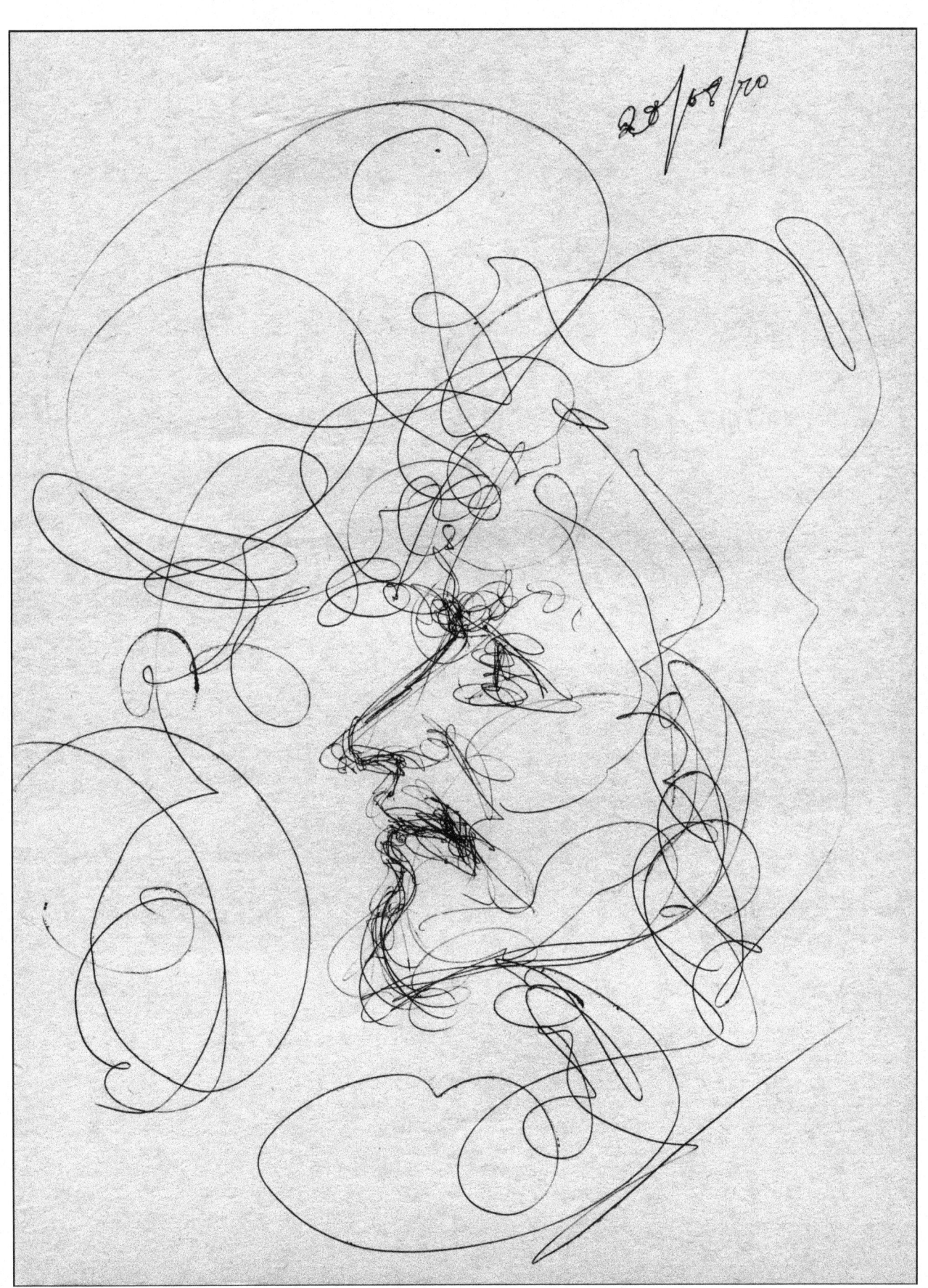

Another drawing which shows how self-assured I was.

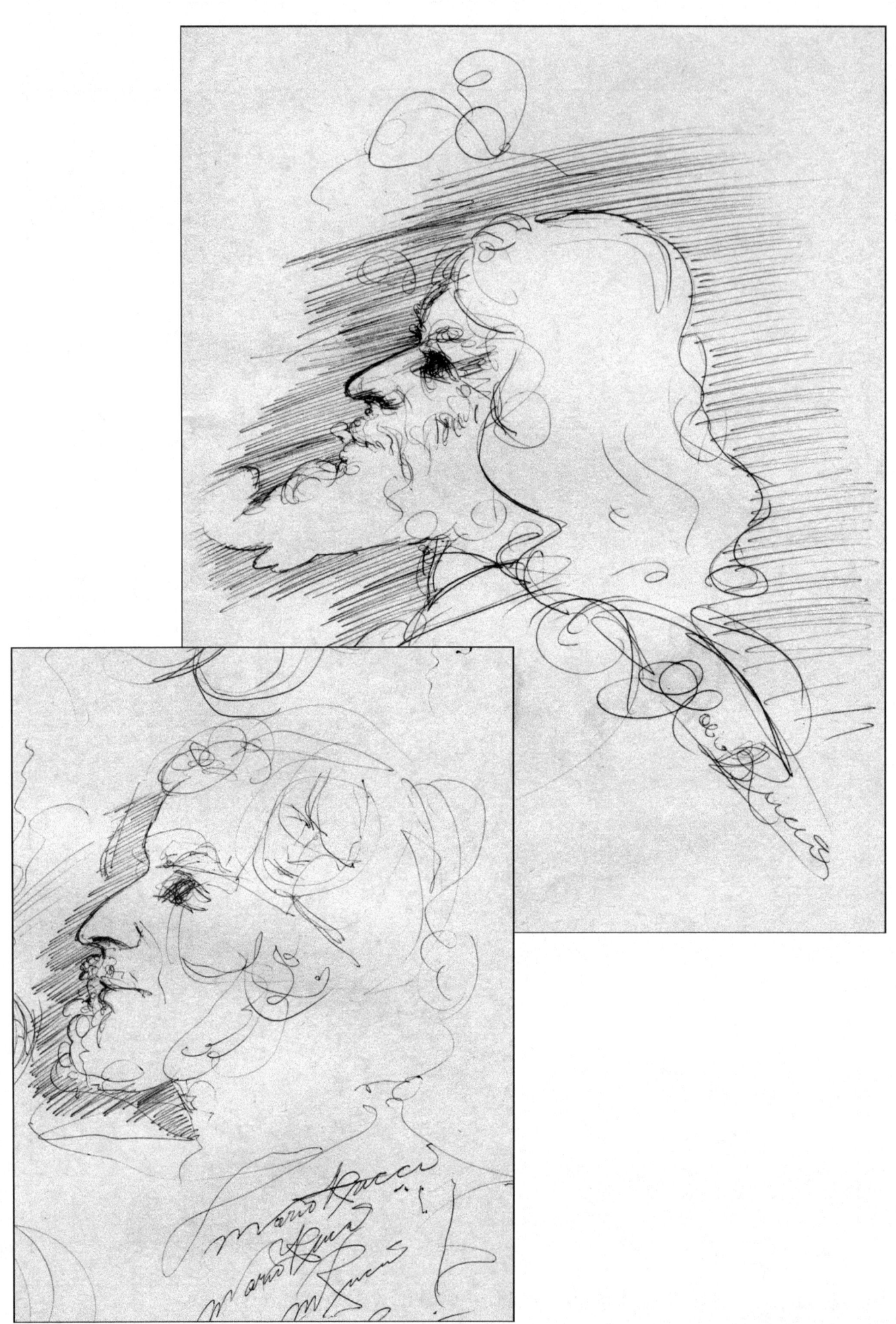

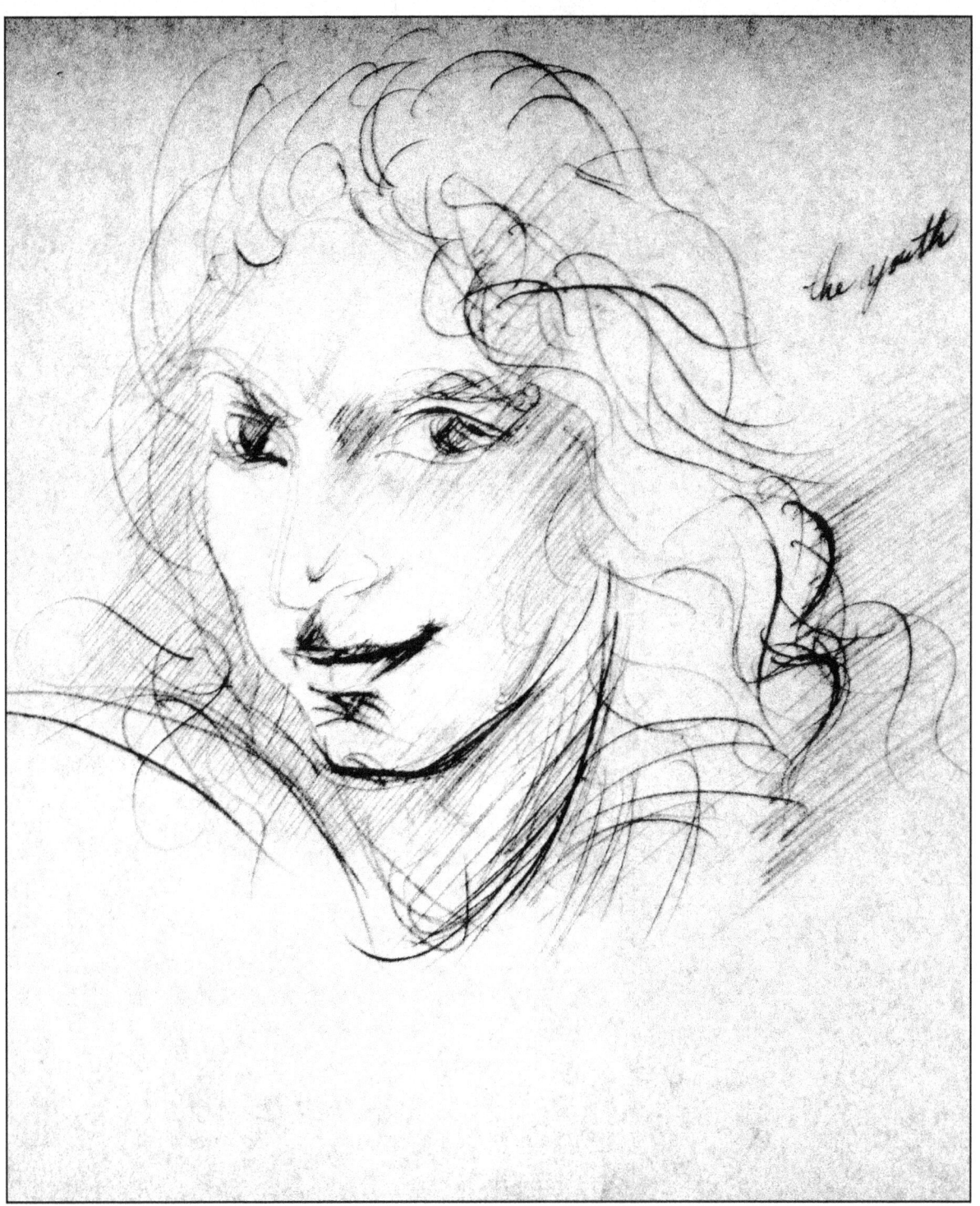

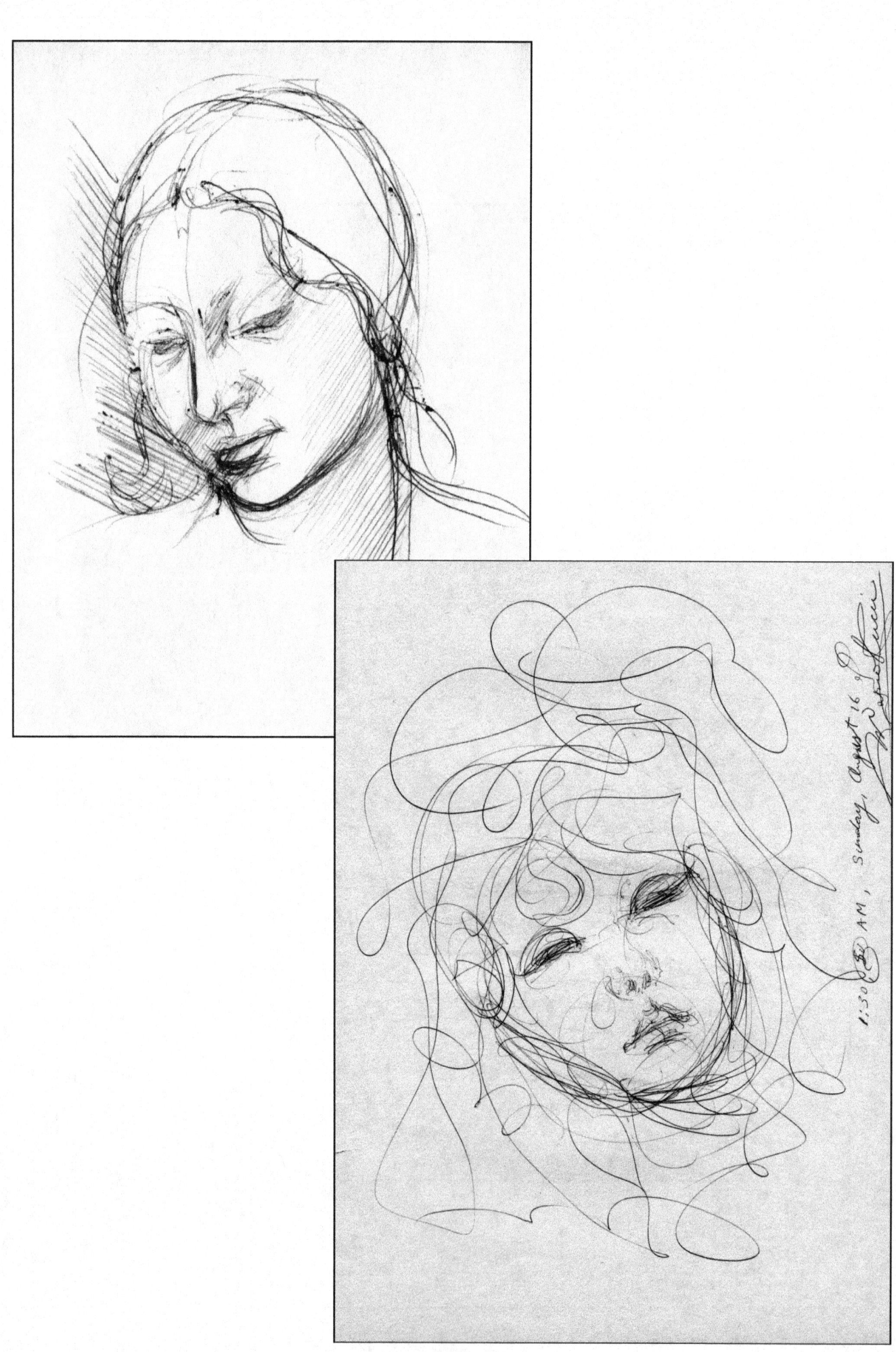

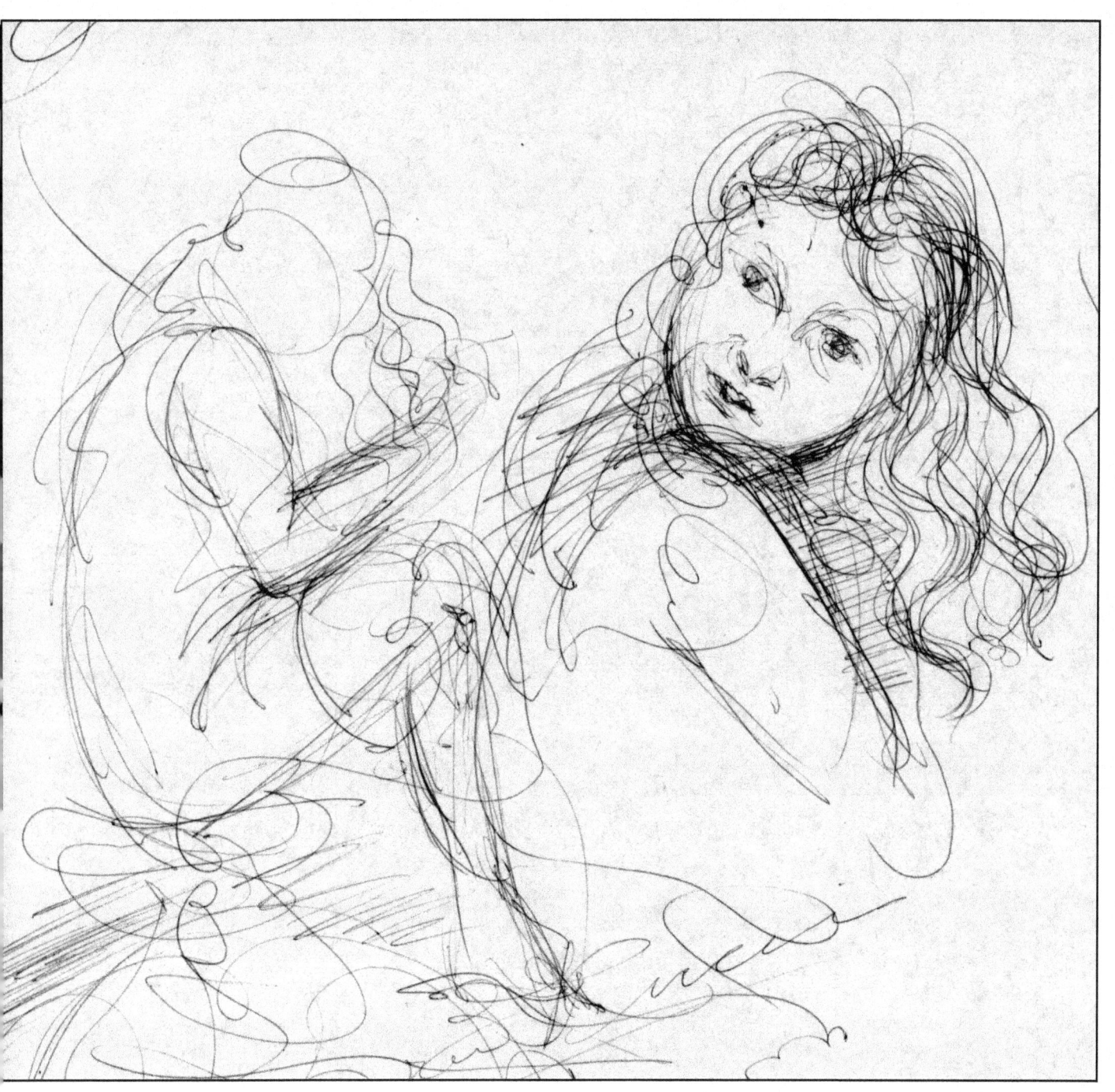

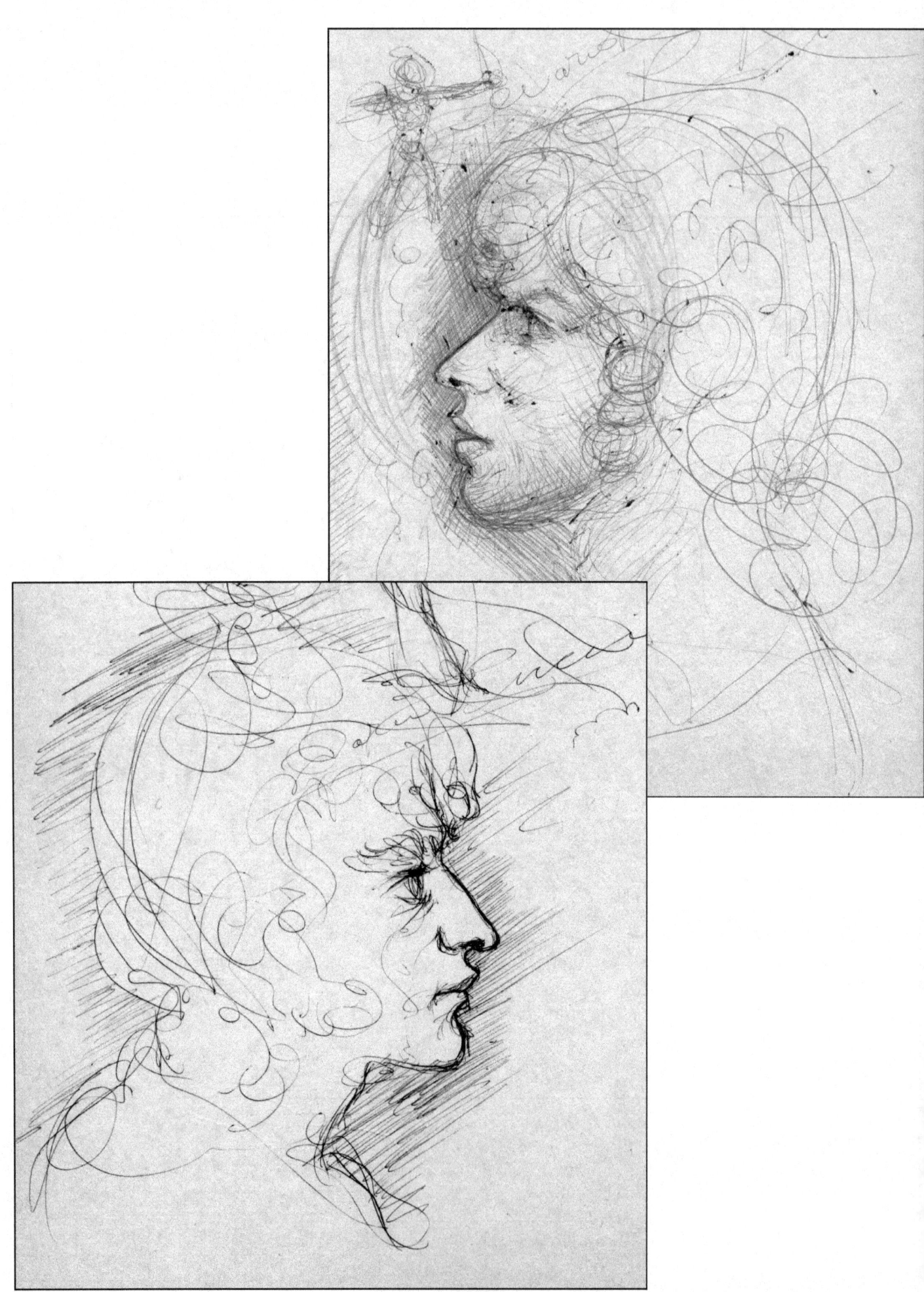

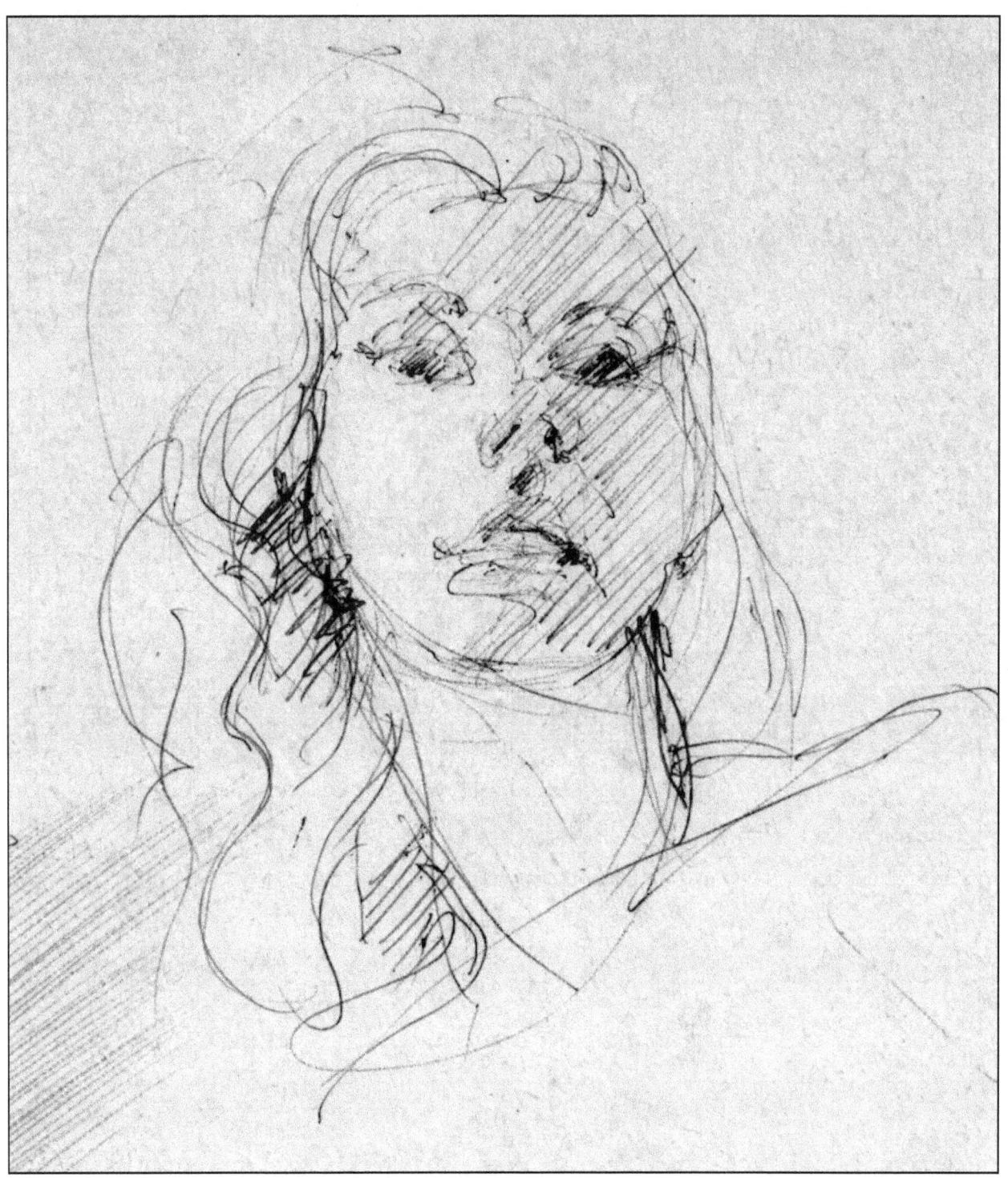

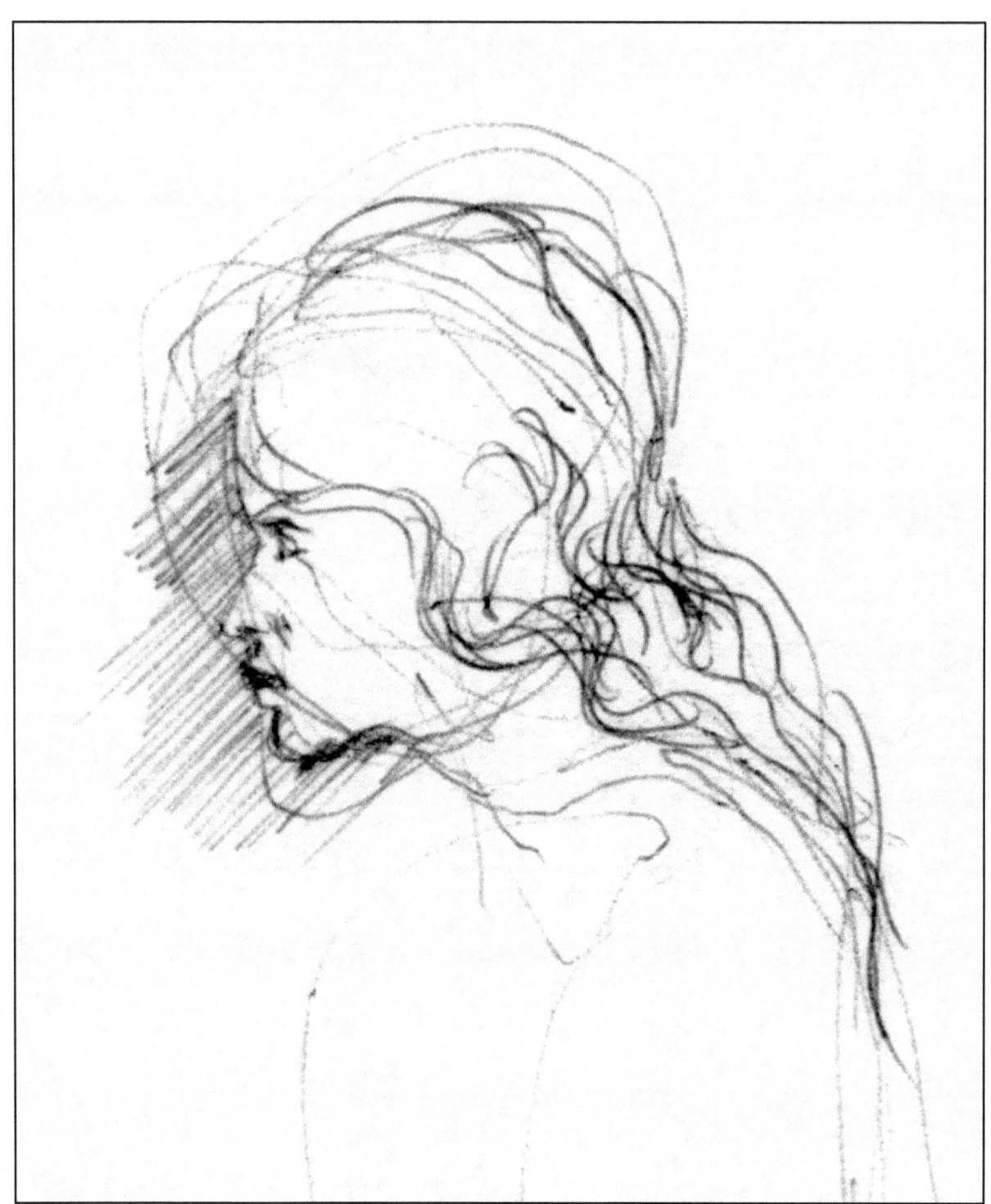

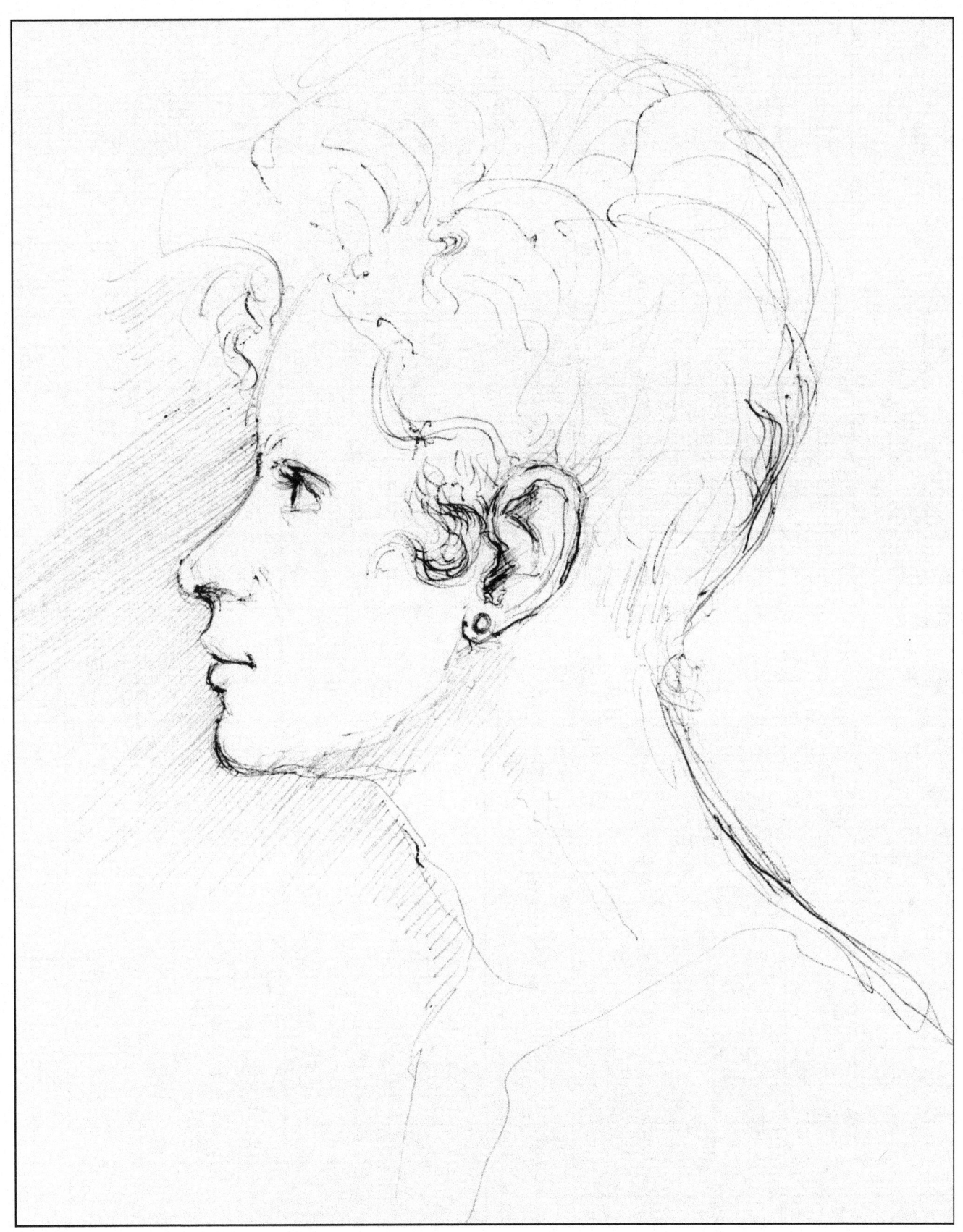

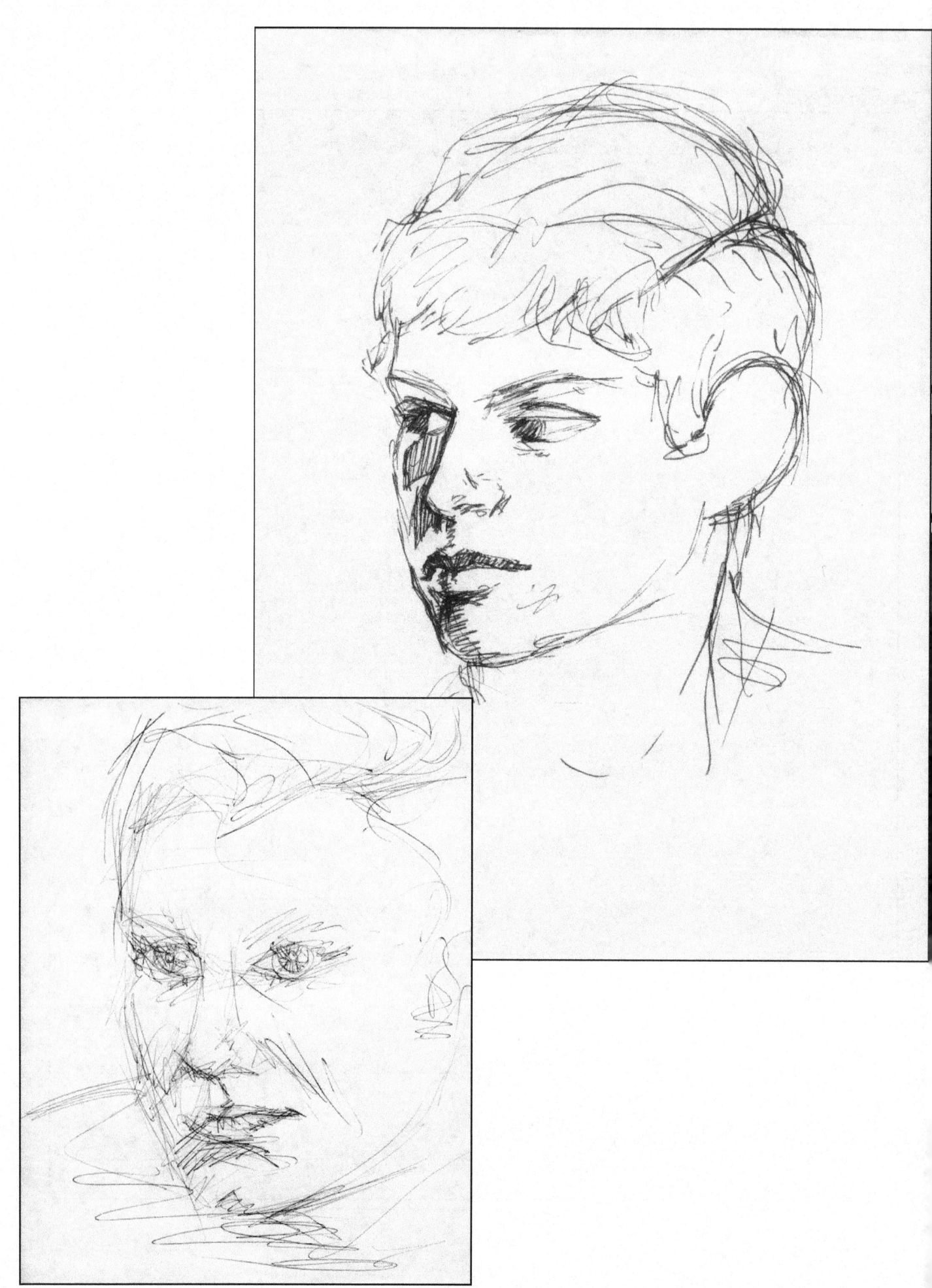

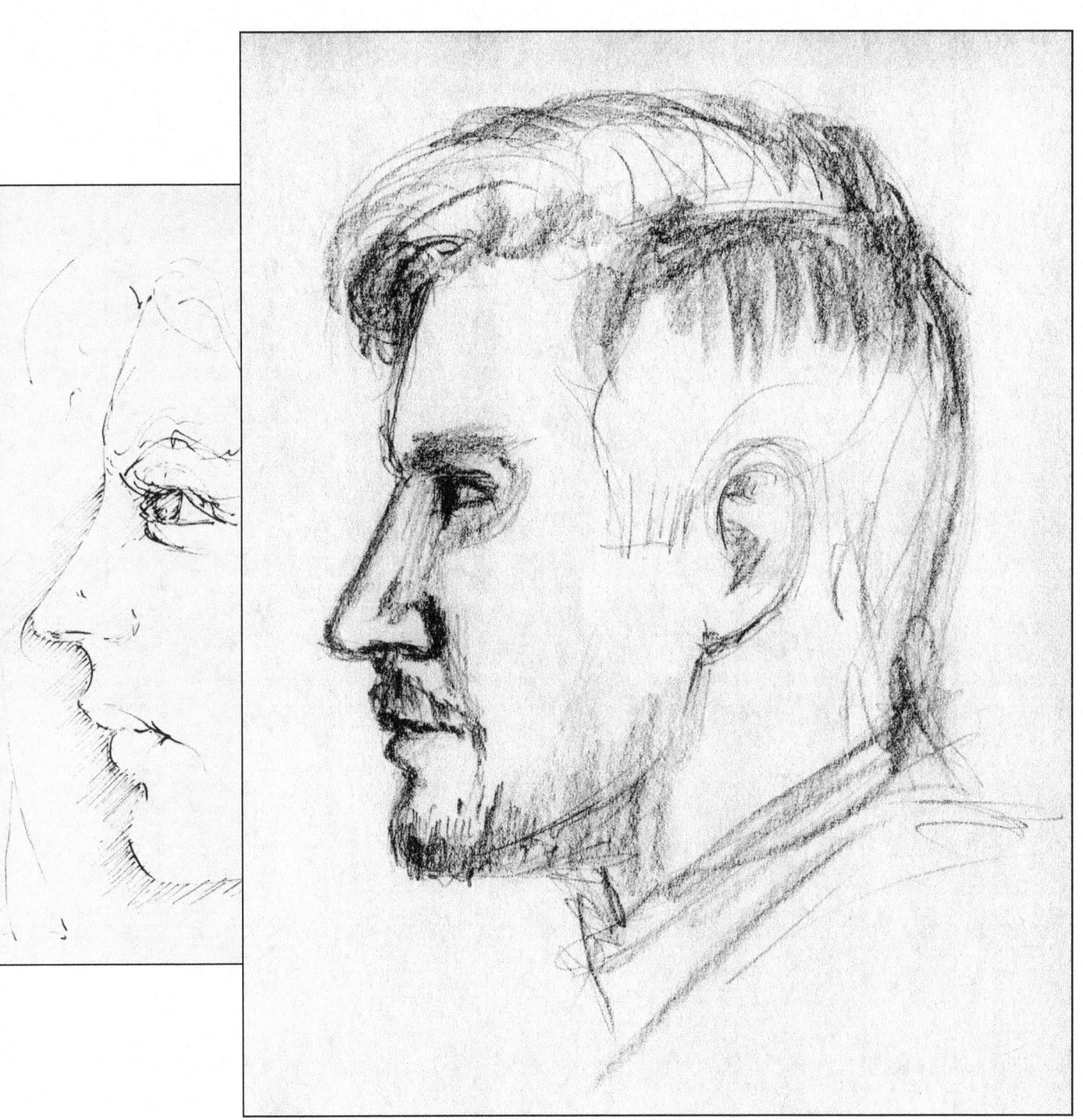

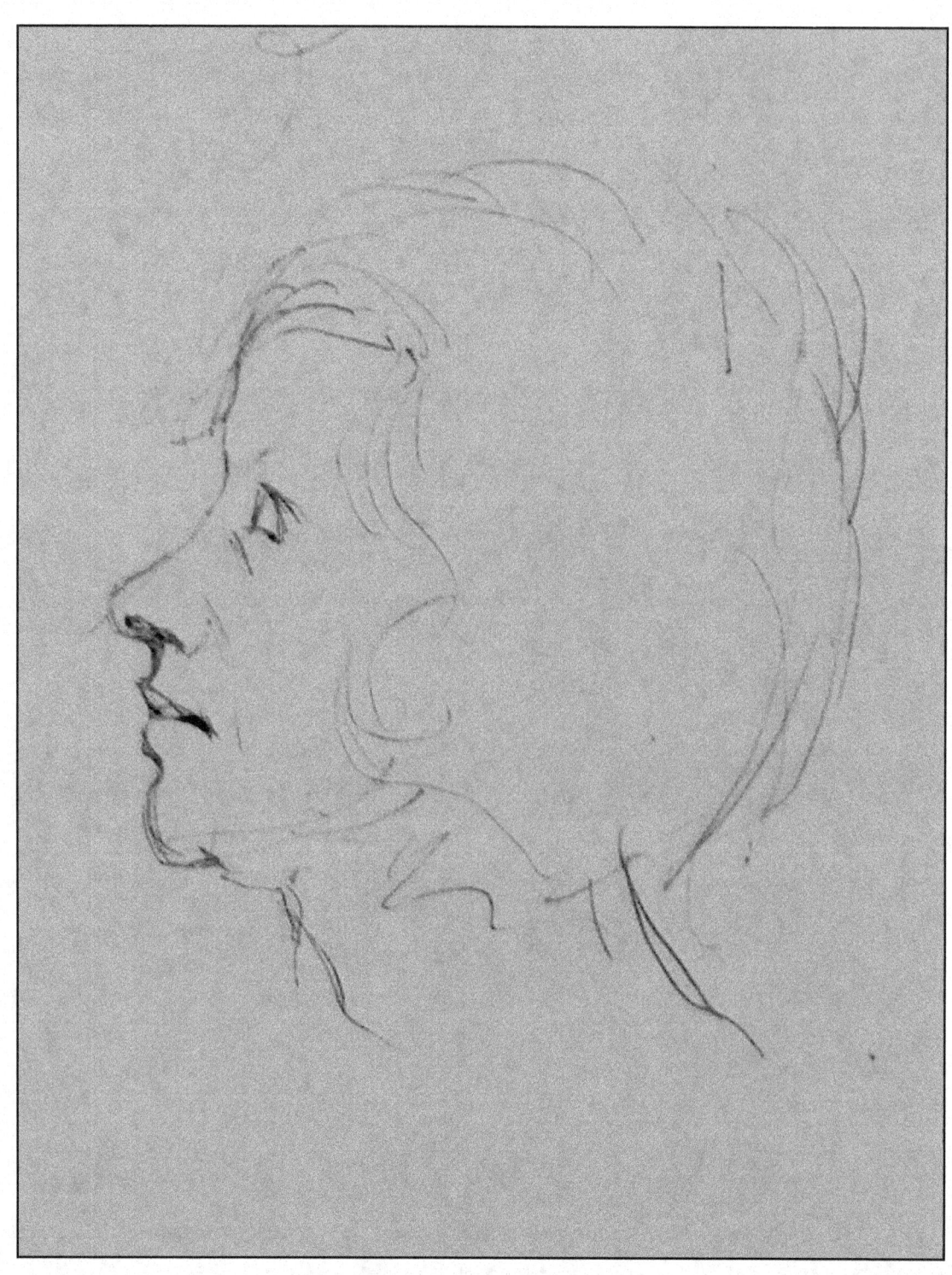

Felt-tipped-Pen Drawing

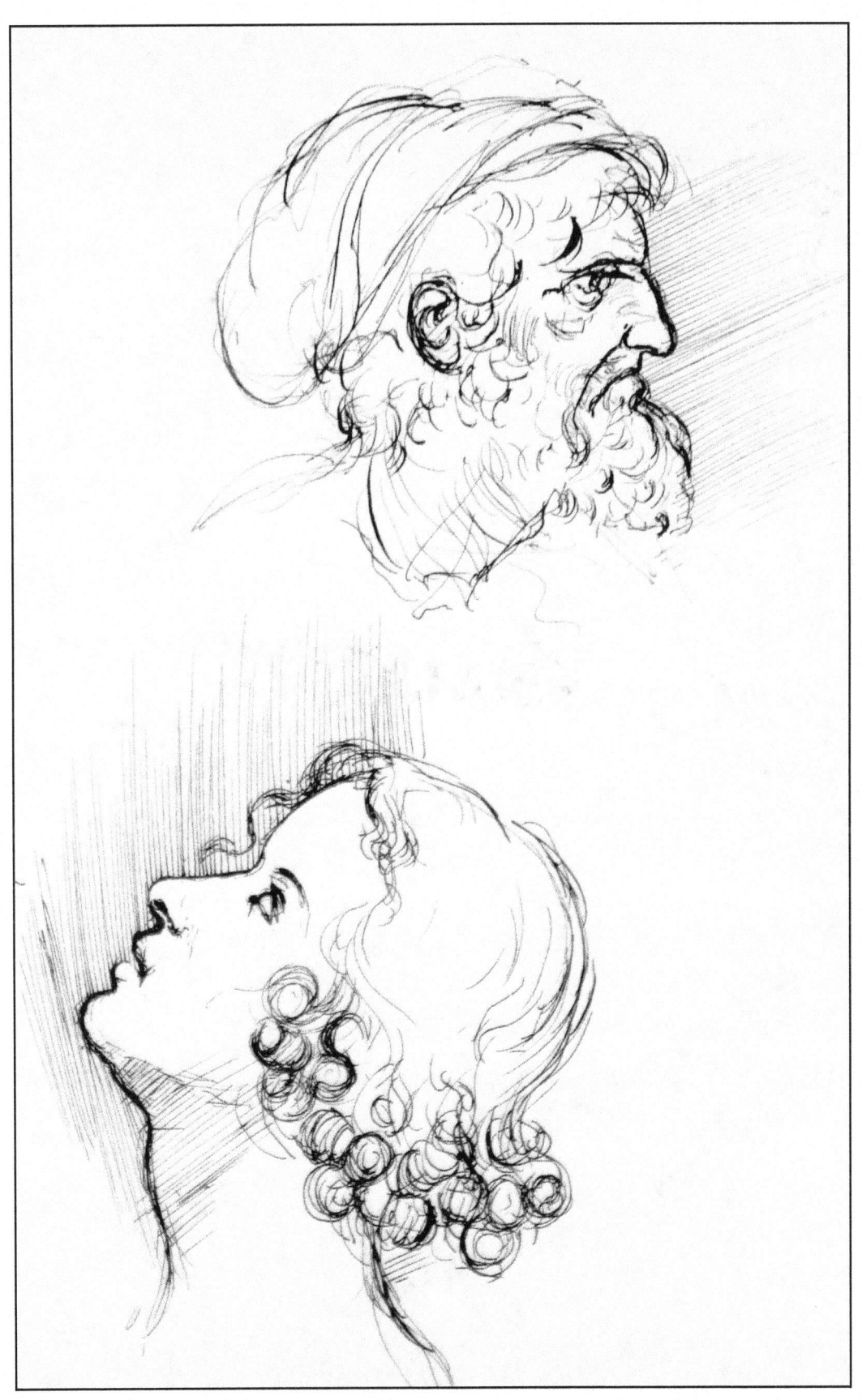

10. Torso

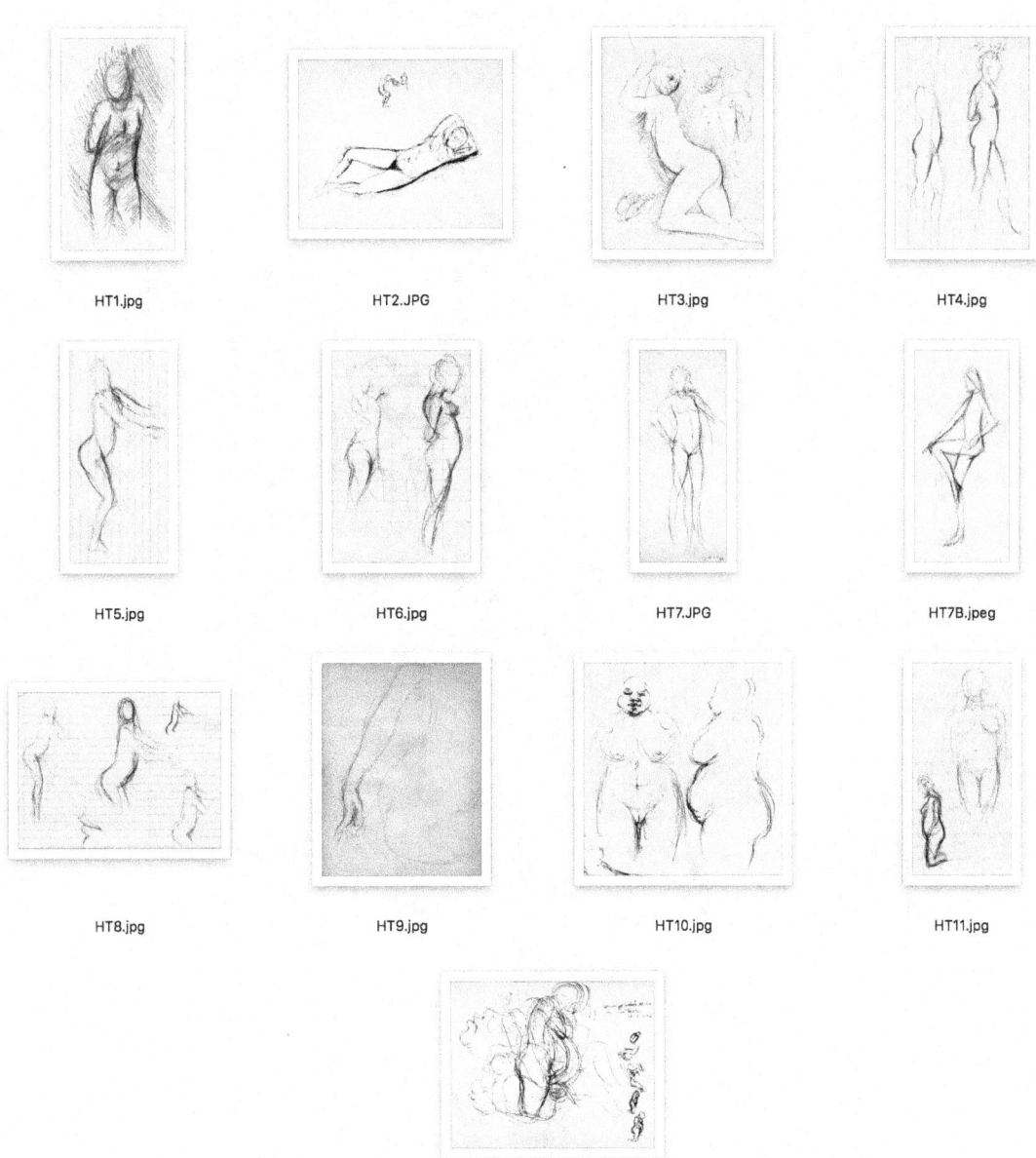

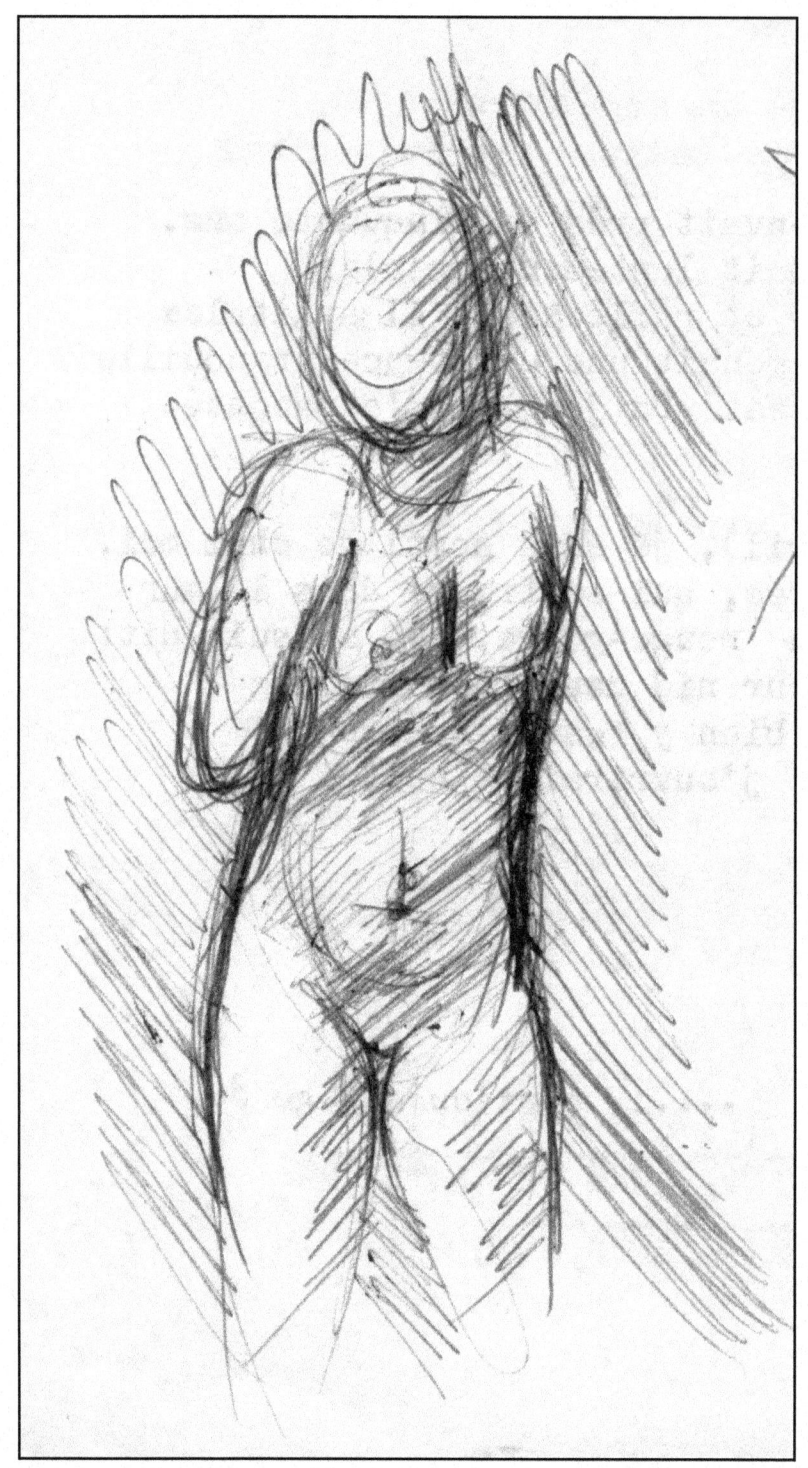

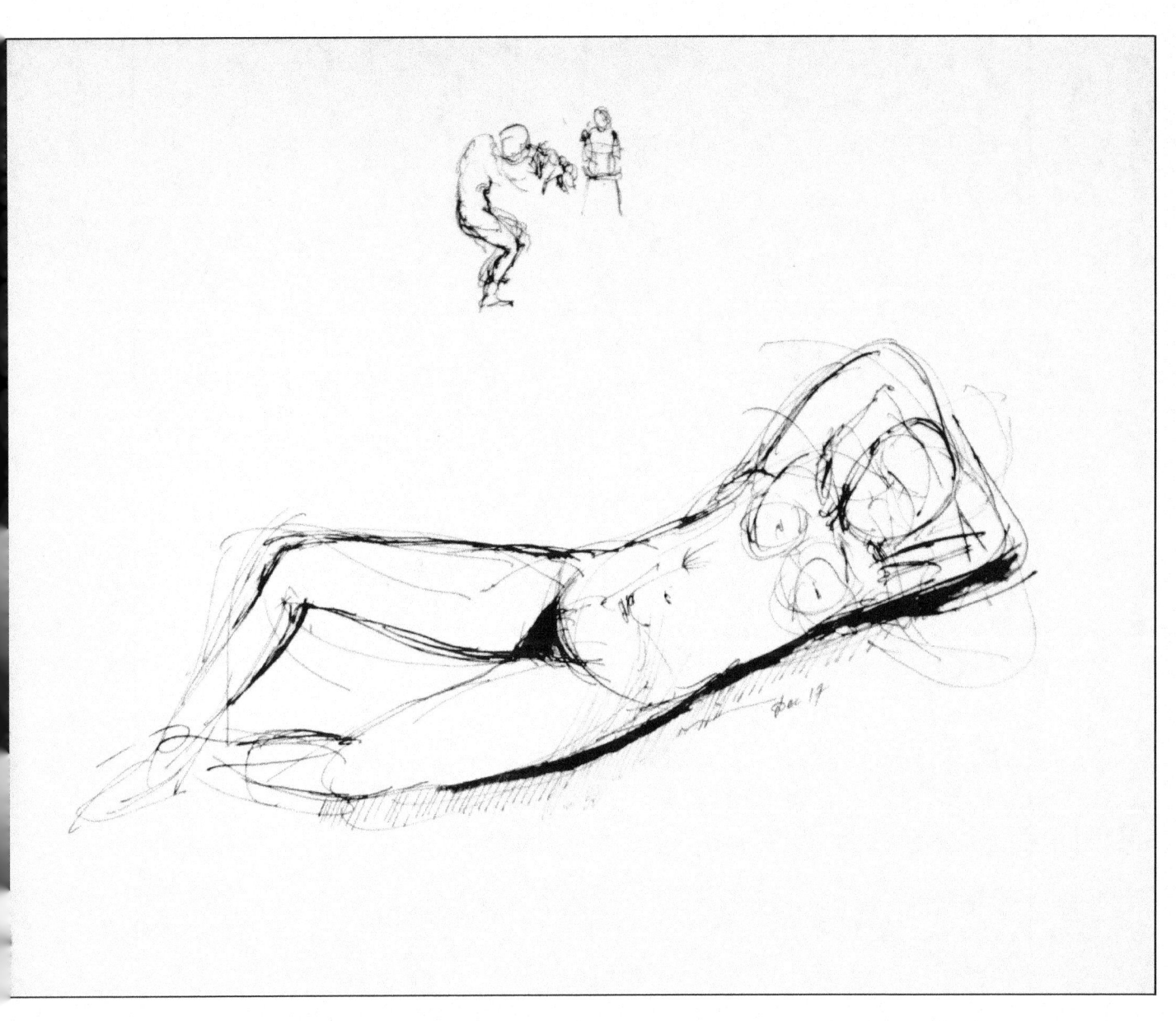

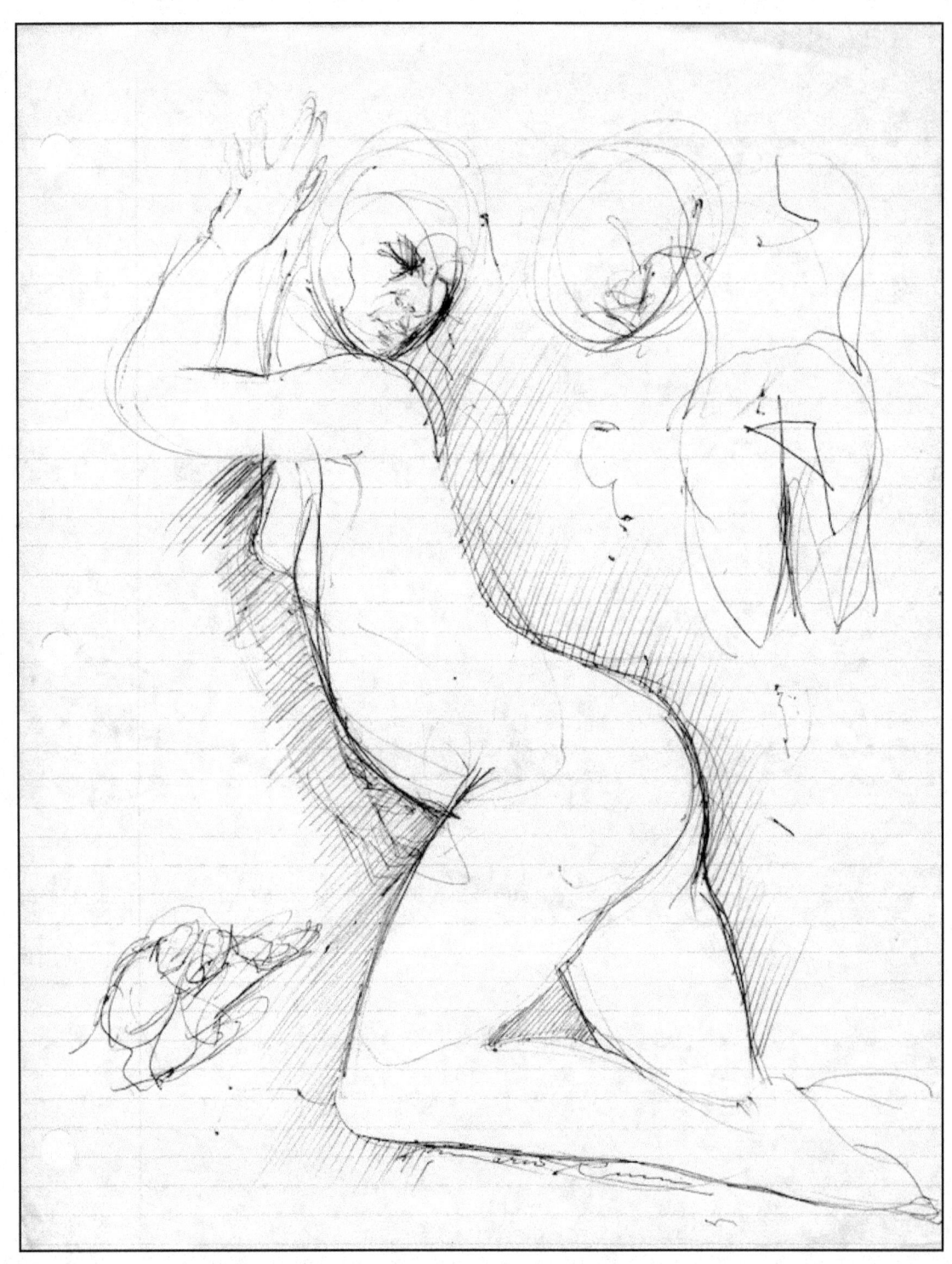

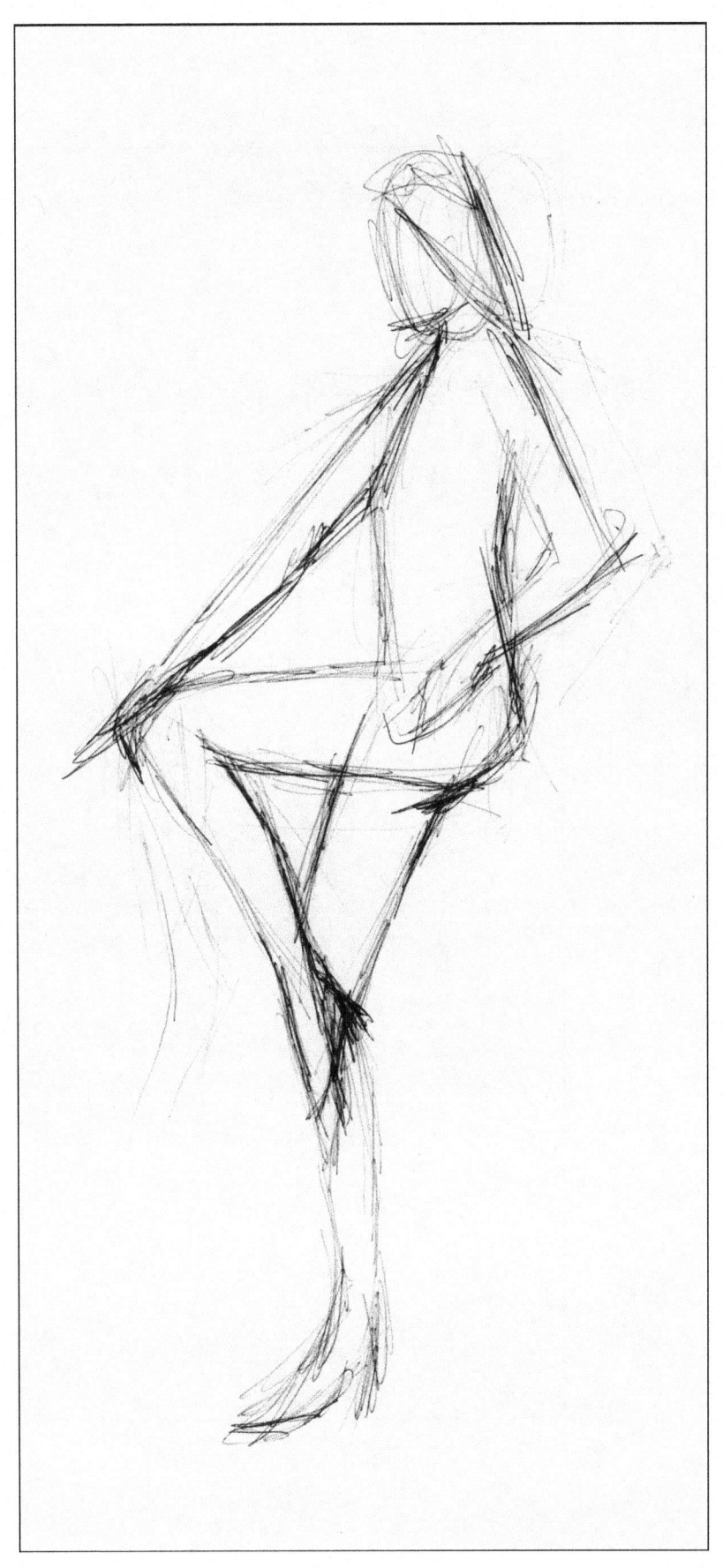

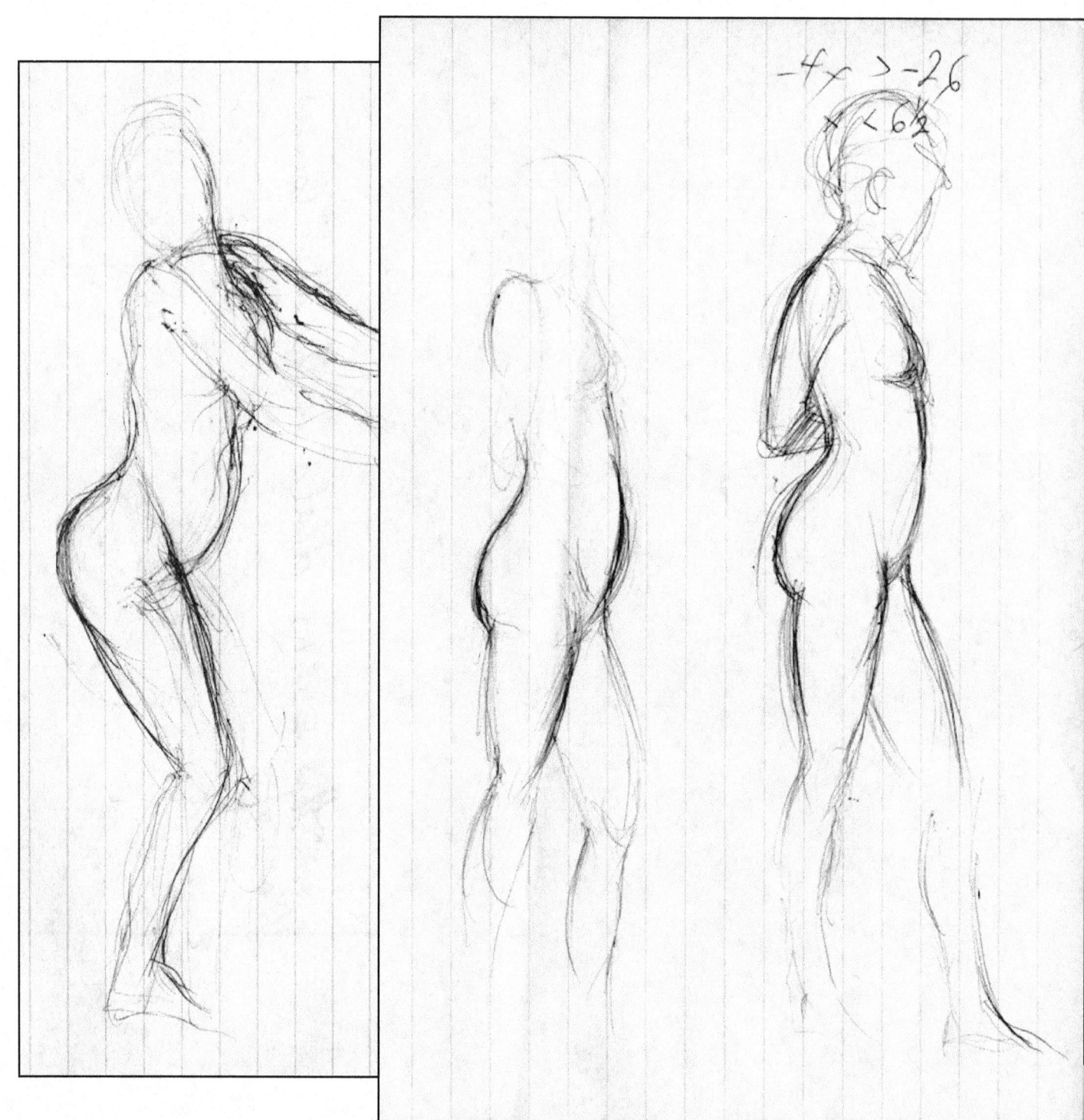

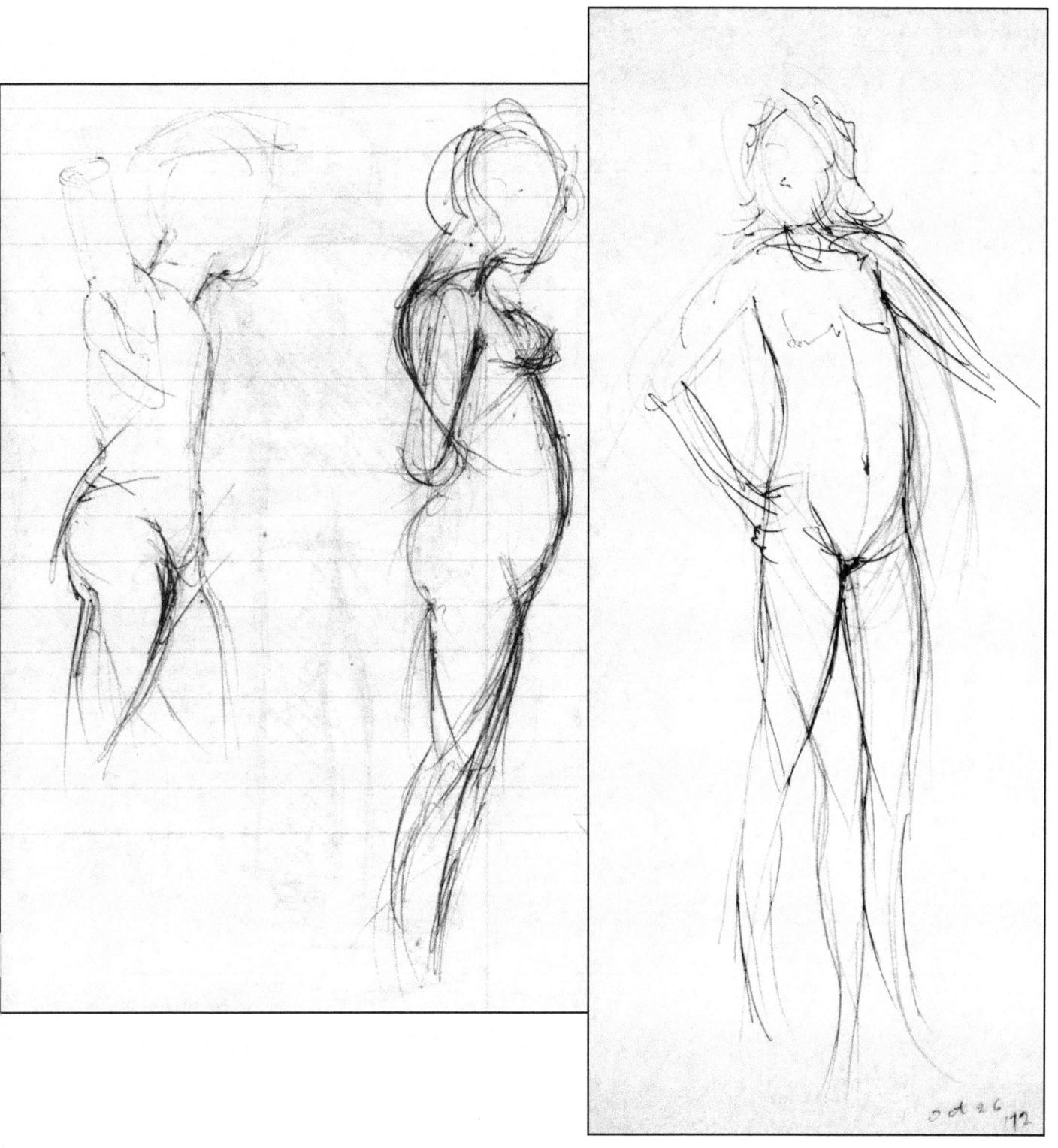

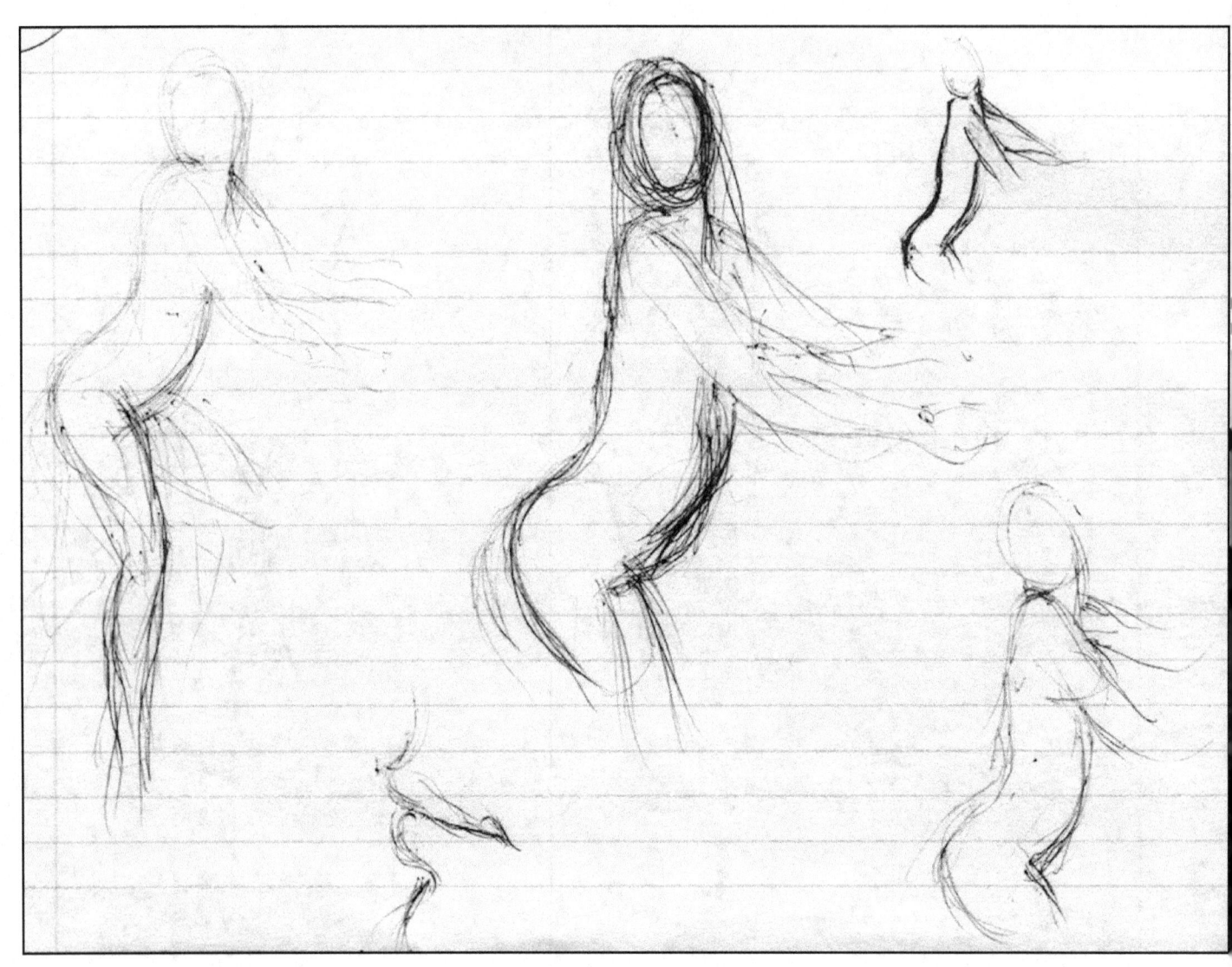

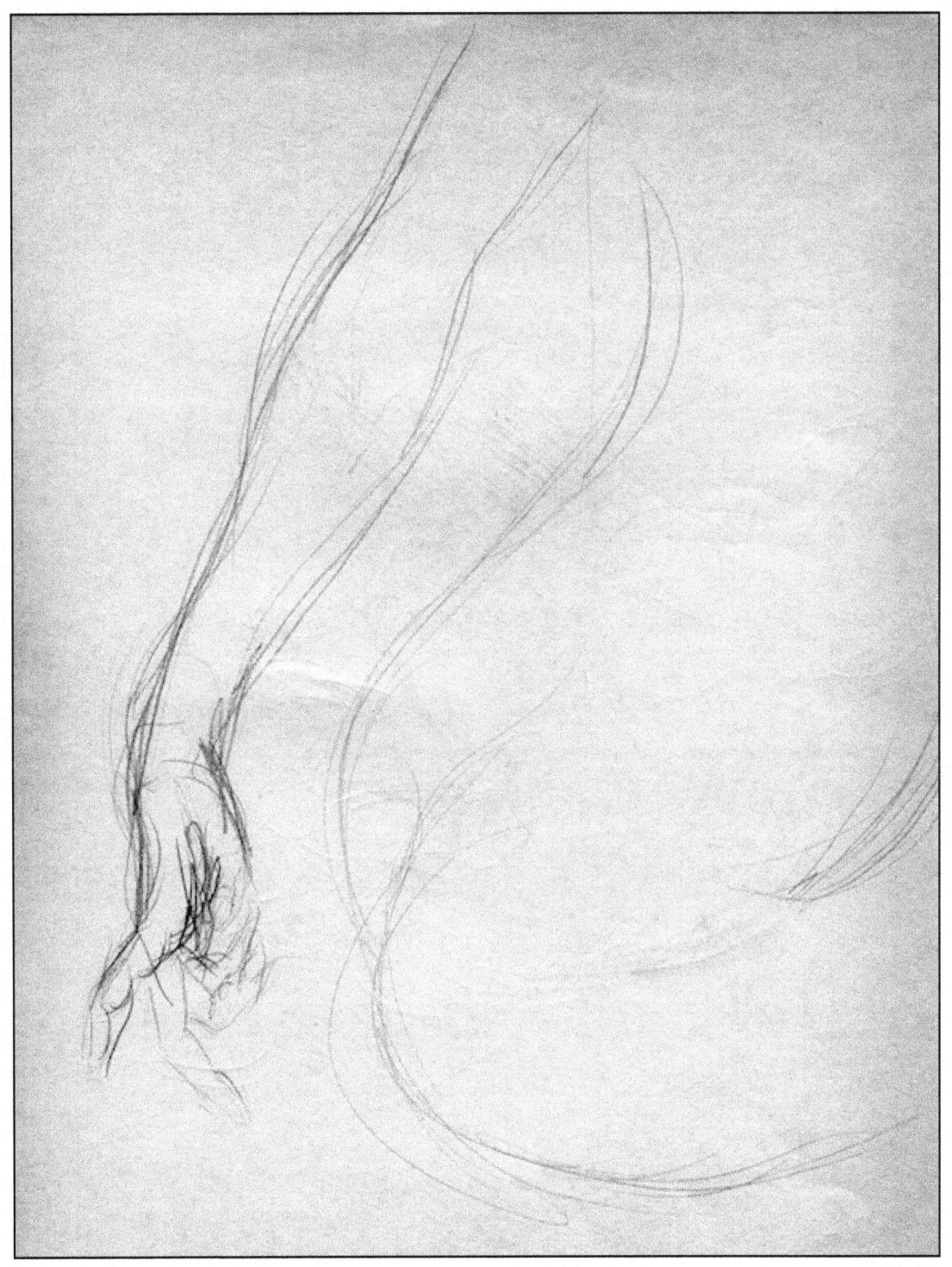

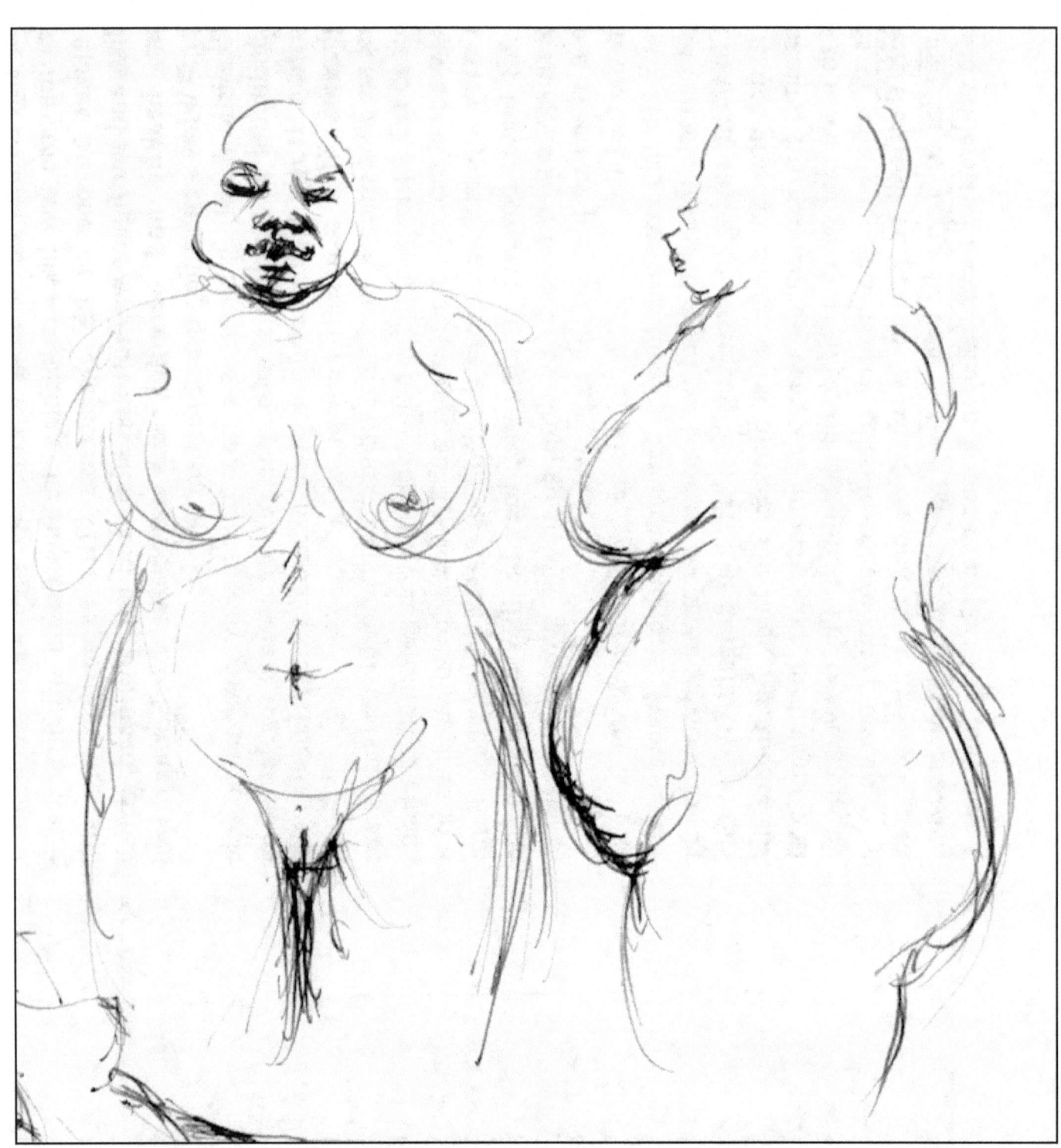

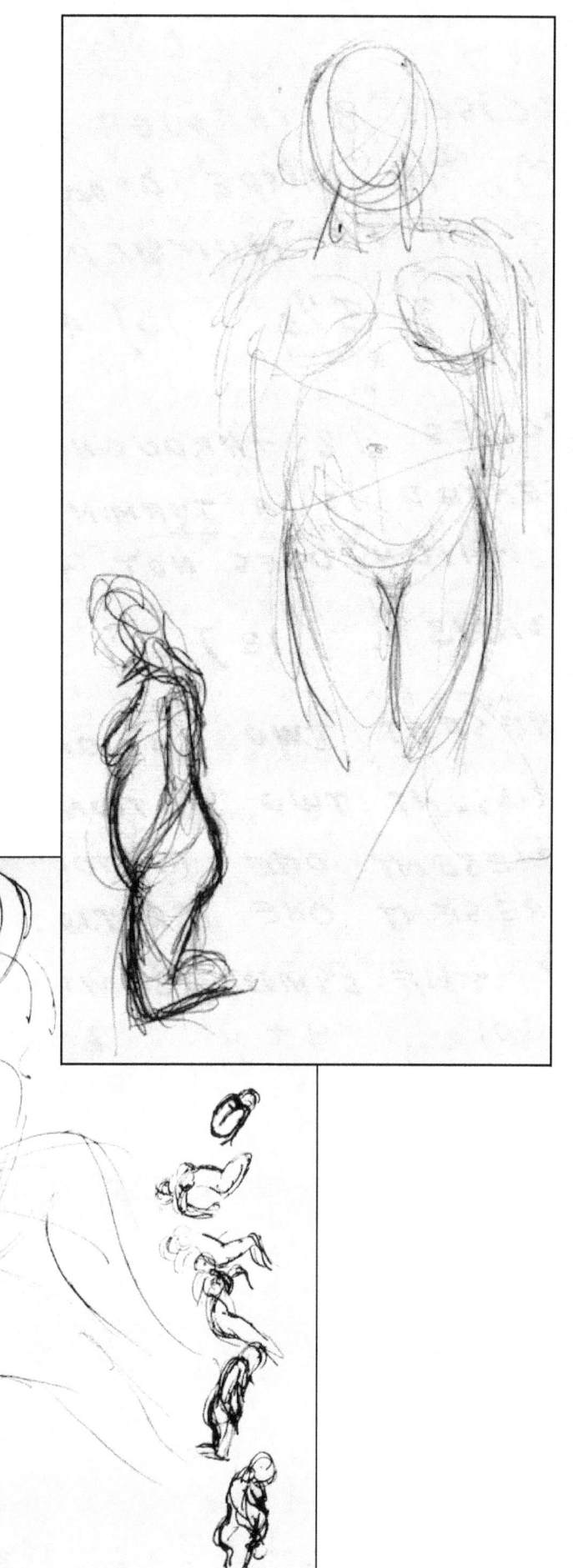

11. Extremities

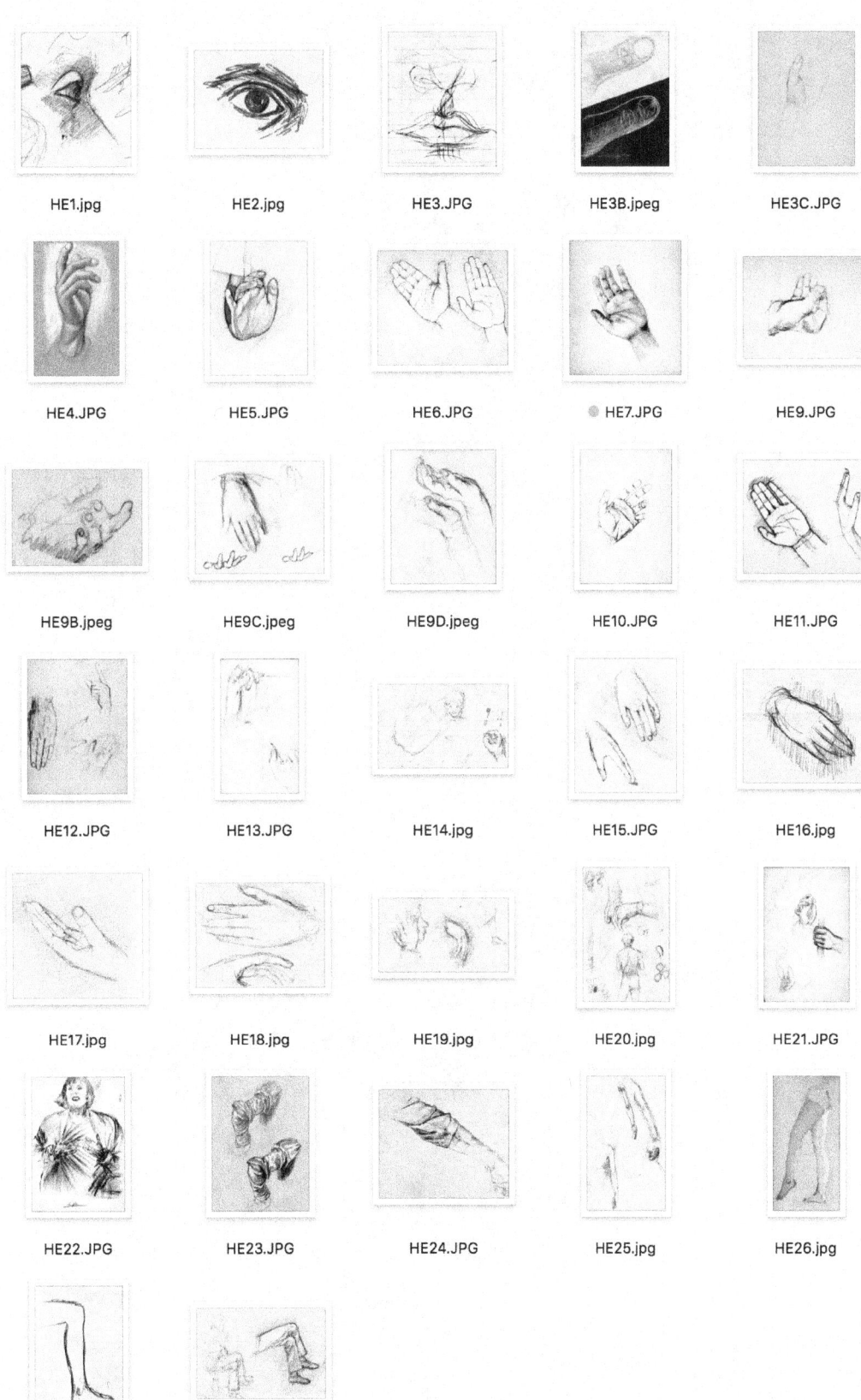

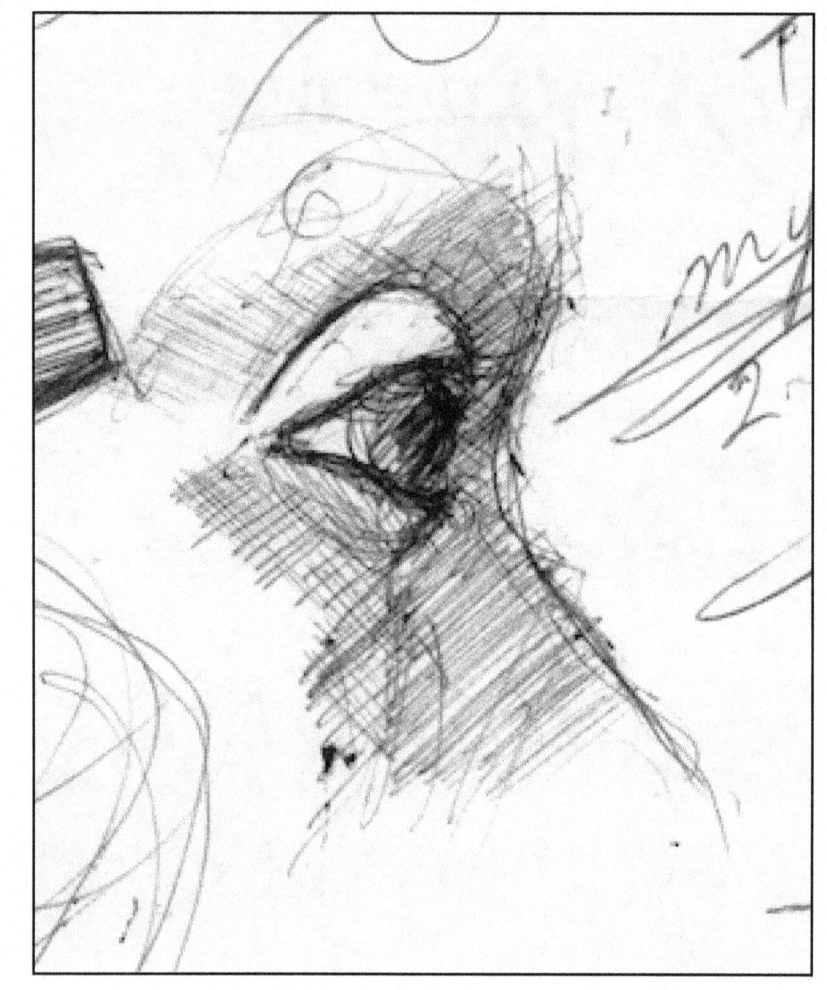

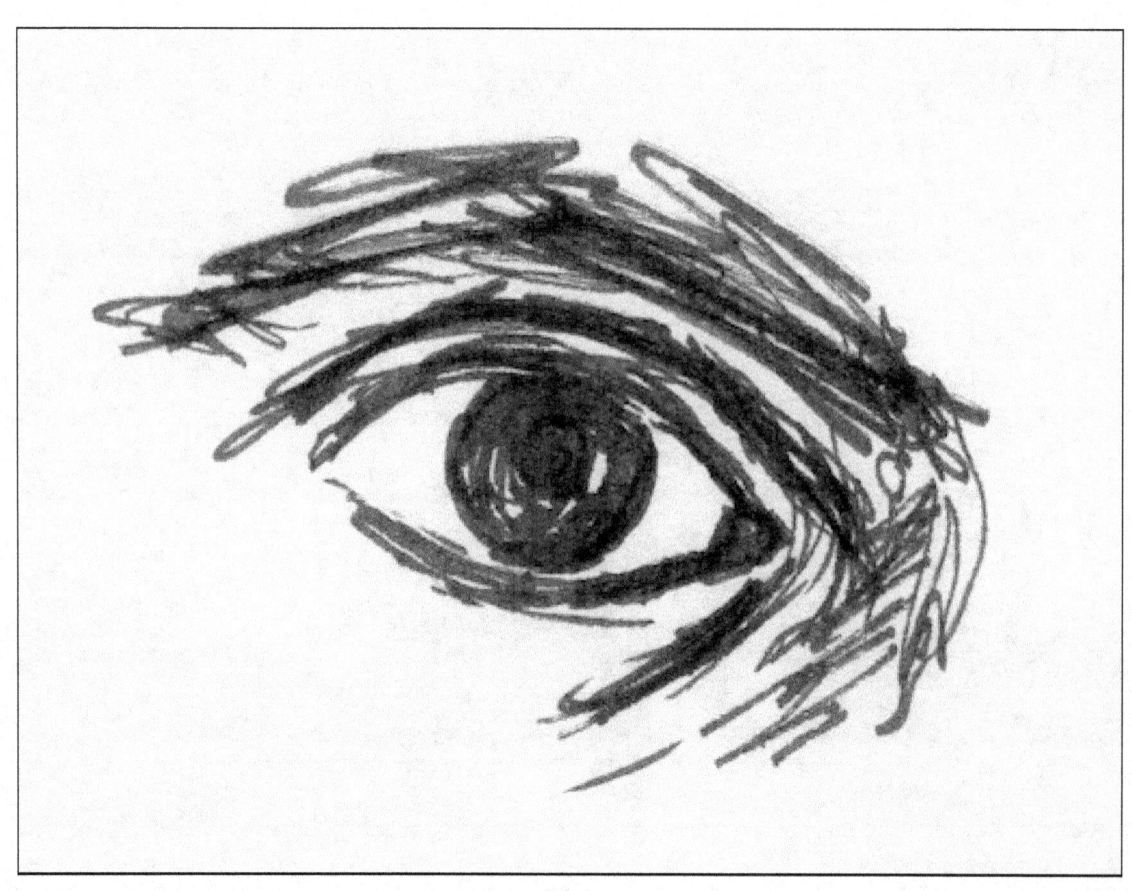

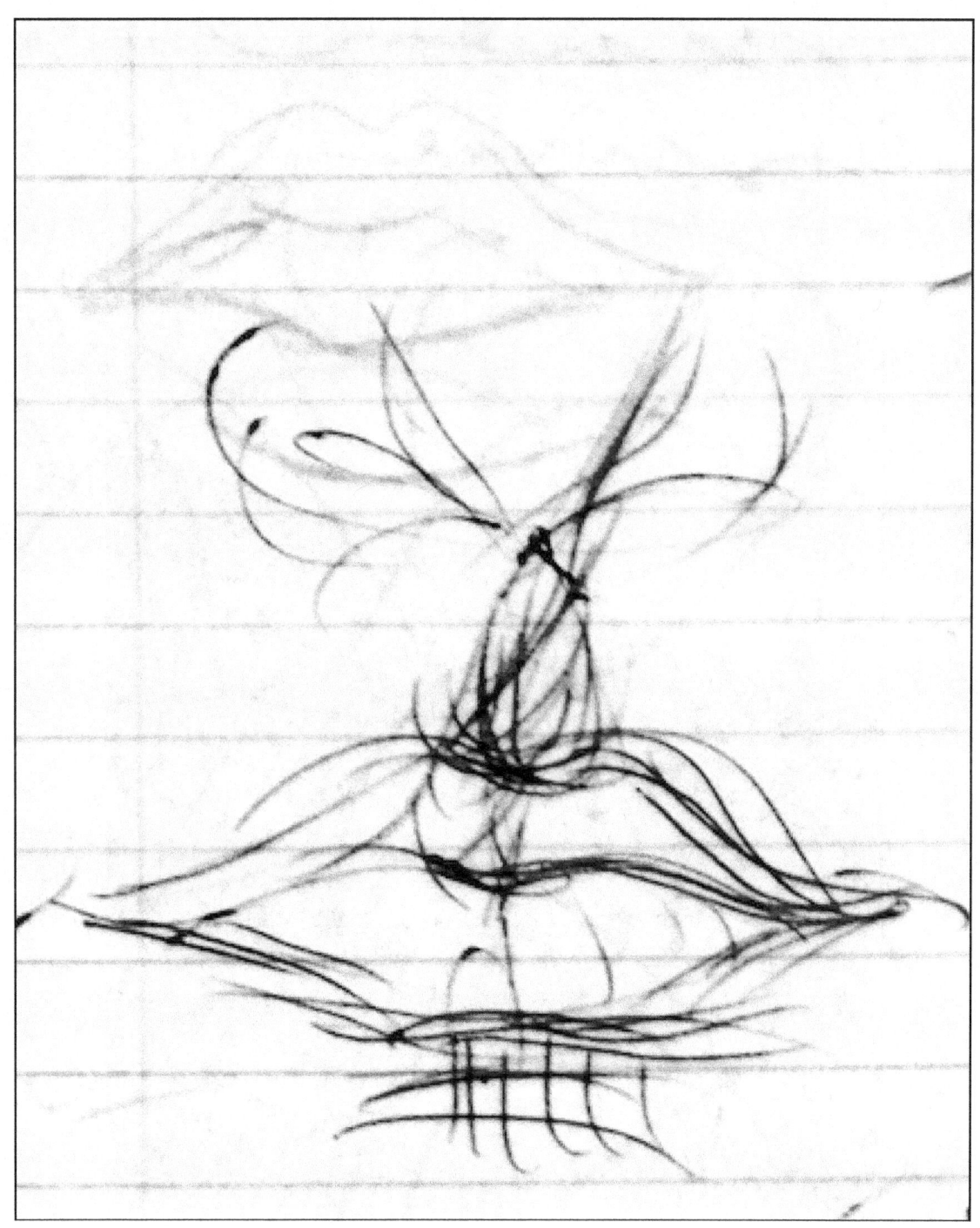

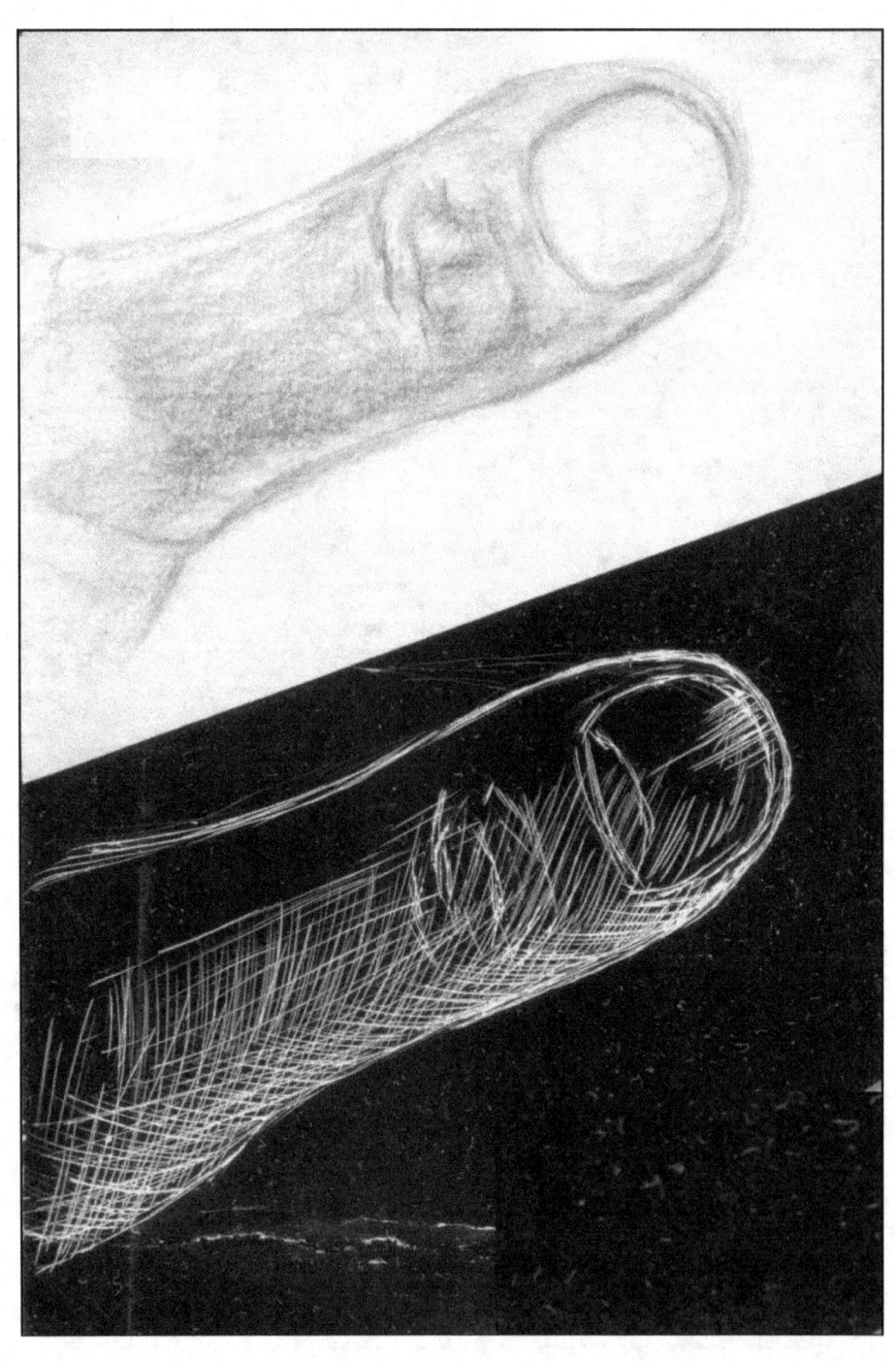

Drawing and Etching my left thumb

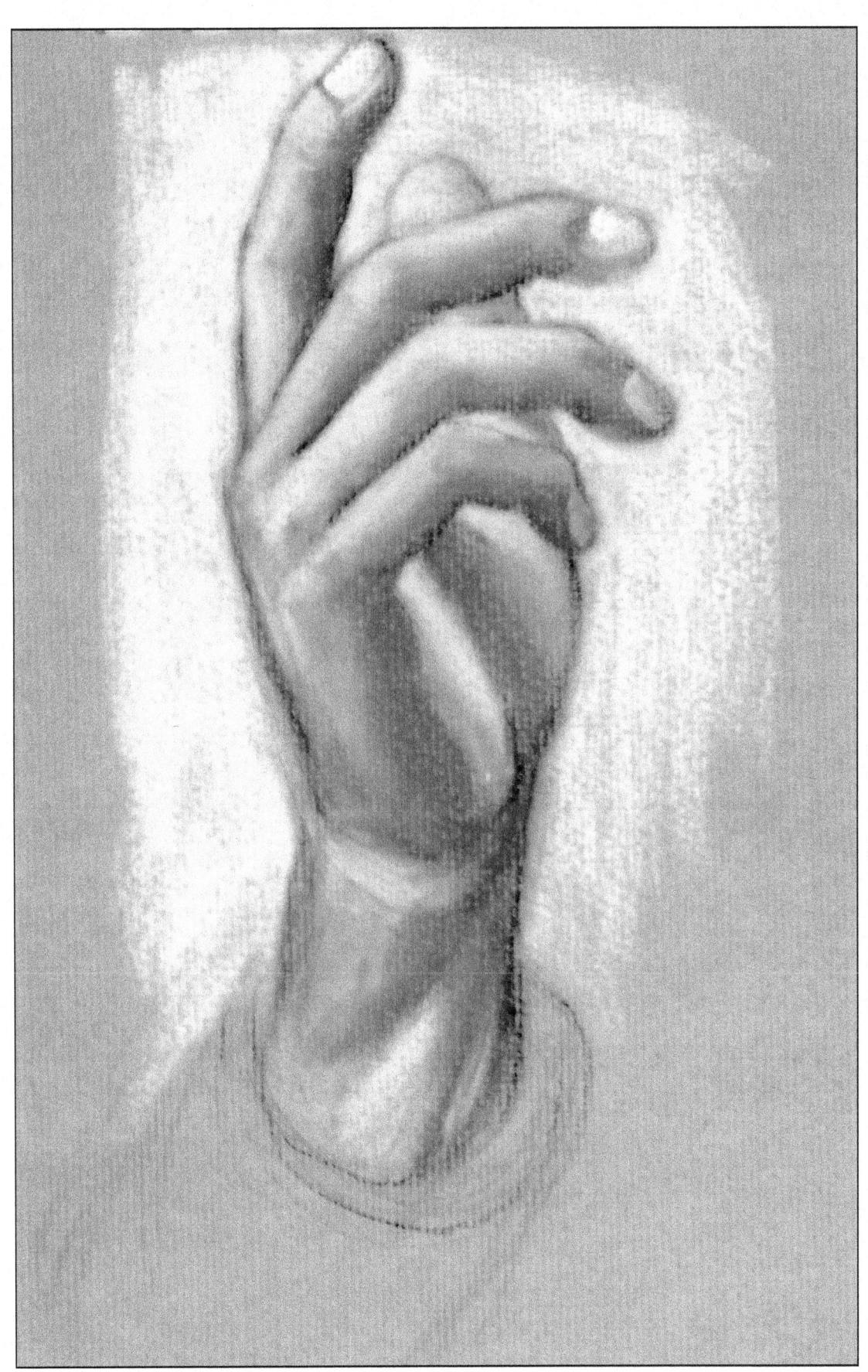

Chalk Drawing on canvas paper

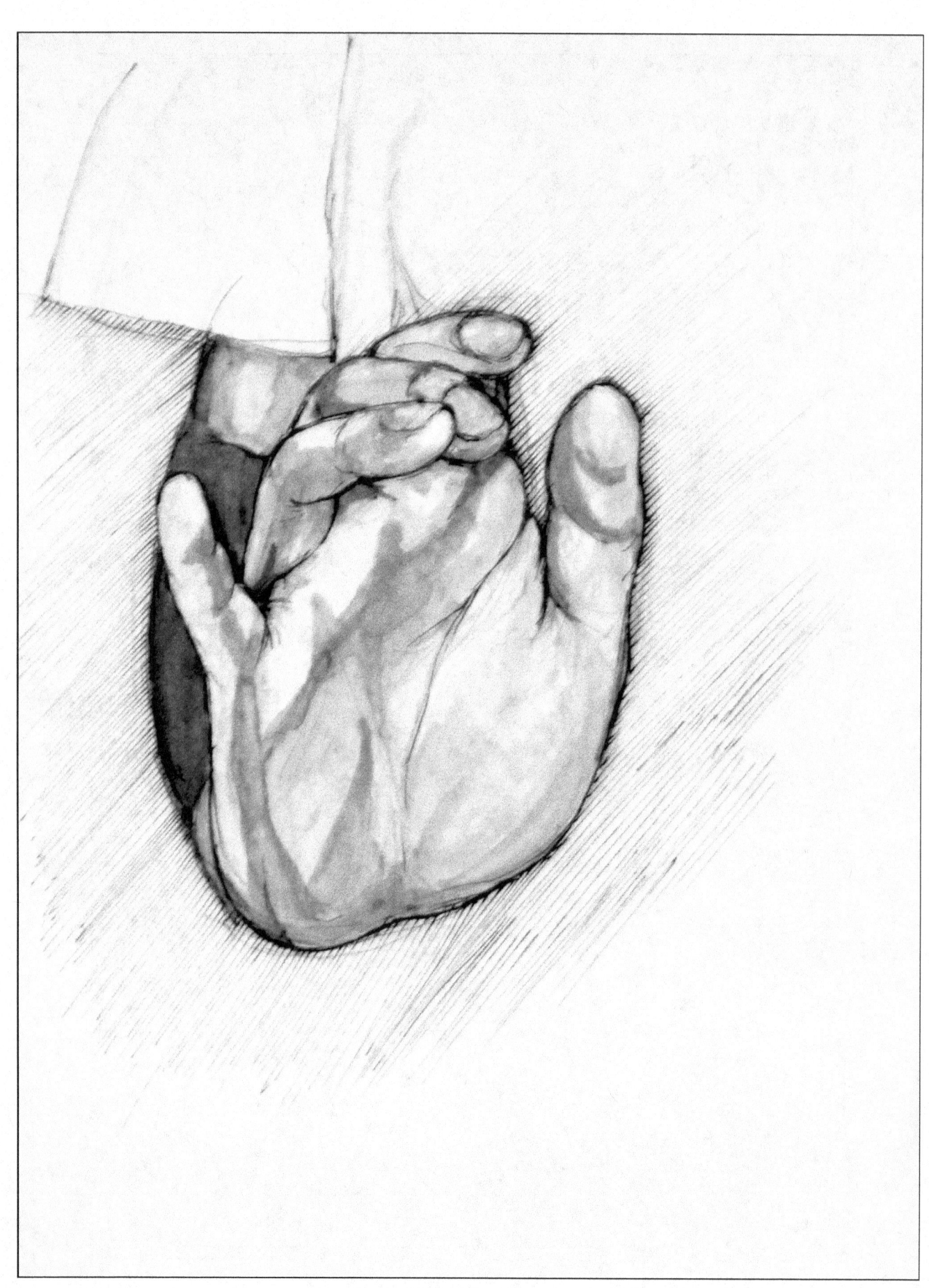

Both Ink Drawing and Ink Painting

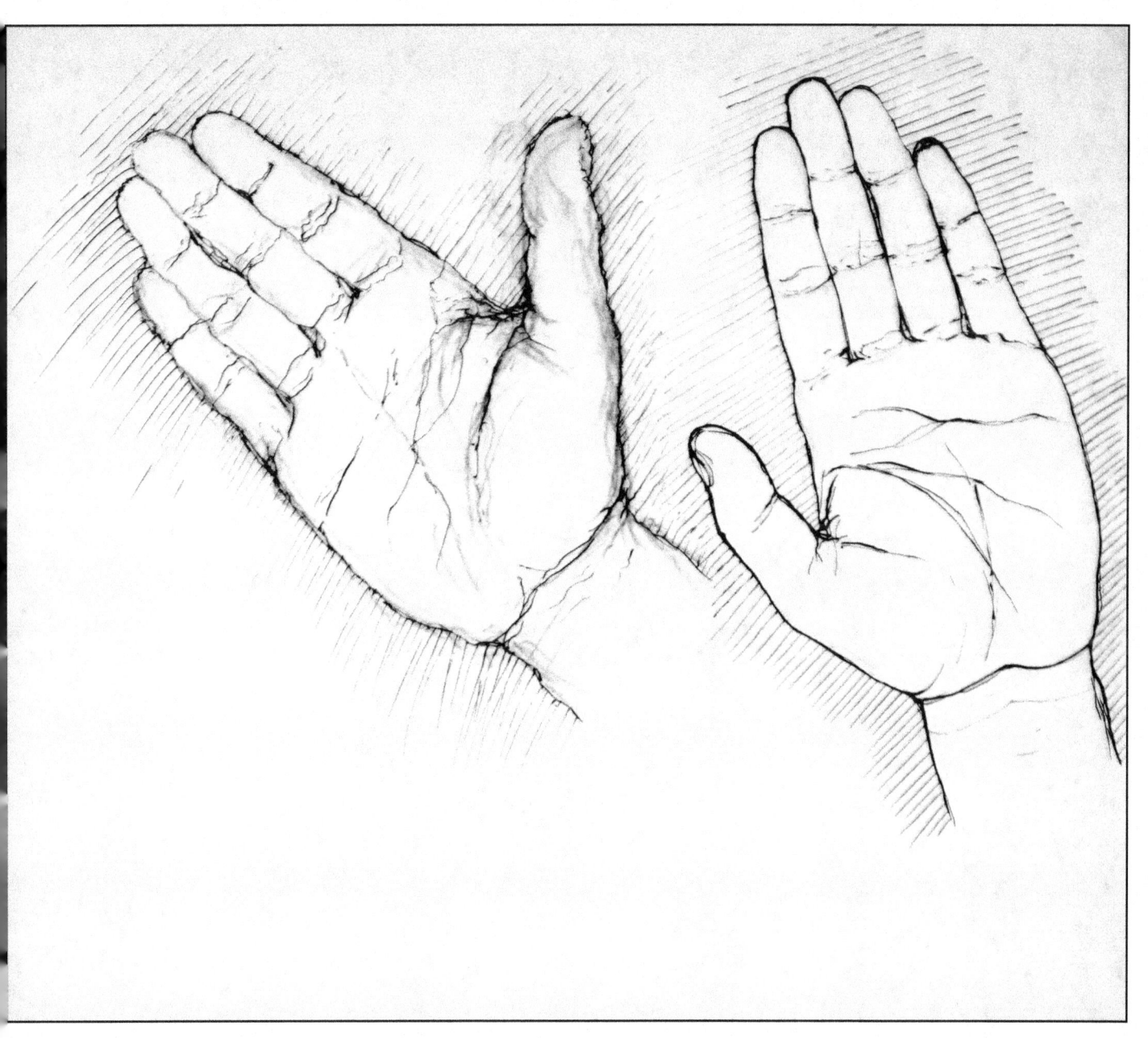

**I drew my left hand with my right hand
and I drew my right hand with my left hand.
Note that I am right-handed.**

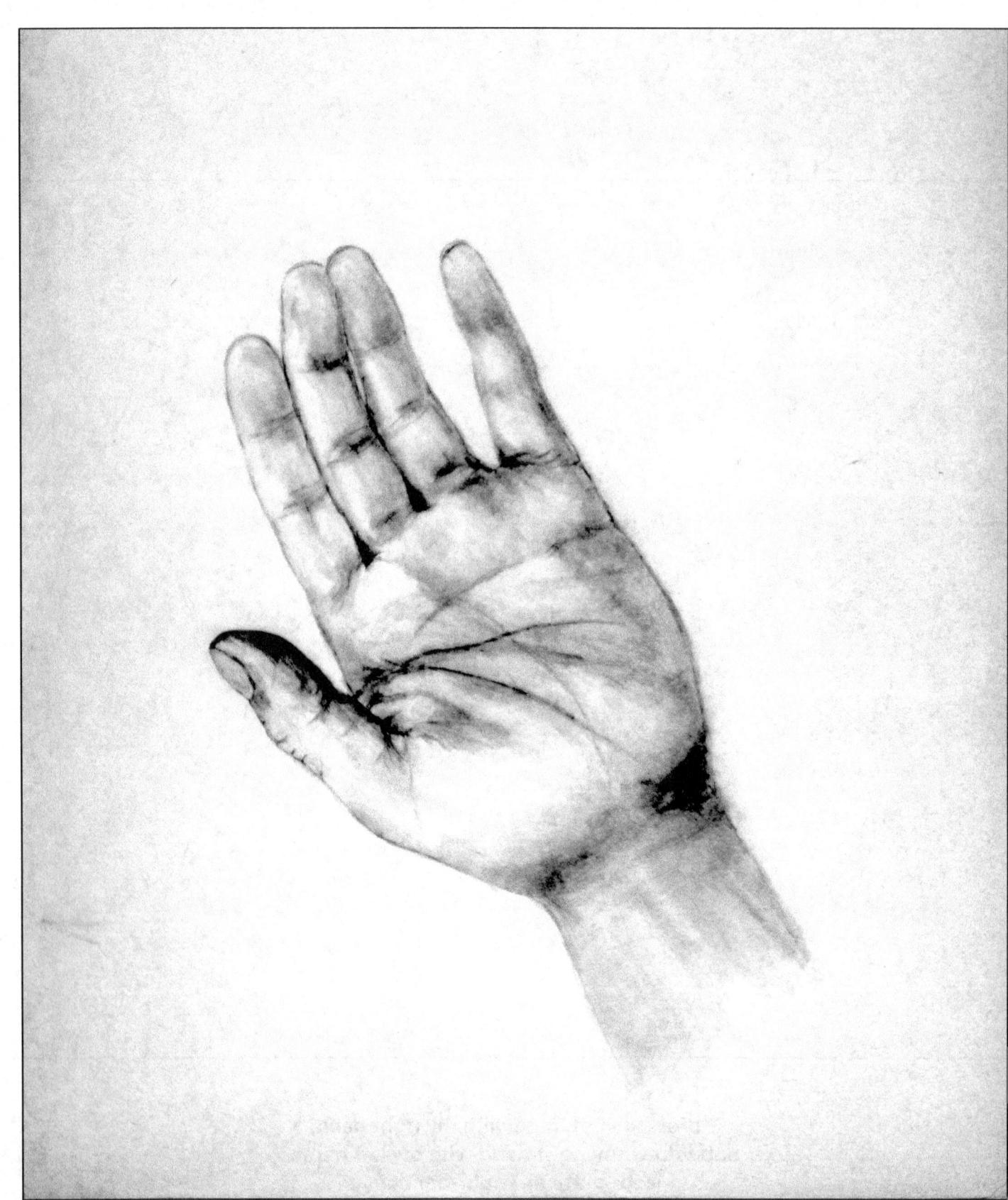

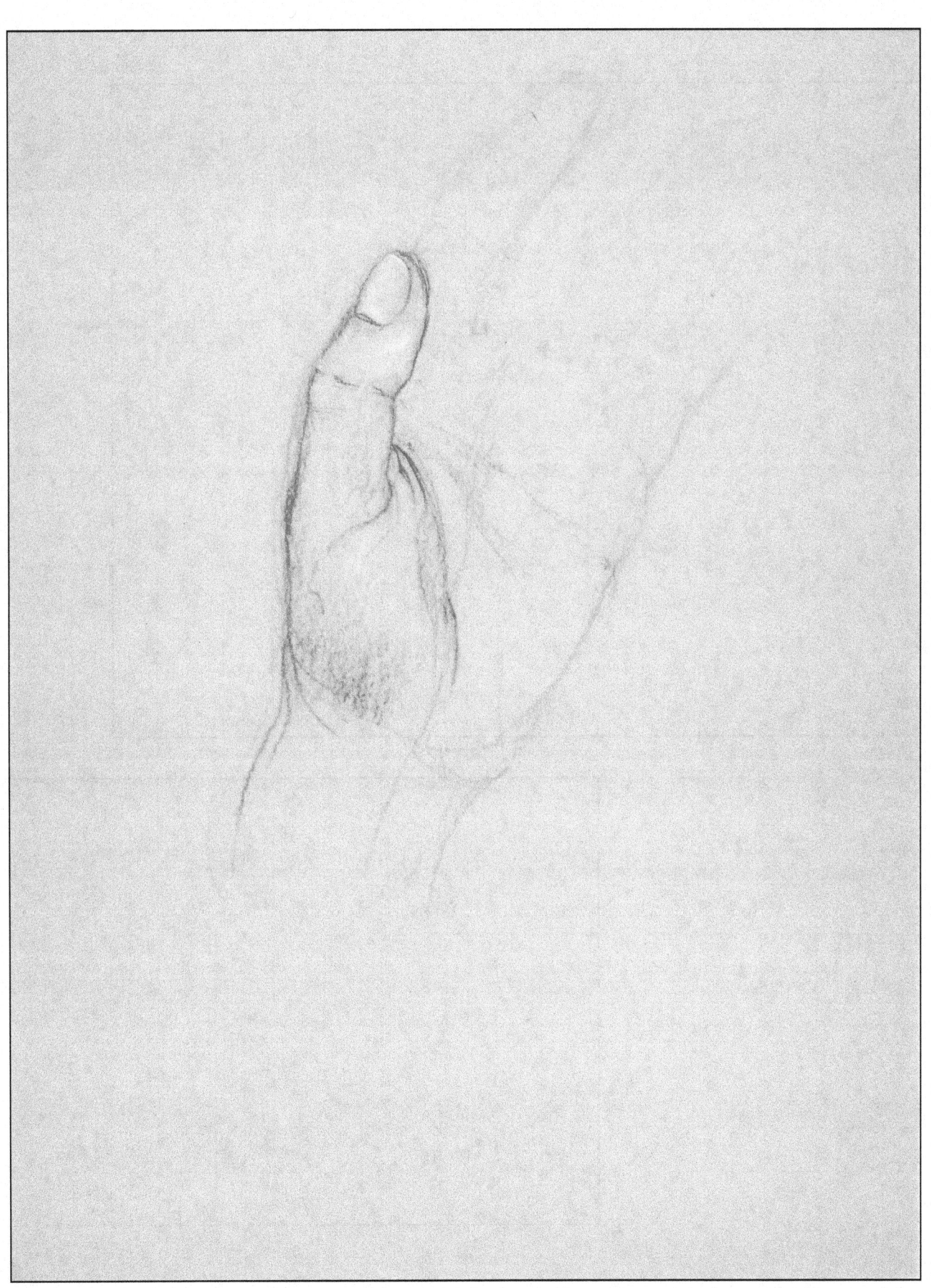

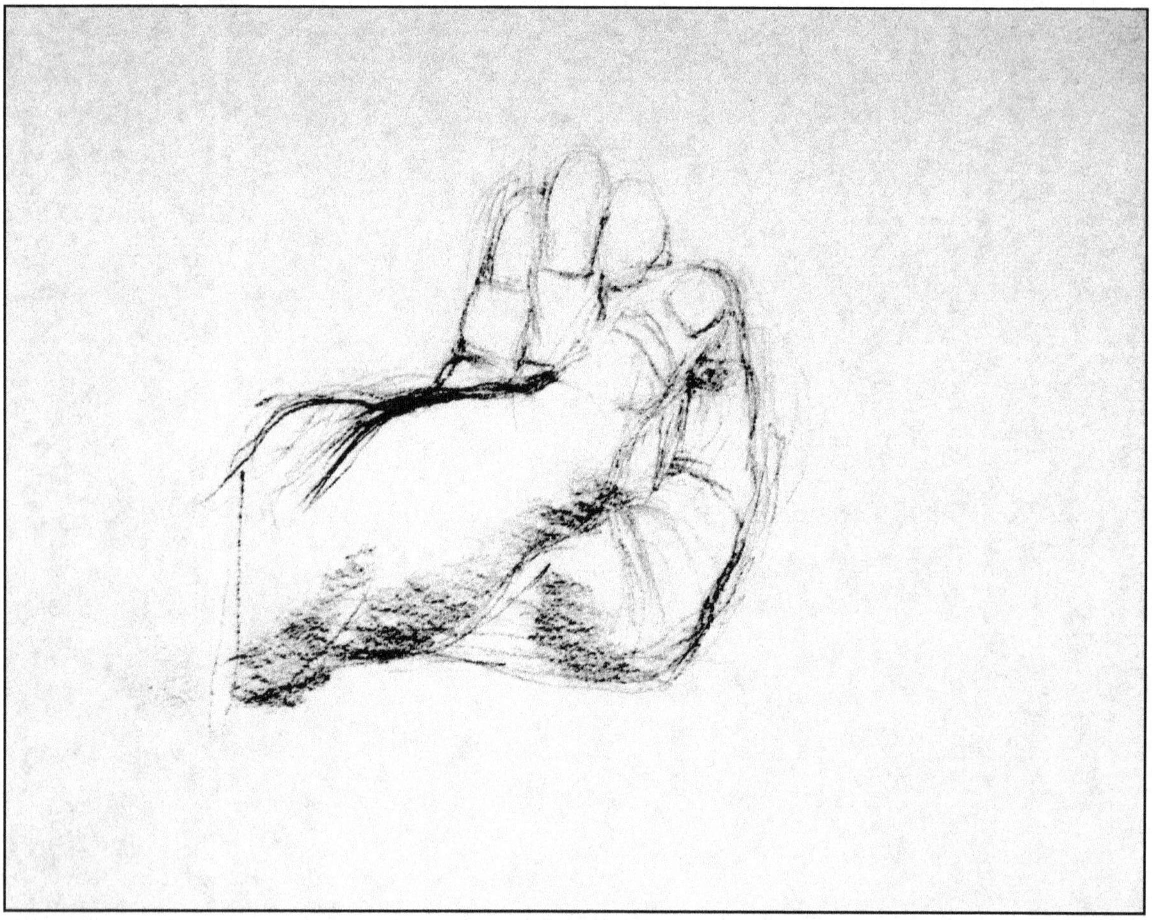

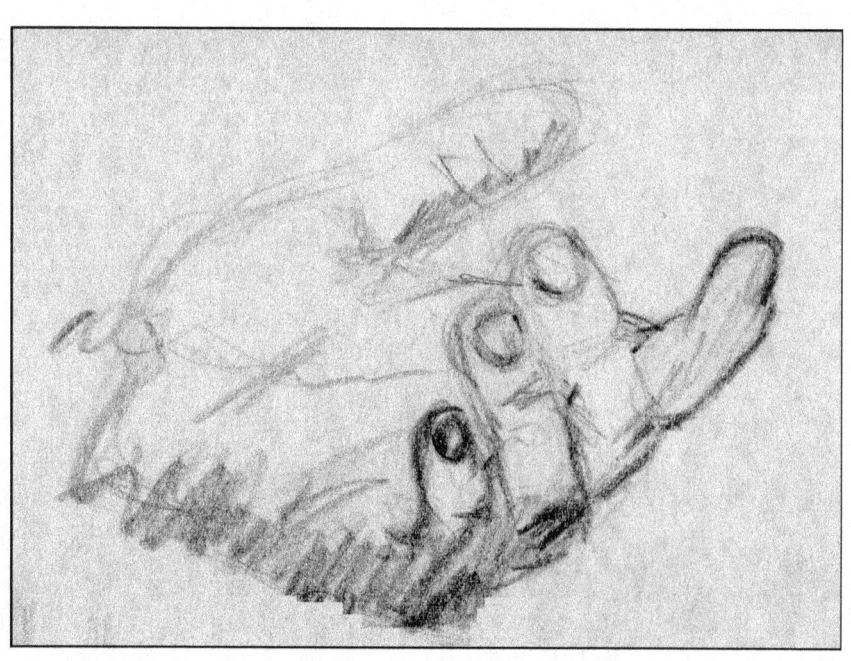

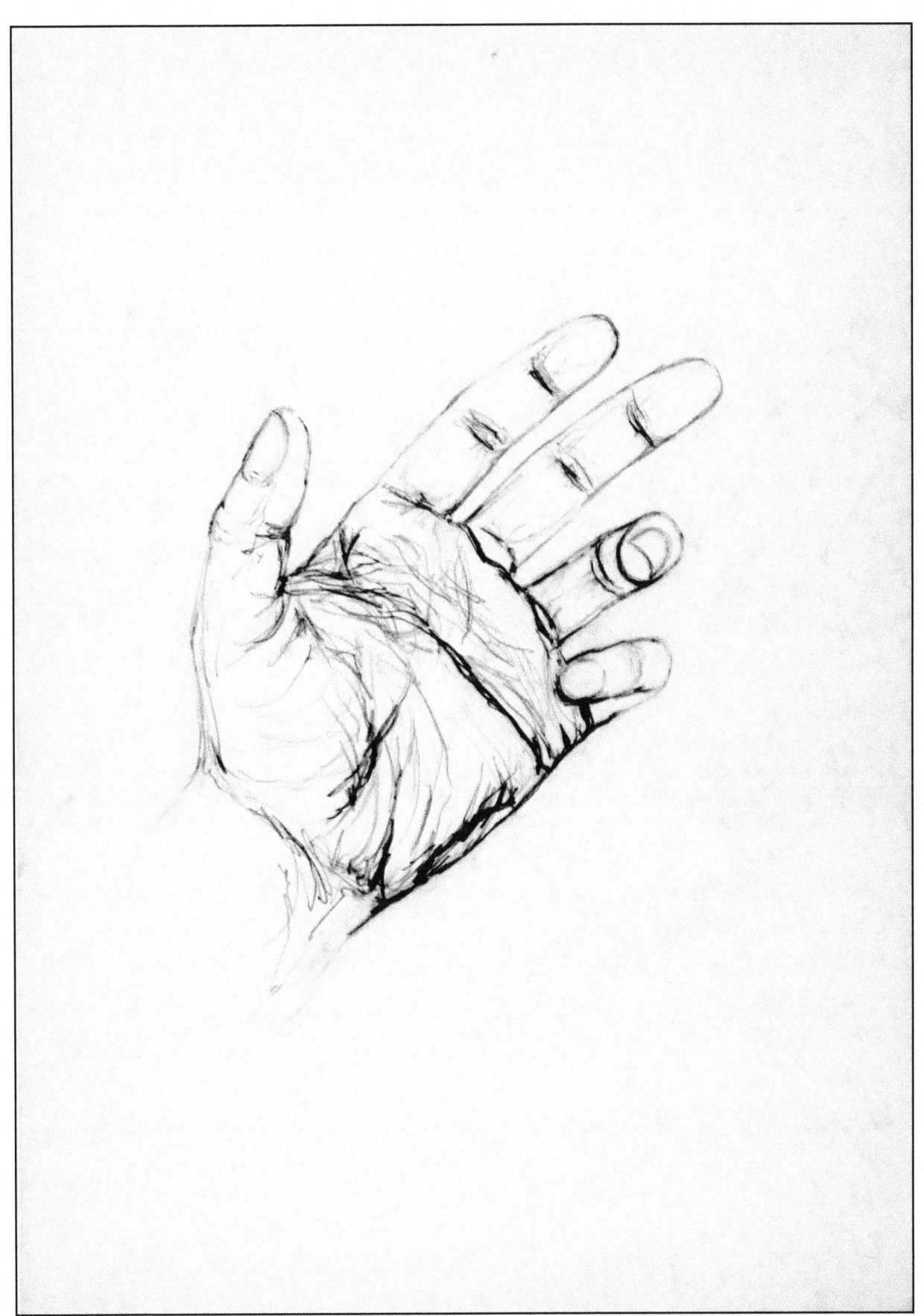

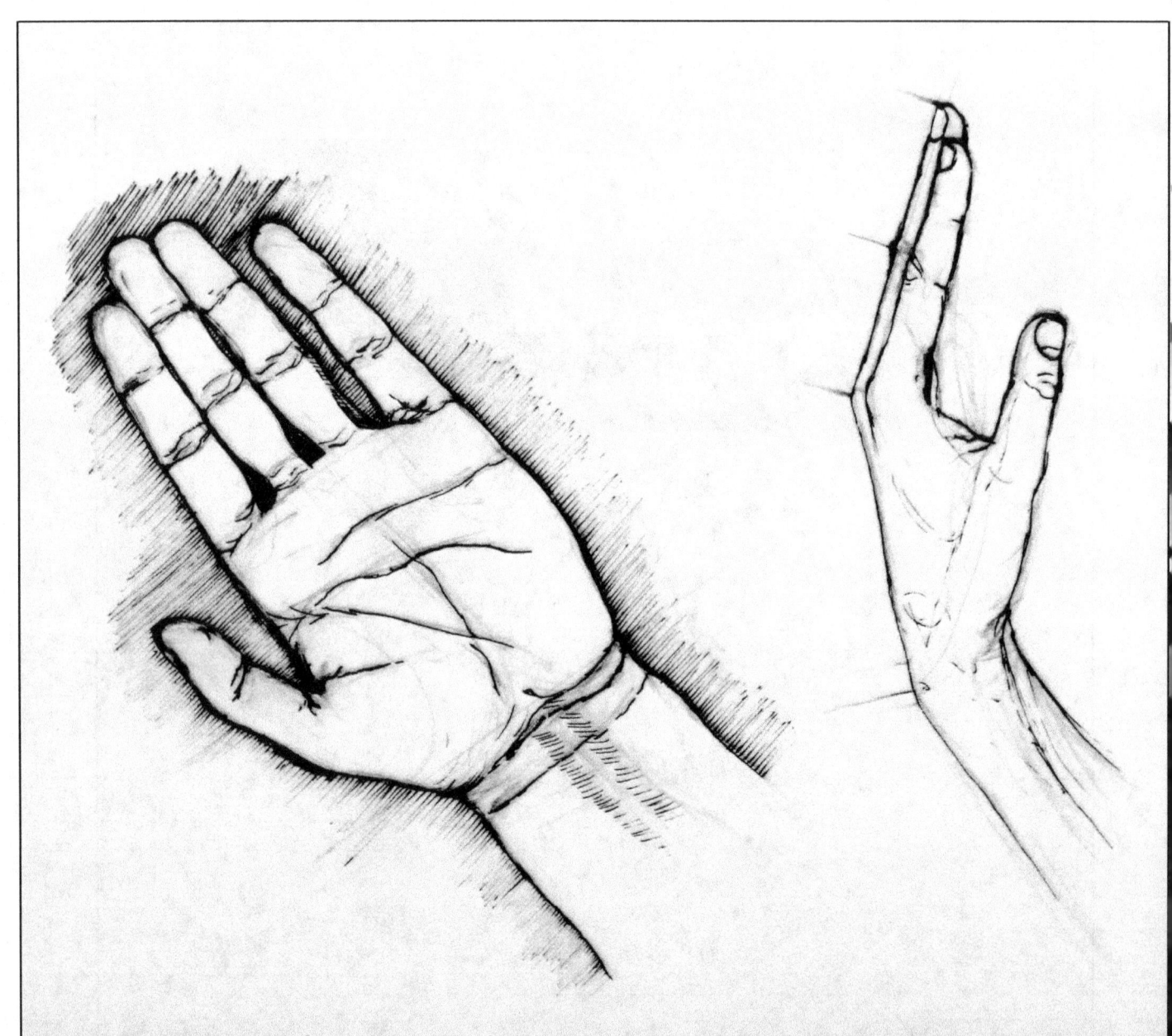

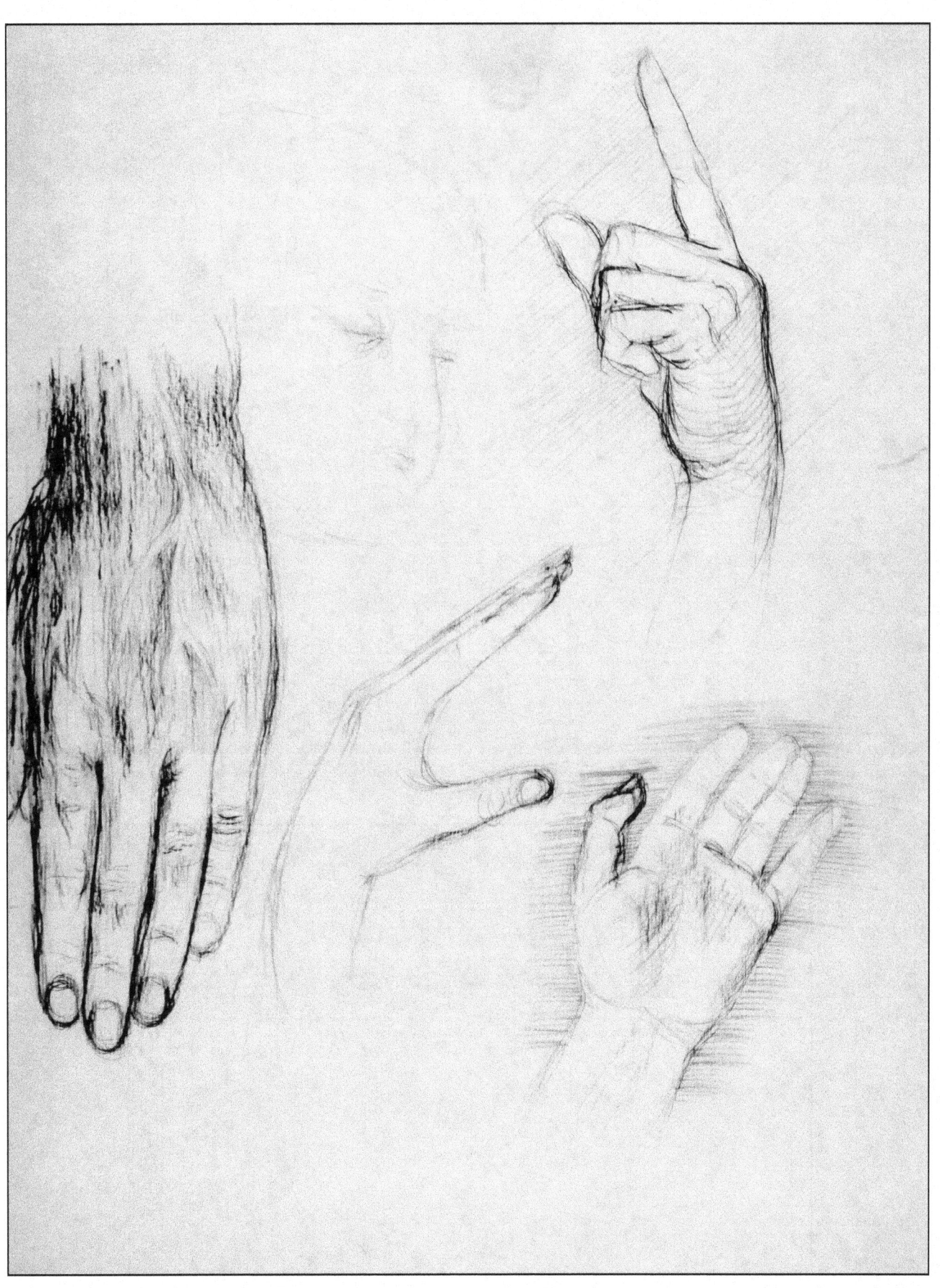

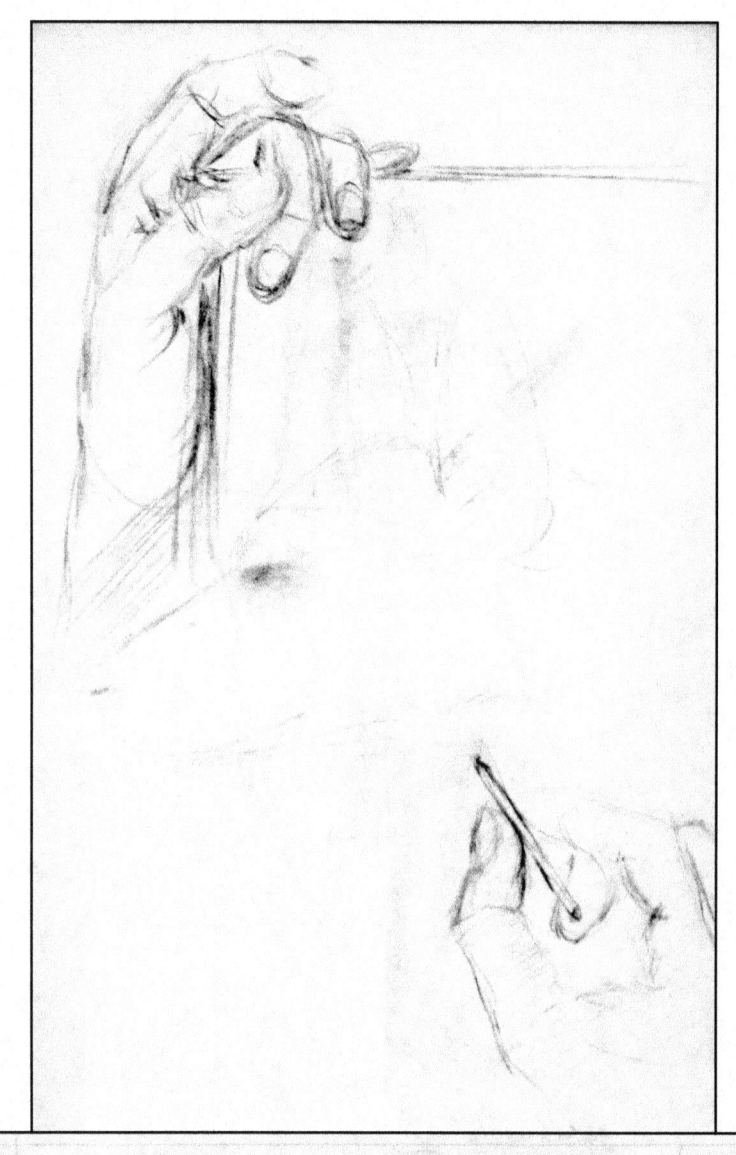
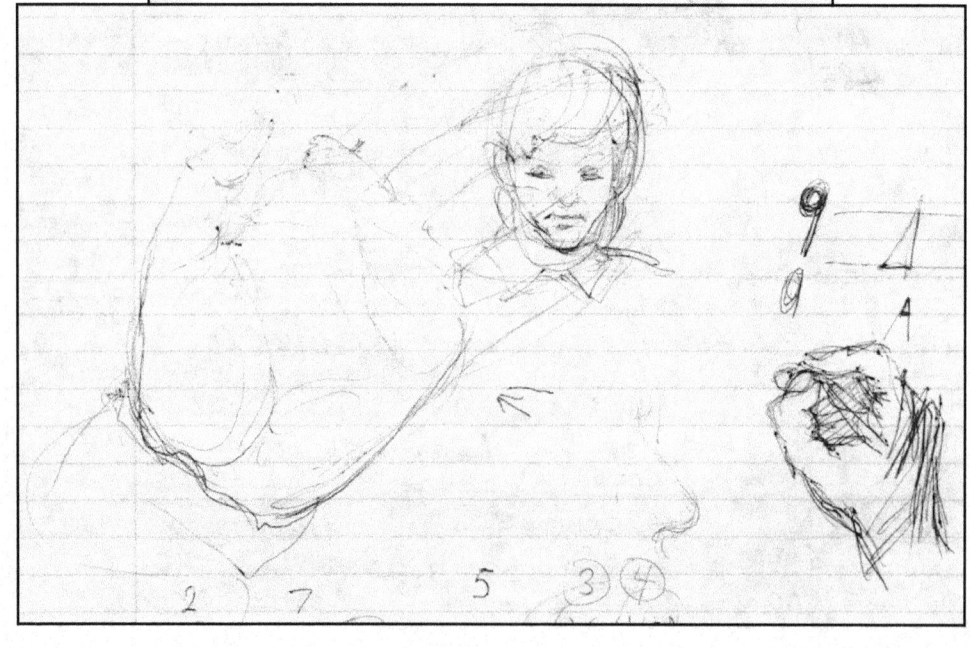

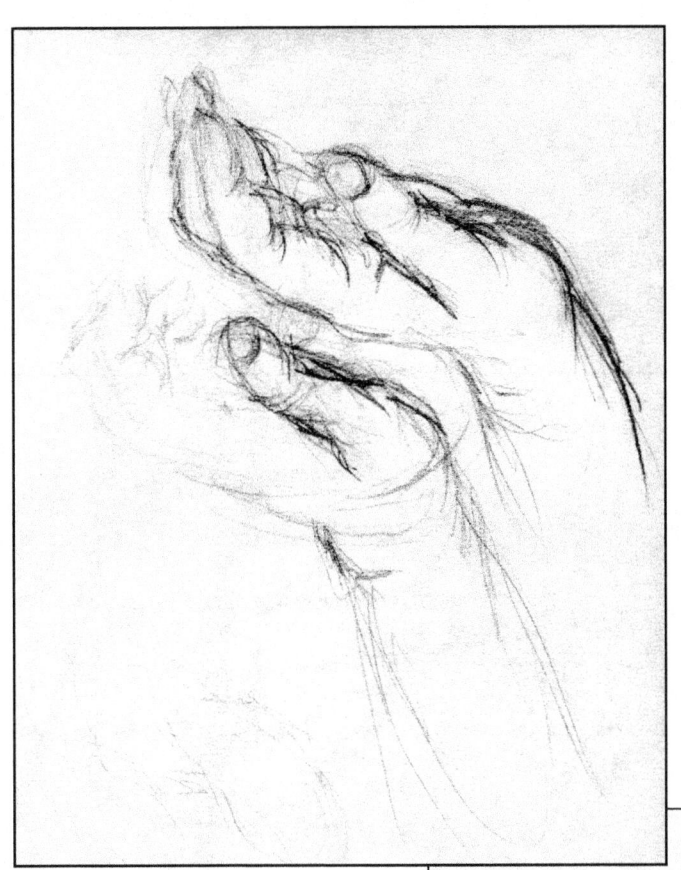
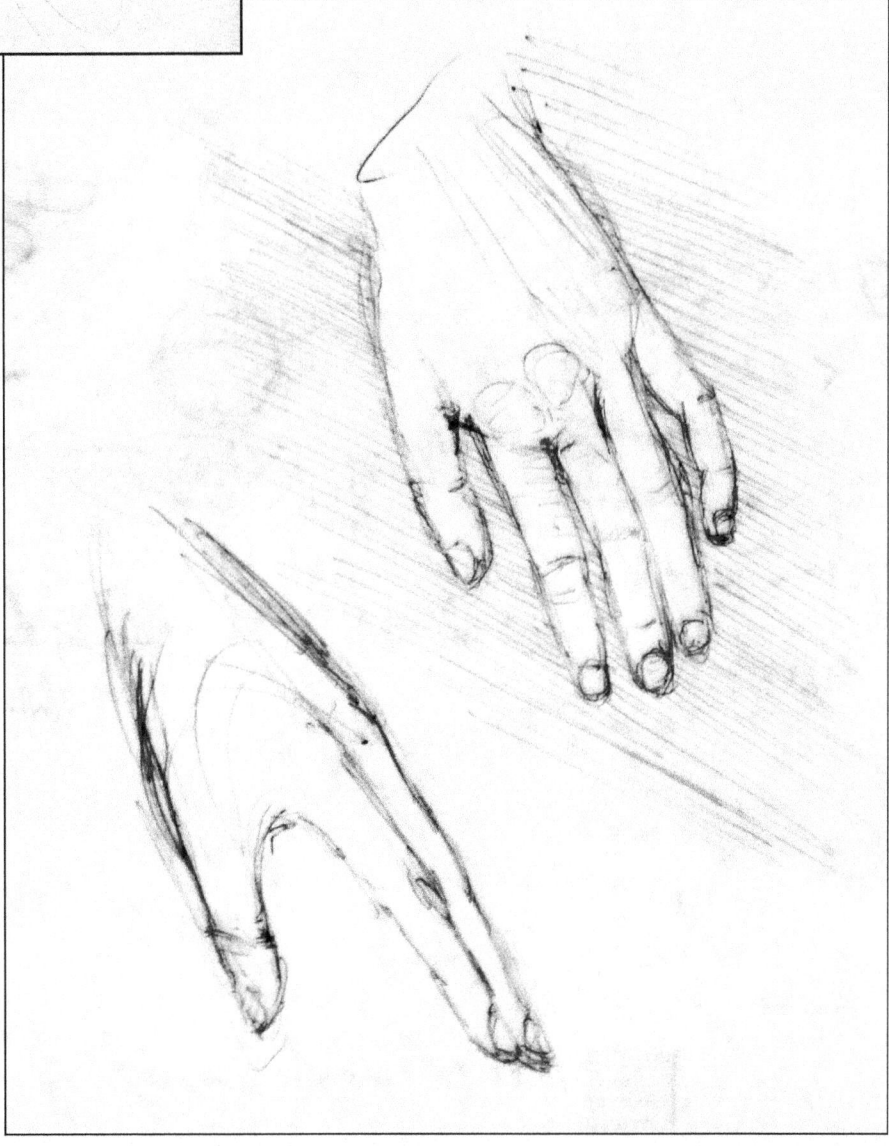

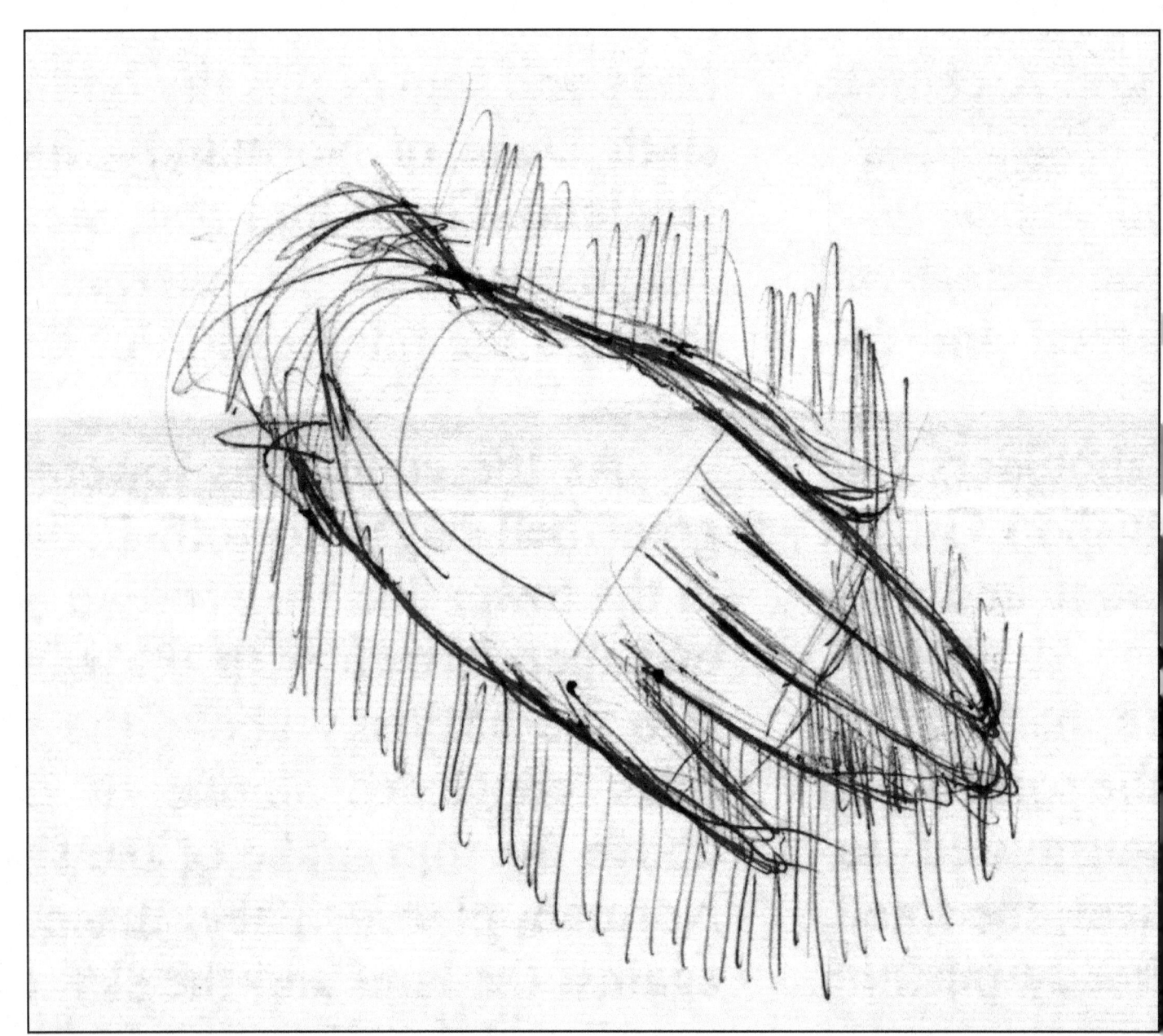

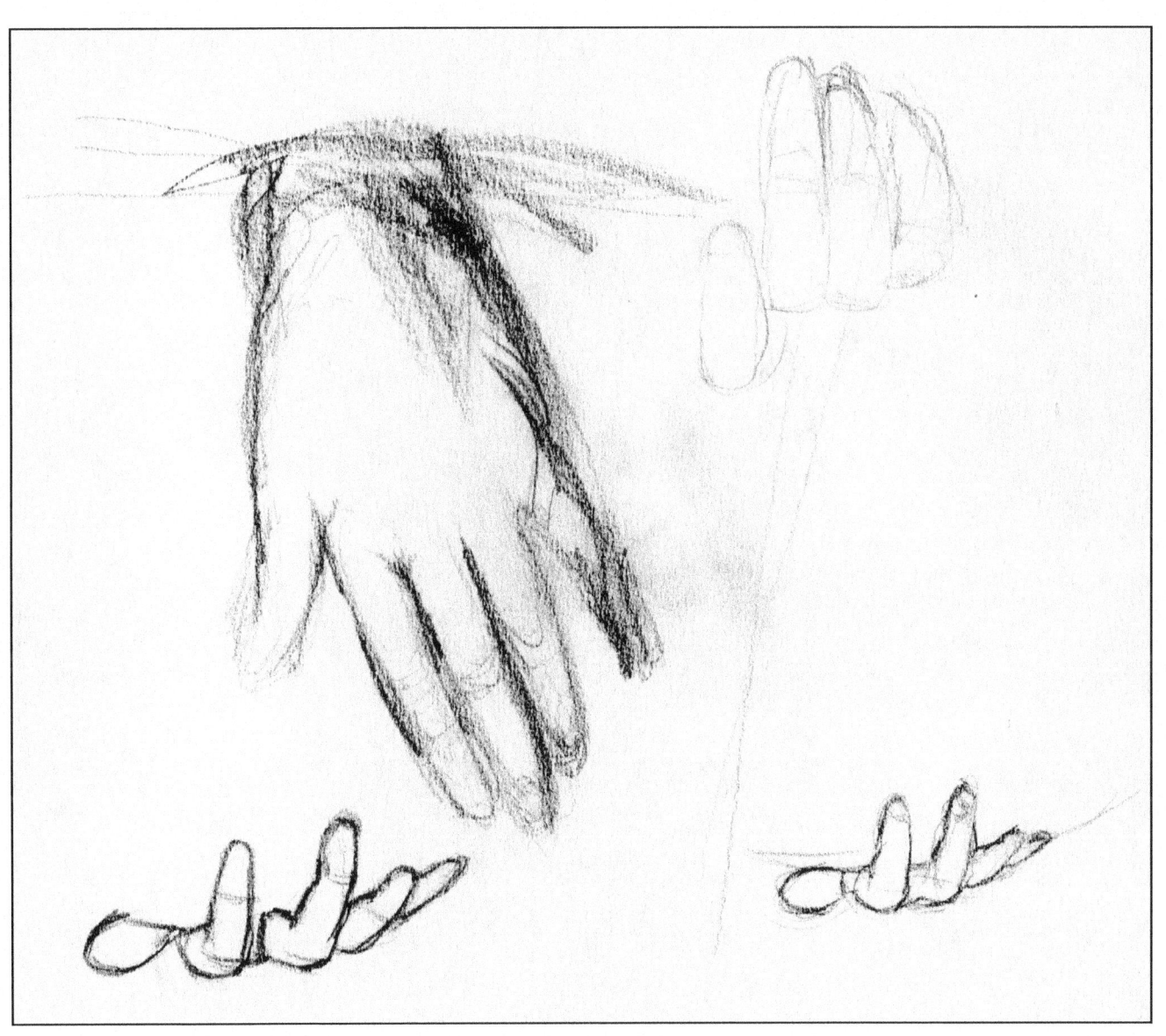

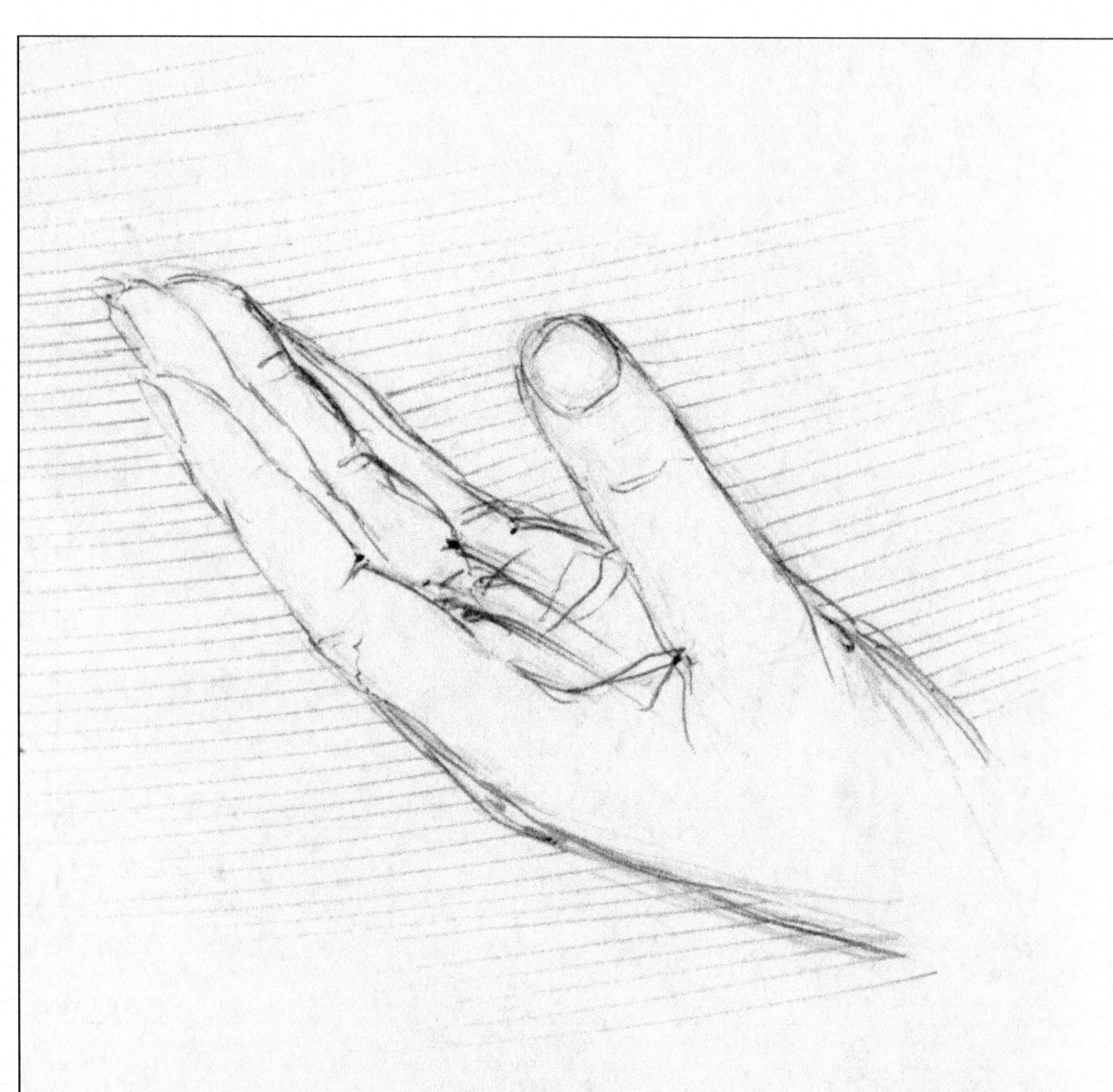

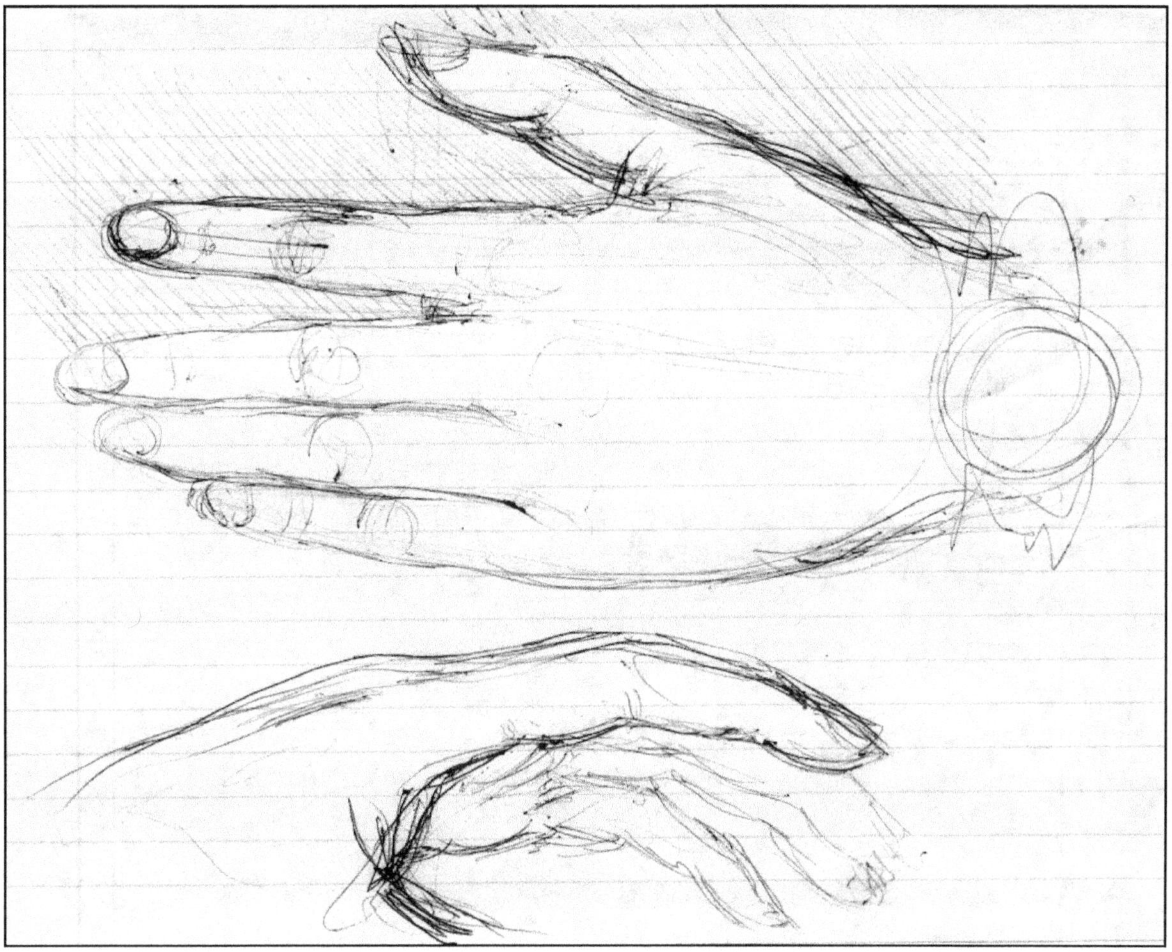

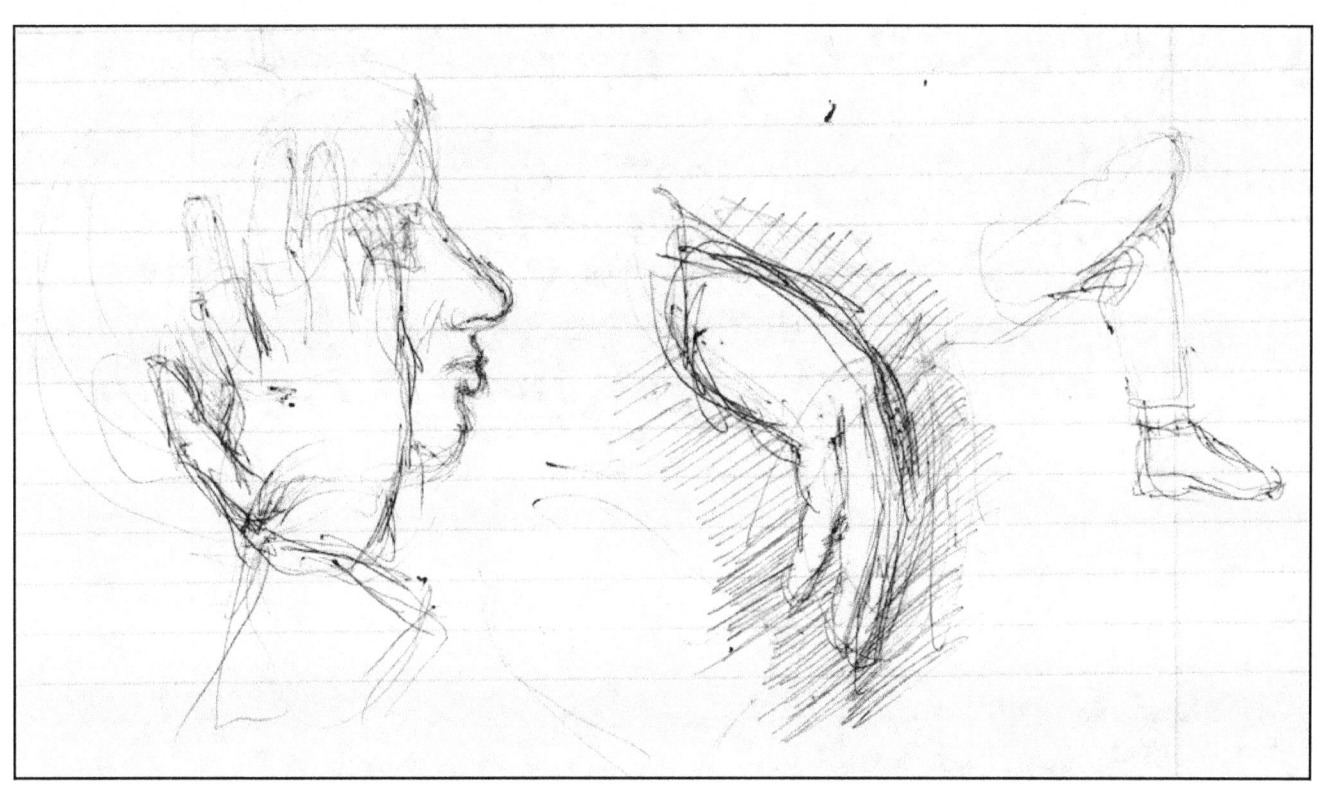

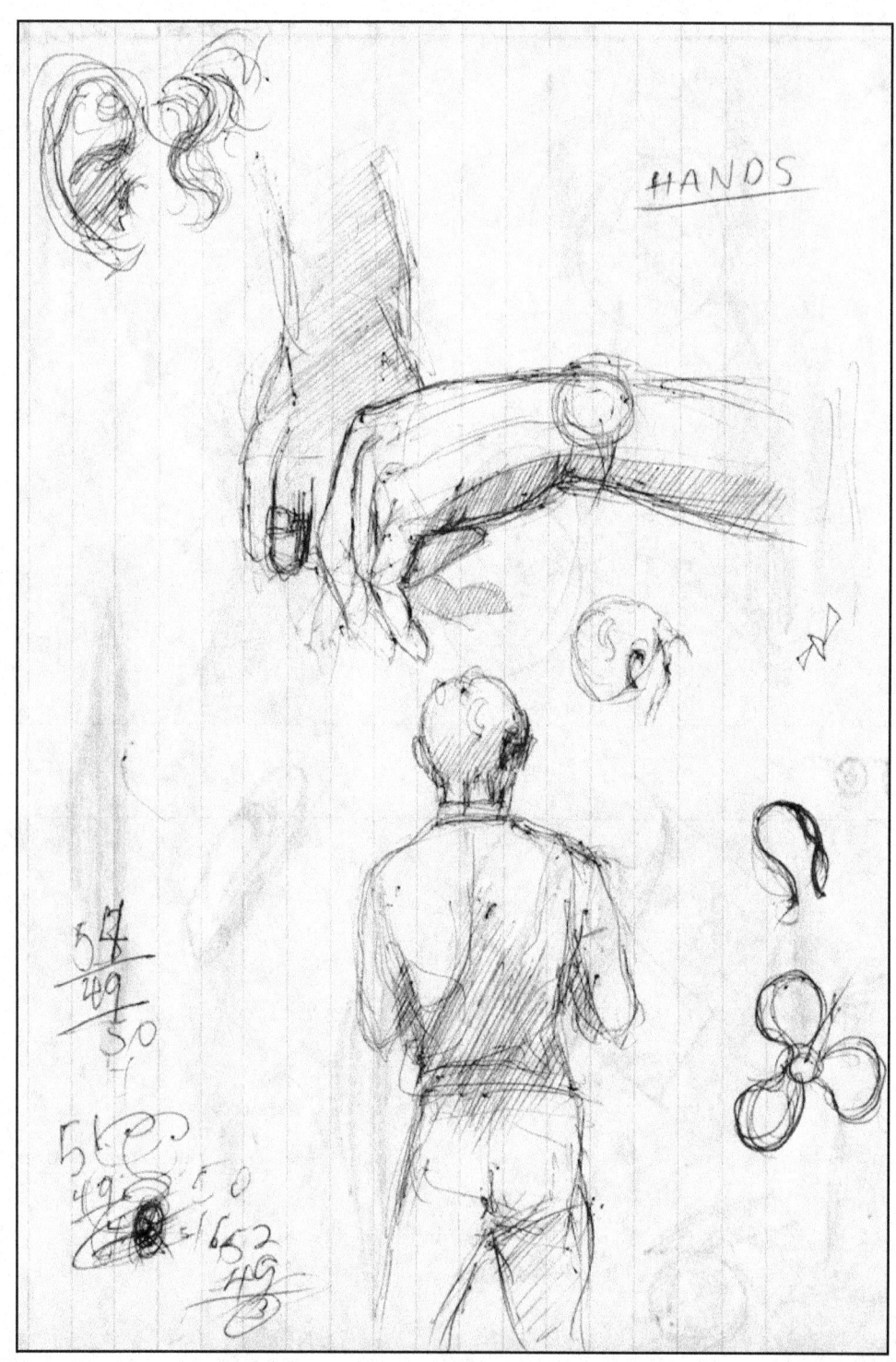

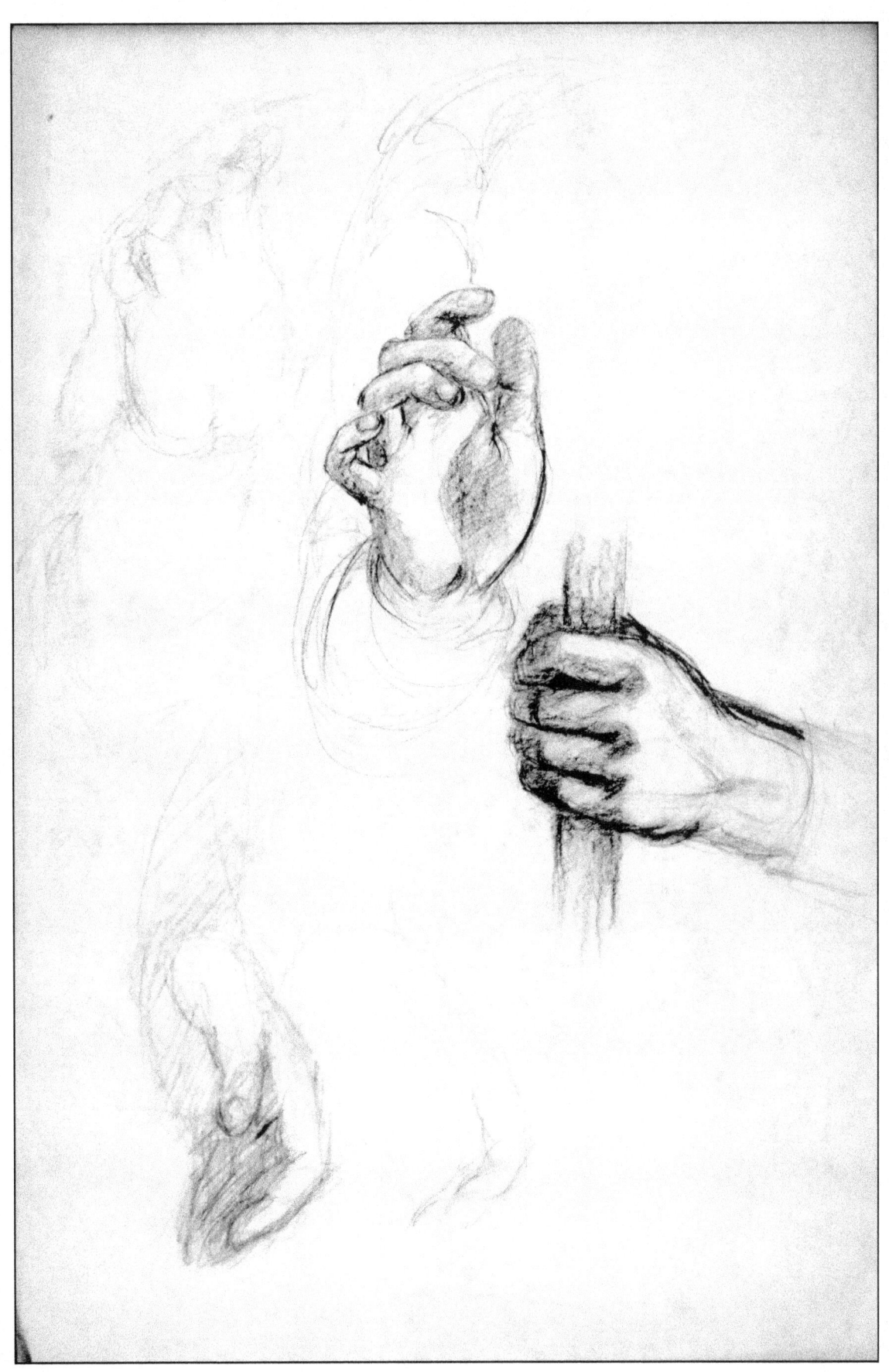

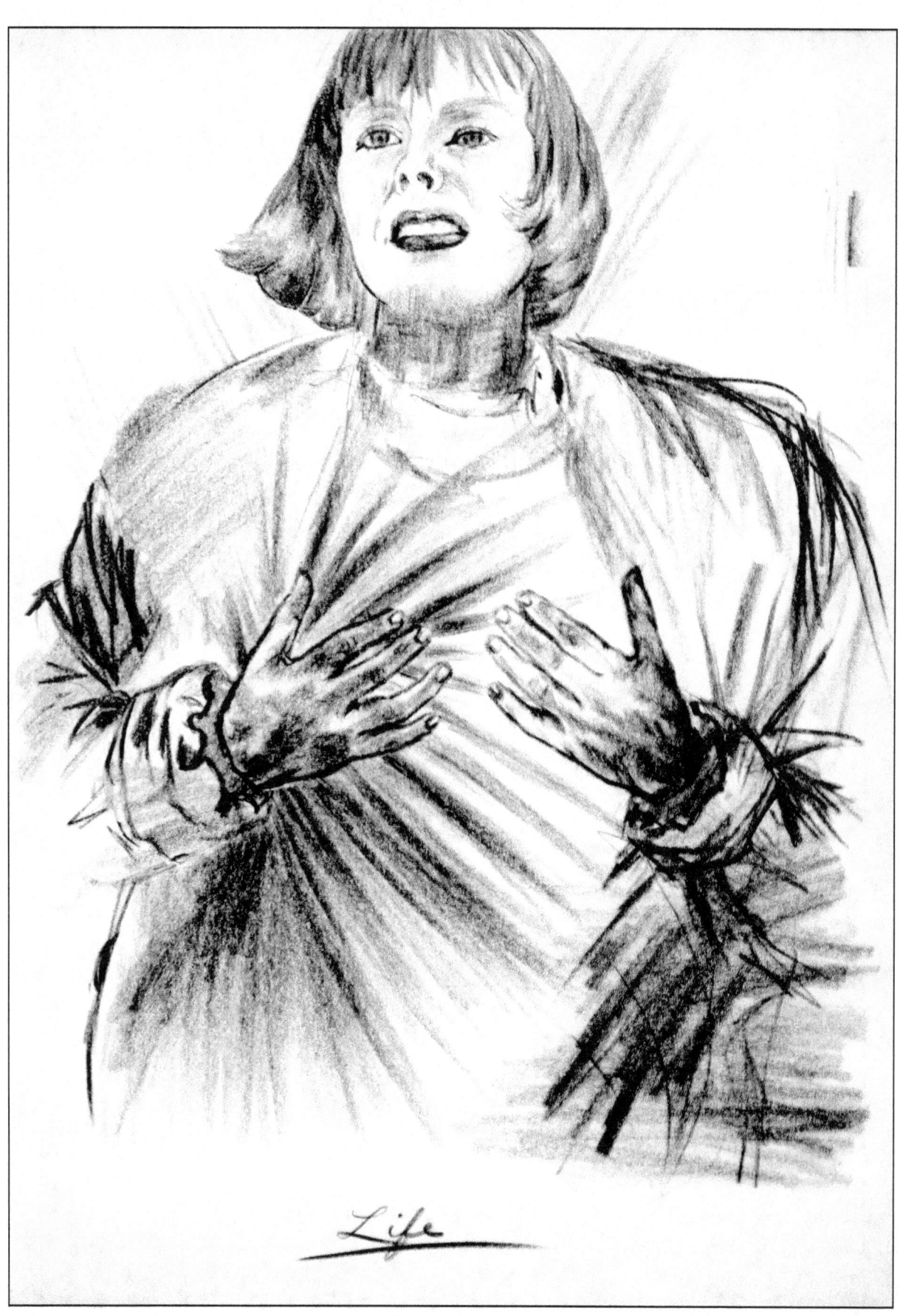

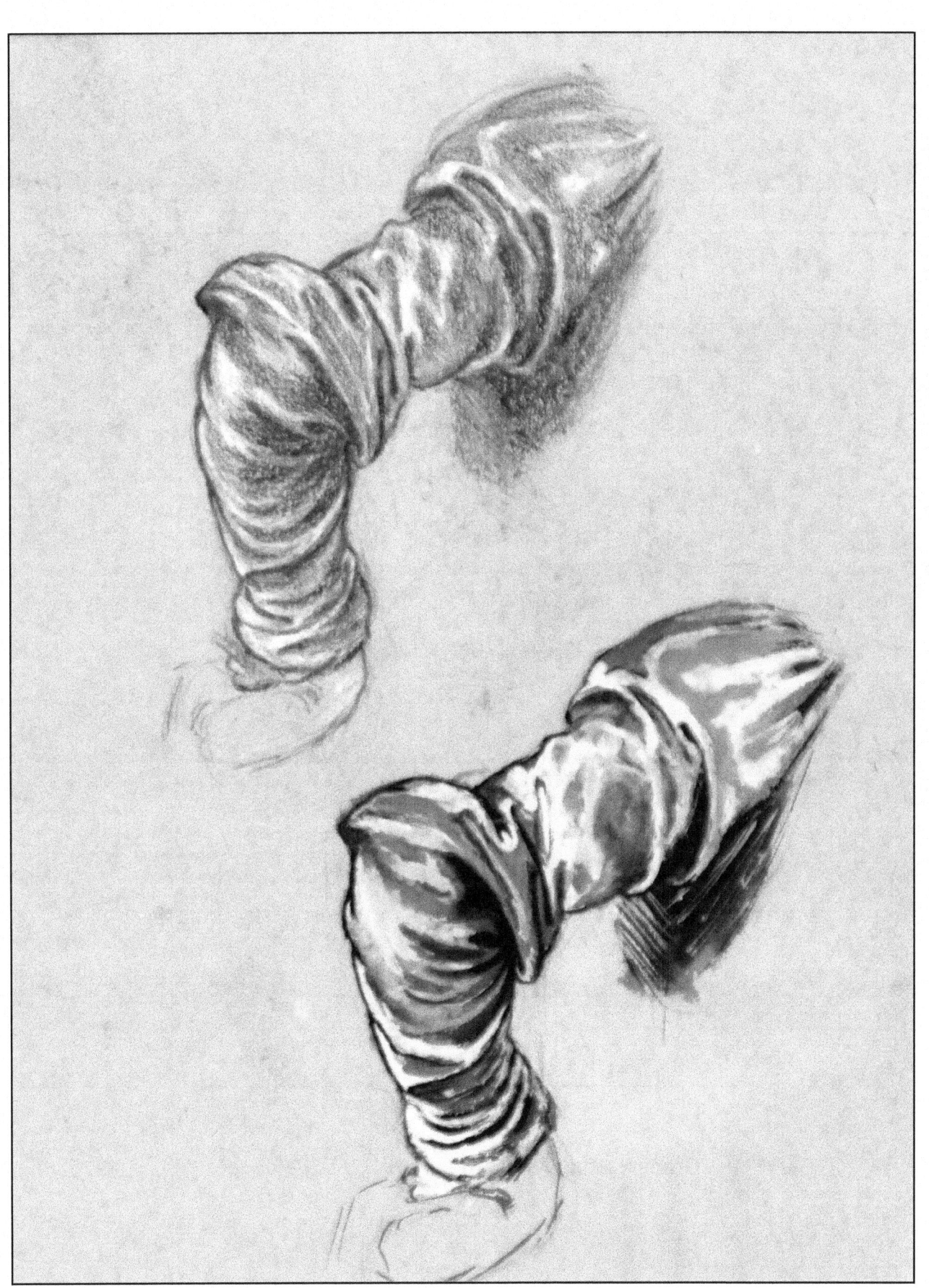

Drapery Study, after Leonardo Da Vinci

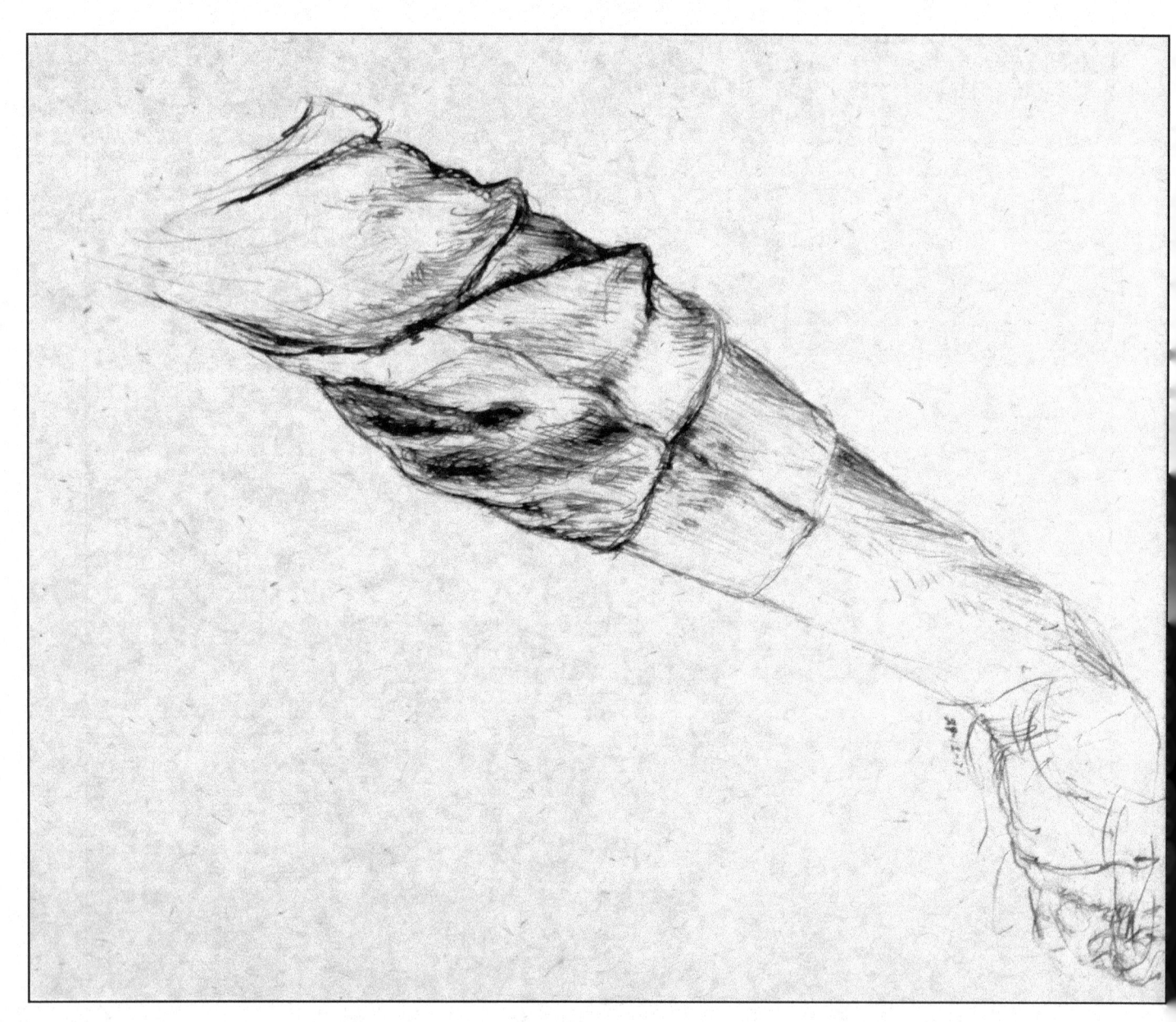

Drapery Study, done in ink, for my left sleeve

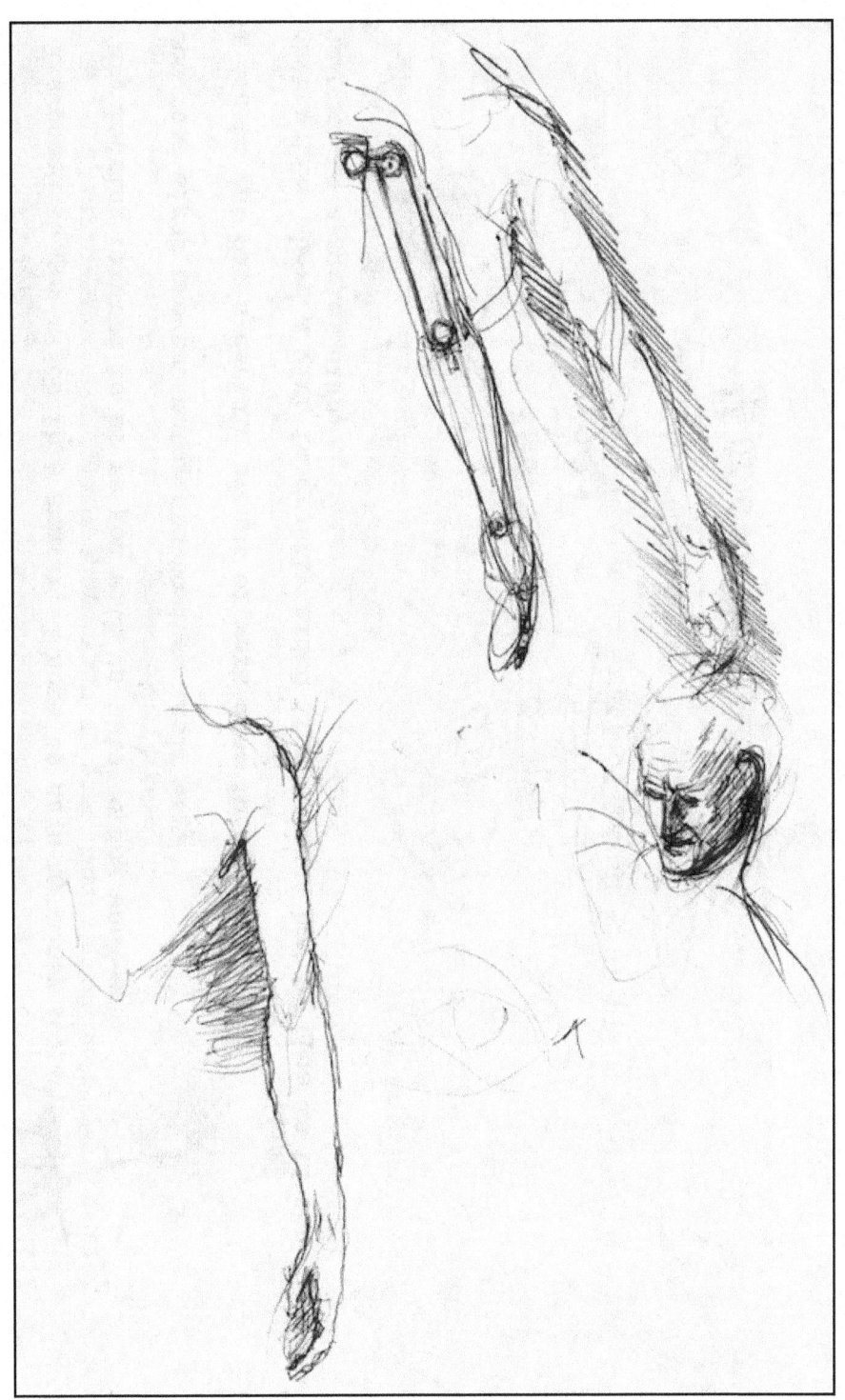

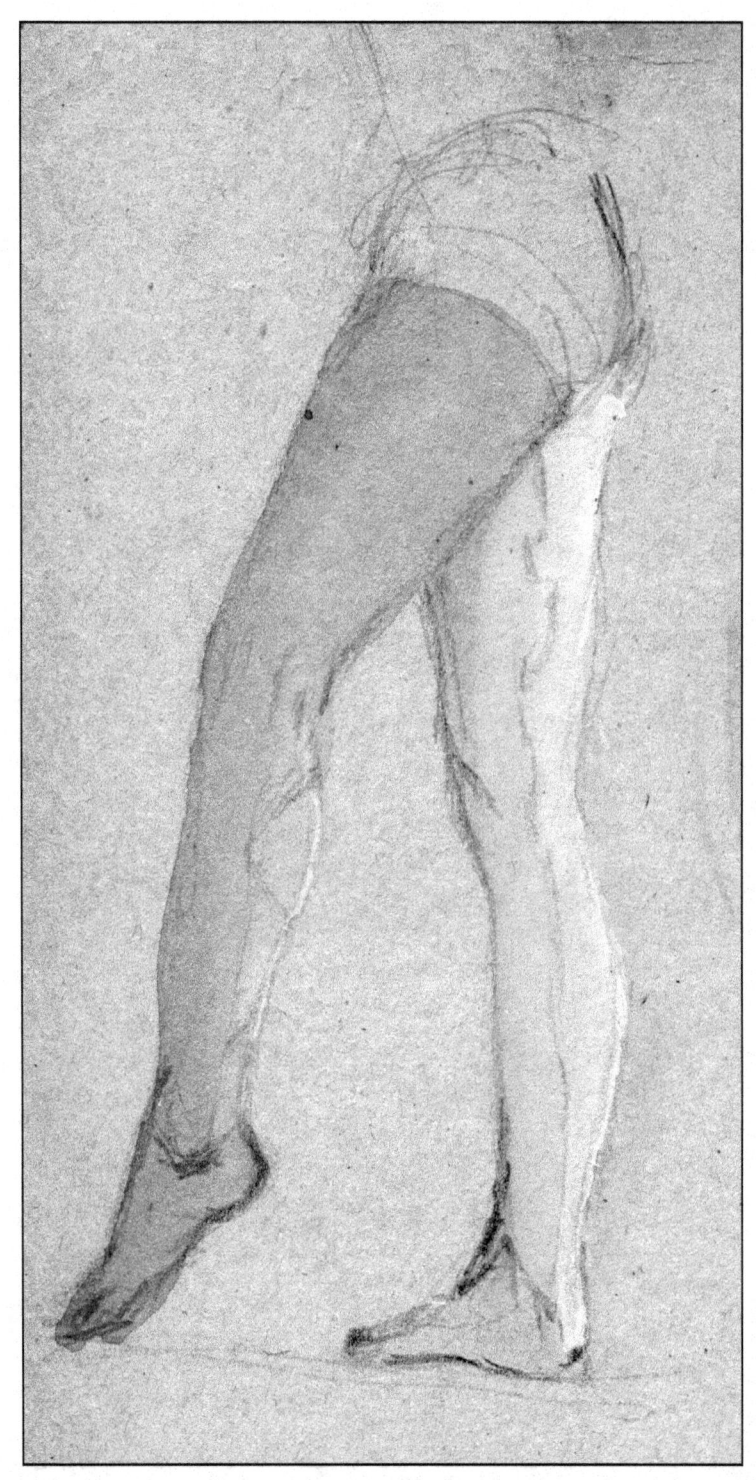

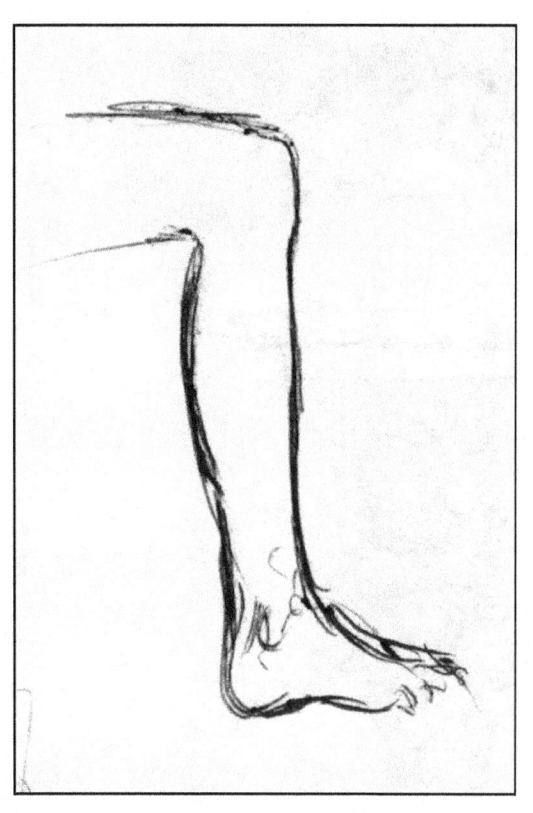

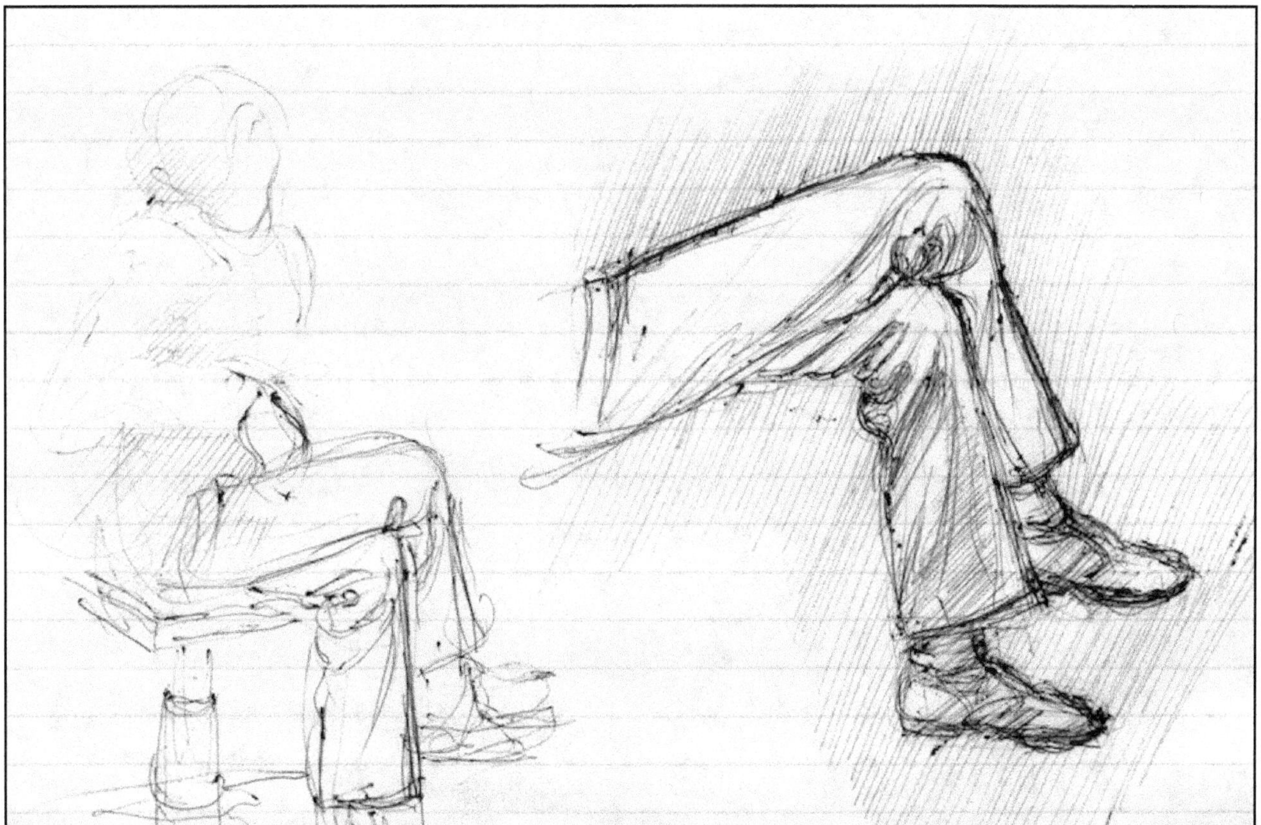

12. Full Figure, Imitation

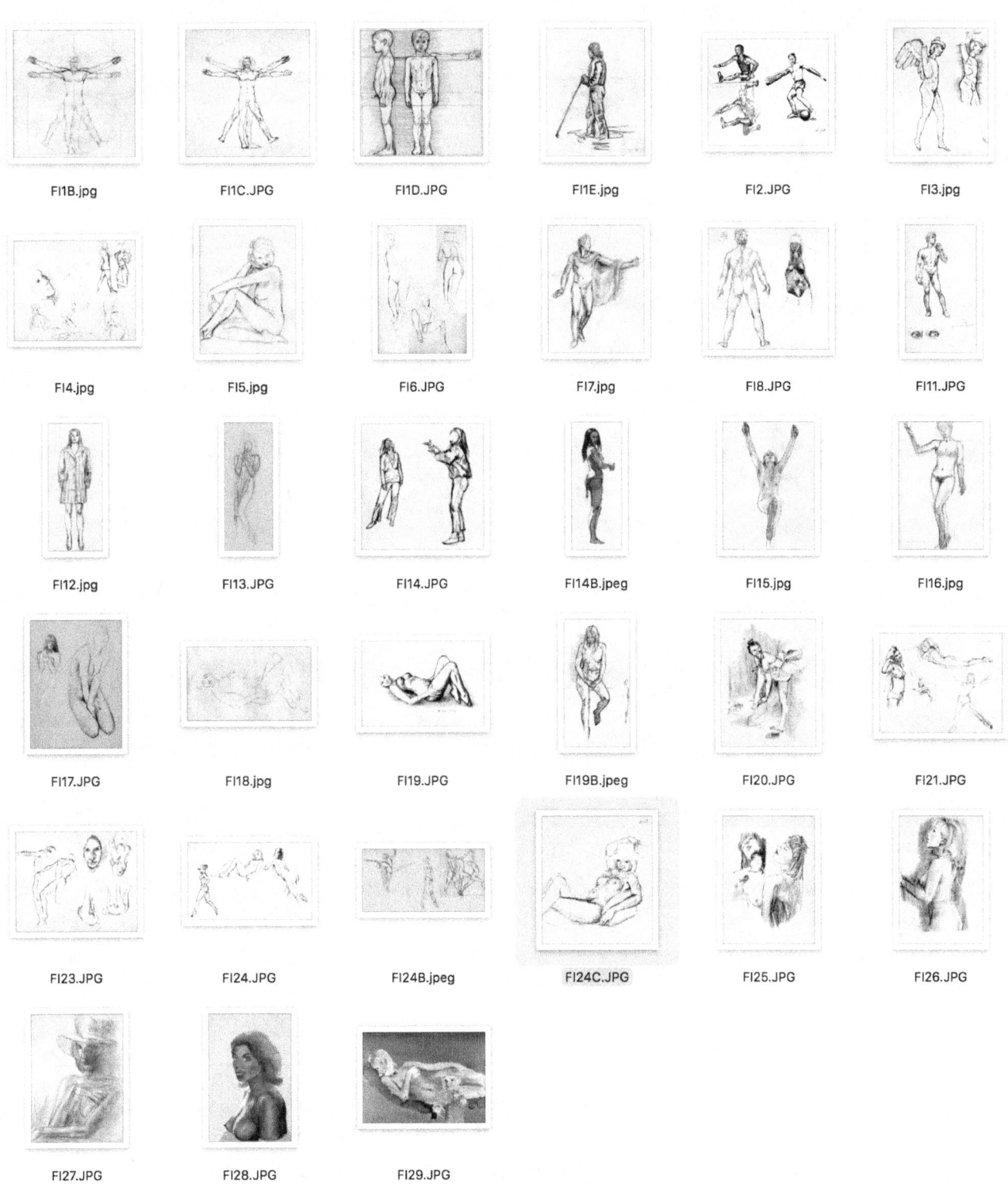

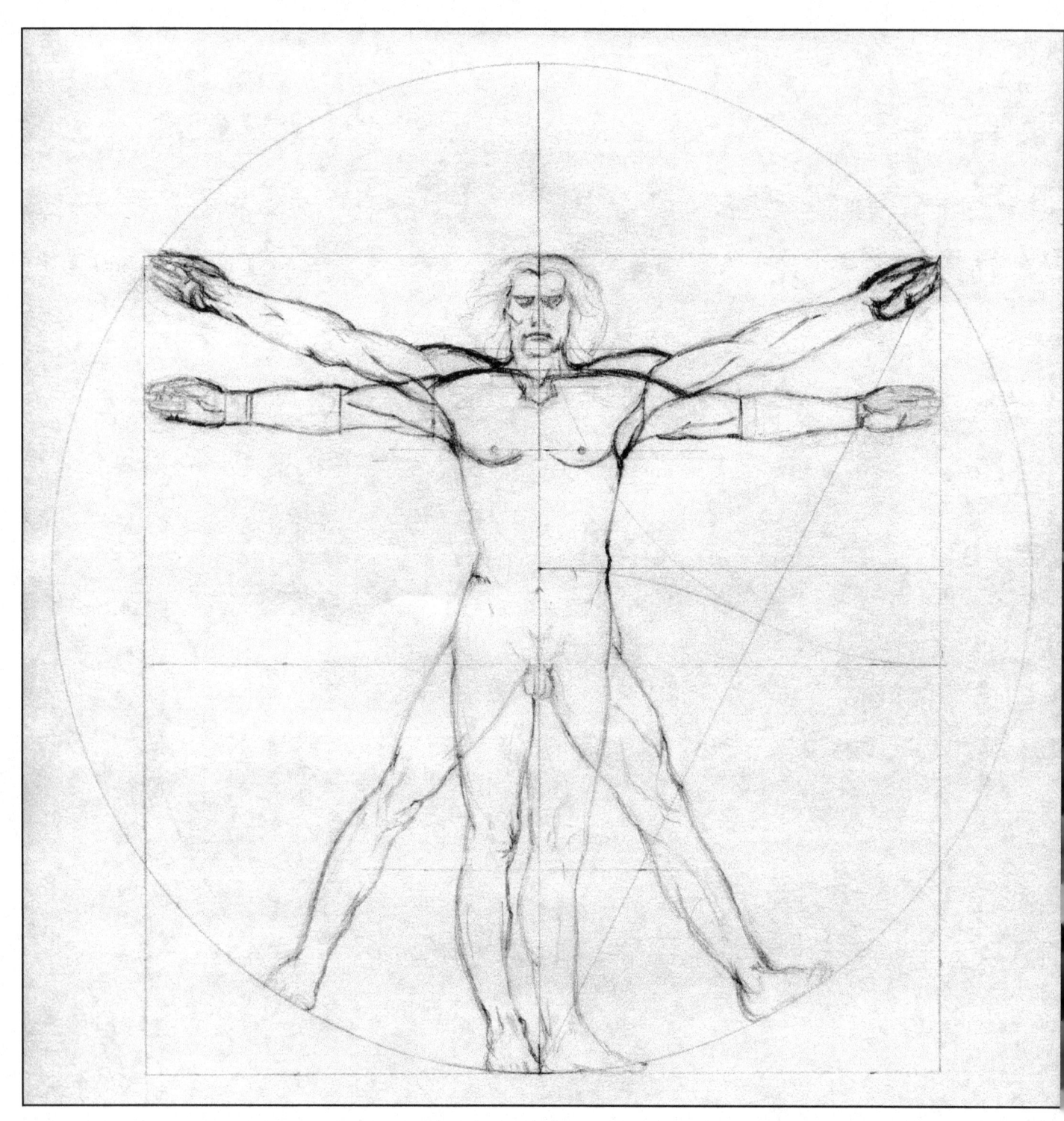

VITRUVIUS' PROPORTIONS OF THE HUMAN FIGURE, after Leonardo da Vinci, my first attempt. Vitruvius was a 1st-century Roman architect, who linked geometry to the human proportions.

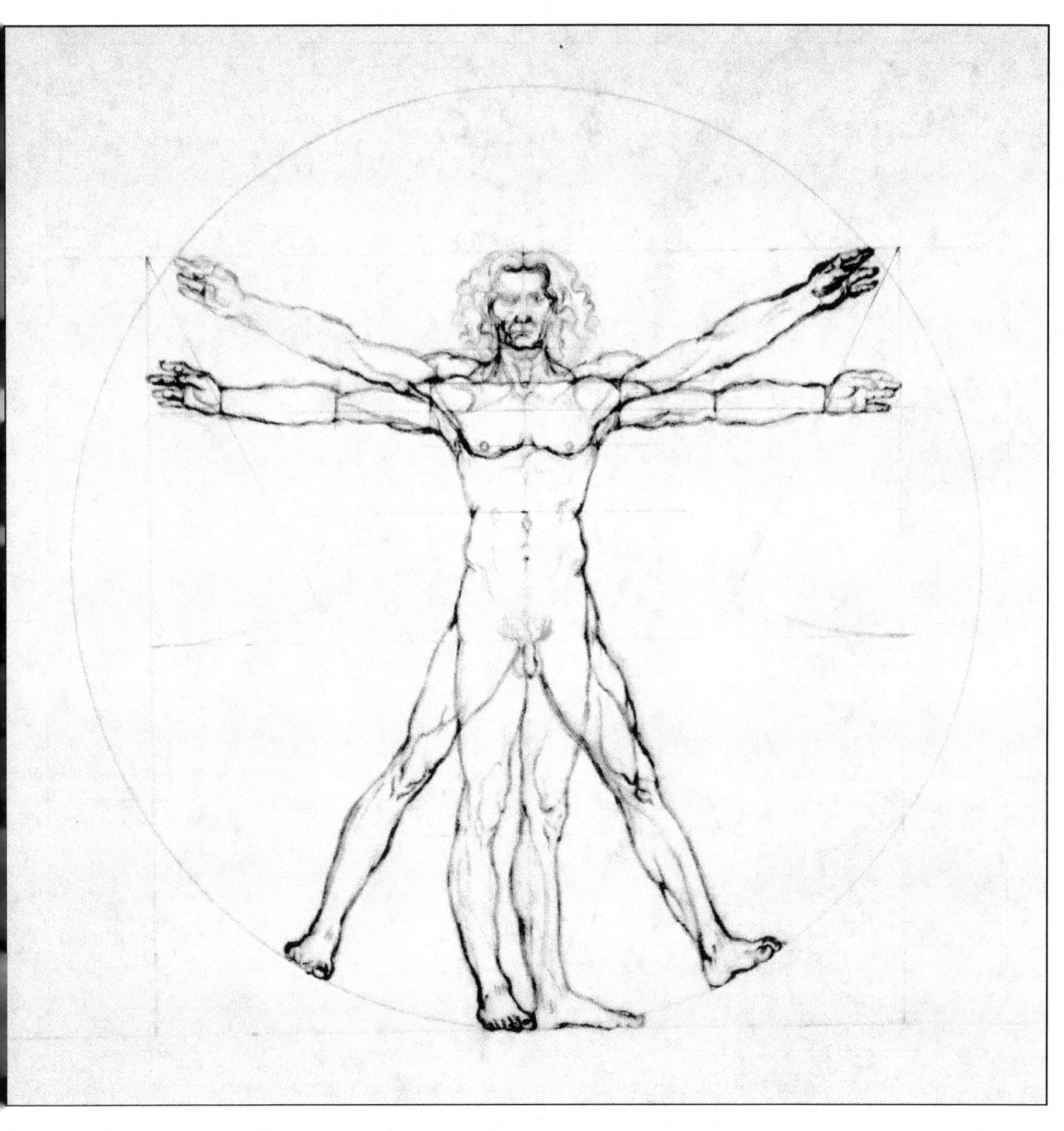

VITRUVIUS' PROPORTIONS OF THE HUMAN FIGURE,
after Leonardo da Vinci, my second and better attempt.

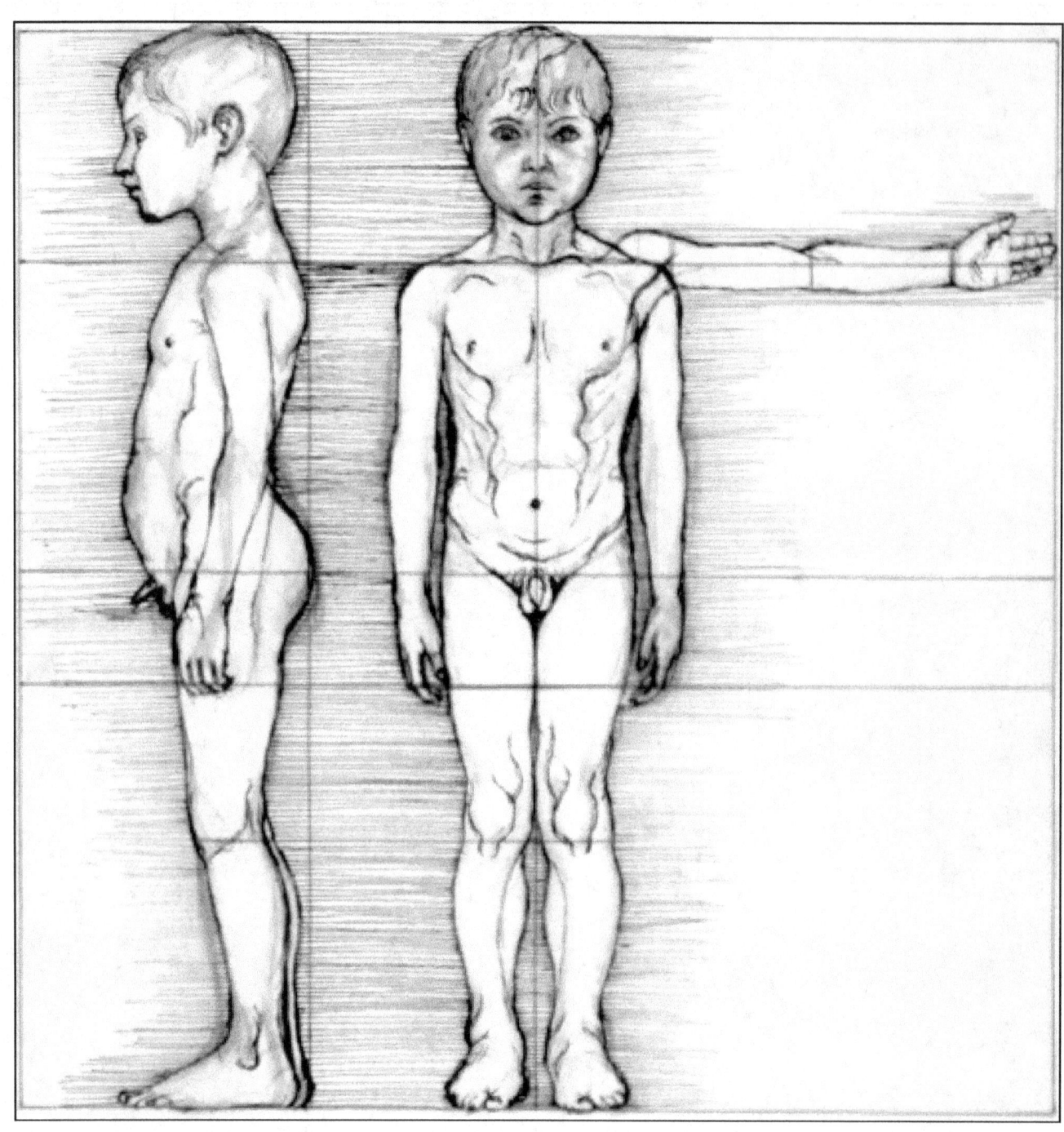

THE PROPORTIONS OF AN 8-YEAR-OLD BOY do not follow those of a grown-up. This counts especially for the head when compared to the length of the body. The distance from the shoulders to the toes can be divided into 2 equal parts when the dividing line passes through the fingers.

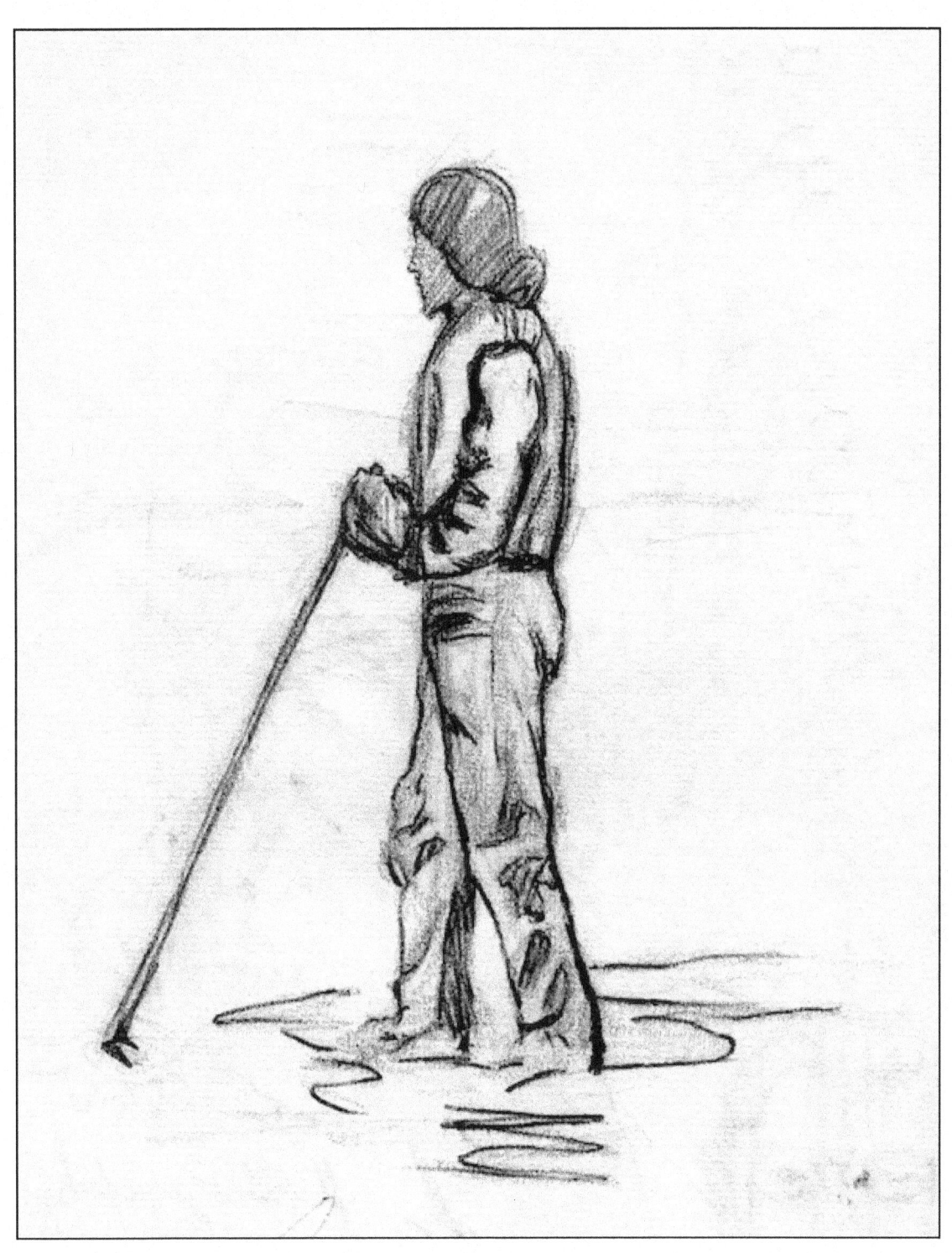

FIGURE FROM A MAGAZINE. One of the few drawings brought over from Italy. It was drawn on a 3"x5" notepad.

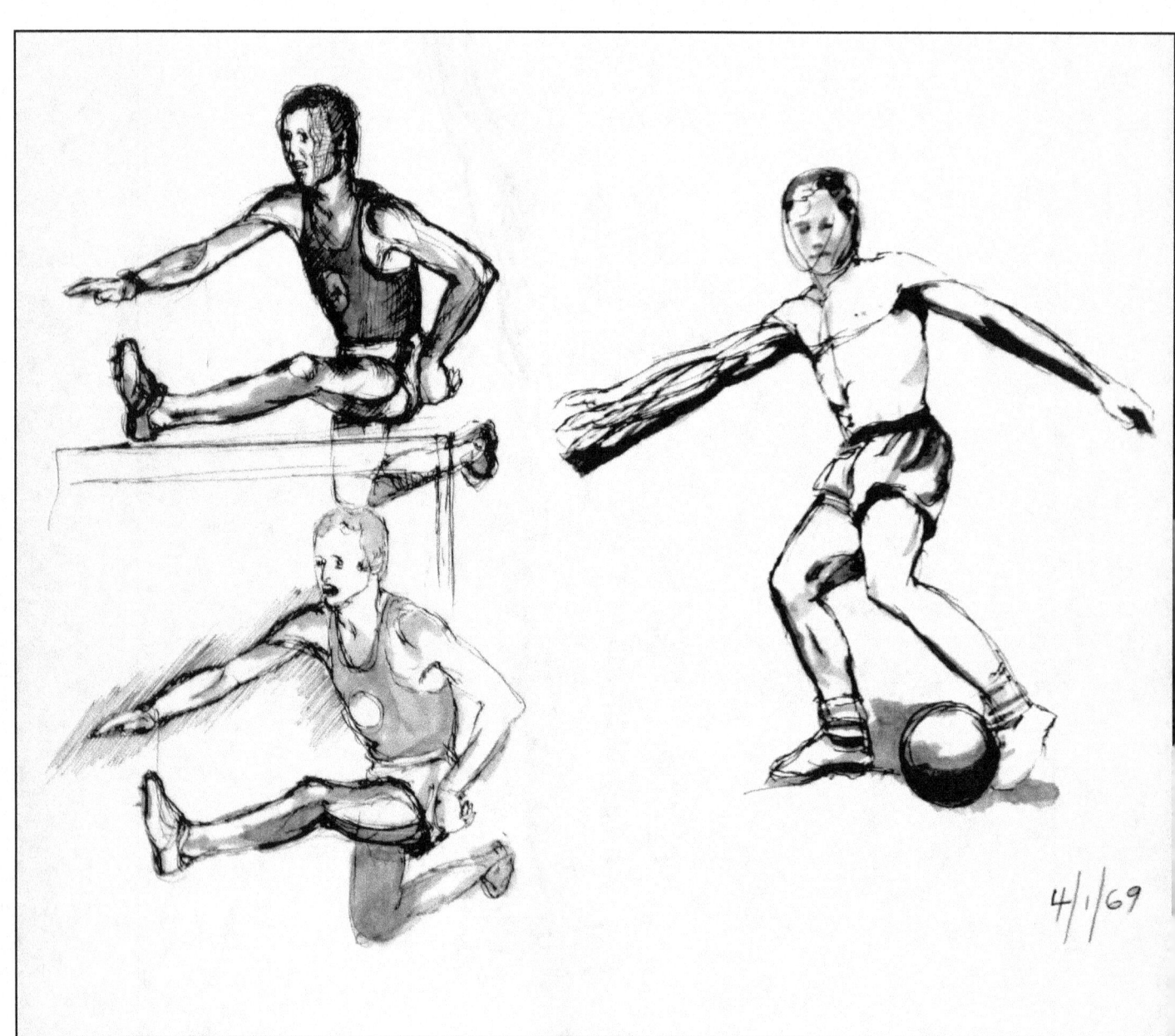

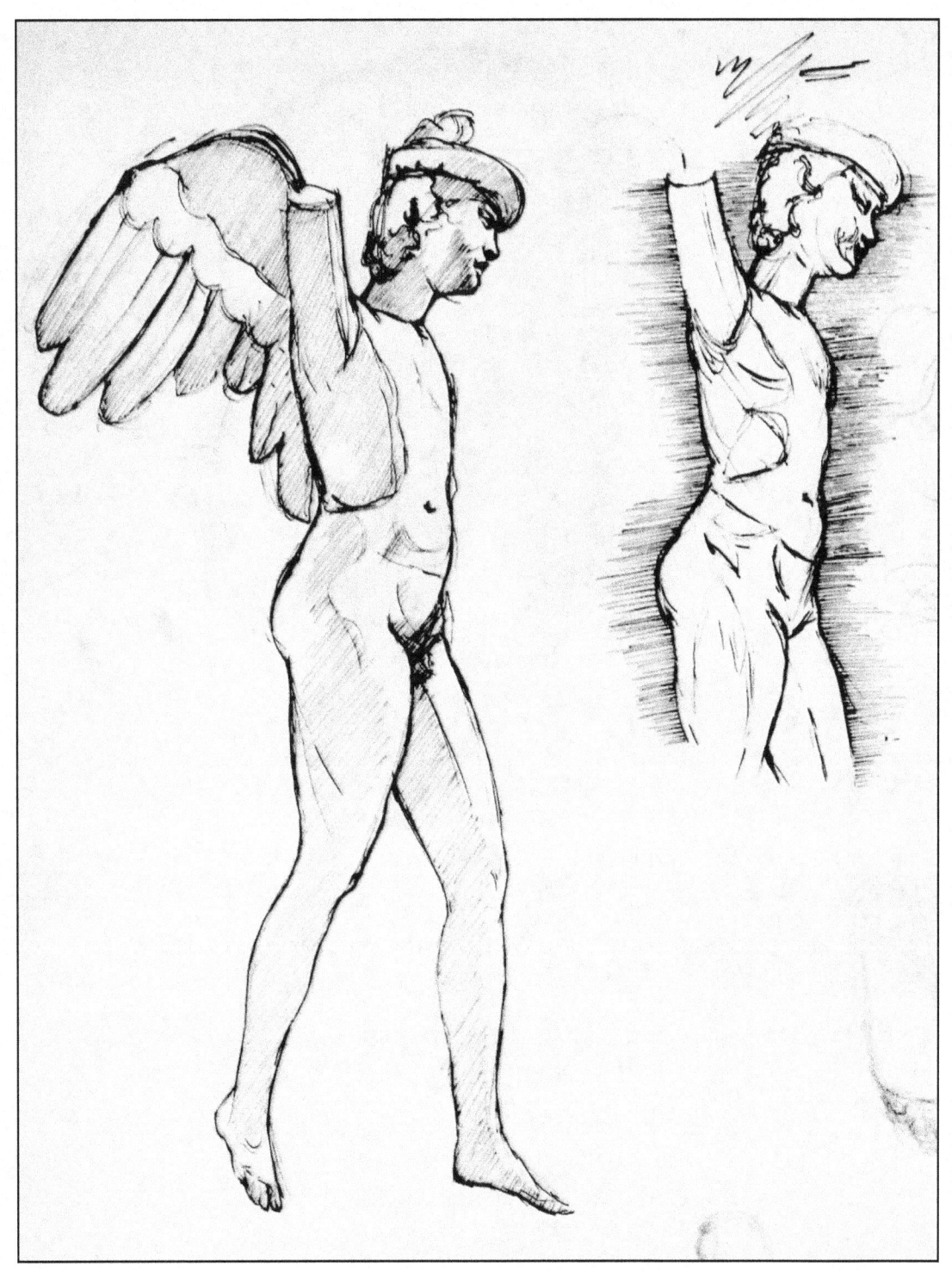

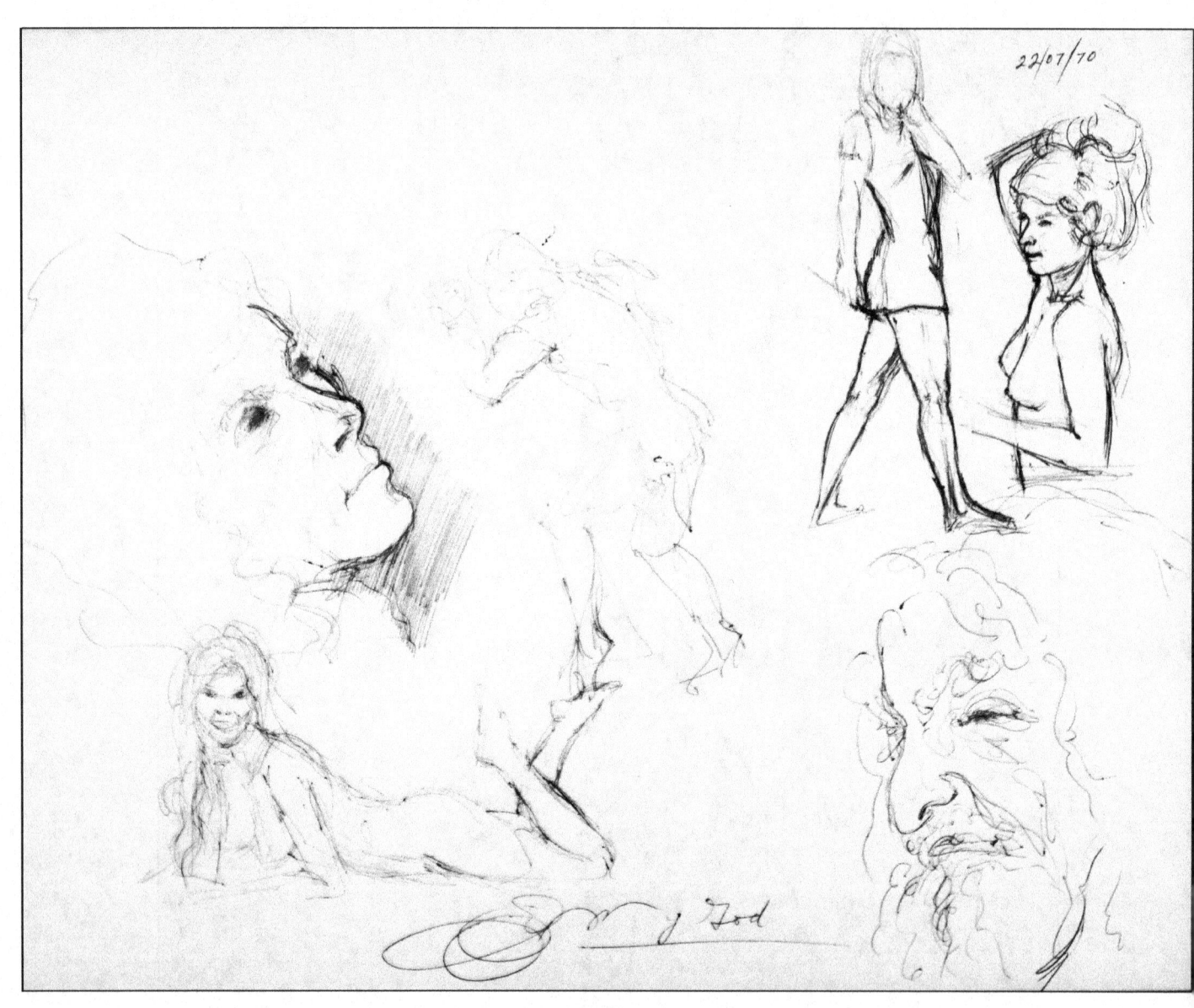

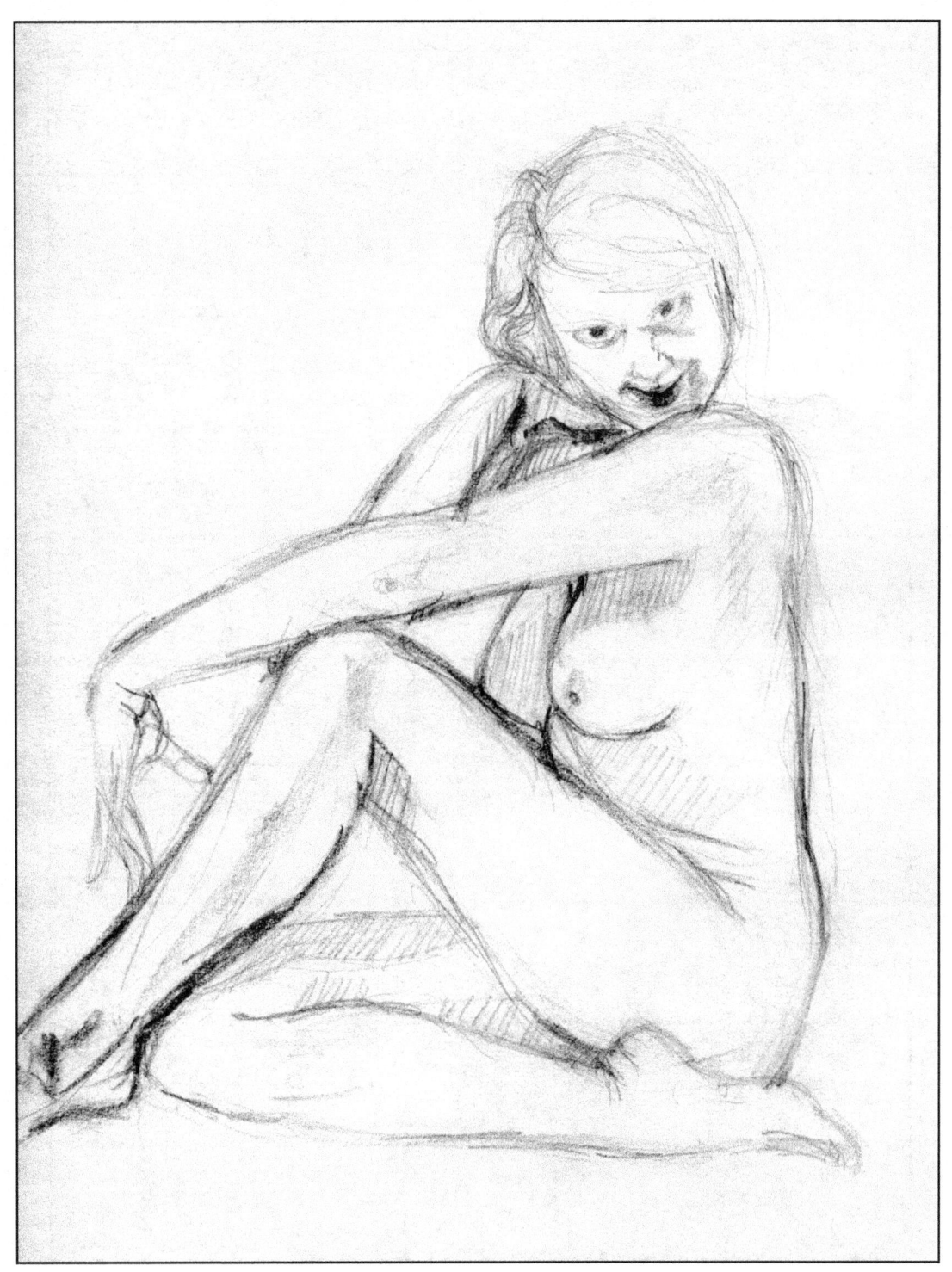

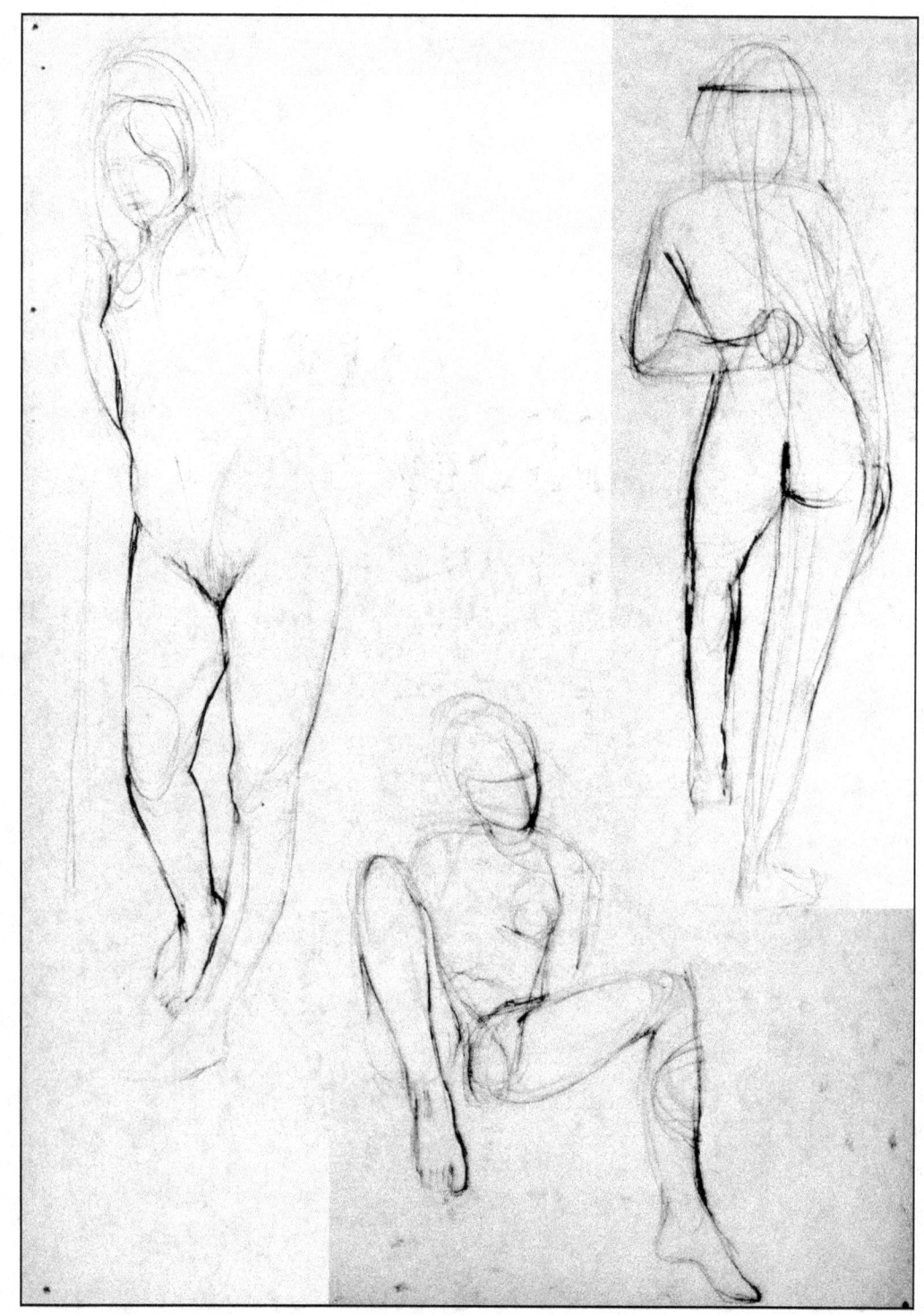

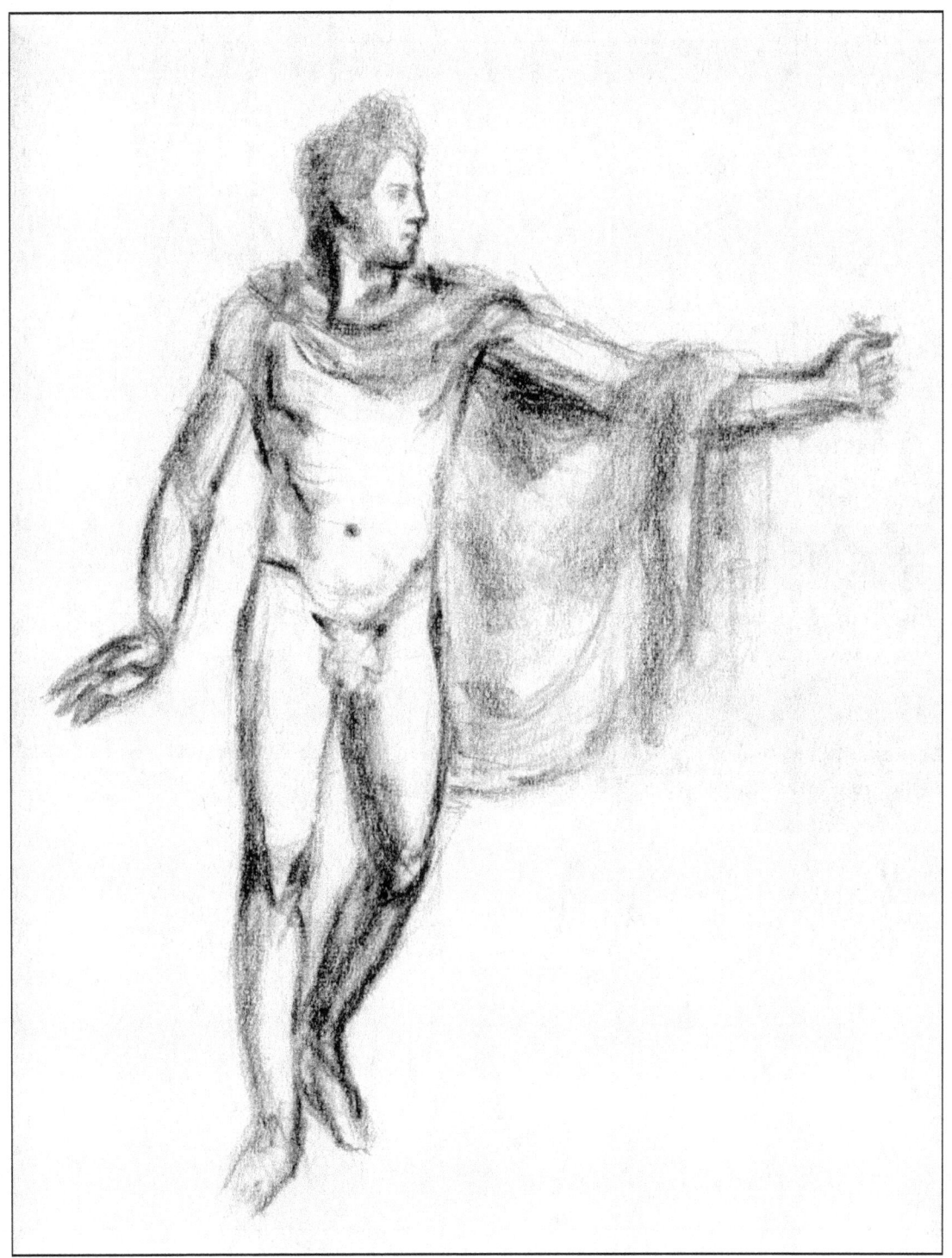

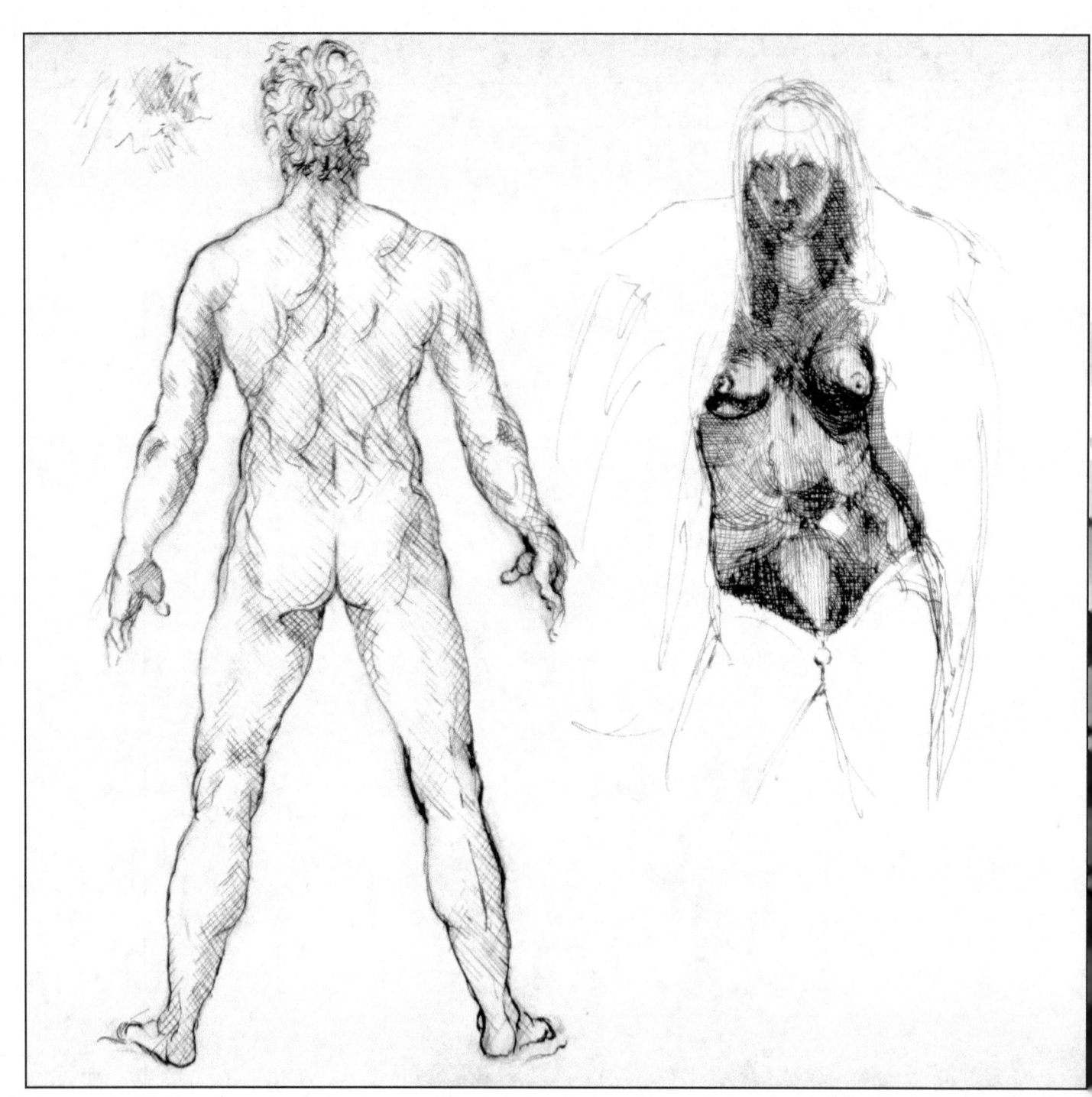

Nib-pen drawing after Leonardo: applied to the drawing of a model

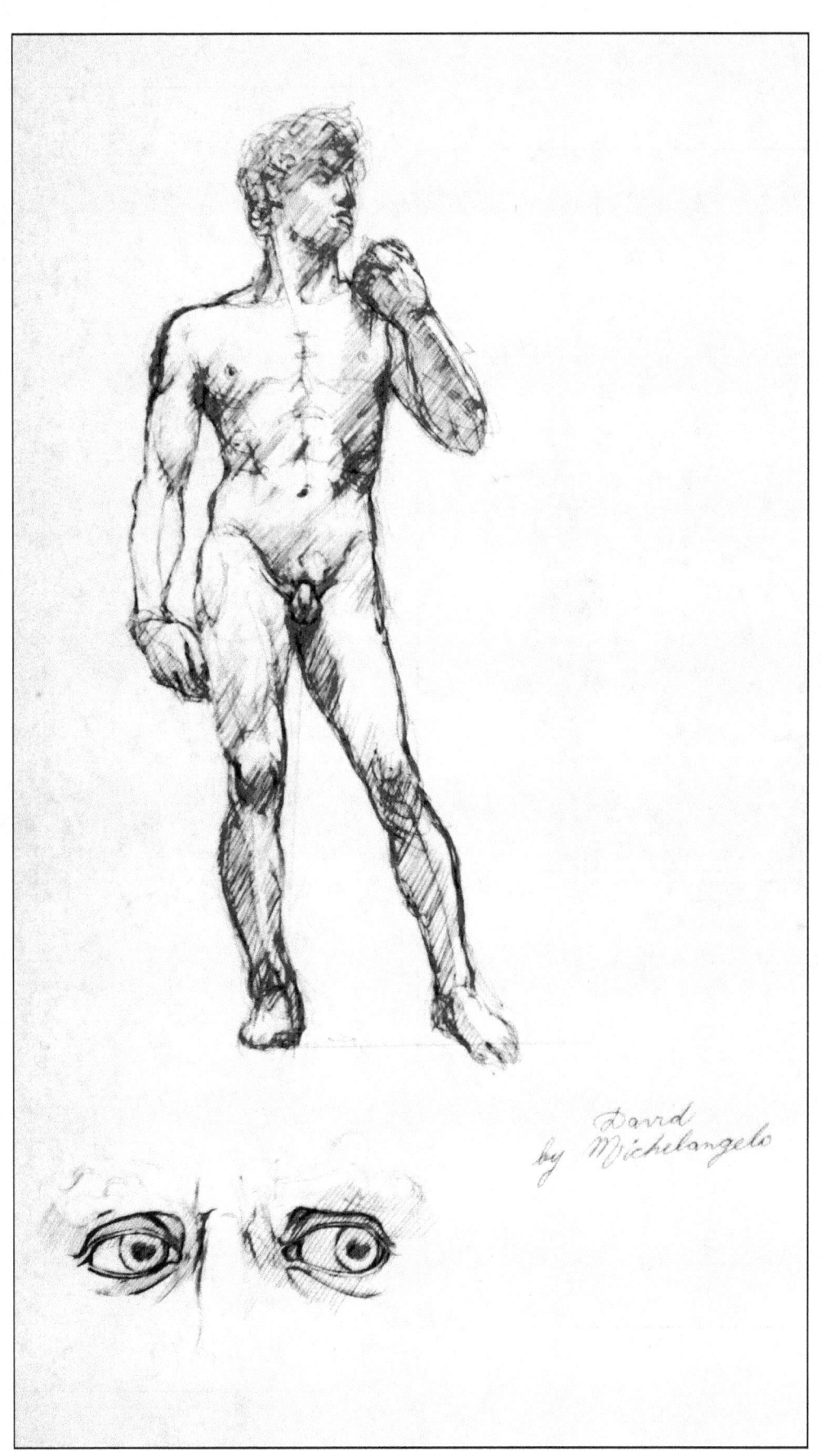

David by Michelangelo

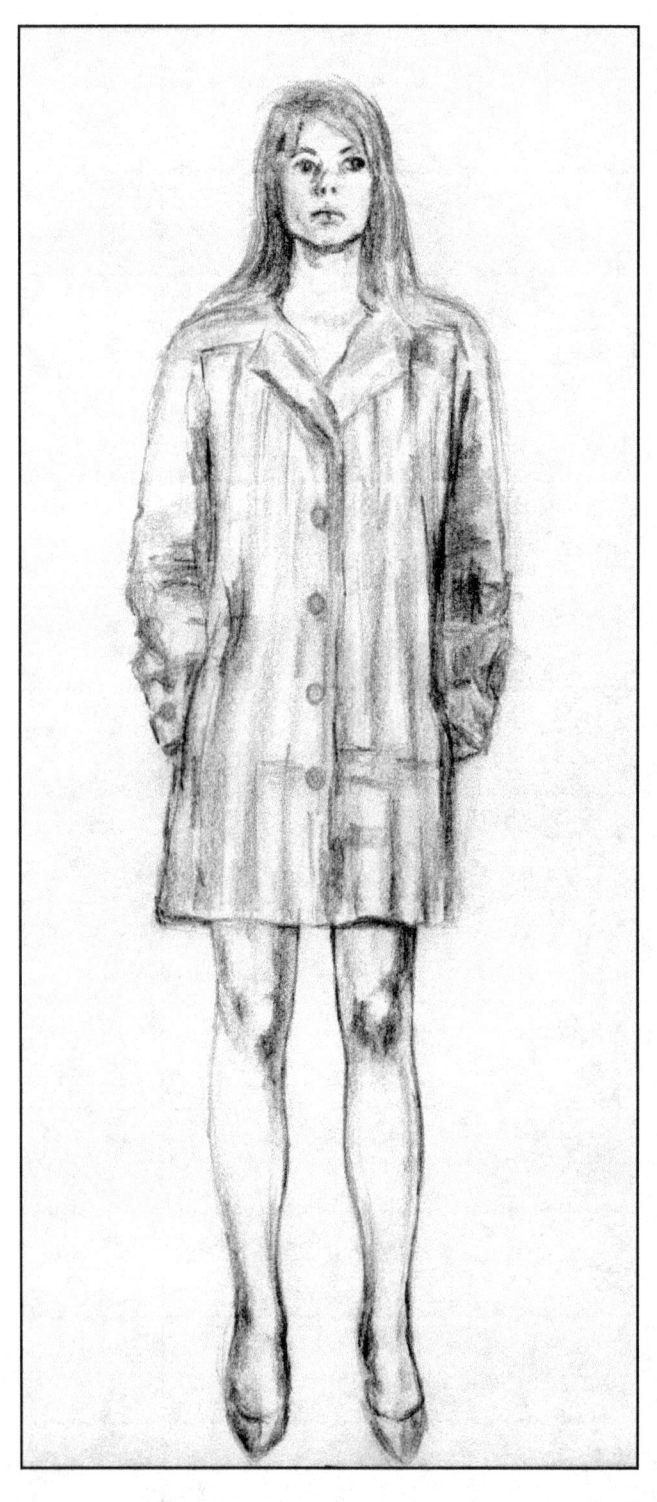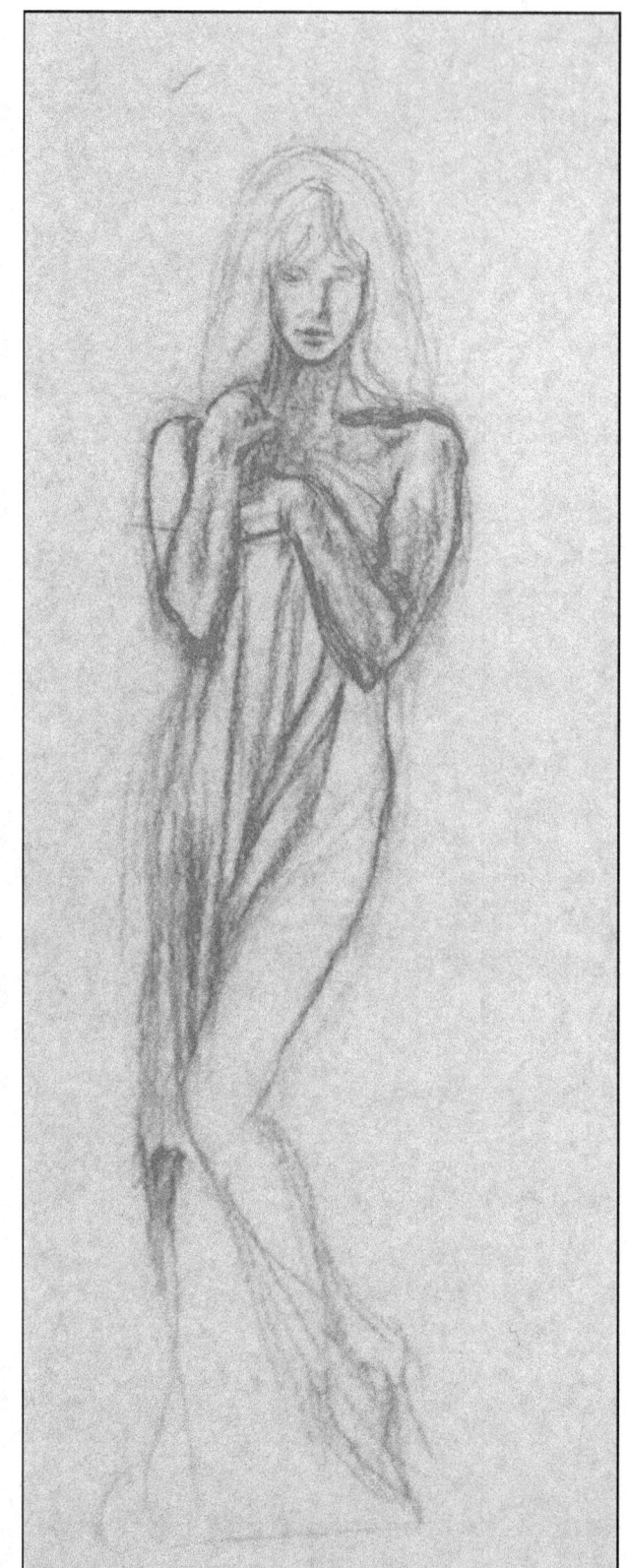

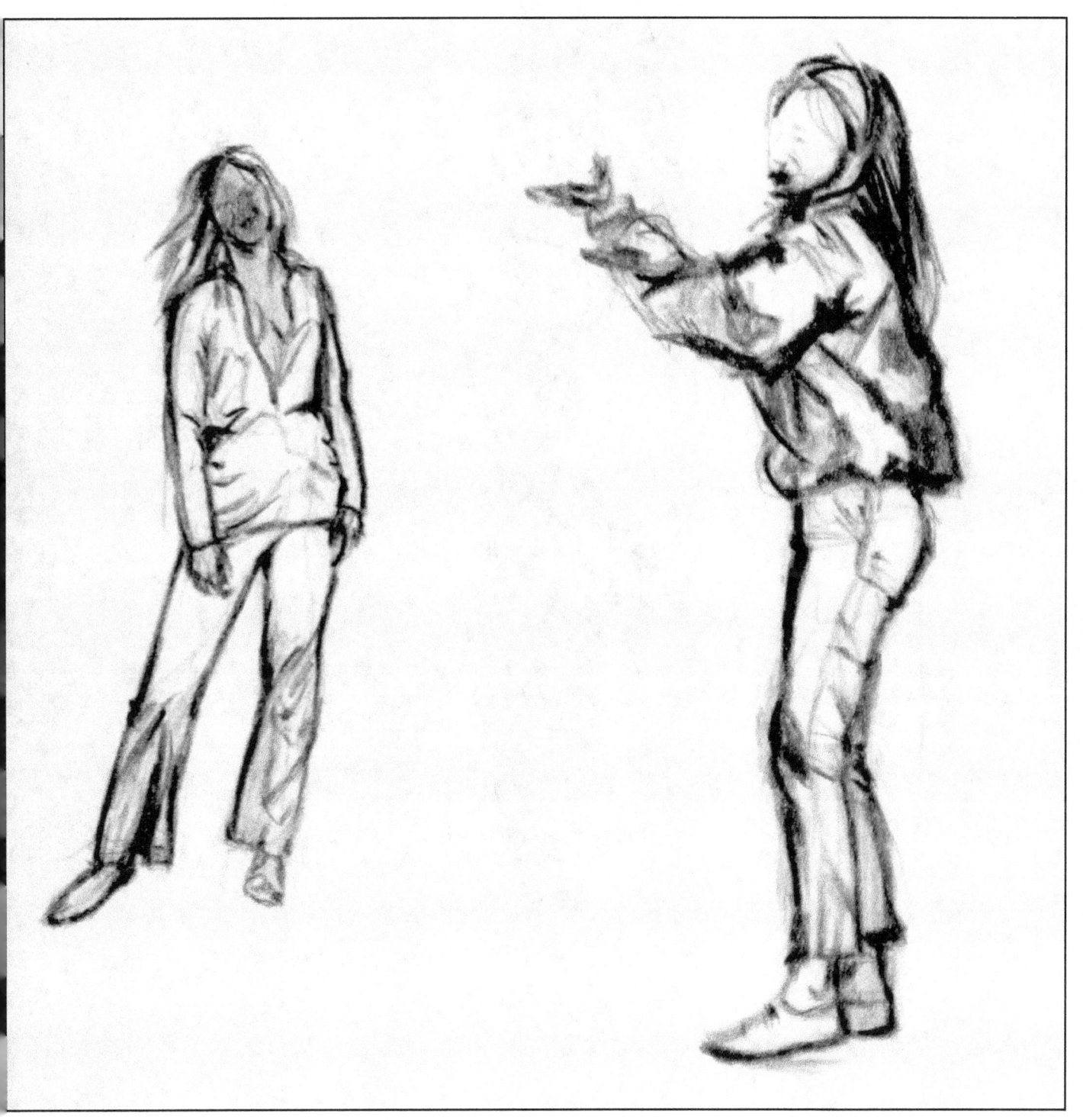

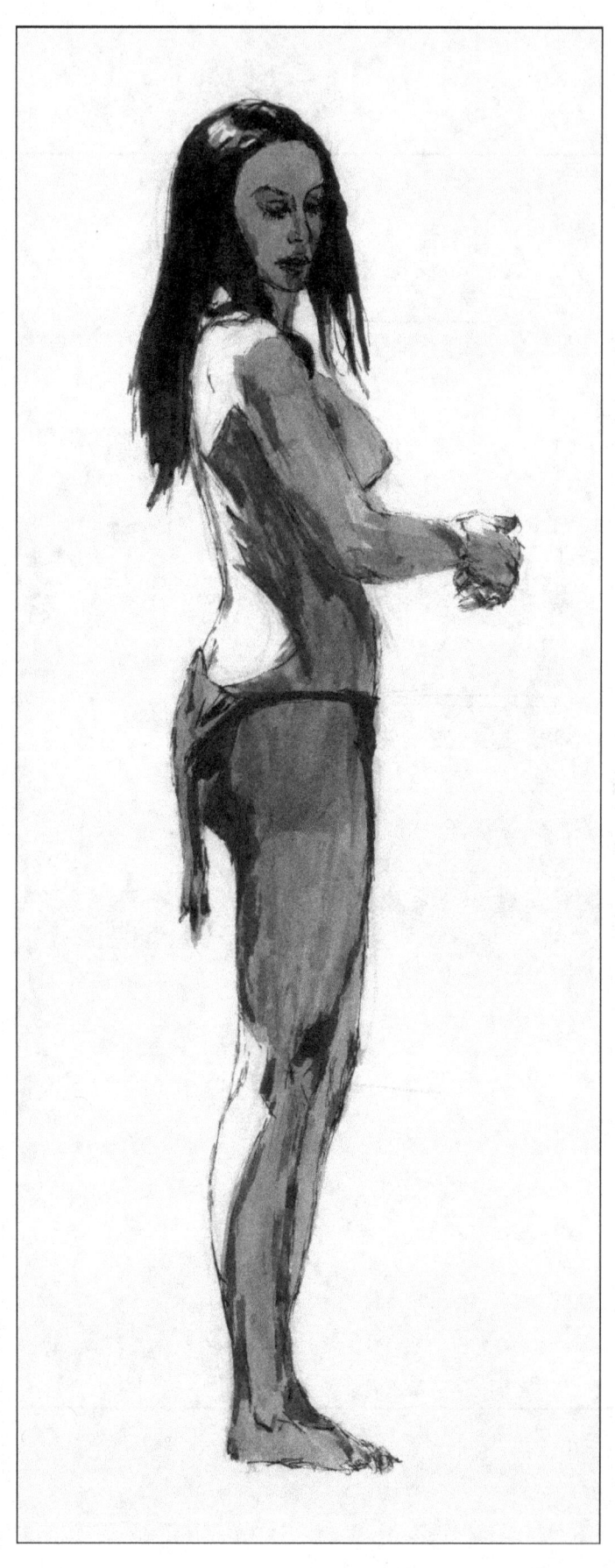

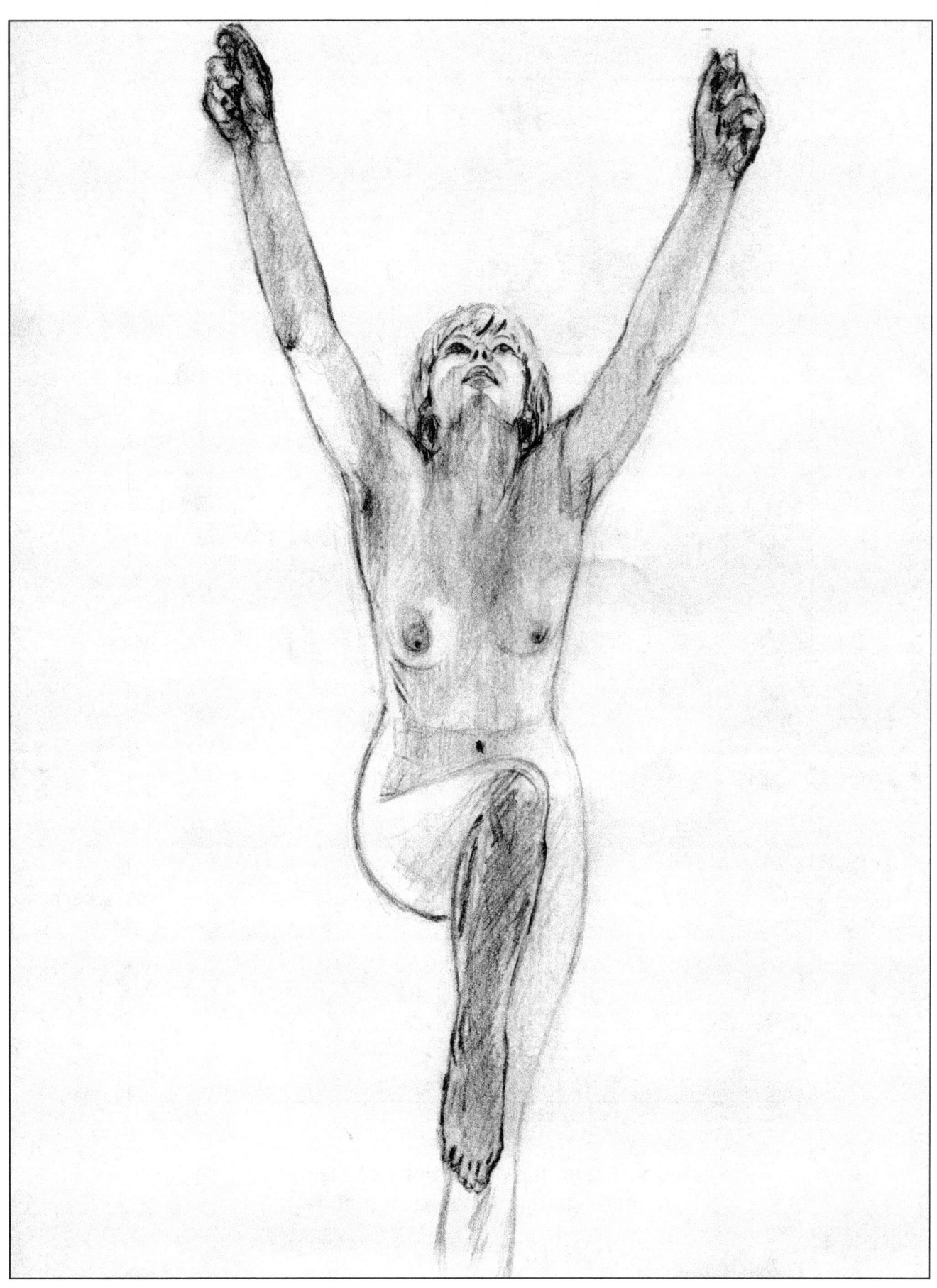

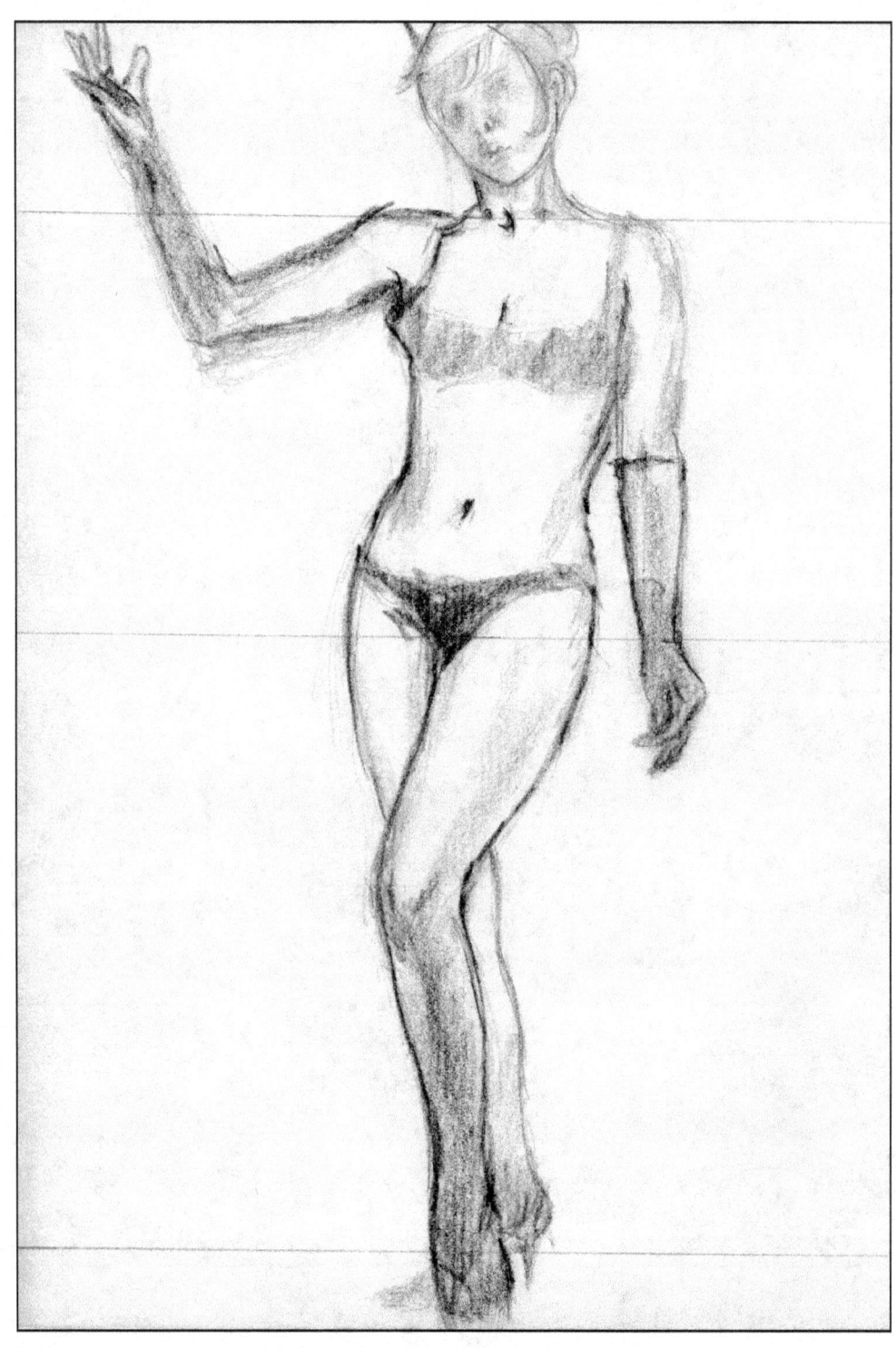

Confirming the proportions of a the human figure in a magazine picture.

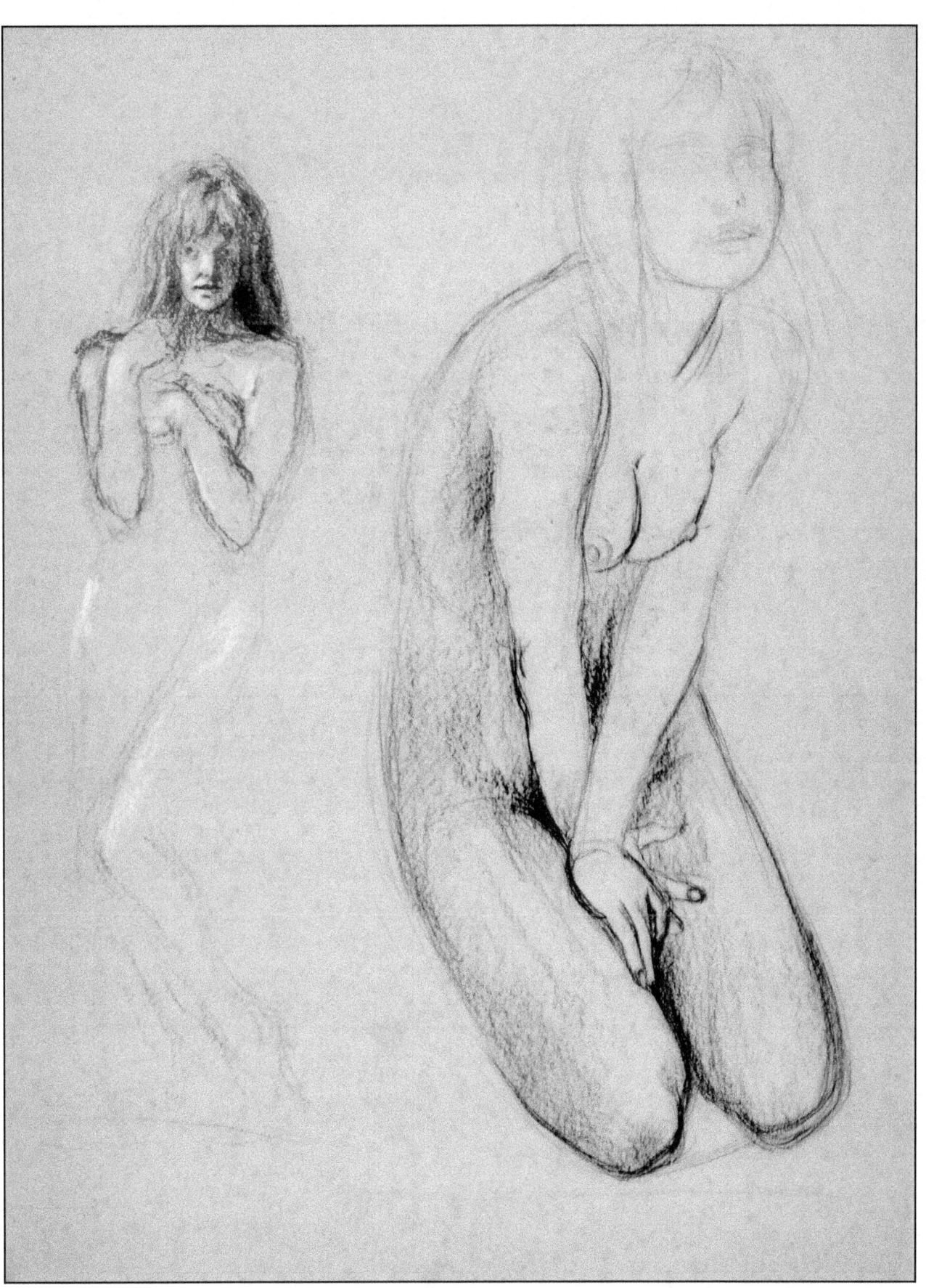

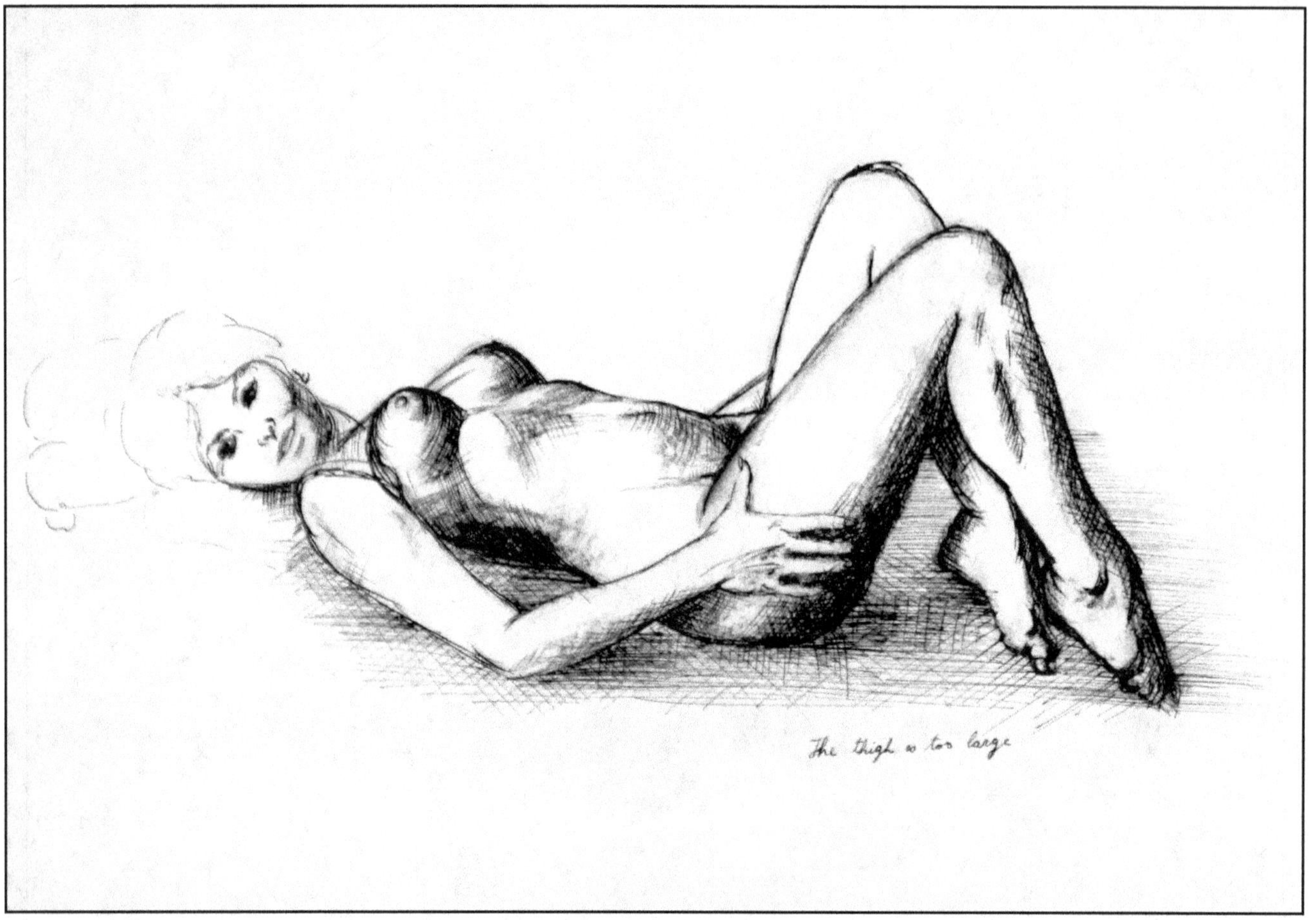

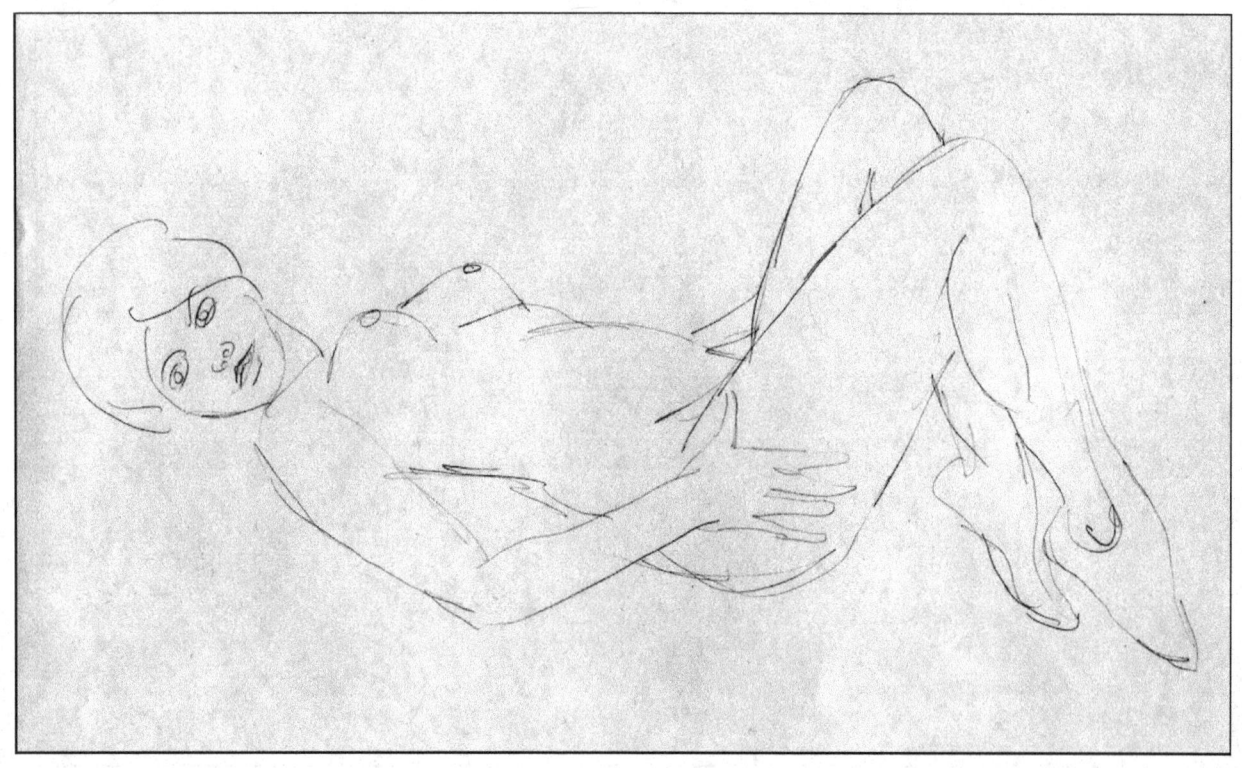

The thigh is too large

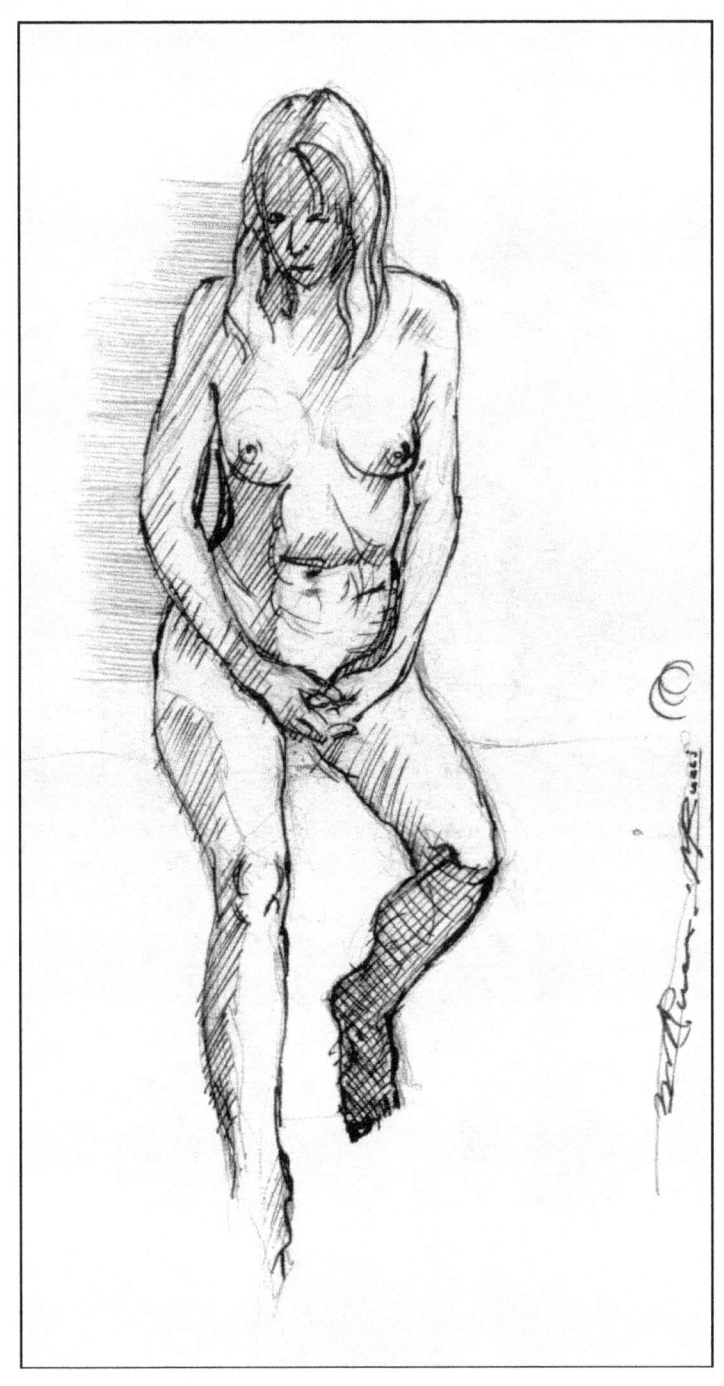

Pencil, nib pen, and ballpoint pen

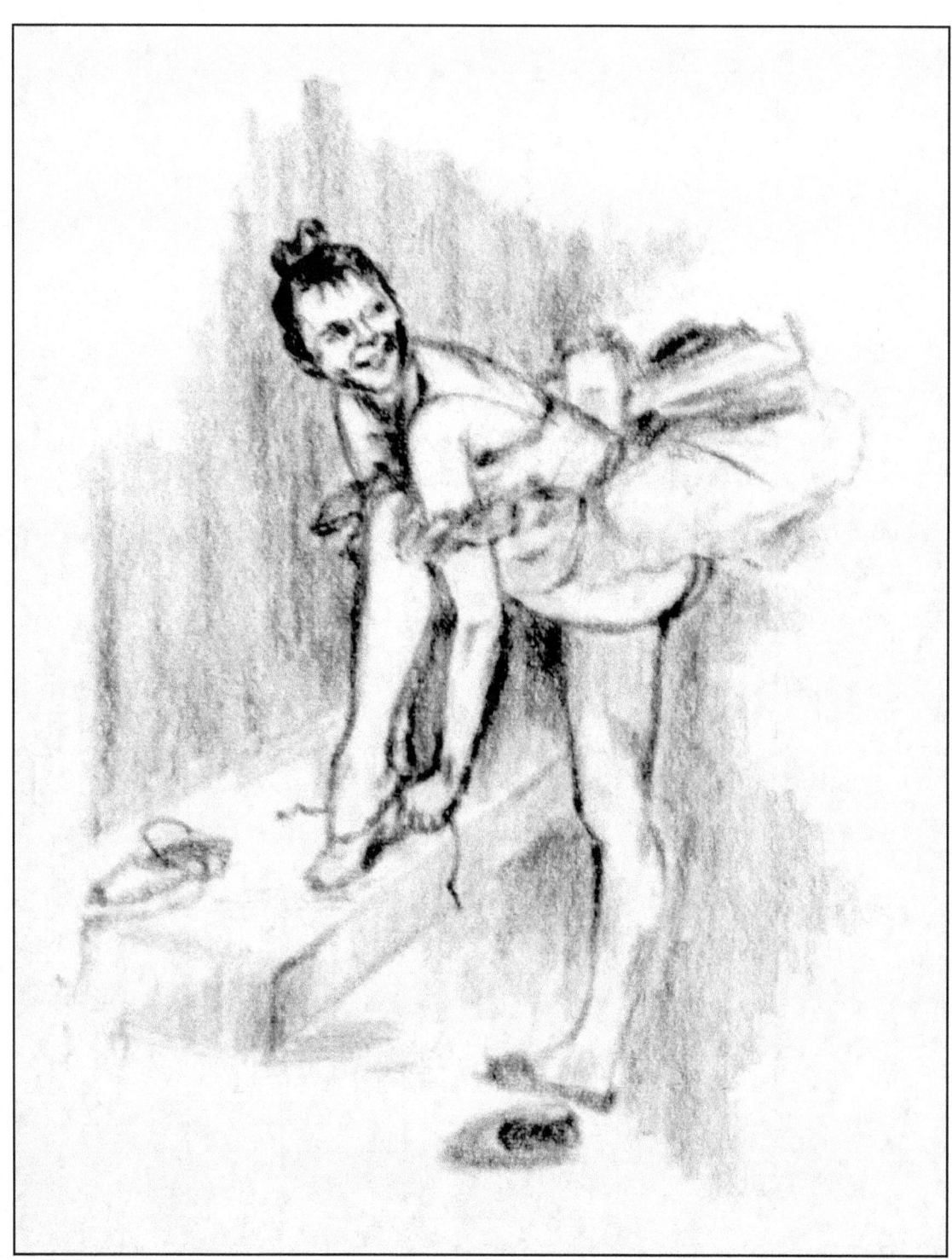

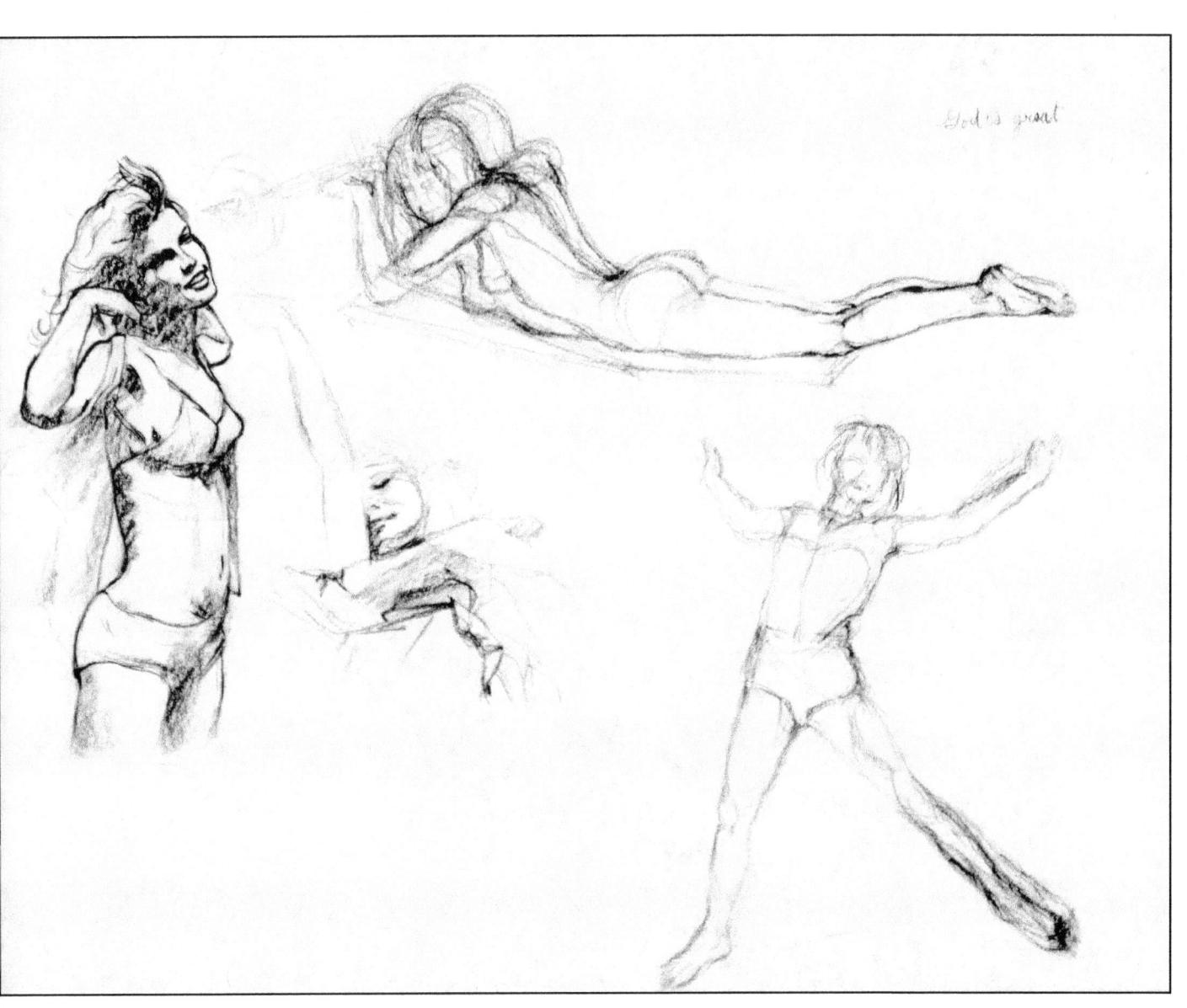

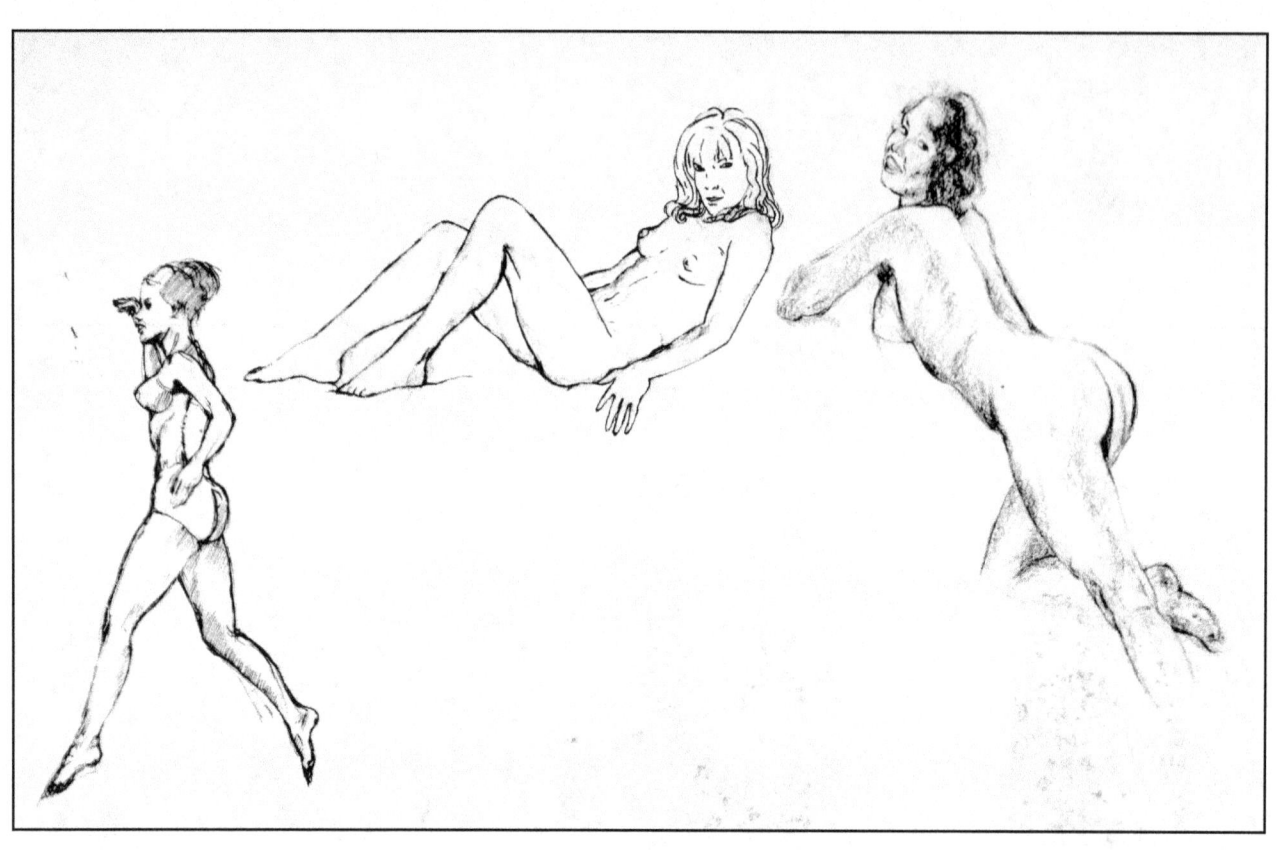

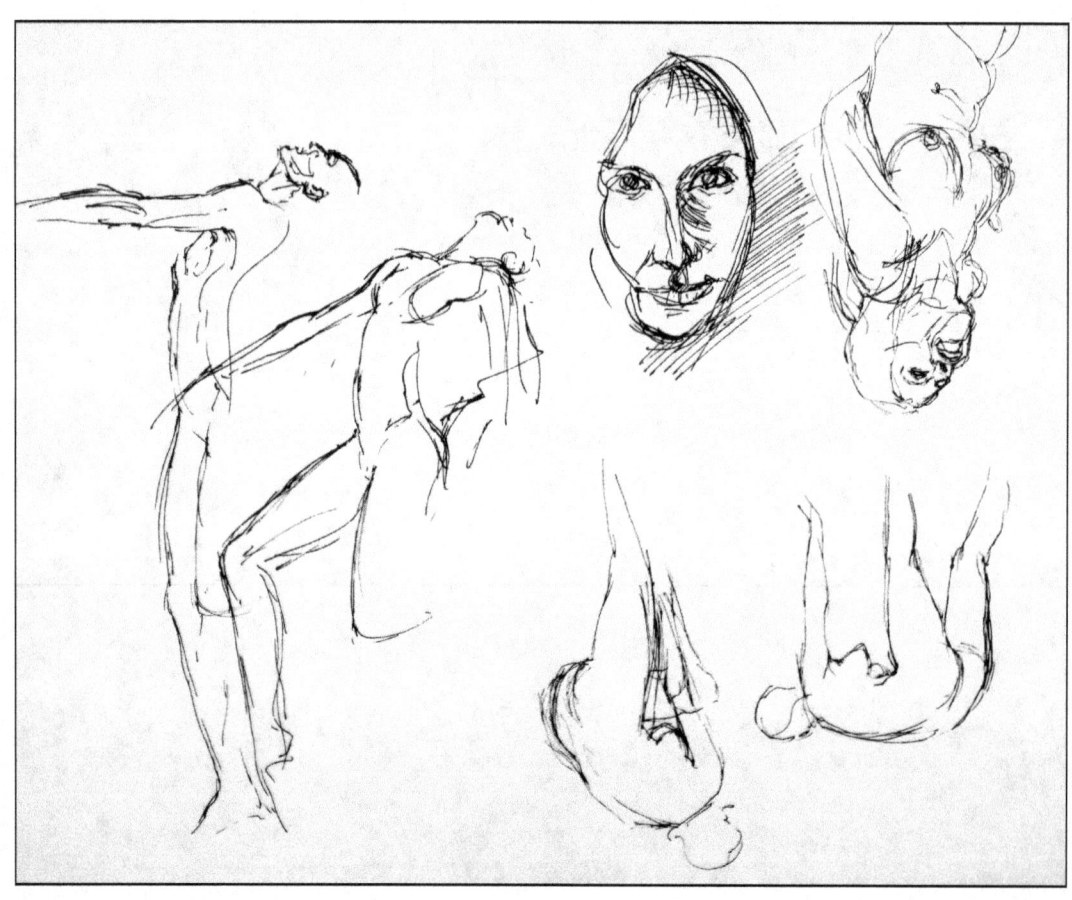

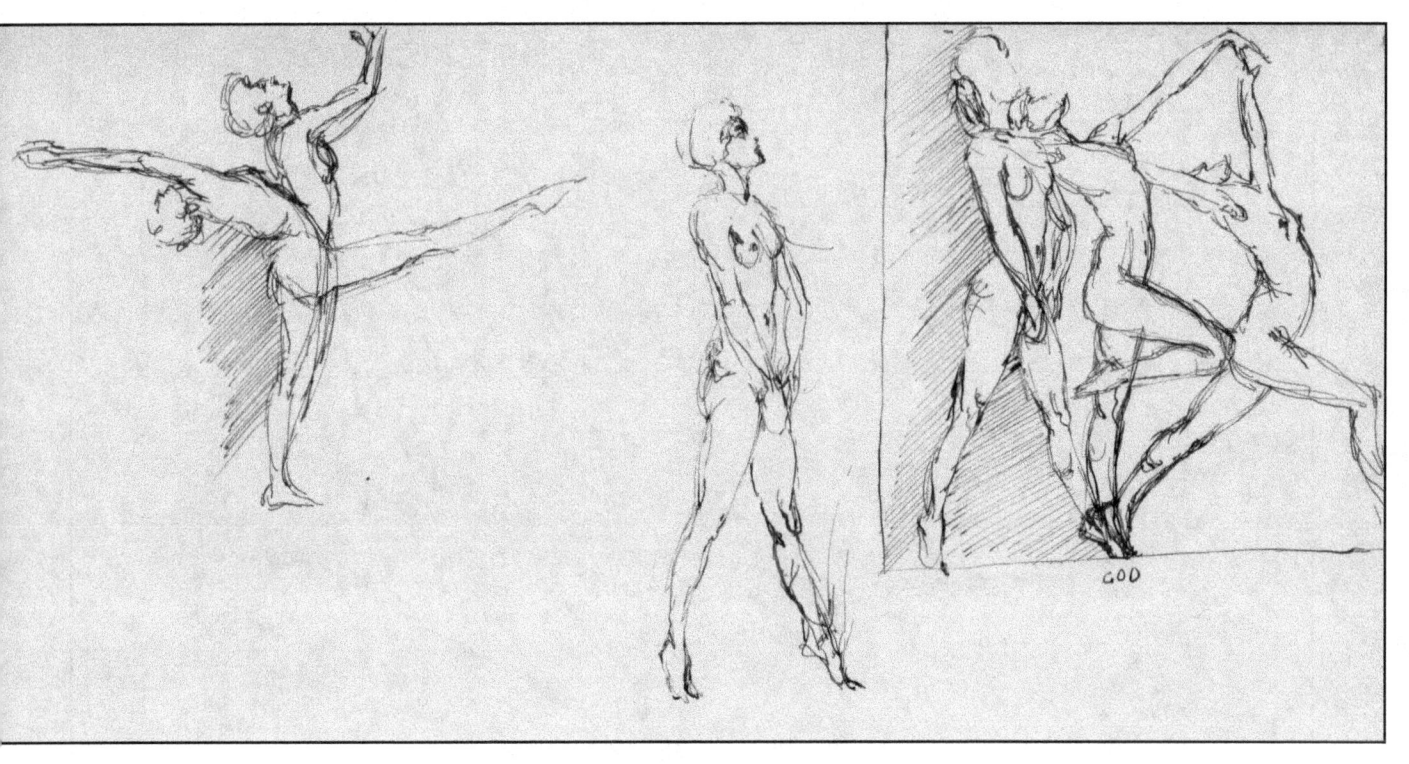

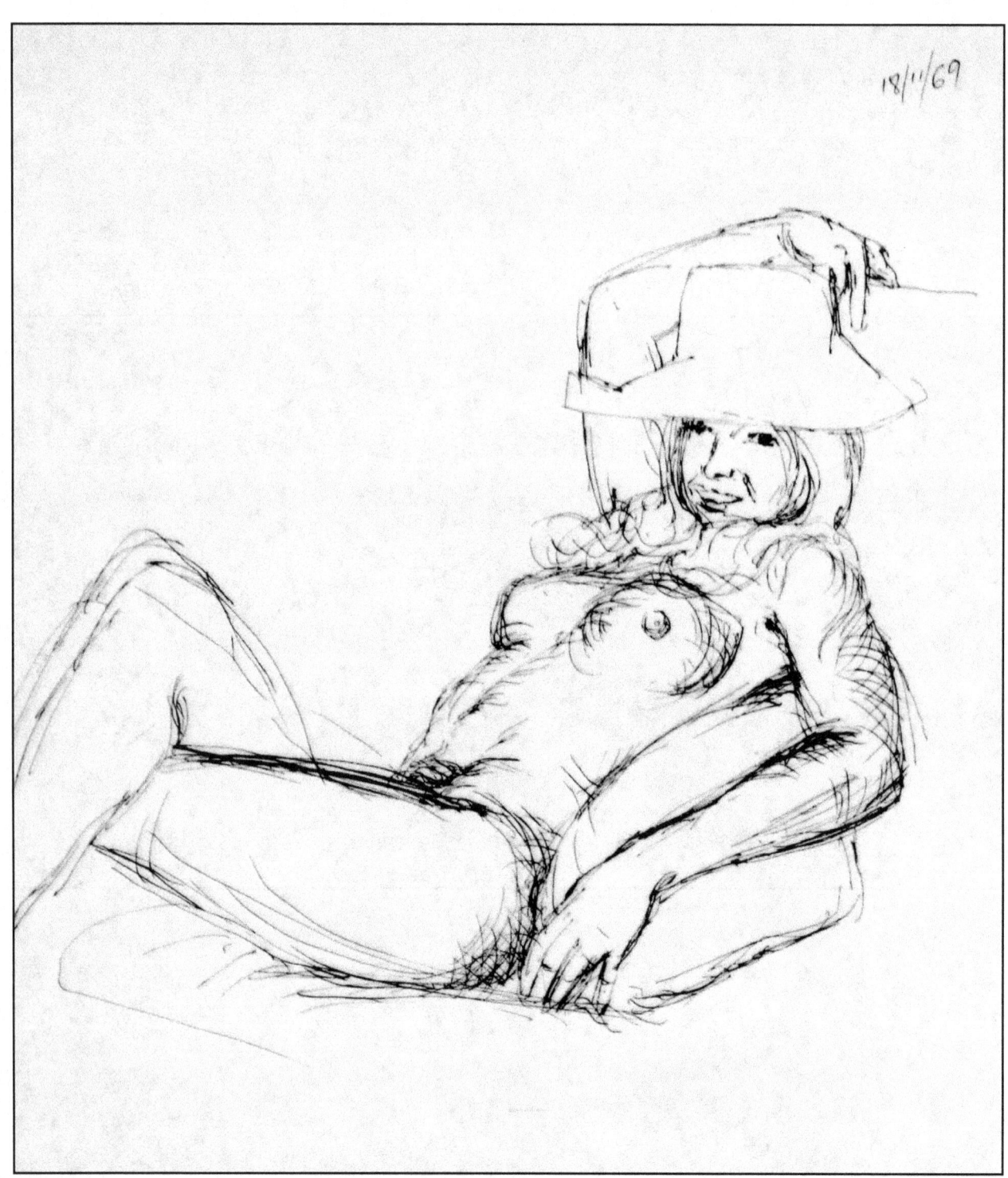

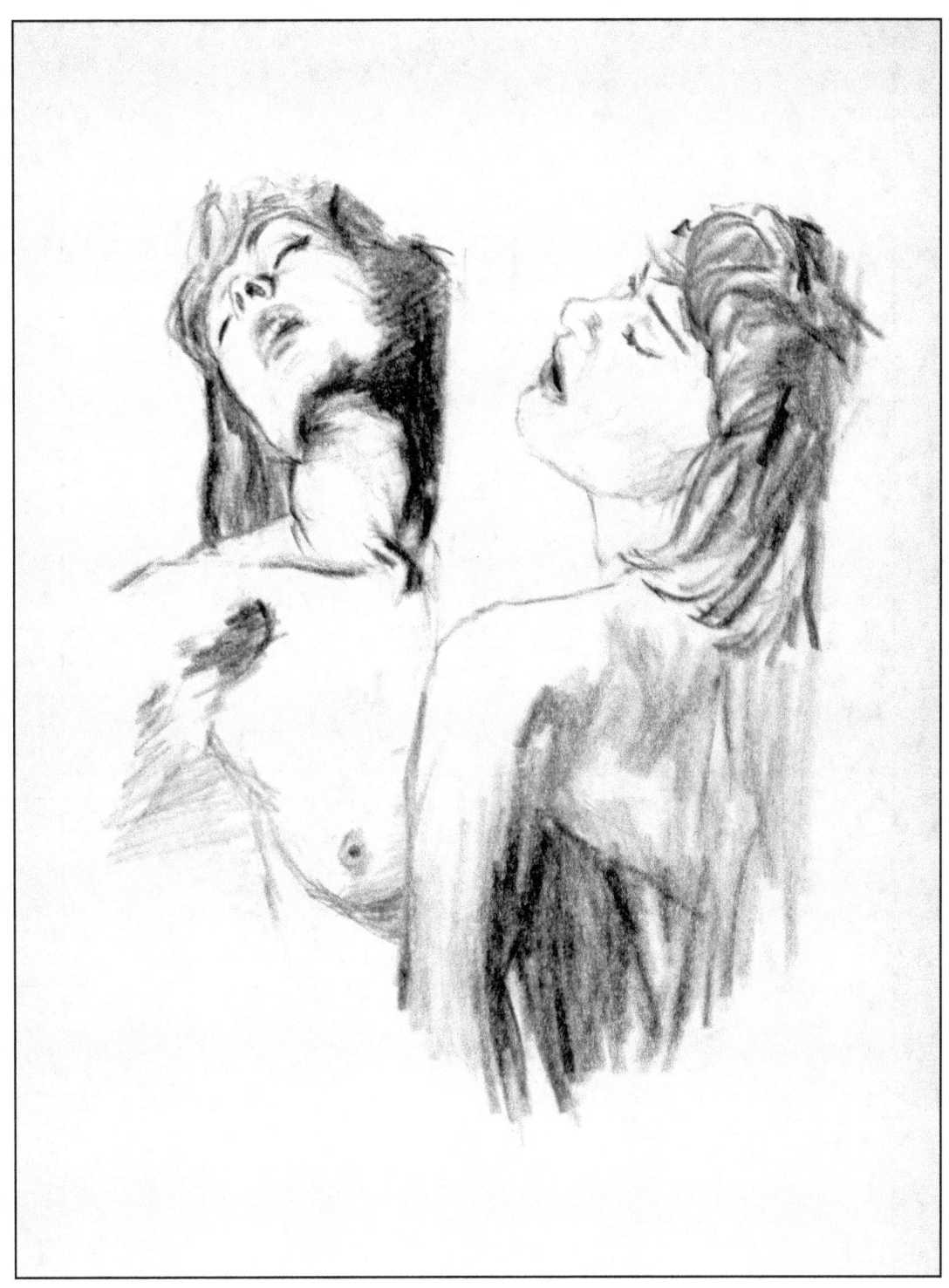

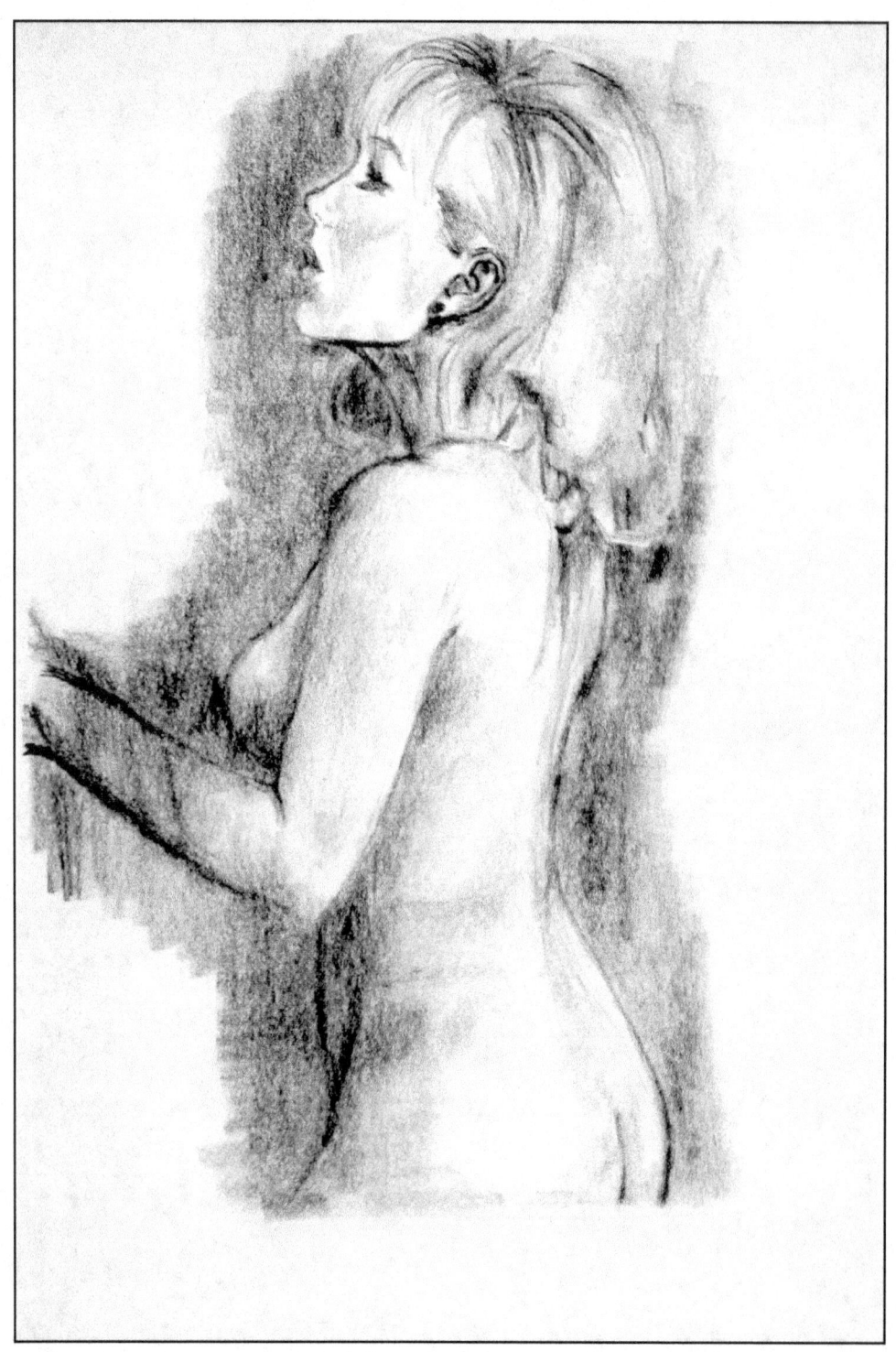

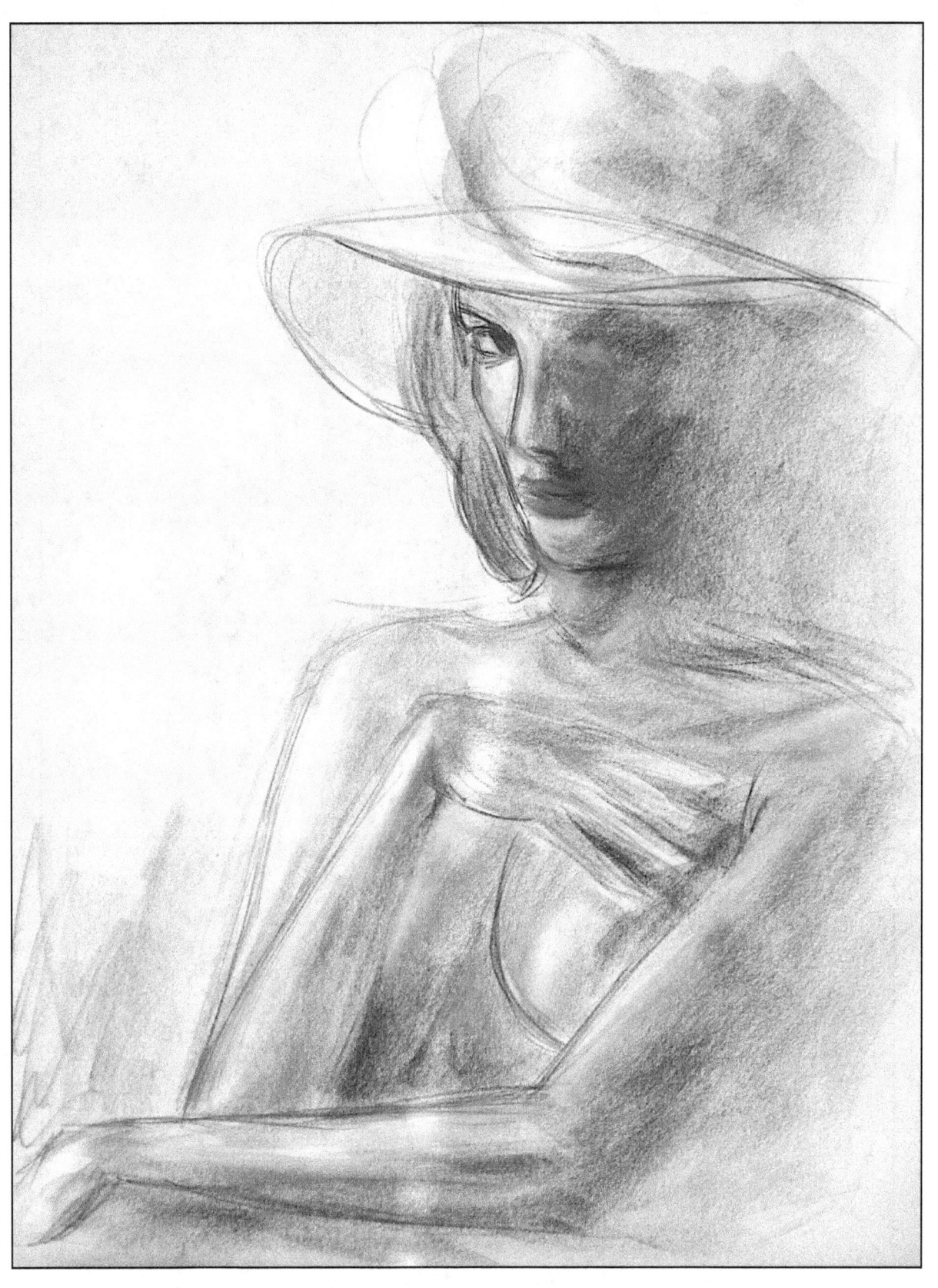

From Photo, Chalk Painting

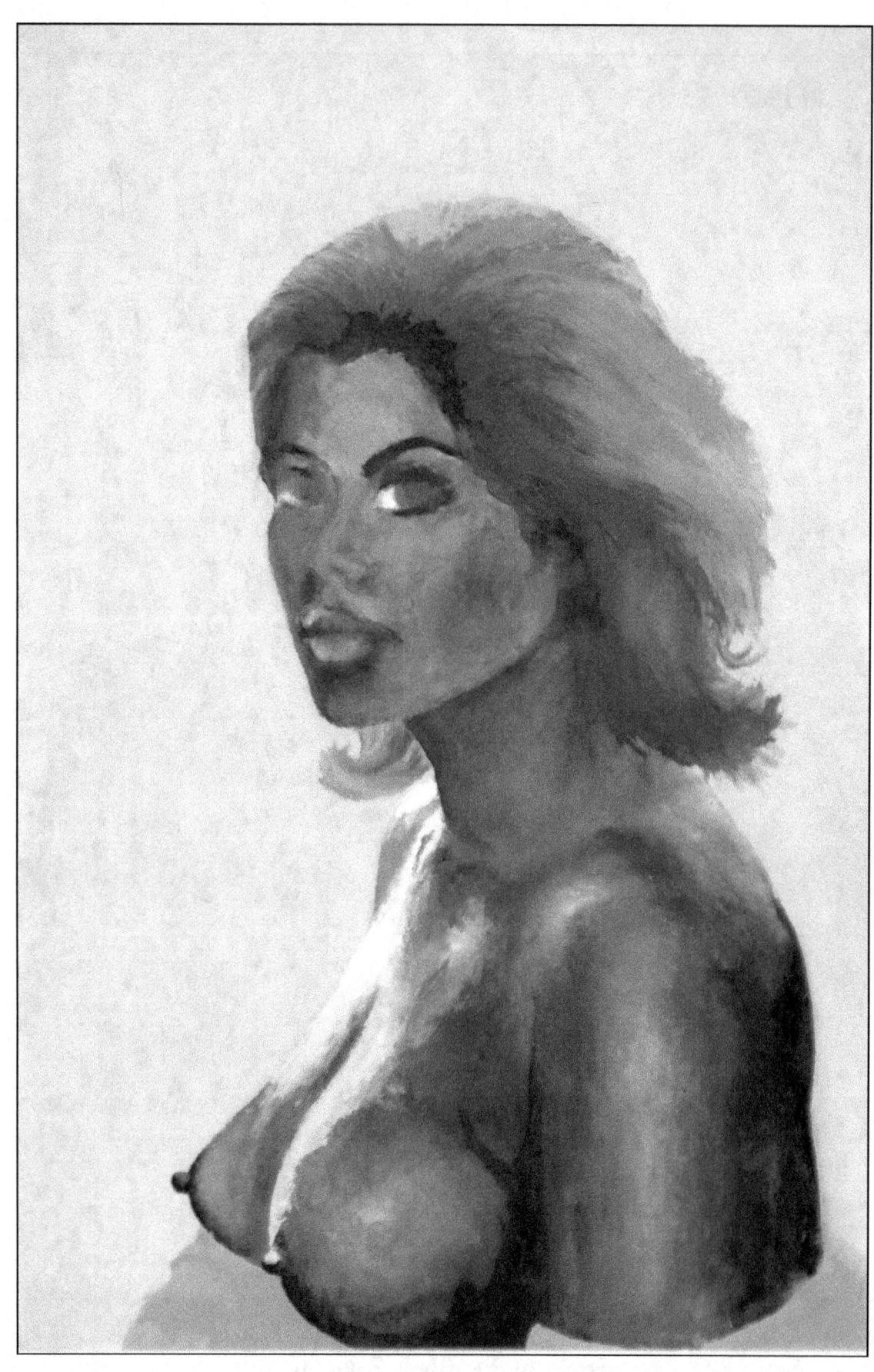

From Photo, Acrylic on Cardboard

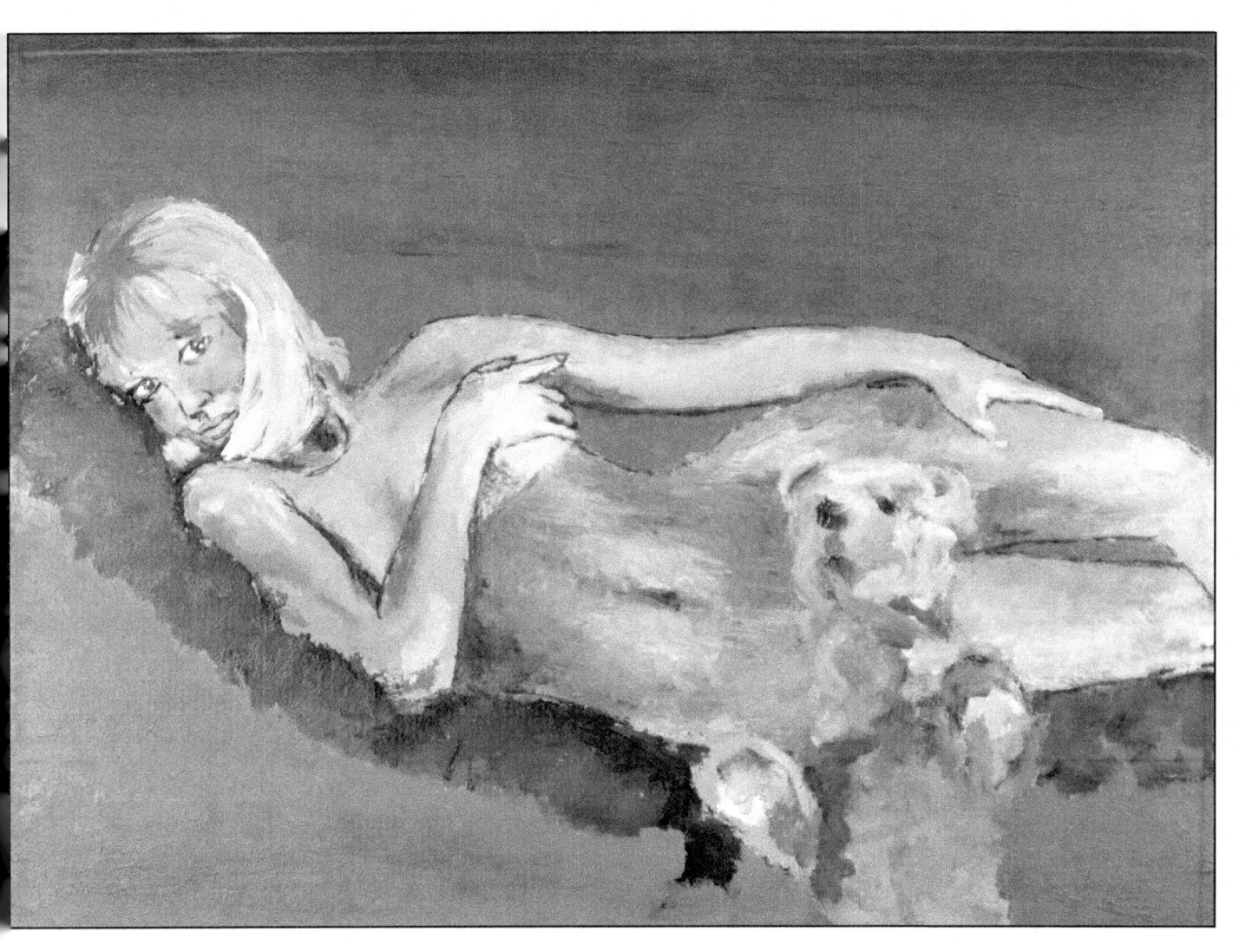

From Photo, Acrylic on Cardboard

13. Full Figure, Observation

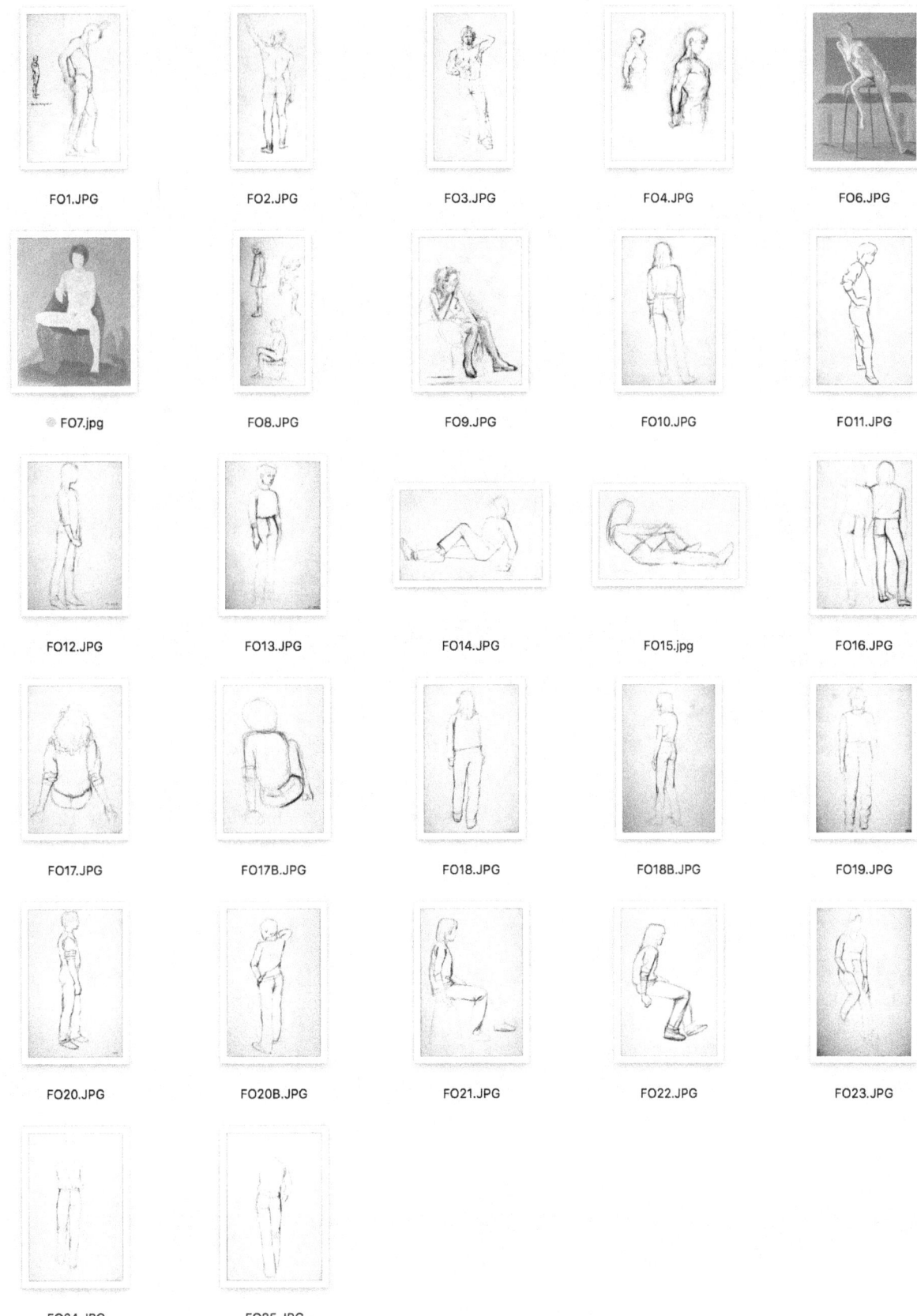

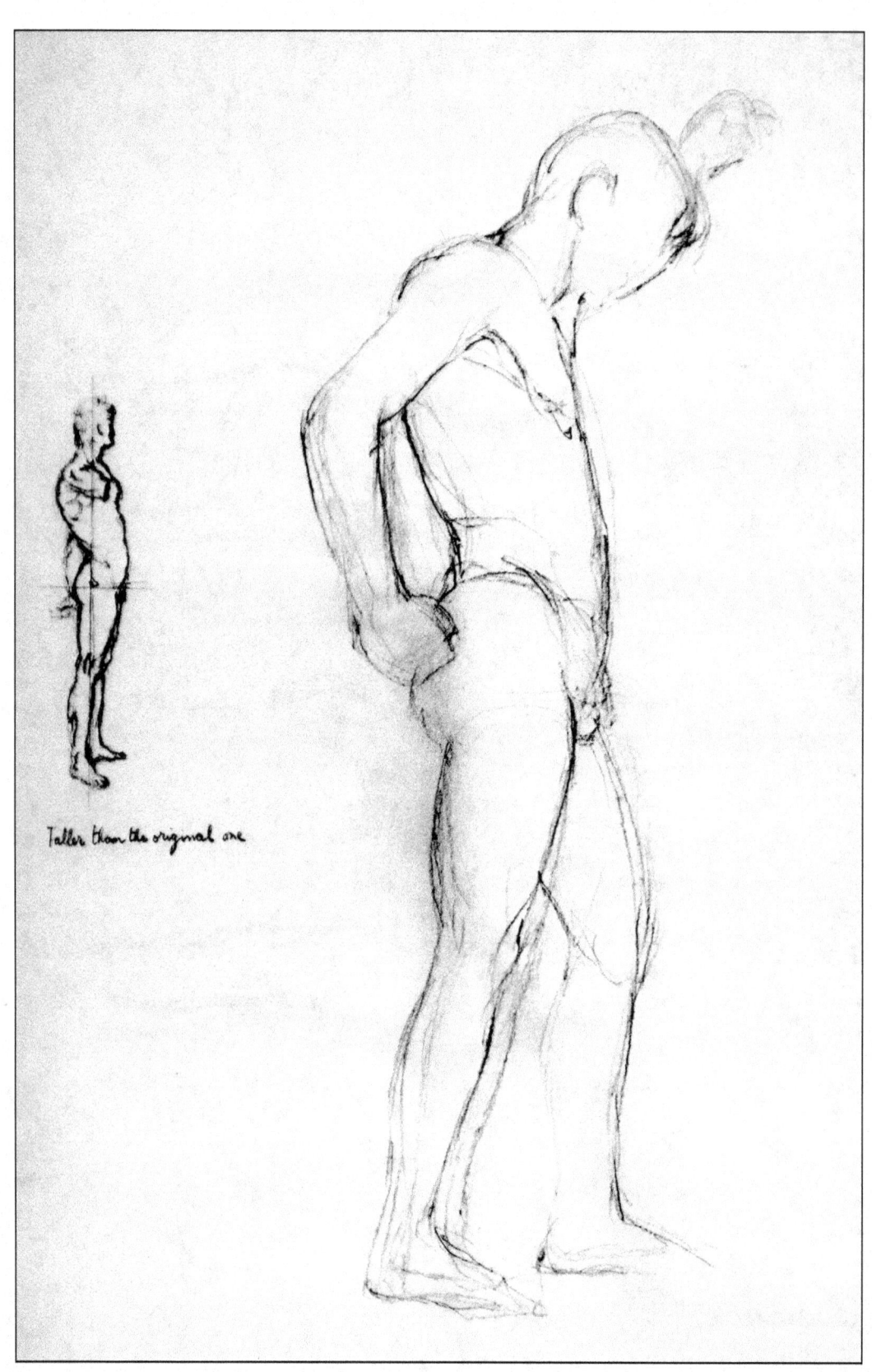

Taller than the original one

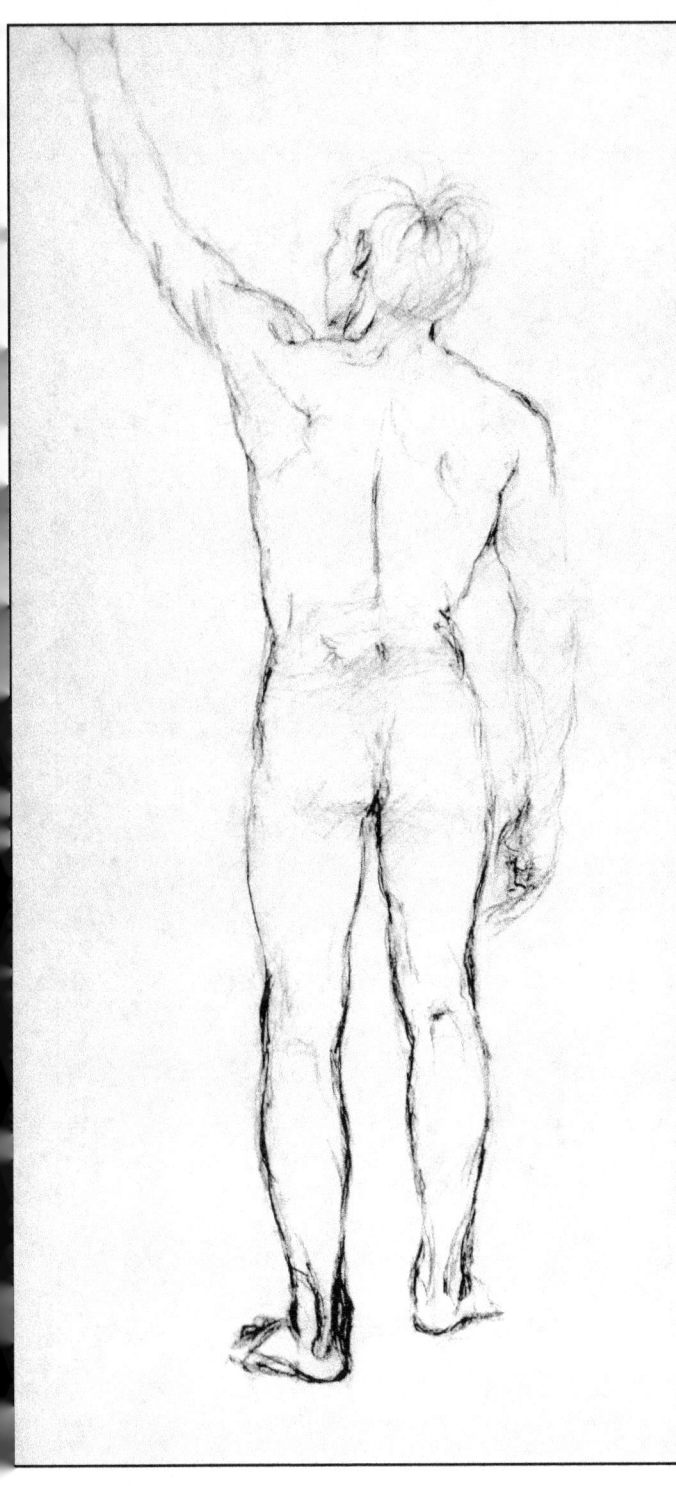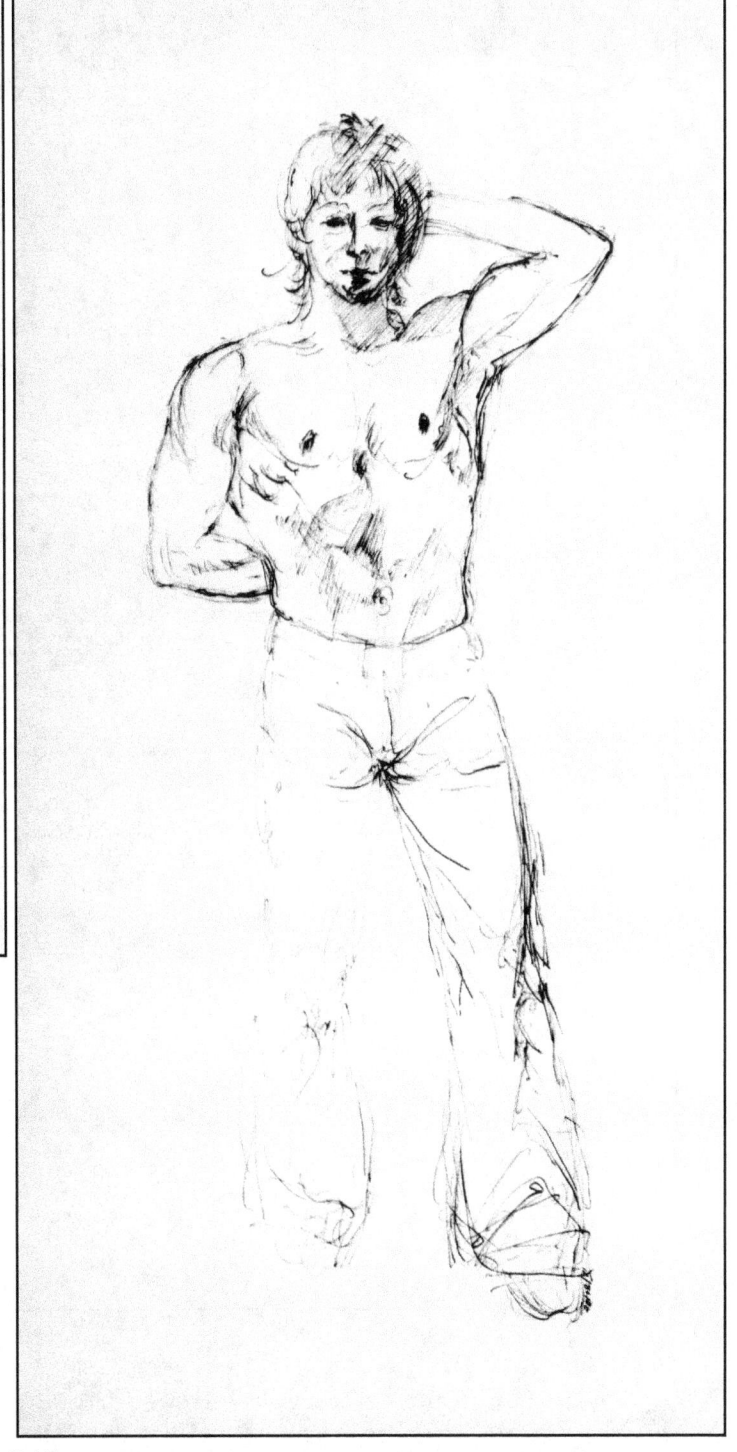

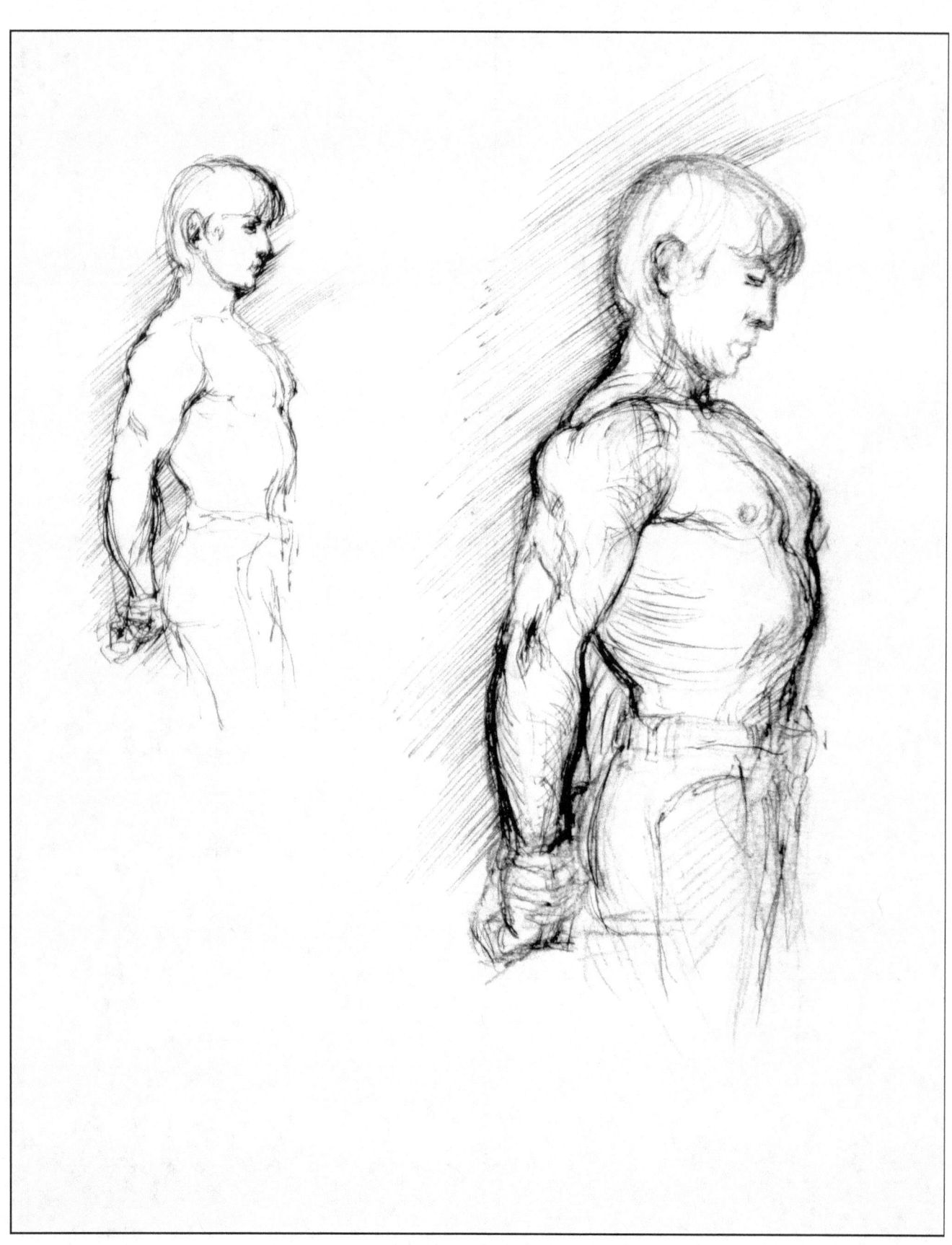

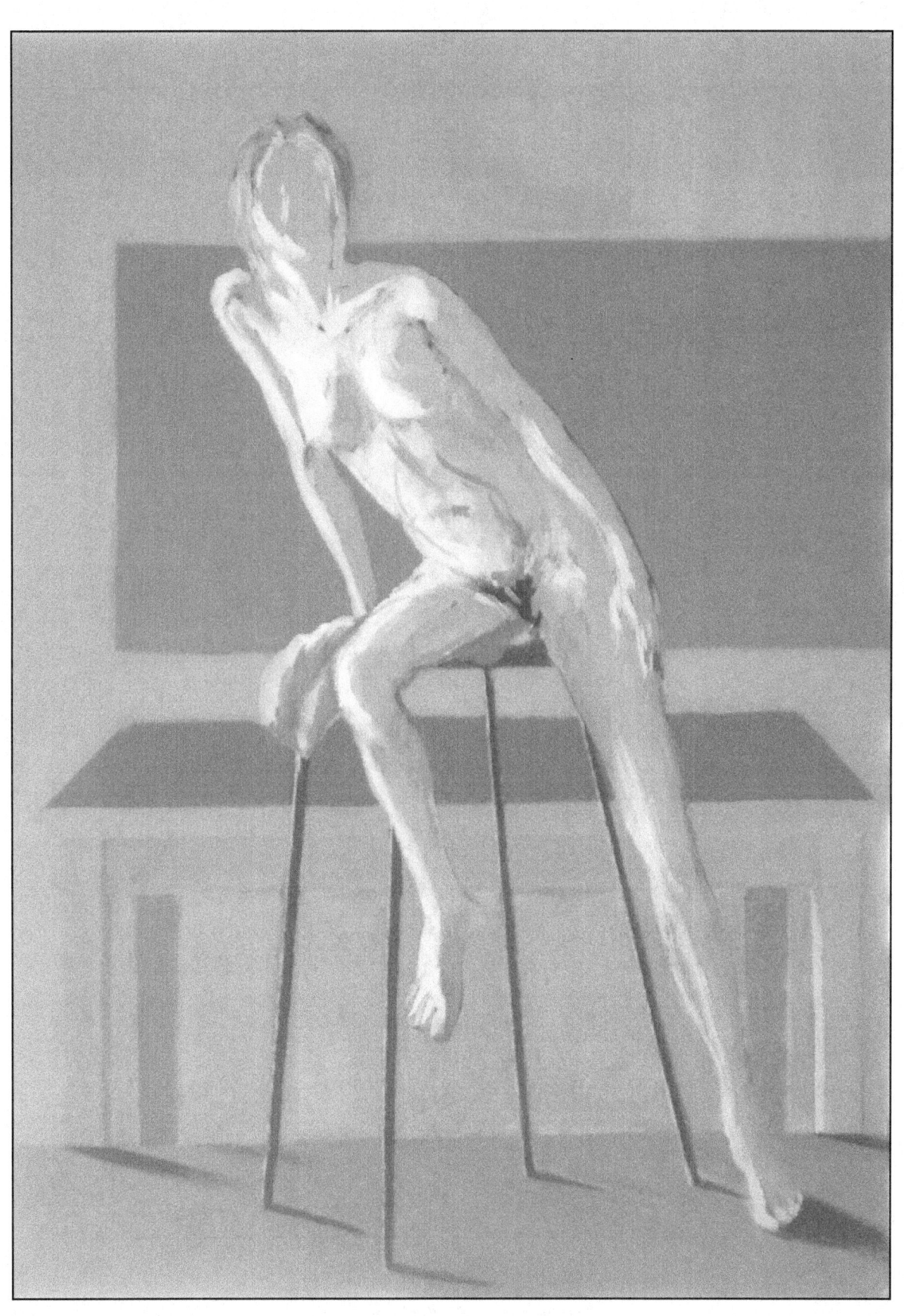

Acrylic on 18"x24" canvas

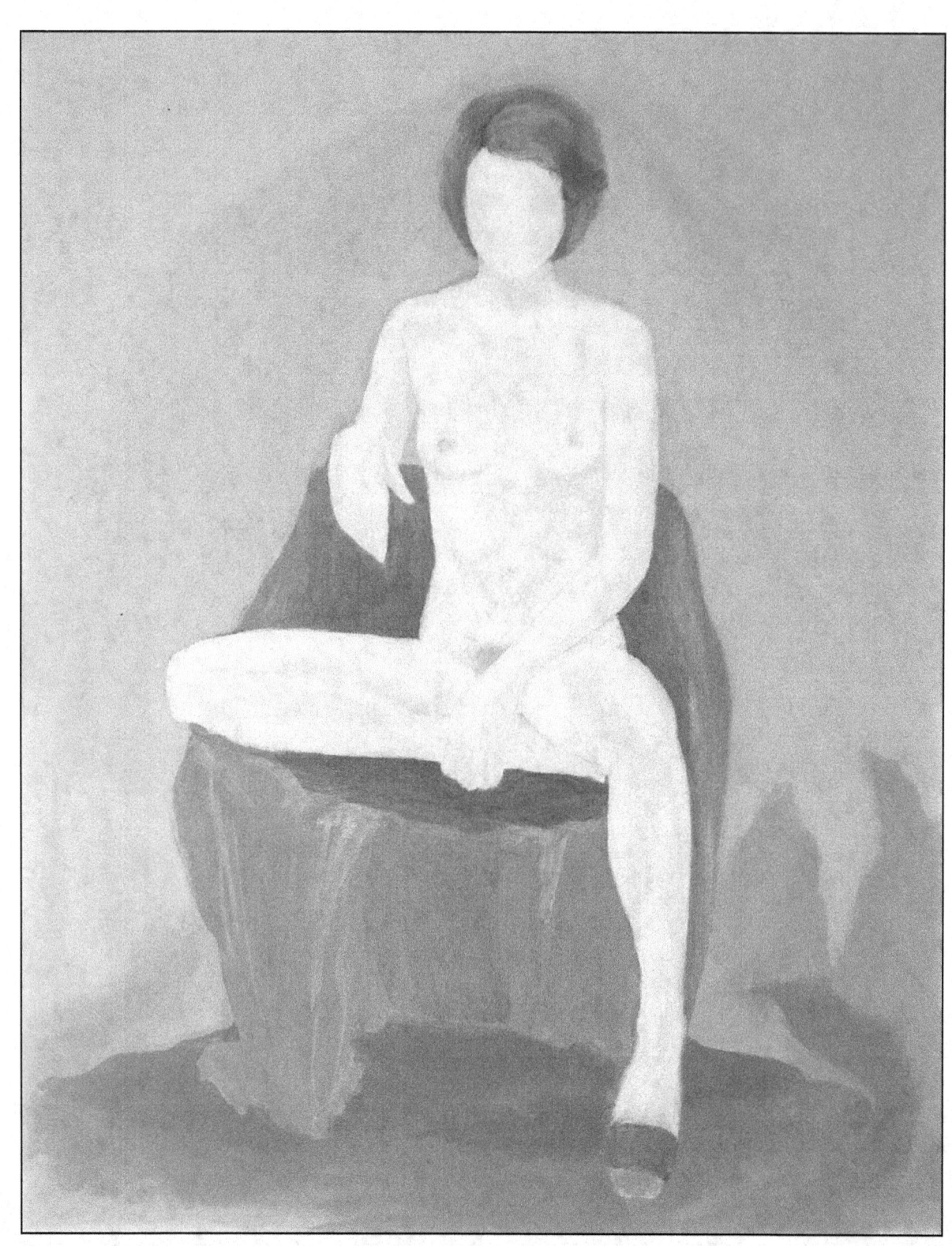

Acrylic on 18"x24" canvas

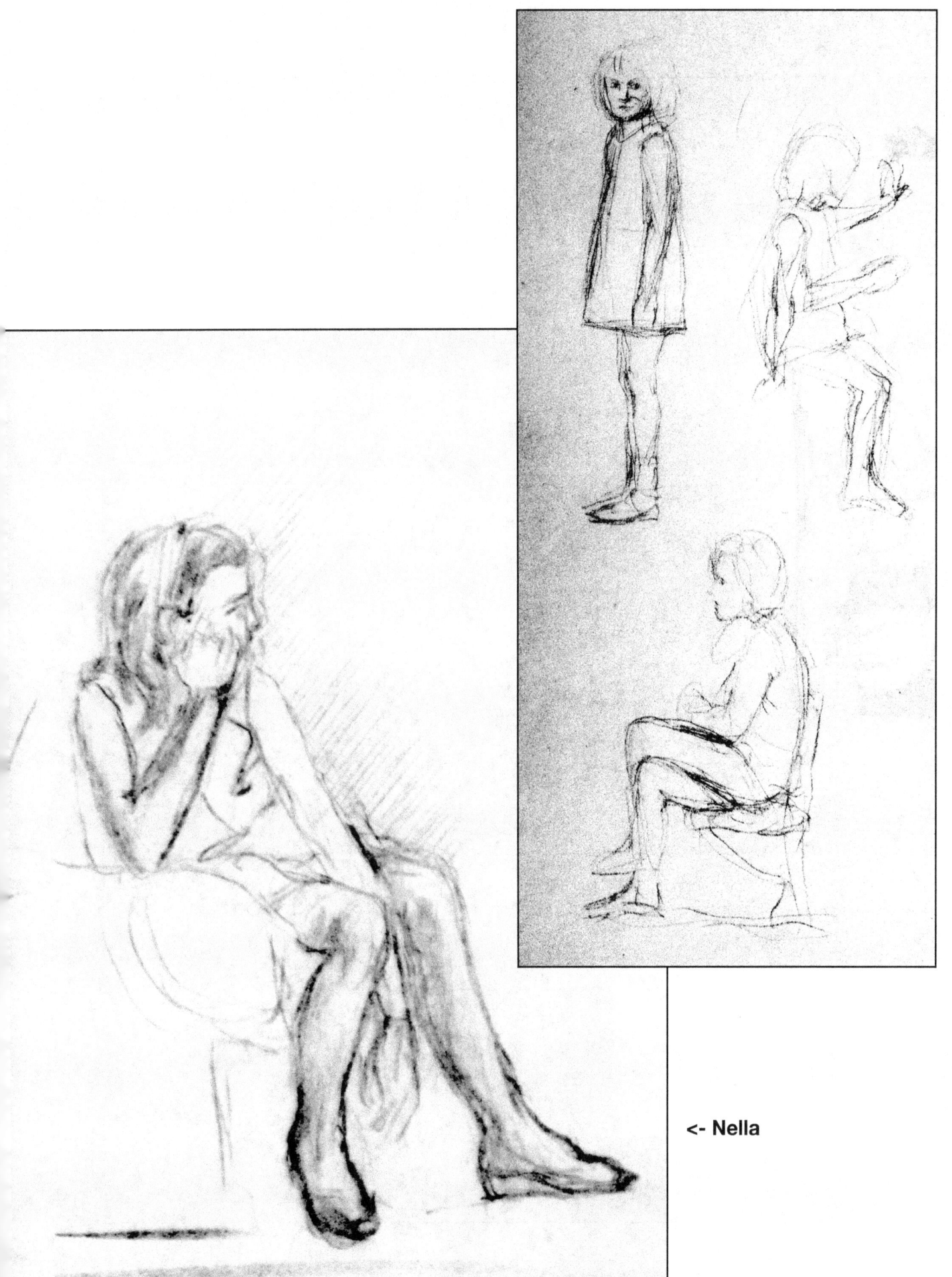

<- Nella

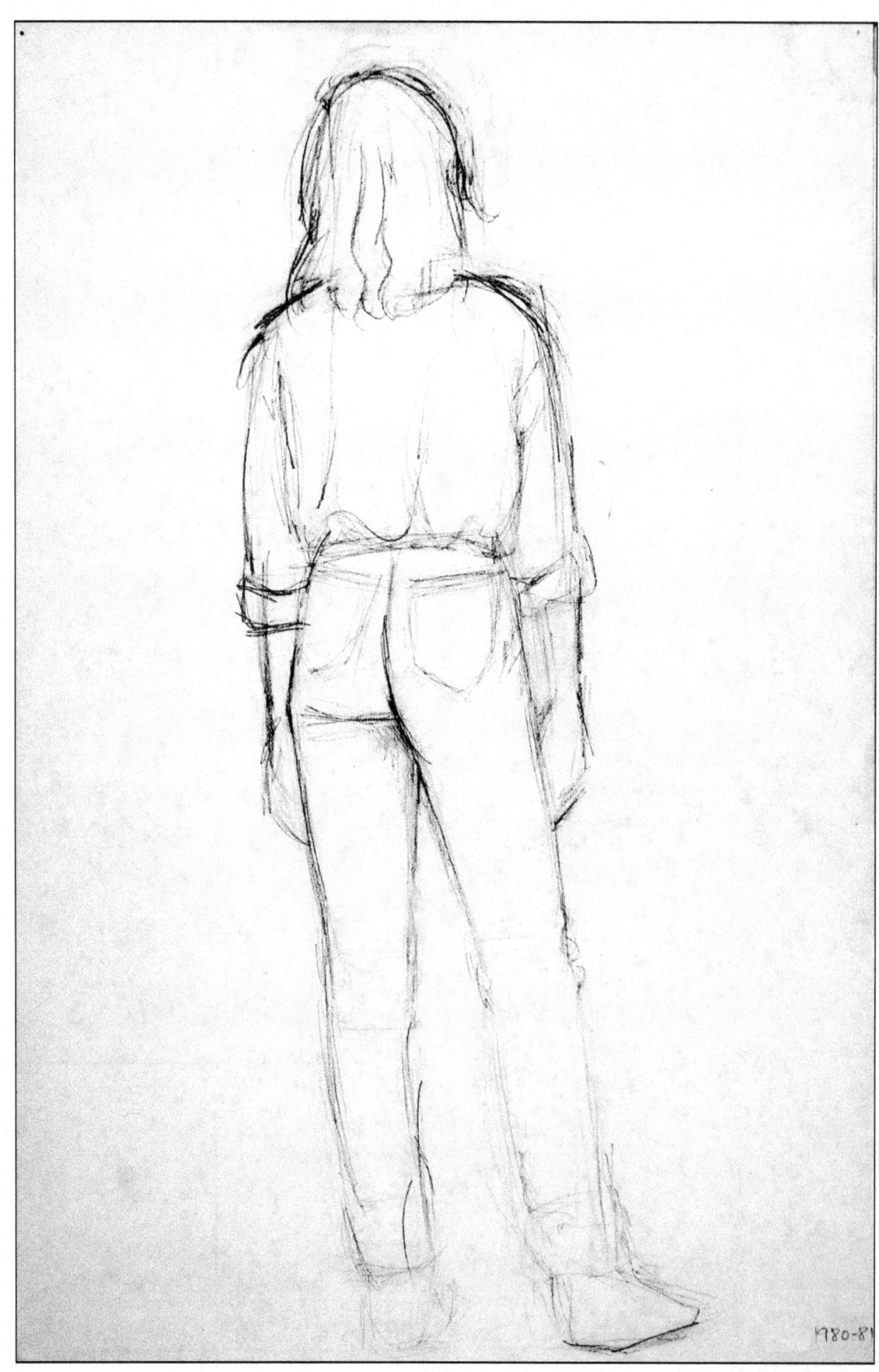

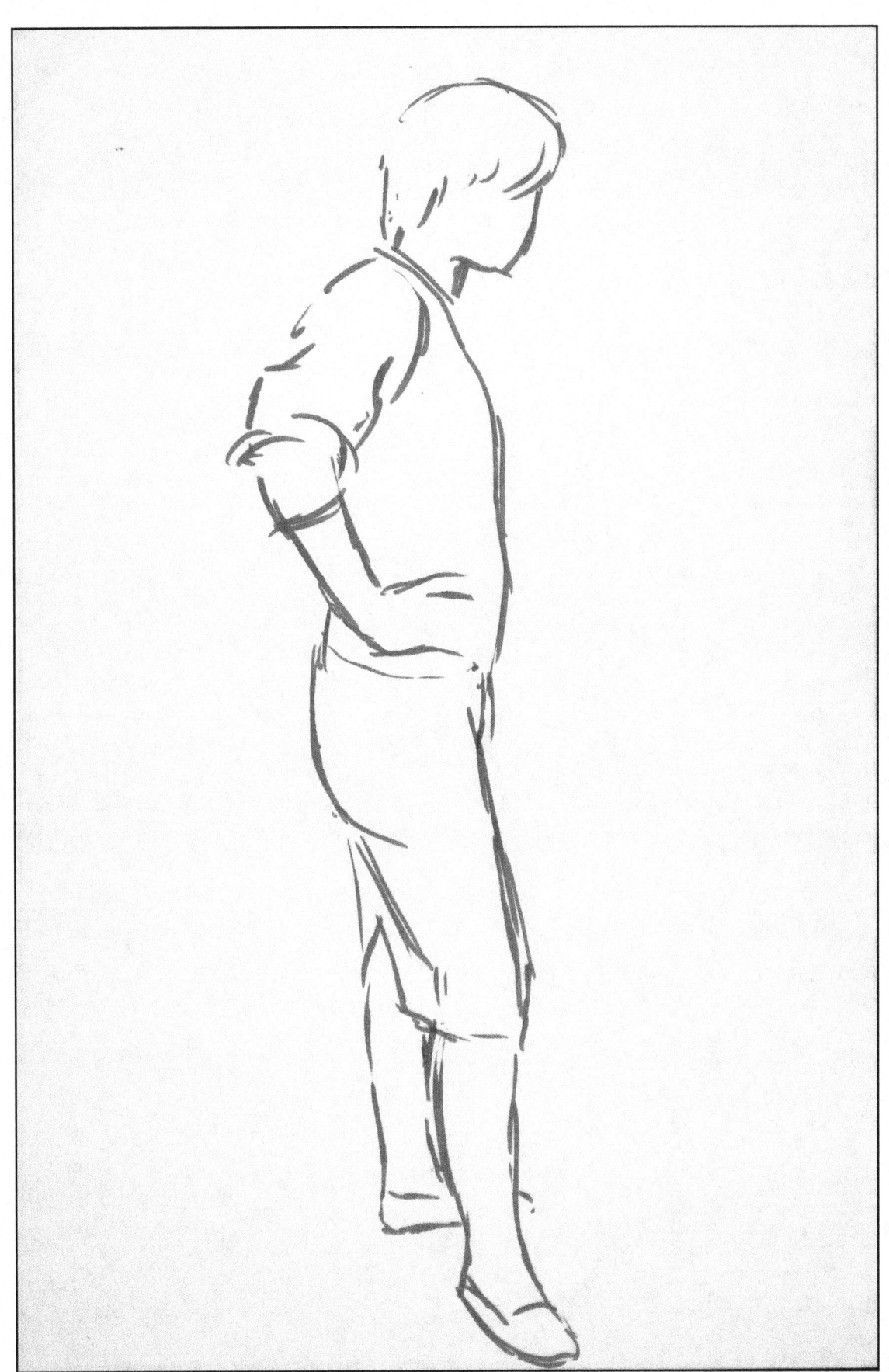

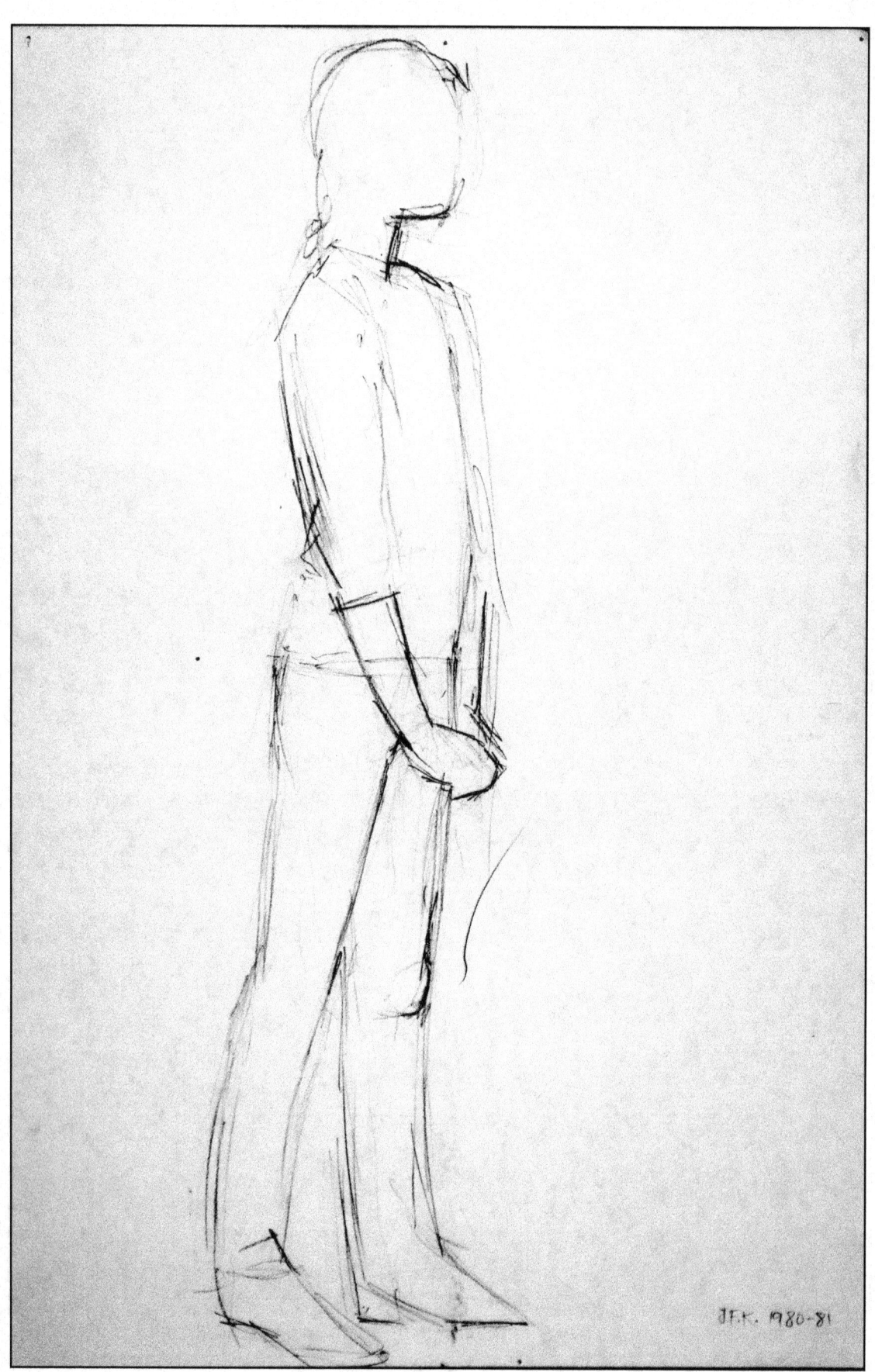

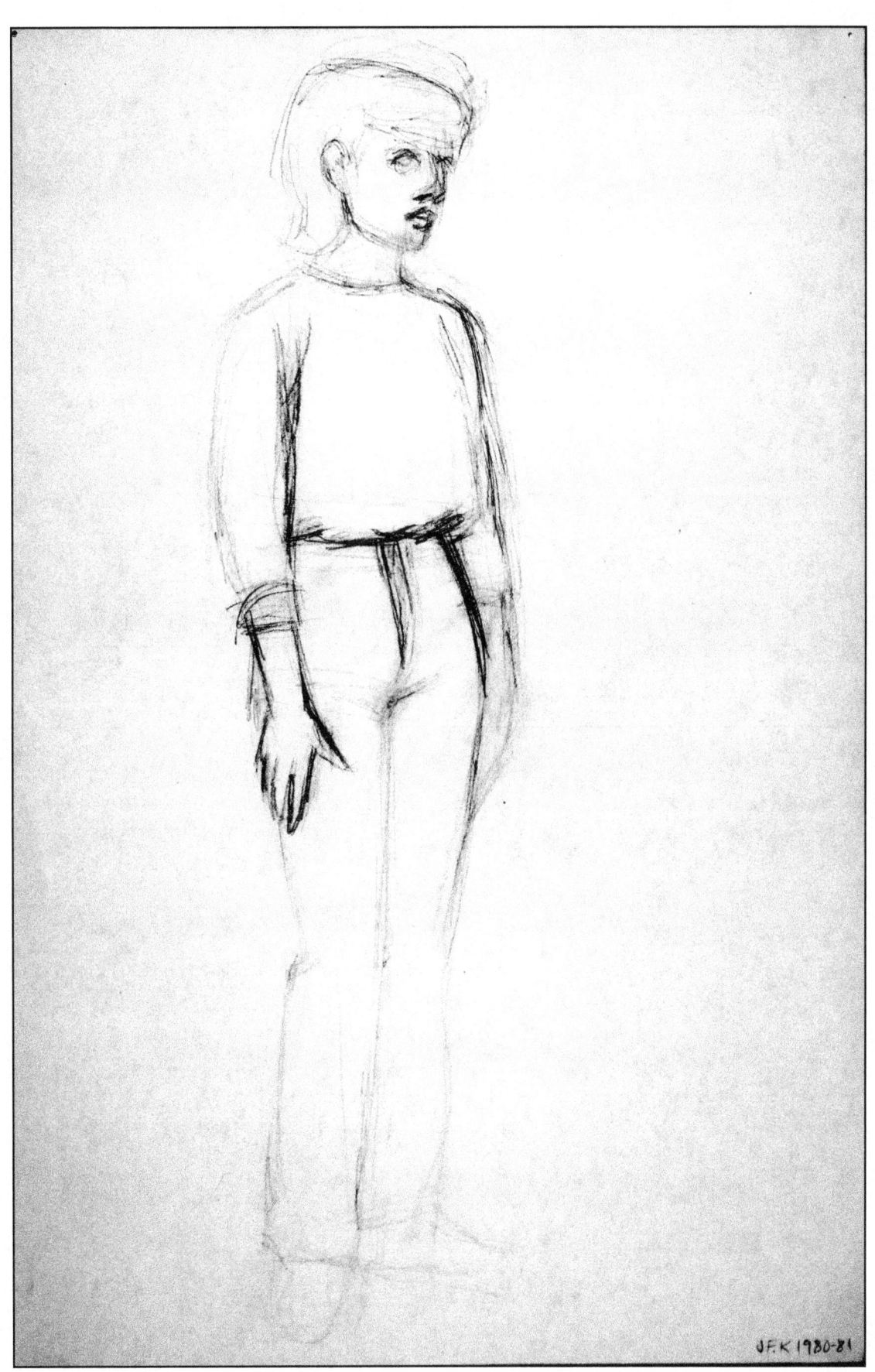

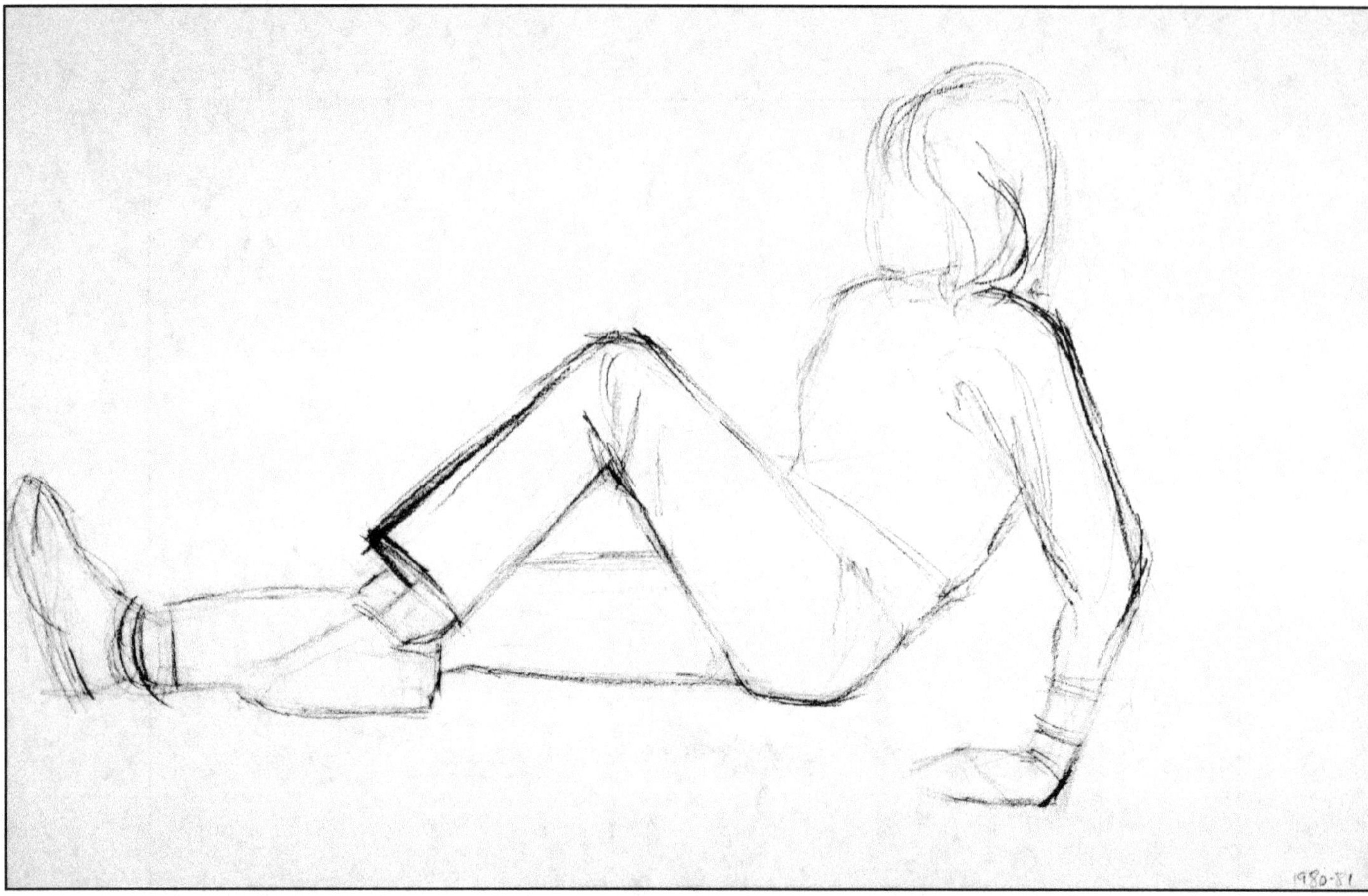

1980-81

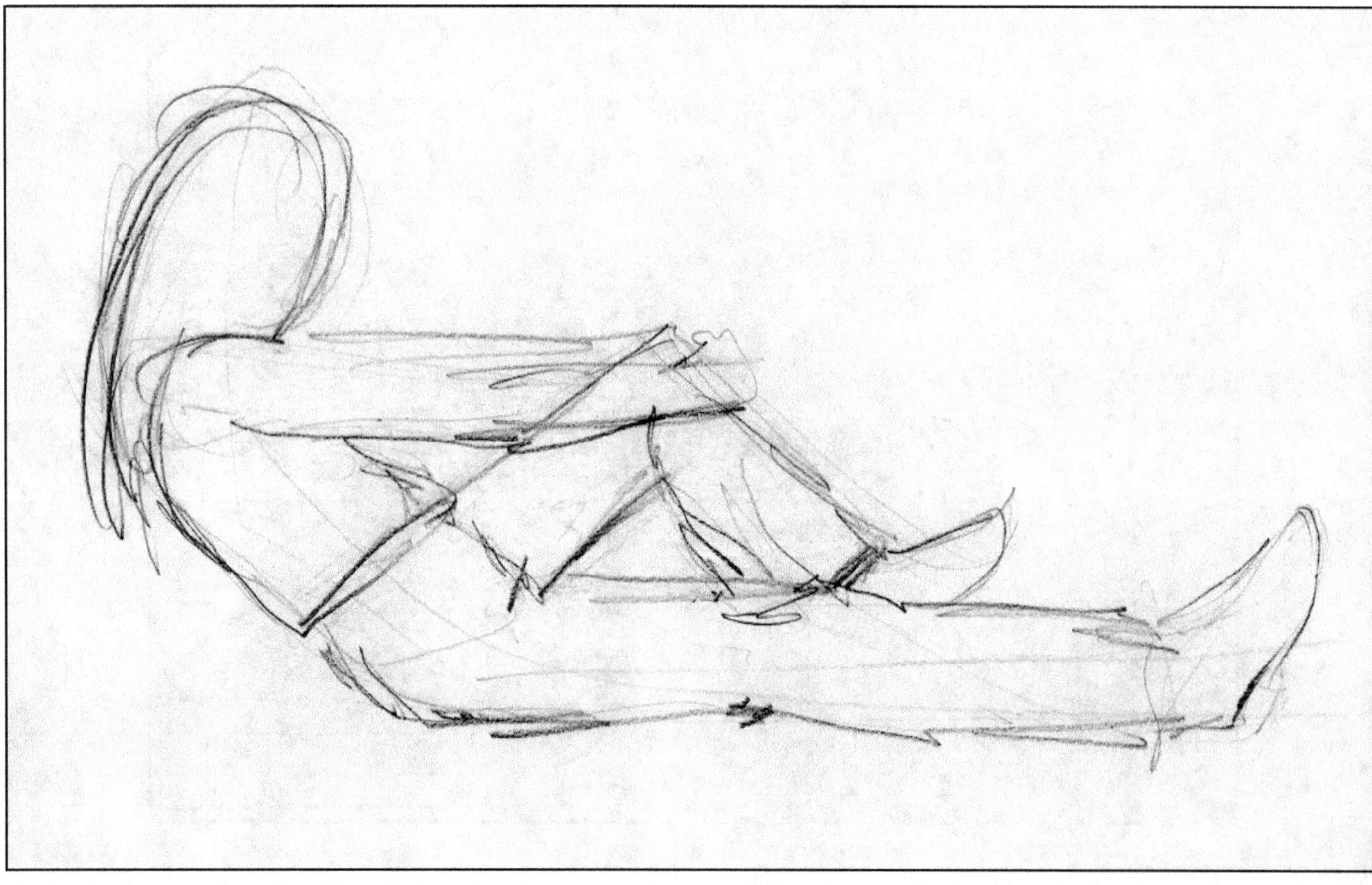

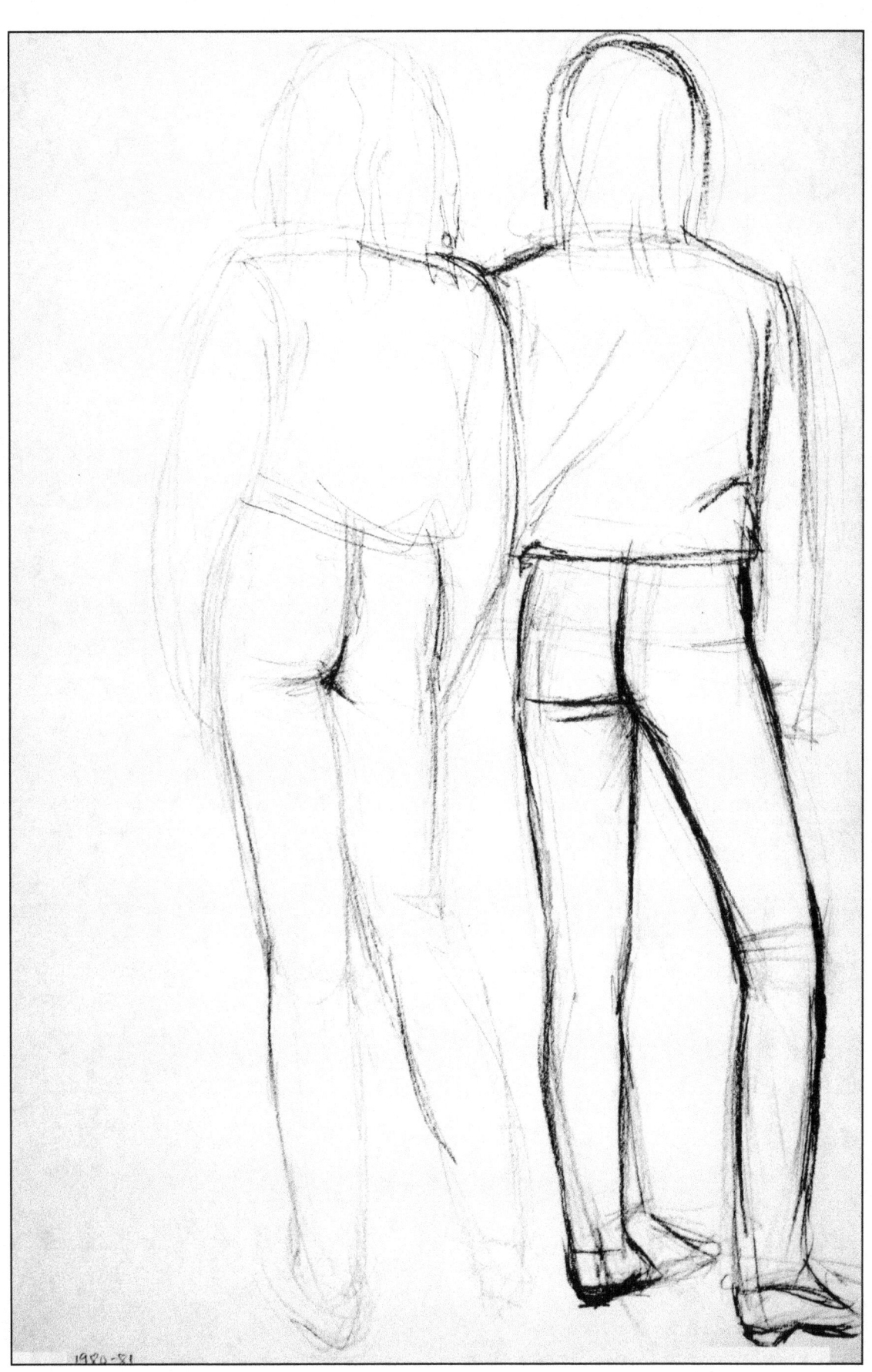

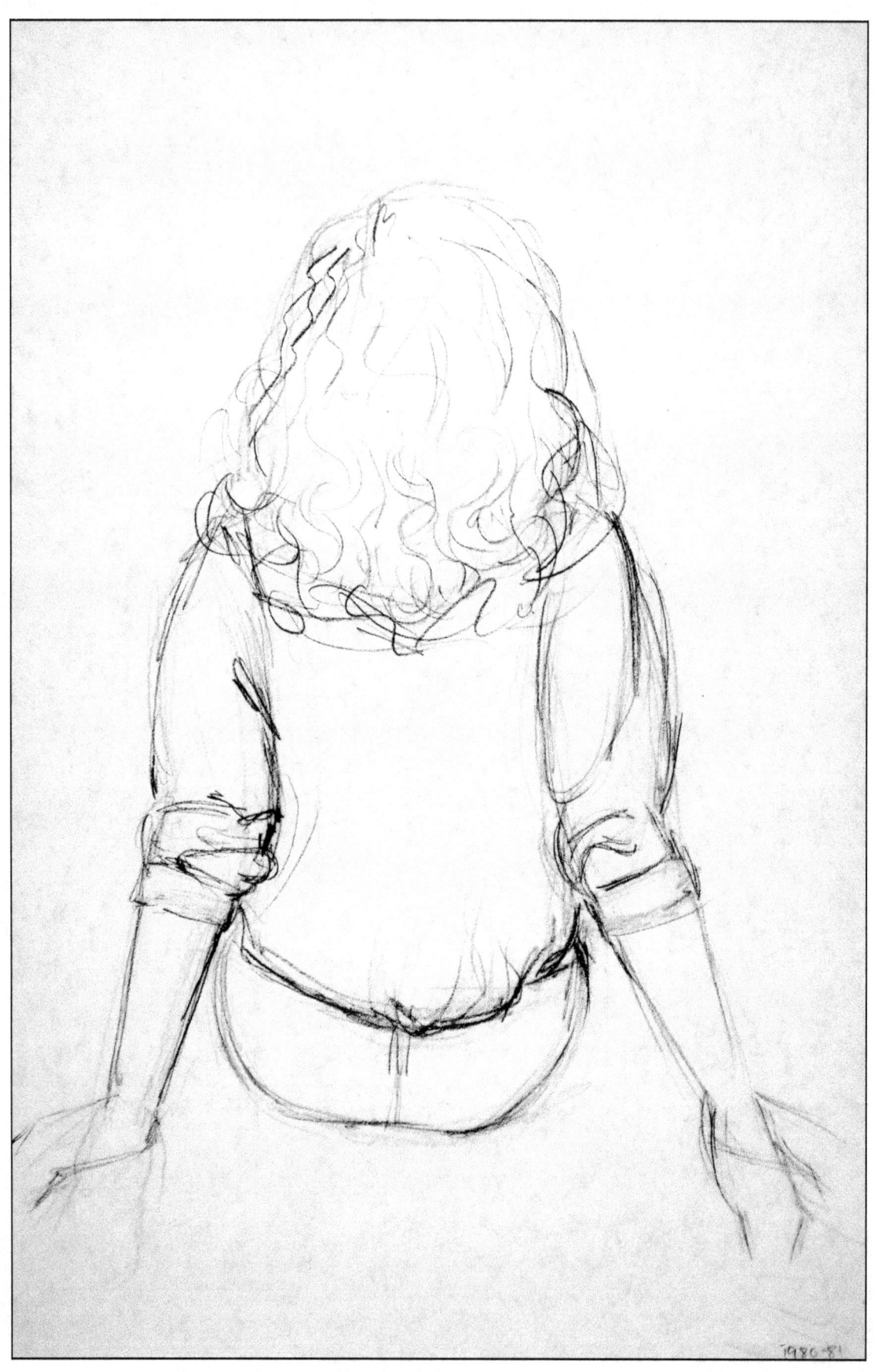

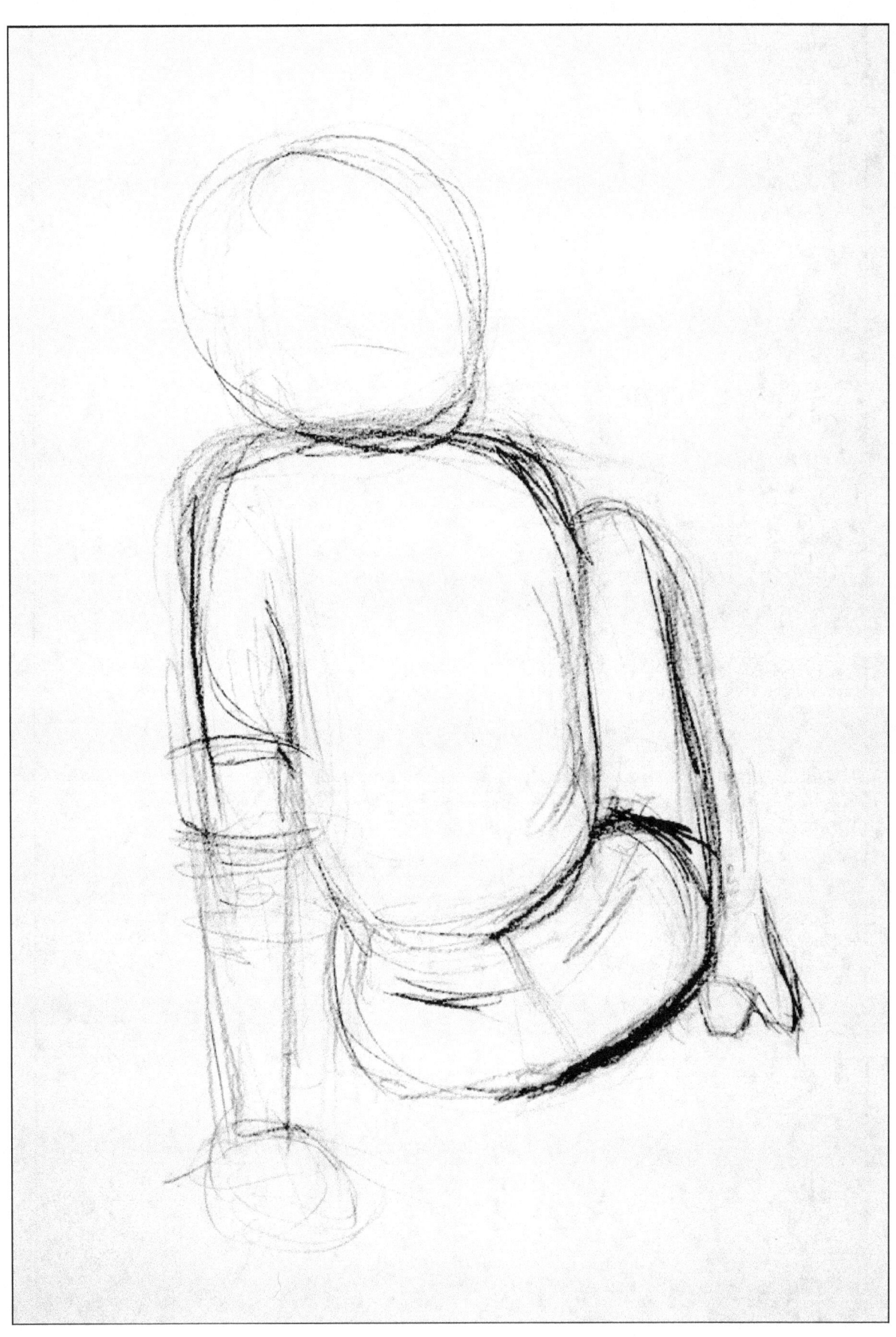

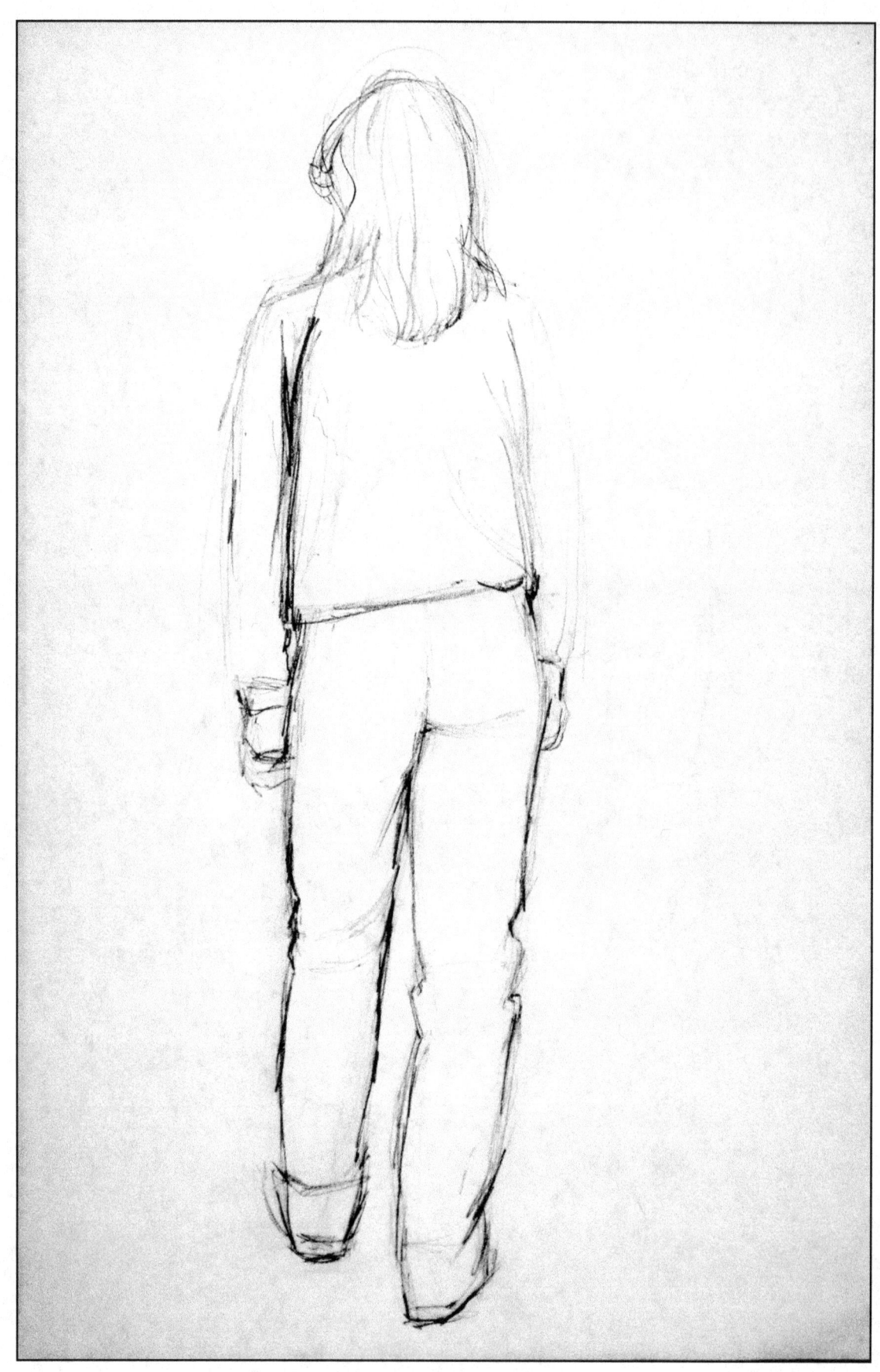

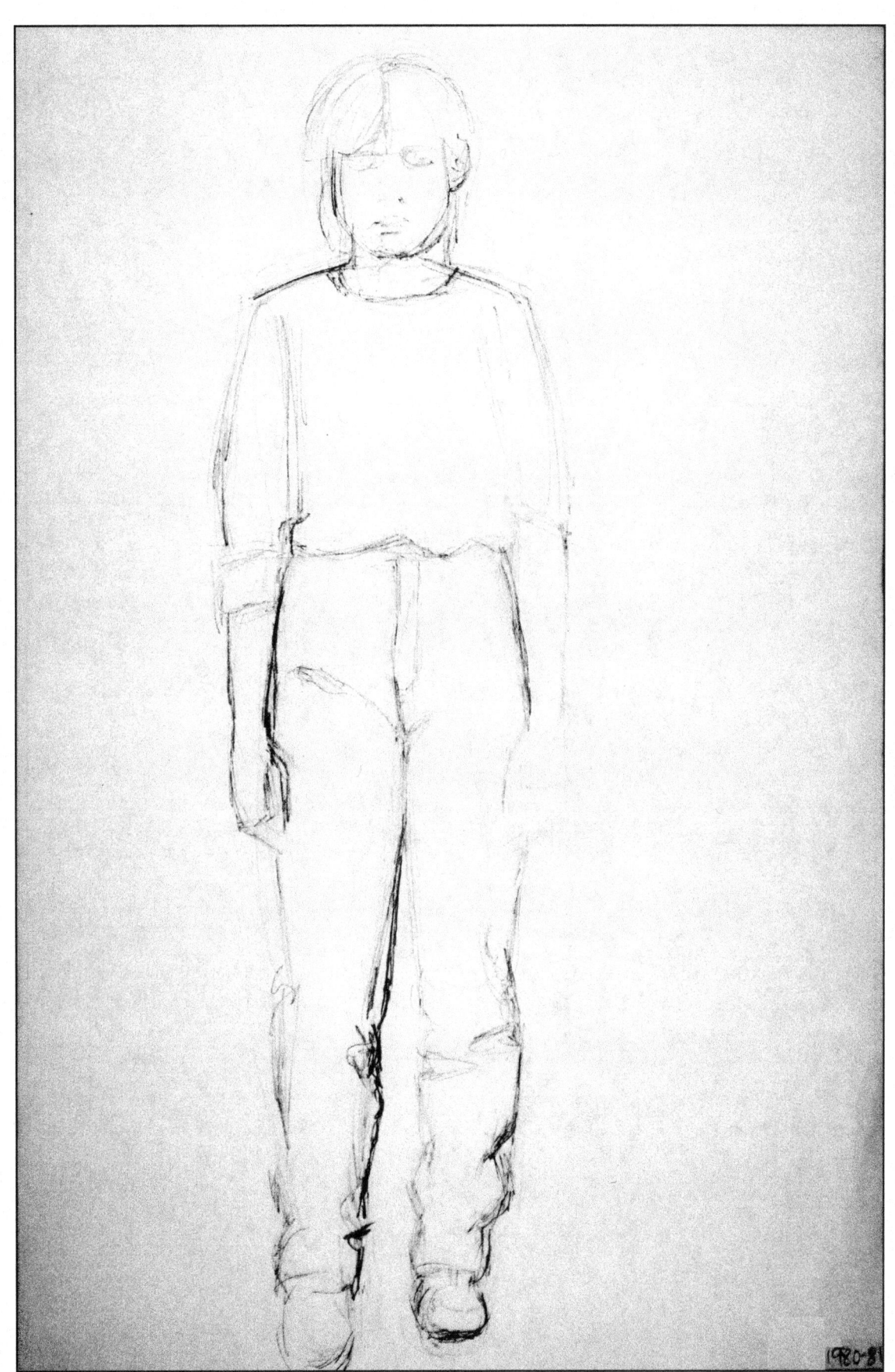

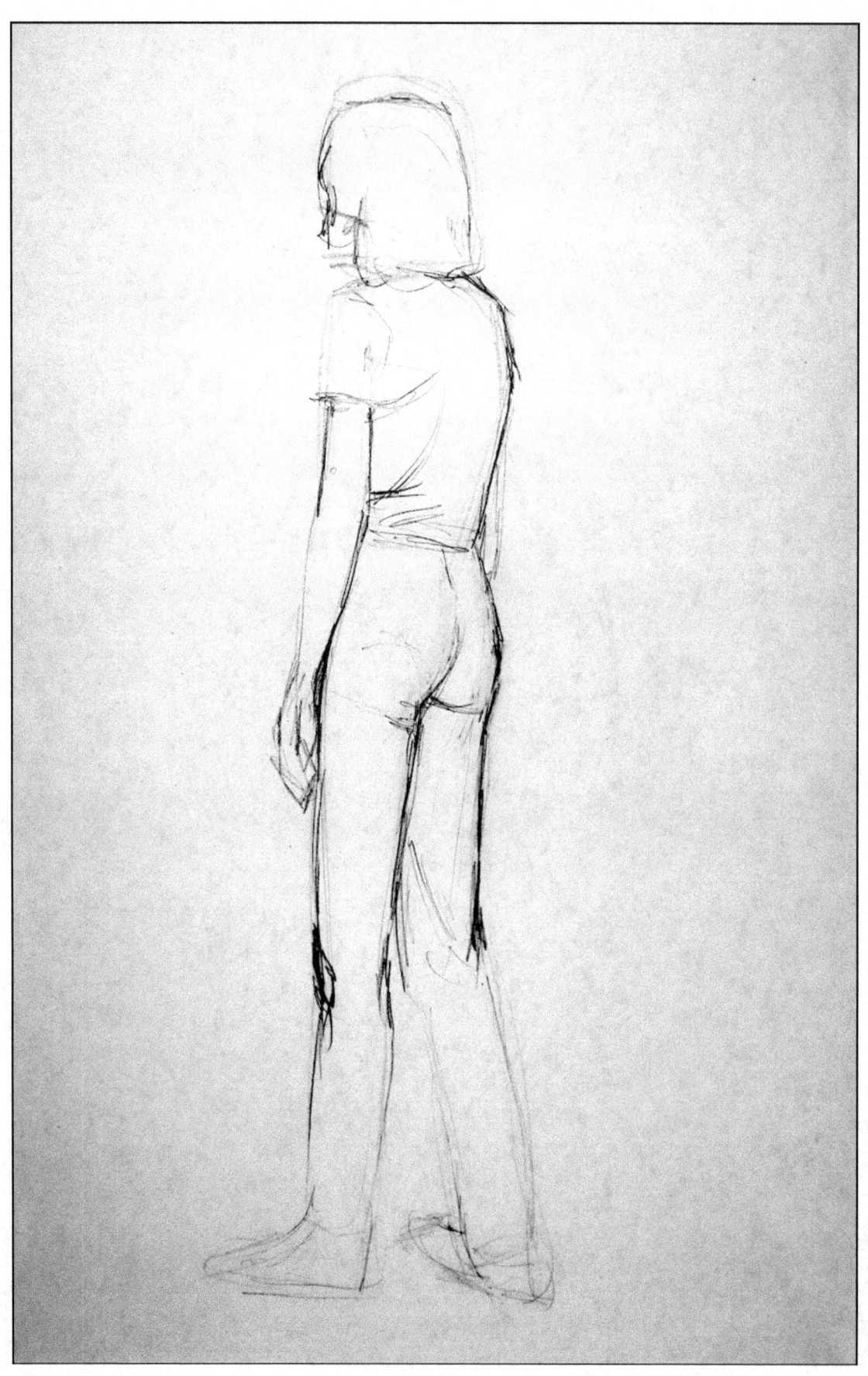

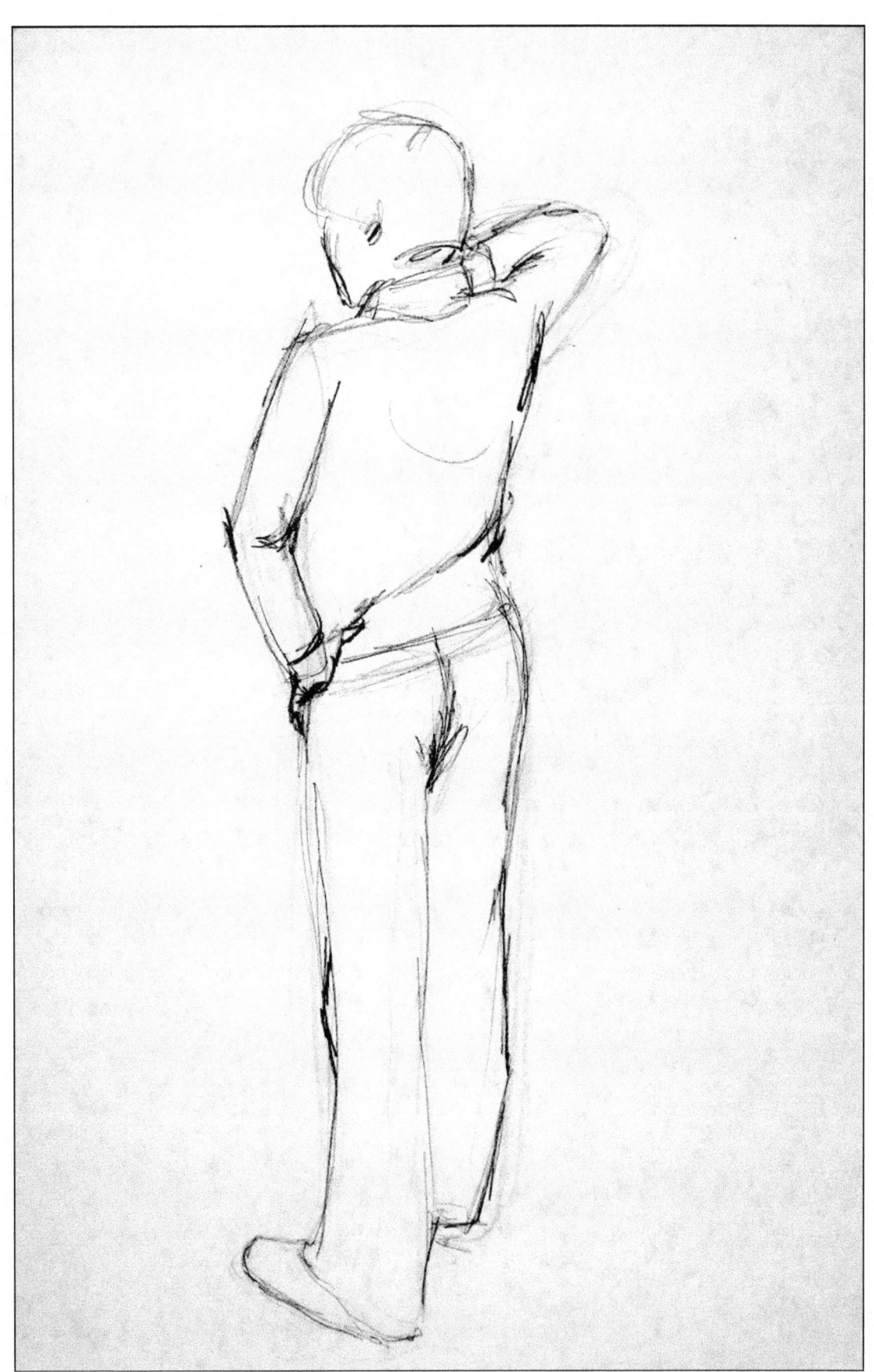

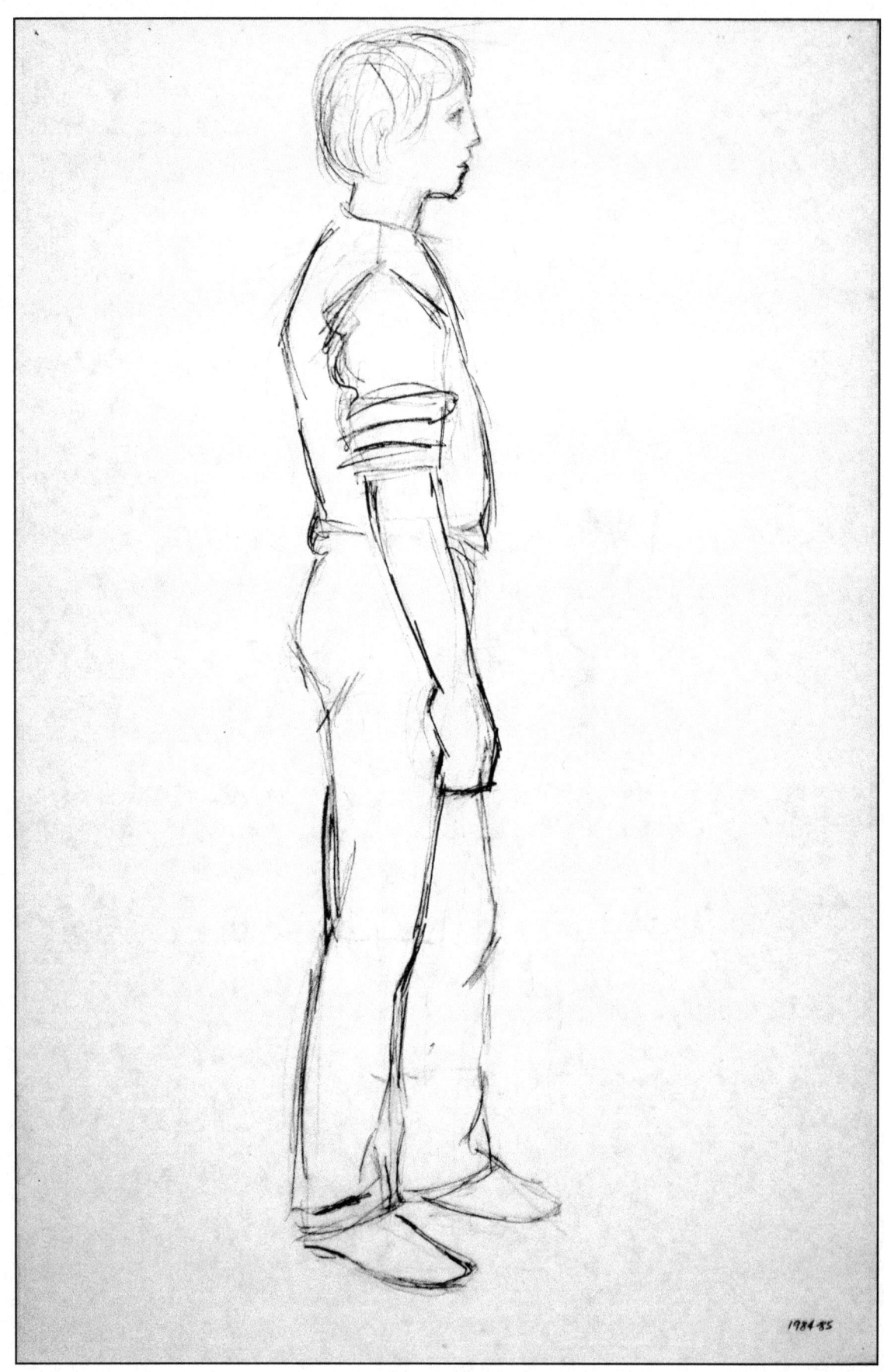

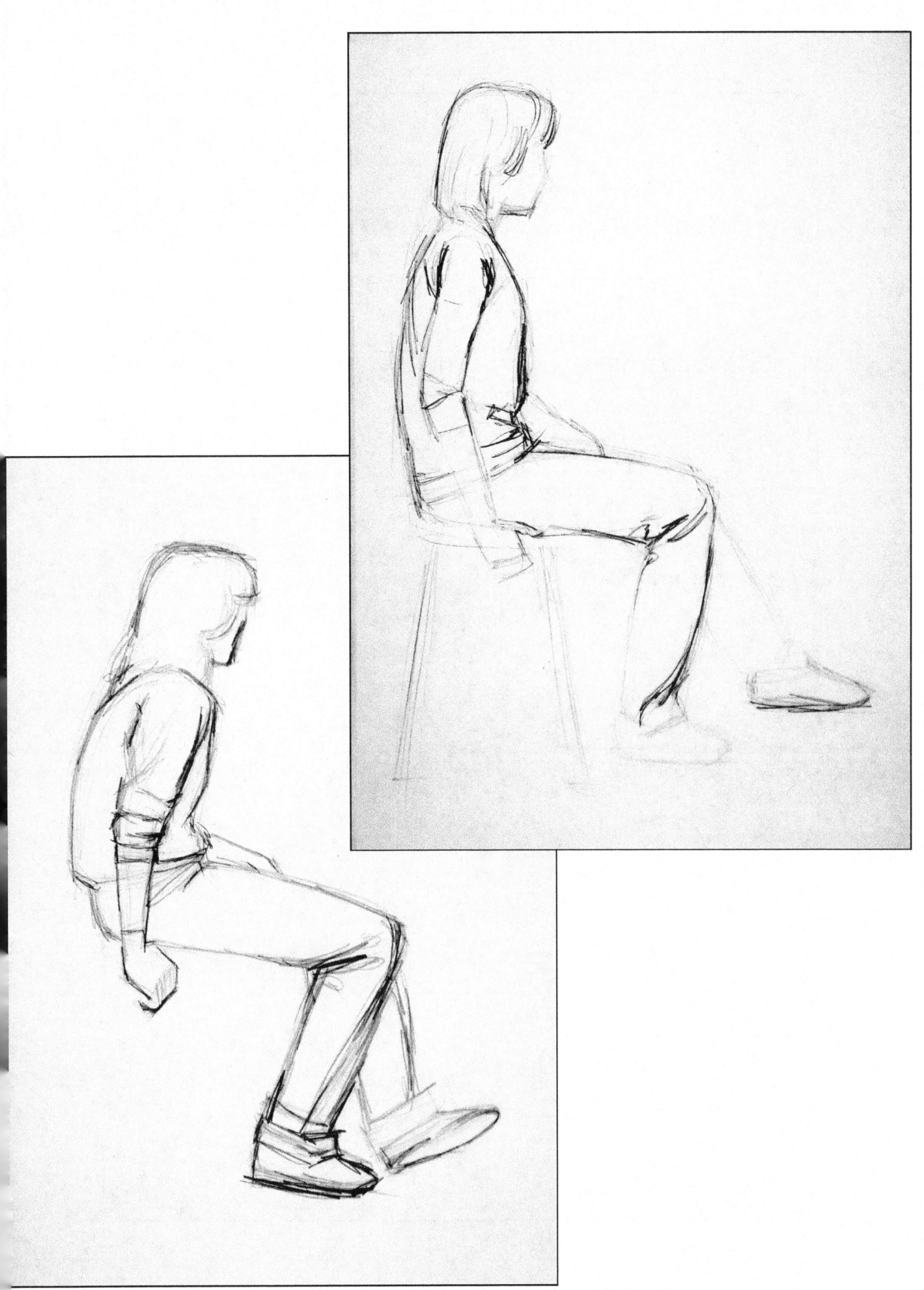

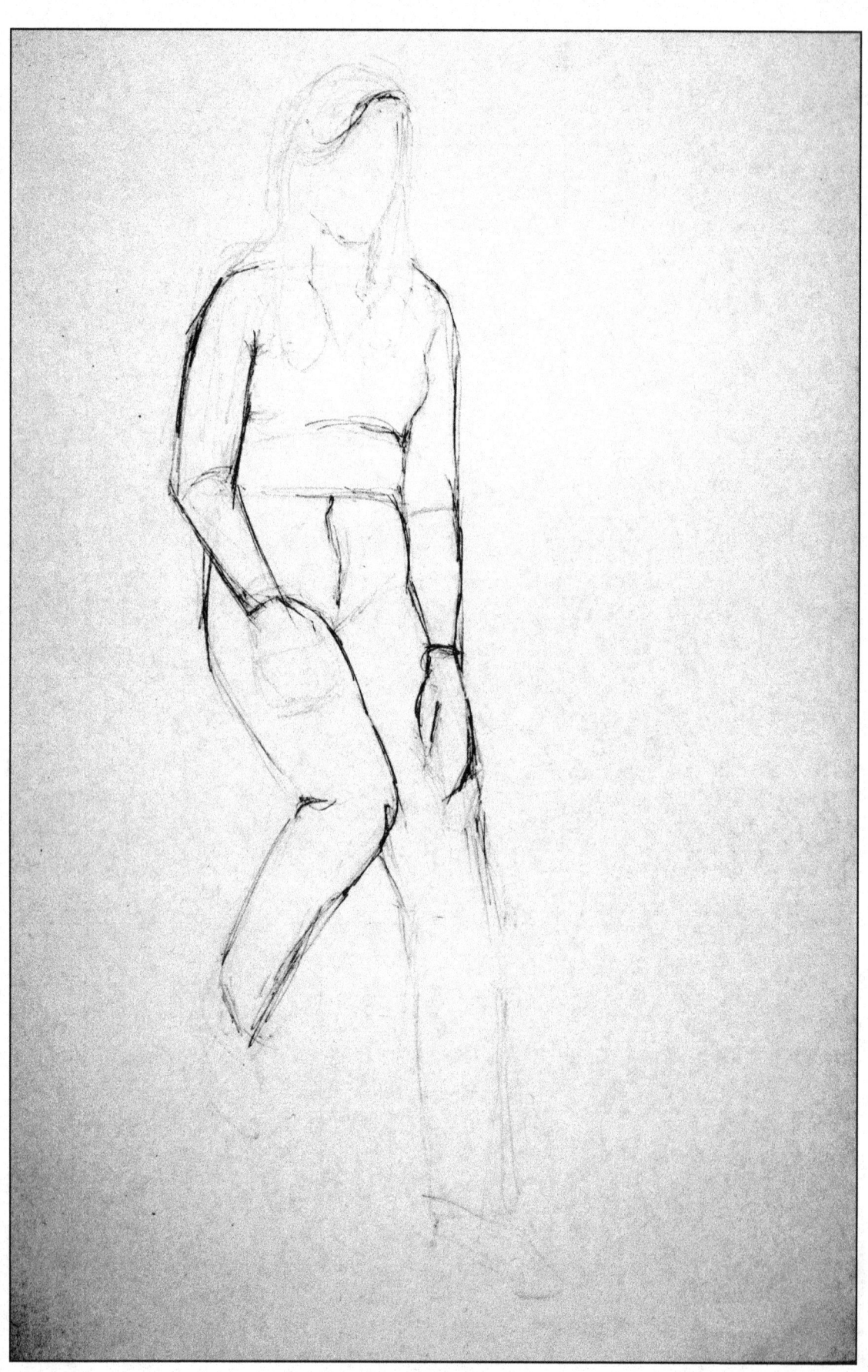

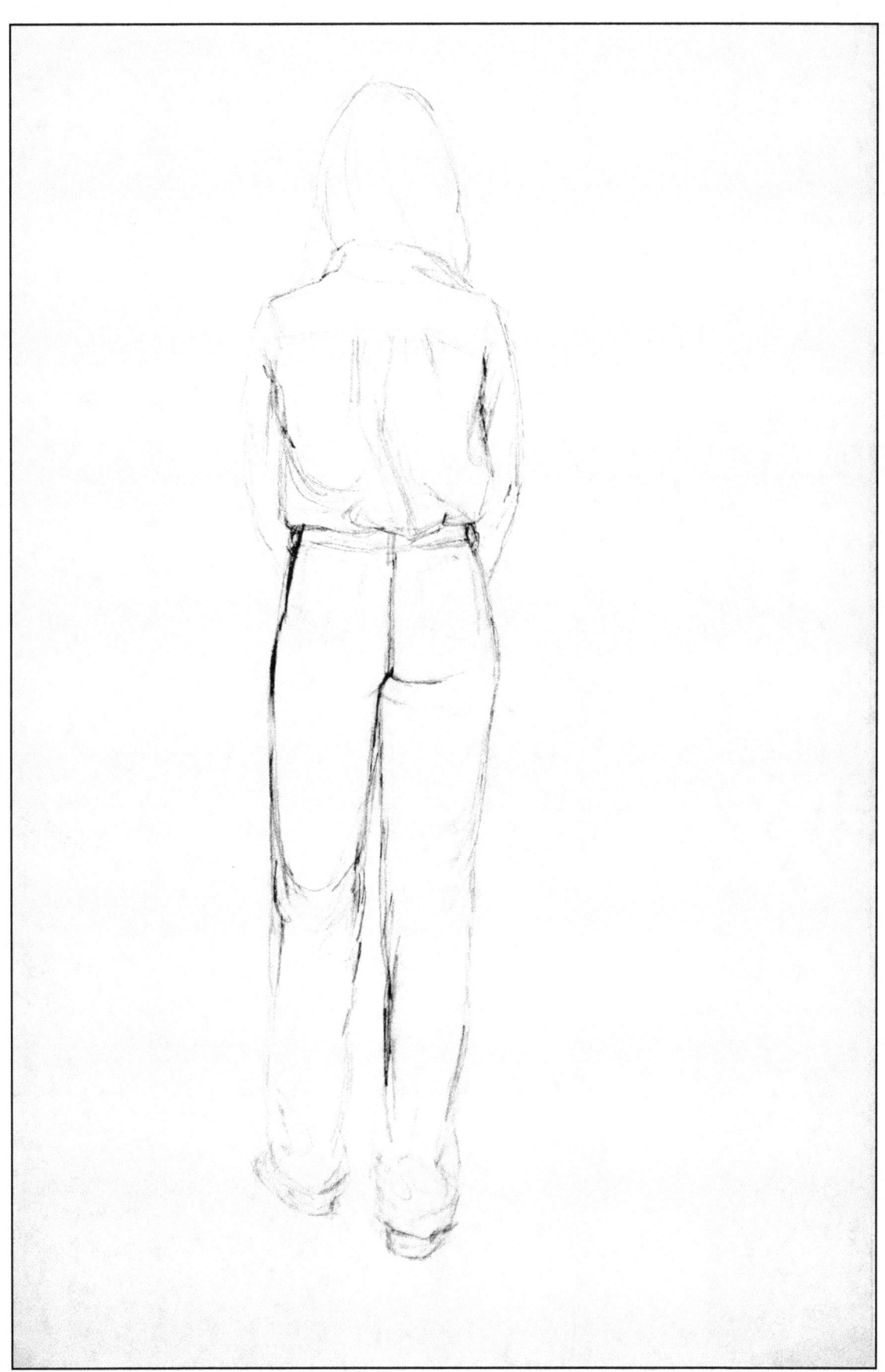

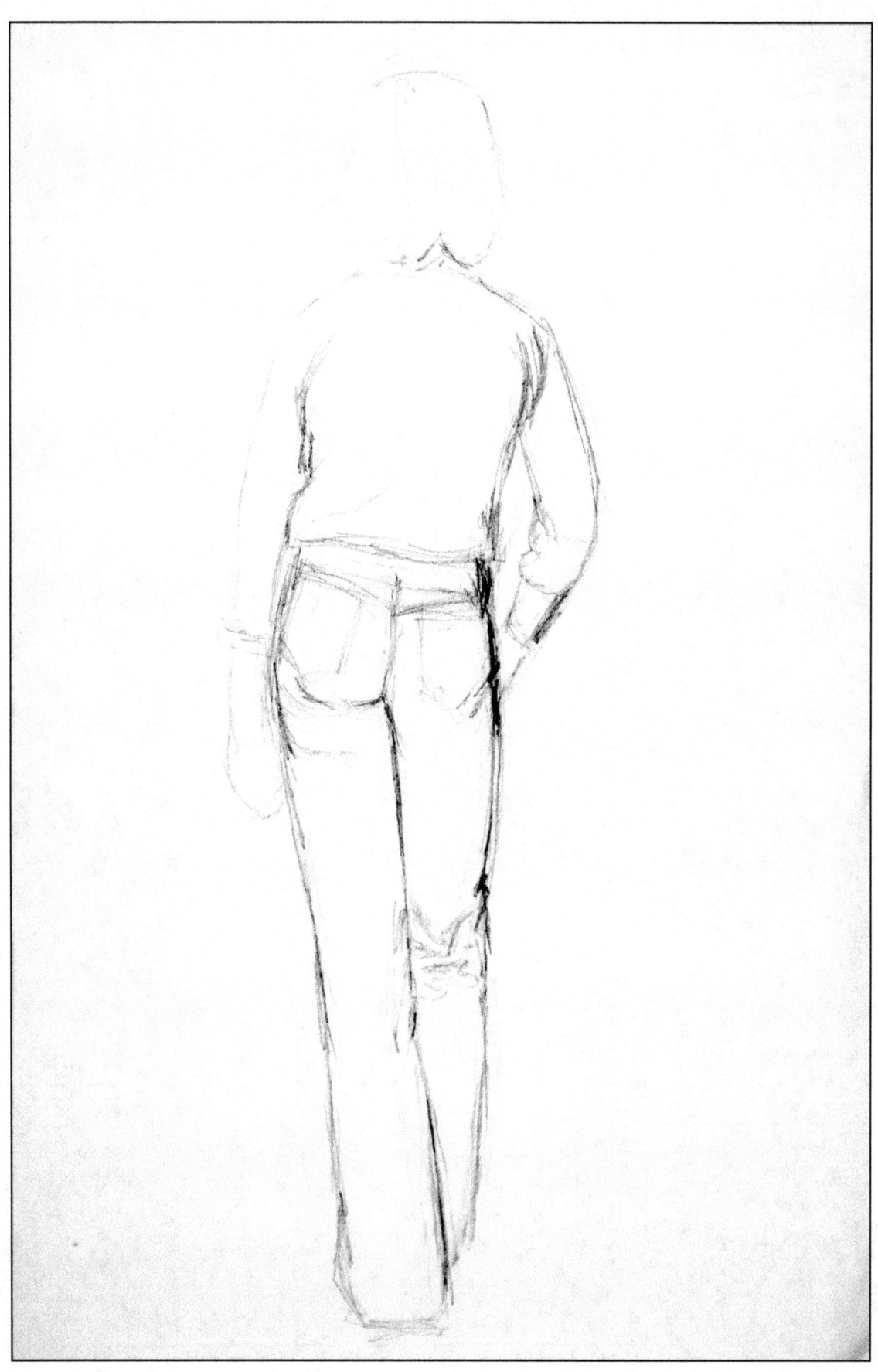

14. Full Figure, Obs/Vis, At School

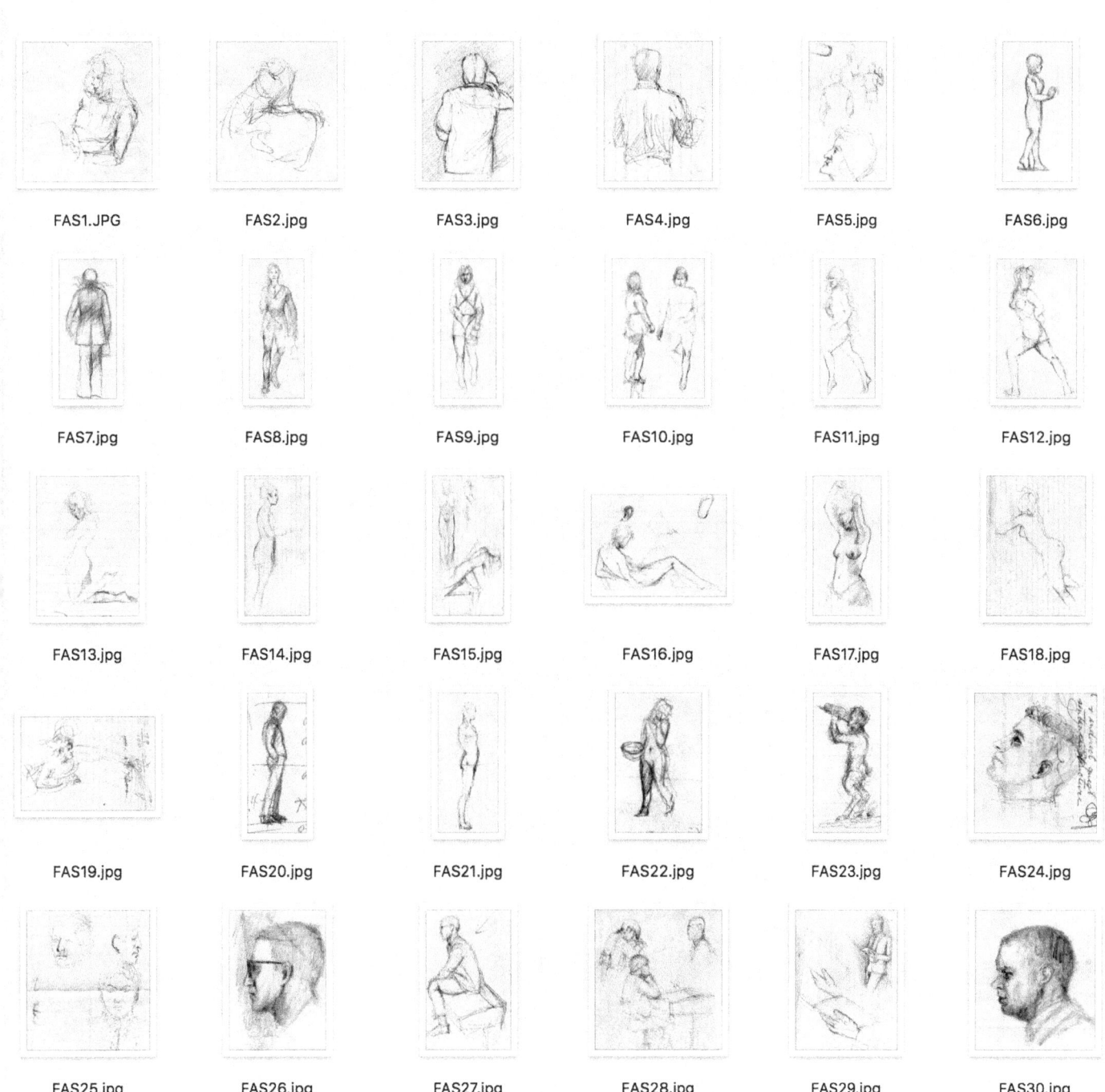

I did these ballpoint-pen drawings when I was in High School, during class.

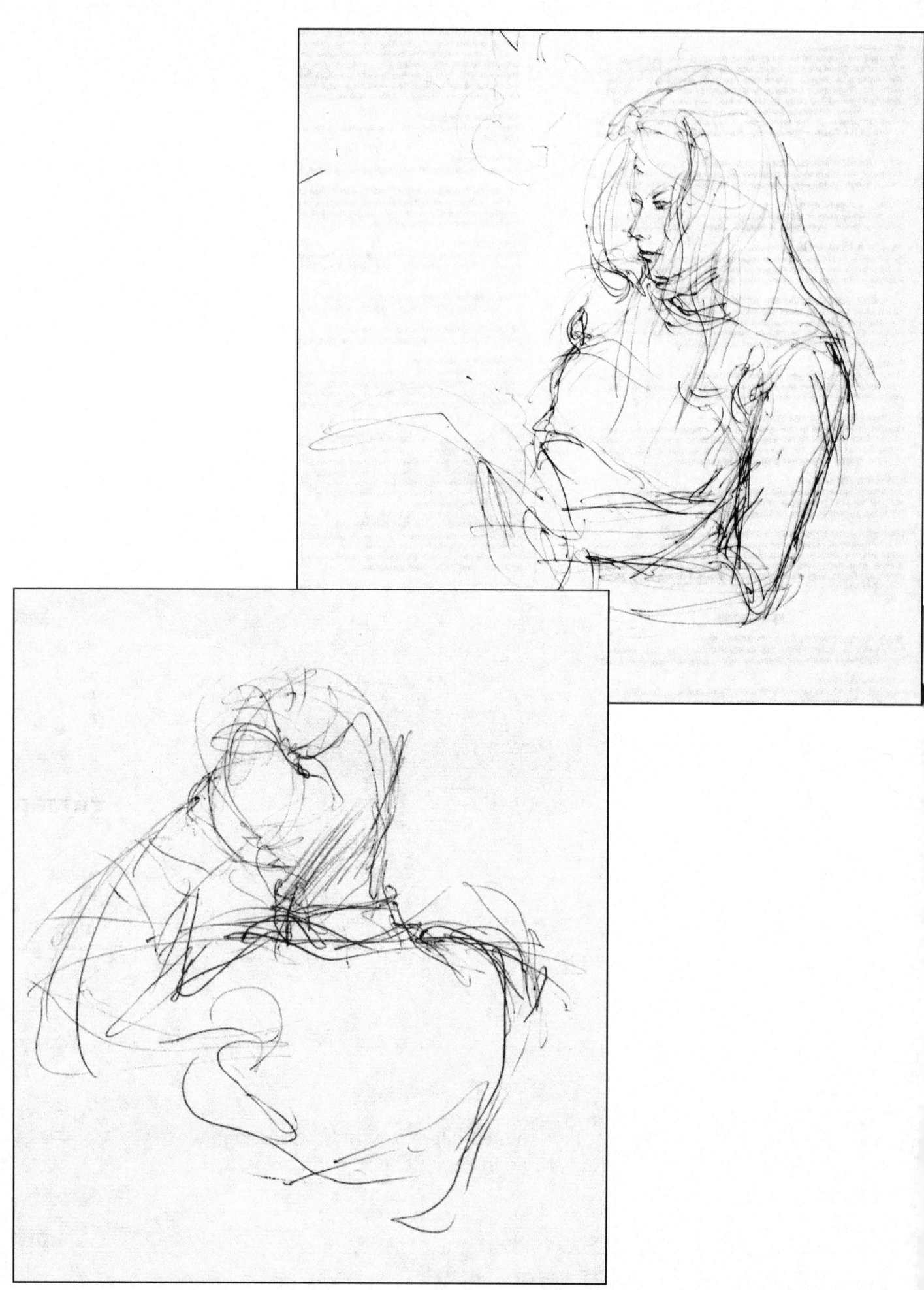

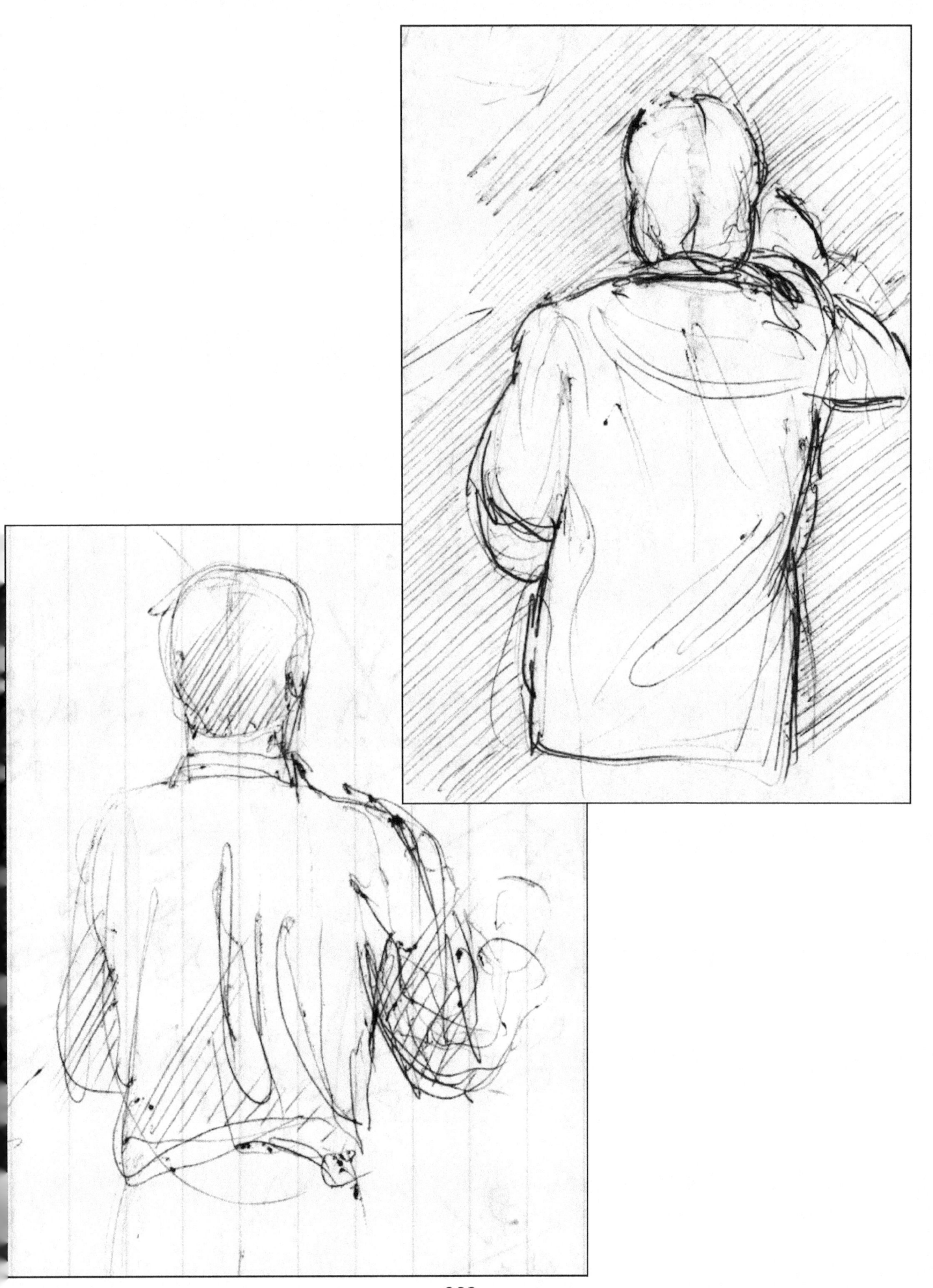

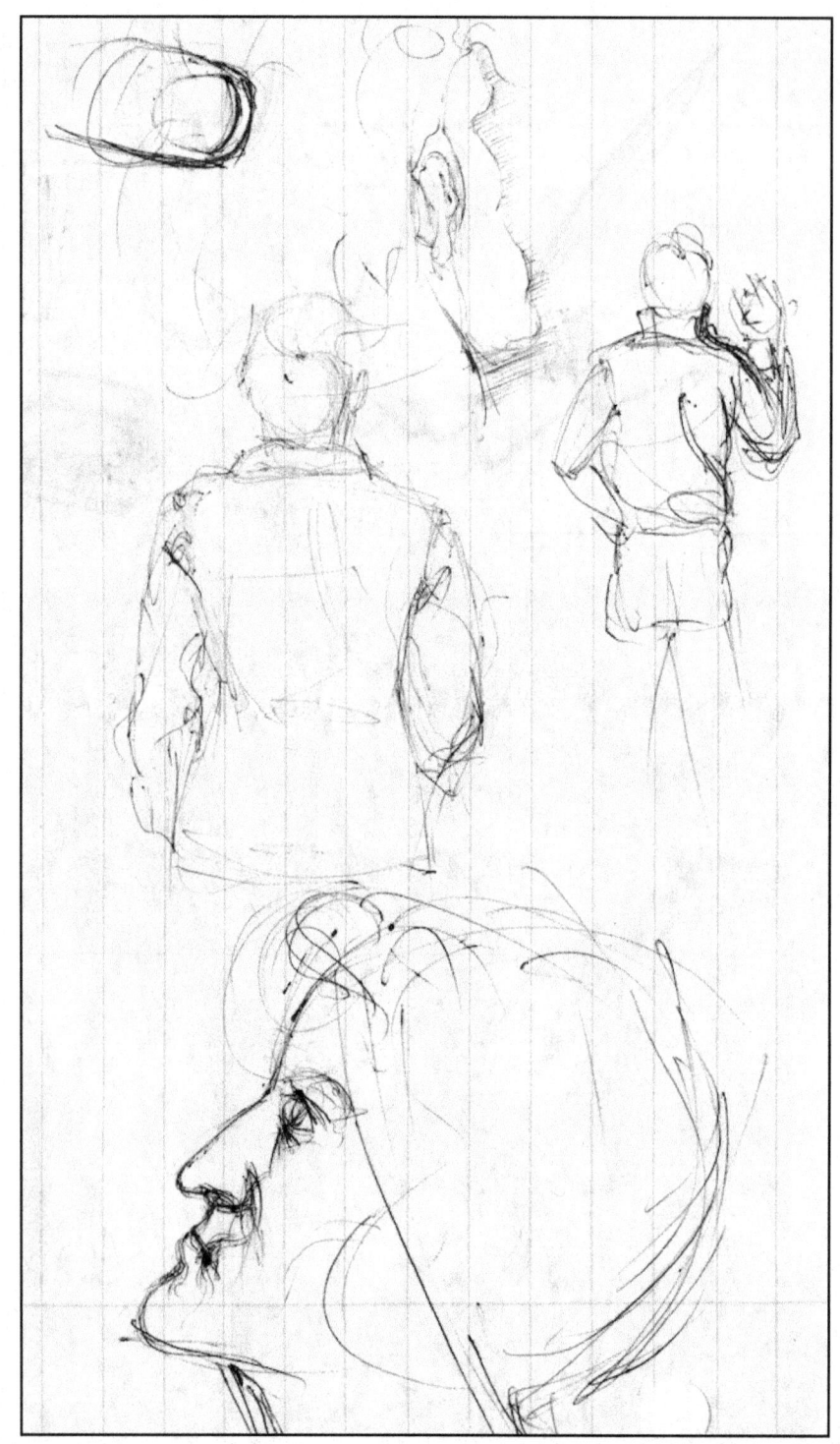

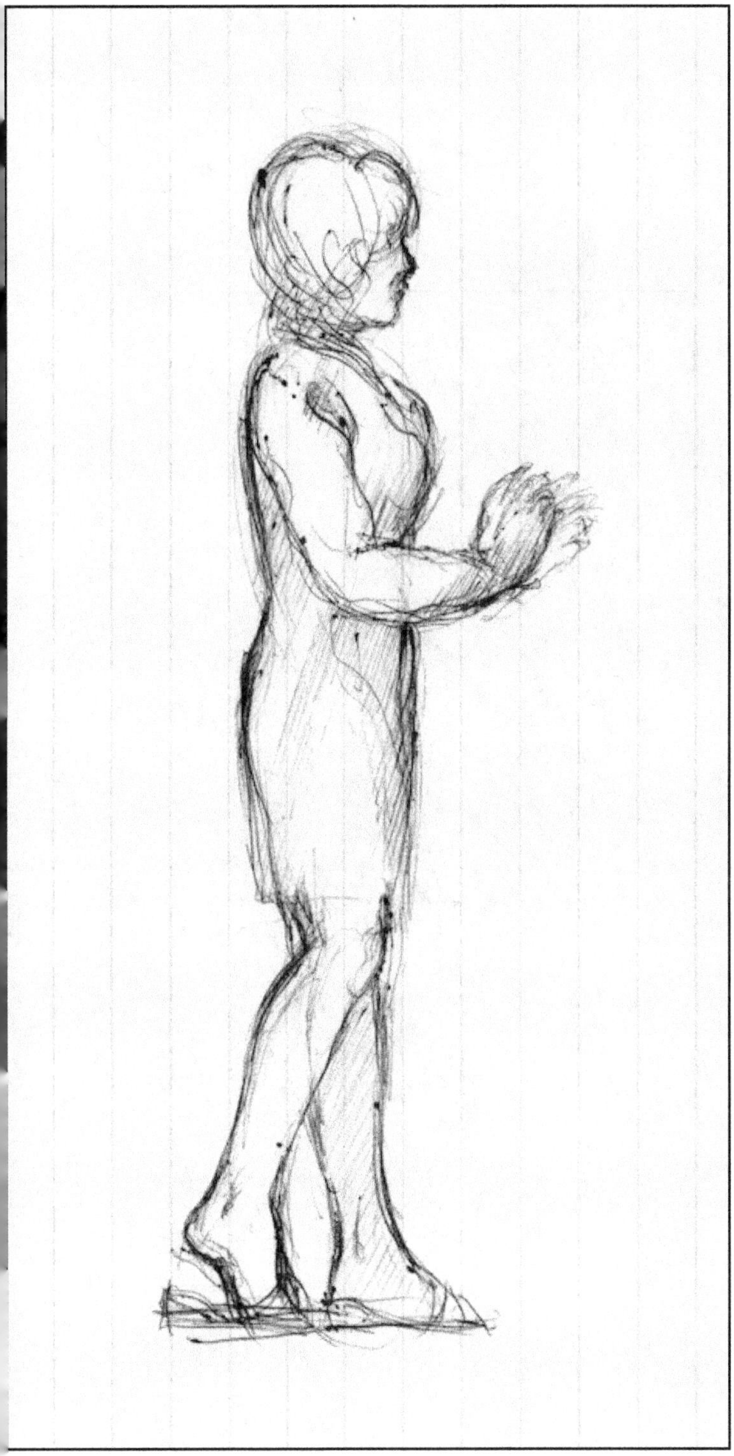

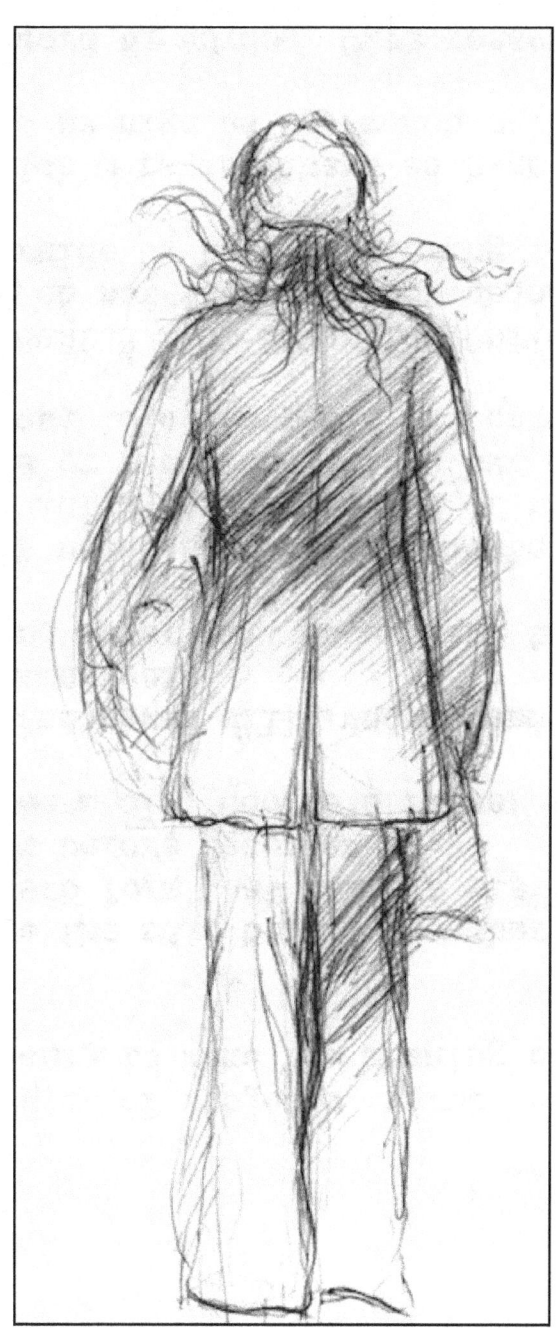

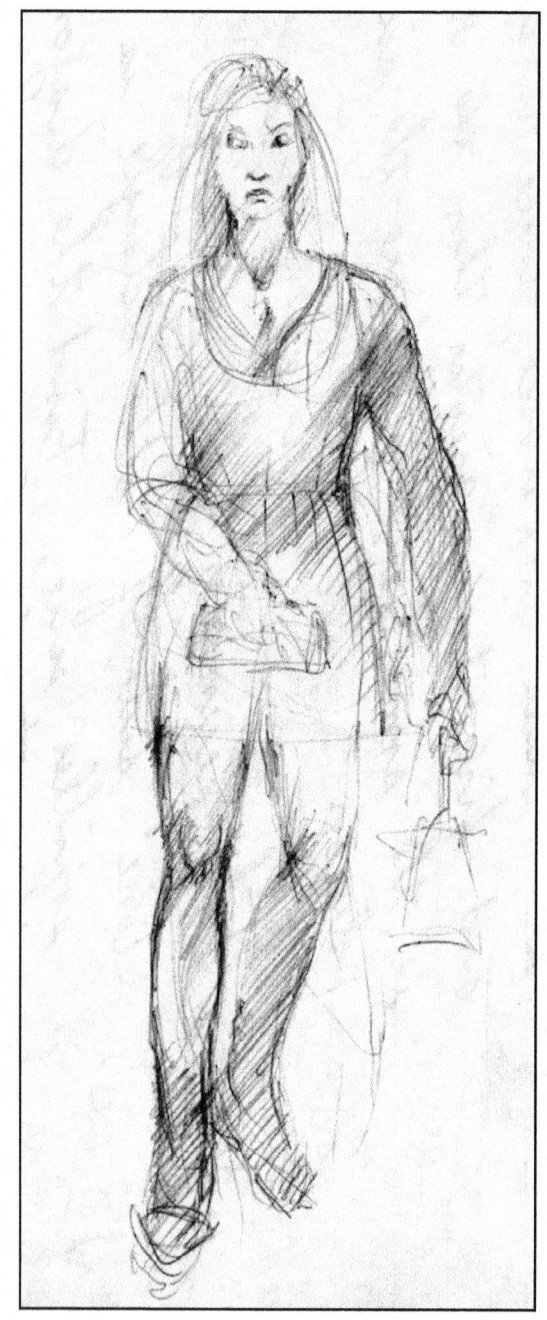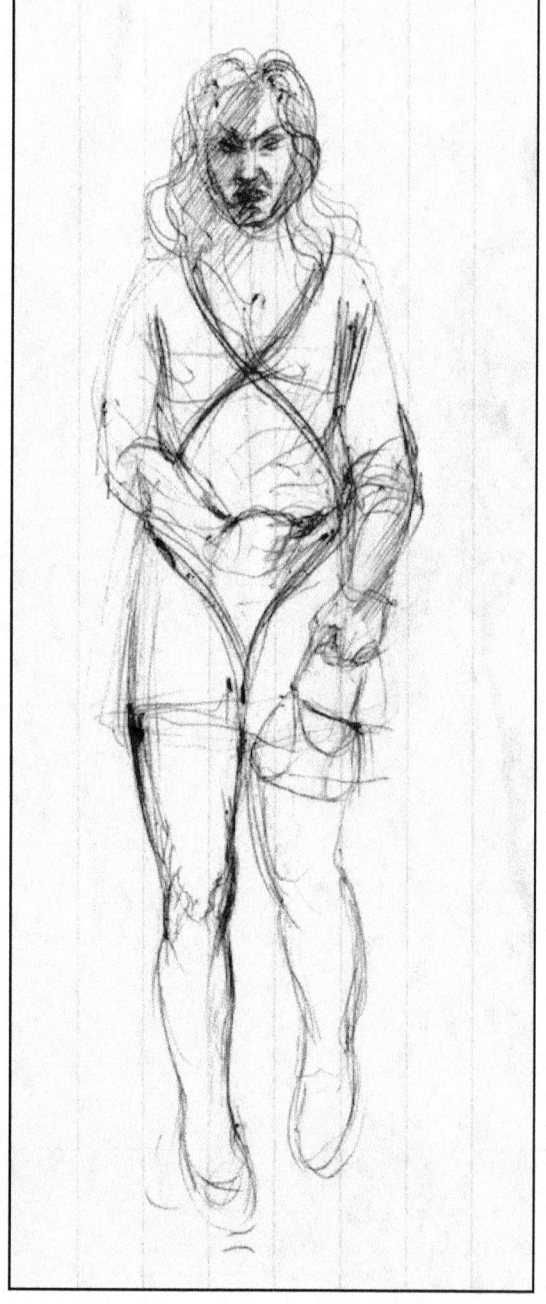

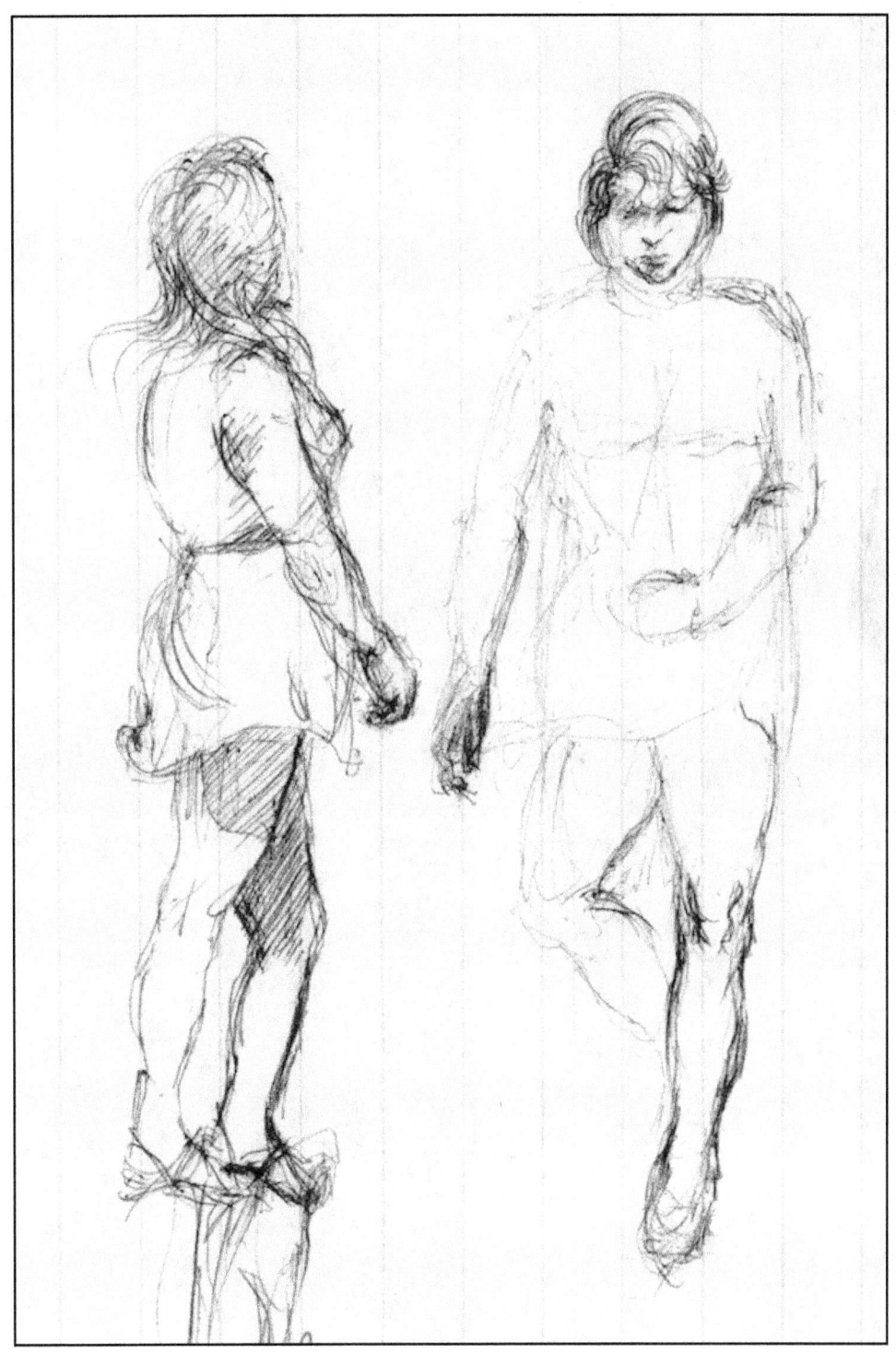

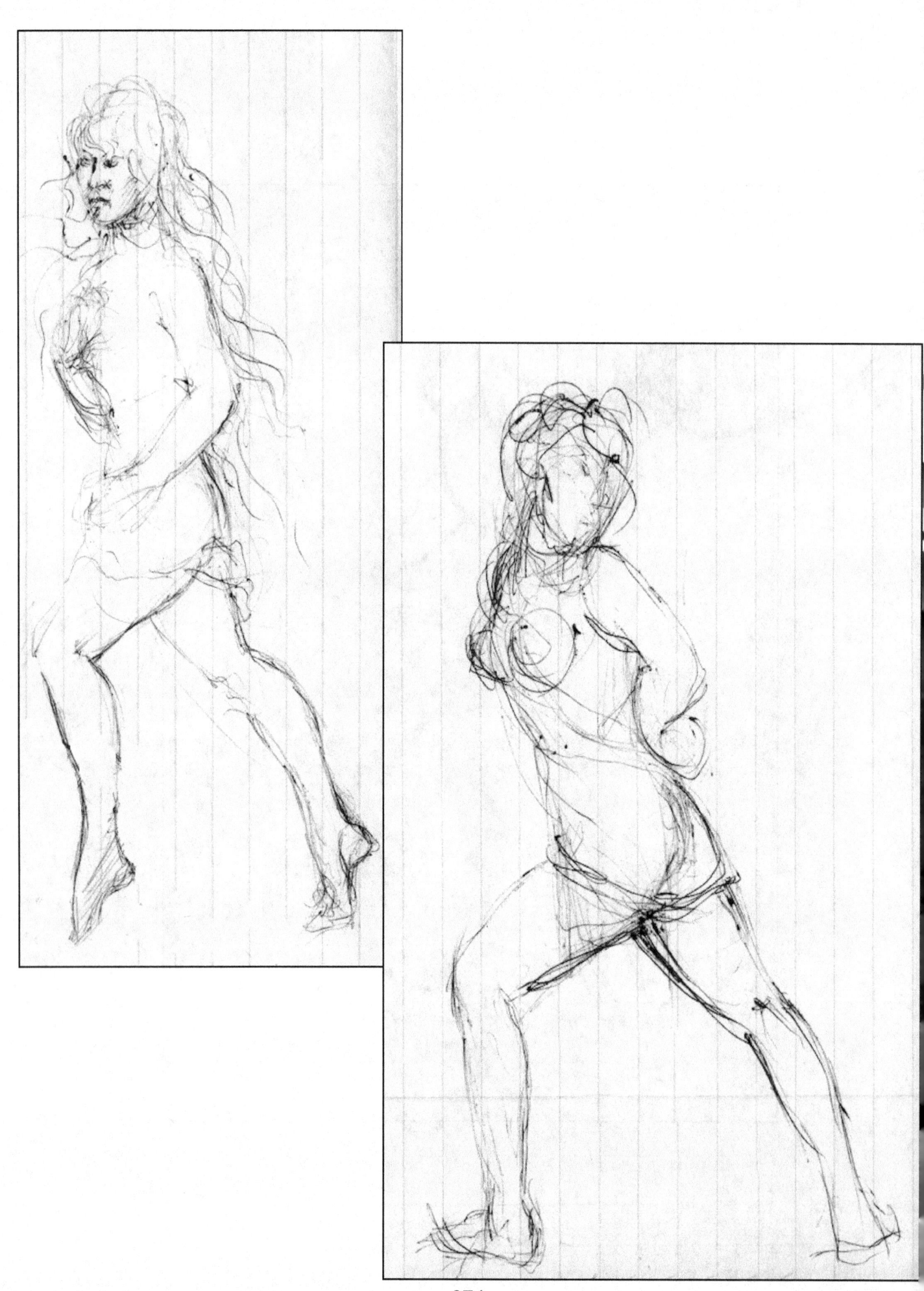

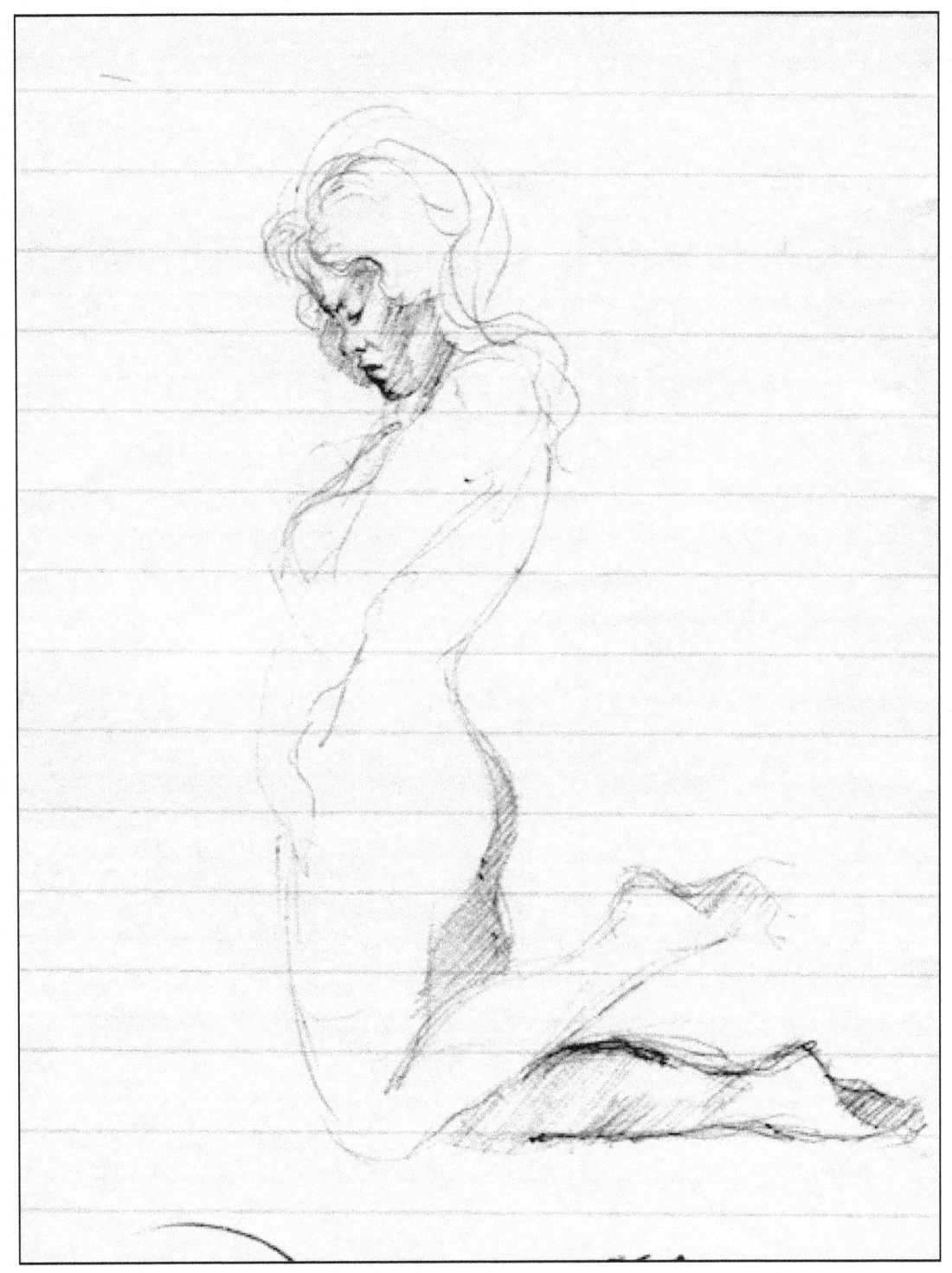

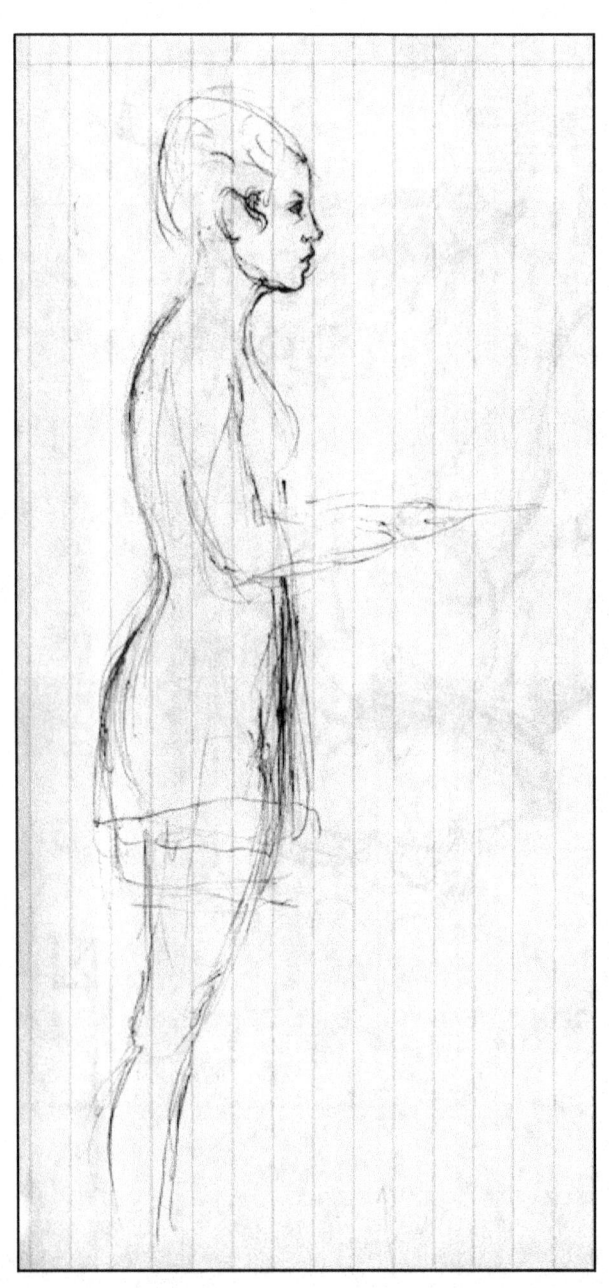
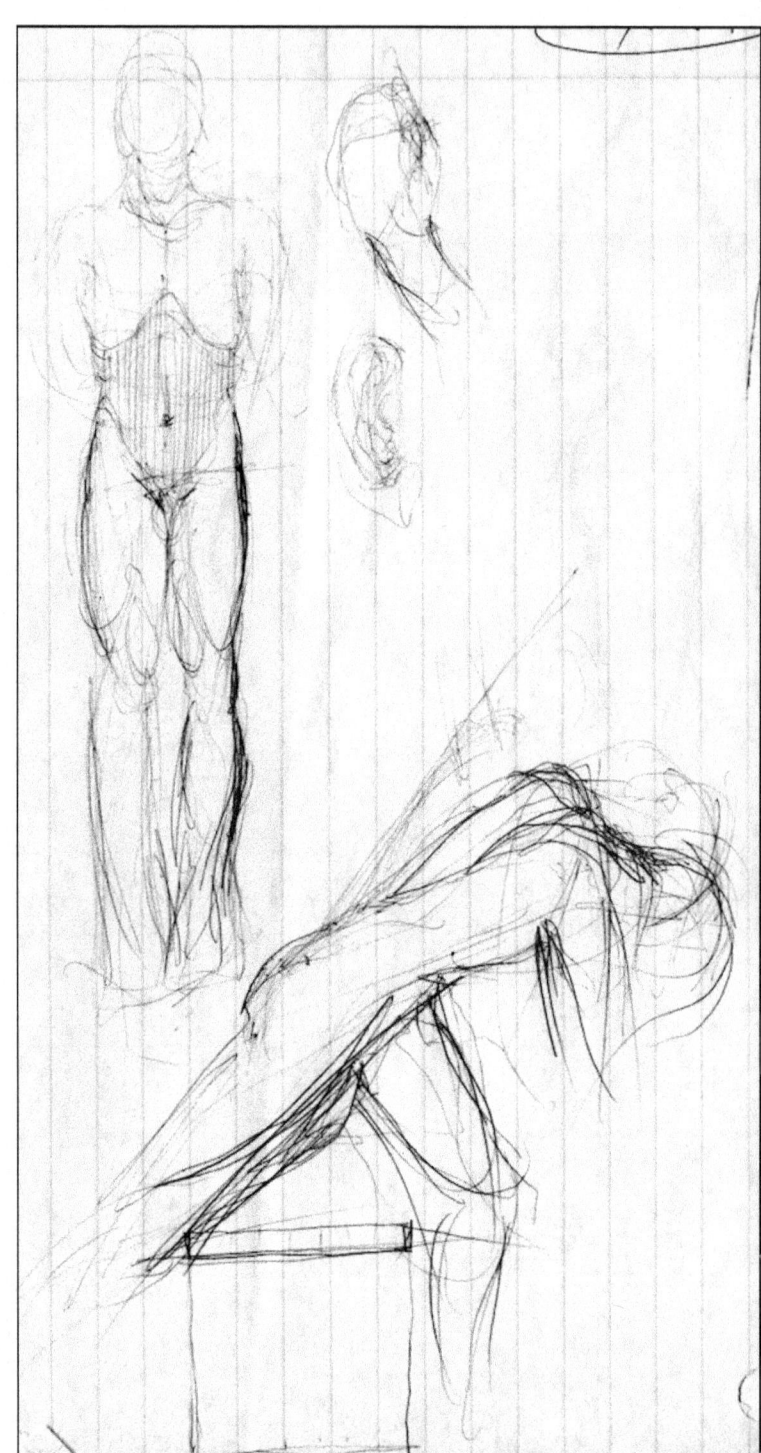

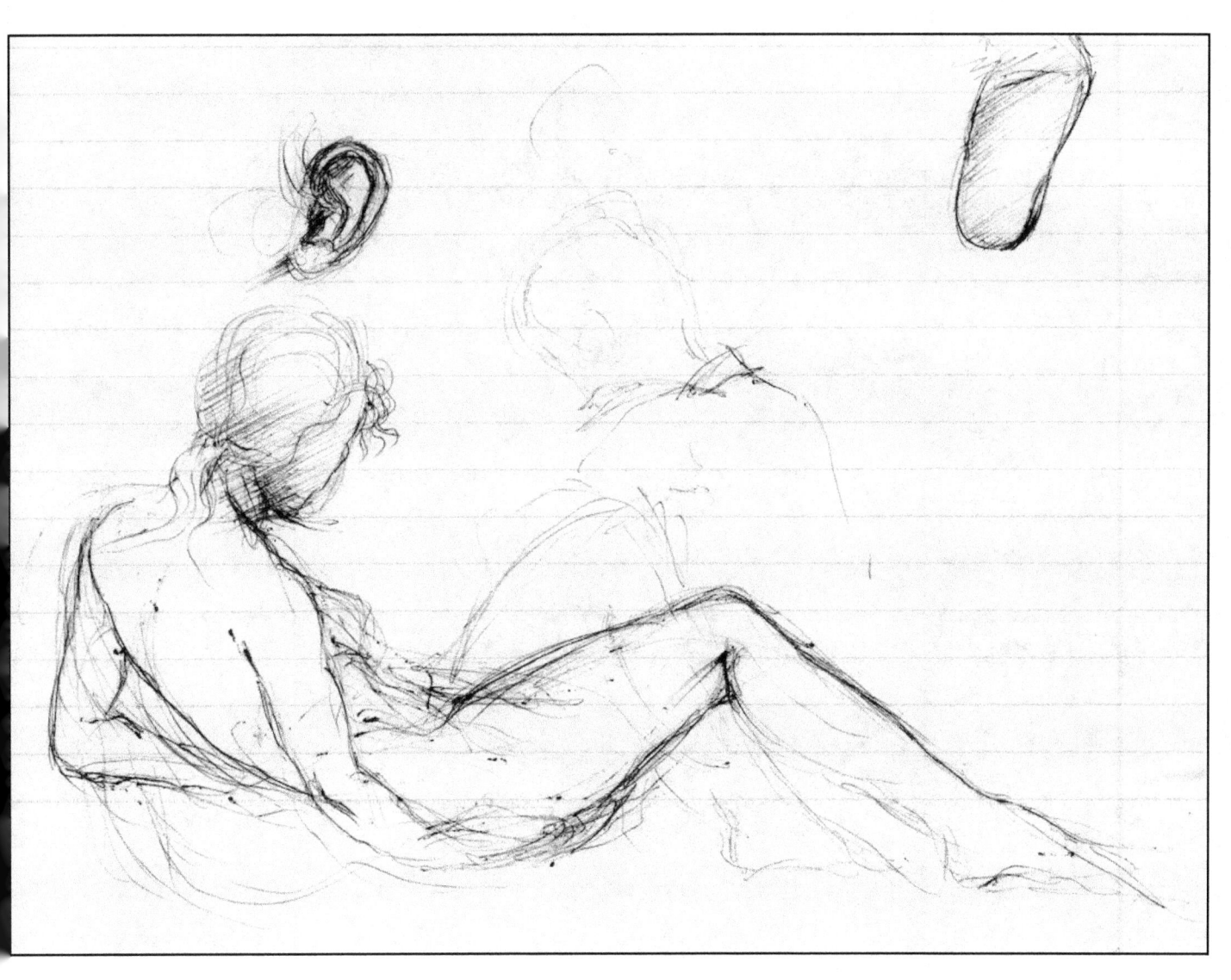

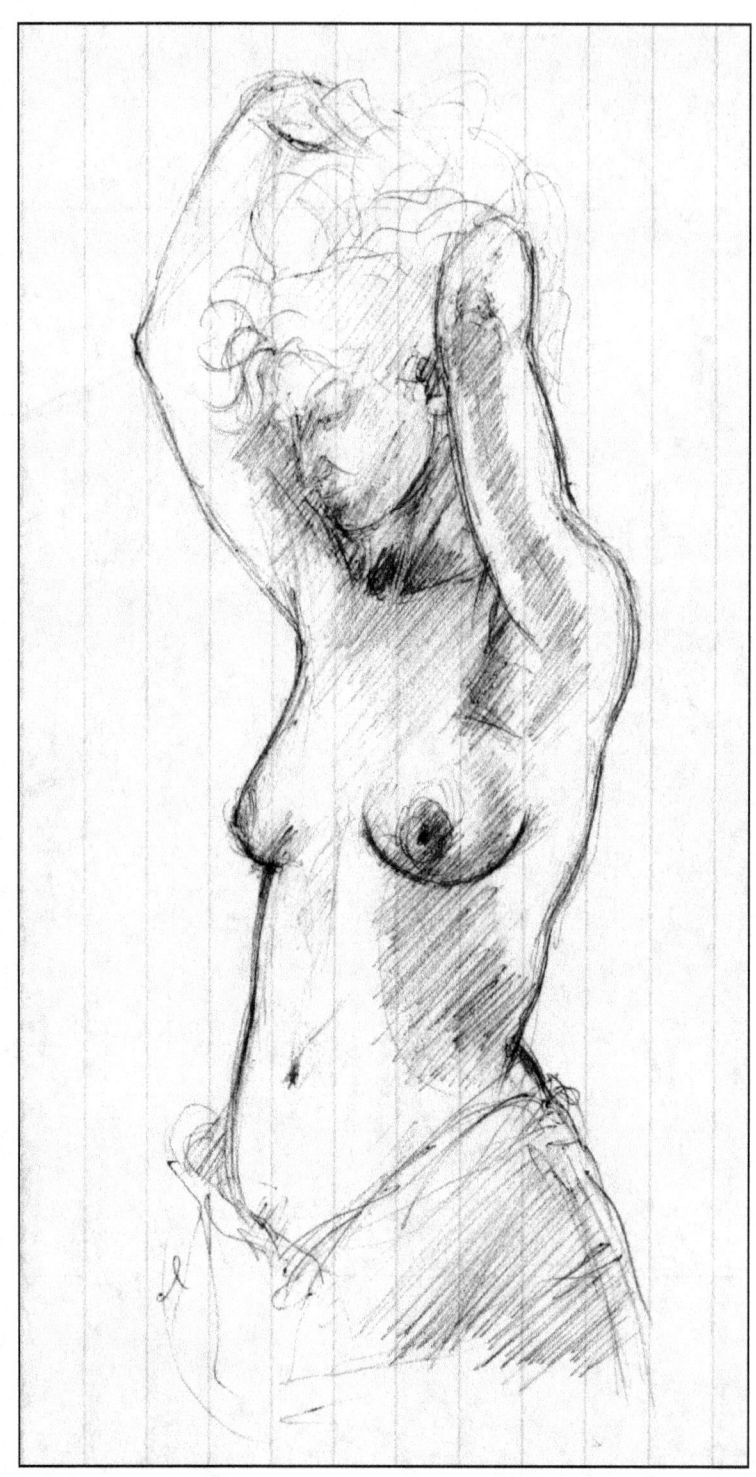

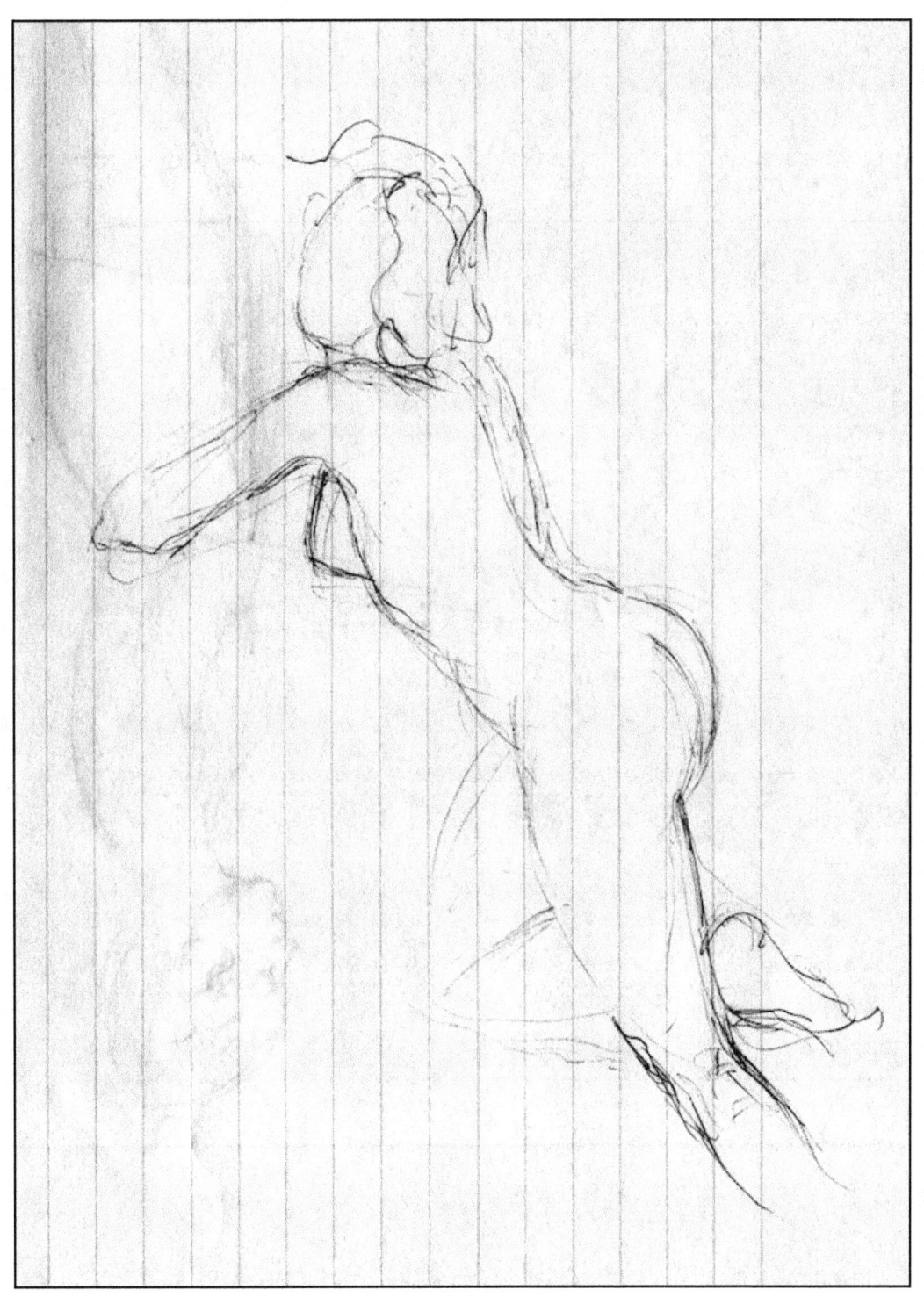

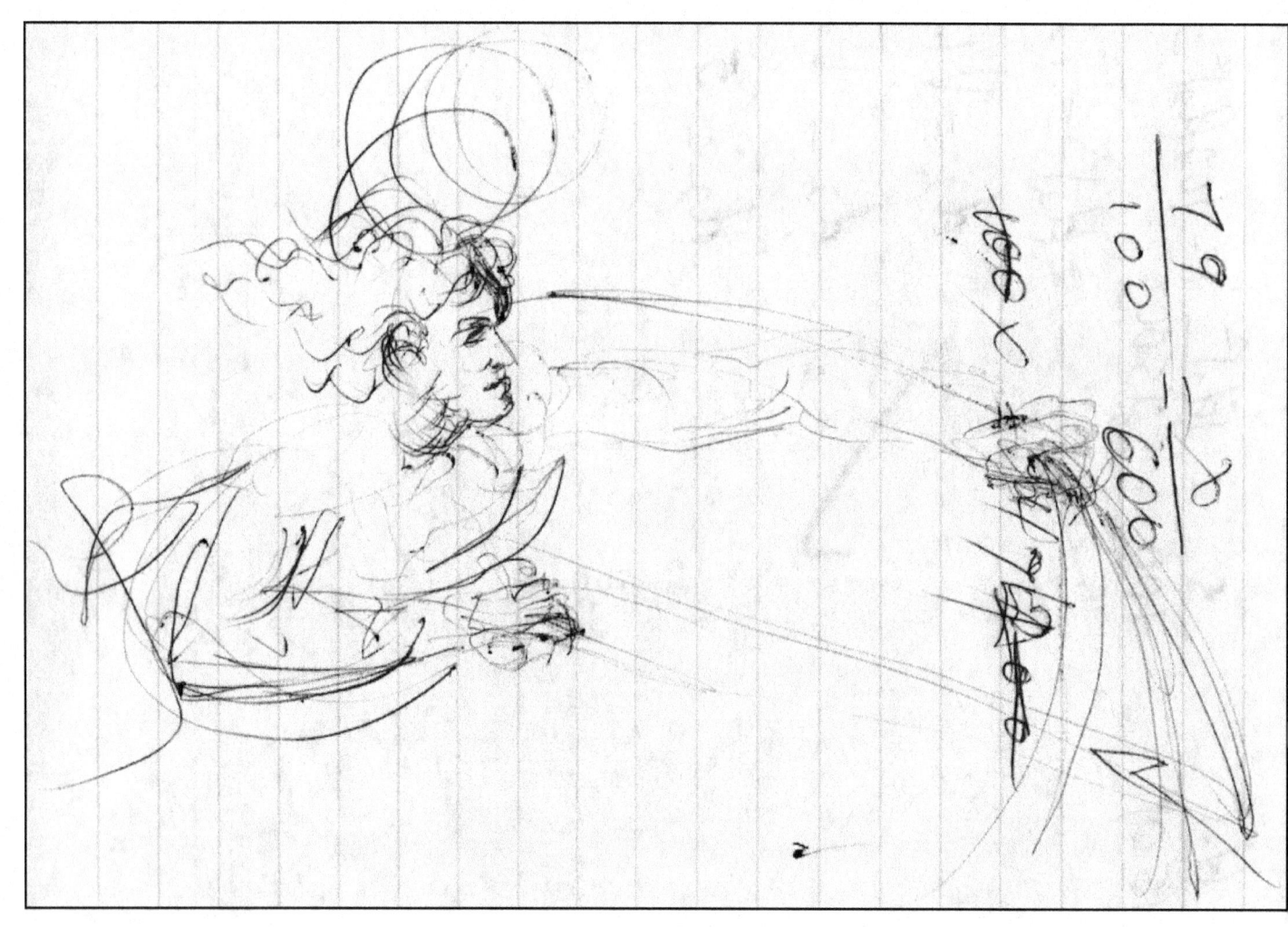

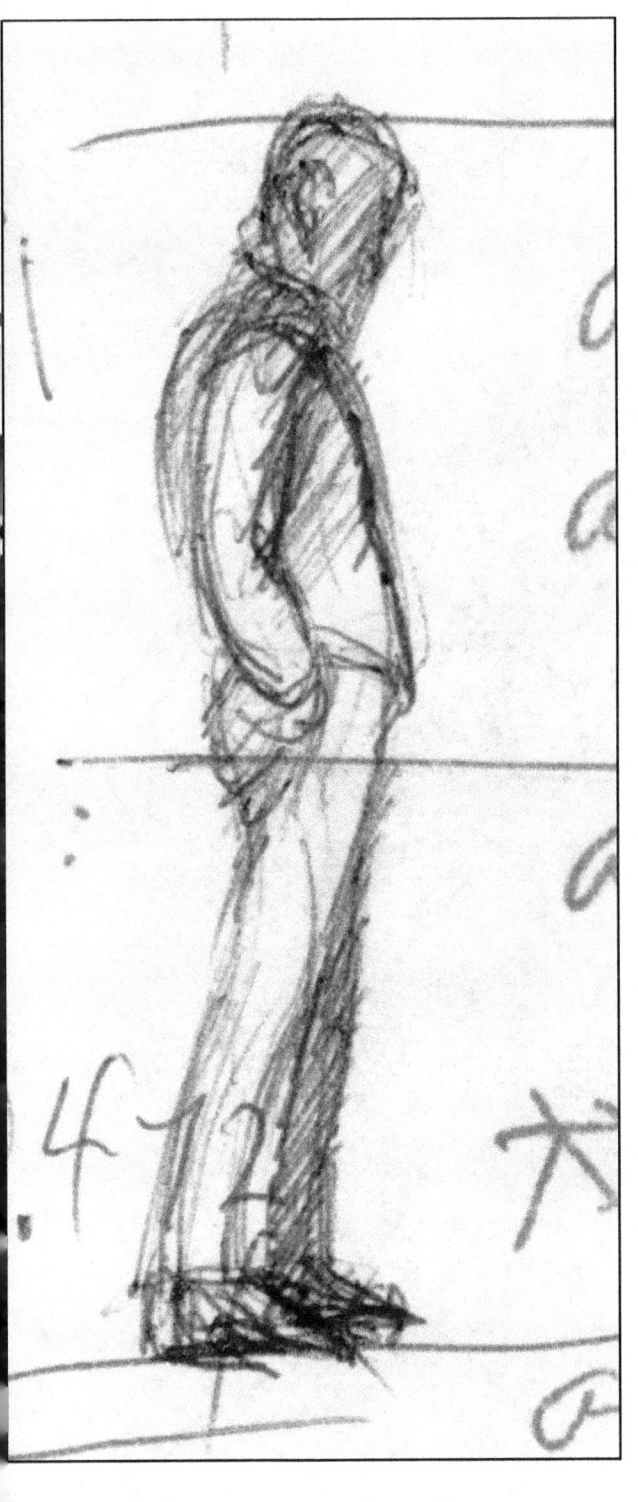
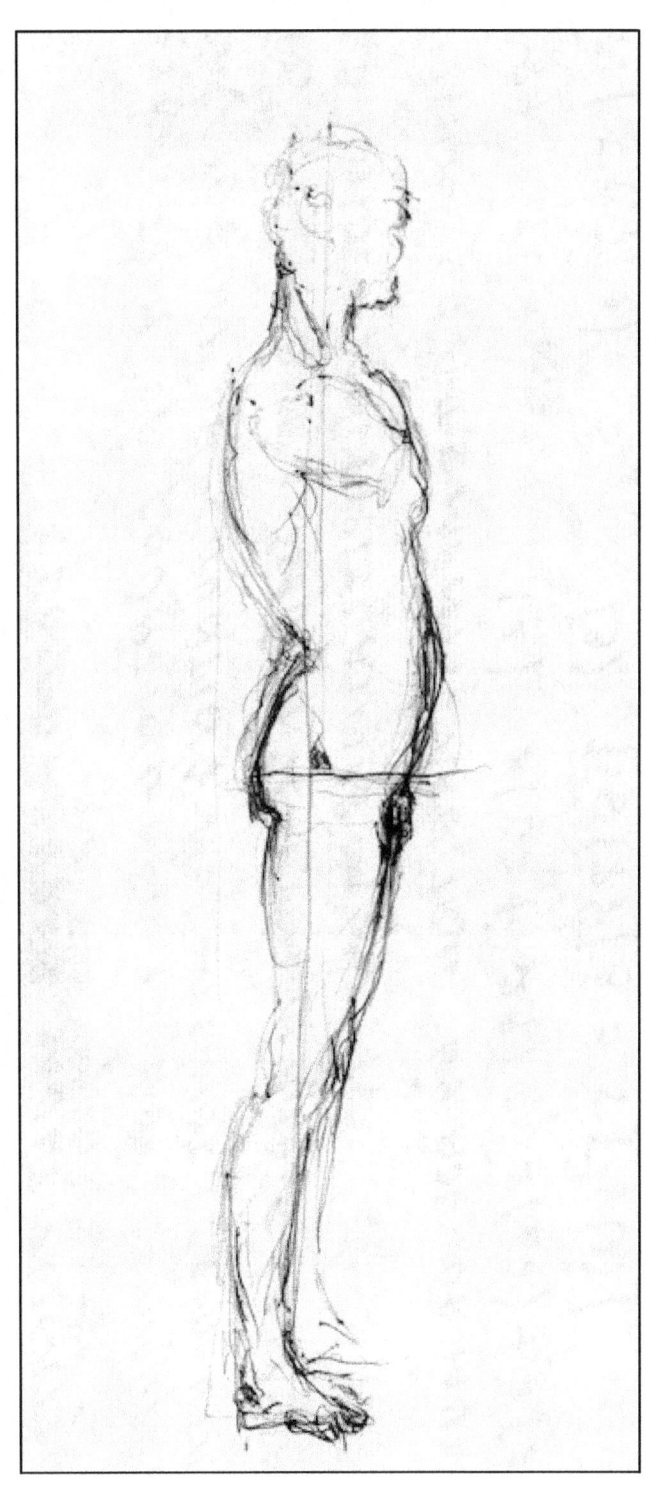

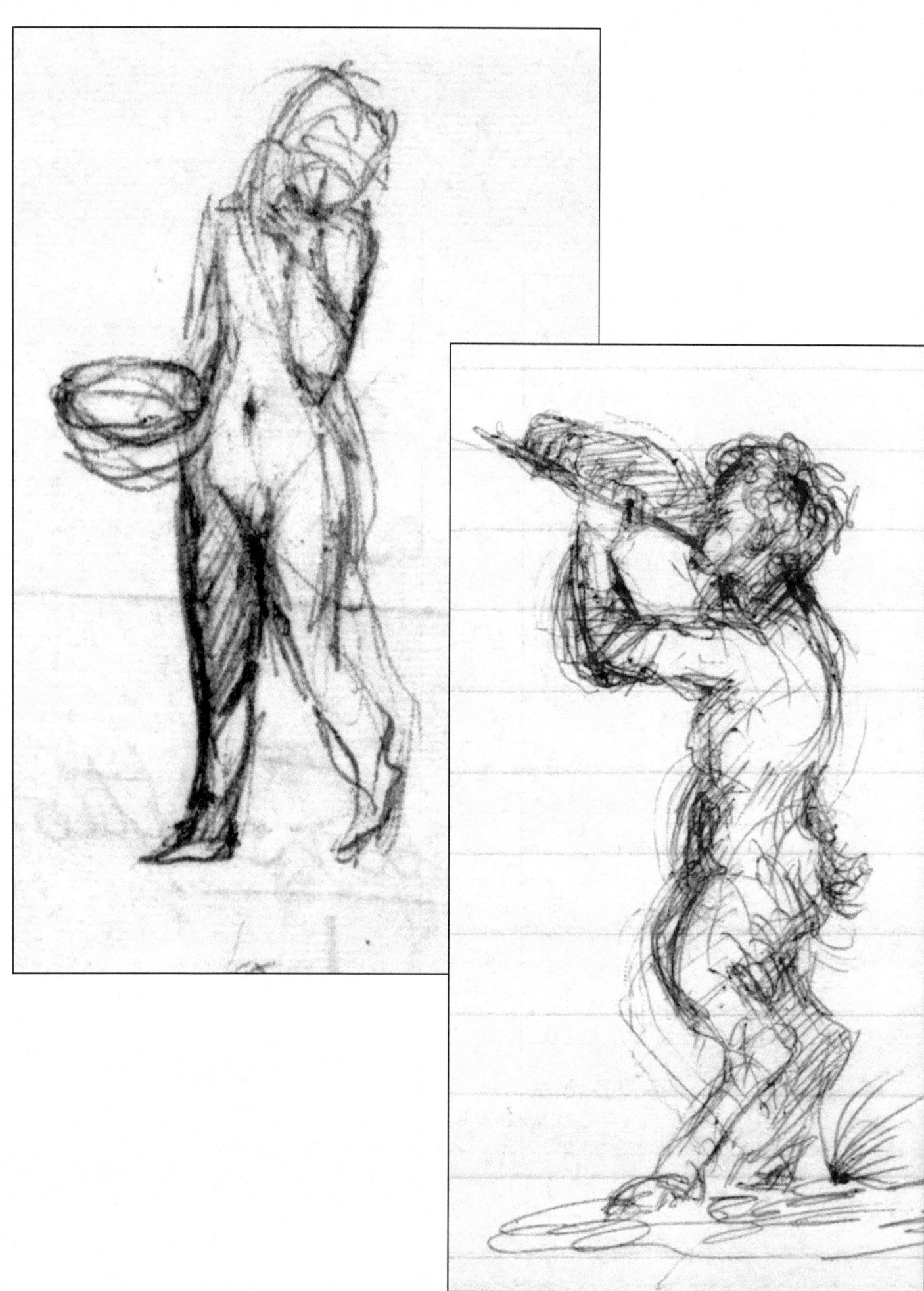

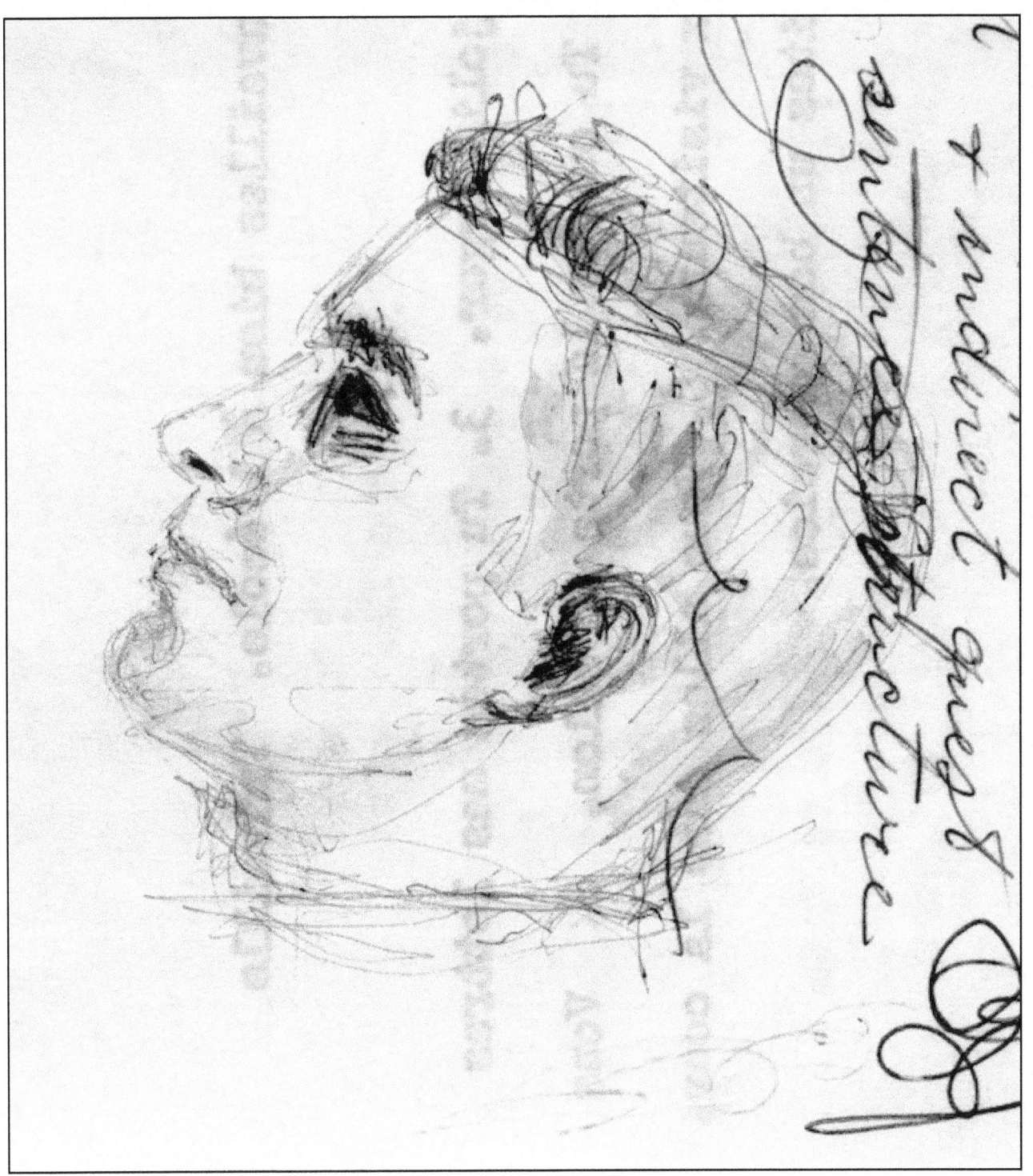

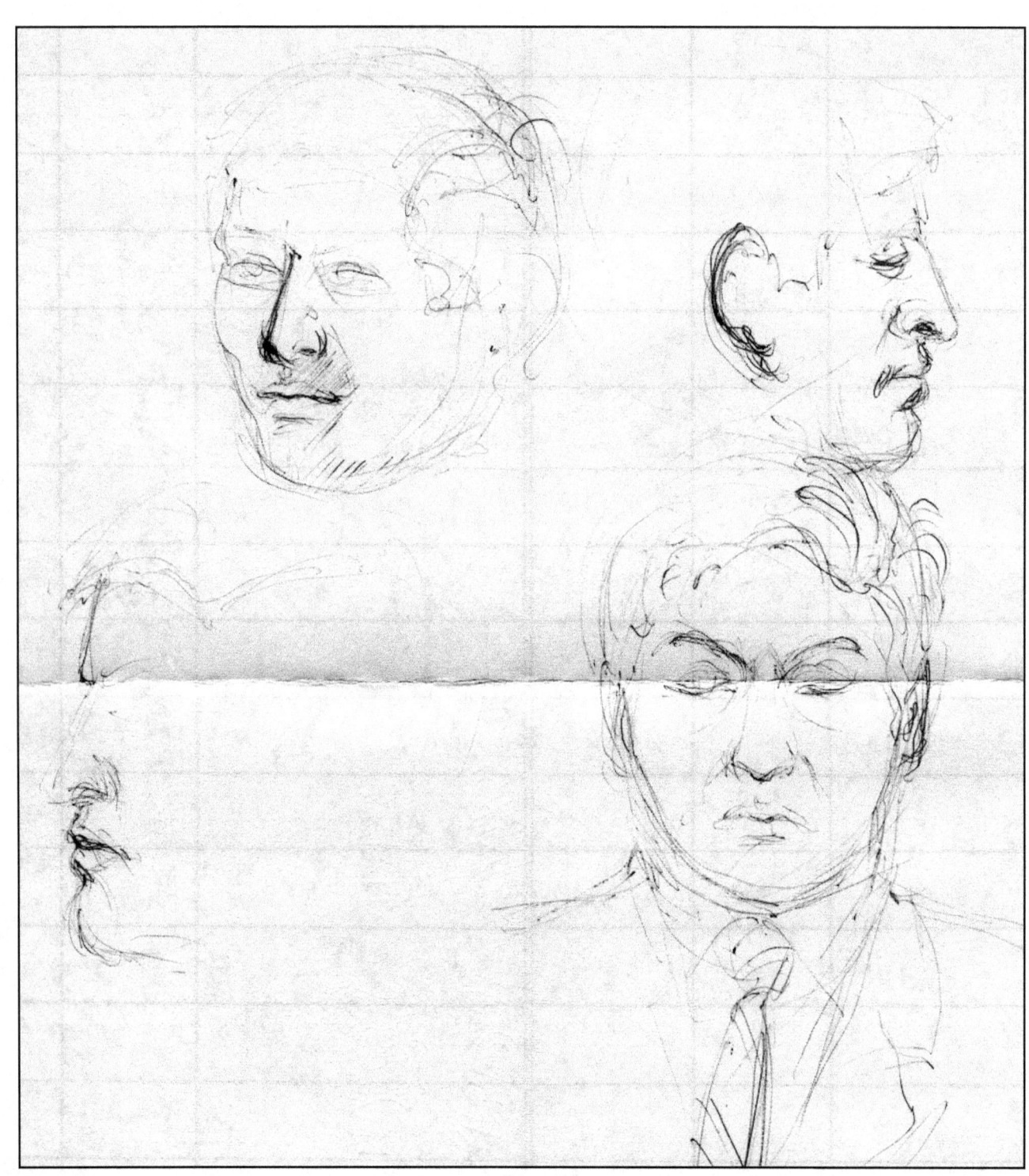

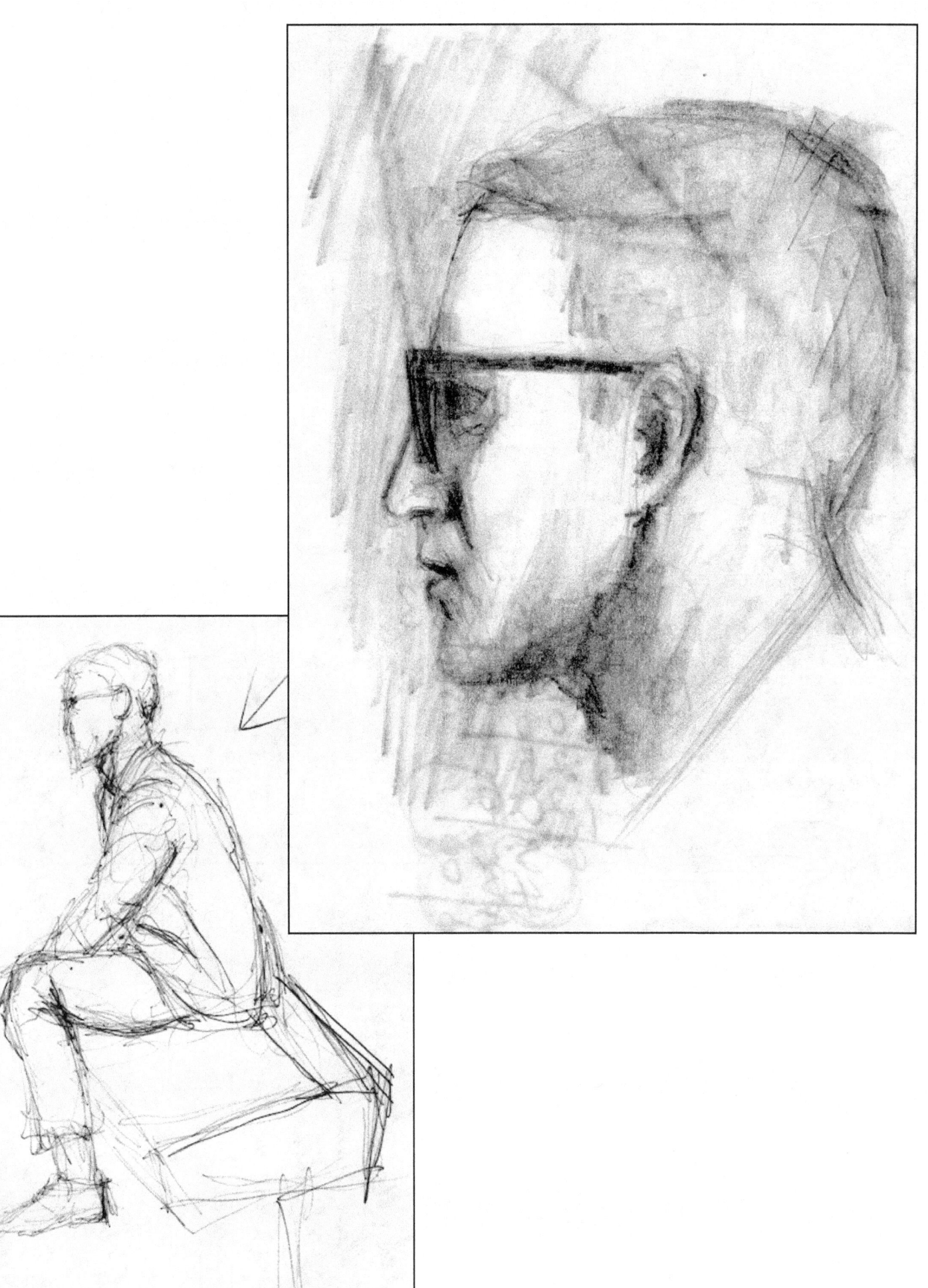

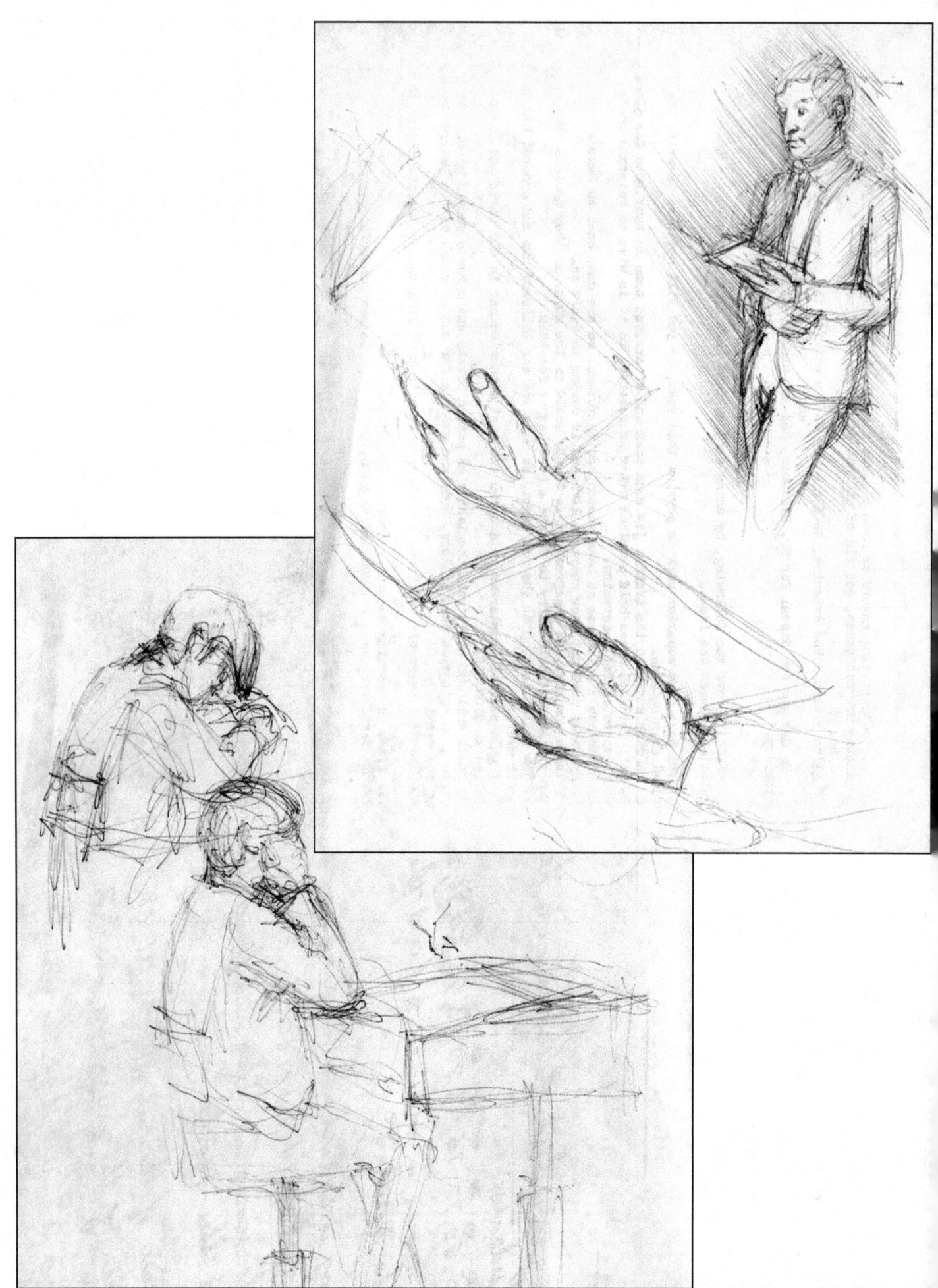

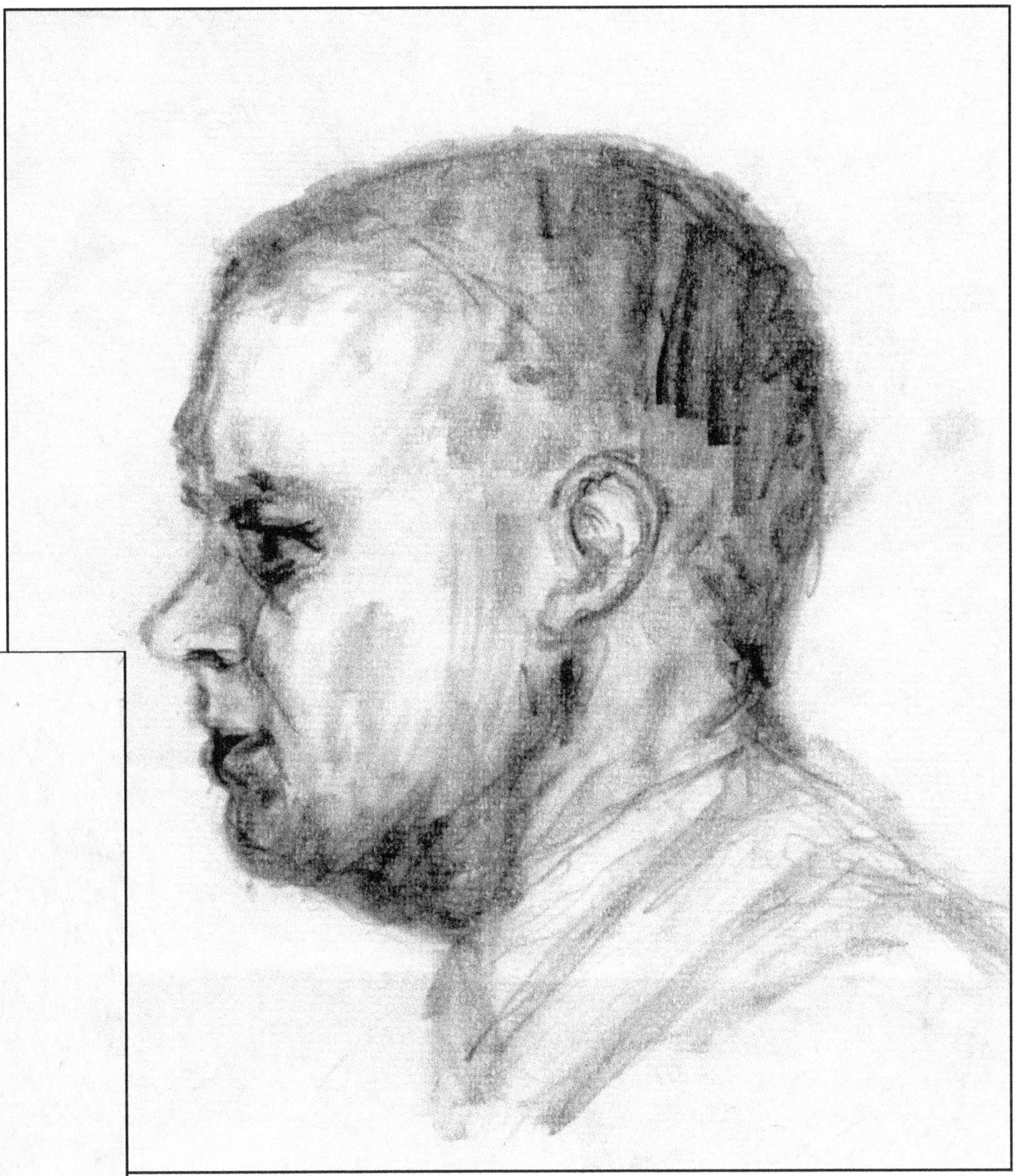

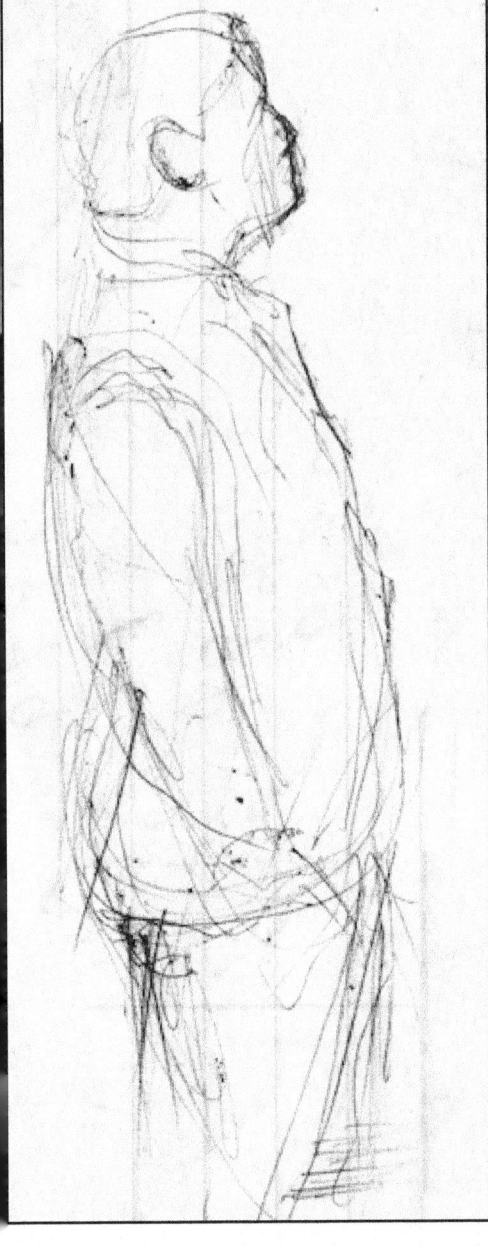

15. Full Figure, Visualization, Other Times

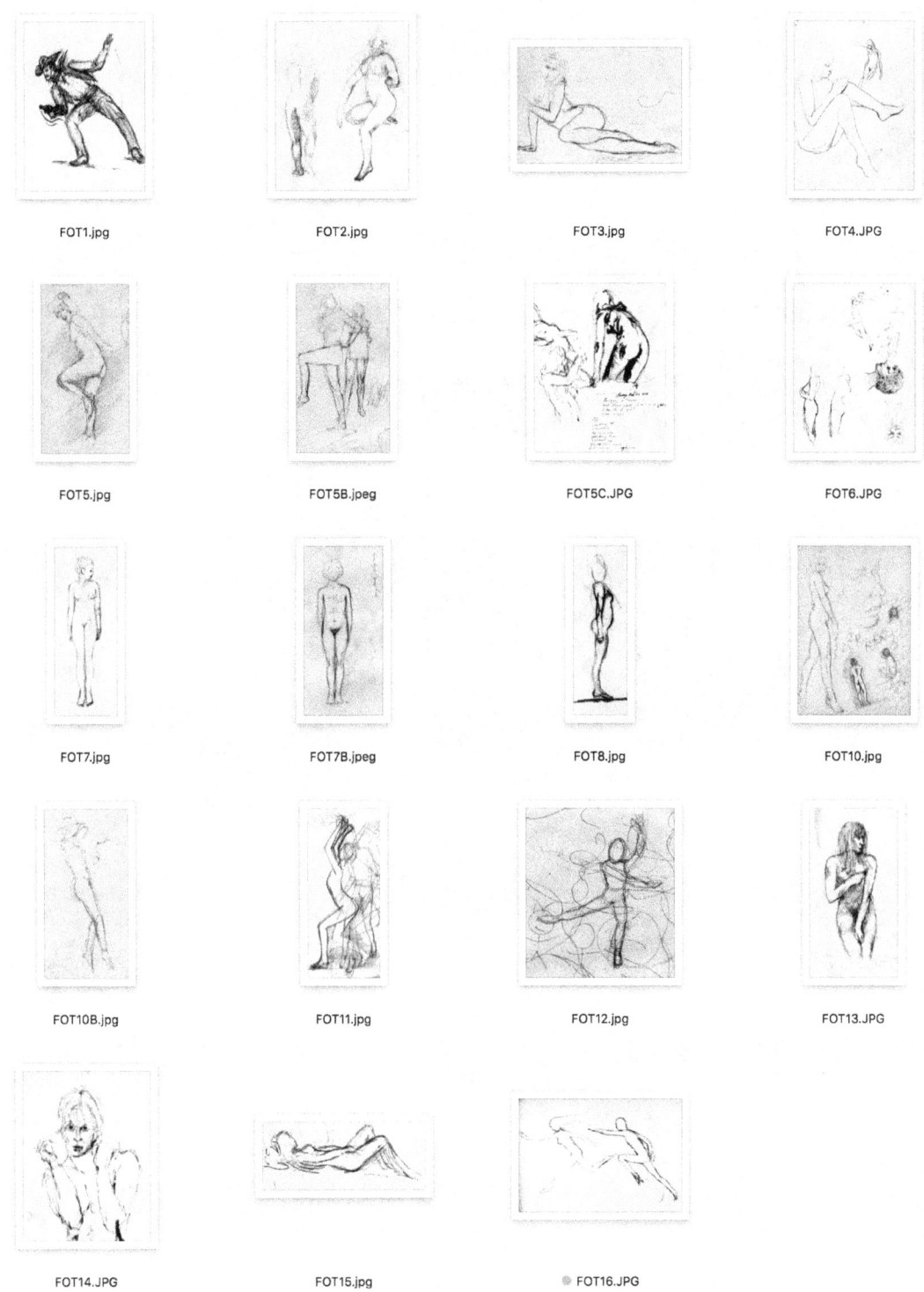

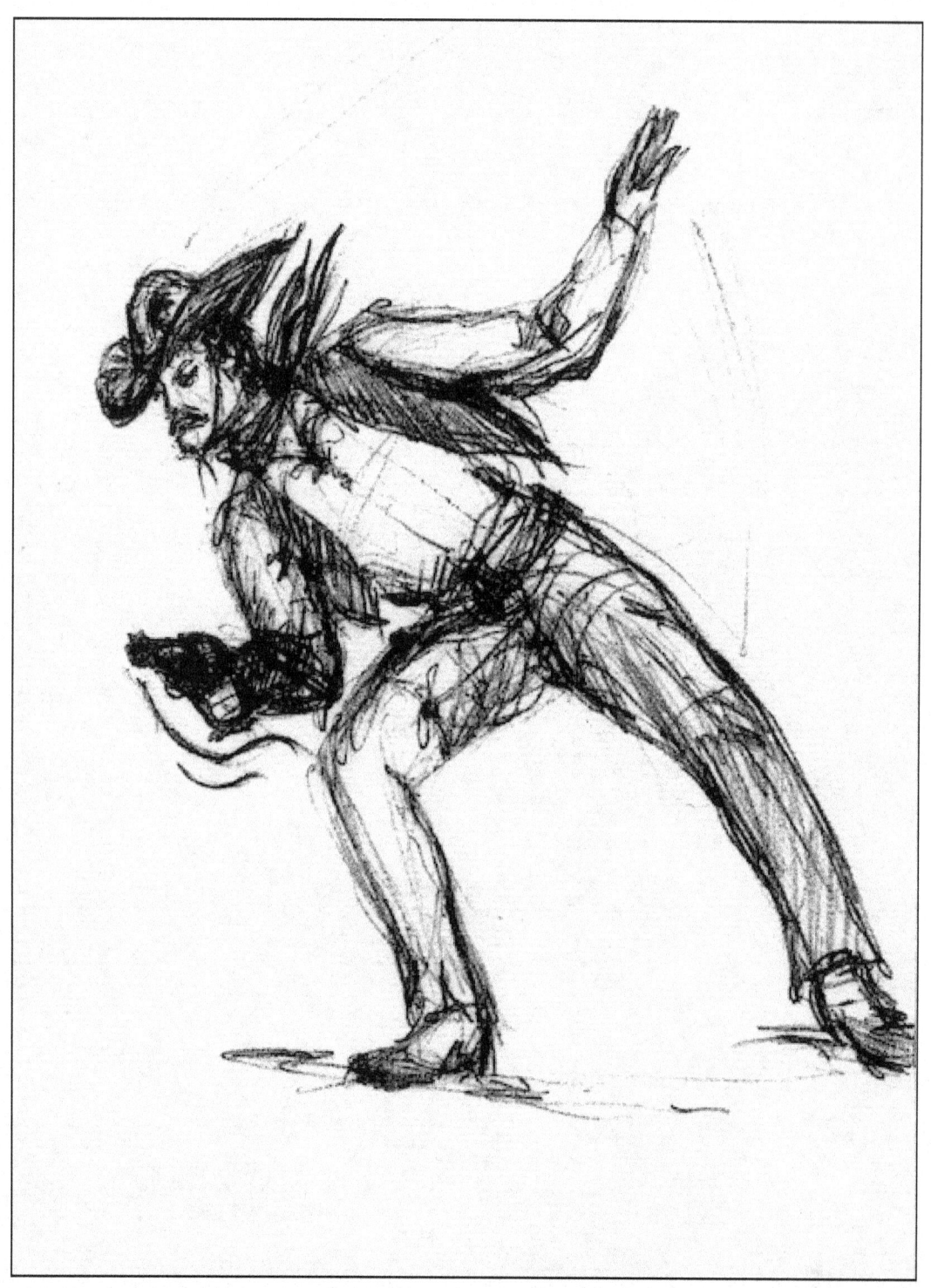

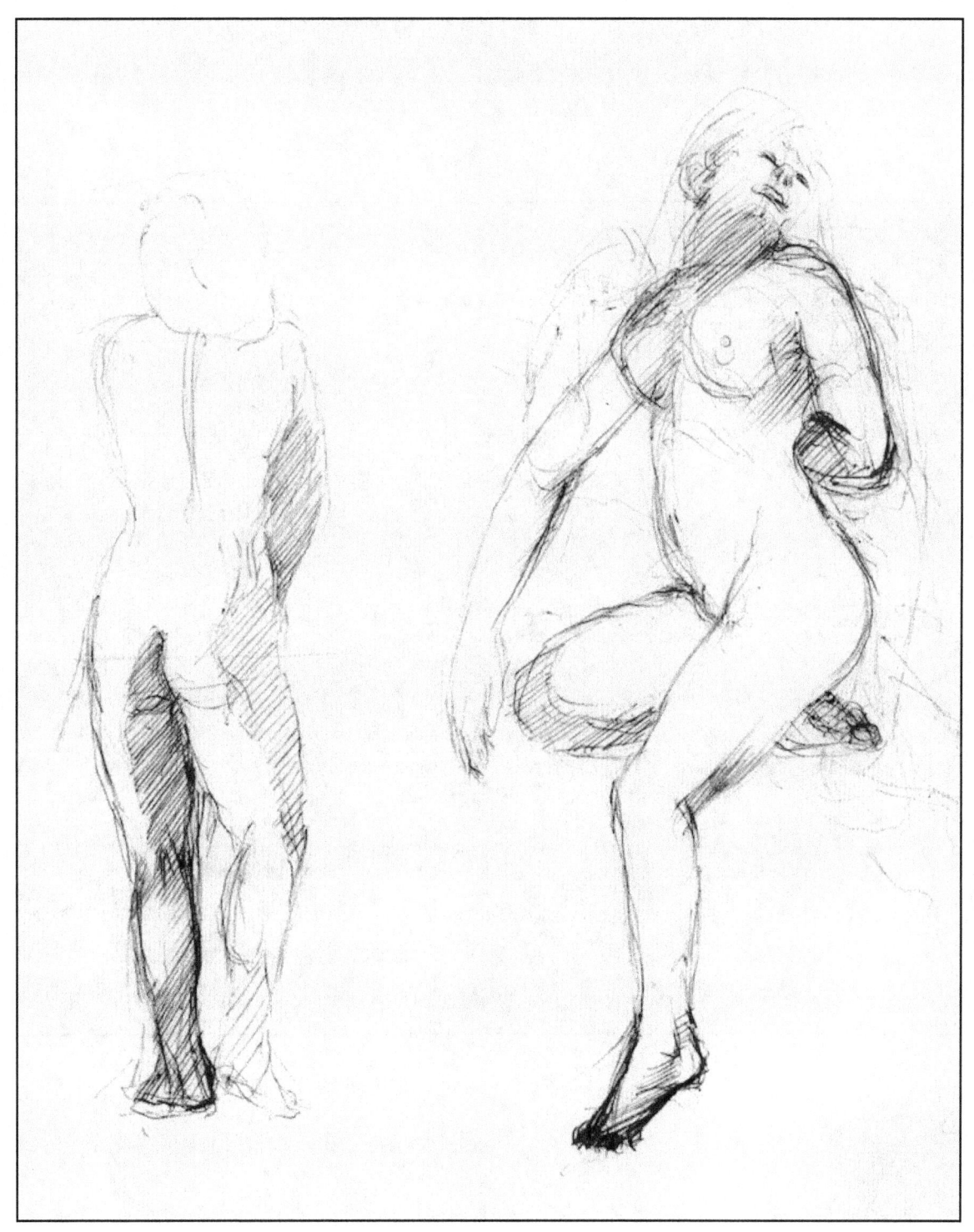

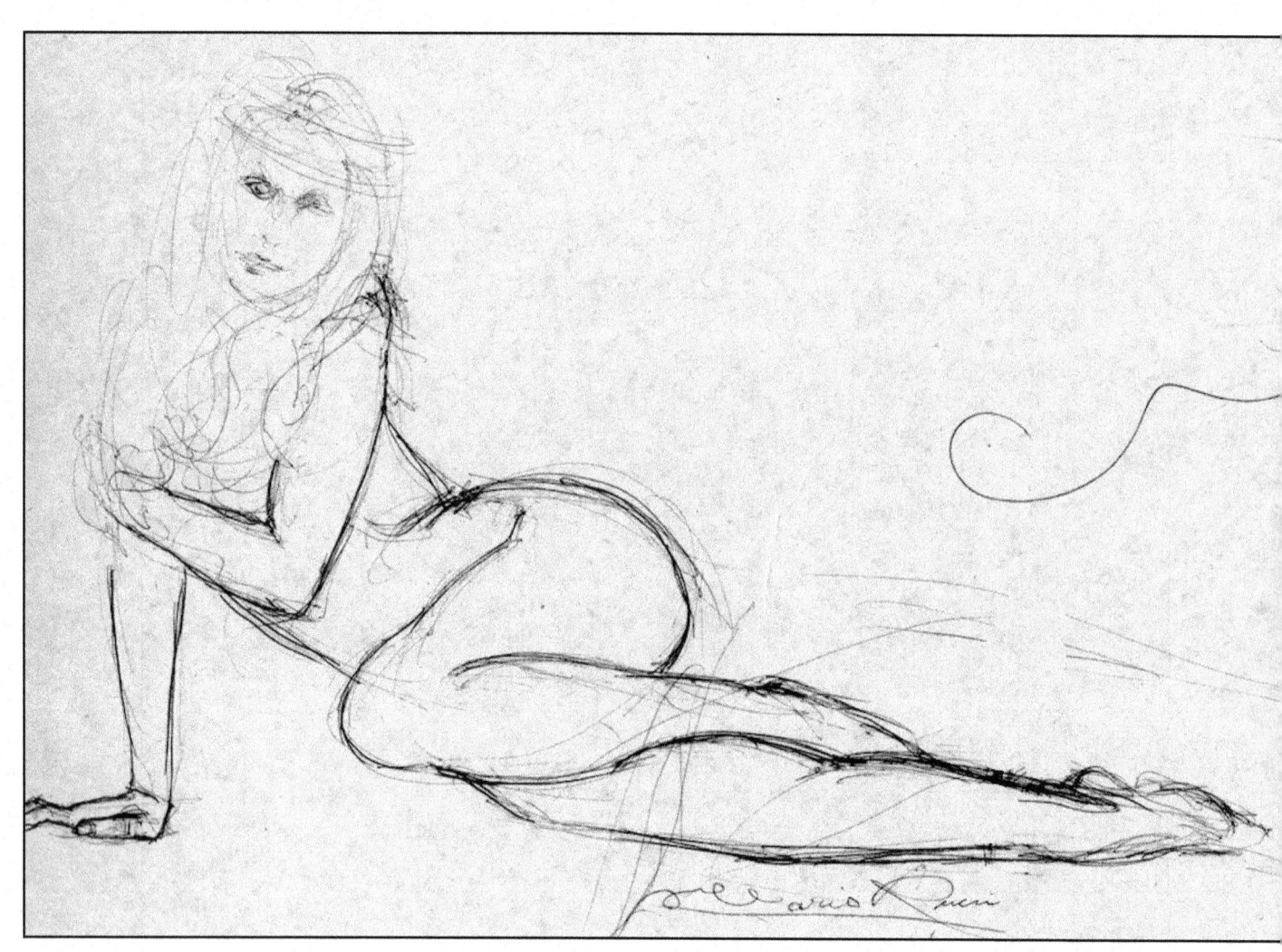

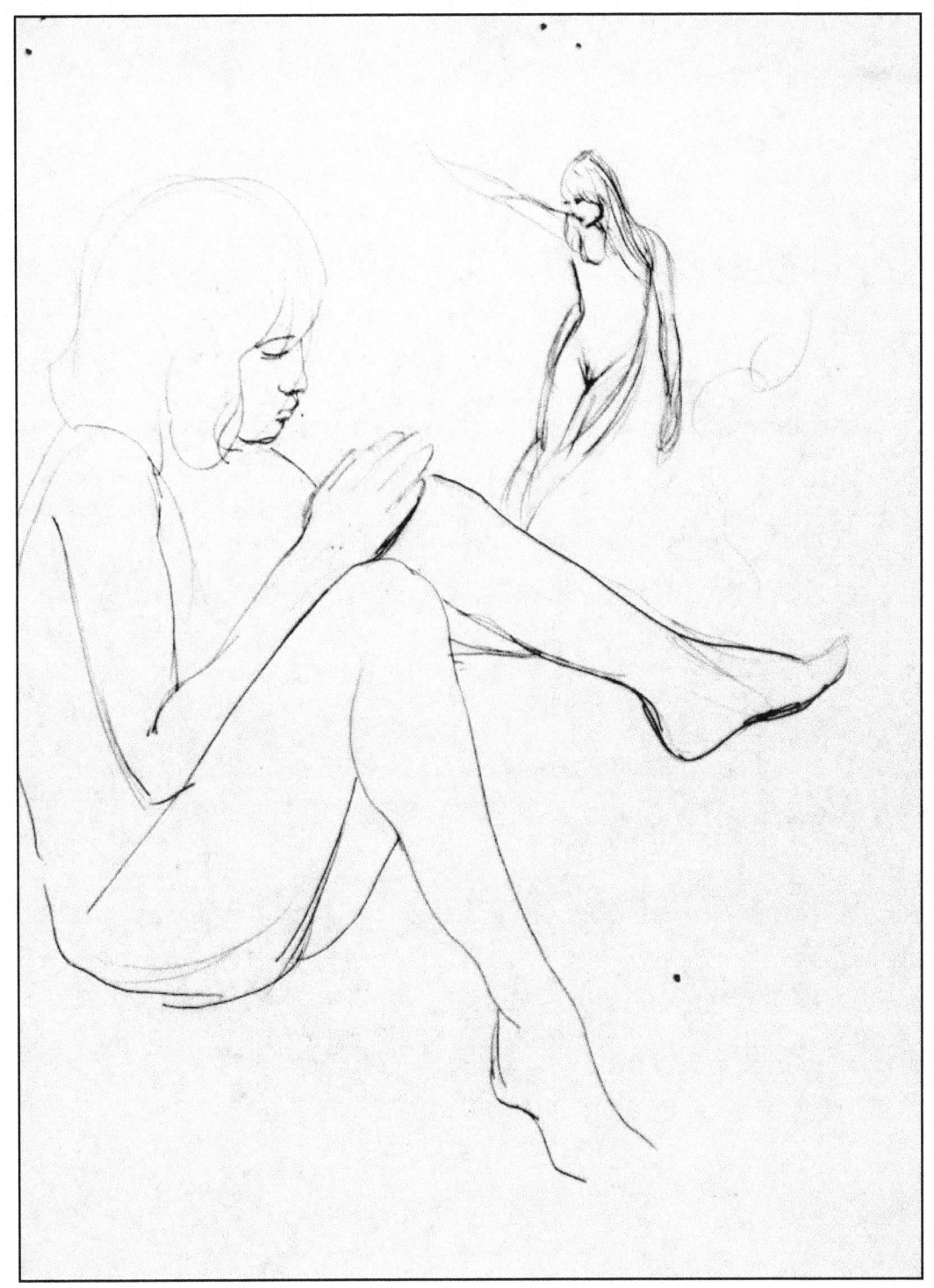

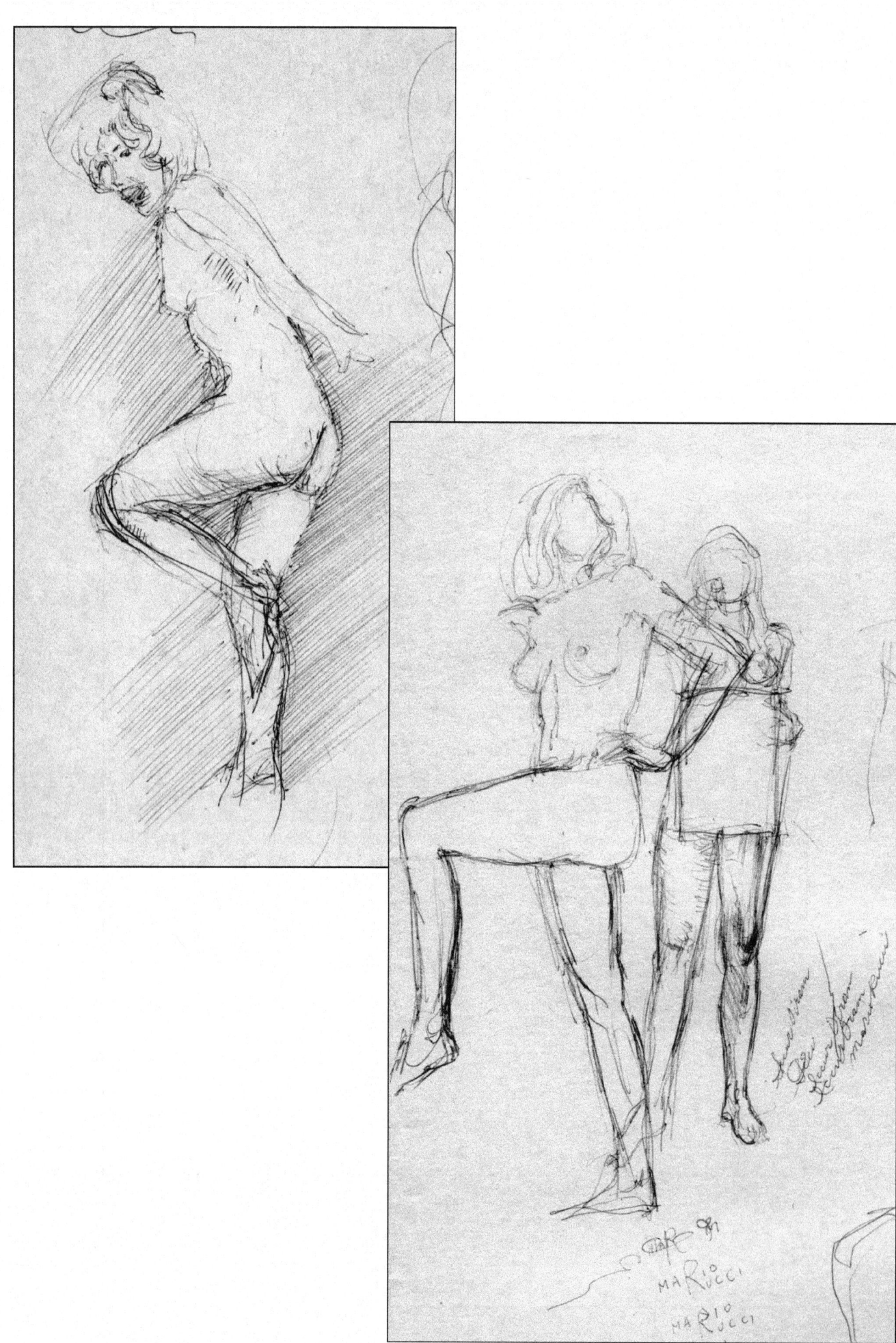

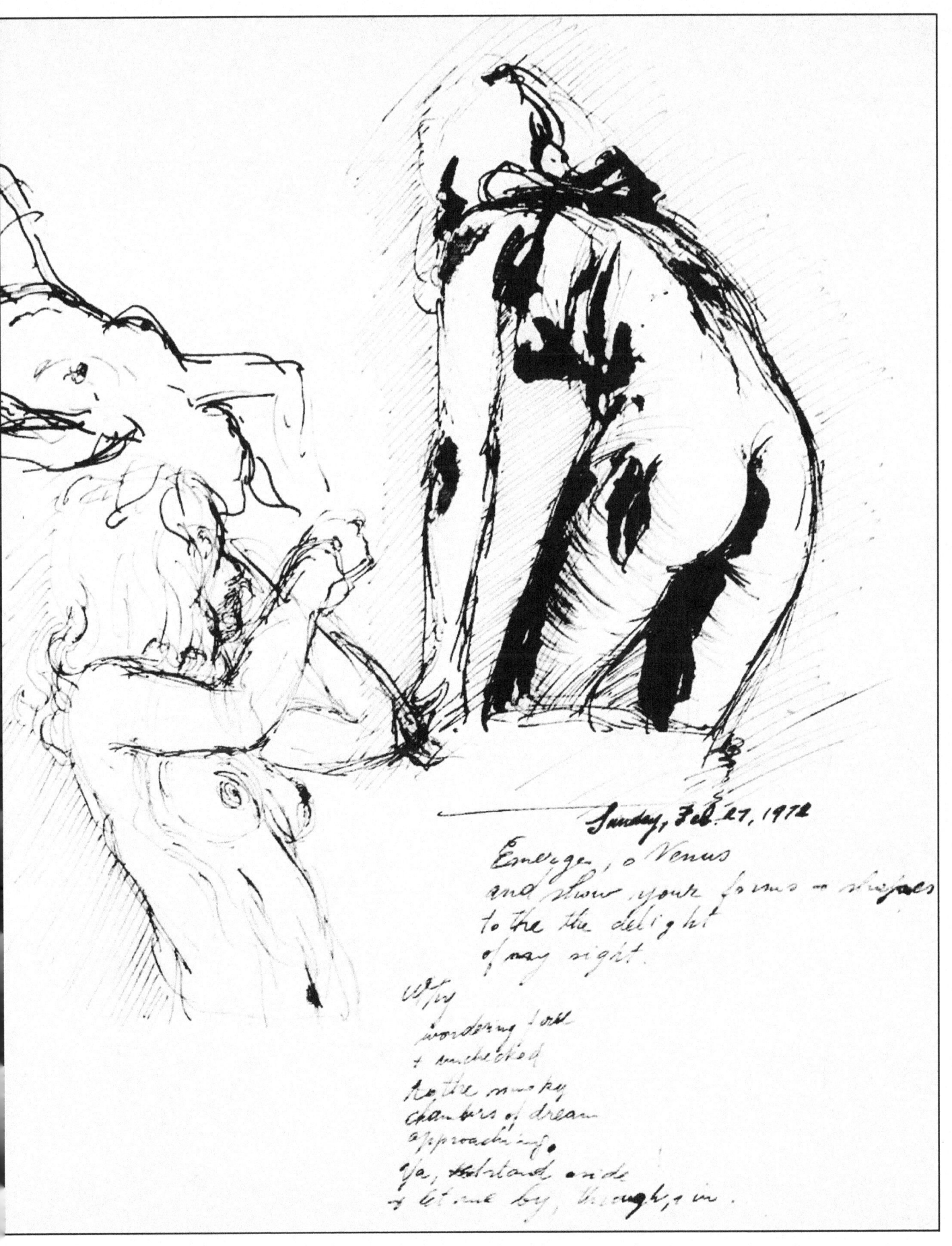

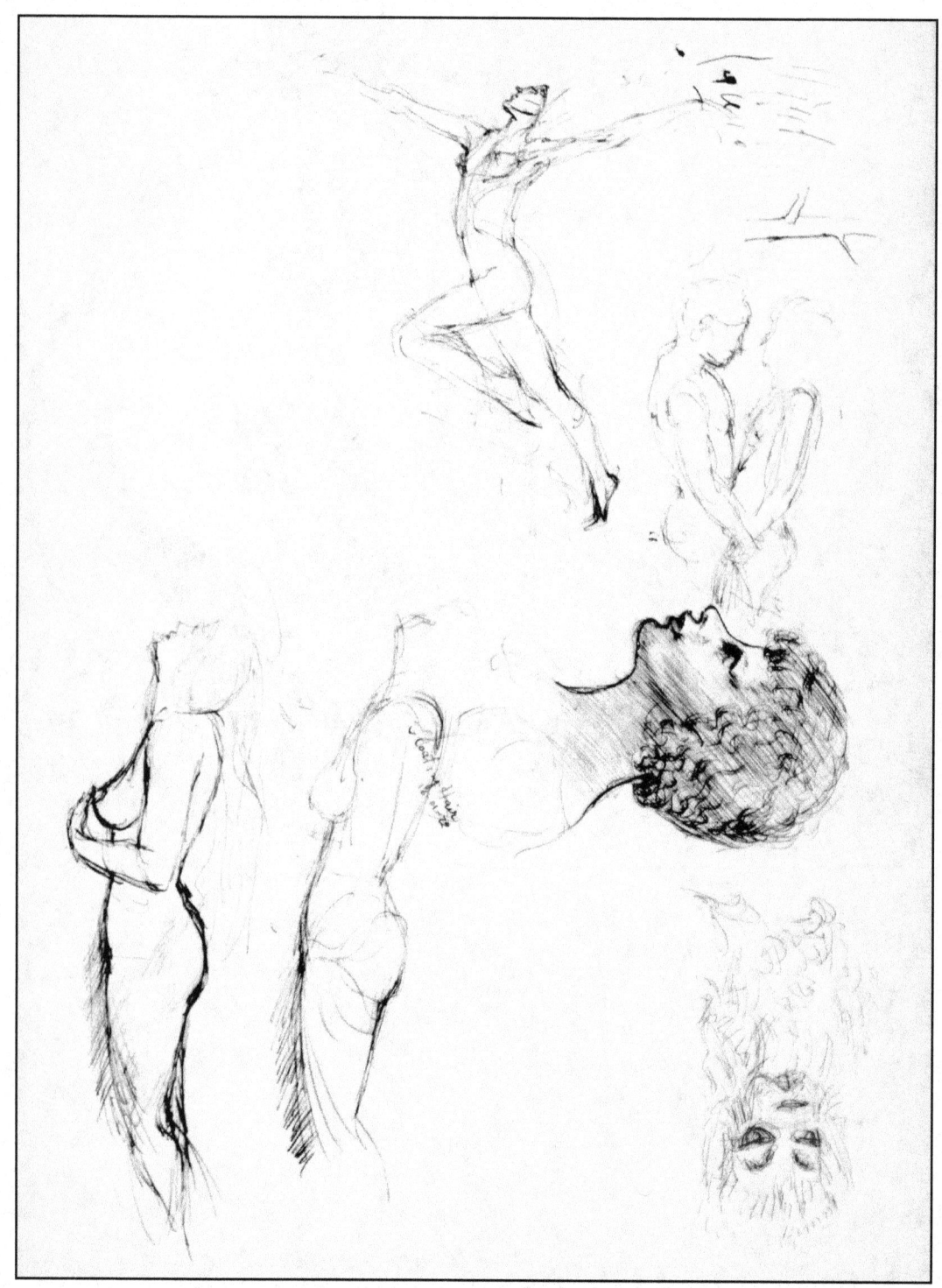

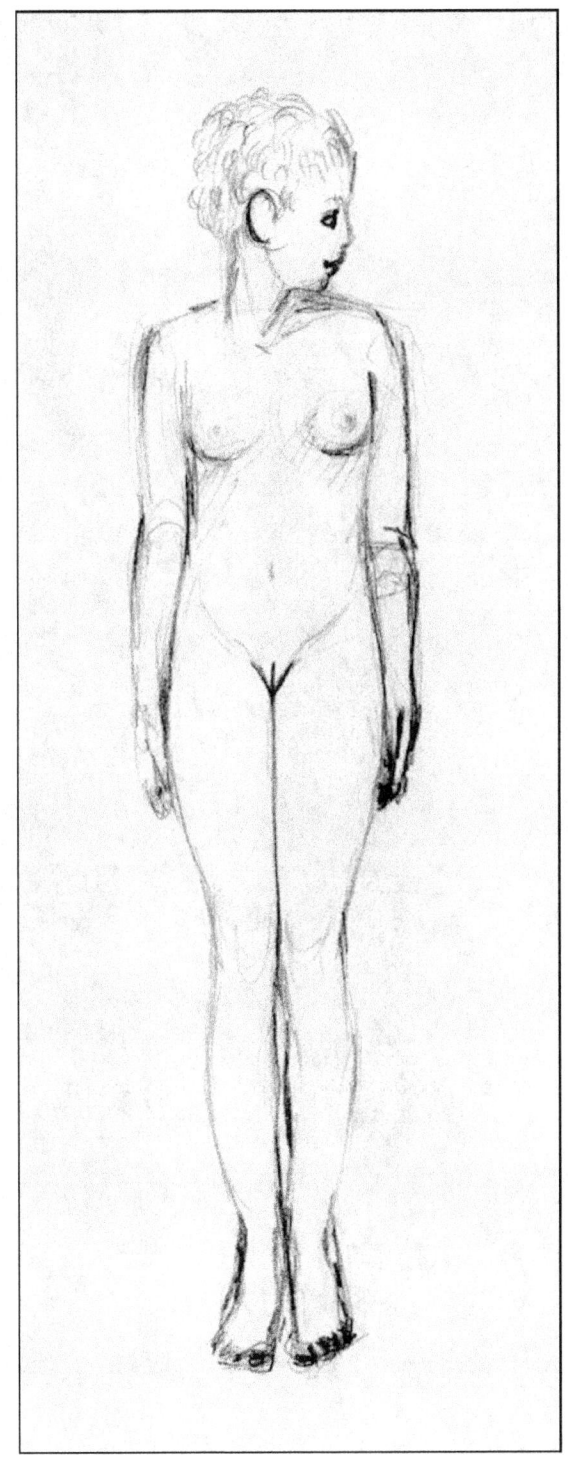
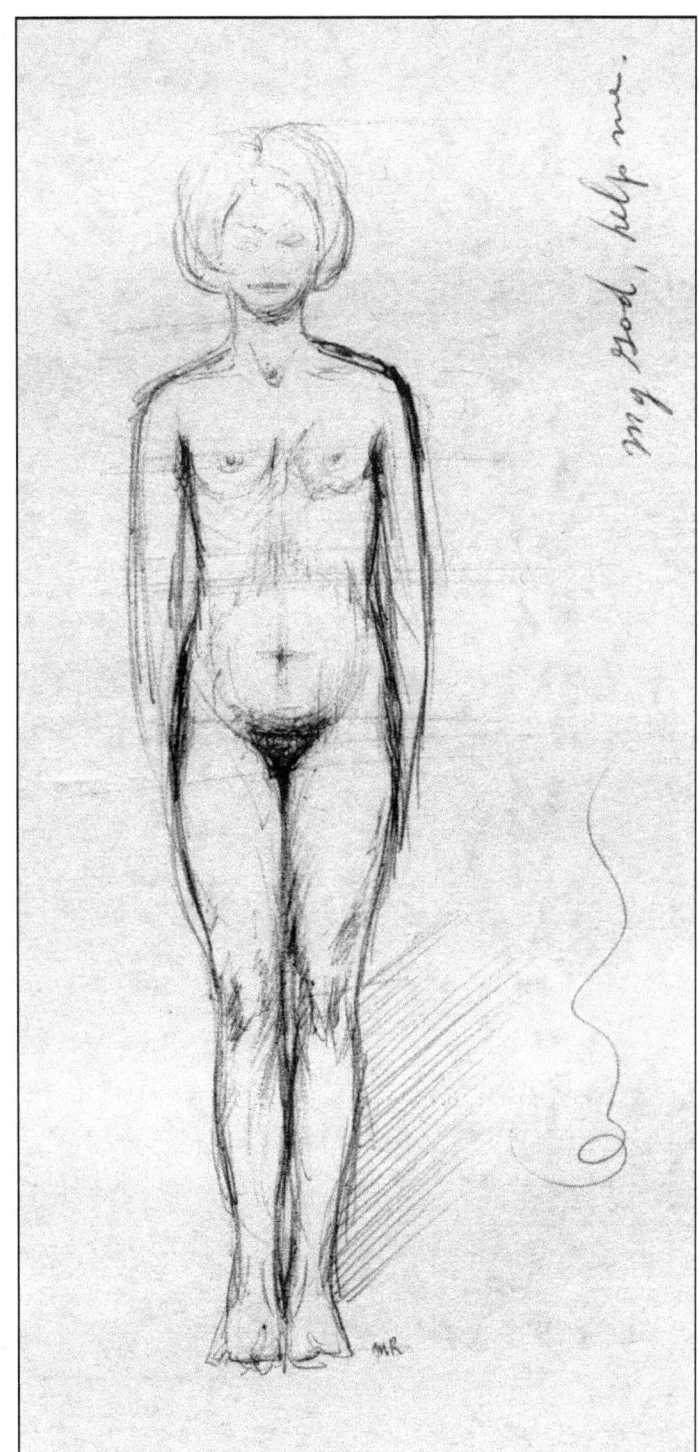

my god, help me.

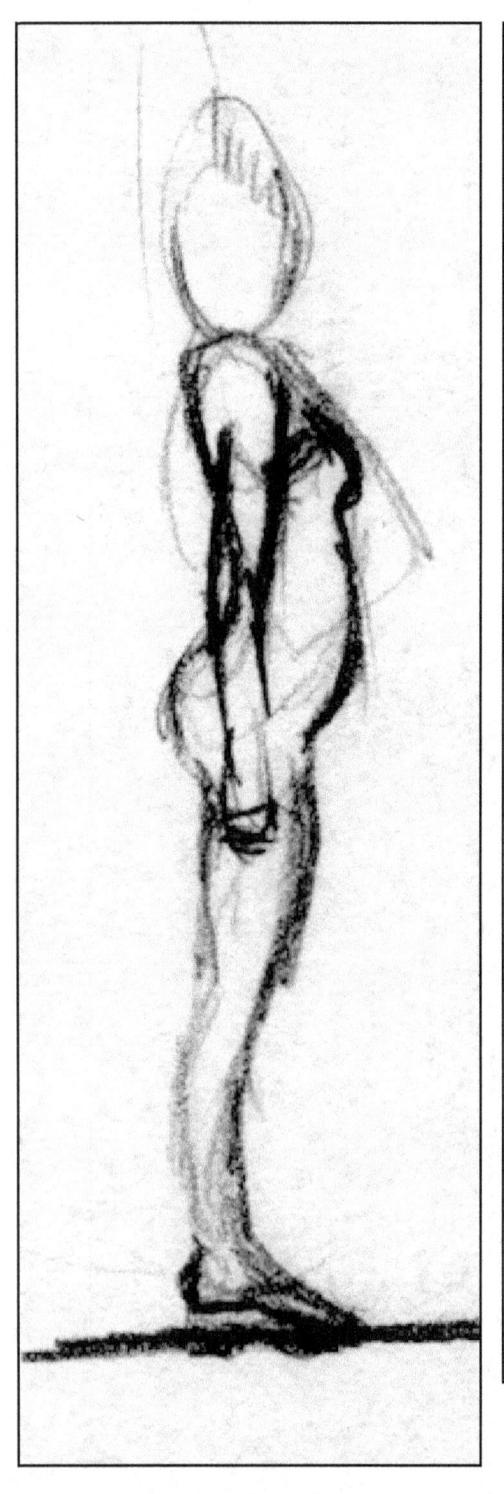

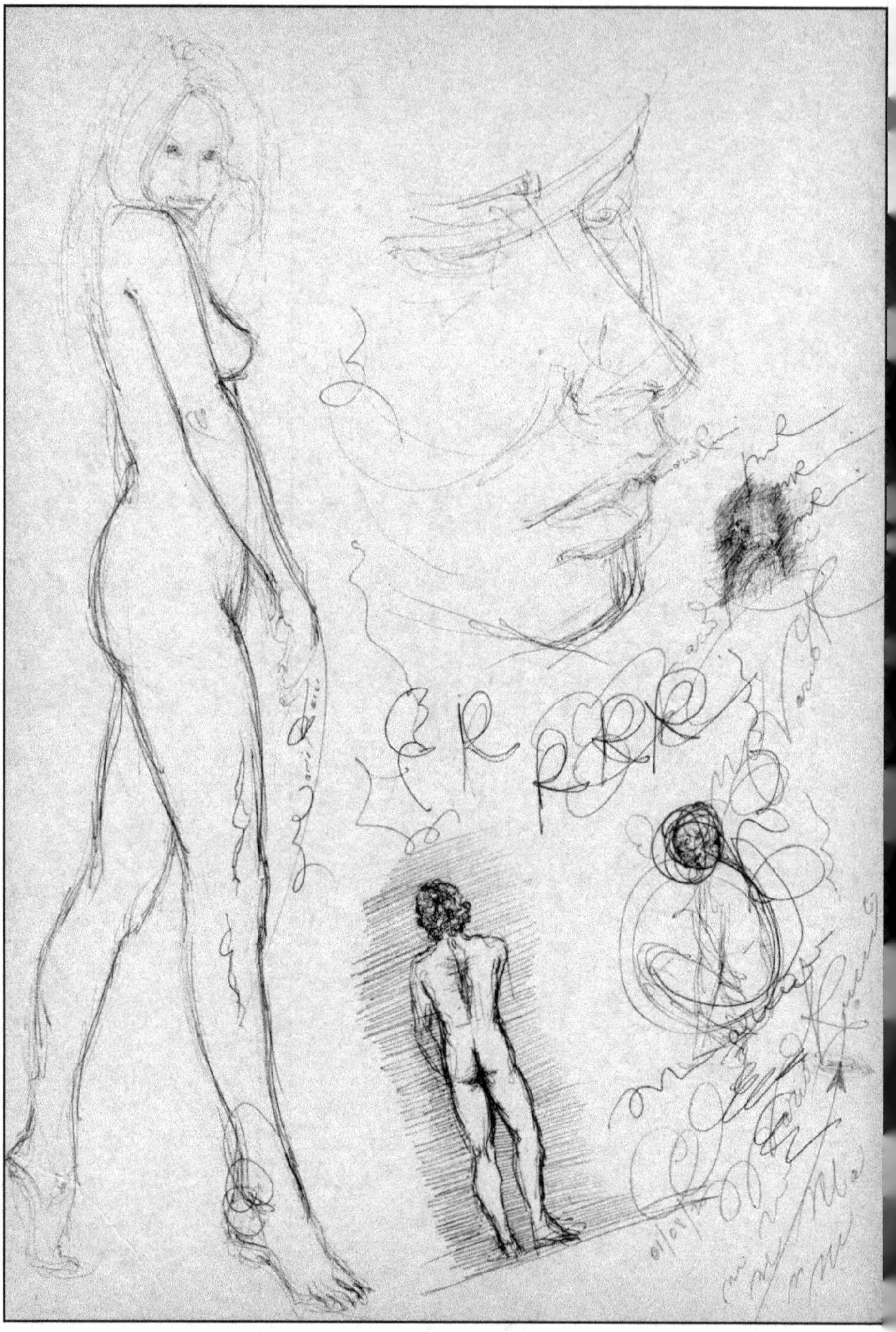

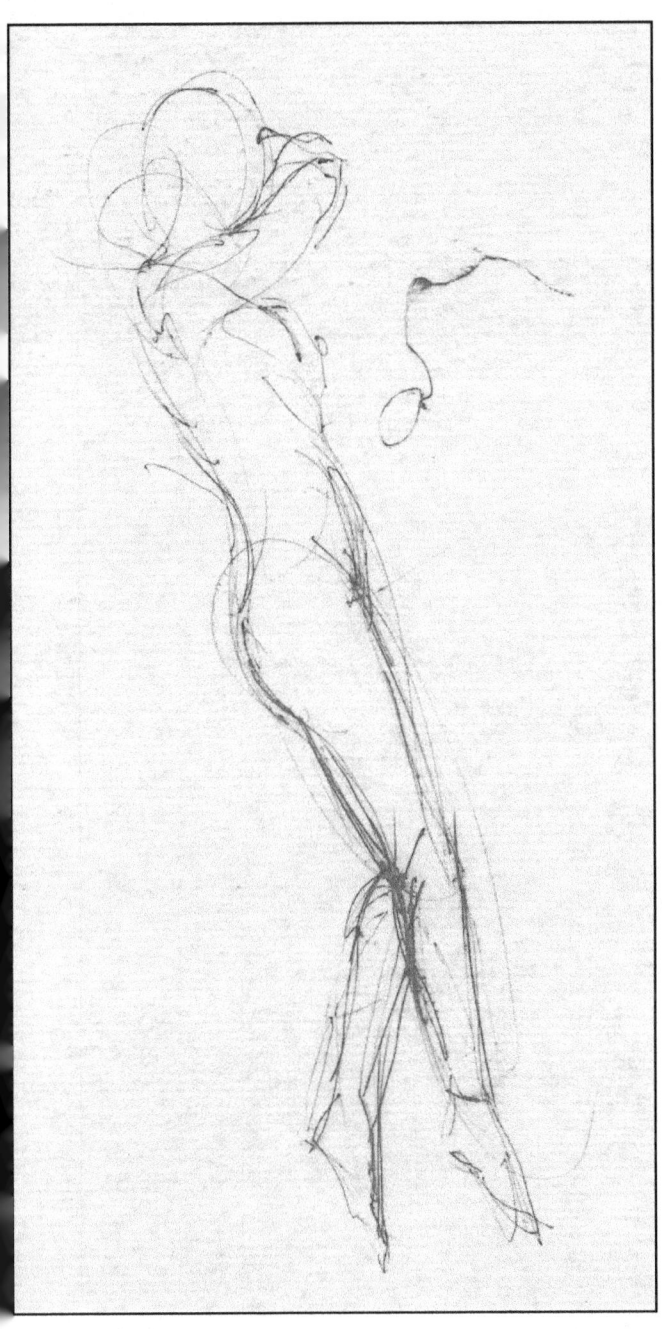
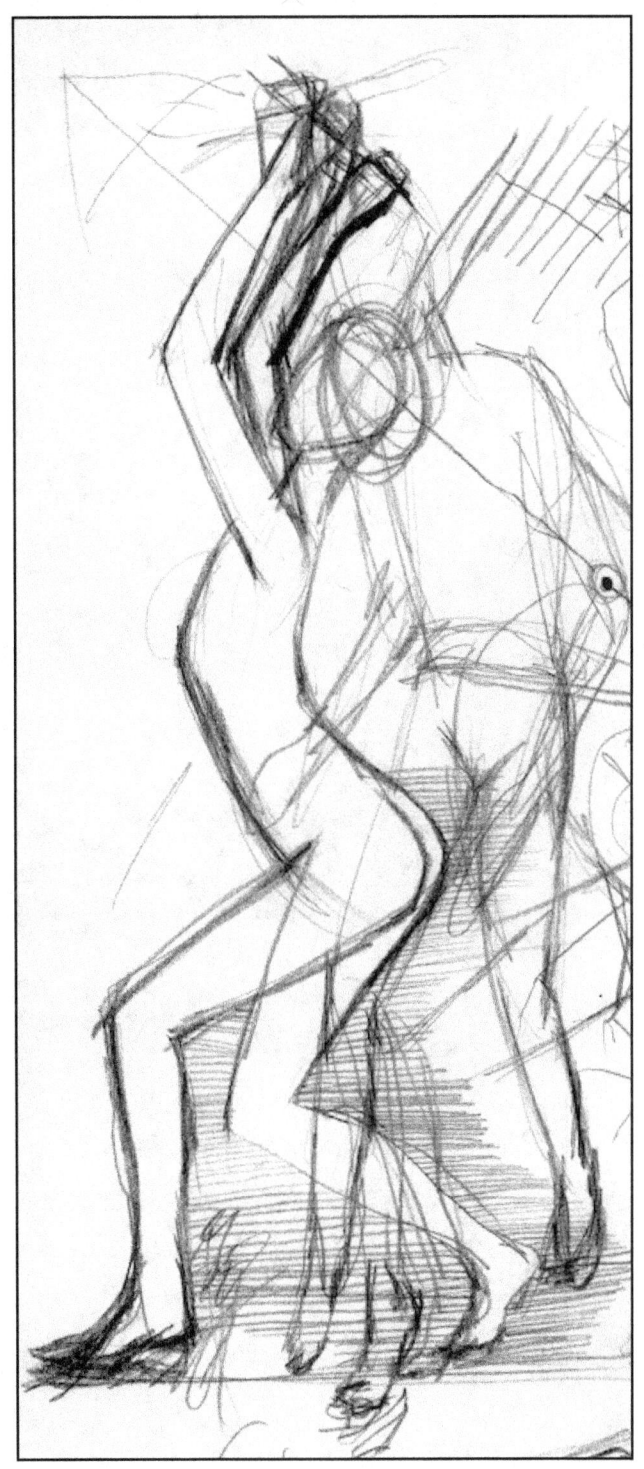

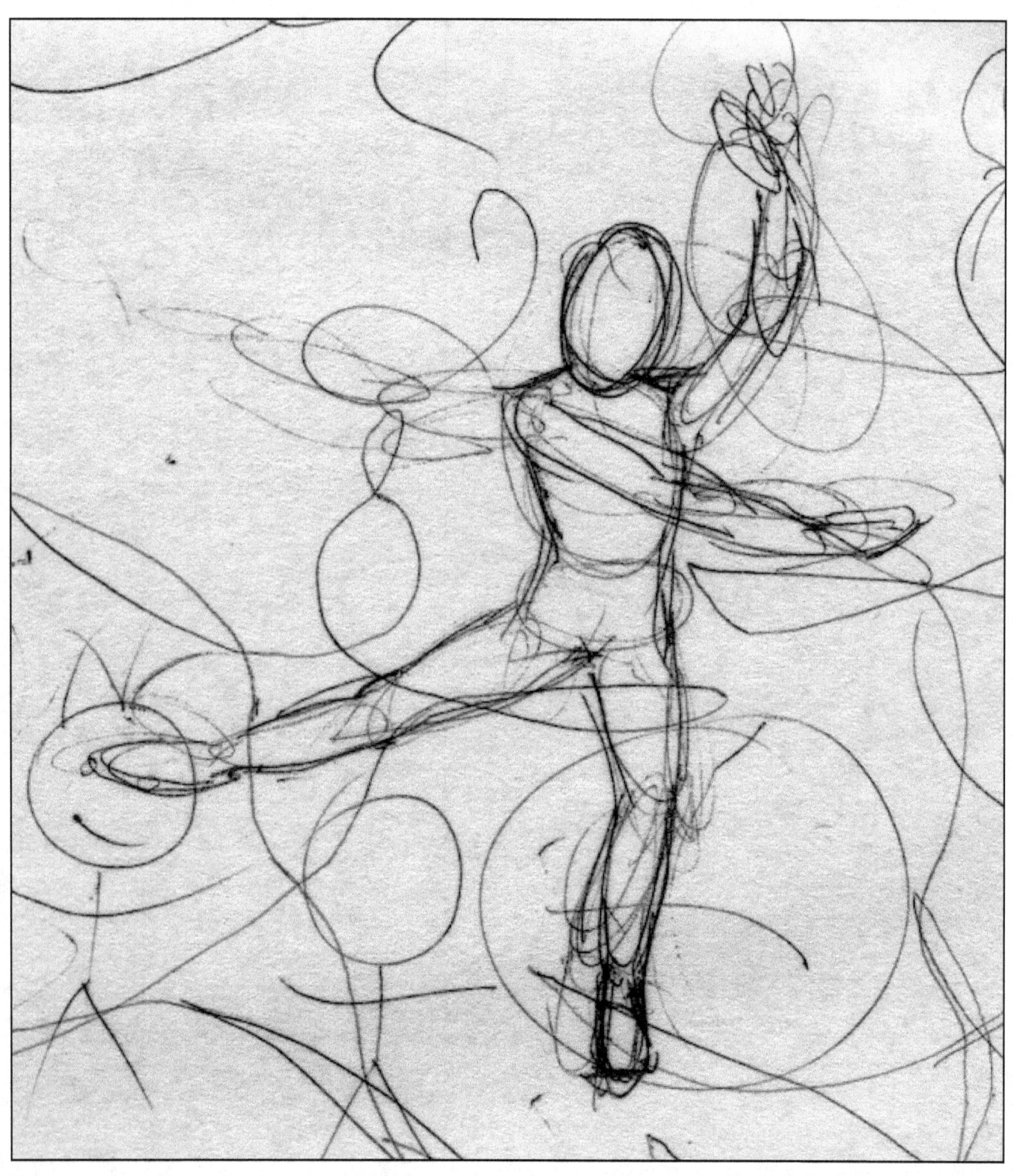

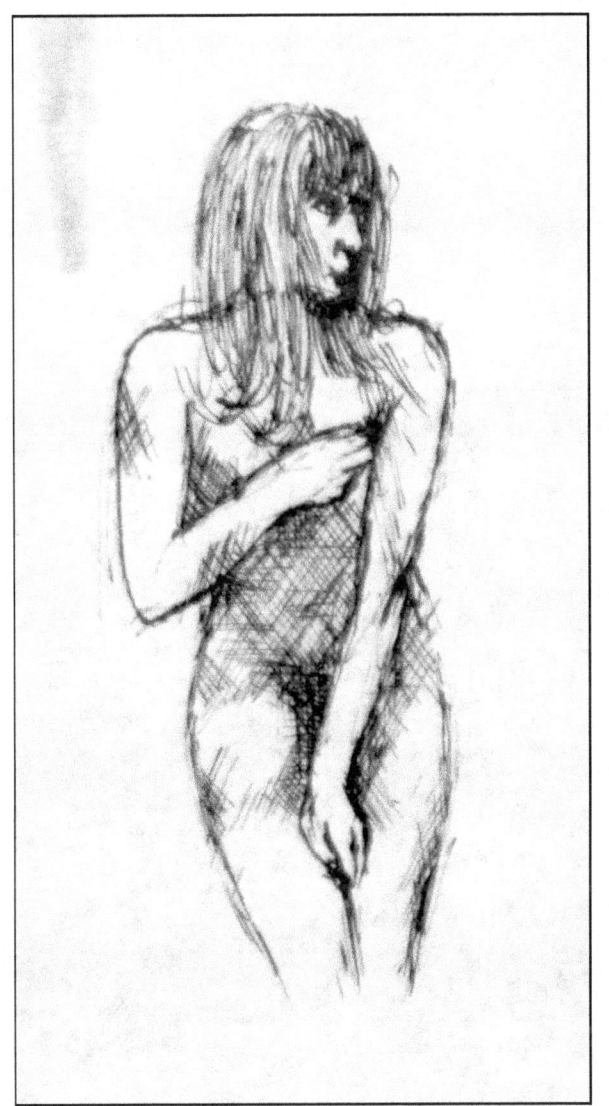
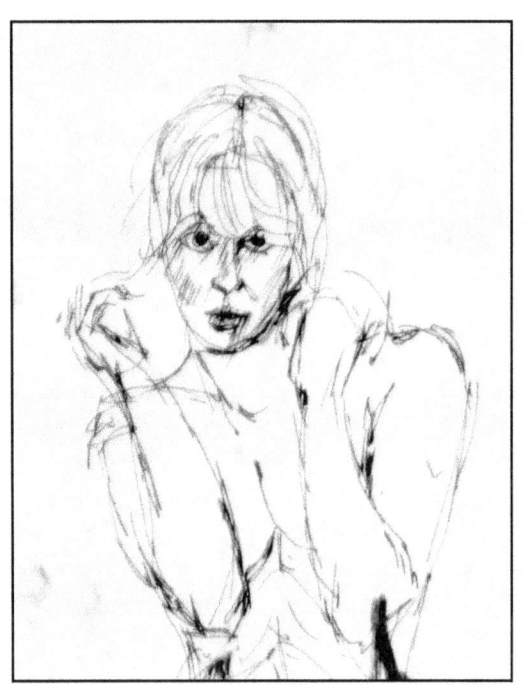
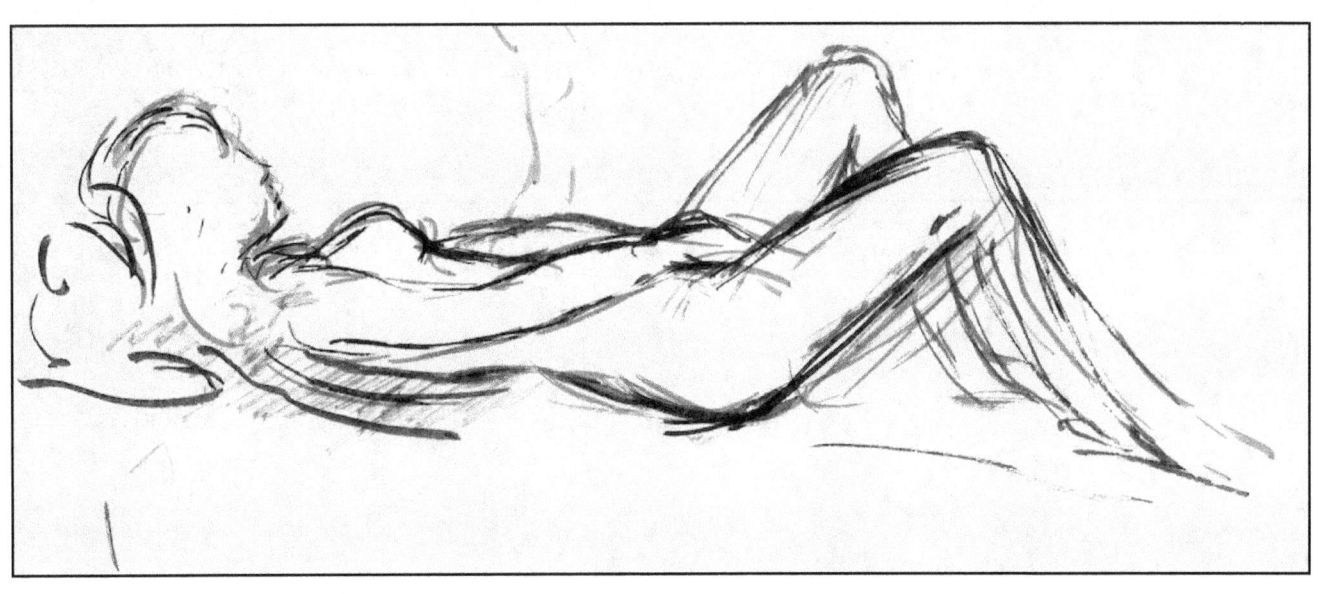

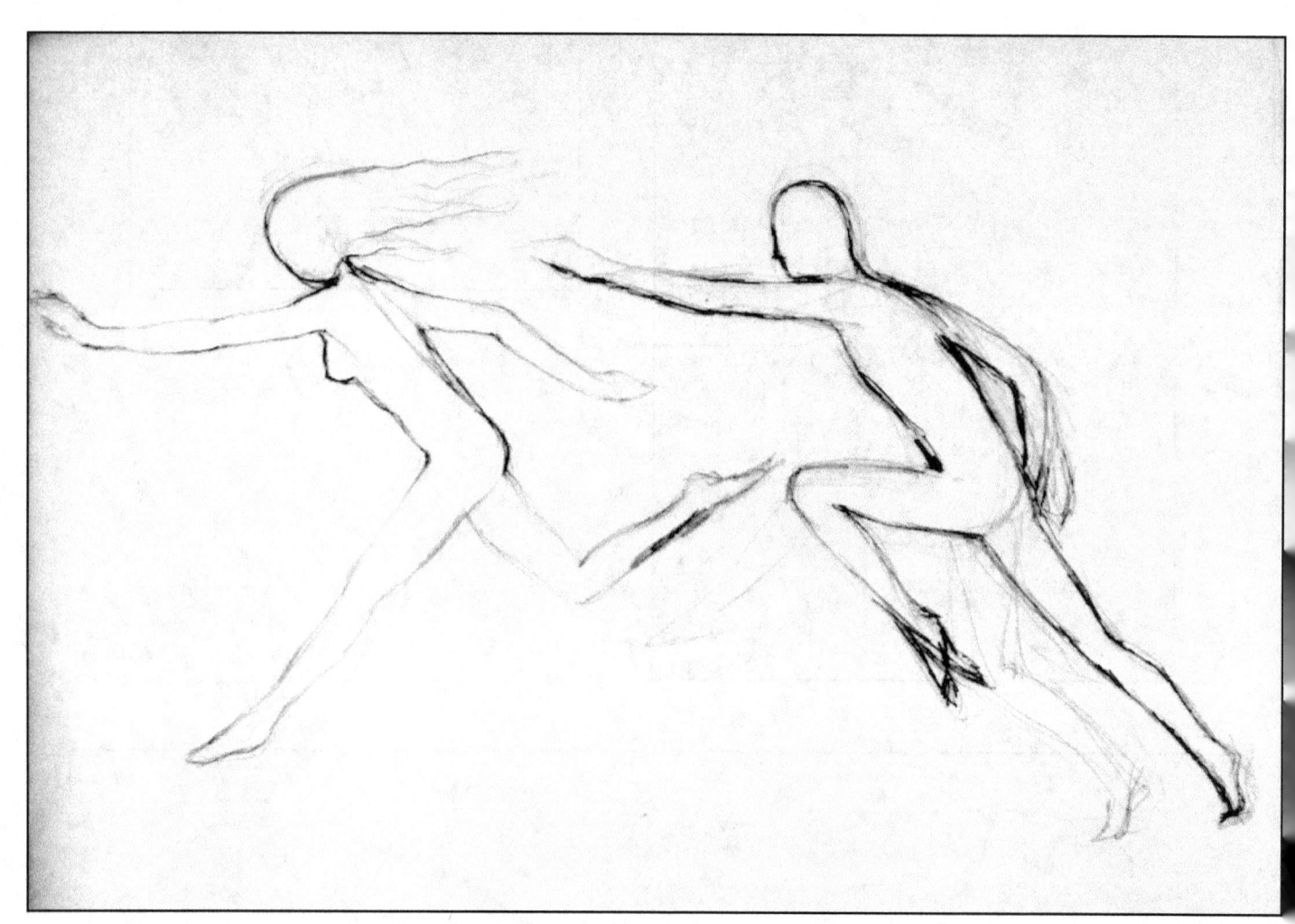

16. HUMAN Composition

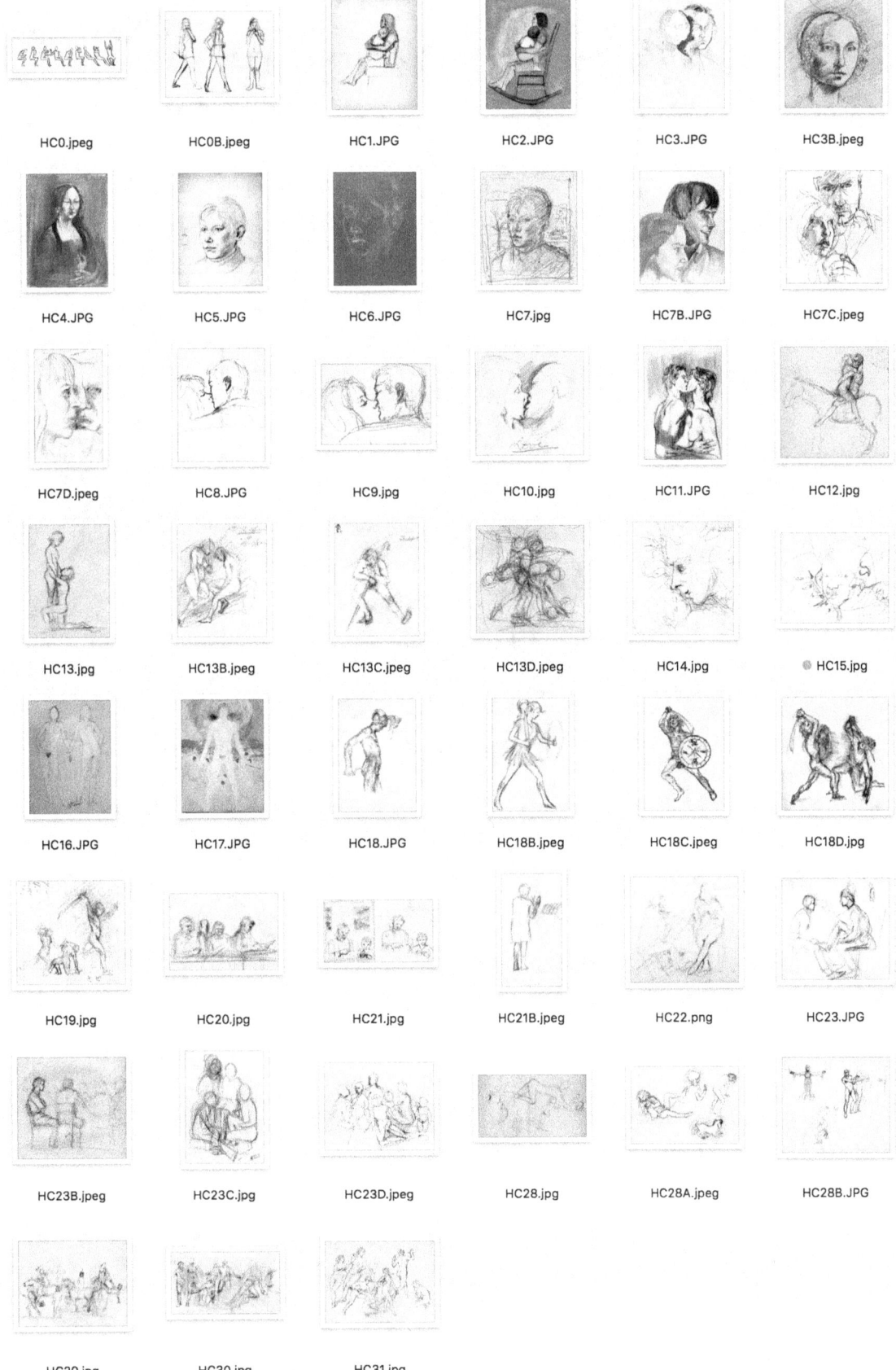

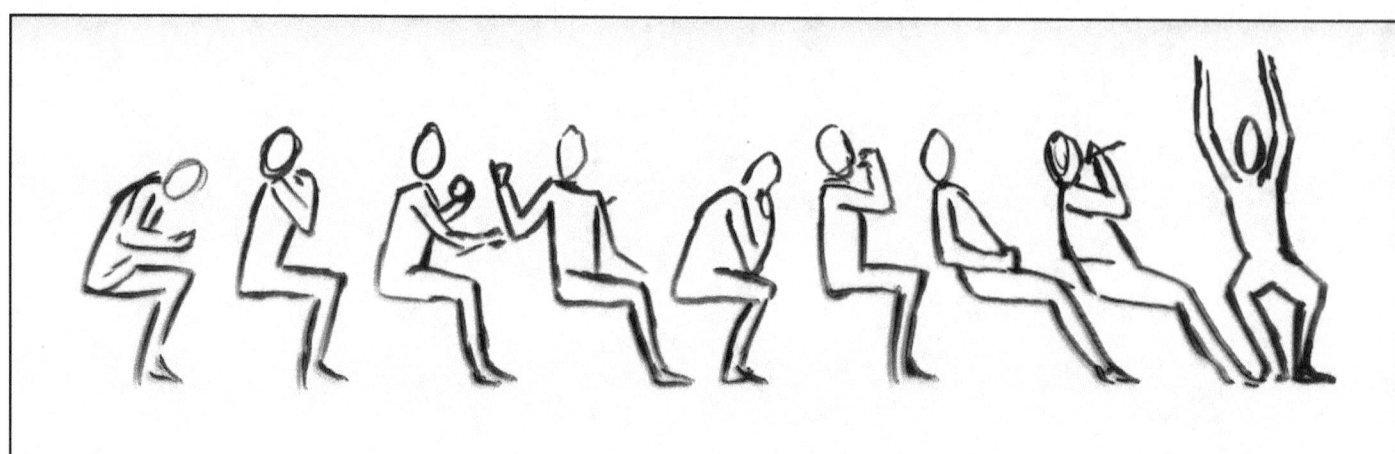

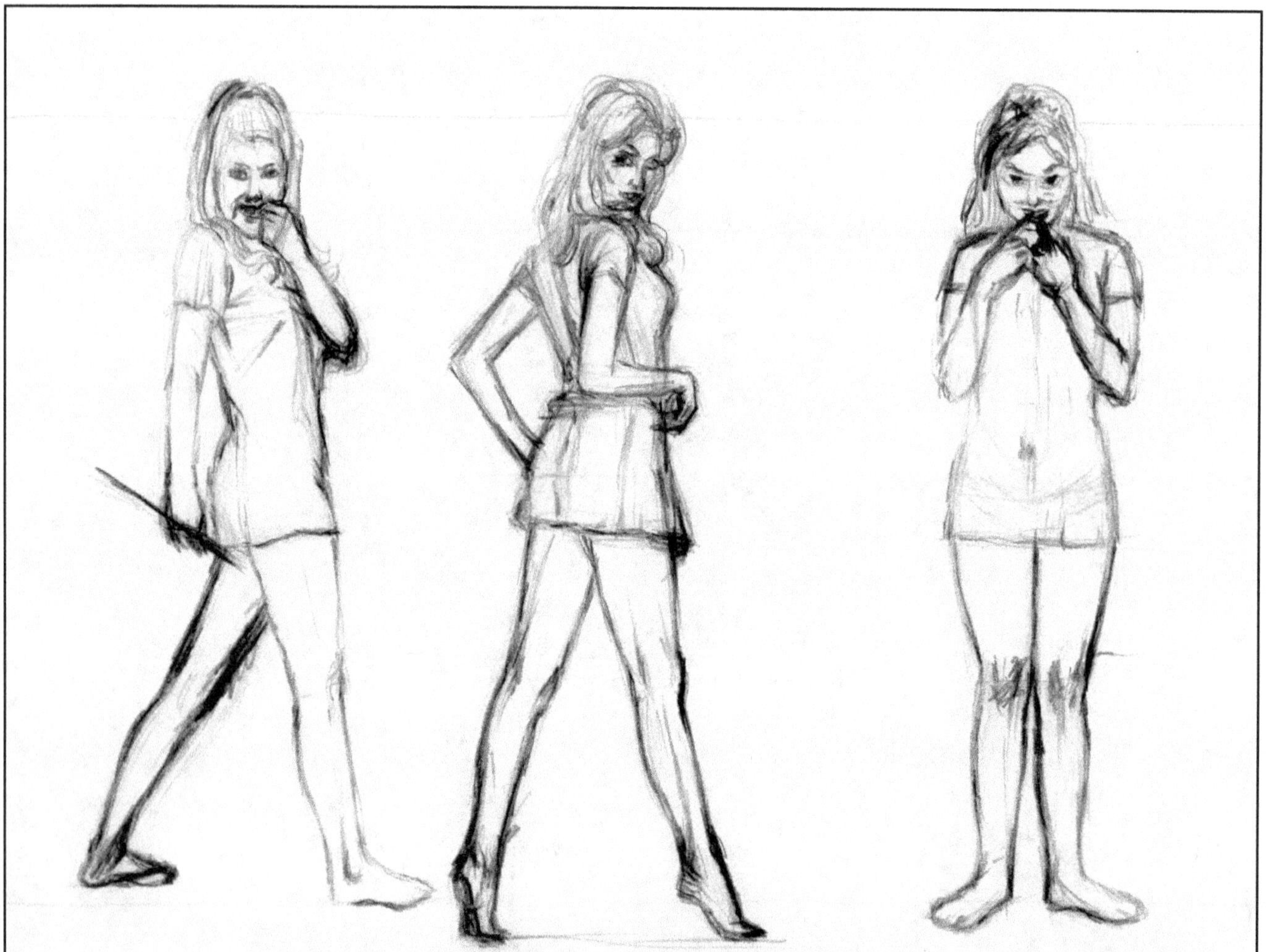

Composition is rectangular, triangular, or circular. The top 2 pictures exemplify what Phidias did with the Parthenon frieze.

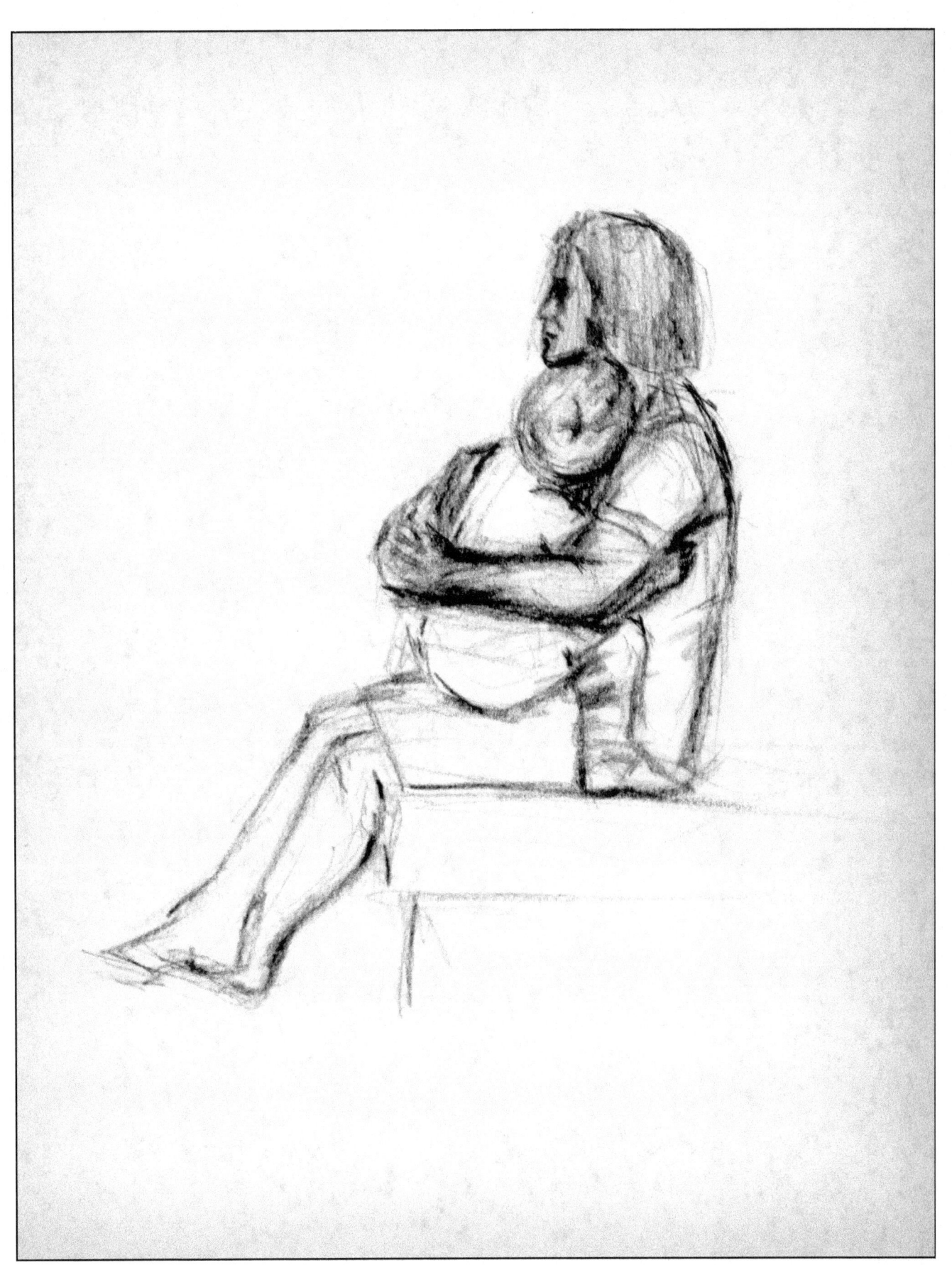

Ilda with Natale

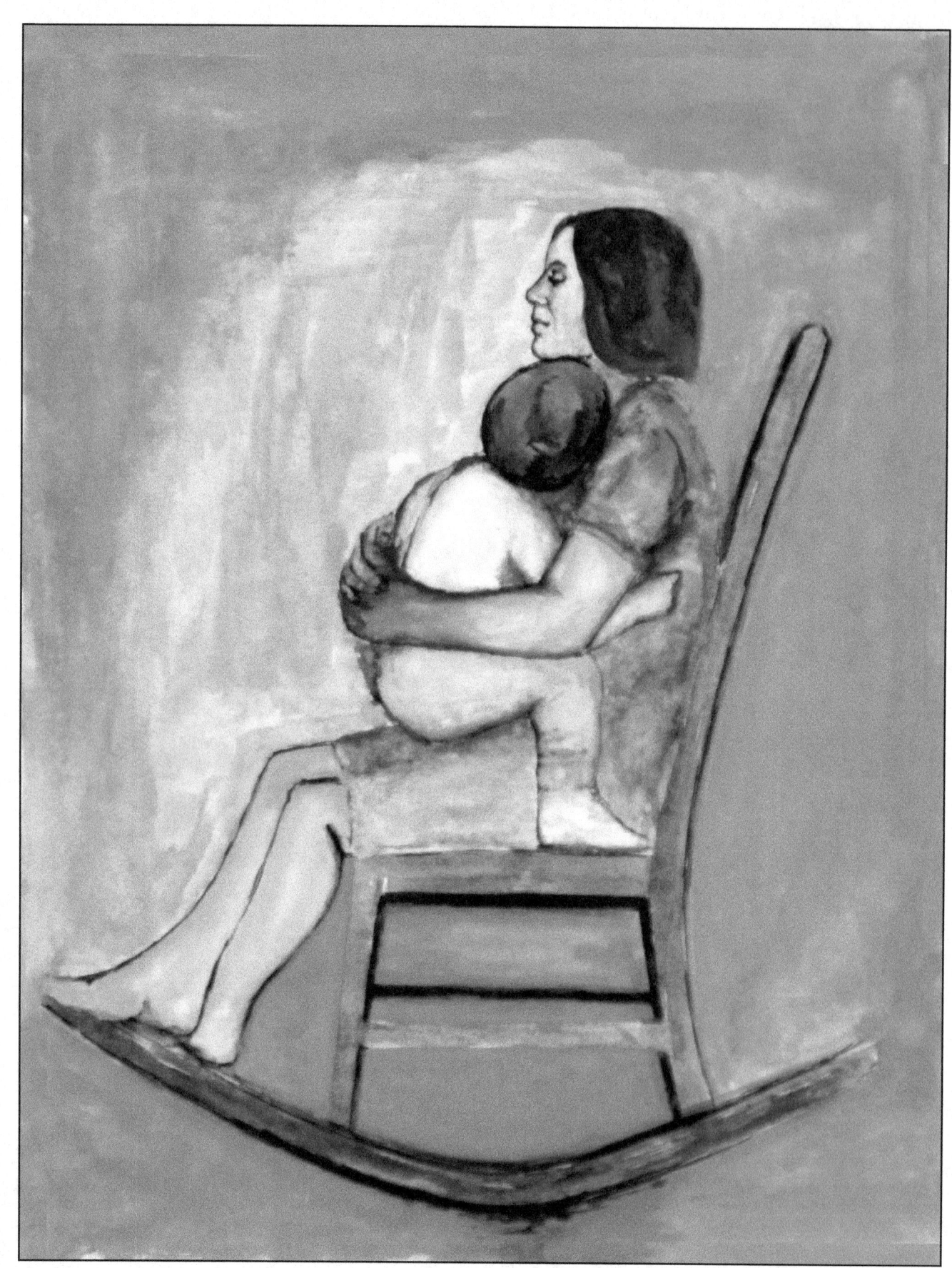

Ilda with Natale

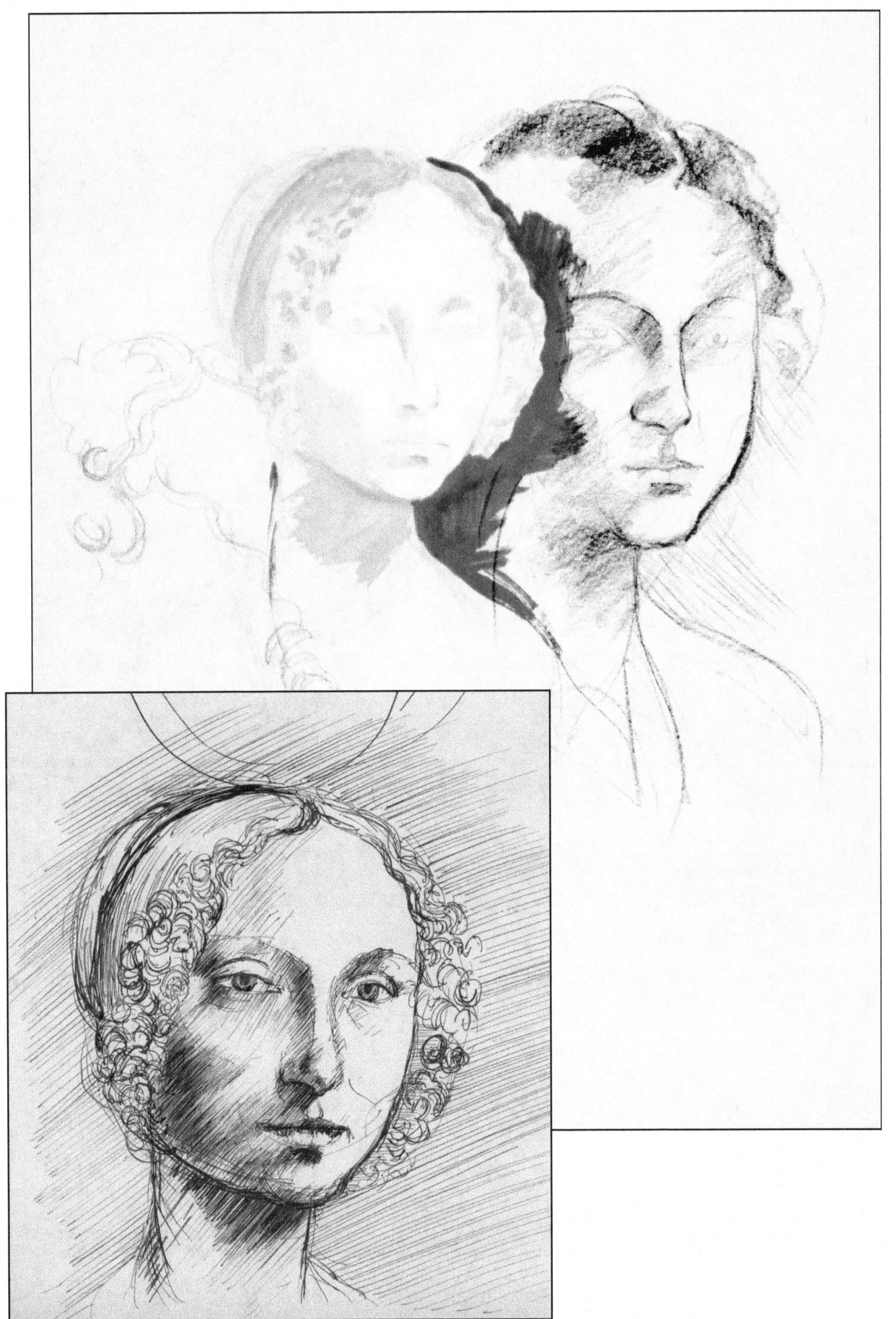

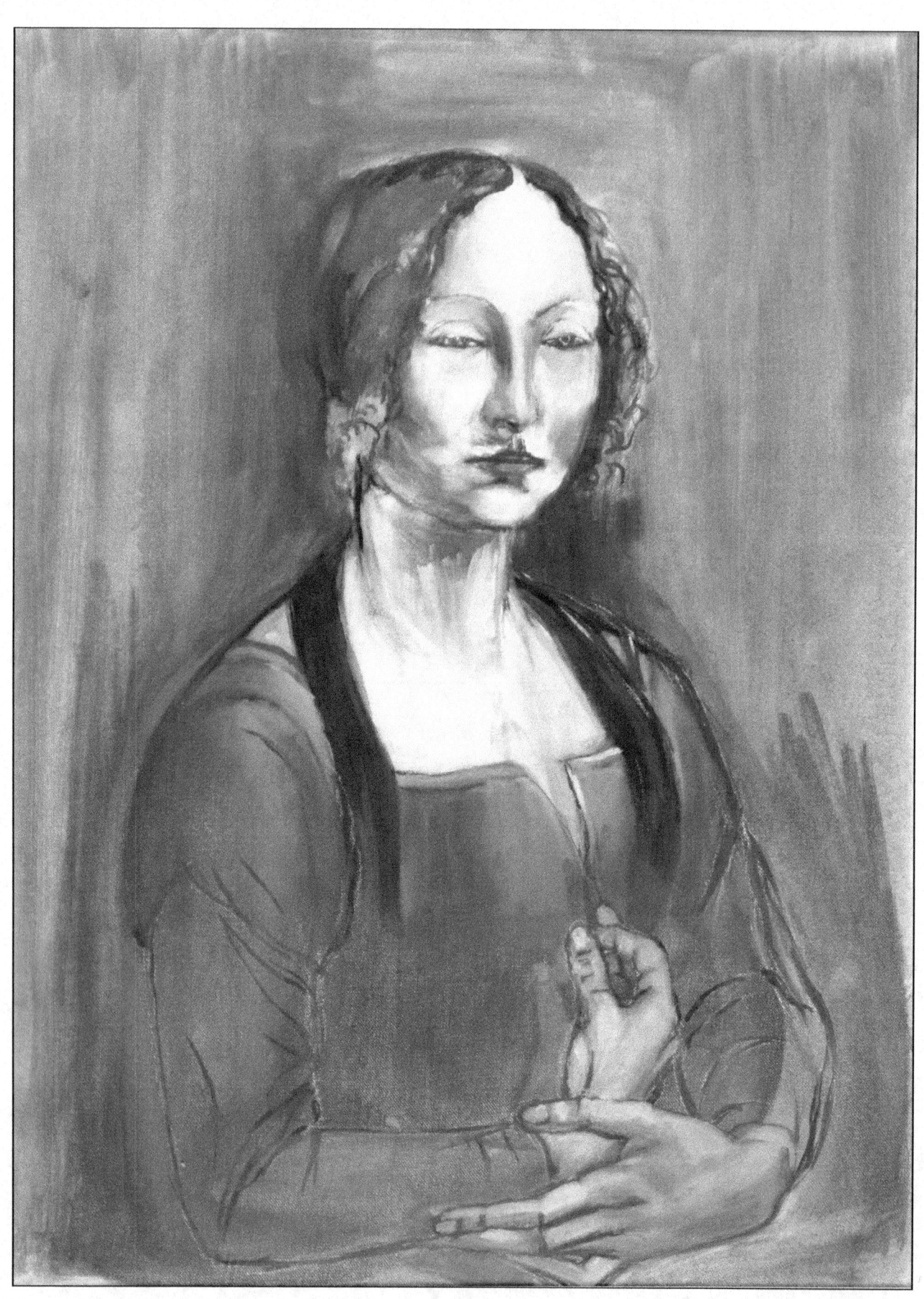

Leonardo's Ginevra de' Benci (with the hands), oil on 18"x24" canvas

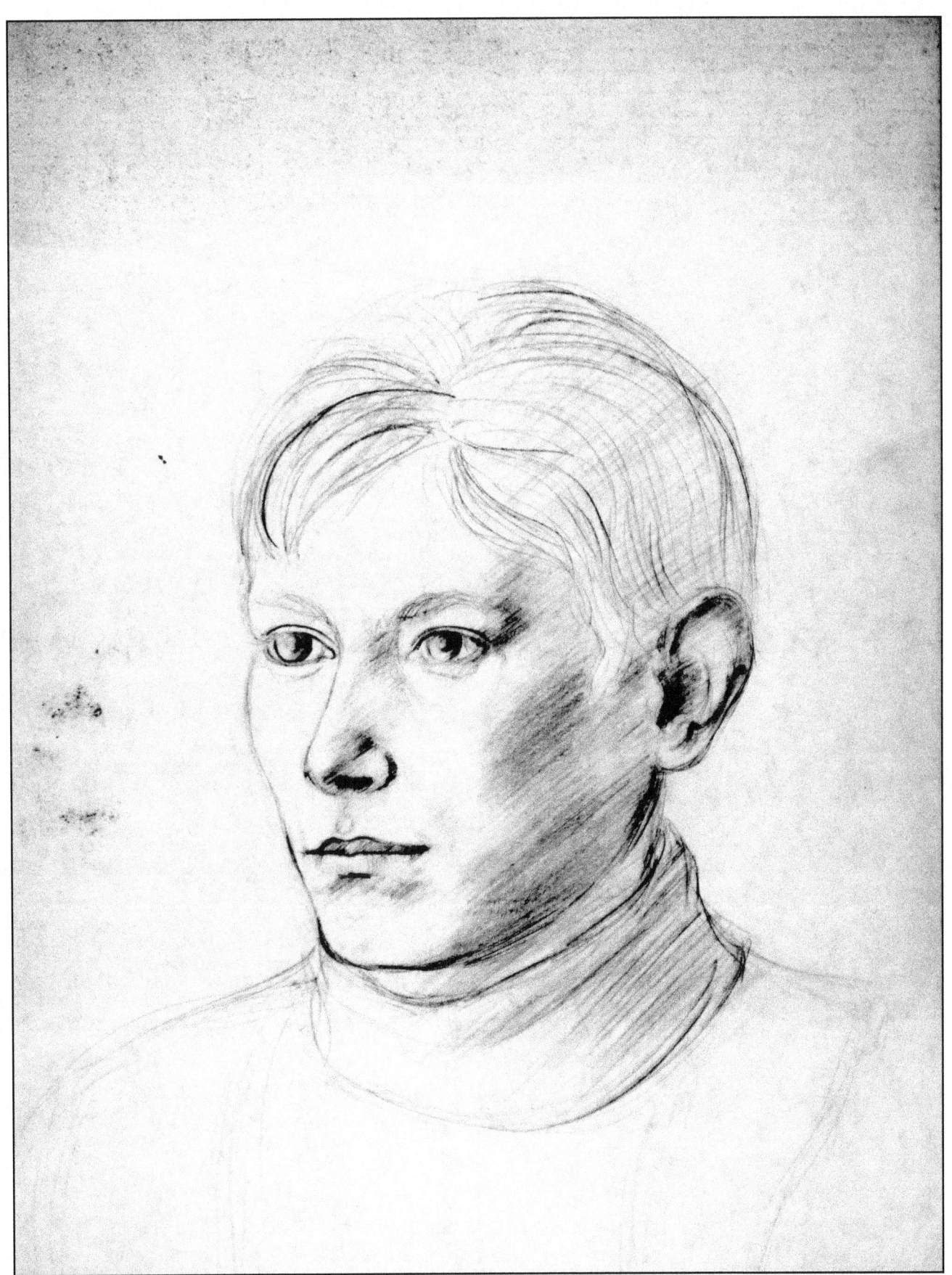

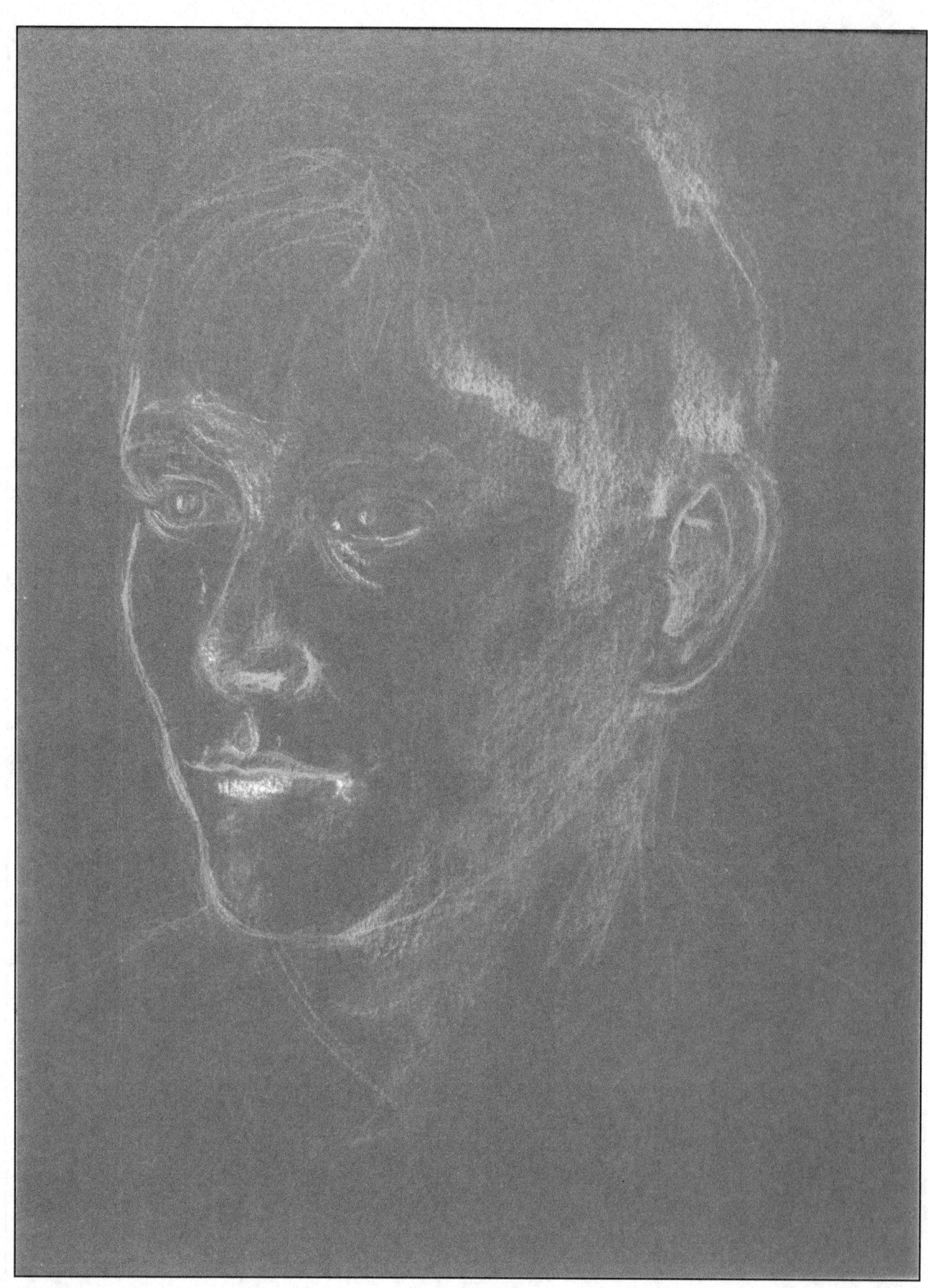

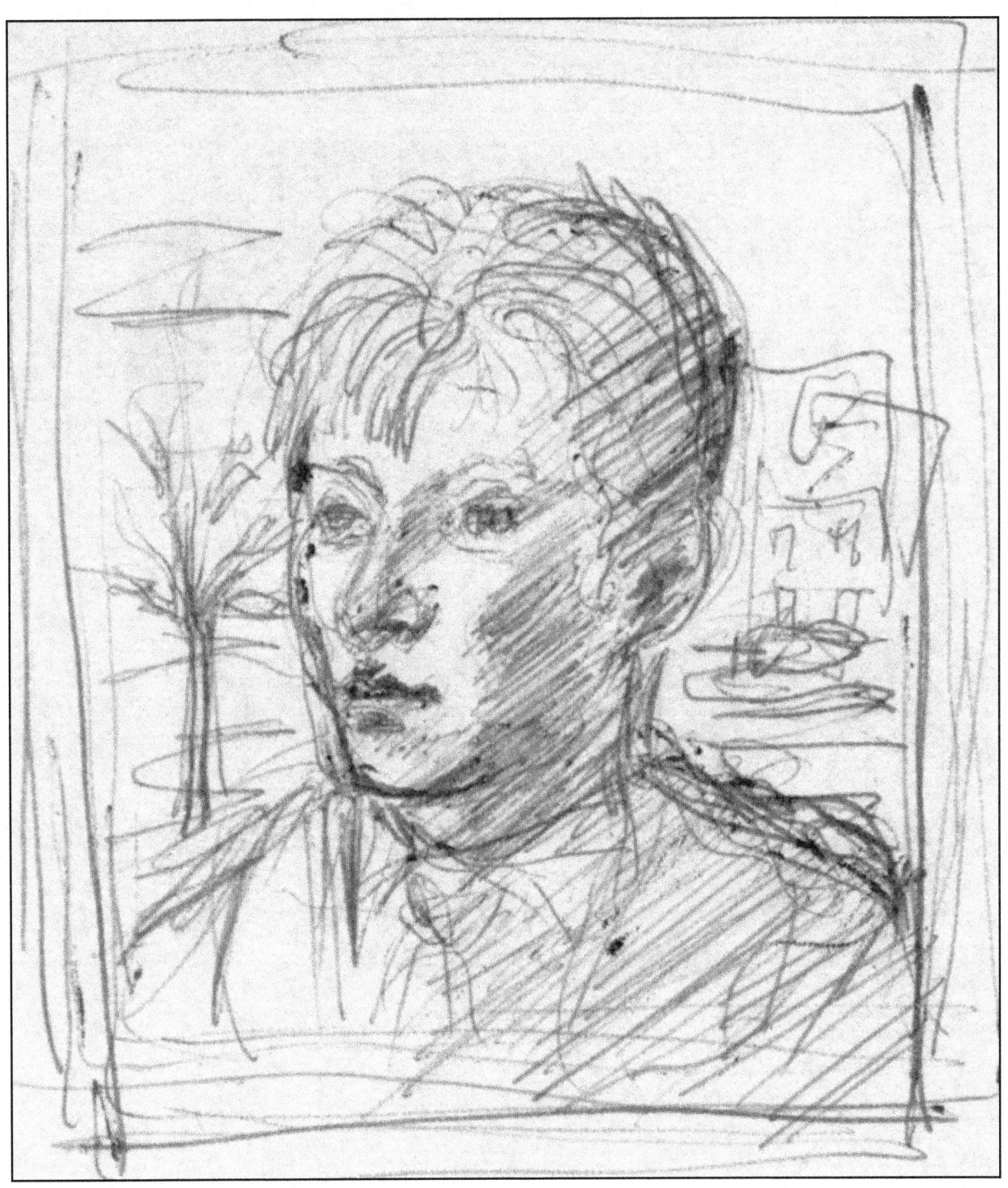

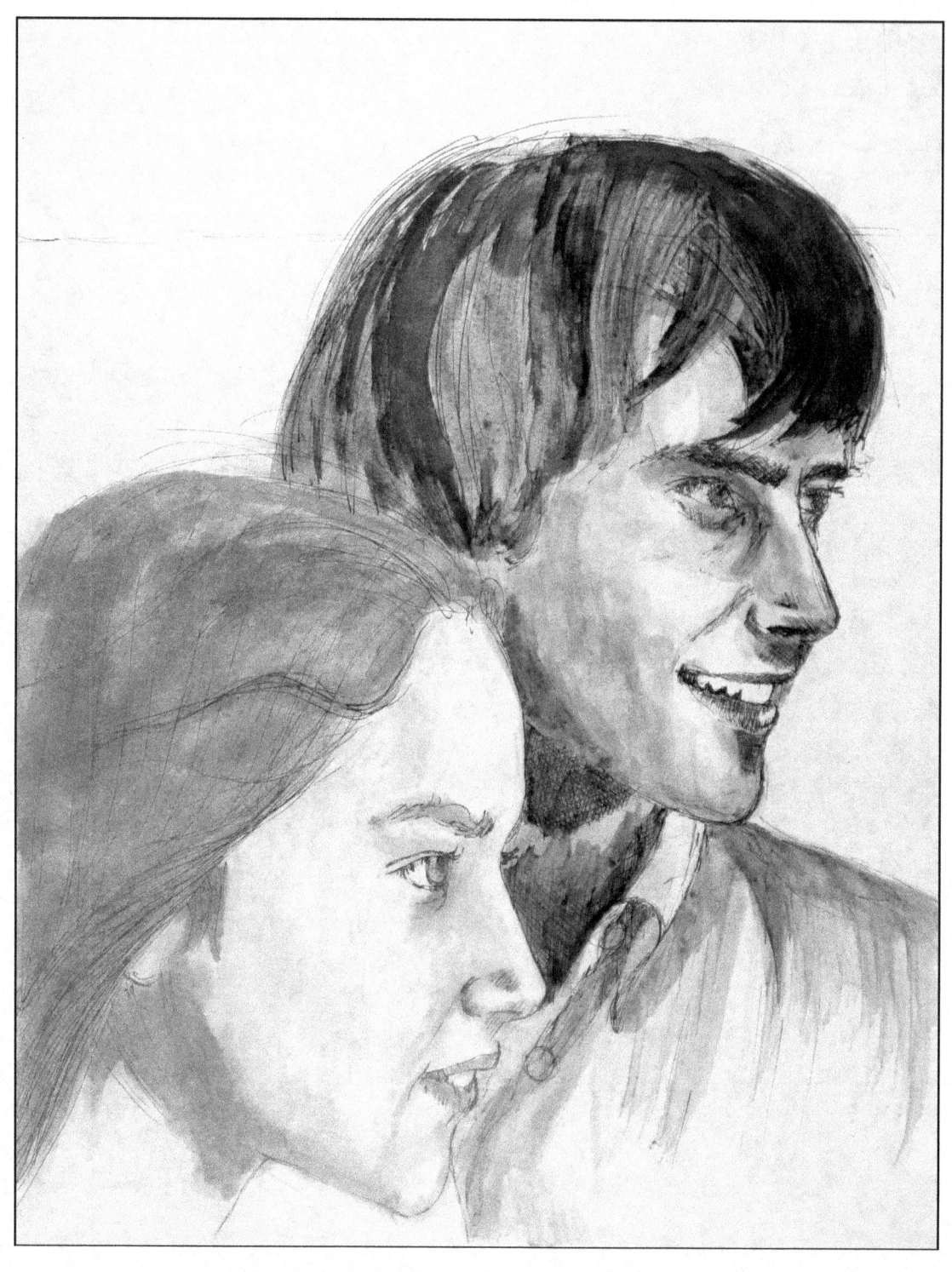

Romeo and Juliet

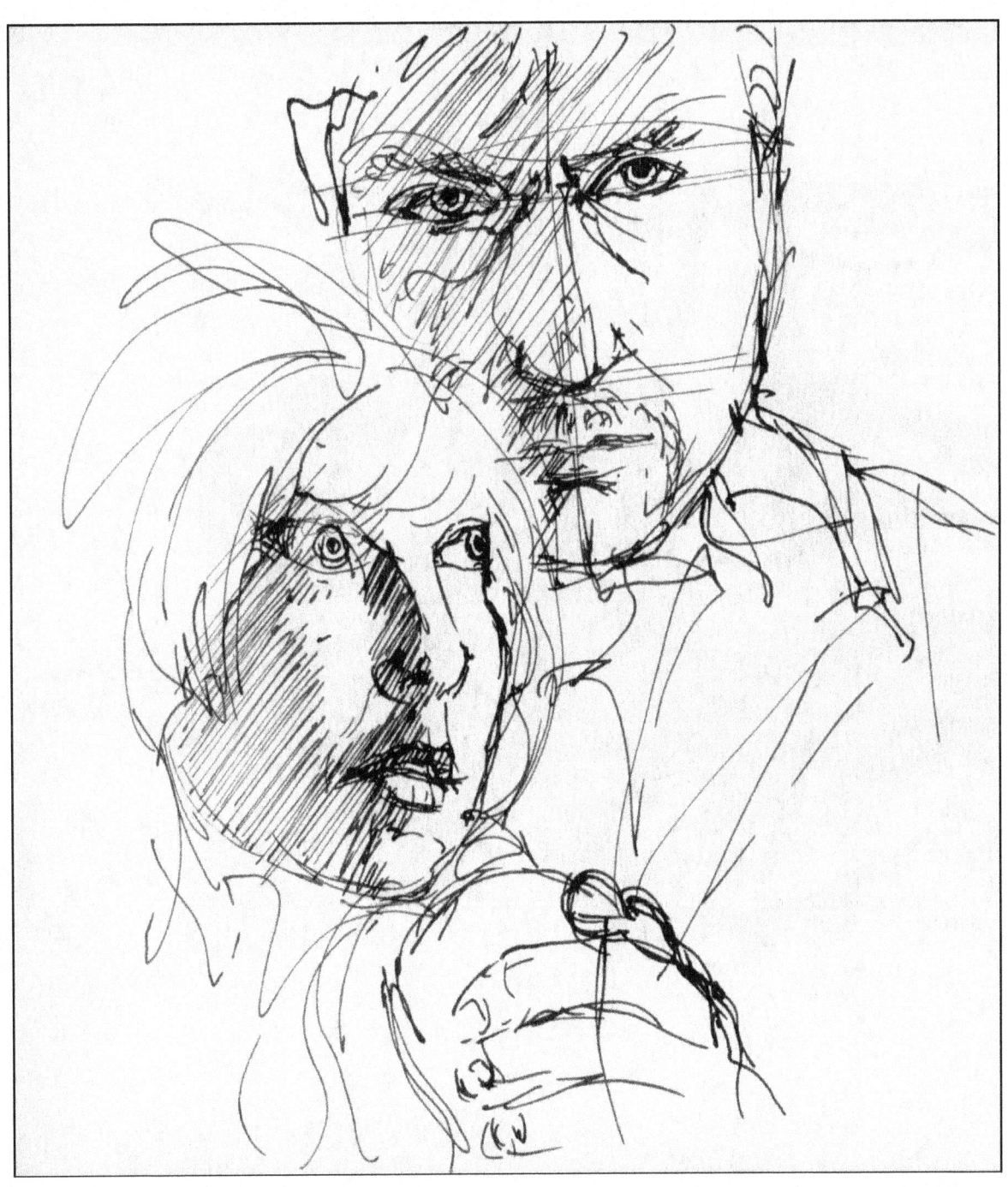

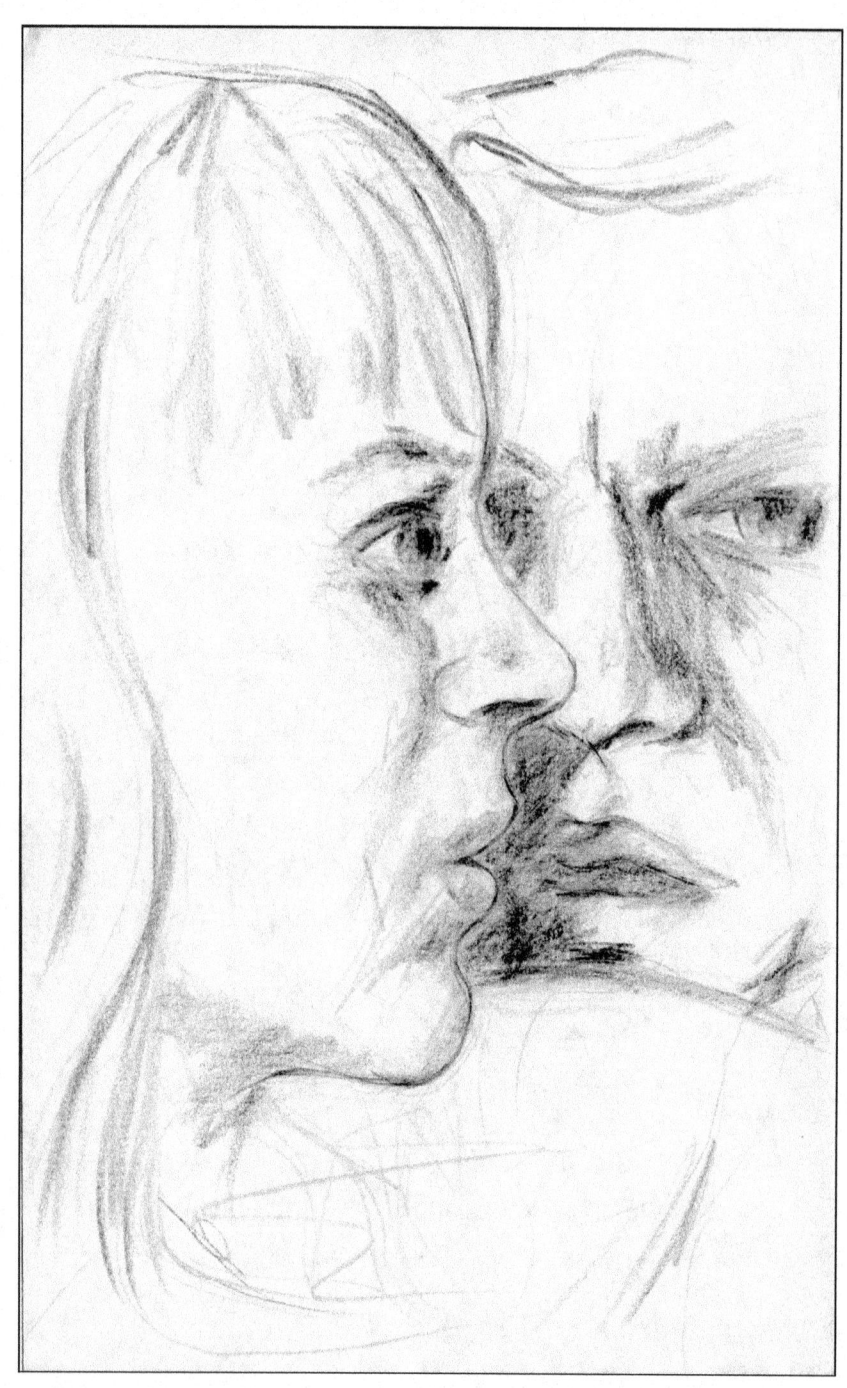

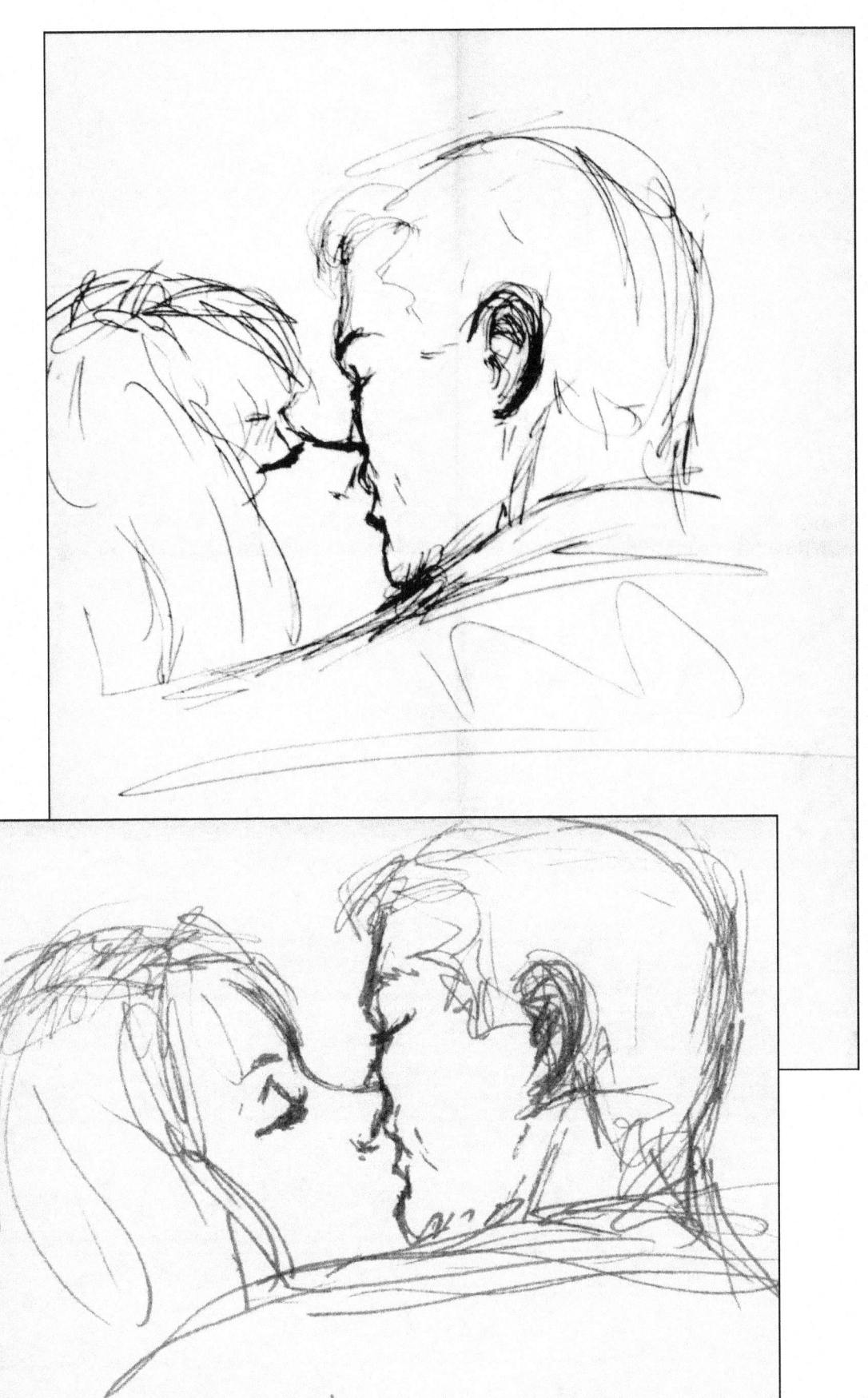

The Kiss

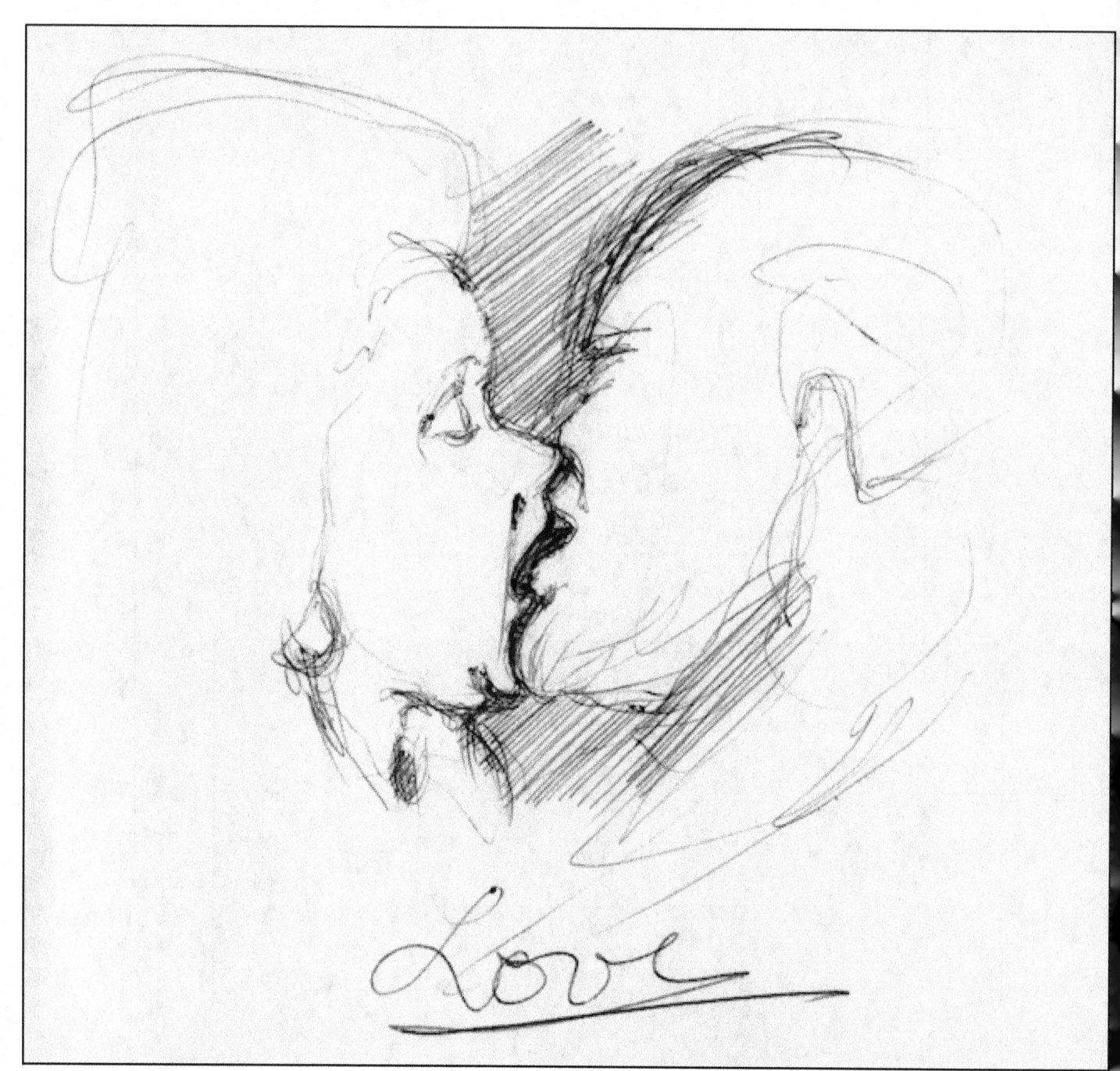

The Kiss

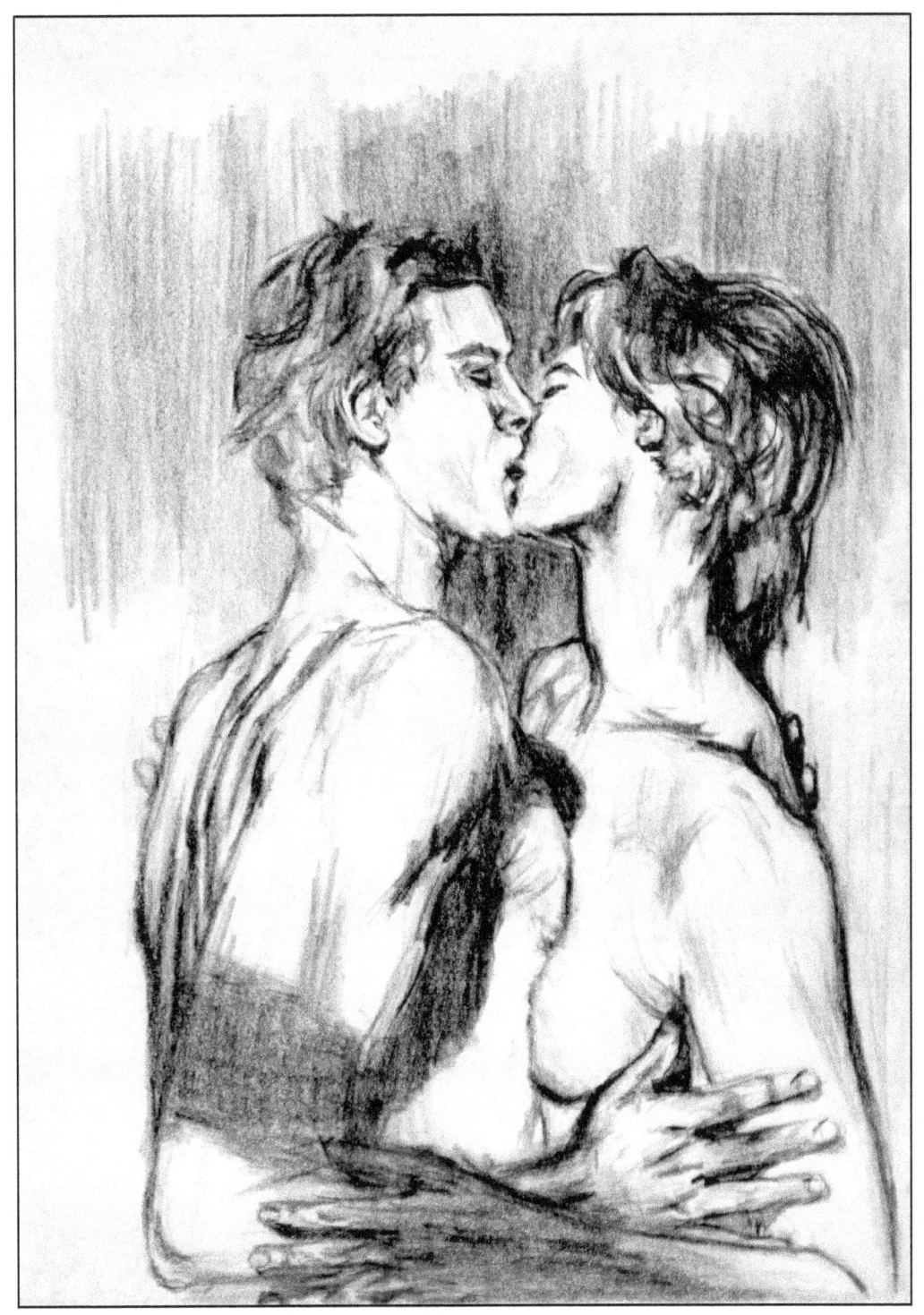

The Kiss

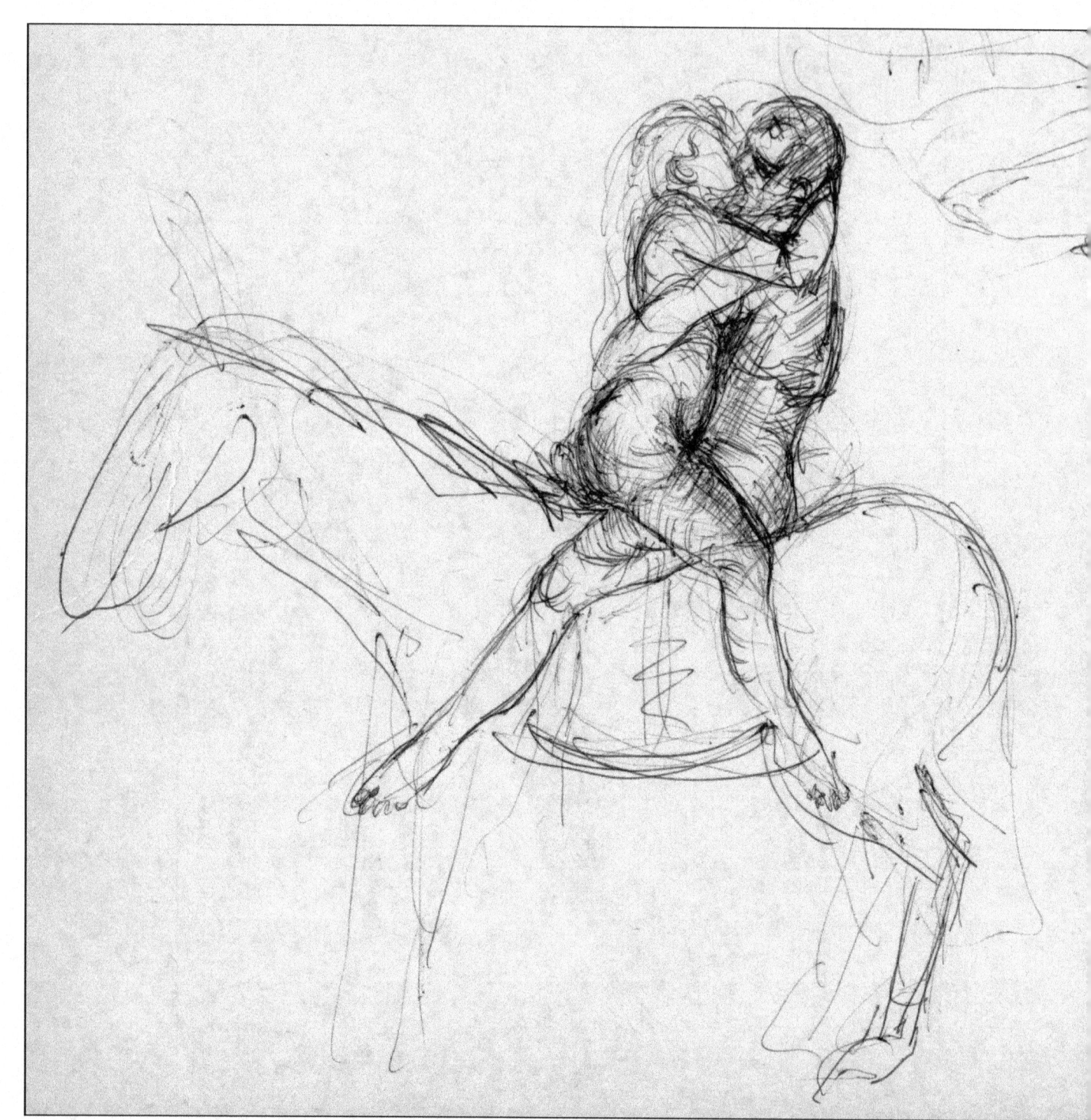

The Kiss

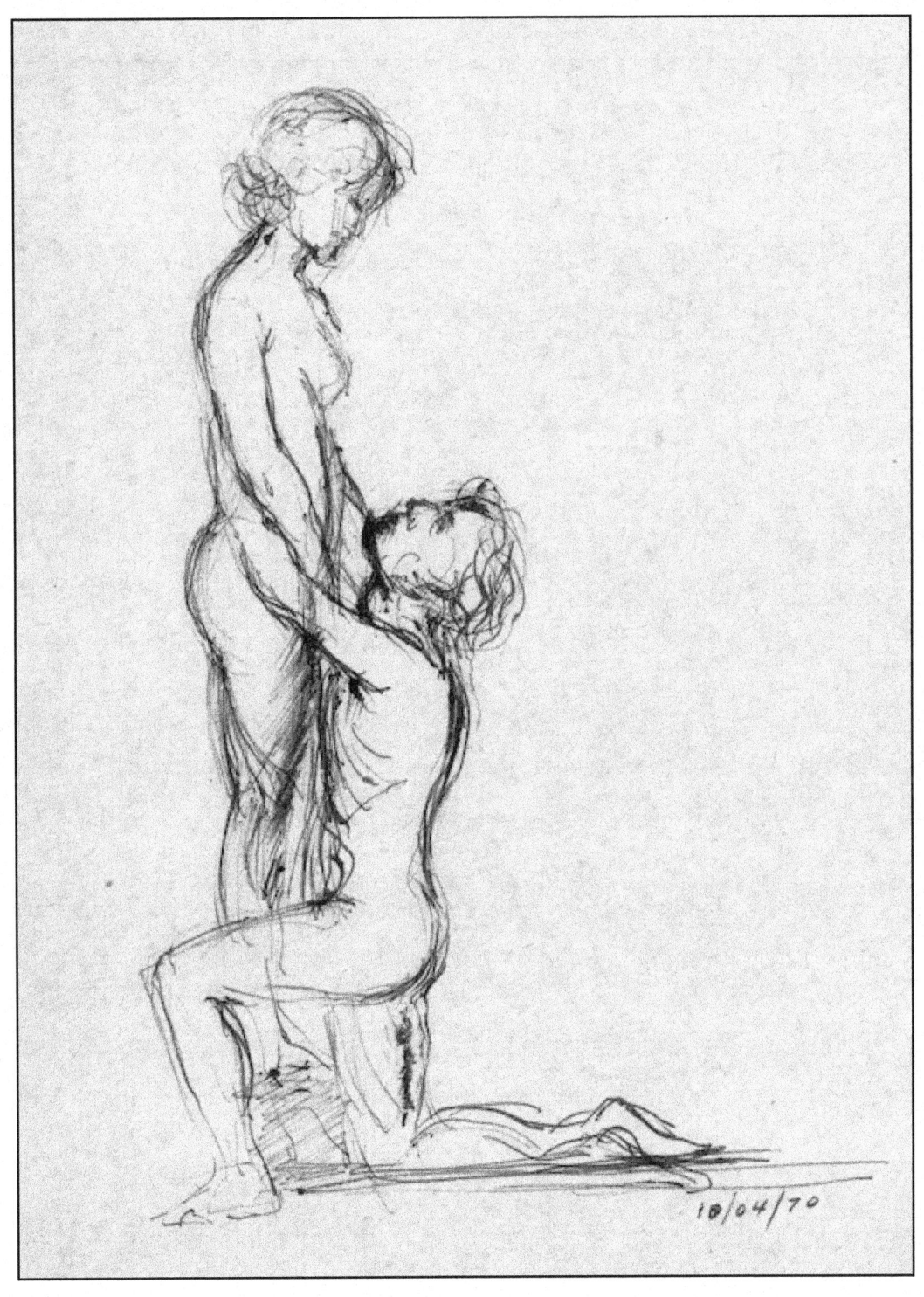

"I love you!"

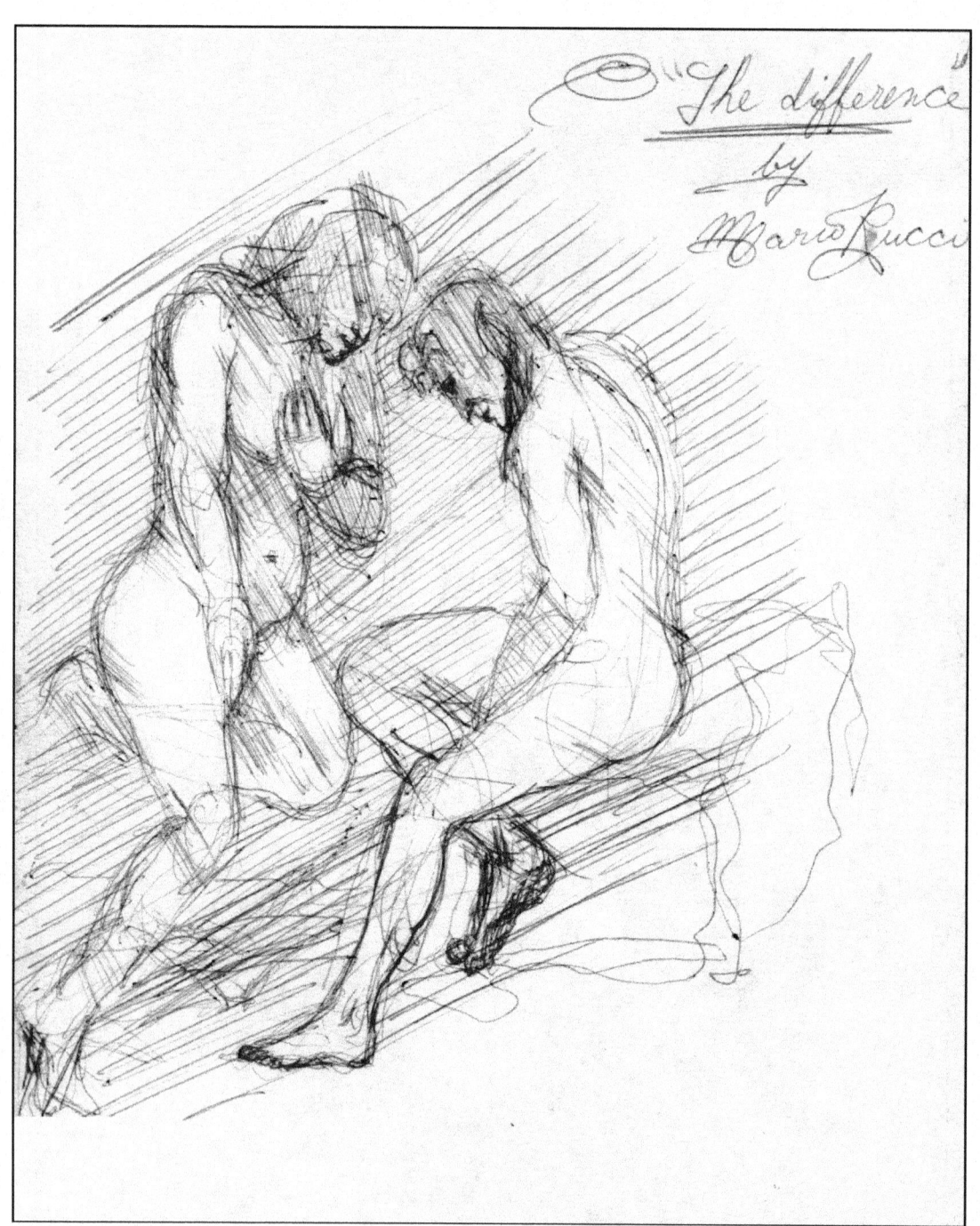

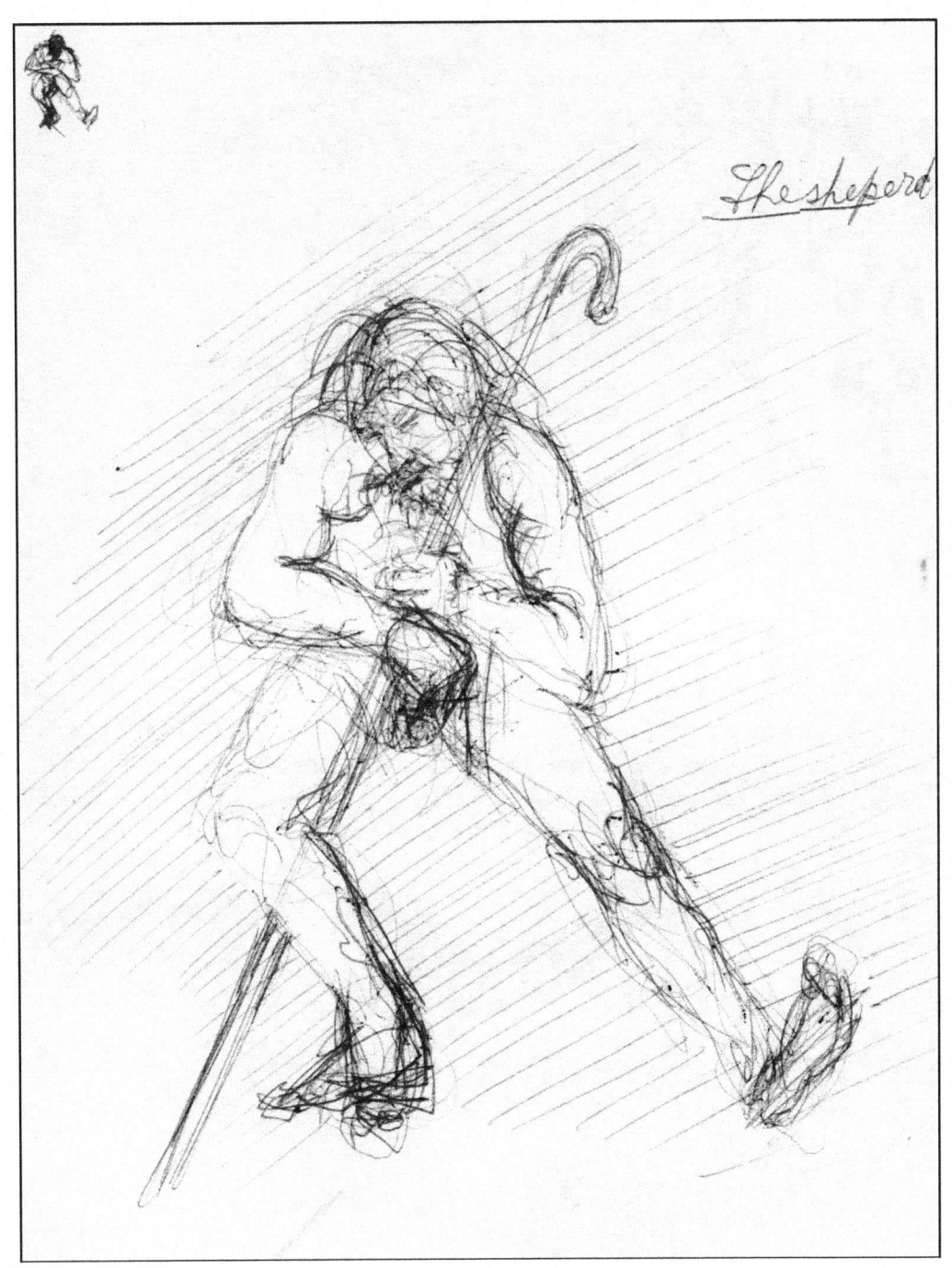

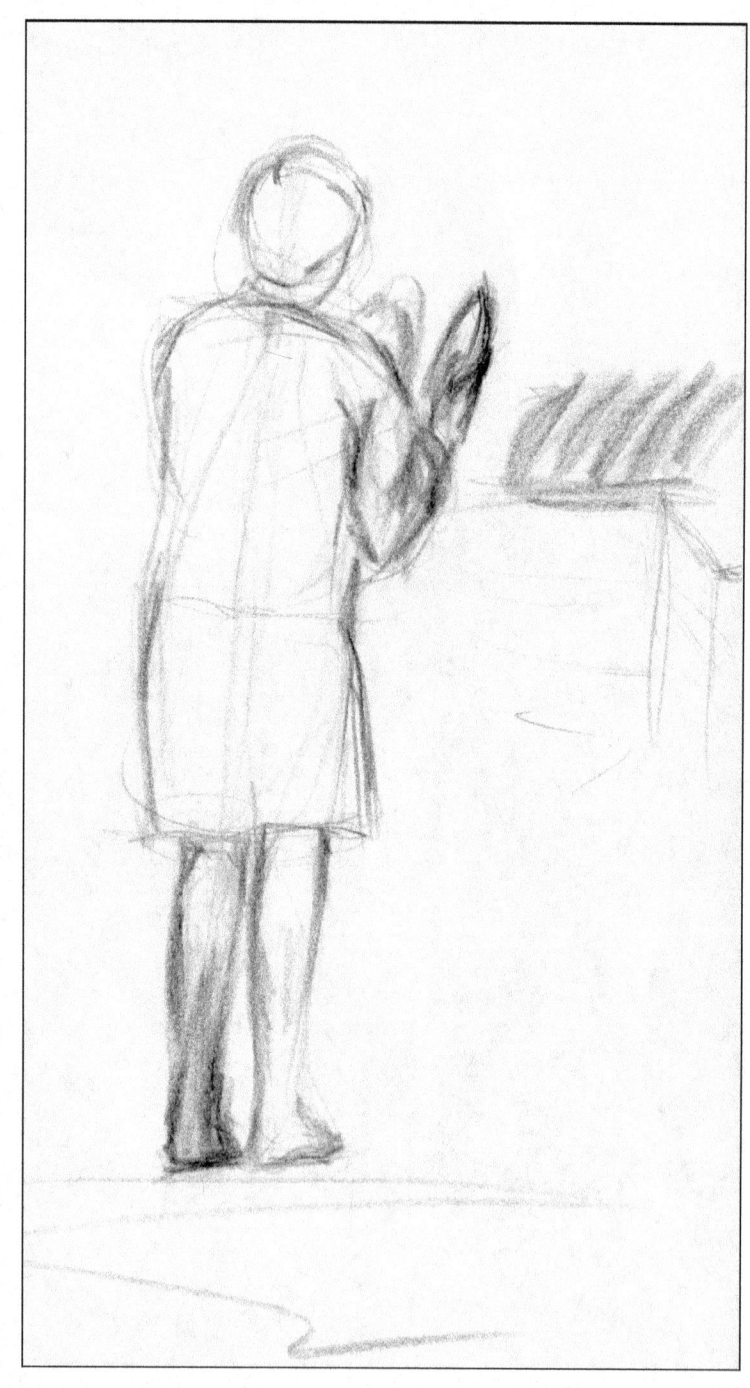

Drying Dishes

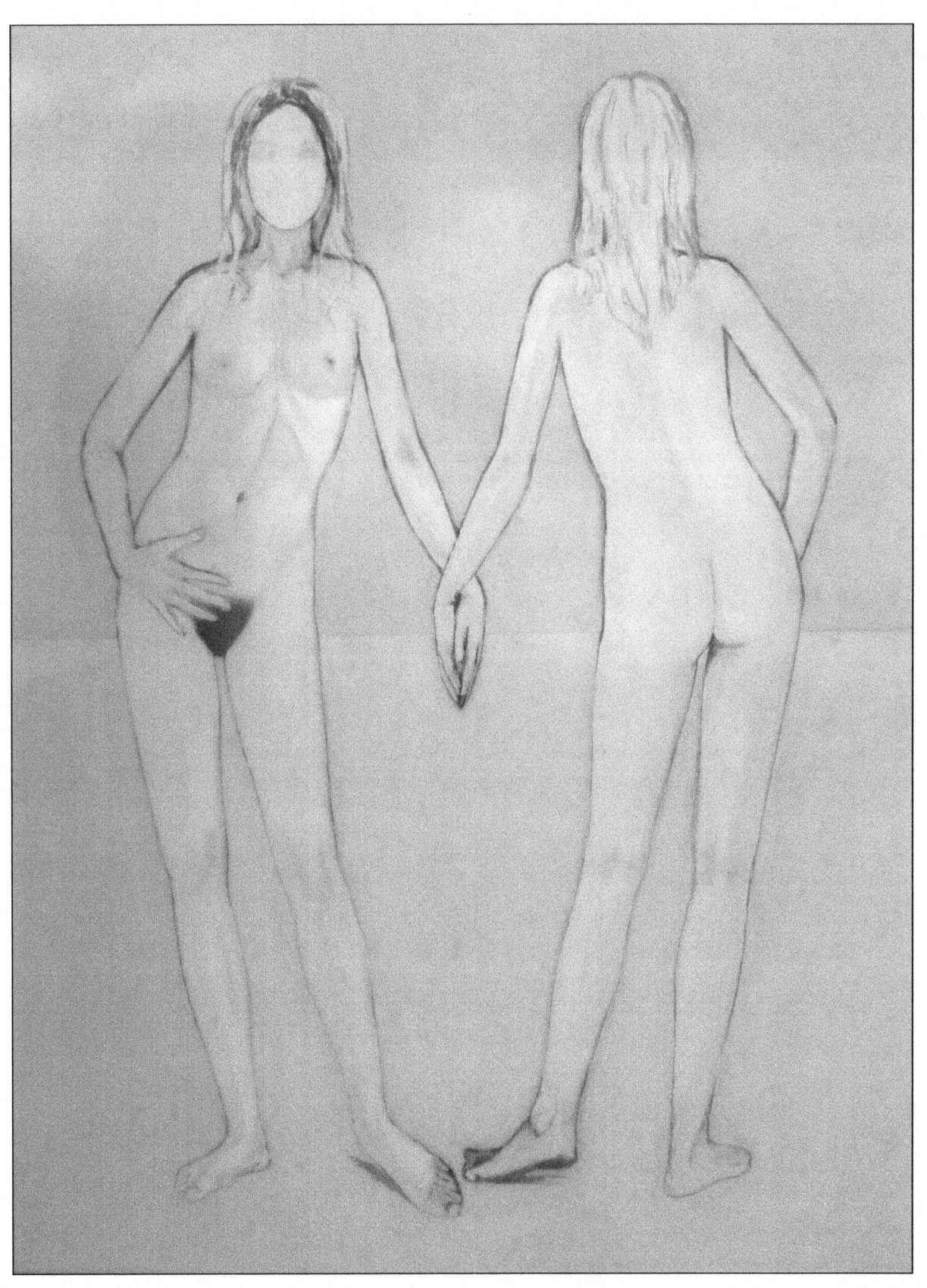

TWINS, acrylic on 30"x40" canvas

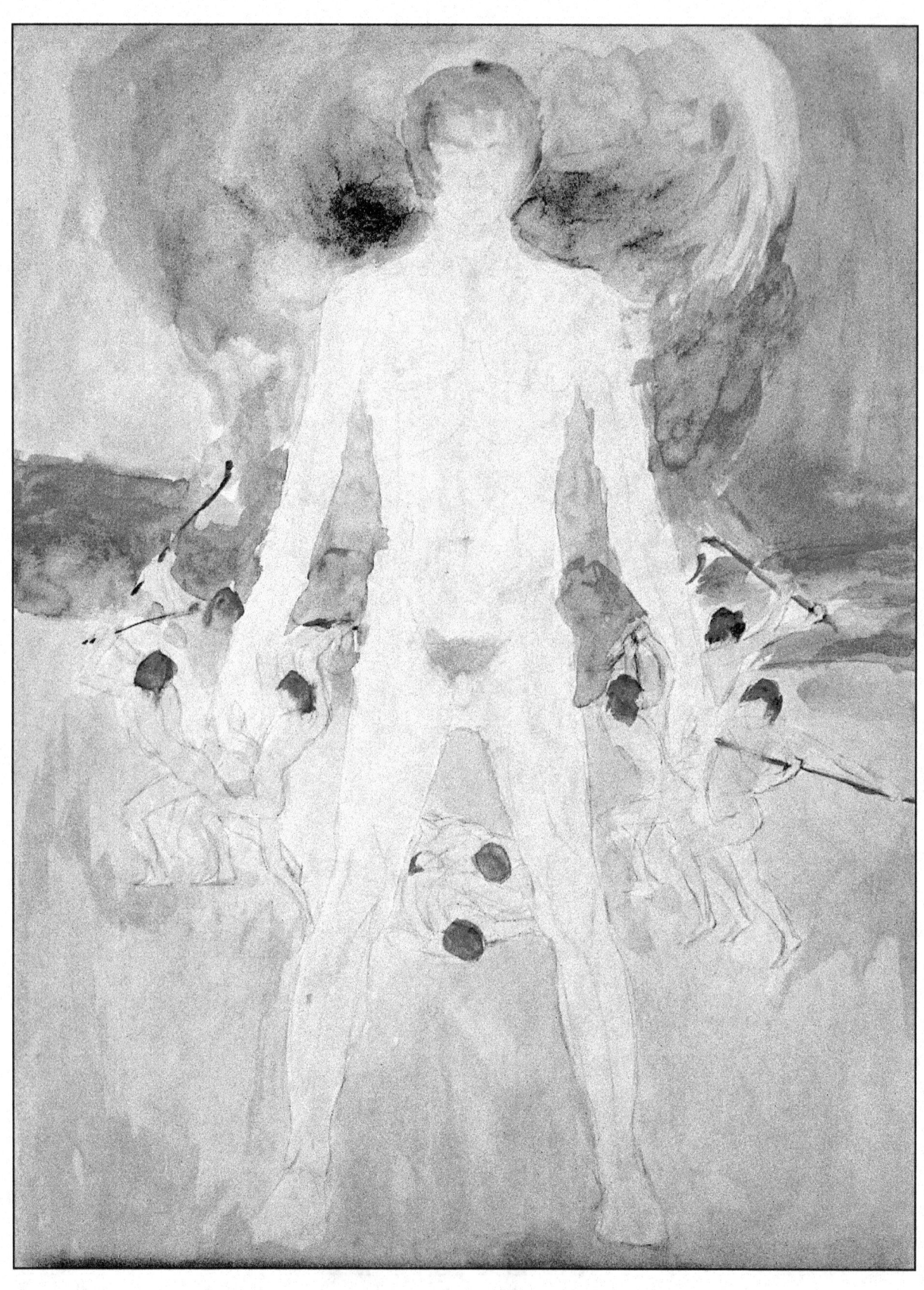

Watercolor, unfinished

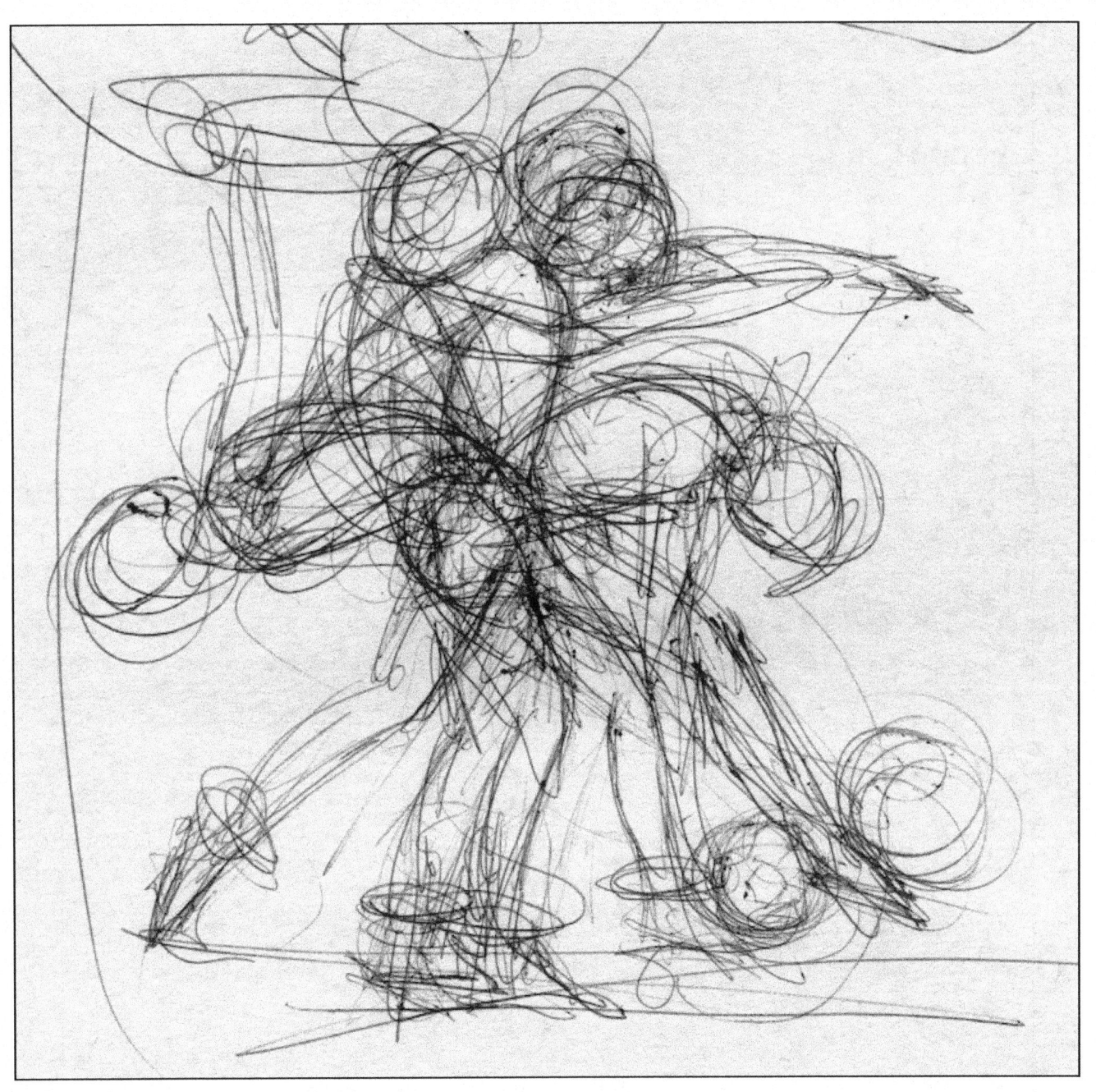

Soccer Player

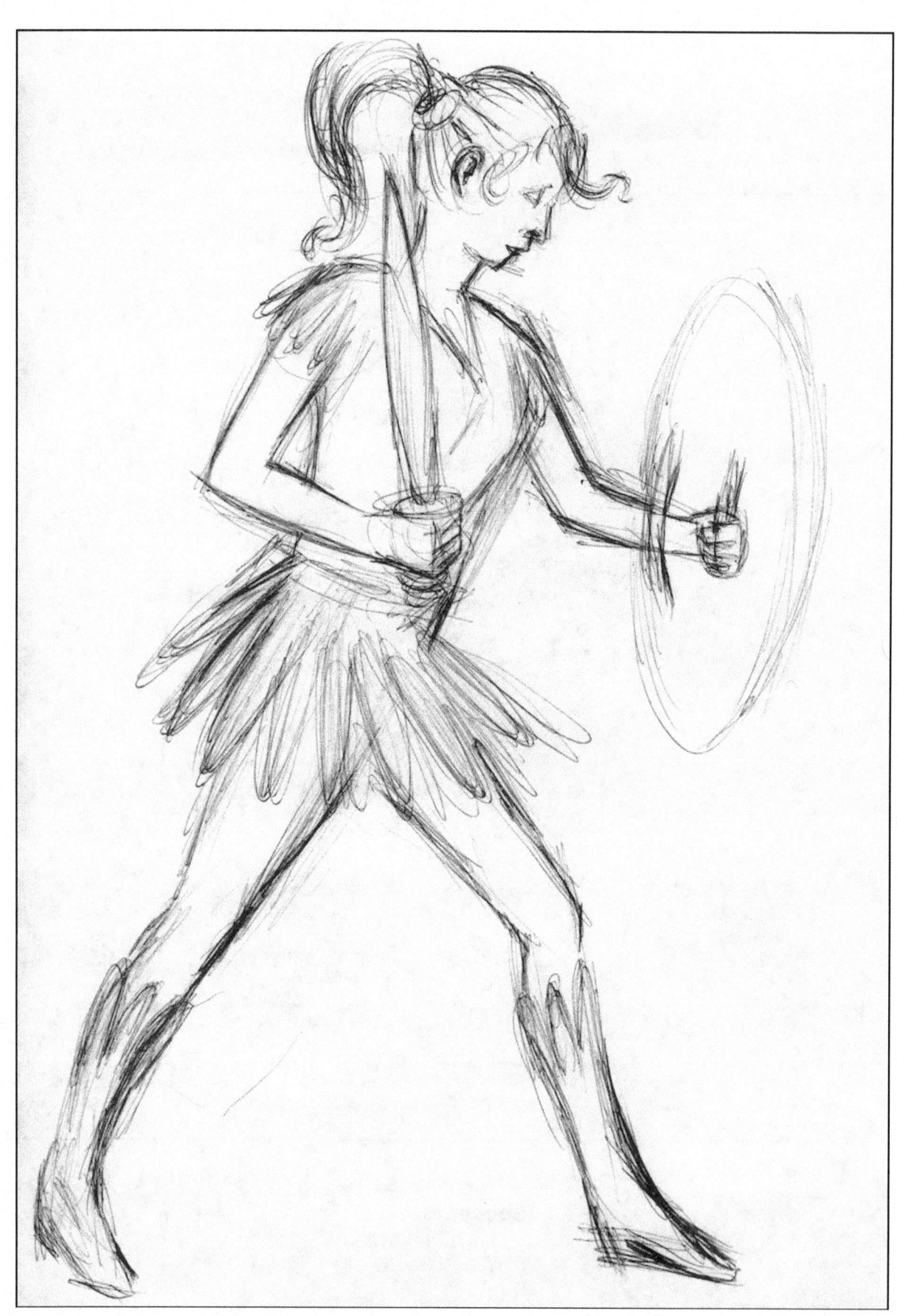

Amazonian Warrior

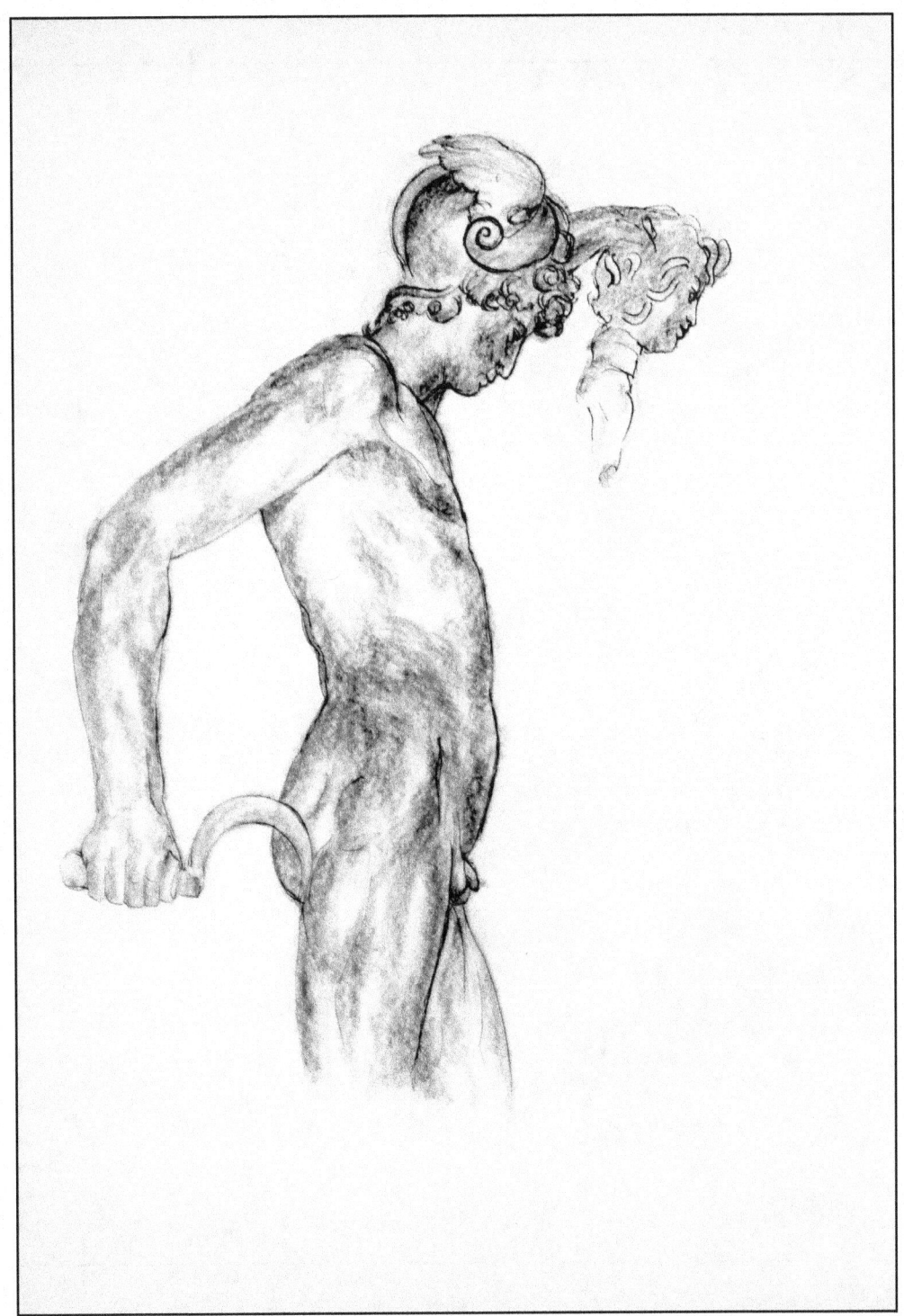

Perseus

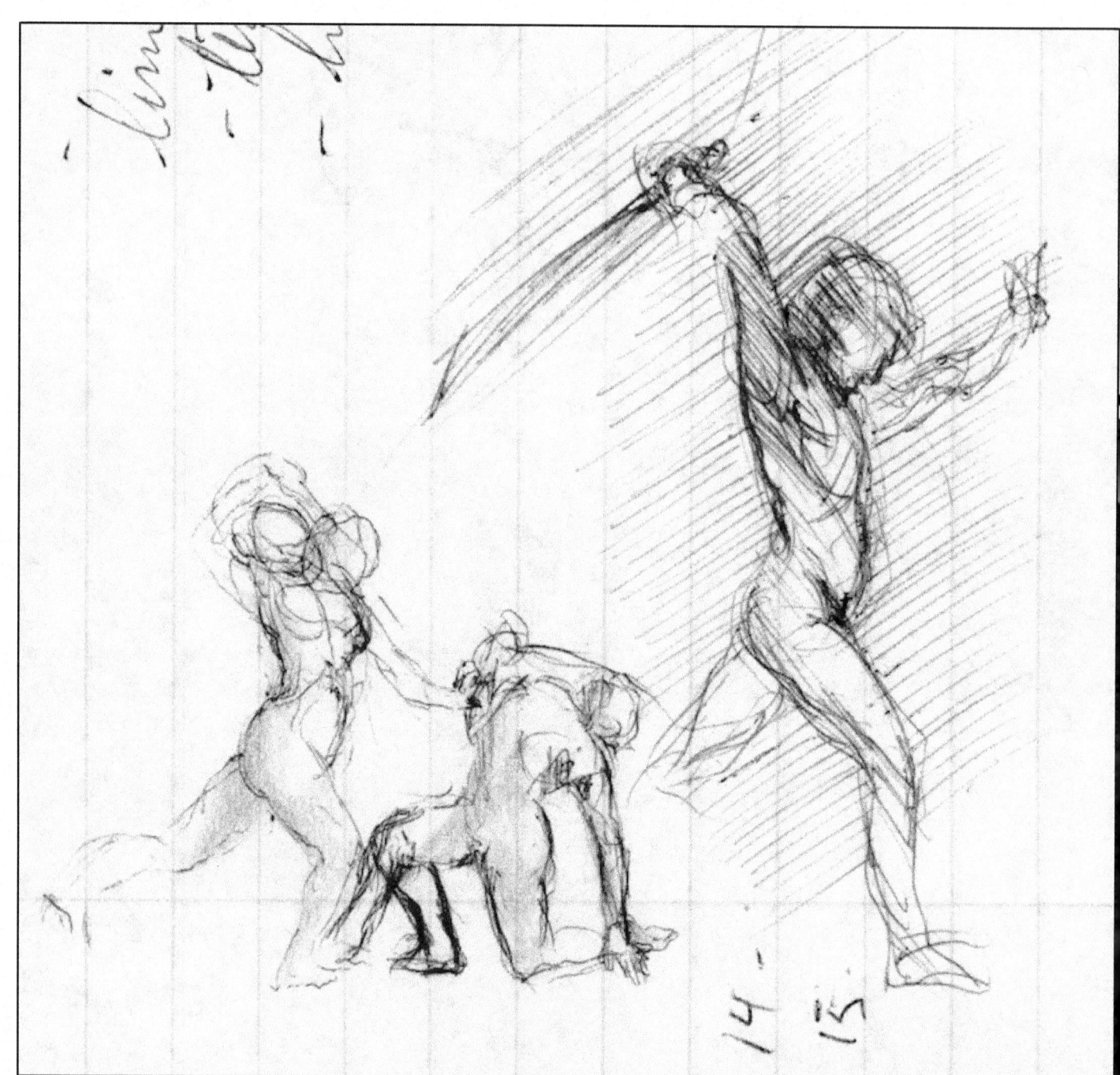

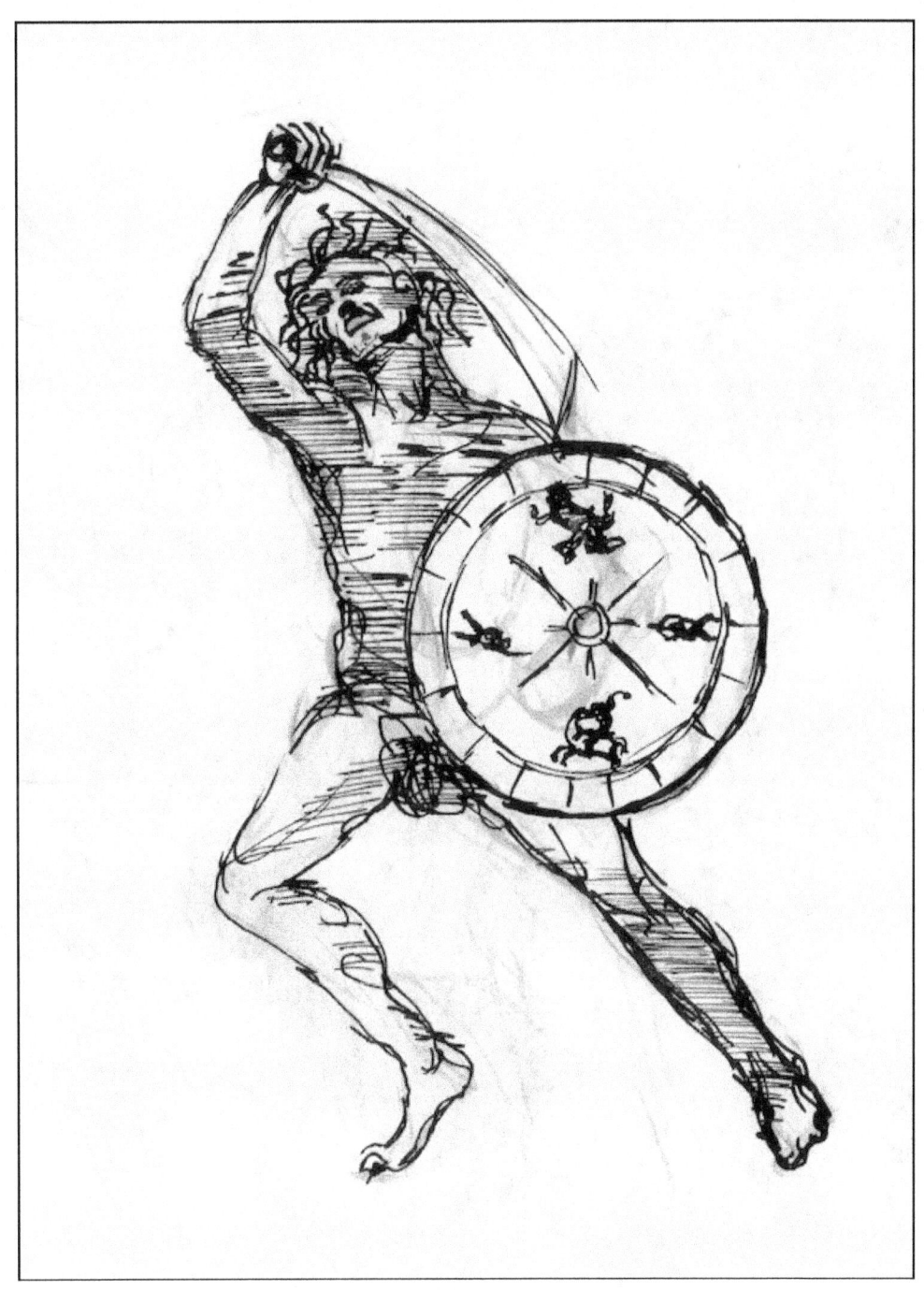

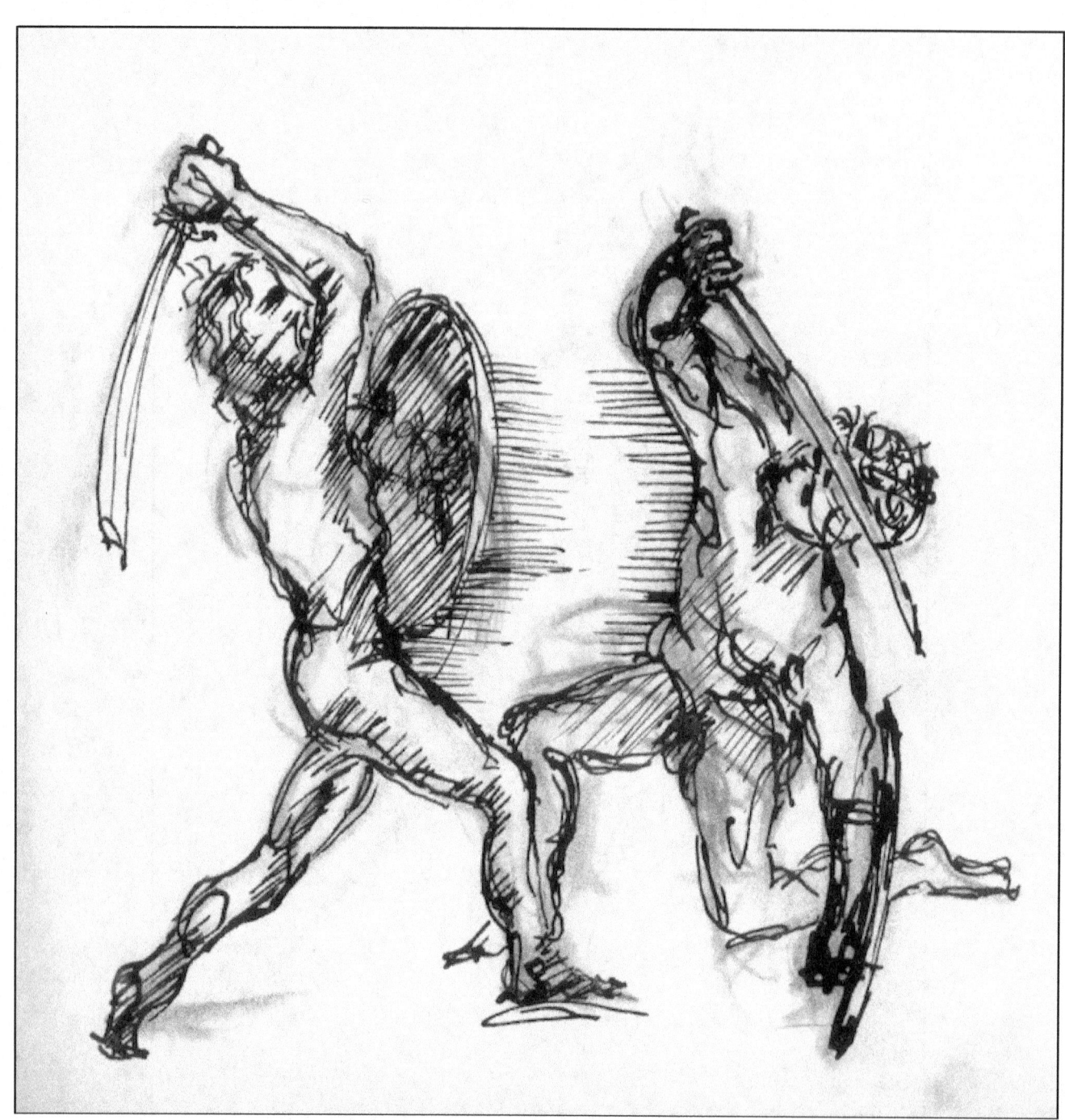

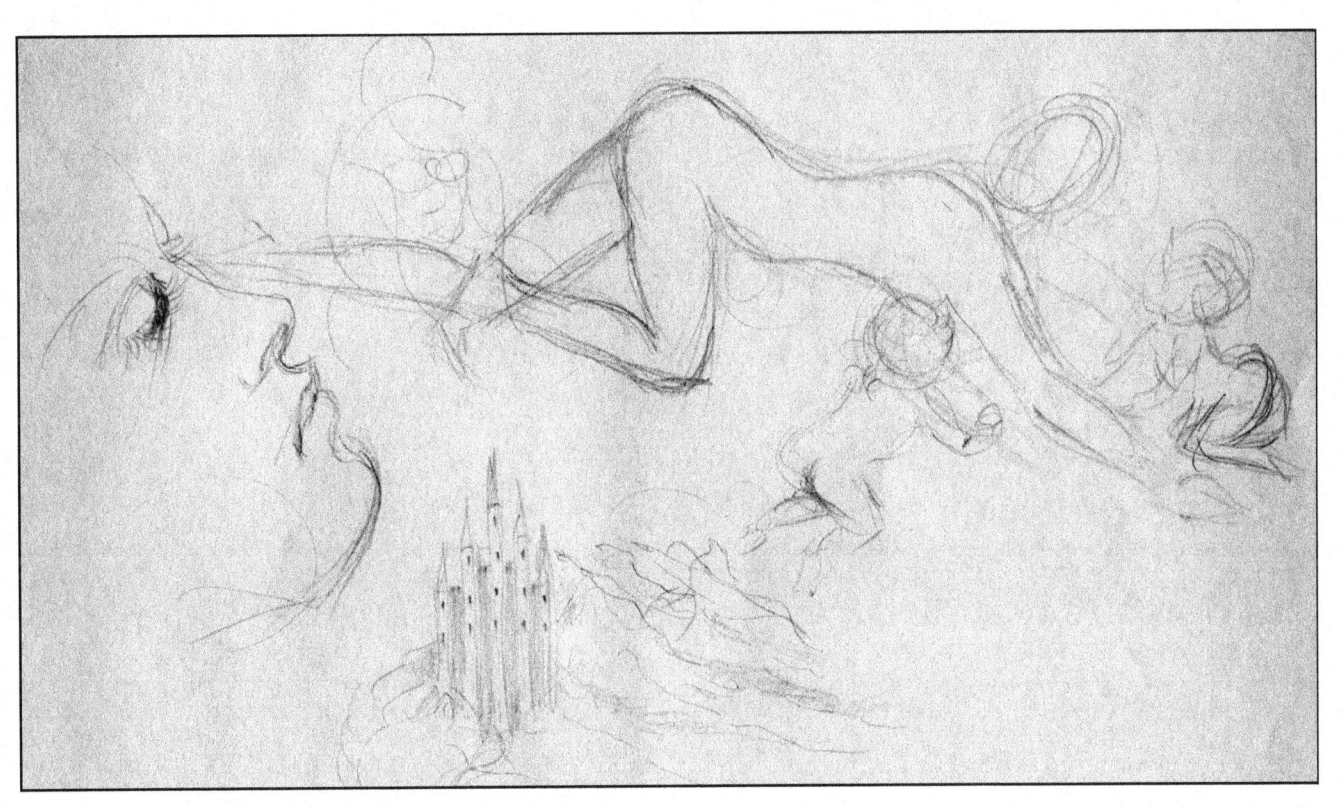

Playing with Children

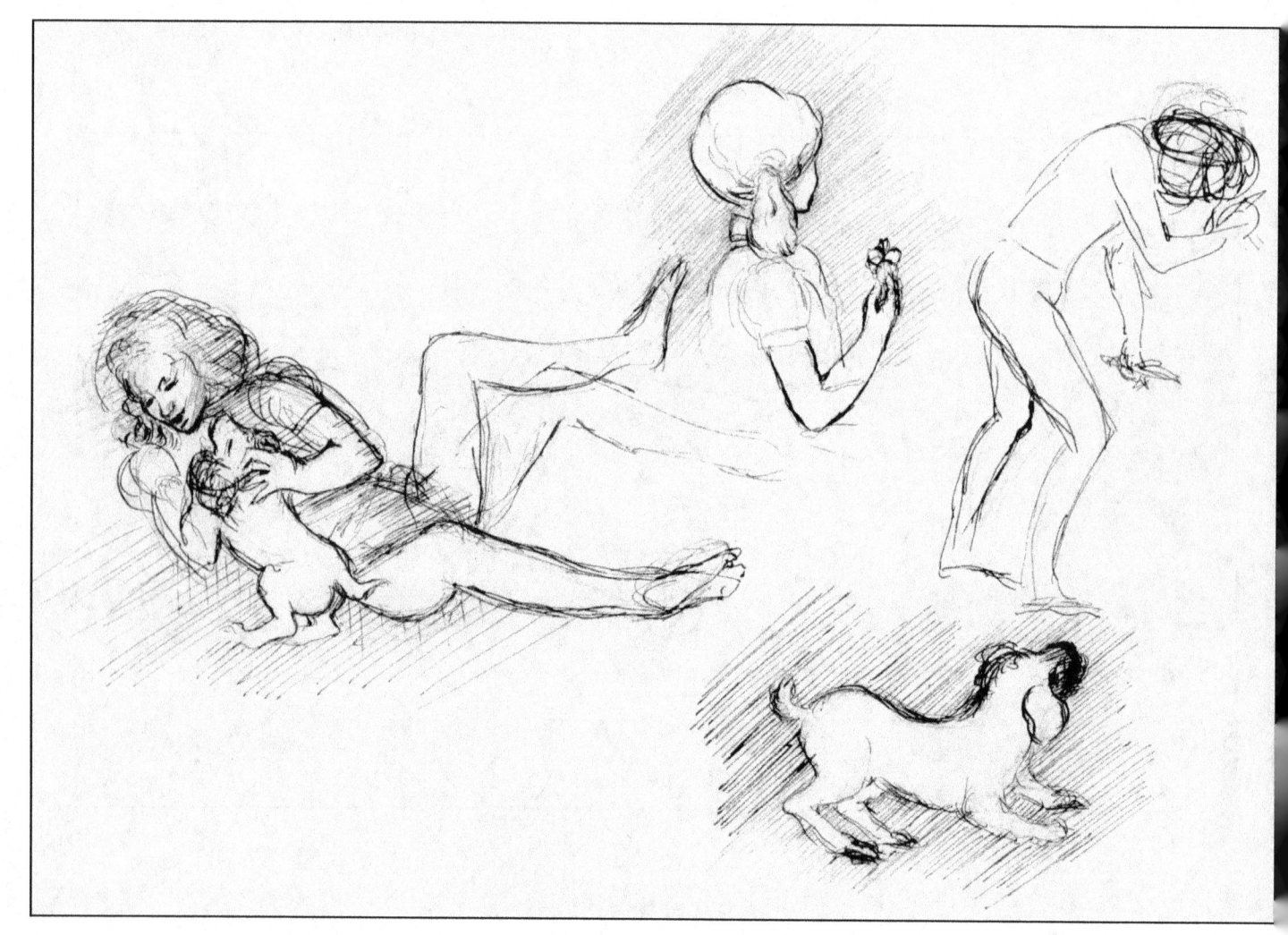

Playing with Dog

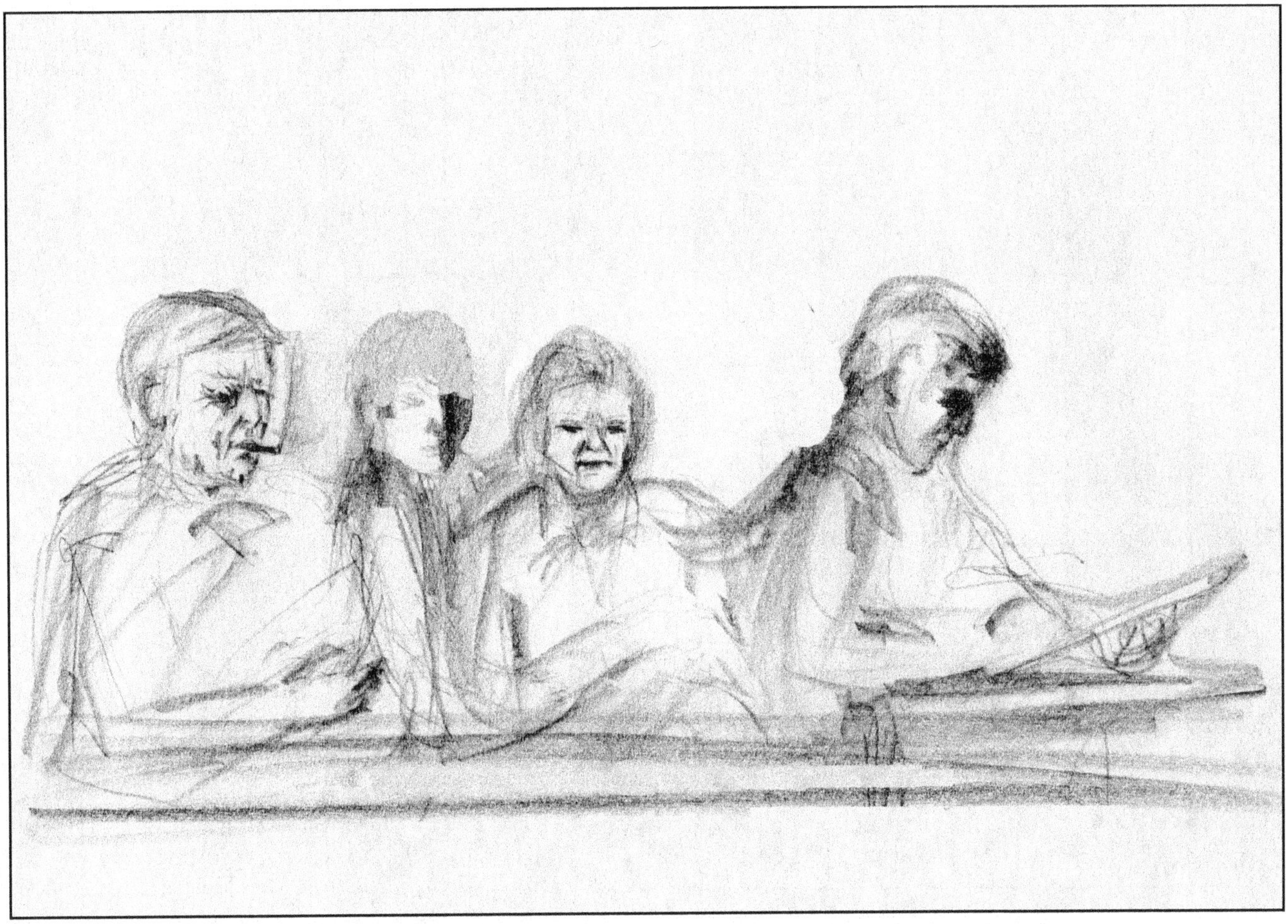

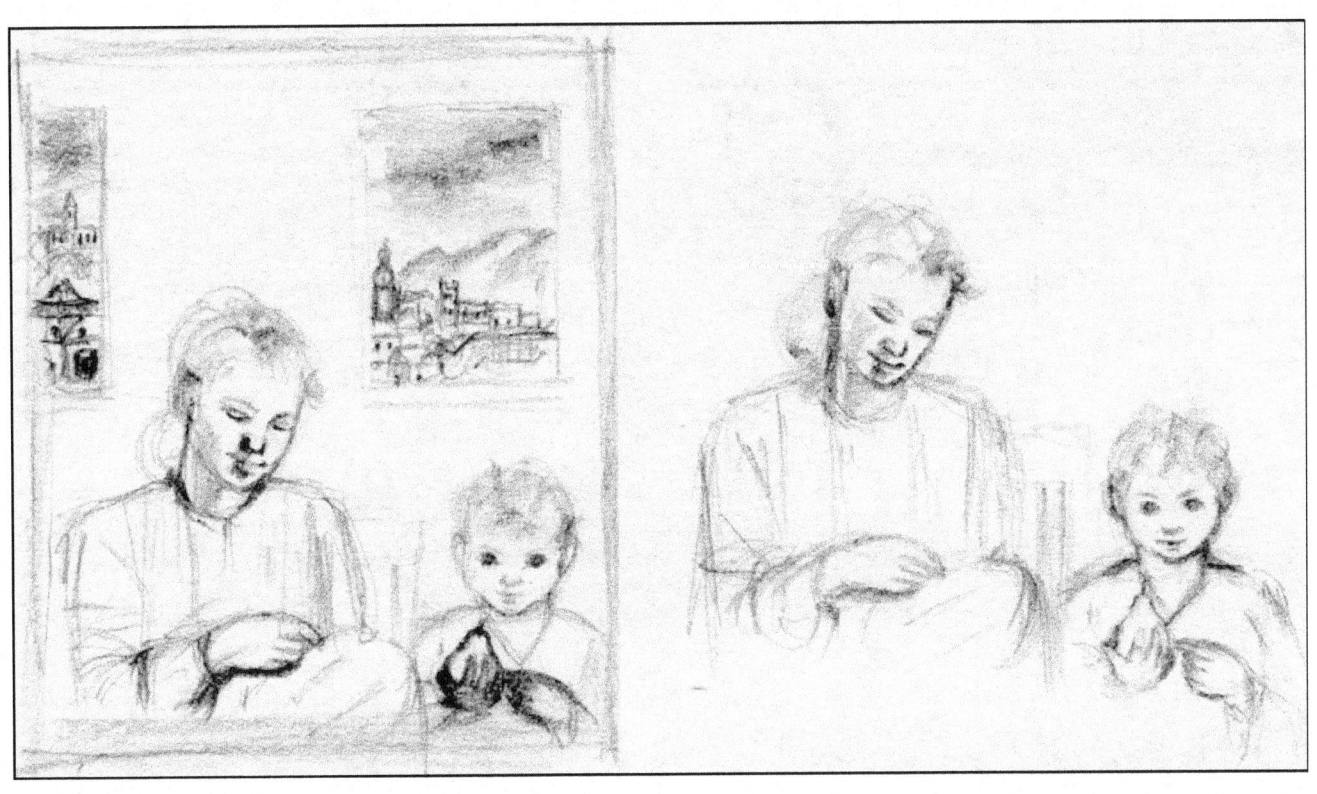

Top: Early Days in Canada; Bottom: Sepino as Backdrop

433

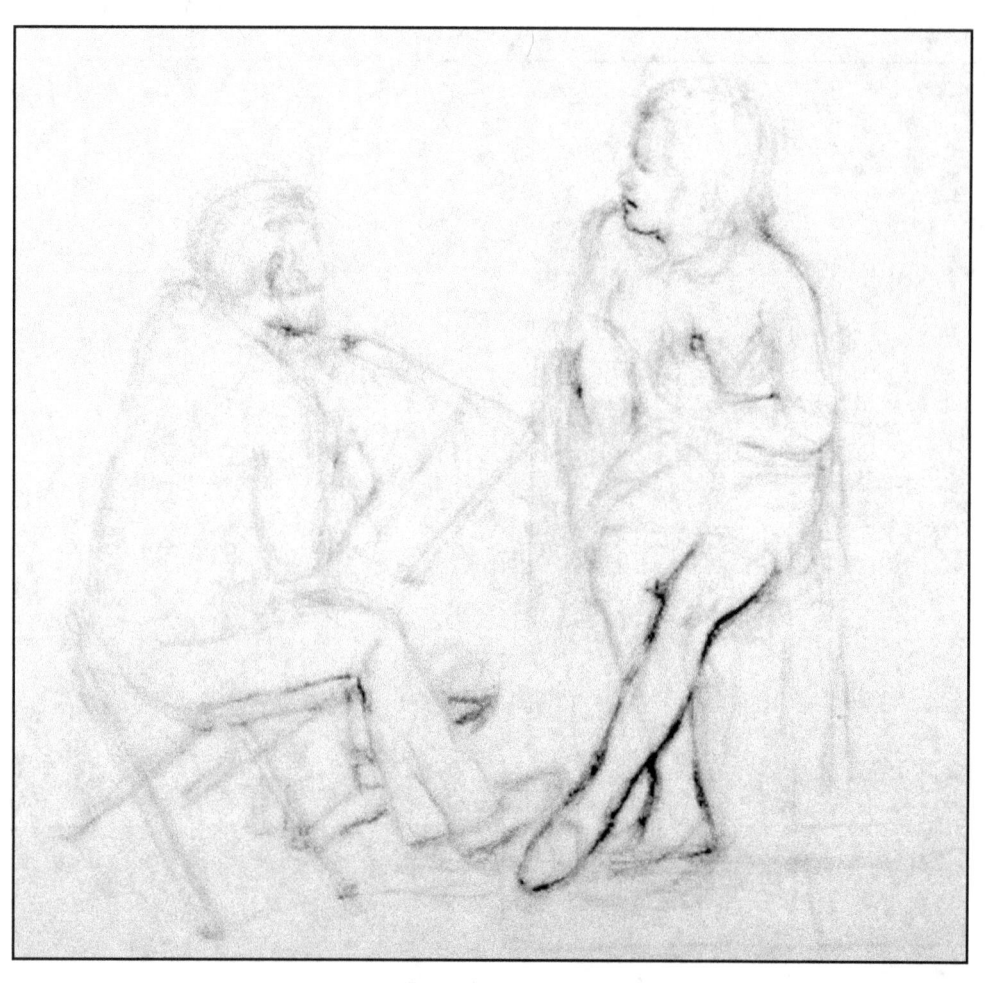

Scenes from My Life

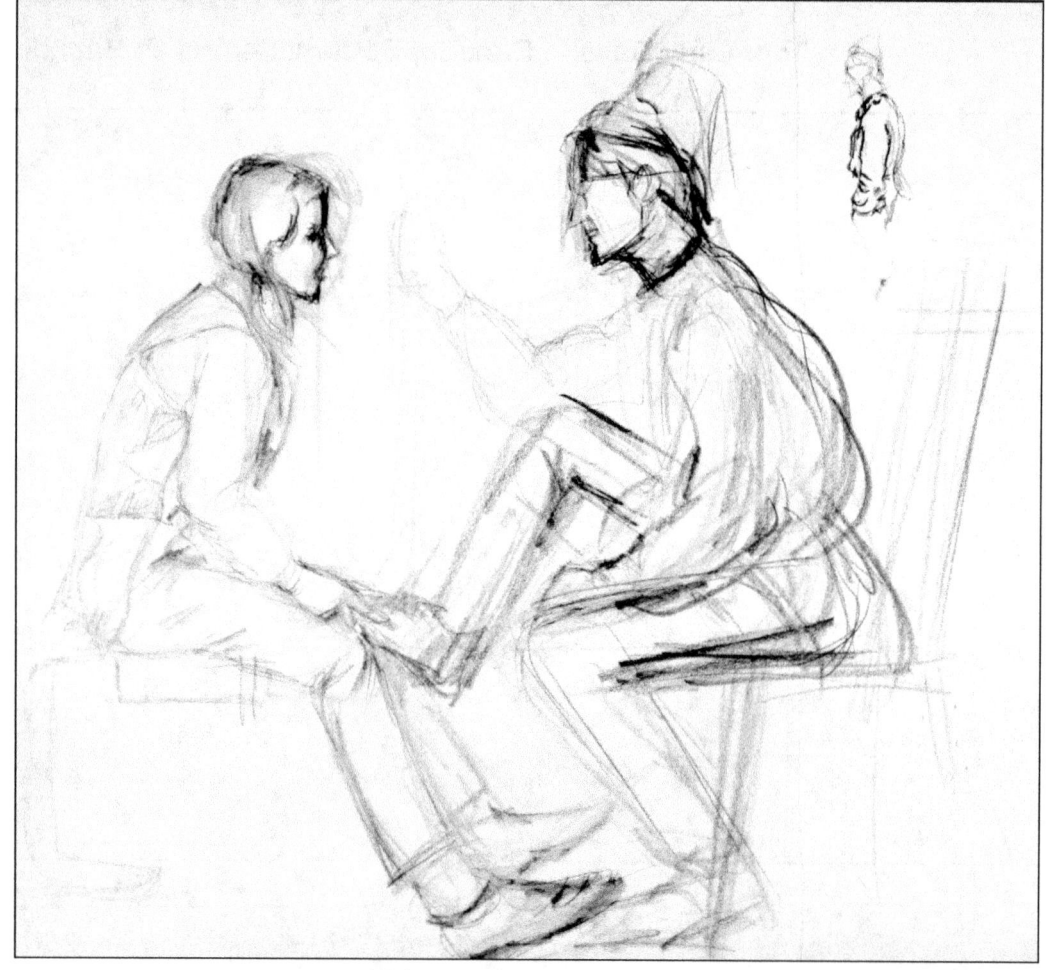

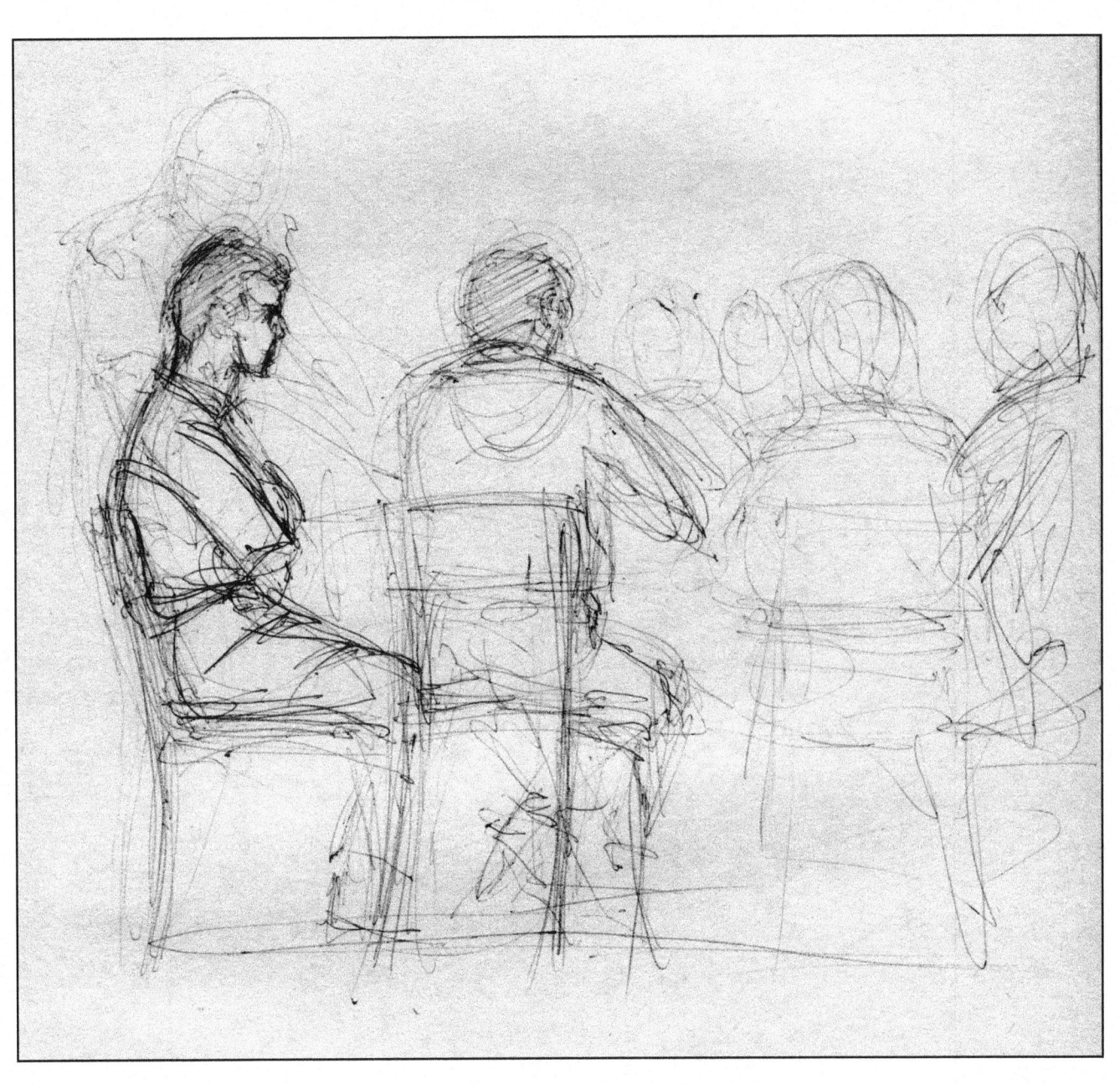

Group of People during Their Lunch Break

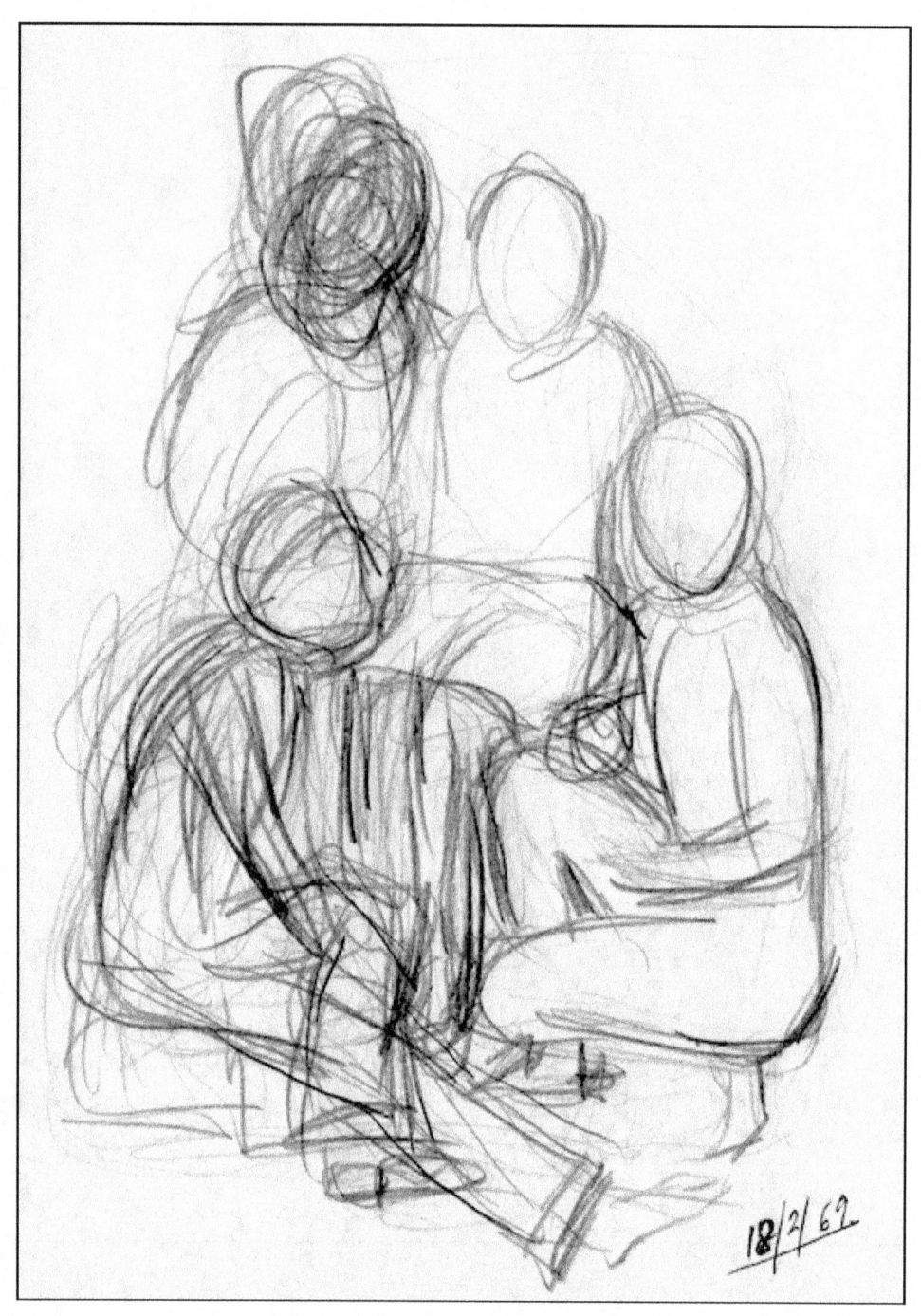

Family Group Blueprint

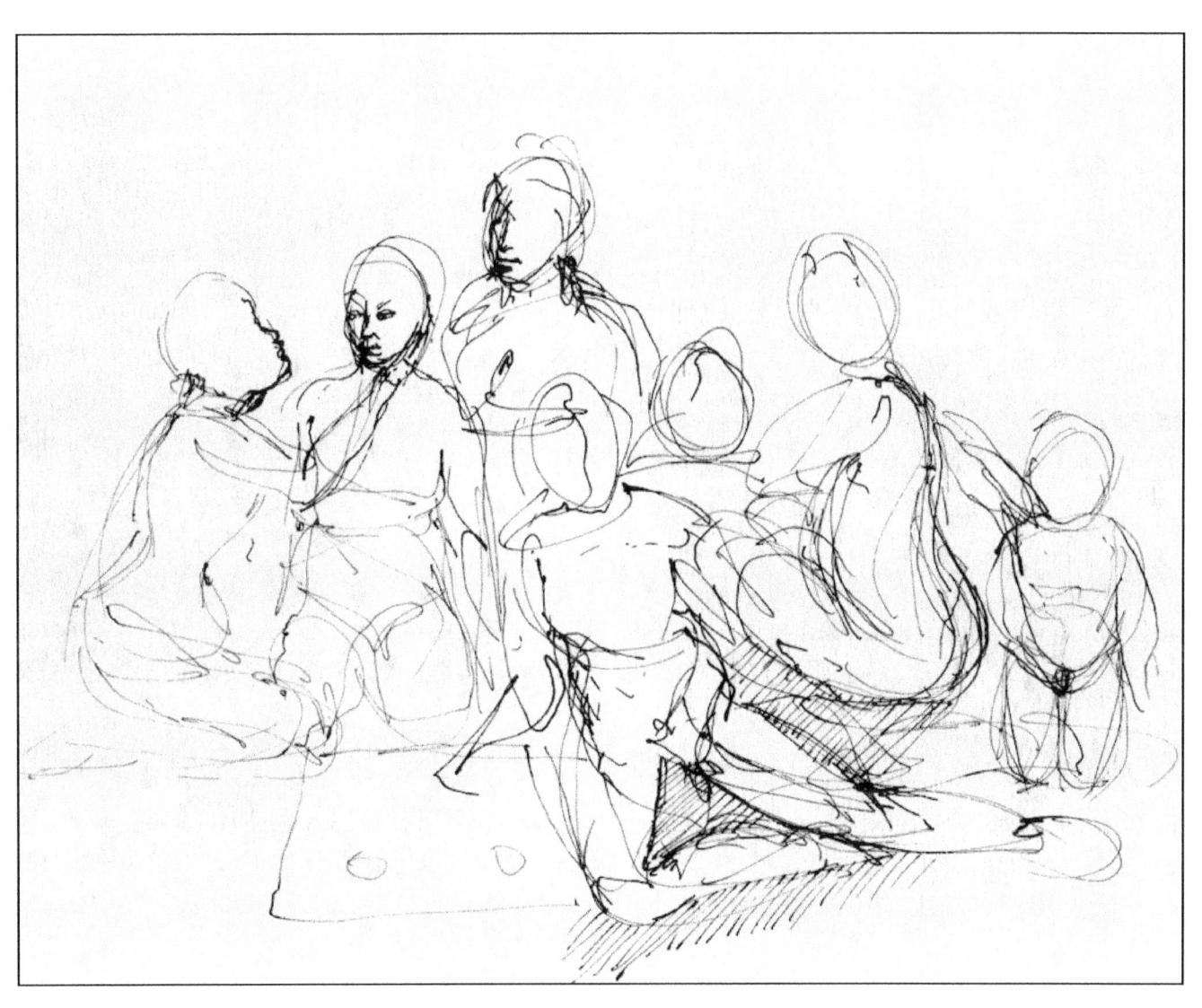

Family Group Blueprint

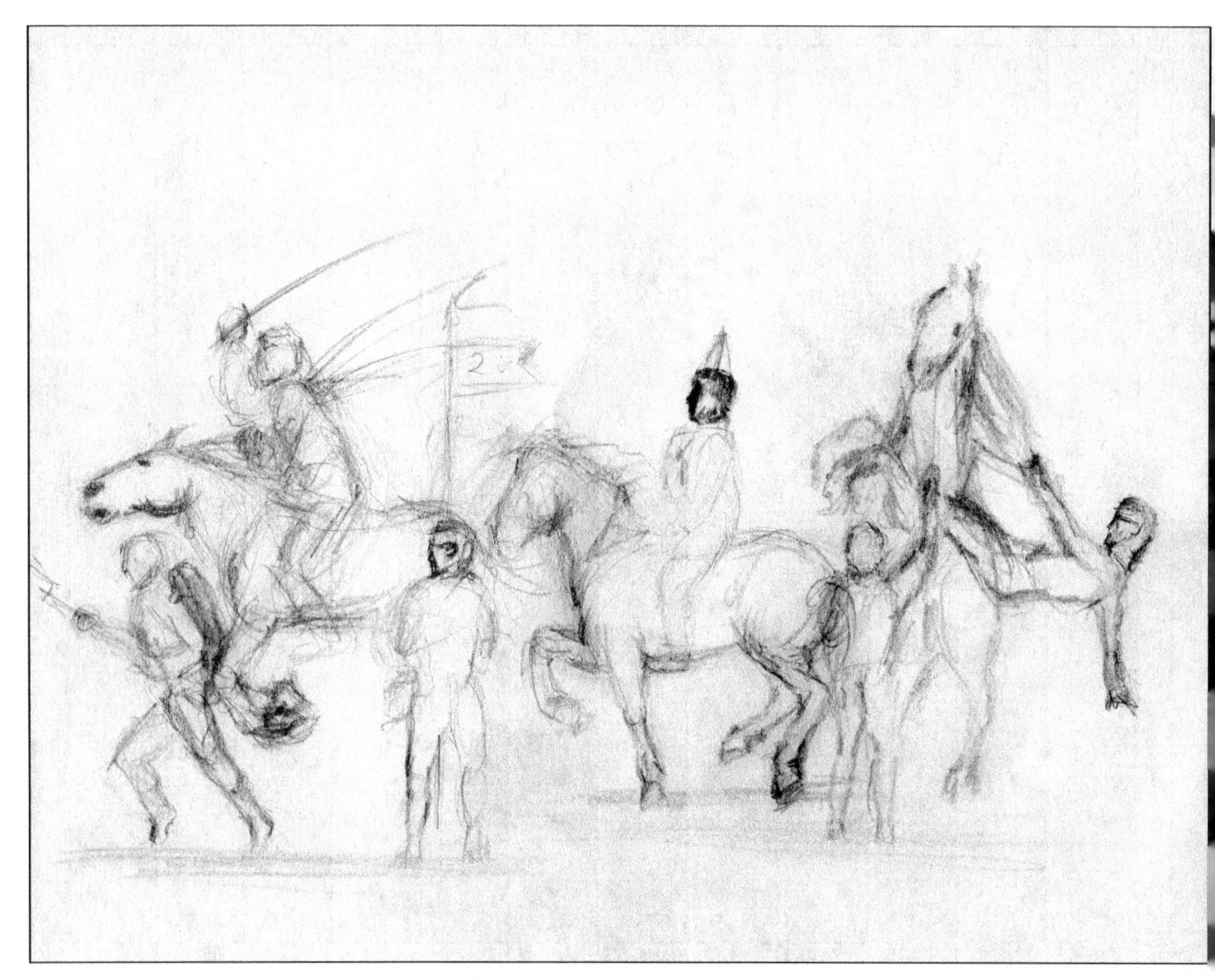

My Teachers in High School: Into Battle!

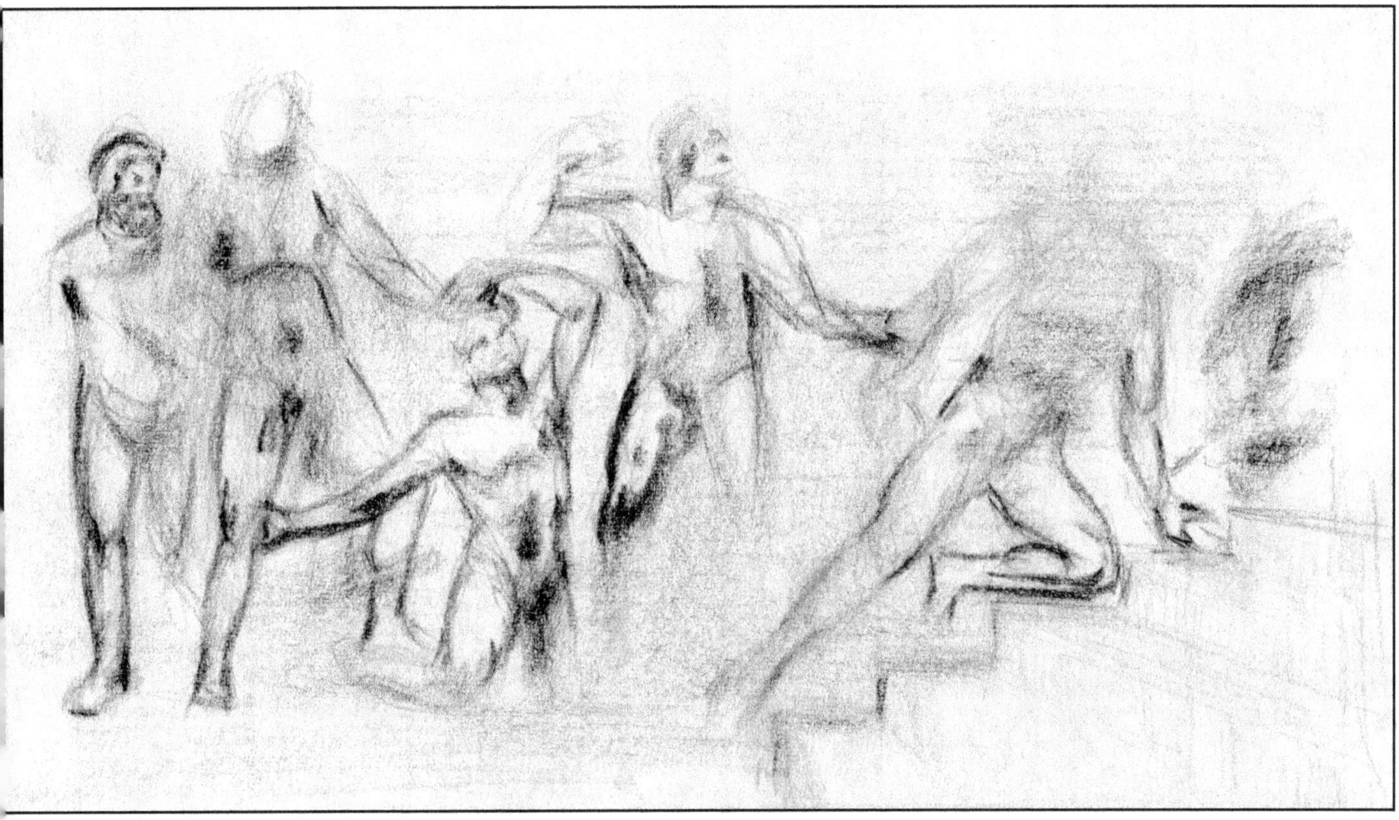

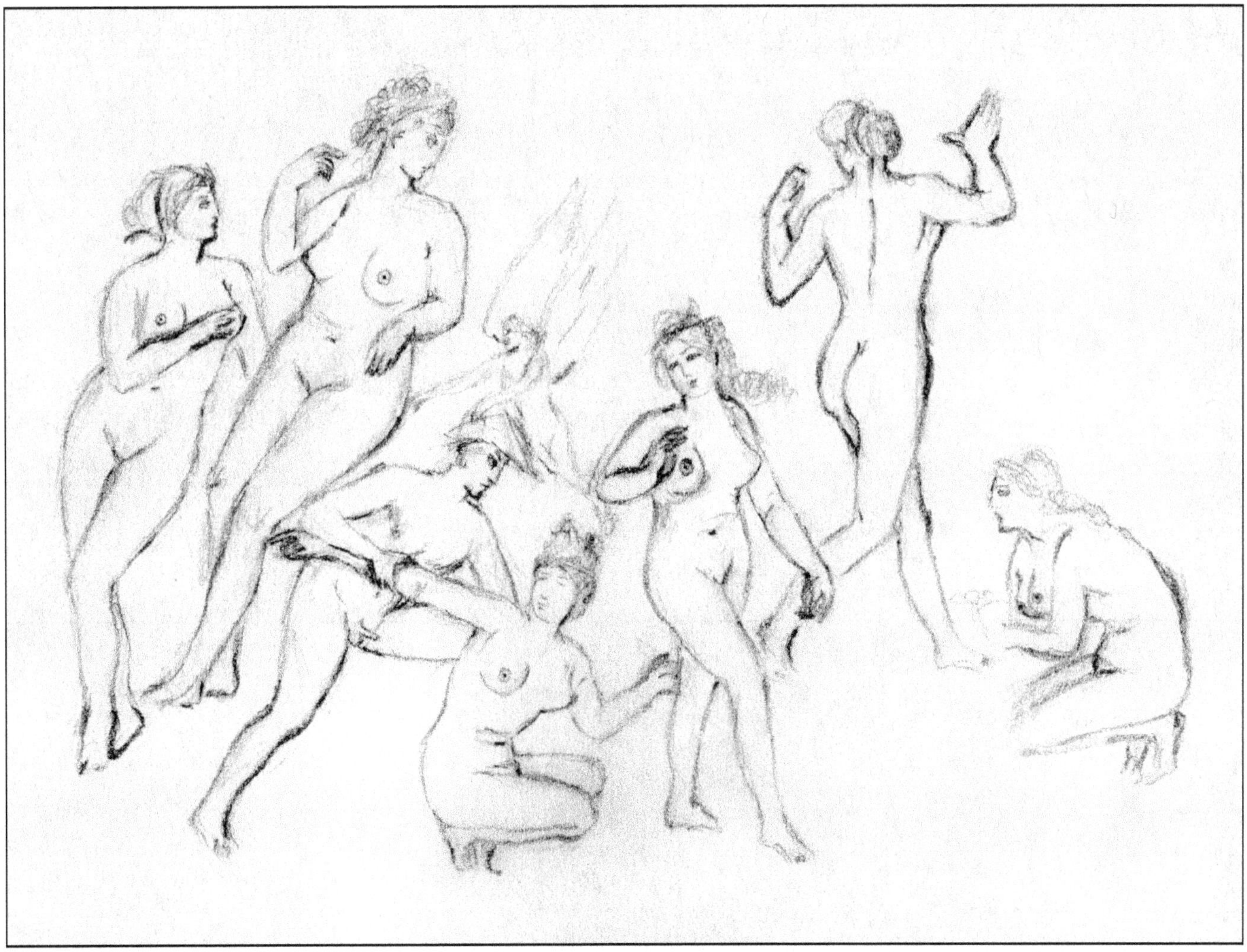

439

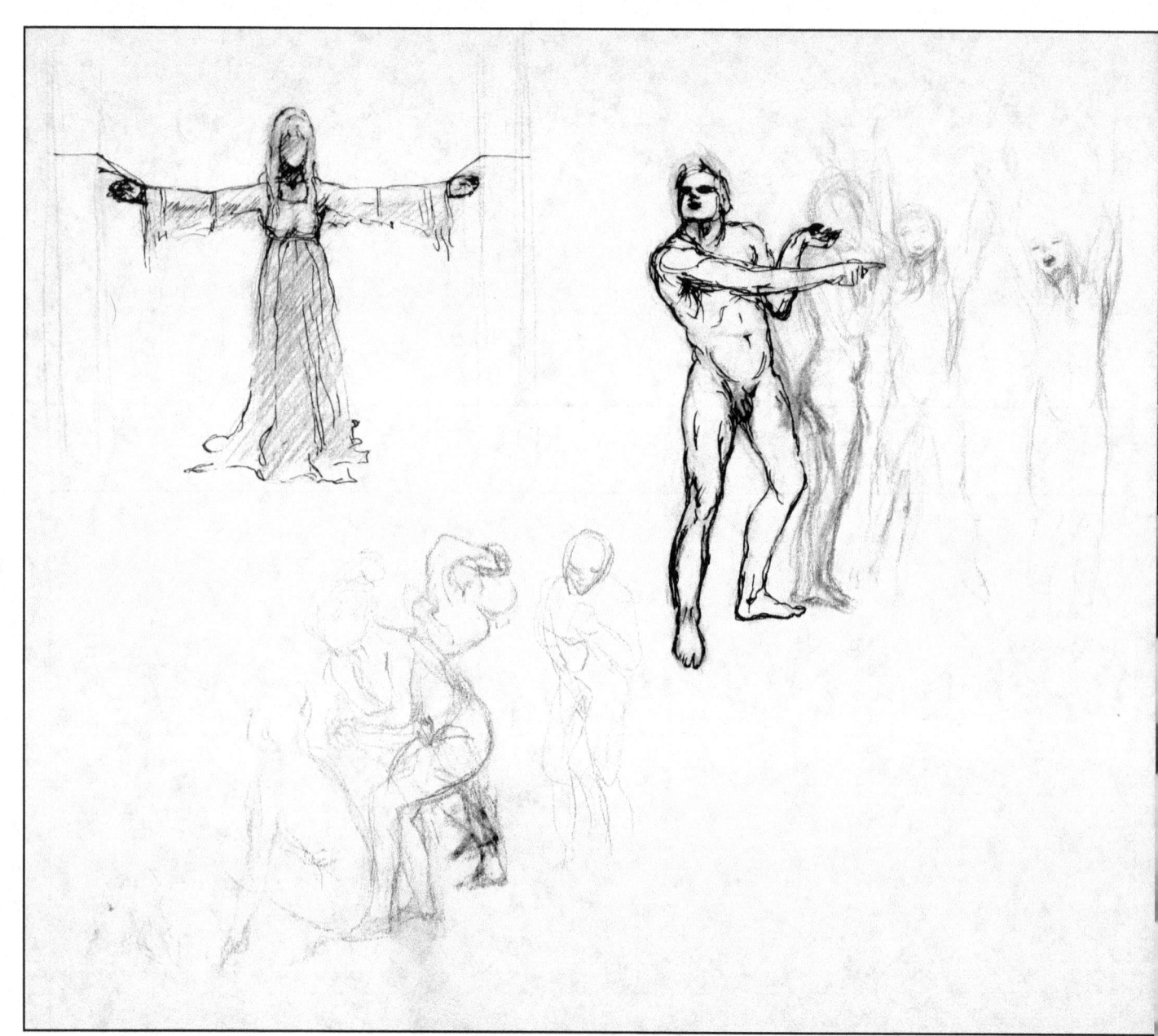

17. HUMAN & ANIMAL Composition

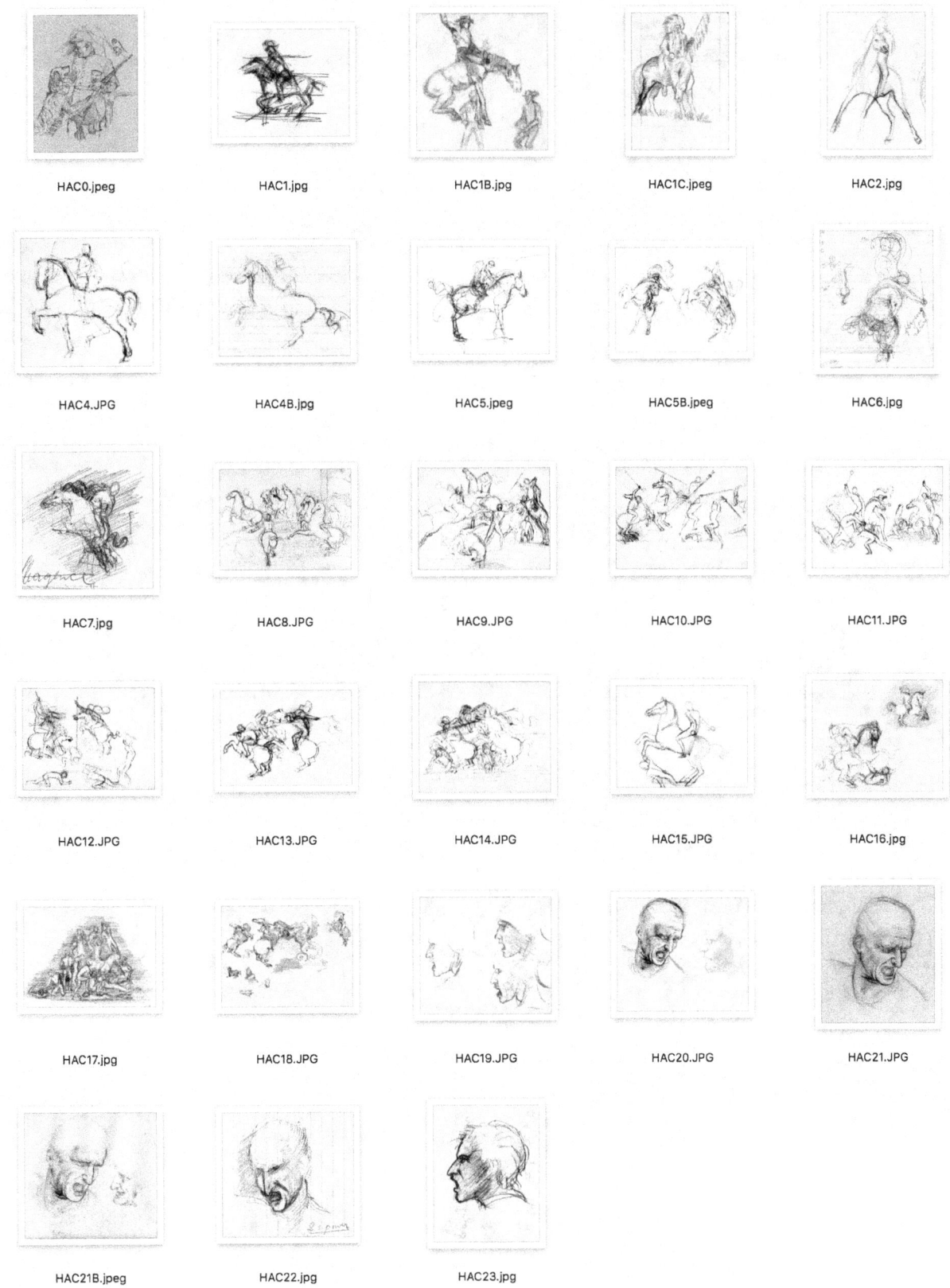

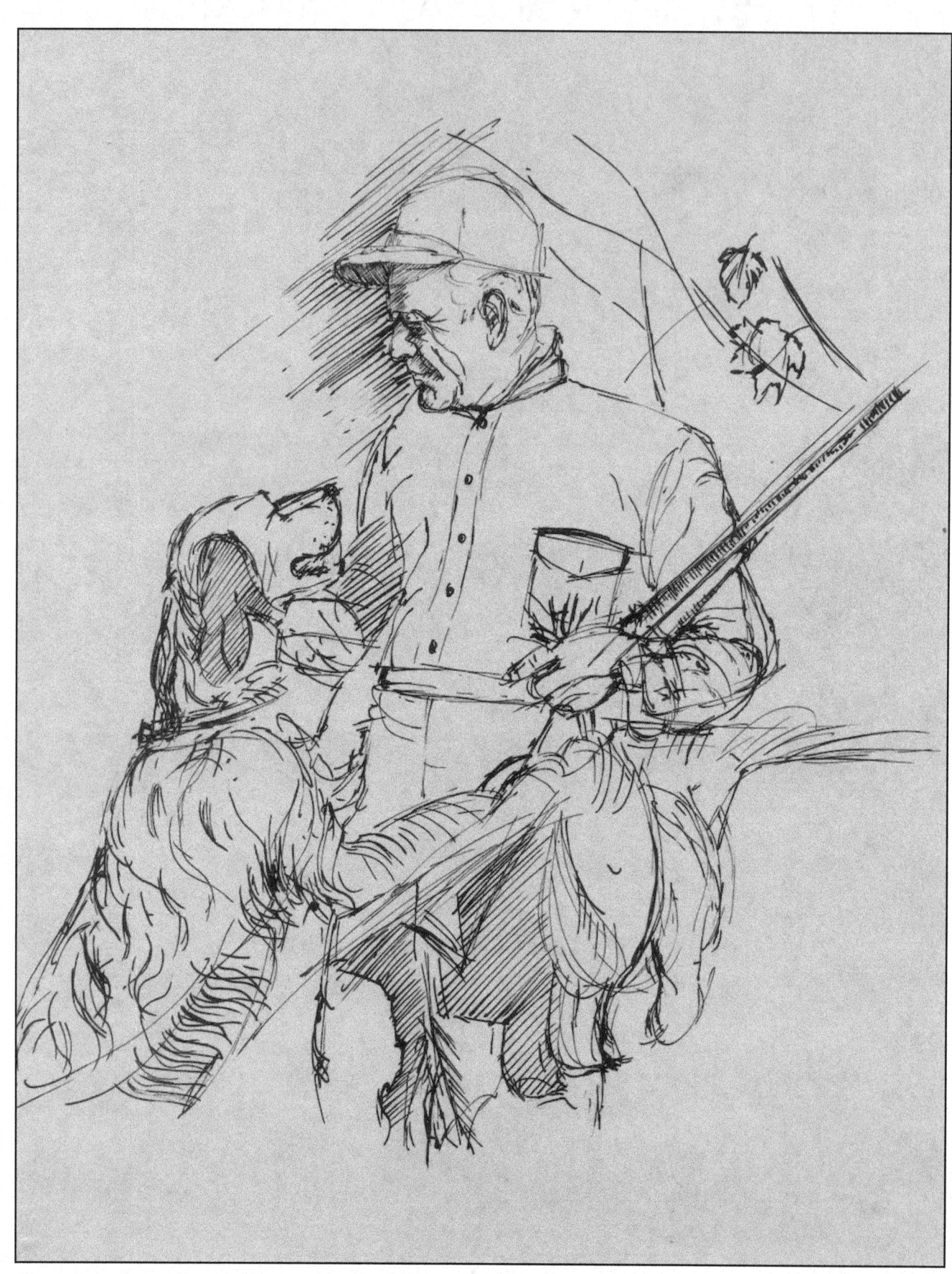

From the Cover of a Copybook

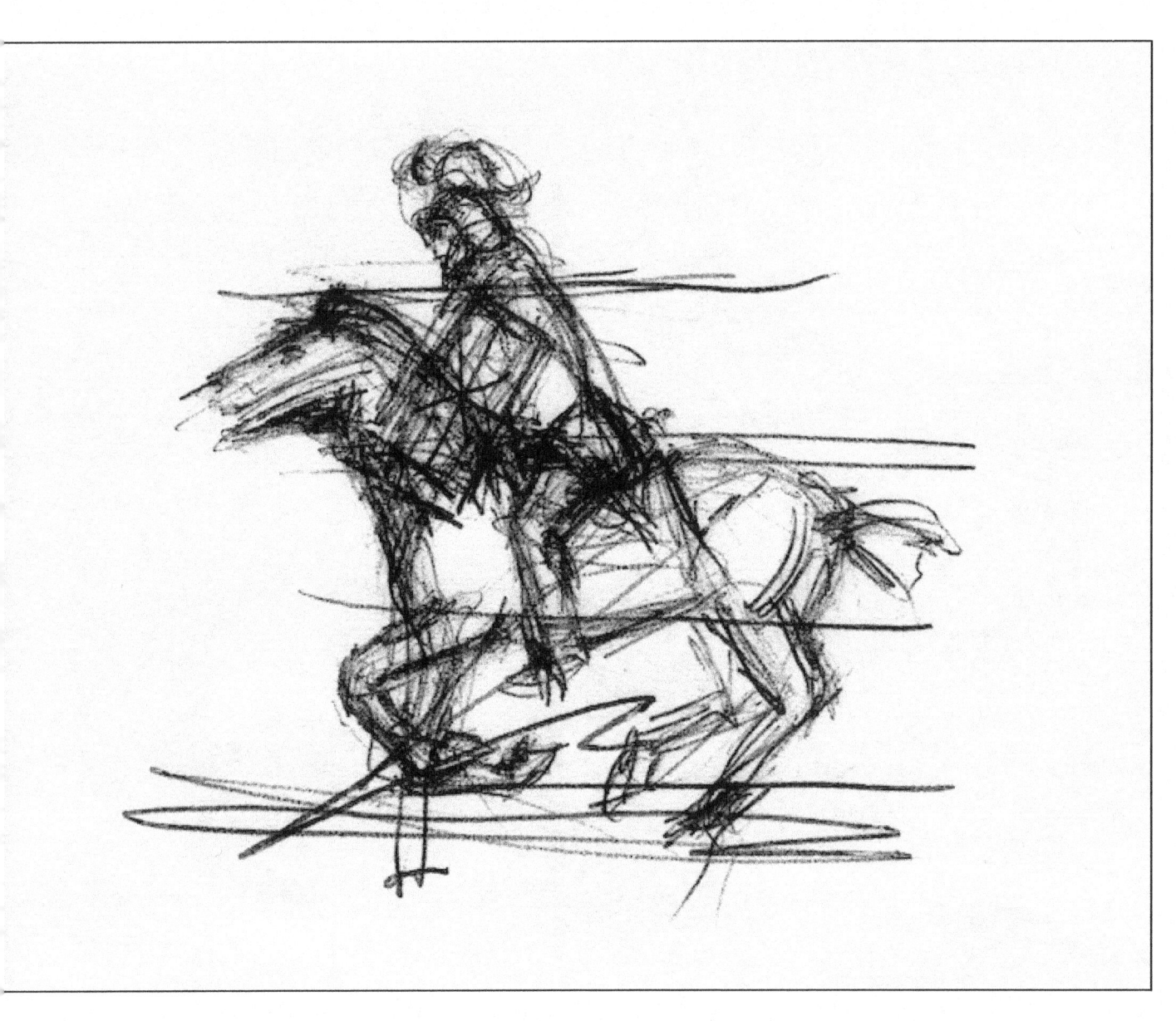

From 3"x5" Notepad, from Italy

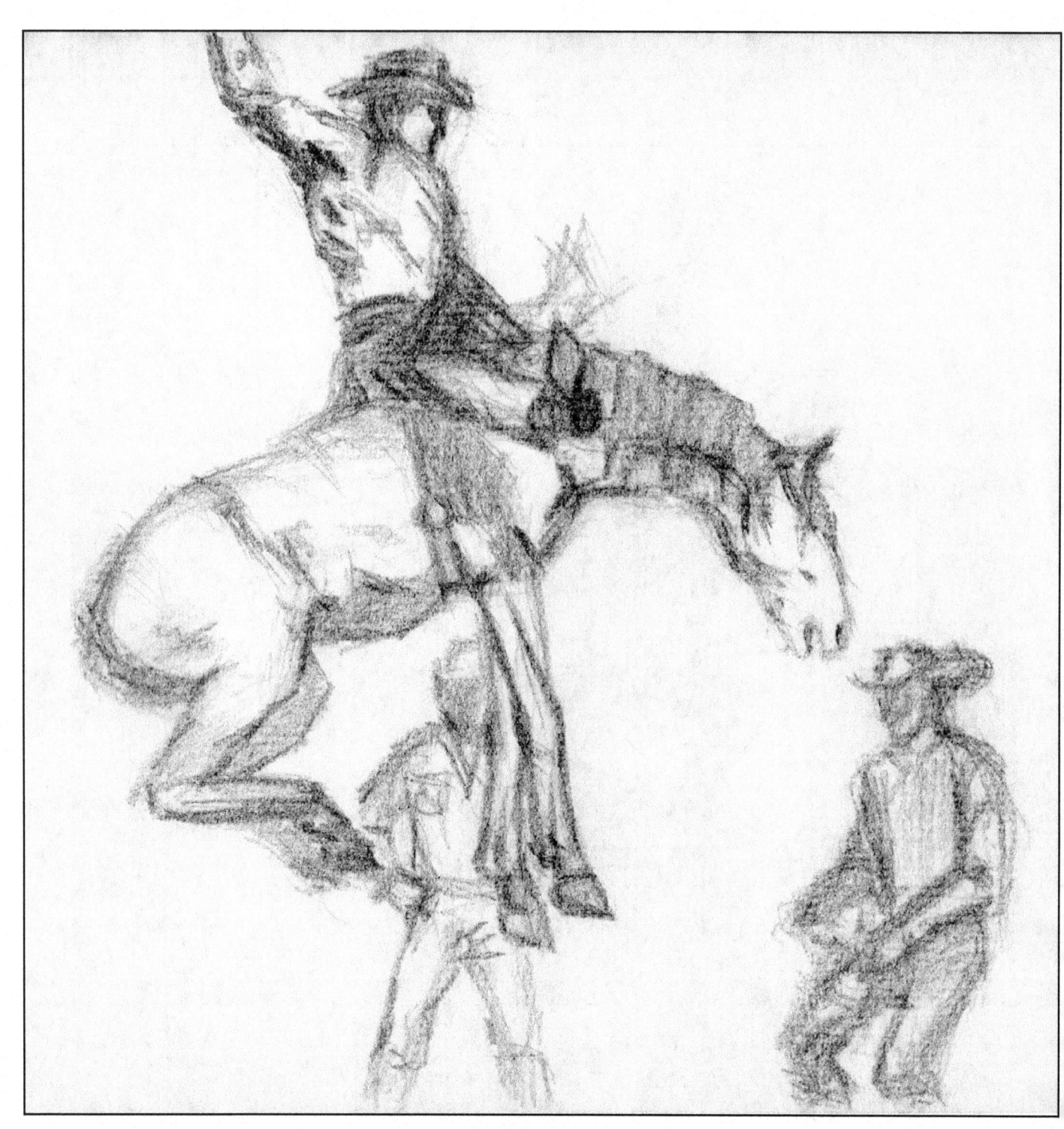

Before Leonardo's Horse

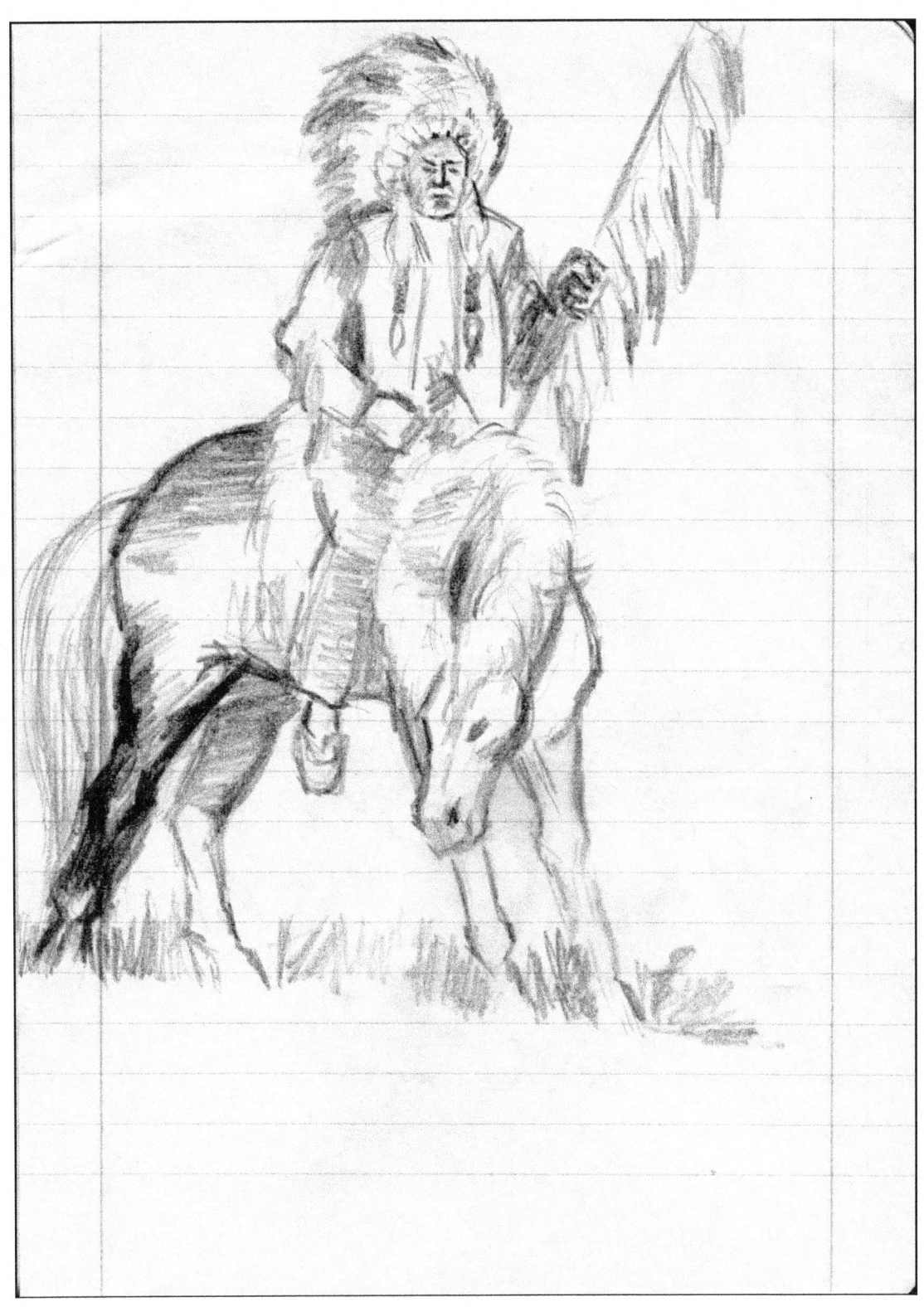

Before Leonardo's Horse

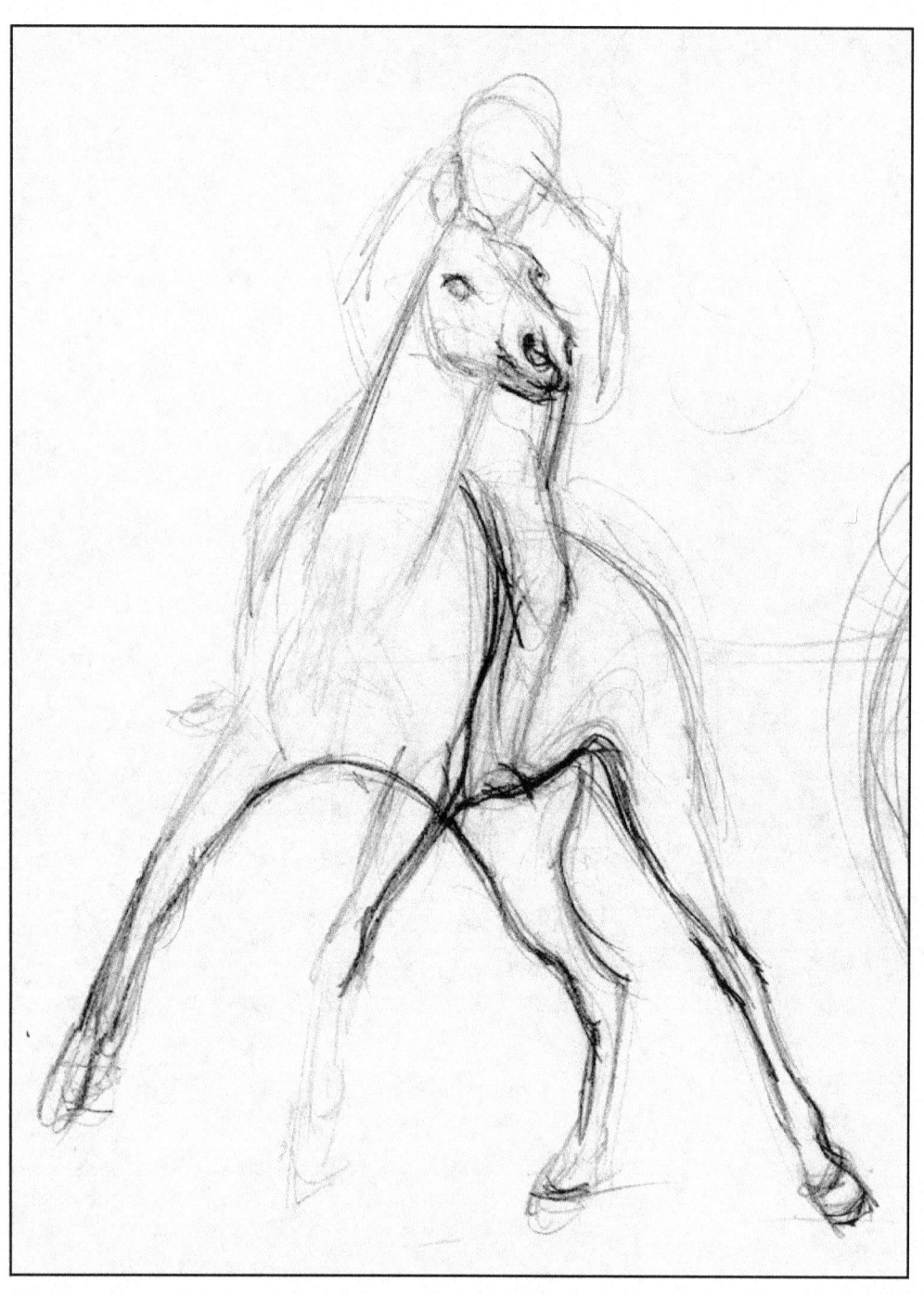

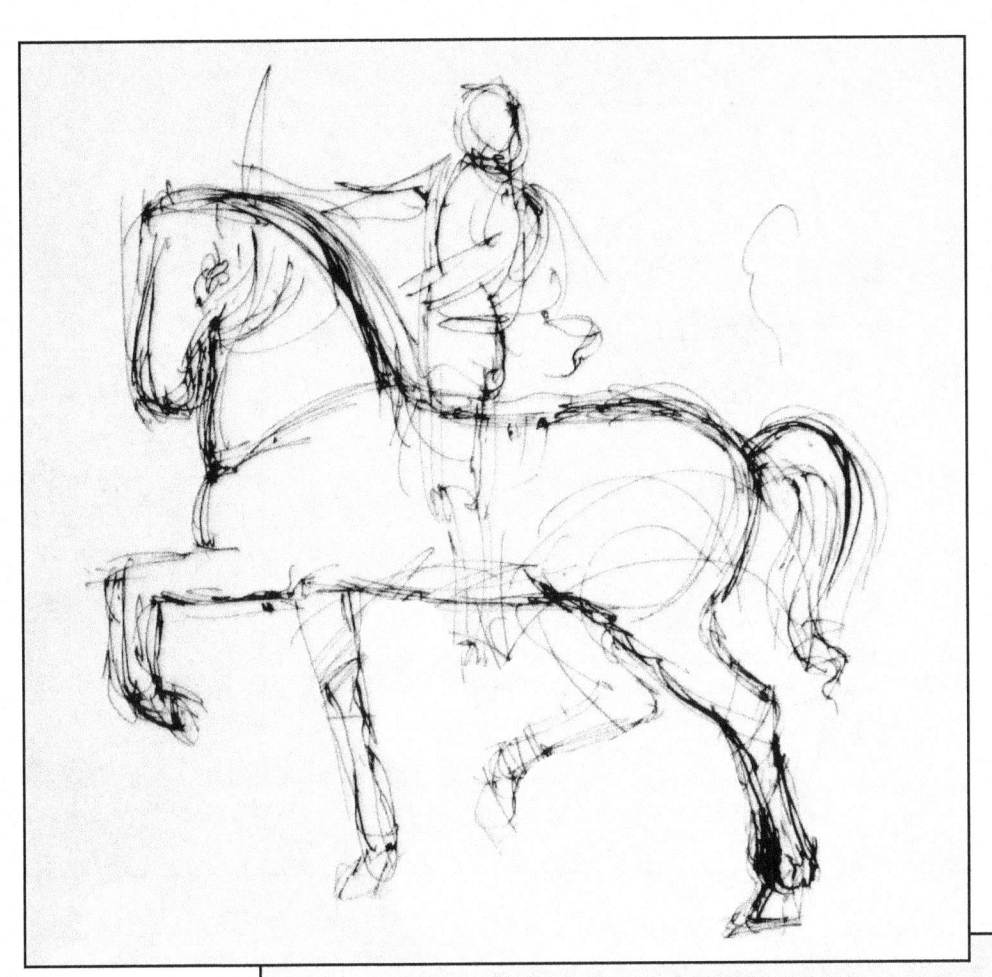
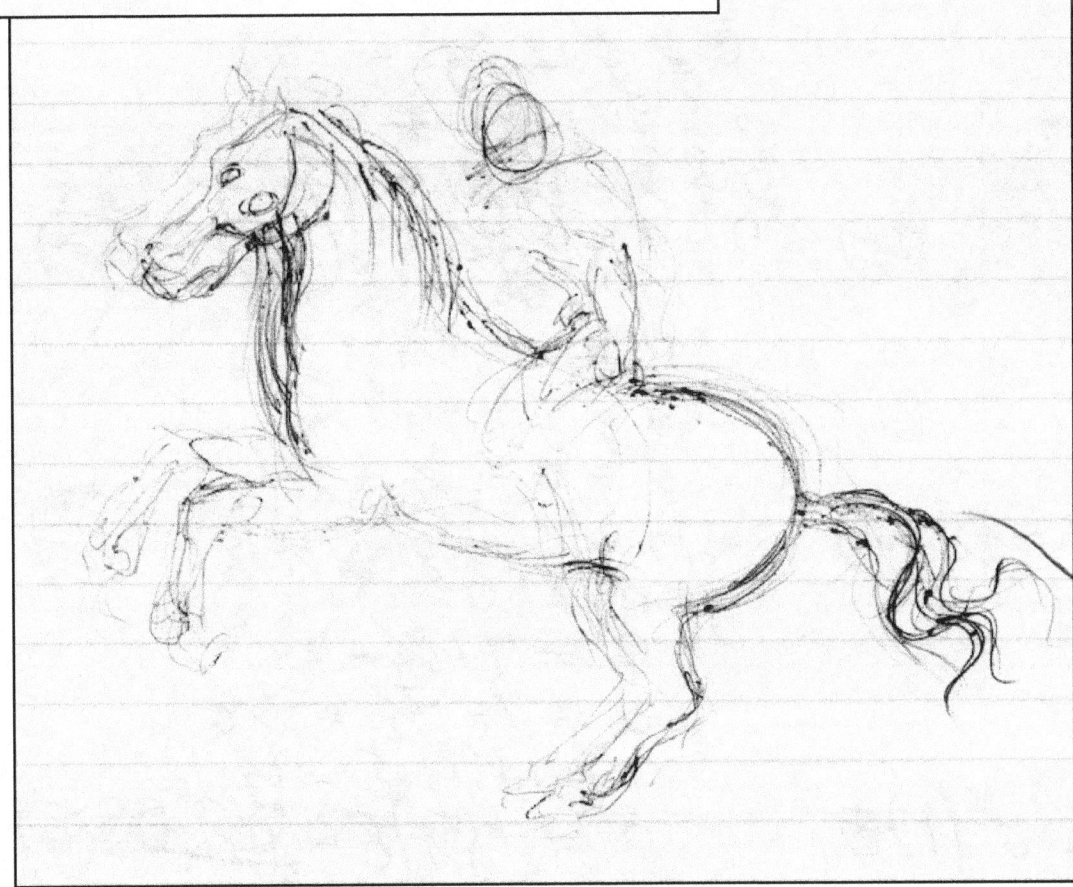

Leonardo's Horse

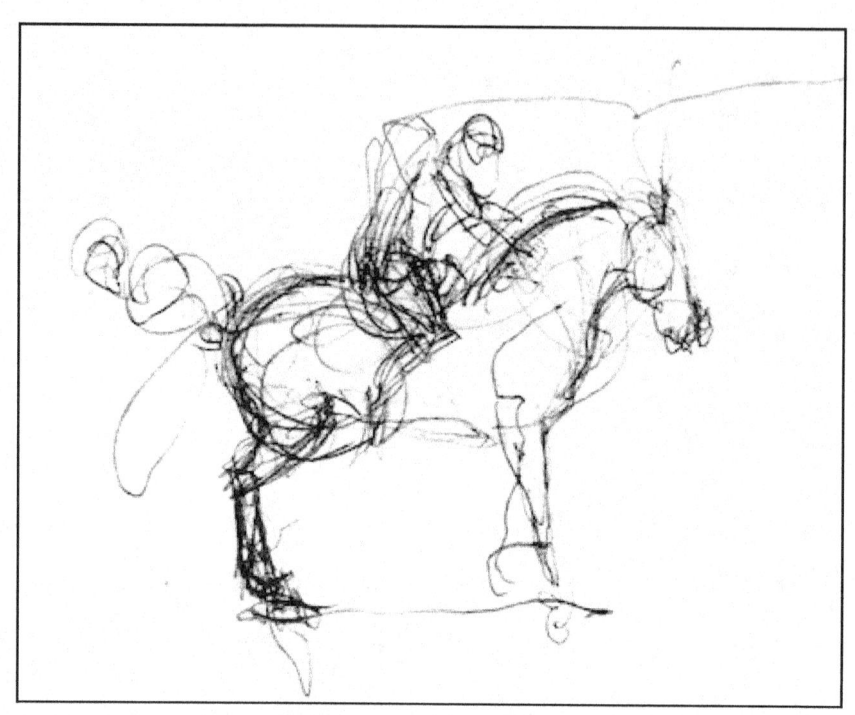
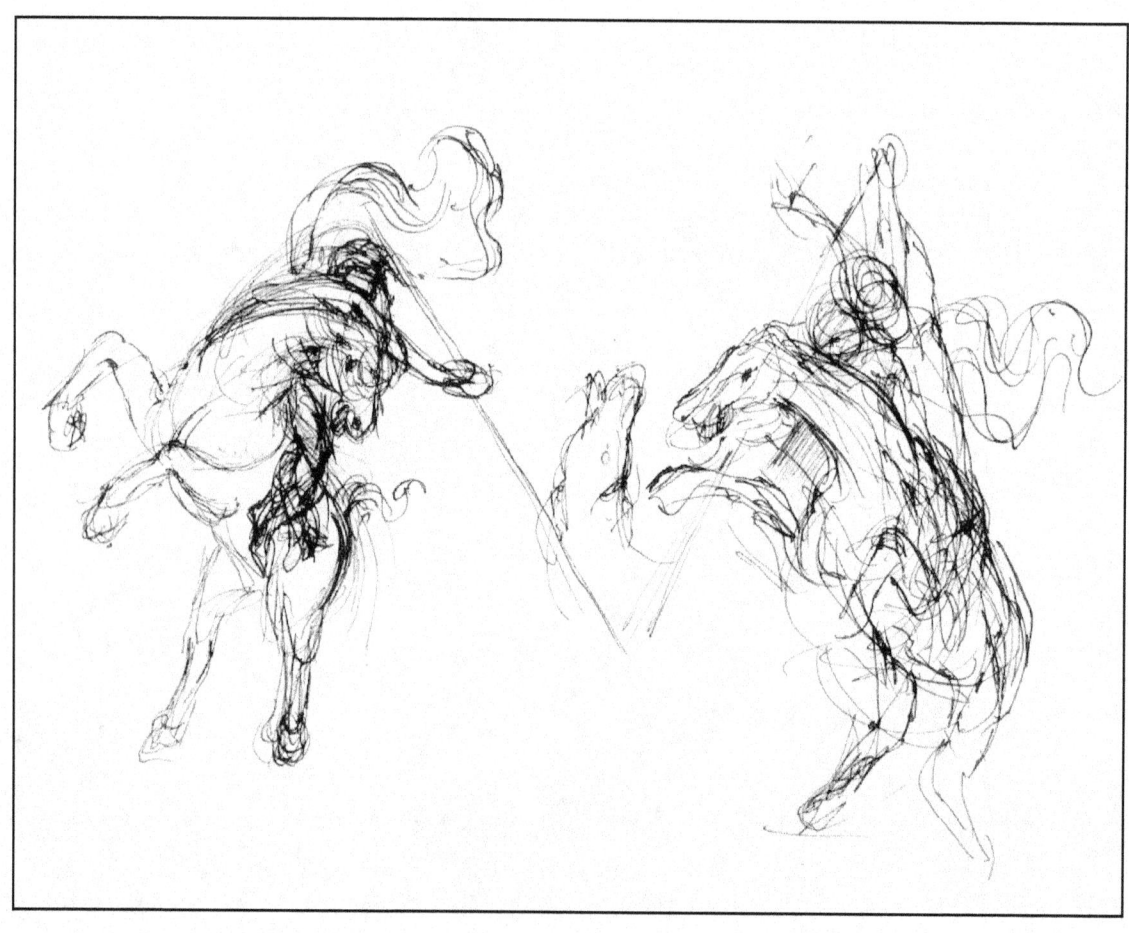

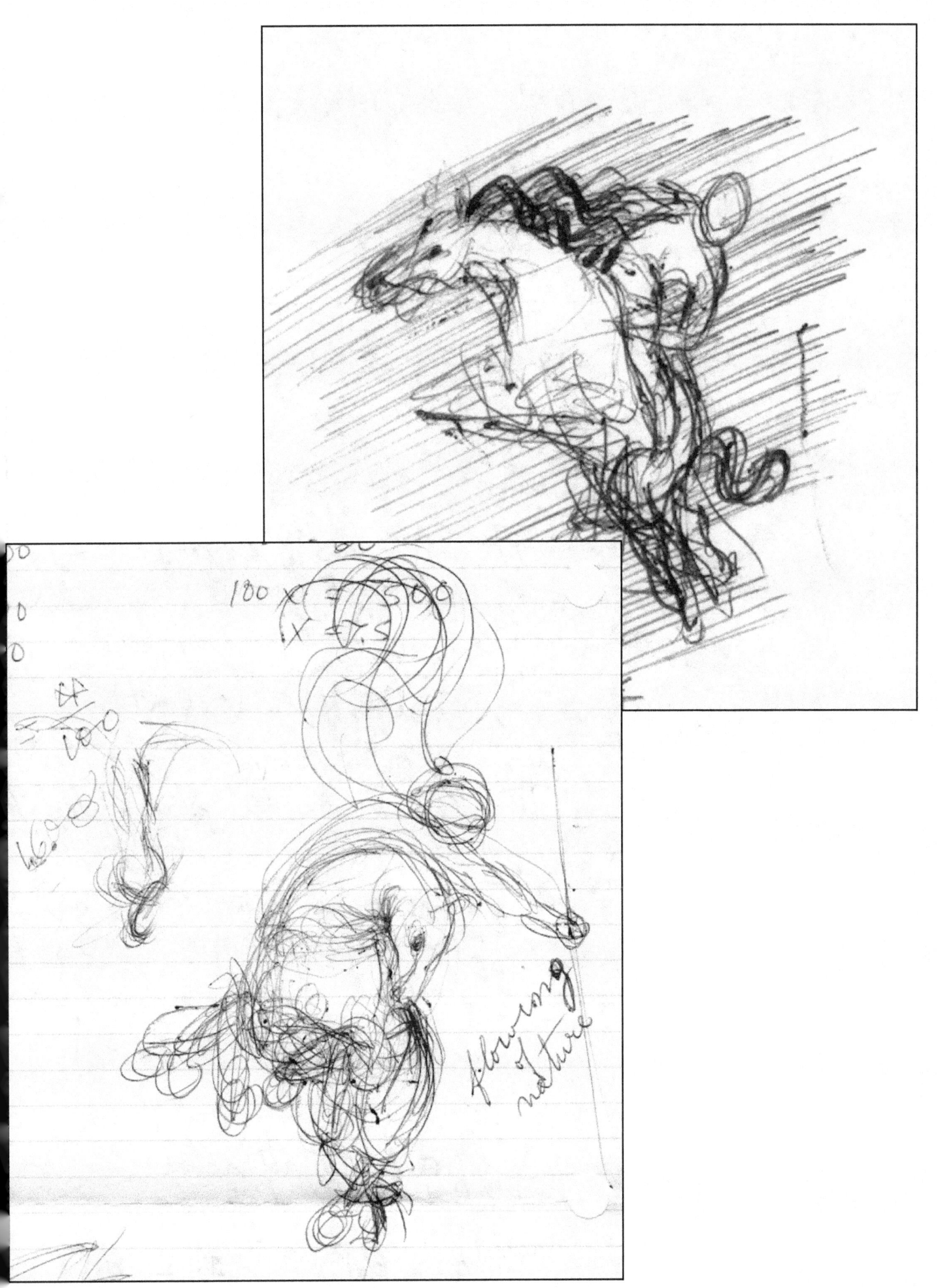

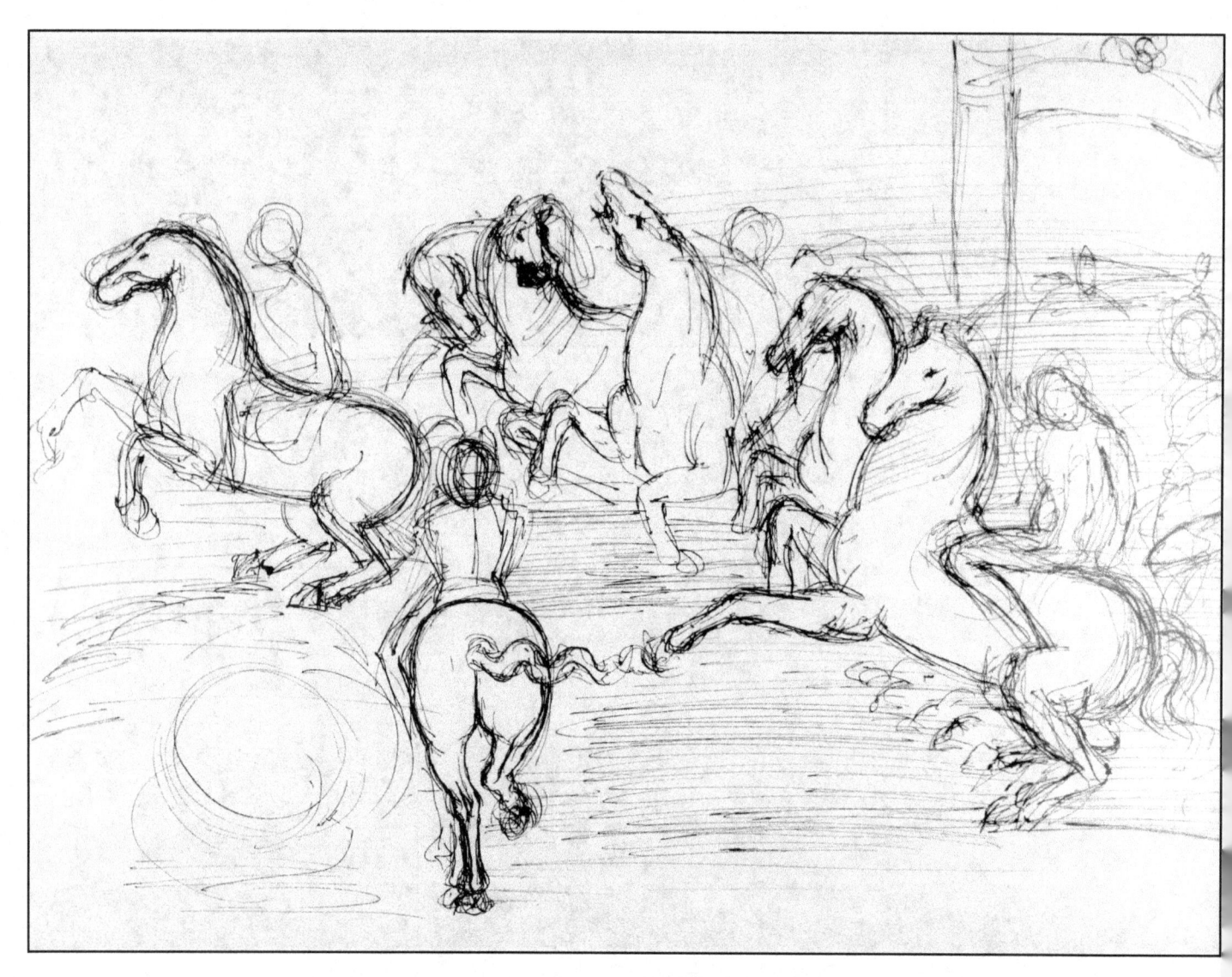

Battle of Anghiari Blueprint, after Leonardo

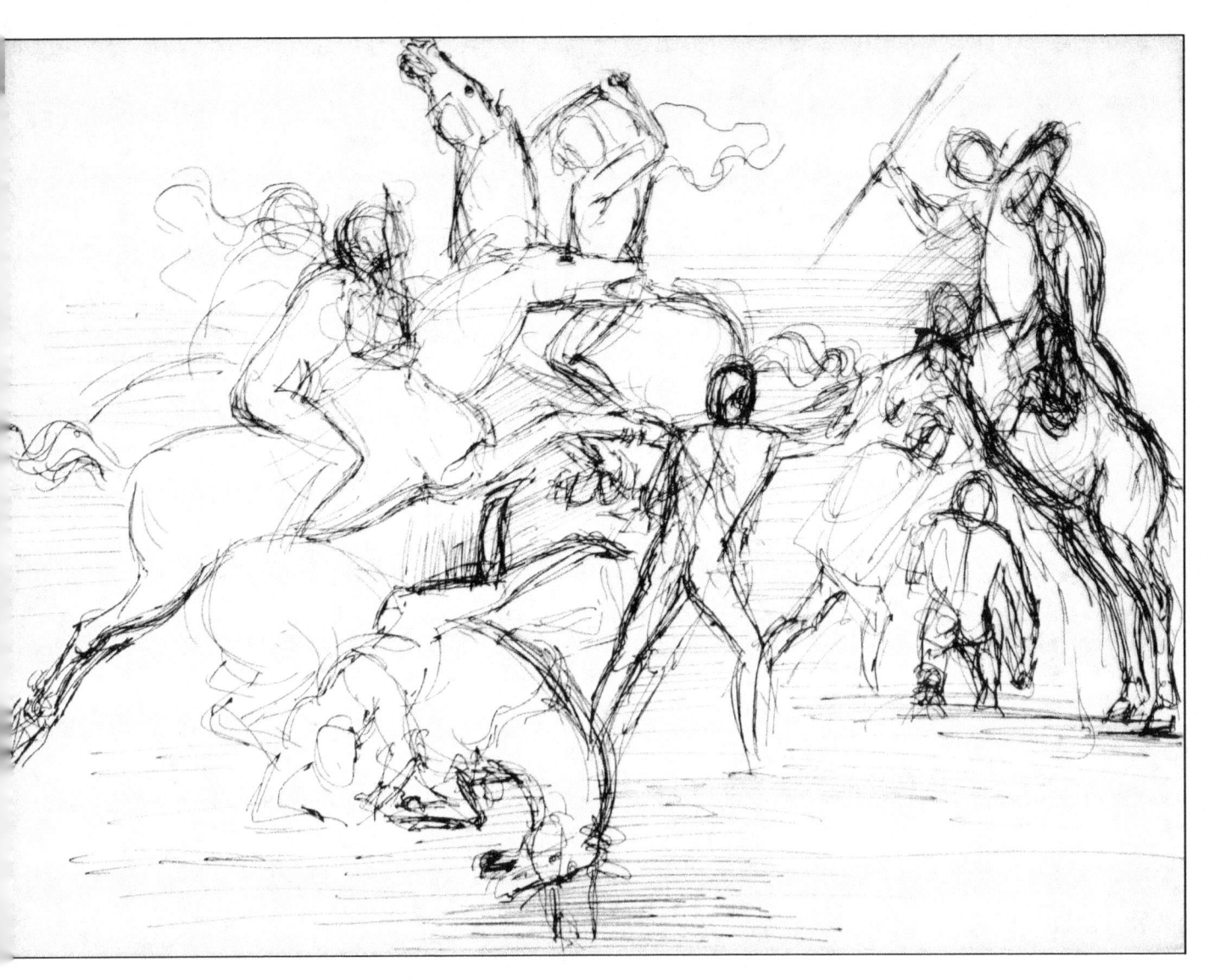

Battle of Anghiari Blueprint, after Leonardo

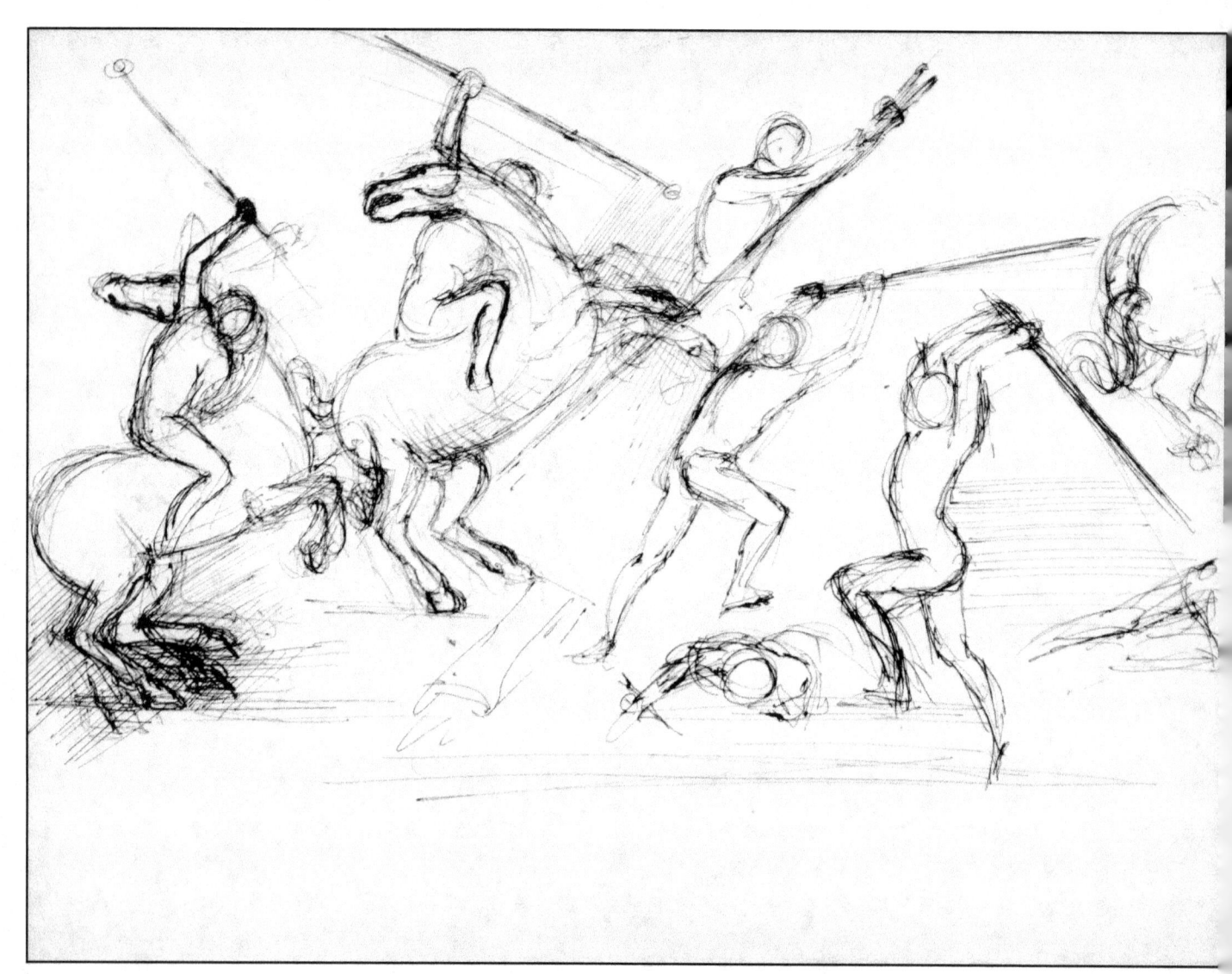

Battle of Anghiari Blueprint, after Leonardo

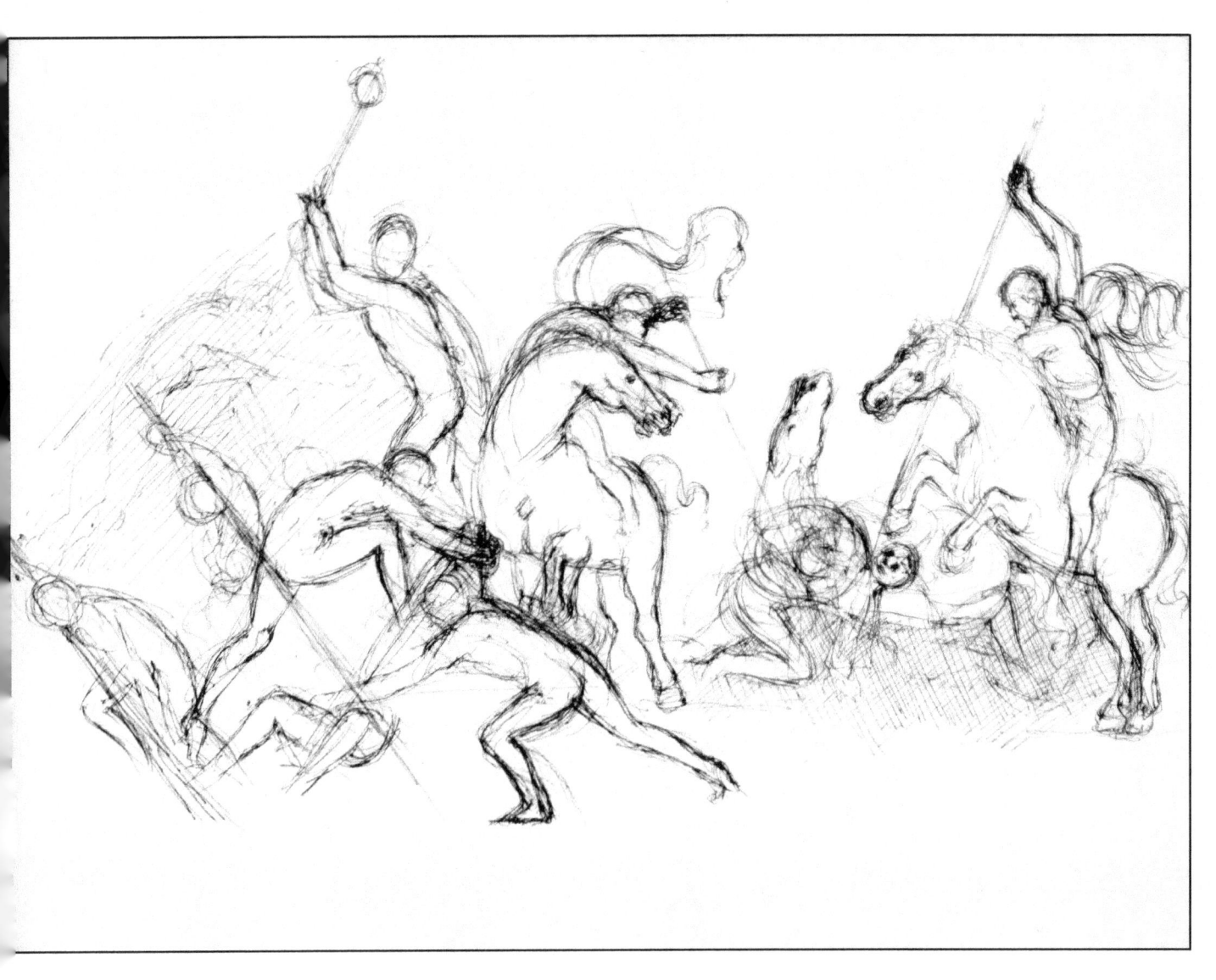

Battle of Anghiari Blueprint, after Leonardo

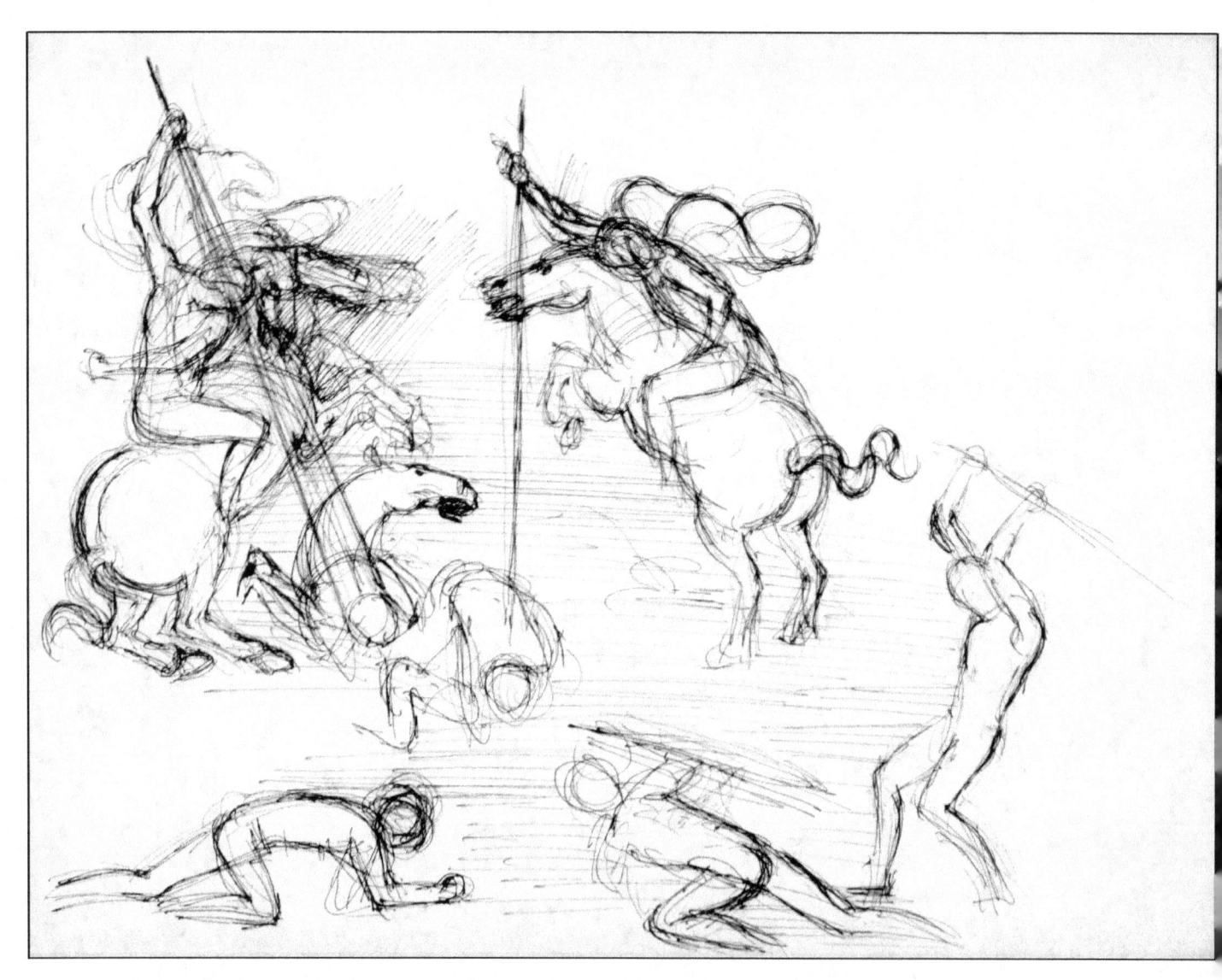

Battle of Anghiari Blueprint, after Leonardo

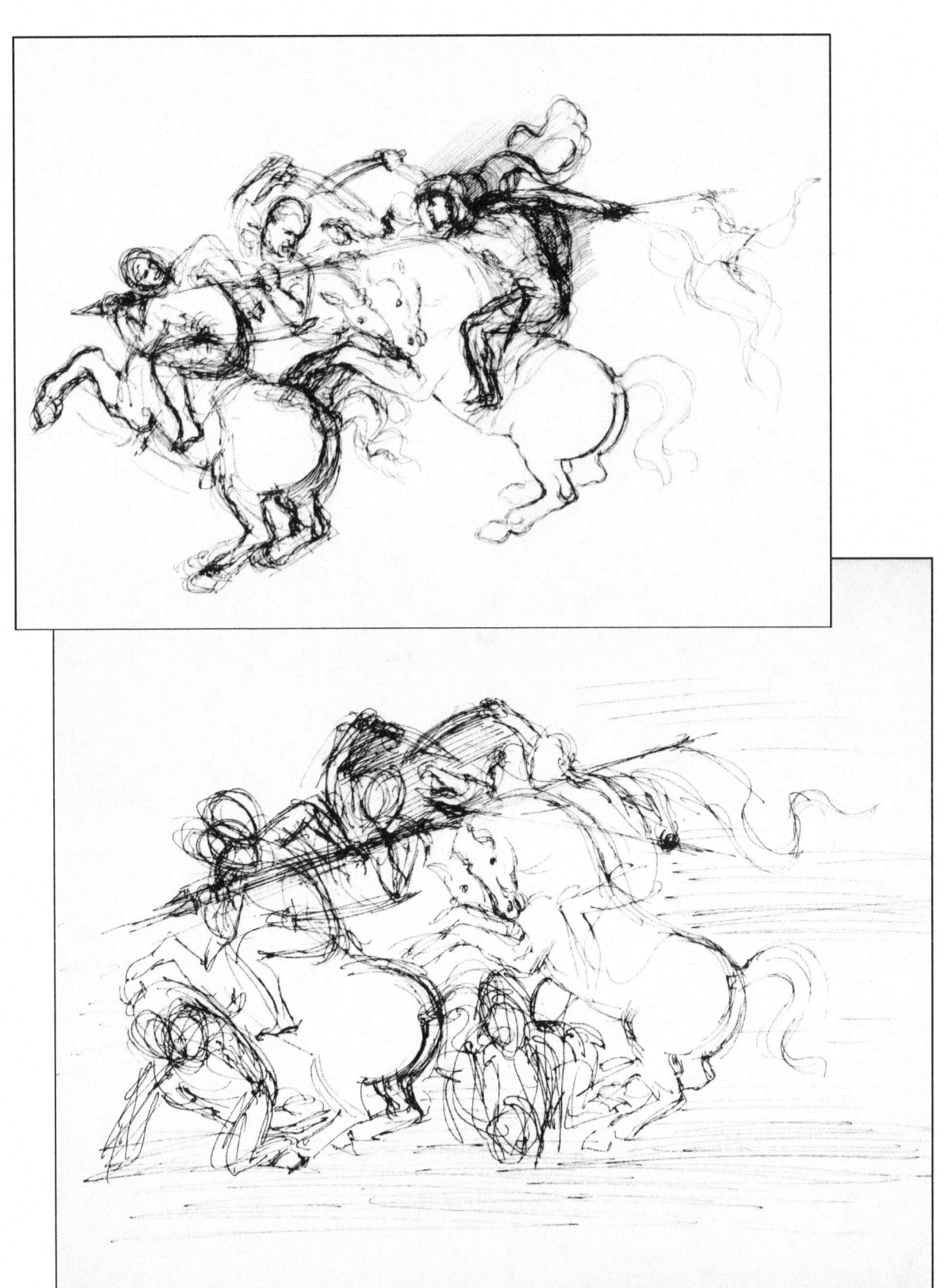

Battle of Anghiari Blueprint, after Leonardo

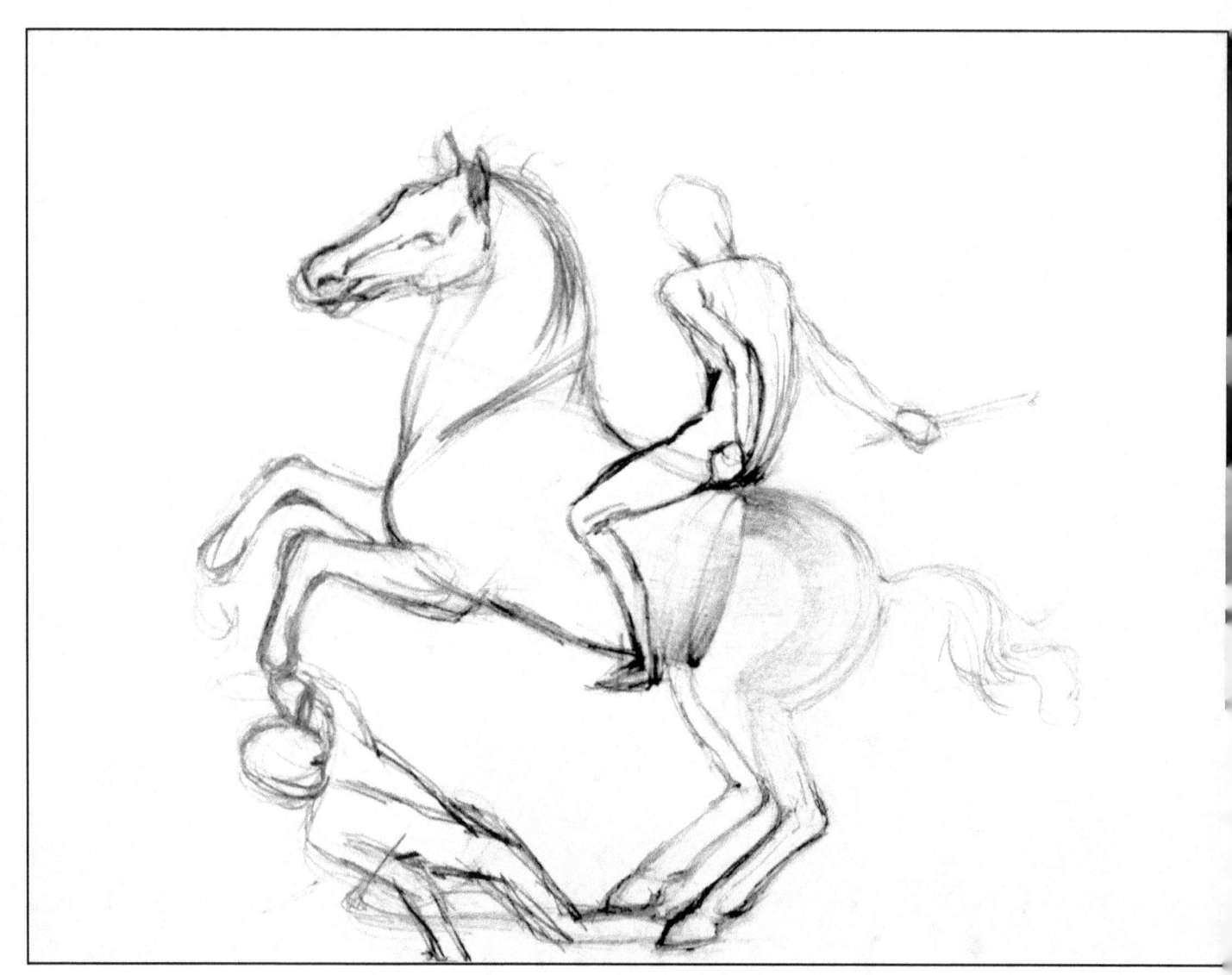

Sforza Monument Blueprint, after Leonardo

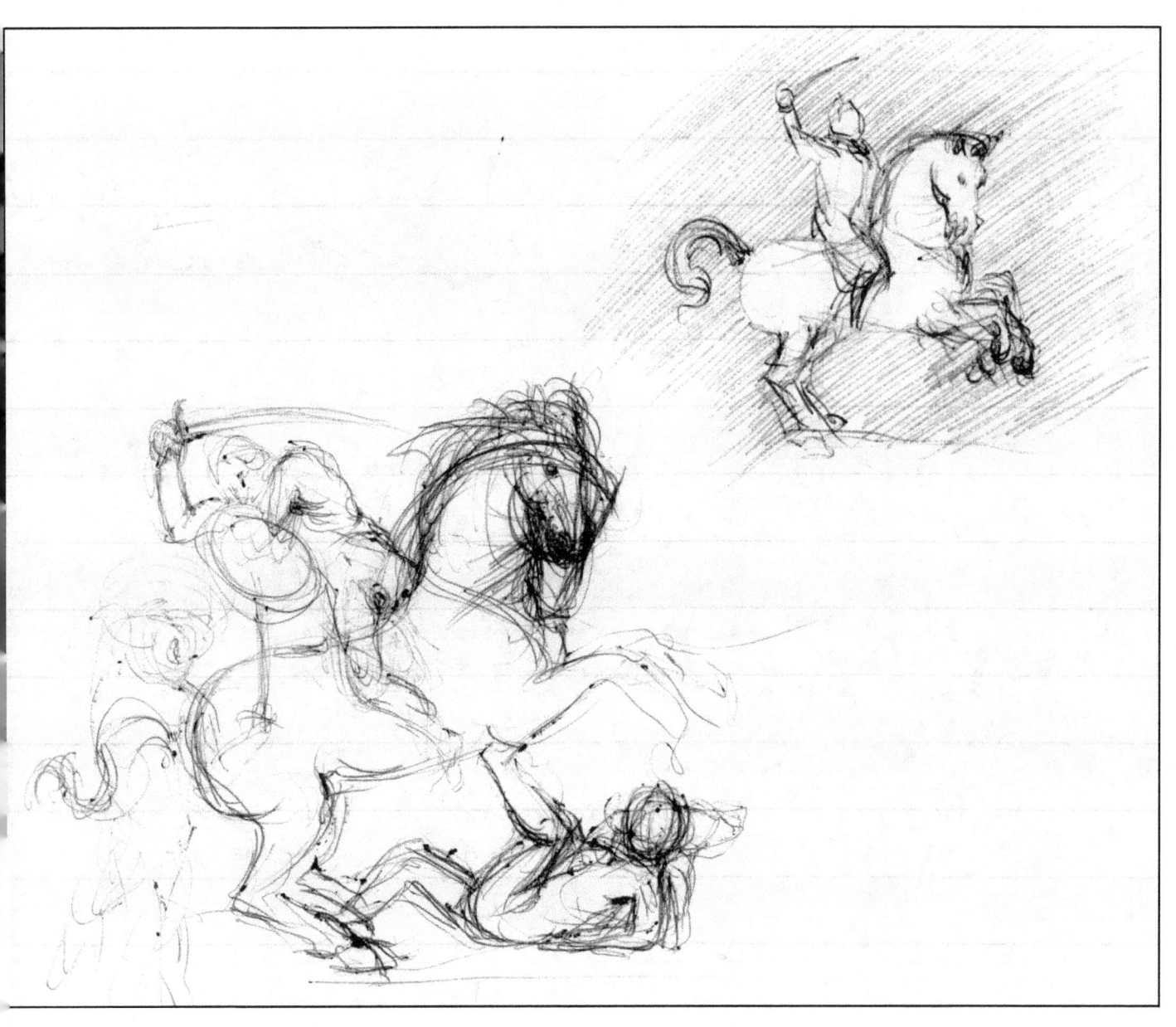

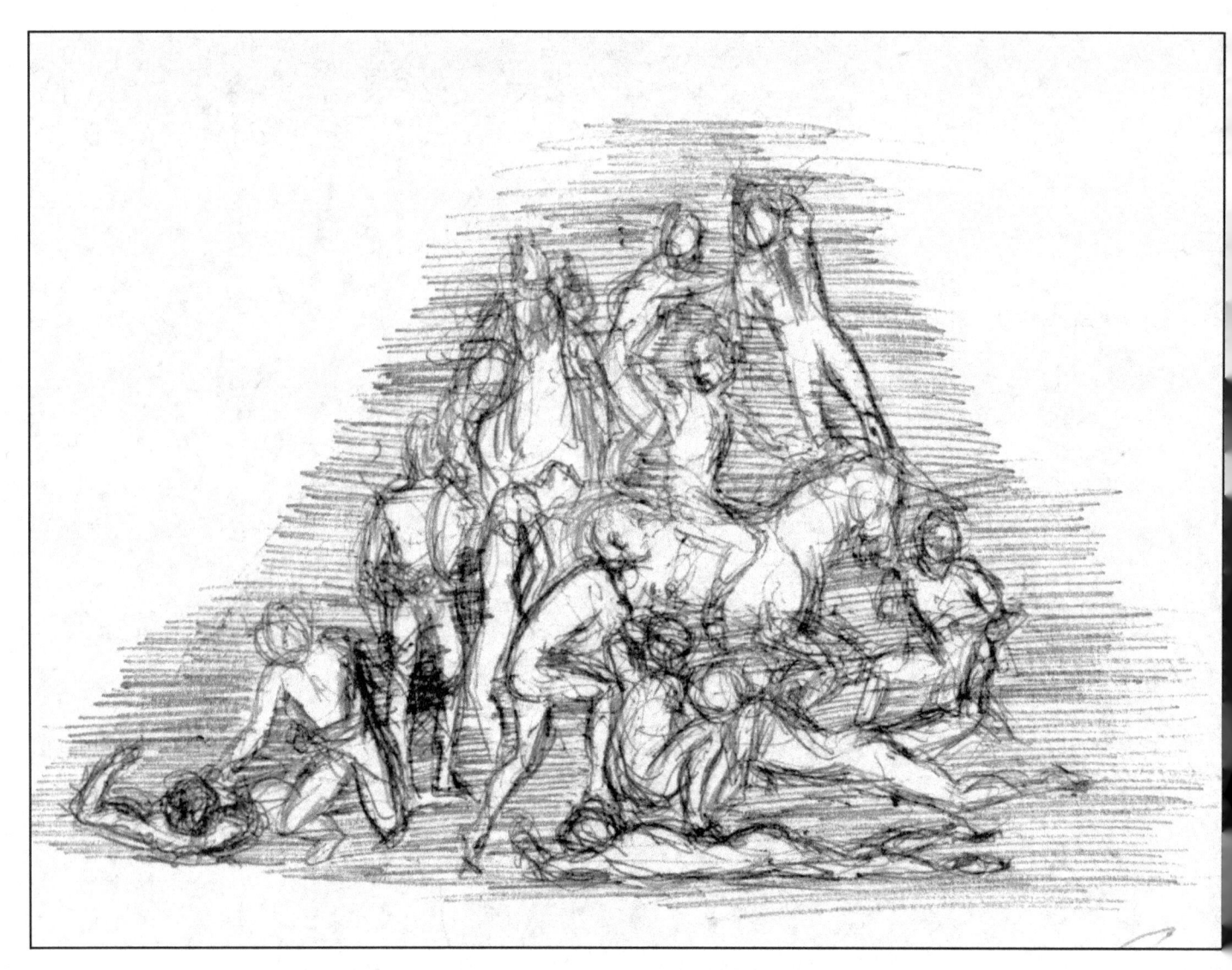

Men and Horses: My Own Blueprint

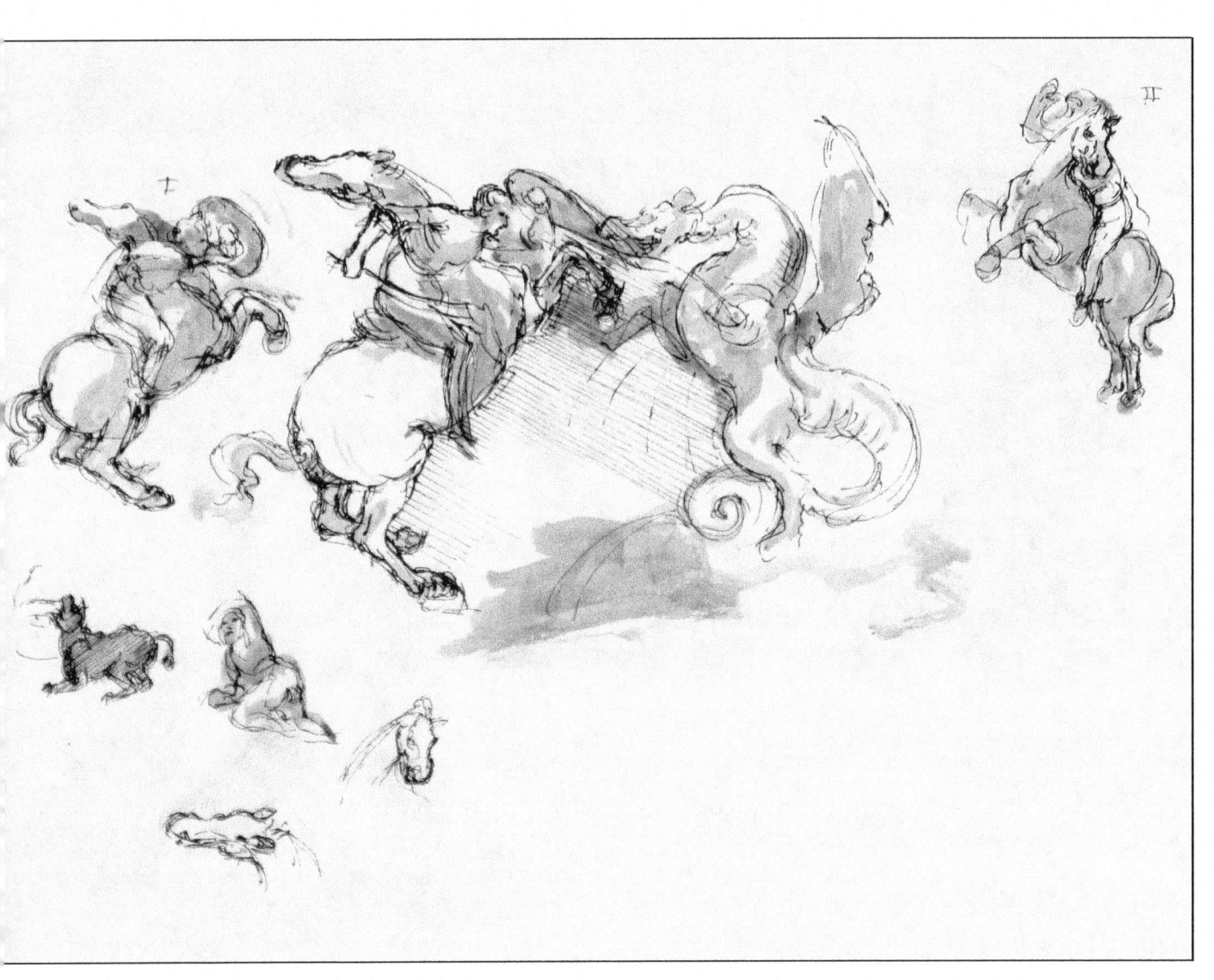

Dragon Fight, after Leonardo

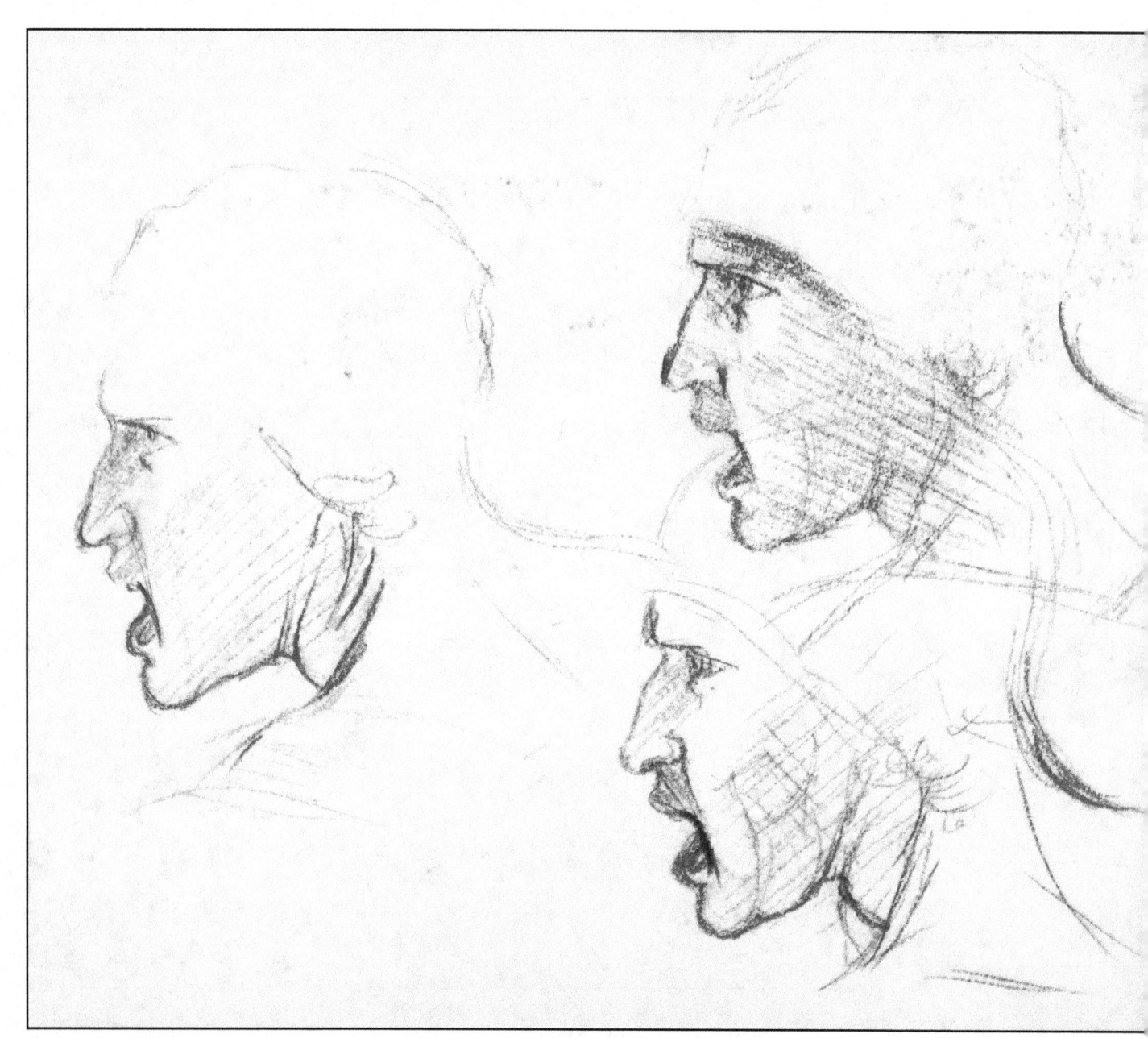

Battle of Anghiari Warrior, after Leonardo

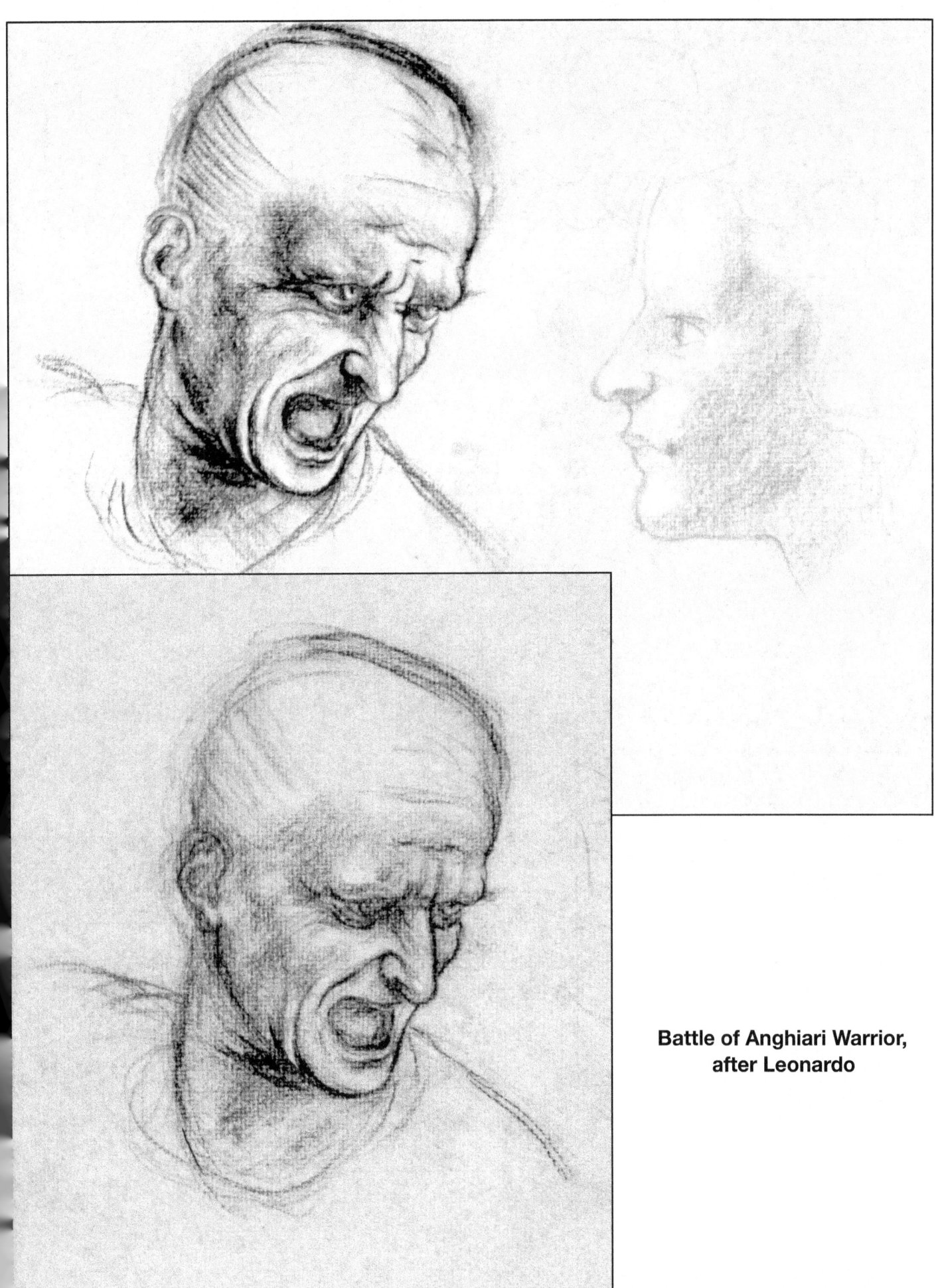

Battle of Anghiari Warrior, after Leonardo

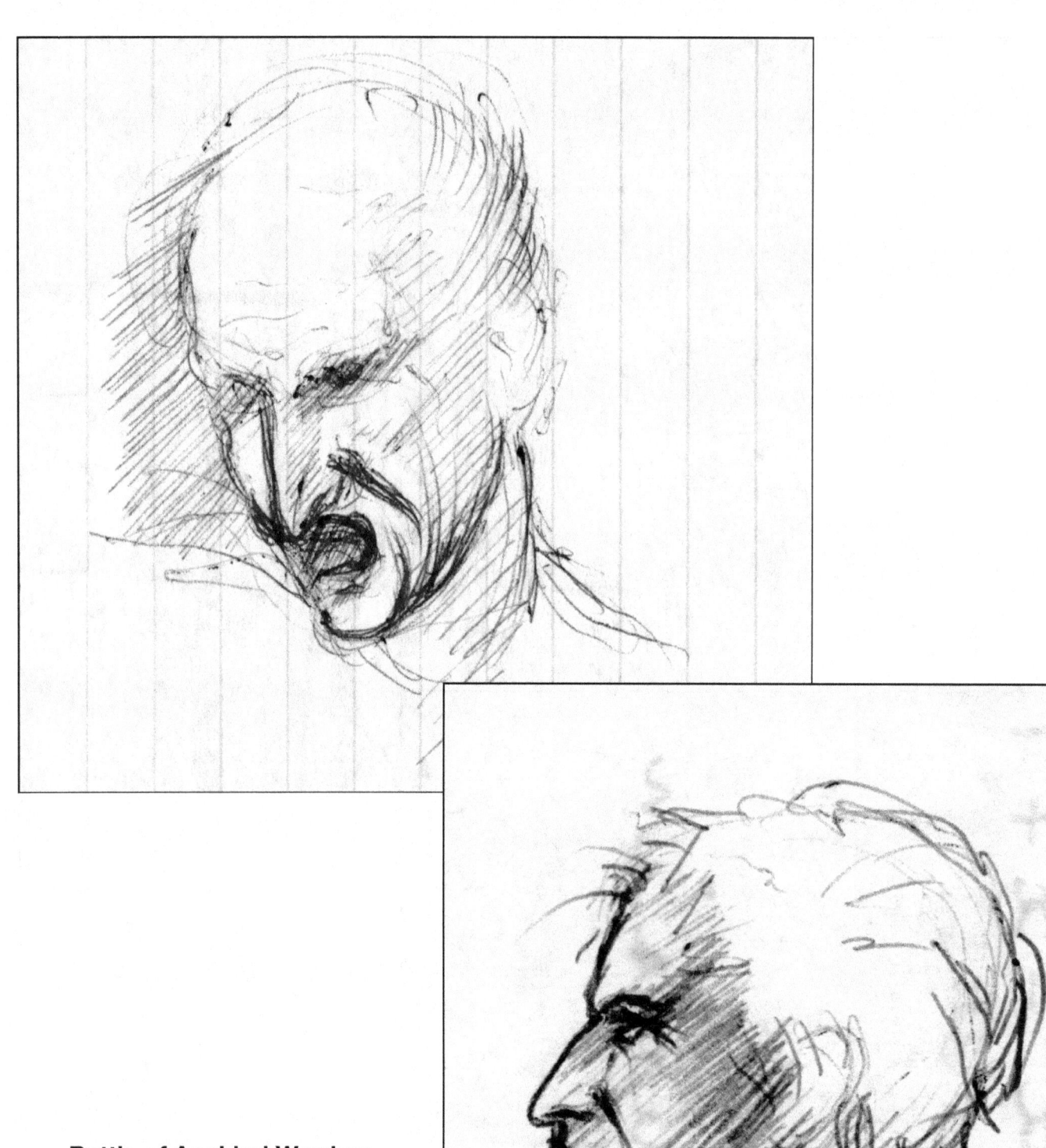

Battle of Anghiari Warriors, from Memory

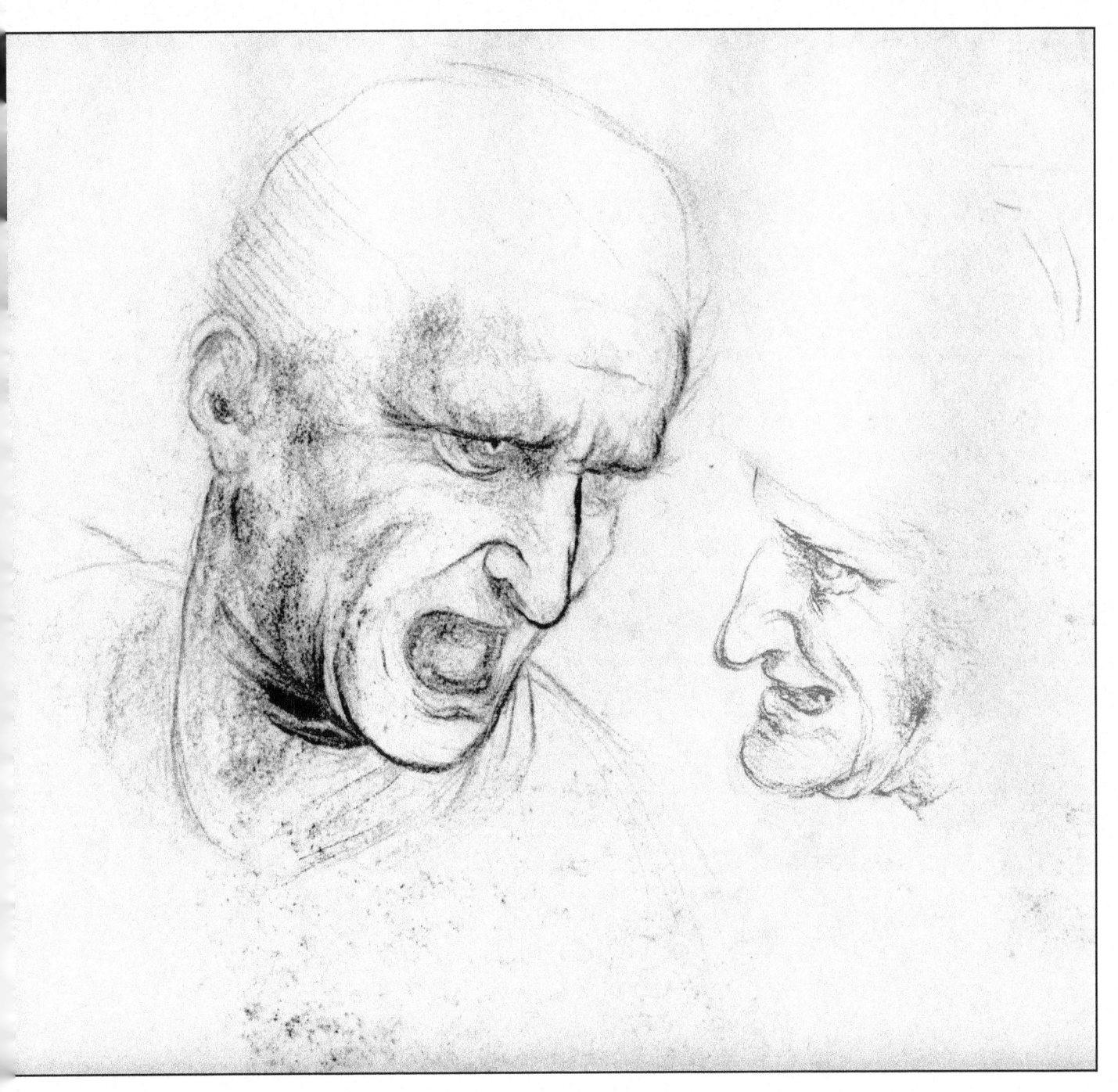

Battle of Anghiari Warriors, after Leonardo

18. HUMAN & DIVINE Composition

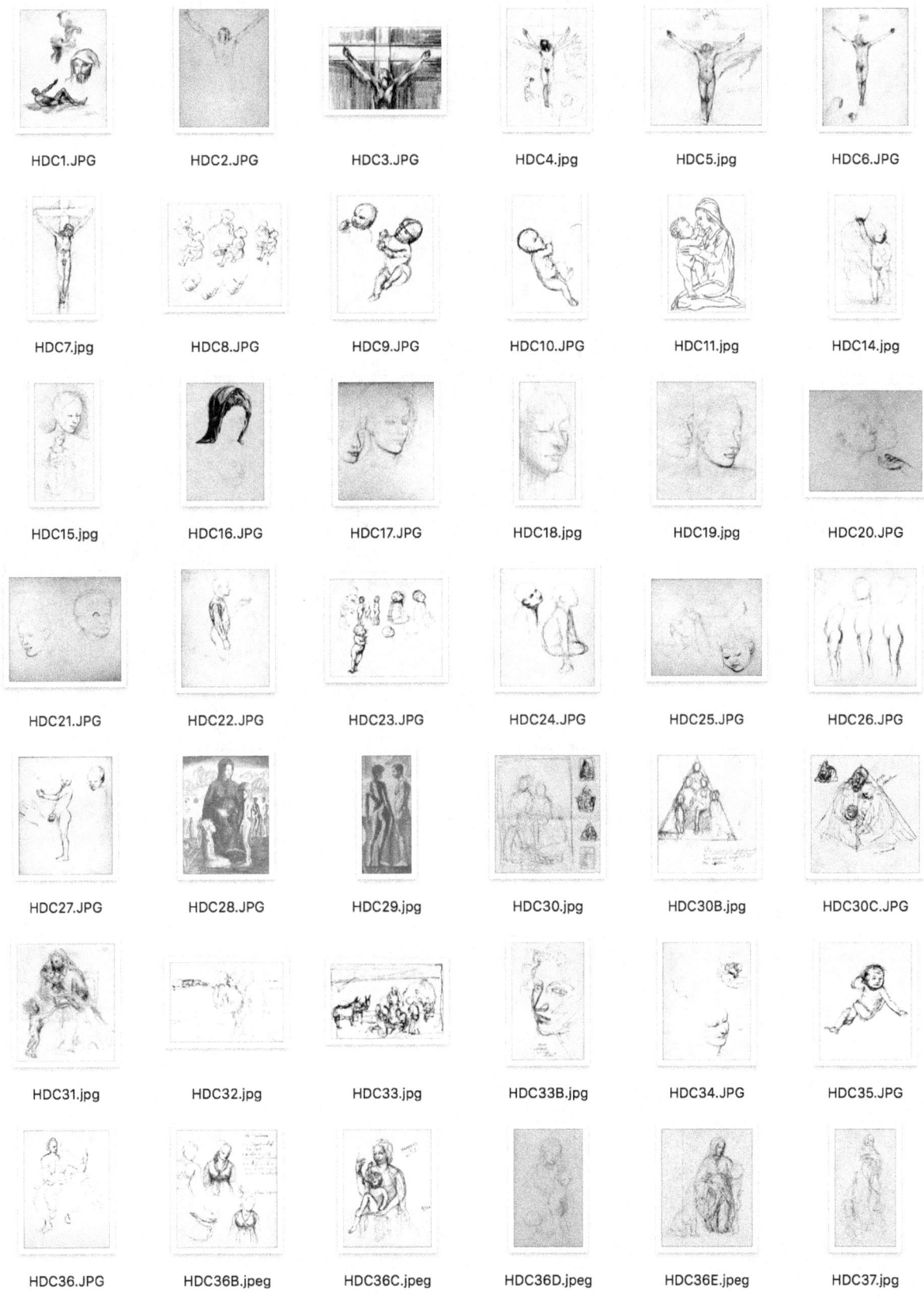

465

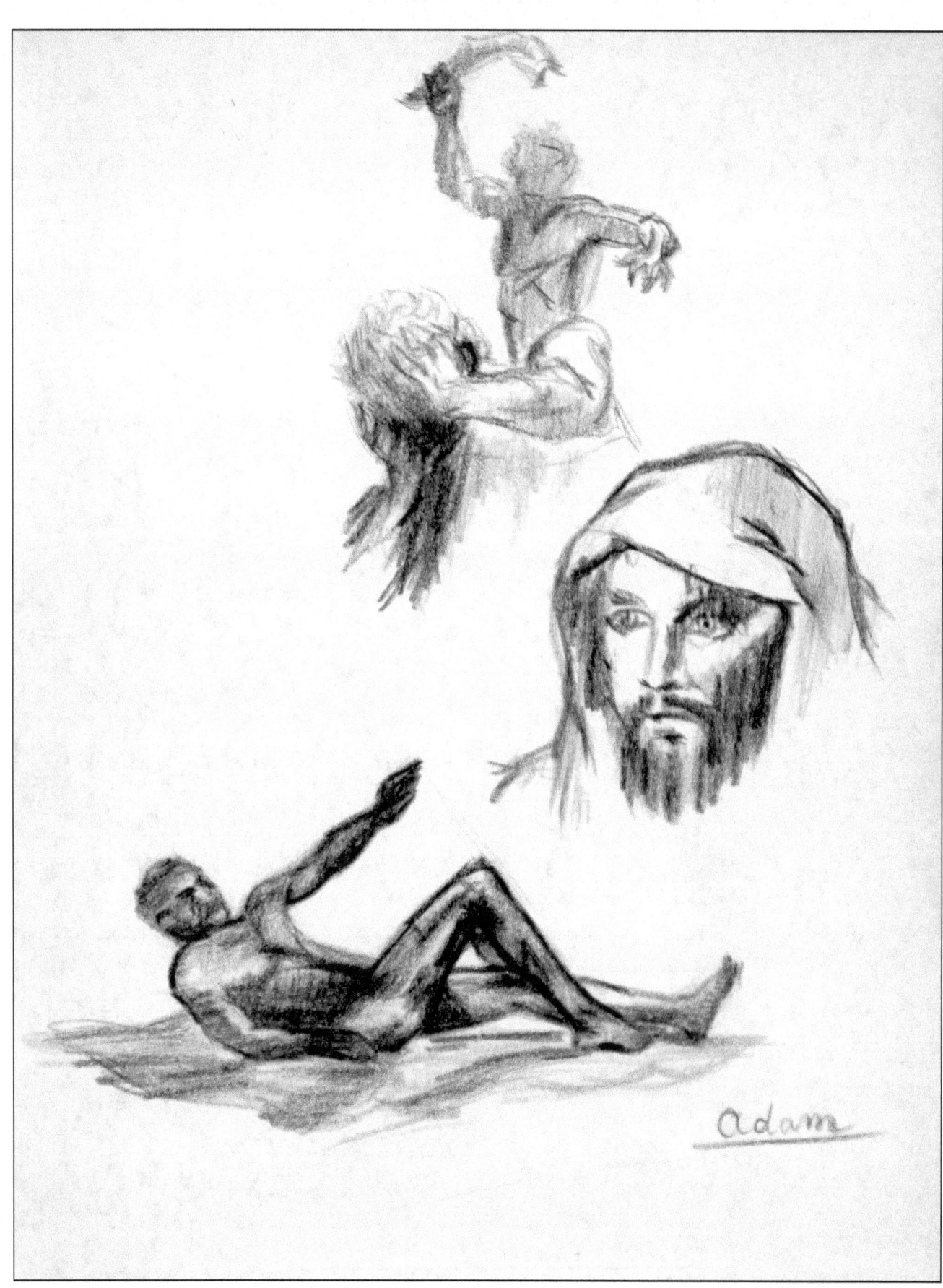

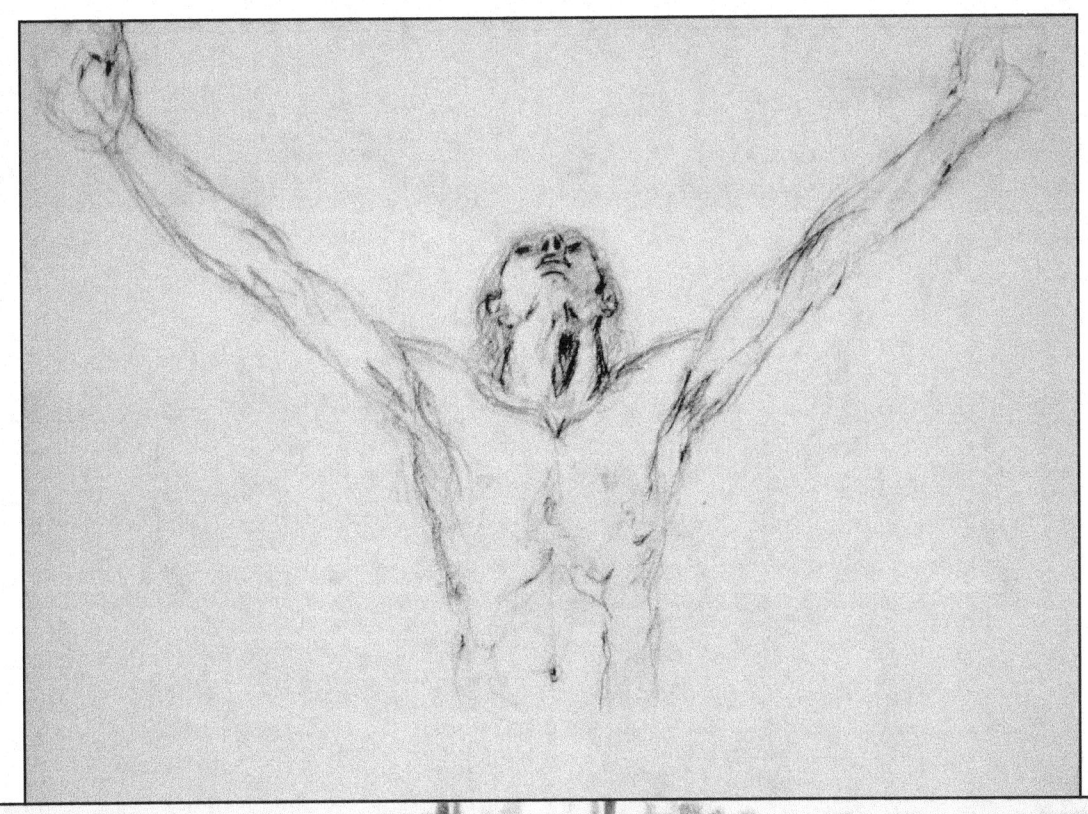
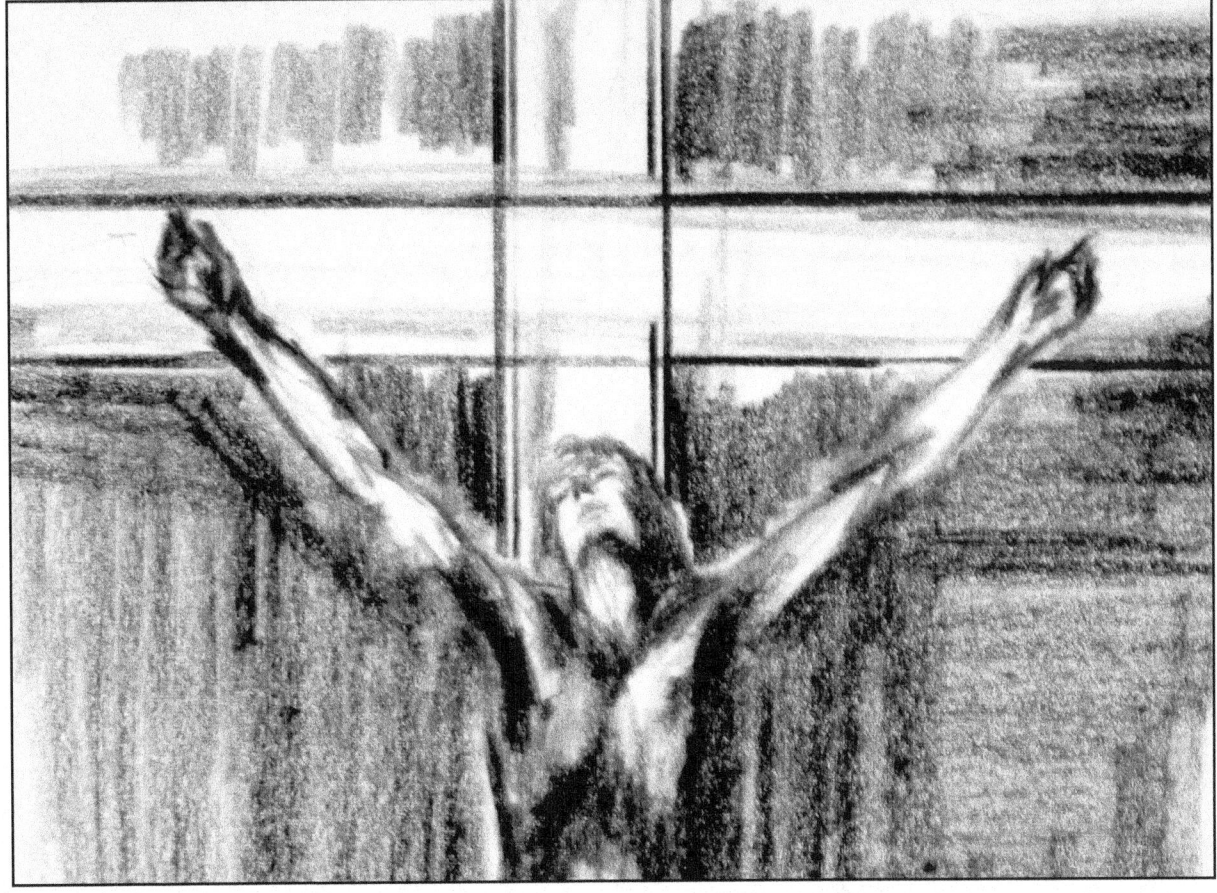

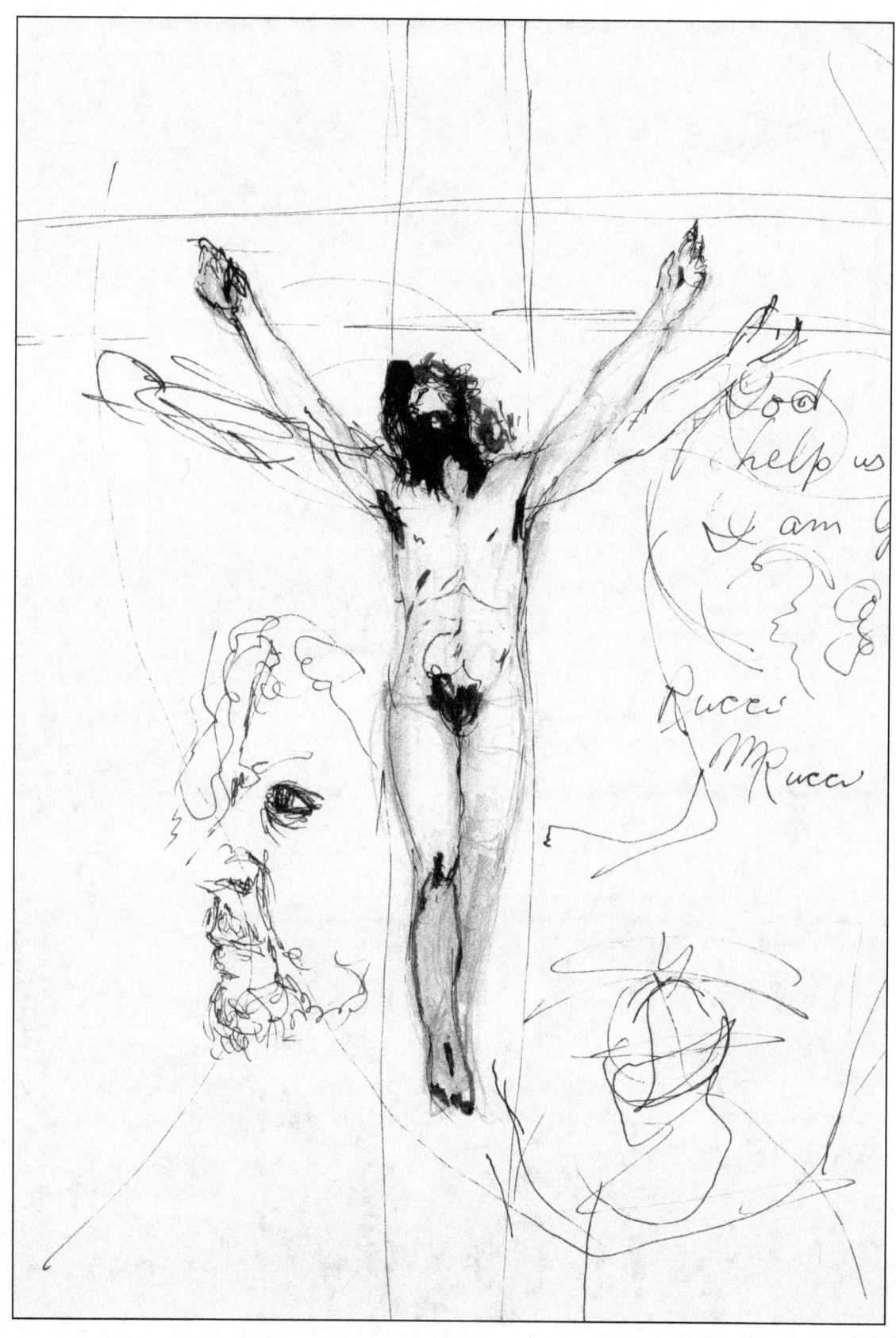

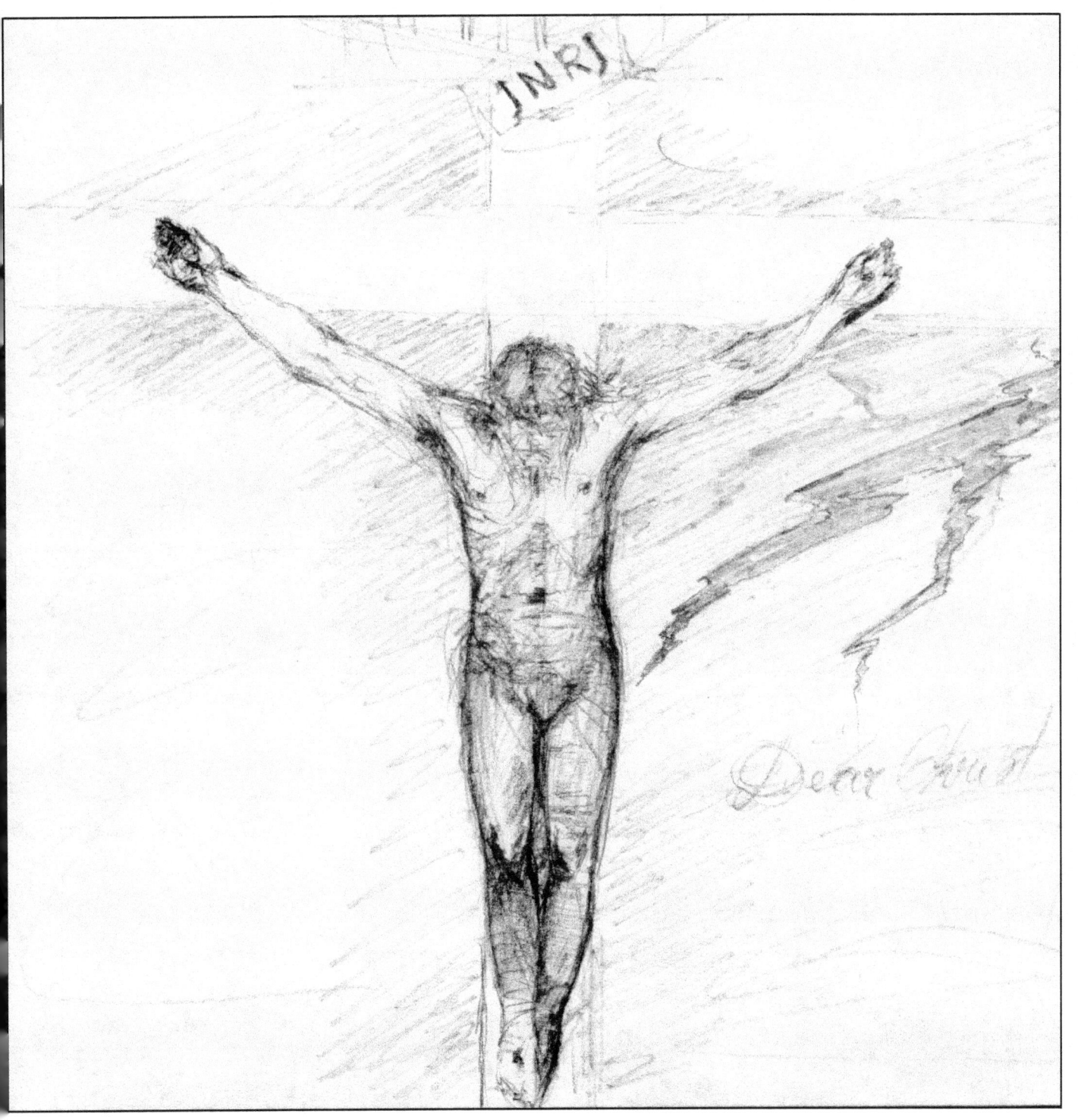

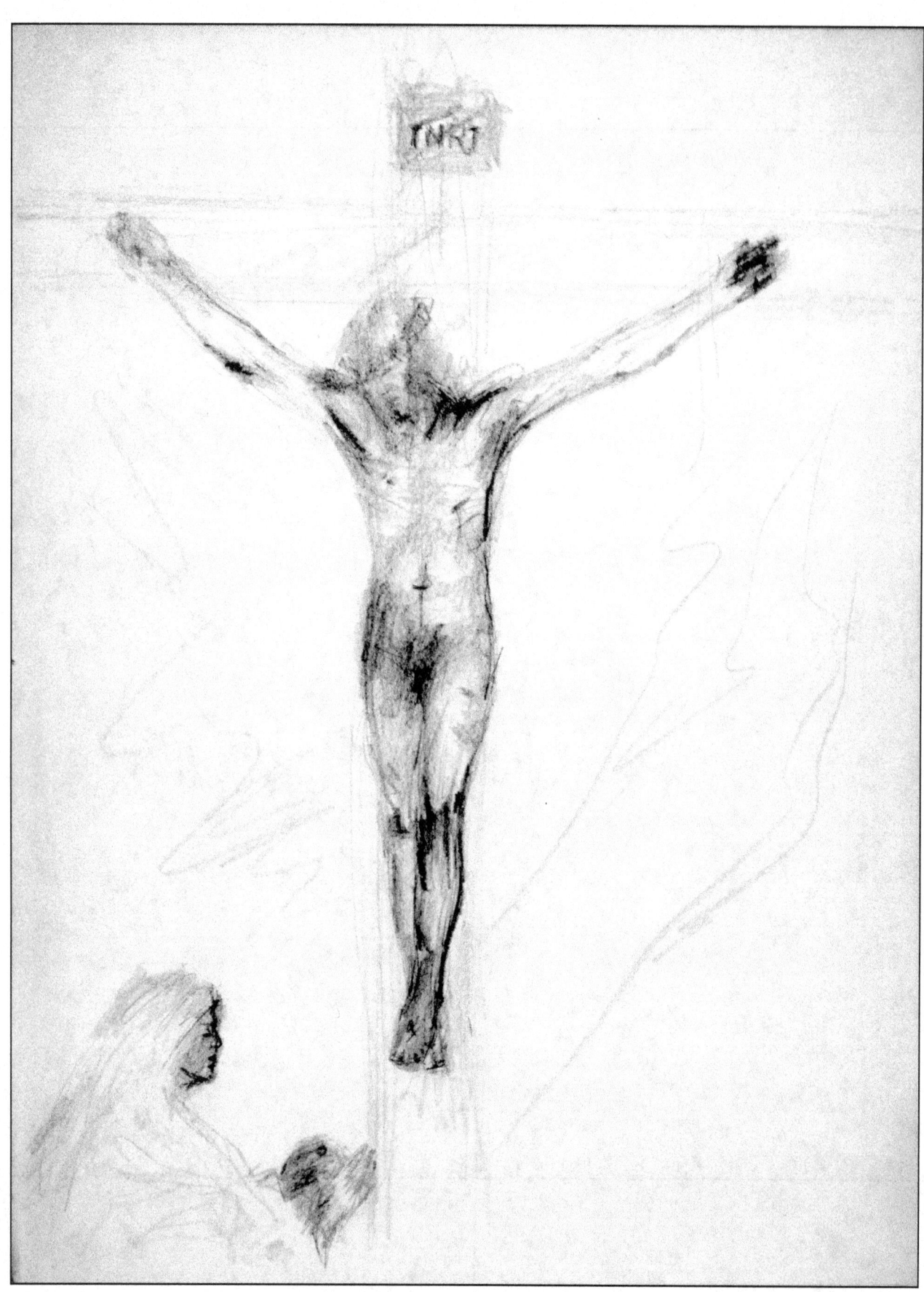

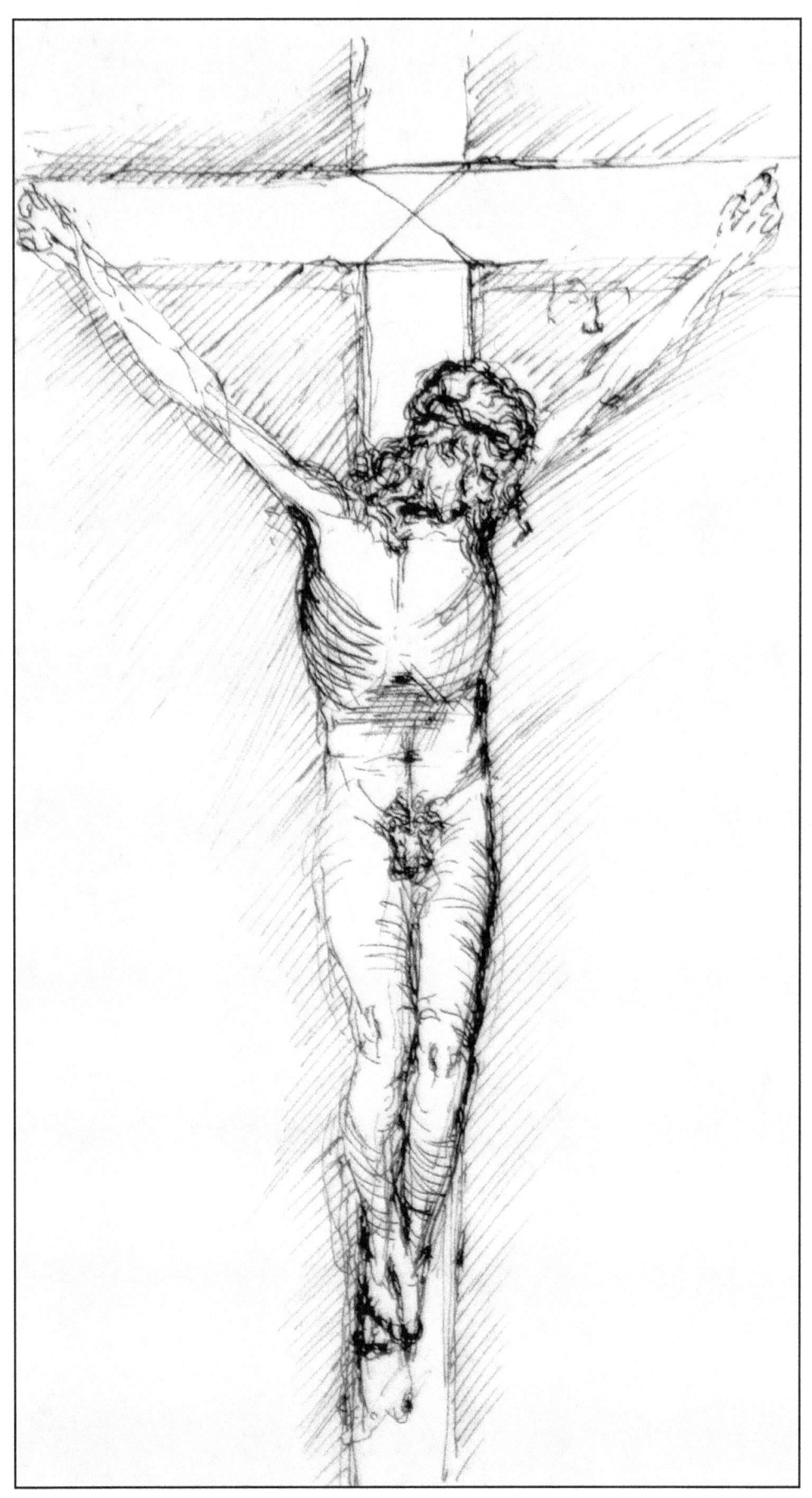

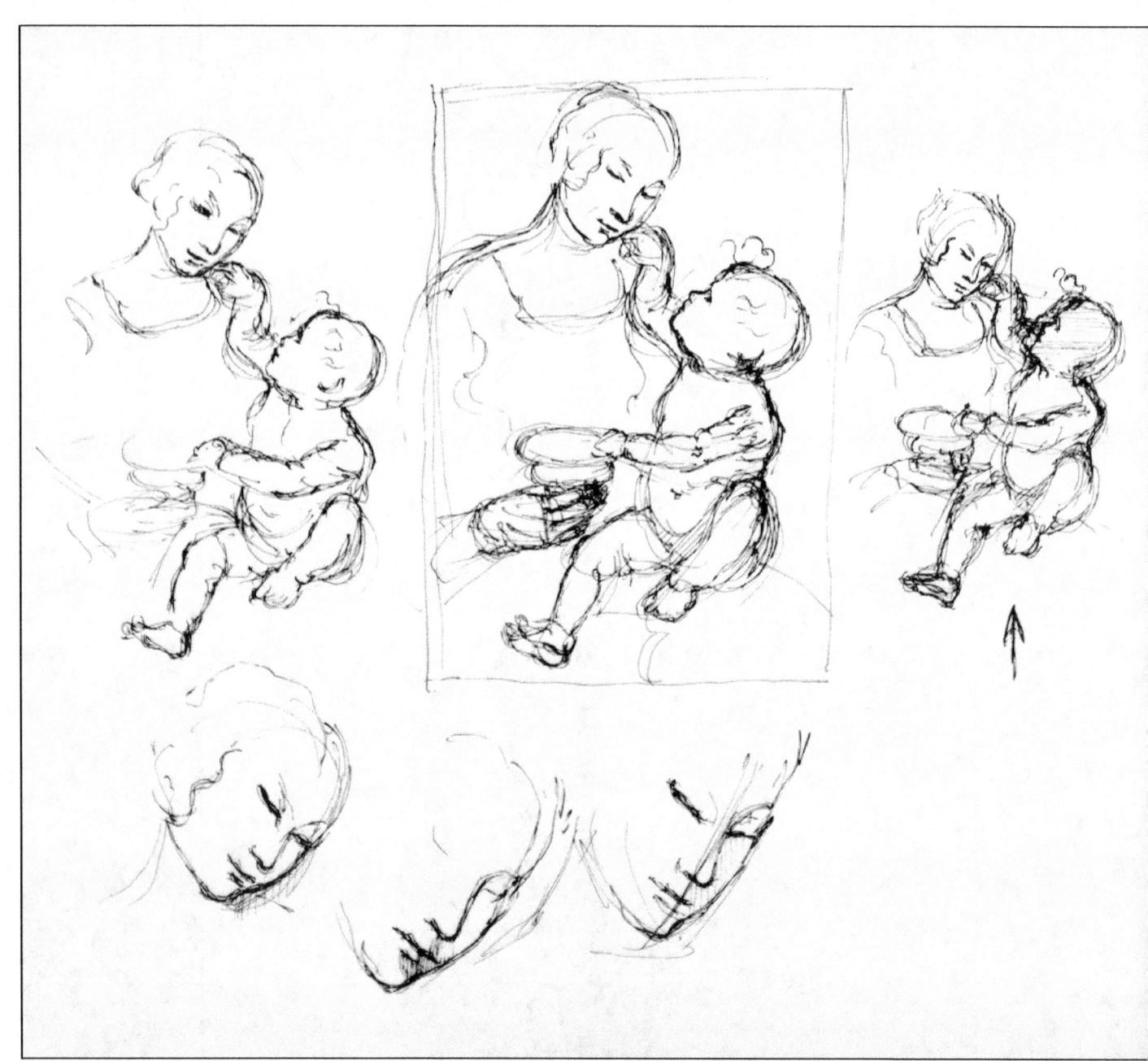

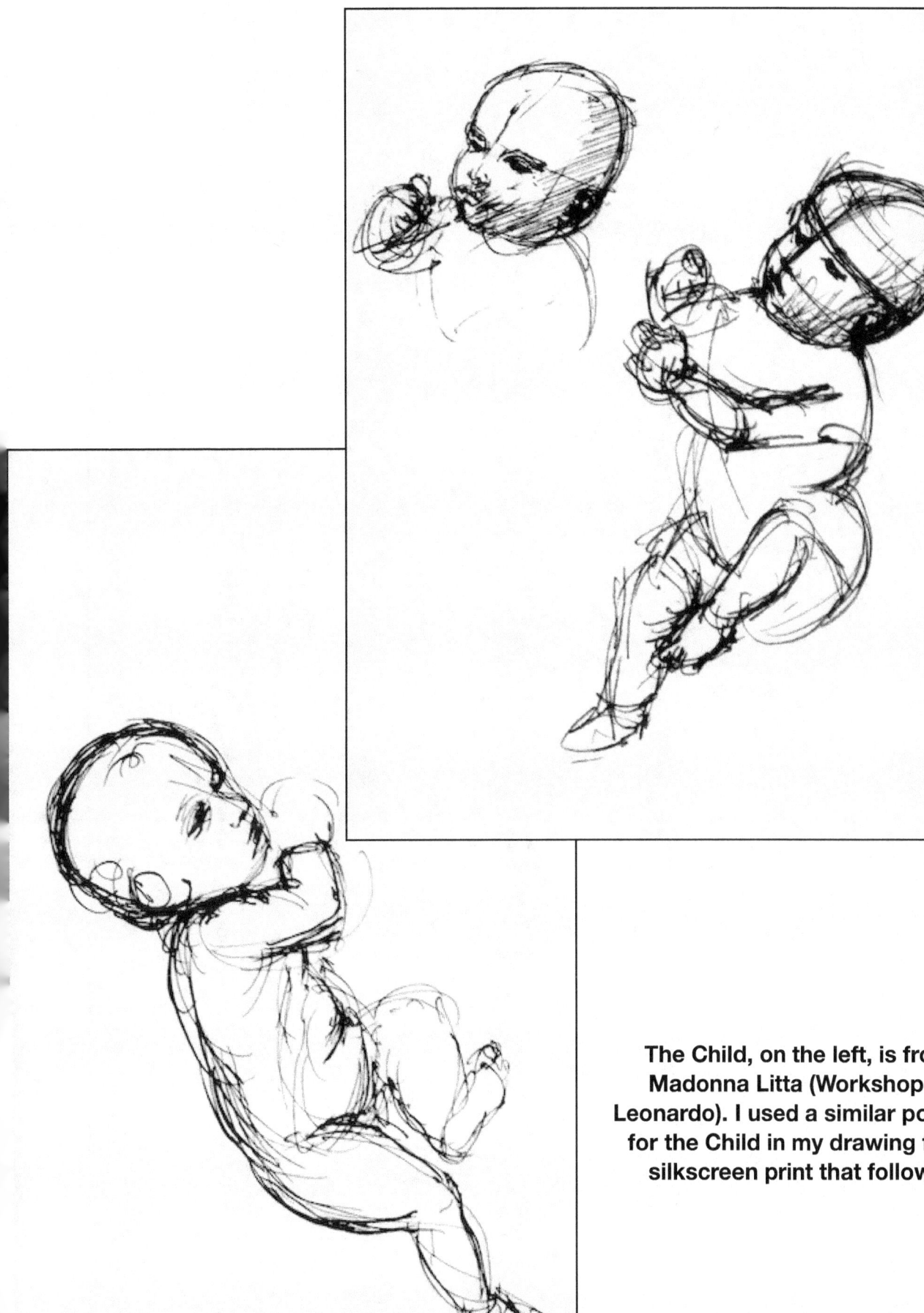

The Child, on the left, is from Madonna Litta (Workshop of Leonardo). I used a similar posture for the Child in my drawing for a silkscreen print that follows.

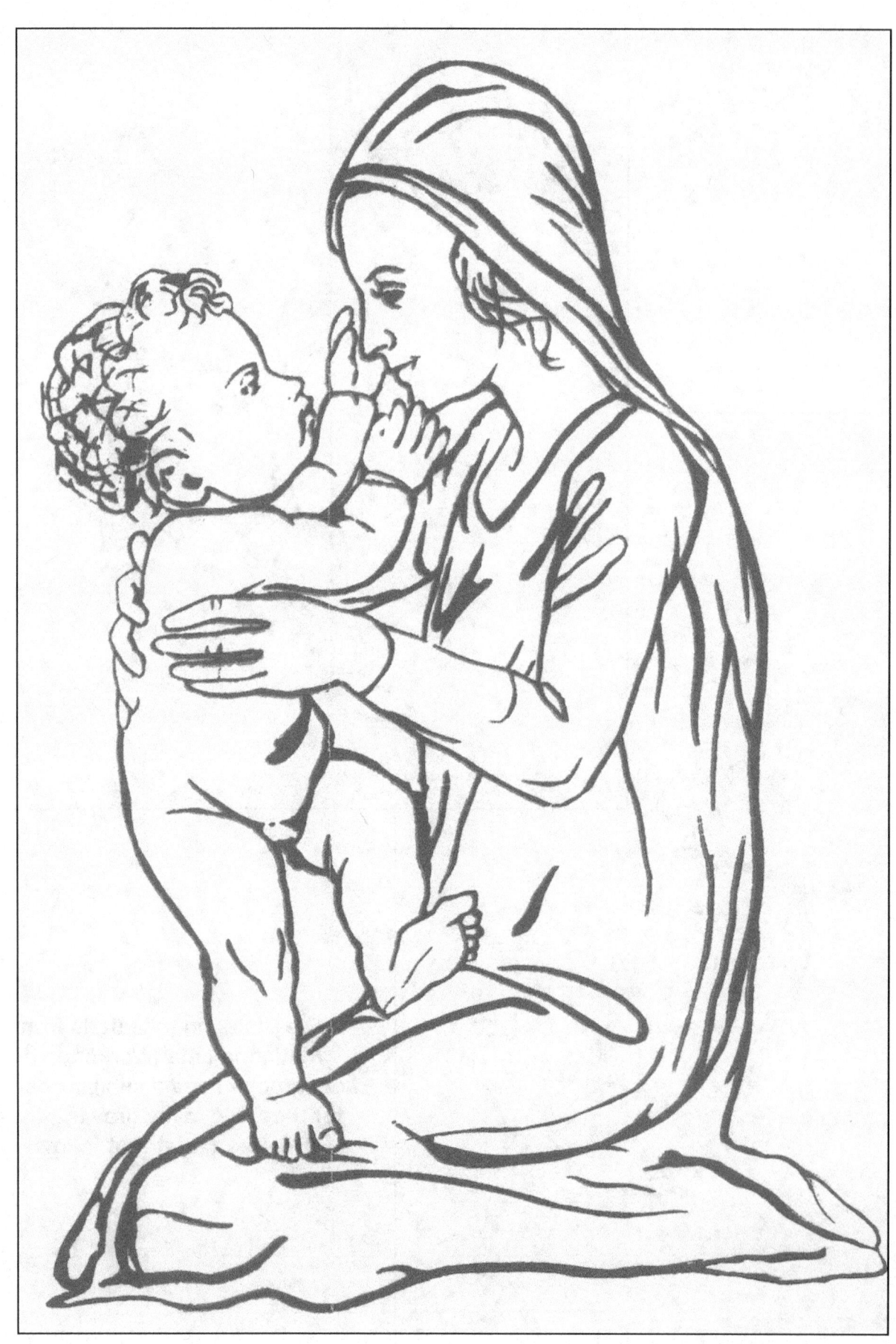

Silkscreen Print (I cut the film but I did not do the printing)

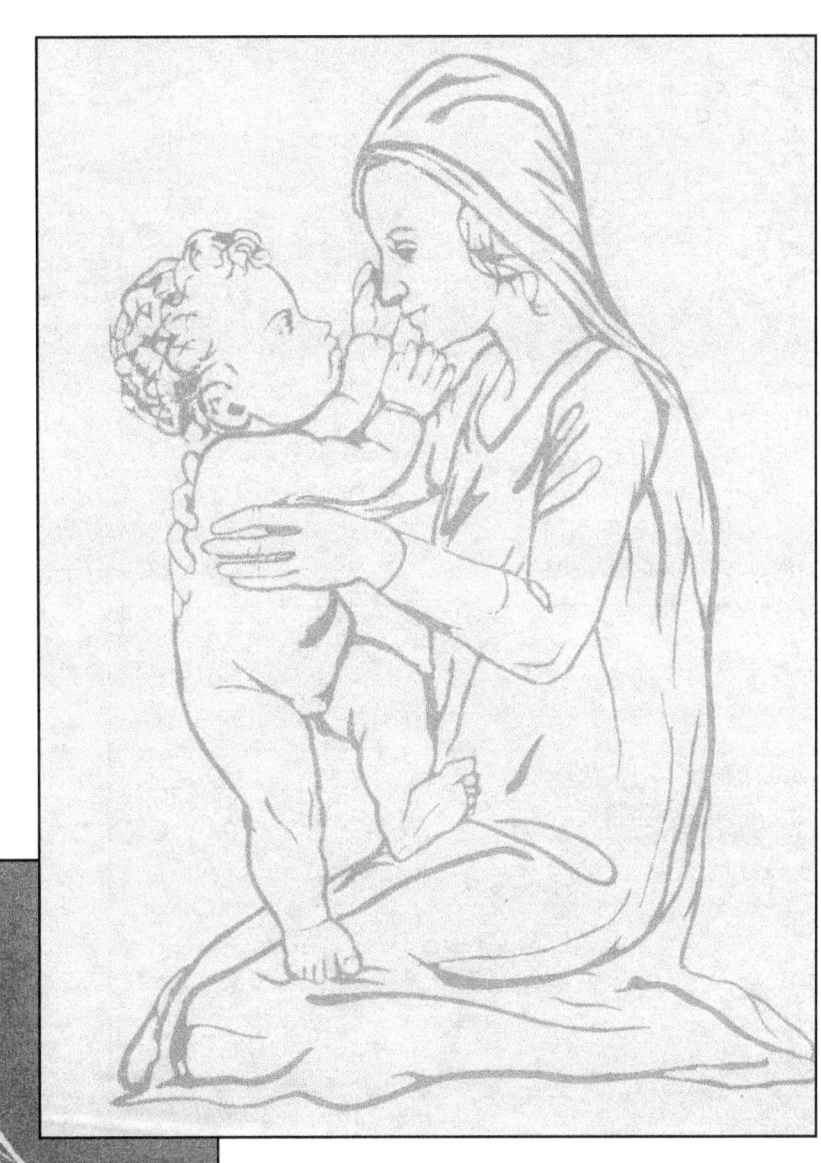

Other Variations of the previous Silkscreen Print

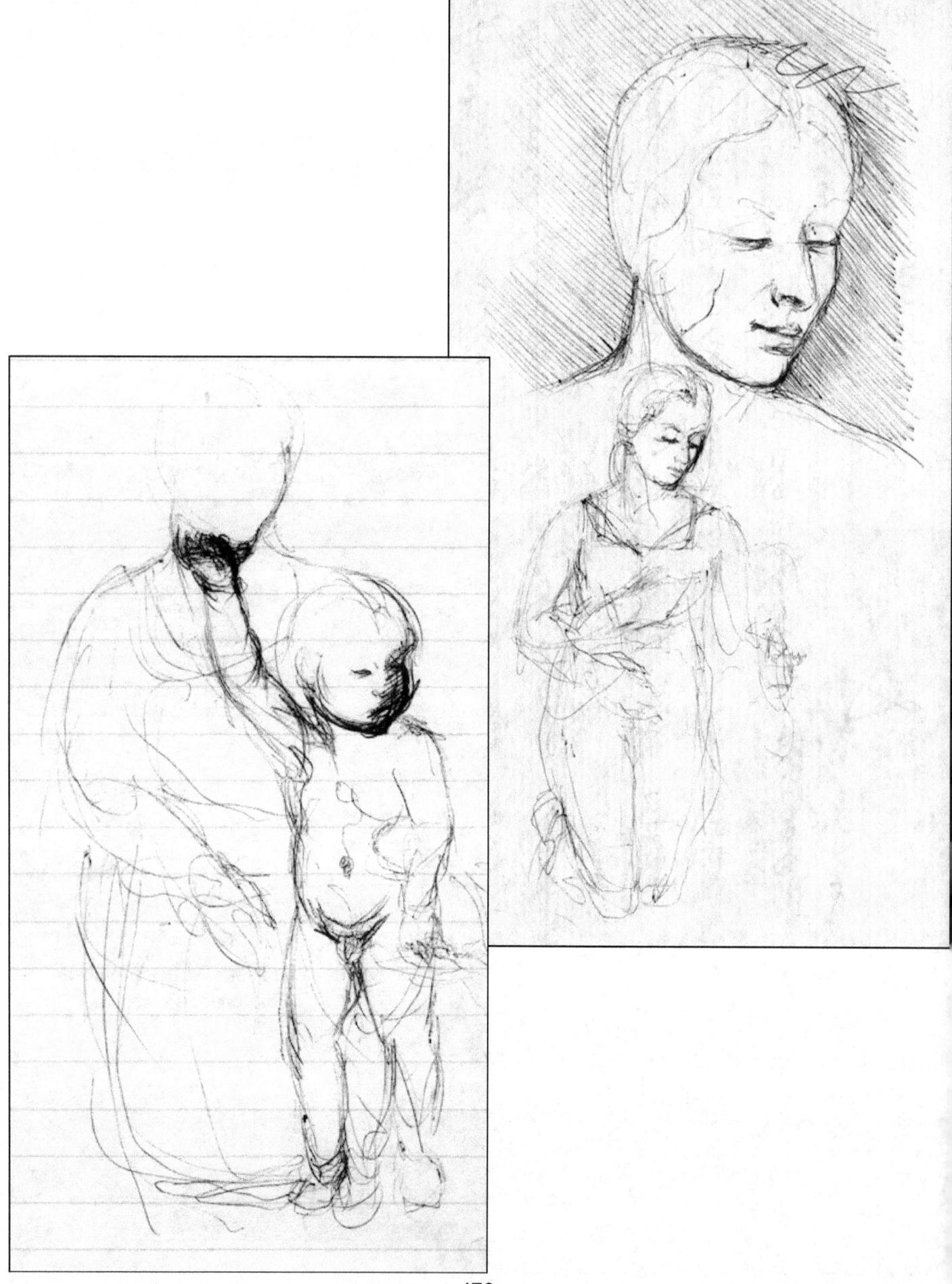

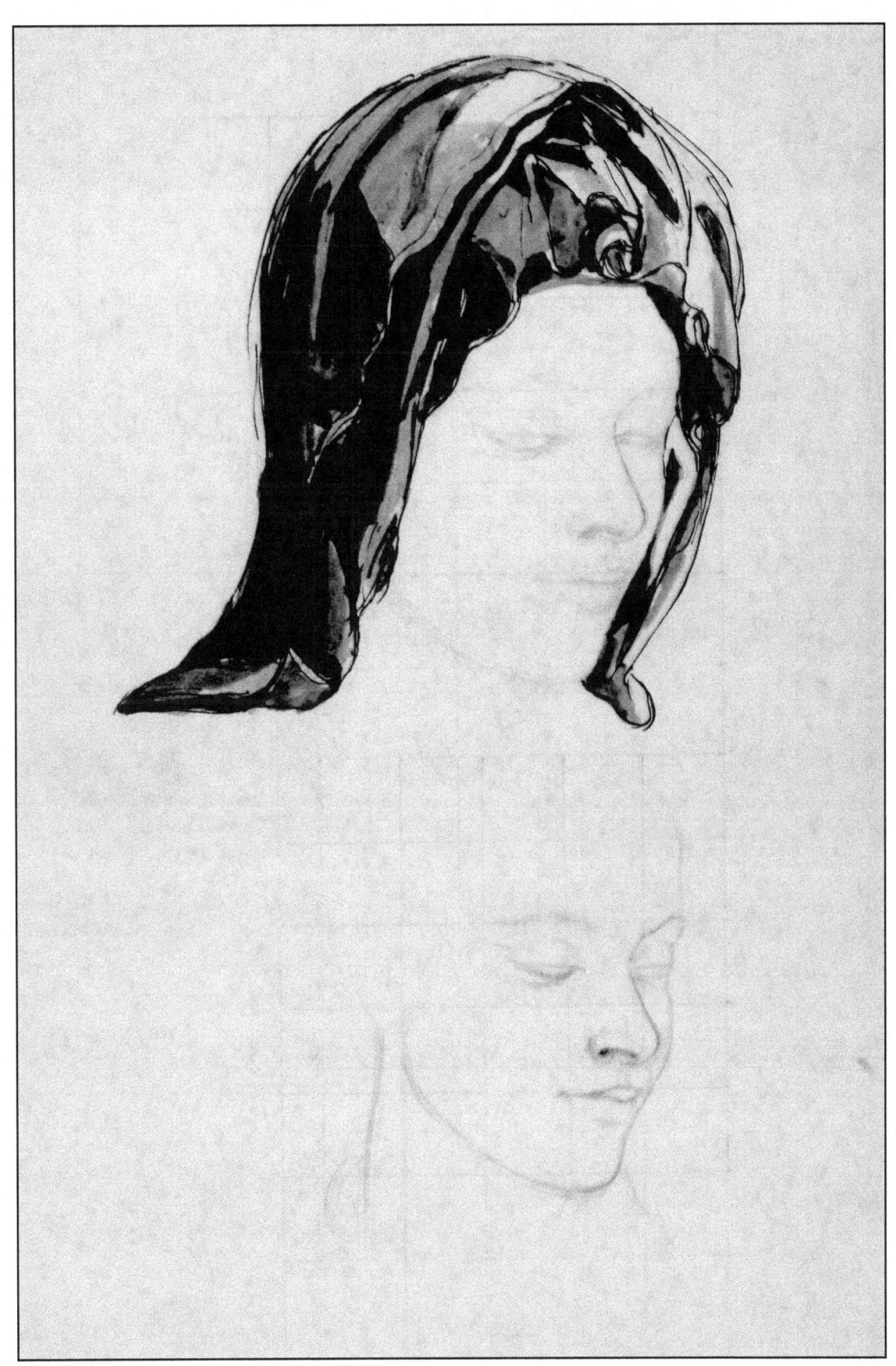

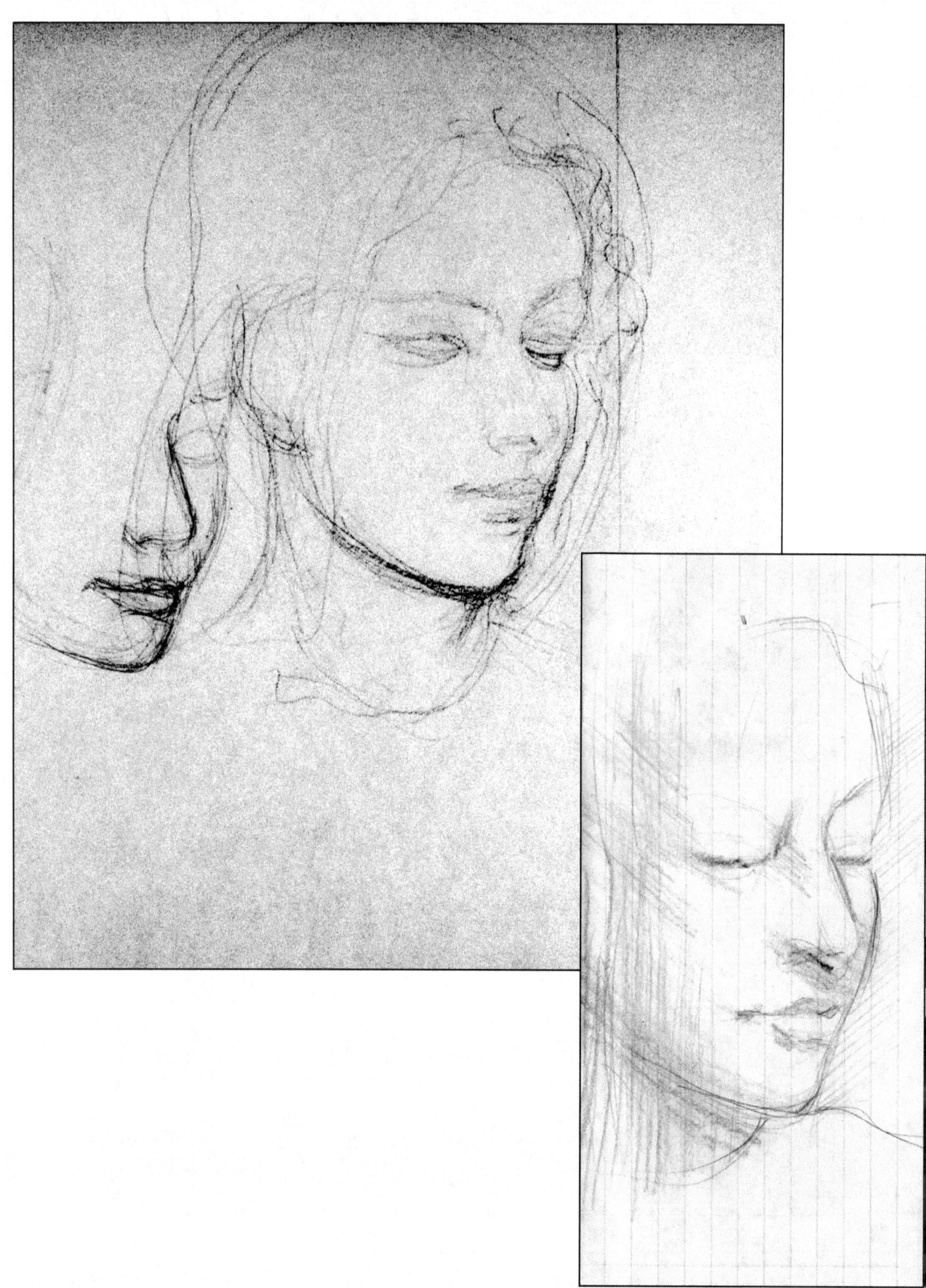

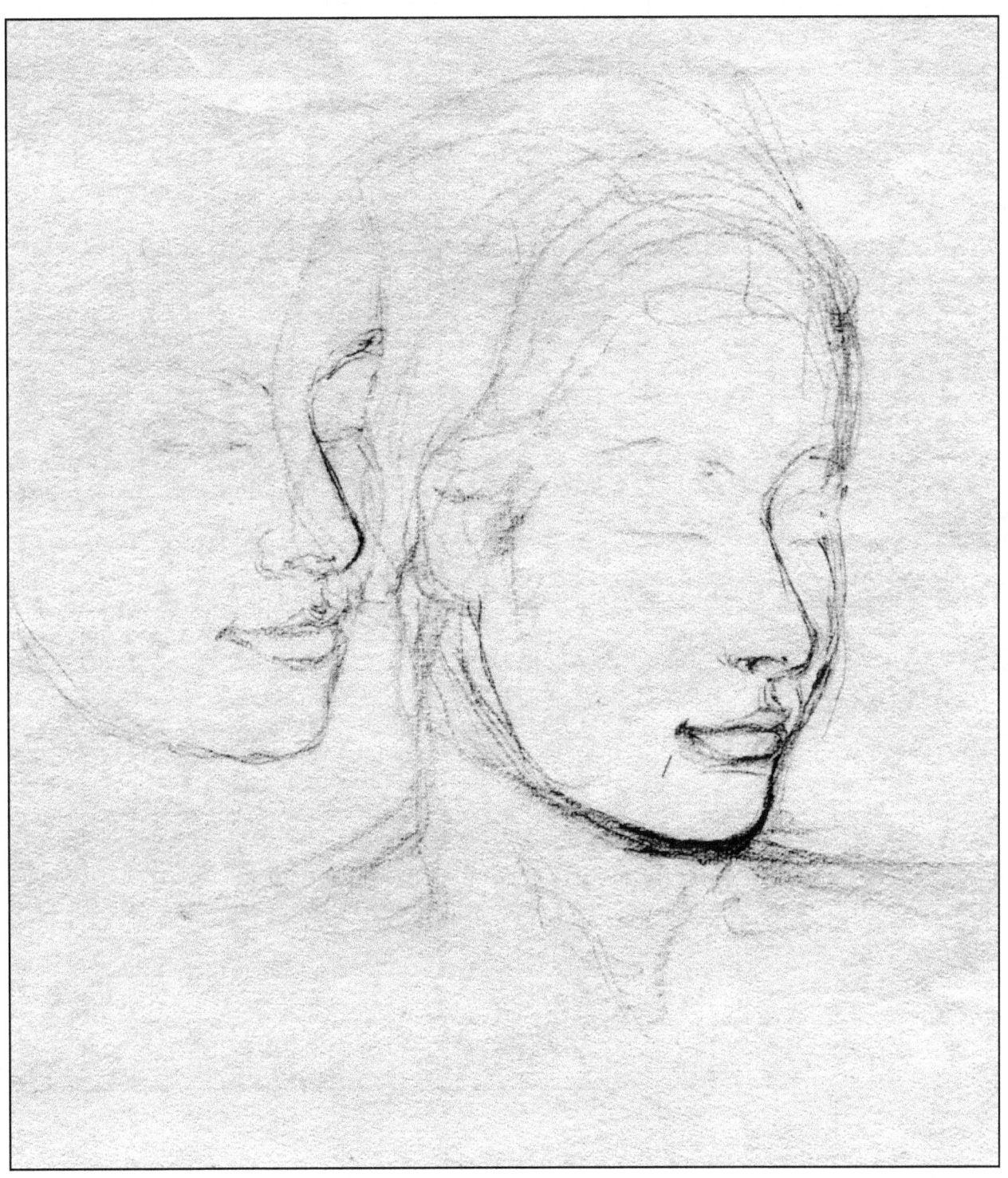

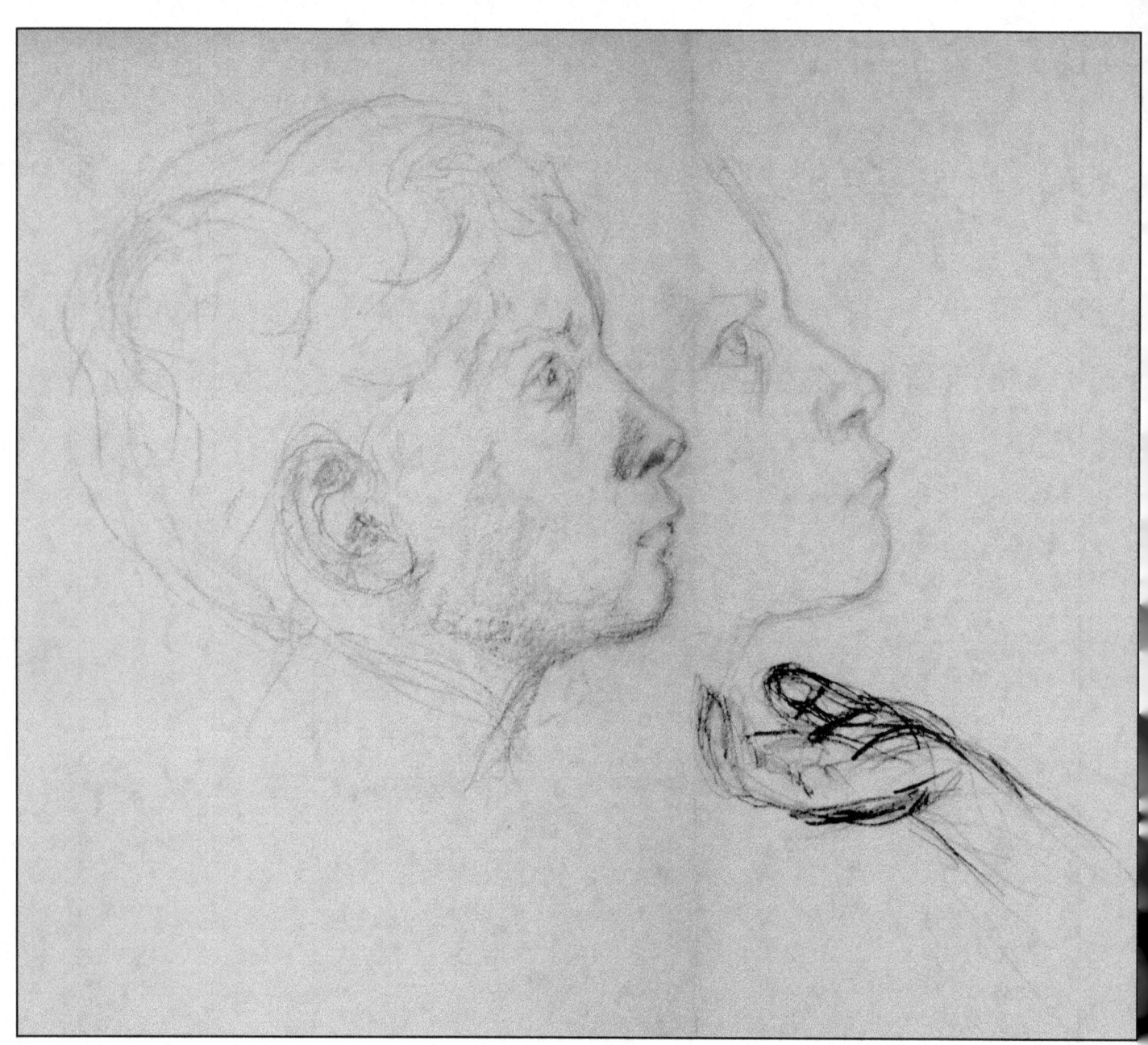

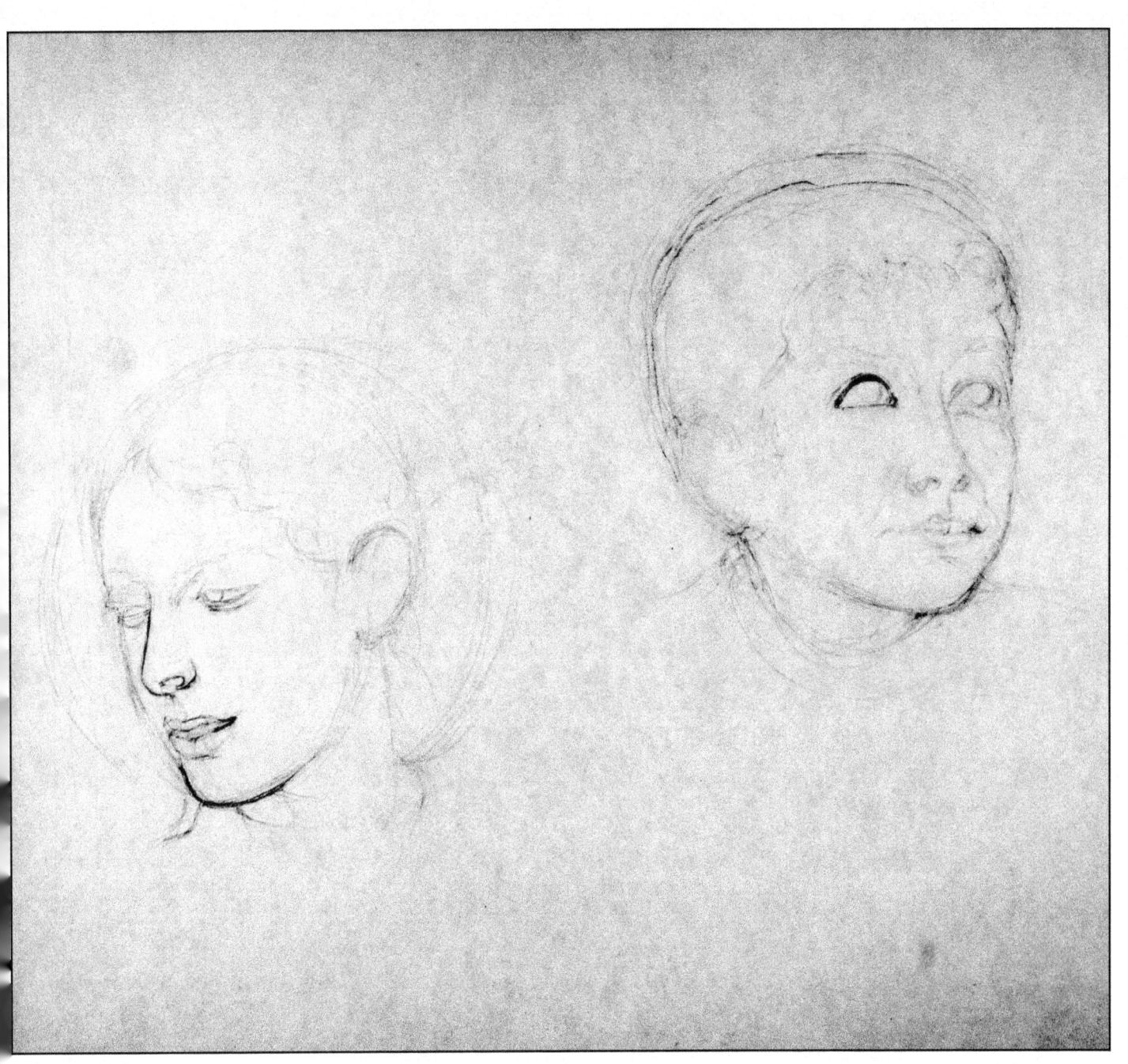

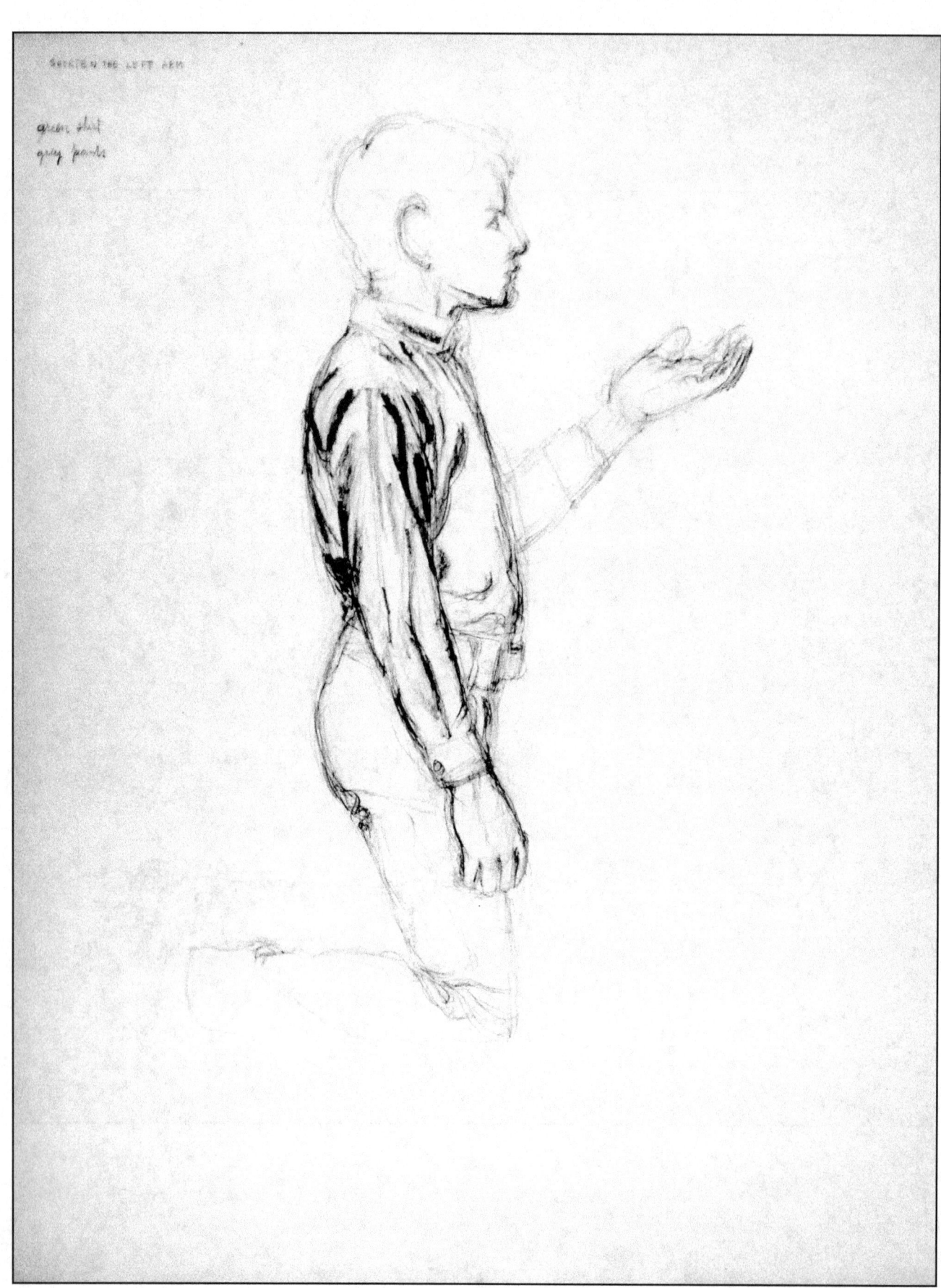

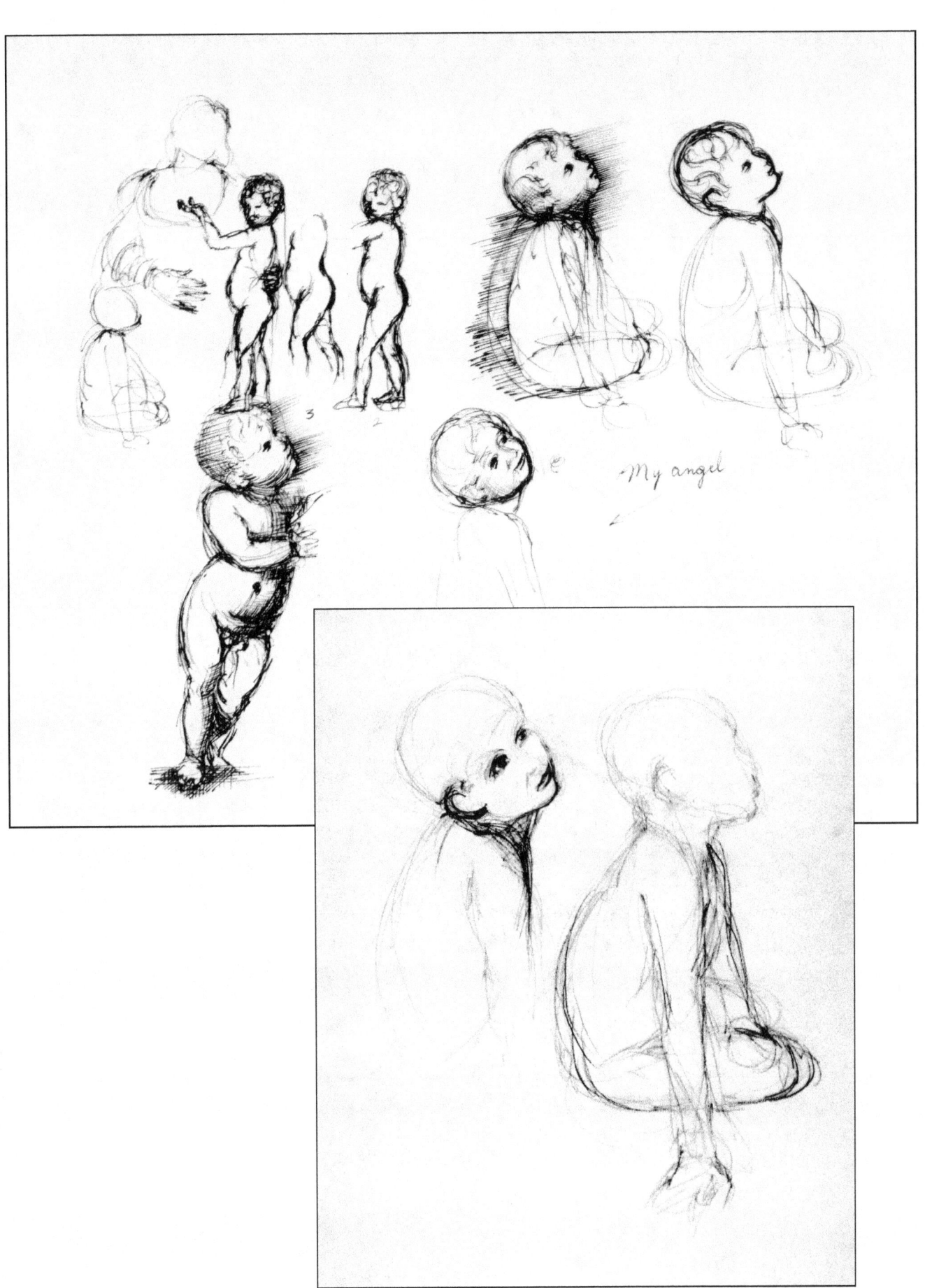

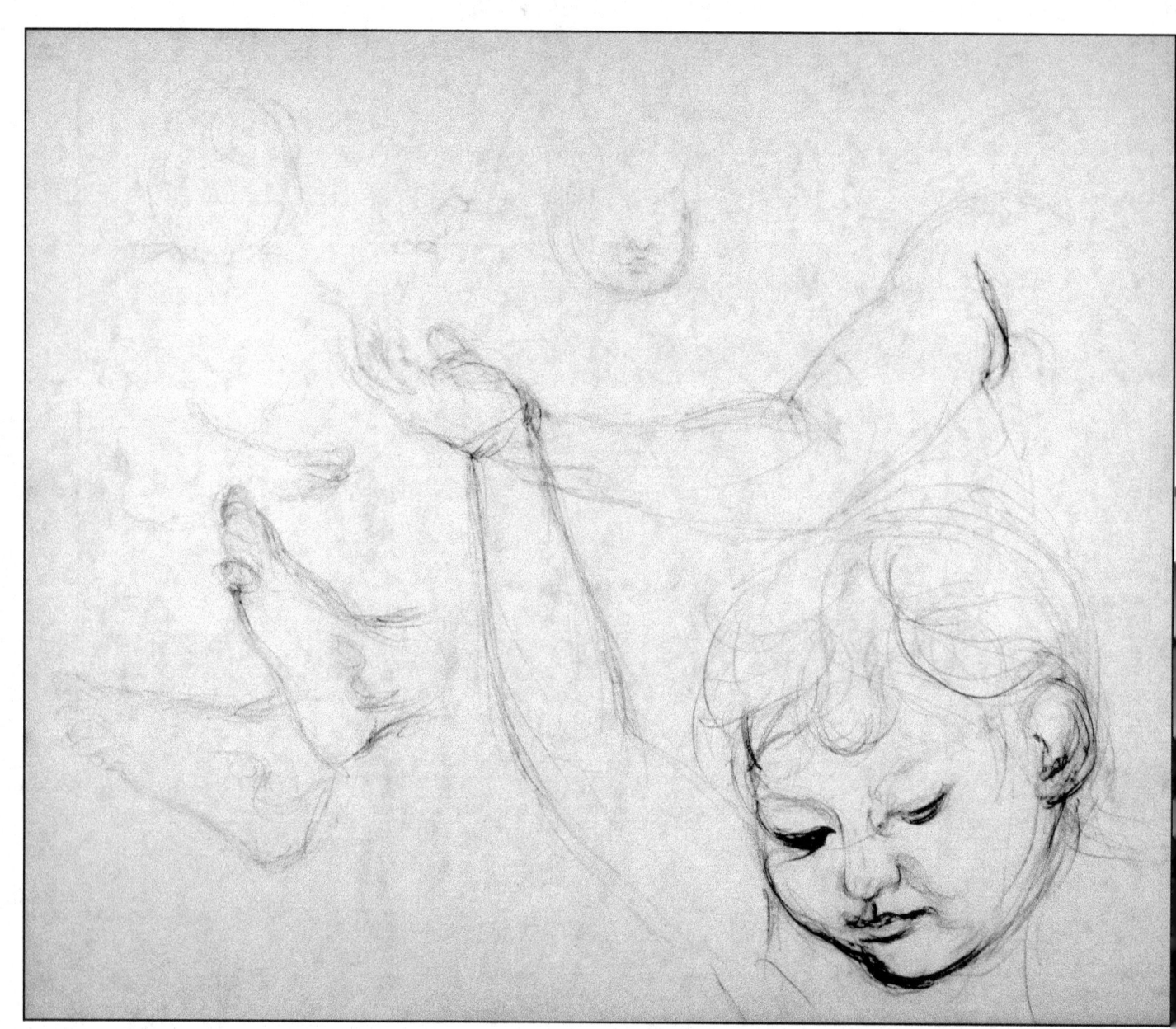

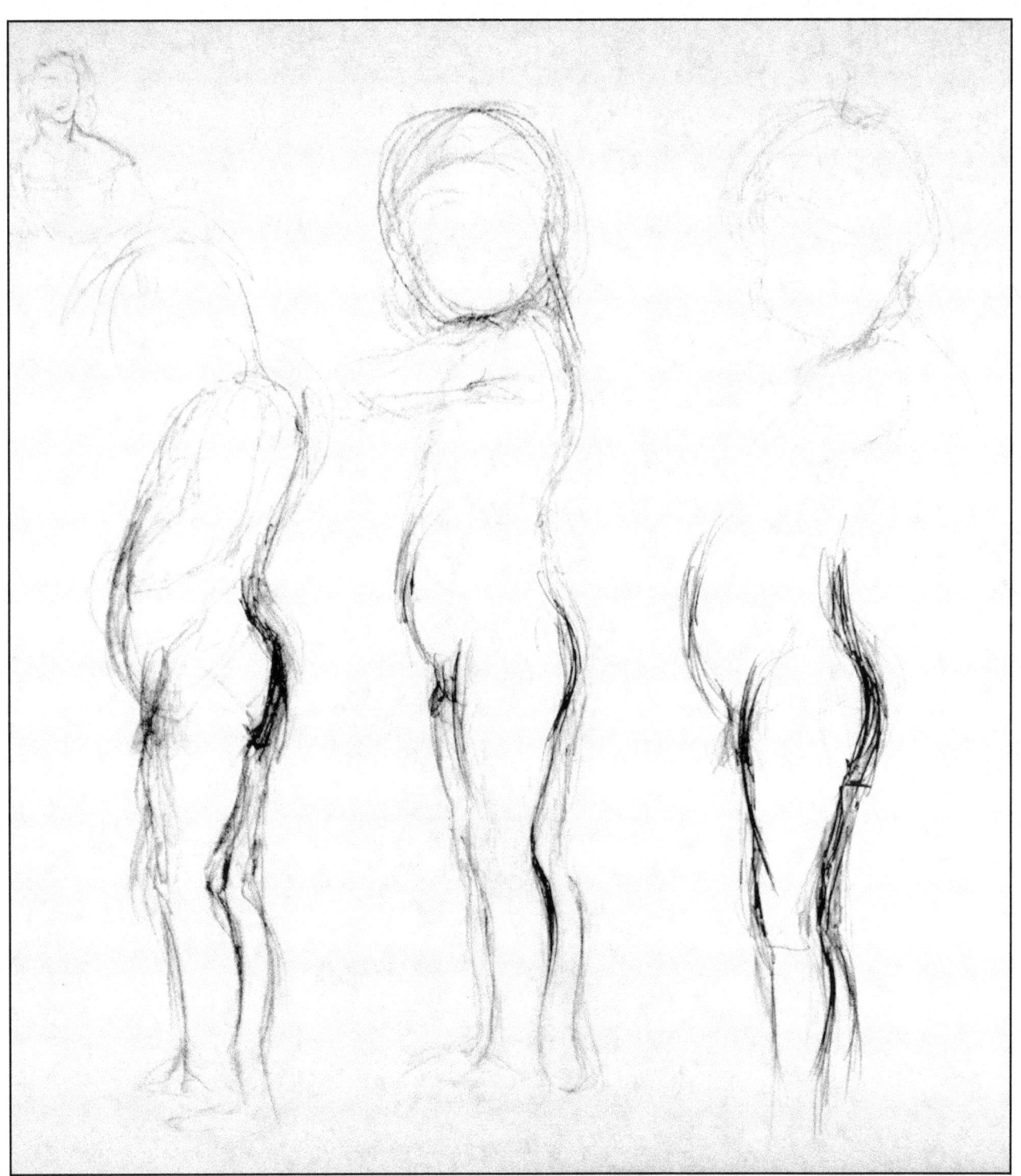

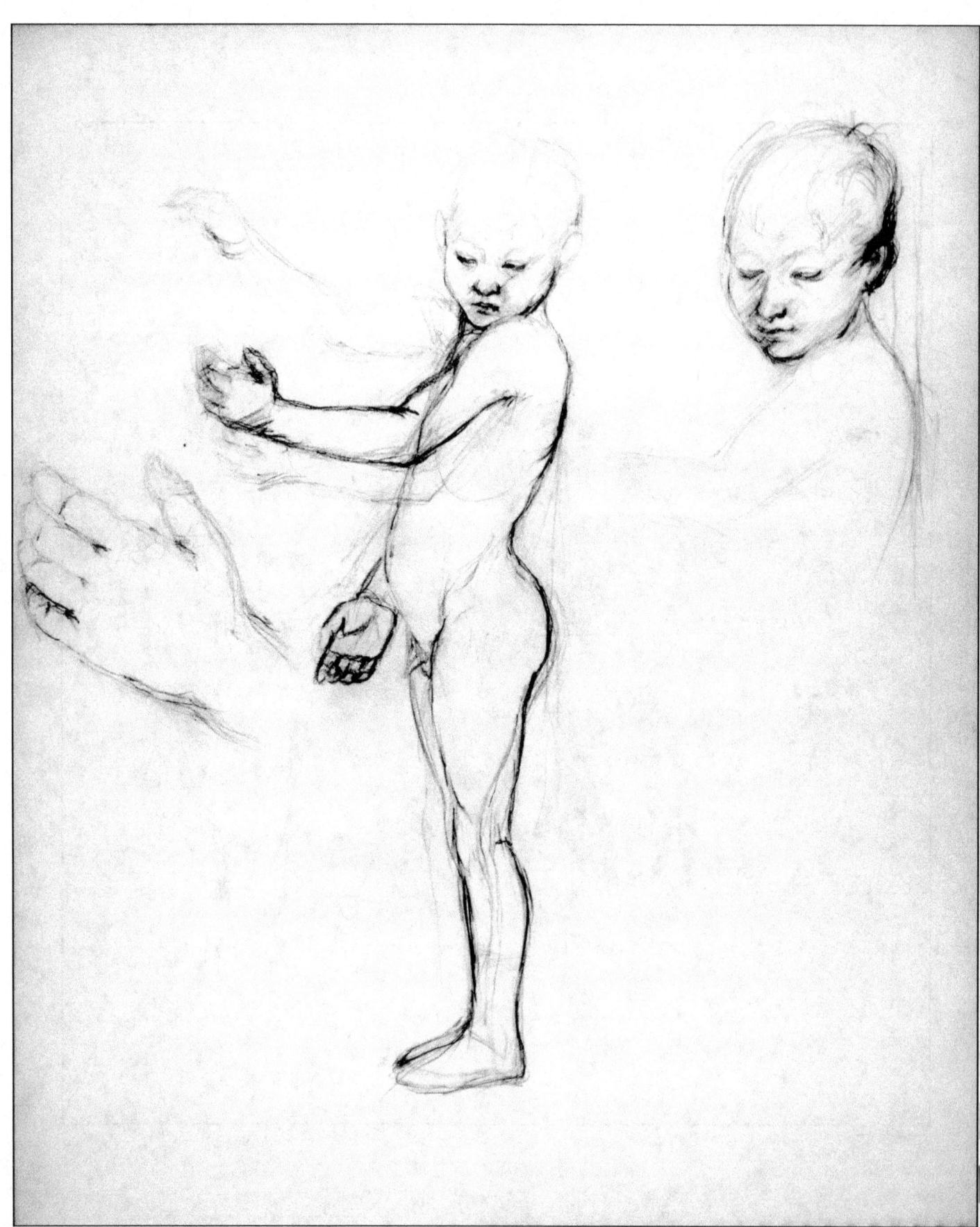

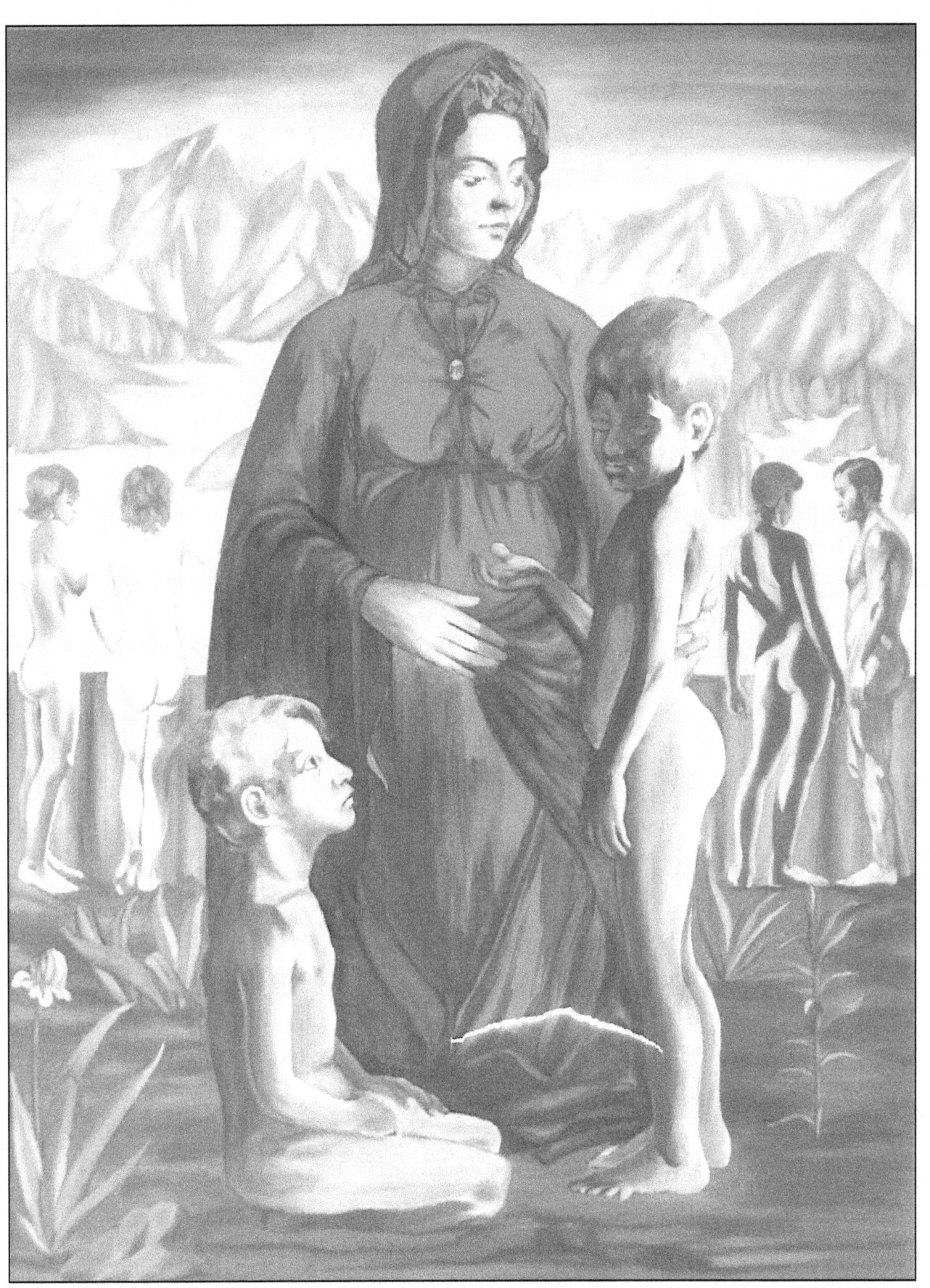

HOLY MOTHER AND CHILD, oil on 30"x40" canvas

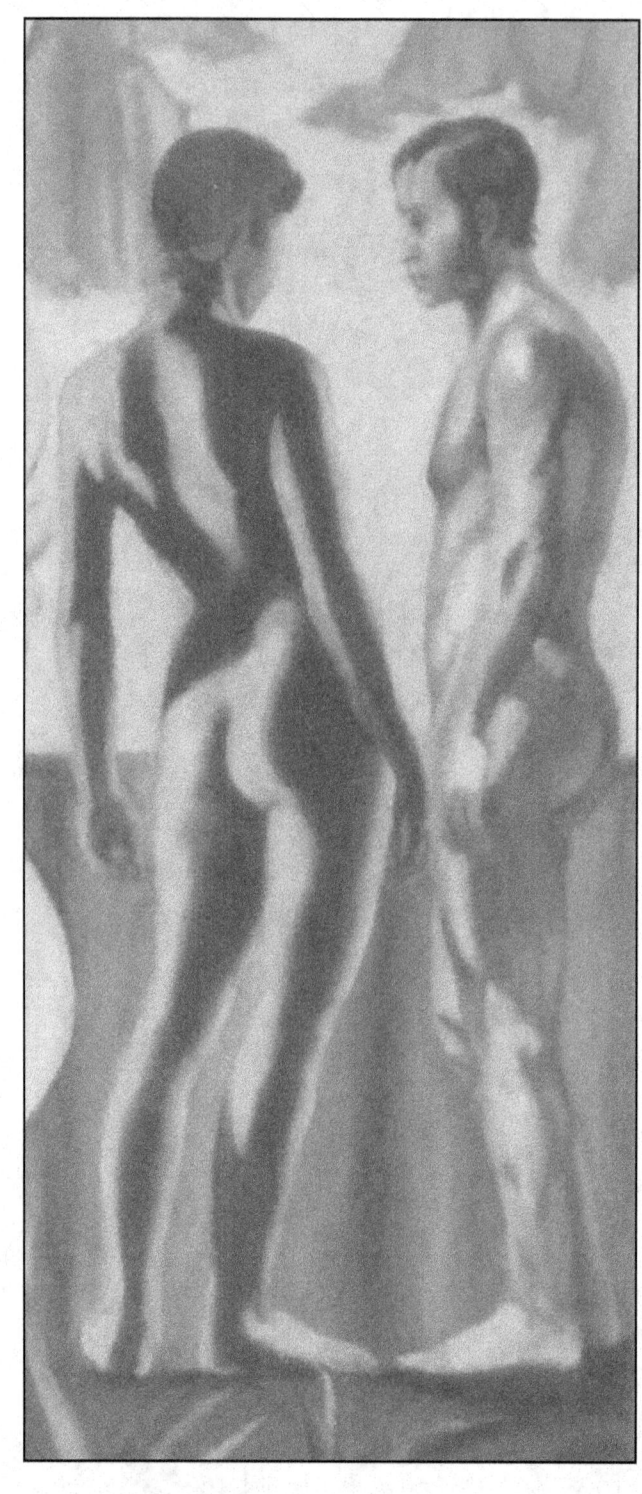

Detail from HOLY MOTHER AND CHILD

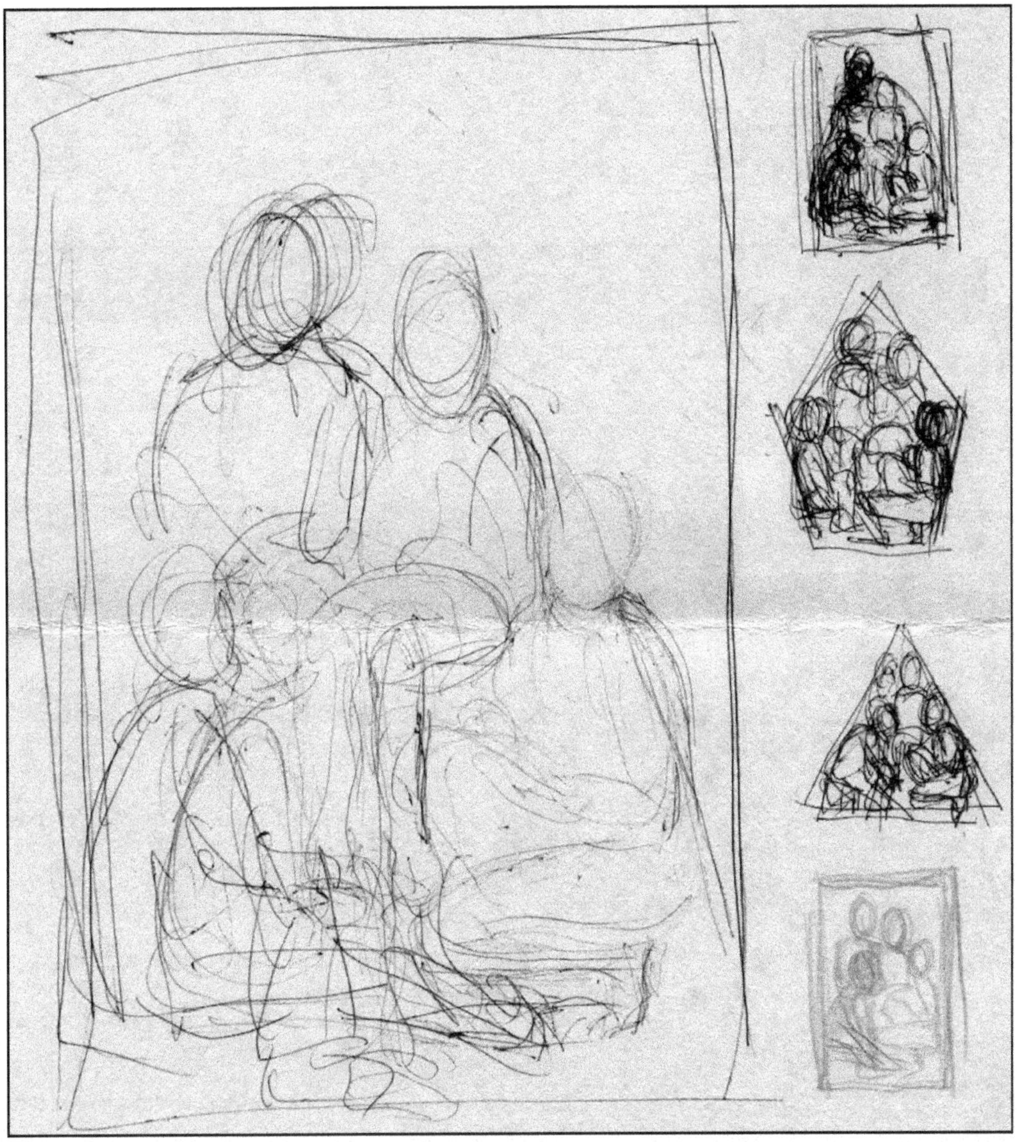

Holy Family Composition Blueprints

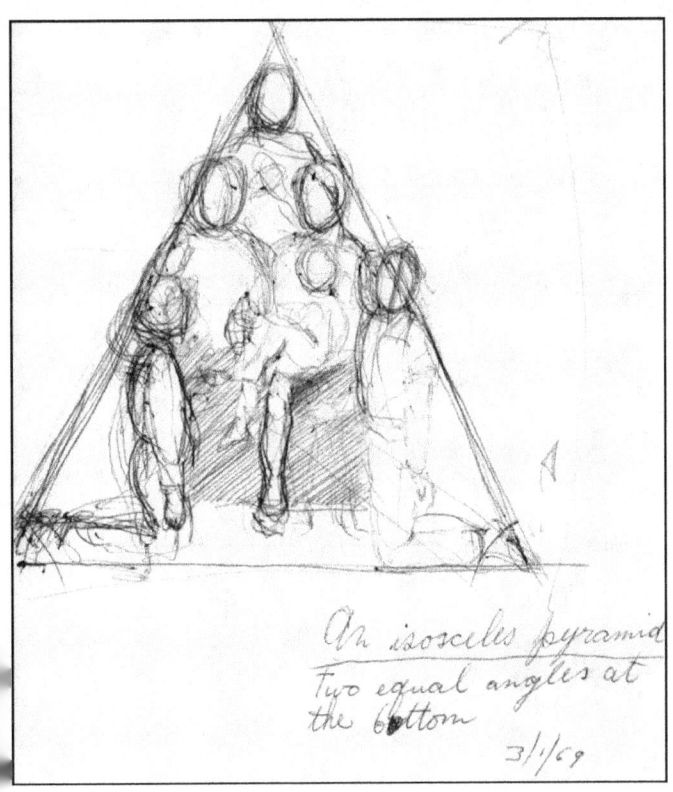

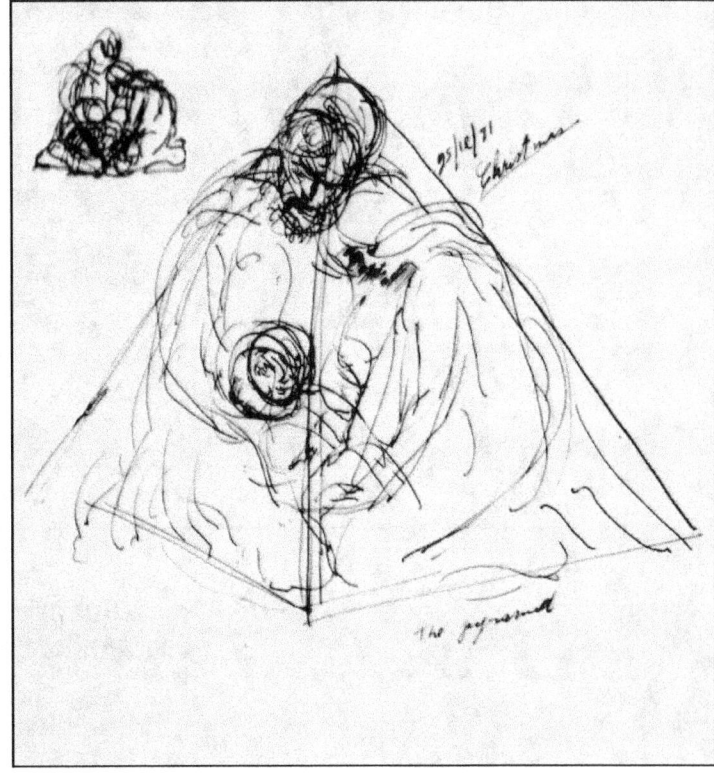

489

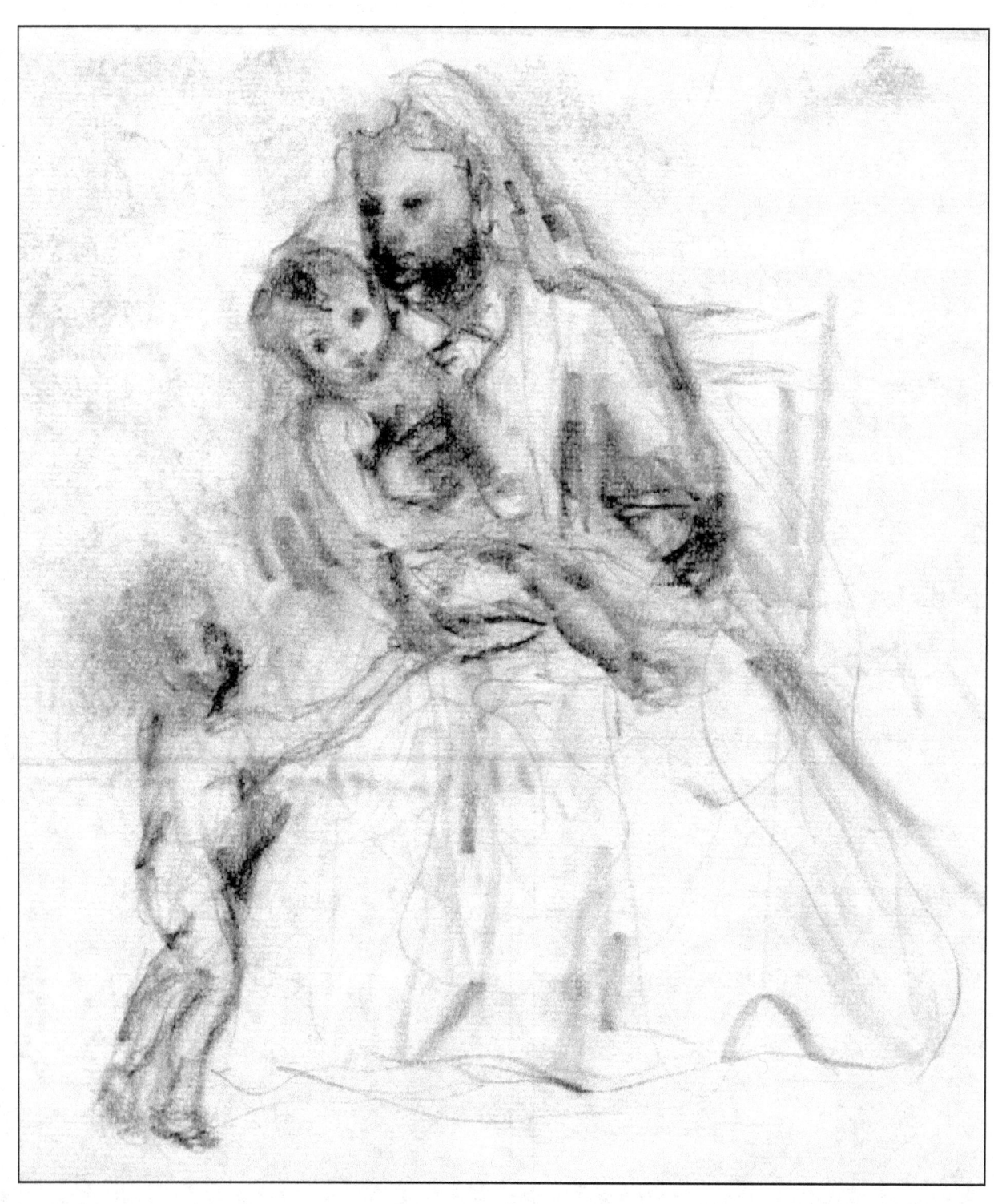

**Blueprint for a
Holy Family Composition**

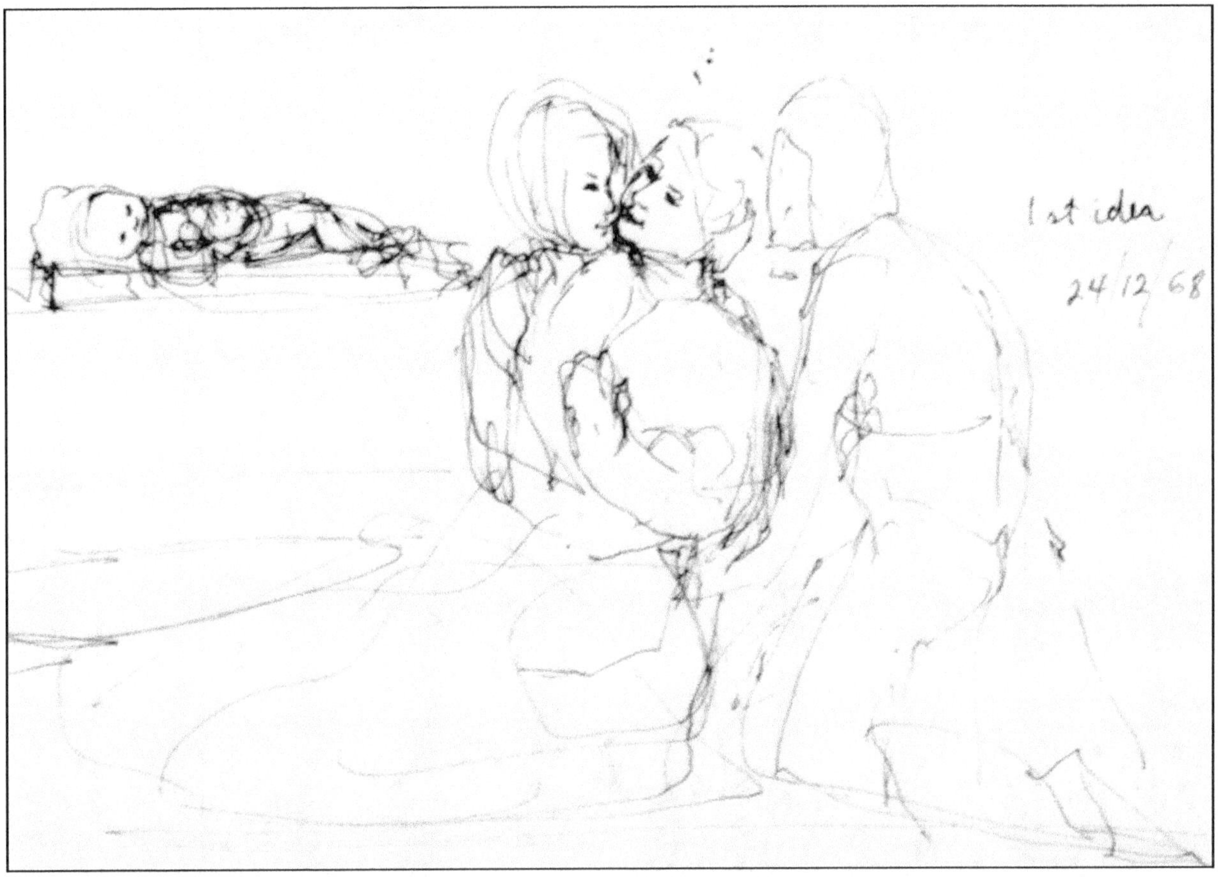

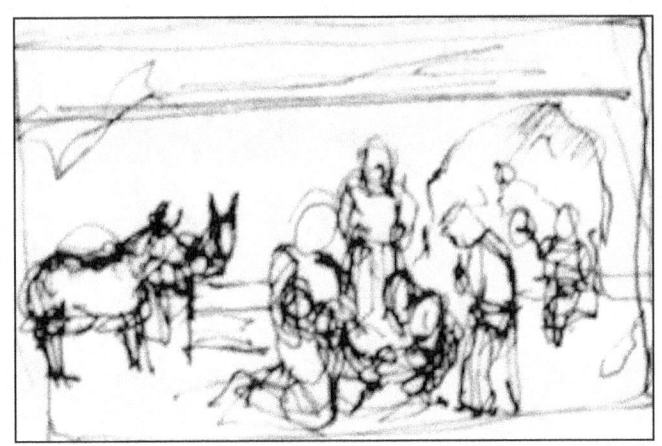

Blueprints for a Nativity Scene

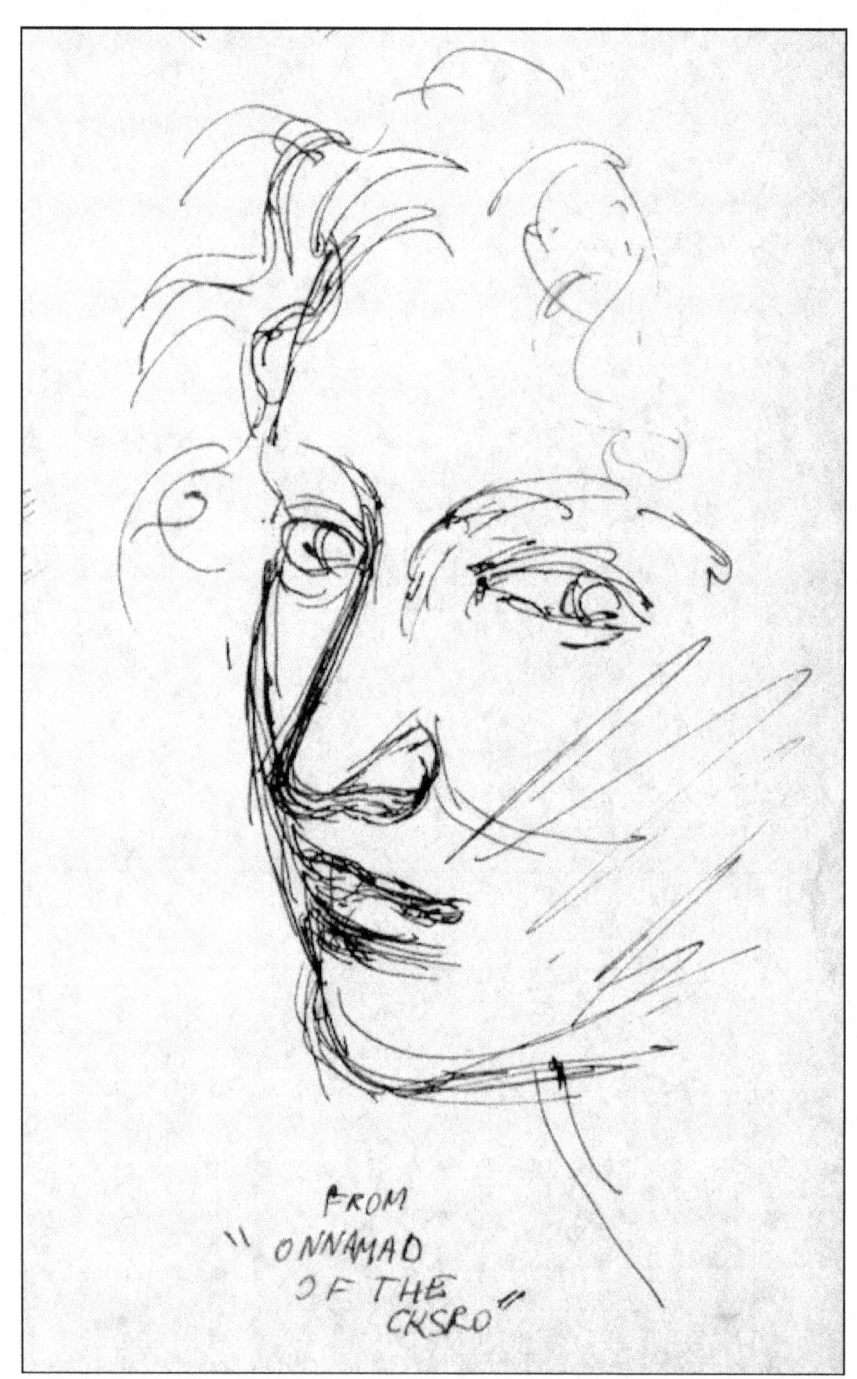

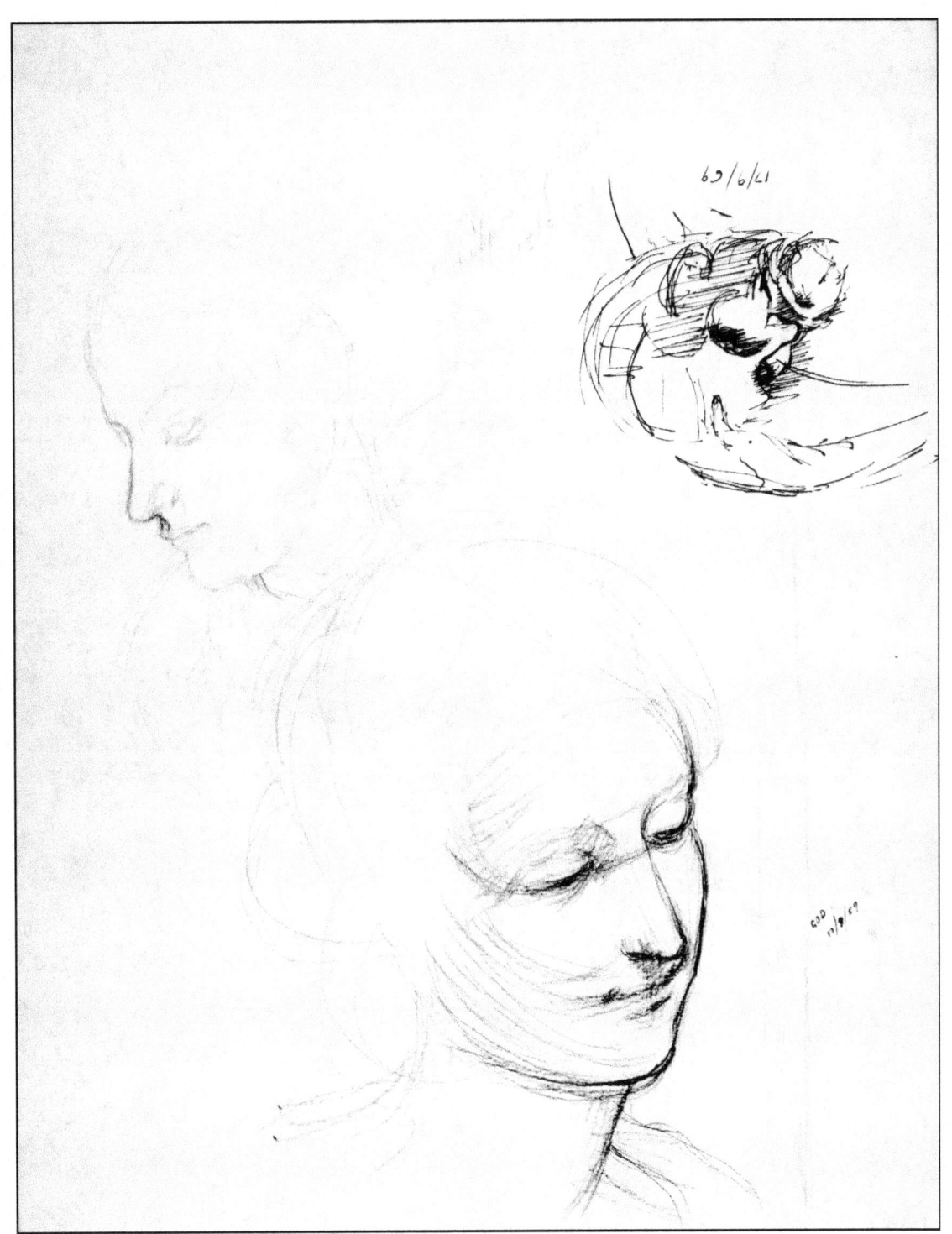

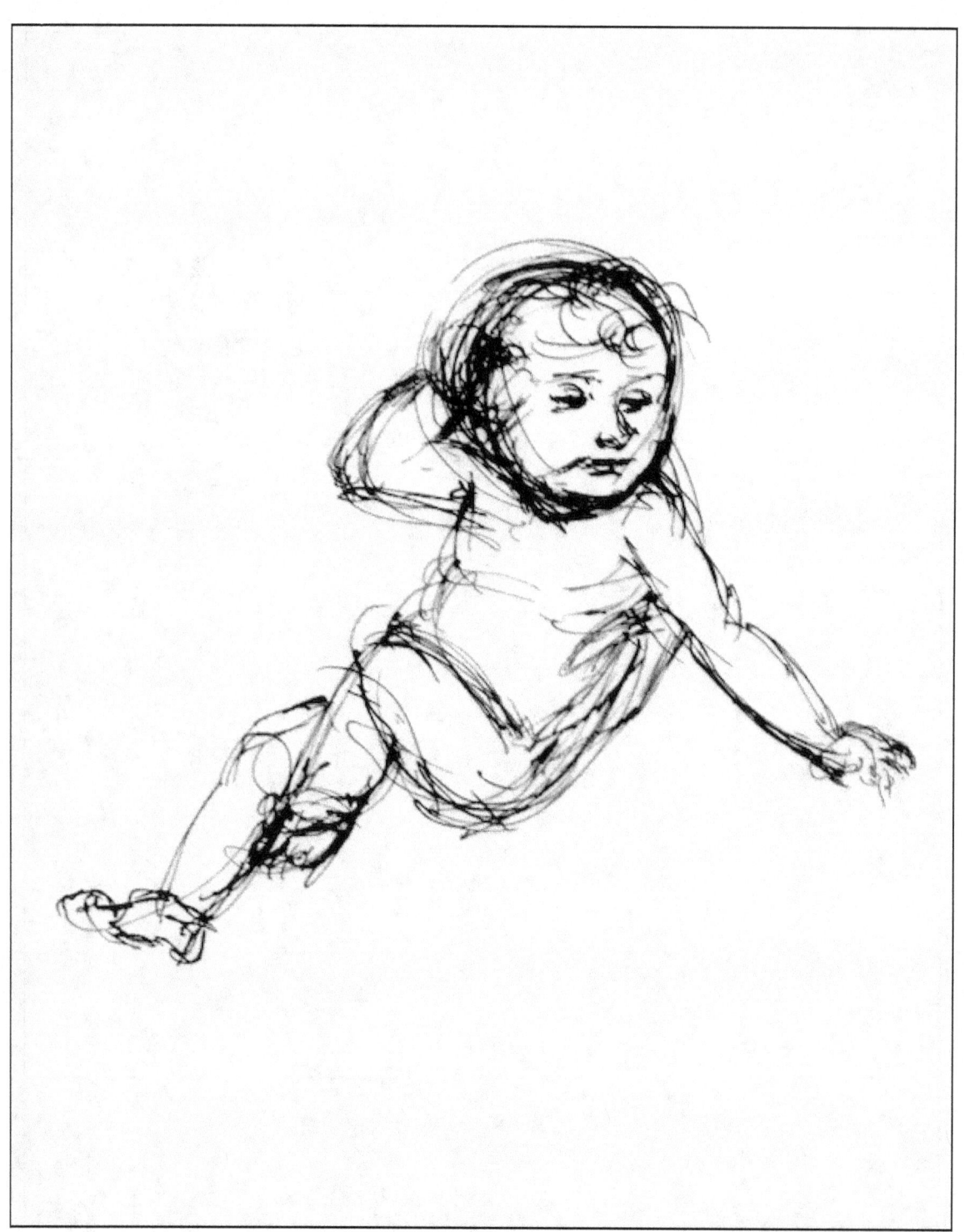

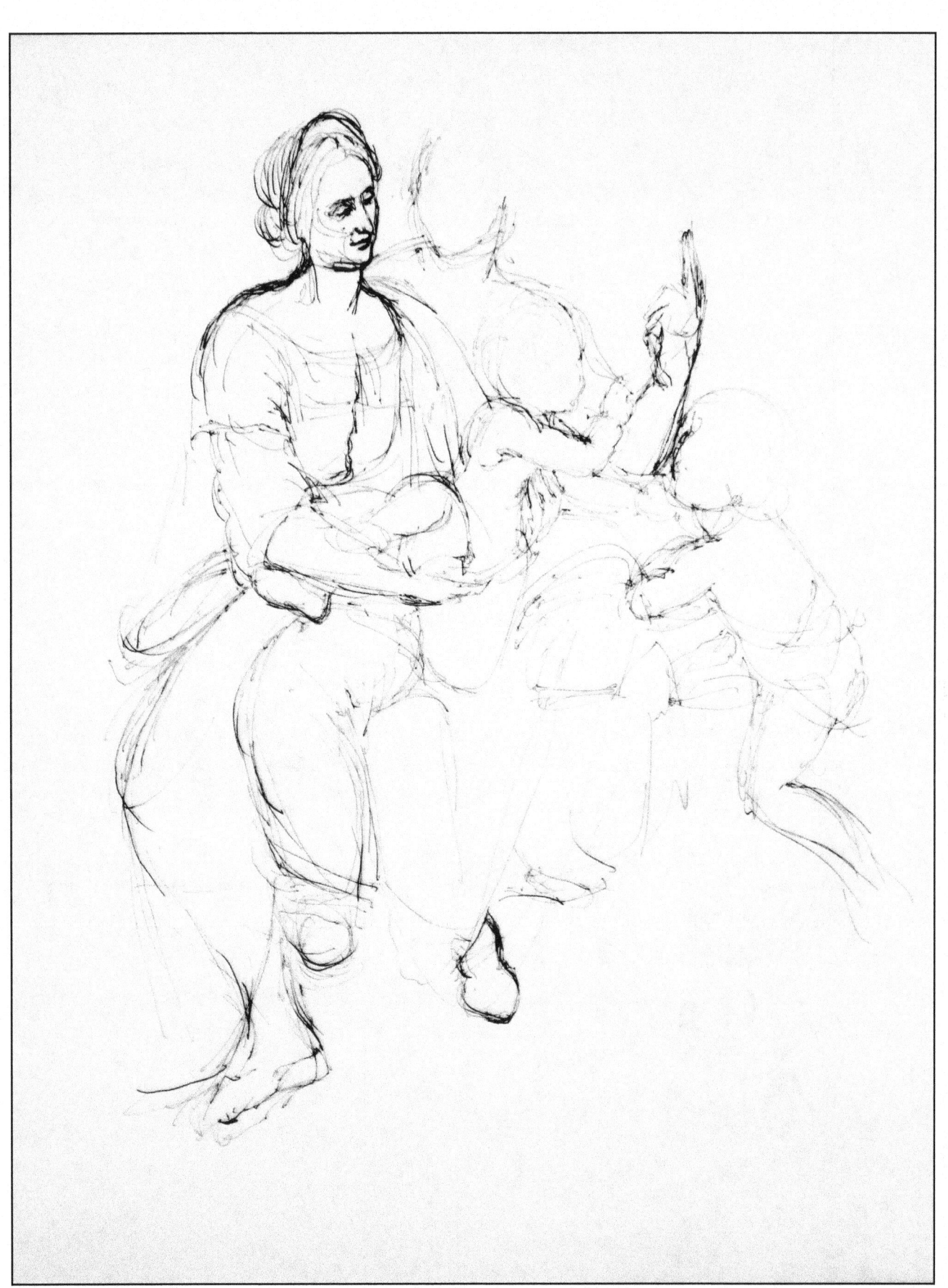

Virgin and Child with St. Anne, after Leonardo

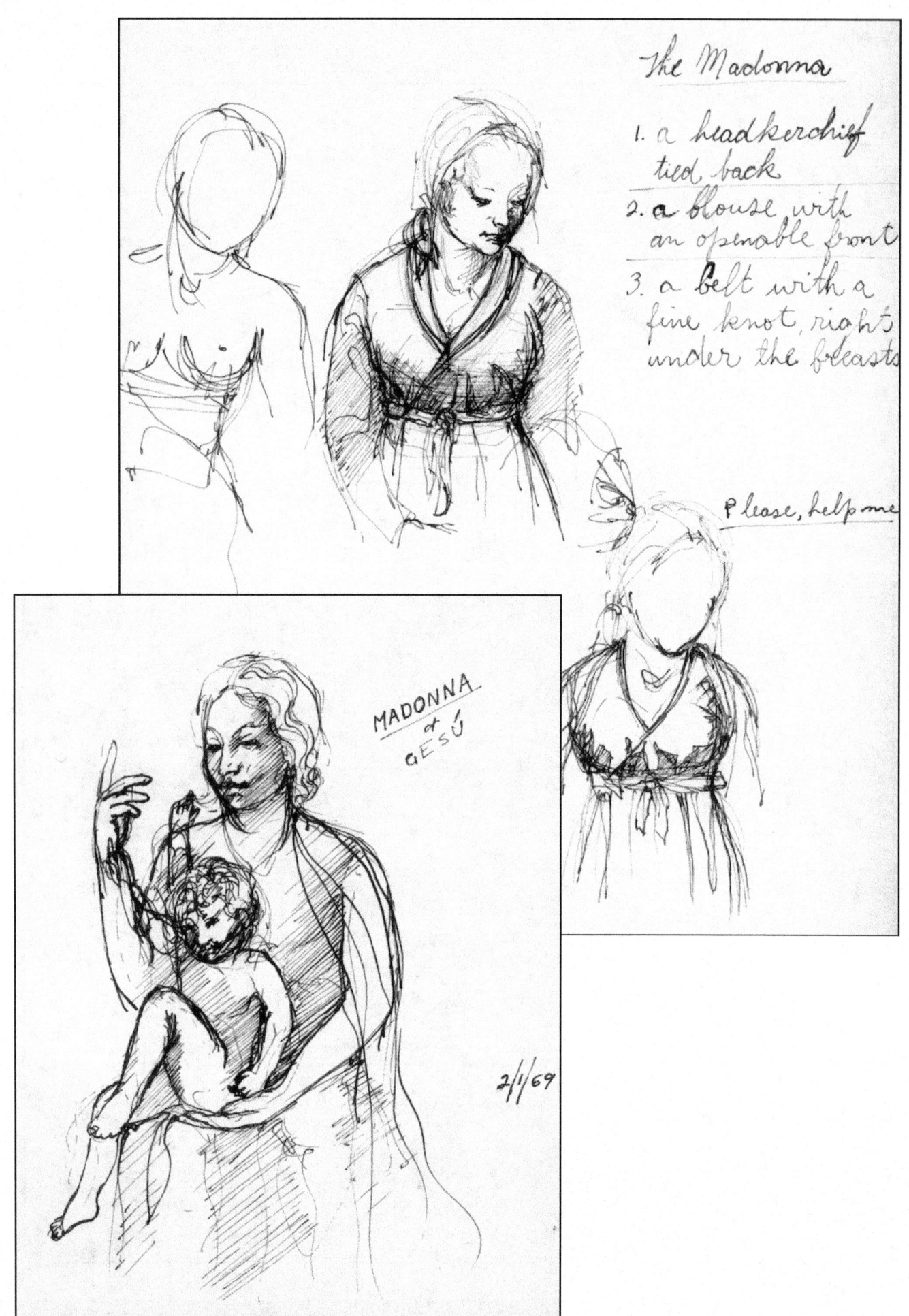

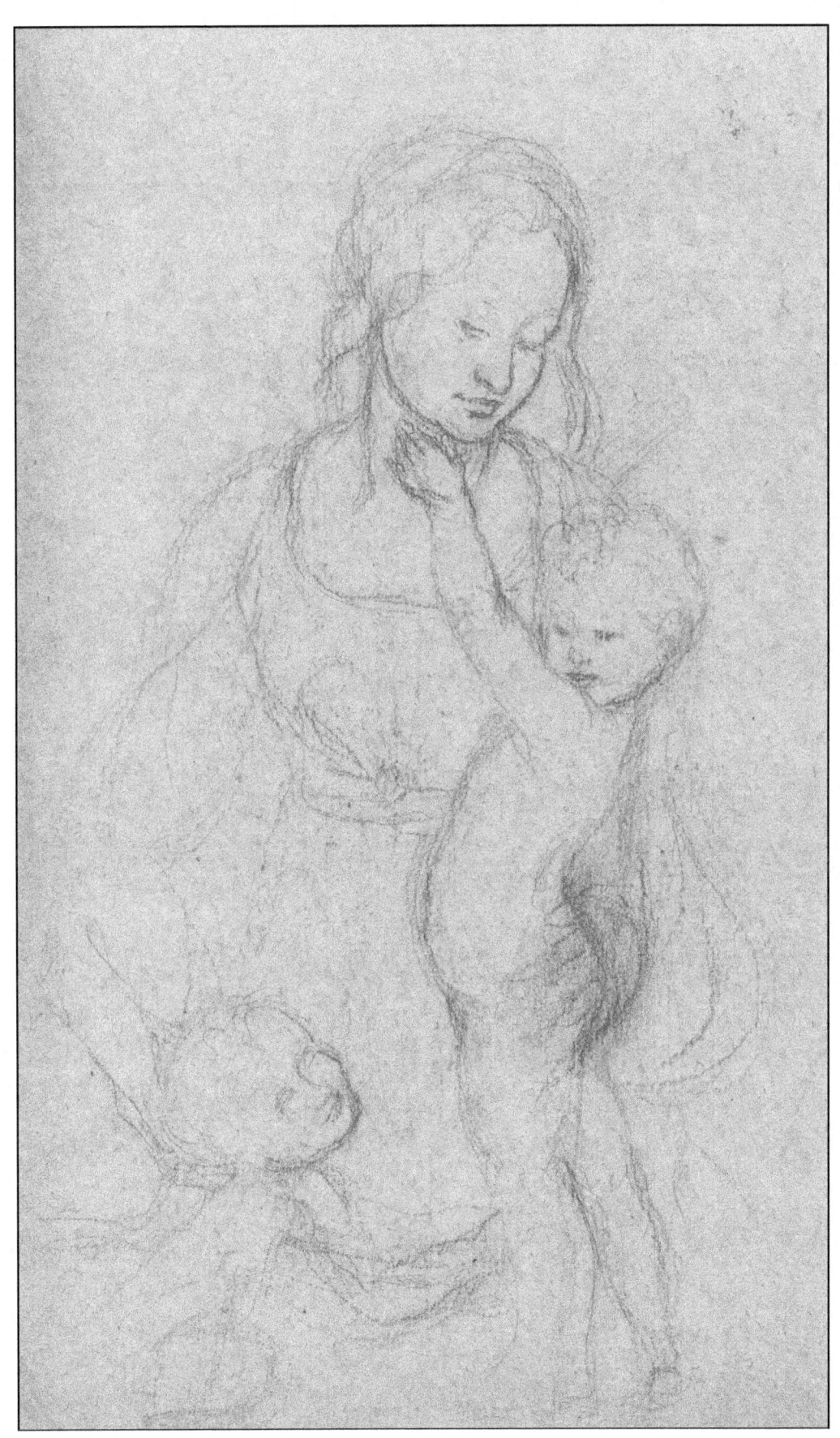

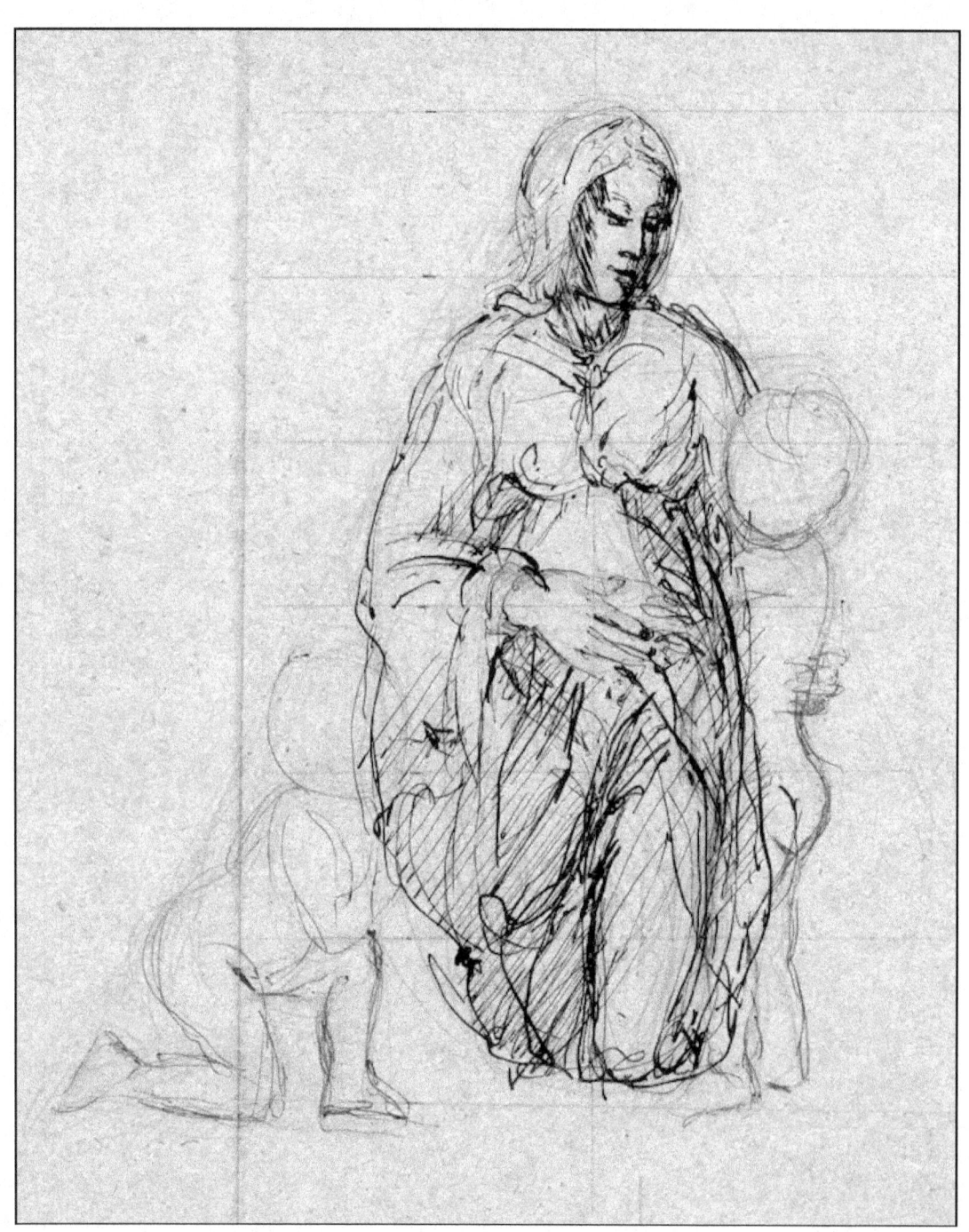

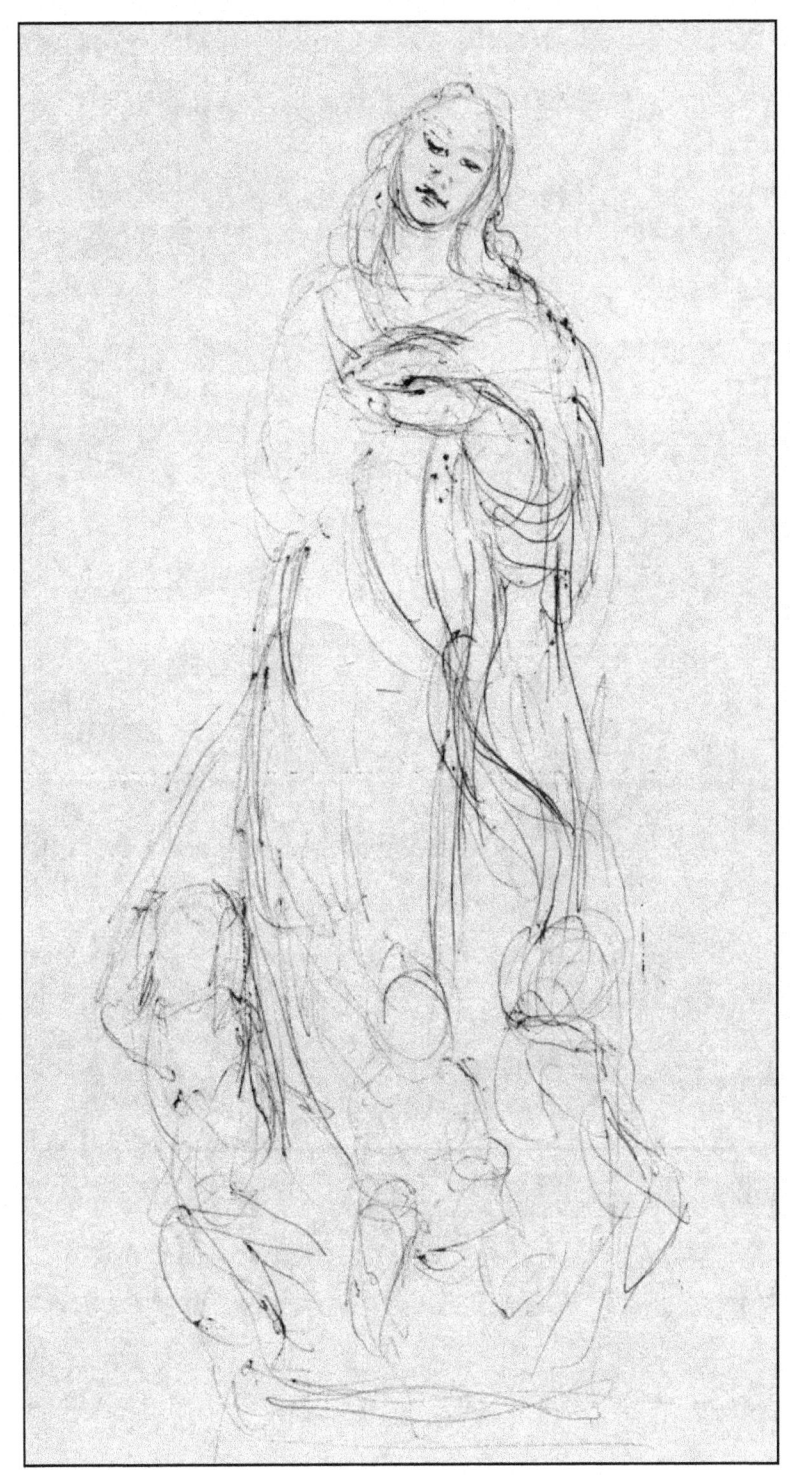

www.ingramcontent.com/pod-product-compliance
Lightning Source LLC
Chambersburg PA
CBHW062059220526
45471CB00010B/3542